BOROWICZ

BUSINESS ETHICS

READINGS AND CASES IN CORPORATE MORALITY

BUSINESS ETHICS

READINGS AND CASES IN CORPORATE MORALITY

SECOND EDITION

W. Michael Hoffman
Bentley College

Jennifer Mills Moore
University of Delaware

McGRAW-HILL PUBLISHING COMPANY

New York St. Louis San Francisco Auckland Bogotá Caracas
Hamburg Lisbon London Madrid Mexico Milan Montreal New Delhi
Oklahoma City Paris San Juan São Paulo Singapore Sydney Tokyo Toronto

This book was set in Times Roman by the College Composition Unit
in cooperation with Waldman Graphics, Inc.
The editors were Judith R. Cornwell and Bernadette Boylan;
the production supervisor was Denise L. Puryear.
The cover was designed by Karen Quigley.
R. R. Donnelley & Sons Company was printer and binder.

BUSINESS ETHICS

Readings and Cases in Corporate Morality

1 2 3 4 5 6 7 8 9 0   DOC DOC   8 9 4 3 2 1 0 9

ISBN 0-07-029328-7

Library of Congress Cataloging-in-Publication Data

Business ethics: readings and cases in corporate morality/W.
  Michael Hoffman, Jennifer Mills Moore—2nd ed.
      p.   cm.
    Includes bibliographies.
    1. Business ethics.   2. Business ethics—Case studies.
  I. Hoffman, W. Michael.   II. Moore, Jennifer Mills.
  HF5387.B873   1990
  174'.4—dc19   89-2429

ABOUT
THE AUTHORS

W. MICHAEL HOFFMAN is the founding director of the Center for Business Ethics at Bentley College in Waltham, Massachusetts, a research and consulting institute and educational forum for the exchange of ideas and information in business ethics. Dr. Hoffman received his Ph.D. in Philosophy at the University of Massachusetts in 1972, and is Professor of Philosophy and Chairman of the Department of Philosophy at Bentley College. Dr. Hoffman has authored or edited ten books and has published over twenty-five articles in professional and scholarly journals. Dr. Hoffman also serves as a consultant on business ethics for corporations and institutions of higher learning; is a past National Endowment for the Humanities Fellow and Consultant; is a lecturer at universities and conferences; and sits on the boards of editors of the *Journal of Business Ethics* and *Business Ethics*.

JENNIFER MILLS MOORE is Assistant Professor of Philosophy at the University of Delaware, where she teaches and does research in business ethics and business law. She has served as Research Associate of the Center for Business Ethics and taught in the Philosophy Department at Bentley College before joining the faculty of the University of Delaware. Dr. Moore received her Ph.D. from Harvard University, and has both published and edited articles and other works in the field of business ethics.

In addition to this anthology, Professors Hoffman and Moore have jointly co-authored articles in business ethics and are co-editors of various publications.

CONTENTS

PREFACE   XV

GENERAL INTRODUCTION: ETHICAL
FRAMEWORKS FOR APPLICATION IN BUSINESS   1

**PART 1   ETHICS AND BUSINESS: FROM THEORY
TO PRACTICE   19**

INTRODUCTION   19

1   Theories of Economic Justice   33

John Rawls, *Justice as Fairness*   34

Robert Nozick, *Distributive Justice*   41

J. J. C. Smart, *Distributive Justice and Utilitarianism*   48

QUESTIONS FOR DISCUSSION   52

**2   Capitalism and Socialism: A Tale
of Two Systems   53**

Irving Kristol, *A Capitalist Conception of Justice*   54

Carl Cohen, *Socialist Democracy*   59

QUESTIONS FOR DISCUSSION   67

3   Ethics and Business Decision Making   68

Verne E. Henderson, *The Ethical Side of Enterprise*   69

Laura L. Nash, *Ethics Without the Sermon*   79

Steven Kelman, *Cost-Benefit Analysis: An Ethical Critique*   90

James V. DeLong and Robert A. Nisbet, *Defending
Cost-Benefit Analysis: Two Replies to Steven Kelman*   97

QUESTIONS FOR DISCUSSION 101

Cases for Part One **103**

The Gift Relationship: From Human Blood to Social Policy by Richard M. Titmuss 104

Training for Ethical Management at Cummins Engine by Michael R. Rion 109

Why Should My Conscience Bother Me? by Kermit Vandivier 116

QUESTIONS FOR DISCUSSION 125

SUPPLEMENTARY READING FOR PART ONE 125

PART 2 THE NATURE OF THE CORPORATION **127**

INTRODUCTION 127

4 Legitimacy, Responsibility, and Liability **143**

George Cabot Lodge, *The Ethical Implications of Ideology* 144

Milton Friedman, *The Social Responsibility of Business Is to Increase Its Profits* 153

Christopher D. Stone, *Why Shouldn't Corporations Be Socially Responsible?* 157

Thomas Donaldson, *The Social Contract: Norms for a Corporate Conscience* 162

Keith Davis, *Five Propositions for Social Responsibility* 165

Anthony F. Buono and Lawrence T. Nichols, *Stockholder and Stakeholder Interpretations of Business' Social Role* 170

W. Michael Hoffman and James V. Fisher, *Corporate Responsibility: Property and Liability* 176

QUESTIONS FOR DISCUSSION 182

5 Identity and Agency **183**

Kenneth Goodpaster and John B. Matthews, Jr., *Can a Corporation Have a Conscience?* 184

Peter A. French, *Corporate Moral Agency* 194

John R. Danley, *Corporate Moral Agency: The Case for Anthropological Bigotry* 202

QUESTIONS FOR DISCUSSION 208

6 Governance and Structure   **209**

SECTION A   BOARD OF DIRECTORS   210

Ralph Nader, Mark Green, and Joel Seligman, *Who
  Rules the Corporation?*   210

Irving S. Shapiro, *Power and Accountability: The
  Changing Role of the Corporate Board of
  Directors*   219

Harold S. Geneen, *Why Directors Can't Protect the
  Shareholders*   226

SECTION B   TAKEOVERS AND CORPORATE
RESTRUCTURING   231

Michael C. Jensen, *Takeovers: Folklore and Science*   231

Robert Kuttner, *The Truth about Corporate Raiders*   240

QUESTIONS FOR DISCUSSION   246

Cases for Part Two   **247**

Corporate Free Speech Is Upheld, First National Bank
  of Boston v. Bellotti.   248

*Directorships of Major U.S. Corporations Tightly
  Interlocked,* Senate Committee on Governmental
  Affairs   253

The Directors Woke Up Too Late at Gulf
  by Wyndham Robertson   254

Oklahoma Meets Wall Street by Paul Hirsch   260

QUESTIONS FOR DISCUSSION   266

SUPPLEMENTARY READING FOR PART TWO   266

PART 3 WORK IN THE CORPORATION   **269**

INTRODUCTION   269

7 Employee Rights and Duties   **287**

David Ewing, *An Employee Bill of Rights*   288

George G. Brenkert, *Privacy, Polygraphs and Work*   294

Joseph R. Des Jardins and Ronald Duska, *Drug Testing
  in Employment*   301

Michael Waldholz, *Drug Testing in the Workplace: Whose Rights Take Precedence?*   309

Donald L. Martin, *Is an Employee Bill of Rights Needed?*   312

Ruth R. Faden and Tom L. Beauchamp, *The Right to Risk Information and the Right to Refuse Health Hazards in the Workplace*   315

QUESTIONS FOR DISCUSSION   322

8   Whistle Blowing   **324**

Richard T. De George, *Whistle Blowing*   325

Gene G. James, *Whistle Blowing: Its Moral Justification*   332

QUESTIONS FOR DISCUSSION   344

9   The Quality of Working Life   **346**

Richard E. Walton, *Alienation and Innovation in the Workplace*   347

Irving Bluestone, *Labor's Stake in Improving the Quality of Working Life*   350

Mike Parker and Dwight Hansen, *The Circle Game*   355

Mitchell Fein, *The Myth of Job Enrichment*   361

Edward Cohen-Rosenthal, *Should Unions Participate in Quality of Working Life Activities?*   366

QUESTIONS FOR DISCUSSION   370

10   Hiring Practices: Preferential Hiring, Reverse Discrimination, and Comparable Worth   **371**

William Bradford Reynolds, *Equal Opportunity, Not Equal Results*   372

Nancy Kubasek and Andrea M. Giampetro, *Moving Forward on Reverse Discrimination*   376

Laura M. Purdy, *In Defense of Hiring Apparently Less Qualified Women*   381

Gerald W. McEntee, *Comparable Worth: A Matter of Simple Justice*   385

Phyllis Schlafly, *Comparable Worth: Unfair to Men and Women*   388

QUESTIONS FOR DISCUSSION   391

Cases for Part Three **393**

DuPont's Policy of Exclusion from the Workplace by
Martha W. Elliott and Tom L. Beauchamp 394

*Roger Boisjoly and The Challenger Disaster: A Case
Study in Management Practice, Corporate Loyalty,
and Business Ethics* by Russell P. Boisjoly and Ellen
Foster Curtis 397

The Eastern Airlines Union-Management Experiment
by John Simmons 404

*High Court Backs a Preference Plan for Blacks in
Jobs: United Steelworkers of America v. Weber* by
Linda Greenhouse 410

QUESTIONS FOR DISCUSSION 416

SUPPLEMENTARY READING FOR PART THREE 416

PART 4 THE CORPORATION IN SOCIETY **419**

INTRODUCTION 419

11 The Consumer **437**

John Kenneth Galbraith, *The Dependence Effect* 438

F. A. von Hayek, *The Non Sequitur of the
"Dependence Effect"* 442

Theodore Levitt, *The Morality (?) of Advertising* 445

David M. Holley, *A Moral Evaluation of Sales
Practices* 452

George G. Brenkert, *Strict Products Liability and
Compensatory Justice* 460

QUESTIONS FOR DISCUSSION 470

12 The Environment **471**

William T. Blackstone, *Ethics and Ecology* 472

Kenneth E. Boulding, *Fun and Games with the Gross
National Product: The Role of Misleading Indicators
in Social Policy* 477

Robert W. Lee, *Conservatives Consider the Crushing
Cost of Environmental Extremism* 482

Larry E. Ruff, *The Economic Common Sense of Pollution* 487

Mark Sagoff, *At the Shrine of Our Lady of Fátima, or Why Political Questions Are Not All Economic* 494

QUESTIONS FOR DISCUSSION 503

13 Regulation **504**

Norman E. Bowie, *Business Codes of Ethics: Window Dressing or Legitimate Alternative to Government Regulation?* 505

Ian Maitland, *The Limits of Business Self-Regulation* 509

George A. Steiner, *New Patterns in Government Regulation of Business* 518

Steven Kelman, *Regulation that Works* 525

QUESTIONS FOR DISCUSSION 529

14 Multinational Business **530**

SECTION A   MULTINATIONALS IN LESS DEVELOPED COUNTRIES 531

Louis Turner, *There's No Love Lost between Multinational Companies and the Third World* 531

Richard T. De George, *Ethical Dilemmas for Multinational Enterprise: A Philosophical Overview* 536

James E. Post, *Ethical Dilemmas of Multinational Enterprise: An Analysis of Nestle's Traumatic Experience with the Infant Formula Controversy* 541

SECTION B   BRIBERY 548

Scott Turow, *What's Wrong with Bribery* 548

Mark Pastin and Michael Hooker, *Ethics and the Foreign Corrupt Practices Act* 550

Robert E. Frederick, *Bribery and Ethics: A Reply to Pastin and Hooker* 554

Henry W. Lane and Donald G. Simpson, *Bribery in International Business: Whose Problem Is It?* 560

SECTION C   SOUTH AFRICA 567

Kenneth N. Carstens, *A Case for Sanctions against South Africa* 567

Patricia H. Werhane, *Moral Justifications for Doing Business in South Africa*   574

QUESTIONS FOR DISCUSSION   579

Cases for Part Four   **581**

Tobacco Advertising, Taxes Come under Attack in Congress by John Robinson   582

The Ford Pinto by W. Michael Hoffman   585

Hooker Chemical and the Love Canal by Timothy S. Mescon and George S. Vozikis   592

A South African Investment by Manuel G. Velasquez, with an update by Timothy Smith   597

QUESTIONS FOR DISCUSSION   603

SUPPLEMENTARY READING FOR PART FOUR   604

PART 5 THE FUTURE CORPORATE ETHOS   **607**

INTRODUCTION   609

15 Developing the Moral Corporation   **615**

Christopher D. Stone, *The Culture of the Corporation*   616

Mark Pastin, *Lessons from High-Profit, High-Ethics Companies: An Agenda for Managerial Action*   624

W. Michael Hoffman, *Developing the Ethical Corporation*   628

QUESTIONS FOR DISCUSSION   634

Case for Part Five   **635**

The Proctor & Gamble Rely Case: A Social Response Pattern for the 1980s? by Archie B. Carroll and Elizabeth Gatewood   636

QUESTIONS FOR DISCUSSION   642

SUPPLEMENTARY READING FOR PART FIVE   642

FURTHER SUGGESTED READING ON BUSINESS ETHICS   643

PREFACE

We began the preface to the first edition of *Business Ethics: Readings and Cases in Corporate Morality* with advice from Cicero's *De Officiis*: "To everyone who proposes to have a good career, moral philosophy is indispensable." Cicero's words are as true and as timely as ever, and the second edition of this text represents our continuing commitment to the union of ethics and business.

The field of business ethics has grown tremendously since 1984, when the first edition was released. At that time, business ethics had just begun to gain momentum. Today it is a mature field. In a 1988 report, the Business Roundtable referred to corporate ethics as "a prime business asset," and corporations have begun to take significant steps toward integrating ethical values into their corporate cultures. The American Assembly of Collegiate Schools of Business has called for grounding in ethics as one of the essential elements of a sound business education. Literature in business ethics continues to grow and deepen.

In the second edition of *Business Ethics,* we have attempted to include both the best new thinking on ethical issues in business and the first edition's time-tested favorites. The goals of the text remain the same. We have tried to be *comprehensive*. In our coverage of the issues, we have selected what we consider to be the most important currently debated moral concerns in the field. We have retained all the topics from the first edition with the exception of price fixing and have added material on employee privacy, drug and polygraph testing, comparable worth, worker health and safety, and hostile takeovers. The sections on advertising, the environment, and bribery have been expanded, and we have updated the section on investment in South Africa. The case material has also been dramatically updated. Many cases from the first edition remain, but we have included timely new cases such as those on tobacco advertising, the space shuttle *Challenger* disaster, and Eastern Airlines' labor–management relations.

As with the first edition, we have tried to be *impartial*. The format of the text, for the most part, is point/counterpoint, and we have included the strongest statements we could find of different perspectives on the issues. We have made an effort to include articles by thinkers from a wide range of constituencies—not just philosophers, but representatives of business, government, labor, law, public interest groups, and a variety of professions.

Finally, we have tried to be *systematic*. We have retained the basic organization of the first edition. We begin with theoretical, structural, or more widely focused issues such as economic justice, the justice of economic systems, and the nature and responsibility of business. These give a framework for discussion and understanding of more specific, concrete issues, such as employee rights, the ethics of marketing and production, environmental ethics, and multinational issues. We conclude with a chapter on the development of the moral corporation of the future. Of course, the book may be used in many different ways. Some instructors may prefer to save the more abstract topics for the end of their course. We believe that the book lends itself readily to organizational variations.

In addition to a general introduction to ethical theory, the text includes an introduction to each part which sets out the major themes of the articles and cases and places them in context. Each part ends with an updated bibliography of supplementary readings, and a longer general bibliography can be found at the end of the text. A new feature of this edition is a set of questions following each chapter and each set of cases. These can be used as a focus for student discussion, for review, or for tests, quizzes, or student assignments. An Instructor's Manual accompanies this second edition. The manual is designed to serve as a resource for instructors. Its features include lecture outlines, teaching aims and suggestions, test questions, and suggestions for structuring the course.

We would like to express our appreciation to Bentley College and the University of Delaware for their support of this and other projects in business ethics. A special thanks also goes to Anne Glynn and Amy Chiari, staff assistants to the Center for Business Ethics, and to Mary Imperatore and Dorothy Milsom, secretaries to the Department of Philosophy at the University of Delaware, for help in the preparation of various stages of this manuscript. Finally, we are obliged to the following scholars for their insightful critical analyses of earlier drafts of this book: L. E. Andrade,

Illinois State University; Paul Camenisch, DePaul University; Tony Crunk, University of Virginia; Diane Dodd-McCue, University of Richmond; Vincent Luizzi, Southwest Texas State University; Lisa Newton, Fairfield University; and Robert Solomon, University of Texas at Austin.

W. Michael Hoffman

Jennifer Mills Moore

BUSINESS ETHICS

READINGS AND CASES IN CORPORATE MORALITY

General Introduction: Ethical Frameworks for Application in Business

Business is a complex fabric of human relationships—relationships between manufacturers and consumers, employers and employees, managers and stockholders, members of corporations and members of the communities in which those corporations operate. These are economic relationships, created by the exchange of goods and services; but they are also *moral* relationships. Questions concerning profit, growth, and technological advance have ethical dimensions: Some of these include the effects of the pollution and depletion of natural resources on society at large, the quality and character of the work environment, and the safety of consumers. As an anthology in business ethics, this text proposes to explore the moral dimension of business.

Ethics may be defined as the study of what is *good* or *right* for human beings. It asks what goals people ought to pursue and what actions they ought to perform. Business ethics is a branch of applied ethics; it studies the relationship of what is good and right to business.

It is often said that business and ethics don't mix. In business, some argue, profit takes first place. Business has its own rules and objectives, and ethical concepts, standards, and judgments are inappropriate to the business context.

But this view is fundamentally mistaken. Business is an economic institution, but like our economy as a whole it has a moral foundation. The free market system is a product of our convictions about the nature of the good life and the good society, about the fair distribution of goods and services, and about what kinds of goods and services to distribute. It is true that the goal of business has been profit, but profit making is not a morally neutral activity. Traditionally, we have encouraged business to pursue profits because we believed—rightly or wrongly—that profit seeking violated no rights and would be best for society as a whole. This conviction has been the source of business' legitimacy, our belief in its right to exist. In the past two decades, the traditional belief in business' contribution to the general welfare has been challenged; for many, business' connection with the moral foundation which justified it no longer seems clear. Distrust of business has increased; recent polls, for example, indicate that Americans believe that the ethical standards of business are lower than those of society as a whole. Many thinkers contend that business faces a true crisis of legitimacy. In such a climate an investigation of business values, of the moral dimension of business, and of the role of business in society becomes urgent. To undertake such an investigation is the task of business ethics. We view this task as taking place on four levels:

1. An ethical investigation of the context in which American business is conducted—that is, capitalism or the free market system. Does the system truly contribute to a good society and reflect our most important social values? In particular, is it a just system? What is economic justice? The selections included in Part One of this text explore the meaning of economic justice and the question of whether capitalism or socialism best embodies that ideal. It also suggests some specific ways in which ethical values have operated or should operate in business decision making.
2. An inquiry, within this broad economic context, into the nature and role of business organizations. Is the function

of business activity simply to make a profit? Does business have other sorts of obligations because of its vast power or relationship to other elements of society? How might corporate structure best reflect the nature and responsibilities of corporations? Such questions are taken up in Part Two of this text.

3. An examination of particular ethical issues which arise in the course of business activity, such as employee rights and duties, quality of working life, hiring practices, advertising and product safety, obligations to the environment, and operating in foreign countries. A range of such issues is covered in Parts Three and Four.

4. An examination and ethical assessment of the values which reside implicitly in business organizations and business activity in general, such as freedom of opportunity, economic growth, and material well-being. We pursue this endeavor throughout the text, and in Part Five we examine the development of a new corporate ethos where the value of ethical business decision making takes on its proper role.

Engaging in ethical reflection on business at each of these levels requires the use of ethical concepts, theories, and standards of judgment. The remainder of this introduction presents some of the most important principles of ethical theory, which could serve as possible frameworks for application in business contexts.

THE AMALGAMATED MACHINERY DILEMMA

Ted Brown is worried. A salesman for Amalgamated Machinery, he has been placed in charge of negotiating an important sale of construction equipment to the government of a small but rapidly developing nation. Deeply in debt, Amalgamated has staked its future on penetrating foreign markets. Ted's potential contract not only is a very large one; it could open the door to even bigger sales in the future. If he lands the contract, Ted's promotion in the firm is practically certain—and he has been convinced he would succeed until he speaks with a powerful government official who is involved in the negotiations. Ted's bid is looked upon very favorably, the official explains, and it is in fact the lowest. A $100,000 "commission fee" payable in cash to the official would clinch the deal. If Ted does not pay the fee, the official regrets that the contract will go to a competitor.

Ted knows that the sale is crucial to the well-being of his company. He believes that his customers would get the best possible deal by buying Amalgamated's equipment. And he knows that $100,000 is a trivial sum beside the potential profits represented by the contract. Yet, although he is aware that such payments are common practice in many countries, he has always felt that they were wrong, and has never before used them to secure a deal.

Ted Brown's dilemma is a fictitious one, but it is not far-fetched. Business people frequently feel torn between their desire to act in the interests of their company and their convictions about what is right. In a study reported by *Business Week* in 1977, 59 percent of the managers at Pitney Bowes and 70 percent of the managers at Uniroyal revealed that they felt pressured to compromise their personal ethical principles to achieve corporate goals.

What is the right decision for Ted to make? What are the most important factors for him to consider in making his decision? How does one determine which are most important? Such questions lead us into the area of ethical theory.

Ted might begin the decision process by considering the potential consequences of his choices. If he refuses to pay the bribe, his company will suffer a severe financial blow; stockholders will take a loss on their investment and some employees may lose their jobs. If he pays the official, his firm will be awarded the contract, he will get his promotion, the government will receive a good price on quality construction equipment, and the official will be $100,000 richer. If we assume that this payment is one of those declared illegal by the 1977 Foreign Corrupt Practices Act, then the scandal which would erupt if the bribe were discovered could hurt the company financially and ruin Ted's career. Provided the payment remains secret, however, it looks as if no harm could result from it.

Yet Ted still feels that bribery is wrong. He reflects that the practice violates the rules of the business game, which decree that one should obtain business only through the fair, free operation of the market system. The payment is also illegal, and although Ted has made no explicit promise, he feels that the rights of a citizen carry with them an obligation to obey the law. On the other hand, he has made a similar implicit promise to act in the best interests of his company.

ETHICAL RELATIVISM

Although we have identified a number of factors relevant to Ted's decision, these seem to have confused rather than simplified his dilemma. Does this mean that there is no rational way of deciding what is right in Ted's situation, that there is no universal standard to which we can appeal, that neither of the choices is better or worse than the other? Ted's colleagues might well challenge his belief that bribery is wrong, pointing out that it is standard practice in the developing nation.

The position that there is no one universal standard or set of standards by which to judge an action's morality is called *ethical relativism*. Ethical relativists may hold that the same act may be morally right for one society and morally wrong for another; or they may hold the more radical position that the same act can be right for one individual and wrong for another. At first glance ethical relativism appears persuasive. But many philosophers contend that it does not stand up well to closer scrutiny. In particular, they hold, it contradicts our everyday ethical experience and the way in which we act and speak about ethical problems and ethical judgments.

One way of stating the position of ethical relativism is to say that it holds that what a person or society *believes* is right *is* right for that person or society. But if this claim is true, it means that what a society believes is right and what is in fact right for that society are one and the same thing. In ordinary life, however, we are continually making distinctions between these two. Several cultures throughout history have believed in slavery, for example. Yet most of us would argue that slavery is not only wrong now, but was wrong then, in spite of cultural mores. Although we know that people's opinions about ethics differ widely, we do not believe that they are all correct. On the contrary, we often praise or blame other people for their ethical standards. We would not do this, it is argued, if we believed that ethical relativism is correct.

We might also ask what constitutes a "society" for the purposes of ethical relativism. If a minority group within a larger culture holds different ethical views from those of the majority, are their views wrong simply because they are in the minority? Or should that group be viewed as a society in its own right with an equally valid set of beliefs? If the minority is to be regarded as a separate society, ought not a dissenting group within the minority be seen in the same way? And should not each individual, as well, be looked upon as a society of sorts with a set of ethical beliefs which are right for himself or herself?

If this version of ethical relativism is true, however, no person can disagree with another person about ethics, because each person's opinion is equally right. In fact, if ethical relativism is true, there *is* no right or wrong in ethics apart from people's beliefs. We have no way of deciding whether one set of beliefs is any better than any other. No one can be mistaken about an ethical problem if ethical relativism is correct, for what a person believes is right *is* right for him or her. Again, these consequences seem to contradict the way we behave in real life since we habitually accuse ourselves and others of making mistakes on ethical issues.

In short, it is argued that if ethical relativism is correct, no comparative moral judgments are possible. We cannot say that any act or belief is better or worse from a moral perspective than any other. Such comparative judgments seem to require the very thing that ethical relativism denies: a universal ethical principle, standard, or framework. But much of our ethical reasoning is the making of comparative judgments. It is the weighing of alternatives, the choice of which values to embrace and the selection of the course of action which best expresses and upholds these values. For this reason some argue that if ethical relativism is true, morality itself is impossible.

Our experience, however, indicates that we do disagree about moral issues, we do make mistakes in ethical choices, and we do make comparative ethical judgments. Moreover, we feel that this ethical dimension is a crucial dimension of human life. Of course, we may be operating under a gigantic illusion. But the fact that our moral experience not only does not support but seems to contradict ethical relativism gives us strong reasons for rejecting the theory.

This does not mean that it is always easy to decide what is right or that there are clear and undisputed criteria for doing so. But it does mean that ethical principles are either right or wrong, and can be attacked or defended with rational arguments. Let us investigate some of these principles and assess their strength as guides to ethical decision making.

As we examine the considerations raised during Ted's reflection on his dilemma, it can be seen that they fall into two distinct groups. One group is concerned with the consequences of Ted's choices—to his company, to the developing nation, to himself, and so on; the other raises issues regarding duties, promises, obligations. Some ethical theorists, called *consequentialists,* hold that the consequences of an action are the sole factors to be taken into account in determining whether that action is right or wrong. For consequentialists, good consequences make right actions. Those who conclude that Ted ought to pay the official because more benefit than harm would result from his action are making a judgment based on consequentialist standards. Others, called *deontologists* (a term derived from the Greek word meaning duty), deny the consequentialist claim. Not all actions which produce good results are right actions, deontologists argue, and some right actions may even produce unpleasant results for ourselves and others. A right action is right not solely because of its consequences, but because it satisfies the demands of justice, because it respects the rights of others, or because we have promised to perform it. Ted is expressing deontological reservations when he feels that in spite of the good consequences it might produce, succumbing to the demands of the government official is wrong.

Consequentialist and deontological theories represent two different processes for making ethical judgments. All of us operate under some such theory, although we rarely make the theory explicit to ourselves and often fail to apply it systematically. Spelled out and applied consistently, ethical theories can serve as guidelines for disciplined and informed ethical decision making. Below we examine two consequentialist theories—egoism and utilitarianism—and the deontological theory of Immanuel Kant.

ETHICAL EGOISM

Ethical egoism states that every person ought always to act so as to promote the greatest possible balance of good over evil for himself or herself. From an egoistic perspective, an act contrary to one's self-interest is an immoral act. That this is true does not mean that an egoist never takes the interests of others into account. On the contrary; most egoists argue that others' interests should be respected, because treating others well promotes our self-interest in the long run.

An egoist, then, would advise Ted to act in his own best interest—or, in his capacity as an agent of Amalgamated Machinery, in the best interest of the company. If Ted takes this advice, it need not mean that he will bribe the government official. Egoists strive to maximize long-term, not merely short-term, benefits; Ted may decide that the risks to his reputation and that of his company override the potential benefits of the payment. Or he may decide that the guilt he would suffer for having compromised his personal beliefs would outweigh the pleasure he would receive from his promotion, although it is difficult to see why he would feel guilty for doing the right (that is, the egoistic) thing.

Does egoism have a special place in business decision making? If the good mentioned in the egoist maxim is interpreted to mean profit or efficiency, ethical egoism might be seen as the standard by which business and businesspeople have traditionally judged their behavior in a free market system. Some have interpreted economist Milton Friedman's claim that the only obligation of business is to increase its profits as an expression of this traditional view. Following this interpretation, Friedman is arguing not that "good ethics is good business," but that "good business is good ethics." He sees altruistic acts on the part of business as a violation of business' function and obligations. This does not mean that business should be prohibited from performing acts which benefit others. If a business makes costly improvements in the working conditions of its employees, for example, in order to increase productivity, decrease turnover, and improve long-run efficiency, it would win the ethical egoist's approval.

Ethical egoism is often found in conjunction with a theory termed *psychological egoism*. While ethical egoism is a normative theory stating how people *ought* to behave, psychological egoism is a descriptive theory which claims that people *do in fact* act solely to promote their own interest. It is important to distinguish between the two theories, but it is also easy to see their connection: If psychological egoism is true, it is difficult to see how people could behave other than egoistically. To tell them that they ought to do so is futile. It looks as if ethical egoism is the only viable ethical theory if psychological egoism is correct.

Is psychological egoism correct, however? Most of us believe that we have observed people performing acts in order to benefit others; we probably feel that we have performed such acts ourselves. Psychological egoism counters this belief with the assertion that even people who perform acts which benefit others do so for their own satisfaction. One might argue that psychological egoism has mistaken the satisfaction which accompanies an act which benefits others for the motive of that act. Although we may receive happiness or pleasure from doing things for others, it does not follow that the pleasure is the motive or object of our action, that we want to do things for others because of the pleasure we will receive. Perhaps the benevolent act itself is our goal, and we receive pleasure from it because we wanted to do it.

Psychological egoism has often been advanced in support of ethical egoism. But some argue that what it does is make ethical egoism—and, ultimately, all ethics—superfluous. If people always act in their own self-interest, it is not necessary to tell them that they ought to do so. We do not advise stones to fall to the earth when dropped or rivers to flow downstream. Nor does it make much sense to tell people that they ought to do what they are incapable of doing. Traditionally, ethics has assumed that clashes between different interests are bound to occur. If this is true, there will be times when the right thing to do is to sacrifice one's own interest for the interests of others. But psychological egoism asserts that people are not capable of such actions. If psychological egoism is correct, ethical reflection and ethical rules seem futile.

Whether psychological egoism is true or not, the suggestion that interests may clash points to some problems with ethical egoism itself as a moral theory. Some egoists attempt to circumvent these problems with the claim that, ultimately, interests do not conflict, and that apparent oppositions can be resolved by free exchange among interested parties. But even one committed to this view could not deny that *perceived* conflicts of interest occur frequently. Some critics claim that ethical egoism provides no way of settling competing claims when they do arise, no way of determining whether one interest is more important than another. In part this is because in an egoistic society, no one occupies a *disinterested* position, which is the same reason an egoist is not equipped to give advice or to pass moral judgments on other people's actions. One could even say that an egoist cannot consistently advise others to be egoists and to pursue their own self-interest. If one is truly committed to egoism one should tell others that they ought to maximize the egoist's well-being, and not their own. Ethical egoism, then, appears self-contradictory.

It is often argued that people ought to behave egoistically because if they do, it will promote the general welfare. It is important, however, to note that this defense of ethical egoism is not itself an egoistic one. It implies that there is a different, nonegoistic basis for the rightness or wrongness of actions—their consequences for society as a whole. We have moved from egoism to utilitarianism.

UTILITARIANISM

This section examines primarily the utilitarianism of Jeremy Bentham (1748–1832), generally acknowledged as the founder of utilitarianism. Bentham argued that when evaluating an action or making a choice one ought to take into account not only the consequences of that action to oneself, but its consequences for all those affected by the act as well. Utilitarianism as Bentham conceived it, then, states that people ought to act so as to promote the greatest *total* balance of good over evil, or the greatest good for the greatest number.

Utilitarians come in two varieties. *Act utilitarians* hold that in every situation one ought to act so as to maximize total good, even if doing so means violating a rule which, when followed, generally promotes social welfare. Such rules, act utilitarians argue, are simply guidelines: They can—in fact, they must—be broken if to do so leads to the public good. *Rule utilitarians,* on the other hand, use the utilitarian principle to develop rules which they believe are in the public interest. They claim that one should obey these rules even when doing so does not lead to the best consequences, for the presence of the rule itself and consistent adherence to it does promote the general welfare.

A rule utilitarian might argue, for example, that laws against bribery are in the best interest of society. For this reason, Ted ought not to bribe the government official, even though in his particular case to agree to the bribe would produce more good than harm. An act utilitarian would counter that although it is often in the best interests of society to obey the rule against bribery, Ted's case is an exception. To insist that he obey the law violates the fundamental demand of utilitarianism that we maximize total good. An act utilitarian would probably advise Ted to pay the official.

We can see the utilitarian principle at work in the technique of cost-benefit analysis, a decision-making process familiar to businesspeople and often used as a guide to fair public policy decisions. Utilitarianism for Bentham is, in fact, a species of cost-benefit analysis, in which the painful consequences of an act are subtracted from the pleasurable ones, and the total reveals the act's moral quality.

Not all utilitarians agree as to what constitutes the "good" they believe should be maximized. Some claim that there are a number of different goods; truth, beauty, health, peace, and freedom might count as some of them. As a *hedonistic utilitarian,* Bentham believes that ultimately there is only one good—pleasure or happiness—and that right actions are those which maximize total pleasure or happiness.

If hedonistic utilitarianism is to work, we must find an accurate way of measuring people's pleasure or happiness so as to arrive at a sum total. But this task is more difficult than it might seem, and an examination of these measurement problems reveals some weaknesses in utilitarianism as a moral theory. How exactly does one go about measuring the costs and benefits of an action? What is to be the unit of measurement? Some thinkers have suggested that, ultimately, all costs and benefits can be expressed in terms of dollars. But what about things that are not bought and sold, and therefore have no price on the market? How do we quantify such benefits as job satisfaction, equality, or the cost of a human life?

Bentham himself proposed a less rigorous measurement device which he termed the hedonic calculus. By taking into account the intensity, duration, certainty or uncertainty, nearness or remoteness, fecundity, purity, and extent of the happiness produced by an act, he claimed, one could determine individual units of happiness and subtract from them units of unhappiness to arrive at a quantitative total.

But is Bentham's calculus really adequate? Can the attempt to quantify the process of ethical judgment ever be satisfactory? Suppose for a moment that Ted does not really have to pay the government official in order to obtain the contract he wants, but that he could secure it by honest means. Suppose also that the hedonic calculus has revealed no difference in the sum total of happiness produced by either act. If Ted decides not to pay the official, the pleasure received by his company because of the savings is balanced by the official's unhappiness at his loss and vice versa. Bentham's version of utilitarianism would, in this case, see no difference between the two acts. Although by making one choice Ted is obtaining the sale honestly and by making the other he is not, the hedonic calculus has no means of taking this fact into account. Hedonistic utilitarianism would judge the two acts morally identical, because they produce the same sum total of good.

John Stuart Mill (1806–1873) objected to this failure of Bentham's utilitarianism to take account of the difference between an honest and a dishonest act which produce the same results. The problem with the hedonic calculus, he believed, was that it did not recognize the fact that pleasure or happiness differs in quality as well as in quantity. Some forms of happiness are more noble than others, he argued; some are achieved by ethical, some by unethical means. Mill thought the failing could be remedied by introducing the element of quality into the hedonic calculus. But his doing so raised as many problems as it solved. The purpose of the hedonic calculus as designed by Bentham was to express the ethical quality of an act in terms of the quantity of happiness it produces. The attempt to reduce quality to quantity is at the core of hedonistic utilitarianism. Mill's introduction of quality into the hedonic calculus suggests that an act can be good or bad independently of the amount of pleasure it produces, and thus contradicts the fundamental principle of utilitarianism. In order to define quality, Mill would have to go outside the bounds of utilitarian theory. As an attempt to revise hedonistic utilitarianism, therefore, Mill's effort seems to fail.

Because introducing the criterion of quality into a utilitarian framework poses so many difficulties, it has been argued that utilitarianism justifies—and perhaps even demands—acts which seem to us to be unjust or immoral. Imagine, for example, a group of thugs who receive their enjoyment from molesting small children. If the hedonic calculus revealed that the thugs receive more personal pleasure from their actions than their victims receive pain, would the thugs win utilitarian approval? Another way of expressing this objection to utilitarianism is to make the claim that people have *rights* which ought not to be violated even when doing so results in a greater sum total of good. It is argued that utilitarianism is incapable of respecting such rights, because they can always be overridden in favor of an act or rule which maximizes total good.

A final objection to utilitarianism is that while it insists that total good be maximized, it tells us nothing about the distribution of this good. There seems to be no reason for utilitarians to disapprove of a slave-owning society, for example, if it could be shown that such a society provided a larger sum of goodness than one in which all people are treated as equals. A familiar criticism of capitalism is that the rich become richer at the expense of the poor; although the sum total of well-being may be maximized, the system is *unjust*. As was the case with rights, utilitarianism seems to have no place in its framework for justice. Claims of justice are always subordinate to the imperative to maximize the balance of good over evil.

It seems to be true that the consequences of an action play an important part in determining whether that action is right or wrong. But egoism's failure to acknowledge that it is sometimes our duty to perform acts which are not in our own interest and utilitarianism's inability to take into account rights and justice suggest that the rightness of an action does not depend solely upon its consequences—for ourselves or for others. Other nonconsequentialist factors may also have a bearing on the moral quality of actions. For an approach which does take such factors into account we turn to the deontological theory of Immanuel Kant.

KANT'S CATEGORICAL IMPERATIVE

In contrast to the consequentialists, Immanuel Kant (1724–1804) holds that one ought to perform right actions not because they will produce good results, but because it is our *duty* to do so. For Kant, moral commands are *categorical imperatives;* that is, they are absolute and unconditional, binding for us regardless of the consequences obedience to them brings about. Ultimately, Kant argues, there is only one categorical imperative. Below we discuss two of his major formulations of this ethical principle.

In our discussion of relativism above, we noted the need for a universal moral principle or set of principles for use in making ethical judgments. For Kant this idea of universality is at the heart of morality, and it serves as the litmus test for immoral action in his first expression of the categorical imperative. In making an ethical decision about action, Kant holds, we should ask ourselves whether we would be willing to have everyone take that action. If we are not willing to permit the universal practice of the action, it is immoral. Kant claims that an act is not moral unless it can be made into a universal law.

If I am contemplating a deceptive advertisement in order to sell a product, for example, I must be willing to endorse a world in which all people lie when it seems to their advantage to do so. Not only would we not wish to see unethical behavior practiced universally; according to Kant, many principles cannot even be *conceived* of as universal. If everyone were entitled to lie, one would never be able to tell if a person is lying or telling the truth. Under such circumstances, the very practice of truth telling is undermined and lying ceases to be advantageous.

Kant would advise Ted not to pay the government official in order to obtain his contract, not because to do so would produce bad consequences, but because the universal practice of bribery would undermine the very basis of business itself. Other rules governing business practices might be justified on similar grounds. Cheating, stealing, breaking contracts, price-fixing, and so on erode the moral backdrop of business and make business activity impossible. If everyone engages in such activities, there is no longer any advantage in doing so. Kant's analysis reveals that the unethical person exempts himself or herself from moral laws without being willing to grant similar privileges to others. He or she is in effect a parasite on the very ethical system he or she violates. Unethical behavior is possible and advantageous only in an *ethical* society. When universalized, it contradicts itself. We should act only on those principles, Kant maintains, which we would be willing to see become universal law.

In a second formulation of the categorical imperative, Kant turns his attention to the rights of human beings. One ought always to act, he claims, so as to treat all human beings as ends in themselves, and never only as means to an end. Both egoism and utilitarianism seem to violate this principle. For the egoist, others have value only insofar as they promote the egoist's self-interest; for the utilitarian, every person appears to be a means for the maximization of good. Kant recognizes that we must often use others as means to an end, as we do, for example, when we hire them to do a job for us. But he emphasizes that they also have a value in and of themselves which we have a duty to respect.

Kant's respect for persons derives from the fact that they are capable of recognizing and choosing to obey moral laws, and he insists upon a close connection between freedom and morality. In a denial of psychological egoism, Kant claims that human beings are the only creatures capable of performing an act not because it is to their advantage, but because duty requires it. It is in making choices based on duty that we take full possession of our freedom, argues Kant. Kant turns his attention away, then, from the *products* of our choice—their results for oneself or for others— and toward the *process* of choice itself. To act out of duty in obedience to the categorical imperative is for Kant what it means to be moral.

Although it offers some significant advantages over consequentialism, Kant's theory is not without its difficulties. An attempt to apply the first formulation of the categorical imperative to actual problems reveals its imprecisions. We have stated above that Kant would prohibit Ted from bribing the official to obtain his contract, because bribery cannot be adopted as a universal practice without contradiction. But suppose that the act Ted chooses to put to Kant's test is not bribery in general, but bribery with qualifications, such as bribery to save one's company from bankruptcy or bribery which secures the best deal for a client. It is less clear whether Ted would be willing to permit these acts on the part of other companies or whether they contradict themselves when universalized. To express the principle of one's action accurately and to test it is not an easy task. It might be possible to describe immoral actions in so specific a way that they would pass Kant's tests, even if, when couched in general terms, they violate the categorical imperative.

A second criticism often directed at Kant is that although he provides us with a rational basis for rights and duties, he does not take into account that duties can conflict, and he does not offer a framework for resolving such conflicts. Businesspeople often feel torn between their duty to their company and their duty to society at large, for example. Although Kant would undoubtedly acknowledge that every person has a right to nondiscriminatory treatment in hiring, he might also assert that those who have been unfairly treated in the past have a right to be compensated for the injustice. What do we do, however, if the only way of compensating minorities and the disadvantaged turns out to involve discrimination against white males? Both compensating the victims of past injustice and refraining from injustice in the present seem commanded by the categorical imperative. What should we do when faced with such conflicts? Consequentialists would argue that deontologists provide no satisfactory answer to this question.

CONCLUSION

Each of the ethical theories we have considered appears to have some weaknesses. Because they identify the rightness of an act with the good results it produces, consequentialist theories can overlook claims of rights and justice and the intrinsic worth of all human beings. Kant's theory seems ambiguous in places and it fails to tell us how to deal with the problem of conflicting rights, conflicting duties. Whether these theories are totally incompatible is an ongoing debate and probably stated in their most extreme form they are. There may be ways, however, of drawing fruitfully on each theory in constructing a moral framework from which to make judgments in business. We are not suggesting that one adopt a naive eclecticism, extracting inconsistent parts from each, but one might find meaningful aspects to each position in formulating a comprehensive moral point of view. Utilitarianism, for example, could act as a check on each individual's pursuit of his or her own self-interest; Kantianism suggests some limits beyond which we ought not to go, even to maximize the sum total of good; conflicts between duties and rights which cannot be resolved within a Kantian framework might be illuminated by consequentialist reflection.

A sense of the relationship among ethical theories will become clearer as we begin to explore the issues which follow. Business can serve as a field for testing the strength of ethical theories and their ability to shed light on concrete problems. The further development of such a dialogue between theory and practice is one of the purposes served by a study of business ethics.

PART ONE

Ethics and Business: From Theory to Practice

In exploring the ethical dimensions of business activity it is not always enough to focus attention on specific ethical problems. Such issues as the rights and duties of employees, product liability, and the responsibility of business to the environment arise in the context of a comprehensive economic system which deeply influences our values and structures the range of choices available to us. Often we will find that the most important ethical question is not "What is right or wrong in this particular situation?" but rather "What is the ethical status of a situation which forces such a choice on the agent?" or "How can it be restructured to provide a more satisfactory climate for ethical decision making?" Some ethical problems are not isolated, but systemic; for this reason Chapter 2 of this part examines the free market system itself from an ethical perspective. What we seek when we evaluate economic systems ethically, at least in part, is a framework for business transactions and decisions, a set of procedures which, if followed, will generally bring about just results. Justice of this kind—called procedural justice—can be illustrated by the familiar method of dividing a piece of cake between two children: Assuming that the two should receive equal slices, if one child cuts the cake and the other chooses the first slice, justice should be served. Not all just procedures produce as completely just results as this one does. But in choosing an economic system we look for one which provides as much justice as possible. Traditionally, it has been held in America that capitalism is such a system; critics challenge this claim. An examination of this controversy requires a clear conception of what justice is, and Chapter 1 provides the groundwork for such a conception by presenting three important theories of economic justice.

Even if the free market system is a just one it may not mean that every event which occurs according to the rules of the system is just. Just procedures are not always sufficient to ensure just results. Suppose, for example, that a person owns one of the five waterholes on an island and that the other four unexpectedly dry up, leaving the owner with a monopoly over the water supply and the opportunity to charge exorbitantly high prices for water. It might be argued that even if the owner of the waterhole acquired it legally, did not conspire to monopolize, and allowed his prices to be determined by the fluctuations of the market, this situation is unjust. Although procedural justice may be necessary to bring about ethical outcomes, it may not be sufficient *by itself* to do so. Although a just economic system is essential for an ethical business climate, we may also find it necessary to examine the relationships and transactions which take place within the system and to make ethical reasoning a part of business decision making at a more specific, less general level. Chapter Three suggests some ways in which this might be done.

DISTRIBUTIVE JUSTICE

Questions of economic justice arise when people find themselves in competition for scarce resources—wealth, income, jobs, food, housing. If there are not enough of society's benefits—and too many of society's burdens—to satisfy everyone, we must ask how to distribute these benefits and burdens fairly. One of the most important problems of economic justice, then, is that of the fair distribution of limited commodities.

What does it mean to distribute things justly or fairly? To do justice is to give each person what he or she deserves or is owed. If those who have the most in a society deserve the most and those who have the least deserve the least, that society is a just one. If not, it is unjust. But what makes one person more, another less, deserving?

Philosophers have offered a wide range of criteria for determining who deserves what. One suggestion is that everyone deserves an equal share. Others hold that benefits and burdens should be distributed on the basis of need, merit, effort or hard work, or contribution to society. John Rawls, Robert Nozick, and J. J. C. Smart each emphasize one or more of these criteria in constructing a theory of economic justice.

The theory of economic justice underlying American capitalism has tended to emphasize contribution to society, along with merit and hard work, as the basis of distribution. We do not expect everyone to end up with an equal share of benefits and burdens under a capitalist system. But supporters of capitalism hold that those who receive more do so because of their greater contribution, and that for this reason the inequalities are just. Recalling the Kantian ethical principles examined in the general introduction to the text, however, it might be argued that rewarding people on the basis of what they contribute to the general welfare implies treating them as means to an end rather than as ends in themselves and overlooks the intrinsic value of persons. Each person's contribution, furthermore, depends largely on inborn skills and qualities and circumstances which permit the development of these traits. Ought people to be rewarded in proportion to accidents of birth over which they have no control? Some philosophers, like John Rawls, think not.

As an egalitarian, Rawls believes that there are no characteristics which make one person more deserving than another; there are no differences between people which justify inequalities in the distribution of social benefits and burdens. Everyone deserves an equal share. That this is true does not mean that Rawls finds all inequalities unjust; but his theory permits only inequalities which benefit everyone and to which everyone has an equal opportunity.

Rawls' principles of distribution are just, he claims, because they are the principles which would be chosen by a group of rational persons designing a society—providing they are ignorant of their own abilities, preferences, and eventual social position. We ought to choose our principles of justice, Rawls argues, from behind a "veil of ignorance"—a position strikingly similar to that of the child who cuts the cake evenly, unsure of which piece he or she will eventually have. Although all those in Rawls' hypothetical situation seek to protect their own interest, they are prevented from choosing a principle of distribution which will benefit themselves at the expense of others. Thus they are likely to reject a utilitarian principle of justice under which the happiness of a few might be sacrificed to maximize total well-being or a notion of justice in which distribution depends in part upon luck, skill, natural endowments, or social position. Rawls believes that they would select egalitarian principles.

Some critics have challenged Rawls' claim that rational persons acting from behind a veil of ignorance would choose egalitarian principles of justice. Rawls assumes that all people are egoists, and he fails to take account of the gamblers among us. Others ask whether the choice of egalitarian principles by uninformed egoists is really enough to justify them ethically. A possible defense of Rawls' argument involves an appeal to the Kantian ethical principle examined in the introduction to the text. Kant held that one test of the ethical acceptability of a principle is whether it can be made into a universal law without contradiction. By placing us behind a hypothetical veil of ignorance, Rawls asks us to choose principles of justice which apply to ourselves and all others equally. As a universal law, Rawls seems to be saying, only the egalitarian theory of justice is fully consistent.

Because he gives everyone a voice in what the principle of justice is to be, and because equal treatment seems to recognize every person's intrinsic worth, Rawls' theory of justice also seems to satisfy the second Kantian test, the treatment of all people as ends in themselves. It is not clear, however, that the egalitarian way is the only way to treat people as ends in themselves. Robert Nozick's libertarianism, which emphasizes individual rights instead of equal distribution, might also be susceptible to a Kantian defense.

Unlike Rawls, Nozick focuses his attention not on what each person ends up with, but on how each person acquired what he or she has. Justice for Nozick is historical; it resides in the *process* of acquisition. A theory of justice thus consists of setting forth rules for just acquisition, and something which has been justly acquired justly belongs to its owner even if this means that some people will receive a far greater share of benefits or burdens than others.

Nozick objects to the attempt to bring about justice by imposing a preconceived pattern of distribution such as the egalitarian one because he believes that no such pattern can be realized without violating people's rights. As the word *libertarian* suggests, the right most heavily emphasized by Nozick is that of freedom, or noninterference. Interference, he holds, is permitted only when the rights of others are being violated. Second is the right to property which has been justly acquired. Under a libertarian theory of justice, taxation to redistribute and equalize wealth is a violation of human rights, an appropriation of the fruit of other people's freedom akin to forced labor. One might also look upon it as the treatment of others as means. The only way to treat people as ends in themselves, a libertarian might argue, is to grant them freedom from coercion. The only just pattern of distribution, libertarians claim, is not a pattern at all, but the product of a multitude of free, individual choices.

Critics of the libertarian theory generally attack what they view as its truncated conception of human rights. It may be true, they say, that persons have rights of noninterference. But surely there are other human rights more positive in nature. If persons have a right to life, for example, it could be argued that they also have a right to certain things they need in order to live: food, clothing, shelter, and so on. If this is true, their right to these things might sometimes override someone else's right to noninterference. For example, Nozick himself admits that it is unjust for one person to appropriate the entire supply of something necessary for life, as in the example of the waterhole mentioned above. If it is correct that there are positive rights which supersede the right to noninterference, libertarianism needs reexamining.

J. J. C. Smart's utilitarian theory of justice differs from both Nozick's and Rawls' in that it neither attempts to make distribution conform to a specific pattern nor focuses on the process by which distribution takes place. As a utilitarian, Smart is concerned with the maximization of happiness or pleasure, and approves of any distribution of goods which accomplishes this goal. Thus utilitarian justice could be compatible with either an equal or an unequal distribution of goods, depending on which of the two is shown to provide the greatest total happiness. Although in general Smart believes that an egalitarian distribution of benefits and burdens is the most likely to maximize happiness, he is in no way committed to equality as a principle of distribution; on the contrary, if he were to find that extreme inequalities were what maximized happiness or that the sum total of happiness would be increased if a few were sacrificed for the good of the greatest number, he would be committed to these strategies. Utilitarianism, in short, is interested in the *maximization* of happiness and not in its distribution.

Some thinkers find utilitarianism's stress on the sum total of happiness to be incompatible with the very idea of justice, and Smart admits that justice is only a subordinate interest for utilitarians. Under utilitarianism, people may be denied what they deserve because that denial increases total happiness.

JUSTICE AND ECONOMIC SYSTEMS

Rawls, Nozick, and Smart offer three different theories of economic justice. They have made no claims, however, about how their principles of justice might best be embodied in an economic system. Rawls, for example, might assert that his theory is compatible with both capitalism and socialism. In Chapter 2 we examine the soundness of the concepts of justice underlying two quite different economic systems. Irving Kristol offers a defense of what he views as the capitalist conception of justice; Carl Cohen's article presents the basic tenets of socialism.

Perhaps the two most important characteristics of capitalism are (1) the private ownership of the means of production (as opposed to common or government ownership), such that most of us must work for others and earn wages to make a living, and (2) a free market system, in which prices and wages are not controlled by the government or by a small, powerful group, but are allowed to fluctuate. The key word here is freedom. Essential to the system is free competition: Workers must be able to move freely from job to job as they choose, and everyone must be free to enter the market to buy and sell. It is on this second characteristic which Kristol focuses in his discussion of capitalism.

Clearly, a free market system will not provide everyone with an equal share of social benefits and burdens; indeed, the conception of justice that lies at the heart of capitalism, Kristol claims, is a fundamentally *anti*egalitarian one. Equality of rights and equality of opportunity are essential to capitalism, but the system makes no guarantee of economic equality. It is interesting to note that Kristol does not believe that equality of opportunity requires us to give special compensation to the disadvantaged, as Rawls does. For Kristol, equality of opportunity means only that there are no *official* barriers to opportunity. Luck will thus play an important role in success under a capitalist system.

But the fact that capitalism is consistent with economic inequality, Kristol argues, does not make it unfair. He claims that the only way to achieve economic equality is through the redistribution of wealth by a centralized government authority—a solution that violates individual liberty. Like Nozick, Kristol defends the capitalist conception of justice because he believes that it best respects people's rights and maximizes freedom.

Capitalism not only protects liberty, Kristol argues. Even though inequalities do exist in a capitalist system, everyone, or nearly everyone, is better off than he or she would be under a different economic system. A capitalist economy maximizes efficiency, for example, and provides a far greater range of goods and services than a planned economy does. If capitalism truly benefits everybody, as Kristol claims, it might win approval not only from Nozick, but from Rawls and Smart as well.

Does everyone really benefit under a capitalist system, however? Some critics argue that the truth of this claim depends on the freedom of the market—a freedom, they hold, that is largely illusory. Because of limitations due to lack of education, poverty, or social position, it is claimed, workers are not free to move from job to job and can thus become trapped in work that is hazardous or low-paying. The influence of powerful, giant corporations skews the market: Individuals are not able to compete on the same terms as large conglomerates, and thus competition is not truly free. Kristol's picture of capitalism, critics might say, fails to take account of the very real constraints felt by people even in a free market system. For this reason it is not clear that every person is better off in a capitalist economy.

These objections do not challenge the *concept* of justice presented by Kristol; they suggest only that capitalist systems fail to achieve the justice they claim. But criticisms have also been leveled at the idea of justice that underlies capitalism. Capitalist justice as Kristol describes it ignores claims of need, for example. People are free to give to others in a capitalist economy, but the needy have no real right to demand that their needs be satisfied. Thus, critics have concluded, capitalism sanctions poverty and extreme inequalities and pits human beings against each other in a fierce competitive struggle. Even if everyone does benefit from a capitalist economy, it might be argued, it is not clear that everyone receives what he or she *deserves*—the criterion we referred to earlier as the earmark of justice.

Capitalism not only fails to reward people equally, Kristol tells us; it also fails to reward them in proportion to their merit, hard work, or contribution to society. In a capitalist system, people are rewarded solely for their contribution to the economy as defined by the market. Again, for Kristol this is one of the strengths of an admittedly imperfect system, for to achieve distributions according to criteria such as merit or hard work would require restrictions on freedom and centralized planning on a scope and scale that he could not tolerate.

In contrast, Carl Cohen explains, socialists believe that extensive planning should be undertaken in the interest of social justice. In part, it is because capitalism is hostile to such planning that socialists reject it.

According to Cohen, socialists object to capitalism because it is consistent with a high degree of inequality. Placing ownership in private hands, socialists believe, creates a class system in which wealth is concentrated in the hands of a few, and the rich get richer at the expense of the poor. These inequalities lead to inequalities in liberty and power as well. According to socialists, Cohen explains, a capitalist society can never be truly democratic, even in a democratic political system, because the wealthy few are far more free and powerful than others.

These problems can be solved, socialists claim, by public ownership of the means of production and careful, systematic planning. Public ownership would eliminate the need for private profit, decrease prices, and allow enterprises to better serve the public. Planning would direct the economy for the public interest, rather than allow it to be controlled randomly by the self-interested actions of a few. Socialists do not believe that planning will interfere with individual liberty and democracy, Cohen explains. Rather, socialists are committed to *democratic* planning in which the people vote to determine economic goals and directions. In fact, socialism as Cohen presents it sees itself as more democratic than capitalism, because it involves the extension of democracy from the political into the economic arena.

Richard Titmuss provides us with the unusual opportunity to compare the advantages of market and nonmarket systems of distribution with respect to one essential commodity—human blood. He compares blood distribution in the United States, which at the time of his study had a predominantly market system of blood distribution, with Great Britain, where a voluntary donor system prevails. Although we would expect a pure market system to maximize efficiency and to provide a good quality product at a good price, Titmuss states, a commercialized blood market fails on both counts. It is far more likely to distribute contaminated blood than a voluntary donor system, it produces far greater waste, and the effort to control these problems can inflate the price of blood by a factor of five to fifteen. Higher prices mean that in some cases, the poor cannot afford the blood they need. In addition, argues Titmuss, a commercialized blood system encourages lack of trust, discord, and action from self-interest, and allows us to feel that we have no obligation to give to others; it discourages the expression of altruism and erodes a sense of community.

Titmuss' findings raise a range of questions concerning distributive justice and systems of distribution, some of which have already been touched upon by Rawls, Nozick, Smart, Kristol, and Cohen. Is a free market system a just means of distributing scarce commodities? Is blood, an essential for human life, something to which everyone has a right regardless of the workings of the market? Do Titmuss' results reveal some fundamental weaknesses in market systems of distribution or is blood too unique a commodity for them to be conclusive?

FROM THEORY TO PRACTICE

In Chapter 3 we turn from an examination of the justice of economic systems to an investigation of ethical business decision making within the system, at a concrete, specific level. Kermit Vandivier's discussion of his own part in the B.F. Goodrich aircraft brake scandal highlights the importance of such an investigation. Striking in Goodrich's decision to market a defective brake are the lack of clarity concerning corporate values, the evasion of responsibility, and the refusal or inability to engage in ethical reflection exhibited by those involved. Although Vandivier and his associates recognized that they were trapped in an ethical dilemma, they lacked the tools to state this dilemma clearly and to make their concerns impact upon corporate policy in an effective way.

Verne Henderson, Laura Nash, and Steven Kelman discuss some ways in which ethical concerns can be and have been significant in business decisions. Henderson offers a conceptual framework for use in clarifying the ethical dimensions of a situation. He believes that the incorporation of ethical concerns into a hierarchy of multiple goals, the selection of appropriate methods for achieving these goals, the development of an awareness of motives, and a review of the potential consequences of an act comprise a decision-making process which could enable business managers to remain sensitive to the interests of all their constituencies. Nash focuses on the process of clarifying corporate values and embedding them in company policy. She offers a list of twelve questions which, when asked regularly on a companywide basis, can help to build a cohesive corporate "character," create an ethical strategy for the corporation, and implement a corporate "conscience." Some of her questions, such as "What is your intention in making this decision?" and "How does this intention compare with the probable results?," echo concerns of Henderson's. Others are reminiscent of Kant's principles, discussed in the general introduction to the text: "How would you define the problem if you stood on the other side of the fence?" or "Under what conditions would you allow exceptions to your stand?" If Henderson's and Nash's guidelines had been incorporated into B.F. Goodrich's corporate policy, they might have clarified Vandivier's dilemma considerably. "Training for Ethical Management at Cummins Engine" describes one company's attempt to integrate some of the ethical principles mentioned in this part into management decisions. Cummins Engine starts with the rule "do not harm" and refines it to arrive at a fully developed notion of responsibility and a list of basic moral principles.

Kelman sees in an already widely used technique for business decision making—cost-benefit analysis—a close resemblance to the utilitarian principle examined in the general introduction. He uses theoretical ethics to illuminate cost-benefit analysis and to argue for his claim that it should not be used as the sole tool in making ethical decisions. Commitment to cost-benefit analysis as Kelman describes it implies the belief that costs and benefits should be totaled and weighed against each other in making a decision, that an act should not be undertaken unless its benefits exceed its costs, and that benefits and costs must be assigned dollar values so that they can be compared on a common scale.

We have already encountered the primary objections to utilitarianism in the introduction to the text; Kelman reiterates some of these. Utilitarianism identifies what is right with what maximizes benefits and minimizes costs, Kelman explains. But he argues that there are instances—those which involve the breaking of a promise, for example, or the violation of a human right—in which an act may be wrong even if its benefits outweigh its costs. Kelman cites examples to illustrate his claim that the utilitarian principle permits or even requires some actions which we are inclined to feel are morally repugnant.

Kelman also challenges the possibility of placing dollar values on nonmarket items such as clean air, health and safety, and human life. And even if it were possible to determine prices for these goods which truly reflect their value to society, he holds, it would not be advisable to do so. Certain items like life and health are "priceless," he argues, and the very act of placing a price on them may lower their perceived value in society. Kelman fears that placing a price on things declares that they are for sale; thus a worker's health may be traded because its dollar value is less than that of the equipment required to protect it. Cost-benefit analysis is particularly inappropriate, Kelman argues, when such "specially valued things" are at stake.

But what happens when a decision must be made which balances the claims of more than one specially valued thing? A decision about environmental quality, for example, may be more than a trade-off between clean air and profits; it may also impact on the jobs of a number of workers. Moreover, people specially value a variety of different goods. How are we to decide whose claims receive preference? Critics James DeLong and Robert Nisbet point out that Kelman has failed to provide guidelines for decision making in such areas. Only some form of cost-benefit analysis, they argue, can settle competing claims regarding specially valued things. Readers interested in pursuing the issue of cost-benefit analysis might wish to look at Mark Sagoff's article on the environment in Chapter 12, Kelman's discussion of government regulation in Chapter 13, and the Ford Pinto case—one of the most famous examples of the use of cost-benefit analysis—at the end of Part Four.

CHAPTER 1

Theories of Economic Justice

READINGS FOR CHAPTER ONE

John Rawls
Justice as Fairness
34

Robert Nozick
Distributive Justice
41

J.J.C.Smart
Distributive Justice and Utilitarianism
48

Justice as Fairness

John Rawls*

THE MAIN IDEA OF THE THEORY OF JUSTICE

My aim is to present a conception of justice which generalizes and carries to a higher level of abstraction the familiar theory of the social contract as found, say, in Locke, Rousseau, and Kant. In order to do this we are not to think of the original contract as one to enter a particular society or to set up a particular form of government. Rather, the guiding idea is that the principles of justice for the basic structure of society are the object of the original agreement. They are the principles that free and rational persons concerned to further their own interests would accept in an initial position of equality as defining the fundamental terms of their association. These principles are to regulate all further agreements: they specify the kinds of social cooperation that can be entered into and the forms of government that can be established. This way of regarding the principles of justice I shall call justice as fairness.

Thus we are to imagine that those who engage in social cooperation choose together, in one joint act, the principles which are to assign basic rights and duties and to determine the division of social benefits. Men are to decide in advance how they are to regulate their claims against one another and what is to be the foundation charter of their society. Just as each person must decide by rational reflection what constitutes his good, that is, the system of ends which it is rational for him to pursue, so a group of persons must decide once and for all what is to count among them as just and unjust. The choice which rational men would make in this hypothetical situation of equal liberty, assuming for the present that this choice problem has a solution, determines the principles of justice.

In justice as fairness the original position of equality corresponds to the state of nature in the traditional theory of the social contract. This original position is not, of course, thought of as an actual historical state of affairs, much less as a primitive condition of culture. It is understood as a purely hypothetical situation characterized so as to lead to a certain conception of justice. Among the essential features of this situation is that no one knows his place in society, his class position or social status, nor does any one know his fortune in the distribution of natural assets and abilities, his intelligence, strength, and the like. I shall even assume that the parties do not know their conceptions of the good or their special psychological propensities. The principles of justice are chosen behind a veil of ignorance. This ensures that no one is advantaged or disadvantaged in the choice of principles by the outcome of natural chance or the contingency of social circumstances. Since all are similarly situated and no one is able to design principles to favor his particular condition, the principles of justice are the result of a fair agreement or bargain. For given the circumstances of the original position, the symmetry of everyone's relations to each other, this initial situation is fair between individuals as moral persons, that is, as rational beings with their own ends and capable, I shall assume, of a sense of justice. The original position is, one might say, the appropriate initial status quo, and thus the fundamental agreements reached in it are fair. This explains the propriety of the name "justice as fairness": it conveys the idea that the principles of justice are agreed to in an initial situation that is fair. The name does not mean that the concepts of justice and fairness are the same, any more than the phrase

*Conant University Professor of Philosophy, Harvard University.

''poetry as metaphor'' means that the concepts of poetry and metaphor are the same.

Justice as fairness begins, as I have said, with one of the most general of all choices which persons might make together, namely, with the choice of the first principles of a conception of justice which is to regulate all subsequent criticism and reform of institutions. Then, having chosen a conception of justice, we can suppose that they are to choose a constitution and a legislature to enact laws, and so on, all in accordance with the principles of justice initially agreed upon. Our social situation is just if it is such that by this sequence of hypothetical agreements we would have contracted into the general system of rules which defines it.

It may be observed that once the principles of justice are thought of as arising from an original agreement in a situation of equality, it is an open question whether the principle of utility would be acknowledged. Offhand it hardly seems likely that persons who view themselves as equals, entitled to press their claims upon one another, would agree to a principle which may require lesser life prospects for some simply for the sake of a greater sum of advantages enjoyed by others. Since each desires to protect his interests, his capacity to advance his conception of the good, no one has a reason to acquiesce in an enduring loss for himself in order to bring about a greater net balance of satisfaction. In the absence of strong and lasting benevolent impulses, a rational man would not accept a basic structure merely because it maximized the algebraic sum of advantages irrespective of its permanent effects on his own basic rights and interests. Thus it seems that the principle of utility is incompatible with the conception of social cooperation among equals for mutual advantage. It appears to be inconsistent with the idea of reciprocity implicit in the notion of a well-ordered society. Or, at any rate, so I shall argue.

I shall maintain instead that the persons in the initial situation would choose two rather different principles: the first requires equality in the assignment of basic rights and duties, while the second holds that social and economic inequalities, for example inequalities of wealth and authority, are just only if they result in compensating benefits for everyone, and in particular for the least advantaged members of society. These principles rule out justifying institutions on the grounds that the hardships of some are offset by a greater good in the aggregate. It may be expedient but it is not just that some should have less in order that others may prosper. But there is no injustice in the greater benefits earned by a few provided that the situation of persons not so fortunate is thereby improved. The intuitive idea is that since everyone's well-being depends upon a scheme of cooperation without which no one could have a satisfactory life, the division of advantages should be such as to draw forth the willing cooperation of everyone taking part in it, including those less well situated. Yet this can be expected only if reasonable terms are proposed. The two principles mentioned seem to be a fair agreement on the basis of which those better endowed, or more fortunate in their social position, neither of which we can be said to deserve, could expect the willing cooperation of others when some workable scheme is a necessary condition of the welfare of all.[1] Once we decide to look for a conception of justice that nullifies the accidents of natural endowment and the contingencies of social circumstance as counters in quest for political and economic advantage, we are led to these principles. They express the result of leaving aside those aspects of the social world that seem arbitrary from a moral point of view.

The idea of the original position is to set up a fair procedure so that any principles agreed to will be just. Somehow we must nullify the effects of specific contingencies which put men at odds and tempt them to exploit social and natural circumstances to their own advantage. Now in order to do this I assume that the parties are situated behind a veil of ignorance. They do not know how the various alternatives will affect their own particular case and they are obliged to evaluate principles solely on the basis of general considerations.[2] The veil of ignorance enables us to make vivid to ourselves the restrictions that it seems reasonable to impose on arguments for principles of justice, and therefore on these principles themselves. Thus it seems reasonable and generally acceptable that no one should be advantaged or disadvantaged by natural fortune or social circumstances in the choice of principles. It also seems widely agreed that it should be impossible to tailor principles to the circumstances of one's own case. We should insure further that particular inclinations and aspirations, and persons' conceptions of their good do not affect the principles adopted. The aim is to rule out those principles that it would be rational to propose for acceptance, however little the chance of success, only if one knew certain things that are irrelevant from the standpoint of justice. For example, if a man knew that he was wealthy, he might find it rational to advance the principle that various taxes for welfare measures be counted unjust; if he knew that he was poor, he would most likely propose the contrary principle. To represent the desired restrictions one imagines a situation in which everyone is deprived of this sort of information. One excludes the knowledge of those contingencies which sets men at odds and allows them to be guided by their prejudices.

It is assumed, then, that the parties do not know certain kinds of particular facts. First of all, no one knows his place in society, his class position or social status; nor does he know his fortune in the distribution of natural assets and abilities, his intelligence and strength, and the like. Nor, again, does anyone know his conception of the good, the particulars of his rational plan of life, or even the special features of his psychology such as his aversion to risk or liability to optimism or pessimism. More than this, I assume that the parties do not know the particular circumstances of their own society. That is, they do not know its economic or political situation, or the level of civilization and culture

it has been able to achieve. The persons in the original position have no information as to which generation they belong. These broader restrictions on knowledge are appropriate in part because questions of social justice arise between generations as well as within them, for example, the question of the appropriate rate of capital saving and of the conservation of natural resources and the environment of nature. There is also, theoretically anyway, the question of a reasonable genetic policy. In these cases too, in order to carry through the idea of the original position, the parties must not know the contingencies that set them in opposition. They must choose principles the consequences of which they are prepared to live with whatever generation they turn out to belong to. As far as possible, then, the only particular facts which the parties know is that their society is subject to the circumstances of justice and whatever this implies.

The restrictions on particular information in the original position are of fundamental importance. The veil of ignorance makes possible a unanimous choice of a particular conception of justice. Without these limitations on knowledge the bargaining problem of the original position would be hopelessly complicated. Even if theoretically a solution were to exist, we would not, at present anyway, be able to determine it.

THE RATIONALITY OF THE PARTIES

I have assumed throughout that the persons in the original position are rational. In choosing between principles each tries as best he can to advance his interests. But I have also assumed that the parties do not know their conception of the good. This means that while they know that they have some rational plan of life, they do not know the details of this plan, the particular ends and interests which it is calculated to promote. How, then, can they decide which conceptions of justice are most to their advantage? Or must we suppose that they are reduced to mere guessing? To meet this difficulty, I postulate that they would prefer more primary social goods rather than less (i.e., rights and liberties, powers and opportunities, income and wealth and self-respect). Of course, it may turn out, once the veil of ignorance is removed, that some of them for religious or other reasons may not, in fact, want more of these goods. But from the standpoint of the original position, it is rational for the parties to suppose that they do want a larger share, since in any case they are not compelled to accept more if they do not wish to nor does a person suffer from a greater liberty. Thus even though the parties are deprived of information about their particular ends, they have enough knowledge to rank the alternatives. They know that in general they must try to protect their liberties, widen their opportunities, and enlarge their means for promoting their aims whatever these are. Guided by the theory of the good and the general facts of moral psychology, their deliberations are no longer guesswork. They can make a rational decision in the ordinary sense.

The assumption of mutually disinterested rationality, then, comes to this: the persons in the original position try to acknowledge principles which advance their system of ends as far as possible. They do this by attempting to win for themselves the highest index of primary social goods, since this enables them to promote their conception of the good most effectively whatever it turns out to be. The parties do not seek to confer benefits or to impose injuries on one another; they are not moved by affection or rancor. Nor do they try to gain relative to each other; they are not envious or vain. Put in terms of a game, we might say: they strive for as high an absolute score as possible. They do not wish a high or a low score for their opponents, nor do they seek to maximize or minimize the difference between their successes and those of others. The idea of a game does not really apply, since the parties are not concerned to win but to get as many points as possible judged by their own system of ends.

I shall now state in a provisional form the two principles of justice that I believe would be chosen in the original position. The first statement of the two principles reads as follows.

- First: each person is to have an equal right to the most extensive basic liberty compatible with a similar liberty for others.
- Second: social and economic inequalities are to be arranged so that they are both (a) reasonably expected to be to everyone's advantage, and (b) attached to positions and offices open to all.

By way of general comment, these principles primarily apply, as I have said, to the basic structure of society. They are to govern the assignment of rights and duties and to regulate the distribution of social and economic advantages. As their formulation suggests, these principles presuppose that the social structure can be divided into two more or less distinct parts, the first principle applying to the one, the second to the other. They distinguish between those aspects of the social system that define and secure the equal liberties of citizenship and those that specify and establish social and economic inequalities. The basic liberties of citizens are, roughly speaking, political liberty (the right to vote and to be eligible for public office) together with freedom of speech and assembly; liberty of conscience and freedom of thought; freedom of the person along with the right to hold (personal) property; and freedom from arbitrary arrest and seizure as defined by the concept of the rule of law. These liberties are all required to be equal by the first principle, since citizens of a just society are to have the same basic rights.

The second principle applies, in the first approximation, to the distribution of income and wealth and to the design of organizations that make use of differences in authority and responsibility, or chains of command. While the distribution of wealth and income need not be equal, it must be to everyone's advantage, and at the same time, positions of authority and offices of command must be accessible to all. One applies the second principle by holding positions open, and then, subject to this constraint, arranges social and economic inequalities so that everyone benefits.

These principles are to be arranged in a serial order with the first principle prior to the second. This ordering means that a departure from the institutions of equal liberty required by the first principle cannot be justified by, or compensated for, by greater social and economic advantages. The distribution of wealth and income, and the hierarchies of authority, must be consistent with both the liberties of equal citizenship and equality of opportunity.

It is clear that these principles are rather specific in their content, and their acceptance rests on certain assumptions that I must eventually try to explain and justify. For the present, it should be observed that the two principles (and this holds for all formulations) are a special case of a more general conception of justice that can be expressed as follows.

> All social values—liberty and opportunity, income and wealth, and the bases of self-respect—are to be distributed equally unless an unequal distribution of any, or all, of these values is to everyone's advantage.

Injustice, then, is simply inequalities that are not to the benefit of all. Of course, this conception is extremely vague and requires interpretation.

As a first step, suppose that the basic structure of society distributes certain primary goods, that is, things that every rational man is presumed to want. These goods normally have a use whatever a person's rational plan of life. For simplicity, assume that the chief primary goods at the disposition of society are rights and liberties, powers and opportunities, income and wealth. These are the social primary goods. Other primary goods such as health and vigor, intelligence and imagination, are natural goods;

although their possession is influenced by the basic structure, they are not so directly under its control. Imagine, then, a hypothetical initial arrangement in which all the social primary goods are equally distributed: everyone has similar rights and duties, and income and wealth are evenly shared. This state of affairs provides a benchmark for judging improvements. If certain inequalities of wealth and organizational powers would make everyone better off than in this hypothetical starting situation, then they accord with the general conception.

Now it is possible, at least theoretically, that by giving up some of their fundamental liberties men are sufficiently compensated by the resulting social and economic gains. The general conception of justice imposes no restrictions on what sort of inequalities are permissible; it only requires that everyone's position be improved.

The second principle insists that each person benefit from permissible inequalities in the basic structure. This means that it must be reasonable for each relevant representative man defined by this structure, when he views it as a going concern, to prefer his prospects with the inequality to his prospects without it. One is not allowed to justify differences in income or organizational powers on the ground that the disadvantages of those in one position are outweighed by the greater advantages of those in another. Much less can infringements of liberty be counterbalanced in this way. Applied to the basic structure, the principle of utility would have us maximize the sum of expectations of representative men (weighted by the number of persons they represent, on the classical view); and this would permit us to compensate for the losses of some by the gains of others. Instead, the two principles require that everyone benefit from economic and social inequalities.

THE TENDENCY TO EQUALITY

I wish to conclude this discussion of the two principles by explaining the sense in which they express an egalitarian conception of justice. Also I should like to forestall the objection to the principle of fair opportunity that it leads to a callous meritocratic society. In order to prepare the way for doing this, I note several aspects of the conception of justice that I have set out.

First we may observe that the difference principle gives some weight to the considerations singled out by the principle of redress. This is the principle that undeserved inequalities call for redress; and since inequalities of birth and natural endowment are undeserved, these inequalities are to be somehow compensated for.[3] Thus the principle holds that in order to treat all persons equally, to provide genuine equality of opportunity, society must give more attention to those with fewer native assets and to those born into the less favorable social positions. The idea is to redress the bias of contingencies in the direction of equality. In pursuit of this principle greater resources might be spent on the education of the less rather than the more intelligent, at least over a certain time of life, say the earlier years of school.

Now the principle of redress has not to my knowledge been proposed as the sole criterion of justice, as the single aim of the social order. It is plausible as most such principles are only as a prima facie principle, one that is to be weighed in the balance with others. For example, we are to weigh it against the principle to improve the average standard of life, or to advance the common good. But whatever other principles we hold, the claims of redress are to be taken into account. It is thought to represent one of the elements in our conception of justice. Now the difference principle is not of course the principle of redress. It does not require society to try to even out handicaps as if all were expected to compete on a fair basis in the same race. But the difference principle would allocate resources in education, say, so as to improve the long-term expectation of the least favored. If this end is attained by giving more attention to the better endowed, it is permissible; otherwise not. And

in making this decision, the value of education should not be assessed only in terms of economic efficiency and social welfare. Equally if not more important is the role of education in enabling a person to enjoy the culture of his society and to take part in its affairs, and in this way to provide for each individual a secure sense of his own worth.

Thus although the difference principle is not the same as that of redress, it does achieve some of the intent of the latter principle. It transforms the aims of the basic structure so that the total scheme of institutions no longer emphasizes social efficiency and technocratic values. We see then that the difference principle represents, in effect, an agreement to regard the distribution of natural talents as a common asset and to share in the benefits of this distribution whatever it turns out to be. Those who have been favored by nature, whoever they are, may gain from their good fortune only on terms that improve the situation of those who have lost out. The naturally advantaged are not to gain merely because they are more gifted, but only to cover the costs of training and education and for using their endowments in ways that help the less fortunate as well. No one deserves his greater natural capacity nor merits a more favorable starting place in society. But it does not follow that one should eliminate these distinctions. There is another way to deal with them. The basic structure can be arranged so that these contingencies work for the good of the least fortunate. Thus we are led to the difference principle if we wish to set up the social system so that no one gains or loses from his arbitrary place in the distribution of natural assets or his initial position in society without giving or receiving compensating advantages in return.

The natural distribution of talents is neither just nor unjust; nor is it unjust that men are born into society at some particular position. These are simply natural facts. What is just and unjust is the way that institutions deal with these facts. Aristocratic and caste societies are unjust because they make these contingencies the ascriptive basis for belonging to more or less enclosed and privileged social classes. The basic structure of these societies incorporates the arbitrariness found in nature. But there is no necessity for men to resign themselves to these contingencies. The social system is not an unchangeable order beyond human control but a pattern of human action. In justice as fairness men agree to share one another's fate. In designing institutions they undertake to avail themselves of the accidents of nature and social circumstance only when doing so is for the common benefit. The two principles are a fair way of meeting the arbitrariness of fortune; and while no doubt imperfect in other ways, the institutions which satisfy these principles are just.

There is a natural inclination to object that those better situated deserve their greater advantages whether or not they are to the benefit of others. At this point it is necessary to be clear about the notion of desert. It is perfectly true that given a just system of cooperation as a scheme of public rules and the expectations set up by it, those who, with the prospect of improving their condition, have done what the system announces that it will reward are entitled to their advantages. In this sense the more fortunate have a claim to their better situation; their claims are legitimate expectations established by social institutions, and the community is obligated to meet them. But this sense of desert presupposes the existence of the cooperative scheme; it is irrelevant to the question whether in the first place the scheme is to be designed in accordance with the difference principle or some other criterion.

Perhaps some will think that the person with greater natural endowments deserves those assets and the superior character that made their development possible. Because he is more worthy in this sense, he deserves the greater advantages that he could achieve with them. This view, however, is surely incorrect. It seems to be one of the fixed points of our considered judgments that no one deserves his place in the distribution of native endowments, any more than one deserves one's initial starting place in society. The assertion that a man deserves the superior character that enables him to make the effort to cultivate his abilities is equally problematic; for his character depends in large part upon fortunate family and social circumstances for which he can claim no credit. The notion of desert seems not to apply to these cases. Thus the more advantaged representative man cannot say that he deserves and therefore has a right to a scheme of cooperation in which he is permitted to acquire benefits in ways that do not contribute to the welfare of others. There is no basis for his making this claim. From the standpoint of common sense, then, the difference principle appears to be acceptable both to the more advantaged and to the less advantaged individual.

NOTES

1. For the formulation of this intuitive idea I am indebted to Allan Gibbard.
2. The veil of ignorance is so natural a condition that something like it must have occurred to many. The closest express statement of it known to me is found in J. C. Harsanyi, "Cardinal Utility in Welfare Economics and in the Theory of Risk-Taking." *Journal of Political Economy,* vol. 61 (1953). Harsanyi uses it to develop a utilitarian theory.
3. See Herbert Spiegelberg, "A Defense of Human Equality," *Philosophical Review,* vol. 53 (1944), pp. 101, 113–123; and D. D. Raphael, "Justice and Liberty," *Proceedings of the Aristotelian Society,* vol. 51 (1950–1951), pp. 187f.

Distributive Justice

Robert Nozick*

The minimal state is the most extensive state that can be justified. Any state more extensive violates people's rights. Yet many persons have put forth reasons purporting to justify a more extensive state. It is impossible within the compass of this book to examine all the reasons that have been put forth. Therefore, I shall focus upon those generally acknowledged to be most weighty and influential, to see precisely wherein they fail. In this paper we consider the claim that a more extensive state is justified, because necessary (or the best instrument) to achieve distributive justice.

The term "distributive justice" is not a neutral one. Hearing the term "distribution," most people presume that some thing or mechanism uses some principle or criterion to give out a supply of things. Into this process of distributing shares some error may have crept. So it is an open question, at least, whether *re*distribution should take place; whether we should do again what has already been done once, though poorly. However, we are not in the position of children who have been given portions of pie by someone who now makes last minute adjustments to rectify careless cutting. There is no *central* distribution, no person or group entitled to control all the resources, jointly deciding how they are to be doled out. What each person gets, he gets from others who give to him in exchange for something, or as a gift. In a free society, diverse persons control different resources, and new holdings arise out of the voluntary exchanges and actions of persons. There is no more a distrib-

uting or distribution of shares than there is a distributing of mates in a society in which persons choose whom they shall marry. The total result is the product of many individual decisions which the different individuals involved are entitled to make.

THE ENTITLEMENT THEORY

The subject of justice in holdings consists of three major topics. The first is the *original acquisition of holdings,* the appropriation of unheld things. This includes the issues of how unheld things may come to be held, the process, or processes, by which unheld things may come to be held, the things that may come to be held by these processes, the extent of what comes to be held by a particular process, and so on. We shall refer to the complicated truth about this topic, which we shall not formulate here, as the principle of justice in acquisition. The second topic concerns the *transfer of holdings* from one person to another. By what processes may a person transfer holdings to another? How may a person acquire a holding from another who holds it? Under this topic come general descriptions of voluntary exchange, and gift and (on the other hand) fraud, as well as reference to particular conventional details fixed upon in a given society. The complicated truth about this subject (with placeholders for conventional details) we shall call the principle of justice in transfer. (And we shall suppose it also includes principles governing how a person may divest himself of a holding, passing it into an unheld state.)

If the world were wholly just, the following inductive definition would exhaustively cover the subject of justice in holdings.

1. A person who acquires a holding in accordance with the principle of justice in acquisition is entitled to that holding.
2. A person who acquires a holding in accordance with the principle of justice in transfer,

Excerpted from *Anarchy, State, and Utopia,* by Robert Nozick. Copyright © 1974 by Basic Books, Inc. Reprinted by permission of Basic Books, Inc. and Basil Blackwell, Ltd.
*Porter Professor of Philosophy, Harvard University.

from someone else entitled to the holding, is entitled to the holding.

3. No one is entitled to a holding except by (repeated) applications of 1 and 2.

The complete principle of distributive justice would say simply that a distribution is just if everyone is entitled to the holdings they possess under the distribution.

A distribution is just if it arises from another just distribution by legitimate means. The legitimate means of moving from one distribution to another are specified by the principle of justice in transfer. The legitimate first "moves" are specified by the principle of justice in acquisition. Whatever arises from a just situation by just steps is itself just. The means of change specified by the principle of justice in transfer preserve justice. As correct rules of inference are truth-preserving, and any conclusion deduced via repeated application of such rules from only true premises is itself true, so the means of transition from one situation to another specified by the principle of justice in transfer are justice-preserving, and any situation actually arising from repeated transitions in accordance with the principle from a just situation is itself just. The parallel between justice-preserving transformations and truth-preserving transformations illuminates where it fails as well as where it holds. That a conclusion could have been deduced by truth-preserving means from premises that are true suffices to show its truth. That from a just situation a situation *could* have arisen via justice-preserving means does *not* suffice to show its justice. The fact that a thief's victims voluntarily *could* have presented him with gifts does not entitle the thief to his ill-gotten gains. Justice in holdings is historical; it depends upon what actually has happened. We shall return to this point later.

Not all actual situations are generated in accordance with the two principles of justice in holdings: the principle of justice in acquisition and the principle of justice in transfer. Some people steal from others, or defraud them, or en-

slave them, seizing their product and preventing them from living as they choose, or forcibly exclude others from competing in exchanges. None of these are permissible modes of transition from one situation to another. And some persons acquire holdings by means not sanctioned by the principle of justice in acquisition. The existence of past injustice (previous violations of the first two principles of justice in holdings) raises the third major topic under justice in holdings: the rectification of injustice in holdings. If past injustice has shaped present holdings in various ways, some identifiable and some not, what now, if anything, ought to be done to rectify these injustices? What obligations do the performers of injustice have toward those whose position is worse than it would have been had the injustice not been done? Or, than it would have been had compensation been paid promptly? How, if at all, do things change if the beneficiaries and those made worse off are not the direct parties in the act of injustice, but, for example, their descendants? Is an injustice done to someone whose holding was itself based upon an unrectified injustice? How far back must one go in wiping clean the historical slate of injustices? What may victims of injustice permissibly do in order to rectify the injustices being done to them, including the many injustices done by persons acting through their government? I do not know of a thorough or theoretically sophisticated treatment of such issues. Idealizing greatly, let us suppose theoretical investigation will produce a principle of rectification. This principle uses historical information about previous situations and injustices done in them (as defined by the first two principles of justice and rights against interference), and information about the actual course of events that flowed from these injustices, until the present, and it yields a description (or descriptions) of holdings in the society. The principle of rectification presumably will make use of its best estimate of subjunctive information about what would have occurred (or a probability distribution over what might have occurred, using the expected value) if the injustice had not taken place. If the actual description of holdings turns out not to be one of the descriptions yielded by the principle, then one of the descriptions yielded must be realized.

The general outlines of the theory of justice in holdings are that the holdings of a person are just if he is entitled to them by the principles of justice in acquisition and transfer, or by the principle of rectification of injustice (as specified by the first two principles). If each person's holdings are just, then the total set (distribution) of holdings is just. To turn these general outlines into a specific theory we would have to specify the details of each of the three principles of justice in holdings: the principle of acquisition of holdings, the principle of transfer of holdings, and the principle of rectification of violations of the first two principles. I shall not attempt that task here. (Locke's principle of justice in acquisition is discussed below.)

HISTORICAL PRINCIPLES AND END-RESULT PRINCIPLES

The general outlines of the entitlement theory illuminate the nature and defects of other conceptions of distributive justice. The entitlement theory of justice in distribution is *historical;* whether a distribution is just depends upon how it came about. In contrast, *current time-slice principles* of justice hold that the justice of a distribution is determined by how things are distributed (who has what) as judged by some *structural* principle(s) of just distribution. A utilitarian who judges between any two distributions by seeing which has the greater sum of utility and, if the sums tie, applies some fixed equality criterion to choose the more equal distribution, would hold a current time-slice principle of justice. As would someone who had a fixed schedule of trade-offs between the sum of happiness and equality. According to a current time-slice principle, all that needs to be looked at, in judging the justice of a distribution, is who ends up with what; in com-

paring any two distributions one need look only at the matrix presenting the distributions. No further information need be fed into a principle of justice. It is a consequence of such principles of justice that any two structurally identical distributions are equally just. (Two distributions are structurally identical if they present the same profile, but perhaps have different persons occupying the particular slots. My having ten and your having five, and my having five and your having ten are structurally identical distributions.) Welfare economics is the theory of current time-slice principles of justice. The subject is conceived as operating on matrices representing only current information about distribution. This, as well as some of the usual conditions (for example, the choice of distribution is invariant under relabeling of columns), guarantees that welfare economics will be a current time-slice theory, with all of its inadequacies.

Most persons do not accept current time-slice principles as constituting the whole story about distributive shares. They think it relevant in assessing the justice of a situation to consider not only the distribution it embodies, but also how that distribution came about. If some persons are in prison for murder or war crimes, we do not say that to assess the justice of the distribution in the society we must look only at what this person has, and that person has, and that person has,... at the current time. We think it relevant to ask whether someone did something so that he *deserved* to be punished, deserved to have a lower share.

PATTERNING

The entitlement principles of justice in holdings that we have sketched are historical principles of justice. To better understand their precise character, we shall distinguish them from another subclass of the historical principles. Consider, as an example, the principle of distribution according to moral merit. This principle requires that total distributive shares vary directly with moral merit; no person should have a greater share than anyone whose moral merit is greater. Or consider the principle that results by substituting "usefulness to society" for "moral merit" in the previous principle. Or instead of "distribute according to moral merit," or "distribute according to usefulness to society," we might consider "distribute according to the weighted sum of moral merit, usefulness to society, and need," with the weights of the different dimensions equal. Let us call a principle of distribution *patterned* if it specifies that a distribution is to vary along with some natural dimension, weighted sum of natural dimensions, or lexicographic ordering of natural dimensions. And let us say a distribution is patterned if it accords with some patterned principle. The principle of distribution in accordance with moral merit is a patterned historical principle, which specifies a patterned distribution. "Distribute according to I.Q." is a patterned principle that looks to information not contained in distributional matrices. It is not historical, however, in that it does not look to any past actions creating differential entitlements to evaluate a distribution; it requires only distributional matrices whose columns are labeled by I.Q. scores. The distribution in a society, however, may be composed of such simple patterned distributions, without itself being simply patterned. Different sectors may operate different patterns, or some combination of patterns may operate in different proportions across a society. A distribution composed in this manner, from a small number of patterned distributions, we also shall term "patterned." And we extend the use of "pattern" to include the overall designs put forth by combinations of end-state principles.

Almost every suggested principle of distributive justice is patterned: to each according to his moral merit, or needs, or marginal product, or how hard he tries, or the weighted sum of the foregoing, and so on. The principle of entitlement we have sketched is *not* patterned. There is no one natural dimension or weighted sum or combination of a small number of natural dimensions that yields the distributions generated in accordance with the principle of entitlement. The set of holdings that results when some persons receive their marginal products, others win at gambling, others receive a share of their mate's income, others receive gifts from foundations, others receive interest on loans, others receive gifts from admirers, others receive returns on investment, others make for themselves much of what they have, others find things, and so on, will not be patterned.

To think that the task of a theory of distributive justice is to fill in the blank in "to each according to his _____ " is to be predisposed to search for a pattern; and the separate treatment of "from each according to his _____ " treats production and distribution as two separate and independent issues. On an entitlement view these are *not* two separate questions. Whoever makes something, having bought or contracted for all other held resources used in the process (transferring some of his holdings for these cooperating factors), is entitled to it. The situation is *not* one of something's getting made, and there being an open question of who is to get it. Things come into the world already attached to people having entitlements over them. From the point of view of the historical entitlement conception of justice in holdings, those who start afresh to complete "to each according to his _____ " treat objects as if they appeared from nowhere, out of nothing. A complete theory of justice might cover this limited case as well; perhaps here is a use for the usual conceptions of distributive justice.

So entrenched are maxims of the usual form that perhaps we should present the entitlement conception as a competitor. Ignoring acquisition and rectification, we might say:

From each according to what he chooses to do, to each according to what he makes for himself (perhaps with the contracted aid of others) and what others choose to do for him and choose to give him of what they've been given previously (under this maxim) and haven't yet expended or transferred.

This, the discerning reader will have noticed, has its defects as a slogan. So as a summary and great simplification (and not as a maxim with any independent meaning) we have:

From each as they choose, to each as they are chosen.

HOW LIBERTY UPSETS PATTERNS

It is not clear how those holding alternative conceptions of distributive justice can reject the entitlement conception of justice in holdings. For suppose a distribution favored by one of these non-entitlement conceptions is realized. Let us suppose it is your favorite one and let us call this distribution D_1; perhaps everyone has an equal share, perhaps shares vary in accordance with some dimension you treasure. Now suppose that Wilt Chamberlain is greatly in demand by basketball teams, being a great gate attraction. (Also suppose contracts run only for a year, with players being free agents.) He signs the following sort of contract with a team: In each home game, twenty-five cents from the price of each ticket of admission goes to him. (We ignore the question of whether he is "gouging" the owners, letting them look out for themselves.) The season starts, and people cheerfully attend his team's games; they buy their tickets, each time dropping a separate twenty-five cents of their admission price into a special box with Chamberlain's name on it. They are excited about seeing him play; it is worth the total admission price to them. Let us suppose that in one season one million persons attend his home games, and Wilt Chamberlain winds up with $250,000, a much larger sum than the average income and larger even than anyone else has. Is he entitled to this income? Is this new distribution D_2 unjust? If so, why? There is *no* question about whether each of the people was entitled to the control over the resources they held in D_1; because that was the

distribution (your favorite) that (for the purposes of argument) we assumed was acceptable. Each of these persons *chose* to give twenty-five cents of their money to Chamberlain. They could have spent it on going to the movies, or on candy bars, or on copies of *Dissent* magazine, or of *Monthly Review*. But they all, at least one million of them, converged on giving it to Wilt Chamberlain in exchange for watching him play basketball. If D_1 was a just distribution, and people voluntarily moved from it to D_2, transferring parts of their shares they were given under D_1 (what was it for if not to do something with?), isn't D_2 also just? If the people were entitled to dispose of the resources to which they were entitled (under D_1), didn't this include their being entitled to give it to, or exchange it with, Wilt Chamberlain? Can anyone else complain on grounds of justice? Each other person already has his legitimate share under D_1. Under D_1, there is nothing that anyone has that anyone else has a claim of justice against. After someone transfers something to Wilt Chamberlain, third parties *still* have their legitimate shares; *their* shares are not changed. By what process could such a transfer among two persons give rise to a legitimate claim of distributive justice on a portion of what was transferred, by a third party who had no claim of justice on any holding of the others *before* the transfer? To cut off objections irrelevant here, we might imagine the exchanges occurring in a socialist society, after hours. After playing whatever basketball he does in his daily work, or doing whatever other daily work he does, Wilt Chamberlain decides to put in *overtime* to earn additional money. (First his work quota is set; he works time over that.) Or imagine it is a skilled juggler people like to see, who puts on shows after hours.

The general point illustrated by the Wilt Chamberlain example and the example of the entrepreneur in a socialist society is that no end-state principle or distributional patterned principle of justice can be continuously realized without continuous interference with people's lives. Any favored pattern would be transformed into one unfavored by the principle, by people choosing to act in various ways; for example, by people exchanging goods and services with other people, or giving things to other people, things the transferrers are entitled to under the favored distributional pattern. To maintain a pattern one must either continually interfere to stop people from transferring resources as they wish to, or continually (or periodically) interfere to take from some persons resources that others for some reason chose to transfer to them.

Patterned principles of distributive justice necessitate *re*distributive activities. The likelihood is small that any actual freely-arrived-at set of holdings fits a given pattern; and the likelihood is nil that it will continue to fit the pattern as people exchange and give. From the point of view of an entitlement theory, redistribution is a serious matter indeed, involving, as it does, the violation of people's rights. (An exception is those takings that fall under the principle of the rectification of injustices.) From other points of view, also, it is serious.

Taxation of earnings from labor is on a par with forced labor. Some persons find this claim obviously true: taking the earnings of *n* hours labor is like taking *n* hours from the person; it is like forcing the person to work *n* hours for another's purpose. Others find the claim absurd. But even these, *if* they object to forced labor, would oppose forcing unemployed hippies to work for the benefit of the needy. And they would also object to forcing each person to work five extra hours each week for the benefit of the needy. But a system that takes five hours' wages in taxes does not seem to them like one that forces someone to work five hours, since it offers the person forced a wider range of choice in activities than does taxation in kind with the particular labor specified.

Whether it is done through taxation on wages or on wages over a certain amount, or through seizure of profits, or through there being a big *social pot* so that it's not clear what's

coming from where and what's going where, patterned principles of distributive justice involve appropriating the actions of other persons. Seizing the results of someone's labor is equivalent to seizing hours from him and directing him to carry on various activities. If people force you to do certain work, or unrewarded work, for a certain period of time, they decide what you are to do and what purposes your work is to serve apart from your decisions. This process whereby they take this decision from you makes them a *part-owner* of you; it gives them a property right in you. Just as having such partial control and power of decision, by right, over an animal or inanimate object would be to have a property right in it.

LOCKE'S THEORY OF ACQUISITION

We must introduce an additional bit of complexity into the structure of the entitlement theory. This is best approached by considering Locke's attempt to specify a principle of justice in acquisition. Locke views property rights in an unowned object as originating through someone's mixing his labor with it. This gives rise to many questions. What are the boundaries of what labor is mixed with? If a private astronaut clears a place on Mars, has he mixed his labor with (so that he comes to own) the whole planet, the whole uninhabited universe, or just a particular plot? Which plot does an act bring under ownership?

Locke's proviso that there be "enough and as good left in common for others" is meant to ensure that the situation of others is not worsened. I assume that any adequate theory of justice in acquisition will contain a proviso similar to Locke's. A process normally giving rise to a permanent bequeathable property right in a previously unowned thing will not do so if the position of others no longer at liberty to use the thing is thereby worsened. It is important to specify *this* particular mode of worsening the situation of others, for the proviso does not encompass other modes. It does not include the worsening due to more limited opportunities to appropriate, and it does not include how I ''worsen'' a seller's position if I appropriate materials to make some of what he is selling, and then enter into competition with him. Someone whose appropriation otherwise would violate the proviso still may appropriate provided he compensates the others so that their situation is not thereby worsened; unless he does compensate these others, his appropriation will violate the proviso of the principle of justice in acquisition and will be an illegitimate one. A theory of appropriation incorporating this Lockean proviso will handle correctly the cases (objections to the theory lacking the proviso) where someone appropriates the total supply of something necessary for life.

A theory which includes this proviso in its principle of justice in acquisition must also contain a more complex principle of justice in transfer. Some reflection of the proviso about appropriation constrains later actions. If my appropriating all of a certain substance violates the Lockean proviso, then so does my appropriating some and purchasing all the rest from others who obtained it without otherwise violating the Lockean proviso. If the proviso excludes someone's appropriating all the drinkable water in the world, it also excludes his purchasing it all. (More weakly, and messily, it may exclude his charging certain prices for some of his supply.) This proviso (almost?) never will come into effect; the more someone acquires of a scarce substance which others want, the higher the price of the rest will go, and the more difficult it will become for him to acquire it all. But still, we can imagine, at least, that something like this occurs: someone makes simultaneous secret bids to the separate owners of a substance, each of whom sells assuming he can easily purchase more from the other owners; or some natural catastrophe destroys all of the supply of something except that in one person's possession. The total supply could not be permissibly appropriated

by one person at the beginning. His later acquisition of it all does not show that the original appropriation violated the proviso. Rather, it is the combination of the original appropriation *plus* all the later transfers and actions that violates the Lockean proviso.

Each owner's title to his holding includes the historical shadow of the Lockean proviso on appropriation. This excludes his transferring it into an agglomeration that does violate the Lockean proviso and excludes his using it in a way, in coordination with others or independently of them, so as to violate the proviso by making the situation of others worse than their baseline situation. Once it is known that someone's ownership runs afoul of the Lockean proviso, there are stringent limits on what he may do with (what it is difficult any longer unreservedly to call) ''his property.'' Thus a person may not appropriate the only water hole in a desert and charge what he will. Nor may he charge what he will if he possesses one, and unfortunately it happens that all the water holes in the desert dry up, except for his. This unfortunate circumstance, admittedly no fault of his, brings into operation the Lockean proviso and limits his property rights. Similarly, an owner's property right in the only island in an area does not allow him to order a castaway from a shipwreck off his island as a trespasser, for this would violate the Lockean proviso.

Notice that the theory does not say that owners do not have these rights, but that the rights are overridden to avoid some catastrophe. (Overridden rights do not disappear; they leave a trace of a sort absent in the cases under discussion.) There is no such external (and *ad hoc?*) overriding. Considerations internal to the theory of property itself, to its theory of acquisition and appropriation, provide the means for handling such cases.

I believe that the free operation of a market system will not actually run afoul of the Lockean proviso. If this is correct, the proviso will not provide a significant opportunity for future state action.

Distributive Justice and Utilitarianism

J. J. C. Smart*

INTRODUCTION

In this paper I shall not be concerned with the defense of utilitarianism against other types of ethical theory. Indeed I hold that questions of ultimate ethical principle are not susceptible of proof, though something can be done to render them more acceptable by presenting them in a clear light and by clearing up certain confusions which (for some people) may get in the way of their acceptance. Ultimately the utilitarian appeals to the sentiment of generalized benevolence, and speaks to others who feel this sentiment too and for whom it is an over-riding feeling.[1] (This does not mean that he will always act from this over-riding feeling. There can be backsliding and action may result from more particular feelings, just as an egoist may go against his own interests, and may regret this.) I shall be concerned here merely to investigate certain consequences of utilitarianism, as they relate to questions of distributive justice. The type of utilitarianism with which I am concerned is act utilitarianism.

THE PLACE OF JUSTICE IN UTILITARIAN THEORY

The concept of justice as a *fundamental* ethical concept is really quite foreign to utilitarianism. A utilitarian would compromise his utilitarianism if he allowed principles of justice which might

Excerpted from "Distributive Justice and Utilitarianism," published in *Justice and Economic Distribution*, edited by John Arthur and William H. Shaw, Englewood Cliffs, N.J.: Prentice-Hall, 1978. Reprinted by permission of the author.

*Research School of Social Sciences, The Australian National University.

conflict with the maximization of happiness (or more generally of goodness, should he be an "ideal" utilitarian). He is concerned with the maximization of happiness[2] and not with the distribution of it. Nevertheless he may well deduce from his ethical principle that certain ways of distributing the means to happiness (e.g., money, food, housing) are more conducive to the general good than are others. He will be interested in justice in so far as it is a political or legal or quasi-legal concept. He will consider whether the legal institutions and customary sanctions which operate in particular societies are more or less conducive to the utilitarian end than are other possible institutions and customs. Even if the society consisted entirely of utilitarians (and of course no actual societies have thus consisted) it might still be important to have legal and customary sanctions relating to distribution of goods, because utilitarians might be tempted to backslide and favour non-optimific distributions, perhaps because of bias in their own favour. They might be helped to act in a more nearly utilitarian way because of the presence of these sanctions.

As a utilitarian, therefore, I do not allow the concept of justice as a fundamental moral concept, but I am nevertheless interested in justice in a subordinate way, as a *means* to the utilitarian end. Thus even though I hold that it does not matter in what way happiness is distributed among different persons, provided that the total amount of happiness is maximized, I do of course hold that it can be of vital importance that the *means* to happiness should be distributed in some ways and not in others. Suppose that I have the choice of two alternative actions as follows: I can either give $500 to each of two needy men, Smith and Campbell, or else give $1000 to Smith and nothing to Campbell. It is of course likely to produce the greatest happiness if I divide the money equally. For this reason utilitarianism can often emerge as a theory with egalitarian consequences. If it does so this is because of the empirical situation, and not because of any moral commitment to egalitarianism as such. Consider, for example, another empirical situation in which the $500 was replaced by a half-dose of a life saving drug, in which case the utilitarian would advocate giving two half-doses to Smith or Campbell and none to the other. Indeed if Smith and Campbell each possessed a half-dose it would be right to take one of the half-doses and give it to the other. (I am assuming that a whole dose would preserve life and that a half-dose would not. I am also assuming a simplified situation: in some possible situations, especially in a society of nonutilitarians, the wide social ramifications of taking a half-dose from Smith and giving it to Campbell might conceivably outweigh the good results of saving Campbell's life.) However, it is probable that in most situations the equal distribution of the means to happiness will be the right utilitarian action, even though the utilitarian has no ultimate moral commitment to egalitarianism. If a utilitarian is given the choice of two actions, one of which will give 2 units of happiness to Smith and 2 to Campbell, and the other of which will give 1 unit of happiness to Smith and 9 to Campbell, he will choose the latter course.[3] It may also be that I have the choice between two alternative actions, one of which gives −1 unit of happiness to Smith and +9 units to Campbell, and the other of which gives +2 to Smith and +2 to Campbell. As a utilitarian I will choose the former course, and here I will be in conflict with John Rawls' theory, whose maximin principle would rule out making Smith worse off.

UTILITARIANISM AND RAWLS' THEORY

Rawls deduces his ethical principles from the contract which would be made by a group of rational egoists in an 'original position' in which they thought behind a 'veil of ignorance,' so that they would not know who they were or even what generation they belonged to.[4] Reasoning behind this veil of ignorance, they would apply the maximin principle. John Harsanyi earlier used the notion of a contract in such a position of ignorance, but used not the maximin principle but the principle of maximizing expected utility.[5] Harsanyi's method leads to a form of rule utilitarianism. I see no great merit in this roundabout approach to ethics *via* a contrary to fact supposition, which involves the tricky notion of a social contract and which thus appears already to presuppose a moral position. The approach seems also too Hobbesian: it is anthropologically incorrect to suppose that we are all originally little egoists. I prefer to base ethics on a principle of generalized benevolence, to which some of those with whom I discuss ethics may immediately respond. Possibly it might show something interesting about our common moral notions if it could be proved that they follow from what would be contracted by rational egoists in an 'original position,' but as a utilitarian I am more concerned to advocate a normative theory which might replace our common moral notions than I am to explain these notions. Though some form of utilitarianism might be deducible (as by Harsanyi) from a contract or original position theory, I do not think that it either ought to be or need be defended in this sort of way.

Be that as it may, it is clear that utilitarian views about distribution of happiness do differ from Rawls' view. I have made a distinction between justice as a moral concept and justice as a legal or quasi-legal concept. The utilitarian has no room for the former, but he can have strong views about the latter, though *what* these views are will depend on empirical considerations. Thus whether he will prefer a political theory which advocates a completely socialist state, or whether he will prefer one which advocates a minimal state (as Robert Nozick's book does[6]), or whether again he will advocate something between the two, is something which depends on the facts of economics, sociology, and so on. As someone not expert in these fields I have no desire to dogmatize on these empirical matters. (My own private non-expert opinion is that probably neither extreme leads to maximization of happiness, though I have a liking for rather more socialism than exists in Australia or U.S.A. at present.) As a utilitarian my approach to political theory has to be tentative and empirical. Not believing in moral rights as such I can not deduce theories about the best political arrangements by making deductions (as Nozick does) from propositions which purport to be about such basic rights.

Rawls deduces two principles of justice.[7] The first of these is that 'each person is to have an equal right to the most extensive basic liberty compatible with a similar liberty for others,' and the second one is that 'social and economic inequalities are to be arranged so that they are both (a) reasonably expected to be to everyone's advantage, and (b) attached to positions and offices open to all.' Though a utilitarian could (on empirical grounds) be very much in sympathy with both of these principles, he could not accept them as universal rules. Suppose that a society which had no danger of nuclear war could be achieved only by reducing the liberty of one per cent of the world's population. Might it not be right to bring about such a state of affairs if it were in one's power? Indeed might it not be right greatly to reduce the liberty of 100% of the world's population if such a desirable outcome could be achieved? Perhaps the present generation would be pretty miserable and would hanker for their lost liberties. However we must also think about the countless future generations which might exist and be happy provided that mankind can avoid exterminating itself, and we must also think of all the pain, misery and genetic damage which would be brought about by nuclear war even if this did not lead to the total extermination of mankind.

Suppose that this loss of freedom prevented a war so devastating that the whole process of evolution on this planet would come to an end. At the cost of the loss of freedom, instead of the war and the end of evolution there might occur an evolutionary process which was not only long lived but also beneficial: in millions of years there

might be creatures descended from *homo sapiens* which had vastly increased talents and capacity for happiness. At least such considerations show that Rawls' first principle is far from obvious to the utilitarian, though in certain mundane contexts he might accede to it as a useful approximation. Indeed I do not believe that restriction of liberty, in our present society, could have beneficial results in helping to prevent nuclear war, though a case could be made for certain restrictions on the liberty of all present members of society so as to enable the government to prevent nuclear blackmail by gangs of terrorists.

Perhaps in the past considerable restrictions on the personal liberties of a large proportion of citizens may have been justifiable on utilitarian grounds. In view of the glories of Athens and its contributions to civilization it is possible that the Athenian slave society was justifiable. In one part of his paper, 'Nature and Soundness of the Contract and Coherence Arguments,'[8] David Lyons has judiciously discussed the question of whether in certain circumstances a utilitarian would condone slavery. He says that it would be unlikely that a utilitarian could condone slavery as it has existed in modern times. However he considers the possibility that less objectionable forms of slavery or near slavery have existed. The less objectionable these may have been, the more likely it is that utilitarianism would have condoned them. Lyons remarks that our judgments about the relative advantages of different societies must be very tentative because we do not know enough about human history to say what were the social alternatives at any juncture.[9]

Similar reflections naturally occur in connection with Rawls' second principle. Oligarchic societies, such as that of eighteenth century Britain, may well have been in fact better governed than they would have been if posts of responsibility had been available to all. Certainly to resolve this question we should have to go deeply into empirical investigations of the historical facts. (To prevent misunderstanding, I do think that in our present society utilitarianism would imply adherence to Rawls' second principle as a general rule.)

A utilitarian is concerned with maximizing total happiness (or goodness, if he is an ideal utilitarian). Rawls largely concerns himself with certain 'primary goods,' as he calls them. These include 'rights and liberties, powers and opportunities, income and wealth.'[10] A utilitarian would regard these as mere means to the ultimate good. Nevertheless if he is proposing new laws or changes to social institutions the utilitarian will have to concern himself in practice with the distribution of these 'primary goods' (as Bentham did).[11] But if as an approximation we neglect this distinction, which may be justifiable to the extent that there is a correlation between happiness and the level of these 'primary goods,' we may say that according to Rawls an action is right only if it is to the benefit of the least advantaged person. A utilitarian will hold that a redistribution of the means to happiness is right if it maximizes the general happiness, even though some persons, even the least advantaged ones, are made worse off. A position which is intermediate between the utilitarian position and Rawls' position would be one which held that one ought to maximize some sort of trade-off between total happiness and distribution of happiness. Such a position would imply that sometimes we should redistribute in such a way as to make some persons, even the least advantaged ones, worse off, but this would happen less often than it would according to the classical utilitarian theory.

UTILITARIANISM AND NOZICK'S THEORY

General adherence to Robert Nozick's theory (in his *Anarchy, State and Utopia*)[12] would be compatible with the existence of very great inequality indeed. This is because the whole theory is based quite explicitly on the notion of *rights:* in the very first sentence of the preface of his book

we read 'Individuals have rights....' The utilitarian would demur here. A utilitarian legislator might tax the rich in order to give aid to the poor, but a Nozickian legislator would not do so. A utilitarian legislator might impose a heavy tax on inherited wealth, whereas Nozick would allow the relatively fortunate to become even more fortunate, provided that they did not infringe the *rights* of the less fortunate. The utilitarian legislator would hope to increase the total happiness by equalizing things a bit. How far he should go in this direction would depend on empirical considerations. He would not want to equalize things too much if this led to too much weakening of the incentive to work, for example. Of course according to Nozick's system there would be no reason why members of society should not set up a utilitarian utopia, and voluntarily equalize their wealth, and also give wealth to poorer communities outside. However it is questionable whether such isolated utopias could survive in a modern environment, but if they did survive, the conformity of the behaviour of their members to utilitarian theory, rather than the conformity to Nozick's theory, would be what would commend their societies to me.

SUMMARY

In this article I have explained that the notion of justice is not a fundamental notion in utilitarianism, but that utilitarians will characteristically have certain views about such things as the distribution of wealth, savings for the benefit of future generations and for the third world countries and other practical matters. Utilitarianism differs from John Rawls' theory in that it is ready to contemplate some sacrifice to certain individuals (or classes of individuals) for the sake of the greater good of all, and in particular may allow certain limitations of personal freedom which would be ruled out by Rawls' theory. *In practice,* however, the general tendency of utilitarianism may well be towards an egalitarian form of society.

NOTES

1. In hoping that utilitarianism can be rendered acceptable to some people by presenting it in a clear light, I do not deny the possibility of the reverse happening. Thus I confess to a bit of a pull the other way when I consider Nozick's example of an 'experience machine'. See Robert Nozick, *Anarchy, State and Utopia* (Oxford: Blackwell, 1975), pp. 42–45, though I am at least partially reassured by Peter Singer's remarks towards the end of his review of Nozick, *New York Review of Books,* March 6, 1975. Nozick's example of an experience machine is more worrying than the more familiar one of a pleasure inducing machine, because it seems to apply to ideal as well as to hedonistic utilitarianism.

2. In this paper I shall assume a hedonistic utilitarianism, though most of what I have to say will be applicable to ideal utilitarianism too.

3. There are of course difficult problems about the assignment of cardinal utilities to states of mind, but for the purposes of this paper I am assuming that we can intelligibly talk, as utilitarians do, about units of happiness.

4. John Rawls, *A Theory of Justice* (Cambridge, Mass: Harvard University Press, 1971).

5. John C. Harsanyi, 'Cardinal Utility in Welfare Economics and the Theory of Risk-Taking', *Journal of Political Economy,* **61** (1953), 434–435, and 'Cardinal Welfare, Individualistic Ethics, and Interpersonal Comparisons of Utility', *ibid.,* **63** (1955), 309–321. Harsanyi has discussed Rawls' use of the maximin principle and has defended the principle of maximizing expected utility instead, in a paper 'Can the Maximin Principle Serve as a Basis for Morality? A Critique of John Rawls' Theory', *The American Political Science Review,* **69** (1975), 594–606. These articles have been reprinted in John C. Harsanyi, *Essays on Ethics, Social Behavior, and Scientific Explanation* (Dordrecht, Holland: D. Reidel, 1976).

6. Robert Nozick, *Anarchy, State and Utopia.* (See note 1 above.)

7. Rawls, *A Theory of Justice,* p. 60.

8. In Norman Daniels (ed.), *Reading Rawls* (Oxford: Blackwell, 1975), pp. 141–167. See pp. 148–149.

9. Lyons, *op. cit.,* p. 149, near top.

10. Rawls, *op. cit.,* p. 62.

11. On this point see Brian Barry, *The Liberal Theory of Justice* (London: Oxford University Press, 1973), p. 55.

12. See note 1.

QUESTIONS FOR DISCUSSION

1. You have been asked to distribute a sum of money *justly* among the following people. Think of your funds as a pie to be divided into six pieces, and rank the six people listed below from highest (the one to whom you would give the most money) to lowest. You may assign one or more of the candidates an equal rank. Defend your distribution, explaining *why* you think it is just. How would your distribution be assessed by Rawls, Nozick, and Smart?
   a. A man who lives off the interest on his inherited wealth
   b. An unemployed man from the inner city
   c. A single mother of five who works as a rest room attendant during the day and moonlights as a prostitute
   d. A blue-collar worker on an automobile plant assembly line
   e. A high-level manager of a consumer products company, male, married
   f. A married woman who holds an exactly comparable position in a similar consumer products company
2. Rawls argues that just principles are those which would be chosen by rational, self-interested people if they were placed behind a "veil of ignorance." What is the purpose of Rawls' "veil of ignorance"? Do you think that people placed behind such a veil really would choose the principles Rawls claims they would choose?
3. Nozick rejects a system that tries to ensure *equality* among persons, because he believes such a system would inevitably interfere with people's *liberty*. Would people be equally *free* under a Nozickian system of justice? If not, can we call Nozick's theory of justice a truly "libertarian" one?
4. Why does Smart believe that the general tendency of utilitarianism is toward equality? What would be the exceptions to this tendency? What might Rawls and Nozick have to say about Smart's theory of justice?

CHAPTER 2

Capitalism and Socialism: A Tale of Two Systems

READINGS FOR CHAPTER TWO

Irving Kristol
A Capitalist Conception of Justice
54

Carl Cohen
Socialist Democracy
59

A Capitalist Conception of Justice

Irving Kristol*

It is fashionable these days for social commentators to ask, "Is capitalism compatible with social justice?" I submit that the only appropriate answer is "No." Indeed, this is the only possible answer. The term "social justice" was invented in order *not* to be compatible with capitalism.

What is the difference between "social justice" and plain, unqualified "justice?" Why can't we ask, "Is capitalism compatible with justice?" We can, and were we to do so, we would then have to explore the idea of justice that is peculiar to the capitalist system, because capitalism certainly does have an idea of justice.

"Social justice," however, was invented and propagated by people who were not much interested in understanding capitalism. These were nineteenth-century critics of capitalism—liberals, radicals, socialists—who invented the term in order to insinuate into the argument a quite different conception of the good society from the one proposed by liberal capitalism. As it is used today, the term has an irredeemably egalitarian and authoritarian thrust. Since capitalism as a socioeconomic or political system is neither egalitarian nor authoritarian, it is in truth incompatible with "social justice."

Let us first address the issue of egalitarianism. In a liberal or democratic capitalist society there is, indeed, a connection between justice and equality. Equality before the law and equality of political rights are fundamental to a liberal

Excerpted from "A Capitalist Conception of Justice" found in *Ethics, Free Enterprise, and Public Policy: Original Essays on Moral Issues in Business,* edited by Richard T. De George and Joseph A. Pichler. Copyright © 1978 by Oxford University Press, Inc. Reprinted by permission.
*Senior fellow, American Enterprise Institute, and co-editor of *The Public Interest.*

capitalist system and, in historical fact, the ideological Founding Fathers of liberal capitalism all did believe in equality before the law and in some form of equality of political rights. The introduction of the term "social justice" represents an effort to stretch the idea of justice that is compatible with capitalism to cover *economic* equality as well. Proponents of something called "social justice" would persuade us that economic equality is as much a right as are equality before the law and equality of political rights. As a matter of fact, these proponents move in an egalitarian direction so formidably that inevitably *all* differences are seen sooner or later to be unjust. Differences between men and women, differences between parents and children, differences between human beings and animals—all of these, as we have seen in the last ten or fifteen years, become questionable and controversial.

A person who believes in "social justice" is an egalitarian. I do not say that he or she necessarily believes in perfect equality; I do not think anyone believes in perfect equality. But "social justice" advocates are terribly interested in far more equality than a capitalist system is likely to deliver. Capitalism delivers many good things but, on the whole, economic equality is not one of them. It has never pretended to deliver economic equality. Rather, capitalism has always stood for equality of economic opportunity, reasonably understood to mean the absence of official barriers to economic opportunity.

We are now in an egalitarian age when Harvard professors write books wondering whether there is a problem of "social justice" if some people are born of handsome parents and are therefore more attractive than others. This is seriously discussed in Cambridge and in other learned circles. Capitalism is not interested in that. Capitalism says there ought to be no *official* barriers to economic opportunity. If one is born of handsome or talented parents, if one inherits a musical skill, or mathematical skill, or whatever, that is simply good luck. No one can question the person's right to the fruits of such skills. Capitalism believes that, through equal opportunity, each individual will pursue his happiness as he defines it, and as far as his natural assets (plus luck, good or bad) will permit. In pursuit of that happiness everyone will, to use that familiar phrase of Adam Smith, "better his condition."

Thus, capitalism says that equal opportunity will result in everyone's bettering his or her condition. And it does. The history of the world over the past 200 years shows that capitalism did indeed permit and encourage ordinary men and women in the pursuit of their happiness to improve their condition. Even Marx did not deny this. We are not as poor as our grandparents. We are all better off because individuals in pursuit of happiness, and without barriers being put in their way, are very creative, innovative, and adept at finding ways for societies to be more productive, thereby creating more wealth in which everyone shares.

Now, although individuals do better their condition under capitalism, they do not better their conditions equally. In the pursuit of happiness, some will be more successful than others. Some will end up with more than others. Everyone will end up with *somewhat* more than he had—everyone. But some people will end up with a lot more than they had and some with a little more than they had. Capitalism does not perceive this as a problem. It is assumed that since everyone gets more, everyone ought to be content. If some people get more than others, the reason is to be found in their differential contributions to the economy. In a capitalist system, where the market predominates in economic decision making, people who—in whatever way—make different productive inputs into the economy receive different rewards. If one's input into the economy is great, one receives a large reward; if one's input is small, one receives a modest reward. The determination of these rewards is by public preferences and public tastes as expressed in the market. If the public wants basketball players to

make $400,000 a year, then those who are good at basketball can become very, very rich. If the public wants to purchase certain paintings for $1 million or $2 million, then certain artists can become very, very rich. On the other hand, croquet players, even brilliant croquet players, won't better their condition to the same degree. And those who have no particular skill had better be lucky.

This is the way the system works. It rewards people in terms of their contribution to the economy as measured and defined by the marketplace—namely, in terms of the free preferences of individual men and women who have money in their pockets and are free to spend it or not on this, that, or the other as they please. Economic justice under capitalism means the differential reward to individuals is based on their productive input *to the economy*. I emphasize "to the economy" because input is measured by the marketplace.

Is it "just" that Mr. Ray Kroc, chairman of the board of McDonald's, should have made so much money by merely figuring out a new way of selling hamburgers? They are the same old hamburgers, just better made, better marketed. Is it fair? Capitalism says it is fair. He is selling a good product; people want it; it is fair. It is "just" that he has made so much money.

However, capitalism doesn't say only that. It also understands that it is an exaggeration to say that literally *everyone* betters his condition when rewards are based on productive input. There are some people who are really not capable of taking part in the race at all because of mental illness, physical illness, bad luck, and so on. Such persons are simply not able to take advantage of the opportunity that does exist.

Capitalism as originally conceived by Adam Smith was not nearly so heartless a system as it presented itself during the nineteenth century. Adam Smith didn't say that people who could make no productive input into the economy through no fault of their own should be permitted to starve to death. Though not a believer, he was enough of a Christian to know that such a conclusion was not consistent with the virtue of charity. He understood that such people had to be provided for. There has never been any question of that. Adam Smith wrote two books. The book that first made him famous was not *The Wealth of Nations* but *The Theory of Moral Sentiments,* in which he said that the highest human sentiment is sympathy—the sympathy that men and women have for one another as human beings. Although *The Wealth of Nations* is an analysis of an economic system based on self-interest, Adam Smith never believed for a moment that human beings were strictly economic men or women. It took some later generations of economists to come up with that idea. Adam Smith understood that people live in a society, not just in an economy, and that they feel a sense of social obligation to one another, as well as a sense of engaging in mutually satisfactory economic transactions.

In both these books, but especially in *The Theory of Moral Sentiments,* Adam Smith addressed himself to the question, "What do the rich do with their money once they get it?" His answer was that they reinvest some of it so that society as a whole will become wealthier and everyone will continue to be able to improve his or her condition to some degree. Also, however, the rich will engage in one of the great pleasures that wealth affords: the expression of sympathy for one's fellow human beings. Smith said that the people who have money can only consume so much. What are they going to do with the money aside from what they consume and reinvest? They will use it in such a way as to gain a good reputation among their fellow citizens. He said this will be the natural way for wealthy people to behave under capitalism. Perhaps he was thinking primarily of Scotsmen. Still, his perceptiveness is interesting. Although capitalism has long been accused of being an inhumane system, we forget that capitalism and humanitarianism entered the modern world together. Name a modern, humane movement—criminal reform, decent treatment of women, kindness to animals, etc. Where does it originate? They all came from the rising bourgeoisie at the end of the eighteenth century. They were all middle-class movements. The movements didn't begin with peasants or aristocrats. Peasants were always cruel to animals and aristocrats could not care less about animals, or about wives, for that matter. It was the bourgeoisie, the capitalist middle class, that said animals should be treated with consideration, that criminals should not be tortured, that prisons should be places of punishment, yes, but humane places of punishment. It was the generation that helped establish the capitalist idea and the capitalist way of thinking in the world that brought these movements to life. Incidentally, the anti-slavery movement was also founded by middle-class men and women who had a sense of social responsibility toward their fellow citizens.

So it is simply and wholly untrue that capitalism is a harsh, vindictive, soulless system. A man like Adam Smith would never have dreamed of recommending such a system. No, he recommended the economic relations which constitute the market system, the capitalist system, on the assumption that human beings would continue to recognize their social obligations to one another and act upon this recognition with some degree of consistency. Incidentally, he even seems to have believed in a progressive income tax.

However, something very peculiar happened after Adam Smith. Something very odd and very bad happened to the idea of capitalism and its reputation after the first generation of capitalism's intellectual Founding Fathers. The economics of capitalism became a "dismal science." One cannot read *The Wealth of Nations* and have any sense that economics is a dismal science. It is an inquiry into the causes of the wealth of nations that tells people how to get rich. It says, "If you organize your economic activities this way, everyone will get richer." There is nothing pessimistic about that, nothing dismal about that. It was an exhilarating message to the world.

Unfortunately, what gave capitalism a bad name in the early part of the nineteenth century was not the socialist's criticism of capitalism but, I fear, the work of the later capitalist economists. We do not even have a really good intellectual history of this episode because people who write histories of economic thought tend not to be interested in intellectual history, but in economics. For some reason, Malthus and then Ricardo decided that capitalist economics should not deal with the production of wealth but rather with its distribution. Adam Smith had said everyone could improve his condition. Malthus said the situation was hopeless, at least for the lower classes. If the lower classes improved their condition, he argued, they would start breeding like rabbits and shortly they would be right back where they started. Ricardo came along and said that the expanding population could not all be fed because there is a shortage of fertile land in the world. In his view, the condition of the working class over the long term was unimprovable.

This was the condition of capitalist economics for most of the nineteenth century. It is a most extraordinary and paradoxical episode in modern intellectual history. Throughout the nineteenth century, ordinary men and women, the masses, the working class, were clearly improving their condition. There is just no question that the working classes in England were better off in 1860 than they had been in 1810. In the United States there was never any such question and in France, too, it was quite clear that the system was working as Adam Smith had said it would. Yet all the economists of the School of Malthus and Ricardo kept saying. "It cannot happen. Sorry, people, but you're doomed to live in misery. There is nothing we can do about it. Just have fewer children and exercise continence." To which the people said, "Thank you very much. We do not much like this system you are recommending to us," as well they might not.

When the possibility of helping the average man and woman through economic growth is rejected loudly and dogmatically by the leading economists of the day, many will believe it. When they conclude that their condition cannot be improved by economic growth, they will seek to improve it by redistribution, by taking it away from others who have more. It is nineteenth-century capitalist economic thought, with its incredible emphasis on the impossibility of improving the condition of the working class—even as the improvement was obviously taking place—that gave great popularity and plausibility to the socialist critique of capitalism and to the redistributionist impulse that began to emerge. This impulse, which is still so appealing, makes no sense. A nation can redistribute to its heart's content and it will not affect the average person one bit. There just isn't ever enough to redistribute. Nevertheless, once it became "clear" in the nineteenth century that there was no other way, redistribution became a very popular subject.

Because capitalism after Adam Smith seemed to be associated with a hopeless view of the world, it provoked egalitarian impulses. Is it not a natural human sentiment to argue that, if we're all in a hopeless condition, we should be hopeless equally? Let us go down together. If that indeed is our condition, equality becomes a genuine virtue. Egalitarianism became such a plausible view of the world because capitalist apologists, for reasons which I do not understand, kept insisting that this is the nature of capitalism. Those who talk about "social justice" these days do not say that the income tax should be revised so that the rich people will get more, although there may be an economic case for it. (I am not saying there is, even though there might be.) "Social justice," the term, the idea, is intimately wedded to the notion of egalitarianism as a proper aim of social and economic policy, and capitalism is criticized as lacking in "social justice" because it does not achieve this equality. In fact, it does not, cannot, and never promised to achieve this result.

However, I think the more important thrust of the term "social justice" has to do with its authoritarian meaning rather than its egalitarian meaning. The term "social" prefixed before the word "justice" has a purpose and an effect which is to abolish the distinction between the public and the private sectors, a distinction which is absolutely crucial for a liberal society. It is the very definition of a liberal society that there be a public sector and a large, private sector where people can do what they want without government bothering them. What is a "social problem?" Is a social problem something that government can ignore? Would anyone say we have a social problem but it is not the business of government? Of course not.

The term "social justice" exists in order to identify those issues about which government should get active. A social problem is a problem that gives rise to a governmental policy, which is why people who believe in the expansion of the public sector are always inventing, discovering, or defining more and more social problems in our world. The world has not become any more problematic than it ever was. The proliferation of things called "social problems" arises out of an effort to get government more and more deeply involved in the lives of private citizens in an attempt to "cope with" or "solve" these "problems." Sometimes real problems are posed. Rarely are they followed by real solutions.

The idea of "social justice," however, assumes not only that government will intervene but that government will have, should have, and can have an authoritative knowledge as to what everyone merits or deserves in terms of the distribution of income and wealth. After all, if we do not like the inequality that results from the operation of the market, then who is going to make the decision as to the distribution of services and wealth? Some authority must be found to say so-and-so deserves more than so-and-so. Of course, the only possible such authority in the modern world is not the Church but the State. To the degree that one defines "social justice" as a kind of protest against the capitalist distribution of income, one proposes some other mechanism for the distribution of income. Government is the only other mechanism that can make the decisions as to who gets what, as to what he or she "deserves," for whatever reason.

The assumption that the government is able to make such decisions wisely, and therefore that government should make such decisions, violates the very premises of a liberal community. A liberal community exists on the premise that there is no such authority. If there were an authority which knew what everyone merited and could allocate it fairly, why would we need freedom? There would be no point in freedom. Let the authority do its work. Now, we have seen the experience of non-liberal societies, and not all of it is bad. I would not pretend that a liberal society is the only possible good society. If one likes the values of a particular non-liberal society, it may not be bad at all. There are many non-liberal societies I admire: monasteries are non-liberal societies, and I do not say they are bad societies. They are pretty good societies—but they are not liberal societies. The monk has no need for liberty if he believes there is someone else, his superior, who knows what is good for him and what reward he merits.

Once we assume that there is a superior authority who has authoritative knowledge of the common good and of the merits and demerits of every individual, the ground of a liberal society is swept away, because the very freedoms that subsist and thrive in a liberal society all assume that there is no such authoritative knowledge. Now, this assumption is not *necessarily* true. Maybe there is someone who really does have an authoritative knowledge of what is good for all of us and how much we all merit. We who choose a liberal society are skeptical as to the possibility. In any case, we think it is more likely that there will be ten people all claiming to have different versions of what is good for all of us and what we should all get, and therefore we choose to let the market settle it. It is an amicable way of not getting involved in endless philosophical or religious arguments about the nature of the true, the good, and the beautiful.

The notion of a "just society" existing on earth is a fantasy, a utopian fantasy. That is not what life on earth is like. The reason is that the world is full of other people who are different from you and me, alas, and we have to live with them. If they were all like us, we would live fine; but they are not all like us, and the point of a liberal society and of a market economy is to accept this difference and say, "Okay, you be you and I'll be I. We'll disagree, but we'll do business together. We'll mutually profit from doing business together, and we'll live not necessarily in friendship but at least in civility with one another."

I am not saying that capitalism is a just society. I am saying that there is a capitalist conception of justice which is a workable conception of justice. Anyone who promises you a just society on this earth is a fraud and a charlatan. I believe that this is not the nature of human destiny. It would mean that we all would be happy. Life is not like that. Life is doomed not to be like that. But if you do not accept this view, and if you really think that life can indeed be radically different from what it is, if you really believe that justice can prevail on earth, then you are likely to start taking phrases like "social justice" very seriously and to think that the function of politics is to rid the world of its evils: to abolish war, to abolish poverty, to abolish discrimination, to abolish envy, to abolish, abolish, abolish. We are not going to abolish any of those things. If we push them out one window, they will come in through another window in some unforeseen form. The reforms of today give rise to the evils of tomorrow. That is the history of the human race.

If one can be somewhat stoical about this circumstance, the basic precondition of social life, capitalism becomes much more tolerable. However, if one is not stoical about it, if one demands more of life than life can give, then capitalism is certainly the wrong system because capitalism does not promise that much and does not give you that much. All it gives is a greater abundance of material goods and a great deal of freedom to cope with the problems of the human condition on your own.

Socialist Democracy

Carl Cohen*

DEMOCRACY FULFILLED

We socialists agree that democracy is necessary and absolutely right. But it is not enough. Democracy is completed, fulfilled, by socialism—which is simply the democratic control of *all* resources in the community by society *as a whole*.

Socialism makes democratic ideals concrete. In it the collective will of the people is put to the service of the people in their daily lives. Through socialism the common interests of all the citizens are protected, their common needs met.

The name "socialism" has—at least to many American ears—a negative, even threatening, connotation. Yet most ordinary people warmly support—under a different name—many activities that are truly socialist in nature. We all know that some things must be done for the community as a whole. And some things can be undertaken *for* the community only *by* the community, acting *as* a community. Constructive collective action in this spirit is socialism.

How, for example, do we "provide for the common defense"? Why, through social action, of course. Armies and warships cannot be maintained by private groups or individuals. National defense undertaken jointly with democratic consent is only one of many socialist enterprises that no one seriously questions.

Excerpted from *Four Systems*, by Carl Cohen. Copyright © 1982 by Random House, Inc. Reprinted by permission of the publisher.

*Professor of philosophy in The Residential College and The College of Medicine, University of Michigan.

How do we make and enforce the criminal law? Collectively, of course. Citizens can neither establish criminal codes and courts as individuals, nor punish as individuals. That would be the war of each against all, in which the lives of people would indeed prove nasty, poor, brutish, and short. The adoption of laws, and their enforcement, is an essentially *social* activity. Nothing else would be feasible or sane. Everyone grants that; to this extent we are all socialists.

Is not the same true of national foreign policy? We may differ as individuals, but do we not agree upon the need for one community position? And of health regulations? Do we allow the meat packers or the drug manufacturers to decide for themselves what is fit to eat or prescribe? And everyone now agrees on the need for community policies, collective undertakings to protect the environment, our forests and fish, animals and birds. Shall we not have public parks or seashores? Shall we not join to protect our historical treasures and the beauties of our land? Absurd even to ask. To do these things we must, of course, act as a society, because as individuals we are relatively helpless and ineffective. We will succeed, if we succeed at all, cooperatively, because there is absolutely no other way to have successful armies, just courts, or beautiful parks. All democratic experience teaches the need for collective action. Real democracy *is* social democracy, democratic socialism.

While we all practice socialism in many spheres, its applicability to other spheres in which it is equally necessary is widely denied. Sometimes manipulated by the rich and powerful, sometimes blinded by our own slogans, sometimes dreading unreal philosophical ghosts, we fear to take social action where we ought. We fail to complete our democracy.

How can we complete it? Where would collective action have greatest impact on daily life? In the economy, of course. Action as a society is needed most of all in producing and distributing the necessities and comforts of ordinary human life. Socialism is democracy extended to the world of work and money.

SOCIALISM AND POPULAR WILL

All the wealth of the world—the houses and food, the land and lumber and luxuries—is somehow divided and distributed. How is that done? And how should it be done? We socialists try to rethink such fundamental questions: Who gets what? And Why?

Satisfactory answers to these questions must, of course, prove acceptable to the masses. Being democrats above all, we trust the judgment of the people. Their choices, when fully informed, will be rational and fair. We lay it down as a restriction upon ourselves, therefore, that the great changes socialism requires must come only as the honest expression of the will of the citizens, through action by their freely elected representatives. An organic transformation of society can succeed only when genuinely willed by its members. True socialists—unlike some who falsely parade under that banner—never have and never will force their solutions on an unwilling community. Democracies around the world, from India to Sweden, have enthusiastically applied socialist theory to their problems, devising socialist solutions specially suitable to their circumstances. The same basic theory can be applied successfully, with American ingenuity, to American circumstances. Confident that we can prove this to the satisfaction of the citizens concerned, we commit ourselves without reservations to abide by the judgment of the people after the case has been put fairly before them. We compel no one; our socialism is democratic, through and through.

RICH AND POOR

How the wealth of most of the world is now divided is very plain to see. A few people get a great deal, and most people get just barely enough, or a little less than enough, to live decently. Rich and poor are the great classes of society, and everyone knows it well. Early democracies accepted these stark inequities as natural and inevitable. We do not. Some democrats still accept them. Material success (they say) is open to everyone in a system of private enterprise, and rewards properly go to the industrious and the able, those ambitious enough to pull themselves out of poverty by effort and wit. Some succeed, some do not, and most (they conclude) receive their just deserts.

It isn't so. That picture of ''free enterprise'' is a myth and always has been. In fact, by putting control of industry and finance into private hands, free enterprise results in the ownership of more and more by fewer and fewer, making economic justice unattainable for most. For centuries, wherever capitalism has prevailed, the great body of wealth has rested in the pockets of a tiny fraction of the citizens, while the masses are divided between those who just get by on their wages, and those who are unemployed and poor, inadequately housed, and often hungry. That great division, between those who have and those who have not, is the leading feature of a private enterprise economy, even when democratic. Those who have get more, because money and property are instruments for the accumulation of more money and more property. Economic freedom in such a system, for the vast majority, is only the freedom to work for another. Working men and women are free to sweat for paychecks, free to look for another job, and maybe—if their needs are desperate—free to go on welfare. These are false freedoms, not deserving the name.

Why does it work out that way? Will the poor always be with us? Ought each person to look out only for himself or herself and devil take the hindmost? We deny that this is the spirit of a decent society. We do not accept the inevitability of poverty; we do not think a democracy need be a cutthroat enterprise, and we know that cooperative action by the members of a society in their joint interests can protect both the essential freedoms of each individual and the economic well-being of all. That rational cooperation is called socialism.

PARKS AND INDUSTRIES

Consider this vivid contrast. No one questions the appropriateness of public parks—places for play and the enjoyment of nature, owned by the people, and operated by their elected representatives (and those they hire) in everyone's interest. Our parks (national, state, and municipal) are among our proudest possessions. Yes, possessions; we own them, each of us, and though some abuse them thoughtlessly, most of us love them and take satisfaction in their beauty. We do not begrudge the need to tax ourselves to maintain them. We could sell the forests and the land, reduce our tax burden thereby, and leave all citizens to take care of their own recreational needs as well as they can. If unable to pay for access to private parks or clubs, or to afford a private lake or a canyon—well, that would be their lookout. Simply to formulate this attitude is to exhibit its absurdity. Natural beauty and opportunity for relaxation and play for ourselves and our children are deep human needs; we fully understand how vital it is that the limited resources of nature, the lakes and forests, streams and wildlife, be preserved, in part at least, for our common and perpetual enjoyment.

Compare with this the condition of the steel industry. Virtually all of the steel in the United States is produced by three companies: U.S. Steel, Republic Steel, Inland Steel. The private owners of these three companies—a tiny fraction of our citizens—literally possess, own as their private property, the foundries, mills, and other facilities that constitute the literal foundation of almost all other industry. Virtually nothing works without steel. Steel mills are not as pretty as parks, true, but are they any less necessary to the well-being of a people? Can any of us do without steel? Not for a day. Cars, trucks, ships, and trains are made of it. Housing and communication depend utterly upon it. Kitchens and radios, elevators and pens—practically all tools and all conveniences require it. Hardly any activity, public or private, goes on without some use of iron or steel. Then why not exhibit the same community concern for steel that we exhibit for our parks? Why let a few capitalists charge us as they please (since we cannot control them) for what we must have? Why suppose that a fair price for steel includes an enormous profit—over and above all the costs of making and shipping the steel—for the private owners of the mills?

What explains so blind an infatuation with "private enterprise"? Under its spell we allow ourselves to be manipulated by the private owners of the steel foundries, gouged (even in our own homes!) by the private owners of the telephone wires. Oil wells and forests, precious resources from our common earth, are exploited by giant corporations whose ultimate object is profit alone. We must wake to see that productive industry, vital to the life of a society, is properly the possession of that society as a whole, not of private individuals or companies. The principles we apply unhesitatingly to parks apply with equal force to factories. Production as well as recreation can be a source of public pride and satisfaction—when socialized. Socialism is nothing more than the *general* application of collective intelligence.

Every democracy, socialist or not, will seek to protect citizens' political rights—but only socialist democracies protect citizens' *economic* rights. Freedom of speech and assembly are priceless; are not freedom from unemployment and hunger equally so? We think so. The same collective action needed to defend the citizens against aggression from without is needed to organize production rationally and to distribute wealth justly within our own borders. In the economic sphere as much as any other, cooperation and foresight are central. The public ownership of industry is the only way to achieve them.

THE INHUMANITY OF THE MARKET

Socialism is simply economic good sense. The long-term fruits of capitalism have become too bitter: cycles of boom and bust, unemployment and welfare, personal dissatisfaction and business failure. Inflation steals from everyone (except those who can raise prices and rents quickly); depression demoralizes everyone. Disorder and distress are widespread. Our land itself is abused, our water poisoned, and our air fouled. When everything is left "up for grabs," the grabbing will be vicious and the outcome chaotic. There can be no intelligent planning for future needs, no rational distribution of products or materials in short supply, no reasonable deployment of human energies, in an economy in which the fundamental rule is dog-eat-dog. Legislation designed to blunt the fangs can do no more than reduce the depth of a serious wound.

Capitalism relies upon the so-called "market economy." The prices asked or offered for raw materials and finished products it leaves entirely to private parties, individuals or business firms, who enter a supposedly open market. This free market, it is argued, will be self-regulating; supply and demand will rationalize prices, fairness and productivity will be ensured by competition, enterprise encouraged by the hope of profit.

None of this actually works in the way capitalist mythology depicts it. The system relies upon the wisdom and power of economic fairies that never did exist. Nothing in the market is dependable, since everything within it fluctuates in response to unpredictable and uncontrollable factors: the tastes of buyers, the moods of sellers, the special circumstances of either, accidents causing short supply, or fashions transforming reasonable supply into glut.

Rationality and fairness through competition? No claim could be more fraudulent. In a capitalist market prices depend largely upon the relative strengths (or weaknesses) of the traders. If I own all the orchards, and am therefore the seller of all the cherries in the market, you, dear buyer, will pay my price or eat no cherries. Steel, timber, farm machinery are for sale in the market. Go, dear friend, and bargain with the sellers. Anyone tempted to believe capitalist propaganda about the give and take in the market should put it to the test. Reflect upon your own recent experiences as a shopper: You were told the price of the item you looked at—a TV set or a can of beans—and you paid that price or left without. That is how the market works for ordinary folks. Giant firms, manufacturers or chain retailers, may bargain with suppliers on occasion—but even then the stronger get the better deals. Those who control resources and money control the market, manipulating it in their own interests. Those who enter the market (either as buyer or seller) with great needs but little power are squeezed and exploited. The weak get twisted, the strong do the twisting. That's free enterprise.

Fairness? Markets do not know the meaning of the word. All's fair in war—and market competition is perpetual war, through guile and threat, on a thousand fronts. Rewards go to the aggressive, the keys to victory are accumulation, possession, control. And rules for fair dealing? They will be evaded, broken surreptitiously, even ignored—just like the rules of war—when it profits the combatants.

PUBLIC OWNERSHIP

Reasonable human beings can end all this. Production and distribution can be designed for human service. Cooperation is the key. Society must be organized with mutual service and mutual benefit as its fundamental theme. That theme is not alien to us; it lies at the core of our highest moral and religious ideals. We must realize these ideals in practice.

Economic cooperation entails two practical principles: (1) productive property must be publicly owned; and (2) production and distribution must be planned for the common good. *Public ownership* and *planning*—acting upon both we

can readily achieve the substance of democratic socialism.

Public ownership is the base. Public ownership of what? Of the means by which goods are produced and work is carried on. Private persons are not entitled to own the instruments of our common good. A system enabling some to exact profit from the work of others, to wax rich while the glaring needs of others go unmet, is fundamentally corrupt. We would end that corruption by bringing all the elements of the productive economy—the electric utilities and the mines, agriculture and transport, the production of metals and paper and drugs, the airlines and the food chains and the telephone system—under public ownership.

We do not propose to confiscate anything. The capital now held by private owners we would have the community pay for, at a fair price. But we would end the surreptitious confiscation by a few of the common wealth. The people have a right to advance their own general welfare through state action. They have that right in the economic sphere as in every other. Individuals will not be deprived of their personal effects, their houses or cars, their books or boots. Indeed, we seek the enlargement of such private goods for individual satisfaction. Individual human beings, after all, are what government is created to serve. But productive property is our common good, our collective concern. We will move it—justly—from private to public hands.

THE ELIMINATION OF PRIVATE PROFIT

The nationalization of all industry will have two consequences. First, *profit* for some from the work of others will be no more. If there is surplus produced by the operation of the utility companies, or the design of computers, or the distribution of any manufactured goods, let that surplus return to the treasury of the entire community. Let all productive systems be used, we say, not for private enrichment but for public benefit, and for continuing investment in the components of public production themselves. Workers should know that they labor each for all, and that any value they produce beyond what they receive in wages will not be taken from them but returned to them in some form of general benefit. One of those benefits will be the reduction of prices; when profits do not need to be squeezed from an enterprise, the consumer need only be charged the actual cost of that product or service. Goods and services will at last be fairly priced.

Telephone networks, natural gas distribution, and electric power supply are good illustrations of the increase in efficiency. These are all virtual monopolies. It makes no sense to have two telephone systems, or two sets of electric power lines, in the same community. Such essential utilities properly belong to all the members of the community served, all of whom need and use them, and must pay for them. That public agencies, even in a capitalist economy, now regulate the utilities is an explicit recognition of our common interest. Why then should *private* parties be permitted to own the lines and generators of a *public* utility? Why should any small group be permitted to *profit* from the necessary use of these instruments by everyone? Of course they should not. In many democracies the public utilities are already completely owned and operated by the public; actual operations change only little; ownership changes entirely. The result is invariably better service at lower cost. Nothing else is fair.

THE RETURN TO PUBLIC SERVICE

By eliminating the need for private profit, the public ownership of industry proves itself not only cheaper but more satisfying for all. A nationalized economy can be guided by one overriding purpose—the *general* welfare. The need for service overrules the need for a good return. Some services yield little profit, or none; yet the self-governed community can nevertheless provide such service widely to its own members.

Take the railroads as an example. The American public is poorly served, when served at all, by privately owned railroads. They would discontinue every service, passenger or freight, that does not maximize financial return on capital investment. While socialist democracies in Western Europe and elsewhere are perfecting their passenger rail services, rebuilding the roadbeds, introducing high-speed, comfortable, and dependable intercity services, the passenger rail network in the United States, because unprofitable, is allowed to rot. Many American cities—even including former great rail centers—no longer have any rail passenger service at all! The private railroads maintain passenger services only where clearly profitable (as between New York and Washington) or where forced to do so by regulatory agencies—and then they do so grudgingly and poorly. Does the public suffer? ''Not our concern,'' reply the private railroads. ''This is a business. A line that loses money regularly must be cut; our primary responsibility is to our stockholders.'' It is; they are right about that. If the owners of the railroads run them only to make money, they will not run them at all where there is no money to be made. But the fundamental aim of the railroads ought not be to make money; it ought to be to serve the people. It will become that when—but only when—all the people served are stockholders.

SOCIAL PLANNING

Two practical principles, we said earlier, comprise the substance of democratic socialism. Public ownership is the first, the foundation of socialism. Planning production and distribution for the common good is the second, and the fruit of socialism. When all members of the community have equal voice in the management of the economy, the elected representatives of those voices will naturally seek to deploy productive powers rationally. The community, then fully in command of its own affairs, will deliberate carefully in choosing its economic goals and in devising the means to attain them. It will make plans.

All intelligent humans plan. Preparing for the future is the mark of rational beings. Capitalists plan thoughtfully for their own advancement, plan cautiously for the security of their families, plan assiduously for the growth of their businesses. Yet they bitterly attack us for advocating the same foresight in the larger community! In matters close to them they do not cease to think ahead. But they insist that the community as a whole should entrust its future to an "invisible hand" that is somehow to ensure social health and prosperity. Sophisticated in private affairs, their handling of public affairs is simply immature, primitive.

Critics of socialism (it should be noted in fairness) often do recognize the need to plan in some particular sphere of the economy. Doing so, of course, such critics implicitly abandon their devotion to "free" markets. They plan the supplies of oil or gas, the road system, the storage of grain, and the money supply. But if the use of careful planning is appropriate in any single sphere of the economy, it is no less appropriate for the economy as a whole. Capitalists who plan, but are infuriated by planning, are blinded by an ideology from which they cannot free their own minds.

A few wealthy critics of socialism, on the other hand, are more perceptive but less forthright. They recognize the inconsistencies of capitalism, but they reject large-scale planning in their own interests. They know that in a system without rational direction, the private owners of productive capacity are in the best position when stormy times come. They will be able to capitalize on every fortuitous turn of events. That is how they got rich and will get richer. Economic planning will equalize opportunities in ways they do not like. It will deprive them of opportunities to exploit. Planning—from their selfish perspective—is a threat.

PLANNING WORKS

Two great objections to economic planning must be dealt with. The first is the claim that it does not work. This has been repeatedly proved false.

Every individual, and every community, has experienced successful planning. When we construct a budget for our school or business, for our family or our town, we plan. Ought we to cease budgeting? Bad budgets are sometimes devised, true; our aim then is to improve them, not to discard budgeting altogether. The same process of improvement through self-correction can take place on a national scale. Community planning need not be always partial, or short-run. What is clearly in our interest to keep under control we need not leave to chance. Department heads who do not plan for their departments, generals who do not adequately plan their battles, we censure and replace. We have learned how essential it is to plan, through zoning, for the growth of our cities, and how we suffer when we fail to do so. The redevelopment of Western Europe, after World War II, was carefully and very successfully planned under American leadership. Military preparedness would be impossible without planning of the most detailed sort. Thorough planning can bring humankind even to the moon. Good planning is the heart of intelligent policy in every sphere, and it always will be. Without a plan there can hardly be any policy at all.

The effectiveness of rational economic planning has been demonstrated again and again. Many socialist countries, maintaining five- and seven-year economic plans under continual adjustment, have met with phenomenal success. Their rates of economic growth have been markedly greater than that of the unplanned American economy over recent decades. True, percentage growth for the American economy is harder than for some others because of our great size. But other economies, almost the size of our own, have been rapidly overtaking us through planning. Economic planning in Japan, for example, has brought stability, full employment, and security for all citizens. The quality of Japanese goods is high, often higher than our own. The quality of their services is very high, often more complete than our own. We cannot hope to compete successfully with them unless we too are prepared to plan thoughtfully for the future.

PLANNING AND DEMOCRACY

The second major objection to economic planning is the claim that it will cost us our freedom. This is as false as the claim that it does not work, and more pernicious.

Here lies the nub of the conflict between democratic socialists and our private enterprise critics. Freedom, says the critic, is the paramount social value. The freedom of each individual as an economic agent must be curtailed, they argue, by any large-scale economic plan. Once the goals are set, and the role of each economic element fixed, every private person must be sharply restricted in the use of his own resources. What can be bought and what can be sold or invested will be determined by the plan. The individual will be forced to work where, and when, and as the socialist bureaucrats have decided. Economic planning, they conclude, is but a pretty name for economic slavery.

The complaint is entirely unfounded. It is plausible only because it supposes, falsely, that economic planning under socialism will be imposed from above, by arbitrary authorities over whom we will have no control. Not so. Democratic socialism brings *democratic* planning. In an economy that is publicly owned and managed, *we* are the planners. Long-range designs for the allocation of resources, decisions about what is to be produced and how it is to be distributed, will come not from a secret, all-powerful elite but from *public* bodies, publicly selected, acting publicly, and answerable to the general public.

This genuine public accountability is absent, we agree, in some countries calling themselves "socialist." We despise that economic czarism as bitterly as do our capitalist friends. That is a false socialism which betrays the democratic spirit to which we are committed. Free citizens, accustomed to governing their own affairs, jealous of their own ultimate authority, will not be fooled by deceitful talk. They—we!—will know when our most important business is truly under our own control, and we will not stand for any other state of affairs. We will give up none of our freedom to do our own planning for our own needs. To the contrary, real freedom of action will be magnified in a truly *democratic* socialism by its increase of economic security for individuals and economic rationality in the whole society.

DEMOCRACY IN THE WORK PLACE

Democracy calls for participation in the important affairs of one's community. One's community is not only his town, or nation, but also his place of work—the factory or office, the restaurant or construction project. Can we make democracy genuine in such places, in the day-to-day lives of ordinary citizens?

Yes, we can, but only under socialism. Where the ownership of the enterprise is private, and profit-oriented, there must be bosses on the job to represent the owners and protect their profits. The workers are hired, whether by the hour or the month, in the owners' interests; they take orders from the bosses or they are fired. Capitalism inevitably produces authoritarianism in labor-management relations. Collective bargaining, of which capitalists make much, does no more than mitigate the severity of worker subordination.

This authoritarianism can be eliminated, however, if the enterprise is itself community-owned-and-operated. We the people then make the procedural rules, and we can decide to institute democratic processes in the places of work themselves. This dramatic change is not merely utopian; it has already been widely introduced in socialist democracies—in Sweden for example, and even in a few isolated places in the United

States. Where it has been thoughtfully designed, work-place democracy has usually proven very successful. It makes for a happier, healthier, and more productive work force. Men and women on the job regain the sense of personal autonomy that traditional hierarchies do not foster and cannot respect. Through collaboration and co-operation, the workers protect one another from abuse, whether deliberate or inadvertent. And everyone is served because day-to-day participation instills pride in the work force, and provides immediate incentives for energetic work of high quality.

Democracy in the work place does not mean disorder. It does not mean that everyone works when and where and how he or she pleases. It means simply that the members of the work force—knowing themselves as owners as well as consumers and workers—participate with community management in setting work rules, production quotas, hours, and procedures. Of all the ways in which democratic ideals can be realized, this is the most concrete, the most immediate, and the most satisfying. It can be achieved under socialism; on a large scale it can be achieved only under socialism. This by itself is a compelling argument for socialist democracy.

QUESTIONS FOR DISCUSSION

1. Kristol argues for a "capitalist conception of justice." Yet he also states, "'Is capitalism compatible with social justice?' I submit that the only appropriate answer is 'No.'" Is Kristol contradicting himself? What does he mean by a "capitalist conception of justice"? By "social justice"?
2. What does Cohen mean when he says that socialism "completes" democracy? In what way might capitalism be undemocratic?

CHAPTER 3

Ethics and Business Decision Making

READINGS FOR CHAPTER THREE

Verne E. Henderson
The Ethical Side of Enterprise
69

Laura L. Nash
Ethics Without the Sermon
79

Steven Kelman
Cost-Benefit Analysis: An Ethical Critique
90

James V. DeLong
and Robert A. Nisbet
*Defending Cost-Benefit Analysis: Two Replies to
Steven Kelman*
97

The Ethical Side of Enterprise

Verne E. Henderson*

"What! Another article on business ethics? What are they trying to ram down my throat this time?" This is a common reaction by businesspeople to what is becoming the latest fad. Peter Drucker recently called it that and stated flatly that there is no such thing as "business ethics."[1] However, there is an ethical side to enterprise, and Drucker's article convinces me that it is not well understood. In *Death in the Afternoon,* Ernest Hemingway wrote that "What is moral is what you feel good after and what is immoral is what you feel bad after." Ethics is different; it is what you do hoping that others will feel good after.

My experience indicates that business management is particularly wary and sometimes even incensed when ethical issues are raised by spokespeople from the religious community. R.H. Tawney noted the prevalence of that attitude more than half a century ago: "Trade is one thing, religion is another."[2] Yet my conversations with businesspeople reveal their frustrations and concerns: "How can we talk about ethics without raising fanatical religious or denominational flags?" "Can't we find a fresh approach, some new words, or something so that we can talk about a subject we all secretly know is very important?"

As a spokesman from the religious community, I affirm the need to remove religious brand names and denominational labels. Moreover, I believe that this new age of ever-advancing technology will require significant ethical innovation. The word "ethics" should generate a new set of feelings and perceptions.

Ethics in the broadest sense provides the basic conditions of acceptance for any activity. The ethics of a game or sport both implies its purpose and specifies rules of fair play. Business schools, for example, have traditionally focused on what we might call the business side of enterprise (finance, accounting, economics, marketing, forecasting), explaining the rules and imparting winning tactics. The human and the legal sides of enterprise have assumed increasing importance as the rules and tactics have become complex and the unresolved disputes numerous. Out of weariness and frustration, we ask a basic question: Should we play this game at all? Of course, we have to play. Business, after all, is a survival activity, isn't it...putting food on the table? So instead we ask: Can't we play the business game differently? The ethical side of enterprise emerges as this questioning of corporate activity grows in breadth and depth. At the macro level, one may question the legitimacy of both the corporation and capitalism as a viable economic system.[3] This article focuses on the micro level, addressing the specific decisions of enterprise on a variety of issues.

THE NEED TO DEFINE ETHICS

As a senior corporate executive recently described the major problems his firm faces in contemplating joint ventures abroad, it became clear to me that his primary concerns were ethical ones. For instance, how do you establish trust and share risk? How do you deal with two governments that have significant cultural differences? What motivates top management to undertake such complex efforts? These joint ventures are new cultural configurations in the marketplace and, as such, they will cause us to question old values and to establish new ones. The role of the ethicist is to aid the manager in negotiating the uncharted depths of this new environment. But first, the term "ethics" must be defined.

Reprinted from "The Ethical Side of Enterprise," by Verne E. Henderson, *Sloan Management Review,* vol. 23, no. 3, pp. 37–47, by permission of the publisher. Copyright © 1982 by the Sloan Management Review Association. All rights reserved.
*Professor of ethics and social issues, Arthur D. Little Management Education Institute, and president, Revehen Consultants.

A Static Definition

Ethics is commonly defined as a set of principles prescribing a behavior code that explains what is good and right or bad and wrong; it may even outline moral duty and obligations generally. However, given the dynamic environment in which business must operate today, this conventional definition is far too static to be useful. It presumes a consensus about ethical principles that does not exist in this pluralistic age. The absence of such a consensus can be attributed to numerous changes that have occurred over time in the business environment, including the growth of conflicting interest groups, shifts in basic cultural values, the death of the Puritan ethic, and the increasing use of legal criteria in ethical decision making.

Multiple Clients   Edgar Schein cites the increasing number of clients and interests the manager must satisfy: the stockholders, the customer, the community and/or government, the enterprise itself, subordinate employees, peers and colleagues, a superior, and perhaps the standards of a profession.[4] Since these clients may possess different and sometimes conflicting expectations, their ethical assessments of a management decision are also likely to differ. With so many clients and ethical expectations, it is never easy to know what is right or which client to heed. The multiple clients (or constituencies) factor requires a careful balancing of priorities and a situational approach to ethical issues.

Shifting Values   George Lodge argues that a new American ideology has emerged as a result of five major shifts in basic values within the American culture:[5]

1. From rugged individualism to "communitarianism";
2. From property rights to membership rights;
3. From competitive markets as the means to determine consumer needs to broader societal determination of community needs;
4. From limited government planning to expanded and extensive government planning;
5. From scientific specialization to a holistic utilization of knowledge.

These shifts in values can give rise to two types of ethical dilemmas. First, an industry can be divided in its loyalties to both old and new ideologies (i.e., to a free market versus a controlled market). Second, society at large may be divided in its loyalties to the needs of an industry versus the needs of the environment. These are tough choices: open markets or managed markets; industry or the environment. Such shifting values increase individuals' and firms' uncertainty regarding ethical issues. Moreover, this uncertainty is not likely to be resolved by simply choosing one ideology over another or one constituency over another.

Death of the Puritan Ethic   According to Daniel Bell, the "Puritan temper" or "Protestant ethic," which allegedly inspired the spirit of capitalism, is dying.[6] In the past this ethic promoted hard work, thrift, saving, moderation, and equality of opportunity or means. However, commercial success has spawned contradictory values that emphasize leisure, spending, debt accumulation, hedonism, and equality of condition or ends. The major consequence of this change is the erosion of a unifying social ethic. The fact that these two ethical systems exist simultaneously motivates and justifies a schizophrenic life-style where one is encouraged to be "straight" at work but a "swinger" on weekends. It is hardly surprising that managers often concede that their most vexing ethical dilemmas involve personnel.

Identical developments are evident at the corporate level. John K. Galbraith perceives a dichotomy within the production system; he labels one part a planning system and the other a marketing system.[7] The inordinate power of the planning system of large corporations gives them a monopoly over consumer needs; they even determine which needs will be served. If this is true, it means that large corporations have also deserted the Puritan ethic, that their only ethic is survival and self-perpetuation, and that their primary constituency consists of themselves.

The death of the Puritan ethic as the dominant ethical force in society has left us visionless. The individual and the corporation, confronting contradictions which foster uncertainty, turn inward and respond to the one constituency over which they have some sense of certainty and control—themselves. Achievement horizons are shortened: individuals expect rapid promotion, and corporations focus exclusively on quarterly progress.

Lawyers as Priests   We used to be able to look to religion for ethical guidance; the priest would bless and legitimize our enterprise. That is no longer the case. In fact, the entry of brand-name religion into the marketplace seems to divide loyalties further and inhibit ethical discussion. This vacuum has been filled by the legal profession.

Lawyers maintain that they only interpret the law and that they do not make it (at least not until they are elected to legislative office). But, as both practitioners and legislators, lawyers increasingly serve our culture as the priest once did. The law determines what is right and implicitly blesses it. In effect, the equation seems to be: if it's legal, it's ethical.

Yet this equation has its limitations. Christopher Stone argues that neither the "invisible" hand of the market nor a court of law is capable of delineating and enforcing the principles and behavior needed to solve society's problems, although both can play a positive role.[8] In his description of the history of corporations and the law, Stone documents numerous cases in which regulation of business by law has been ineffective. In addition, such regulation is rarely cost-effective, and it usually produces unanticipated and/or unacceptable consequences. Thus, while our growing dependence on the law as a substitute for ethics may be understandable, it is not necessarily desirable.

A Dynamic Definition

In these rapidly changing times, both the underlying purpose and the rules of the business game have become increasingly unclear. One consequence of these changes is that ethics can no longer be viewed as a static code or a set of principles that is understood and agreed upon by all. Charles Powers and David Vogel address this problem by providing a simple but dynamic working definition: "In essence ethics is concerned with clarifying what constitutes human welfare and the kind of conduct necessary to promote it."[9]

The first part of this definition implies both a constellation of values and a process of discussion or debate. While some values will be widely shared, individuals and groups will sometimes differ on "what constitutes human welfare." The Powers and Vogel definition is particularly suitable to the U.S., where no "ultimate authority" issues quick, precise answers. Rather, the process of clarification is an ongoing response to changing values, emerging technological or economic developments, and shifting political forces. For example, government's increasing role as an income transfer agent in recent years signifies a change in the definition of human welfare. The fact that some portion of the national income is distributed on the basis of need rather than merit affirms a particular perception of economic justice. Lester Thurow notes a correlation between environmentalism and income distribution, suggesting that environmentalism is one of the newest consumer wants for those whose basic needs already have been satisfied.[10] This represents a further refinement of the definition of human welfare.

The second part of the Powers and Vogel definition focuses on behavior. Once we have conceptualized or reached some consensus about what constitutes human welfare, the debate then focuses on the kind of conduct necessary to promote that concept of human welfare. For instance, having determined that some national income should be distributed on the basis of need rather than merit, we can use income tax legislation to establish a new code of conduct: taking from some and giving to others. In this way a new ethic is established. Most of the regulation of business that began in the last century can be viewed from this same perspective—a higher state of human welfare was clarified and complementary conduct was subsequently mandated.

New political and economic forces are continually reshaping our perception of the highest state of human welfare and altering our conduct accordingly. At the corporate level, deciding what is good and right or bad and wrong in such a dynamic environment is necessarily "situational." Therefore, instead of relying on a set of fixed ethical principles, we must now develop an ethical process. In order to do this, this article will next outline a conceptual ethical framework and then present an algorithm designed to deal with ethical questions on a situational basis.

A CONCEPTUAL FRAMEWORK

Business executives regularly wrestle with the new factors of the business environment: multiple clients and goals, shifting values and cultural contradictions, and increasing dependence on legal staffs. Although the profit-oriented corporation will naturally focus *primarily* on economic goals, decisions that focus *exclusively* on profit maximization are being challenged. Typically, all of these decisions are fashioned with care in the guarded privacy of corporate offices and boardrooms. This is due in part to the nature of the competitive business game; undoubtedly, some secrecy is also occasioned by less noble motives. Once a product or service reaches the market, these decisions face exposure to public scrutiny.

The process has become even more complex in our turbulent environment. Focusing on legal considerations, let us assume that the vast majority of businesspeople intend to function within the boundaries of the law. Unfortunately, the legal status of an increasing number of manufacturing or marketing decisions is unclear when they are initially conceived and put into operation. Public scrutiny of these decisions (by Congress, a federal or state agency, or perhaps some other client) often raises questions of legality. In cases where some law or legal precedent exists, a clear determination of status can be achieved (although this may take years).

Over time many products and services have fallen from presumed legality into illegality, including cyclamates, DDT, firecrackers, recombinant DNA, and payments to foreign officials and governments. Thus, not only must products and services face final acceptance or rejection by the consumer, but their legal status may change as new information becomes available.

According to our dynamic definition of ethics, ethical issues emerge when our perception of what constitutes human welfare receives or requires clarification. More specifically, ethical issues arise when laws or legal precedents are either unclear or at variance with shifting cultural values. The proliferation of multinational and transnational corporations has provided numerous examples of this process. Positioned between two or more legal/ethical systems, these firms face scrutiny by publics that may differ radically on significant issues: the use and distribution of material resources, the source and exercise of authority, perceptions of time, measurement of productivity, and the use of competition as a motivating force. These differences alter ethical objectives and their complementary customs and legal sanctions.

Many multinationals have been affected by the existence of the Foreign Corrupt Practices Act of 1977. Under this law, of course, it is illegal for U.S. firms to make payments to foreign officials or governments. Yet, some would ar-

Figure 1 A conceptual framework

gue that the Act itself is unethical insofar as it restricts international trade and thereby diminishes both human welfare and our national interest. When the Act was proposed, the Securities and Exchange Commission took the position that secret payments deprived current and prospective stockholders of potentially relevant information about company operations. The Internal Revenue Service questioned the deduction of such payments as business expenses. In effect, the Act was passed to satisfy a constituency that includes an unknown percentage of domestic and foreign consumers, unidentified current and prospective stockholders, and an agency of the federal government (which presumably acts on behalf of taxpayers). But are there consumers, stockholders, and taxpayers who would take a different ethical stance? Probably. None of the available choices satisfies the total constituency; this is characteristic of ethical dilemmas.

The issue of foreign payments illustrates how ethical questions develop from corporate decisions that are privately conceived and executed in advance of public scrutiny and without clear legal or ethical precedent. Aside from blatant corruption and dishonesty, the above process describing the emergence of ethical issues accounts for much of the consternation and confusion about business ethics today. It is the failure to understand and anticipate this process that creates the vast majority of ethical dilemmas.

The conceptual framework described above is summarized in Figure 1. The inner circle of this figure represents corporate decisions before they are revealed to the public. Once these decisions are manifested (middle circle), they may become the subject of considerable public debate. The result of this debate is the codification process (outer circle), in which society determines the legal and ethical status of each decision.

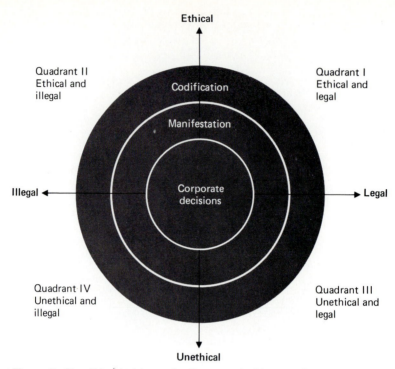

Figure 2 Classifying decisions using the conceptual framework.

One question continually confronts business executives as they privately ponder alternatives: What happens when our decisions become public? This question can be particularly difficult to answer, since the legal and ethical status of a decision may change over time. Decision makers need to answer the question: Into which quadrant of Figure 2 will an issue with ethical implications fall?

Consider the business executive who aspires to function in Quadrant I. When his or her decisions become manifest and codified, they will prove to be both ethical and legal. In the past this was a reasonable expectation for most decision makers. While it is dangerous to make assumptions about the intentions of businesspeople today, it seems that more of their decisions now fall into Quadrants II, III, and IV.

In Quadrant II (ethical and illegal), we find a host of controversial issues that divide the country because their ethical and legal statuses con-

flict: selling marijuana, ''whistle blowing,'' windfall profits, and payments to foreign officials. While many individuals will attempt to resolve such conflicts by focusing on an issue's legal status, the ethical questions surrounding an issue also should be examined. According to our conceptual framework, the ethical perceptions concerning an issue must be addressed before its legal status can be changed. This is a time-consuming task that business has been unwilling or unable to assume on a large scale.

Quadrant III contains another series of controversial subjects—those which are legal but unethical. For example, while the marketing of infant feeding formulas to developing countries is legal, a recent vote at the United Nations called it unethical. (The U.S. abstained from voting.) The following examples are legal as well, but some have questioned their ethical underpinnings: the manufacture of pesticides, the use of laetrile in cancer treatment, plant relocation based on labor cost differentials, and interlocking directorships. As in Quadrant II, it is tempting to focus corporate attention on the legal status of these issues, rather than on their ethical foundation.

In Quadrant IV (unethical and illegal), we find a wide variety of actions that have been censured, including discrimination against minorities and women, occupational hazards, disposal of chemical waste, and political slush funds. In these areas, the laws are clear and ethical support is sufficiently strong to silence open dissent.

While some issues clearly belong in one quadrant or another, there are many others whose status is unclear. How then do we decide which quadrant an issue belongs in? This is determined not only by *which* action is being examined, but also by *how* that action is undertaken. One interesting example is "whistle blowing." To the extent that some forms of whistle blowing are ethical but in clear violation of company rules or expectations, they may be placed in Quadrant II. However, where such behavior jeopardizes trade secrets or national security, we might want to place it in Quadrants III or IV. The fact that whistle blowing may be placed in any of these quadrants underscores the turbulence in our legal and ethical environments.

The conceptual framework presented here depicts a dynamic environment filled with legal and ethical uncertainty. Since decision making in such an environment must frequently be based on situational factors, an algorithm is needed that will allow us to judge each ethical issue on its own merits.

A SITUATIONAL ETHIC ALGORITHM

According to Joseph Fletcher, the basic tenet underlying situation ethics is that circumstances alter cases.[11] This theory maintains that honesty is not always the best policy—it depends on the situation. In Fletcher's judgment, complex, significant ethical decisions are made based on the situation at a given moment in time, and, there-

fore, no two judgments will ever be the same. As the consequences of business decisions become more complex and unpredictable, the situation ethic becomes a necessity. There is a danger, however, that disastrous outcomes will be rationalized too easily as "we did the best we could." Since a situation ethic is without ready-made answers, it is important to develop a rigorous, rational process for examining ethical issues. Such homework should precede the implementation of a decision and serve as the ethical equivalent of a cost-benefit analysis.

Fletcher identifies four factors that can serve as check points in sorting out the ethical dimensions of a given situation.[12] These factors, translated into the business context, are goals, methods, motives, and consequences. Analyzing situations from these four perspectives constitutes an ethical algorithm which can increase our sense of certainty about decisions and ultimately provide a defendable decision-making *process*. Users of the algorithm plug in their own values as they examine goals, methods, motives, and consequences. Careful consideration of these four factors before selecting a course of action is likely to yield a variety of significant insights.

Goals

The goal structure of an organization should be examined from the perspectives of goal multiplicity, constituency priority, and goal compatibility.

Goal Multiplicity While profit maximization (subject to certain constraints) is an implicit goal of most business corporations, many firms simultaneously pursue other goals as well. Moreover, an organization's goal structure is often complicated by the imposition of constraints from outside sources. For example, a firm that relocates to another part of the country in order to maximize profits must consider the reactions of public officials and employees. A company that does business in South Africa must weigh the effect of its actions on the "ethical investor" who is opposed to apartheid. In some cases constraints such as these can eventually function as goals themselves. To the extent that these new goals can be measured, they will figure prominently in the minds of stockholders, employees, the government, and various segments of the population at large. Decision makers must be clear about this multiplicity of goals from the outset, particularly if constraints are incorporated into the goal structure.

Sometimes, however, constraints are not included in the goal structure. Some corporations, for example, treat affirmative action strictly as a constraint. It never becomes part of the goal structure, at least not in a formal sense. Minimum compliance with affirmative action guidelines may be perceived as an acceptable policy, but not as a corporate objective. Such a policy may be difficult to defend publicly, but it illustrates the importance of goal clarity and the handling of constraints.

Constituency Priority Multiple goals can be identified as serving only corporate purposes, a specific national interest, or a minority constituency. Ranking these constituencies in terms of priorities enriches the definition of the goal structure. In most corporations, top priority is usually assigned to the enterprise itself and/or the stockholders to varying degrees. Secondary and lower priorities are given, for example, to a national interest (affirmative action) and a minority constituency (employee satisfaction), respectively. The ranking exercise itself can be illuminating, spotlighting inconsistencies and potential conflicts within the goal structure. In particular, inconsistencies are likely to appear in matching up constituent priority with goal priority. Clarity and management consensus are the operational objectives in this exercise.

Business is not always happy with morality that is legislated by others. Adopting a hierarchy of multiple goals (including those previously perceived as constraints) builds a stronger, broader ethical foundation for enterprise.

Goal Compatibility After a firm has identified and ranked its multiple goals, the goals should be checked for compatibility. Because the ethical side of enterprise is intangible and unpredictable, an organization will frequently find that its goals conflict with one another. For example, one company that was doing business in South Africa publicly adopted the dual goals of modest profit and effective opposition to apartheid.[13] While profit was easy to measure, "effective opposition to apartheid" proved to be a much more nebulous goal. Different groups applying different standards argued that the firm should use significantly different methods to achieve these goals. One suggestion was for the firm to withdraw from South Africa, thereby sacrificing the profit goal entirely. When it finally became clear that the two goals were incompatible, the company was forced to choose between them.

Methods

Before selecting appropriate methods to achieve its goals, a firm must carefully consider the acceptability of various methods to constituents. In addition, the organization should decide whether these methods are intended to maximize goals or merely to satisfy them; whether the methods are essential, incidental, or extraneous to the goals themselves.

Constituent Acceptability Where ethical issues emerge, the firm must consider the acceptability of various methods to its constituents. Today a corporation has more constituencies than ever before. Over time these groups have voiced a greater number of expectations and concerns, which have resulted in much new legislation. Consequently, manufacturing methods must meet new standards of product and employee safety and environmental protection. Increased

SEC and IRS regulation governs investment and marketing activities in foreign countries. The passage of ERISA has regulated the vesting of employee pension benefits. As such changes in regulation and legislation continue, business can help shape them by carefully evaluating the acceptability of its methods to multiple constituencies.

Methods That Satisfy or Maximize Goals   Should the decision maker select methods that satisfy a goal or methods that maximize achievement? How safe is safe? Should a firm simply satisfy affirmative action requirements, or should it make a maximum effort to increase the employment of minorities and women? The fact that corporations have not really confronted and answered these questions has created ethical confusion. For example, such confusion has arisen in the debate over what constitutes excess or windfall profits. What is a fair or ethically acceptable return on investment? Over what period of time? The situation ethic algorithm suggests that businesspeople must confront such questions as part of the decision-making process.

Essential, Incidental, or Extraneous   It has been suggested that the decentralization of management at General Electric under Ralph Cordiner in the 1950s was a major contributor to the pricing conspiracy which ensued.[14] However, the real goals behind GE's decision to decentralize remain shrouded in controversy. Was decentralization absolutely *essential* to goal achievement? Was it *incidental?* Did management believe that it would probably have a positive impact and was worth trying at little risk? Or was it really *extraneous* to the goal itself and more a whim or personal predilection of top management? Such questions are always relevant as a firm attempts to select the most effective methods for achieving its goals.

Formal contractual arrangements and informal commitments to employees may be areas offering a number of significant choices for the future. These include such issues as the vesting of pensions, flextime, educational opportunities and on-the-job training, salary bonuses for production workers, and lifetime work contracts. In each case, business can evaluate whether such changes are essential, incidental, or extraneous to success.

Motives

It is often difficult to distinguish between motives and methods. Simply stated, corporations do not have motives. Rather, individuals have motives which find their way into corporate life through goal and method selection. In some instances, it is readily apparent that the motives of a strong or influential executive are the driving force behind a corporation's goals and methods. What drives a manager or executive to take certain actions? An instinct for survival, an innate competitive urge, a desire for power? Although employees' motives are often difficult to discern, they are the lifeblood of any institution, determining its character, climate, and degree of success. The more influential an employee, the more his or her motives will affect the firm's goals and methods. While we can only infer from an individual's behavior what his or her motives are, there are nevertheless some useful check points in this third step of the ethical algorithm.

Hidden or Known   Do others know what your motives are? As decisions with ethical implications are revealed to the public, the underlying motives of business executives tend to emerge as well. The revelation of these motives often determines the ethical or legal labeling that follows.

Motives of corporate decision makers are often suspect simply because they are somewhat hidden. The invisibility of corporate leaders makes it easy for them to be labeled "greedy" or "power hungry." If there is any substance to such accusations or if decision makers remain silent regarding their motives, the worthy goals or methods of corporate enterprise can be drowned in a sea of outraged voices. The situation ethic does not stipulate that all motives should be revealed at all times. Rather, it argues that executives should know what their motives are and when it is essential to make them public.

Shared or Selfish   In *The Gamesman,* Michael Maccoby identifies four distinct executive types, each distinguished in large measure by his motives: the Craftsman, the Companyman, the Jungle Fighter, and the Gamesman.[15] The Craftsman is absorbed in his creative process; the Companyman bases his identity on that of the firm. The Jungle Fighter is a power seeker; the Gamesman thrives on competitive activities that allow him to mark himself as a winner. In addition to underscoring the critical role that motives play, Maccoby implies that leaders driven by narrow personal or selfish motives are less likely to achieve corporate success, especially over the long term. Executives who question whether their motives are purely selfish or widely shared are moving in the direction of consensus management. Again the situation ethic does not argue that consensus is always desirable or possible, only that it is an important check point in the ethical algorithm.

Value Orientation   Commitments to certain basic values and/or religious beliefs tend to enter corporate life through the motives of key business leaders. It is becoming increasingly important for executives to be able to articulate these values and beliefs in the context of their work life. The value shifts noted by Lodge appear to have received only indirect, inconsistent attention from the business community.[16] It is not clear why business has been silent in this arena. However, it is clear that this silence has had negative effects on the ethical soundness of enterprise. In the future the success of capitalistic enterprise will be largely determined by what business leaders' motives are and by how effectively they can articulate them.

Consequences

In the final step of the ethical algorithm, the firm reviews its goals, methods, and motives and considers the potential consequences of its actions. Each of the multiple goals and methods is matched with one or more consequences. Decision makers must ask: What are the consequences of using a particular method or reaching a specific goal? These potential outcomes can be grouped into several categories.

Time Frames   Most firms will find it instructive to project the consequences of their policies over several different time periods. Of course, the appropriate time frames will vary with each firm's products and goals.

Constituency Impact   Possible consequences must be considered from the perspective of each of the firm's constituencies. This is especially important if ethical and legal precedents are unclear or if new technology is to be introduced.

Exogenous Effects   Firms must also anticipate the probable consequences of the efforts of others. In some companies such a notion is standard marketing practice. These exogenous effects are likely to grow in importance with advancing technology, increasing interdependence, global markets, and shifting values and political climates.

CONCLUSION

Sensitivity to the ethical side of enterprise means searching arduously for decisions and actions that warrant and receive the affirmation of an expanding multifarious constituency. The conceptual framework presented here is one attempt to perceive this constituency in all of its complexity. The ethical algorithm is one means of working with this constituency, rather than against it. The singular importance of enterprise to our daily lives and our collective future demands our careful attention and finest efforts.

NOTES

1. See P. E. Drucker, "Ethical Chic," *Forbes,* 14 September 1981, pp. 160–173.
2. See R. H. Tawney, *Religion and the Rise of Capitalism* (New York: Harcourt & Brace, 1926).
3. See P. Berger, "New Attack on the Legitimacy of Business," *Harvard Business Review,* September–October 1981.
4. See E. H. Schein, "The Problem of Moral Education for the Business Manager" (Paper prepared for the Seventeenth Conference on Science, Philosophy, and Religion, August 1966).
5. See G. C. Lodge, *The New American Ideology* (New York: Alfred A. Knopf, 1979).
6. See D. Bell, *The Cultural Contradictions of Capitalism* (New York: Basic Books, 1976).
7. See J. K. Galbraith, *Economics and the Public Purpose* (Boston: Houghton Mifflin, 1978).
8. See C. D. Stone, *Where the Law Ends: The Social Context of Corporate Behavior* (New York: Harper Torchbooks, 1975).
9. See C. Powers and D. Vogel, *Ethics in the Education of Business Managers* (Hastings-on-Hudson: Institute of Society, Ethics and the Life Sciences, The Hastings Institute, 1980).
10. See L. Thurow, *The Zero-Sum Society* (New York: Basic Books, 1980).
11. See J. Fletcher, *Situation Ethics: The New Morality* (Philadelphia: The Westminster Press, 1966). Dr. Fletcher is former Professor of Ethics at the Episcopal Divinity School, Cambridge, MA).
12. Ibid.
13. See D. T. Verma, "Polaroid in South Africa (A)," #9-372-624 (Boston: Intercollegiate Case Clearing House, 1971).
14. See R. A. Smith, "The Incredible Electrical Conspiracy," *Fortune,* April 1961.
15. See M. Maccoby, *The Gamesman* (New York: Bantam Books, 1976).
16. See Lodge (1979).

Ethics Without the Sermon

Laura L. Nash*

Whether you regard it as an unchecked epidemic or as the first blast of Gabriel's horn, the trend toward focusing on the social impact of the corporation is an inescapable reality that must be factored into today's managerial decision making. But for the executive who asks, "How do we as a corporation examine our ethical concerns?" the theoretical insights currently available may be more frustrating than helpful.

Many executives firmly believe that corporate operations and corporate values are dynamically intertwined. For the purposes of analysis, however, the executive needs to uncoil the business-ethics helix and examine both strands closely.

Unfortunately, the ethics strand has remained largely inaccessible, for business has not yet developed a workable process by which corporate values can be articulated. If ethics and business are part of the same double helix, perhaps we can develop a microscope capable of enlarging our perception of both aspects of business administration—what we do and who we are.

Philosophy has been sorting out issues of fairness, injury, empathy, self-sacrifice, and so on, for more than 2000 years. In seeking to examine the ethics of business, therefore, business logically assumes it will be best served by a "consultant" in philosophy who is already familiar with the formal discipline of ethics.

As the philosopher begins to speak, however, a difficulty immediately arises; corporate executives and philosophers approach problems in radically different ways. The academician ponders the intangible, savors the paradoxical, and embraces the peculiar; he or she speaks in a special language of categorical imperatives and deontological viewpoints that must be taken into consideration before a statement about honesty is agreed to have any meaning.

Like some Triassic reptile, the theoretical view of ethics lumbers along in the far past of Sunday School and Philosophy I, while the reality of practical business concerns is constantly measuring a wide range of competing claims on time and resources against the unrelenting and objective marketplace.

Not surprisingly, the two groups are somewhat hostile. The jokes of the liberal intelligentsia are rampant and weary: "*Ethics and Business*—the shortest book in the world." "Business and ethics—a subject confined to the preface of business books." Accusations from the corporate cadre are delivered with an assurance that rests more on an intuition of social climate than on a certainty of fact: "You do-gooders are ruining America's ability to compete in the world."

What is needed is a process of ethical inquiry that is immediately comprehensible to a group of executives and not predisposed to the utopian, and sometimes anticapitalistic, bias marking much of the work in applied business philosophy today. So I suggest, as a preliminary solution, a set of 12 questions that draw on traditional philosophical frameworks but that avoid the level of abstraction normally associated with formal moral reasoning.

I offer the questions as a first step in a very new discipline. As such, they form a tentative model that will certainly undergo modifications after its parts are given some exercise. Table 1 poses the 12 questions.

To illustrate the application of the questions, I will draw especially on a program at Lex Service Group, Ltd., whose top management prepared a statement of financial objectives and moral values as a part of its strategic planning process. Lex is a British company with opera-

TABLE 1

TWELVE QUESTIONS FOR EXAMINING THE ETHICS OF A BUSINESS DECISION

1 Have you defined the problem accurately?

2 How would you define the problem if you stood on the other side of the fence?

3 How did this situation occur in the first place?

4 To whom and to what do you give your loyalty as a person and as a member of the corporation?

5 What is your intention in making this decision?

6 How does this intention compare with the probable results?

7 Whom could your decision or action injure?

8 Can you discuss the problem with the affected parties before you make your decision?

9 Are you confident that your position will be as valid over a long period of time as it seems now?

10 Could you disclose without qualm your decision or action to your boss, your CEO, the board of directors, your family, society as a whole?

11 What is the symbolic potential of your action if understood? if misunderstood?

12 Under what conditions would you allow exceptions to your stand?

tions in the United Kingdom and the United States. Its sales total about $1.2 billion. In 1978 its structure was partially decentralized, and in 1979 the chairman's policy group began a strategic planning process. The intent, according to its statement of values and objectives, was "to make explicit the sort of company Lex was, or wished to be."

Neither a paralegal code nor a generalized philosophy, the statement consisted of a series of general policies regarding financial strategy as well as such aspects of the company's character as customer service, employee-shareholder responsibility, and quality of management. Its content largely reflected the personal values of Lex's chairman and CEO, Trevor Chinn, whose private philanthropy is well known and whose concern for social welfare has long been echoed in the company's personnel policies.

In the past, pressure on senior managers for high profit performance had obscured some of these ideals in practice, and the statement of strategy was a way of radically realigning various competing moral claims with the financial objectives of the company. As one senior manager remarked to me, "The values seem obvious, and if we hadn't been so gross in the past we wouldn't have needed the statement." Despite a predictable variance among Lex's top executives as to the desirability of the values outlined in the statement, it was adopted with general agreement to comply and was scheduled for reassessment at a senior managers' meeting one year after implementation.

1. Have You Defined the Problem Accurately?

How one assembles the facts weights an issue before the moral examination ever begins, and a definition is rarely accurate if it articulates one's loyalties rather than the facts. The importance of factual neutrality is readily seen, for example, in assessing the moral implications of producing a chemical agent for use in warfare. Depending on one's loyalties, the decision to make the substance can be described as serving one's country, developing products, or killing babies. All of the above may be factual statements, but none is neutral or accurate if viewed in isolation.

Similarly, the recent controversy over marketing U.S.-made cigarettes in Third World countries rarely noted that the incidence of lung cancer in underdeveloped nations is quite low (from one-tenth to one-twentieth the rate for U.S. males) due primarily to the lower life expectancies and earlier predominance of other diseases in these nations. Such a fact does not decide the ethical complexities of this marketing problem,

but it does add a crucial perspective in the assignment of moral priorities by defining precisely the injury that tobacco exports may cause.

Extensive fact gathering may also help defuse the emotionalism of an issue. For instance, local statistics on lung cancer incidence reveal that the U.S. tobacco industry is not now "exporting death," as has been charged. Moreover, the substantial and immediate economic benefits attached to tobacco may be providing food and health care in these countries. Nevertheless, as life expectancy and the standards of living rise, a higher incidence of cigarette-related diseases appears likely to develop in these nations. Therefore, cultivation of the nicotine habit may be deemed detrimental to the long-term welfare of these nations.

According to one supposedly infallible truth of modernism, technology is so complex that its results will never be fully comprehensible or predictable. Part of the executive's frustration in responding to question 1 is the real possibility that the "experts" will find no grounds for agreement about the facts.

As a first step, however, defining fully the factual implications of a decision determines to a large degree the quality of one's subsequent moral position. Pericles' definition of true courage rejected the Spartans' blind obedience in war in preference to the courage of the Athenian citizen who, he said, was able to make a decision to proceed in full knowledge of the probable danger. *A truly moral decision is an informed decision. A decision that is based on blind or convenient ignorance is hardly defensible. One simple test of the initial definition is the question:*

2. How Would You Define the Problem If You Stood on the Other Side of the Fence?

The contemplated construction of a plant for Division X is touted at the finance committee meeting as an absolute necessity for expansion at a cost saving of at least 25 percent. With plans drawn up for an energy-efficient building and an option already secured on a 99-year lease in a new industrial park in Chippewa County, the committee is likely to feel comfortable in approving the request for funds in a matter of minutes.

The facts of the matter are that the company will expand in an appropriate market, allocate its resources sensibly, create new jobs, increase Chippewa County's tax base, and most likely increase its returns to the shareholders. To the residents of Chippewa County, however, the plant may mean the destruction of a customary recreation spot, the onset of severe traffic jams, and the erection of an architectural eyesore. These are also facts of the situation, and certainly more immediate to the county than utilitarian justifications of profit performance and rights of ownership from an impersonal corporation whose headquarters are 1000 miles from Chippewa County and whose executives have plenty of acreage for their own recreation.

The purpose of articulating the other side, whose needs are understandably less proximate than operational considerations, is to allow some mechanism whereby calculations of self-interest (or even of a project's ultimate general beneficence) can be interrupted by a compelling empathy for those who might suffer immediate injury or mere annoyance as a result of a corporation's decisions. Such empathy is a necessary prerequisite for shouldering voluntarily some responsibility for the social consequences of corporate operations, and it may be the only solution to today's overly litigious and anarchic world.

There is a power in self-examination: with an exploration of the likely consequences of a proposal, taken from the viewpoint of those who do not immediately benefit, comes a discomfort or an embarrassment that rises in proportion to the degree of the likely injury and its articulation. Like Socrates as gadfly, who stung his fellow citizens into a critical examination of their conduct when they became complacent, the discomfort of the alternative definition is meant to prompt a disinclination to choose the expedient over the most responsible course of action.

Abstract generalities about the benefits of the profit motive and the free market system are, for some, legitimate and ultimate justifications, but when unadorned with alternative viewpoints, such arguments also tend to promote the complacency, carelessness, and impersonality that have characterized some of the more injurious actions of corporations. The advocates of these arguments are like the reformers in Nathaniel Hawthorne's short story "Hall of Fantasy" who "had got possession of some crystal fragment of truth, the brightness of which so dazzled them that they could see nothing else in the whole universe."

In the example of Division X's new plant, it was a simple matter of defining the alternate facts; the process rested largely on an assumption that certain values were commonly shared (no one likes a traffic jam, landscaping pleases more than an unadorned building, and so forth). But the alternative definition often underscores an inherent disparity in values or language. To some, the employment of illegal aliens is a criminal act (fact 1); to others, it is a solution to the 60 percent unemployment rate of a neighboring country (fact 2). One country's bribe is another country's redistribution of sales commissions.

When there are cultural or linguistic disparities, it is easy to get the facts wrong or to invoke a pluralistic tolerance as an excuse to act in one's own self-interest: "That's the way they do things over there. Who are we to question their beliefs?" This kind of reasoning can be both factually inaccurate (many generalizations about bribery rest on hearsay and do not represent the complexities of a culture) and philosophically inconsistent (there are plenty of beliefs, such as those of the environmentalist, which the same generalizers do not hesitate to question).

3. How Did This Situation Occur in the First Place?

Lex Motor Company, a subsidiary of Lex Service Group, Ltd., had been losing share at a 20 percent rate in a declining market; and Depot B's performance was the worst of all. Two nearby Lex depots could easily absorb B's business, and closing it down seemed the only sound financial decision. Lex's chairman, Trevor Chinn, hesitated to approve the closure, however, on the grounds that putting 100 people out of work was not right when the corporation itself was not really jeopardized by B's existence. Moreover, seven department managers, who were all within 5 years of retirement and had had 25 or more years of service at Lex, were scheduled to be made redundant.

The values statement provided no automatic solution for it placed value on both employees' security and shareholders' interest. Should they close Depot B? At first Chinn thought not: Why should the little guys suffer disproportionately when the company was not performing well? Why not close a more recently acquired business where employee service was not so large a factor? Or why not wait out the short term and reduce head count through natural attrition?

As important as deciding the ethics of the situation was the inquiry into its history. Indeed, the history gave a clue to solving the dilemma: Lex's traditional emphasis on employee security and high financial performance had led to a precipitate series of acquisitions and subsequent divestitures when the company had failed to meet its overall objectives. After each rationalization, the people serving the longest had been retained and placed at Depot B, so that by 1980 the facility had more managers than it needed and a very high proportion of long-service employees.

So the very factors that had created the performance problems were making the closure decision difficult, and the very solution that Lex was inclined to favor again would exacerbate the situation further!

In deciding the ethics of a situation it is important to distinguish the symptoms from the disease. Great profit pressures with no sensitivity to the cycles in a particular industry, for example, may force division managers to be ruthless with employees, to short-weight customers, or even to fiddle with cash flow reports in order to meet headquarters' performance criteria.

Dealing with the immediate case of lying, quality discrepancy, or strained labor relations—when the problem is finally discovered—is only a temporary solution. A full examination of how the situation occurred and what the traditional solutions have been may reveal a more serious discrepancy of values and pressures, and this will illuminate the real significance and ethics of the problem. It will also reveal recurring patterns of events that in isolation appear trivial but that as a whole point up a serious situation.

Such a mechanism is particularly important because very few executives are outright scoundrels. Rather, violations of corporate and social values usually occur inadvertently because no one recognizes that a problem exists until it becomes a crisis. This tendency toward initial trivialization seems to be the biggest ethical problem in business today. Articulating answers to my first three questions is a way of reversing that process.

4. To Whom and What Do You Give Your Loyalties As a Person and As a Member of the Corporation?

Every executive faces conflicts of loyalty. The most familiar occasions pit private conscience and sense of duty against corporate policy, but equally frequent are the situations in which one's close colleagues demand participation (tacit or explicit) in an operation or a decision that runs counter to company policy. To whom or what is the greater loyalty—to one's corporation? superior? family? society? self? race? sex?

The good news about conflicts of loyalty is that their identification is a workable way of smoking out the ethics of a situation and of discovering the absolute values inherent in it. As one executive in a discussion of a Harvard case study put it, "My corporate brain says this action is O.K., but my noncorporate brain keeps flashing these warning lights."

The bad news about conflicts of loyalty is that there are few automatic answers for placing priorities on them. "To thine own self be true" is a murky quagmire when the self takes on a variety of roles, as it does so often in this complex modern world.

Supposedly, today's young managers are giving more weight to individual than to corporate identity, and some older executives see this tendency as being ultimately subversive. At the same time, most of them believe individual integrity is essential to a company's reputation.

The U.S. securities industry, for example, is one of the most rigorous industries in America in its requirements of honesty and disclosure. Yet in the end, all its systematic precautions prove inadequate unless the people involved also have a strong sense of integrity that puts loyalty to these principles above personal gain.

A system, however, must permit the time and foster the motivation to allow personal integrity to surface in a particular situation. An examination of loyalties is one way to bring this about. Such an examination may strengthen reputations but also may result in blowing the whistle (freedom of thought carries with it the risk of revolution). But a sorting out of loyalties can also bridge the gulf between policy and implementation or among various interest groups whose affiliations may mask a common devotion to an aspect of a problem—a devotion on which consensus can be built.

How does one probe into one's own loyalties and their implications? A useful method is simply to play various roles out loud, to call on one's loyalty to family and community (for example) by asking, "What will I say when my child asks me why I did that?" If the answer is "That's the way the world works," then your loyalties are clear and moral passivity inevitable. But if the question presents real problems, you have begun a demodulation of signals from your conscience that can only enhance corporate responsibility.

5. What Is Your Intention in Making This Decision?

6. How Does This Intention Compare With the Likely Results?

These two questions are asked together because their content often bears close resemblance and, by most calculations, both color the ethics of a situation.

Corporation Buglebloom decides to build a new plant in an underdeveloped minority-populated district where the city has been trying with little success to encourage industrial development. The media approve and Buglebloom adds another star to its good reputation. Is Buglebloom a civic leader and supporter of minorities or a canny investor about to take advantage of the disadvantaged? The possibilities of Buglebloom's intentions are endless and probably unfathomable to the public; Buglebloom may be both canny investor and friend of minority groups.

I argue that despite their complexity and elusiveness, a company's intentions do matter. The "purity" of Buglebloom's motives (purely profit-seeking or purely altruistic) will have wide-reaching effects inside and outside the corporation—on attitudes toward minority employees in other parts of the company, on the wages paid at the new plant, and on the number of other investors in the same area—that will legitimize a certain ethos in the corporation and the community.

Sociologist Max Weber called this an "ethics of attitude" and contrasted it with an "ethics of absolute ends." An ethics of attitude sets a standard to ensure a certain action. A firm policy at headquarters of not cheating customers, for example, may also deter salespeople from succumbing to a tendency to lie by omission or purchasers from continuing to patronize a high-priced supplier when the costs are automatically passed on in the selling price.

What about the ethics of result? Two years later, Buglebloom wishes it had never begun Project Minority Plant. Every good intention has been lost in the realities of doing business in an unfamiliar area, and Buglebloom now has dirty hands: some of those payoffs were absolutely unavoidable if the plant was to open, operations have been plagued with vandalism and language problems, and local resentment at the industrialization of the neighborhood has risen as charges of discrimination have surfaced. No one seems to be benefiting from the project.

The goodness of intent pales somewhat before results that perpetrate great injury or simply do little good. Common sense demands that the "responsible" corporation try to align the two more closely, to identify the probable consequences and also the limitations of knowledge that might lead to more harm than good. Two things to remember in comparing intention and results are that knowledge of the future is always inadequate and that overconfidence often precedes a disastrous mistake.

These two precepts, cribbed from ancient Greece, may help the corporation keep the disparities between intent and result a fearsome reality to consider continuously. The next two questions explore two ways of reducing the moral risks of being wrong.

7. Whom Could Your Decision or Action Injure?

The question presses whether injury is intentional or not. Given the limits of knowledge about a new product or policy, who and how many come into contact with it? Could its inadequate disposal affect an entire community? two em-

ployees? yourself? How might your product be used if it happened to be acquired by a terrorist radical group or a terrorist military police force? Has your distribution system or disposal plan ensured against such injury? Could it ever?

If not, there may be a compelling moral justification for stopping production. In an integrated society where business and government share certain values, possible injury is an even more important consideration than potential benefit. In policymaking, a much likelier ground for agreement than benefit is avoidance of injury through those "universal nos"—such as no mass death, no totalitarianism, no hunger or malnutrition, no harm to children.

To exclude *at the outset* any policy or decision that might have such results is to reshape the way modern business examines its own morality. So often business formulates questions of injury only after the fact in the form of liability suits.

8. Can You Engage the Affected Parties in a Discussion of the Problem Before You Make Your Decision?

If the calculus of injury is one way of responding to limitations of knowledge about the probable results of a particular business decision, the participation of affected parties is one of the best ways of informing that consideration. Civil rights groups often complain that corporations fail to invite participation from local leaders during the planning stages of community development projects and charitable programs. The corporate foundation that builds a tennis complex for disadvantaged youth is throwing away precious resources if most children in the neighborhood suffer from chronic malnutrition.

In the Lex depot closure case I have mentioned, senior executives agonized over whether the employees would choose redundancy over job transfer and which course would ultimately be more beneficial to them. The managers, however, did not consult the employees. There were more than 200 projected job transfers to another town. But all the affected employees, held by local ties and uneasy about possibly lower housing subsidies, refused relocation offers. Had the employees been allowed to participate in the redundancy discussions, the company might have wasted less time on relocation plans or might have uncovered and resolved the fears about relocating.

The issue of participation affects everyone. (How many executives feel that someone else should decide what is in *their* best interest?) And yet it is a principle often forgotten because of the pressure of time or the inconvenience of calling people together and facing predictably hostile questions.

9. Are You Confident That Your Position Will Be As Valid over a Long Period of Time As It Seems Now?

As anyone knows who has had to consider long-range plans and short-term budgets simultaneously, a difference in time frame can change the meaning of a problem as much as spring and autumn change the colors of a tree. The ethical coloring of a business decision is no exception to this generational aspect of decision making. Time alters circumstances, and few corporate value systems are immune to shifts in financial status, external political pressure, and personnel. (One survey now places the average U.S. CEO's tenure in office at five years.)

At Lex, for example, the humanitarianism of the statement of objectives and values depended on financial prosperity. The values did not fully anticipate the extent to which the U.K. economy would undergo a recession, and the resulting changes had to be examined, reconciled, and fought if the company's values were to have any meaning. At the Lex annual review, the managers asked themselves repeatedly whether hard times were the ultimate test of the statement or a clear indication that a corporation had to be able to "afford" ethical position.

Ideally, a company's articulation of its values should anticipate changes of fortune. As the hearings for the passage of the Foreign Corrupt Practices Act of 1977 demonstrated, doing what you can get away with today may not be a secure moral standard, but short-term discomfort for long-term sainthood may require irrational courage or a rational reasoning system or, more likely, both. These 12 questions attempt to elicit a rational system. Courage, of course, depends on personal integrity.

Another aspect of the ethical time frame stretches beyond the boundaries of question 9 but deserves special attention, and that is the timing of the ethical inquiry. When and where will it be made?

The questions offered here do not solve the problem of making time for the inquiry. For suggestions about creating favorable conditions for examining corporate values, drawn from my field research, see Table 2, page 87.

10. Could You Disclose Without Qualm Your Decision or Action to Your Boss, Your CEO, the Board of Directors, Your Family, or Society as a Whole?

The old question, "Would you want your decision to appear on the front page of the *New York Times?*" still holds. A corporation may maintain that there's really no problem, but a survey of how many "trivial" actions it is reluctant to disclose might be interesting. Disclosure is a way of sounding those submarine depths of conscience and of searching out loyalties. It is also a way of keeping a corporate character cohesive. The Lex group, for example, was once faced with a very sticky problem concerning a small but profitable site with unpleasant (although in no way illegal) working conditions, where two men with 30 years' service worked. I wrote up the case for a Lex senior managers' meeting on the promise to disguise it heavily because the executive who supervised the plant was convinced that, if the chairman and the personnel director

TABLE 2	

SHARED CONDITIONS OF SOME SUCCESSFUL ETHICAL INQUIRIES

Freed time frame	Understanding and identifying moral issues takes time and causes ferment, and the executive needs an uninterrupted block of time to ponder the problems.
Unconventional location	Religious groups, boards of directors, and professional associations have long recognized the value of the retreat as a way of stimulating fresh approaches to regular activities. If the group is going to transcend normal corporate hierarchies, it should hold the discussion on neutral territory so that all may participate with the same degree of freedom.
Resource person	The advantage of bringing in an outsider is not that he or she will impose some preconceived notion of right and wrong on management but that he will serve as a midwife for bringing the values already present in the institution out into the open. He can generate closer examination of the discrepancies between values and practice and draw on a wider knowledge of instances and intellectual frameworks than the group can. The resource person may also take the important role of arbitrator—to ensure that one person does not dominate the session with his or her own values and that the dialogue does not become impossibly emotional.
Participation of CEO	In most corporations the chief executive still commands an extra degree of authority for the intangible we call corporate culture, and the discussion needs the perspective of the legitimization by that authority if it is to have any seriousness of purpose and consequence. One of the most interesting experiments in examining corporate policy I have observed lacked the CEO's support, and within a year it died on the vine.
Credo	Articulating the corporation's values and objectives provides a reference point for group inquiry and implementation. Ethical codes, however, when drawn up by the legal department do not always offer a realistic and full representation of management's beliefs. The most important ethical inquiry for management may be the very formulation of such a statement, for the *process* of articulation is as useful as the values agreed on.
Homegrown topics	In isolating an ethical issue, drawing on your own experience is important. Philosophical business ethics has tended to reflect national social controversies, which though relevant to the corporation may not always be as relevant—not to mention as easily resolved—as some internal issues that are shaping the character of the company to a much greater degree. Executives are also more likely to be informed on these issues.
Resolution	In all the programs I observed except one, there was a point at which the inquiry was slated to have some resolution: either a vote on the issue, the adoption of a new policy, a timetable for implementation, or the formulation of a specific statement of values. The one program observed that had no such decision-making structure was organized simply to gather information about the company's activities through extrahierarchical channels. Because the program had no tangible goals or clearly articulated results, its benefits were impossible to measure.

knew the plant's true location, they would close it down immediately.

At the meeting, however, as everyone became involved in the discussion and the chairman himself showed sensitivity to the dilemma, the executive disclosed the location and spoke of his own feelings about the situation. The level of mutual confidence was apparent to all, and by other reports it was the most open discussion the group had ever had.

The meeting also fostered understanding of the company's values and their implementation. When the discussion finally flagged, the chairman spoke up. Basing his views on a full knowledge of the group's understanding of the problem, he set the company's priorities. "Jobs over fancy conditions, health over jobs," Chinn said, "but we always *must disclose*." The group decided to keep the plant open, at least for the time being.

11. What Is the Symbolic Potential of Your Action If Understood? If Misunderstood?

Jones Inc., a diversified multinational corporation with assets of $5 billion, has a paper manufacturing operation that happens to be the only major industry in Stirville, and the factory has been polluting the river on which it is located. Local and national conservation groups have filed suit against Jones Inc. for past damages, and the company is defending itself. Meanwhile, the corporation has adopted plans for a new waste-efficient plant. The legal battle is extended and local resentment against Jones Inc. gets bitter.

As a settlement is being reached, Jones Inc. announces that, as a civic-minded gesture, it will make 400 acres of Stirville woodland it owns available to the residents for conservation and recreation purposes. Jones' intention is to offer a peace pipe to the people of Stirville, and the company sees the gift as a symbol of its own belief in conservation and a way of signaling that value to Stirville residents and national conservation groups. Should Jones Inc. give the land away? Is the symbolism significant?

If the symbolic value of the land is understood as Jones Inc. intends, the gift may patch up the company's relations with Stirville and stave off further disaffection with potential employees as the new plant is being built. It may also signal to employees throughout the corporation that Jones Inc. places a premium on conservation efforts and community relations.

If the symbolic value is misunderstood, however, or if completion of the plant is delayed and the old one has to be put back in use—or if another Jones operation is discovered to be polluting another community and becomes a target of the press—the gift could be interpreted as nothing more than a cheap effort to pay off the people of Stirville and hasten settlement of the lawsuit.

The Greek root of our word *symbol* means both signal and contract. A business decision—whether it is the use of an expense account or a corporate donation—has a symbolic value in signaling what is acceptable behavior within the corporate culture and in making a tacit contract with employees and the community about the rules of the game. How the symbol is actually perceived (or misperceived) is as important as how you intend it to be perceived.

12. Under What Conditions Would You Allow Exceptions to Your Stand?

If we accept the idea that every business decision has an important symbolic value and a contractual nature, then the need for consistency is obvious. At the same time, it is also important to ask under what conditions the rule of the game may be changed. What conflicting principles, circumstances, or time constraints would provide a morally acceptable basis for making an exception to one's normal institutional ethos? For instance, how does the cost of the strategy to develop managers from minority groups over the long term fit in with short-term hurdle rates? Also to be considered is what would mitigate a clear case of employee dishonesty.

Questions of consistency—if you would do X, would you also do Y?—are yet another way of eliciting the ethics of the company and of oneself, and can be a final test of the strength, idealism, or practicality of those values. A last example from the experience of Lex illustrates this point and gives temporary credence to the platitude that good ethics is good business. An article in the Sunday paper about a company that had run a series of racy ads, with pictures of half-dressed women and promises of free merchandise to promote the sale of a very mundane product, sparked an extended examination at Lex of its policies on corporate inducements.

One area of concern was holiday giving. What was the acceptable limit for a gift—a bottle of whiskey? a case? Did it matter only that the company did not *intend* the gift to be an inducement, or did the mere possibility of inducement taint the gift? Was the cut-off point absolute? The group could agree on no halfway point for allowing some gifts and not others, so a new value was added to the formal statement that prohibited the offering or receiving of inducements.

The next holiday season Chinn sent a letter to friends and colleagues who had received gifts of appreciation in the past. In it he explained that, as a result of Lex's concern with "the very complex area of business ethics," management had decided that the company would no longer send any gifts, nor would it be appropriate for its employees to receive any. Although the letter did not explain Lex's reasoning behind the decision, apparently there was a large untapped consensus about such gift giving: by return mail Chinn received at least twenty letters from directors, general managers, and chairmen of companies with which Lex had done business congratulating him for his decision, agreeing with the new policy, and thanking him for his holiday wishes.

The 12 questions are a way to articulate an idea of the responsibilities involved and to lay them open for examination. Whether a decisive

policy is also generated or not, there are compelling reasons for holding such discussions:

The process facilitates talk as a group about a subject that has traditionally been reserved for the privacy of one's conscience. Moreover, for those whose consciences twitch but don't speak in full sentences, the questions help sort out their own perceptions of the problem and various ways of thinking about it.

The process builds a cohesiveness of managerial character as points of consensus emerge and people from vastly different operations discover that they share common problems. It is one way of determining the values and goals of the company, and that is a key element in determining corporate strategy.

It acts as an information resource. Senior managers learn about other parts of the company with which they may have little contact.

It helps uncover ethical inconsistencies in the articulated values of the corporation or between these values and the financial strategy.

It helps uncover sometimes dramatic differences between the values and the practicality of their implementation.

It helps the CEO understand how the senior managers think, how they handle a problem, and how willing and able they are to deal with complexity. It reveals how they may be drawing on the private self to the enhancement of corporate activity.

In drawing out the private self in connection with business and in exploring the significance of the corporation's activities, the process derives meaning from an environment that is often characterized as meaningless.

It helps improve the nature and range of alternatives.

It is cathartic.

The situations for testing business morality remain complex. But by avoiding theoretical inquiry and limiting the expectations of corporate goodness to a few rules for social behavior that are based on common sense, we can develop an ethic that is appropriate to the language, ideology, and institutional dynamics of business decision making and consensus. This ethic can also offer managers a practical way of exploring those occasions when their corporate brains are getting warning flashes from their noncorporate brains.

Cost-Benefit Analysis: An Ethical Critique

Steven Kelman*

At the broadest and vaguest level, cost-benefit analysis may be regarded simply as systematic thinking about decision-making. Who can oppose, economists sometimes ask, efforts to think in a systematic way about the consequences of different courses of action? The alternative, it would appear, is unexamined decision-making. But defining cost-benefit analysis so simply leaves it with few implications for actual regulatory decision-making. Presumably, therefore, those who urge regulators to make greater use of the technique have a more extensive prescription in mind. I assume here that their prescription includes the following views:

1. There exists a strong presumption that an act should not be undertaken unless its benefits outweigh its costs.
2. In order to determine whether benefits outweigh costs, it is desirable to attempt to express all benefits and costs in a common scale or denominator, so that they can be compared with each other, even when some benefits and costs are not traded on markets and hence have no established dollar values.
3. Getting decision-makers to make more use of cost-benefit techniques is important enough to warrant both the expense required to gather the data for improved cost-benefit estimation and the political efforts needed to give the activity higher priority compared to other activities, also valuable in and of themselves.

My focus is on cost-benefit analysis as applied to environmental, safety, and health regulation. In that context, I examine each of the above propositions from the perspective of formal ethical theory, that is, the study of what actions it is morally right to undertake. My conclusions are:

1. In areas of environmental, safety, and health regulation, there may be many instances where a certain decision might be right even though its benefits do not outweigh its costs.
2. There are good reasons to oppose efforts to put dollar values on non-marketed benefits and costs.
3. Given the relative frequency of occasions in the areas of environmental, safety, and health regulation where one would not wish to use a benefits-outweigh-costs test as a decision rule, and given the reasons to oppose the monetizing of non-marketed benefits or costs that is a prerequisite for cost-benefit analysis, it is not justifiable to devote major resources to the generation of data for cost-benefit calculations or to undertake efforts to "spread the gospel" of cost-benefit analysis further.

I

How do we decide whether a given action is morally right or wrong and hence, assuming the desire to act morally, why it should be undertaken or refrained from? Like the Molière character who spoke prose without knowing it, economists who advocate use of cost-benefit analysis for public decisions are philosophers without knowing it: the answer given by cost-benefit analysis,

Excerpted from "Cost-Benefit Analysis: An Ethical Critique," *Regulation*, January–February 1981. Reprinted by permission of the publisher.
*Kennedy School of Government, Harvard University.

that actions should be undertaken so as to max-imize net benefits, represents one of the classic answers given by moral philosophers—that given by utilitarians. To determine whether an action is right or wrong, utilitarians tote up all the pos-itive consequences of the action in terms of hu-man satisfaction. The act that maximizes attain-ment of satisfaction under the circumstances is the right act. That the economists' answer is also the answer of one school of philosophers should not be surprising. Early on, economics was a branch of moral philosophy, and only later did it become an independent discipline.

Before proceeding further, the subtlety of the utilitarian position should be noted. The posi-tive and negative consequences of an act for sat-isfaction may go beyond the act's immediate con-sequences. A facile version of utilitarianism would give moral sanction to a lie, for instance, if the satisfaction of an individual attained by tell-ing the lie was greater than the suffering imposed on the lie's victim. Few utilitarians would agree. Most of them would add to the list of negative consequences the effect of the one lie on the ten-dency of the person who lies to tell other lies, even in instances when the lying produced less satisfaction for him than dissatisfaction for oth-ers. They would also add the negative effects of the lie on the general level of social regard for truth-telling, which has many consequences for future utility. A further consequence may be added as well. It is sometimes said that we should include in a utilitarian calculation the feeling of dissatisfaction produced in the liar (and perhaps in others) because, by telling a lie, one has "done the wrong thing." Correspondingly, in this view, among the positive consequences to be weighed into a utilitarian calculation of truth-telling is sat-isfaction arising from "doing the right thing." This view rests on an error, however, because it *assumes* what it is the purpose of the calculation to *determine*—that telling the truth in the in-stance in question is indeed the right thing to do. Economists are likely to object to this point, ar-guing that no feeling ought "arbitrarily" to be

excluded from a complete cost-benefit calcula-tion, including a feeling of dissatisfaction at do-ing the wrong thing. Indeed, the economists' cost-benefit calculations would, at least ideally, include such feelings. Note the difference be-tween the economist's and the philosopher's cost-benefit calculations, however. The econo-mist may choose to include feelings of dissatis-faction in his cost-benefit calculation, but what happens if somebody asks the economist, "Why is it right to evaluate an action on the basis of a cost-benefit test?" If an answer is to be given to that question (which does not normally preoc-cupy economists but which does concern both philosophers and the rest of us who need to be persuaded that cost-benefit analysis is right), then the circularity problem reemerges. And there is also another difficulty with counting feelings of dissatisfaction at doing the wrong thing in a cost-benefit calculation. It leads to the perverse re-sult that under certain circumstances a lie, for example, might be morally right if the individual contemplating the lie felt no compunction about lying and morally wrong only if the individual felt such a compunction!

This error is revealing, however, because it begins to suggest a critique of utilitarianism. Util-itarianism is an important and powerful moral doctrine. But it is probably a minority position among contemporary moral philosophers. It is amazing that economists can proceed in unani-mous endorsement of cost-benefit analysis as if unaware that their conceptual framework is highly controversial in the discipline from which it arose—moral philosophy.

Let us explore the critique of utilitarianism. The logical error discussed before appears to sug-gest that we have a notion of certain things be-ing right or wrong that *predates* our calculation of costs and benefits. Imagine the case of an old man in Nazi Germany who is hostile to the re-gime. He is wondering whether he should speak out against Hitler. If he speaks out, he will lose his pension. And his action will have done noth-ing to increase the chances that the Nazi regime will be overthrown: he is regarded as somewhat eccentric by those around him, and nobody has ever consulted his views on political questions. Recall that one cannot add to the benefits of speaking out any satisfaction from doing "the right thing," because the purpose of the exercise is to determine whether speaking out *is* the right thing. How would the utilitarian calculation go? The benefits of the old man's speaking out would, as the example is presented, be nil, while the costs would be his loss of his pension. So the costs of the action would outweigh the benefits. By the utilitarians' cost-benefit calculation, it would be *morally wrong* for the man to speak out.

To those who believe that it would not be morally wrong for the old man to speak out in Nazi Germany, utilitarianism is insufficient as a moral view. We believe that some acts whose costs are greater than their benefits may be morally right and, contrariwise, some acts whose benefits are greater than their costs may be morally wrong.

This does not mean that the question whether benefits are greater than costs is morally irrelevant. Few would claim such. Indeed, for a broad range of individual and social decisions, whether an act's benefits outweigh its costs is a sufficient question to ask. But not for all such decisions. These may involve situations where certain duties—duties not to lie, break promises, or kill, for example—make an act wrong, even if it would result in an excess of benefits over costs. Or they may involve instances where people's rights are at stake. We would not permit rape even if it could be demonstrated that the rapist derived enormous happiness from his act, while the victim experienced only minor displeasure. We do not do cost-benefit analyses of freedom of speech or trial by jury. The Bill of Rights was not RARGed.* As the United Steelworkers noted in

_____

Editor's note: The Regulatory Analysis Review Group (RARG) was created by President Carter to improve the cost-benefit analysis of regulatory policy. It was subsequently disbanded by President Reagan.

a comment on the Occupational Safety and Health Administration's economic analysis of its proposed rule to reduce worker exposure to carcinogenic coke-oven emissions, the Emancipation Proclamation was not subjected to an inflationary impact statement. The notion of human rights involves the idea that people may make certain claims to be allowed to act in certain ways or to be treated in certain ways, even if the sum of benefits achieved thereby does not outweigh the sum of costs. It is this view that underlies the statement that "workers have a right to a safe and healthy work place" and the expectation that OSHA's decisions will reflect that judgment.

In the most convincing versions of nonutilitarian ethics, various duties or rights are not absolute. But each has a *prima facie* moral validity so that, if duties or rights do not conflict, the morally right act is the act that reflects a duty or respects a right. If duties or rights do conflict, a moral judgment, based on conscious deliberation, must be made. Since one of the duties nonutilitarian philosophers enumerate is the duty of beneficence (the duty to maximize happiness), which in effect incorporates all of utilitarianism by reference, a non-utilitarian who is faced with conflicts between the results of cost-benefit analysis and non-utility-based considerations will need to undertake such deliberation. But in that deliberation, additional elements, which cannot be reduced to a question of whether benefits outweigh costs, have been introduced. Indeed, depending on the moral importance we attach to the right or duty involved, cost-benefit questions may, within wide ranges, become irrelevant to the outcome of the moral judgment.

In addition to questions involving duties and rights, there is a final sort of question where, in my view, the issue of whether benefits outweigh costs should not govern moral judgment. I noted earlier that, for the common run of questions facing individuals and societies, it is possible to begin and end our judgment simply by finding out if the benefits of the contemplated act outweigh the costs. This very fact means that one way to show the great importance, or value, attached to an area is to say that decisions involving the area should not be determined by cost-benefit calculations. This applies, I think, to the view many environmentalists have of decisions involving our natural environment. When officials are deciding what level of pollution will harm certain vulnerable people—such as asthmatics or the elderly—while not harming others, one issue involved may be the right of those people not to be sacrificed on the altar of somewhat higher living standards for the rest of us. But more broadly than this, many environmentalists fear that subjecting decisions about clean air or water to the cost-benefit tests that determine the general run of decisions removes those matters from the realm of specially valued things.

II

In order for cost-benefit calculations to be performed the way they are supposed to be, all costs and benefits must be expressed in a common measure, typically dollars, including things not normally bought and sold on markets, and to which dollar prices are therefore not attached. The most dramatic example of such things is human life itself; but many of the other benefits achieved or preserved by environmental policy—such as peace and quiet, fresh-smelling air, swimmable rivers, spectacular vistas—are not traded on markets either.

Economists who do cost-benefit analysis regard the quest after dollar values for non-market things as a difficult challenge—but one to be met with relish. They have tried to develop methods for imputing a person's "willingness to pay" for such things, their approach generally involving a search for bundled goods that *are* traded on markets and that vary as to whether they include a feature that is, *by itself,* not marketed. Thus, fresh air is not marketed, but houses in different parts of Los Angeles that are similar except for the degree of smog are. Peace and quiet is not

marketed, but similar houses inside and outside airport flight paths are. The risk of death is not marketed, but similar jobs that have different levels of risk are. Economists have produced many often ingenious efforts to impute dollar prices to non-marketed things by observing the premiums accorded homes in clean air areas over similar homes in dirty areas or the premiums paid for risky jobs over similar nonrisky jobs.

These ingenious efforts are subject to criticism on a number of technical grounds. It may be difficult to control for all the dimensions of quality other than the presence or absence of the non-marketed thing. More important, in a world where people have different preferences and are subject to different constraints as they make their choices, the dollar value imputed to the non-market things that most people would wish to avoid will be lower than otherwise, because people with unusually weak aversion to those things or unusually strong constraints on their choices will be willing to take the bundled good in question at less of a discount than the average person. Thus, to use the property value discount of homes near airports as a measure of people's willingness to pay for quiet means to accept as a proxy for the rest of us the behavior of those least sensitive to noise, of airport employees (who value the convenience of a near-airport location) or of others who are susceptible to an agent's assurances that "it's not so bad." To use the wage premiums accorded hazardous work as a measure of the value of life means to accept as proxies for the rest of us the choices of people who do not have many choices or who are exceptional risk-seekers.

A second problem is that the attempts of economists to measure people's willingness to pay for non-marketed things assume that there is no difference between the price a person would require for *giving up* something to which he has a preexisting right and the price he would pay to *gain* something to which he enjoys no right. Thus, the analysis assumes no difference between how much a homeowner would need to be paid in order to give up an unobstructed mountain view that he already enjoys and how much he would be willing to pay to get an obstruction moved once it is already in place. Available evidence suggests that most people would insist on being paid far more to assent to a worsening of their situation than they would be willing to pay to improve their situation. The difference arises from such factors as being accustomed to and psychologically attached to that which one believes one enjoys by right. But this creates a circularity problem for any attempt to use cost-benefit analysis to determine *whether* to assign to, say, the homeowner the right to an unobstructed mountain view. For willingness to pay will be different depending on whether the right is assigned initially or not. The value judgment about whether to assign the right must thus be made first. (In order to set an upper bound on the value of the benefit, one might hypothetically assign the right to the person and determine how much he would need to be paid to give it up.)

Third, the efforts of economists to impute willingness to pay invariably involve bundled goods exchanged in *private* transactions. Those who use figures garnered from such analysis to provide guidance for *public* decisions assume no difference between how people value certain things in private individual transactions and how they would wish those same things to be valued in public collective decisions. In making such assumptions, economists insidiously slip into their analysis an important and controversial value judgment, growing naturally out of the highly individualistic microeconomic tradition—namely, the view that there should be no difference between private behavior and the behavior we display in public social life. An alternative view—one that enjoys, I would suggest, wide resonance among citizens—would be that public, social decisions provide an opportunity to give certain things a higher valuation than we choose, for one reason or another, to give them in our private activities.

Thus, opponents of stricter regulation of health risks often argue that we show by our daily risk-taking behavior that we do not value life in-

finitely, and therefore our public decisions should not reflect the high value of life that proponents of strict regulation propose. However, an alternative view is equally plausible. Precisely because we fail, for whatever reasons, to give lifesaving the value in everyday personal decisions that we in some general terms believe we should give it, we may wish our social decisions to provide us the occasion to display the reverence for life that we espouse but do not always show. By this view, people do not have fixed unambiguous "preferences" to which they give expression through private activities and which therefore should be given expression in public decisions. Rather, they may have what they themselves regard as "higher" and "lower" preferences. The latter may come to the fore in private decisions, but people may want the former to come to the fore in public decisions. They may sometimes display racial prejudice, but support antidiscrimination laws. They may buy a certain product after seeing a seductive ad, but be skeptical enough of advertising to want the government to keep a close eye on it. In such cases, the use of private behavior to impute the values that should be entered for public decisions, as is done by using willingness to pay in private transactions, commits grievous offense against a view of the behavior of the citizen that is deeply engrained in our democratic tradition. It is a view that denudes politics of any independent role in society, reducing it to a mechanistic, mimicking recalculation based on private behavior.

Finally, one may oppose the effort to place prices on a non-market thing and hence in effect incorporate it into the market system out of a fear that the very act of doing so will reduce the thing's perceived value. To place a price on the benefit may, in other words, reduce the value of that benefit. Cost-benefit analysis thus may be like the thermometer that, when placed in a liquid to be measured, itself changes the liquid's temperature.

Examples of the perceived cheapening of a thing's value by the very act of buying and selling it abound in everyday life and language. The disgust that accompanies the idea of buying and selling human beings is based on the sense that this would dramatically diminish human worth. Epithets such as ''he prostituted himself,'' applied as linguistic analogies to people who have sold something, reflect the view that certain things should not be sold because doing so diminishes their value. Praise that is bought is worth little, even to the person buying it. A true anecdote is told of an economist who retired to another university community and complained that he was having difficulty making friends. The laconic response of a critical colleague—''If you want a friend why don't you buy yourself one''— illustrates in a pithy way the intuition that, for some things, the very act of placing a price on them reduces their perceived value.

The first reason that pricing something decreases its perceived value is that, in many circumstances, non-market exchange is associated with the production of certain values not associated with market exchange. These may include spontaneity and various other feelings that come from personal relationships. If a good becomes less associated with the production of positively valued feelings because of market exchange, the perceived value of the good declines to the extent that those feelings are valued. This can be seen clearly in instances where a thing may be transferred both by market and by non-market mechanisms. The willingness to pay for sex bought from a prostitute is less than the perceived value of the sex consummating love. (Imagine the reaction if a practitioner of cost-benefit analysis computed the benefits of sex based on the price of prostitute services.)

Furthermore, if one values in a general sense the existence of a non-market sector because of its connection with the production of certain valued feelings, then one ascribes added value to any non-marketed good simply as a repository of values represented by the non-market sector one wishes to preserve. This seems certainly to be the case for things in nature, such as pristine streams or undisturbed forests: for many people who value them, part of their value comes from their position as repositories of values the non-market sector represents.

The second way in which placing a market price on a thing decreases its perceived value is by removing the possibility of proclaiming that the thing is ''not for sale,'' since things on the market by definition are for sale. The very statement that something is not for sale affirms, enhances, and protects a thing's value in a number of ways. To begin with, the statement is a way of showing that a thing is valued for its own sake, whereas selling a thing for money demonstrates that it was valued only instrumentally. Furthermore, to say that something cannot be transferred in that way places it in the exceptional category—which requires the person interested in obtaining that thing to be able to offer something else that is exceptional, rather than allowing him the easier alternative of obtaining the thing for money that could have been obtained in an infinity of ways. This enhances its value. If I am willing to say ''You're a really kind person'' to whoever pays me to do so, my praise loses the value that attaches to it from being exchangeable only for an act of kindness.

In addition, if we have already decided we value something highly, one way of stamping it with a cachet affirming its high value is to announce that it is ''not for sale.'' Such an announcement does more, however, than just reflect a preexisting high valuation. It signals a thing's distinctive value to others and helps us persuade them to value the thing more highly than they otherwise might. It also expresses our resolution to safeguard that distinctive value. To state that something is not for sale is thus also a source of value for that thing, since if a thing's value is easy to affirm or protect, it will be worth more than an otherwise similar thing without such attributes.

If we proclaim that something is not for sale, we make a once-and-for-all judgment of its special value. When something is priced, the issue of its perceived value is constantly coming up, as a standing invitation to reconsider that original judgment. Were people constantly faced with questions such as "how much money could get you to give up your freedom of speech?" or "how much would you sell your vote for if you could?", the perceived value of the freedom to speak or the right to vote would soon become devastated as, in moments of weakness, people started saying "maybe it's not worth *so much* after all." Better not to be faced with the constant questioning in the first place. Something similar did in fact occur when the slogan "better red than dead" was launched by some pacifists during the Cold War. Critics pointed out that the very posing of this stark choice—in effect, "would you *really* be willing to give up your life in exchange for not living under communism?"—reduced the value people attached to freedom and thus diminished resistance to attacks on freedom.

Finally, of some things valued very highly it is stated that they are "priceless" or that they have "infinite value." Such expressions are reserved for a subset of things not for sale, such as life or health. Economists tend to scoff at talk of pricelessness. For them, saying that something is priceless is to state a willingness to trade off an infinite quantity of all other goods for one unit of the priceless good, a situation that empirically appears highly unlikely. For most people, however, the word priceless is pregnant with meaning. Its value-affirming and value-protecting functions cannot be bestowed on expressions that merely denote a determinate, albeit high, valuation. John Kennedy in his inaugural address proclaimed that the nation was ready to "pay any price [and] bear any burden... to assure the survival and the success of liberty." Had he said instead that we were willing to "pay a high price" or "bear a large burden" for liberty, the statement would have rung hollow.

III

An objection that advocates of cost-benefit analysis might well make to the preceding argument should be considered. I noted earlier that, in cases where various non-utility-based duties or rights conflict with the maximization of utility, it is necessary to make a deliberative judgment about what act is finally right. I also argued earlier that the search for commensurability might not always be a desirable one, that the attempt to go beyond expressing benefits in terms of (say) lives saved and costs in terms of dollars is not something devoutly to be wished.

In situations involving things that are not expressed in a common measure, advocates of cost-benefit analysis argue that people making judgments "in effect" perform cost-benefit calculations anyway. If government regulators promulgate a regulation that saves 100 lives at a cost of $1 billion, they are "in effect" valuing a life at (a minimum of) $10 million, whether or not they say that they are willing to place a dollar value on a human life. Since, in this view, cost-benefit analysis "in effect" is inevitable, it might as well be made specific.

This argument misconstrues the real difference in the reasoning processes involved. In cost-benefit analysis, equivalencies are established *in advance* as one of the raw materials for the calculation. One determines costs and benefits, one determines equivalencies (to be able to put various costs and benefits into a common measure), and then one sets to toting things up—waiting, as it were, with bated breath for the results of the calculation to come out. The outcome is determined by the arithmetic; if the outcome is a close call or if one is not good at long division, one does not know how it will turn out until the calculation is finished. In the kind of deliberative judgment that is performed without a common measure, no establishment of equivalencies occurs in advance. Equivalencies are not aids to the decision process. In fact, the decision-maker might not even be aware of what the "in effect" equivalencies were, at least before they are revealed to him afterwards by someone pointing out what he had "in effect" done. The decision-maker would see himself as simply having made a deliberative judgment; the "in effect" equivalency number did not play a causal role in the decision but at most merely reflects it. Given this, the argument against making the process explicit is the one discussed earlier in the discussion of problems with putting specific values on things that are not normally quantified—that the very act of doing so may serve to reduce the value of those things.

My own judgment is that modest efforts to assess levels of benefits and costs are justified, although I do not believe that government agencies ought to sponsor efforts to put dollar prices on nonmarket things. I also do not believe that the cry for more cost-benefit analysis in regulation is, on the whole, justified. If regulatory officials were so insensitive about regulatory costs that they did not provide acceptable raw material for deliberative judgments (even if not of a strictly cost-benefit nature), my conclusion might be different. But a good deal of research into costs and benefits already occurs—actually, far more in the U.S. regulatory process than in that of any other industrial society. The danger now would seem to come more from the other side.

Defending Cost-Benefit Analysis: Two Replies to Steven Kelman

James V. DeLong*

Steven Kelman's "Cost-Benefit Analysis—An Ethical Critique" presents so many targets that it is difficult to concentrate one's fire. However, four points seem worth particular emphasis:

1. The decision to use cost-benefit analysis by no means implies adoption of the reduction-

From *Regulation*, March–April 1981. Reprinted by permission of the publisher.
*Attorney, Washington, D.C.

ist utilitarianism described by Kelman. It is based instead on the pragmatic conclusion that any value system one adopts is more likely to be promoted if one knows something about the consequences of the choices to be made. The effort to put dollar values on noneconomic benefits is nothing more than an effort to find some common measure for things that are not easily comparable when, in the real world, choice must be made. Its object is not to write a computer program but to improve the quality of difficult social choices under conditions of uncertainty, and no sensible analyst lets himself become the prisoner of the numbers.

2. Kelman repeatedly lapses into "entitlement" rhetoric, as if an assertion of a moral claim closes an argument. Even leaving aside the fundamental question of the philosophical basis of those entitlements, there are two major problems with this style of argument. First, it tends naturally toward all-encompassing claims.

   Kelman quotes a common statement that "workers have a right to a safe and healthy workplace," a statement that contains no recognition that safety and health are not either/or conditions, that the most difficult questions involve gradations of risk, and that the very use of entitlement language tends to assume that a zero-risk level is the only acceptable one. Second, entitlement rhetoric is usually phrased in the passive voice, as if the speaker were arguing with some omnipotent god or government that is maliciously withholding the entitlement out of spite. In the real world, one person's right is another's duty, and it often clarifies the discussion to focus more precisely on who owes this duty and what it is going to cost him or her. For example, the article posits that an issue in government decisions about acceptable pollution levels is "the right" of such vulnerable groups as asthmatics or the elderly "not to be sacrificed on the altar of somewhat higher living standards for the rest of us." This defends the entitlement by assuming the costs involved are both trivial and diffused. Suppose, though, that the price to be paid is not "somewhat higher living standards," but the jobs of a number of workers?

Kelman's counter to this seems to be that entitlements are not firm rights, but only presumptive ones that prevail in any clash with nonentitlements, and that when two entitlements collide the decision depends upon the "moral importance we attach to the right or duty involved." So the above collision would be resolved by deciding whether a job is an entitlement and, if it is, by then deciding whether jobs or air have greater "moral importance."

I agree that conflicts between such interests present difficult choices, but the quantitative questions, the cost-benefit questions, are hardly irrelevant to making them. Suppose taking X quantity of pollution from the air of a city will keep one asthmatic from being forced to leave town and cost 1,000 workers their jobs? Suppose it will keep 1,000 asthmatics from being forced out and cost one job? These are not equivalent choices, economically or morally, and the effort to decide them according to some abstract idea of moral importance only obscures the true nature of the moral problems involved.

3. Kelman also develops the concept of things that are "specially valued," and that are somehow contaminated if thought about in monetary terms. As an approach to personal decision making, this is silly. There are many things one specially values—in the sense that one would find the effort to assign a market price to them ridiculous—which are nonetheless affected by economic factors. I may specially value a family relationship, but how often I phone is influenced by long-distance rates. I may specially value music, but be affected by the price of records or the cost of tickets at the Kennedy Center.

When translated to the realm of government decisions, however, the concept goes beyond silliness. It creates a political grotesquerie. People specially value many different things. Under Kelman's assumptions, people must, in creating a political coalition, recognize and accept as legitimate everyone's special value, without concern for cost. Therefore, everyone becomes entitled to as much of the thing he specially values as he says he specially values, and it is immoral to discuss vulgar questions of resource limitations. Any coalition built on such premises can go in either of two directions: It can try to incorporate so many different groups and interests that the absurdity of its internal contradictions becomes manifest. Or it can limit its membership at some point and decide that the special values of those left outside are not legitimate and should be sacrificed to the special values of those in the coalition. In the latter case, of course, those outside must be made scapegoats for any frustration of any group member's entitlement, a requirement that eventually leads to political polarization and a holy war between competing coalitions of special values.

4. The decisions that must be made by contemporary government indeed involve painful choices. They affect both the absolute quantity and the distribution not only of goods and benefits, but also of physical and mental suffering. It is easy to understand why people would want to avoid making such choices and would rather act in ignorance than with knowledge and responsibility for the consequences of their choices. While this may be understandable, I do not regard it as an acceptable moral position. To govern is to choose, and government officials—whether elected or appointed—betray their obligations to the welfare of the people who hired them if they adopt a policy of happy ignorance and nonresponsibility for consequences.

The article concludes with the judgment that the present danger is too much cost-benefit analysis, not too little. But I find it hard to believe, looking around the modern world, that its major problem is that it suffers from an excess of rationality. The world's stock of ignorance is and will remain quite large enough without adding to it as a matter of deliberate policy.

Robert A. Nisbet*

A considerable distance separates Steven Kelman's views and mine on, first, the appositeness of cost-benefit analysis and, second, the historical context in which we live. No matter: his thoughtful and gracefully written article ex-z presses a point of view that is widespread and must not be disregarded by those of us who see the matter somewhat differently.

1. I question Kelman's use of "utilitarianism." It seems to me that he has in mind, rather, Bentham's notable (or notorious) hedonic calculus—which does indeed posit that the morally right act is always the one that maximizes satisfaction. Granted that utilitarian theory was originated by Bentham, with the assistance of James Mill. But there is much warrant and precedent for taking it as we find it in John Stuart Mill's *Utilitarianism.*

   Mill, like Bentham and the great English utilitarians of the late nineteenth century, believes the end of government should be to accomplish the greatest possible good for the greatest possible number. But Mill will have none of the hedonic calculus. "He who saves a fellow creature from drowning does what is morally right, whether his motive be duty, or the hope of being paid for his trouble; he who betrays a friend that trusts him is guilty of a crime, even if his object be to serve another friend to whom he is under greater obligation." And there is more: "It is confessedly

unjust," says Mill, "to break faith with anyone, to violate an engagement, either express or implied, or disappoint expectations raised by our own conduct...." So much for Kelman's illustrations with respect to the irrelevance or impiety of cost-benefit assessment.

In addition, the conviction that utility ought to be the ultimate standard of value is, for Mill, quite compatible with the belief that "certain social utilities...are vastly more important and therefore more absolute and imperative than any others are as a class"—and, further, that these utilities should be and are "guarded by a sentiment not only different in degree but in kind." Mill lists a number of such "utilities," chief among them liberty. Were he living today, he might very well—in fact, probably would—add conservation of resources to his list of overriding utilities.

2. That leads me to Kelman's worthy insistence that there are certain values in life for which cost-benefit assessment is inappropriate, even immoral or illogical. I dare say there are, most of them being highly subjective and egocentric. But consider so subjective a state of mind as, say, one's love of another human being. We stipulate the crassness and venality of claiming to love another if the loved one's exclusive attraction is an abundance of worldly goods. There have been other ages, however, not without honor, and there are even now peoples whose morality must be presumed at least as elevated as ours who take a less subjective (and romantic) view of this matter than we contemporary Americans do. In many a newspaper in India we find advertisements for spouses, with everything from a Ph.D. to a given number of cows put on the negotiation counter. Marriages are not to be allowed, in such a culture, to run the risk of foundering on mere human passion—call it love—and on subjective assessment free of cost-benefit analysis. Marriage is too serious in the Hindu's mind, too sacred, too vital. I do not recommend the Hindu dogma of marriage to this

---

Excerpted from *Regulation,* March–April 1981. Reprinted by permission of the publisher.

*Albert Schweitzer Professor Emeritus in the Humanities, Columbia University.

generation of Americans, but from all I have been able to discover from Indian records, as many happy marriages proceed from naked cost-benefit analysis there as from whatever most marriages proceed from in the United States. In fact, I know of virtually nothing, really, in mankind's history, however sacred—birth, marriage, and death foremost—that has not been and is not today in many places subjected to cost-benefit consideration.

To take a less universal crisis of the human condition, the care of the handicapped is, I believe, an obligation of any civilized society. But are we being callous to see economic disaster ahead if we dismiss altogether cost-benefit criteria in our search for ways of increasing their mobility? Is it inhumane to look for other ways of helping wheelchair users than by spending tens of millions on ramps and lifts?

Or take the environment. As far as I am concerned, laws against pollution and resource depletion are always called for, within reasonable limits. And doubtless some parts of the wilderness should be maintained as nearly as possible in their pristine state. But not, I would argue, with such zeal that even prospecting for vital fuels and minerals is outlawed. There is no evidence in this area—or elsewhere, for that matter—of the surfeit of cost-benefit balancing Kelman seems to have observed. With memory fresh of the Alaskan wilderness bill that President Carter signed, I am obliged to conclude that proper balance lies a long way ahead of us—meaning a balance under which private industry has a great deal more leeway than it now has to explore, mine, or otherwise develop these areas. We should remember that serious environmental-

ism (conservation, as it was called then) began under such prescient minds as Theodore Roosevelt and Gifford Pinchot, who repeatedly declared that the purpose of conservation was *not* idle preservation but rather to prevent wanton desolation and to guarantee a future in which people could continue to rise in the scale of economy and civilization.

Unoccupied land is exactly a place where cost-benefit analysis is vital—in the sheer interest of the large numbers of underprivileged among us, including the young not yet established in a career and most emphatically blacks, Hispanics, and other minorities whose rise to middle-class status is among the highest items on our national social agenda. What they, and all others who are currently disadvantaged and in need of channels of upward mobility, require most is economic growth and increased productivity. For without the certain prospect of a vast number of new jobs in the private sector, much of the foundation for what we call the American way of life is destroyed. It is truly unfortunate that the once noble conservation movement in this country has fallen, for the most part, into the hands of those less interested in the welfare of posterity than in the preservation of a wilderness that has become an end in itself, a source of happiness for a tiny few who, I fear, love the wilderness above man. Environmentalism is rapidly becoming the socialism, not of fools, but of the middle and upper classes.

In sum, I agree with Kelman that there assuredly are considerations of the quality of life which should be free of cost-benefit analysis. But I am too avid a student of the great civilizations of past and present to believe that there are very many of these considerations.

QUESTIONS FOR DISCUSSION

1. Henderson distinguishes between actions that are legal and actions that are ethical. What is the difference between legality and morality? What concerns have to be considered if we intend to act ethically, rather than simply legally?
2. Select what you take to be the most important guidelines offered by Henderson and Nash and explain how they might have clarified the situations of Vandivier in particular and B.F. Goodrich in general in the case, "Why Should My Conscience Bother Me?"
3. Explain the similarities and the differences between the cost-benefit analysis described by Kelman and utilitarianism (see general introduction). Why does Kelman believe that utilitarianism is inadequate? Cost-benefit analysis?
4. Turn to the cost-benefit analysis performed by the Ford Motor Company in the Pinto case in Part Four. How might Kelman respond to this example? How might DeLong and Nisbet reply?

Ethics and Business: From Theory to Practice

CASES FOR PART ONE

Richard M. Titmuss
The Gift Relationship: From Human Blood to Social Policy
104

Michael R. Rion
Training for Ethical Management at Cummins Engine
109

Kermit Vandivier
Why Should My Conscience Bother Me?
116

The Gift Relationship: From Human Blood to Social Policy

Richard M. Titmuss*

The starting point of this study is human blood. [It] originated, and grew over many years of introspection, from a series of value questions formulated within the context of attempts to distinguish the "social" from the "economic" in public policies and in those institutions and services with declared "welfare" goals.[1] Could, however, such distinctions be drawn and the territory of social policy at least broadly defined without raising issues about the morality of society and of man's regard or disregard for the needs of others? Why should men not contract out of the "social" and act to their own immediate advantage? Why give to strangers?—a question provoking an even more fundamental moral issue: Who is my stranger in the relatively affluent, acquisitive and divisive societies of the twentieth century? What are the connections, then, if obligations are extended, between the reciprocals of giving and receiving and modern welfare systems?

The choice of blood as an illustration and case study was no idle academic thought; it was deliberate. Short of examining humankind itself and the institution of slavery—of men and women as market commodities—blood as a living tissue may now constitute in Western societies one of the ultimate tests of where the "social" begins and the "economic" ends. If blood is considered in theory, in law, and is treated in practice as a trading commodity, then ultimately human hearts, kidneys, eyes and other organs of the body may also come to be treated as commodities to be bought and sold in the marketplace.

Profitable competition for blood "is a healthy

thing," it is argued by some in the United States. It improves services, increases supplies of blood, and is the answer to a "shiftless, socialistic approach."[2] If competition for blood were eliminated, it is warned, it would "be the entering wedge for the destruction of our entire antimonopoly structure," and would threaten the interests of "great pharmaceutical companies."[3]

The payment of donors and competition for blood should be introduced in Britain, urged two economists in a publication of the Institute of Economic Affairs in London in 1968.[4] Productivity would rise; supplies of blood would increase; "a movement towards more efficiency in the economy as a whole." The Editor, Mr. Arthur Seldon, in a preface said that the authors "have made an unanswerable case for a trial period in which the voluntary donor is supplemented by the fee-paid donor so that the results can be judged in practice, and not prejudged by doctrinaire obfuscation."

In essence, these writers, American and British, are making an economic case against a monopoly of altruism in blood and other human tissues. They wish to set people free from the conscience of obligation. Although their arguments are couched in the language of price elasticity and profit maximization they have far-reaching implications for human values and all "social service" institutions. They legitimate, for instance, the great increase since 1967 in the number of commercial hospitals in the United States.

The moral issues that are raised extend far beyond theories of pricing and the operations of the marketplace. Moreover, they involve the foundations of professional freedom in medical care and other service relationships with people, the concept of the hospital and the university as non-profit making institutions, and the legal doctrine in the United States of charitable immunity. Charity in that country would be subject under competitive conditions to the same laws of restraint and warranty and have the same freedoms as business men in the private market.

Adapted by permission of the publisher from *The Gift Relationship* by Richard M. Titmuss. Copyright © 1972, George Allen and Unwin, Ltd.

*Formerly in the Department of Social Administration, London School of Economics.

THE KANSAS CITY CASE

All these issues were crystallized and debated in the now-famous Kansas City case of 1962. Before we pursue them it is instructive to review the causes and implications of this particular event. Briefly, the facts are these.[5]

In 1953 a meeting in the City of doctors, pathologists, hospital administrators and local citizens decided to form a non-profit making community blood bank. There was a need for more blood, which the local hospital blood banks were not fully supplying, and the local branch of the American Red Cross was at the time channelling the blood it collected to the Armed Forces in Korea. For the next two years there were endless disputes among the various interests involved (which need not concern us here) about power, institutional control and finance. Then, in May 1955, a commercial blood bank (calling itself the Midwest Blood Bank and Plasma Center) started operations.

The bank was owned and operated by a man and his wife. He had completed grade school, had no medical training, and had previously worked as a banjo teacher, secondhand car salesman and photographer. The blood bank procedures seem to have been actually directed by his wife. She called herself an R.N. but was not licensed as a nurse in either Kansas or Missouri, and did not show any evidence of experience or training in blood banking. Originally there had been a third partner but he had been chased out of the bank by the husband with a gun. A medical director was appointed to comply with public health regulations. He was aged 78, a general practitioner with no training in blood banking. The bank was inspected and licensed by the Federal authority, the National Institutes of Health.

It was situated in a slum area, displayed a sign reading "Cash Paid for Blood," drew blood from donors described as "Skid-Row derelicts," and was said by one witness to have "worms all over the floor." In 1958 another commercial bank, the World Blood Bank, Inc., was established in Kansas City and also began operations.

From 1955 onwards pressures of various kinds were brought to bear on relatives of hospital patients, members of associations and trade unions to provide blood on a replacement basis to these commercial banks. But local hospitals refused to accept blood from these sources to discharge patients' blood fees. These and other developments seem to have forced a solution to the disputes over the control of the non-profit community blood bank, and in April 1958 it commenced operations. Subsequently, it appears from the evidence that practically all the large local hospitals entered into blood supply contracts with the Community Bank and ceased operating their own banks. The Community Bank thus had a virtual monopoly.

The two commercial banks then complained to the Federal Trade Commission alleging restraint of trade. In July 1962, after an investigation lasting several years, the Commission issued a complaint against the Community Blood Bank and its officers, directors, administrative director and business manager; the Kansas City Area Hospital Association and its officers, directors, and executive director; three hospitals individually and as representatives of the forty members of the Hospital Association; sixteen pathologists, and two hospital administrators.

The complaint charged the respondents with having entered into an agreement or planned course of action to hamper and restrain the sale and distribution of human blood in interstate commerce. They were charged with conspiring to boycott a commercial blood bank in the sale and distribution of blood in commerce, and that the conspiracy was to the injury of the public and unreasonably restricted and restrained interstate commerce in violation of Section 5 of the Federal Trade Commission Act of 1952. This Section of the Act declares that "uniform methods of competition in commerce, and unfair or deceptive acts or practices in commerce, are declared unlawful." Violation of a Commission "cease and desist order," after it becomes final, subjects the violator to civil penalties up to $5,000 for each day that the violation continues.

The respondents appealed. After lengthy hearings before an Examiner for the Commission in 1963, a further appeal and more hearings before the full Trade Commission of five members, a ruling was issued in October 1966. By a majority of three to two the Commission decided that the Community Blood Bank and the hospitals, doctors and pathologists associated with it were illegally joined together in a conspiracy to restrain commerce in whole human blood.

In January 1969 the Federal Trade Commission's ruling of 1966 in the Kansas City case was set aside by the Eighth U.S. Circuit Court of Appeals in St. Louis.[6] Up to the end of 1969 no appeal had been made to the Supreme Court.

Though this may be the end of this particular case the fact that it happened is one illustration among many of the increasing commercialization of the blood banking system and of hospital and medical services in general. This trend must logically lead to more and more recourse to the laws and practices of the marketplace. There is no inconsistency in this development. If blood as a living human tissue is increasingly bought and sold as an article of commerce, and profit accrues from such transactions, then it follows that the laws of commerce must, in the end, prevail.

Having said this we must point out that although attempts have been made to value human life,[7] no money values can be attached to the presence or absence of a spirit of altruism in a society. Altruism in giving to a stranger does not begin and end with blood donations. It may touch every aspect of life and affect the whole fabric of values. Its role in satisfying the biological need to help—particularly in modern societies—is another unmeasurable element. In this study we have used human blood as an indicator, perhaps the most basic and sensitive indicator of social values and human relationships that could be found for a comparative study. If dollars or pounds exchange for blood then it may be morally acceptable for a myriad of other human activities and relationships also to exchange for dollars or pounds. Economists may fragment systems and values; other people do not.

We do not know and could never estimate in economic terms the social costs to American society of the decline in recent years in the voluntary giving of blood. It is likely that a decline in the spirit of altruism in one sphere of human activities will be accompanied by similar changes in attitudes, motives and relationships in other spheres.

Once man begins to say, as he sees that dollars exchange for blood supplies from Skid Row and a poor and often coloured population of sellers, "I need no longer experience (or suffer from) a sense of responsibility (or sin) in not giving to my neighbour" then the consequences are likely to be socially pervasive. There is nothing permanent about the expression of reciprocity. If the bonds of community giving are broken the result is not a state of value neutralism. The vacuum is likely to be filled by hostility and social conflict.

BLOOD DISTRIBUTION IN THE UNITED STATES VERSUS BRITAIN

In comparing commercialized blood market systems in the United States with a voluntary system functioning as an integral part of the National Health Service in Britain we consider four sets of criteria. These are basic criteria which economists would themselves apply in attempting to assess the relative advantages and disadvantages of different systems. They exclude, therefore, the much wider and unquantifiable social, ethical and philosophical aspects which, as this study has demonstrated, extend far beyond the narrower confines of blood distribution systems judged simply in economic and financial terms.

These four criteria which to some extent overlap are, briefly stated: (1) economic efficiency; (2) administrative efficiency; (3) price—the cost per unit to the patient; (4) purity, potency and safety—or quality per unit.

On all four criteria, the commercialized blood market fails. In terms of economic efficiency it is highly wasteful of blood; shortages, chronic and acute, characterize the demand and supply position and make illusory the concept of equilibrium; the market also involves heavy external costs. It is administratively inefficient; the so-called mixed pluralism of the American market results in more bureaucratization, avalanches of paper and bills, and much greater administrative, accounting and computer overheads. These wastes, disequilibria and inefficiencies are reflected in the price paid by the patient (or consumer); the cost per unit of blood varying in the United States between £10 and £20 (at the official rate of exchange in 1969) compared with £1 6s. (£2 if processing costs are included) in Britain—five to fifteen times higher. And, finally, in terms of quality, commercial markets are much more likely to distribute contaminated blood; in other words, the risks for the patient of disease and death in the form of serum hepatitis are substantially higher.

Paradoxically—or so it may seem to some—the more commercialized a blood distribution system becomes (and hence more wasteful, inefficient and dangerous) the more will the gross national product be inflated. In part, and quite simply, this is the consequence of statistically "transferring" an unpaid service (voluntary blood donors, voluntary workers in the service, unpaid time) with much lower external costs to a monetary and measurable paid activity involving costlier externalities. Similar effects on the gross national product would ensue if housewives were paid for housework or childless married couples were financially rewarded for adopting children or hospital patients cooperating for teaching purposes charged medical students. The gross national product is also inflated when commercial markets accelerate "blood obsolescence"—or waste; the waste is counted because someone has paid for it.

What *The Economist* described in its 1969 survey of the American economy as the great "efficiency gap" between that country and Britain[8] clearly does not apply in the field of human blood. On the economic and technical criteria employed in this study in relation to blood distribution systems such a conclusion needs to be reversed; the voluntary socialized system in Britain is economically, professionally, administratively and qualitatively more efficient than the mixed, commercialized and individualistic American system.

Another myth, the Paretian myth of consumer sovereignty, has also to be shattered. In commercial blood markets the consumer is not king. He has less freedom to live unharmed; little choice in determining price; is more subject to shortages in supply; is less free from bureaucratization; has fewer opportunities to express altruism; and exercises fewer checks and controls in relation to consumption, quality and external costs. Far from being sovereign, he is often exploited.

Those who suffer most and have the largest bills of all to pay are haemophiliacs. It is estimated that the incidence in the United States is 1 in 10,000 of the male population (lower estimates have been made for Britain). The fact that the disease is not only hereditary but may occur as a consequence of one of the most frequent mutations in medicine, means that the incidence may be expected to increase rather than decrease throughout the world.

Modern medical treatment now consists of human plasma and a variety of concentrated blood products. A ten-day course of treatment with these substances—say for a dental extraction—may require gifts from 60 blood donors each involving a potential risk of infecting the patient with hepatitis. In Britain, these products are prepared under the auspices of the National Blood Transfusion Service and are supplied at no cost to the patient under the National Health Service. They are not sold—or priced—commercially. The blood is given by voluntary donors.[9]

In the United States, where clinically some of the products are considered to be less satisfactory, they are produced and marketed commercially. At retail prices ruling in 1966, the cost to an average adult of a ten-day course of treatment with human plasma products was about $2250. In 1969 it was reported: "Many patients require plasma or plasma concentrate therapy three times a month or more. By the end of the year, this patient has a staggering plasma bill. In families of two or more haemophiliac youngsters, the financial burden is even more acute. The financial aspects alone can cause family problems and disruption. Patients often relate guilt feelings because of the financial burden they cause their families."[10] They are also continually reminded by these market forces that for their survival from one bleeding episode to the next they are dependent on blood supplies from strangers. They are "bad risks"; noninsurable by the private market in the United States; not acceptable by profit-making hospitals.

It has been estimated that if all the needs of haemophiliac patients in the United States were fully met they would require about one-eighth of all the blood collected each year in the country—or about 1,000,000 pints.

In England, where it is estimated that there are more than 2000 patients with severe haemorrhagic disorders, the problems they face are in no way comparable to those confronting similar patients in the United States. They would not wish to emigrate. While there are serious difficulties in the technical production of adequate quantities of the appropriate blood products (which use only certain of the valuable constituents of plasma) there is no shortage of blood, and no problems for the patient in paying for the blood and medical treatment.

Let me conclude by quoting from Alexander Solzhenitsyn's great work *Cancer Ward*,[11] banned in the Soviet Union. Shulubin, a cancer patient in a hospital in Central Asia, is talking to Kostoglotov, a former prisoner in a labour camp now in exile as a patient in the same hospital. "He (Shulubin) spoke very distinctly, like a master giving a lesson.

'We have to show the world a society in which all relationships, fundamental principles and laws flow directly from moral ethics, and from them *alone*. Ethical demands would determine all calculations: how to bring up children, what to prepare them for, to what purpose the work of grown-ups should be directed, and how their leisure should be occupied. As for scientific research, it should only be conducted where it doesn't damage ethical morality, in the first instance where it doesn't damage the researchers themselves.'"

Kostoglotov then raises questions. "'There has to be an economy, after all, doesn't there? That comes before everything else.' 'Does it?' said Shulubin. 'That depends. For example, Vladimir Solovyov argues rather convincingly that an economy could and should be built on an ethical basis.'

'What's that? Ethics first and economics afterwards?' Kostoglotov looked bewildered."

NOTES

1. For an earlier attempt to define the territory of social policy and the roles and functions of the social services, see the writer's *Commitment to Welfare* (1968) and particularly Chapter 1.
2. Countless statements of such opinions have been made in the United States in recent years. See, as one example, R. E. Dice, "Paid Donor Programs," *Proc. A.M.A. Conference on Blood and Blood Banking,* Chicago, 1964. Reference should also be made to *Hearings Before the Subcommittee on Antitrust and Monopoly of the Committee of the Judiciary,* United States Senate, 88th Congress, on S. 2560 (U.S. Government Printing Office, 1964), and *Hearing Before the Subcommittee on Antitrust and Monopoly of the Committee of the Judiciary,* United States Senate, 90th Congress, S. 1945 (U.S. Government Printing Office, 1967).
3. R. Carlinger, general manager, Pioneer Blood Service, Inc., New York. Statement before the Senate Subcommittee on Antitrust and Monopoly, August 1, 1967 (*Hearings on* S. 1945, op. cit., 1967, pp. 51–56).
4. M. H. Cooper and A. J. Culyer, *The Price of Blood,* Hobart Paper 41, The Institute of Economic Affairs, 1968.
5. They are taken from: Federal Trade Commission, Washington Final Order (8519), October 26, 1966;

Hearings on S. 2560, op. cit., 1964, and *Hearings on* S. 1945, op. cit, 1967; W. E. Whyte, "Federal Trade Commission Versus the Community Blood Bank of Kansas City et al.," *Proc. A.M.A. Conference on Blood and Blood Banking,* Chicago, 1964.

6. A.M.A. *News,* January 27, 1969.

7. See, for example, T. W. Schultz, "Investment in Human Capital," *Am. Econ. Rev.,* 51, March 1, 1961.

8. *The Economist,* U.S.A. Report, May 10, 1969.

9. R. Biggs and R. G. Macfarlane, *Treatment of Haemophilia and other Coagulation Disorders,* Blackwell, Oxford, 1966.

10. C. Taylor, "Haemophilic Center at Work," *Rehabilitation Record,* Vol. 10, No. 2, March–April 1969, pp. 1–6. A study of 177 haemophiliac patients by the university Department of Psychiatry in Sheffield in 1968 failed to confirm American findings that haemophilia is liable to cause marked psychiatric symptoms. There was also no evidence of acute financial and occupational difficulties (BBI. G. Bronks, and E. K. Blackburn, "A Socio-Medical Study of Haemophilia and Related States," *Brit. J. prev. soc. Med.,* 1968, Vol. 22, pp. 68–72).

11. Vol. 2, translated by N. Bethell and D. Burg, Bodley Head, London, 1969.

Training for Ethical Management at Cummins Engine

Michael R. Rion*

Some years ago a *New Yorker* cartoon featured several somber businessmen clustered around the chief executive's desk, consternation re-

---

Excerpted from "Training for Ethical Management at Cummins Engine," by Michael R. Rion, published in *Doing Ethics in Business: New Ventures in Management Development,* edited by Donald G. Jones. Copyright© 1982 by Oelgeschlager, Gunn & Hain, Publishers, Inc., Cambridge: MA. Reprinted with permission of the publisher.

*Former corporate responsibility director, Cummins Engine Company and now president, Hartford Seminary.

flected on their faces. The executive presses the intercom to say, "Miss Dugan, will you send someone in here who can distinguish right from wrong?" Too frequently, this vignette symbolizes the perception of managers that ethics is someone else's business, not necessarily irrelevant to management decisions but certainly not part of the manager's competence. But ethics cannot be integrated effectively into management decisions unless line managers accept responsibility for the moral dimension of their decisions as well as economic features. Ms. Dugan ought no more to send in someone who can tell right from wrong than she should someone who can tell a profitable sale from an unprofitable one. To that end, in-house training in ethics and management is an important strategy. This [essay] discusses one such program, recently developed at Cummins Engine Company, Inc.

BACKGROUND

Cummins is a major worldwide designer and manufacturer of diesel engines, with annual sales of nearly $2 billion and nearly 23,000 employees worldwide. A successful producer, whose engines are widely acclaimed in the industry, the company also has a strong tradition of social responsibility. Top management, from the founding of the company, committed the firm to ethical business practices, support for the local community, and respect for all stakeholders whose lives or interests are affected by company action. Like any increasingly complex organization, Cummins does not meet its goals with perfect accuracy and the problems of sustaining and implementing ethical management arise regularly. Nevertheless, the company has a deserved reputation as a leader in socially responsible ethical business management.

A staff group devoted to responsibility concerns is one manifestation of Cummins' effort to sustain its commitment to ethical management. Currently, a public affairs group includes government and community relations, environmental management, and corporate responsibility. The mission of the corporate responsibility department is, broadly conceived, to support the company's efforts to make ethically responsible decisions. This means many things: development of ethical practice policies; staff support for top management; *ad hoc* and more regular consultation with line managers on particular issues they raise; and monitoring of certain policies already in place.

Those efforts convinced staff members a few years ago that further effort was necessary to emphasize line manager responsibility for the ethical dimensions of decisions. No staff support can possibly cover the array of issues managers face daily, and the department's role is conceived as support *to* line managers, *not* their conscience. A call to Ms. (or Mr.) Dugan occasionally is understandable, but corporate responsibility could never, and should never, replace the responsibility of line managers. Accordingly, a pilot training project was inaugurated as one effort to strengthen the capacity of managers to resolve ethical issues in their work. This context is important to understanding the project since it has programmatic as well as educational goals. More specifically, the project aims:

To increase the confidence and competence of individual managers dealing with ethical issues.

To develop a network of managers who, over time, can be mutually supportive in strengthening the ethical dimension of managerial decisions.

To expand or "leverage" the resources of the corporate responsibility department through greater interaction with line managers and their issues.

A PILOT PROJECT

Since December 1979, four groups of managers each attended a pilot series of three day-long workshops on ethics and management. Evalua-

tions of the program were encouraging, and it is being continued on a regular basis. A brief description follows.

Groups of eighteen to twenty-four managers were selected from middle and upper management. Concerns in selecting the initial groups included finding interested individuals, providing diversity of organizational functions in each group, and avoiding participation by subordinates and their supervisors in the same group. Participation was entirely voluntary and enthusiastic. Indeed, numerous managers inquired about the program along the way, and there will be little difficulty in recruiting participants for future series.

Each group attended three day-long workshops, spread over approximately six months. The interim periods between the sessions were used for individual meetings with the instructor and for development of case material for succeeding workshops. Staggering the series also enabled the experience from each session of a series to be used in revising the subsequent series.

The structure of the three workshops is based upon its stated learning goals:

1. To increase recognition of ethical dimensions in management decisions.
2. To acquire concepts and methods for ordering and analysis of ethical issues.
3. To strengthen the capacity for resolution of ethical issues in management decisions.

These goals represent the process of ethical judgment, and the entire process is experienced with cases in each session. The emphasis, however, is sequential: the first session focuses upon recognition, the second upon ordering and analysis, the third upon judgment. Although some of the normative ethical content of the workshop is discussed below, a brief summary of the sessions may be helpful here. Session 1 includes development of an adequate definition of ethics; discussion of the goals, successes, and failures of ethical management at Cummins; exploration of the sources of moral disagreement, and assessment of Cummins' explicit policies on ethical practices. Session 2 is devoted largely to apprehending and appling a conceptual framework for ordering and analyzing moral responsibility. Finally, Session 3 is devoted exclusively to analysis of several participant cases; the aim is both to hone judgment skills and to explore in greater depth certain moral concepts relevant to the cases selected.

NORMATIVE CONTENT

What follows now is the author's own normative approach that is incorporated into the training design.[1] Comments are necessary at three levels: social-economic structure, institutional ethical commitments, and individual ethical judgment in managerial roles.

1. The Social Context of Management Ethics

Managers wield significant power affecting the lives of various ''stakeholders''—employees, customers, suppliers, stockholders, governments, and communities. To say that managers should simply maximize profits as agents of shareholders presumes that the market dynamics are effective and relatively quick to respond. If so, it is *possible* that competitive pressure would prevent the worst abuses. The truth, however, is that this assumption is invalid for a whole range of corporate decisions. And, when the assumption is false, the injunction becomes dangerous. If managers are ignoring realms of corporate impact removed from market constraints, immense injury can occur to employees, customers, communities, and the public interest. There is no ready theory as refined as the free-market model to take its place, but in corporate offices the reality of managerial discretion and influence is evident.

Management ethics, and particularly management training in ethics, must take as its imme-

diate base the realities of managerial discretion and seek to provide ethically sound and practically helpful guidance in exercising that discretion with sensitivity to human dignity and human values. The underlying assumption is that, without a clear social theory or public policy to provide more adequate accountability for corporate power, business corporations hold a kind of public trust—society requires business enterprise for human well-being, and individual corporations derive their power ultimately from society's consent that the business is fulfilling its public trust. Part of this task is learning how to avoid harm and respect stakeholders.

This point does not diminish the importance of the broader issues of appropriate political-economic structures. Managers, as citizens and as corporate representatives, must engage in discussions of these issues as our society searches for more adequate models. In the meantime, corporate managers should not be harming people, and in its simplest terms, that is the narrow task that management ethics sets for itself within the larger debate.

2. Institutional Ethics and Ethos

The institutional context for the exercise of managerial judgment is a critical feature of ethical management, and one not readily affected by training. Although much research is needed on the institutional requisites for an ethically responsible corporation, a number of elements seem essential. Firm and visible top management commitment, and especially a history of such commitment, is essential to keeping ethical dimensions of management on the agenda of operating managers. Staff support is useful, and policies and codes of conduct have a place, as does recruitment policy. Management ethics training is a single component, ineffective without a supportive institutional context. Such training needs to examine the peculiar context of an institution, but its focus will be upon equipping managers better to fulfill institutional goals if those goals include ethical management. If not, the training may help individuals, but its impact will be lost unless it is part of a wider strategy to reshape an unfavorable ethos.

3. Ethical Judgment in Management

Understanding the managerial role and the kinds of decisions that face managers is essential to teaching ethics for management. As Charles Powers and David Vogel point out, management, unlike other professions, finds its *raison d'être* in organizational purposes and needs rather than in independently inspiring goals such as health or justice.[2] The manager's role responsibility is essentially a formal one, receiving content only through the particular goals and directions of a specific organization; hence the importance of the particular institutional ethos. But individual character and judgment are not thereby imprisoned in organizational conformity. At the extremes, individual and corporate identity can diverge to the point of resignation, perhaps in protest, or converge in deadening acquiescence, but most managers find sufficient compatibility with corporate goals to carry on *and* sufficient ambiguity and leeway in corporate policies to allow for creative individual judgment. Parallels between ethics and business judgment may be instructive.

Corporate goals determine the general direction and criteria of business judgments—what markets deserve priority, whether pricing is premium or competitive, what standards by which to judge potential return on investment, and so on. The manager must effectively integrate these criteria with the complexity and detail of specific decisions, and here his or her education, ingenuity, and common sense determine the outcome. The same holds true for the ethical dimension of managerial judgment. Corporate goals and policy may set general expectations and even some specific guidance, but individual understanding of concepts such as fairness and honesty will be decisive in the manager's decision

to select a particular supplier or to discuss certain issues in a negotiation.

Few managers have frequent opportunity to pass judgment on major corporate goals and strategies, but all managers deal both with specific details and with precedent-setting policy decisions at their own level. Ethical considerations are nearly always present. In the "big issues," such as investment in South Africa or closing a plant, they are most clearly on the agenda; in the routine decisions of individual managers fulfilling their particular organizational roles, ethical issues likewise abound but are not as often recognized. When they are recognized, the ethical dimensions may confound the decisionmaker because the legitimacy and conceptual tools of ethics are not as readily accepted as are those of finance or marketing or production. Ethics may seem relative, vague, or irrelevant. The managers have a decision to make, with pressures from all sides, and without any formal education in the field, ethical considerations will enter the decision only through implicit dimensions of character and generalized feelings of what is fair or right.

If ethics is to be taught effectively to managers, these characteristics must be taken into account—managerial role responsibilities in the institutional context, continual pressure for decisions, and the frequent lack of clarity about ethical reasoning. Ethics, understood as the principles and process of reasoning about moral responsibility, must be taught in ways that link clearly to institutional roles and to the particularities of business decisions and in ways that encourage a sense of confidence and competence on the part of the individual manager.

The most pressing questions a manager faces—in ways questions of *role* responsibility—are *whether* he or she is indeed responsible for a particular issue, and if so, *what* does that responsibility entail? What may be most useful is a framework for reasoning through these questions, a framework that determines the relevance of substantive principles and enables their application in concrete circumstances. The framework used here is as follows.[3]

NEGATIVE AND AFFIRMATIVE RESPONSIBILITIES

A distinction between negative and affirmative responsibilities offers initial guidance in determining one's moral responsibility. Simply put, *the responsibility not to harm others is more stringent than the responsibility positively to help others*. Virtually all ethical systems, even in different cultures, acknowledge a *moral minimum that prohibits doing injury to another person and, as a corollary, requires corrective action when harm is inflicted*.

The distinction applies to corporate action. Much of the debate and criticism surrounding the notion of "corporate social responsibility" has focused on affirmative responsibilities such as corporate contributions to charitable programs, extra costs to enhance architectural beauty or employee well-being, or "donation" of executives' time for community groups. These actions may be laudable and can certainly be conceived as moral responsibilities rooted in respect for persons. But they do represent affirmative choices open to debate depending upon the circumstances and one's view of morality and the role of corporations. In contrast, there are fewer disputes that corporations should not knowingly market unsafe products (the definition of "unsafe," of course, occasions significant debate).

A first "cut" in applying ethics, then, is the simple injunction: *do no harm*. What does this enjoin? While a precise definition will lead to disagreements about human nature and needs, a reasonably specific range of considerations offers a core definition despite inevitable ambiguities at the edges. The harm that can be done to persons and to institutions includes the following:

1. Material injury, including direct assault; impairment of health; deprivation of food, clothes, and shelter; economic loss.
2. Deprivation of freedom, including political rights and personal choices.

3. Violation of certain moral principles such as promise-keeping, truth-telling, and justice.

In undergraduate and graduate courses, this definition would spark debates leading into the theories of Rawls and Nozick and a whole range of social philosophical issues. As a framework for managers reasoning through problems, however, the definition provides sufficient material to assist the analysis.

To recapitulate, a fundamental moral principle is to avoid injuring others, and understanding "injury" often requires careful analysis. Furthermore, we are obliged to correct or compensate for injury that we have caused. But even if we are scrupulous in avoiding injury, we do not exhaust the range of moral action, for there are occasions when we ought to prevent or correct injury caused by others, and there are also numerous affirmative responsibilities.

Responding to Injury Caused by Others: The "Kew Gardens Principle"

The distinction between negative and affirmative responsibilities is meant to indicate that certain responsibilities ("do no harm") are more stringent and of higher priority than others ("help others"). An important middle step between the two are instances where we have the opportunity to prevent or correct harm that others inflict. We do not violate the "do no harm" principle if we fail to act, but in the face of clear need, it sometimes seems that offering aid is more than mere generosity.

What is at stake here is how to determine when an agent is responsible to act. It has been said already that one is responsible to act to correct self-caused injury. A set of considerations known collectively as the "Kew Gardens Principle" helps to decide when one is likewise responsible to act in the circumstances like those described above (i.e., where the injury is not self-caused). The principle takes its name from a murder in the Kew Gardens section of New York that was witnessed by thirty to forty bystanders, none of whom so much as screamed or called police. The principle seeks to clarify why we would ordinarily believe that rendering assistance under such circumstances is morally obligatory.

The Kew Gardens Principle

To the degree that each of the four factors below holds, the agent has an increased moral obligation to aid another:

1. *Need*   There is a clear need for aid; (for example, a harm has been or is about to be done).

2. *Proximity*   The agent is "close" to the situation, not necessarily in space but certainly in terms of notice; that is, he or she knows of the need or could reasonably be held responsible for knowing of it.

3. *Capability*   The agent has some means by which to aid the person in need without undue risk to the agent.

4. *Last Resort*   No one else is likely to help. The first three factors create a presumption to aid the person in need. This presumption is strengthened to the degree that the agent is likely to be the only one who will render help. Given our propensity to fail to act on the false assumption that others will do so, it is important both to assess this consideration carefully and to give the other three factors greater weight.

The Kew Gardens principle is generally applicable in managerial decisions as a "rough and ready" tool to guide considerations about moral responsibility. When claims are pressed upon managers by various stakeholders, the four considerations outlined may be useful in sorting through whether the managers are obliged to act (there may be affirmative responsibilities that lead them to act, but here the question is whether they have a more stringent obligation to respond). Disagreements are bound to arise here, but the Kew Gardens principle at least provides a framework for working through the issues. Over a whole range of managerial questions, the principle may prove helpful in limiting and defining managerial moral responsibility.

AFFIRMATIVE MORAL RESPONSIBILITY

The preceding discussion focuses upon the most stringent moral obligations that embody respect for persons: avoidance of harm, correcting self-caused injury, and coming to the aid of those harmed by others. These are the most stringent precisely because they are minimal; without adherence to these obligations, more generous deeds would be of no avail. But general compliance with negative injunctions does not exhaust moral responsibility, for respect for persons yields principles of doing good as well as not doing evil. Where there is human need, or the opportunity for human growth, ethical concern rooted in respect for persons can call forth response. Negative injunctions focus narrowly upon human needs bound up directly with the agent's actions and define a generally realizable set of obligations. In contrast, affirmative responsibilities extend to all human needs and open up a range of actions beyond the resources and capacities of the individual agent.

Beyond negative responsibilities, then, people must choose the moral commitments they intend to pursue and those that they cannot or do not wish to pursue. A simple example is personal charitable giving. From among the numerous solicitations received each year from worthy organizations, donors must choose the organizations to which to devote their limited funds. This choice need not reflect negatively on the worth of the charities declined, for it follows from the donors' limited resources and their commitments and interests. So it is with the full range of possible affirmative moral responsibilities. Individuals choose from among a multitude of potential projects and charitable acts limited patterns of commitment that express both their moral sensitivities and their unique identities. Individuals might argue about the appropriateness of particular choices. Unlike negative injunctions where there are some clear ways to understand individual responsibility, affirmative responsibilities cover such a wide range and relate as much to the agents' values and personal identity as to independent considerations that resolution of such disputes is difficult.

There are parallels here to the affirmative moral responsibilities of corporations and, thus, of their managerial decisionmakers. Here, as well, negative injunctions are more clear while affirmative responsibilities can unfold a range of actions that, if vigorously pursued, could pull the corporation away from its primary task and exhaust its resources. Like individuals, corporations have limited resources and distinctive identities that are reflected in their limited affirmative moral commitments. The amount and nature of corporate charitable contributions, extra fringe benefits for employees, and corporate championing of particular social causes illustrate the variety of such commitments. Resolving disagreements about a corporation's commitments is as difficult as it is for individuals, for again it is a matter of corporate values and role as much as one of independent assessment of the options.

The point is not to discount affirmative responsibilities because of their extent and the difficulty of determining which ones are appropriate. These considerations actually underscore the importance of going beyond negative injunctions to embody fully moral commitments. But these same considerations also indicate the necessity to view particular affirmative responsibilities as less stringent than negative injunctions.

SPECIFIC MORAL PRINCIPLES

The discussion to this point outlines a way of understanding moral responsibility. Within that framework, specific moral principles give further definition to *particular responsibilities*. A reasonably thorough list of moral principles includes:

Promise-keeping

Truth-telling

Reparation (compensating for previous wrongful acts)

Gratitude

Justice

Beneficence (doing good, preventing or removing evil)

Nonmaleficence (refraining from doing evil)

Morally virtuous self-development

The relationship of these substantive principles to the responsibility framework is sketched in Table 3. Development of specific principles can take place within this context.

Once this general framework is apprehended, the most fruitful learning—for both practical and theoretical purposes—comes from working through cases and parsing the meaning of relevant concepts. In this way, links between ethical theory and concrete problems can be built that illumine both practice and principle.

NOTES

1. I am indebted to Charles Powers and to Jon Gunneman, whose contribution to my understanding of management ethics is far greater than subsequent footnoted references could suggest.

2. Charles W. Powers and David Vogel, *Ethics in the Education of Business Managers* (Hastings-on-Hudson, N.Y.: Institute of Society, Ethics, and the Life Sciences, The Hastings Center, 1980), pp. 2–4.

3. The approach described is clearly more formalist than consequential, and this normative "bias" is made clear to participants in the course of the program. The framework owes much to the discussion in John G. Simon; Charles W. Powers; and Jon P. Gunnemann, *The Ethical Investor* (New Haven: Yale University Press, 1972), Chapter 2.

		TABLE 3		
MORAL RESPONSIBILITIES				
Negative responsibilities				**Affirmative responsibilities**
Correcting self-caused injury	Avoiding injury	Correcting injury caused by others		
Reparation	Do no harm (nonmaleficence)	Beneficence as preventing or removing harm		Beneficence as doing good Developing moral virtue
	Compliance with promise-keeping truth-telling gratitude justice			
	(Concept of responsibilities to stakeholders in most relevant here)	Kew Gardens principle aids in determining responsibility		

← Increasing stringency of Obligation

Why Should My Conscience Bother Me?

Kermit Vandivier*

The B.F. Goodrich Co. is what business magazines like to speak of as "a major American corporation." It has operations in a dozen states and as many foreign countries, and of these far-flung facilities, the Goodrich plant at Troy, Ohio, is not the most imposing. It is a small, one-story building, once used to manufacture airplanes. Set in the grassy flatlands of west-central Ohio, it employs only about six hundred people. Nevertheless, it is one of the three largest manufacturers of aircraft wheels and brakes, a leader in a most profitable industry. Goodrich wheels and

Excerted from "Why Should My Conscience Bother Me?" by Kermit Vandivier, from *In the Name of Profit*, edited by Robert Heilbroner. Copyright© 1972 Doubleday, a divisionBantam, Doubleday, Dell Publishing Group, Inc. Reprinted with permission.
*Staff writer, *Daily News,* Troy, Ohio.

brakes support such well-known planes as the F111, the C5A, the Boeing 727, the XB70 and many others. Its customers include almost every aircraft manufacturer in the world.

Contracts for aircraft wheels and brakes often run into millions of dollars, and ordinarily a contract with a total value of less than $70,000, though welcome, would not create any special stir of joy in the hearts of Goodrich sales personnel. But purchase order P-23718, issued on June 18, 1967, by the LTV Aerospace Corporation, and ordering 202 brake assemblies for a new Air Force plane at a total price of $69,417, was received by Goodrich with considerable glee. And there was good reason. Some ten years previously, Goodrich had built a brake for LTV that was, to say the least, considerably less than a rousing success. The brake had not lived up to Goodrich's promises, and after experiencing considerable difficulty, LTV had written off Goodrich as a source of brakes. Since that time, Goodrich salesmen had been unable to sell so much as a shot of brake fluid to LTV. So in 1967, when LTV requested bids on wheels and brakes for the new A7D light attack aircraft it proposed to build for the Air Force, Goodrich submitted a bid that was absurdly low, so low that LTV could not, in all prudence, turn it down.

Goodrich had, in industry parlance, "bought into the business." Not only did the company not expect to make a profit on the deal; it was prepared, if necessary, to lose money. For aircraft brakes are not something that can be ordered off the shelf. They are designed for a particular aircraft, and once an aircraft manufacturer buys a brake, he is forced to purchase all replacement parts from the brake manufacturer. The $70,000 that Goodrich would get for making the brake would be a drop in the bucket when compared with the cost of the linings and other parts the Air Force would have to buy from Goodrich during the lifetime of the aircraft. Furthermore, the company which manufactures brakes for one particular model of an aircraft quite naturally has the inside track to supply other brakes when the planes are updated and improved.

Thus, that first contract, regardless of the money involved, is very important, and Goodrich, when it learned that it had been awarded the A7D contract, was determined that while it may have slammed the door on its own foot ten years before, this time, the second time around, things would be different. The word was soon circulated throughout the plant: "We can't bungle it this time. We've got to give them a good brake, regardless of the cost."

There was another factor which had undoubtedly influenced LTV. All aircraft brakes made today are of the disk type, and the bid submitted by Goodrich called for a relatively small brake, one containing four disks and weighing only 106 pounds. The weight of any aircraft part is extremely important. The lighter a part is, the heavier the plane's payload can be. The four-rotor, 106-pound brake promised by Goodrich was about as light as could be expected, and this undoubtedly had helped move LTV to award the contract to Goodrich.

The brake was designed by one of Goodrich's most capable engineers, John Warren. A tall, lanky blond and a graduate of Purdue, Warren

had come from the Chrysler Corporation seven years before and had become adept at aircraft brake design. The happy-go-lucky manner he usually maintained belied a temper which exploded whenever anyone ventured to offer any criticism of his work, no matter how small. On these occasions, Warren would turn red in the face, often throwing or slamming something and then stalking from the scene. As his coworkers learned the consequences of criticizing him, they did so less and less readily, and when he submitted his preliminary design for the A7D brake, it was accepted without question.

Warren was named project engineer for the A7D, and he, in turn, assigned the task of producing the final production design to a newcomer to the Goodrich engineering stable, Searle Lawson. Just turned twenty-six, Lawson had been out of the Northrup Institute of Technology only one year when he came to Goodrich in January 1967. Like Warren, he had worked for a while in the automotive industry, but his engineering degree was in aeronautical and astronautical sciences, and when the opportunity came to enter his special field, via Goodrich, he took it. At the Troy plant, Lawson had been assigned to various "paper projects" to break him in, and after several months spent reviewing statistics and old brake designs, he was beginning to fret at the lack of challenge. When told he was being assigned to his first "real" project, he was elated and immediately plunged into his work.

The major portion of the design had already been completed by Warren, and major assemblies for the brake had already been ordered from Goodrich suppliers. Naturally, however, before Goodrich could start making the brakes on a production basis, much testing would have to be done. Lawson would have to determine the best materials to use for the linings and discover what minor adjustments in the design would have to be made.

Then, after the preliminary testing and after the brake was judged ready for production, one whole brake assembly would undergo a series of grueling, simulated braking stops and other severe trials called qualification tests. These tests are required by the military, which gives very detailed specifications on how they are to be conducted, the criteria for failure, and so on. They are performed in the Goodrich plant's test laboratory, where huge machines called dynamometers can simulate the weight and speed of almost any aircraft. After the brakes pass the laboratory tests, they are approved for production, but before the brakes are accepted for use in military service, they must undergo further extensive flight tests.

Searle Lawson was well aware that much work had to be done before the A7D brake could go into production, and he knew that LTV had set the last two weeks in June, 1968, as the starting dates for flight tests. So he decided to begin testing immediately. Goodrich's suppliers had not yet delivered the brake housing and other parts, but the brake disks had arrived, and using the housing from a brake similar in size and weight to the A7D brake, Lawson built a prototype. The prototype was installed in a test wheel and placed on one of the big dynamometers in the plant's test laboratory. The dynamometer was adjusted to simulate the weight of the A7D and Lawson began a series of tests, "landing" the wheel and brake at the A7D's landing speed, and braking it to a stop. The main purpose of these preliminary tests was to learn what temperatures would develop within the brake during the simulated stops and to evaluate the lining materials tentatively selected for use.

During a normal aircraft landing the temperatures inside the brake may reach 1000 degrees, and occasionally a bit higher. During Lawson's first simulated landings, the temperature of his prototype brake reached 1500 degrees. The brake glowed a bright cherry-red and threw off incandescent particles of metal and lining material as the temperature reached its peak. After a few such stops, the brake was dismantled and the linings were found to be almost completely disintegrated. Lawson chalked this first failure up

to chance and, ordering new lining materials, tried again.

The second attempt was a repeat of the first. The brake became extremely hot, causing the lining materials to crumble into dust.

After the third such failure, Lawson, inexperienced though he was, knew that the fault lay not in defective parts or unsuitable lining material but in the basic design of the brake itself. Ignoring Warren's original computations, Lawson made his own, and it didn't take him long to discover where the trouble lay—the brake was too small. There simply was not enough surface area on the disks to stop the aircraft without generating the excessive heat that caused the linings to fail.

The answer to the problem was obvious but far from simple—the four-disk brake would have to be scrapped, and a new design, using five disks, would have to be developed. The implications were not lost on Lawson. Such a step would require the junking of all the four-disk-brake subassemblies, many of which had now begun to arrive from the various suppliers. It would also mean several weeks of preliminary design and testing and many more weeks of waiting while the suppliers made and delivered the new subassemblies.

Yet, several weeks had already gone by since LTV's order had arrived, and the date for delivery of the first production brakes for flight testing was only a few months away.

Although project engineer John Warren had more or less turned the A7D over to Lawson, he knew of the difficulties Lawson had been experiencing. He had assured the young engineer that the problem revolved around getting the right kind of lining material. Once that was found, he said, the difficulties would end.

Despite the evidence of the abortive tests and Lawson's careful computations, Warren rejected the suggestion that the four-disk brake was too light for the job. Warren knew that his superior had already told LTV, in rather glowing terms, that the preliminary tests on the A7D brake were very successful. Indeed, Warren's superiors weren't aware at this time of the troubles on the brake. It would have been difficult for Warren to admit not only that he had made a serious error in his calculations and original design but that his mistakes had been caught by a green kid, barely out of college.

Warren's reaction to a five-disk brake was not unexpected by Lawson, and, seeing that the four-disk brake was not to be abandoned so easily, he took his calculations and dismal test results one step up the corporate ladder.

At Goodrich, the man who supervises the engineers working on projects slated for production is called, predictably, the projects manager. The job was held by a short, chubby and bald man named Robert Sink. A man truly devoted to his work, Sink was as likely to be found at his desk at ten o'clock on Sunday night as ten o'clock on Monday morning. His outside interests consisted mainly of tinkering on a Model-A Ford and an occasional game of golf. Some fifteen years before, Sink had begun working at Goodrich as a lowly draftsman. Slowly, he worked his way up. Despite his geniality, Sink was neither respected nor liked by the majority of the engineers, and his appointment as their supervisor did not improve their feelings about him. They thought he had only gone to high school. It quite naturally rankled those who had gone through years of college and acquired impressive specialties such as thermodynamics and astronautics to be commanded by a man whom they considered their intellectual inferior. But, though Sink had no college training, he had something even more useful: a fine working knowledge of company politics.

Puffing upon a Meerschaum pipe, Sink listened gravely as young Lawson confided his fears about the four-disk brake. Then he examined Lawson's calculations and the results of the abortive tests. Despite the fact that he was not a qualified engineer, in the strictest sense of the word, it must certainly have been obvious to Sink that Lawson's calculations were correct and that a four-disk brake would never have worked on the A7D.

But other things of equal importance were also obvious. First, to concede that Lawson's calculations were correct would also mean conceding that Warren's calculations were incorrect. As projects manager, he not only was responsible for Warren's activities, but, in admitting that Warren had erred, he would have to admit that he had erred in trusting Warren's judgment. It also meant that, as projects manager, it would be he who would have to explain the whole messy situation to the Goodrich hierarchy, not only at Troy but possibly on the corporate level at Goodrich's Akron offices. And, having taken Warren's judgment of the four-disk brake at face value (he was forced to do this since, not being an engineer, he was unable to exercise any engineering judgment of his own), he had assured LTV, not once but several times, that about all there was left to do on the brake was pack it in a crate and ship it out the back door.

There's really no problem at all, he told Lawson. After all, Warren was an experienced engineer, and if he said the brake would work, it would work. Just keep on testing and probably, maybe even on the very next try, it'll work out just fine.

Lawson was far from convinced, but without the support of his superiors there was little he could do except keep on testing. By now, housings for the four-disk brake had begun to arrive at the plant, and Lawson was able to build up a production model of the brake and begin the formal qualification tests demanded by the military.

The first qualification attempts went exactly as the tests on the prototype had. Terrific heat developed within the brakes and, after a few, short, simulated stops, the linings crumbled. A new type of lining material was ordered and once again an attempt to qualify the brake was made. Again, failure.

On April 11, the day the thirteenth test was completed, I became personally involved in the A7D situation.

I had worked in the Goodrich test laboratory for five years, starting first as an instrumentation engineer, then later becoming a data analyst and technical writer. As part of my duties, I analyzed the reams and reams of instrumentation data that came from the many testing machines in the laboratory, then transcribed it to a more usable form for the engineering department. And when a new-type brake had successfully completed the required qualification tests, I would issue a formal qualification report.

Qualification reports were an accumulation of all the data and test logs compiled by the test technicians during the qualification tests, and were documentary proof that a brake had met all the requirements established by the military specifications and was therefore presumed safe for flight testing. Before actual flight tests were conducted on a brake, qualification reports had to be delivered to the customer and to various government officials.

On April 11, I was looking over the data from the latest A7D test, and I noticed that many irregularities in testing methods had been noted on the test logs.

Technically, of course, there was nothing wrong with conducting tests in any manner desired, so long as the test was for research purposes only. But qualification test methods are clearly delineated by the military, and I knew that this test had been a formal qualification attempt. One particular notation on the test logs caught my eye. For some of the stops, the instrument which recorded the brake pressure had been deliberately miscalibrated so that, while the brake pressure used during the stops was recorded as 1000 psi (the maximum pressure that would be available on the A7D aircraft), the pressure had actually been 1100 psi!

I showed the test logs to the test lab supervisor, Ralph Gretzinger, who said he had learned from the technician who had miscalibrated the instrument that he had been asked to do so by Lawson. Lawson, said Gretzinger, readily admitted asking for the miscalibration, saying he had been told to do so by Sink.

I asked Gretzinger why anyone would want to miscalibrate the data-recording instruments.

"Why? I'll tell you why," he snorted. "That brake is a failure. It's way too small for the job, and they're not ever going to get it to work. They're getting desperate, and instead of scrapping the damned thing and starting over, they figure they can horse around down here in the lab and qualify it that way."

An expert engineer, Gretzinger had been responsible for several innovations in brake design. It was he who had invented the unique brake system used on the famous XB70. A graduate of Georgia Tech, he was a stickler for detail and he had some very firm ideas about honesty and ethics. "If you want to find out what's going on," said Gretzinger, "ask Lawson, he'll tell you."

Curious, I did ask Lawson the next time he came into the lab. He seemed eager to discuss the A7D and gave me the history of his months of frustrating efforts to get Warren and Sink to change the brake design. "I just can't believe this is really happening," said Lawson, shaking his head slowly. "This isn't engineering, at least not what I thought it would be. Back in school, I thought that when you were an engineer, you tried to do your best, no matter what it cost. But this is something else."

He sat across the desk from me, his chin propped in his hand. "Just wait," he warned. "You'll get a chance to see what I'm talking about. You're going to get in the act, too, because I've already had the word that we're going to make one more attempt to qualify the brake, and that's it. Win or lose, we're going to issue a qualification report!"

I reminded him that a qualification report could only be issued after a brake had successfully met all military requirements, and therefore, unless the next qualification attempt was a success, no report would be issued.

"You'll find out," retorted Lawson. "I was

already told that regardless of what the brake does on test, it's going to be qualified.'' He said he had been told in those exact words at a conference with Sink and Russell Van Horn.

This was the first indication that Sink had brought his boss, Van Horn, into the mess. Although Van Horn, as manager of the design engineering section, was responsible for the entire department, he was not necessarily familiar with all phases of every project, and it was not uncommon for those under him to exercise the what-he-doesn't-know-won't-hurt-him philosophy. If he was aware of the full extent of the A7D situation, it meant that matters had truly reached a desperate stage—that Sink had decided not only to call for help but was looking toward that moment when blame must be borne and, if possible, shared.

Also, if Van Horn had said, ''regardless what the brake does on test, it's going to be qualified,'' then it could only mean that, if necessary, a false qualification report would be issued! I discussed this possibility with Gretzinger, and he assured me that under no circumstances would such a report ever be issued.

''If they want a qualificaton report, we'll write them one, but we'll tell it just like it is,'' he declared emphatically. ''No false data or false reports are going to come out of this lab.''

On May 2, 1968, the fourteenth and final attempt to qualify the brake was begun. Although the same improper methods used to nurse the brake through the previous tests were employed, it soon became obvious that this too would end in failure.

When the tests were about half completed, Lawson asked if I would start preparing the various engineering curves and graphic displays which were normally incorporated in a qualification report. ''It looks as though you'll be writing a qualification report shortly,'' he said.

I flatly refused to have anything to do with the matter and immediately told Gretzinger what I had been asked to do. He was furious and re-

peated his previous declaration that under no circumstances would any false data or other matter be issued from the lab.

''I'm going to get this settled right now, once and for all,'' he declared. ''I'm going to see Line [Russell Line, manager of the Goodrich Technical Services Section, of which the test lab was a part] and find out just how far this thing is going to go!'' He stormed out of the room.

In about an hour, he returned and called me to his desk. He sat silently for a few moments, then muttered, half to himself, ''I wonder what the hell they'd do if I just quit?'' I didn't answer and I didn't ask him what he meant. I knew. He had been beaten down. He had reached the point when the decision had to be made. Defy them now while there was still time—or knuckle under, sell out.

''You know,'' he went on uncertainly, looking down at his desk, ''I've been an engineer for a long time, and I've always believed that ethics and integrity were every bit as important as theorems and formulas, and never once has anything happened to change my beliefs. Now this.... Hell, I've got two sons I've got to put through school and I just....'' His voice trailed off.

He sat for a few more minutes, then, looking over the top of his glasses, said hoarsely, ''Well, it looks like we're licked. The way it stands now, we're to go ahead and prepare the data and other things for the graphic presentation in the report, and when we're finished, someone upstairs will actually write the report.

''After all,'' he continued, ''we're just drawing some curves, and what happens to them after they leave here, well, we're not responsible for that.''

He was trying to persuade himself that as long as we were concerned with only one part of the puzzle and didn't see the completed picture, we really weren't doing anything wrong. He didn't believe what he was saying, and he knew I didn't believe it either. It was an embarrassing and shameful moment for both of us.

I wasn't at all satisfied with the situation and decided that I too would discuss the matter with Russell Line, the senior executive in our section.

Tall, powerfully built, his teeth flashing white, his face tanned to a coffee-brown by a daily stint with a sun lamp, Line looked and acted every inch the executive. He was a crossword-puzzle enthusiast and an ardent golfer, and though he had lived in Troy only a short time, he had been accepted into the Troy Country Club and made an official of the golf committee. He commanded great respect and had come to be well liked by those of us who worked under him.

He listened sympathetically while I explained how I felt about the A7D situation, and when I had finished, he asked me what I wanted him to do about it. I said that as employees of the Goodrich Company we had a responsibility to protect the company and its reputation if at all possible. I said I was certain that officers on the corporate level would never knowingly allow such tactics as had been employed on the A7D.

"I agree with you," he remarked, "but I still want to know what you want me to do about it."

I suggested that in all probability the chief engineer at the Troy plant, H. C. "Bud" Sunderman, was unaware of the A7D problem and that he, Line, should tell him what was going on.

Line laughed, good-humoredly. "Sure, I could, but I'm not going to. Bud probably already knows about this thing anyway, and if he doesn't, I'm sure not going to be the one to tell him."

"But why?"

"Because it's none of my business, and it's none of yours. I learned a long time ago not to worry about things over which I had no control. I have no control over this."

I wasn't satisfied with this answer, and I asked him if his conscience wouldn't bother him if, say, during flight tests on the brake, something should happen resulting in death or injury to the test pilot.

"Look," he said, becoming somewhat exasperated, "I just told you I have no control over this thing. Why should my conscience bother me?"

His voice took on a quiet, soothing tone as he continued. "You're just getting all upset over this thing for nothing. I just do as I'm told, and I'd advise you to do the same."

He had made his decision, and now I had to make mine.

I made no attempt to rationalize what I had been asked to do. It made no difference who would falsify which part of the report or whether the actual falsification would be by misleading numbers or misleading words. Whether by acts of commission or omission, all of us who contributed to the fraud would be guilty. The only question left for me to decide was whether or not I would become a party to the fraud.

Before coming to Goodrich in 1963, I had held a variety of jobs, each a little more pleasant, a little more rewarding than the last. At forty-two, with seven children, I had decided that the Goodrich Company would probably be my "home" for the rest of my working life. The job paid well, it was pleasant and challenging, and the future looked reasonably bright. My wife and I had bought a home and we were ready to settle down into a comfortable, middle-age, middle-class rut. If I refused to take part in the A7D fraud, I would have to either resign or be fired. The report would be written by someone anyway, but I would have the satisfaction of knowing I had had no part in the matter. But bills aren't paid with personal satisfaction, nor house payments with ethical principles. I made my decision. The next morning, I telephoned Lawson and told him I was ready to begin on the qualification report.

In a few minutes, he was at my desk, ready to begin. Before we started, I asked him, "Do you realize what we are going to do?"

"Yeah," he replied bitterly, "we're going to screw LTV. And speaking of screwing," he continued, "I know now how a whore feels, because that's exactly what I've become, an engineering whore. I've sold myself. It's all I can do to look at myself in the mirror when I shave. I make me sick.''

I was surprised at his vehemence. It was obvious that he too had done his share of soul-searching and didn't like what he had found. Somehow, though, the air seemed clearer after his outburst, and we began working on the report.

I had written dozens of qualification reports, and I knew what a ''good'' one looked like. Resorting to the actual test data only on occasion, Lawson and I proceeded to prepare page after page of elaborate, detailed engineering curves, charts, and test logs, which purported to show what had happened during the formal qualification tests. Where temperatures were too high, we deliberately chopped them down a few hundred degrees, and where they were too low, we raised them to a value that would appear reasonable to the LTV and military engineers. Brake pressure, torque values, distances, times—everything of consequence was tailored to fit the occasion.

Occasionally, we would find that some test either hadn't been performed at all or had been conducted improperly. On those occasions, we ''conducted'' the test—successfully, of course—on paper.

For nearly a month we worked on the graphic presentation that would be a part of the report. Meanwhile, the fourteenth and final qualification attempt had been completed, and the brake, not unexpectedly, had failed again.

During that month, Lawson and I talked of little else except the enormity of what we were doing. The more involved we became in our work, the more apparent became our own culpability. We discussed such things as the Nuremberg trials and how they related to our guilt and complicity in the A7D situation. Lawson often expressed his opinion that the brake was downright dangerous and that, once on flight tests, ''anything is liable to happen.''

I saw his boss, John Warren, at least twice during that month and needled him about what we were doing. He didn't take the jibes too kindly but managed to laugh the situation off as ''one of those things.'' One day I remarked that what we were doing amounted to fraud, and he pulled out an engineering handbook and turned to a section on laws as they related to the engineering profession.

He read the definition of fraud aloud, then said, ''Well, technically I don't think what we're doing can be called fraud. I'll admit it's not right, but it's just one of those things. We're just kinda caught in the middle. About all I can tell you is, do like I'm doing. Make copies of everything and put them in your SYA file.''

''What's an 'SYA' file?'' I asked.

''That's a 'save your ass' file.'' He laughed.

On June 5, 1968, the report was officially published and copies were delivered in person to the Air Force and LTV. Within a week, flight tests were begun at Edwards Air Force Base in California. Searle Lawson was sent to California as Goodrich's representative. Within approximately two weeks, he returned because some rather unusual incidents during the tests had caused them to be canceled.

His face was grim as he related stories of several near crashes during landings—caused by brake troubles. He told me about one incident in which, upon landing, one brake was literally welded together by the intense heat developed during the test stop. The wheel locked, and the plane skidded for nearly 1500 feet before coming to a halt. The plane was jacked up and the wheel removed. The fused parts within the brake had to be pried apart.

Lawson had returned to Troy from California that same day, and that evening, he and others of the Goodrich engineering department left for Dallas for a high-level conference with LTV.

That evening I left work early and went to see my attorney. After I told him the story, he advised that, while I was probably not actually guilty of fraud, I was certainly part of a conspiracy to defraud. He advised me to go to the Federal Bureau of Investigation and offered to arrange an appointment. The following week he took me to the Dayton office of the FBI, and after I had been warned that I would not be immune from prosecution, I disclosed the A7D matter to one of the agents. The agent told me to say nothing about the episode to anyone and to report any further incident to him. He said he would forward the story to his superiors in Washington.

A few days later, Lawson returned from the conference in Dallas and said that the Air Force, which had previously approved the qualification report, had suddenly rescinded that approval and was demanding to see some of the raw test data taken during the tests. I gathered that the FBI had passed the word.

Finally, early in October 1968, Lawson submitted his resignation, to take effect on October 25. On October 18, I submitted my own resignation, to take effect on November 1. In my resignation, addressed to Russell Line, I cited the A7D report and stated: "As you are aware, this report contained numerous deliberate and willful misrepresentations which, according to legal counsel, constitute fraud and expose both myself and others to criminal charges of conspiracy to defraud....The events of the past seven months have created an atmosphere of deceit and distrust in which it is impossible to work...."

On October 25, I received a sharp summons to the office of Bud Sunderman. As chief engineer at the Troy plant, Sunderman was responsible for the entire engineering division. Tall and graying, impeccably dressed at all times, he was capable of producing a dazzling smile or a hearty chuckle or immobilizing his face into marble hardness, as the occasion required.

I faced the marble hardness when I reached his office. He motioned me to a chair. "I have your resignation here," he snapped, "and I must say you have made some rather shocking, I might even say irresponsible, charges. This is very serious."

Before I could reply, he was demanding an explanation "I want to know exactly what the fraud is in connection with the A7D and how you can dare accuse this company of such a thing!"

I started to tell some of the things that had happened during the testing, but he shut me off saying, "There's nothing wrong with anything we've done here. You aren't aware of all the things that have been going on behind the scenes. If you had known the true situation, you would never have made these charges." He said that in view of my apparent "disloyalty" he had decided to accept my resignation "right now," and said it would be better for all concerned if I left the plant immediately. As I got up to leave he asked me if I intended to "carry this thing further."

I answered simply, "Yes," to which he replied, "Suit yourself." Within twenty minutes, I had cleaned out my desk and left. Forty-eight hours later, the B. F. Goodrich Company recalled the qualification report and the four-disk brake, announcing that it would replace the brake with a new, improved, five-disk brake at no cost to LTV.

Ten months later, on August 13, 1969, I was the chief government witness at a hearing conducted before Senator William Proxmire's Economy in Government Subcommittee of the Congress's Joint Economic Committee. I related the A7D story to the committee, and my testimony was supported by Searle Lawson, who followed me to the witness stand. Air Force officers also testified, as well as a four-man team from the General Accounting Office, which had conducted an investigation of the A7D brake at the request of Senator Proxmire. Both Air Force and GAO investigators declared that the brake was dangerous and had not been tested properly.

Testifying for Goodrich was R. G. Jeter, vice-president and general counsel of the company, from the Akron headquarters. Representing the Troy plant was Robert Sink. These two denied any wrongdoing on the part of the Goodrich Company, despite expert testimony to the contrary by Air Force and GAO officials. Sink was quick to deny any connection with the writing of the report or of directing any falsifications, claiming to be on the West Coast at the time. John Warren was the man who supervised its writing, said Sink.

As for me, I was dismissed as a high-school graduate with no technical training, while Sink testified that Lawson was a young, inexperienced engineer. "We tried to give him guidance," Sink testified, "but he preferred to have his own convictions."

About changing the data and figures in the report, Sink said: "When you take data from several different sources, you have to rationalize among those data what is the true story. This is part of your engineering know-how." He admitted that changes had been made in the data, "but only to make them more consistent with the overall picture of the data that is available."

Jeter pooh-poohed the suggestion that anything improper occurred, saying: "We have thirty-odd engineers at this plant...and I say to you that it is incredible that these men would stand idly by and see reports changed or falsified....I mean you just do not have to do that working for anybody....Just nobody does that."

The four-hour hearing adjourned with no real conclusion reached by the committee. But, the following day the Department of Defense made sweeping changes in its inspection, testing and reporting procedures. A spokesman for the DOD said the changes were a result of the Goodrich episode.

The A7D is now in service, sporting a Goodrich-made five-disk brake, a brake that works very well, I'm told. Business at the Goodrich plant is good. Lawson is now an engineer for LTV and has been assigned to the A7D project. And I am now a newspaper reporter.

At this writing, those remaining at Goodrich are still secure in the same positions, all except Russell Line and Robert Sink. Line has been rewarded with a promotion to production superintendent, a large step upward on the corporate ladder. As for Sink, he moved up into Line's old job.

QUESTIONS FOR DISCUSSION

1. In "The Gift Relationship," Titmuss documents a case of market failure in the distribution of human blood, and argues that a voluntary, nonmarket system is both more efficient and fairer. What are the reasons for the failure of the market system in this case? Can you draw any conclusions about market versus nonmarket systems of distribution in general from the case, or is human blood too unusual a product to permit generalization? What makes blood "special"?

2. Why is the B.F. Goodrich aircraft brake case entitled "Why Should My Conscience Bother Me?" *Should* Russell Line's conscience have bothered him if a test pilot had been injured or killed? Should Kermit Vandivier's? Why or why not? What makes a person morally responsible for an action or event?

3. How would you use the framework developed at Cummins Engine to solve the ethical dilemma faced by Kermit Vandivier in the B.F. Goodrich case?

SUPPLEMENTARY READING FOR PART ONE

Action, H. B. *The Morals of Markets: An Ethical Exploration.* London: Longman Group Limited, 1971.

Arthur, John, and William H. Shaw, eds. *Justice and Economic Distribution.* Englewood Cliffs, N.J.: Prentice-Hall, 1978.

Bell, Daniel, and Irving Kristol, eds. *Capitalism Today.* New York: Basic Books, 1970.

Bowie, Norman. *Towards a New Theory of Distributive Justice.* Amherst, Mass.: University of Massachusetts Press, 1971.

Buchanan, Allen E. *Ethics, Efficiency and the Market.* Totowa, N.J.: Rowman & Allenheld, 1985.

Daniels, Norman, ed. *Reading Rawls: Critical Studies of a Theory of Justice.* New York: Basic Books, 1976.

Drucker, Peter. "What Is 'Business Ethics'?" *The Public Interest,* vol. 63, Spring 1981, pp. 18–36.

Dworkin, Gerald, Gordon Bermanto, and Peter G. Brown, eds. *Markets and Morals*. Washington, D.C.: Hemisphere Publishing, 1977.

Freeman, R. Edward, and Daniel R. Gilbert, Jr. *Corporate Strategy and the Search for Ethics*. Englewood Cliffs, N.J.: Prentice-Hall, 1988.

Harrington, Michael. *Socialism*. New York: Saturday Review Press, 1974.

Hayek, F. A. *Law, Legislation and Liberty,* vols. 1–3. Chicago, Ill.: University of Chicago Press, 1976.

Heilbroner, Robert L. *Between Capitalism and Socialism*. New York: Random House, 1970.

———. *Marxism: For and Against*. New York: W. W. Norton, 1980.

Held, Virginia. *Property, Profits and Economic Justice*. Belmont, Calif.: Wadsworth Publishing, 1980.

Hoffman, W. Michael, and Jennifer Moore. "What Is Business Ethics: A Reply to Peter Drucker." *Journal of Business Ethics,* vol. 4, November 1982.

Jones, Donald, ed. *Doing Ethics in Business*. Cambridge, Mass.: Oelgeschlager, Gunn & Hain, 1982.

Kipnis, Kenneth, and Diana T. Meyers. *Economic Justice*. Totowa, N.J.: Rowman and Allenheld, 1985.

Novak, Michael. *The Spirit of Democratic Capitalism*. New York: Simon & Schuster, 1982.

Nozick, Robert. *Anarchy, State and Utopia*. New York: Basic Books, 1974.

Paul, Jeffrey, ed. *Reading Nozick: Essays on Anarchy, State and Utopia*. Totowa, N.J.: Rowman and Allenheld, 1981.

Phelps, E. S. *Altruism, Morality and Economic Theory*. New York: Russell Sage, 1975.

Posner, Richard A. *The Economics of Justice,* 2d ed. Cambridge, Mass.: Harvard University Press, 1983.

Rawls, John. *A Theory of Justice*. New York: Bobbs-Merrill, 1966.

Schein, Edgar H. "The Problem of Moral Education for the Business Manager." *Moral Education,* vol. 8, *1,* pp. 3–14.

Schweickart, David. *Capitalism or Worker Control? An Ethical and Economic Appraisal*. New York: Praeger, 1980.

Wuthnow, Robert. "The Moral Crisis in American Capitalism." *Harvard Business Review,* March–April 1982, pp. 76–84.

PART TWO

The Nature of the Corporation

In Part One we examined the ethical dimensions of the economic system in which business operates. Here, we turn attention to the nature and role of the corporation within that system. Reflection on the nature of the corporation is important, in part, because our understanding of the corporation shapes our beliefs about the corporation's responsibilities. If we hold that a corporation is a privately owned enterprise designed to make a profit, for example, we are likely to have a narrower view of corporate responsibility than if we hold it to be a quasi-public institution. In Chapter 4 we approach the problem of the nature of the corporation from the perspective of the corporate social responsibility debate.

It is not clear that we can attribute any responsibilities to corporations at all, however, unless we can look upon them as moral agents in some sense. Does it make sense to regard corporations as moral agents, analogous to individuals? Who or what is "Gulf Oil" or "Ford Motor Company"? Chapter 5 explores these and other questions about the identity and agency of corporations.

Finally, we investigate the nature of the corporation from the perspective of its internal structure and governance; in particular, we focus on the corporate board of directors.

Who should sit on the board? What is and what should be the relationship between the board, management, and stockholders? How far should the board's power extend? Such questions regarding the role and composition of the board of directors are taken up in Chapter 6.

THE CORPORATE SOCIAL RESPONSIBILITY DEBATE

Traditionally it has been held that the major responsibility of business in American society is to produce goods and services and to sell them for a profit. This conception of business' role has been one of the cornerstones of its legitimacy—that is, society's belief in the right of business to exist. Recently, however, the traditional view has been questioned. Increasingly, business is being asked not only to refrain from harming society, but to contribute actively and directly to public well-being; it is expected not only to obey a multitude of legal requirements, but also to go beyond the demands of the law and exercise *moral* judgment in making its decisions. What are the reasons for the changing conception of corporate social responsibility?

George Cabot Lodge views the classical conception of the role and responsibility of business as part of a comprehensive ideology, and he points to a radical shift in American ideology as the source of the problem of corporate social responsibility. Traditional ideology, Lodge believes, no longer fits reality, yet it is to this ideology which we still look for legitimacy and in terms of which we still view corporate obligation. We have not yet explicitly recognized the ideology which would legitimize the modern corporation. Since ideology is the source of our ethical standards, Lodge claims, the result of the shift is a crisis of legitimacy and confusion about the responsibilities of the corporation. The old ideology as set forth by Lodge is an individualistic one which stresses personal struggle and fulfillment and the sanctity of private property rights. It views the community as nothing more than the sum total of the individuals who make it up. Consequently, the welfare of the community is identified with the sum of the welfares of its members, and the pursuit of individual satisfaction is considered the only regulatory device needed to produce the public good. Government regulation is kept to the minimum needed to guard individual freedom.

In the context of the traditional ideology, businesses are understood as pieces of private property, instruments of their owners designed primarily to make money. Because the pressure of an "invisible hand" ensures that each entrepreneur's pursuit of his own profit will result in the good of the whole, and because businesses are the property of their owners to do with as they please, business has no other responsibility than to perform its economic function well. As economist Milton Friedman, one of the most forceful exponents of the traditional ideology, puts it, "the social responsibility of business is to increase its profits."

Why has the old ideology begun to erode and a new one begun to take its place? One answer is that today's giant corporations no longer seem to fit the old model. Usually we associate ownership with control, but the modern corporation is owned by shareholders who have little or no psychological or operational involvement in it. Some thinkers have argued that corporations can no longer accurately be viewed as private property. As ownership separates from control, corporations come to seem less like mere instruments of their owners and more like autonomous entities capable of their own goals and decisions.

The tremendous impact on and power over our society exerted by corporations also casts doubt on their private character. Thinkers such as Keith Davis argue that social power inevitably implies social responsibility, and suggest that those who fail to exercise a responsibility commensurate with their power will lose that power. As the power of business has grown, we have become increasingly aware of the external costs—pollution, hazardous products, job dissatisfaction—corporations have passed on to society at large. These costs in turn call into question a basic assumption of the old ideology: the identity of individual and social well-being.

The corporation's evolution away from the kind of enterprise described in the traditional American ideology brings the question of corporate responsibility into sharp focus. Lodge offers us two alternatives: We can explicitly acknowledge the new, "communitarian" ideology which is already reflected in the operational realities of our institutions, and specify corporate obligations on its basis, or we can attempt to make reality fit the old ideology once again. Some, such as Christopher Stone, Anthony Buono and Lawrence Nichols, Keith Davis, and Thomas Donaldson, take the first option, arguing that corporations are no longer merely economic institutions but sociological institutions as well; Milton Friedman opts for the second alternative.

Although Friedman agrees with Lodge that the notion of corporate social responsibility emerges from a new ideology, he does not find this a convincing reason to support the notion. On the contrary; Friedman holds fast to the traditional values of a free market system and rejects the idea of corporate social responsibility because he feels it is "fundamentally subversive" of these values. For Friedman, the sole social responsibility of business is to increase its profits, while staying within the legal "rules of the game."

It is important to realize that Friedman is not claiming that the corporation has *no* responsibilities or obligations. Rather, he is arguing that corporations are directly responsible only to one set of people—their shareholders. Regardless of the actual relationship between ownership and control in the modern corporation, Friedman believes they *ought* not to be separate. Because the shareholders own the corporation and hire managers to run it for them, Friedman argues, managers are "fiduciaries" of the shareholders—they have an obligation to act in shareholders' interest, namely, to make a profit. To demand that corporate managers exercise responsibility to society at large is to ask them to violate their obligations to shareholders.

Managers who assume "social responsibility," Friedman argues, are actually using shareholders' money to solve social problems without their permission. They are in effect "taxing" shareholders, but because they are private employees rather than publicly elected officials, their actions lack authority and legitimacy. Behind Friedman's argument lies a conviction that each social institution exists to perform a particular function. The legitimacy of corporate activity depends on executives fulfilling and confining themselves to the role of agents serving the interests of shareholders. "Social responsibility" is the job of government, not business.

In "Why Shouldn't Corporations Be Socially Responsible?" Christopher Stone critically examines several arguments which might be used to support Friedman's position. It is often suggested that management has made a promise to maximize the profits of corporate stockholders and ought to stand by its promise but, argues Stone, this is simply not the case. There is no explicit promise or contract between managers and shareholders. Nor is it true that managers are bound by an implicit contract because they have been hired by the owners of the corporation. In reality, says Stone, shareholders have neither much power nor much interest in selecting the management of the corporation.

Even if such a contract did exist, Stone continues, it would not mean that management has an obligation to maximize profits in *every possible way,* or that the contract would supersede all other obligations. Business may have an obligation not to sell products that are dangerous to consumers, for example—such as the Ford Pinto—even if by doing so it will make a profit. A contract which required one to subordinate all moral considerations to considerations of profit would be an immoral contract, one which undermines the basis of contract itself. If such a promise *had* been made, argues Stone, it would be morally right to break it.

There seems to be no firm basis, Stone concludes, for the claim that management's *only* obligation is to produce a profit for corporate shareholders. To be sure, managers may have this obligation, but that does not relieve them of all other responsibilities. There are obligations more fundamental than the one Friedman describes; these may include responsibilities to consumers, employees, the surrounding community, and future generations.

In "Five Propositions for Social Responsibility," Keith Davis argues that the social power of business gives rise to social obligations. Business is not isolated from the rest of society; it is a social entity and plays a crucial part in promoting society's well-being. Because of its tremendous power, Davis argues, business is obligated to calculate the social costs and benefits, as well as the economic costs and benefits, of its actions. As a good "citizen," business must not only refrain from harm, but also contribute actively to solving social problems in areas where it has the necessary competence. Finally, Davis sounds a warning note: the "Iron Law of Responsibility," he claims, decrees that those who do not use their power responsibly will eventually lose it.

Thomas Donaldson echoes some of these themes in "The Social Contract: Norms for a Corporate Conscience." He focuses on the idea of an implied contract between business and society in an attempt to specify what the social obligations of business might be. According to Donaldson, the very *right* of corporations to exist and operate is granted to them by society. It is society which recognizes productive organizations as single agents with special status under the law and which permits them to use natural resources and hire employees. In return, society should be permitted to demand at least that the benefits of authorizing the existence of corporations outweigh the liabilities. If Donaldson is correct, the corporation is a social entity—not merely an economic one—from the moment of its inception. His social contract theory implies that the legitimacy of corporate activity lies in the successful exercise of social responsibility.

In Friedman, on the one hand, and Stone, Davis, and Donaldson, on the other, we see two quite different interpretations of business' social role. Anthony Buono and Laurence Nichols refer to these two positions as the "stockholder model" and the "stakeholder model." Adherents of the stockholder model, such as Friedman, believe that the sole purpose of the corporation is to make a profit for its shareholders. Stakeholder theorists, in contrast, believe that the corporation has not just one but many purposes. The corporation should be operated not merely for the benefit of shareholders, but for all "stakeholders"—all those whose contributions are necessary for the success of the firm. Buono and Nichols argue that both long-term self-interest and ethical duty require the adoption of the stakeholder model.

We began our discussion of corporate social responsibility with a consideration of the decay of the traditional American ideology. One of the cornerstones of that ideology is the notion of private property. In their article, W. Michael Hoffman and James Fisher return to the concept of property, this time in the context of corporate liability.

Friedman claims that the corporation is a piece of private property, and that the exercise of social responsibility takes away corporate profits from those who rightfully own them— the shareholders. Lodge and others hold that corporations no longer operate as purely private institutions; therefore, one might argue that the benefits which flow from them ought to be shared collectively. Hoffman and Fisher point out that both Friedman and Lodge are assuming that property, whether private or public, is only a good; they have overlooked the fact that it can be a liability as well. Once this is understood it is no longer clear that the notion of the corporation as private property ought to be abandoned. That the corporation is private property means not only that the public may be excluded from benefiting from its profits; it also means that the public has a right to be excluded from liability for any negative effects it may cause. Thus the idea of private property allows us to hold the corporation accountable in a way in which that of public property does not.

Hoffman and Fisher also suggest that there may be some things that cannot remain private property because of the inability of individual owners to accept the liabilities. Such things, therefore, if they are to exist at all, must become public property, and all their benefits and liabilities shared collectively.

THE CORPORATION AS A MORAL AGENT

The authors included in Chapter 4 examined the issue of whether the corporation ought to have moral responsibilities and offered suggestions as to what these might be. They did not, however, ask whether the corporation is the kind of entity which is capable of having responsibilities at all. Normally we associate moral responsibility with individual persons. But corporations are not individual persons; they are collections of individuals who work together to establish corporate policy, make corporate decisions, and execute corporate actions. In the 1978 *First National Bank of Boston v. Bellotti* decision the U.S. Supreme Court granted corporations the right to free speech—a right we ordinarily attribute only to individuals. It might be argued that if corporations are to receive the rights accorded persons, they should also be treated as full-fledged individuals in every way. Dissenting opinion, on the other hand, claimed that corporations are not persons, and that therefore the decision was inappropriate.

What does it mean to say that the Ford Motor Company or Gulf Oil is responsible for a particular action? Who is to blame for an immoral corporate action? Does it make sense to look at the corporation as a moral agent, analogous to a person? And if not, does this mean that we cannot judge corporate actions according to ethical standards?

Kenneth Goodpaster and John Matthews argue that there is an analogy between individual and organizational behavior, and that for this reason corporate conduct can be evaluated in moral terms. Some thinkers have claimed that only persons are capable of moral responsibility in the fullest sense, because such responsibility presupposes the ability to reason, to have intentions, and to make autonomous choices. But although the corporation is not a person in a literal sense, Goodpaster and Matthews respond, it is made up of persons. For this reason, we can project many of the attributes of individual human beings to the corporate level. We already speak of corporations having goals, values, interests, strategies. Why, ask Goodpaster and Matthews, shouldn't we also speak of the corporate conscience?

Thinkers who assume that corporations cannot exercise moral responsibility advocate trust in the "invisible hand" of the market system to "moralize" the actions of corporations. Milton Friedman is one of these. Others feel that the "hand of government" is required to ensure moral corporate behavior. Both of these views, however, fail to locate the source of responsible corporate action in the corporation itself. Both rely upon systems and forces external to the corporation. Goodpaster and Matthews argue for a third alternative: endowing the corporation with a conscience analogous to that of an individual, recognizing the ability of corporations to exercise independent moral judgment, and locating the responsibility for corporate behavior in the hands of corporate managers. This "hand of management" alternative, they admit, is not without its problems—and it requires more thorough analysis on both the conceptual and practical levels. But Goodpaster and Matthews believe that it is the best alternative of the three because it provides a framework for an inventory of corporate responsibilities and accepts corporations as legitimate members of the moral community.

Peter French develops the analogy between individual persons and corporations in detail in his article. One of the most important elements in the notion of responsibility, French points out, is that of intention. In general we do not hold persons morally responsible for unintentional acts. If we wish the idea of corporate responsibility to make sense, we must be able to discover a corporate intention. But how can a collective intend? French suggests that we make use of what he calls the Corporate Internal Decision (CID) Structure to understand the meaning of corporate intention.

The CID Structure has two major components: an organizational flowchart which indicates the "rules of the game"—the levels of responsibility within the corporate hierarchy (French calls this "the grammar of corporate decision making")—and a corporate policy which includes the beliefs, principles, and goals of the organization. Some have argued that it is precisely these characteristics that make corporations nonmoral and fundamentally different from individuals. Here French uses them in the service of corporate responsibility. A decision is a corporate decision—intended by the corporation—if it has been made in accordance with the operational flowchart and if it reflects corporate policy.

It is a crucial aspect of French's theory that a corporate intention or decision is not identical with the intentions or decisions of those within the organization. It is true that corporate action is dependent on the action of individuals in that a corporation cannot act without some human being acting. French holds that the CID Structure literally "incorporates" the actions of individuals. A corporate act is different from the acts of which it is incorporated, just as the activity of an organism is different from the activity of its parts.

If French is correct, corporations must be regarded as genuine, independent moral agents, on an equal footing with human beings. It is precisely this feature of French's position which John Danley attacks. Corporate and individual agency are *not* the same, argues Danley. The reasons in favor of "anthropological bigotry" become clear when we focus on the "moral moves" which take place after an agent has done something—especially on those of blame and punishment.

French holds that only those actions which are done in accordance with the organizational flowchart and guided by corporate policy can be counted as "corporate acts." Presumably corporate policy includes the provisions of the corporate charter, which grants corporations the right to do business as long as they obey the law. But if the members of the corporation voted to act illegally, then, Danley claims, their decision could not be described as a "corporate action" at all. It is unclear whether corporations can ever act illegally under French's theory.

Even if corporations can perform illegal acts, it is difficult to see how moral sanctions can be applied to them. Only individuals can be punished. Fines can be levied on corporations, but ultimately individuals—stockholders, consumers, employees—pay the cost. If French is correct in saying that a corporate act is not identical with the acts of individuals, however, it does not make sense to go inside the corporation to punish an individual: This is to punish a person for something he did not do. Either corporations cannot be punished at all under French's theory, Danley argues, or individuals are made to suffer in their place, and are thus relegated to the status of second-rate citizens of the moral community. French's organismic view of the corporation, concludes Danley, has some serious drawbacks. He suggests that a machine, the activities of which are dependent on persons, is a more adequate model for understanding corporate morality.

CORPORATE ACCOUNTABILITY AND THE BOARD OF DIRECTORS

Central to the issue of corporate legitimacy, responsibility, and liability taken up in Chapter 4 is the issue of corporate accountability. To whom ought corporations to be accountable? How can such accountability be implemented? The authors included in Chapter 6 look not to regulations imposed on the corporation from outside, but on the corporate internal structure itself for answers to these questions. Because historically the board of directors has been conceived of as one important locus of corporate accountability and because suggestions for changes in the role, election, and staffing of boards have been at the heart of several important proposals for reform, it is appropriate that they focus their attention on the nature, role, and composition of corporate boards.

Traditionally, corporate governance has been conceived on a rough analogy with the American political system. As the owners of the corporation, shareholders elect representatives—the board of directors—to establish broad objectives and direct corporate activities. The directors in turn select corporate officers to execute their policies. Management is thus accountable to the board of directors, and the board to shareholders.

But it is increasingly unclear that this picture represents the reality of corporate governance. Such thinkers as Ralph Nader, Mark Green, and Joel Seligman hold that management really controls the election of board members through its power over the machinery of proxy voting. The board, they claim, does not provide a check on the power of management; it does not really make policies or select executive officers, but routinely rubber-stamps the decisions of management.

The case of multimillion-dollar bribery by Gulf Oil executives included in this part of the text lends some credence to these claims. Gulf's board remained ignorant for more than a year after the disclosure of the payments that the company's chief executive officer and chairman of the board had been personally involved. Once aware of the payments, it seemed to be unclear about its loyalties and reluctant to exercise its authority over management.

Furthermore, as a 1978 press release from the Senate Committee on Governmental Affairs indicates, corporate boards are so tightly interlocked that what power they do have is concentrated in the hands of a small elite. The overwhelming potential for conflicts of interest further impedes boards' ability to check management power.

Nader, Green, and Seligman see an urgent need for a truly effective board which will make accountable the unbridled power of management. Their suggestions for achieving this goal include a revamping of the shareholder electoral system; the institutionalizing of a new profession, that of the professional director who devotes full time to supervising the activities of the corporation; and the prohibition of interlocking directorates.

Still other issues of corporate governance are raised by the vast power of the corporation in modern society. The traditional model of corporate governance assumes that the most important constituency of the corporation is its shareholders, and that it is primarily to shareholders that the corporation ought to be accountable. But perhaps this is not so. The view that the crucial form of corporate accountability is accountability to shareholders is based on the assumption that the corporation is a piece of private property; the shareholders are the owners of the corporation and therefore the corporation is answerable only to them. But we have already noted that this assumption has been challenged. Lodge has claimed that the corporation is not private property, but is really a public institution. If this is true, presumably there ought to be some way to represent all relevant constituencies of the corporation in its internal structure. Milton Friedman has argued that to ask corporations to exercise "social" power is to make them into miniature governments; but Nader, Green, and Seligman claim that corporations do in fact exert such power and that they *are* governments in a sense for this reason. To ask corporations to be accountable only to stockholders is to permit governments to exist without the consent of the governed, an idea which is fundamentally at odds with the political philosophy of the United States. The election of "public interest directors," each of whom is placed in charge of overseeing such areas as consumer protection, employee welfare, and shareholder rights, may be one way to ensure corporate accountability to those whom it affects. And Nader, Green, and Seligman propose that the board should be made up only of "outside" directors—persons who have no other relationship to the corporation.

The interpretation of the corporation as a public institution is precisely what Irving Shapiro objects to in his essay on corporate governance. Corporations are not analogous to governments, he argues. They are private enterprises formed to execute the essential task of providing goods and services—a task, Shapiro suggests, government could not perform efficiently. The corporation has an important external locus of accountability government does not: the competition engendered by the free market system. For these reasons Shapiro defends the rationale behind the present system of corporate governance; he does not believe that a radical overhaul is required.

Shapiro does not look favorably on proposals that the board contain more "outside" directors or representatives of various interest groups. Although independence of judgment is crucial in a corporate director, he fears that outside directors may lack the depth of understanding of an industry's problems necessary for informed decision making. Such directors might find themselves dependent on the explanations of the chief executive officer, and thus unable to exert adequate control over management activities. And although the presence of public interest directors on the board could generate a healthy tension, it might also lead to conflicts of interest and paralysis. A clear division of labor between boards of directors and management and a conscientious execution of their respective tasks, Shapiro concludes, are all that is necessary to produce an effective system of corporate governance that ensures accountability.

Like Shapiro, Harold Geneen sees the corporation primarily as a piece of private property run for the benefit of its shareholders. But he disagrees that todays' boards are generally effective in protecting shareholders' interests. The reason is the predominance of large numbers of "inside" directors on the board—those who are also members of upper management—and the common practice of having the CEO also serve as board chair. "Inside" directors, Geneen argues, have a direct conflict of interest. Because they are members of management, they cannot objectively monitor and evaluate management's performance as their role as board member demands. As CEO, the chair of the board has a tremendous amount of power over the other inside directors, who are subordinates. The CEO needs to persuade only a few outside directors in order to get the approval needed for decisions. Dissenting voices of outside directors are easily drowned out by the monolithic voice of management. Because even outside board members depend on management for valuable "perks," and because board members are almost completely protected from personal liability for their decisions, there is little incentive for them to "rock the boat" by criticizing management. Geneen suggests that corporations take immediate steps to develop truly independent boards. The responsibilities of boards and of management, he argues, should be separate and distinct. The board should be made up of qualified outsiders.

TAKEOVERS AND CORPORATE RESTRUCTURING

One of the most controversial business-related issues in recent years is the unprecedented increase in mergers and takeovers, especially hostile takeovers. The colorful jargon of the hostile takeover scene—terms like "sharks," "greenmail," "white knights," "golden parachutes," "scorched earth policies"—has taken root in the national imagination.

The growth of the takeover business raises both questions about corporate accountability and questions about the nature and purpose of the corporation.

Proponents of unrestricted takeovers, such as Michael Jensen, argue that they make managers more accountable to shareholders. Takeover targets, he claims, are usually companies managed by executives who have failed to maximize their value and whose share price is therefore lower than it ought to be. Shareholders who sell their shares to raiders or friendly "suitors" at higher than market value are best seen as "voting" out the old management in favor of a new one. The higher share price represents the belief of the new management that they can increase the firm's value. Jensen approves of "golden parachutes," huge severance payments offered to incumbent management after a takeover, because they encourage managers to act in the interest of the shareholders rather than trying to retain their power. Even controversial takeover defenses like selling the company's most valuable assets ("selling the crown jewels"), Jensen believes, are generally good for shareholders. In addition to benefiting shareholders, Jensen argues, unrestricted takeovers help to allocate capital more efficiently and thus are good for society as a whole.

Robert Kuttner challenges Jensen's picture of takeover targets as poorly managed companies whose shareholders "vote" out incumbent management. Most targeted companies, he claims, are well run; and shareholders are not doing anything like "voting" when they sell their shares to a raider—they are simply trying to gain a short-term profit. Kuttner believes that the new emphasis on takeovers has had serious harmful effects on society. The new emphasis forces managers to emphasize short-term share price rather than long-term growth, productivity, quality, or product price—the traditional bases of competition. Fear of takeover encourages managers to go heavily into debt, making the firm more vulnerable to periodic down-turns in the market. The negative effects of increased takeovers on other stakeholders, such as employees and local communities, have been highly publicized. The case "Oklahoma Meets

Wall Street'' describes the impact of a hostile takeover attempt on a small U.S. town. Most importantly, Kuttner asks,
is maximizing wealth for shareholders the sole measure of
success for a firm or a business practice? The questions he
raises lead us back to the central issues of this part of the
book: What is the nature of a corporation? Who are its constituents, other than managers and shareholders? What
should society expect in return for the many legal privileges
and immunities conferred on corporations?

CHAPTER 4

Legitimacy, Responsibility, and Liability

READINGS FOR CHAPTER FOUR

George Cabot Lodge
The Ethical Implications of Ideology
144

Milton Friedman
The Social Responsibility of Business Is to Increase Its Profits
153

Christopher D. Stone
Why Shouldn't Corporations Be Socially Responsible?
157

Thomas Donaldson
The Social Contract: Norms for a Corporate Conscience
162

Keith Davis
Five Propositions for Social Responsibility
165

Anthony F. Buono and Lawrence T. Nichols
Stockholder and Stakeholder Interpretations of Business' Social Role
170

W. Michael Hoffman and James V. Fisher
Corporate Responsibility: Property and Liability
176

The Ethical Implications of Ideology

George Cabot Lodge*

Business is said to lack a sense of social responsibility, but what is "responsibility" after all? At the least, it is, as philosopher Charles Frankel says, "the product of definite social arrangements." From such arrangements flow the do's and don'ts that constitute the more or less coercive framework by which a community assesses and controls behavior. Today the framework is in disarray. Sufficient perhaps to enable us to identify clear-cut villanies and to punish the scoundrels who perpetrate them, it is of less help in appraising the actions of many managers who in their own judgement and that of many of their peers consider their conduct justifiable and well-meaning even while large segments of public opinion believe it to be inhumane, irresponsible or corrupt.

In examining this difference of opinion it will be useful to bear in mind Frankel's "definite social arrangements." I shall call such arrangements ideology, meaning a framework of ideas which a community uses to define values and to make them explicit. Ideology is the source of legitimacy of institutions, and the justification for the authority of those who manage them. Ideology can be conveniently seen as a bridge which a community uses to get from timeless, universal, non-controversial notions such as survival, justice, economy, self-fulfillment and self-respect to the application of these notions in the real world.

Excerpted from "The Connection Between Ethics and Ideology" found in *Proceedings of the First National Conference on Business Ethics,* edited by W. Michael Hoffman (Waltham, Mass: The Center For Business Ethics, Bentley College, 1977). Reprinted by permission of the publisher and author.

*Business, Government, and Competition Area, Harvard Business School.

The real world is made up of populations—concentrated or dispersed; of natural elements and resources—air, water, earth, oil, minerals, etc.; of institutions—General Motors, government, OPEC, the Palestine Liberation Organization. As the real world changes—either by events such as people moving to New York City or by revelation, such as of the inexorable relationships emerging between population, oil, food and money in the world—so the definition of values within the real world changes, and so ideology changes. Frequently, however, there is a lag. Communities have a propensity to linger with an old ideology after its institutions have perforce departed from it. The status quo tends to use the old ideas to justify itself.

The real world of America is plainly vastly different today from what is was 20 or 50 or 100 years ago. Consequently the traditional ideology of America has also changed—for better or for worse. We are living with a new reality. Thus there are new constraints on how we define values and make them explicit. We are in transit from one ideology to another and many of the ethical dilemmas we face are the result of this transition.

Two things have happened: First, the traditional ideology of America has become inconsistent with the real world. Secondly, great institutions have departed from the traditional ideology, contributing thereby to its subversion and replacement.

We are thus looking for legitimacy and authority to ideas which are increasingly inconsistent with practice and reality. Theoretically there are two possibilities: 1) returning to the old ideology, making practice and reality conform, or 2) recognizing explicitly the new ideology and making the best of it, aligning our behavior with it, hopefully preserving what is most valuable of the old. As a practical matter, the first choice is impossible. We must do the second. Until we do so institutions will lack legitimacy; the powerful will be drained of authority; the definition of values will be unclear and what many consider unethical behavior will abound.

THE TRADITIONAL IDEOLOGY OF THE UNITED STATES

Our traditional ideology is not at all hard to identify. It is composed of five great ideas that first came to America in the eighteenth century, having been set down in seventeenth century England as "natural" laws by John Locke, among others. These ideas found fertile soil in the vast, underpopulated wilderness of America and served us well for a hundred years or so. They are now in an advanced state of erosion. The Lockean Five are:

1. *Individualism.* This is the atomistic notion that the community is no more than the sum of the individuals in it. It is the idea that fulfillment lies in an essentially lonely struggle in what amounts to a wilderness where the fit survive—and where, if you do not survive, you are somehow unfit. Closely tied to individualism is the idea of *equality,* in the sense implied in the phrase "equal opportunity," and the idea of *contract,* the inviolate device by which individuals are tied together as buyers and sellers. In the political order in this country, individualism evolved into *interest group pluralism,* which became the preferred means of directing society.
2. *Property rights.* Traditionally, the best guarantee of individual rights was held to be the sanctity of property rights. By virtue of this concept, the individual was assured freedom from the predatory powers of the sovereign.
3. *Competition—consumer desire.* Adam Smith most eloquently articulated the idea that the uses of property are best controlled by each individual proprietor competing in an open market to satisfy individual consumer desires. It is explicit in U.S. antitrust law and practice.
4. *Limited state.* In reaction to the powerful hierarchies of medievalism, the conviction grew that the least government is the best government. We do not mind how big government may get, but we are reluctant to allow it authority or focus. And whatever happens the cry is, "Don't let it plan—particularly down there in Washington. Let it be responsive to crises and to interest groups. Whoever pays the price can call the tune."
5. *Scientific specialization and fragmentation.* This is the corruption of Newtonian mechanics which says that, if we attend to the parts, as experts and specialists, the whole will take care of itself.

There are a number of powerful American myths associated with these ideas: John Wayne as the frontiersman; rags to riches with Horatio Alger; and, most fundamentally, *the myth of material growth and progress.*

Implicit in individualism is the notion that man has the will to acquire power, that is, to control external events, property, nature, the economy, politics or whatever. Under the concept of the limited state, the presence of this will in the human psyche meant the guarantee of progress through competition, notably when combined with the Darwinian notion that the inexorable processes of evolution are constantly working to improve on nature.

Scientific specialization has been part of this "progress," fragmenting knowledge and society while straining their adaptability. This splintering has brought us at least one hideous result: an amoral view of progress "under which nuclear ballistic missiles definitely represent progress over gunpowder and cannonballs, which in turn represent progress over bows and arrows."[1] This treacherous myth places no apparent limit on the degree to which man can gain dominion over his environment, nor does it stipulate any other ideological criteria for defining progress.

It can be argued that while the Lockean Five may be valid as ideals, in practice we have often departed from them. For example, history is replete with examples of business going to "the limited state'' and seeking protection or favor. While this might be justified in the name of property rights, it had the effect of forcing the government into an active, planning mode. Or one might cite the many examples in America of ethnic communities with a high sense of interdependency, organic social constructs instead of the atomistic conglomerations of Locke. Immigrants did indeed bring a strong sense of community with them but it must be admitted that over time this sense weakened for want of nourishment from the surrounding social system. Whatever may have been our historic inconsistencies with the traditional ideology, it seems true that for most of our history it served as the principal justification for our institutional life and behavior. Departures from it were exceptional and every effort was made to minimize their significance.

Today, as I have indicated, the exceptions are overwhelming. The old ideas perform less and less well as definers of values in the real world, and many of our most important institutions have either radically departed from the old ideology or are in the process of doing so in the name of obedience to the law, efficiency, economies of scale, consumer desire, productivity, crisis and necessity.

Although many small enterprises remain comfortably and acceptably consistent with the Lockean Five and hopefully can remain so, the managers of large institutions in both the so-called private and public sectors are forced not to practice what they preach. It is this gap between the behavior of institutions and what they sometimes thoughtlessly claim as a source of authority that causes trauma. If we were to ask, what then is the ideology which would legitimize the behavior of these institutions, we would, I think, come up with five counterparts to the Lockean Five.

THE NEW IDEOLOGY

They are:

1. *Communitarianism.* The community—New York City, for example—is more than the sum of the individuals in it. It has special and urgent needs as a community, and the survival and the self-respect of the individuals in it depend on the recognition of those needs. There are few who can get their kicks à la John Wayne, although many try. Individual fulfillment for most depends on a place in a community, an identity with a whole, participation in an organic social process. And further: If the community, the factory, or the neighborhood is well designed, its members will have a sense of identity with it. They will be able to make maximum use of their capacities. If it is poorly designed, people will be correspondingly alienated and frustrated. In the complex and highly organized America of today, few can live as Locke had in mind.

Both corporations and unions have played leading roles in the creation of the circumstances which eroded the old idea of individualism and created the new. But invariably they have been ideologically unmindful of what they have done. Therefore, they have tended to linger with the old forms and assumptions even after those have been critically altered.

A central component of the old notion of individualism is the so-called Protestant ethic: hard work, thrift, delayed gratification and obedience to authority. Business has extolled these virtues on the production side of things even as it has systematically undercut them on the marketing side. Advertising departments spend millions reminding us that the good life entails immediate gratification of our most lurid desires, gratification which we can buy now and pay for later. Leisure and luxury are touted as the hallmark of happiness.[2]

Our former social policy attempted to guarantee that each worker have equal opportunity. The lawyers enforcing equal employment legislation, however, have taken quite a different tack. In the case of AT&T, for example, they argued that discrimination had become institutionalized; it had become endemic to the AT&T community, and women, for example, had been slotted into certain tasks. When this kind of argument is being accepted, it is no longer necessary to prove individual discrimination in order to get redress.

The government then moved to change the makeup of the whole of AT&T so as to provide, in effect, for *equality of representation* at all levels. Without any specific charge having been brought, the company in turn agreed to upgrade 50,000 women and 6,600 minority group workers and—perhaps most significantly—to hire 4,000 men to fill traditionally female jobs such as operator and clerk. The company also agreed to pay some $15 million in compensation. Thus the issue became one of *equality of result* not of opportunity; a communitarian idea had superseded an individualistic one.

2. *Rights and duties of membership.* A most curious thing has happened to private property— it has stopped being very important. After all, what difference does it really make today whether a person *owns* or just *enjoys* property? He may get certain psychic kicks out of owning a jewel or a car or a TV set or a house—but does it really make a difference whether he owns or rents?

Even land, that most basic element of property, has gone beyond the bounds of the traditional ideology. "Land," agreed the United Nations Commission on Human Settlements in 1976, "because of the crucial role it plays in human settlements, cannot be treated as an ordinary asset controlled by individuals and subject to the pressures and inefficiencies of the market."[3]

Today there is a new right which clearly supersedes property rights in political and social importance. It is the right to survive—to enjoy income, health, and other rights associated with membership in the American community or in some component of that community, including a corporation.

These rights derive not from any individualistic action or need; they do not emanate from a contract. They are rather communitarian rights that public opinion holds to be consistent with a good community. This is a revolutionary departure from the old Lockean conception under which only the fit survive.

The utility of property as a legitimizing idea has eroded as well. It is now quite obvious that our large public corporations are not private property at all. The 1,500,000 shareholders of General Motors do not and cannot control, direct, or in any real sense be responsible for "their" company. Furthermore, the vast majority of them have not the slightest desire for such responsibility. They are investors pure and simple, and if they do not get a good return on their investment, they will put their money elsewhere.

Campaign GM and other similar attempts at stockholder agitation represent heroic but naively conservative strategies to force shareholders to behave like owners and thus to legitimize corporations as property. But such action is clearly a losing game. And it is a peculiar irony that James Roche, as GM chairman, branded such agitation as radical, as the machinations of "an adversary culture...antagonistic to our American ideas of private property and individual responsibility." In truth, of course, GM is the radical; Nader et alia were acting as conservatives, trying to bring the corporation back into ideological line.

But, the reader may ask, if GM and the hundreds of other large corporations like it are not property, then what are they? The best we can say is that they are some sort of collective, floating in philosophic limbo, dangerously vulnerable to the charge of illegitimacy and to the charge that they are not amenable to community control. Consider how the management of this nonproprietary institution is selected. The myth is that the stockholders select the board of directors which in turn selects the management. This is not true, however.

Management selects the board, and the board, generally speaking, blesses management.

Managers thus get to be managers according to some mystical, circular process of questionable legitimacy. Under such circumstances it is not surprising that "management's rights" are fragile and its authority waning. Alfred Sloan warned us of this trend in 1927:

There is a point beyond which diffusion of stock ownership must enfeeble the corporation by depriving it of virile interest in management upon the part of some one man or group of men to whom its success is a matter of personal and vital interest. And conversely at the same point the public interest becomes involved when the public can no longer locate some tangible personality within the ownership which it may hold responsible for the corporation's conduct.[4]

We have avoided this profound problem because of the unquestioned effectiveness of the corporate form per se. In the past, when economic growth and progress were synonymous, we preferred that managers be as free as possible from stockholder interference, in the name of efficiency. But today the definition of efficiency, the criteria for and the limitations of growth, and the general context of the corporation are all much less sure. So the myth of corporate property is becoming a vulnerability.

3. *Community need.* It was to the notion of community need that ITT appealed in 1971 when it sought to prevent the Justice Department from divesting it of Hartford Fire Insurance. The company lawyers said, in effect: "Don't visit that old idea of competition on us. The public interest requires ITT to be big and strong at home so that it can withstand the blows of Allende in Chile, Castro in Cuba, and the Japanese in general. Before you apply the antitrust laws to us, the Secretary of the Treasury, the Secretary of Commerce, and the Council of Economic Advisers should meet to decide what, in the light of our balance-of-payments problems and domestic

economic difficulties, the national interest is."[5]

Note that here again it was the company arguing the ideologically radical case. The suggestion was obvious: ITT is a partner with the government—indeed with the Cabinet—in defining and fulfilling the community needs of the United States. There may be some short-term doubt about who is the senior partner, but partnership it is. This concept is radically different from the traditional idea underlying the antitrust laws—namely that the public interest emerges *naturally* from free and vigorous competition among numerous aggressive, individualistic, and preferably small companies attempting to satisfy consumer desires.

4. *Active, planning state.* It follows that the role of the state is changing radically—it is becoming the setter of our sights and the arbiter of community needs. Inevitably, it will take on unprecedented tasks of coordination, priority setting, and planning in the largest sense. It will need to become far more efficient and authoritative, capable of making the difficult and subtle tradeoffs which now confront us—for example, between environmental purity and energy supply.

Government is already big in the United States, probably bigger in proportion to our population than even in those countries which we call "socialist." Some 16 percent of the labor force now works for one or another governmental agency, and by 1980 it will be more. Increasingly, U.S. institutions live on government largess—subsidies, allowances, and contracts to farmers, corporations, and universities—and individuals benefit from social insurance, medical care, and housing allowances. The pretense of the limited state, however, means that these huge allocations are relatively haphazard, reflecting the crisis of the moment and the power of interest groups rather than any sort of coherent and objective plan.

If the role of government were more precisely and consciously defined, the government could be smaller in size. To a great extent, the plethora of bureaucracies today is the result of a lack of focus and comprehension, an ironic bit of fallout from the old notion of the limited state. With more consciousness we could also consider more fruitfully which issues are best left to local or regional planning and which, in fact, transcend the nation-state and require a more global approach.

5. *Holism—interdependence.* Finally, and perhaps most fundamentally, the old idea of scientific specialization has given way to a new consciousness of the interrelatedness of all things. Spaceship earth, the limits of growth, the fragility of our life-supporting biosphere have dramatized the ecological and philosophical truth that everything is related to everything else. Harmony between the works of man and the demand of nature is no longer the romantic plea of conservationists. It is an absolute rule of survival, and thus it is of profound ideological significance, subverting in many ways all of the Lockean ideas.

ETHICAL APPLICATIONS

Many of the ethical issues of our time can be better understood if we view them in the light of this ideological transition.

In the aftermath of Watergate came the disclosure that scores of America's most important corporations had violated the Corrupt Practices Act, making illegal contributions to political campaigns and payoffs to many politicians for presumed favors. While in general it is wrong to violate the law, there are plainly exceptions to the rule as the experience of prohibition demonstrates; there are also degrees of wrongness. Political payoffs are in a sense a perfectly natural result of the traditional ideology. If the institution of government is held in low repute, if it is indeed regarded essentially as a necessary evil

and if its direction is supposed to arise from the pulling and hauling of innumerable interest groups, then it is natural that those groups will tend to use every means, fair or foul, to work their will. It is the way the system works. How do we change the system? We provide government with a more revered status, we acknowledge that it has a central role in the definition of the needs of the community and in the determination of priorities, and that this role requires a certain objective distance from special interests. We then restrict the practice of lobbying, insulate government from pressure groups and charge it with the responsibility of acting coherently in the national interest. Even as we do this we can sense the predictable threats which the Communitarian state brings: elitism, unresponsiveness and perhaps an increasing partnership between government and large corporations, replacing the adversary relationship inherent in the traditional ideology and evolving possibly into a form of corporate statism which could erode essential elements of democracy.

So without excusing the illegality of those making and receiving the payoffs or in any sense minimizing their ethical flabbiness, we must acknowledge that perhaps more important is the systemic weakness which their behavior exposed. Of equal importance is an awareness of the consequences of correcting that weakness and a precise recognition of our choices.

In this connection one of the most important uses of ideological analysis is that it helps to make explicit the full range of possibilities flowing from a change in practice. There is a propensity in any society for these possibilities to be obscured or muted by those who are seeking the change. It is perfectly possible for the United States to get the worst of Communitarianism unless we are fully alert to the choices which the transition requires of us.

Take, for example, the natural gas crisis that paralyzed the country in the winter of 1977; throwing one and a half million persons out of work and causing suffering and even death in many communities. Who and what is to blame? Some say it is regulation; others argue that it is greedy companies seeking to maximize short term profits. It is pointless and superfluous to look for villains in this matter. The problem is systemic. Sooner or later government will perceive the energy problem as the holistic one that it is and begin to offer some coherent leadership. Until it does, catastrophe will mount as will unethical behavior.

It would seem clear that the ethical corporate executive would address reality, urge government to do the coherent planning required, offer to assist—careful not to dominate or dictate—and then proceed to implement the plan with the efficiency for which U.S. corporations are justly respected. Only in this way can the investment decisions of the oil companies, for example, be both intelligent and just.

The means of achieving our energy needs can be varied. Competition in the market place may work for some of them; but clearly for others regulation and/or some sort of partnership arrangement with government will be required. Perhaps the use of a federal charter would be practical as a way of providing a broad framework for legitimate activity with a minimum of unnecessary intervention. What stands in the way of such a course of action is principally a good deal of irrelevant ideology on the part of government, business and the public in general.

The Lockheed case raises other issues of government-business relationships. In August 1975, Lockheed, a major U.S. defense contractor, admitted it had made under-the-table payments totaling at least $22 million since 1970. Part of the payments, particularly those made in Japan, were used to promote the sales of the L-1011 Tri-Star jet liner. Difficulties with both producing and selling the L-1011 had placed the company on the brink of bankruptcy in 1971 when Congress bailed it out agreeing to guarantee a $250 million loan. At the time Congress established a Loan Guarantee Board with broad powers of supervision over Lockheed. Manage-

ment defended its questionable foreign payments, arguing that they were necessary to consummate foreign sales especially of the L-1011. The company also believed that such practices were "consistent with practices engaged in by numerous other companies abroad, including many of its competitors, and are in keeping with business practices in many foreign countries."[6]

Daniel J. Haughton, then chairman of Lockheed's Board, told the Senate Subcommittee on Multinational Corporations, that French competition in wide-bodied aircraft was especially serious. He submitted a newspaper article reporting that the French Defense Ministry had indulged in a variety of payments and "sweeteners" to make it the world's largest arms exporter next to the U.S. and USSR. His point was that in the interests of Lockheed's shareholders he had to do the same.

A central issue in this case is certainly the relationship between Lockheed and the U.S. Government. There are many connections. Lockheed is a major defense contractor. It is answerable to the Loan Guarantee Board of which the Secretary of the Treasury is chairman. It is a major exporter of military aircraft. The evidence suggests that these relationships with government were and still are vague and unclear.

The government was prepared to help the company when Lockheed's banks went to bat for it in 1971 but afterwards there is little to suggest that the Loan Guarantee Board did much supervising. There is evidence that President Nixon and presumably the U.S. Government were active in persuading Japan to purchase L-1011's, but we do not know whether anyone in government knew about the $7 million paid to Yoshio Kodama for the sale of Lockheed's products there. Haughton's reference to the French is interesting. The French government obtaining business for French industry around the world in the French national interest is one matter. Lockheed bribing foreign officials in the interest of Lockheed's shareholders is clearly another. Was Lockheed acting in the national interest or its shareholder's interest? Haughton said the latter but by inference his use of the French example suggests that he was thinking of the former.

Here again clarity and explicitness are essential. The question of what U.S. business sells in the way of military equipment around the world is surely infused with the national interest. It relates to our defense posture, our diplomatic alliances and our balance of payments. Haughton's problem may well have been as much a matter of the definition of the terms of his company's partnership with government as it was of ethics.

The go-it-alone propensity of business was particularly prevalent at the end of the 1960s, manifesting itself in rampant "social responsibility" mixed with a sense of corporate omnipotence. Those were the days, for example, when powerful white urban business leaders got together supremely confident that with their wisdom and resources they could solve the problems of racism, poverty and blight that infested the cities. I heard one suggest that sending mobile libraries down through Harlem would do the trick. What these men seemed to forget or ignore was that they had neither the right nor the competence to introduce permanent irreversible changes into the social and political milieu around them. The task of renovating the ghetto was above all else a political one in which they could of course play a role but only as the political realities had been faced and dealt with. They were part of a system and it was the system which was malfunctioning.

Failure to observe this fact led to waste and bitterness. Indeed with the most ethical intentions some business leaders were downright unethical. I had a friend who owned a small paper company, employing 500 workers, located on the banks of a turgid New England stream. Seventeen paper companies dumped their effluent into this stream. In the spring of 1969 we celebrated Earth Day at Harvard. We all wore little buttons with green smiles on them. It was a beautiful day;

the Charles River stunk and its banks were embroidered with beer cans and we had seminars galore. My friend came down and he really got religion—harmony with nature, holism and all the rest. He went back determined to clean up his effluent. He spent $2.5 million doing so. A few months later I read that he had gone broke, so I went up to see him. I asked him what he had learned. He was, it seemed, encased in a kind of angelic halo as he spoke of the necessity of clean water and sacrificing material things for spiritual ends. When I pointed out that the water was no cleaner, he said, "Well, that's those 17 other fellows upstream."

"How are they going to get the word?" I asked.

"Oh, they will learn from my example."

I think he thought that somehow the divinity of his image would ooze osmotically upstream.

I said, "Did it occur to you to go to the state, maybe to the several states bordering the river, perhaps even to the Environmental Protection Agency in Washington and seek strict standards, enforced, so that when you went clean everybody would go clean and the water would run clear and there would be something for your people out of work and maybe even a little something for you?"

"Oh, no," he said. "That's not the American way. Private enterprise can do the job. That's the social responsibility of business. We can't have those bureaucrats doing the job."

There is something noble, I suppose, about anyone who puts principle ahead of profits—if he knows what he is doing. That is, if my friend had said to himself, "Before I violate any one of the Lockean Five, I would rather die or go broke," we would call him a martyr. We might suggest something about the tactics of martyrdom—how it is better to have followers than not—but we would admire him. But if, on the other hand, he did what he did unmindful of the visceral control which the old ideology exerted over his perceptions and decision-making, then all we can say is that he was an ignorant, irresponsible, unethical manager who had no business managing anything.

Another problem in business leaders saying that, acting alone, they can solve our community problems is that unsophisticated people will tend to believe them, and will consequently blame business when the problems persist. Anger and violence are apt to follow.

Inside the corporation, ethical questions abound about the proper relationship between employers and employees. Work, it is said, is dehumanizing, alienating, and boring. The old notions of managerial authority rooted in property rights and contract no longer seem to be acceptable. Consequently many firms are moving away from the old notions to new ones of consensus and rights and duties of membership in which the right to manage actually comes from the managed. Consensual arrangements naturally threaten the old institutions attached to the contract both in management and labor. Trade unions are particularly anxious about the new development.

The new approaches will come easier—and more ethically—if we are mindful of the radical implications of what we are doing. The old institutions need to be treated gently so that their resistance will be minimized. There may after all be an important role for unions in the new consensual arrangements. Workers' participation in management can be made more effective by a properly functioning union. But both management and labor need to learn new techniques. Also, the new way is not without its own threats and dangers. The idea of the contract after all emerged to protect the individual from the worst abuses of ancient and medieval communitarianism. Unless we are careful, hideous injustice can be perpetrated in the name of consensus; all sorts can be excluded, for example, the weak, the black, the white, women, men, or those we merely do not like.

In conclusion, it is worth emphasizing that perhaps the most appalling ethical problems which we may face are those associated with the new ideology. How can we preserve and protect some of the most cherished attributes of the old as we move inexorably toward the new? How can we safeguard individual rights in the face of communitarianism, the rights of privacy and choice and liberty; how can we avoid the grim excesses of centralized, authoritarian, impersonal bureaucracy; how can we insure democracy at all levels of our political system; and how can we enliven efficiency as the definition of what is a cost and what is a benefit becomes increasingly obscure? The general answer to these questions is alertness, consciousness of what is happening. This is no time to sing the old hymns. Rather it is essential to compose new ones. It is after all not beyond the realm of possibility that we could find ourselves marching stolidly into a Communitarian prison lustily singing Lockean hymns.

The specific answers must flow from specific situations. The ethical manager will be realistic about both the situation and the roles and functions of business, government and other institutions in dealing with it. He will also bear in mind the long-term interests of the persons and communities which he affects, having the courage to place those interests above his own short-term preoccupations. He will see his problems in the context of all of their relationships, employing his skills as a generalist to help produce appropriately systemic solutions.

NOTES

1. Gunter Stent, *The Coming of the Golden Age: A View of the End of Progress* (Garden City, Natural History Press, 1969), p. 90.
2. See Daniel Bell, "The Cultural Contradictions of Capitalism," *The Public Interest,* Fall 1970, pp. 38–39.
3. Quoted in *The New York Times,* June 7, 1976.
4. Quoted in Herman E. Drooss and Charles Gilbert, *American Business History* (Englewood Cliffs: Prentice Hall, 1972), p. 264.
5. See *Hearings Before the Committee on the Judiciary, United States Senate, 92nd Congress, Second Session on Nomination of Richard G. Klein-*

dienst of Arizona to be Attorney General (Washington, Government Printing Office, 1972).

6. "Lockheed Says It Paid $22 Million to Get Contracts," *The Wall Street Journal*, August 4, 1975.

The Social Responsibility of Business Is to Increase Its Profits

Milton Friedman*

When I hear businessmen speak eloquently about the "social responsibilities of business in a free-enterprise system," I am reminded of the wonderful line about the Frenchman who discovered at the age of 70 that he had been speaking prose all his life. The businessmen believe that they are defending free enterprise when they declaim that business is not concerned "merely" with profit but also with promoting desirable "social" ends; that business has a "social conscience" and takes seriously its responsibilities for providing employment, eliminating discrimination, avoiding pollution and whatever else may be the catchwords of the contemporary crop of reformers. In fact they are—or would be if they or anyone else took them seriously—preaching pure and unadulterated socialism. Businessmen who talk this way are unwitting puppets of the intellectual forces that have been undermining the basis of a free society these past decades.

The discussions of the "social responsibilities of business" are notable for their analytical looseness and lack of rigor. What does it mean to say that "business" has responsibilities? Only people can have responsibilities. A corporation is an artificial person and in this sense may have artificial responsibilities, but "business" as a whole cannot be said to have responsibilities, even in this vague sense. The first step toward clarity in examining the doctrine of the social responsibility of business is to ask precisely what it implies for whom.

Presumably, the individuals who are to be responsible are businessmen, which means individual proprietors or corporate executives. Most of the discussion of social responsibility is directed at corporations, so in what follows I shall mostly neglect the individual proprietors and speak of corporate executives.

In a free-enterprise, private-property system, a corporate executive is an employee of the owners of the business. He has direct responsibility to his employers. That responsibility is to conduct the business in accordance with their desires, which generally will be to make as much money as possible while conforming to the basic rules of the society, both those embodied in law and those embodied in ethical custom. Of course, in some cases his employers may have a different objective. A group of persons might establish a corporation for an eleemosynary purpose—for example, a hospital or a school. The manager of such a corporation will not have money profit as his objectives but the rendering of certain services.

In either case, the key point is that, in his capacity as a corporate executive, the manager is the agent of the individuals who own the corporation or establish the eleemosynary institution, and his primary responsibility is to them.

Needless to say, this does not mean that it is easy to judge how well he is performing his task. But at least the criterion of performance is straightforward, and the persons among whom a voluntary contractual arrangement exists are clearly defined.

Of course, the corporate executive is also a person in his own right. As a person, he may have many other responsibilities that he recog-

*Senior research fellow, Hoover Institute on War, Revolution, and Peace, Stanford University, and Nobel Prize–winning economist.

nizes or assumes voluntarily—to his family, his conscience, his feelings of charity, his church, his clubs, his city, his country. He may feel impelled by these responsibilities to devote part of his income to causes he regards as worthy, to refuse to work for particular corporations, even to leave his job, for example, to join his country's armed forces. If we wish, we may refer to some of these responsibilities as "social responsibilities." But in these respects he is acting as a principal, not an agent; he is spending his own money or time or energy, not the money of his employers or the time or energy he has contracted to devote to their purposes. If these are "social responsibilities," they are the social responsibilities of individuals, not of business.

What does it mean to say that the corporate executive has a "social responsibility" in his capacity as businessman? If this statement is not pure rhetoric, it must mean that he is to act in some way that is not in the interest of his employers. For example, that he is to refrain from increasing the price of the product in order to contribute to the social objective of preventing inflation, even though a price increase would be in the best interests of the corporation. Or that he is to make expenditures on reducing pollution beyond the amount that is in the best interests of the corporation or that is required by law in order to contribute to the social objective of improving the environment. Or that, at the expense of corporate profits, he is to hire "hard-core" unemployed instead of better qualified available workmen to contribute to the social objective of reducing poverty.

In each of these cases, the corporate executive would be spending someone else's money for a general social interest. Insofar as his actions in accord with his "social responsibility" reduce returns to stockholders, he is spending their money. Insofar as his actions raise the price to customers, he is spending the customers' money. Insofar as his actions lower the wages of some employees, he is spending their money.

The stockholders or the customers or the employees could separately spend their own money on the particular action if they wished to do so. The executive is exercising a distinct "social responsibility," rather than serving as an agent of the stockholders or the customers or the employees, only if he spends the money in a different way than they would have spent it.

But if he does this, he is in effect imposing taxes, on the one hand, and deciding how the tax proceeds shall be spent, on the other.

This process raises political questions on two levels: principle and consequences. On the level of political principle, the imposition of taxes and the expenditure of tax proceeds are governmental functions. We have established elaborate constitutional, parliamentary and judicial provisions to control these functions, to assure that taxes are imposed so far as possible in accordance with the preferences and desires of the public—after all, "taxation without representation" was one of the battle cries of the American Revolution. We have a system of checks and balances to separate the legislative function of imposing taxes and enacting expenditures from the executive function of collecting taxes and administering expenditure programs and from the judicial function of mediating disputes and interpreting the law.

Here the businessman—self-selected or appointed directly or indirectly by stockholders—is to be simultaneously legislator, executive and jurist. He is to decide whom to tax by how much and for what purpose, and he is to spend the proceeds—all this guided only by general exhortations from on high to restrain inflation, improve the environment, fight poverty and so on and on.

The whole justification for permitting the corporate executive to be selected by the stockholders is that the executive is an agent serving the interests of his principal. This justification disappears when the corporate executive imposes taxes and spends the proceeds for "social" purposes. He becomes in effect a public employee, a civil servant, even though he remains in name an employee of a private enterprise. On grounds of political principle, it is intolerable that such civil servants—insofar as their actions in the name of social responsibility are real and not just window-dressing—should be selected as they are now. If they are to be civil servants, then they must be elected through a political process. If they are to impose taxes and make expenditures to foster "social" objectives, then political machinery must be set up to make the assessment of taxes and to determine through a political process the objectives to be served.

This is the basic reason why the doctrine of "social responsibility" involves the acceptance of the socialist view that political mechanisms, not market mechanisms, are the appropriate way to determine the allocation of scarce resources to alternative uses.

On the grounds of consequences, can the corporate executive in fact discharge his alleged "social responsibilities"? On the other hand, suppose he could get away with spending the stockholders' or customers' or employees' money. How is he to know how to spend it? He is told that he must contribute to fighting inflation. How is he to know what action of his will contribute to that end? He is presumably an expert in running his company—in producing a product or selling it or financing it. But nothing about his selection makes him an expert on inflation. Will his holding down the price of his product reduce inflationary pressure? Or, by leaving more spending power in the hands of his customers, simply divert it elsewhere? Or, by forcing him to produce less because of the lower price, will it simply contribute to shortages? Even if he could answer these questions, how much cost is he justified in imposing on his stockholders, customers and employees for this social purpose? What is his appropriate share and what is the appropriate share of others?

And, whether he wants to or not, can he get away with spending his stockholders', customers' or employees' money? Will not the stockholders fire him? (Either the present ones or

those who take over when his actions in the name of social responsibility have reduced the corporation's profits and the price of its stock.) His customers and his employees can desert him for other producers and employers less scrupulous in exercising their social responsibilities.

This facet of "social responsibility" doctrine is brought into sharp relief when the doctrine is used to justify wage restraint by trade unions. The conflict of interest is naked and clear when union officials are asked to subordinate the interest of their members to some more general purpose. If the union officials try to enforce wage restraint, the consequence is likely to be wildcat strikes, rank-and-file revolts and the emergence of strong competitors for their jobs. We thus have the ironic phenomenon that union leaders—at least in the U.S.—have objected to Government interference with the market far more consistently and courageously than have business leaders.

The difficulty of exercising "social responsibility" illustrates, of course, the great virtue of private competitive enterprise—it forces people to be responsible for their own actions and makes it difficult for them to "exploit" other people for either selfish or unselfish purposes. They can do good—but only at their own expense.

Many a reader who has followed the argument this far may be tempted to remonstrate that it is all well and good to speak of Government's having the responsibility to impose taxes and determine expenditures for such "social" purposes as controlling pollution or training the hard-core unemployed, but that the problems are too urgent to wait on the slow course of political processes, that the exercise of social responsibility by businessmen is a quicker and surer way to solve pressing current problems.

Aside from the question of fact—I share Adam Smith's skepticism about the benefits that can be expected from "those who affected to trade for the public good"—this argument must be rejected on grounds of principle. What it amounts to is an assertion that those who favor the taxes and expenditures in question have failed to per-suade a majority of their fellow citizens to be of like mind and that they are seeking to attain by undemocratic procedures what they cannot at-tain by democratic procedures. In a free soci-ety, it is hard for ''evil'' people to do ''evil,'' especially since one man's good is another's evil.

I have, for simplicity, concentrated on the spe-cial case of the corporate executive, except only for the brief digression on trade unions. But pre-cisely the same argument applies to the newer phenomenon of calling upon stockholders to re-quire corporations to exercise social responsi-bility (the recent G.M. crusade for example). In most of these cases, what is in effect involved is some stockholders trying to get other stockhold-ers (or customers or employees) to contribute against their will to ''social'' causes favored by the activists. Insofar as they succeed, they are again imposing taxes and spending the proceeds.

The situation of the individual proprietor is somewhat different. If he acts to reduce the re-turns of his enterprise in order to exercise his ''social responsibility,'' he is spending his own money, not someone else's. If he wishes to spend his money on such purposes, that is his right, and I cannot see that there is any objection to his doing so. In the process, he, too, may im-pose costs on employees and customers. How-ever, because he is far less likely than a large corporation or union to have monopolistic power, any such side effects will tend to be mi-nor.

Of course, in practice the doctrine of social responsibility is frequently a cloak for actions that are justified on other grounds rather than a reason for those actions.

To illustrate, it may well be in the long-run interest of a corporation that is a major employer in a small community to devote resources to pro-viding amenities to that community or to improv-ing its government. That may make it easier to attract desirable employees, it may reduce the wage bill or lessen losses from pilferage and sab-otage or have other worthwhile effects. Or it may

be that, given the laws about the deductibility of corporate charitable contributions, the stockhold-ers can contribute more to charities they favor by having the corporation make the gift than by doing it themselves, since they can in that way contribute an amount that would otherwise have been paid as corporate taxes.

In each of these—and many similar—cases, there is a strong temptation to rationalize these actions as an exercise of ''social responsibility.'' In the present climate of opinion, with its wide-spread aversion to ''capitalism,'' ''profits,'' the ''soulless corporation'' and so on, this is one way for a corporation to generate goodwill as a by-product of expenditures that are entirely justi-fied in its own self-interest.

It would be inconsistent of me to call on cor-porate executives to refrain from this hypocrit-ical window-dressing because it harms the foun-dations of a free society. That would be to call on them to exercise a ''social responsibility''! If our institutions, and the attitudes of the public make it in their self-interest to cloak their ac-tions in this way, I cannot summon much indig-nation to denounce them. At the same time, I can express admiration for those individual pro-prietors or owners of closely held corporations or stockholders of more broadly held corpora-tions who disdain such tactics as approaching fraud.

Whether blameworthy or not, the use of the cloak of social responsibility, and the nonsense spoken in its name by influential and prestigious businessmen, does clearly harm the foundations of a free society. I have been impressed time and again by the schizophrenic character of many businessmen. They are capable of being ex-tremely far-sighted and clear-headed in matters that are internal to their businesses. They are incredibly short-sighted and muddle-headed in matters that are outside their businesses but af-fect the possible survival of business in general. This short-sightedness is strikingly exemplified in the calls from many businessmen for wage and price guidelines or controls or income policies.

There is nothing that could do more in a brief period to destroy a market system and replace it by a centrally controlled system than effective governmental control of prices and wages.

The short-sightedness is also exemplified in speeches by businessmen on social responsibility. This may gain them kudos in the short run. But it helps to strengthen the already too prevalent view that the pursuit of profits is wicked and immoral and must be curbed and controlled by external forces. Once this view is adopted, the external forces that curb the market will not be the social consciences, however highly developed, of the pontificating executives; it will be the iron fist of Government bureaucrats. Here, as with price and wage controls, businessmen seem to me to reveal a suicidal impulse.

The political principle that underlies the market mechanism is unanimity. In an ideal free market resting on private property, no individual can coerce any other, all cooperation is voluntary, all parties to such cooperation benefit or they need not participate. There are no values, no "social" responsibilities in any sense other than the shared values and responsibilities of individuals. Society is a collection of individuals and of the various groups they voluntarily form.

The political principle that underlies the political mechanism is conformity. The individual must serve a more general social interest—whether that be determined by a church or a dictator or a majority. The individual may have a vote and say in what is to be done, but if he is overruled, he must conform. It is appropriate for some to require others to contribute to a general social purpose whether they wish to or not.

Unfortunately, unanimity is not always feasible. There are some respects in which conformity appears unavoidable, so I do not see how one can avoid the use of the political mechanism altogether.

But the doctrine of "social responsibility" taken seriously would extend the scope of the political mechanism to every human activity. It does not differ in philosophy from the most explicitly collectivist doctrine. It differs only by professing to believe that collectivist ends can be attained without collectivist means. That is why, in my book "Capitalism and Freedom," I have called it a "fundamentally subversive doctrine" in a free society, and have said that in such a society, "there is one and only one social responsibility of business—to use its resources and engage in activities designed to increase its profits so long as it stays within the rules of the game, which is to say, engages in open and free competition without deception or fraud."

Why Shouldn't Corporations Be Socially Responsible?

Christopher D. Stone*

The opposition to corporate social responsibility comprises at least four related though separable positions. I would like to challenge the fundamental assumption that underlies all four of them. Each assumes in its own degree that the managers of the corporation are to be steered almost wholly by profit, rather than by what they think proper for society on the whole. Why should this be so? So far as ordinary morals are concerned, we often expect human beings to act in a fashion that is calculated to benefit others, rather than themselves, and commend them for it. Why should the matter be different with corporations?

From *Where the Law Ends* by Christopher D. Stone, New York: Harper & Row, pp. 80–87. Copyright © 1975 by Christopher D. Stone. Reprinted by permission of Harper & Row, Publishers, Inc.

*Crocker Professor of Law, University of Southern California.

THE PROMISSORY ARGUMENT

The most widespread but least persuasive arguments advanced by the "antiresponsibility" forces take the form of a moral claim based upon the corporation's supposed obligations to its shareholders. In its baldest and least tenable form, it is presented as though management's obligation rested upon the keeping of a promise—that the management of the corporation "promised" the shareholders that it would maximize the shareholders' profits. But this simply isn't so.

Consider for contrast the case where a widow left a large fortune goes to a broker, asking him to invest and manage her money so as to maximize her return. The broker, let us suppose, accepts the money and the conditions. In such a case, there would be no disagreement that the broker had made a promise to the widow, and if he invested her money in some venture that struck his fancy for any reason other than that it would increase her fortune, we would be inclined to advance a moral (as well, perhaps, as a legal) claim against him. Generally, at least, we believe in the keeping of promises; the broker, we should say, had violated a promissory obligation to the widow.

But that simple model is hardly the one that obtains between the management of major corporations and their shareholders. Few if any American shareholders ever put their money into a corporation upon the express promise of management that the company would be operated so as to maximize their returns. Indeed, few American shareholders ever put their money directly *into* a corporation at all. Most of the shares outstanding today were issued years ago and found their way to their current shareholders only circuitously. In almost all cases, the current shareholder gave his money to some prior shareholder, who, in turn, had gotten it from B, who, in turn, had gotten it from A, and so on back to the purchaser of the original issue, who, many years before, had bought the shares through an underwriting syndicate. In the course of these transactions, one of the basic elements that exists in the broker case is missing: The manager of the corporation, unlike the broker, was never even offered a chance to refuse the shareholder's "terms" (if they were that) to maximize the shareholder's profits.

There are two other observations to be made about the moral argument based on a supposed promise running from the management to the shareholders. First, even if we do infer from all the circumstances a "promise" running from the management to the shareholders, but not one, or not one of comparable weight running elsewhere (to the company's employees, customers, neighbors, etc.), we ought to keep in mind that as a moral matter (which is what we are discussing here) sometimes it is deemed morally justified to break promises (even to break the law) in the furtherance of other social interests of higher concern. Promises can advance moral arguments, by way of creating presumptions, but few of us believe that promises, per se, can end them. My promise to appear in class on time would not ordinarily justify me from refusing to give aid to a drowning man. In other words, even if management *had* made an express promise to its shareholders to "maximize your profits," (a) I am not persuaded that the ordinary person would interpret it to mean "maximize *in every way you can possibly get away with,* even if that means polluting the environment, ignoring or breaking the law"; and (b) I am not persuaded that, even if it were interpreted as so blanket a promise, most people would not suppose it ought—morally—to be broken in some cases.

Finally, even if, in the face of all these considerations, one still believes that there is an overriding, unbreakable, promise of some sort running from management to the shareholders, I do not think that it can be construed to be any stronger than one running to *existent* shareholders, arising from *their* expectations as measured by the price *they* paid. That is to say, there is nothing in the argument from promises that would wed us to a regime in which management was bound to maximize the income of shareholders. The argument might go so far as to support compensation for existent shareholders if the society chose to announce that henceforth management would have other specified obligations, thereby driving the price of shares to a lower adjustment level. All future shareholders would take with "warning" of, and a price that discounted for, the new "risks" of shareholding (i.e., the "risks" that management might put corporate resources to *pro bonum* ends).

THE AGENCY ARGUMENT

Related to the promissory argument but requiring less stretching of the facts is an argument from agency principles. Rather than trying to infer a promise by management to the shareholders, this argument is based on the idea that the shareholders designated the management their agents. This is the position advanced by Milton Friedman in his *New York Times* article. "The key point," he says, "is that...the manager is the agent of the individuals who own the corporation...."[1]

Friedman, unfortunately, is wrong both as to the state of the law (the directors are *not* mere agents of the shareholders)[2] and on his assumption as to the facts of corporate life (surely it is closer to the truth that in major corporations the shareholders are *not,* in any meaningful sense, selecting the directors; management is more often using its control over the proxy machinery to designate who the directors shall be, rather than the other way around).

What Friedman's argument comes down to is that for some reason the directors ought morally to consider themselves more the agents for the shareholders than for the customers, creditors, the state, or the corporation's immediate neighbors. But why? And to what extent? Throwing in terms like "principal" and "agent" begs the fundamental questions.

What is more, the "agency" argument is not only morally inconclusive, it is embarrassingly at odds with the way in which supposed "agents" actually behave. If the managers truly considered themselves the agents of the shareholders, as agents they would be expected to show an interest in determining how their principals wanted them to act—and to act accordingly. In the controversy over Dow's production of napalm, for example, one would expect, on this model, that Dow's management would have been glad to have the napalm question put to the shareholders at a shareholders' meeting. In fact, like most major companies faced with shareholder requests to include "social action" measures on proxy statements, it fought the proposal tooth and claw.[3] It is a peculiar agency where the "agents" will go to such lengths (even spending tens of thousands of dollars of their "principals'" money in legal fees) to resist the determination of what their "principals" want.

THE ROLE ARGUMENT

An argument so closely related to the argument from promises and agency that it does not demand extensive additional remarks is a contention based upon supposed considerations of *role*. Sometimes in moral discourse, as well as in law, we assign obligations to people on the basis of their having assumed some role or status, independent of any specific verbal promise they made. Such obligations are assumed to run from a captain to a seaman (and vice versa), from a doctor to a patient, or from a parent to a child. The antiresponsibility forces are on somewhat stronger grounds resting their position on this basis, because the model more nearly accords with the facts—that is, management never actually promised the shareholders that they would maximize the shareholders' investment, nor did the shareholders designate the directors their agents for this express purpose. The directors and top management are, as lawyers would say, fiduciaries. But what does this leave us? So far as the directors are fiduciaries of the shareholders in a legal sense, of course they are subject to the legal limits on fiduciaries—that is to say, they cannot engage in self-dealing, "waste" of corporate assets, and the like. But I do not understand any proresponsibility advocate to be demanding such corporate largesse as would expose the officers to legal liability; what we are talking about are expenditures on, for example, pollution control, above the amount the company is required to pay by law, but less than an amount so extravagant as to constitute a violation of these legal fiduciary duties. (Surely no court in America today would enjoin a corporation from spending more to reduce pollution than the law requires.) What is there about assuming the role of corporate officer that makes it immoral for a manager to involve a corporation in these expenditures? A father, one would think, would have stronger obligations to his children by virtue of his status than a corporate manager to the corporation's shareholders. Yet few would regard it as a compelling moral argument if a father were to distort facts about his child on a scholarship application form on the grounds that he had obligations to advance his child's career; nor would we consider it a strong moral argument if a father were to leave unsightly refuse piled on his lawn, spilling over into the street, on the plea that he had obligations to give every moment of his attention to his children, and was thus too busy to cart his refuse away.

Like the other supposed moral arguments, the one from role suffers from the problem that the strongest moral obligations one can discover have at most only prima facie force, and it is not apparent why those obligations should predominate over some contrary social obligations that could be advanced.

Then too, when one begins comparing and weighing the various moral obligations, those running back to the shareholder seem fairly weak by comparison to the claims of others. For one thing, there is the consideration of alternatives. If the shareholder is dissatisfied with the direction the corporation is taking, he can sell out, and if he does so quickly enough, his losses may

be slight. On the other hand, as Ted Jacobs observes, "those most vitally affected by corporate decisions—people who work in the plants, buy the products, and consume the effluents—cannot remove themselves from the structure with a phone call."[4]

THE "POLESTAR" ARGUMENT

It seems to me that the strongest moral argument corporate executives can advance for looking solely to profits is not one that is based on a supposed express, or even implied promise to the shareholder. Rather, it is one that says, if the managers act in such fashion as to maximize profits—if they act *as though* they had promised the shareholders they would do so—then it will be best for all of us. This argument might be called the polestar argument, for its appeal to the interests of the shareholders is not justified on supposed obligations to the shareholders per se, but as a means of charting a straight course toward what is best for the society as a whole.

Underlying the polestar argument are a number of assumptions—some express and some implied. There is, I suspect, an implicit positivism among its supporters—a feeling (whether its proponents own up to it or not) that moral judgments are peculiar, arbitrary, or vague—perhaps even "meaningless" in the philosophic sense of not being amenable to rational discussion. To those who take this position, profits (or sales, or price-earnings ratios) at least provide some solid, tangible standard by which participants in the organization can measure their successes and failures, with some efficiency, in the narrow sense, resulting for the entire group. Sometimes the polestar position is based upon a related view—not that the moral issues that underlie social choices are meaningless, but that resolving them calls for special expertise. "I don't know any investment adviser whom I would care to act in my behalf in any matter except turning a profit.... The value of these specialists...lies in their limitations; they ought not allow themselves to see so much of the world that they become distracted."[5] A slightly modified point emphasizes not that the executives lack moral or social expertise per se, but that they lack the social authority to make policy choices. Thus, Friedman objects that if a corporate director took "social purposes" into account, he would become "in effect a public employee, a civil servant....On grounds of political principle, it is intolerable that such civil servants...should be selected as they are now."[6]

I do not want to get too deeply involved in each of these arguments. That the moral judgments underlying policy choices are vague, I do not doubt—although I am tempted to observe that when you get right down to it, a wide range of actions taken by businessmen every day, supposedly based on solid calculations of "profit," are probably as rooted in hunches and intuition as judgments of ethics. I do not disagree either that, ideally, we prefer those who have control over our lives to be politically accountable; although here, too, if we were to pursue the matter in detail we would want to inspect both the premise of this argument, that corporate managers are not *presently* custodians of discretionary power over us anyway, and also its logical implications: Friedman's point that "if they are to be civil servants, then they must be selected through a political process"[7] is not, as Friedman regards it, a *reductio ad absurdum*—not, at any rate, to Ralph Nader and others who want publicly elected directors.

The reason for not pursuing these counterarguments at length is that, whatever reservations one might have, we can agree that there is a germ of validity to what the "antis" are saying. But their essential failure is in not pursuing the alternatives. Certainly, *to the extent* that the forces of the market and the law can keep the corporation within desirable bounds, it may be better to trust them than to have corporate managers implementing their own vague and various notions of what is best for the rest of us. But are the "antis" blind to the fact that there are circumstances in which the law—and the forces of the market—are simply not competent to keep the corporation under control? The shortcomings of these traditional restraints on corporate conduct are critical to understand, not merely for the defects they point up in the "antis'" position. More important, identifying where the traditional forces are inadequate is the first step in the design of new and alternative measures of corporate control.

NOTES

1. *New York Times,* September 12, 1962, sect. 6, p. 33, col. 2.
2. See, for example, *Automatic Self-Cleansing Filter Syndicate Co. Ltd. v. Cunninghame* (1906) 2 Ch. 34.
3. "Dow Shalt Not Kill," in S. Prakash Sethi, *Up Against the Corporate Wall,* Englewood Cliffs, N.J.: Prentice-Hall, 1971), pp. 236–266, and the opinion of Judge Tamm in *Medical Committee for Human Rights v.* S.E.C., 432 F.2d 659 (D.C. Cir. 1970), and the dissent of Mr. Justice Douglas in the same case in the U.S. Supreme Court, 404 U.S. 403, 407–411 (1972).
4. Theodore J. Jacobs, "Pollution, Consumerism, Accountability," *Center Magazine* 5, 1 (January–February 1971): 47.
5. Walter Goodman, "Stocks Without Sin," *Harper's,* August 1971, p. 66.
6. *New York Times,* September 12, 1962, sec. 6, p. 122, col. 3.
7. Ibid., p. 122, cols. 3–4.

The Social Contract: Norms for a Corporate Conscience

Thomas Donaldson*

In a speech to the Harvard Business School in 1969, Henry Ford II stated:

> The terms of the contract between industry and society are changing.... Now we are being asked to serve a wider range of human values and to accept an obligation to members of the public with whom we have no commercial transactions.

The "contract" to which Henry Ford referred concerns a corporation's *indirect* obligations. It represents not a set of formally specified obligations, but a set of binding, abstract ones. A social contract for business, if one exists, is not a typewritten contract in the real world, but a metaphysical abstraction not unlike the "social contract" between citizens and government that philosophers have traditionally discussed. Such a contract would have concrete significance, for it would help to interpret the nature of a corporation's indirect obligations, which are notoriously slippery.

The aim of this paper is to discover a corporation's indirect obligations by attempting to clarify the meaning of business's so-called "social contract." The task is challenging. Although people speak frequently of such a contract, few have attempted to specify its meaning. Although businesspeople, legislators, and academics offer examples of supposed infractions of the "contract," few can explain what justifies the contract itself.

Corporations, unlike humans, are artifacts, which is to say *we* create them. We *choose* to

From *Corporations and Morality,* Copyright © 1982, pp. 36–54. Adapted by permission of Prentice-Hall, Inc., Englewood Cliffs, N.J.
*Wirtenberger Professor of Ethics, Loyola University of Chicago.

create corporations and we might choose either not to create them or to create different entities. Corporations thus are like political states in their need for justification.

The social contract has typically (though not always) been applied to governments. Is there any reason to suppose it is applicable to economic institutions? To productive organizations such as General Motors? One reason for doing so is that companies like General Motors are social giants. They affect the lives of millions of people, influence foreign policy, and employ more people than live in many countries of the world. Equally important is the fact that General Motors exists only through the cooperation and commitment of society. It draws its employees from society, sells its goods to society, and is given its status by society. All of this may suggest the existence of an implied agreement between it and society. If General Motors holds society responsible for providing the condition of its existence, then for what does society hold General Motors responsible? What are the terms of the social contract?

The simplest way of understanding the social contract is in the form: "We (the members of society) agree to do X, and you (the productive organizations) agree to do Y." Applying this form to General Motors (or any productive organization) means that the task of a social contract argument is to specify X, where X refers to the obligations of society to productive organizations, and to specify Y, where Y refers to the obligations of productive organizations to society.

It is relatively easy in this context to specify X, because what productive organizations need from society is:

1. Recognition as a single agent, especially in the eyes of the law.
2. The authority: (a) to own or use land and natural resources, and (b) to hire employees.

It may appear presumptuous to assume that productive organizations must be warranted by society. Can one not argue that any organization has a *right* to exist and operate? That they have this right *apart* from the wishes of society? When asking such questions, one must distinguish between claims about rights of mere organizations and claims about rights of organizations with special powers, such as productive organizations. A case can be made for the unbridled right of the Elks Club, whose members unite in fraternal activities, to exist and operate (assuming it does not discriminate against minorities or women); but the same cannot be said for Du Pont Corporation, which not only must draw on existing stores of mineral resources, but must find dumping sites to store toxic chemical by-products. Even granted that people have an inalienable right to form and operate organizations, and even granted that this right exists apart from the discretion of society, the productive organization requires special status under the law and the opportunity to use society's resources: two issues in which every member of society may be said to have a vested interest.

Conditions 1 and 2 are obviously linked to each other. In order for a productive organization to use land and hire employees (conditions of 2), it must have the authority to perform those acts as if it were an individual agent (the condition of 1). The philosophical impact of 1 should not be exaggerated. To say that productive organizations must have the authority to act as individual agents is not necessarily to affirm that they are abstract, invisible persons. Rather it is a means of stating the everyday fact that productive organizations must, for a variety of purposes, be treated as individual entities. For example, a corporation must be able to hire new employees, to sign contracts, and to negotiate purchases without getting the O.K. from *all* its employees and stockholders. The corporation *itself*, not its stockholders or managers, must be considered to be the controller of its equipment and land; for its stockholders or managers may leave, sell their shares, or die. If they do, the organization still controls its resources; it still employs its work force, and it still is obliged to honor its previous contracts and commitments.

Defining the *Y* side of the contract is as difficult as defining the *X* side is easy. It is obvious that productive organizations must be allowed to exist and act. But it is not obvious precisely why societies should allow them to exist, that is, what specific benefits society should hope to gain from the bargain. What specific functions should society expect from productive organizations? What obligations should it impose? Only one assumption can be made readily: that the members of society should demand at a minimum that the benefits from authorizing the existence of productive organizations outweigh the detriments of doing so. This is nothing other than the expectation of all voluntary agreements: that no party should be asked to conclude a contract which places him or her in a position worse than before.

Two principal classes of people stand to benefit or be harmed by the introduction of productive organizations: (1) people who consume the organizations' products, i.e., consumers; and (2) people who work in such organizations, i.e., employees. The two classes are broadly defined and not mutually exclusive. "Consumer" refers to anyone who is economically interested; hence virtually anyone qualifies as a consumer. "Employee" refers to anyone who contributes labor to the productive process of a productive organization, including managers, laborers, part-time support personnel, and (in corporations) members of the board of directors.

From the standpoint of our hypothetical consumers, productive organizations promise to *enhance the satisfaction of economic interests*. That is to say, people could hope for the introduction of productive organizations to better satisfy their interests for shelter, food, entertainment, transportation, health care, and clothing. The prima facie benefits for consumers include:

1. Improving efficiency through:
   a. Maximizing advantages of specialization.
   b. Improving decision-making resources.

c. Increasing the capacity to use or acquire expensive technology and resources.
2. Stabilizing levels of output and channels of distribution.
3. Increasing liability resources.

From the standpoint of consumers, productive organizations should minimize:

1. Pollution and the depletion of natural resources.
2. The destruction of personal accountability.
3. The misuse of political power.

Productive organizations should also be viewed from the standpoint of their effects on people as workers, that is, from the standpoint of their effects upon individual laborers and craftsmen in the state of individual production who opt to work for productive organizations.

It is not difficult to discover certain prima facie benefits, such as the following:

1. Increasing income potential (and the capacity for social contributions).
2. Diffusing personal liability.
3. Adjusting personal income allocation.

From the standpoint of workers, productive organizations should minimize:

1. Worker alienation.
2. Lack of worker control over work conditions.
3. Monotony and dehumanization of the worker.

Thus the social contract will specify that these negative consequences be minimized.

Finally, a caveat must be made concerning justice. Society will grant productive organizations the conditions necessary for their existence only if they agree not to violate certain minimum standards of justice—however these are to be specified. For example, it would refuse to enact the contract if it knew that the existence of productive organizations would systematically reduce a given class of people to an inhuman existence, subsistence poverty, or enslavement.

This point, in turn, provides a clue to one of the specific tenets of the contract. Although the contract might allow productive organizations to undertake actions requiring welfare trade-offs, it would prohibit organizational acts of injustice. It might allow a corporation to lay off, or reduce the salaries of, thousands of workers in order to block skyrocketing production costs; here, worker welfare would be diminished while consumer welfare would be enhanced. But it is another matter when the company commits gross injustices in the process—for example, if it lies to workers, telling them that no layoffs are planned merely to keep them on the job until the last minute. Similarly, it is another matter when the organization follows discriminatory hiring policies, refusing to hire blacks or women, in the name of "consumer advantage." These are clear injustices of the kind that society would want to prohibit as a condition of the social contract. We may infer, then, that a tenet of the social contract will be that productive organizations are to remain within the bounds of the general canons of justice.

Determining what justice requires is a notoriously difficult task. The writings of Plato, Aristotle, and more recently, John Rawls, have shed considerable light on this subject, but unfortunately we must forego a general discussion of justice here. At a minimum, however, the application of the concept of justice to productive organizations appears to imply *that productive organizations avoid deception or fraud, that they show respect for their workers as human beings, and that they avoid any practice that systematically worsens the situations of a given group in society*. Despite the loud controversy over what justice means, most theorists would agree that justice means at least this much for productive organizations.

Our sketch of a hypothetical social contract is now complete. By utilizing the concept of rational people existing in a state of individual production, we have indicated the terms of a contract which they would require for the introduction of productive organizations. The questions asked in the beginning were: Why should corporations exist at all? What is the fundamental justification for their activities? How can we measure their performance, to say when they have performed poorly or well? A social contract helps to answer these questions. Corporations considered as productive organizations exist to enhance the welfare of society through the satisfaction of consumer and worker interests, in a way which relies on exploiting corporations' special advantages and minimizing disadvantages. This is the *moral foundation* of the corporation when considered as a productive organization. The social contract also serves as a tool to measure the performance of productive organizations. That is, when such organizations fulfill the terms of the contract, they have done well. When they do not, then society is morally justified in condemning them.

Productive organizations (whether corporations or not) that produce quality goods at low prices, that reject government favoritism, and that enhance the well-being of workers receive high marks by the standards of the social contract. Those that allow inefficiency, charge high prices, sell low-quality products, and fail to enhance the well-being of workers receive low marks. The latter organizations have violated the terms of the social contract. They must reform themselves, or lose their moral right to exist.

Five Propositions for Social Responsibility

Keith Davis*

Business's need for social response and social responsibility has been discussed loudly and at length. What does it all mean? One way to understand the issues is to examine the basic propositions offered in the social responsibility debate.

Modern society presents business with immensely complicated problems. Technology has advanced to a level that tests intellectual capacities, markets have become more complex and international in scope, and difficult new problems of social issues and social responsibility have arisen. In earlier periods, the mission of business was clear. It was strictly an economic one—to produce the best quality of goods and services at the lowest possible price and to distribute them effectively. The accomplishment of this mission was remarkably effective, so effective that large numbers of the population found their minimum economic needs reasonably satisfied and began to turn their thoughts toward other needs.

Beginning in the 1950s, the public's mood shifted sharply toward social concerns, and this mood was reflected in extensive social demands made on institutions. Since business interacts extensively with all of society, perhaps more of these demands were made on business than any other institution. By sticking strictly to its economic role in the past, business had left the social side of its activities largely untended and was unprepared to deal effectively with social issues. However, the public also was unprepared for its new role as social protagonist, and, as a result, churning and ferment have marked discussion of social priorities, how they are to be accomplished, and what role business should play in this accomplishment.

After more than twenty years of controversy, the debate over business and social issues has now reached some maturity. Out of this maturity, a degree of uniform support is developing for certain social propositions to guide the conduct of business as well as of other institutions. These guidelines apply to a greater or lesser degree according to individual circumstances, but the important point is that they do apply. Intel-

Excerpted from "Five Propositions for Social Responsibility," by Keith Davis, *Business Horizons*, Vol. XVIII, No. 3, June 1975, pp. 19–24. Copyright © 1975 by School of Business, Indiana University. Reprinted with permission.
*Emeritus professor of management, Arizona State University.

ligent businessmen will take heed of these guidelines if they wish to avoid unnecessary confrontations with society. This article examines five of these guidelines which are supported by a degree of consensus. These guidelines collectively will be called the social responsibility mode.

SOCIAL RESPONSIBILITY AND POWER

One basic proposition is that *social responsibility arises from social power*. Modern business has immense social power in such areas as minority employment and environmental pollution. If business has the power, then a just relationship demands that business also bear responsibility for its actions in these areas. Social responsibility arises from concern about the consequences of business's acts as they affect the interests of others. Business decisions do have social consequences. Businessmen cannot make decisions that are solely economic decisions, because they are interrelated with the whole social system. This situation requires that businessmen's thinking be broadened beyond the company gate to the whole social system. Systems thinking is required.

Social responsibility implies that a business decision maker in the process of serving his own business interests is obliged to take actions that also protect and enhance society's interests. The net effect is to improve the quality of life in the broadest possible way, however quality of life is defined by society. In this manner, harmony is achieved between business's actions and the larger social system. The businessman becomes concerned with social as well as economic outputs and with the total effect of his institutional actions on society.

Business institutions that ignore responsibility for their social power are threatened by what Keith Davis and Robert L. Blomstrom call the Iron Law of Responsibility: "In the long run, those who do not use power in a manner which society considers responsible will tend to lose it."[1] The record of history has supported operation of this law as one institution after another has found its power either eroded or overthrown when it fails to use power responsibly. The implication for business is that, if it wishes to retain its viability and significance as a major social institution, then it must give responsible attention to social issues.

The fundamental assumption of this model is that society has entrusted to business large amounts of society's resources to accomplish its mission, and business is expected to manage these resources as a wise trustee for society. In addition to the traditional role of economic entrepreneurship, business now has a new social role of trusteeship. As trustee for society's resources, it serves the interests of all claimants on the organization, rather than only those of owners, or consumers, or labor.

AN OPEN SYSTEM INTERFACE

A second basic proposition is that *business shall operate as a two-way open system with open receipt of inputs from society and open disclosure of its operations to the public*. An open interface in both directions is essential. Business has been charged with consistently turning a deaf ear toward many of the inputs directed toward it. The executive suite has been geared to send messages but not to receive them. Under the best of conditions, business has offered an untrained ear to social inputs so that it misunderstood the message or heard only selected parts.

The social responsibility model expects business to turn both a sensitive and a trained ear to social needs and wants. If these inputs do not flow freely from society, perhaps because of society's past frustrations with communication efforts, business will seek them just as avidly as it seeks market information for traditional economic purposes. Business must know what is going on in society if business is to respond to social needs.

With regard to business communication outputs, the charge is that most outward communication has been a public relations facade, usually revealing the good but rarely the bad about business products or operations. The social responsibility model, however, postulates a policy of full disclosure in which both product and social data about a firm are available in the same way that economic data are now available. To accomplish the objective of full disclosure the social audit is proposed.[2] Such an audit would serve the same purpose in social areas that an accounting audit serves in economic areas. It is a necessary instrument to determine whether a business has been using its social assets responsibly. It shows where progress has been made and where deficiencies remain. It is a useful guide to management for improving its performance, a check and balance on mismanagement of resources, and an open disclosure to those with a bona fide interest in social performance.

The model of the social audit is, of course, an ideal. At the present, it is hardly operational and decades may pass before it reaches the proficiency of today's accounting audits, but it is a justifiable model in support of an open business system. Though the ideal of open communication probably can never be reached fully because of inherent difficulties in the communication process, the social responsibility model postulates that considerable improvement is both possible and necessary.

Some aspects of consumerism are examples of the beginning of open disclosure. For example, the public has insisted that installment debt charges be fully disclosed, that grocery prices allow comparative price shopping, that containers not be misleading, and that labels disclose the dangers of products.

CALCULATION OF SOCIAL COSTS

A third basic proposition is that *social costs as well as benefits of an activity, product, or service shall be thoroughly calculated and considered in order to decide whether to proceed with it.* In the past, business has been required to consider only two factors in deciding whether to proceed with an activity. These factors were technical feasibility and economic profitability. If they were favorable, the activity was launched. Now business has a third factor to consider—the social effect of an activity. Only if all factors are favorable is it safe to proceed.

In making these kinds of decisions, both short- and long-run costs must be considered. For example, a firm that builds row upon row of look-alike houses may be saving $500 on each house and passing along $400 of the saving to each buyer, thus serving consumer interests. In the long run, however, this kind of construction may encourage the rapid development of a city slum. In this instance, the lack of a long-range outlook may result in serious social costs.

Long-run cost data need to be diligently sought; business cannot assume that if nothing negative is evident, there is no problem. The automobile industry, for example, is faulted for the myopic vision that prevented it from perceiving the serious environmental problems that developed from automobile emissions. Even though it was a transportation expert on which the public depended, the industry was unable to foresee and prevent the environmental degradation that resulted from its products. Similarly, the chemical industry did not foresee the health-damaging effects of vinyl chloride gas even though it was known as a powerful chemical.

If better forecasting cannot be developed, then is it worthwhile to initiate potentially damaging activities even when they bring short-run benefits? In the future, for example, extreme caution may be required for introduction of new products from dangerous chemical families.

In sum, the expectation of the social responsibility model is that a detailed cost/benefit analysis will be made prior to determining whether to proceed with an activity and that social costs will be given significant weight in the decision-making process. Almost any business action will entail some social costs. The basic question is whether the benefits outweigh the costs so that there is a net social benefit. Many questions of judgment arise, and there are no precise mathematical measures in the social field, but rational and wise judgments can be made if the issues are first thoroughly explored.

For major business projects, such as the doubling of a plant's capacity and employment in a suburban area, the social responsibility model implies that society may eventually require social impact statements comparable with today's environmental impact statements. Then affected parties could become involved in considering a project before decisions have been made. In other instances, such as the introduction of new drugs, the public wants the government to act in the public's interest through regulatory agencies.

What is being threatened is the business decision-making process itself. Business is expected to make responsible decisions based on thorough examination of costs and benefits and, if necessary, only after those groups affected have been involved, such as a community. If business cannot establish a track record of responsible decisions, then the Iron Law of Responsibility will force business to share its decision-making powers with government and representatives of affected interest groups. Business will have a less free hand in making decisions with a social impact.

THE USER PAYS

A fourth basic proposition is that the *social costs of each activity, product, or service shall be priced into it so that the consumer (user) pays for the effects of his consumption on society.* This philosophy holds that a fair consumer price for a product or service is one that includes all costs of production, including social costs. Historically, society or someone else has had to bear these social costs while the consumer benefited from reduced product prices.

Consider the case of the environment. For the most part, the environment has been an economic free good that a business could use, pass-ing much of the saving on to the consumer. It was a public common available to all without substantial charge. The strip miner could mine coal without the cost of restoring the topsoil, thus providing cheaper electricity for consumers. The steelmaker could use oxygen from the air for his blast furnace without paying society a penny for it, and he also could use the air as a dumping ground for his wastes. Similarly, he could draw water from the river and discharge his wastes into it without paying for this service.

Society placed no economic value on these public commons. They were free goods. Therefore, both the businessman and his customers avoided paying for degradation of the common, and these costs were transferred to society as social costs. This was not a serious problem as long as the load on the common was light, but when it became heavy, society found itself burdened with costs that it did not wish to bear. The social responsibility model assumes that generally society should not bear these costs. The consumer should pay for his consumption, including social costs of preventing pollution. That is a fair price; any other would be unfair to the public or to innocent third parties.

The philosophy that the user pays is a general guide, not a hard and fast rule. There will be many exceptions including instances when the costs are unknown at the time the user makes his purchase or when the costs are so minimal that they will be ignored. In other cases, a remedy may not be technologically feasible and so no costs are established, for example, the removal of sulfate chemicals from the stacks of coal-burning electrical generating stations. Technology is not available for the complete removal of these pollutants, so some are allowed and no additional charge is transmitted to the consumer. Thus he buys his electricity more cheaply than he could if total removal were technologically feasible and the removal equipment required. In other instances, the government may underwrite part of the costs in the name of the public interest, passing costs on to taxpayers rather than to users of that particular product or service.

Nevertheless, the general philosophy that the user pays still applies. The reasoning is that since his consumption incurs the social cost, he should bear as much of it as possible. If the added costs discourage his consumption, the result is still beneficial because certain social costs are avoided.

SOCIAL RESPONSIBILITIES AS CITIZENS

A fifth basic proposition is that *beyond social costs business institutions as citizens have responsibilities for social involvement in areas of their competence where major social needs exist.* The four preceding propositions concern social costs directly caused by business. In the fifth proposition, business actions are only indirectly related to certain social problems, but nevertheless business is obliged to help solve them.

The fifth proposition is based essentially on the reasoning that business is a major social institution that should bear the same kinds of citizenship costs for society that an individual citizen bears. Business will benefit from a better society just as any citizen will benefit; therefore, business has a responsibility to recognize social problems and actively contribute its talents to help solve them.

Such involvement is expected of any citizen, and business should fulfill a citizenship role. Business will not have primary responsibility for solving problems, but it should provide significant assistance. For example, business did not directly cause educational problems, but it does stand to gain some benefit from their solution; therefore, it has some responsibility to help develop and apply solutions.

A MATTER OF HARMONY

The thrust of the foregoing propositions is that business, like any individual, needs to act responsibly regarding the consequences of its actions. The socially responsible organization behaves in such a way that it protects and improves the social quality of life along with its own quality of life. In essence, quality of life refers to the degree to which people live in harmony with their inner spirit, their fellow man, and nature's physical environment. Business has a significant effect on each of these, particularly the last two. It can support harmony among people as well as in the environment if it will take the larger system's view.

Although quality of life embraces harmony, it is not a static concept that seeks to preserve a utopian status quo. Rather, it is a dynamic concept in which people live harmoniously with the changes occurring in nature and in themselves. It is, however, a utopian concept in the sense that most people use it as an ultimate goal that they realize probably will never be obtained absolutely. It is essentially a set of criteria by which judgments may be made about social progress. The social responsibility model seeks to improve the quality of life through its five propositions.

Certain observations can be made concerning the implementation of the social responsibility model.

First, it applies to all organizations. Although this discussion has been presented in the context of business, the social responsibility model does not single out business for special treatment. All organizations have equal responsibilities for the consequences of their actions.

Similarly, social responsibility applies to all persons in all of their life roles, whether employee, camper, renter, or automobile driver. An individual who tosses his rubbish along a roadside is just as irresponsible as a business that pours pollutants into a river. The individual may argue that his offense is less in magnitude, but when his rubbish is added to all the rest, it becomes a massive offense against the public interest.

As a matter of fact, quality of life will be improved less than people expect if only business is socially responsible. Substantial improvement will be achieved only when most organizations and persons act in socially responsible ways.

Second, the movement toward greater social responsibility is not a fad but a fundamental change in social directions. Business executives will do their organizations grievous damage if they assume social responsibility is merely something to be assigned to a third assistant with action to be taken only when absolutely necessary and when the organization is backed into a corner.

Social responsibility is here to stay despite its intangibles and imponderables. As stated earlier, business probably has been a significant cause of the rise of social responsibility ideas because it did its economic job so well that it released people from economic want, freeing them to pursue new social goals.

Third, social response by business will increase business's economic costs. Social responsibility is not a free ride or a matter of simple goodwill. Actions such as the reduction of pollution take large amounts of economic resources. The costs are there. It is true that some of these costs are transferred from other segments of society, so society as a whole may not bear higher costs for some actions; however, these costs are brought into the business system and, in most instances, will flow through in the form of higher prices.

This situation is likely to put further strain on business-consumer relations. It may even lead to consumer demands for less social involvement in the short run, but the long-run secular trend toward more social involvement is likely to remain.

NOTES

1. Keith Davis and Robert L. Blomstrom, *Business and Society: Environment and Responsibility,* 3rd ed. (New York: McGraw-Hill Book Company, 1975), p. 50. Italics in original. A number of analysts believe that the desirable course of events is for business to lose a substantial part of its power. That is a separate issue not treated in this article,

but for details the reader is referred to the review of Richard Barnet and Ronald Muller's *Global Reach: The Power of the Multinational Corporation,* in William G. Ryan, ''The Runaway Global Corporation,'' *Business Horizons* (February 1975), pp. 91–95.

2. Further discussion of the social audit is found in Raymond A. Bauer and Dan H. Fenn, Jr., *The Corporate Social Audit* (New York: The Russell Sage Foundation, 1972); and John J. Corson and George A. Steiner, *Measuring Business's Social Performance: The Corporate Social Audit* (New York: Committee for Economic Development, 1975). The social audit for business originally was proposed by Howard R. Bowen, *Social Responsibilities of the Businessman* (New York: Harper & Brothers, 1953), pp. 155–156.

━━━━━━━━━━━━━━━━━━━━━━━━

Stockholder and Stakeholder Interpretations of Business' Social Role

Anthony F. Buono*

Lawrence T. Nichols †

There was a time, in the not too distant past, when a U.S. president could proclaim that, ''The business of America is business'' and feel assured that everyone listening to him would understand the reference. The underlying belief was that what was good for such economic bastions as General Motors was good for our country. It was virtually inconceivable that anyone who was not somehow ''misguided'' would question the adequacy of a system that had been so success-

Original essay. Copyright © 1990 by A. Buono and L. Nichols. Printed with permission of the authors.

*Department of Management, Bentley College.

†Department of Sociology and Anthropology, University of West Virginia.

ful in providing so much in the way of goods, income, and wealth for so many people.[1]

Today the situation is quite different. Most people would probably agree that business is still the dominant social institution in our country. It is becoming increasingly difficult, however, to reach consensus on the specific mission of the corporate sector. Indeed, despite many of the historic achievements of our business system, U.S. corporations and their leaders have suffered severe losses of public support and confidence.[2] Over the past two decades, business organizations and their management have faced many new demands which are based on changing societal expectations about the appropriate role of the corporation in the larger society. Current attitudes toward IBM, which is generally viewed as the new bastion of U.S. economic power, exemplify much of this tension and uneasiness. IBM is described in such extremes as a "major resource," "singlehandedly...defending America's trade imbalance" to being a "malevolent force because of its stranglehold on the [computer] industry."[3] As reflected by these divergent views, the question on many people's minds seems to be, "What is the proper business of business?"

STOCKHOLDER AND STAKEHOLDER MODELS OF THE CORPORATION

One way of clarifying our understanding of the tensions underlying business's social role is to assess the relationship between corporations and the different social groups that are affected by the corporations' operation: stockholders, employees, unions, customers, suppliers, local communities, public and special interest groups, government agencies, and so forth. The exact nature of the bond between corporations and these groups, as one might expect, is quite variable in intensity, duration, and significance. This has given rise to two opposed perspectives on business's role—the stockholder and stakeholder models of corporate activity.

Stockholder Model

Throughout most of our history, the *stockholder model* has been the norm. Based on this traditional business gospel, a corporation is essentially viewed as a piece of private property owned by those who hold its stock. These individuals elect a board of directors, whose responsibility is to serve the best interests of the owners. This model assumes that the interactions between business organizations and the different groups affected by their operations (employees, consumers, suppliers) are most effectively structured as marketplace transactions. The forces of supply and demand, the pressures of a competitive market, will ensure the best use of business and its economic resources. In essence, the board of directors and its appointed managers are fiduciary agents or trustees for the owners. The directors and managers fulfill their social obligations when they operate in the best financial interests of the stockholders, in other words, when they act to maximize profits.

Stakeholder Model

In contrast to the stockholder view, a new perspective, referred to as the *stakeholder model*, suggests that corporations are servants of the larger society. This approach acknowledges that there are expanding demands being placed on business organizations which include a wider variety of groups not traditionally defined as part of the corporation's immediate self-interest. In a narrow sense, stakeholders are those identifiable groups or individuals on which an organization depends for its survival, sometimes referred to as primary stakeholders—stockholders, employees, customers, suppliers, and key government agencies. On a broader level, however, a stakeholder is any identifiable group or individual who can affect or is affected by organizational performance in terms of its products, policies, and work processes. In this sense, public interest groups, protest groups, local communities, government agencies, trade associations, competitors, unions, and the press are also organizational stakeholders.[4] Stockholders continue to occupy a place of prominence, but profit goals are to be pursued within the broader context of the public interest. Businesses are socially responsible when they consider and act on the needs and demands of these different stakeholders.

Motives

In addition to the tension created by the stockholder and stakeholder models of corporate performance, arguments about business's social role inevitably include the question of motives: Should business operate in its own *self-interest* or should it consider broader *social or moral duties?* A number of prominent economists, for instance, argue that the pursuit of profit is and must always remain the most fundamental social responsibility of any business, provided that such activity occurs within accepted moral and legal rules. The corporation is a highly specialized social instrument, designed for the explicit purpose of creating wealth. Business must therefore operate in its own self-interest. Proponents of the social or moral view rebut these arguments by underscoring the ideal of a social contract for business, the corporation's character as servant of the larger society. Because businesses are socially created, they are bound to attempt whatever tasks society imposes on them.

INTERPRETATIONS OF BUSINESS'S SOCIAL ROLE

These two debates—the distinction between stockholder and stakeholder views and whether business should act in its own self-interest or in the interests of the larger society—reflect four competing interpretations of business's responsibilities to the larger society:

1. *Productivism:* Social responsibility refers to corporate behavior which is justified in terms of *rational self-interest* and the direct fulfillment of *stockholder* interests.
2. *Philanthropy:* Social responsibility refers to corporate behavior which is justified in terms of *moral duty* and the direct fulfillment of *stockholder* interests.
3. *Progressivism:* Social responsibility refers to corporate behavior which is justified in terms of *rational self-interest* and the direct fulfillment of *stakeholder* interests.
4. *Ethical Idealism:* Social responsibility refers to corporate behavior which is justified in terms of *moral duty* and the direct fulfillment of *stakeholder* interests.

Their interrelationships are illustrated in Figure 3.

Productivism

Productivism is a traditional, fundamentalist view of business's social role. The basic premise of this view is that business exists in order to fulfill a specific societal function—to produce wealth.[5]

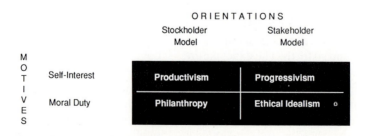

Figure 3 Interpretations of Business's Social Role

Since this task is critically important for any society, people in business should take pride in their function. When business organizations observe safe and sound practices and maximize profits while minimizing losses they are serving the common good and operating in a responsible manner. The concept of social responsibility must, therefore, be rather narrowly interpreted and cannot include social welfare projects, however well intentioned, which divert business from its basic set of activities.

Many of the arguments against a broader interpretation of business's social role and responsibilities are built on a productivist rationale. Based on this view, organizations do not have any right to use corporate funds to support charitable causes. Others suggest that expanded notions of responsibility create inefficiency in our businesses. Since one of the strengths of our economic system is clear-cut, well-focused goals, it is irresponsible to place additional burdens on business that would create ambiguous goals and diffuse its resources and expertise.

Philanthropy

Philanthropy shares most of the assumptions of productivism but departs from it on the nature and extent of corporate duties. According to the philanthropic perspective, corporations have obligations to society which go beyond considerations of profit and loss. The basic market forces of supply and demand, therefore, are not the only factors that business people should consider. Due to the power concentrated in the corporate sector, business has a social obligation to undertake certain activities *for their own sake*. Although such moral duties extend beyond organizational stockholders, they are justified on the basis of *indirectly* improving the position of the stockholders and the company through a strengthening of the larger society.[6]

Philanthropic activities have deep historical roots in U.S. business. In addition to providing financial support to civic, educational, health, social welfare, and arts and cultural organizations, businesses often lend the services of their members to local causes, donate the use of their facilities to community groups, and organize company-run volunteer projects to sponsor various charities. Many large corporations even have philanthropic advisory committees which attempt to set priorities based on community and organizational needs, improve the process of screening and selecting grant recipients, and monitor and evaluate recipient performance. In the early 1980s, the Business Roundtable published a statement encouraging the business community to increase its activities and contributions for educational, health, welfare, and cultural activities.[7] Within the bounds of this view, however, social responsibility does *not* go beyond such well-defined and controlled donations and volunteer activities.

Progressivism

Progressivism defines self-interest in broader, longer-term ways. Often referred to as "enlightened self-interest" or "enlightened egoism," this orientation suggests that business accept a limited role as an agent of social change and engage in various activities that will sustain public confidence. Specific policies might include affirmative action programs, environmental protection, energy conservation, and efforts to hire the hard-core unemployed. Due to basic changes in business's environment and the rise in influence of different stakeholders, this broader interpretation of social responsibility is defended as being in the long-term interests of the firm as well as the larger society. It is still influenced by self-interest in that the goal is to guarantee the continued profitability of business while minimizing further encroachment by government and criticism by stakeholders.

The influence of the progressivist view of social responsibility is reflected in the growth and development of such organizational practices as issues management and public affairs.[8] These roles reflect an evolution of the older "public relations" function, with greater emphases on information gathering, environmental analysis, and appropriate modifications to company policies and strategies. The orientation of both issues management and public affairs is toward more *direct* interaction between an organization and its stakeholders.

Ethical Idealism

Those groups and individuals who hold an ethical idealist interpretation of social responsibility call for a full reinterpretation and reassessment of the mission of business. Due to basic problems inherent in our society (such as selfishness, materialism, short-sightedness, wastefulness), the moderate reforms proposed by other interpretations of business's social role are not sufficient to treat the malaise that exists in our society. Since our basic problems are moral not technical, the nature of our economic system must be questioned and reevaluated. Ethical idealists feel that corporate activity will not be fully responsible until a sense of altruism has transformed business practice and a new spirit restores our lost sense of community, self-realization, and service.

Examples of ethical idealist interpretations of corporate responsibility include: (1) the movement toward employee ownership where local communities are intimately involved in organizational decision making; (2) the creation of "co-corps," organizations focused on service rather than profit, operated for the benefit of the public instead of stockholders; (3) the Nader group's calls for "constitutionalizing the corporation" that would replace state chartering with federal chartering, provide an expanded "bill of rights" for all employees, and influence significant shifts in labor-management power relations; and (4) the dozens of populist lobbying groups that push for social reform in business.[9] An important point is that although an ethical idealist interpretation of social responsibility may be rare among business

people, it is relatively common among many public interest stakeholder groups.

THE CORPORATION AND ITS EVOLVING ROLE IN SOCIETY

Although arguments over the appropriate role of business and its relationship to the larger society have always existed, today's debate is urgent and widespread. Corporate horror stories seem to unfold in the news media on virtually a daily basis. It is estimated that over the past 10 years, two-thirds of the *Fortune* 500 companies have been involved in some type of illegal or unethical activity.[10] A *New York Times*/CBS News poll found that 55 percent of those interviewed think that most corporate executives are dishonest in their business dealings. Moreover, two-thirds of the sample felt that government was not doing enough to catch these individuals and that for those who were caught, punishment was too lenient.[11] To come to some conclusion about the proper role of business is essential for the survival of both business and society.

We believe that the well-being of business and society requires the adoption of a stakeholder model. This need not mean that business must abandon its interest in profits or adopt an exclusively "ethical idealist" position. The stakeholder model also leaves room for a "progressivist" stance. Concern for stakeholders and interest in profits are not mutually exclusive. The stakeholder model is preferable to the stockholder model for several reasons:

1. The stockholder model has failed to deal adequately with contemporary societal problems and the true complexities of economic transactions and interactions.
2. It is in the long-term interest of business to take a broader view of its responsibilities. If business does not become accountable for its actions on its own, growing stakeholder pressures will ensure government-imposed accountability.

3. Understanding and satisfying the needs of stakeholders is important to the well-being of the firm. Being aware of the multiple forces that influence events allows us to be in a better position to make corporate decisions. In today's highly competitive economic and social environment, no important stakeholder can be ignored.

4. The stakeholder model is in keeping with our notions of fairness. Employees, consumers, communities, etc. are not just instruments for enriching stockholders. They have legitimate goals and interests of their own. Business has an obligation to treat its stakeholders with a sense of fairness and justice and to acknowledge their fundamental rights, not simply because it will be in its own vested interest in the long term, but because it is the ethical position to take as well.

NOTES

[*Author's note*: This essay is based on A. F. Buono & L. T. Nichols, *Corporate Policy, Values and Social Responsibility* (New York: Praeger, 1985).]

1. For a good summary of this period and the subsequent change in attitudes and orientations, see G. F. Cavanagh, *American Business Values* (Englewood Cliffs, N.J.: Prentice-Hall, 1984).

2. See F. W. Steckmest, *Corporate Performance: The Key to Public Trust* (New York: McGraw-Hill, 1982); D. O. Friedrichs, "The Legitimacy Crisis in the United States: A Conceptual Analysis," *Social Problems*, vol. 27, *5*, 1980, 540–555; and R. B. Reich, "On the Brink of an Anti-Business Era," *New York Times*, April 12, 1987, p. F3.

3. See the commentary, "Is IBM Good for America?" *Business and Society Review*, no. 56, Winter 1986, pp. 4–16.

4. R. E. Freeman, *Strategic Management: A Stakeholder Approach* (Boston: Pitman, 1984); and R. E. Freeman and D. L. Reed, "Stockholders and Stakeholders: A New Perspective on Corporate Governance," *California Management Review*, vol. *25* (Spring 1983), pp. 88–106.

5. For a fuller explanation and defense of the productivist view see Milton Friedman's "The Social Responsibility of Business Is to Increase Its Profits" found in W. M. Hoffman and J. M. Moore (eds.), *Business Ethics* (New York: McGraw-Hill, 1990). See also F. Hayek, *Studies in Philosophy, Politics and Economics* (Chicago: University of Chicago Press, 1967).

6. H. Lindsell, *Free Enterprise: A Judeo-Christian Defense* (Wheaton Ill. Tyndale House, 1982). For a fuller discussion of the underlying social contract, see Thomas Donaldson's essay "The Social Contract" found in Hoffman and Moore, *Business Ethics*.

7. See Steckmest, *Corporate Performance*, pp. 150–151.

8. J. F. Coates, V. T. Coates, J. Jarratt, and L. Heinz, *Issues Management: How You Can Plan, Organize and Manage for the Future* (Mt. Airy, Mdt. Lomond Publications, 1986); and L. E. Preston, *Social Issues and Public Policy in Business and Management* (College Park: Center for Business and Public Policy, University of Maryland, 1986).

9. See M. Carney and D. Shearer, *Economic Democracy: The Challenge of the 1980s* (Armonk, N.Y.: M. E. Sharpe, 1980); A. Collier, "The Co-Corp: Big Business Can Re-Form Itself," *Harvard Business Review*, vol. 57, *6*, 1979, pp. 121–134; and R. Nader, M. Green, and J. Seligman (eds.), *Taming the Giant Corporation* (N.Y.: Norton, 1976).

10. Reported in S. Gellerman, "Why 'Good' Managers Make Bad Ethical Choices," *Harvard Business Review*, vol. 64, *4*, 1986, p. 85.

11. See A. Clymer, "Low Marks for Executive Honesty," *New York Times*, June 9, 1985, pp. F1, F6; and R. Nader, "White Collar Fraud: America's Crime Without Criminals," *New York Times*, May 19, 1985, p. F3.

Corporate Responsibility: Property and Liability

W. Michael Hoffman*
James V. Fisher†

I

Daniel Bell suggested in the early seventies that the question of social responsibility would be the crux of a debate that would serve as a turning point for the corporation in modern society.[1] This thought has been echoed recently by George Lodge in his book *The New American Ideology*. Bell and Lodge are the most recent in a line of social theorists who portray our society—and particularly the world of business—as in the midst of one of the great transformations of Western civilization. Old ideas that once legitimized our institutions are eroding in the face of changing operational realities. And one of the most important of these ideas being challenged is that of private property.[2] For example Lodge says:

> A curious thing has happened to private property— it has stopped being very important. After all, *what difference* does it really make today *whether a person owns or just enjoys property?*...The value of property as a legitimizing idea and basis of authority has eroded as well. It is obvious that our large public corporations are not private property at all....It was to (the) notion of *community need,* for example, that ITT appealed in 1971 when it sought to prevent the Justice Department from divesting it of Hartford Fire Insurance....Note that here, *as so often happens, it was the company that argued the ideologically radical case.*[3] [Emphasis added]

A longer version of this paper was presented at the Ethics and Economics Conference, University of Delaware, Nov. 12, 1977. Copyright © 1977 by W. Michael Hoffman and James V. Fisher. Reprinted by permission of the authors.

*Director, Center for Business Ethics, Bentley College.
†Formerly in the Department of Philosophy, Bentley College; now a psychoanalyst in London, England.

At the heart of the entire debate is the question of the nature of the corporation. Is the corporation primarily an instrument of owners or is it an autonomous enterprise which can freely decide where its economic and moral responsibilities lie? This question arose with the advent of the megacorporation and its *de facto* separation of ownership and control. Stockholding owners today have little or no direct control over what they "own," control being for all practical purposes totally in the specially trained hands of management. With this operational shift of power to management, corporate objectives have enlarged to include at least a recognition of social obligations other than providing the greatest possible financial gain or advantage for their stockholders. But herein lie questions not only as to what these corporate social obligations are and how they are to be acted upon, but more importantly, as to what conceptually justifies and legitimizes the corporation itself now that private property theory is said to have eroded. Answers to the former clearly are dependent on answers to the latter.

Through a variety of rather slippery normative moves, corporate revisionists like Galbraith seem to argue that the great corporation must now simply be regarded as no longer a private but really a public institution. This would, presumably, provide a basis for corporate social responsibility that goes significantly beyond Friedman's "one and only one" social responsibility of business—to increase its profits.[4] Such a "corporate revolution" would appear to mean that the corporation is moving away (whether consciously or unconsciously) from legitimizing itself as *private property* to legitimizing itself as more like *common property*. In fact, perhaps the modern corporation should be seen as an exemplification of the philosophical unsoundness of private property, a strange development, to be sure, since the theory of private property has ostensibly been the essential pillar of capitalism itself.

It is important to note that the analysis which we have just sketched has focused almost exclusively on the issue of *control*. Traditionally, three elements have characterized property: the right to control, to benefit from, and to alienate (to sell or dispose of) something. An analysis of property which focuses exclusively on *control*, however, is seriously deficient, and a somewhat different picture of the question of corporate social responsibility begins to emerge when one focuses on the property rights of benefit and alienation. Clearly there are dangers to a society in the midst of radical change if it proceeds to discard basic legitimizing ideas of such social import as that of private property before it carefully considers the logic of that move.

It is an interesting fact to ponder that no fully adequate explication of a theory of justification of property acquisition has yet been achieved in modern Western social philosophy. By fully adequate is meant (a) a theory which goes beyond the "justification" that possession *is* ownership, i.e., that having an enforceable claim to something is to be understood as having the power to enforce that claim, and (b) a theory which is reasonably congruent with social realities. The lack of a fully adequate theory of property, however, does not preclude examination of the notion of property itself.

In this paper our primary interest is with the internal logic of the notion of property. The logic of *private property,* it will be argued, indicates a class of things which cannot become (or at least remain) private property, and thus the concept of private property suggests an inevitable transition from (some kinds of) private property to common property. Moreover, the theory of the "managerial revolution" will be seen to result in a gerrymandered definition of private property rather than in an innocent discarding of the idea. The social analysts who have focused on corporate control have made an important empirical observation, but, in reference to the issue of the relation of the corporation, private property, and social responsibility, they have generated serious conceptual confusion. Nor have the philosophers helped very much.

II

The property rights of control, benefit, and alienation always imply the right to exclude. Since we intend to focus on the right to benefit, the following is proposed as a working definition of *private property* in order to clarify and highlight the logic of the notion of property.[5]

> *Something (x) is the private property of someone (S) if and only if S has the right to exclude all others from the use or benefit of x.*

The right to alienate will be considered directly, though no attempt will be made in this paper to develop a satisfactory definition integrating the errant element of control.

Common property, on the other hand, must be defined in such a way as to include the individual rights of those who share ownership as well as the collective right of the owners to exclude all others.

> *Something (x) is the common property of two or more people (S_1, S_2, etc.) if and only if S_1, S_2, etc. together have the right to exclude all others from the use or benefit of x, and S_1, S_2, etc. each has the right not to be excluded from the use or benefit of x.*

These definitions which emphasize the right to exclude or the right not to be excluded are, it will be argued, incomplete. There is, in fact, a *double-edged* exclusion which will become obvious when we consider the right to alienate or dispose of something.

To elaborate further the concept of common property, let us consider what it means for something to be common property. Suppose an apple tree is the common property of S_1, S_2, etc., and suppose further that it is autumn and the apple tree in question is now full of ripe apples. If S_1 were to pick one of those ripe apples and eat it, and assuming no prior agreement to refrain from eating any apples (say, for example, to save them all for pressing cider), then it would make little sense for S_2 to say to S_1: "You had no right to eat that apple since it was common property and you have now excluded the rest of us from the use or benefit of it.'' Here being common property would appear to mean (again in the absence of some specific agreement) that while S_1 had indeed excluded S_2 from the use or benefit of that apple, nevertheless S_2 had not been excluded from the use or benefit of the apple tree—at least as long as there is another ripe apple for S_2. The problem becomes somewhat more complicated if that autumn the apple tree in question were to have borne only one edible apple (each gets one bite?), but clearly any individual commoner's right not to be excluded cannot be taken to mean an *absolute* preclusion of any other individual commoner's actual use of the common property. What this suggests is that any notion of common property is incomplete without some (implicit or explicit) procedure for ''fair-taking/using.''

III

We can talk about at least three modes in which an individual makes a claim (at least a *de facto* claim) to *own* something: (1) taking possession; (2) use; and (3) alienating or *disowning* it. We will elaborate (1) briefly and then move to (3), since it is of greatest interest for the argument being developed in this paper.

Under the first category, taking possession, at least three elements can be distinguished: directly grasping something physically—what is referred to in legal contracts as ''taking possession;'' shaping, forming, or developing something; and taking possession by simply marking something as one's own. Note the function of the concept of intention in all three of these activities. Not only is it a necessary element in ownership, its scope extends beyond the immediate relation to the thing itself. Thus the claim to ownership extends to not only such things as unknown parts (mineral deposits, etc.) and organic results (eggs, the offspring, etc.), but also connections made by chance subsequent to the original acquisition (alluvial deposits, jetsam, etc.). This is even more explicit when I take pos-

session by shaping or forming something. By shaping or forming it, I take more than just the immediate constituents into my possession. This applies to the organic (breeding of cattle, etc.) as well as to the reshaping of raw materials and the ''forces of nature.'' The point that needs to be emphasized is that marking something as my own is an action that extends my intention to ownership beyond the immediate thing itself, a principle that has been long accepted in legal theory and in social practice (and in fact is at the basis of our patent laws, etc.).

It is with the third category, however, that we come to the most interesting move. In a sense when I *disown* something (e.g., by selling it) I intend the thing in its entirety (I intend, so to speak, to be rid of it) and so presuppose the claim that it is/was most completely my own.

It is at this point that we can see clearly the missing half of our definitions of property. Note that it is generally held that there are two ways of *disowning* something:

1. I may yield it to the intention (will) of another, i.e., to another's claim to ownership (usually in exchange for something I deem valuable, though it may be an outright gift as long as the recipient accepts it as his or her own); or
2. I may abandon it (as *res nullius,* the property of no one? or as now the common property of all?).

The first option is clear enough and if we pursued that discussion the questions would center around the issue of what constitutes a fair exchange. But what about the second option? Where does the logic of disowning lead us? Consider the following case:

Suppose S, being perceptive and industrious, notes that there is a good market for tiger skins (well tanned, handsome to the eye, and luxurious to the touch). Furthermore, there are wild tigers in S's vicinity and the tigers may rightfully be appropriated by anyone and thus become the private property of the one who appropriates them (there being plenty of tigers in the vicinity relative to the number of people, etc.). By virtue of S's physical strength, cunning, and dexterity (as well as industriousness), S is able to capture several of these tigers intending to breed them in captivity for their very fine skins. Suppose further that S is successful initially in breeding the tigers, but it soon develops that they do not live long enough in captivity to grow to a size to produce sufficiently luxurious skins. But S is undaunted and eventually, by ingenuity and much hard labor, is successful in breeding stock that is long-lived, very handsome and adequately large.

Let's suppose further that as a result of this ingenious breeding process S produces a tiger, we can call it T_n, which has two very special and advantageous characteristics: (a) T_n regularly sheds its skin, leaving each time a very fine tiger skin ready to be tanned and sold; and (b) T_n appears to be immune to the aging process and even impervious to anything which might harm or even kill it. T_n appears to be indestructible, a source, it seems, of an infinite number of fine tiger skins.

Can it be doubted that T_n is the private property of S, that S has the right to exclude all others from the use or benefit of T_n? If anything could ever satisfy the traditional property accounts like those of Kant, Locke, and Hegel, surely S's ownership of T_n could.

Now let's imagine that one day T_n begins to show signs of a developing nasty temperament, and finally it becomes painfully clear to S that T_n is a serious danger to S (far outweighing the amazing advantages which T_n manifests), and as well a danger to those in S's immediate living unit, S's neighbors, and even S's whole community. But T_n is indestructible (or at least no one has yet found a way to do away with T_n). What is S to do? The danger is critical.

Aha! S, using what precautions are possible, takes T_n one day to the village green and in the presence of the (not too happy) villagers makes the following announcement: "I, S, who have rightfully acquired this tiger, T_n, as my private property, do here and now publicly renounce, relinquish, and abandon my property in T_n." We are assuming, of course, that S has attempted to transfer property in T_n to someone else, to yield S's property in T_n to the will of another and so into

that person's possession, but understandably has found no takers.

Imagine then that the next day S's neighbor appears at S's door, cut and scratched and bearing the remains of a flock of sheep which had been destroyed during the night. "Look what your tiger has done," says the neighbor to S. "My tiger?" responds S. "I renounced and abandoned my property in that tiger yesterday. That's not *my* tiger." No doubt we would be more than a little sympathetic with the neighbor's reply: "The hell it's not *your* tiger!"

It is interesting to observe that Kant, Locke, and Hegel (to name only a few) all treat property *only* as if it were a good, i.e., as if the right to exclude all others was something always desirable (note our use of the term "goods"). Why is it that these pillars of modern Western social and political philosophy have apparently ignored what we might call the "garbage factor"? (Which is not to say that those involved with the practice of law and politics have likewise ignored this factor.) Is it because we no longer live in an age when people commonly throw their garbage out the window? Or because there are now so many of us? Or because of such things as radioactive nuclear wastes and breeder reactors? No matter. It is in any case clear that the initial definition of private property must now be revised along the following lines:

1a. x is S's private property if and only if S has the right to exclude all others from the use or benefit of x AND

1b. *each of these others has the right to be excluded from liability for the maleficence of* x.

The term "liability" ("responsibility" does equally as well) is chosen for etymological reasons—the root of "liability" being *ligare*, to bind. It is not intended in any technical legal sense. This is what we may call the *double-edged exclusionary definition* of private property.

What will become obvious on reflection is that *if S's property is S's in precisely the same sense and for the same reason that S's action is S's, then the discussion of morality is also a discussion of property.*

Consider for a moment the question of the relation of intention to responsibility. In one sense I cannot be held responsible for an act that was not, in some significant sense, intentional. But I doubt that we want to take this in the strictest sense, i.e., that I have a right to recognize as my action—and to accept responsibility for—only those aspects of the deed of which I was conscious in my aim and which were contained in my original purpose. Surely, even though one may intend only to bring about a single, immediate state of affairs, there are consequences which are implicit within that state of affairs or connected with it empirically of which I ought to be aware and for which I am therefore morally responsible.

There is a clear parallel between how we deal with the question of someone's liability and how we deal with the beneficial additions to someone's property (by nature, chance, etc.) which, though subsequent to the time and intention of the acquisition of that property, are judged to be *part* of that property. It is directly analogous to the distinction between having an action imputed to me and being responsible for the consequences of an action. I may be responsible for a criminal act, though it does not follow that the thing done may be directly imputed to me. To apply this to our case of T_n, we might say that on the one hand we do not want to confuse S with T_n, though on the other hand we may want to hold S responsible for the consequences that follow.

Hegel observes: "To act is to expose oneself to bad luck. Thus bad luck has a right over me and is an embodiment of my own will (intention)."[6]

It is fair, we think, to paraphrase Hegel: "To acquire property is to expose oneself to bad luck."

The case of T_n, we argue, demonstrates that we are inclined to hold T_n's owner liable for the consequences, an inclination that finds expression in positive legislation in contemporary society. If we hold S liable for T_n, it is clear that what we are saying is that not only does S have rights in reference to T_n, but all others do as well. All the story of T_n does is to make explicit that the *double-edged exclusionary definition* represents what has always been, and indeed must be, implicit in the notion of private property.

The abandonment mode of disowning makes sense, then, *only if* property is *only* considered a good. Or rather we might say, it is morally justified only if what is abandoned *is* good. If it is acknowledged that property also entails liability for maleficence, then it follows (especially where the negative consequences of something are serious) that such a mode of disowning is really tantamount to ascribing to the thing in question the *de facto* status of common property of all—and that without the express (or implied) consent of those to whom the liability is transferred. Or perhaps we should say that the thing in question *ought* to be the common property of all, since in fact the negative consequences may fall more heavily on some than on others. Note that the definition of common property must also be revised to pick up the double-edged aspect.

2a. x *is the common property of* S_1, S_2, *etc., if and only if* S_1, S_2, *etc. together have the right to exclude all others from the use or benefit of* x, *and* S_1, S_2, *etc. each has the right not to be excluded from the use or benefit of* x.

2b. *BUT not the right to be excluded from liability for the maleficence of* x.

IV

Given this interpretation of the logic of the notion of property, now reconsider a view which is current these days among some social theorists and popularized in Lodge's eclectic *The New American Ideology:* the view that the notion of (private) property is passé in our "postindustrial" era. Here Lodge suggests, as we have indicated above, that "(t)he value of property as a legitimizing idea and basis of authority has eroded...(and that it) is obvious that our large public corporations are not private property at all."

This "ideological" change, reflecting the operational changes in management practice in large "public" corporations, has been characterized as a *managerial revolution*. If we are to use a metaphor like "revolution" here, then it might be said that the managerial revolution is a revolution, to be sure, a revolution in the concept of property. That is, what seems to be implicit in the theory of the managerial revolution is not a move away from the notion of private property to some new basis of legitimation for the modern corporation, but rather a radical change in the concept of property itself. The implicit change (or revolution) is a *gerrymandering* of the concept of property out of parts of the concepts of private and common property. It would then appear to be something like the following:

1a. *S has the right to exclude all others from the use or benefit of* x *BUT*
2b. *these others do not have the right to be excluded from liability for the maleficence of* x.

This is, of course, a bit oversimplified, but recent cases like that of the Lockheed and Chrysler Corporations suggest that it is not far off the mark in characterizing our contemporary situation. We should entertain such (implicit) proposals for a gerrymandered definition of private property, we suggest, with considerable hesitation and even skepticism. Too easily giving up the notion of private property runs the danger of giving up the right to hold accountable for *x* those people who have the sole right to the use or benefit of *x*. What would be more rational (and not merely conceptually conservative, we are arguing) is to say that *when all others are to be held liable for S's* x, *then each of those others should also have the right not to be excluded from the use or benefit of* x—in other words, that *x* becomes common property. Or, one might say, logically some kind of social revolution is what is called for, not a conceptual revolution.

One of the many questions which now arise concerns the problem of symmetry (or fairness). Why should it be considered right to put a limit on liability (or to recognize a *de facto* limit, e.g., bankruptcy laws, etc.), but not to have some sort of similar limit on the use or benefits? (But would that not turn private property rights into common property rights, i.e., some procedure for fair taking/using?) The question becomes especially critical in situations where the negative consequences of something are actual while the benefits only potential. Thus, for example, S may declare the intention to assume liability for *x* commensurate with the potential benefits from *x* (or even commensurate with the total assets of S), but how does this help when the negative consequences are actual and the benefits only potential (or when the potential negative effects far outweigh the potential benefits)?

Lest one think that this a purely hypothetical situation, consider the case of the 1957 Price-Anderson Act.

> In 1954, when the government decided to encourage electric utilities to venture into nuclear power, the companies at first were enthusiastic; but after studying the consequences of a possible major nuclear accident, they and such equipment manufacturers as General Electric and Westinghouse backed off. They feared damage claims that could bankrupt them. Insurers refused then and refuse now to provide full coverage. And so the utilities told Congress they would build nuclear plants only if they first were to be immunized from full liability. Congress responded with the Price-Anderson Act of 1957. Because of this law—a law that legalized financial unaccountability—nuclear power technology exists and is growing today.... In 1965, when it recommended that the Price-Anderson Act be renewed, the Congressional Joint Committee on Atomic Energy "reported that one of the Act's objectives had been achieved—the deterrent to industrial participation in the atomic energy program

had been removed by eliminating the threat of large liability claims.''...In December 1975...Congress voted to extend the law for ten more years.[7]

In the face of such policies we have attempted to demonstrate that the logic of property leads one from the notion of private property (the right to exclude) with a kind of inevitability to the notion of common property (the right not to be excluded)—unless one proposes gerrymandering the concept of private property. At least this is true with respect to certain kinds of things which have traditionally been seen to fall within the range of what can rightfully become (and remain) private property. A more elaborate specification of what kinds of things these might be is a topic that goes much beyond the scope of this paper. And, of course, there remains the task of filling out our incomplete notion of common property, i.e., formulating the principles for procedures for fair-taking and fair-using.

NOTES

1. Daniel Bell, *The Coming of Post-Industrial Society: A Venture in Social Forecasting* (New York: Basic Books, 1973), p. 291.

2. The classic analysis which generated much of the contemporary discussion is A. A. Berle, Jr., and G. G. Means, *The Modern Corporation and Private Property* (New York: The Macmillan Company, 1932). See also A. A. Berle, Jr., *Power Without Property* (London: Sidgwick and Jackson, 1959).

3. George C. Lodge, *The New American Ideology* (New York: Alfred A. Knopf, Inc., 1975), pp. 17–19. Also see his article ''The Connection between Ethics and Ideology'' delivered at Bentley College's ''First National Conference on Business Ethics,'' published in the Conference *Proceedings,* edited by W. Michael Hoffman, Center for Business Ethics, 1977.

4. Milton Friedman, *Capitalism and Freedom* (Chicago: University of Chicago Press, 1962), p. 133.

5. These definitions are adapted from C. B. Macpherson, ''A Political Theory of Property,'' in *Democratic Theory: Essays in Retrieval* (Oxford: Clarendon Press, 1973), p. 128.

6. Hegel, *Philosophy of Right,* trans. T. M. Knox (Oxford University Press, 1952), § 119A

7. Morton Mintz and Jerry S. Cohen, *Power, Inc.* (New York: The Viking Press, 1976), pp. 513f. Other such liability exclusionary examples could be cited.

QUESTIONS FOR DISCUSSION

1. Would Friedman be more likely to agree or disagree with the Supreme Court's decision in *First National Bank of Boston v. Bellotti?* Explain.
2. Does the Supreme Court's decision more closely reflect what Lodge calls the ''traditional ideology'' or the ''new ideology''?
3. What are the main limitations on what Stone calls Friedman's ''agency argument''? Take into account not only Stone, but Davis, Donaldson, and Buono and Nichols as well.
4. According to Hoffman and Fisher, what are the advantages of the traditional emphasis on private property rights? What do Hoffman and Fisher mean when they claim that the contemporary notion of property is ''gerrymandered''?

CHAPTER 5

Identity and Agency

READINGS FOR CHAPTER FIVE

Kenneth E. Goodpaster and John B. Matthews, Jr.
Can a Corporation Have a Conscience?
184

Peter A. French
Corporate Moral Agency
194

John R. Danley
Corporate Moral Agency: The Case for Anthropological Bigotry
202

Can a Corporation Have a Conscience?

Kenneth E. Goodpaster*

John B. Matthews, Jr.†

During the severe racial tensions of the 1960s, Southern Steel Company (actual case, disguised name) faced considerable pressure from government and the press to explain and modify its policies regarding discrimination both within its plants and in the major city where it was located. SSC was the largest employer in the area (it had nearly 15,000 workers, one-third of whom were black) and had made great strides toward removing barriers to equal job opportunity in its several plants. In addition, its top executives (especially its chief executive officer, James Weston) had distinguished themselves as private citizens for years in community programs for black housing, education, and small business as well as in attempts at desegregating all-white police and local government organizations.

SSC drew the line, however, at using its substantial economic influence in the local area to advance the cause of the civil rights movement by pressuring banks, suppliers, and the local government:

> As individuals we can exercise what influence we may have as citizens," James Weston said, "but for a corporation to attempt to exert any kind of economic compulsion to achieve a particular end in a social area seems to me to be quite beyond what a corporation should do and quite beyond what a corporation can do. I believe that while gov-

Reprinted by permission of the *Harvard Business Review*. Excerpts from "Can a Corporation Have a Conscience?" by Kenneth E. Goodpaster and John B. Matthews, Jr. (January–February 1982). Copyright © 1982 by the President and Fellows of Harvard College; all rights reserved.

*General Management Area, Harvard Business School.

†Wilson Professor of Business Administration, Harvard Business School.

ernment may seek to compel social reforms, any attempt by a private organization like SSC to impose its views, its beliefs, and its will upon the community would be repugnant to our American constitutional concepts and that appropriate steps to correct this abuse of corporate power would be universally demanded by public opinion.

Weston could have been speaking in the early 1980s on any issue that corporations around the United States now face. Instead of social justice, his theme might be environmental protection, product safety, marketing practice, or international bribery. His statement for SSC raises the important issue of corporate responsibility. Can a corporation have a conscience?

Weston apparently felt comfortable saying it need not. The responsibilities of ordinary persons and of "artificial persons" like corporations are, in his view, separate. Persons' responsibilities go beyond those of corporations. Persons, he seems to have believed, ought to care not only about themselves but also about the dignity and well-being of those around them—ought not only to care but also to act. Organizations, he evidently thought, are creatures of, and to a degree prisoners of, the systems of economic incentive and political sanction that give them reality and therefore should not be expected to display the same moral attributes that we expect of persons.

Others inside business as well as outside share Weston's perception. One influential philosopher—John Ladd—carries Weston's view a step further:

> "It is improper to expect organizational conduct to conform to the ordinary principles of morality," he says. "We cannot and must not expect formal organizations, or their representatives acting in their official capacities, to be honest, courageous, considerate, sympathetic, or to have any kind of moral integrity. Such concepts are not in the vocabulary, so to speak, of the organizational language game."[1]

In our opinion, this line of thought represents a tremendous barrier to the development of business ethics both as a field of inquiry and as a practical force in managerial decision making. This is a matter about which executives must be philosophical and philosophers must be practical. A corporation can and should have a conscience. The language of ethics does have a place in the vocabulary of an organization. There need not be and there should not be a disjunction of the sort attributed to SSC's James Weston. Organizational agents such as corporations should be no more and no less morally responsible (rational, self-interested, altruistic) than ordinary persons.

We take this position because we think an analogy holds between the individual and the corporation. If we analyze the concept of moral responsibility as it applies to persons, we find that projecting it to corporations as agents in society is possible.

DEFINING THE RESPONSIBILITY OF PERSONS

When we speak of the responsibility of individuals, philosophers say that we mean three things: someone is to blame, something has to be done, or some kind of trustworthiness can be expected.

We apply the first meaning, what we shall call the *causal* sense, primarily to legal and moral contexts where what is at issue is praise or blame for a past action. We say of a person that he or she was responsible for what happened, is to blame for it, should be held accountable. In this sense of the word, *responsibility* has to do with tracing the causes of actions and events, of finding out who is answerable in a given situation. Our aim is to determine someone's intention, free will, degree of participation, and appropriate reward or punishment.

We apply the second meaning of *responsibility* to rule following, to contexts where individuals are subject to externally imposed norms often associated with some social role that people play. We speak of the responsibilities of parents to children, of doctors to patients, of lawyers to clients, of citizens to the law. What is socially expected and what the party involved is to answer for are at issue here.

We use the third meaning of *responsibility* for decision making. With this meaning of the term, we say that individuals are responsible if they are trustworthy and reliable, if they allow appropriate factors to affect their judgment; we refer primarily to a person's independent thought processes and decision making, processes that justify an attitude of trust from those who interact with him or her as a responsible individual.

The distinguishing characteristic of moral responsibility, it seems to us, lies in this third sense of the term. Here the focus is on the intellectual and emotional processes in the individual's moral reasoning. Philosophers call this "taking a moral point of view" and contrast it with such other processes as being financially prudent and attending to legal obligations.

To be sure, characterizing a person as "morally responsible" may seem rather vague. But vagueness is a contextual notion. Everything depends on how we fill in the blank in "vague for _____ purposes."

In some contexts the term "six o'clockish" is vague, while in others it is useful and informative. As a response to a space-shuttle pilot who wants to know when to fire the reentry rockets, it will not do, but it might do in response to a spouse who wants to know when one will arrive home at the end of the workday.

We maintain that the processes underlying moral responsibility can be defined and are not themselves vague, even though gaining consensus on specific moral norms and decisions is not always easy.

What, then, characterizes the processes underlying the judgment of a person we call morally responsible? Philosopher William K. Frankena offers the following answer:

"A morality is a normative system in which judgments are made, more or less consciously, [out of a] consideration of the effects of actions...on the lives of persons...including the lives of others besides the person acting....David Hume took a similar position when he argued that what speaks in a moral judgment is a kind of sympathy....A little later,...Kant put the matter somewhat better by characterizing morality as the business of respecting persons as ends and not as means or as things...."[2]

Frankena is pointing to two traits, both rooted in a long and diverse philosophical tradition:

1. *Rationality.* Taking a moral point of view includes the features we usually attribute to rational decision making, that is, lack of impulsiveness, care in mapping out alternatives and consequences, clarity about goals and purposes, attention to details of implementation.

2. *Respect.* The moral point of view also includes a special awareness of and concern for the effects of one's decisions and policies on others, special in the sense that it goes beyond the kind of awareness and concern that would ordinarily be part of rationality, that is, beyond seeing others merely as instrumental to accomplishing one's own purposes. This is respect for the lives of others and involves taking their needs and interests seriously, not simply as resources in one's own decision making but as limiting conditions which change the very definition of one's habitat from a self-centered to a shared environment. It is what philosopher Immanuel Kant meant by the "categorical imperative" to treat others as valuable in and for themselves.

It is this feature that permits us to trust the morally responsible person. We know that such a person takes our point of view into account not merely as a useful precaution (as in "honesty is the best policy") but as important in its own right.

These components of moral responsibility are not too vague to be useful. Rationality and respect affect the manner in which a person approaches practical decision making: they affect the way in which the individual processes information and makes choices. A rational but not respectful Bill Jones will not lie to his friends *unless* he is reasonably sure he will not be found out. A rational but not respectful Mary Smith will defend an unjustly treated party *unless* she thinks it may be too costly to herself. A rational *and* respectful decision maker, however, notices—and cares—whether the consequences of his or her conduct lead to injuries or indignities to others.

Two individuals who take "the moral point of view" will not of course always agree on ethical matters, but they do at least have a basis for dialogue.

PROJECTING RESPONSIBILITY TO CORPORATIONS

Now that we have removed some of the vagueness from the notion of moral responsibility as it applies to persons, we can search for a frame of reference in which, by analogy with Bill Jones and Mary Smith, we can meaningfully and appropriately say that corporations are morally responsible. This is the issue reflected in the SSC case.

To deal with it, we must ask two questions: Is it meaningful to apply moral concepts to actors who are not persons but who are instead made up of persons? And even if meaningful, is it advisable to do so?

If a group can act like a person in some ways, then we can expect it to behave like a person in other ways. For one thing, we know that people organized into a group can act as a unit. As business people well know, legally a corporation is considered a unit. To approach unity, a group usually has some sort of internal decision structure, a system of rules that spell out authority relationships and specify the conditions under which certain individuals' actions become official actions of the group.[3]

If we can say that persons act responsibly only if they gather information about the impact of

their actions on others and use it in making decisions, we can reasonably do the same for organizations. Our proposed frame of reference for
thinking about and implementing corporate responsibility aims at spelling out the processes
associated with the moral responsibility of individuals and projecting them to the level of organizations. This is similar to, though an inver-
sion of, Plato's famous method in the *Republic,*
in which justice in the community is used as a
model for justice in the individual.

Hence, corporations that monitor their employment practices and the effects of their production processes and products on the environment and human health show the same kind
of rationality and respect that morally responsible individuals do. Thus, attributing actions,
strategies, decisions, and moral responsibilities to corporations as entities distinguishable
from those who hold offices in them poses no
problem.

And when we look about us, we can readily
see differences in moral responsibility among corporations in much the same way that we see differences among persons. Some corporations
have built features into their management incentive systems, board structures, internal control
systems, and research agendas that in a person
we would call self-control, integrity, and con-
scientiousness. Some have institutionalized
awareness and concern for consumers, employees, and the rest of the public in ways that others clearly have not.

As a matter of course, some corporations attend to the human impact of their operations and
policies and reject operations and policies that
are questionable. Whether the issue be the health
effects of sugared cereal or cigarettes, the safety
of tires or tampons, civil liberties in the corporation or the community, an organization reveals
its character as surely as a person does.

Indeed, the parallel may be even more dramatic. For just as the moral responsibility displayed by an individual develops over time from
infancy to adulthood,[4] so too we may expect to
find stages of development in organizational character that show significant patterns.

EVALUATING THE IDEA OF MORAL PROJECTION

Concepts like moral responsibility not only make
sense when applied to organizations but also provide touchstones for designing more effective
models than we have for guiding corporate policy.

Now we can understand what it means to invite SSC as a corporation to be morally responsible both in-house and in its community, but
should we issue the invitation? Here we turn to
the question of advisability. Should we require
the organizational agents in our society to have
the same moral attributes we require of ourselves?

Our proposal to spell out the processes associated with moral responsibility for individuals
and then to project them to their organizational
counterparts takes on added meaning when we
examine alternative frames of reference for corporate responsibility.

Two frames of reference that compete for the
allegiance of people who ponder the question of
corporate responsibility are emphatically opposed to this principle of moral projection—what
we might refer to as the "invisible hand" view
and the "hand of government" view.

The Invisible Hand

The most eloquent spokesman of the first view
is Milton Friedman (echoing many philosophers
and economists since Adam Smith). According
to this pattern of thought, the true and only social responsibilities of business organizations are
to make profits and obey the laws. The workings of the free and competitive marketplace will
"moralize" corporate behavior quite independently of any attempts to expand or transform
decision making via moral projection.

A deliberate amorality in the executive suite
is encouraged in the name of systemic morality:

the common good is best served when each of us and our economic institutions pursue not the common good or moral purpose, advocates say, but competitive advantage. Morality, responsibility, and conscience reside in the invisible hand of the free market system, not in the hands of the organizations within the system, much less the managers within the organizations.

To be sure, people of this opinion admit, there is a sense in which social or ethical issues can and should enter the corporate mind, but the filtering of such issues is thorough: they go through the screens of custom, public opinion, public relations, and the law. And, in any case, self-interest maintains primacy as an objective and a guiding star.

The reaction from this frame of reference to the suggestion that moral judgment be integrated with corporate strategy is clearly negative. Such an integration is seen as inefficient and arrogant, and in the end both an illegitimate use of corporate power and an abuse of the manager's fiduciary role. With respect to our SSC case, advocates of the invisible hand model would vigorously resist efforts, beyond legal requirements, to make SSC right the wrongs of racial injustice. SSC's responsibility would be to make steel of high quality at least cost, to deliver it on time, and to satisfy its customers and stockholders. Justice would not be part of SSC's corporate mandate.

The Hand of Government

Advocates of the second dissenting frame of reference abound, but John Kenneth Galbraith's work has counterpointed Milton Friedman's with insight and style. Under this view of corporate responsibility, corporations are to pursue objectives that are rational and purely economic. The regulatory hands of the law and the political process rather than the invisible hand of the marketplace turns these objectives to the common good.

Again, in this view, it is a system that provides the moral direction for corporate decision making—a system, though, that is guided by political managers, the custodians of the public purpose. In the case of SSC, proponents of this view would look to the state for moral direction and responsible management, both within SSC and in the community. The corporation would have no moral responsibility beyond political and legal obedience.

What is striking is not so much the radical difference between the economic and social philosophies that underlie these two views of the source of corporate responsibility but the conceptual similarities. Both views locate morality, ethics, responsibility, and conscience in the systems of rules and incentives in which the modern corporation finds itself embedded. Both views reject the exercise of independent moral judgment by corporations as actors in society.

Neither view trusts corporate leaders with stewardship over what are often called noneconomic values. Both require corporate responsibility to march to the beat of drums outside. In the jargon of moral philosophy, both views press for a rule-centered or a system-centered ethics instead of an agent-centered ethics. These frames of reference countenance corporate rule-following responsibility for corporations but not corporate decision-making responsibility.

The Hand of Management

To be sure, the two views under discussion differ in that one looks to an invisible moral force in the market while the other looks to a visible moral force in government. But both would advise against a principle of moral projection that permits or encourages corporations to exercise independent, noneconomic judgment over matters that face them in their short- and long-term plans and operations.

Accordingly, both would reject a third view of corporate responsibility that seeks to affect the thought processes of the organization itself—a sort of ''hand of management'' view—since neither seems willing or able to see the engines of profit regulate themselves to the degree that would be implied by taking the principle of moral projection seriously. Cries of inefficiency and moral imperialism from the right would be matched by cries of insensitivity and illegitimacy from the left, all in the name of preserving us from corporations and managers run morally amok.

Better, critics would say, that moral philosophy be left to philosophers, philanthropists, and politicians than to business leaders. Better that corporate morality be kept to glossy annual reports, where it is safely insulated from policy and performance.

The two conventional frames of reference locate moral restraint in forces external to the person and the corporation. They deny moral reasoning and intent to the corporation in the name of either market competition or society's system of explicit legal constraints and presume that these have a better moral effect than that of rationality and respect.

Although the principle of moral projection, which underwrites the idea of a corporate conscience and patterns it on the thought and feeling processes of the person, is in our view compelling, we must acknowledge that it is neither part of the received wisdom, nor is its advisability beyond question or objection. Indeed, attributing the role of conscience to the corporation seems to carry with it new and disturbing implications for our usual ways of thinking about ethics and business.

Perhaps the best way to clarify and defend this frame of reference is to address the objections to the principle found in the last pages of this article. There we see a summary of the criticisms and counterarguments we have heard during hours of discussion with business executives and business school students. We believe that the replies to the objections about a corporation having a conscience are convincing.

LEAVING THE DOUBLE STANDARD BEHIND

We have come some distance from our opening reflection on Southern Steel Company and its role in its community. Our proposal—clarified, we hope, through these objections and replies—suggests that it is not sufficient to draw a sharp line between individuals' private ideas and efforts and a corporation's institutional efforts but that the latter can and should be built upon the former.

Does this frame of reference give us an unequivocal prescription for the behavior of SSC in its circumstances? No, it does not. Persuasive arguments might be made now and might have been made then that SSC should not have used its considerable economic clout to threaten the community into desegregation. A careful analysis of the realities of the environment might have disclosed that such a course would have been counterproductive, leading to more injustice than it would have alleviated.

The point is that some of the arguments and some of the analyses are or would have been moral arguments, and thereby the ultimate decision that of an ethically responsible organization. The significance of this point can hardly be overstated, for it represents the adoption of a new perspective on corporate policy and a new way of thinking about business ethics. We agree with one authority, who writes that ''the business firm, as an organic entity intricately affected by and affecting its environment, is as appropriately adaptive . . . to demands for responsible behavior as for economic service.''[5]

The frame of reference here developed does not offer a decision procedure for corporate managers. That has not been our purpose. It does, however, shed light on the conceptual foundations of business ethics by training attention on the corporation as a moral agent in society. Legal systems of rules and incentives are insufficient, even though they may be necessary, as frameworks for corporate responsibility. Taking conceptual cues from the features of moral responsibility normally expected of the person in our opinion deserves practicing managers' serious consideration.

The lack of congruence that James Weston saw between individual and corporate moral responsibility can be, and we think should be, overcome. In the process, what a number of writers have characterized as a double standard—a discrepancy between our personal lives and our lives in organizational settings—might be dampened. The principle of moral projection not only helps us to conceptualize the kinds of demands that we might make of corporations and other organizations but also offers the prospect of harmonizing those demands with the demands that we make of ourselves.

IS A CORPORATION A MORALLY RESPONSIBLE "PERSON"?

Objection 1 to the Analogy

Corporations are not persons. They are artificial legal constructions, machines for mobilizing economic investments toward the efficient production of goods and services. We cannot hold a corporation responsible. We can only hold individuals responsible.

Reply

Our frame of reference does not imply that corporations are persons in a literal sense. It simply means that in certain respects concepts and functions normally attributed to persons can also be attributed to organizations made up of persons. Goals, economic values, strategies, and other such personal attributes are often usefully projected to the corporate level by managers and researchers. Why should we not project the functions of conscience in the same way? As for holding corporations responsible, recent criminal prosecutions such as the case of Ford Motor Company and its Pinto gas tanks suggest that

society finds the idea both intelligible and useful.

Objection 2

A corporation cannot be held responsible at the sacrifice of profit. Profitability and financial health have always been and should continue to be the "categorical imperatives" of a business operation.

Reply

We must of course acknowledge the imperatives of survival, stability, and growth when we discuss corporations, as indeed we must acknowledge them when we discuss the life of an individual. Self-sacrifice has been identified with moral responsibility in only the most extreme cases. The pursuit of profit and self-interest need not be pitted against the demands of moral responsibility. Moral demands are best viewed as containments—not replacements—for self-interest.

This is not to say that profit maximization never conflicts with morality. But profit maximization conflicts with other managerial values as well. The point is to coordinate imperatives, not deny their validity.

Objection 3

Corporate executives are not elected representatives of the people, nor are they anointed or appointed as social guardians. They therefore lack the social mandate that a democratic society rightly demands of those who would pursue ethically or socially motivated policies. By keeping corporate policies confined to economic motivations, we keep the power of corporate executives in its proper place.

Reply

The objection betrays an oversimplified view of the relationship between the public and the private sector. Neither private individuals nor private corporations that guide their conduct by ethical or social values beyond the demands of law should be constrained merely because they are not elected to do so. The demands of moral responsibility are independent of the demands of political legitimacy and are in fact presupposed by them.

To be sure, the state and the political process will and must remain the primary mechanisms for protecting the public interest, but one might be forgiven the hope that the political process will not substitute for the moral judgment of the citizenry or other components of society such as corporations.

Objection 4

Our system of law carefully defines the role of agent or fiduciary and makes corporate managers accountable to shareholders and investors for the use of their assets. Management cannot, in the name of corporate moral responsibility, arrogate to itself the right to manage those assets by partially noneconomic criteria.

Reply

First, it is not so clear that investors insist on purely economic criteria in the management of their assets, especially if some of the shareholders' resolutions and board reforms of the last decade are any indication. For instance, companies doing business in South Africa have had stockholders question their activities, other companies have instituted audit committees for their boards before such auditing was mandated, and mutual funds for which "socially responsible behavior" is a major investment criterion now exist.

Second, the categories of "shareholder" and "investor" connote wider time spans than do immediate or short-term returns. As a practical matter, considerations of stability and long-term return on investment enlarge the class of principals to which managers bear a fiduciary relationship.

Third, the trust that managers hold does not and never has extended to "any means available" to advance the interests of the principals. Both legal and moral constraints must be understood to qualify that trust—even, perhaps, in the name of a larger trust and a more basic fiduciary relationship to the members of society at large.

Objection 5

The power, size, and scale of the modern corporation—domestic as well as international—are awesome. To unleash, even partially, such power from the discipline of the marketplace and the narrow or possibly nonexistent moral purpose implicit in that discipline would be socially dangerous. Had SSC acted in the community to further racial justice, its purposes might have been admirable, but those purposes could have led to a kind of moral imperialism or worse. Suppose SSC had thrown its power behind the Ku Klux Klan.

Reply

This is a very real and important objection. What seems not to be appreciated is the fact that power affects when it is used as well as when it is not used. A decision by SSC not to exercise its economic influence according to "noneconomic" criteria is inevitably a moral decision and just as inevitably affects the community. The issue in the end is not whether corporations (and other organizations) should be "unleashed" to exert moral force in our society but rather how critically and self-consciously they should choose to do so.

The degree of influence enjoyed by an agent, whether a person or an organization, is not so much a factor recommending moral disengagement as a factor demanding a high level of moral awareness. Imperialism is more to be feared when moral reasoning is absent than when it is present. Nor do we suggest that the "discipline of the marketplace" be diluted; rather, we call for it to be supplemented with the discipline of moral reflection.

Objection 6

The idea of moral projection is a useful device for structuring corporate responsibility only if our understanding of moral responsibility at the level of the person is in some sense richer than our understanding of moral responsibility on the level of the organization as a whole. If we are not clear about individual responsibility, the projection is fruitless.

Reply

The objection is well taken. The challenge offered by the idea of moral projection lies in our capacity to articulate criteria or frameworks of reasoning for the morally responsible person. And though such a challenge is formidable, it is not clear that it cannot be met, at least with sufficient consensus to be useful.

For centuries, the study and criticism of frameworks have gone on, carried forward by many disciplines, including psychology, the social sciences, and philosophy. And though it would be a mistake to suggest that any single framework (much less a decision mechanism) has emerged as the right one, it is true that recurrent patterns are discernible and well enough defined to structure moral discussion.

In the body of the article, we spoke of rationality and respect as components of individual responsibility. Further analysis of these components would translate them into social costs and benefits, justice in the distribution of goods and services, basic rights and duties, and fidelity to contracts. The view that pluralism in our society has undercut all possibility of moral agreement is anything but self-evident. Sincere moral disagreement is, of course, inevitable and not clearly lamentable. But a process and a vocab-

ulary for articulating such values as we share is no small step forward when compared with the alternatives. Perhaps in our exploration of the moral projection we might make some surprising and even reassuring discoveries about ourselves.

Objection 7

Why is it necessary to project moral responsibility to the level of the organization? Isn't the task of defining corporate responsibility and business ethics sufficiently discharged if we clarify the responsibilities of men and women in business as individuals? Doesn't ethics finally rest on the honesty and integrity of the individual in the business world?

Reply

Yes and no. Yes, in the sense that the control of large organizations does finally rest in the hands of managers, of men and women. No, in the sense that what is being controlled is a cooperative system for a cooperative purpose. The projection of responsibility to the organization is simply an acknowledgment of the fact that the whole is more than the sum of its parts. Many intelligent people do not an intelligent organization make. Intelligence needs to be structured, organized, divided, and recombined in complex processes for complex purposes.

Studies of management have long shown that the attributes, successes, and failures of organizations are phenomena that emerge from the coordination of persons' attributes and that explanations of such phenomena require categories of analysis and description beyond the level of the individual. Moral responsibility is an attribute that can manifest itself in organizations as surely as competence or efficiency.

Objection 8

Is the frame of reference here proposed intended to replace or undercut the relevance of the "invisible hand" and the "government hand" views, which depend on external controls?

Reply

No. Just as regulation and economic competition are not substitutes for corporate responsibility, so corporate responsibility is not a substitute for law and the market. The imperatives of ethics cannot be relied on—nor have they ever been relied on—without a context of external sanctions. And this is true as much for individuals as for organizations.

This frame of reference takes us beneath, but not beyond, the realm of external systems of rules and incentives and into the thought processes that interpret and respond to the corporation's environment. Morality is more than merely part of that environment. It aims at the projection of conscience, not the enthronement of it in either the state or the competitive process.

The rise of the modern large corporation and the concomitant rise of the professional manager demand a conceptual framework in which these phenomena can be accommodated to moral thought. The principal of moral projection furthers such accommodation by recognizing a new level of agency in society and thus a new level of responsibility.

Objection 9

Corporations have always taken the interests of those outside the corporation into account in the sense that customer relations and public relations generally are an integral part of rational economic decision making. Market signals and social signals that filter through the market mechanism inevitably represent the interests of parties affected by the behavior of the company. What, then, is the point of adding respect to rationality?

Reply

Representing the affected parties solely as economic variables in the environment of the company is treating them as means or resources and not as ends in themselves. It implies that the only voice which affected parties should have in organizational decision making is that of potential buyers, sellers, regulators, or boycotters. Besides, many affected parties may not occupy such roles, and those who do may not be able to signal the organization with messages that effectively represent their stakes in its actions.

To be sure, classical economic theory would have us believe that perfect competition in free markets (with modest adjustments from the state) will result in all relevant signals being "heard," but the abstractions from reality implicit in such theory make it insufficient as a frame of reference for moral responsibility. In a world in which strict self-interest was congruent with the common good, moral responsibility might be unnecessary. We do not, alas, live in such a world.

The element of respect in our analysis of responsibility plays an essential role in ensuring the recognition of unrepresented or underrepresented voices in the decision making of organizations as agents. Showing respect for persons as ends and not mere means to organizational purposes is central to the concept of corporate moral responsibility.

NOTES

1. See John Ladd, "Morality and the Ideal of Rationality in Formal Organizations," *The Monist*, October 1970, p. 499.
2. See William K. Frankena, *Thinking About Morality* (Ann Arbor: University of Michigan Press, 1980), p. 26.
3. See Peter French, "The Corporation as a Moral Person," *American Philosophical Quarterly*, July 1979, p. 207.
4. A process that psychological researchers from Jean Piaget to Lawrence Kohlberg have examined carefully; see Jean Piaget, *The Moral Judgement of the Child* (New York: Free Press, 1965) and Lawrence

Kohlberg, *The Philosophy of Moral Development* (New York: Harper & Row, 1981).
5. See Kenneth R. Andrews, *The Concept of Corporate Strategy,* revised edition (Homewood, Ill.: Dow Jones–Irwin, 1980), p. 99.

Corporate Moral Agency

Peter A. French*

1. In one of his *New York Times* columns of not too long ago Tom Wicker's ire was aroused by a Gulf Oil Corporation advertisement that "pointed the finger of blame" for the energy crisis at all elements of our society (and supposedly away from the oil company). Wicker attacked Gulf Oil as the major, if not the sole, perpetrator of that crisis and virtually every other social ill, with the possible exception of venereal disease. I do not know if Wicker was serious or sarcastic in making all of his charges; I have a sinking suspicion that he was in deadly earnest, but I have doubts as to whether Wicker understands or if many people understand what sense such ascriptions of moral responsibility make when their subjects are corporations. My interest is to argue for a theory that accepts corporations as members of the moral community, of equal standing with the traditionally acknowledged residents—biological human beings—and hence treats Wicker-type responsibility ascriptions as unexceptionable instances of a perfectly proper sort without having to paraphrase them. In short, I shall argue that corporations should be treated as full-fledged moral persons

From "The Corporation as a Moral Person" by Peter A. French. Paper presented at the Ethics and Economics Conference, University of Delaware, November 11, 1977. Copyright © 1977 by Peter A. French. Reprinted by permission of the author.
*Department of Philosophy, Trinity University.

and hence that they can have whatever privileges, rights, and duties as are, in the normal course of affairs, accorded to moral persons.

2. There are at least two significantly different types of responsibility ascriptions that I want to distinguish in ordinary usage (not counting the laudatory recommendation, "He is a responsible lad.") The first type pins responsibility on someone or something, the who-dun-it or what-dun-it sense. Austin has pointed out that it is usually used when an event or action is thought by the speaker to be untoward. (Perhaps we are more interested in the failures rather than the successes that punctuate our lives.)

   The second type of responsibility ascription, parasitic upon the first, involves the notion of accountability.[1] "Having a responsibility" is interwoven with the notion "Having a liability to answer," and having such a liability or obligation seems to imply (as Anscombe has noted[2]) the existence of some sort of authority relationship either between people, or between people and a deity, or in some weaker versions between people and social norms. The kernel of insight that I find intuitively compelling is that for someone to legitimately hold someone else responsible for some event, there must exist or have existed a responsibility relationship between them such that in regard to the event in question the latter was answerable to the former. In other words, a responsibility ascription of the second type is properly uttered by someone Z if he or she can hold X accountable for what he or she has done. Responsibility relationships are created in a multitude of ways, e.g., through promises, contracts, compacts, hirings, assignments, appointments, by agreeing to enter a Rawlsian original position, etc. The "right" to hold responsible is often delegated to third parties; but importantly, in the case of moral responsibility, no delegation occurs because no person is excluded from the relationship: moral responsibility relationships hold reciprocally and without prior agreements among all moral persons. No special arrangement needs to be established between parties for anyone to hold someone morally responsible for his or her acts or, what amounts to the same thing, every person is a party to a responsibility relationship with all other persons as regards the doing or refraining from doing of certain acts: those that take descriptions that use moral notions.

Because our interest is in the criteria of moral personhood and not the content or morality, we need not pursue this idea further. What I have maintained is that moral responsibility, although it is neither contractual nor optional, is not a class apart but an extension of ordinary, garden-variety responsibility. What is needed in regard to the present subject, then, is an account of the requirements in *any* responsibility relationship.[3]

3. A responsibility ascription of the second type amounts to the assertion that the person held responsible is the cause of an event (usually an untoward one) and that the action in question was intended by the subject or that the event was the direct result of an intentional act of the subject. In addition to what it asserts, it implies that the subject is liable to account to the speaker (who the speaker is or what the speaker is, a member of the "moral community," a surrogate for that aggregate). The primary focus of responsibility ascriptions of the second type is on the subject's intentions rather than, though not to the exclusion of, occasions.[4]

4. For a corporation to be treated as a responsible agent it must be the case that some things that happen, some events, are describable in a way that makes certain sentences true, sentences that say that some of the things a corporation does were intended by the corporation itself. That is not accomplished if attributing intentions to a corporation is only a shorthand way of attributing intentions to the biological persons who comprise, for example, its board of directors. If that were to turn out to be the case, then on metaphysical

if not logical grounds there would be no way to distinguish between corporations and mobs. I shall argue, however, that a corporation's CID Structure (the *Corporate Internal Decision* Structure) is the requisite redescription device that licenses the predication of corporate intentionality.

It is obvious that a corporation's doing something involves or includes human beings' doing things and that the human beings who occupy various positions in a corporation usually can be described as having reasons for *their* behavior. In virtue of those descriptions they may be properly held responsible for their behavior, *ceteris paribus*. What needs to be shown is that there is sense in saying that corporations, and not just the people who work in them, have reasons for doing what they do. Typically, we will be told that it is the directors, or the managers, etc. that really have the corporate reasons and desires, etc. and that although corporate actions may not be reducible without remainder, corporate intentions are always reducible to human intentions.

5. Every corporation must have an internal decision structure. The CID Structure has two elements of interest to us here: (1) an organizational or responsibility flow chart that delineates stations and levels within the corporate power structure and (2) corporate decision recognition rule(s) (usually embedded in something called "corporate policy"). The CID Structure is the personnel organization for the exercise of the corporation's power with respect to its ventures, and as such its primary function is to draw experience from various levels of the corporation into a decision-making and ratification process. When operative and properly activated, the CID Structure accomplishes a subordination and synthesis of the intentions and acts of various biological persons into a corporate decision. When viewed in another way the CID Structure licenses the descriptive transformation of events seen under another aspect as the

acts of biological persons (those who occupy various stations on the organizational chart) as corporate acts by exposing the corporate character of those events. A functioning CID Structure *incorporates* acts of biological persons. For illustrative purposes, suppose we imagine that an event E has at least two aspects, that is, can be described in two nonidentical ways. One of those aspects is "Executive X's doing *y*" and one is "Corporation C's doing *z*." The corporate act and the individual act may have different properties: indeed they have different causal ancestors though they are causally inseparable.[5]

Although I doubt he is aware of the metaphysical reading that can be given to this process, J. K. Galbraith rather neatly captures what I have in mind when he writes in his recent popular book on the history of economics:

From [the] interpersonal exercise of power, the interaction...of the participants, comes the *personality* of the corporation.[6]

I take Galbraith here to be quite literally correct, but it is important to spell out how a CID Structure works this "miracle."

In philosophy in recent years we have grown accustomed to the use of games as models for understanding institutional behavior. We all have some understanding of how rules of games make certain descriptions of events possible that would not be so if those rules were nonexistent. The CID Structure of a corporation is a kind of constitutive rule (or rules) analogous to the game rules with which we are familiar. The organization chart of, for example, the Burlington Northern Corporation distinguishes "players" and clarifies their rank and the interwoven lines of responsibility within the corporation. The Burlington chart lists only titles, not unlike King, Queen, Rook, etc. in chess. What it tells us is that anyone holding the title "Executive Vice President for Finance and Administration" stands in a certain relationship to anyone holding the ti-

tle "Director of Internal Audit" and to anyone holding the title "Treasurer," etc. Also it expresses, or maps, the interdependent and dependent relationships that are involved in determinations of corporate decisions and actions. In effect, it tells us what anyone who occupies any of the positions is vis-à-vis the decision structure of the whole. The organizational chart provides what might be called the grammar of corporate decision-making. What I shall call internal recognition rules provide its logic.[7]

Recognition rules are of two sorts. Partially embedded in the organizational chart are the procedural recognitors: we see that decisions are to be reached collectively at certain levels and that they are to be ratified at higher levels (or at inner circles, if one prefers the Galbraithean model). A corporate decision is recognized internally not only by the procedure of its making, but by the policy it instantiates. Hence every corporation creates an image (not to be confused with its public image) or a general policy, what G. C. Buzby of the Chilton Company has called the "basic belief of the corporation,"[8] that must inform its decisions for them to be properly described as being those of that corporation. "The moment policy is side-stepped or violated, it is no longer the policy of that company."[9]

Peter Drucker has seen the importance of the basic policy recognitors in the CID Structure (though he treats matters rather differently from the way I am recommending). Drucker writes:

Because the corporation is an institution it must have a basic policy. For it must subordinate individual ambitions and decisions to the *needs* of the corporation's welfare and survival. That means that it must have a set of principles and a rule of conduct which limit and direct individual actions and behavior.[10]

6. Suppose, for illustrative purposes, we activate a CID Structure in a corporation, Wicker's favorite, the Gulf Oil Corporation. Imag-

ine then that three executives X, Y, and Z have the task of deciding whether or not Gulf Oil will join a world uranium cartel (I trust this may catch Mr. Wicker's attention and hopefully also that of Jerry McAfee, current Gulf Oil Corporation president). X, Y, and Z have before them an Everest of papers that have been prepared by lower echelon executives. Some of the reports will be purely factual in nature, some will be contingency plans, some will be in the form of position papers developed by various departments, some will outline financial considerations, some will be legal opinions, and so on. Insofar as these will all have been processed through Gulf's CID Structure system, the personal reasons, if any, individual executives may have had when writing their reports and recommendations in a specific way will have been diluted by the subordination of individual inputs to peer group input even before X, Y, and Z review the matter. X, Y, and Z take a vote. Their taking of a vote is authorized procedure in the Gulf CID Structure, which is to say that under these circumstances the vote of X, Y, and Z can be redescribed as the corporation's making a decision: that is, the event "X Y Z voting" may be redescribed to expose an aspect otherwise unrevealed, that is quite different from its other aspects, e.g., from X's voting in the affirmative.

But the CID Structure, as already suggested, also provides the grounds in its nonprocedural recognitor for such an attribution of corporate intentionality. Simply, when the corporate act is consistent with the implementation of established corporate policy, then it is proper to describe it as having been done for corporate reasons, as having been caused by a corporate desire coupled with a corporate belief and so, in other words, as corporate intentional.

An event may, under one of its aspects, be described as the conjunctive act "X did a (or as X intentionally did a) and Y did a (or as Y intentionally did a) and Z did a (or as Z in-

tentionally did a)" (where $a =$ voted in the affirmative on the question of Gulf Oil joining the cartel). Given the Gulf CID Structure—formulated in this instance as the conjunction of rules: when the occupants of positions A, B, and C on the organizational chart unanimously vote to do something and if doing that something is consistent with an implementation of general corporate policy, other things being equal, then the corporation has decided to do it for corporate reasons—the event is redescribable as "the Gulf Oil Corporation did j for corporate reasons f" (where j is "decided to join the cartel" and f is any reason [desire + belief] consistent with basic policy of Gulf Oil, e.g., increasing profits) or simply as "Gulf Oil Corporation intentionally did j." This is a rather technical way of saying that in these circumstances the executives voting are, given its CID Structure, also the corporation deciding to do something, and that regardless of the personal reasons the executives have for voting as they do, and even if their reasons are inconsistent with established corporate policy or even if one of them has no reason at all for voting as he does, the corporation still has reasons for joining the cartel; that is, joining is consistent with the inviolate corporate general policies as encrusted in the precedent of previous corporate actions and its statements of purpose as recorded in its certificate of incorporation, annual reports, etc. The corporation's only method of achieving its desires or goals is the activation of the personnel who occupy its various positions. However, if X voted affirmatively purely for reasons of personal monetary gain (suppose he had been bribed to do so), that does not alter the fact that the corporate reason for joining the cartel was to minimize competition and hence pay higher dividends to its shareholders. Corporations have reasons because they have interests in doing those things that are likely to result in realization of their established corporate goals re-

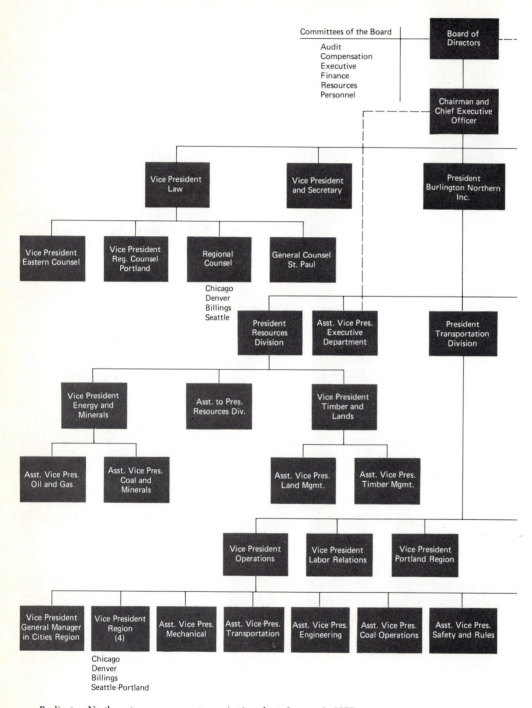

Burlington Northern top management organization chart, January 1, 1977.

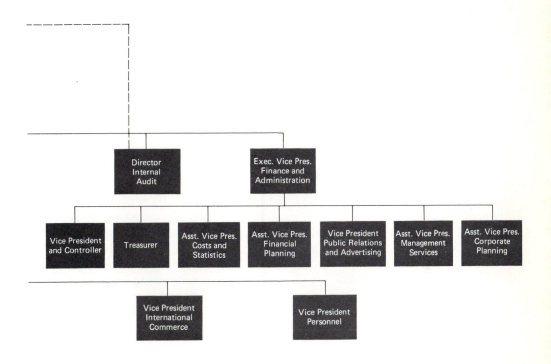

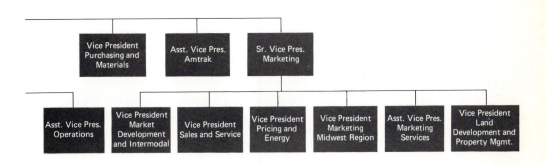

gardless of the transient self-interest of directors, managers, etc. If there is a difference between corporate goals and desires and those of human beings, it is probably that the corporate ones are relatively stable and not very wide ranging, but that is only because corporations can do relatively fewer things than human beings, being confined in action predominately to a limited socioeconomic sphere. It is, of course, in a corporation's interest that its component membership view the corporate purposes as instrumental in the achievement of their own goals. (Financial reward is the most common way this is achieved.)

It will be objected that a corporation's policies reflect only the current goals of its directors. But that is certainly not logically necessary nor is it in practice totally true for most large corporations. Usually, of course, the original incorporators will have organized to further their individual interests and/or to meet goals which they shared. But even in infancy the melding of disparate interests and purposes gives rise to a corporate long-range point of view that is distinct from the intents and purposes of the collection of incorporators viewed individually. Also corporate basic purposes and policies, as already mentioned, tend to be relatively stable when compared to those of individuals and not couched in the kind of language that would be appropriate to individual purposes. Furthermore, as histories of corporations will show, when policies are amended or altered it is usually only peripheral issues and matters of style that are involved. Radical policy alteration constitutes a new corporation. This point is captured in the incorporation laws of such states as Delaware. ("Any power which is not enumerated in the charter or which cannot be inferred from it is *ultra vires*[11] of the corporation.") Obviously underlying the objection is an uneasiness about the fact that corporate intent is dependent upon policy and purpose that is but an artifact of the sociopsy-

chology of a group of biological persons. Corporate intent seems somehow to be a tarnished, illegitimate, offspring of human intent. But this objection is a form of the anthropocentric bias that pervades traditional moral theory. By concentrating on possible descriptions of events and by acknowledging only that the possibility of describing something as an agent depends upon whether or not it can be properly described as having done something for a reason, we avoid the temptation of trying to reduce all agents to human referents.

The CID Structure licenses redescriptions of events as corporate and attributions of corporate intentionality while it does not obscure the private acts of executives, directors, etc. Although X voted to support the joining of the cartel because he was bribed to do so, X did not join the cartel: Gulf Oil Corporation joined the cartel. Consequently, we may say that X did something for which he should be held morally responsible, yet whether or not Gulf Oil Corporation should be held morally responsible for joining the cartel is a question that turns on issues that may be unrelated to X's having accepted a bribe.

Of course Gulf Oil Corporation cannot join the cartel unless X or somebody who occupies position A on the organization chart votes in the affirmative. What that shows, however, is that corporations are collectivities. That should not, however, rule out the possibility of their having metaphysical status and being thereby full-fledged moral persons.

This much seems to me clear: We can describe many events in terms of certain physical movements of human beings and we also can sometimes describe those events as done for reasons by those human beings, but further we also can sometimes describe those events as corporate and still further as done for corporate reasons that are qualitatively different from whatever personal reasons, if any, component members may have for doing what they do.

Corporate agency resides in the possibility of CID Structure licensed redescription of events as corporate intentional. That may still appear to be downright mysterious, although I do not think it is, for human agency, as I have suggested, resides in the possibility of description as well. On the basis of the foregoing analysis, however, I think that grounds have been provided for holding corporations *per se* to account for what they do, for treating them as metaphysical persons *qua* moral persons.

A. A. Berle has written:

The medieval feudal power system set the "lords spiritual" over and against the "lords temporal." These were the men of learning and of the church who in theory were able to say to the greatest power in the world: "You have committed a sin; therefore either you are excommunicated or you must mend your ways." The lords temporal could reply: "I can kill you." But the lords spiritual could retort: "Yes that you can, but you cannot change the philosophical fact." In a sense this is the great lacuna in the economic power system today.[12]

I have tried to fill that gap by providing reasons for thinking that the moral world is not necessarily composed of homogeneous entities. It is sobering to keep in mind that the Gulf Oil Corporation certainly knows what "You are held responsible for payment in full of the amount recorded on your statement" means. I hope I have provided the beginnings of a basis for an understanding of what "The Gulf Oil Corporation should be held responsible for destroying the ecological balance of the bay" means.

NOTES

1. For which there are good lexical grounds. See *Oxford English Dictionary*, especially entry, Accountability.

2. G. E. M. Anscombe, "Modern Moral Philosophy," *Philosophy* 33, 1958, pp. 1–19.

3. For a more detailed discussion, see my *Foundations of Corporate Responsibility*, forthcoming. In that book I show that the notion of the juristic person does not provide a sufficient account. For example, the deceased in a probate case cannot be *held* responsible in the relevant way by anyone, even though the deceased is a juristic person, a subject of rights.

4. L. Austin, "Three Ways of Spilling Ink," in *Philosophical Papers* (Oxford: Clarendon Press, 1970), p. 273. "In considering responsibility, few things are considered more important than to establish whether a man *intended* to do A, or whether he did A intentionally." Moreover, to be the subject of a responsibility ascription of the second type, to be a party in responsibility relationships, hence to be a moral person, the subject must be, at minimum, what I shall call a Davidsonian agent. If corporations are moral persons, they will be non-eliminatable Davidsonian agents. See, for example, Donald Davidson, "Agency," in *Agent, Action, and Reason*, ed. Binkley, Bronaugh and Marros (Toronto: University of Toronto Press, 1971).

5. The causal inseparability of these acts I hope to show is a product of the CID Structure, X's doing y is not the cause of C's doing z nor is C's doing z the cause of X's doing y, although if X's doing y causes Event E then C's doing z causes E and vice versa.

6. John Kenneth Galbraith, *The Age of Uncertainty* (Boston: Houghton Mifflin, 1977), p. 261.

7. By "recognition rule(s)" I mean what Hart, in another context, calls "conclusive affirmative indication" that a decision on act has been made or performed for corporate reasons. H. L. A. Hart, *The Concept of Law* (Oxford: Clarendon Press, 1961), Chap. VI.

8. G. C. Buzby, "Policies—A Guide to What a Company Stands For," *Management Record* (March 1962), p. 5.

9. Ibid.

10. Peter Drucker, *Concept of the Corporation* (New York: John Day Co., 1946/1972), pp. 36–37.

11. Beyond the legal competence.

12. A. A. Berle, "Economic Power and the Free Society," *The Corporate Take-Over*, ed. Andrew Hacker (Garden City, N.Y.: Doubleday, 1964), p. 99.

[*Author's note:* I am grateful to Professors Donald Davidson, J. L. Mackie, Howard Wettstein, and T. E. Uehling for their helpful comments on earlier versions of this paper. I wish also to acknowledge the support of the University of Minnesota Graduate School.]

Corporate Moral Agency: The Case for Anthropological Bigotry

John R. Danley*

In "Corporate Moral Agency,"[1] Peter A. French argues for a position, increasingly popular, which would accept "corporations as members of the moral community, of equal standing with the traditionally acknowledged residents—biological human beings." This is but one implication of accepting the claim that one can legitimately ascribe moral responsibility to corporations. To put the matter somewhat differently, again in French's words, "corporations should be treated as full-fledged moral persons and hence...have whatever privileges, rights, and duties as are, in the normal course of affairs, accorded to moral persons."

Unwilling to rest content with the usual assaults on prejudices against real persons based on race, creed, sex, religion, or national origin, French is among those[2] seeking to open yet another new front. The struggle is now being extended beyond real persons to eliminate discrimination against a particular class of *personae fictae,* fictitious persons, namely the corporation. Before too hastily endorsing this new "corporate" liberation movement let us pause for reflection. If after serious consideration we do vote to admit these peculiar entities into our rather exclusivist and elitist community of moral be-

From *Action and Responsibility: Bowling Green Studies in Applied Philosophy,* vol. II, 1980. Reprinted by permission of the publisher.
*Department of Philosophy, Southern Illinois University.

ings, we should insist on their having equal standing with the rest of us run-of-the-mill featherless bipeds. After all, what moral neighborhood worthy of the name would allow second-class citizens? After examining the case for admission, however, I find myself driven to the uncomfortable position of defending apartheid, biological apartheid that is, of defending anthropological bigotry. I contend that corporations should not be included in the moral community; they should not be granted full-fledged moral status. Within this emotionally charged atmosphere it is tempting to employ the standard *ad hominems* of bigotry ("Think of the value of your property"; or, "Before you know it your daughter will bring a corporation home to dinner"; "What about the children?"; and so forth), but I will attempt to ward off these temptations. My claim is that the corporatist programs of the kind represented by French would seriously disturb the logic of our moral discourse. Indeed, the corporatist position, while offering no substantial advantages, would entail the reduction of biological persons to the status of second-class citizens. Let us turn now to the dispute.

I

There is little doubt that we often speak of corporations as being responsible for this or that sin or charitable act, whether of microscopic or cosmic proportions. The question is what we mean when we speak in that way. Sometimes all we mean is that the corporation is the cause of such and such. In these instances we are isolating a cause for an event or state of affairs, an exercise not much more (or less) troublesome than saying "The icy pavement caused the accident." The debate revolves around a fuller sense of "responsibility," a sense which includes more than the idea of "causing to happen." In this richer sense, we ascribe responsibility only if the event or state of affairs caused was also intended by the agent.

When the concept of responsibility is unpacked in this fashion, the traditionalists appear to have victory already in hand. Whatever else we may say of them, collective entities are surely not the kinds of things capable of intending. Individuals within the corporation can intend, lust, have malice aforethought, and so forth, but the corporation cannot. Traditionalists, like myself, maintain that only persons, i.e., entities with particular physical and mental properties, can be morally responsible. Corporations lack these. For the traditionalists, to speak of corporations being responsible is simply elliptical for speaking of certain individuals within the corporation being responsible. On this point, and perhaps this one alone, I do not believe Milton Friedman[3] to be in error.

Undaunted by this venerable line of reasoning, the corporatists proceed to press their case. Although it is French's view that I am treating, I am concerned not so much with the details of his argument as with the general outlines of the corporatist position. Using French's theory as representative, however, provides us with one of the most forceful, sophisticated theories developed. French has worked for years in the area of collective responsibility.[4] His strategy is to accept the traditionalists' analysis of "responsibility," and then to attempt to show that some sense can be made of ascribing "intentions" to a corporation.

The key to making some sense of corporate "intentions" is what French calls the Corporate Internal Decision Structure, the CID. The CID is that which allows one, "licenses" one, to redescribe the actions of certain individuals within a corporation as actions of the corporation. Although the notion is complicated, a CID contains two elements which are particularly relevant:

1. an organization or responsibility flow chart delineating stations and levels within the corporate power structure and
2. corporate decision recognition rules.

As French puts it, the organizational chart provides the grammar for corporate decision making; the recognition rules provide the logic. The purpose of the organizational chart is to locate which procedures will count as decisions for the corporation, and who may or must participate in those procedures. The recognition rules, we are informed, are of two sorts. The first sort are procedural recognitors, "partially embedded in the organizational chart." What these amount to, it seems, are directives more explicit than those contained in the chart, expanding upon it. The second sort of recognition rules are expressed primarily in corporate policy.

Employing the cumbersome apparatus of the CID, some acts may now be described in two non-identical ways, or so it is claimed.

> One of these...is 'Executive X's doing y' and one is 'Corporation C's doing z.' The corporate act, and the individual act may have different properties; indeed, they have different causal ancestors though they are causally inseparable.

The effect of this, of course, is that when certain individuals as specified by the organizational chart, engage in certain procedures as specified by the organizational chart and some recognition rules, and act in accordance with other recognition rules (corporate policy), then French claims we can redescribe the action as a corporate act, an intentional corporate act. It is critical to the corporatist position that the two descriptions are non-identical. Saying that "Corporation C did z" is not reducible to the statement that "Executives X, Y, and Z, voted to do y," even though y and z are the same. Since they are non-identical the traditionalist is supposedly prevented from ascribing responsibility only to these individuals. The acts of the individuals are necessary for a corporate act but not identical with it.

Like a child with a new toy, one is strongly inclined by the glitter of this technical hardware to dismantle it, to try to find out how it all works, to see whether it really fits together, to see how and whether it can handle hard cases. To be sure, there are some problems which one can detect immediately. Let me mention two. First of all, it is unclear what French means by an organizational chart. Since his examples are those of nice neat black lines and boxes on a page, like the ones found in business textbooks and corporate policy manuals, one is left with the impression that this is what he has in mind. If so, there are severe difficulties. Most everyone is aware of the extent to which corporate reality departs from the ethereal world of black lines and boxes. Will French maintain that any decisions made by the managers of corporations which do not conform to the organizational chart are not decisions of the corporation? Biting the bullet here may be the best course but it is probable that most decisions are not strictly corporate decisions then. Few corporations act at all, if this criterion is used. French needs a more positivistic interpretation[5] of the organizational chart, one which would insure that the flow chart realistically captured the actual procedures and personages holding the powers. The difficulty with this modification, however, is that the CID begins to lose its function as a normative criterion by which to determine which acts are corporate acts and which are not. The positivistic interpretation would mean that a corporate act is whatever some powerful person within the corporation manages to get others in the corporation to perform, or gets others outside to accept as a corporate act. That will not work at all. The CID appears nestled upon the familiar horns of a dilemma. At least more work is necessary here.

There is a second difficulty. A basic component of the CID must be the corporate charter. Recently the general incorporation charters have become little more than blank tablets for the corporation to engage in business for "any lawful purpose," although some aspects of the organizational chart and a few recognition rules are delineated. Even these permissive rules of recognition have pertinence for French. Suppose every aspect of the CID was followed except that the board of directors voted unanimously to engage the corporation in some unlawful activity. According to the charter, a part of the CID, this is not possible. One could not redescribe such an act as a corporate act. This result of this is that corporations can never act illegally. Unlike the Augustinian doctrine that for fallen man it is not possible not to sin, the French doctrine appears to be that for the corporation it is not possible to sin at all.

These are but two of many queries which might be addressed to French's proposal. However, it is not my concern to dwell on such technical points here, lest we be distracted from the larger issue. Suppose, for the sake of argument, that we accept some mode of redescribing individual acts such that one could identify these acts as constituting a corporate intentional act. Accept French's. Would that establish the corporatist case? I think not. French tips his hand, for instance, when he writes that what "needs to be shown is that there is sense in saying that corporations, and not just the people who work in them, have reasons for doing what they do." But, obviously, French needs to show much more. All that is established by a device which redescribes, is that there is *a sense* in saying that corporations have intentions. The significant question is whether that sense of "intend" is the one used by the traditionalists when explicating "responsibility," and when denying that corporations can have intentions. The traditionalists can easily, and quite plausibly, claim that the corporatist is equivocating on "intend." The sense in which a corporation intends is much different from that in which a biological person intends. The corporatist has further laid the foundation for this charge by finding it necessary to construct the apparatus so that the sense of "intend" involved can be made clear. The more clearly this sense of "intend" is articulated, the more clearly it diverges from what we usually mean by "intend." The arbitrariness of constructing a sense of "intend" should be evident when we consider the possibility of ascribing intentions to numerous other entities, such as plants, animals, or machines. One could go to extraordinary lengths to provide a sense for attributing intentionally to many of these. Yet, few would contend that it was very similar to what we mean in attributing "intention" to humans.

Consider a computer programmed to play chess which learns from previous mistakes. There is a sense in which the computer intends to respond P-K4 to my king pawn opening, but is this the same sense of "intend" as when I intended P-K4? Furthermore, even ascribing an intention to the computer by no means entails that we would be ready to ascribe responsibility to it. The point is that it remains for the corporatist to demonstrate the relationship between the sense of "intend" and the sense involved in ascriptions of responsibility to humans. Hence, a rather difficult task remains for the corporatist before the case is made.

II

Thus far I have established only that the corporatist has failed to establish the position. I must admit that I am not entirely enamored of the preceding line of argument. The dispute smacks of the theological controversies concerning whether "wisdom" or "goodness" when attributed to God have the same sense as when predicated of humans. Nonetheless, the corporatist has moved the debate in that direction by attempting to equate two markedly different senses. There are, fortunately, other factors to be considered in evaluating the corporatist position. These factors appear when one expands the focus of attention beyond the narrow conditions for ascribing "responsibility," and begins to examine the concept as it functions in the broader context of moral discourse.

Much hangs in the balance when ascribing "responsibility." Affixing responsibility is a prelude to expressing approbation or disapprobation—praise or blame. When the agent responsible is praised, that is the final move in the moral game. (Morality never pays very well.) But, when the responsibility is affixed and the agent in question is blame worthy, that is far from the end of

the matter. In this case, affixing responsibility and expressing disfavor is itself a prelude to many further permissible or obligatory moves. Minimally, the blameworthy party is expected to express regret or remorse. More importantly, the agent may be required to pay compensation or be subject to punishment. Ascribing responsibility opens the door for these major moral moves. (There are other door openers as well, for example, the notion of cause in strict liability.) Any understanding of the concept of responsibility is incomplete without incorporating the role it plays in relation to these other moral moves. It is this which is lacking from the previous discussion of "intend." Such an analysis cannot be provided here. What can be done, however, is to sketch briefly how ascribing responsibility to corporations effectively blocks these moves, sundering many of the threads which tie "responsibility" so intimately with concepts like remorse, regret, compensation, or punishment. Let me elaborate.

An indication of the consequences of admitting the corporation into the moral community have been foreshadowed by admission into the legal corpus as a person. That legacy is an odious one, marred by an environment within which the corporation has enjoyed nearly all of the benefits associated with personhood while shouldering but few of the burdens or risks. Much the same would result from admission into the moral world. That legacy is not solely to be explained by jaundiced justices or bad judicial judgments, but is a natural consequence of attempting to pretend that the corporation is just another pretty face. While the law early began holding the corporation liable (read: responsible) for certain specified acts, and the scope of things for which it was liable has dramatically increased over the years, there has been a hesitancy to judge that corporations could be subject to most criminal statutes. One of the major stumbling blocks was just the one which is the subject of this paper. It was clear that many of the criminal statutes required criminal intent, or a criminal state of mind, and unable to locate the corporate mind, it was judged that the corporation was not subject to these. The relevance of proposals such as French's is that the justices would now have a method for determining when the corporation acts with intent, with malice aforethought, with premeditation or out of passion. What I am anxious to bring to light, however, is that these proposals offer no advantage over the traditionalist view and in fact create further problems. Consider now the moral moves involved in extracting compensation from, or punishing, a guilty person. How is one to make these moral moves against a corporate person? One cannot. An English jurist put the point well in an often quoted quip to the effect that corporations have no pants to kick, no soul to damn. We may concur with the sentiment of that jurist who concluded that "by God they ought to have both," but they have neither, although French has given them a surrogate soul, the CID.

The corporation cannot be kicked, whipped, imprisoned, or hanged by the neck until dead. Only individuals of the corporation can be punished. What of punishment through the pocketbook, or extracting compensation for a corporate act? Here too, the corporation is not punished, and does not pay the compensation. Usually one punishes the stockholders who in the present corporate climate have virtually no control over corporate actions. Or, if the corporation can pass on the cost of a fiscal punishment or compensation, it is in the end the consumer who pays for the punishment or compensation. If severe enough, hitting the pocketbook may result in the reduction of workforce, again resting the burden on those least deserving, more precisely, on those not responsible at all. Sooner or later, usually sooner, someone hits upon the solution of punishing those individuals of the corporation most directly responsible for the corporate act. There are also moral difficulties associated with this alternative. For example, many top executives are protected through insurance policies, part of the perks of the job.

That would be satisfactory if the intent is simply to compensate, but it neutralizes any deterrent or retributive effect. But let us pass over these considerations and examine more closely these recommendations to "go inside" the corporation to punish an individual, whether stockholder, employee, agent, manager, or director of the corporation.

For the traditionalist there is little difficulty. The traditionalist recognizes the corporation as a legal fiction which for better or worse may have equal protection under the law of other persons, but the traditionalist may accept those legal trappings as at best a useful way of treating the corporation for legal purposes. For the traditionalist it makes moral sense for the law to go inside the corporation. After all, morally the corporation is not responsible; only individuals are. As long as those within the corporation pay for the deed, there is no theoretical difficulty.

What of the corporatist's position? The single advantage is that the adoption of that position would mean that some sense could be made of pointing an accusing finger or raising a fist in moral outrage at a fictitious person, a behavior which might otherwise appear not only futile but ridiculous. In the new corporatist scheme the behavior would no longer be ridiculous, only futile. The disadvantages, on the other hand, are apparent when one attempts to follow the responsibility assignment with the normally attendant moral moves as I have just shown. Either those moves are blocked entirely, since one may find no method by which to punish, or the moves are diverted away from the genuine culprit (the fictitious moral agent) and directed toward someone inside the corporation (non-fictitious moral agent). Either alternative is unacceptable. The former would entail that some citizens of the moral community, namely corporate persons, were not subject to the full obligations of membership. That reduces biological members to the status of second-class citizens, shouldering as they do all the burdens. The latter alternative, "going inside," is equally offensive. This alternative means that biological agents are sacrificed vicariously for the sins of the corporation. This solution not only reduces the biological agents to second-class citizens, but would make scapegoats or worse, sacrificial lambs, of them. Thus would the admission of the corporation into the moral community threaten to disturb the logic associated with the ascription of responsibility.

In addition to these problems, the corporatists face other theoretical obstacles. It is not clear that "going inside" a corporation is often, if ever, intelligible, given the analysis of a corporate act. To counter the traditionalist's claim that only individuals are responsible, French claims that the corporate act is not identical with the acts of individuals in the corporation. Given this, how is it possible now to reverse that claim and hold individuals responsible for something which they did not do? All they did at most was to vote for the corporation to do something, or to pay for something to be done on behalf of the corporation. The claim that individual acts and corporate acts are not identical opens the door to criminalless crime, a possibility admitted openly by French in another earlier paper. French there notes that a collective entity may be responsible yet no individual in that collectivity be responsible. Far from being an extreme case, that outcome may include all corporate acts. As mentioned above, such an alternative is unacceptable. But, again, can one make intelligible going inside to make one or more individuals responsible? In order to do so the corporatist must shift ground and concede that the individual acts and the corporate acts are identical, or perhaps that the individuals, by voting on a course of illegal or immoral action, coerced the hapless corporation to go along with the deed.

III

Although I have offered what I take to be a satisfactory defense of the traditionalist position, I would like to close by suggesting an alternative model for viewing the corporation. An alternative is needed because the corporatist's model has largely succeeded in warping many of our intuitions and is reinforced not only by legal idioms, but by managerial vocabulary. In many a corporatist's eye the corporation is an organism, and perhaps even much like a biological person. It has a brain, nerve receptors, muscle, it moves, reproduces, expands, develops, grows, in some periods the "fat is cut off," processes information, makes decisions, and so on. It adjusts to the environment. Such a metaphor may be useful but we have now begun to be victimized by the metaphorical model. Unfortunately, reformers have found it useful to accept that language and that model. It is useful to personify and then to vilify. The model, I fear, stands behind many attempts to endow the corporation with moral agency and personhood.

A more adequate model, especially for those who are reform minded, I would maintain provides a different perspective from which to view contemporary trends. The corporation is more like a machine than an organism.[6] Like machines they are human inventions, designed by humans, modified by humans, operated by humans. Like many machines they are controlled by the few for the benefit of the few. They are no longer simple, easily understandable, organizations, but as complicated as the latest piece of electronic hardware. It takes years of training to learn how to operate and direct one. Like machines they are created, yet they create and shape humans.

If a complicated machine got out of hand and ravaged a community, there seems something perverse about expressing our moral outrage and indignation to the machine. More appropriately, our fervor should be addressed to the operators and to the designers of the machine. They, not the machines, are morally responsible. To ascribe responsibility to such machines, no matter how complicated, is tantamount to mistaking the created for the creator. This mystification is a contemporary form of animism. Such is the case for anthropological bigotry.

NOTES

1. The basic argument of the article appears in a more detailed version in French's forthcoming book *Foundations of Corporate Responsibility*. I have not had the opportunity to consult that book. See also his article in the *American Philosophical Quarterly*, Vol. 13, No. 3, 1976.

2. Of those who apparently espouse this view to some degree are Norman Bowie and Tom L. Beauchamp in *Ethical Theory and Business* (Englewood Cliffs, N.J., Prentice-Hall, Inc., 1979) e.g. Chapter 1 and comments on page 128 and Christopher Stone in *Where The Law Ends* (Harper Colophon, New York, 1975).

3. See *Capitalism and Freedom,* (Chicago, IL, University of Chicago Press, 1962), pp. 133–136.

4. One of French's earliest works is "Morally Blaming Whole Populations," which appears in *Philosophy, Morality, and International Affairs* (New York, Oxford University Press, 1974) edited by Virginia Held et al., pp. 266–285.

5. The positive interpretation is suggested by, among other things, French's references to Austin and H. L. A. Hart. The distinction between organizational chart and recognition rules also resembles the positivistic distinction between secondary and primary rules.

6. Although I do not follow Ladd's argument, one good example of taking this alternative model seriously is demonstrated in his "Morality and the Ideal of Rationality in Formal Organizations," in *The Monist,* Vol. 54 (October 1970), pp. 488–516.

QUESTIONS FOR DISCUSSION

1. What do Goodpaster and Matthews mean when they say that the "invisible hand" view and the "hand of government" view of the corporation are "conceptually similar"? How does their proposed "hand of management" view differ?

2. Consolidated Industries, Inc., a chemical company, has a company policy containing the clause, "Consolidated Industries, Inc., regards the safety of employees, consumers, and the surrounding community as of paramount importance. All reasonable precautions must be taken to make the operation of our plants as safe as possible." One day, carelessness at Consolidated's Topeka, Alabama, plant results in an explosion and a chemical leak, causing injury and death to hundreds of people. Under French's view, is Consolidated Industries morally responsible for the action? Would Consolidated Industries be morally responsible if its company policy were different? How would Danley respond to these questions?

CHAPTER 6

Governance and Structure

READINGS FOR CHAPTER SIX

Section A   Board of Directors

Ralph Nader, Mark Green and Joel Seligman
Who Rules The Corporation?
210

Irving S. Shapiro
Power and Accountability: The Changing Role of the Corporate Board of Directors
219

Harold S. Geneen
Why Directors Can't Protect the Shareholders
226

Section B   Takeovers and Corporate Restructuring

Michael C. Jensen
Takeovers: Folklore and Science
231

Robert Kuttner
The Truth about Corporate Raiders
240

Section A
Board of Directors

Who Rules the Corporation?

Ralph Nader *
Mark Green †
Joel Seligman ‡

All modern state corporation statutes describe a common image of corporate governance, an image pyramidal in form. At the base of the pyramid are the shareholders or owners of the corporation. Their ownership gives them the right to elect representatives to direct the corporation and to approve fundamental corporate actions such as mergers or bylaw amendments. The intermediate level is held by the board of directors, who are required by a provision common to nearly every state corporation law "to manage the business and affairs of the corporation." On behalf of the shareholders, the directors are expected to select and dismiss corporate officers; to approve important financial decisions; to distribute profits; and to see that accurate periodic reports are forwarded to the shareholders. Finally, at the apex of the pyramid are the corporate officers. In the eyes of the law, the officers are the employees of the shareholder owners. Their authority is limited to those responsibilities which the directors delegate to them.

In reality, this legal image is virtually a myth. In nearly every large American business corporation, there exists a management autocracy. One

man—variously titled the President, or the Chairman of the Board, or the Chief Executive Officer—or a small coterie of men rule the corporation. Far from being chosen by the directors to run the corporation, this chief executive or executive clique chooses the board of directors and, with the acquiescence of the board, controls the corporation.

The common theme of many instances of mismanagement is a failure to restrain the power of these senior executives. A corporate chief executive's decisions to expand, merge, or even violate the law can often be made without accountability to outside scrutiny. There is, for example, the detailed disclosures of the recent bribery cases. Not only do these reports suggest how widespread corporate foreign and domestic criminality has become; they also provide a unique study in the pathology of American corporate management.

At Gulf Corporation, three successive chief executive officers were able to pay out over $12.6 million in foreign and domestic bribes over a 15-year period without the knowledge of "outside" or non-employee directors on the board. At Northrop, chairman Thomas V. Jones and vice president James Allen were able to create and fund the Economic and Development Corporation, a separate Swiss company, and pay $750,000 to Dr. Hubert Weisbrod, a Swiss attorney, to stimulate West German jet sales without the knowledge of the board or, apparently, other senior executives. At 3M, chairman Bert Cross and finances vice president Irwin Hansen ordered the company insurance department to pay out $509,000 for imaginary insurance and the bookkeeper to fraudulently record the payments as a "necessary and proper" business expense for tax purposes. Ashland Oil Corporation's chief executive officer, Orwin E. Atkins, involved at least eight executives in illegally generating and distributing $801,165 in domestic political contributions, also without question.

The legal basis for such a consolidation of power in the hands of the corporation's chief ex-

Excerpted from Ralph Nader, Mark Green, and Joel Seligman, *Taming the Giant Corporation* (New York: W. W. Norton, 1976). Copyright © 1976 by Ralph Nader. Reprinted by permission.

*Founder of Public Citizen, Inc. and Center for the Study of Responsive Law.

†President, Democracy Project.

‡School of Law, University of Michigan.

ecutive is the proxy election. Annually the shareholders of each publicly held corporation are given the opportunity of either attending a meeting to nominate and elect directors or returning proxy cards to management or its challengers signing over their right to vote. Few shareholders personally attend meetings. Sylvan Silver, a Reuters correspondent who covers over 100 Wilmington annual meetings each year, described representative 1974 meetings in an interview: At Cities Service Company, the 77th largest industrial corporation with some 135,000 shareholders, 25 shareholders actually attended the meeting; El Paso Natural Gas with 125,000 shareholders had 50 shareholders; at Coca Cola, the 69th largest corporation with 70,000 shareholders, 25 shareholders attended the annual meeting; at Bristol Meyers with 60,000 shareholders a like 25 shareholders appeared. Even "Campaign GM," the most publicized shareholder challenge of the past two decades, attracted no more than 3,000 of General Motors' 1,400,000 shareholders, or roughly two-tenths of one percent.

Thus, corporate directors are almost invariably chosen by written proxies. Yet management so totally dominates the proxy machinery that corporate elections have come to resemble the Soviet Union's euphemistic "Communist ballot"—that is, a ballot which lists only one slate of candidates. Although federal and state laws require the annual performance of an elaborate series of rituals pretending there is "corporate democracy," in 1973, 99.7 percent of the directorial elections in our largest corporations were uncontested.

THE BEST DEMOCRACY MONEY CAN BUY

The key to management's hegemony is money. Effectively, only incumbent management can nominate directors—because it has a nearly unlimited power to use corporate funds to win board elections while opponents must prepare separate proxies and campaign literature entirely at their own expense.

There is first management's power to print and post written communications to shareholders. In a typical proxy contest, management will "follow up" its initial proxy solicitation with a bombardment of five to ten subsequent mailings. As attorneys Edward Aranow and Herb Einhorn explain in their treatise, *Proxy Contests for Corporate Control*:

> Perhaps the most important aspect of the follow-up letter is its role in the all-important efforts of a soliciting group to secure the *latest-dated* proxy from a stockholder. It is characteristic of every proxy contest that a large number of stockholders will sign and return proxies to one faction and then change their minds and want to have their stock used for the opposing faction.

The techniques of the Northern States Power Company in 1973 are illustrative. At that time, Northern States Power Company voluntarily employed cumulative voting, which meant that only 7.2 percent of outstanding shares was necessary to elect one director to Northern's 14-person board. Troubled by Northern's record on environmental and consumer issues, a broadly based coalition of public interest groups called the Citizens' Advocate for Public Utility Responsibility (CAPUR) nominated Ms. Alpha Snaby, a former Minnesota state legislator, to run for director. These groups then successfully solicited the votes of over 14 percent of all shareholders, or more than twice the votes necessary to elect her to the board.

Northern States then bought back the election. By soliciting proxies a second, and then a third time, the Power Company was able to persuade (or confuse) the shareholders of 71 percent of the 2.8 million shares cast for Ms. Snaby to change their votes.

Larger, more experienced corporations are usually less heavyhanded. Typically, they will begin a proxy campaign with a series of "build-up" letters preliminary to the first proxy solicitation. In Campaign GM, General Motors elevated this strategy to a new plateau by encasing the Project on Corporate Responsibility's single

100-word proxy solicitation within a 21-page booklet specifically rebutting each of the Project's charges. The Project, of course, could never afford to respond to GM's campaign. The postage costs of soliciting GM's 1,400,000 shareholders alone would have exceeded $100,000. The cost of printing a document comparable to GM's 21-page booklet, mailing it out, accompanied by a proxy statement, a proxy card, and a stamped return envelope to each shareholder might have run as high as $500,000.

Nor is it likely that the Project or any other outside shareholder could match GM's ability to hire "professional" proxy solicitors such as Georgeson & Company, which can deploy up to 100 solicitors throughout the country to personally contact shareholders, give them a campaign speech, and urge them to return their proxies. By daily tabulation of returned proxies, professional solicitors are able to identify on a day-by-day basis the largest blocks of stock outstanding which have yet to return a favorable vote.

THE STATE OF THE BOARD

But does not the board of directors with its sweeping statutory mandate "to manage the business and affairs of every corporation" provide an internal check on the power of corporate executives? No. Long ago the grandiloquent words of the statutes ceased to have any operative meaning. "Directors," William O. Douglas complained in 1934, "do not direct." "[T]here is one thing all boards have in common, regardless of their legal position," Peter Drucker has written. *"They do not function."* In Robert Townsend's tart analysis, "[M]ost big companies have turned their boards of directors into nonboards.... In the years that I've spent on various boards I've never heard a single suggestion from a director (made as a director *at* a board meeting) that produced any result at all."

Recently these views are corroborated by Professor Myles Mace of the Harvard Business School, the nation's leading authority on the per-

formance of boards of directors. In *Directors—Myth and Reality,* Mace summarized the results of hundreds of interviews with corporate officers and directors.

Directors do not establish the basic objectives, corporate strategies or broad policies of large and medium-size corporations, Mace found. Management creates the policies. The board has a right of veto but rarely exercises it. As one executive said, "Nine hundred and ninety-nine times out of a thousand, the board goes along with management...." Or another, "I can't think of a single time when the board has failed to support a proposed policy of management or failed to endorse the recommendation of management."

The board does not select the president or other chief executive officers. "What is perhaps the most common definition of a function of the board of directors—namely, to select the president—was found to be the greatest myth," reported Mace. "The board of directors in most companies, except in a crisis, does not select the president. The president usually chooses the man who succeeds him to that position, and the board complies with the legal amenities in endorsing and voting his election." A corporate president agreed: "The former company president tapped me to be president, and I assure you that I will select my successor when the time comes." Even seeming exceptions such as RCA's 1975 ouster of Robert Sarnoff frequently turn out to be at the instigation of senior operating executives rather than an aroused board.

The board's role as disciplinarian of the corporation is more apparent than real. As the business-supported Conference Board conceded, "One of the most glaring deficiencies attributed to the corporate board...is its failure to monitor and evaluate the performance of the chief executive in a concrete way." To cite a specific example, decisions on executive compensation are made by the president—with perfunctory board approval in most situations. In the vast majority of corporations, Professor Mace found, the compensation committee, and the board which approves the recommendations of the compensation committee, "are not decision-making bodies."

Exceptions to this pattern become news events. In reporting on General Motors' 1971 annual shareholders' meeting, the *Wall Street Journal* noted that, "The meeting's dramatic highlight was an impassioned and unprecedented speech by the Rev. Leon Sullivan, GM's recently appointed Negro director, supporting the Episcopal Church's efforts to get the company out of South Africa. It was the first time that a GM director had ever spoken against management at an annual meeting." Now Rev. Sullivan is an unusual outside director, being General Motor's first black director and only "public interest" director. But what makes Leon Sullivan most extraordinary is that he was the first director in *any* major American corporation to come out publicly against his own corporation when its operations tended to support apartheid.

REVAMPING THE BOARD

The modern corporation is akin to a political state in which all powers are held by a single clique. The senior executives of a large firm are essentially not accountable to any other officials within the firm. These are precisely the circumstances that, in a democratic political state, require a separation of powers into different branches of authority. As James Madison explained in the *Federalist No. 47*:

> The accumulation of all powers, legislative, executive, and judiciary, in the same hands, whether of one, a few or many, and whether hereditary, self-appointed, or elective, may justly be pronounced the very definition of tyranny. Were the federal constitution, therefore, really chargeable with this accumulation of power, or with a mixture of powers, having a dangerous tendency to such an accumulation, no further arguments would be necessary to inspire a universal reprobation of the system.

A similar concern over the unaccountability of business executives historically led to the elevation of a board of directors to review and check the actions of operating management. As a practical matter, if corporate governance is to be reformed, it must begin by returning the board to this historical role. The board should serve as an internal auditor of the corporations, responsible for constraining executive management from violations of law and breach of trust. Like a rival branch of government, the board's function must be defined as separate from operating management. Rather than pretending directors can "manage" the corporation, the board's role as disciplinarian should be clearly described. Specifically, the board of directors should:

- establish and monitor procedures that assure that operating executives are informed of and obey applicable federal, state, and local laws;
- approve or veto all important executive management business proposals such as corporate by-laws, mergers, or dividend decisions;
- hire and dismiss the chief executive officer and be able to disapprove the hiring and firing of the principal executives of the corporation; and
- report to the public and the shareholders how well the corporation has obeyed the law and protected the shareholders' investment.

It is not enough, however, to specify what the board should do. State corporations statutes have long provided that "the business and affairs of a corporation shall be managed by a board of directors," yet it has been over a century since the boards of the largest corporations have actually performed this role. To reform the corporation, a federal chartering law must also specify the manner in which the board performs its primary duties.

First, to insure that the corporation obeys federal and state laws, the board should designate executives responsible for compliance with these laws and require periodic signed reports describing the effectiveness of compliance procedures.

Mechanisms to administer spot checks on compliance with the principal statutes should be created. Similar mechanisms can insure that corporate "whistle blowers" and nonemployee sources may communicate to the board—in private and without fear of retaliation—knowledge of violations of law.

Second, the board should actively review important executive business proposals to determine their full compliance with law, to preclude conflicts of interest, and to assure that executive decisions are rational and informed of all foreseeable risks and costs. But even though the board's responsibility here is limited to approval or veto of executive initiatives, it should proceed in as well-informed a manner as practicable. To demonstrate rational business judgment, the directorate should require management "to prove its case." It should review the studies upon which management relied to make a decision, require management to justify its decision in terms of costs or rebutting dissenting views, and, when necessary, request that outside experts provide an independent business analysis.

Only with respect to two types of business decisions should the board exceed this limited review role. The determination of salary, expense, and benefit schedules inherently possesses such obvious conflicts of interest for executives that only the board should make these decisions. And since the relocation of principal manufacturing facilities tends to have a greater effect on local communities than any other type of business decision, the board should require management to prepare a "community impact statement." This public report would be similar to the environmental impact statements presently required by the National Environmental Policy Act. It would require the corporation to state the purpose of a relocation decision; to compare feasible alternative means; to quantify the costs to the local community; and to consider methods to mitigate these costs. Although it would not prevent a corporation from making a profit-maximizing decision, it would require the corporation to minimize the costs of relocation decisions to local communities.

To accomplish this restructuring of the board requires the institutionalization of a new profession: the full-time "professional" director. Corporate scholars frequently identify William O. Douglas' 1940 proposal for "salaried, professional experts [who] would bring a new responsibility and authority to directorates and a new safety to stockholders" as the origin of the professional director idea. More recently, corporations including Westinghouse and Texas Instruments have established slots on their boards to be filled by full-time directors. Individuals such as Harvard Business School's Myles Mace and former Federal Reserve Board chairman William McChesney Martin consider their own thoroughgoing approach to boardroom responsibilities to be that of a "professional" director.

To succeed, professional directors must put in the substantial time necessary to get the job done. One cannot monitor the performance of Chrysler's or Gulf's management at a once-a-month meeting; those firms' activities are too sweeping and complicated for such ritual oversight. The obvious minimum here is an adequate salary to attract competent persons to work as full-time directors and to maintain the independence of the board from executive management.

The board must also be sufficiently staffed. A few board members alone cannot oversee the activities of thousands of executives. To be able to appraise operating management, the board needs a trim group of attorneys, economists, and labor and consumer advisors who can analyze complex business proposals, investigate complaints, spot-check accountability, and frame pertinent inquiries.

The board also needs timely access to relevant corporate data. To insure this, the board should be empowered to nominate the corporate financial auditor, select the corporation's counsel, compel the forwarding and preservation of corporate records, require all corporate executives or representatives to answer fully all board questions respecting corporate operations, and dismiss any executive or representative who fails to do so.

This proposed redesign for corporate democracy attempts to make executive management accountable to the law and shareholders without diminishing its operating efficiency. Like a judiciary within the corporation, the board has ultimate powers to judge and sanction. Like a legislature, it oversees executive activity. Yet executive management substantially retains its powers to initiate and administer business operations. The chief executive officer retains control over the organization of the executive hierarchy and the allocation of the corporate budget. The directors are given ultimate control over a narrow jurisdiction: Does the corporation obey the law, avoid exploiting consumers or communities, and protect the shareholders' investment? The executive contingent retains general authority for all corporate operations.

No doubt there will be objections that this structure is too expensive or that it will disturb the "harmony" of executive management. But it is unclear that there would be any increased cost in adopting an effective board. The true cost to the corporation could only be determined by comparing the expense of a fully paid and staffed board with the savings resulting from the elimination of conflicts of interest and corporate waste. In addition, if this should result in a slightly increased corporate expense, the appropriateness must be assessed within a broader social context: should federal and state governments or the corporations themselves bear the primary expense of keeping corporations honest? In our view, this cost should be placed on the corporations as far as reasonably possible.

It is true that an effective board will reduce the "harmony" of executive management in the sense that the power of the chief executive or seniors executives will be subject to knowledgeable review. But a board which monitors rather than rubber-stamps management is exactly what is necessary to diminish the unfettered authority of the corporate chief executive or ruling clique. The autocratic power these individuals presently possess has proven unacceptably dangerous: it has led to recurring violations of law, conflicts of interest, productive inefficiency, and pervasive harm to consumers, workers, and the community environment. Under normal circumstances there should be a healthy friction between operating executives and the board to assure that the wisest possible use is made of corporate resources. When corporate executives are breaking the law, there should be no "harmony" whatsoever.

ELECTION OF THE BOARD

Restructuring the board is hardly likely to succeed if boards remain as homogeneously white, male, and narrowly oriented as they are today. Dissatisfaction with current selection of directors is so intense that analysts of corporate governance, including Harvard Law School's Abram Chayes, Yale political scientist Robert Dahl, and University of Southern California Law School Professor Christopher Stone, have each separately urged that the starting point of corporate reform should be to change the way in which the board is elected.

Professor Chayes, echoing John Locke's principle that no authority is legitimate except that granted "the consent of the governed," argues that employees and other groups substantially affected by corporate operations should have a say in its governance:

> Shareholder democracy, so-called, is misconceived because the shareholders are not the governed of the corporations whose consent must be sought.... Their interests are protected if financial information is made available, fraud and overreaching are prevented, and a market is maintained in which their shares may be sold. A priori, there is no reason for them to have any voice, direct or representational, in [corporate decision making]. They are no more affected than nonshareholding neighbors by these decisions....

A more spacious conception of 'membership,' and one closer to the facts of corporate life, would include all those having a relation of sufficient intimacy with the corporation or subject to its powers in a sufficiently specialized way. Their rightful share in decisions and the exercise of corporate power would be exercised through an institutional arrangement appropriately designed to represent the interests of a constituency of members having a significant common relation to the corporation and its power.

Professor Dahl holds a similar view: "[W]hy should people who own shares be given the privileges of citizenship in the government of the firm when citizenship is denied to other people who also make vital contributions to the firm?" he asks rhetorically. "The people I have in mind are, of course, employees and customers, without whom the firm could not exist, and the general public, without whose support for (or acquiescence in) the myriad protections and services of the state the firm would instantly disappear...." Yet Dahl finds proposals for interest group representation less desirable than those for worker self-management. He also suggests consideration of codetermination statutes such as those enacted by West Germany and ten other European and South American countries under which shareholders and employees separately elect designated portions of the board.

From a different perspective, Professor Stone has recommended that a federal agency appoint "general public directors" to serve on the boards of all the largest industrial and financial firms. In certain extreme cases such as where a corporation repeatedly violates the law, Stone recommends that the federal courts appoint "special public directors" to prevent further delinquency.

There are substantial problems with each of those proposals. It seems impossible to design a general "interest group" formula which will assure that all affected constituencies of large industrial corporations will be represented and that all constituencies will be given appropriate weight. Even if such a formula could be designed, however, there is the danger that consumer or community or minority or franchisee representatives would become only special pleaders for their constituents and otherwise lack the loyalty or interest to direct generally. This defect has emerged in West Germany under codetermination. Labor representatives apparently are indifferent to most problems of corporate management that do not directly affect labor. They seem as deferential to operating executive management as present American directors are. Alternatively, federally appointed public directors might be frozen out of critical decision-making by a majority of "privately" elected directors, or the appointing agency itself might be biased.

Nonetheless, the essence of the Chayes-Dahl-Stone argument is well taken. The boards of directors of most major corporations are, as CBS's Dan Rather criticized the original Nixon cabinet, too much like "twelve grey-haired guys named George." The quiescence of the board has resulted in important public and, for that matter, shareholder concerns being ignored.

An important answer is structural. The homogeneity of the board can only be ended by giving to each director, in addition to a general duty to see that the corporation is profitably administered, a separate oversight responsibility, a separate expertise, and a separate constituency so that each important public concern would be guaranteed at least one informed representative on the board. There might be nine corporate directors, each of whom is elected to a board position with one of the following oversight responsibilities:

1. Employee welfare
2. Consumer protection
3. Environmental protection and community relations
4. Shareholder rights
5. Compliance with law
6. Finances
7. Purchasing and marketing

8. Management efficiency
9. Planning and research

By requiring each director to balance responsibility for representing a particular social concern against responsibility for the overall health of the enterprise, the problem of isolated "public" directors would be avoided. No individual director is likely to be "frozen out" of collegial decision-making because all directors would be of the same character. Each director would spend the greater part of his or her time developing expertise in a different area; each director would have a motivation to insist that a different aspect of a business decision be considered. Yet each would simultaneously be responsible for participating in all board decisions, as directors now are. So the specialized area of each director would supplement but not supplant the director's general duties.

To maintain the independence of the board from the operating management it reviews also requires that each federally chartered corporation shall be directed by a purely "outside" board. No executive, attorney, representative, or agent of a corporation should be allowed to serve simultaneously as a director of that same corporation. Directorial and executive loyalty should be furthered by an absolute prohibition of interlocks. No director, executive, general counsel, or company agent should be allowed to serve more than one corporation subject to the Federal Corporate Chartering Act.

Several objections may be raised. First, how can we be sure that completely outside boards will be competent? Corporate campaign rules should be redesigned to emphasize qualifications. This will allow shareholder voters to make rational decisions based on information clearly presented to them. It is also a fair assumption that shareholders, given an actual choice and role in corporate governance, will want to elect the men and women most likely to safeguard their investments.

A second objection is that once all interlocks are proscribed and a full-time outside board required, there will not be enough qualified directors to staff all major firms. This complaint springs from that corporate mentality which, accustomed to 60-year-old white male bankers and businessmen as directors, makes the norm a virtue. In fact, if we loosen the reins on our imagination, America has a large, rich, and diverse pool of possible directorial talent from academics and public administrators and community leaders to corporate and public interest lawyers.

But directors should be limited to four two-year terms so that boards do not become stale. And no director should be allowed to serve on more than one board at any one time. Although simultaneous service on two or three boards might allow key directors to "pollinize" directorates by comparing their different experiences, this would reduce their loyalty to any one board, jeopardize their ability to fully perform their new directorial responsibilities, and undermine the goal of opening up major boardrooms to as varied a new membership as is reasonable.

The shareholder electoral process should be made more democratic as well. Any shareholder or allied shareholder group which owns .1 percent of the common voting stock in the corporation or comprises 100 or more individuals and does not include a present executive of the corporation, nor act for a present executive, may nominate up to three persons to serve as directors. This will exclude executive management from the nomination process. It also increases the likelihood of a diverse board by preventing any one or two sources from proposing all nominees. To prevent frivolous use of the nominating power, this proposal establishes a minimum shareownership condition.

Six weeks prior to the shareholders' meeting to elect directors, each shareholder should receive a ballot and a written statement on which each candidate for the board sets forth his or her qualifications to hold office and purposes for seeking office. All campaign costs would be borne by the corporation. These strict campaign and funding rules will assure that all nominees will have an equal opportunity to be judged by the shareholders. By preventing directorates from being bought, these provisions will require board elections to be conducted solely on the merit of the candidates.

Finally, additional provisions will require cumulative voting and forbid "staggered" board elections. Thus any shareholder faction capable of jointly voting approximately 10 percent of the total number of shares cast may elect a director.

A NEW ROLE FOR SHAREHOLDERS

The difficulty with this proposal is the one that troubled Juvenal two millennia ago: *Quis custodiet ipsos custodes,* or Who shall watch the watchmen? Without a full-time body to discipline the board, it would be so easy for the board of directors and executive management to become friends. Active vigilance could become routinized into an uncritical partnership. The same board theoretically elected to protect shareholder equity and internalize law might instead become management's lobbyist.

Relying on shareholders to discipline directors may strike many as a dubious approach. Historically, the record of shareholder participation in corporate governance has been an abysmal one. The monumental indifference of most shareholders is worse than that of sheep; sheep at least have some sense of what manner of ram they follow. But taken together, the earlier proposals—an outside, full-time board, nominated by rival shareholder groups and voted on by beneficial owners—will increase involvement by shareholders. And cumulative voting insures that an aroused minority of shareholders—even one as small as 9 or 10 percent of all shareholders—shall have the opportunity to elect at least one member of the board.

But that alone is hardly sufficient. At a corporation the size of General Motors, an aggregation of 10 percent of all voting stock might require the allied action of over 200,000 individuals—which probably could occur no

more than once in a generation. To keep directors responsive to law and legitimate public concerns requires surer and more immediate mechanisms. In a word, it requires arming the victims of corporate abuses with the powers to swiftly respond to them. For only those employees, consumers, racial or sex minorities, and local communities harmed by corporate depradations can be depended upon to speedily complain. By allowing any victim to become a shareholder and by permitting any shareholder to have an effective voice, there will be the greatest likelihood of continuing scrutiny of the corporation's directorate.

Shareholders are not the only ones with an incentive to review decisions of corporate management; nor, as Professors Chayes and Dahl argue, are shareholders the only persons who should be accorded corporate voting rights. The increasing use by American corporations of technologies and materials that pose direct and serious threats to the health of communities surrounding their plants requires the creation of a new form of corporate voting right. When a federally chartered corporation engages, for example, in production or distribution of nuclear fuels or the emission of toxic air, water, or solid waste pollutants, citizens whose health is endangered should not be left, at best, with receiving money damages after a time-consuming trial to compensate them for damaged property, impaired health, or even death.

Instead, upon finding of a public health hazard by three members of the board of directors or 3 percent of the shareholders, a corporate referendum should be held in the political jurisdiction affected by the health hazard. The referendum would be drafted by the unit triggering it—either the three board members or a designate of the shareholders. The affected citizens by majority vote will then decide whether the hazardous practice shall be allowed to continue. This form of direct democracy has obvious parallels to the initiative and referendum procedures familiar to many states—except that the election will be paid for by a business corporation and will not necessarily occur at a regular election.

This type of election procedure is necessary to give enduring meaning to the democratic concept of "consent of the governed." To be sure, this proposal goes beyond the traditional assumption that the only affected or relevant constituents of the corporation are the shareholders. But no longer can we accept the Faustian bargain that the continued toleration of corporate destruction of local health and property is the cost to the public of doing business. In an equitable system of governance, the perpetrators should answer to their victims.

Power and Accountability: The Changing Role of the Corporate Board of Directors

Irving S. Shapiro*

The proper direction of business corporations in a free society is a topic of intense and often heated discussion. Under the flag of corporate governance there has been a running debate about the performance of business organizations, together with a flood of proposals for changes in the way corporate organizations are controlled.

It has been variously suggested that corporate charters be dispensed by the Federal Government as distinct from those of the states (to tighten the grip on corporate actions); that only outsiders unconnected to an enterprise be allowed to sit on its board of directors or that, as a minimum, most of the directors should qualify

as "independent"; that seats be apportioned to constituent groups (employees, women, consumers and minorities, along with stockholders); that boards be equipped with private staffs, beyond the management's control (to smoke out facts the hired executives might prefer to hide or decorate); and that new disclosure requirements be added to existing ones (to provide additional tools for outside oversight of behavior and performance).

Such proposals have come from the Senate Judiciary Committee's antitrust arm; from regulatory agency spokesmen, most notably the current head of the Securities and Exchange Commission, Harold Williams, and a predecessor there, William Cary; from the professoriat in schools of law and business; from the bench and bar; and from such observers of the American scene as Ralph Nader and Mark Green.[1]

Suggestions for change have sometimes been offered in sympathy and sometimes in anger. They have ranged from general pleas for corporations to behave better, to meticulously detailed reorganization charts. The span in itself suggests part of the problem: "Corporate Governance" (like Social Responsibility before it) is not a subject with a single meaning, but is a shorthand label for an array of social and political as well as economic concerns. One is obliged to look for a way to keep discussion within a reasonable perimeter.

There appears to be one common thread. All of the analyses, premises, and prescriptions seem to derive in one way or another from the question of accountability: Are corporations suitably controlled, and to whom or what are they responsible? This is the central public issue, and the focal point for this paper.

One school of opinion holds that corporations cannot be adequately called to account because there are systemic economic and political failings. In this view, nothing short of a major overhaul will serve. What is envisioned, at least by many in this camp, are new kinds of corporate organizations constructed along the lines of dem-

---

Excerpted from a paper presented in the Fairless Lecture Series, Carnegie-Mellon University, Oct. 24, 1979. Reprinted by permission.

*Former chair of the board, E.I. du Pont de Nemours & Company.

ocratic political institutions. The guiding ideology would be communitarian, with the needs and rights of the community emphasized in preference to profit-seeking goals now pursued by corporate leaders (presumably with Darwinian abandon, with natural selection weeding out the weak, and with society left to pick up the external costs).

BOARDS CHANGING FOR BETTER

Other critics take a more temperate view. They regard the present system as sound and its methods of governance as morally defensible. They concede, though, that changes are needed to reflect new conditions. Whether the changes are to be brought about by gentle persuasion, or require the use of a two-by-four to get the mule's attention, is part of the debate.

This paper sides with the gradualists. My position, based on a career in industry and personal observation of corporate boards at work, is that significant improvements have been made in recent years in corporate governance, and that more changes are coming in an orderly way; that with these amendments, corporations are accountable and better monitored than ever before; and that pat formulas or proposals for massive "restructuring" should be suspect. The formula approach often is based on ignorance of what it takes to run a large enterprise, on false premises as to the corporate role in society, or on a philosophy that misreads the American tradition and leaves no room for large enterprises that are both free and efficient.

The draconian proposals would almost certainly yield the worst of all possibilities, a double-negative tradeoff: They would sacrifice the most valuable qualities of the enterprise system to gain the least attractive features of the governmental system. Privately owned enterprises are geared to a primary economic task, that of joining human talents and natural resources in the production and distribution of goods and services. That task is essential, and two centuries of national experience suggest these conclusions: The United States has been uncommonly successful at meeting economic needs through reliance on private initiative; and the competitive marketplace is a better course-correction device than governmental fiat. The enterprise system would have had to have failed miserably before the case could be made for replacing it with governmental dictum.

Why should the public have any interest in the internal affairs of corporations? Who cares who decides? Part of the answer comes from recent news stories noting such special problems as illegal corporate contributions to political campaigns, and tracking the decline and fall of once-stout companies such as Penn Central. Revelations of that kind raise questions about the probity and competence of the people minding the largest stores. There is more to it than this, though. There have always been cases of corporate failures. Small companies have gone under too, at a rate far higher than their larger brethren.[2] Instances of corruption have occurred in institutions of all sizes, whether they be commercial enterprises or some other kind.

Corporate behavior and performance are points of attention, and the issue attaches to size, precisely because people do not see the large private corporation as entirely private. People care about what goes on in the corporate interior because they see themselves as affected parties whether they work in such companies or not.

There is no great mystery as to the source of this challenge to the private character of governance. Three trends account for it. First is the growth of very large corporations. They have come to employ a large portion of the workforce, and have become key factors in the nation's technology, wealth and security. They have generated admiration for their prowess, but also fear of their imputed power.

The second contributing trend is the decline of owner-management. Over time, corporate shares have been dispersed. The owners have hired managers, entrusted them with the power to make decisions, and drifted away from involvement in corporate affairs except to meet statutory requirements (as, for example, to approve a stock split or elect a slate of directors).

That raises obvious practical questions. If the owners are on the sidelines, what is to stop the managers from remaining in power indefinitely, using an inside position to control the selection of their own bosses, the directors? Who is looking over management's shoulder to monitor performance?

The third element here is the rise in social expectations regarding corporations. It is no longer considered enough for a company to make products and provide commercial services. The larger it is, the more it is expected to assume various obligations that once were met by individuals or communities, or were not met at all.

With public expectations ratcheting upward, corporations are under pressure to behave more like governments and embrace a universe of problems. That would mean, of necessity, that private institutions would focus less on problems of their own choice.

If corporations succumbed to that pressure, and in effect declared the public's work to be their own, the next step would be to turn them into institutions accountable to the public in the same way that units of government are accountable.

But the corporation does not parallel the government. The assets in corporate hands are more limited and the constituents have options. There are levels of appeal. While the only accountability in government lies within government itself—the celebrated system of checks and balances among the executive, legislative, and judicial branches—the corporation is in a different situation: It has external and plural accountability, codified in the law and reinforced by social pressure. It must "answer" in one way or another to all levels of government, to competitors in the marketplace who would be happy to have the chance to increase their own market share, to employees who can strike or quit, and to con-

sumers who can keep their wallets in their pockets. The checks are formidable even if one excludes for purposes of argument the corporation's initial point of accountability, its stockholders (many of whom do in fact vote their shares, and do not just use their feet).

The case for major reforms in corporate governance rests heavily on the argument that past governmental regulation of large enterprises has been impotent or ineffectual. This is an altogether remarkable assertion, given the fact that the nation has come through a period in which large corporations have been subjected to an unprecedented flood of new legislation and rule making. Regulation now reaches into every corporate nook and cranny—including what some people suppose (erroneously) to be the sanctuary of the boardroom.

Market competition, so lightly dismissed by some critics as fiction or artifact, is in fact a vigorous force in the affairs of almost all corporations. Size lends no immunity to its relentless pressures. The claim that the largest corporations somehow have set themselves above the play of market forces or, more likely, make those forces play for themselves, is widely believed. Public opinion surveys show that. What is lacking is any evidence that this is so. Here too, the evidence goes the other way. Objective studies of concentrated industries (the auto industry, for instance) show that corporate size does not mean declining competitiveness, nor does it give assurance that the products will sell.

Everyday experience confirms this. Consider the hard times of the Chrysler Corporation today, the disappearance of many once-large companies from the American scene, and the constant rollover in the membership list of the "100 Largest," a churning process that has been going on for years and shows no signs of abating.[3]

If indeed the two most prominent overseers of corporate behavior, government and competition, have failed to provide appropriate checks and balances, and if that is to be cited as evidence that corporations lack accountability, the burden of proof should rest with those who so state.

The basics apply to Sears Roebuck as much as to Sam's appliance shop. Wherever you buy the new toaster, it should work when it is plugged in. Whoever services the washing machine, the repairman should arrive at the appointed time, with tools and parts.

Special expectations are added for the largest firms, however. One is that they apply their resources to tasks that invite economies of scale, providing goods and services that would not otherwise be available, or that could be delivered by smaller units only at considerable loss of efficiency. Another is that, like the elephant, they watch where they put their feet and not stamp on smaller creatures through clumsiness or otherwise.

A second set of requirements can be added, related not to the markets selected by corporations individually, but to the larger economic tasks that must be accomplished in the name of the national interest and security. In concert with others in society, including big government, big corporations are expected to husband scarce resources and develop new ones, and to foster strong and diverse programs of research and development, to the end that practical technological improvements will emerge and the nation will be competitive in the international setting.

Beyond this there are softer but nonetheless important obligations: To operate with respect for the environment and with careful attention to the health and safety of people, to honor and give room to the personal qualities employees bring to their jobs, including their need to make an identifiable mark and to realize as much of their potential as possible; to lend assistance in filling community needs in which corporations have some stake; and to help offset community problems which in some measure corporations have helped to create.

This is not an impossible job, only a difficult one. Admitting that the assignment probably is not going to be carried out perfectly by any or-

ganization, the task is unlikely to be done even half well unless some boundary conditions are met. Large corporations cannot fulfill their duties unless they remain both profitable and flexible. They must be able to attract and hold those volunteer owners; which is to say, there must be the promise of present or future gain. Companies must have the wherewithal to reinvest significant amounts to revitalize their own capital plants, year after year in unending fashion. Otherwise, it is inevitable that they will go into decline versus competitors elsewhere, as will the nation.

Flexibility is no less important. The fields of endeavor engaging large business units today are dynamic in nature. Without an in-and-out flow of products and services, without the mobility to adapt to shifts in opportunities and public preferences, corporations would face the fate of the buggywhip makers.

Profitability and flexibility are easy words to say, but in practice they make for hard decisions. A company that would close a plant with no more than a passing thought for those left unemployed would and should be charged with irresponsibility; but a firm that vowed never to close any of its plants would be equally irresponsible, for it might be consigning itself to a pattern of stagnation that could ultimately cost the jobs of the people in all of its plants.

The central requirement is not that large corporations take the pledge and bind themselves to stated actions covering all circumstances, but that they do a thoughtful and informed job of balancing competing (and ever changing) claims on corporate resources, mediating among the conflicting (also changing) desires of various constituencies, and not giving in to any one-dimensional perspective however sincerely felt. It is this that describes responsible corporate governance.

Certainly, corporations do not have the public mandate or the resources to be what Professor George Lodge of the Harvard Business School would have them be, which is nationally chartered community-oriented collectives.[4] Such a mission for corporations would be tolerable to society only if corporations were turned into mini-governments—but that takes us back to the inefficiency problem noted earlier. The one task governments have proven they almost always do badly is to run production and distribution organizations. The only models there are to follow are not attractive. Would anyone seriously argue that the public would be ahead if General Motors were run along the lines of Amtrak, or Du Pont were managed in the manner of the U.S. Postal System?

Once roles are defined, the key to success in running a large corporation is to lay out a suitable division of labor between the board and the management, make that division crystal clear on both sides, and staff the offices with the right people. Perhaps the best way to make that split is to follow the pattern used in the U.S. Constitution, which stipulates the powers of the Federal Government and specifies that everything not covered there is reserved to the states or the people thereof. The board of directors should lay claim to five basic jobs, and leave the rest to the paid managers.

The duties the board should not delegate are these:

1. The determination of the board policies and the general direction the efforts of the enterprise should take.
2. The establishment of performance standards—ethical as well as commercial—against which the management will be judged, and the communication of these standards to the management in unambiguous terms.
3. The selection of company officers, and attention to the question of succession.
4. The review of top management's performance in following the overall strategy and meeting the board's standards as well as legal requirements.
5. The communication of the organization's goals and standards to those who have a sig-

nificant stake in its activities (insiders and outsiders both) and of the steps being taken to keep the organization responsive to the needs of those people.

The establishment of corporate strategy and performance standards denotes a philosophy of active stewardship, rather than passive trusteeship. It is the mission of directors to see that corporate resources are put to creative use, and in the bargain subjected to calculated risks rather than simply being tucked into the countinghouse for safekeeping.

That in turn implies certain prerequisites for board members of large corporations which go beyond those required of a school board member, a trustee of a charitable organization, or a director of a small, local business firm. In any such assignments one would look for personal integrity, interest and intelligence, but beyond these there is a dividing line that marks capability and training.

The stakes are likely to be high in the large corporation, and the factors confronting the board and management usually are complex. The elements weighing heavily in decisions are not those with which people become familiar in the ordinary course of day-to-day life, as might be the case with a school board.

Ordinarily the management of a corporation attends to such matters as product introductions, capital expansions, and supply problems. This in no way reduces the need for directors with extensive business background, though. With few exceptions, corporate boards involve themselves in strategic decisions and those involving large capital commitments. Directors thus need at least as much breadth and perspective as the management, if not as much detailed knowledge.

If the directors are to help provide informed and principled oversight of corporate affairs, a good number of them must provide windows to the outside world. That is at least part of the rationale for outside directors, and especially for directors who can bring unique perspective to the group. There is an equally strong case, though, for directors with an intimate knowledge of the company's business, and insiders may be the best qualified to deliver that. What is important is not that a ratio be established, but that the group contain a full range of the competences needed to set courses of action that will largely determine the long-range success of the enterprise.

BOARDS NEED WINDOWS

The directors also have to be able and willing to invest considerable time in their work. In this day and age, with major resources on the line and tens of thousands of employees affected by each large corporation, there should be no seat in the boardroom for people willing only to show up once a month to pour holy water over decisions already made. Corporate boards need windows, not window dressing!

There are two other qualities that may be self-evident from what has been said, but are mentioned for emphasis. Directors must be interested in the job and committed to the overall purpose of the organization. However much they may differ on details of accomplishment, they must be willing to work at the task of working with others on the board. They ought to be able to speak freely in a climate that encourages open discussion, but to recognize the difference between attacking an idea and attacking the person who presents it. No less must they see the difference between compromising tactics to reach consensus and compromising principles.

Structures and procedures, which so often are pushed to the fore in discussions of corporate governance, actually belong last. They are not unimportant, but they are subordinate.

Structure follows purpose, or should, and that is a useful principle for testing some of the proposals for future changes in corporate boards. Today, two-thirds to three-quarters of the directors of most large corporations are outsiders, and it is being proposed that this trend be pushed

still farther, with the only insider being the chief executive officer, and with a further stipulation that he not be board chairman. This idea has surfaced from Harold Williams, and variations on it have come from other sources.

The idea bumps into immediate difficulties. High-quality candidates for boards are not in large supply as it is. Conflicts of interest would prohibit selection of many individuals close enough to an industry to be familiar with its problems. The disqualification of insiders would reduce the selection pool to a still smaller number, and the net result could well be corporate boards whose members were less competent and effective than those now sitting.

Experience would also suggest that such a board would be the most easily manipulated of all. That should be no trick at all for a skillful CEO, for he would be the only person in the room with a close, personal knowledge of the business.

The objective is unassailable: Corporate boards need directors with independence of judgment; but in today's business world, independence is not enough. In coping with such problems as those confronting the electronics corporations beset by heavy foreign competition, or those encountered by international banks which have loans outstanding in countries with shaky governments, boards made up almost entirely of outsiders would not just have trouble evaluating nuances of the management's performance; they might not even be able to read the radar and tell whether the helmsman was steering straight for the rocks.

If inadequately prepared individuals are placed on corporate boards, no amount of sincerity on their part can offset the shortcoming. It is pure illusion to suppose that complex business issues and organizational problems can be overseen by people with little or no experience in dealing with such problems. However intelligent such people might be, the effect of their governance would be to expose the people most affected by the organization—employees, owners, customers, suppliers—to leadership that would be (using the word precisely) incompetent.

It is sometimes suggested that the members of corporate boards ought to come from the constituencies—an employee-director, a consumer-director, an environmentalist-director, etc. This Noah's Ark proposal, which is probably not to be taken seriously, is an extension of the false parallel between corporations and elected governments. The flaw in the idea is all but self evident: People representing specific interest groups would by definition be committed to the goals of their groups rather than any others; but it is the responsibility of directors (not simply by tradition but as a matter of law as well) to serve the organization as a whole. The two goals are incompatible.

If there were such boards they would move at glacial speed. The internal political maneuvering would be Byzantine, and it is difficult to see how the directors could avoid an obvious challenge of accountability. Stockholder suits would pop up like dandelions in the spring.

One may also question how many people of ability would stand for election under this arrangement. Quotas are an anathema in a free society, and their indulgence here would insult the constituencies themselves—a woman on the board not because she is competent but only because she is female; a black for black's sake; and so on ad nauseam.

A certain amount of constituency pleading is not all bad, as long as it is part of a corporate commitment. There is something to be said for what Harold Williams labels "tension," referring to the divergence in perspective of those concerned primarily with internal matters and those looking more at the broader questions. However, as has been suggested by James Shepley, the president of Time, Inc., "tension" can lead to paralysis, and is likely to do so if boards are packed with groups known to be unsympathetic to the management's problems and business realities.

As Shepley commented, "The chief executive would be out of his mind who would take a risk-laden business proposition to a group of directors who, whatever their other merits, do not really understand the fine points of the business at hand, and whose official purpose is to create 'tension.'"[5]

Students of corporate affairs have an abundance of suggestions for organizing the work of boards, with detailed structures in mind for committees on audit, finance, and other areas; plus prescriptions for membership. The danger here is not that boards will pick the wrong formula—many organization charts could be made to work—but that boards will put too much emphasis on the wrong details.

The idea of utilizing a committee system in which sub-groups have designated duties is far more important than the particulars of their arrangement. When such committees exist, and they are given known and specific oversight duties, it is a signal to the outside world (and to the management) that performance is being monitored in a no-nonsense fashion.

It is this argument that has produced the rule changes covering companies listed on the New York Stock Exchange, calling for audit committees chaired by outside directors, and including no one currently active in management. Most large firms have moved in that direction, and the move makes sense, for an independently minded audit committee is a potent instrument of corporate oversight. Even a rule of that kind, though, has the potential of backfiring.

Suppose some of the directors best qualified to perform the audit function are not outsiders? Are the analytical skills and knowledge of career employees therefore to be bypassed? Are the corporate constituencies well served by such an exclusionary rule, keeping in mind that all directors, insiders or outsiders, are bound by the same legal codes and corporate books are still subject to independent, outside audit? It is scarcely a case of the corporate purse being placed in the hands of the unwatched.

Repeatedly, the question of structure turns on the basics: If corporations have people with competence and commitment on their boards, structure and process fall into line easily; if people with the needed qualities are missing or the performance standards are unclear, corporations are in trouble no matter whose guidebook they follow. Equally, the question drives to alternatives: The present system is surely not perfect, but what is better?

By the analysis presented here the old fundamentals are still sound, no alternative for radical change has been defended with successful argument, and the best course appears to be to stay within the historical and philosophical traditions of American enterprise, working out the remaining problems one by one.

NOTES

1. U.S. Senate, Committee on the Judiciary Subcommittee on Antitrust, Monopoly & Business Rights; Address by Harold M. Williams, *Corporate Accountability,* Fifth Annual Securities Regulation Institute, San Diego, California (January 18, 1978); W. Cary, A *Proposed Federal Corporate Minimum Standards Act,* 29 Bus. Law. 1101 (1974) and W. Cary, *Federalism & Corporate Law: Reflections Upon Delaware,* 83 Yale L.J., 663 (1974); D. E. Schwartz, *A Case for Federal Chartering of Corporations,* 31 Bus. Law. 1125 (1976); M. A. Eisenberg, *Legal Modes of Management Structure in the Modern Corporation; Officers, Directors & Accountants,* 63 Calif. L. Rev. 375 (1975); A. J. Goldberg, *Debate on Outside Directors, New York Times,* October 29, 1972 (§3, p. 1); Ralph Nader & Mark Green, *Constitutionalizing the Corporation: The Case for Federal Chartering of Giant Corporations* (1976).
2. *See* "Sixty Years of Corporate Ups, Downs & Outs," *Forbes,* September 15, 1977, p. 127 et seq.
3. *See* Dr. Betty Bock's Statement before Hearings on S.600, Small and Independent Business Protection Act of 1979, April 25, 1979.
4. G. Lodge, *The New American Ideology* (1975).
5. Shepley, *The CEO Goes to Washington,* Remarks to Fortune Corporation Communications Seminar, March 28, 1979.

Why Directors Can't Protect the Shareholders

Harold S. Geneen*

Among the boards of directors of *Fortune* 500 companies, I estimate that 95% are not fully doing what they are legally, morally, and ethically supposed to do. And they couldn't even if they wanted to.

The board of directors of any company is supposed to represent the interests of the owners—the shareholders. In doing this, the board's primary function is to oversee and evaluate the performance of management in running the company, and if that performance is not satisfactory, to do something about it. That does not mean the board is supposed to run the company. The board's responsibility is to sit in judgment on the management, especially on the performance of the chief executive, and to reward, punish, or replace the management as the board sees fit. That is what is supposed to happen. That is what may appear to happen. But it doesn't.

Typically, the boardroom of a large company is the most exquisitely expensive room in the building, hidden behind closed doors, hushed in silent splendor. You can count the number of board members by the empty chairs around the great polished table. The table is oval so that all who sit there can be deemed equal. Most of the time the boardroom is empty: these important people use it only 12 times a year.

Excerpted from "The Board of Directors" from *Managing* by Harold S. Geneen with Alvin Moscow. Copyright © 1984 by Harold S. Geneen and Alvin Moscow, Inc. Reprinted by permission of Doubleday, a division of Bantam, Doubleday, Dell Publishing Group, Inc.

*Former chair and chief executive officer, ITT Corporation.

The first Tuesday or the second Thursday of every month, the members show up. On entering the room, each is handed a sealed envelope. Soon, the minutes of the previous meeting are read and approved. Perhaps the directors then adjourn temporarily so that the executive committee of the board can meet separately to discuss management salaries and changes in company personnel. When the whole board reconvenes, the chief executive presents an overall view of the company's activities and results that month. If he is so inclined he may go into details, or he may turn the explaining over to a subordinate. Whatever the results, management always reports in effect how good they have been and are and will be, despite whatever intolerable conditions hover over the economy or the marketplace. They never tell you that they've done a lousy job or that they were beaten by a more efficient or smarter competitor. Never? Well, hardly ever.

What can an outside director do? He can ask a question about what troubles him. It will be answered logically, if not in great detail. If the director questions the answer, he will be given more detail. He will be told that management's answer comes not from the chief executive alone but from those in the company right down to the division involved in the problem. They know more than the director does about anything concerning the company. If one stubborn director continues, he is likely to be embarrassed by what he doesn't know. If he persists, he is casting himself in the role of a troublemaker, and no one likes a troublemaker. So what is the director to do, except sit back in his chair, taste his cold coffee, and desist.

Management does 90% to 95% of the talking. Outside board members, who are not part of the management, sit there and listen; then they go to lunch, and then go home and open the envelopes that contain their fees.

Nominally, outside directors are elected by the stockholders; actually, in most instances they serve at the pleasure of the chief executive. They are nominated by a committee of the outside board members, but the nominations have to pass the scrutiny of the chief executive. If he says, ''I cannot work with that man,'' that man will not be nominated. If there ever is a conflict between a board member and the chief executive, who stays and who goes? It is well known and accepted that only those men and women who can ''get along'' are elected to the board and stay on it.

One might also ask how independent board members can be if they accept all the perks heaped on them by the management they are to judge. Isn't there a fundamental conflict of interest here? Certainly the board would object if the company's purchasing agent accepted free dinners and trips abroad from suppliers. If a board member is dependent on the same kinds of perks, how can he act independently? I have a feeling that most board fees are too high for the work done to earn them and too low for the work that should be done.

If the board of directors is really there to represent the interests of the stockholders, what is the chief executive doing on the board? Doesn't *he* have a conflict of interest? He's the professional manager. He cannot represent the shareholders and impartially sit in judgment on himself. He should not. Nevertheless, in every corporation that I know of, the chief executive is a member of the board. In more than three-quarters of the *Fortune* 500 corporations, the chief executive sits as chairman of the board.

I wore both hats in my day at ITT, and they felt great: chief executive officer and chairman of the board. No crime was involved. But it was not fair to the interests of the stockholders. The unfairness goes deeper. Since the chief executive is not alone on the board of directors and is ordinarily backed up by his top management team, in most companies the chief executive needs to persuade only one or two outside directors to obtain a majority. Certainly, none of the inside directors would substantially challenge his boss in the boardroom.

That is not to say that the chief executive does not have the best interests of the stockholders in his heart or mind. Generally he does, but conflicts of interest can arise. The point is that there are few if any genuine checks or balances on the power of the chief executive in large public corporations.

Oh, yes, the board sets the salary, bonuses, and fringe benefits of the chief executive and can fire him. But how often have you heard of a board removing a chief executive for being inadequate? I doubt if more than a handful of the *Fortune* 500 chief executives have been removed from office in any given year. Have they all been performing so marvelously over these years of declining American industrial performance? I doubt it. When do the directors ever cut a chief executive's salary? When disaster strikes, when the ground heaves, the walls buckle, and the roof caves in, when the wreckage is all around them. Then the board, if it survives, sits up and acts. I suspect the directors take action not out of concern for the stockholder, but because of a sudden awakening of self-interest: as fiduciaries, they may be in legal jeopardy. Even so, how many companies have gone belly up without their boards of directors having attempted any semblance of remedial action? Too often the board has no idea of the trouble the company is in, or finds out about it too late.

A board of directors can and occasionally does say no to a specific management request, if and when it disagrees with a particular expansion plan, a research project, or a merger. But suppose some members of the board come to the conclusion that the chief executive is inadequate for the job, or that he is competent but not as good as someone else might be. First of all, that is a difficult, complex decision to reach: there are no set standards of measurement to which they can turn with assurance. How can they form a fair judgment if nearly all their information comes from the chief executive himself? He does not readily tell them about his mistakes. No chief executive would tolerate board members going behind his back and seeking information from his subordinates, even if they would talk, which is unlikely.

Nevertheless, suppose several outside directors come to the conclusion that on a scale of one to ten their man is only a four. The directors have the power to fire him, pay him three months' or three years' salary according to his contract, and to go out and find someone better to head the company. But they hesitate to confront management and destroy the harmony of the board's relationship to the chief executive. They are concerned, too, with the talk it will cause among security analysts, lending institutions, and investors. The talk will get around that there is something wrong with the company.

In most large corporations the board has also given up its prerogative of determining the pay of top management. Outside consulting firms are routinely called in, and they set the parameters of corporate salaries. Their yardstick is not performance but rather the size of the company and what the fellow down the street is paying in a similar situation. Boards of directors accept those recommendations almost without fail.

If the company is not in trouble, top management automatically gets, say, a 10% salary increase. If one man did particularly well, he gets 15%. Hardly a year goes by without increases for top management. Hefty stock options are handed out almost automatically. When the stock market goes up, everyone cashes in; when it goes down, the board issues new options at lower prices. But except when a company is on or over the threshold of bankruptcy, have you ever heard of a chief executive whose salary was reduced? Even in a disastrous year, when his bonus will be a bit less than in better times, his salary will stay the same. Or maybe improve. In a survey of 100 corporations in 1982, 55 had declining profits, but the chief executives of nearly half of those 55 received increases in compensation.

The chief executive himself handles compensation matters in management ranks quite differently. He and his top managers hold long, intense meetings, reviewing the performance of the men who report to them. Targets have been set and results are measured against those targets. But at the very top, at the board level, there are no such performance reviews of the men who are running the company.

Every diligent board of directors should address itself on behalf of the shareholders to this key question: What is the standard of performance of the company's management—not what the company earned last year or this year, but what the company *should* have earned?

Today's boards are ineffectual because their opinions are based on what they have been told by the company's management. Individually, no director would invest his own money or his bank's money on the basis of what somebody told him. He would go out and do his own checking.

Directors run virtually no personal risk for any amount of complacency, cronyism, or outright neglect of their duties. While the law holds them responsible as fiduciaries to the stockholders, the courts have interpreted that responsibility very leniently. A director would rarely be found liable unless cupidity, a clear conflict of interest, or gross negligence (a vague concept) could be proved. Even then he is usually further protected by his company's indemnification and insurance policies, which in effect guarantee that any damages assessed against him will be paid by the company.

In the old days, the system worked because boards of directors were composed mainly of self-made, independently well-off businessmen who never feared to speak their minds. Usually they served for the honor and public prestige of serving, and were compensated only with a $20 gold piece at the end of each board meeting. Today's board fees, plus stock options, pension plans, and perks, can add up to $100,000 or more a year for a director of a large corporation. In a medium-size company, compensation can range anywhere from $30,000 to $60,000. To my mind, that kind of money should *obligate* a director to earn

it. If he fails to do his job, he should be at some personal risk for the consequences.

One way to reintroduce personal independence on a board of directors would be to strip away some of the protections given to members of the board. What's wrong with holding directors personally responsible—in terms of money from their own pockets up to some reasonable limit? Maybe the amount of his or her risk should have some relationship to how much he or she is being paid. Wouldn't some multiple of those fees and perks—say, ten times the total annual compensation and fringe benefits—have a sobering effect? Thus, a director taking in $100,000 a year would be liable up to a maximum of $1 million. On the other hand, a director who chose to serve for the honor of it and a $20 honorarium for each meeting would limit his liability.

If a board of directors as a whole is to do its duty, the directors must regain their objectivity in viewing the management's performance. In a company where the founder or majority stock owner is chairman of the board, you will find that kind of objectivity and scrutiny. Whenever their own money is involved, board members will not hesitate to ask all sorts of questions of the managers running the company, and they won't be satisfied if performance does not come up to expectations.

Perhaps the best way for a board of directors to regain its independence would be to take all the internal management members off the board, including the chief executive. The chief executive and his management team would continue to attend board meetings, but they would be there to report and to explain to the board what they did in managing the company and why. The board would have the clear responsibility to see that the management was doing a satisfactory job. Each group—board and management—would then have separate and distinct responsibilities.

The chief executive's role would become one of convincing the board that his recommendations are solid and should be supported on their merits. He would still be running the company. If he's a good man and his judgments are sound, he should have no difficulty persuading his board to support him. If an honest difference of opinion arises, then the advocacy system of putting forth all the facts, opinions, and feelings of everyone in the boardroom should result in an agreement on the best answer.

I can already hear the loud cries of protest. No chief executive wants someone looking over his shoulder all the time! Of course he doesn't. But the board already calls for an independent auditor to check management's financial figures—so why shouldn't the board also hire an independent management auditor to check policies and performance? The auditor might be an individual, it might be a team of management consultants. Whoever did such auditing would have no power to tell the chief executive or anyone else in management what to do. He would be there purely to audit. His loyalty would be to the board. He would report his findings to the directors, just as Price Waterhouse and Arthur Andersen submit their audits. It would be for the board to use that information and to take whatever action it sees fit. The board would then have a much needed, independent source of information. In fact, I would guess that such a professional adviser would have to say very little at a board meeting. His just being there and "in the know" would oblige the chief executive to be more objective in his presentations to the board.

With an informed board of outsiders, led by one of its members as chairman, the quality and intensity of board meetings would rise to a level not seen for many years. The best way ever devised for seeking the truth in any given situation is advocacy: presenting the pros and cons from different, informed points of view and digging down deep into the facts.

If a company wanted to go a step further, perhaps the board should be telling management how well it expects the company to perform for the year ahead, rather than the other way around. If a board reviewed with a chief executive what the board expected of management before a fiscal year started, not afterward, what do you think would happen? The process would, I maintain, lead to a much better evaluation of the short- and long-term objectives of the company. My guess is that that chief executive would go back to his management team and say, "Look, fellows, the directors think we ought to do better. They think we ought to do 10% better and I can tell you their reasons. Maybe their assumptions will prove wrong; maybe ours will. But we're just going to have to stretch ourselves to try to make that 10%." Management must manage. That's the message and it must come from the board.

What are the dangers of giving so much added power to the board? As long as the board's actions are open to the scrutiny of the shareholders and its actions are reported in the company's annual report, I do not foresee problems that cannot be overcome. The chief executive does not have to accept the board's advice. If he comes to an impasse with an unreasonable board, he can offer to resign and issue a statement on their dispute. He would be protected from an unreasonable board by his contract guarantees of severance pay, plus public opinion.

I would hope that a growing awareness of the problem, once it is discussed frankly and openly in public, would induce boards of directors to insist on their own initiative upon a clear separation of powers from management. The chairman of the board should be an outside director. He should report to the stockholders at the annual meeting, not to the chief executive, who is appointed by and should report to the board.

If boards of directors fail to take action, the day may come when Congress will see the need to pass legislation or the Securities and Exchange Commission to issue a regulation to make it illegal for a chief executive of a company to also serve as chairman of its board. That would go a long way toward ending what should be perceived as a clear-cut, basic conflict of interest on boards as they are constituted today.

**Section B
Takeovers and Corporate
Restructuring**

Takeovers: Folklore and Science

Michael C. Jensen*

From 1981 to 1983, the number of large U.S. corporate acquisitions grew at a rate roughly double that of the 1970s and even exceeded the one realized during the famous merger wave of the 1960s. The drama of 2,100 annual takeovers valued at more than $1 million—much of it played out in heated, public battles—has generated an enormous amount of criticism, not only from politicians and the media but also from high-level corporate executives.

Commenting in the *Wall Street Journal* on the Bendix and Martin Marietta takeover battle, for example, Lee Iacocca, chairman of Chrysler, argued:

"It's not a merger. It's a three-ring circus. If they're really concerned about America, they'd stop it right now. It's no good for the economy. It wrecks it. If I were in the banking system I'd say no more [money] for conglomerates for one year."

A former director at Bendix added:

"I think...it's the kind of thing corporate America ought not to do, because the poor stockholder is the one whose interest is being ignored in favor of the egos of directors and executives.

Reprinted by permission of the *Harvard Business Review*. Excerpts from "Takeovers: Folklore and Science" by Michael C. Jensen (November–December 1984). Copyright © 1984 by the President and Fellows of Harvard College; all rights reserved.
*Control Area, Harvard Business School and LaClare Professor of Finance and Business Administration, University of Rochester.

And who the hell is running the show—the business of making brakes and aerospace equipment—while all of this is going on?"

In a 1984 *New York Times* piece on the "surge of corporate mergers," Felix Rohatyn noted:

"All this frenzy may be good for investment bankers now, but it's not good for the country or investment bankers in the long run. We seem to be living in a 1920s, jazz age atmosphere."

Just as the public outcry over excesses on Wall Street in the early 1930s led to the Glass-Steagall Act regulating banking, so the latest criticisms of mergers have brought enormous political pressure to bear on Congress to restrict takeovers. The July 1983 report of the SEC Advisory Committee on Tender Offers contained 50 recommendations for new regulations. Democratic Representative Peter Rodino has cosponsored a bill that would require advance notice of proposed acquisitions resulting in assets of $5 billion and 25,000 employees and a judgment by the Antitrust Division of the Justice Department or the FTC whether such acquisitions "serve the public interest."

The popular view underlying these proposals is wrong, however, because it ignores the fundamental economic function that takeover activities serve. In the corporate takeover market, management teams compete for the right to control—that is, to manage—corporate resources. Viewed in this way, the market for control is an important part of the managerial labor market, which is very different from, and has higher stakes than, the normal labor market. After all, potential chief executive officers do not simply leave their applications with personnel officers. Their on-the-job performance is subject not only to the normal internal control mechanisms of their organizations but also to the scrutiny of the external market for control.

Imagine that you are the president of a large billion-dollar corporation. Suddenly, another management team threatens your job and prestige by trying to buy your company's stock. The whole world watches your performance. Putting yourself in this situation leads to a better understanding of the reasons behind the rhetoric, maneuverings, and even lobbying in the political and regulatory sectors by managers for protection from unfriendly offers.

The Bendix attempt to take control of Martin Marietta in 1982 gained considerable attention because of Marietta's unusual countertakeover offer for Bendix, called the "Pac-Man defense," whose principle is: "My company will eat yours before yours eats mine."[1] Some describe this kind of contest as disgraceful. I find it fascinating because it makes clear that the crucial issue is not whether the two companies will merge but which managers will be in control.

At the end of the contest, Bendix held 67% of Martin Marietta while Martin Marietta held 50% of Bendix. United Technologies then entered as Martin Marietta's friend and offered to buy Bendix. But it was Allied, coming in late, that finally won the battle with its purchase of all of Bendix's stock, 39% of Martin Marietta's, and a promise not to buy more. When the dust had cleared, shareholders of Bendix and Martin had both won; their respective shares gained roughly 38% in value (after adjusting for marketwide stock price change). Allied's shareholders, on the other hand, lost approximately 8.6%.[2]

Given the success and history of the modern corporation, it is surprising how little the media, the legal and political communities, and even business executives understand the reasons behind the complexities and subtleties of takeover battles. Prior to the last decade, the academic community made little progress in redressing this lack of understanding. But research efforts in business schools across the country have recently begun to overcome it.

In this article I summarize the most important scientific evidence refuting the myths that swirl around the controversy. The research shows that:

- Takeovers of companies by outsiders do not harm shareholders of the target company; in fact, they gain substantial wealth.
- Corporate takeovers do not waste resources; they use assets productively.
- Takeovers do not siphon commercial credit from its uses in funding new plant and equipment.
- Takeovers do not create gains for shareholders through creation of monopoly power.
- Prohibition of plant closings, layoffs, and dismissals following takeovers would reduce market efficiency and lower aggregate living standards.
- Although managers are self-interested, the environment in which they operate gives them relatively little leeway to feather their nests at shareholders' expense. Corporate control-related actions of managers do not generally harm shareholders, but actions that eliminate actual or potential takeover bids are most suspect as exceptions to this rule.
- Golden parachutes for top-level executives are, in principle, in the interest of shareholders. Although the practice can be abused, the evidence indicates that shareholders gain when golden parachutes are adopted.
- In general, the activities of takeover specialists benefit shareholders.

Before exploring the evidence, I consider why shareholders are the most important constituency of the modern corporation and why their interests must be held paramount when discussing the current wave of acquisitions and mergers.

THE NATURE OF THE CORPORATION

Stockholders are commonly portrayed as one group in a set of equal constituencies, or "stakeholders," of the company. In fact, stockholders are not equal with these other groups because they are the ultimate holders of the rights to organization control and therefore must be the focal point for any discussion concerning it.

The public corporation is the nexus for a complex set of voluntary contracts among customers, workers, managers, and the suppliers of materials, capital, and risk bearing. The rights of the interacting parties are determined by law, the corporation's charter, and the implicit and explicit contracts with each individual.

Corporations, like all organizations, vest control rights in the constituency bearing the residual risk.[3] (Residual risk is the risk associated with the difference between the random cash inflows and outflows of the organization.) In partnerships and privately held companies, for example, these residual claims and the organizational control rights are restricted to major decision agents (directors and managers); in mutuals and consumer cooperatives, to customers; and in supplier cooperatives, to suppliers.

Corporations are unique organizations because they make no restrictions on who can own their residual claims and this makes it possible for customers, managers, labor, and suppliers to avoid bearing any of the corporate residual risk. Because stockholders guarantee the contracts of all constituents, they bear the corporation's residual risk. The absence of restrictions on who can own corporate residual claims allows specialization in risk bearing by those investors who are most adept at the function. As a result, the corporation realizes great efficiencies in risk bearing that reduce costs substantially and allow it to meet market demand more efficiently than other organizations.

Although the identities of the bearers of residual risk may differ, all business organizations vest organizational control rights in them. For control to rest in any other group would be equivalent to allowing that group to "play poker" with someone else's money and would create inefficiencies that lead to the possibility of failure. Stockholders as the bearers of residual risk hold the right to control of the corporation, although they delegate much of this control to a board of directors who normally hire, fire, and set the compensation of at least the CEO.

Proof of the efficiency of the corporate organizational form shows dramatically in market performance. In principle, any marketer can supply goods and services. In reality, all organizational forms compete for consumers, managers, labor, and supplies of capital and other goods. Those that supply the goods demanded by customers at the lowest price win out. The dominance of the corporate form of organization in large-scale nonfinancial activities indicates that it is winning much of this competition.

ACQUISITION FOLKLORE

Takeovers can be carried out through mergers, tender offers, and proxy fights, or sometimes through elements of all three. A tender offer made directly to the stockholders to buy some or all of their shares for a specified price during a specified time period does not require the approval of the target company's management or board of directors. A merger, however, is negotiated with the company's management and, when approved by its board of directors, is submitted to the shareholders for approval. In a proxy contest the votes of the stockholders are solicited, generally for the election of a new slate of directors.

Takeovers frequently begin with what is called a "friendly" merger offer from the bidder to the target management and board. If management turns down the offer, the bidder can, and often does, take the offer directly to the shareholders in the form of a tender offer. At this point, target company managers usually oppose the offer by issuing press releases condemning it as outside the shareholders' best interest, by initiating court action, by requesting antitrust action against the bidder, by starting a countertakeover move for the bidder, and by other actions designed to make the target company a less desirable acquisition.

Target company management often casts about for a "white knight"—a friendly merger partner who will protect the "maiden" from the advances of the feared raider and, more important, who will pay a higher price. When the company doesn't find a white knight, and an unfriendly bidder takes it over, its leaders will likely look for new jobs. The takeover process penalizes incompetent or self-serving managers whose actions have lowered the market price of their corporation's stock. Although the process operates with a lag, the forces are strong and persistent. Of course—as a result of economies of scale or other efficiencies—some efficient managers lose their jobs after a takeover through no fault of their own.

This kind of romantic language has been used to offer comic relief, but it contributes to the atmosphere of folklore that surrounds a process fundamental to the corporate world. The resulting myths and misunderstandings distort the public's perception and render a meaningful dialogue impossible.

Folklore: Takeovers Harm the Shareholders of Target Companies.

Fact: The pejorative term *raider* used to label the bidding company in an unfriendly takeover suggests that the bidder will buy control of a company, pillage it, and leave the stockholders with only a crumbling shell.

More than a dozen studies have painstakingly gathered evidence on the stock price effect of successful takeovers.[4] According to these studies, companies involved in takeovers experience abnormal increases in their stock prices for approximately one month surrounding the initial announcement of the takeover. (Abnormal stock price changes are stock price changes customarily adjusted by regression analysis to eliminate the effects of marketwide forces on all corporations.)[5] Target company shareholders gain 30% from tender offers and 20% from mergers.

The shareholders of bidding companies, on the other hand, earn only about 4% from tender offers and nothing from mergers. If the much

feared raiding has taken place, it seems to be of a peculiar, Robin Hood variety.

In sum, contrary to the argument that merger activity wastes resources without benefiting stockholders, stockholders earn substantial gains in successful takeovers. In the Texaco takeover of Getty, for example, Getty Oil shareholders realized abnormal stock price gains of $4.7 billion, or 78.6% of the total equity value, and Texaco shareholders, abnormal returns of $1.3 billion or 14.5%. Gains for both totaled $6 billion, 40% of the sum of their equity values. Gulf stockholders earned abnormal returns of $6.2 billion (79.9%) from the Socal takeover, and Socal stockholders earned $2.8 billion (22.6%). The total gains of $9 billion in this merger represent a 44.6% increase in the total equity values of both companies.

In light of these shareholder benefits, the cries to eliminate or restrain unfriendly takeovers seem peculiar (and in some cases self-serving). In a January 5, 1983 *Wall Street Journal* article, Peter Drucker called for such controls: "The question is no longer whether unfriendly takeovers will be curbed but only when and how." He went on to say:

"The recent shoot-out between Bendix and Martin Marietta has deeply disturbed even the staunchest laissez-faire advocates in the business community. And fear of the raider and his unfriendly takeover bid is increasingly distorting business judgment and decisions. In company after company the first question is no longer: Is this decision best for the business? But, will it encourage or discourage the raider?"

Such arguments may comfort concerned managers and board members who want protection from the discipline of competition in the market for managers. But they are based on false premises. The best way to discourage the competing manager (that's what *raider* means) is to run a company to maximize its value. "Will this decision help us obtain maximum market value?" is the only logically sensible interpretation of "What is best for the business?"

Folklore: Takeover Expenditures Are Wasted.

Fact: Purchase prices in corporate takeovers represent the transfer of wealth from the stockholders of bidding companies to those of target organizations, not the consumption of wealth. In a takeover, the resources represented in the cash received by the target shareholders can still be used to build new plant and equipment or for R&D.

The only resources consumed are those used to arrange the transaction, such as the time and fees of managers, lawyers, economists, and financial consultants. These expenses are often large in dollar terms; the financial fees of the U.S. Steel/Marathon Oil merger were more than $27 million, and those received by four investment banking firms in the Getty takeover hit a record by exceeding $47 million. But they are a tiny fraction of the dollar value of the acquisition; total financial and legal fees usually amount to only about .7%. More significantly, they help shareholders achieve their much larger gains of 4% to 30%.

In fact, the stock price change is the best measure of the takeover's future impact on the organization. The vast scientific evidence on the theory of efficient markets indicates that, in the absence of inside information, a security's market price represents the best available estimate of its true value. The evidence shows that market prices incorporate all current public information about future cash flows and the value of individual assets in an unbiased way. Stock prices change, of course, in response to new information about individual assets. Because market prices are efficient, however, the new information is equally likely to cause them to decrease or increase, after allowing for normal returns. Positive stock price changes, then, indicate a *rise* in the total profitability of the merged companies. Furthermore, because evidence indicates it does not come from the acquisition of market power, this increased profitability must come from the company's improved productivity.

Folklore: By Merging Competitors, Takeovers Create a Monopoly That Will Raise Product Prices, Produce Less, and Thereby Harm Consumers.

Fact: The evidence from four studies of the issue indicates that takeover gains come not from the merger's creation of monopoly market power but from its productive economies and synergy.

If the gains did come from the creation of companies with monopolistic powers, industry competitors would benefit, in turn, from the higher prices and would enjoy significant increases in profits and stock prices. Furthermore, the stock prices of rivals would fall if the FTC or the Antitrust Division of the Justice Department cancelled or challenged the merger.

The evidence indicates, however, that competitors gain when two other companies in the same industry merge. But these gains are not related to the creation of monopolistic power or industry concentration. Moreover, the stock prices of competitors do not fall on announcement of antitrust prosecution or cancellation of the acquisition. This evidence supports the hypothesis that takeover gains stem from real economies in production and distribution realized through the takeover and that it signals the availability of similar gains for rival companies.[6]

In fact, the evidence raises serious doubts about the wisdom of FTC or Justice Department policies concerning mergers. The cancellation of an acquisition erases virtually all the stock price increases occurring on its announcement—with no apparent offsetting benefits to anyone.[7]

Folklore: Consolidating Facilities after a Takeover Leads to Plant Closings, Layoffs, and Employee Dismissals—All At Great Social Cost.

Fact: No evidence with which I am familiar indicates that takeovers produce more plant closings, layoffs, and dismissals than would otherwise have occurred.

This charge raises a serious question, however, about the proper criteria for evaluation of the social desirability of takeovers. The standard efficiency yardstick measures increases in the aggregate real standard of living. By these criteria the wealth gains from takeovers (and their associated effects) are good as long as they do not come from the creation of monopolistic market power. Therefore, even if takeovers lead to plant closings, layoffs, and dismissals, their prohibition or limitation would generate real social costs and reduce aggregate human welfare because of the loss of potential operating economies.

Some observers may not agree that the standard efficiency criterion is the best measure of social desirability. But the adoption of any other criterion threatens to paralyze innovation. For example, innovations that increase standards of living in the long run initially produce changes that reduce the welfare of some individuals, at least in the short run. The development of efficient truck and air transport harmed the railroads and their workers; the rise of television hurt the radio industry. New and more efficient production, distribution, or organizational technology often imposes similar short-term costs.

The adoption of new technologies following takeovers enhances the overall real standard of living but reduces the wealth of those individuals with large investments in older technologies. Not surprisingly, such individuals and companies, their unions, communities, and political representatives will lobby to limit or prohibit takeovers that might result in new technologies. When successful, such politics reduce the nation's standard of living and its standing in international competition.

MANAGER-SHAREHOLDER CONFLICTS

The interests of managers and shareholders conflict on many, but certainly not all, issues. The divergence intensifies if the company becomes the target of an unfriendly takeover. During a takeover top managers of target companies can lose both their jobs and the value of their talents, knowledge, and income that are particular to the organization. Threatened with these losses, such officers may try to reduce the probability of a successful unfriendly takeover and benefit themselves at the expense of shareholders.

Management Struggles

The attempt by Carter Hawley Hale to acquire Marshall Field is an interesting example of a management struggle to retain control. Marshall Field, a high-quality department and specialty store chain, enjoyed less growth than other retailers but consistently rejected merger bids. In early 1978, Carter Hawley Hale, another retailer, offered $42 per share for Marshall Field stock, which was selling for less than $20. Resisting, Marshall Field filed a lawsuit that argued the acquisition would violate securities and antitrust laws. It informed shareholders that the asking price was inadequate and made several defensive acquisitions that aggravated potential antitrust problems and made it less attractive to Carter Hawley. Marshall Field's board authorized top officials to take "such action as they deemed necessary" to defeat the offer. After Carter Hawley withdrew the offer, Marshall Field's stock fell back to $20 per share.

In April 1984, another retailer, The Limited, tried to take over Carter Hawley Hale, whose stock then experienced abnormal gains of 49% in the ensuing conflict. Carter Hawley filed suit against The Limited, claiming securities law violations and antitrust problems, and gave up 33% of its voting rights through the sale of $300 million of convertible preferred stock to General Cinema Corporation. Carter Hawley then gave General Cinema a six-month option to buy the Waldenbook chain, one of its most profitable subsidiaries, and repurchased 51% of its own shares.

As a result The Limited withdrew its offer in May and Carter Hawley stockholders lost $363 million—the entire 49% abnormal stock price gain.

Both of these cases show what happens to stock prices when acquisition bids fail. The average abnormal stock price changes surrounding unsuccessful takeover bids are uniformly small and negative, ranging from −1% to −5%. The exception is the 8% positive return to shareholders of companies subjected to unsuccessful proxy contests. It is interesting that a proxy contest causes an abnormal stock price gain even when the challengers fail, perhaps because the contest threat motivates incumbent managers to change their strategies.

Uncoordinated, independent decisions by individual shareholders regarding the acceptance or rejection of a tender offer can cause most of the takeover gains to go to bidding company stockholders.[8] If target managers act as the agents for all target shareholders in negotiating with the bidder for a higher price, however, this "free rider" problem can be alleviated.

Empirical evidence also indicates that some managerial opposition benefits target shareholders. For example, on the failure of a tender offer, target stock prices do not on average immediately lose the 30% average increase in price they earned when the offer was made. In fact, they generally stay up, apparently in anticipation of future bids. And target companies that receive at least one more bid in the two years following the failure of a tender offer on average realize another 20% increase in price. Those targets that do not receive another bid, however, lose the entire initial price increase.[9] Apparently, a little opposition in a merger battle is good, but too much can be disastrous if it prohibits takeover of the company.

Golden Parachutes

Some companies provide compensation in employment contracts for top-level managers in the event that a takeover occurs—that is, golden parachutes. Allied agreed, for example, to make up the difference for five years between Bendix CEO William Agee's salary in subsequent employment and his former annual $825,000 salary in the event of a change in control at Bendix. Much confusion exists about the propriety and desirability of golden parachutes, even among senior executives.

But the detractors fail to understand that the parachutes protect stockholders as well as managers. Think about the problem in the following way: top-level managers and the board of directors act as stockholders' agents in deals involving hundreds of millions of dollars. If the alternative providing the highest value to stockholders is sale to another company and the retirement of the current management team, stockholders do not want the managers to block a bid in fear of losing their own jobs. Stockholders may be asking managers to sacrifice position and wealth to negotiate the best deal for them.

Golden parachutes are clearly desirable when they protect stockholders' interests. Like anything else, however, they may be abused. For example, a stockholder doesn't want to pay managers so much for selling the company that they hurry to sell at a low price to the first bidder. But that is a problem with the details of the parachute's contractual provisions and not with the existence of the parachute itself. An analysis of 90 companies shows that adoption of golden parachutes on average has no negative effect on stock prices and provides some evidence of positive effects.[10]

The thing that puzzles me about most golden parachute contracts is that they pay off only when the manager leaves his job and thus create an unnecessary conflict of interest between shareholders and executives. Current shareholders and the acquiring company will want to retain the services of a manager who has valuable knowledge and skills. But the officer can collect the golden parachute premium only by leaving; the contract rewards him or her for taking an action that may well hurt the business. As the bidder assimilates the knowledge that turnover among valuable top-level managers after the acquisition is highly likely, it will reduce its takeover bid. A company can eliminate this problem by making the award conditional on transfer of control and not on the manager's exit from the company.

Selling the "Crown Jewels"

Another often criticized defensive tactic is the sale of a major division by a company faced with a takeover threat. Some observers claim that such sales prove that managers will do anything to preserve their tenure, even to the extent of crippling or eliminating major parts of the business that appear attractive to outside bidders. Such actions have been labeled a "scorched earth policy."

Studies of the effects of corporate spinoffs, however, indicate they generate significantly positive abnormal returns.[11] Moreover, when target managers find a white knight to pay more for the entire company than the initial, hostile bidder, shareholders clearly benefit.

In the same way, when an acquirer is interested mainly in a division rather than the whole company, shareholders benefit when target management auctions off the unit at a higher price. Brunswick's sale of its Sherwood Medical Industries division to American Home Products shows how the sale of a crown jewel can benefit shareholders. Whittaker Corporation made a hostile takeover bid for Brunswick in early 1982. In defense, Brunswick sold a key division, Sherwood Medical, to American Home Products through a negotiated tender offer for 64% of Brunswick's shares. American Home Products then exchanged these shares with Brunswick for Sherwood's stock. Because its main interest lay in acquiring Sherwood, Whittaker withdrew its offer.[12]

The value of the Whittaker offer to Brunswick shareholders ranged from $605 million to $618 million, depending on the value assigned to the convertible debentures that were part of the offer. The total value to Brunswick shareholders of the management strategy, selling off the Sherwood division, was $620 million. Moreover, because of the structure of the transaction, the cash proceeds went directly to the Brunswick shareholders through the negotiated tender offer. The $620 million value represents a gain of $205 million (49%) on the total equity value of Brunswick prior to the initial Whittaker offer. The Brunswick shareholders were $2 million to $15 million better off with the management strategy, hardly evidence of a scorched-earth policy.

Takeover Artists

Recently, criticism has been directed at corporate takeover specialists who are said to take advantage of a company's vulnerability in the market and thus ultimately harm shareholders. While acting in their own interests, however, these specialists also act as agents for shareholders of companies with entrenched managers. Returning to the Marshall Field story, for example, Carl Icahn launched a systematic campaign to acquire the chain after it had avoided takeover. When it looked as if he would achieve the goal, Marshall Field initiated a corporate auction and merged with BATUS (British American Tobacco Company, U.S.) for $30 per share in 1982. After adjustment for inflation, that price was slightly less than the $20 price of Field's stock in 1977, when it defeated Carter Hawley's $42 offer.

Takeover specialists like Icahn risk their own fortunes to dislodge current managers and reap part of the value increases available from redeploying the assets or improving the management. Evidence from a study of 100 such instances indicates that when such specialists announce the purchase of 5% or more of a company's shares, the stockholders of that company on average earn significantly positive abnormal returns of about 6%.[13]

THE EFFECTIVENESS OF THE MARKET

The corporation has contributed much to the enhancement of society's living standards. Yet the details of how and why this complex institution functions and survives are poorly understood, due in part to the complexity of the issues involved and in part to the political controversy that historically surrounds it. Much of this controversy reflects the actions of individuals and groups that wish to use the corporation's assets for their own purposes, without purchasing them.

One source of the controversy comes from the separation between managers and shareholders—a separation necessary to realize the large efficiencies in risk bearing that are the corporation's comparative advantage. The process by which internal control mechanisms work so that professional managers act in the shareholders' interest is subtle and difficult to observe. When internal control mechanisms are working well, the board of directors will replace top-level managers whose talents are no longer the best ones available for the job.[14]

When these mechanisms break down, however, stockholders receive some protection from the takeover market, where alternative management teams compete for the rights to manage the corporation's assets. This competition can take the form of mergers, tender offers, or proxy fights.

Scientific evidence indicates that activities in the market for corporate control almost uniformly increase efficiency and shareholders' wealth. Yet there is an almost continuous flow of unfavorable publicity and calls for regulation and restriction of unfriendly takeovers. Many of these appeals arise from managers who want protection from competition for their jobs and others who desire more controls on corporations. The result, in the long run, may be a further weakening of the corporation as an organizational form and a reduction in human welfare.

NOTES

1. For further analysis, see Leo Herzel and John R. Schmidt, "SEC is Probing 'Double Pac-Man' Takeover Defense," *Legal Times*, April 18, 1983, p. 27.

2. For further insight, see Claude W. McAnally, III, "The Bendix-Martin Marietta Takeover and Stockholder Returns," unpublished masters thesis, Massachusetts Institute of Technology, 1983.

3. The only exception is the nonprofit organization, against which there are no residual claims.

4. For a summary, see Michael C. Jensen and Richard S. Ruback, "The Market for Corporate Control: The Scientific Evidence," *Journal of Financial Economics,* April 1983, p. 5.

5. Financial economists have used abnormal price changes or abnormal returns to study the effects of various events on security prices since Eugene F. Fama, Lawrence Fisher, Michael C. Jensen, and Richard Roll used them to measure the impact of stock splits in "The Adjustment of Stock Prices to New Information," *International Economic Review,* February 1969, p. 1.

6. B. Espen Eckbo, "Horizontal Mergers, Collusion, and Stockholder Wealth," *Journal of Financial Economics,* April 1983, p. 241; Robert Stillman, "Examining Antitrust Policy Towards Horizontal Mergers," *Journal of Financial Economics,* April 1983, p. 225.

7. Peggy Wier, "The Costs of Antimerger Lawsuits: Evidence from the Stock Market," *Journal of Financial Economics,* April 1983.

8. See S. Grossman and O. Hart, "Takeover Bids, the Free-Rider Problem, and the Theory of the Corporation," *Bell Journal of Economics,* Spring 1980, p. 42; and Michael Bradley, "Interfirm Tender Offers and the Market for Corporate Control," *Journal of Business,* October 1980, p. 345.

9. Michael Bradley, Anand Desai, and E. Han Kim, "The Rationale Behind Interfirm Tender Offers: Information or Synergy?" *Journal of Financial Economics,* April 1983.

10. Richard A. Lambert and David F. Larcker, "Golden Parachutes, Executive Decision-Making and Shareholder Wealth," *Journal of Accounting and Economics,* forthcoming.

11. See Katherine Schipper and Abbie Smith, "Effects of Recontracting on Shareholder Wealth: The

Case of Voluntary Spin-offs," *Journal of Financial Economics,* December 1983, p. 437; Gailen Hite and James Owers, "Security Price Reactions Around Corporate Spin-off Announcements," *Journal of Financial Economics,* December 1983, p. 409.

12. For a further analysis, see Leo Herzel and John R. Schmidt, "Shareholders Can Benefit from Sale of 'Crown Jewels,'" *Legal Times,* October 24, 1983, p. 33.

13. For analysis of the effects of purchases by six so-called raiders, Bluhdorn, Icahn, Jacobs, Lindner, Murdock, and Posner, see Clifford G. Holderness and Dennis Sheehan, "The Evidence on Six Controversial Investors," University of Rochester Managerial Economics Research Center Working Paper No. MERC 84-06 (Rochester, N.Y.: August 1984).

14. For evidence on the relation between poor performance and executive turnover, see Anne Coughlan and Ronald Schmidt, "Executive Compensation, Management Turnover and Firm Performance: An Empirical Investigation," *Journal of Accounting and Economics,* forthcoming.

[*Author's note:* I am indebted to Armen Alchian, Karl Brunner, Harry DeAngelo, Leo Herzel, Charles Plosser, Richard Rosett, Robert Sproull, Alan Underberg, and Ned Wass for comments and assistance.]

The Truth about Corporate Raiders

Robert Kuttner*

Not long ago, the corporate raiders Irwin Jacobs and T. Boone Pickens addressed an overflow crowd of Harvard Business School students. Pickens and Jacobs make their livings borrowing money and attempting to seize control of corporations, or cashing in their shares for a fast profit once they have set off a bidding war. Pick-

From *The New Republic* (January 20, 1986). Copyright © 1986. Reprinted with permission.
*Economics editor, *The New Republic*.

ens made $89 million for failing to take over Phillips Petroleum. The B-school kids were about as euphoric as people who study balance sheets ever get. The mood was more like a rock concert than a financial seminar. You almost expected Pickens to perform an act of arbitrage right there on stage, to wild applause.

Judging by the eager reception, raiders present a splendid role model for the business student of the 1980s. They offer a much faster career track than the tamer brands of management, entrepreneurship, and bond-peddling. Intriguingly, they also serve as the business school version of populists. For, according to Pickens and his many admirers in the academy, the financial press, and the brokerage houses, raiders are the invisible hand incarnate. They embody the democratic virtue of enhancing corporate accountability, the capitalist virtue of maximizing value for shareholders, and the social virtue of forcing the redeployment of assets on reluctant corporate managers. Thus the raider offers not only fame and fortune, but the commodity most highly prized by capitalists ever since the Protestant reformation: virtue itself.

Is corporate raiding truly so virtuous? There is the semblance of a debate about that, but the debate is oddly muted. After all, the raiders' adversaries, in the short run, are incumbent corporate management. As *Newsweek's* Robert Samuelson wrote in a representative column lauding Pickens, "Can you imagine a group less deserving of help? I can't."

Indeed. Introducing Jacobs and Pickens to Harvard, the attorney Ira Millstein intoned: "The alternatives are these: Do we wish to tilt the playing field to the managers? Or to the raiders?" When the issue is posed that way, as it normally is, one is tempted to shrug: a plague on both their houses.

The trouble is that the question is far too narrow, and it begs several other questions: What is the nature of a corporation? Who are its constituents, other than managers and shareholders? What is the best way of making corporations accountable to their various constituencies? What should society expect in return for the many legal privileges and immunities conferred on corporations? What sort of regime of corporate control maximizes the long-term goals of productivity growth and fair distribution of rewards for the whole economy? These questions, in turn, raise other chestnuts of economic theory: What is the relationship of individual utility to social utility? And what should society do when auction markets fail to produce the best of all possible worlds?

Pickens is only the most swashbuckling player in the takeover casino. The more usual hostile takeover occurs when one large corporation, such as GAF, offers to buy the shares of another large corporation, such as Union Carbide, at a premium price, over the objections of the incumbent board and managers, who will doubtless lose their jobs. A reverse variation, lately in vogue, is the management buy-out, in which incumbent management adopts the same maneuver, preemptively. In almost all cases, raiders use borrowed money.

The takeover game is accelerating for several reasons. First, the current regulatory climate is exceptionally lax. In more normal times, many fashionable takeover techniques might be prohibited as inherently manipulative. But in the laissez-faire 1980s, no regulator is disposed to interfere with the presumed genius of the market. Second, tender offers produce great short-run gains for people who trade stocks. Any time a bidding war for a publicly traded firm breaks out, current stockholders in that firm can look forward to quick windfall gains when they tender their shares to the raider. The more raiding, the more run-ups. Third, recent changes in tax law provide large subsidies for takeovers that employ borrowed money. Interest on the new debt is tax-deductible, of course. More important, the new owner may take the huge accelerated depreciation write-offs that were instituted in President Reagan's 1981 tax cut, and may do so based on the new high value of the corporation's as-

sets set by the buyer's own purchase price. This means that almost any corporation that hasn't traded hands since 1981 is worth more to potential buyers than to its current owners.

Finally, the middlemen making the immense profits on the transactions—lawyers, investment bankers, institutional investors—are people of substantial political influence. They like coherent ground rules, but above all they want the game to continue. To the extent that the SEC has been involved at all, it has acted to expedite the game, in line with the prevailing theory that shareholders benefit.

There is nothing new about shrewd middlemen netting windfall profits from purely financial or speculative rearrangements of assets. The previous peak of financial innovation in the service of speculative borrowing, ominously enough, was in the late 1920s. Critics dating back to Veblen have long called attention to the difference between entrepreneurs whose bag of tricks is purely ''financial'' and those who create real economic wealth. ''Speculators,'' wrote Keynes, ''may do no harm as bubbles on a steady stream of enterprise. But the position is serious when enterprise becomes the bubble on a whirlpool of speculation.''

What is truly new about the current wave of speculative takeovers is the widespread approbation. The raiding phenomenon occurs at a historical moment when resurgent laissez-faire dominates philosophical assumptions. The widespread approval of hostile takeovers reflects the philosophical triumph of the ''Chicago'' school of economics, whose worldview is predicated on the assumption that markets must know what they are doing. Nearly all the economists weighing hostile takeovers sound like Chicago economists. Even the proposed remedies for abuses are almost entirely market remedies. In the Chicago view, the only test that is really necessary is whether the raiding game boosts share prices.

The *1985 Economic Report of the President* includes an entire chapter defending hostile takeovers. The chapter is pure Chicago economic theory, right down to its title, "The Market for Corporate Control," which is borrowed from a famous article of two decades ago by Professor Henry Manne, who argued that corporate takeover battles should be understood as markets no different from other markets. Manne and his disciples contend that whole corporations are simply commodities, "like apples." The management team that can command the highest price is, by definition, the highest-valued team, and hence deserves to win.

In the story told by the *Economic Report of the President,* hostile takeovers, no matter how implausible or disruptive, are therefore an unmitigated good. The proof of this is simply that takeover battles increase the price paid to shareholders of the target company, which must mean that the takeover team will wring more performance out of the assets than the old managers. Otherwise, the report argues, it would have been irrational for the raider to pay a premium. Raiders, therefore, increase society's real wealth. So valuable is this service that the middleman rake-off by investment bankers and lawyers pales into insignificance. In fact, says the report, the only real abuses are management's defensive tactics, which serve management's own interests at the expense of the shareholders.

The report reads very much like a term paper in a University of Chicago economics class; and it suggests that the debate about the social benefit of hostile takeovers is really two debates—one about the appropriate regulatory framework for corporate ownership and control, the other about how to think about economics. For the Chicago school, which has dominated this debate, there is one simple answer to all economic questions: the more nearly all economic life resembles an auction, the more efficient and hence socially superior it is. If corporations are perpetually on the block, any dislocation, insecurity, middleman windfall, or speculative overreaching is outweighed by the prospect that assets are being redeployed to their highest and

best use. The apotheosis of this view is the work of Michael Jensen, a financial economist and takeover advocate, who wrote in a recent issue of *Harvard Business Review,* "The takeover market provides a unique, powerful, and impersonal mechanism to accomplish the major restructuring and redeployment of assets required by changes in technology and consumer preference.... Scientific evidence indicates that activities in the market for corporate control almost uniformly increase efficiency and shareholders' wealth."

Jensen's scientific evidence boils down to the fact that raiders bid up stock values of target companies (by an average of about 30 percent). This, of course, must be true by definition; nobody would tender shares to a raider who merely matched the market price. Jensen goes on to argue that raiders are prepared to pay premiums because they must be able to produce some "synergy" that the prior managers had failed to exploit. (In Chicago-babble, "must be" is the preferred verb form.) Even if a bidder buys a company only to sell off its assets, this is also a social good, because the assets ultimately wind up in the hands of someone better able to exploit them. Jensen also contends that when an acquiring corporation goes deeply into debt in order to buy a target company, leaving the newly combined firm with a substantial debt that can be three or four times its total equity, this sort of "leveraging up" is also a good thing, because the burden of meeting payments forces executives to work harder.

Jensen even likes "golden parachutes"—the multimillion-dollar consolation prizes paid to executives who lose out in takeovers. He argues that they remove one source of opposition to a more fluid market in corporate control.

Is this picture true, or only convenient? Is maximization of shareholder value in the short run the only test of economic worth? Share prices, after all, were soaring in mid-1929, but this didn't necessarily reflect an underlying healthy economy. Is the hostile takeover the only way, or the best way, of redeploying physical and human capital, and of keeping managers disciplined? Are takeover battles the most efficient form of the ''creative destruction'' that Schumpeter said was a crucial element of capitalism?

Evidence is beginning to accumulate that the easy speculative takeovers of the 1980s have substantial negative effects on particular firms and on the economy as a whole. The evidence is messy, anecdotal, and institutional; it lacks the conceptual neatness (and the political constituency) of the Chicago view. But it seems to discredit both the takeover game and the financial economists' view of the corporate arena as nothing but an auction.

One effect of takeovers is accelerating debt. In the aggregate, the ''leveraged buy-out'' boom is one more realm where the American economy is sailing forward on an ocean of speculative borrowing. According to the New York Stock Exchange, $89 billion in corporate equity was converted into debt last year. The debt-equity ratio of U.S. corporations has increased from 57 percent in 1961 to more than 81 percent in 1984, and eight points of that increase occurred in just the last year. Debt is fine in a rising market when real interest rates are falling. But how will these over-leveraged companies perform in the next recession?

Beyond the problem of excessive borrowing, one also must consider what the casino mentality does to the entire corporate culture. In a world where whole corporations are prey, the manager who plans for the long term is a sucker. Raiders posing as populists neatly appropriate the widespread criticism of managers as myopic oafs worried only about this quarter's earnings. But for managers, takeover fears only intensify the obsession with the quarterly bottom line. For when reported profits drop, the stock may become undervalued, making it an easier target. Takeover worries also lead prudent managers to get rid of cash cushions, to raid pension funds, and to throw overboard anything that might make them a target. Often managers deliberately turn a swan

back into an ugly duckling in order to make the firm less attractive to a potential raider. In cases like CBS's successful defense against Ted Turner, or Walt Disney's defense against Saul Steinberg, the target firm ends up uglifying itself by selling off some of its most profitable divisions, or taking on crippling debt, which depresses its own earnings for years to come.

The claim that target firms are poorly managed underperformers is not borne out by the facts. A study by Professor Louis Lowenstein of the Columbia University Law School looked at all of the industrial firms that were targets of hostile takeovers during 1981. He found that they enjoyed a return on equity of 16 percent—well above average. This finding only reflects common sense. Raiders are after good firms that happen to have depressed stock prices; they are not interested in paying premium prices for lemons.

There is also increasing evidence that many shotgun mergers turn out to be bad deals. The synergy fails to materialize. The acquiring firm discovers that it overpaid, and later sells off the assets of the target firm, often for a loss. There is a long catalog of cases in which the acquiring firm, understandably, knew less about what it was buying than the established management, and proved to be an even worse manager.

The proof that raiders often overpay is that the parent firm's own stock subsequently declines. Several recent studies reveal that hostile takeovers indeed bid up the price of the target firm (as they would have to), but over time they tended to depress the performance of the raiding firm. A study by Professor Frederick Scherer of Swarthmore College found that target companies had nearly double the average rate of profitability, pre-merger, but a sharp decline, post-merger.

Another intriguing phenomenon that gives the lie to the Chicago interpretation of the efficiency of hostile takeovers is the latest fad, the management buy-out. Managers have found that two can play this game. The same device available to raiders—borrowing money and buying stock—is available to managers. Lately many managers have preemptively taken their companies private, using the same sort of junk-bond financing as raiders. Now, obviously if the social justification for an unfriendly takeover is the claim that incumbent management was doing a poor job, the same claim cannot possibly apply when that same incumbent management buys out the shareholders. On the contrary, there is a pretty fair presumption that if management is taking advantage of its privileged information to buy out undervalued stock, then it is violating its fiduciary duty to its own shareholders. And there is some evidence that a management preparing to go private can subtly act to drive down the stock price—for example, by overfunding its pension plan to depress quarterly earnings—in order to buy the stock back at a bargain later on. When management swoops in to buy the company, the invisible hand at work is that of Alex Portnoy, not Adam Smith.

Setting aside assumptions and getting down to cases, often the only factor that makes the deal pay at all is the tax angle. In his study of management buy-outs, Professor Lowenstein found that without the tax subsidy the return on equity in a sample of 28 management buy-outs would have been a paltry six percent.

Hostile takeovers, in sum, do produce gains for three kinds of people—stockholders who happen to hold shares in a target company on the eve of a bidding war; middlemen (investment bankers and lawyers made $100 million in the Pantry Pride takeover of Revlon); and executives looking to increase their own status. But contrary to the Chicago view of financial markets, they don't automatically translate into gains to the national welfare. Here we have a double case of market failure. The first market failure is a familiar theorem, one that won the Nobel Prize in economics for Professor Herbert Simon: the self-interest of a corporate executive should not be mistaken for the self-interest of the company. Executives are notorious empire builders, and

there is no quicker road to empire than a big merger.

The second kind of market failure is even more fundamental. It is the failure of the stock market to accurately reflect the true "worth" of a given firm on a given day. The main characteristic of the stock market is that it fluctuates. Studies show that the fluctuations in share prices vastly overstate actual variations in a firm's profitability.

The stock market, by its very nature, is a traders' market, where prices reflect the expectation traders impute to other traders as much as they reflect the real value of the underlying corporate assets. Often the total value of a firm's shares is substantially less than its liquidation value, or the price it would fetch in a negotiated sale. But that is no proof that the present managers are inferior to the raiders. The shares may be depressed for any number of reasons, ranging from lack of consumer confidence about the economy as a whole to current high interest rates pulling money into the bond market, to investor pessimism about a particular industry. Oil companies were takeover targets because the stock market valued their shares at a price that translated to about three dollars a barrel. Yet often, because of the vagaries of the takeover game, a very badly managed company, such as Texaco, winds up taking control of a well-managed firm, such as Getty. If the legal rules that make possible an orderly corporate and financial marketplace suddenly provide that any firm with undervalued shares is up for grabs whenever a prospective raider can borrow enough money, then the entire real economy is turned into a speculative casino, in which rearranging assets yields greater rewards than building them.

What should be done about all this? If you buy the Chicago/Reagan administration view, nothing should be done. But even if the evidence troubles you, the remedy remains elusive. The reform proposals currently under debate fall into two categories—pro-raider and pro-manager, exactly the formulation Attorney Millstein began with. This is hardly surprising, because raiders and managers are the ones with seats at the political table. There is no Productivity PAC lobbying Congress and the SEC.

If you think that corporate management needs more security, then there are devices that can frustrate raiding. You can require that the boards of directors of both the target firm and the acquiring firm approve any tender offer. You can prohibit ''two-tier'' tender offers, in which a raider purposely induces a stampede by offering a better price to the first shareholders who tender their stock than to the rest. You can amend the Williams Act of 1968, which regulates tender offers, by lengthening the time the offer must be open. You can also provide that any short-run profit a raider makes from his stock holdings must be returned to the company.

On the other hand, if you think that raiding exemplifies the invisible hand, you can lubricate the takeover market in various ways. You can make management buy-outs more difficult. You can prohibit golden parachutes, non-voting stock gimmicks, preferential sell-offs to ''white knights,'' and other brands of ''shark repellent'' now in vogue. Unocal managed to fight off Boone Pickens by buying its own shares in a ''self-tender'' that excluded Pickens from the offer. Chicagoans think this should be illegal.

The best regulation currently on the table is the one recently proposed by the Federal Reserve Board, which wants to extend its ''margin'' requirements to corporate takeovers. These rules limit how much you can borrow to buy corporate stock. It is a little odd that if you want to speculate in 100 shares of IBM, you must put up 50 percent of your own funds, but if you want to borrow all of the money necessary to take over the entire company, no problem. Extending margin requirements would keep managers under the threat of tender offers, but damp down the excessive leverage, and thereby also take away some of the tax advantages. However, the Federal Reserve Board of Governors split three-to-two on this plan, and two new Reagan appoin-

tees will soon create an administration majority on the Fed. The administration released comments Christmas week opposing the Fed's margin proposal.

Even the best remedies now on the table beg the larger question of what we expect from corporations, and how they should be governed. The cure for T. Boone Pickens is not greater security for corporate managers, just as the remedy for lazy entrenched management is not necessarily Pickens.

Since the classic 1932 work of Adolf Berle and Gardner Means, *The Modern Corporation and Private Property,* it has been widely recognized that a big corporation seldom reflects its storybook structure of share-holding owners who monitor, hire, and fire salaried executives and boards of directors. Control, as the saying goes, is separated from ownership. In practice, most corporations are run by managers and by passive, self-selecting boards of directors. The lack of corporate accountability to shareholders—and, by extension, to society—has troubled generations of reformers. Critics in the mode of Ralph Nader have proposed to democratize the corporation by increasing the power of its outside (nonmanagement) directors, and its shareholders. Against this history, the hostile takeover is the Chicago version of social revolution; it deftly outflanks the progressive critics with a radically classic version of shareholder democracy, and without recourse to government regulation.

But the Chicago remedy is a mite too radical, for it ignores the fact that corporations are not just fluid collections of assets, but sets of relationships. Moreover, ''the market'' that exists in the real world is not a grand casino, but a set of legal rules and social norms that makes practical capitalism possible. Without conventions like money, bankruptcy, legally enforceable contracts, federally sanctioned and regulated banks and stock markets, there would be no marketplace. And once you admit that these markets depend on society's rules, it becomes legitimate to discuss variations on those rules. The market is often virtuous, but in a civil polity it can never be the sole virtue or the sole standard of virtue.

In the Chicago view, any private transaction, such as a contract or the sale of shares, is presumed to be voluntary, while any public intervention is presumed to be coercive. But that assumption, when you get down to cases, is often nonsensical. A worker with 20 years on the job and ties to the community is hardly a free contracting party with power equal to his employer's. By the same token, a pension fund, confronted with a take-it-or-leave-it tender offer, is not free to sell or not sell. Private transactions can be intensely coercive; and public regulation can lessen coercion, and hence increase choice.

Everybody wants a competitive marketplace, but there are better ways of stimulating competition than by putting entire corporations on a perennial auction block. Surely it is healthier for corporations to compete in the usual way—on the basis of the quality and price of their products and services, on the price their shares command in the financial marketplace—than by chronically threatening to acquire each other. If we had more product competition and price competition, we wouldn't have to rely on the threat of takeovers to allocate resources efficiently.

In Germany and Japan, the two industrial economies with the highest long-term productivity growth, hostile takeovers simply don't exist. The control of the corporation is not subject to an auction, yet product competition and innovation are fierce. Interestingly too, German industry and Japanese industry are much more highly leveraged than ours. They rely heavily on debt financing, yet in an institutionally stable context where the debt goes for investment in new technology, not for takeover wars.

The threat of takeovers is a very poor version of shareholder democracy. In the Chicago model, the only corporate citizens who need to be served are shareholders, who change overnight as investors trade shares. But in the real world, workers and managers and the communities where they live have some long-term stake in the viability of an enterprise. Real corporate democracy would place managers under more scrutiny from outside directors, and would include some participatory rights for employees. It is more than a little ironic that the latest device for sheltering a corporation from raiders is to give a large block of stock to the one group unlikely to sell capriciously—the workers. Boone Pickens may be performing a service for genuine corporate democracy after all: he may force the corporations to pay more attention to their most loyal constituency, their own employees.

QUESTIONS FOR DISCUSSION

1. Nader, Green, and Seligman quote Peter Drucker's comment, "[T]here is one thing all boards have in common, regardless of their legal position. *They do not function.*" What are the traditional functions of the corporate board? According to Nader, Green, and Seligman and Geneen, how do most boards fail to fulfill these functions? How would Nader, Green, and Seligman like to see the function of the board changed?

2. Pan American Products is a manufacturer of industrial equipment. It employs 10,000 people in its factories, many of which are the primary source of jobs in the communities in which the factories operate. The firm is in good financial shape; its stock is selling for $50 a share. In addition, Pan American prides itself on the quality of its products and its loyalty to employees and customers. US Products, a long-time rival of Pan American, has begun a hostile takeover by making a tender offer for Pan American stock at $58 a share. US Products has a poor reputation in the area of quality control and has broken up the other companies it has bought and sold off the pieces. Does Pan American's management team have a right to try to keep their company out of the hands of US Products? Defend your answer. What implications, if any, does this example have on the problem of hostile takeovers in general?

THE NATURE OF THE CORPORATION

CASES FOR PART TWO

First National Bank of Boston v. Bellotti
Corporate Free Speech Is Upheld
248

Senate Committee on Governmental Affairs
*Directorships of Major U.S. Corporations
Tightly Interlocked*
253

Wyndham Robertson
The Directors Woke Up Too Late at Gulf
254

Paul Hirsch
Oklahoma Meets Wall Street
260

Corporate Free Speech Is Upheld, First National Bank of Boston v. Bellotti

If the speakers here were not corporations, no one would suggest that the state could silence their proposed speech. It is the type of speech indispensable to decision making in a democracy, and this is no less true because the speech comes from a corporation rather than from an individual.

Justice Lewis F. Powell, Jr.

Ideas which are not a product of individual choice are entitled to less First Amendment protection. Indeed, what some have considered to be the principal function of the First Amendment, the use of communication as a means of self-expression, self-realization and self-fulfillment, is not at all furthered by corporate speech.

Justice Byron R. White

WASHINGTON—The U.S. Supreme Court yesterday struck down a Massachusetts law that prohibited banks and business corporations from spending corporate funds to publicize political views not related to their companies' business purposes.

In a 5–4 decision defining the free-speech rights of corporations for the first time, the high court overturned a Massachusetts Supreme Judicial Court decision against the First National Bank of Boston and four other businesses in the state that wanted to spend money in 1976 to express their opposition to a referendum proposal to amend the state constitution.

The proposed amendment, which was defeated, would have authorized the legislature to enact a graduated personal income tax.

Justice Lewis Powell, writer for the majority, said yesterday that the First Amendment to the Constitution was not meant to abridge

"speech indispensable to decision making in a democracy" simply because "the speech comes from a corporation rather than an individual."

In the main dissenting opinion, Justice Byron R. White said the decision raises "considerable doubt" that the Court would uphold laws in 31 states that restrict corporate political activities. Most of the laws ban corporate contributions to candidates for state offices.

White said the ruling also "clearly raises great doubt" that the Court would uphold the Corrupt Practices Act, the 1907 law with which Congress made it a crime for a corporation, a national bank, or a labor union to contribute money in connection with congressional or presidential elections.

States should be free to draw distinctions between corporations and individuals, White said. "Ideas which are not a product of individual choice are entitled to less First Amendment protection," he said.

Powell was joined by Chief Justice Warren F. Burger and Justices Potter Stewart, Harry A. Blackmun, and John Paul Stevens.

White's dissent was joined by Justices Thurgood Marshall and William J. Brennan, Jr. Justice William H. Rehnquist wrote his own dissenting opinion, emphasizing states' regulatory rights over corporations.

"A state grants to a business corporation the blessings of potentially perpetual life and limited liability to enhance its efficiency as an economic entity," Rehnquist wrote.

"It might reasonably be concluded that those properties, so beneficial in the economic sphere, pose special dangers in the political sphere," he said.

Joining First National in the court challenge were the New England Merchants National Bank, the Gillette Co., Digital Equipment Corp., and Wyman-Gordon Co.

The statute involved prohibited corporations from making contributions or expenditures to influence the vote on any referendum unless it

---

Excerpted from United Press International and AP news-features. "Reaction" from *The Boston Globe* (April 27, 1978). Reprinted by permission of UPI, AP, and *The Boston Globe*.

"materially" affects any of the companies' property, business or assets. When the five firms announced plans in 1976 to spend money to make their opposition known to the income tax, the state attorney general's office announced it would prosecute.

Violation of the law carried a possible corporation fine of up to $50,000 and a one-year prison sentence or $10,000 fine to individual company officers.

Yesterday's ruling was the first to confront the issue whether a corporation—defined by Chief Justice John Marshall in 1819 as "an artificial being, invisible, intangible and existing only in contemplation of law"—has a protected liberty to engage in political activities.

Reaction: "It's a Major Blow to Consumers"

James B. Ayres *

Lawrence Collins †

The Supreme Court decision upholding the right of corporations to spend their money to speak out on political issues will make it harder for citizens' groups to win referendum questions involving corporate interests, a spokesman for the Massachusetts Public Interest Research Group (MassPIRG) said yesterday.

Peter S. Rider, MassPIRG staff counsel, said the bottle industry spent more than $5 million to kill the bottle referendum last year, permissible under the state law which allows a corporation with a direct interest in a referendum to advertise.

"But," said Rider, "What happens on a broad-reaching referendum such as a proposal to classify property tax levies according to business or residential use? You have the potential for virtually unlimited spending."

Rep. Lois G. Pines (D–Newton), who has led a drive for six years to ban nondeposit bottles and cans in Massachusetts and who last year saw a statewide referendum on the issue defeated by 21,000 votes, expressed shock at the high court's decision.

"This is a major disappointment," Pines said. "I think it has a potentially devastating effect on government. It will mean that big business interests will have more clout than ever before. It's a major blow to consumers or just ordinary people."

First Asst. Atty. Gen. Thomas R. Kiley, who argued the Commonwealth's case before the Supreme Court last November, yesterday said he "naturally is disappointed."

"We haven't seen the full decision yet, so I couldn't even speculate on the possible impact it might have on the state's political scene," said Kiley. "But it is a very significant case."

The U.S. Chamber of Commerce, however, hailed the decision as a great victory for the business community.

"The opinion clears business of the charge that the appearance or possibility of corruption will inevitably result if business speaks out on public issues," Chamber President Richard Lesher said.

The "decision also casts doubt about the legality of lobby reform proposals which single out activities of business for special treatment and regulation," Lesher contended.

On the other hand, Common Cause Senior Vice President Fred Wertheimer called the court's decision "just plain wrong."

Wertheimer said the decision "sets the stage for massive corporate expenditures in initiative campaigns throughout the country and seriously undermines the integrity of the initiative process."

More bluntly, an AFL-CIO spokesman termed the decision, "a victory for the best freedom of speech that money can buy."

*Reporter for *The Boston Globe*.
†Former reporter for *The Boston Globe*.

Excerpts from High Court Opinions

FROM MAJORITY OPINION
BY JUSTICE POWELL

In sustaining a state criminal statute that forbids certain expenditures by banks and business corporations for the purpose of influencing the vote on referendum proposals, the Massachusetts Supreme Judicial Court held that the First Amendment rights of a corporation are limited to issues that materially affect its business, property, or assets. The Court rejected appellants' claim that this statute abridged freedom of speech in violation of the First and Fourteenth Amendments....

The Court below framed the principal question in this case as whether and to what extent corporations have First Amendment rights. We believe that the Court posed the wrong question. The Constitution often protects interests broader than those of the party seeking their vindication. The First Amendment, in particular, serves significant social interests. The proper question therefore is not whether corporations have First Amendment rights and, if so, whether they are co-extensive with those of natural persons. Instead, the question must be whether [the statute in question] abridges expression that the First Amendment was meant to protect. We hold that it does....

In appellants' view the enactments of a graduated personal income tax, as proposed to be authorized by constitutional amendment, would have a seriously adverse effect on the economy of the state. The importance of the referendum issue to the people and government of Massachusetts is not disputed. Its merits, however, are the subject of sharp disagreement....

If the speakers here were not corporations, no one would suggest that the state could silence their proposed speech. It is the type of speech indispensable to decision making in a democracy, and this is no less true because the speech comes from a corporation rather than from an individual.

Nor do our recent commercial speech cases lend support to appellee's business interest theory. They illustrate that the First Amendment goes beyond the protection of the press and the self-expression of individuals to prohibit government from limiting the stock of information from which members of the public may draw. A commercial advertisement is constitutionally protected not so much because it pertains to the seller's business as because it furthers the social interest in the free flow of commercial information.

We thus find no support in the First or Fourteenth Amendments, or in the decisions of this Court, for the proposition that speech that otherwise would lie within the protection of the First Amendment loses that protection simply because its source is a corporation that cannot prove, to the satisfaction of a court, a material effect on its business or property....

If a legislature may direct business corporations to stick to business, it also may limit other corporations—religions, charitable, or civic—to their respective business when addressing the public. Such power in government to channel the expression of views is unacceptable under the First Amendment....

If appellee's arguments were supported by record or legislative findings that corporate advocacy threatened imminently to undermine democratic processes, thereby denigrating, rather than serving First Amendment interest, these arguments would merit our consideration. But there has been no showing that the relative voice of corporations has been overwhelming or even significant in influencing referendums in Massachusetts or that there has been any threat to the confidence of the citizenry in government.

Nor are appellee's arguments inherently persuasive or supported by the precedents of this Court. Referendums are held on issues, not candidates for public office. The risk of corruption perceived in cases involving candidate elections simply is not present in a popular vote on a public issue.

FROM CONCURRING MAJORITY BY CHIEF JUSTICE BURGER

I joined the opinion and judgment of the Court but write separately to raise some questions likely to arise in this area in the future.

A disquieting aspect of Massachusetts' position is that it may carry the risk of infringing on the First Amendment rights of those who employ the corporate form—as most do—to carry on the business of mass communications, particularly the large media conglomerates. This is because of the difficulty, and perhaps impossibility, of distinguishing, either as a matter of fact or constitutional law, media corporations from corporations such as the appellants in this case.

Making traditional use of the corporate form, some media enterprises have amassed vast wealth and power and conduct many activities, some directly related—and some not—to their publishing and broadcasting activities. Today, a corporation might own the dominant newspaper in one or more large metropolitan centers, television and radio stations in those same centers and others, a newspaper chain, news magazines with nationwide circulation, national or worldwide wire news services, and substantial interests in book publishing and distribution enterprises. Corporate ownership may extend vertically, to pulp timberlands to insure an adequate continuing supply of newsprint and to trucking and steamship lines for the purpose of transporting the newsprint to the presses.

Such activities would be logical economic auxiliaries to a publishing conglomerate. Ownership also may extend beyond to business activities unrelated to the task of publishing newspapers and magazines or broadcasting radio and television programs. Obviously, such far-reaching ownership would not be possible without the state-provided corporate form and its ''special rules relating to such matters as limited liability,

perpetual life, and the accumulation, distribution, and taxation of assets....''

The meaning of the Press Clause, as a provision separate and apart from the Speech Clause, is implicated only indirectly by this case. Yet Massachusetts' position poses serious questions. The evolution of traditional newspapers into modern corporate conglomerates in which the daily dissemination of news by print is no longer the major part of the whole enterprise suggests the need for caution in limiting the First Amendment rights of corporations as such. Thus, the tentative probings of this brief inquiry are wholly consistent, I think, with the Court's refusal to sustain [a] serious and potentially dangerous restriction on the freedom of political speech.

FROM DISSENTING OPINION BY JUSTICE WHITE

... The issue is whether a state may prevent corporate management from using the corporate treasury to propagate views having no connection with the corporate business. The Court commendably enough squarely faces the issue but unfortunately errs in deciding it. The Court invalidates the Massachusetts statute and holds that the First Amendment guarantees corporate managers the right to use not only their personal funds but also those of the corporation to circulate fact and opinion, irrelevant to the business placed in their charge and necessarily representing their own personal or collective views about political and social questions. I do not suggest for a moment that the First Amendment requires a state to forbid such use of corporate funds, but I do strongly disagree that the First Amendment forbids state interference with managerial decisions of this kind.

By holding that Massachusetts may not prohibit corporate expenditures or contributions made in connection with referendums involving issues having no material connection with the corporate business the Court not only invalidates the statute, which has been on the books in one form or another for many years, but also casts considerable doubt upon the constitutionality of legislation passed by some states restricting corporate political activity as well as upon the federal Corrupt Practices Act. The Court's fundamental error is its failure to realize that the state's regulatory interests, in terms of which the alleged curtailment of First Amendment rights accomplished by the statute must be evaluated, are themselves derived from the First Amendment. ...Although in my view the choice made by the state would survive even the most exacting scrutiny, perhaps a rational argument might be made to the contrary. What is inexplicable is for the Court to substitute its judgment as to the proper balance for that of Massachusetts where the state has passed legislation reasonably designed to further First Amendment interests in the context of the political arena where the expertise of legislation is at its peak and that of judges is at its very lowest. Moreover, the result reached today in critical respects marks a drastic departure from the Court's prior decisions which have protected against governmental infringement the very First Amendment interests which the Court now deems inadequate to justify the Massachusetts statute.

...Indeed, what some have considered to be the principal function of the First Amendment, the use of communication as a means of self-expression, self-realization, and self-fulfillment, is not at all furthered by corporate speech.

The state has not interfered with the prerogatives of corporate management to communicate about matters that have material impact on the business affairs entrusted to them, however much individual stockholders may disagree on economic or ideological grounds.

Nor has the state forbidden management from formulating and circulating its views at its own expense or at the expense of others, even where the subject at issue is irrelevant to corporate business affairs. But Massachusetts has chosen to forbid corporate management from spending corporate funds in referendum elections absent from demonstrable effect of the issue on the economic life of the company. In short, corporate management may not use corporate monies to promote what does not further corporate affairs but in the last analysis are purely personal views of the management, individually or as a group.

This is not only a policy which a state may adopt consistent with the First Amendment but one which protects the very freedoms that the court has held to be guaranteed by the First Amendment. In *Board of Education v. Barnette* the Court struck down a West Virginia statute which compelled children enrolled in public school to salute the flag and pledge allegiance to it on the grounds that the First Amendment prohibits public authorities from requiring an individual to express support for or agreement with the cause with which he disagrees or concerning which he prefers to remain silent. Subsequent cases have applied this principle to prohibit organizations to which individuals are compelled to belong as a condition of employment from using compulsory dues to support candidates, political parties, or other forms of political expression with which members disagree or do not wish to support.

I would affirm the judgment of the Supreme Judicial Court of the Commonwealth of Massachusetts.

FROM DISSENTING OPINION BY JUSTICE REHNQUIST

This Court decided at an early date with neither argument nor discussion that a business corporation is a "person" entitled to the protection of the Equal Protection clause of the Fourteenth Amendment. Likewise it soon became accepted that the property of a corporation was protected under the Due Process Clause of that same amendment. ...I can see no basis for concluding that the liberty of the corporation to engage in political activity with regard to matters having no material effect on its business is necessarily incidental to the purpose for which the Commonwealth permitted these corporations to be organized or submitted within its boundaries.

Nor can I disagree with the Supreme Judicial Court's factual finding that no such effect has been shown by these appellants. Because the statute as construed provides at least as much protection as the Fourteenth Amendment requires, I believe it is constitutionally valid.

It is true, as the Court points out, that recent decisions of this Court have emphasized the interest of the public in receiving the information offered by the speaker seeking protection. The free flow of information is in no way diminished by the Commonwealth's decision to permit the operation of business corporations with limited rights of political expression. All natural persons who owe their existence to a higher sovereign than the Commonwealth remain as free as before to engage in political activity.

I would affirm the judgment of the Supreme Judicial Court.

Directorships of Major U.S. Corporations Tightly Interlocked

For the first time in over a decade, a Congressional committee has taken a comprehensive look at interlocking directorships among the Nation's largest corporations.

Initiated by the late Sen. Lee Metcalf (D–Mont.) as chairman of the Subcommittee on Reports, Accounting and Management, the study, prepared by the subcommittee's staff, identifies and analyzes 530 direct and 12,193 indirect interlocks among 130 of the nation's top industrials, financial institutions, retailing organizations, transportation companies, utilities, and broad-

Senate Committee on Governmental Affairs press release, April 23, 1978.

casting companies. The companies in the study represented about 25 percent of the assets of all U.S. corporations.

The study disclosed an extraordinary pattern of directorate concentration:

- 123 of these major firms each connected on an average with half of the other major companies in the study.
- The 13 largest firms not only were linked together, but accounted for 240 direct and 5,547 indirect interlocks, reaching an average of more than 70 percent of the other 117 corporations. The 13 largest corporations ranked by assets were: American Telephone and Telegraph, BankAmerica, Citicorp, Chase Manhattan, Prudential, Metropolitan Life, Exxon, Manufacturers Hanover, J.P. Morgan, General Motors, Mobil, Texaco, and Ford.
- The leading competitors in the fields of automotives, energy, telecommunications, and retailing met extensively on boards of America's largest financial institutions, corporate customers, and suppliers.
- The largest commercial bankers clustered on major insurance company boards and insurance directors joined on the banking company boards.
- A direct interlock occurs when two companies have a common director. An indirect interlock occurs when two companies each have a director on the board of a third company.
- The nation's largest airlines and electric utilities were substantially interlocked with major lending institutions.
- The boardrooms of four of the largest banking companies (Citicorp, Chase Manhattan, Manufacturers Hanover, and J.P. Morgan), two of the largest insurance companies (Prudential and Metropolitan Life) and three of the largest nonfinancial companies (AT&T, Exxon, and General Motors) looked like virtual summits for leaders in American business.

These patterns of director interrelationships imply an overwhelming potential for antitrust abuse and possible conflicts of interest which could affect prices, supply and competition, and impact on the shape and direction of the American economy, said the staff.

Use of the Senate Computer Center enabled the staff to compile master lists of the direct and indirect interlocks among the major companies studied for the year 1976. These lists and accompanying computer analyses are included in the study, along with directorships of officials of the Business Council, Conference Board and Business Roundtable. The study also identifies 256 directors who each sat on the boards of from six to thirteen corporations and the 74 persons who each sat on from three to six of the 130 major corporations.

The subcommittee staff recommended, among other things, that Congress consider:

1. Prohibiting interlocking directorates between corporations with over $1 billion in sales or assets. The proscription would apply to all lines of business, including regulated and non-regulated enterprises. It would be a flat prohibition against multiple management representation involving two or more companies above the $1 billion threshold. Such legislation, said the staff, may be more palatable to both the business and the political sectors since it seeks to reach concentration by restructuring the composition of corporate boards rather than the corporate organizations themselves.
2. Amending the Clayton Act to prohibit all types of horizontal interlocks between actual and potential competitors and vertical interlocks between a company and its customers, suppliers and sources of credit and capital. Such prohibitions, said the staff, may have to be specially tailored to meet the interlock problems within regulatory jurisdictions, but in the nonregulated areas, they should be given sweeping effect.
3. In cooperation with regulatory agencies, legislate a Business in the Sunshine Act requiring open corporate board meetings, subject to closure when trade secrets, privileged and/

or special financial information or personnel matters are to be discussed.

Regulatory agencies, the staff proposed, should

1. Adopt rules requiring public representation on the boards of large corporations, and
2. Collect and make public current and complete reports on interlocking directorships of companies under their jurisdiction.

Commenting on the disarray of Federal records regarding corporate ownership and control, the staff said that prosecutors and the average citizen should "no longer have to hunt and pick their way through incomplete and inaccurate Government and private information sources. Computerization is far enough advanced to provide a central and up-to-date source for that information."

The Securities and Exchange Commission should take a lead role in collecting and disseminating such data, the staff suggested, adding that the executive branch could require such action under the Federal Reports Act if cooperation among regulatory agencies was not forthcoming.

The Directors Woke Up Too Late at Gulf

Wyndham Robertson*

Sister Jane Scully had just returned from a winter visit to Florida. It had not been altogether a pleasure trip. The Roman Catholic nun, president of Carlow College in Pittsburgh, had also been, since April of 1975, a member of the board of directors of Gulf Oil Corp., the eighth-largest industrial company in the nation and for a time one of the most troubled companies anywhere. For her trip, Sister Jane had taken along a 364-page volume—a detailed account of how Gulf had handed out more than $12 million to national and international political figures.

The report was written after a nine-month investigation demanded by the Securities and Exchange Commission as part of a consent judgment settling a suit against Gulf last year. The investigation was headed by John J. McCloy, eighty-one, the distinguished lawyer and public servant, and two outside directors. Sister Jane had felt she needed to get away for a while to ponder the McCloy report and, as she puts it, borrowing from campus vernacular, "to get my head together." She came home to Pittsburgh with "strong feelings." So, forthrightly, last January 11, she paid a Sunday visit to Bob Rawls Dorsey, sixty-three, the man who had invited her to join Gulf's board and of whom she remains "very fond."

At that point Dorsey was the chairman and chief executive officer of Gulf, but his days in the job were numbered. The polished Texan was not yet resigned to his fate, but Sister Jane, whose head was by now thoroughly together, knew precisely where she stood. "I told him," she said recently, "that I felt there had to be some management changes—and that would certainly include him—in order to restore a sense of rectitude to the corporation." Asked how Dorsey responded, she replied, "He didn't say anything. Just, 'Thank you for your views.'"

At an emotional six-hour meeting on the following day, Gulf's board of directors decided, without ever taking a vote, that Dorsey and three other officers of the company should resign their positions. As Sister Jane recalls the session, "Most of that meeting was devoted to philosophical speculation about the role of the corporate citizen." She believes the board took strong action in the conviction that it had "an obligation to society" to restore the credibility of the com-

pany. As the discussion wore on into the evening, she says, "People were speaking from the heart and expressing their deepest values."

Perhaps. But it can be argued that the board had been slow to summon those values. Two and a half years had passed since August of 1973, when Dorsey called a special meeting to tell the board that Gulf's Washington lobbyist, Claude Wild Jr., had given $100,000 in corporate cash to Richard Nixon's 1972 campaign. During that long hiatus, the directors displayed questionable judgment. For example, there is no evidence that, until the SEC stepped in, the directors pressed very hard to find out who in management was responsible for authorizing the illegal payments. And they released a principal culprit—Claude Wild himself—from all liability to the corporation in what may have been, at least partly, an effort to keep the dimensions of the scandal hidden.

THE VEIL OF POLITENESS

Why did the directors behave as they did? In part, because they were led astray by the management. Gulf's general counsel and lawyers retained by the company withheld from the board some devastating details that they had turned up while looking into the company's transgressions. And Dorsey kept secret from the board, for more than a year and a half after the scandal broke, the fact that he had personally authorized the largest political payments—$4 million to the party backing President Park Chung Hee of Korea.

Beyond that, the board's temporizing seems to have flowed from the inherently ambiguous relationship between the directors and the chief executive whose actions they were supposed to oversee. There is nothing disreputable about Gulf's directors—the nine outsiders include such men as James Higgins, chairman of the Mellon Bank, the archetype of the hardworking, conscientious businessman. But most of the outside directors were personal friends of Dorsey, and the three insiders on the board were dependent upon him for their advancement.

Under these conditions, familiar in many corporations large and small, the directors found it difficult to pierce the veil of politeness by aggressively questioning the chief executive or usurping his reins. And for a long time, Gulf's directors seemed not to sense that their interests and those of management might be at odds. They traveled a long and rutted road with Dorsey, generally following his lead—until it took them into litigious territory that threatened their own reputations and fortunes. As a result, the effects of the scandal have been dragged out, the corporation is still struggling to clean itself up, and the directors have exposed themselves to serious personal liability.

Gulf's initial investigation began in July, 1973, soon after Claude Wild owned up to Dorsey that he had given that $100,000 to the Nixon campaign. Wild was compelled to confess after Common Cause, the "citizens' lobby," won its fight to spring "Rose Mary's Baby"—a previously undisclosed list of campaign contributors held by Nixon's secretary, Rose Mary Woods. Dorsey says this was the first he had learned about Gulf's illegal political activities in the U.S. To this day, however, no one but Dorsey and his closest confidants can be sure whether that is true.

THE FIRST REVELATIONS

Shortly after Wild delivered his news, Gulf retained a Pittsburgh law firm, Eckert, Seamans, Cherin & Mellott, to represent the corporation before the Watergate Special Prosecution, which was investigating illegal contributions. At the board meeting on August 1, after Dorsey revealed the $100,000 contribution, the directors ordered a partner in the firm, Cloyd Mellott, to make a "thorough investigation" and report back at their meeting the following month. For reasons that are not clear, Mellott didn't report back until four months later.

But throughout August, both he and, presumably, Dorsey learned plenty—mainly from Claude Wild. Wild, fifty-two, is the son of a former Humble Oil lobbyist in Austin who was himself well connected politically.

On August 2, 1973, the day after the special board meeting, Mellott, one of his partners, Thomas Wright, and Gulf's general counsel, Merle Minks, met with Wild. According to Wright, Wild said he had been receiving $300,000 or $400,000 every year in cash from one William Viglia, who brought the funds from the Bahamas. Wild sent about half of this to subordinates in Pennsylvania, Louisiana, Texas, California, and other states for distribution to politicians there.

He did not give details of the contributions made by the subordinates, but he gave the lawyers an earful about what he did with *his* share. His first assignment was to funnel $50,000 to Lyndon Johnson in the early Sixties, and after that he passed money along to such well-known politicians as Hugh Scott, Henry Jackson, Wilbur Mills, and Hubert Humphrey. He also told the lawyers, according to Wright, that because politicians did not like their names showing up on expense accounts, he used some of the cash for entertaining.

IT HAPPENED IN A WATER CLOSET

On the following day, the same three lawyers and a second in-house counsel found out a little more from William Viglia. A small, elderly, and nervous man, Viglia had lived in Nassau since 1959 and kept the books for Bahamas Exploration Ltd., a largely dormant Gulf subsidiary that held a few exploration licenses and paid annual fees to keep them, but hadn't explored for years.

Every year, Bahamas Ex, as it was called, got an average of $400,000 from another subsidiary, Gulf Petroleum, S.A. Viglia said he took this money out in cash, and at intervals of about three weeks carried $25,000, often in his pocket, for delivery to Wild. Viglia assumed that the transfers of money between the two subsidiaries had been requested over the years by the various Gulf controllers. The transfers were made to a Bahamian bank account in the name of Bahamas Ex, but this account was kept secret, and deposits and withdrawals were never reflected on the internal records of the company. Viglia told the lawyers that he was instructed to destroy the bank statements and canceled checks after examining them for accuracy. As the McCloy report later described the process, in a phrase that appears to have sprung from the quill of its octogenarian editor, Viglia "tore [the records] up and flushed them in a water closet."

All of this, it should be remembered, the lawyers learned a mere two days after the board's August 1 meeting. Yet the first time the directors knew that the payments exceeded $100,000 was more than three months later, and at that time they learned only of an additional $25,000. In November, after a series of meetings with the Watergate Special Prosecution, Gulf and Wild pleaded guilty in U.S. District Court to violations of the federal Corrupt Practices Act. Gulf was charged with making the Nixon contribution, plus payments of $10,000 to Senator Jackson and $15,000 to Congressman Mills for their 1972 presidential campaigns. The company requested the return of the payments and got the money back. Gulf was fined $5,000 and Wild, $1,000.

THE BAD NEWS CAME SLOWLY

Though Mellott had been asked to report to the board in September, 1973, he didn't get around to it until December. When he finally appeared, his prepared remarks—which he says he read "practically verbatim"—show that he confined himself mainly to a description of the 1972 presidential-campaign payments, which were already public knowledge. But he also revealed that he had turned up "various other contributions in connection with federal elections since January 1, 1968," and that other political contributions may have been made from corporate funds "possibly beginning as early as 1960." He disclosed no details about these payments other than to say that "the amounts involved were substantial."

Mellott apparently volunteered very little of what he knew. For example, his written remarks don't mention that the contributions passed through a systematic mechanism, nor do they reveal recipients other than the three whose names were already well known. Two months later, in February, 1974, Mellott made a second report, and it was only under questioning from the board that he disclosed that "the total amount involved since 1960 would be approximately $4.8 million."

Mellott made a third and, apparently, final report to the board on June 11. At that time he repeated the figure of $4.8 million, told of 1968 contributions to Nixon's and Humphrey's presidential campaigns, and ran through a list of dollar amounts expended since 1968 for various political cocktail parties and fund-raising dinners. This was, almost exactly, the same accounting of illegal payments that he had given the Watergate Special Prosecution *eight months earlier*. These contributions to federal elections added up to only $345,000. As for the rest, he said, "we are advised by Mr. Wild" that it went to candidates in the states, other political dinners and cocktail parties, business and charitable gifts, entertainment, and expenses of delivering the funds. Wild had received and dispensed $4.1 million, either to federal officials or to bagmen in the states. But according to Mellott, Wild had no records to account for it.

Dorsey himself, during all this time, kept from the directors the biggest political payments of all—that $4 million in Korea. It is still unclear whether these payments to President Park's political party were legal or illegal under Korean law, but the McCloy committee said that Dorsey did not even consider the question at the time. In any case, they were obviously something the directors ought to have been told about in order to help them determine who was responsible for Gulf's political payments and what should be done about them.

As it happened, the money for Korea, like the payments in the U.S., had been charged to the books of Bahamas Ex, and one of the lawyers at Eckert, Seamans, saw an entry about it early in the investigation. He didn't know what the money was for, however, and Viglia told him that the actual funds—as opposed to the bookkeeping entry itself—never passed through the subsidiary. Mellott apparently never brought any of this to the board's attention. Nor did the lawyers, or anyone in Gulf's management, call in Price Waterhouse, the company's auditors, who could have tracked down that payment in short order. Moreover, the directors apparently didn't share with the auditors what Mellott *had* told them. Although the board's audit committee met with Price Waterhouse five times in 1974, the partner in charge of the account says the firm didn't know that the illegal payments exceeded $125,000 until "early 1975."

The board had to wait until May, 1975—or nearly two years—to find out about the Korean payments. Dorsey told the directors just before he was forced to tell the world, in testifying before the Senate subcommittee on multinational corporations. As a footnote to history, it is instructive to observe that Dorsey's self-assured bearing and straightforward testimony to the committee obviously impressed the Senators. One of them, Charles Percy, was moved to make a statement that is today heavy with irony. Said Percy: "I think if President Nixon had done what you have done, originally, and just owned up to everything, and laid it on the line...I think he would have finished his term." Of course, one of Dorsey's problems, and one of the problems facing his directors, was that he *hadn't* laid it on the line, originally.

WAS A DIRECTOR DOZING?

While a lot was withheld from the directors, it is at least clear that they were told, as early as December of 1973, that the $125,000 was only the tip of an iceberg. And by the following June they had learned the scope, if not the details, of the domestic payments. What is far less clear is how closely the directors were paying attention. One who apparently missed a lot was James Walton, forty-five, a graduate of Yale and the Harvard Business School. Walton worked for Gulf for ten years before becoming president of the Carnegie Institute, the Pittsburgh cultural center. His mother was the daughter of one of Gulf's founders, and he is the only member of the founding family now on the board.

Last fall Walton testified under oath in connection with a shareholders' suit and insisted that Eckert, Seamans had never reported any payments beyond the $125,000. A portion of his testimony went like this:

Q. Did you at some point learn that there was more than had been reported to you by Eckert, Seamans?
A. Than the $125,000?
Q. Yes.
A. Yes.
Q. When?
A. The spring of 1975.

The testimony is more than a little puzzling, because over a year earlier, Mellott had told the board that the payments were substantially greater. Moreover, Walton said that when the board finally did learn of the larger payments, it was Dorsey, not Mellott, who told them. Perhaps the kindest interpretation that can be put on Walton's answers is that he was woefully confused.

When Mellott reported to the directors in December of 1973 and again in February, he advised them that they had to decide what action to take, if any, with respect to the illegal payments. He told them they could seek recovery from both the recipients and from any officer or employee who participated. He also advised that they had no "absolute duty" to bring a lawsuit. So long as they acted "honestly, in good faith, and for what they believed to be in the best interests of Gulf," he believed a business judgment not to litigate could be successfully defended against a shareholder's derivative action. (By February this was no hypothetical matter, as several shareholders' lawyers had written threatening letters demanding action from the board.)

THE BOARD FACES THE FULL DISCLOSURES

The SEC started to investigate Gulf in October and quickly turned up the off-the-books account and the Korean payments. On March 13 of last year, the SEC issued an injunction that ordered the McCloy investigation, and on the same day Gulf admitted publicly that it had spent more than $10 million of corporate funds on political activities. With that, shareholders began to sue and the directors awakened to the idea that their interests and those of management could be quite different. Sister Jane, who joined the board in April of 1975, described her experience almost a year later: "I was aware throughout his last year of a growing tension—almost a paranoia—among the board members. There was increasing uneasiness from the time I joined until January, when we did something about it."

Several board members—most notably Nathan Pearson, financial adviser to the Paul Mellon family—became extremely cautious about authorizing seemingly routine corporate actions. They may have felt that management had led them astray once and they weren't going to let it happen again. Pearson, a towering man of sixty-four, was a member of the McCloy committee and was presumably learning things that offended what one longtime friend calls his "New England conscience." While he and others picked nits with management, Dorsey became increasingly testy. Not a reflective man by nature, and often given to arrogance, Dorsey was impatient with what he regarded as the directors' growing preoccupation with details he felt were the prerogative of management.

At the two board meetings following the SEC injunction, the directors started second-guessing a lot of decisions. The board had been enjoined against filing proxy or registration statements that failed to disclose material information about unlawful payments. Not knowing how much they still *didn't* know, the directors worried that the McCloy investigation would turn up information that could later be used to prove they hadn't made full disclosure. So in the spring of last year, despite Dorsey's urging, they refused to sign the SEC registration statement necessary to effect a new stock-option plan. And some of them argued for canceling the 1975 annual meeting for fear that the proxy statement could be challenged for failing to make adequate disclosure.

The McCloy report concluded that since 1960 Gulf and its subsidiaries had made payments to politicians and government officials in the U.S. and abroad, both legal and illegal, of more than $12 million. The committee said the figure was "subject to some increase." For example, it was "possible that for a number of years as much as $1,000,000 annually" may have found its way to Korean political figures and parties. Gulf's chief financial officer, Harold Hammer, argued strenuously in early 1975 that an additional $2 million paid out in Italy, ostensibly for nonpolitical purposes, should be added in. (The McCloy report, citing a lack of evidence, disagreed with Hammer.) Hammer thinks his criticism was the reason Dorsey later stripped him of virtually all of his corporate responsibilities. This year, after Dorsey left, Hammer again became Gulf's principal financial officer.

The shareholders' lawyers are pushing for restitution, of course, and they say they don't care where the money comes from, so long as it flows back into Gulf. They occasionally point out that some of the directors who are defendants in the suits are themselves very well-to-do. All together, the lawyers are asking for some $14.8 million in restitution—plus the more than $3 million that Gulf says it has spent on all its investigations. Jerry McAfee, Dorsey's successor, calls the litigation a "sword of Damocles." He says the directors "have been through hell."

In some ways it is easy to sympathize and to conclude that, but for the grace of God, any well-meaning director could find himself in the same position. Gulf's directors—who incidentally are paid more than $20,000 annually to do their jobs—erred, as others might have, by treating as a routine matter something that was anything but.

In discussing the problem of illegal campaign contributions, the McCloy committee said: "It is hard to escape the conclusion that a sort of 'shut-eye sentry' attitude prevailed upon the part of both the responsible corporate officials and the recipients as well as on the part of those charged with enforcement responsibilities." The key phrase is from a Kipling poem, "The Shut-Eye Sentry," which contains these lines:

> But I'd shut my eyes in the sentry-box,
>   So I didn't see nothin' wrong.

If there is a lesson for directors in the Gulf episode, it is that, as surrogate sentries for the shareholders, they must be alert at the watch. And if they doze, they are apt to be rudely awakened by unfriendly lawyers rapping loudly on the box.

████████████████████████

Oklahoma Meets Wall Street

Paul Hirsch*

"We're still in business," said spokesman Steve Milburn. He said despite the fact that the company has shut down its famous oil well on the state capital

From "Introduction: Oklahoma Meets Wall Street," *Pack Your Own Parachute: How to Survive Mergers, Takeovers, and Other Corporate Disasters* by Paul Hirsch. Copyright © 1987, Addison-Wesley Publishing Company, Inc. Reading, MA. Reprinted with permission. Quotes reprinted by permission of *The New York Times*, Inc., 1985, 1986. All rights reserved.
Quotes reprinted by permission of *The New York Times*, Inc., 1985, 1986. All rights reserved.
*Department of Sociology and Business Policy, University of Chicago.

grounds in Oklahoma City, along with its historic Burbank Field wells in Osage county, Phillips still has 8,000 producing wells in the U.S.

Bartlesville Examiner-Enterprise

August 1986

Phillips Petroleum was on the ropes. The giant oil company dropped nearly 10,000 people between 1985 and 1987, close to 25 percent of its work force worldwide. Bartlesville, Oklahoma, its affluent, largely white-collar headquarters city of 38,000, was especially hard hit.

"Anyone with the brains God gave a grasshopper is not buying a house in Bartlesville," said one Phillips manager in summer 1986. Two of the only retailers with something to smile about were the local U-Haul and Ryder truck renters, whose volume always goes up "as people pack up to move on... 'If you wanted a truck today, you couldn't get one,'" said Gordon Brown, owner of Bartlesville Auto Supply. Social workers noticed a different kind of increase—in the amount of anxiety and tension among Phillips employees as they saw their job prospects dwindling. Even before the waves of layoffs and early retirements, Jerry Poppenhouse, art director at Phillips, told a reporter, "The mood now is, 'Who's going to be next?'" Another manager and Bartlesville resident added, "Outsiders don't understand that even if you aren't laid off, or your co-workers aren't, you still go to church or scouts or soccer with someone who is."

Phillips Petroleum, the nation's seventeenth largest industrial corporation and eighth biggest oil producer, was cash poor. Deeply in debt, it had to raise vast sums of money very quickly. Asked which of the company's far-flung operations might be for sale in 1985, Chairman and Chief Executive Officer William Douce said, "All of them—and that's no joke." This included oil fields in Africa, Alaska, the Gulf of Mexico, and the North Sea around Holland—where Phillips had been the first to discover oil that helped Europe become less dependent on supplies from the Middle East. All or parts of these were soon sold, along with coal and geothermal facilities in Texas, Utah, Nevada, and California. In addition to selling off petroleum reserves and other properties, Phillips axed or delayed some big research and exploration projects.

Cutting back its work force and payroll was another policy Phillips adopted to raise cash. Nearly every employee was offered incentives to quit voluntarily before the company moved on to layoffs and terminations. People fifty-five or older were promised a larger pension if they signed up for early retirement immediately. A majority of long-service managers at all levels took the offer. Some were ready and welcomed the opportunity. But others felt rejected, helpless, and all alone.

"Some simply have resigned themselves to resigning," said one. "I mean to retiring without knowing if they would be able to get another job and if they will need one...Many would rather still be working, and not only just for the money." Another recent retiree added:

The ones I feel sorry for are those still in their middle fifties. Fifty-five is early to retire. There's no other work here right now, though if you want to go to California or New York you can probably start over. But it's not just a matter of getting in your car and going. Say you're a homeowner. If you were transferred the company would take it off your hands. But you're retired now. You have this real estate you can't dispose of. Right now I don't think you can even rent out many of the houses for sale. It's a tough situation.

In spite of these hardships, Phillips employees and Bartlesville residents still considered themselves "lucky." Only seventeen months earlier, Phillips had won a crucial victory for them. It succeeded, against strong odds, in keeping the company independent and in Oklahoma. In an extraordinary four-month period etched in the memory of Bartlesville's small population, corporate raiders T. Boone Pickens and Carl Icahn

each attempted to purchase Phillips Petroleum from its shareholders. "How would you feel," asked one Bartlesville citizen, "if Godzilla and Frankenstein both stomped through your town?"

To beat them back, Phillips had repurchased much of its own stock and taken on billions of dollars in new debt to pay for it. Both current and former employees knew why the company had to raise so much cash. They knew their pain stemmed from the bills falling due for this victory. If employment was down here, many said, look at what happened to people at the other companies that tangled with T. Boone Pickens or blew themselves up to avoid him.

"Look at Gulf and its white knight, Chevron," exclaimed one Phillips staffer. "I have a good friend at Chevron. In another year or two they'll be operating both companies with the same number of employees Chevron had when they took Gulf over. That's 50 percent fewer people working than when the two companies were running separately." Before driving Gulf into Chevron's embrace, Pickens had made profitable runs on Cities Service (in neighboring Tulsa), Superior Oil, Supron Energy, and General American Oil (which chose to be acquired by Phillips in 1983, rather than be taken over by Pickens's Mesa Petroleum Company). None of these companies exists independently any longer. "The other companies all lost their identities, and we feared that," commented another Phillips veteran. "Everybody's pleased Phillips was able to retain it. We're grateful the company is still intact."

Soon after Phillips repulsed its invaders, one of its computer engineers, A. J. Lafaro, received an unusual request from Los Angeles, home of Unocal ("76") Oil. Pickens had selected Unocal as his next takeover target, and some of its employees remembered a "Boonebuster" T-shirt worn all over Bartlesville during the time Phillips was fighting the same battle. Lafaro had designed it at about the same time that the movie *Ghostbusters* was a big success. He superimposed the international symbol for "No" over a picture of Mr. Pickens, who also purchased some to give as Christmas presents. Unocal employees now wanted them for their impending struggle. Said one Phillips official, "Believe me, if they're going through anything like what we went through, they could use [them]!"

The "Boonebuster" shirt is only one example of the enthusiasm and commitment Bartlesville citizens showed for Phillips during its bitter fights to stay independent. The community was shocked, angered, and scared at the possibility of losing any or all of the company to a corporate takeover. Here was the largest employer in the state brought to its knees, with its fate hinging on maneuvers in far-away boardrooms on Wall Street. "I get the feeling that a bunch of strangers are out there playing Russian roulette with the future of this community—this state, really—and I don't like it," said Josef Derryberry, a jeweler in Bartlesville.

At a crisis forum of 8,000 residents, speakers discussing what the loss of Phillips would mean to the community and nation included the area's school superintendent, the director of the National Institute for Petroleum and Energy Research, the Sears manager at a newly built shopping mall, a former vice president of what had been the Cities Service Oil Company, student officers from the local high school, and the Osage Indian chief on whose nearby land Frank Phillips had originally struck oil. Rudy Taylor, a newspaper publisher in neighboring Caney, Kansas, received a standing ovation when he said:

Without Phillips, we'd just be Mayberry R.F.D., and with Phillips we have a lot of confidence in our future and we have a world of ideas on how we can improve our little corner of the world... Our chief industry in Caney, Kansas, is Phillips Petroleum Company; it's been that way for over a half century and... because of their influence our community is a progressive one. We feel the Phillips influence in our schools, and in our places of business and in our churches and our lodges... We're in this fight with you and we're in it to win. Let's do it!"

Looking back on the community's outpouring of support, a Phillips manager later commented:

Farming and oil are the lifeblood of this part of the country. And farming was already in bad shape. Bartlesville has no other appreciable industry that I am aware of. It's pretty much Phillips, and if Phillips goes or starts trimming down, everything turns down. The impact on the community if Phillips were to go is that others would just vanish. Bartlesville would be a ghost town. But as long as there is some nucleus of Phillips here, there will be the Phillips people and there will be these other people from the supporting communities in surrounding areas who will come to Bartlesville.

Christmas in Bartlesville, 1984, turned out to be a happy one. On Christmas eve, just three weeks after Pickens launched his takeover bid, he and Phillips announced a settlement. "We were very pleased Phillips maintained its identity," recalls one retiree, "but at the same time I think people resented Mr. Pickens making the profit he did." In financial terms, Phillips agreed to repurchase the 8.9 million shares in the company Pickens had accumulated, for $10 a share more than they had cost him. This yielded a gross profit of $89 million for Pickens on shares he had held for roughly six weeks. Phillips would also pay Pickens and his group $25 million more to cover expenses they ran up in making their run on the company.

But this was only the beginning. The settlement also required Phillips to present an expensive plan at its next annual meeting designed to raise its shares' value for other investors as well. The company would propose to buy back 38 percent of all its stock. (Pickens had only owned about 6 percent, or less than one-sixth of the additional amount the company agreed to repurchase.) To remove Pickens's takeover threat and satisfy his demands, Phillips had spent $57 million in three weeks and was now committed to borrowing nearly $3 *billion* to cover its proposed stock buyback program.

As the dust settled from one battle and the new year got under way, Phillips next heard from

Carl Icahn, perhaps Wall Street's most feared financier and corporate raider. Icahn was buying big blocks of the company's stock and demanding Phillips pay more for the shares it proposed to buy back. He had substantial support from what *New York Times* writer Daniel Cuff called "those cold and distant institutions that own 47 percent of Phillips [stock] and hold the key to its future." On February 5, 1985, Icahn offered to buy Phillips from its shareholders for a higher price. Now in its second battle in two months, there was little doubt at Phillips or in Bartlesville this time about the company's fate if it lost this ownership contest. Pickens at least said he would move to Bartlesville and run the company if he gained control. Financial analyst George Sneed's chilling interpretation of Icahn's intentions made Pickens sound like a long-lost friend:

> Icahn and his backers have no interest in buying Phillips Petroleum Company to operate it. They would liquidate the company if they get control of it. They are trying to force the price up and if they can get Phillips merged or bought out at a higher price, that is what they want...There is an awful lot of stock in the hands of short-term speculators and they absolutely do not care what happens to Bartlesville.

While local residents disliked both corporate raiders, Icahn was generally deemed even less trustworthy and more dangerous than Pickens. Jeweler Josef Derryberry again spoke for many when he said he could not trust Icahn's remarks about his plans for Phillips: "One moment you'll keep Phillips in Bartlesville and the next moment you say you'll sell it to the highest bidder. There's only one business I know of that you can sell and keep it too," he said. Asked to compare people's reactions to Icahn and Pickens, a Phillips manager recalled:

> Pickens wasn't too well liked, but Icahn, well we really had to campaign against him...Pickens was a petroleum man. But Icahn, and there were several with him, had made quite a reputation and a

lot of money just moving parts of companies around. They were both looked at in a different way. I think in Bartlesville they both were considered SOB's, but Boone at least was Mr. SOB.

Not everyone agrees. As one retail merchant, whose business has still not recovered, sees it, "We put Icahn and Pickens in the same classification. One was an easterner, one a southwesterner. You know, it doesn't make any difference whether you got shit on your boots or wear a bow tie. If you're a corporate raider looking for a quick profit, who cares who he is?"

On March 5, 1985, Phillips assured its independence for the foreseeable future by meeting Icahn's terms. It "sharply improved the terms" of its offer to repurchase much of the company's stock from its shareholders. To pay for it, the company took on more debt. Published estimates of Mr. Icahn's gross profit from his roughly six-week investment in Phillips stock range from $30 million to $75 million. The company also paid an additional $25 million of Icahn's expenses from their takeover fight. These included payments to "a consortium of private and institutional investors, including such active raiders as the Canadian Belzberg family, Saul Steinberg, and the Leucadia National Corporation, [which, for holding aside] $1.5 billion for about two weeks [to loan Icahn if he had needed it], received $5,625,000 in fees and never had to put up a nickel." In return, Phillips got agreements from Carl Icahn and his main Wall Street backer, Drexel Burnham Lambert, Inc., to stop trying to buy the company. Phillips' outlay, for the three months of legal and financial services it bought itself and its raiders, exceeded $200 million. Irwin Jacobs, one of Icahn's best-known allies in the just-finished battle, summed it up very well: "Phillips has bought its independence, and the town of Bartlesville can rest easy tonight."

Once again, Phillips employees and Bartlesville were relieved the company stayed independent and intact. The city had recently been in the news for mailing heart-shaped Valentine's

Day cookies with the Phillips 66 shield on them to Icahn and large shareholders during the latest battle. But the mood was less joyful and more subdued than when the contest with Pickens ended. Now, Bartlesville heaved "a collective sigh of relief. 'Conservative optimism' is how the editor of the local paper describes the mood," reported the *Christian Science Monitor*. A Phillips manager recalls:

> After a while people had just sort of gotten used to it. A little jaded, probably more fatalistic. Yeah, we might be taken over. Another one just showed up with more threats, so they'll fight it out. Much of the outrage and shock was probably used up in the struggle with Pickens. Everyone was still upset, but people just got on with other things as the fights dragged on.

Six weeks after Phillips settled with Icahn, David Oakley, owner of the city's Pontiac-Buick dealership, reported that car sales were improving. "People are convinced now that there is going to be a community, although they're not sure if they're going to have a job," he said.

To remain independent and keep raiders at bay, Phillips had taken a very high stakes gamble. This was that its oil and gas, combined with the sale of assets, would keep generating enough cash to cover payments due on the billions it borrowed to buy back 50 percent of its stock.

In less than a year, the company's debt had tripled from $2.8 to $8.6 billion. Its credit rating had been lowered. Phillips's interest payments for 1985 zoomed to $846 million, more than double its earnings. Company officials, and some oil industry experts, downplayed the seriousness of the situation. Phillips planned to reduce its debt quickly by *selling at least $2 billion in assets*. "They've got salable stuff coming out their ears...[and] could get rid of $2 billion without blinking," said one industry analyst. Company Chairman William Douce acknowledged that "it's a pretty good debt load for a while, but we have a strong cash flow and that's really the name of the game." After leading his company through the two brutal takeover wars, Douce referred to himself as a "born-again debtor." "We can remain strong and vital, no question," he said.

Others were less optimistic about the firm's chances for a quick comeback. "Phillips has mortgaged its future. The price of independence is a mountain of debt," said Sanford Margoshes, senior oil analyst at Shearson/American Express. He believed that "this is a company where some of the glow has been extinguished." Many observers called Phillips's debt, now between 75 and 80 percent of its total capital, "staggering." They predicted management's energy would be absorbed more by cutting debt and expenses than by competing hard for new oil fields and customers. Phillips is "definitely a weaker competitor," said Lawrence Funkhauser, Chevron's vice president for exploration and production. "They've got a period of four or five years to get back to where they were before Pickens attacked them." Amoco's chief economist, Ted Eck, also commented, "It's hard to see how you could be a superaggressive exploration company when you've got 75 percent debt."

The most critical wild card in Phillips's high-stakes gamble would be the price of oil. The cash flow it needed to pay off its huge debt required a minimum price of $20 per barrel. After the big stock buyback, the *Washington Post* reported:

> About the only thing analysts believe could put Phillips' rebuilding efforts out of kilter would be an unexpected drop in the price of oil. In setting up its restructuring, Phillips has assumed an average oil price for the next few years of about $27 a barrel, and a worst-case scenario of about $20 a barrel.

"If the price of oil goes down, Phillips is going to be in trouble," said oil analyst Fred Leuffer. Another analyst, who asked not to be identified, added, "If oil prices went down to $20 a barrel, Phillips faced financial peril." The experts' consensus tied Phillips's recovery to these magic numbers. If they fell below $20, that would mean lower prices for the assets Phillips needed to sell, and less cash from the sale of its own oil and gasoline. Since the company had to repay its steep loans, no matter what, the missing balance would have to come from elsewhere if oil prices did drop.

Within five months of Phillips's successful fights to stay independent, oil prices started a plunge toward $10 a barrel. The company's strategy of "borrow now, pay later" began to unravel. Its high debt and cash-poor position left it without any of the "rainy day" money companies need to tide themselves over during hard times. Phillips was more vulnerable to falling prices than any other oil company (except Unocal, which had followed Phillips's example by also going into deep debt to fight off another bid by T. Boone Pickens). Two *Wall Street Journal* reports show how precarious the company's financial position became by the summers of 1985 and 1986:

> Bob Crawford raises his voice to be heard over a thumping oil pump he has just lubricated in the Phillips Petroleum Co. oil field here [in Shidler, Oklahoma]. "If oil prices drop farther, Phillips will have to liquidate this field and me with it," he says. For Phillips and several other major oil companies, "the crunch" came mainly from taking on massive increases in debt at a time when oil prices were slumping. The result is a double-edged sword that threatens to seriously reduce both revenue and profit in the industry.
>
> The heavy debt, low-price bug has made no big oil company sicker than Phillips. Just last year, Phillips was weathering the energy slump quite nicely. Its profit rose 12%, and its debt load was one of the lightest around. But the company's bitter takeover battles with Messrs. Pickens and Icahn earlier this year changed all that. To fend them off, Phillips borrowed $4.5 billion, raising its debt-to-equity ratio to a staggering 80%. That's easily the highest among the majors, and analysts are worried, particularly in light of falling prices.
>
> "They're over my danger line," says Kurt Wulff, a Donaldson, Lufkin & Jenrette analyst...Living on the edge is proving painful for

the nation's eighth biggest oil company. (August 9, 1985)

> Most energy-related companies have been forced to cut costs sharply because of the oil price plunge, but Unocal and Phillips are in especially difficult positions..."they're hanging on with bloody fingers at this point," says [analyst] Alan Edgar...
>
> For its part, Phillips has taken drastic steps in light of lower oil prices. Its work force has been cut by 3,400 employees, to 21,900, since the first of the year. (July 28, 1986)

In Bartlesville, Phillips acknowledged that by summer 1985, it was using up oil reserves faster than it was replacing them. "If we continued that way, it would make us self-liquidating," said Bill Thompson, vice president for planning and development. "It's like having a house that takes four gallons of paint and you've got only three—the house will look like hell." A common feeling managers expressed was that budget reductions were cutting into the bone of their operations. For example:

> Staffing and operations have been cut back to a point where I can no longer function smoothly. This happened just as markets became chaotic because of falling oil prices. So now we are missing business we should be getting because we just can't handle it. And it's not because people are lazy or stupid, people are working very hard at nights and on weekends. I work feverishly all day and then bring a briefcase full of work home and work until 10:30 or so every night, and still can't keep up. If things stay like this, Phillips has a serious problem, because we can't continue as we are.

Referring back to the takeover battles, the same manager says, "We've done the equivalent of somebody who was threatened by a mugger, sitting there slashing your wrist so you scare them off with all the blood. We don't have the strength to go out and lift weights anymore. We've had to pull back our operations and try to conserve cash as much as possible."

Mr. Pickens was not convinced the company's operations had been streamlined far enough. His recommendations in both summer 1985 and 1986 reportedly suggested that Phillips should continue "slimming the...payroll" and "cut their costs and trim exploration budgets before cutting dividends further."

Phillips Petroleum has retained its independence, but the price of victory was very high for the company, its employees, and the people of Bartlesville. Many jobs were lost, and for those remaining the company is a much leaner "home away from home." The takeover battles also left scars on the community at large. One of the city's leading retailers believes the experience "destroyed a part of" its spirit. John Norell, president of a Phillips research subsidiary, wrote in a letter to the U.S. House Energy and Commerce Committee, "There is something fundamentally wrong in America that a $16 billion company who is financially strong and interested in long-range developments for itself, the country, and humanity on one day can then on the next day, after a run on it by Mr. T. Boone Pickens, be *reduced to a debt-ridden, short term, and cost-cutting entity.*"

Oil industry analyst Sanford Margoshes spoke for many when he said, "As a member of the planet I would say one should not be pleased with a proliferation of this type of development."

QUESTIONS FOR DISCUSSION

1. In *First National Bank of Boston v. Bellotti,* the Supreme Court upheld the right of corporations to speak out on issues unrelated to the purposes of their business. Does this decision suggest that the corporation may be regarded as a "person"? What are the implications of this decision for corporate social responsibility?
2. What does Justice Rehnquist mean when he claims in his dissenting opinion that free expression and the free flow of information are "in no way diminished" by the Massachusetts law restricting the speech of corporations?
3. Is the Gulf Oil scandal evidence that corporate boards of directors do not function properly? Would any of the reforms suggested by Nader, Green, and Seligman or Geneen have helped to prevent the scandal? Explain.
4. What would Michael Jensen be likely to say about the impact of T. Boone Pickens' and Carl Icahn's takeover attempts on Bartlesville, Oklahoma? Robert Kuttner?

SUPPLEMENTARY READING FOR PART TWO

Berger, Peter L. "New Attack on the Legitimacy of Business." *Harvard Business Review,* September–October 1981, pp. 82–89.

Brown, Courtney. *Putting the Corporate Board to Work.* New York: MacMillan, 1976.

Buchholz, Rogene A. *Essentials of Public Policy for Management.* Englewood Cliffs, N.J.: Prentice-Hall, 1985.

Commons, Dorman L. *Tender Offer: The Sneak Attack in Corporate Takeovers.* Berkeley: University of California Press, 1985.

Dill, William R., ed. *Running the American Corporation.* Englewood Cliffs, N.J.: Prentice-Hall, 1978.

Donaldson, Thomas. *Corporations and Morality.* Englewood Cliffs, N.J.: Prentice-Hall, 1982.

Eisenberg, Melvin Aron. *The Structure of the Corporation.* Boston: Little, Brown, 1976.

Freeman, R. Edward. *Strategic Management: A Stakeholder Approach.* Boston: Pitman, 1984.

French, Peter. *Collective and Corporate Responsibility.* New York: Columbia University Press, 1984.

Friedman, Milton. *Capitalism and Freedom.* Chicago: University of Chicago Press, 1962.

Green, Mark, et al. "The Case for a Corporate Democracy Act." *Business and Society Review,* vol. 34, Summer 1980, pp. 55–58.

Herman, Edward S. *Corporate Control, Corporate Power.* New York: Cambridge University Press, 1981.

Hoffman, W. Michael, et al., eds. *Corporate Governance and Institutionalizing Ethics.* Lexington, Mass.: Lexington Books, 1983.

Ladd, John. "Morality and the Ideal of Rationality in Formal Organizations." *Monist,* vol. 54, 1970, pp. 489–499.

Lehman, Craig. "Takeovers and Takeover Defenses: Some Utilities of the Free Market," in Tom L. Beauchamp and Norman E. Bowie, eds. *Ethical Theory and Business,* 3d ed. Englewood Cliffs, N.J.: Prentice-Hall, 1988.

Levitt, Theodore. "The Dangers of Corporate Social Responsibility." *Harvard Business Review,* September–October 1958, pp. 41–50.

Lodge, George C. *The New American Ideology.* New York: Alfred A. Knopf, 1979.

May, Larry. *The Morality of Groups.* Notre Dame, Ind.: University of Notre Dame Press, 1987.

Nader, Ralph, Mark Green, and Joel Seligman. *Taming the Giant Corporation.* New York: W. W. Norton, 1976.

Newton, Lisa. "The Hostile Takeover: An Opposition View," in Tom L. Beauchamp and Norman E. Bowie, eds. *Ethical Theory and Business,* 3d ed. Englewood Cliffs, N.J.: Prentice-Hall, 1988.

The Role and Composition of the Board of Directors of the Large Publicly Owned Corporation. Statement of the Business Roundtable, January 1978.

Schwartz, Donald C. "The Case for Federal Chartering of Corporations." *Business and Society Review,* Winter 1973–1974, pp. 52–58.

Stone, Christopher D. "Public Directors Merit a Try." *Harvard Business Review,* March–April 1976, pp. 20–39.

Tuleja, Tad. *Beyond the Bottom Line.* New York: Penguin Books, 1985.

Velasquez, Manuel. "Why Corporations Are Not Morally Responsible for Anything They Do." *Business and Professional Ethics Journal,* vol. 2, Spring 1983, pp. 1–18.

Weidenbaum, Murray. *Strengthening the Corporate Board.* St. Louis: Washington University, Center for Study of American Business, 1985.

Work in the Corporation

In Part Two we examined the notion that business organizations have obligations not only, or even primarily, to their shareholders, but also to other stakeholders in the firm. One of the most important of these groups of stakeholders is the corporation's employees. They provide the productive and decision-making power of the business; in a very real sense, they *are* the corporation.

What obligations hold between a company and its employees? The traditional view of the relation between employer and employee has been that it is a free agreement or contract between the two parties for their mutual benefit. According to this contract, the primary responsibility of the employer is to pay fair wages. In return, employees owe the company loyalty, obedience, and satisfactory job performance. Either party can terminate the contract at any time, and traditionally, this power to terminate has been thought sufficient to protect the interests of both employers and employees. Like the traditional understanding of the corporation itself, however, this simple model of employer-employee relations has been challenged. Some thinkers argue that the employee's interests are not sufficiently protected by the right to quit. In the past two decades a strong interest has emerged in securing more extensive rights for employees to protect them from potential abuses of power in the workplace. In Chapter 7, we examine the rights and duties of employees, with a special focus on the employee rights movement and on the issues of privacy and health and safety. The rights of free speech and dissent in the workplace have also received increasing attention, as "whistle-blowing" incidents—cases in which employees go above the head of their supervisor or to the public to reveal corporate wrongdoing—have become more and more common. We devote Chapter 8 to the ethical issues raised by the practice of whistle blowing.

In 1971 a study on work in America commissioned by the Department of Health, Education and Welfare reported that a large majority of Americans are dissatisfied with work. Since then several other studies have supported this finding. Comparisons with work styles in Japan and West Germany, where productivity is particularly high, have also raised questions about the quality of working life in the United States. In the past decade, issues surrounding work have received a growing amount of attention. The selections included in Chapter 9 address questions of job satisfaction and the quality of working life.

In Chapter 10 we turn to an area of business-employee relations that has already been the subject of much legislation—that of discrimination in the workplace. The elimination of discrimination is essential both to a truly free society and to a truly efficient market. As a major social institution, business has a significant role to play in the perpetuation or termination of discrimination in U.S. society. But how should business exercise this role? Is "preferential hiring" the answer? A policy of compensating according to "comparable worth"? Both of these issues are examined in our selections.

EMPLOYEE RIGHTS AND DUTIES

Until recently, employee rights have been restricted to those specified in the contract between employee and employer; generally, these had to do with wages, job description, hours, pension, and other benefits. If an employee did not like the treatment he or she received at the hands of an employer, did not wish to carry out an order, or disagreed with company policy, he or she could leave the job. Conversely, employers were permitted to fire employees for any reason or for no reason at all. Both parties, then, were free to terminate their contract at any time; but because jobs have usually been harder to find than employees, many felt that employers held the power and that employees were relatively powerless and required protection.

Today corporations are subject to laws governing minimum wages and maximum hours, specifying health and safety standards, and forbidding discrimination in hiring, firing, and promotion. An employer cannot fire an employee for union activity. But within these limits, argues David Ewing in his ''An Employee Bill of Rights,'' corporations retain a great deal of power over their employees. The structure of most business organizations is still an authoritarian one. The relationship of employer to employee remains that of a superior to a subordinate.

According to Ewing, employees in the workplace lack many of the most basic civil liberties guaranteed by the Constitution. A number of corporations give their employees lie detector tests, collect extensive information about them, and attempt to dictate their behavior off the job. For the most part, employees are permitted little control over matters that directly affect their work lives. They can be fired for dissenting from company views or for refusing to execute an order, even if they believe that the order is immoral or illegal. Frequently there is no grievance procedure within the organization and no means of ensuring that employees receive just treatment. In effect, Ewing holds, the workplace represents a ''black hole'' in American rights; most citizens are virtually rightless from nine to five.

The civil liberties specified in the Bill of Rights were designed to protect citizens against possible abuses of power by government. But many corporations today have bigger ''populations'' than the largest of the original thirteen colonies, Ewing points out. The gross annual income of some

of the largest conglomerates exceeds the gross national product of such countries as Austria, Norway, and Greece. When
corporate power reaches the magnitude of a mini-
government, argues Ewing, it is necessary to protect those
subject to that power by an explicit recognition of their rights.
His proposed employee bill of rights, which would guarantee employees the rights of free speech, dissent, privacy,
and due process, represents one way in which this task might
be accomplished.

One of the most hotly discussed employee rights in recent years has been the right to privacy. Employers have
long been free to search employees' desks or lockers and to
control their time at work. But today, advances in technology allow employers to probe much more deeply into what
used to be the private realm. Lie detector or polygraph tests,
drug tests, detailed medical examinations, computerized systems of supervision, and extensive psychological tests are
only some examples of the technologies that may threaten
employee privacy.

Because U.S. business loses millions of dollars each year
from employee theft and sabotage, it is not surprising that
employers wish to find a way to "test" for honesty and loyalty. Polygraph tests, which attempt to determine if a subject is telling the truth through an examination of physiological responses, claim to do just this. The use of polygraphs
has been greatly restricted by a 1988 Federal law but it is
still permitted in investigating thefts and sabotages, and unrestricted use is permitted in the public sector. George Brenkert argues that the use of polygraph tests is unethical, because it violates employees' right to privacy. Polygraph tests
violate privacy in two ways, argues Brenkert. Often they
give employers information to which they are not entitled—
information about the employee's sex life, medical history,
behavior off the job, fantasies, desires, etc., that is not directly relevant to their job performance. And even when
the information obtained *is* job relevant, Brenkert claims, it
is obtained by an intrusive method. Polygraphs attempt to
circumvent our normal mechanisms of self-protection and
turn part of ourselves—the part over which we have no con-

trol—against the rest of us. Finally, Brenkert points out, polygraph tests are notoriously inaccurate and thus run a significant chance of harming honest employees.

Like employee theft, drug use by employees has been estimated to cost business millions of dollars in the form of lowered productivity, absenteeism, employee error, etc. Drug use also carries the risk of serious physical injury to consumers, the public, or employees themselves. To counter these problems, many companies have instituted programs to test applicants and/or current employees for drug use. Over 30 percent of *Fortune* 500 firms, as well as numerous smaller companies, now employ some kind of drug test. Are such programs a threat to employee privacy? Joseph Des Jardins and Ronald Duska argue that they are. Drawing on the guidelines set out by Brenkert, Des Jardins and Duska argue that employers do have a right to information that is directly related to job performance. But drug use, they claim, is not directly relevant. People use drugs differently, and drugs can have varied effects. Some drug users will be impaired on the job, but others will not. The commonly used drug tests, moreover, do not give much information about impairment. They show only the presence of the drug's metabolite in the urine and not the kind of drug, the amount that is present, or how long ago the drug was taken. An astute supervisor can spot impairment in the form of absenteeism, carelessness, low productivity, or psychological problems. If these problems do arise, the supervisor may discipline the employee for these reasons alone. There is no need to inquire into the employee's use of drugs. However, if no performance problems show up, there is no impairment—the employee *is* doing the job. Again, drug testing is not necessary. Des Jardins and Duska conclude that if what the employer is truly interested in is performance, drug test results are either superfluous or irrelevant. Testing is only justified, they argue, in jobs in which drug use poses a "clear and present" danger to others. In a *Wall Street Journal* interview conducted by Michael Waldholz, two corporate executives debate the acceptability of drug testing, touching on several of the issues raised by Des Jardins and Duska.

Not all thinkers believe that steps should be taken to protect employee rights. Donald Martin, for example, argues that an employee bill of rights such as that suggested by Ewing is not necessary. Citizens need a bill of rights to protect them against the government, Martin acknowledges, but this is because the cost of moving to a different country is very high. The cost of changing jobs, however, he claims, is relatively low. The ability of employees to move from job to job thus is enough to protect their interests. If personal liberty is restricted on the job, Martin argues, it is not because employers are tyrannizing employees, but because employee rights are costly and employees have "chosen" fewer rights in exchange for higher earning power. An employee bill of rights would not only be expensive, it would also limit the freedom of employees to trade their rights for higher salaries. Martin would probably favor letting job market forces decide whether polygraph testing and drug testing are acceptable. The case "DuPont's Policy of Exclusion from the Workplace" highlights some of the issues raised by Martin. In this case, one of the questions is whether DuPont should protect women of childbearing age from health risks against their will, or whether the women should be allowed to take risks in order to obtain the same high-paying jobs as men.

If employees are to protect their rights effectively by exercising their power to change jobs, at the very least they must have adequate information about the ways in which their jobs may threaten their interests. This is particularly difficult in the area of health and safety risks, since employees may not know the risks they face until it is too late to avoid them. The Occupational Safety and Health Administration (OSHA) sets minimum standards for safety in the workplace, but no job can be entirely riskfree. Ruth Faden and Tom Beauchamp argue that employees have a right to know about the health and safety risks they face on the job. Their article explores the extent of employees' right to know and the corresponding duty of an employer to disclose the relevant information. Faden and Beauchamp also point out that the right to know is not effective unless it is accompanied by a real ability to alter working conditions, either by changing jobs, filing complaints with OSHA, or refusing to perform unusually hazardous assignments.

WHISTLE BLOWING

Occasionally an employee discovers, or is asked to participate in, an activity he or she believes to be unethical or illegal. In such a situation the employee may choose to "blow the whistle" or reveal the activity, either to someone higher up within the corporation (usually called "internal" whistle blowing) or to the public ("external" whistle blowing). Readers will recall Kermit Vandivier's dilemma at B. F. Goodrich in Part One. In "Roger Boisjoly and the Challenger Disaster," Boisjoly must decide whether to blow the whistle on Morton Thiokol over his concerns about the safety of the space shuttle *Challenger*.

Do employees have the right, or perhaps even the obligation, to blow the whistle on corporate wrongdoing? Should they receive legal protection from such retaliations by their employer as firing, blackballing, or attacks on professional integrity? Some, such as Ralph Nader, recommend not only that whistle blowing receive protection but that it be actively encouraged as a means of improving corporate responsibility. Others are violently opposed to whistle blowing, feeling that it violates the duties of employees to their employer. States James M. Roche, chairman of General Motors Corporation:

> Some of the enemies of business now encourage an employee to be disloyal to the enterprise. They want to create suspicion and disharmony and pry into the proprietary interests of the business: However this is labeled—industrial espionage, whistle blowing, or professional responsibility—it is another tactic for spreading disunity and creating conflict.

Legally, an employee is regarded as the agent of the corporation for which he or she works. Agency law states that employees have a duty to obey the directions of their employers, to act solely in their employers' interests in all matters related to their employment, and to refrain from disclosing confidential information that, if revealed, might harm their employers. The law does not require employees to carry out commands which are illegal or immoral, but neither does it authorize them to reveal such commands to the public or (for the most part) protect them from reprisals if they do so.

Richard De George argues that because it is a form of disloyalty, and because it can cause harm to the firm, whistle blowing needs moral justification. De George believes that whistle blowing is only morally permissible under certain conditions: when serious (physical) harm is threatened and when the employee has already exhausted channels within the corporation in an attempt to correct the problem. De George regards whistle blowing as a supererogatory, self-sacrificing or heroic act and believes that employees very rarely have an *obligation* to blow the whistle. For such an obligation to be present, De George believes, an employee must have documented evidence of serious potential harm and good reason to believe that blowing the whistle will really succeed in averting the harm. The best solution to the problem of whistle blowing in the workplace, claims De George, is to encourage channels of communication and response inside the corporation so that employees are not forced to be "moral heroes."

Gene James believes that De George's criteria are too strict. Harms such as sexual harassment, fraud, or invasion of privacy may also justify blowing the whistle, he believes, even though these do not involve the physical harm that De George finds necessary. James also believes that whistle blowing is more often obligatory than De George admits. Employees who are aware of the potentially harmful consequences of a corporate act and who fail to blow the whistle, James holds, bear part of the responsibility for those consequences. In these cases, the duty to blow the whistle outweighs both the risk of job loss and the duty of loyalty to the corporation.

It is not always clear that a dissenting employee *is* being disloyal to the corporation. In many cases corporations could have saved themselves thousands of dollars in lawsuits and a tarnished public image by responding to dissenting employees. In part, whether a dissenting employee is acting in the interest of the corporation depends upon how broadly we interpret the nature, function, and goals of business. If the function of business is to produce a reliable product and refrain from harming its "stakeholders" as well as making a profit, then it could be argued that top management—and not Roger Boisjoly or Kermit Vandivier—acted against the interests of their companies.

THE QUALITY OF WORKING LIFE

> I start the automobile, the first welds... the welding gun's got a square handle with a button on the top for high voltage and a button on the bottom for low.... I stand in one spot, about a two- or three-feet area, all night. The only time a person stops is when the line stops. We do about thirty-two jobs per car, per unit. Forty-eight units an hour, eight hours a day. Thirty-two times forty-eight times eight. Figure it out. That's how many times I push that button.... Repetition is such that if you were to think about the job itself, you'd slowly go out of your mind.... I don't understand why more guys don't flip. Because you're nothing but a machine when you hit this type of thing. They give better care to that machine than they will to you. They'll have more respect, give more attention to that machine.... If that machine breaks down, there's somebody out there to fix it right away. If I break down, I'm just pushed over to the other side until another man takes my place. The only thing they have in their mind is to keep that line running.

The feelings of this spot welder at a Ford assembly plant are not unique. Thousands of Americans hold jobs in which they experience fragmentation, repetition, the feeling of being a mere cog in a machine. Most statistics indicate that job dissatisfaction in America is increasing. The 1971 task force report to the secretary of Health, Education and Welfare reported that only 24 percent of all blue-collar workers would choose the same type of work if they could make the choice again.

Nor is the dissatisfaction confined to blue-collar workers, although they are the primary focus of the readings included in this chapter. One executive describes his job:

> I don't know of any situation in the corporate world where an executive is completely free and sure of his job from moment to moment.... The danger starts as soon as you become a district manager. You have men working for you and you have a boss above—

you're caught in a squeeze....There's always the insecurity. You bungle a job. You're fearful of losing a big customer. You're fearful so many things will appear on your record, stand against you. You're always fearful of the big mistake. You've got to be careful when you go to corporation parties. Your wife, your children have got to behave properly. You've got to fit in the mold. You've got to be on guard....The executive is a lonely animal in the jungle who doesn't have a friend....

I left that world because suddenly the power and the status were empty. I'd been there, and when I got there it was nothing....So when the corporation was sold, my share of the sale was such...I didn't have to go back into the jungle. I don't have to fight to the top. I've been to the mountain top....It isn't worth it.

Richard Walton groups such feelings of meaninglessness, powerlessness, and repetitiveness under the heading of "alienation." Alienation occurs when workers have no control over their work processes, when they lack a sense of purpose and a sense of the finished product of their work, and when work ceases to be a means of self-expression and becomes merely the task of carrying out the purposes of another. When we hire someone to perform a task for us, we are treating that person as a means to accomplish our end. The fact that we offer payments in return for the job, however, is a recognition of the fact that the person we have hired is also what Kant would call an end in himself or herself, a person with his or her own goals, purposes, and desires. Designing jobs so that employees can achieve self-expression and self-fulfillment is another, perhaps equally important, way of recognizing employees' intrinsic value as people. The major complaint of the spot welder quoted above is that he is treated not as a person, but as an object.

Although it begins at the workplace, explains Walton, alienation places a heavy toll on society at large in the form of mental health problems, absenteeism, high turnover rates, frequent strikes, sabotage, lack of commitment to work and a decline in the quality of services and products. As characterized by Walton, alienation is a deep-rooted and pervasive problem which requires thoughtful, systematic solutions.

Walton sees the search for innovations to reduce alienation, however, as an opportunity not only to enhance the quality of working life but also to increase productivity. His conviction that overcoming alienation in the workplace can be rewarding both to workers and to business is supported by statistics from the HEW Work in America study mentioned above. At Corning Glass, for example, changes which gave workers more autonomy decreased rejects from 28 to 1 percent, decreased absenteeism from 8 to 1 percent, and increased productivity. Redesign of work at Norway's *Norsk Hydro* fertilizer company decreased production costs per ton by 30 percent and decreased absenteeism from 7 to 4 percent. The percentage of workers expressing satisfaction rose from 58 to 100 percent.

How do we go about decreasing alienation? Proposed solutions include structuring jobs to give workers more challenge, more mobility, more variety, and a greater sense of accomplishment. Often this involves decreasing specialization and replacing assembly lines with teams of three or four workers who assemble an entire unit of machinery. Other important suggestions are increased democracy in the workplace, with more worker participation in running the business, and more cooperation between workers and management. Another suggestion is giving workers a bigger "stake" in the business through stock ownership or profit-sharing plans. Any of or all these may be included in what union leader Irving Bluestone calls a "quality of working life program."

Bluestone claims that the workforce has changed dramatically in the past few decades and that the workplace must change to meet it. He sees increased democracy in the workplace as the most important goal of a quality of working life (QWL) program, and calls for union support of QWL. Bluestone regards QWL as an extension of, not a departure from, the traditional goal of unions. QWL programs, he claims, benefit both unions and management. Benefits include lowered absenteeism and turnover, fewer disciplinary actions against employees, a decrease in grievances filed by employees, and improved product quality.

Mike Parker and Dwight Hansen are more sceptical about the benefits of QWL programs for workers and unions. They fear that the programs upset the traditional adversarial relationship between unions and management, eroding the power of the unions. Because they emphasize cooperation between workers and management, Parker and Hansen believe, QWL programs undercut union solidarity and divide workers against each other, undermining the power to act collectively which has been the mainstay of workers since unionism began. They believe that the cooperation offered by QWL may be a new form of manipulation, a way for management to bypass the influence of the union and go directly to the shop floor. Parker and Hansen claim that QWL programs have been used to wring concessions from workers, concessions that have not been outweighed by the benefits of QWL. Ultimately, they conclude, the nature of the economic relationship between workers and management dooms QWL: Management's job is to cut the costs of production, and workers are merely one of those costs. "The Eastern Airlines Union-Management Experiment" describes a QWL experiment at Eastern Airlines and gives the reader a chance to evaluate Bluestone's and Parker and Hansen's claims.

Mitchell Fein argues against QWL programs for different reasons. He questions the assumption of thinkers like Walton and Bluestone that participation and personal fulfillment are essential characteristics of a satisfying job. Not all workers want more autonomy, more challenge, and more variety in their work, he argues. If they did, there would be more union emphasis on QWL programs at the bargaining table. In fact, he believes, most workers are satisfied with their jobs. Fein fears that workers will suffer because management will impose preconceived ideas on them about what makes work satisfying, and he suggests that QWL programs represent an exploitation of workers' job satisfaction for gains in productivity.

Edward Cohen-Rosenthal is a moderate voice in the QWL debate. He believes that the interests of workers and management are too often seen as conflicting, when they are actually complementary. This means that although QWL programs can be used as tools for union-busting or manipulation, it is possible to construct a program that benefits both workers and management. Possible drawbacks of QWL programs for workers include job loss from increased productivity, violations of the union contract, and erosion of the protective power of the union. But with true commitment, a program can lead to greater representation of worker concerns, higher job satisfaction, lower stress, fewer grievances, and the preservation of jobs.

PREFERENTIAL HIRING

Few people would take issue with the goal of equal opportunity for all Americans. Equal opportunity in the workplace is especially important, because denying people access to good jobs also denies them access to a decent standard of living, social status, power, and personal development. When people are denied jobs because of some characteristic—such as sex or race—which is irrelevant to their capacity to perform satisfactorily, they are not being given an equal opportunity, but are being discriminated against. Discrimination is not only unjust; it also undermines the possibility of a free market system. The market cannot be "free" if people do not have an equal opportunity to enter it. Without equal opportunity, the market cannot work efficiently. Comparisons of annual income, job title, and proportional representation in the highest and lowest economic positions between white males and women and minorities show that racial and sexual discrimination is being practiced in our society and that this discrimination has decreased only slightly in recent years.

Title VII of the Civil Rights Act of 1964 prohibits discrimination on the basis of race, color, religion, sex, or national origin. The act also established the Equal Employment Opportunity Commission, which has the power to enforce compliance with Title VII. Business has responded with a range of strategies, from "passive nondiscrimination" to the establishment of hard quotas specifying the number of women or minorities that must be hired. One of the most frequently used and controversial strategies is "preferential hiring." Preferential hiring may be defined as a policy of preferring the female or minority candidate over the white male in cases in which both candidates are qualified. The term "affirmative action" is sometimes used interchangeably with "preferential hiring."

Because preferential hiring involves giving preference to certain applicants *because* they are female or members of minority groups, some feel that it is a form of reverse discrimination—that is, that it deprives applicants who are *not* members of disadvantaged groups of their right to equal consideration. Is preferential hiring, or "affirmative action," unjust?

William Bradford Reynolds, Assistant Attorney General under the Reagan Administration, argues that affirmative action programs are only justified under special circumstances and that general policies of preferential hiring are unfair. The chief function of affirmative action programs, argues Reynolds, should be to broaden applicant pools and encourage training programs so that everyone has an "equal opportunity" to be considered for a job. Affirmative action programs may also be used to provide "make-whole relief" to victims of discrimination—that is, to compensate victims so that they are as nearly as possible in the position that they would have been in if there had been no discrimination. But preferential hiring policies benefit not only victims, but *all* members of a disadvantaged group. Those who have not personally been victims of discrimination do not deserve compensation, Reynolds believes. Such preferential hiring policies are also unfair to third parties, for example, white males, who are deprived of their chance at an equal opportunity in order to provide advantages for others. Reynolds believes that it is fair to ask white males to help pay the employer's debt to those who have actually been victims of discrimination, because the white males have been beneficiaries of that discrimination. But, he claims, it is not fair to make them sacrifice for those who have *not* personally been wronged. Finally, Reynolds argues, disproportions in the number of women and minorities in certain jobs may be due not to discrimination, but to factors like interest, skills, and hard work. In a free market society, we cannot expect the kind of proportional representation of race and gender in different jobs that some would like to see.

Nancy Kubasek and Andrea Giampetro argue that while affirmative action may seem to violate the command to "treat equals equally," and thus may seem unjust, it does not do so. They argue that although the official barriers to equal opportunity have been removed, many others remain: Blacks live in separate neighborhoods from whites, almost always poorer ones with fewer social services. Their schools are usually inferior to those in white neighborhoods. Because they lead lives largely segregated from whites, blacks have less chance to meet whites and have greatly lowered chances when jobs are filled through the "old-boy" network or casual contact. The separate lives of blacks and whites also mean that many whites do not feel comfortable with blacks, and people tend to hire who they feel most comfortable with. Kubasek and Giampetro claim that these subtle social forces put blacks at a systematic competitive disadvantage and give whites a consistent competitive edge. If Kubasek and Giampetro are right, then even blacks who have not experienced actual incidents of discrimination need help if they are to have an "equal opportunity" to compete. And because blacks and whites are not yet true equals, affirmative action plans do not violate the principle that we should treat equals equally. Finally, Kubasek and Giampetro argue that policies of preferential hiring are not unfair to whites. Affirmative action does not place whites at a competitive disadvantage, they claim; it merely takes away the competitive edge that whites did not earn and would not have had if competition had been fair all along. Once the competitive disadvantage of blacks is overcome, they believe, there will no longer be a need for policies of preferential hiring.

Laura Purdy claims that women, too, suffer from a systematic competitive disadvantage. Citing empirical studies to support her claims, Purdy argues that both men and women perceive women as less qualified than they really are. Our society has conditioned us not to regard women as a source of authority, creativity, leadership, etc., and thus we frequently do not "see" these things in women even when they are there. If this claim is correct, Purdy argues, then ordinary affirmative action programs that prefer women when they are equally as qualified as a male job candidate will still not overcome women's disadvantage. Purdy believes employees are justified in hiring women who seem *less* qualified than their male competition, because she believes that they are really more qualified than our social biases make them seem.

United Steelworkers of America v. Weber gives the reader a chance to explore some of the ethical issues surrounding affirmative action programs. In this case, the U.S. Supreme Court declared that the preferential admission of minorities into a U.S. Steel training program was declared to be consistent with Title VII, and not an unlawful form of discrimination. In the most recent affirmative action case at this writing, the Supreme Court declared that it was lawful for a company to promote a woman with a slightly lower score on an employee evaluation scale over a man with a slightly higher score in order to remedy a clear imbalance between the percentage of women in an area's labor pool and those working for the company.

Affirmative action policies are designed to increase the proportion of women and blacks in jobs traditionally held by white males and to improve their access to those jobs. Although there has been a significant increase in the numbers of women entering male-dominated professions, however, most women remain in traditionally female-dominated jobs, and almost all these jobs are low-paying. Women still earn only 60 percent of what men earn. Interestingly, once a traditionally male job becomes predominantly female, the status and salary of that job goes down. Positions such as secretary or bank teller, both of which used to be held mostly by men, are examples. Also, many jobs held by women that demand considerable skill and training are paid less well than unskilled jobs held by men. Nurses are paid less than truck drivers. Child care workers are paid less than mail carriers.

Some argue these differences are due to the workings of the market. Others see them as a form of sex-based wage discrimination, charging that society devalues the work of women simply because women perform it. One proposed solution to these problems is a policy of "comparable worth." Under comparable worth, a company would pay equal salaries for work that is of "comparable value" to the company. If the work performed by secretaries, a predominantly female position, is found to be of comparable value with the work performed by lathe operators, who are usually men, the secretaries would be eligible for a "comparable worth raise." Comparable worth has been extremely controversial doctrine.

Phyllis Schlafly argues that a nationwide policy of comparable worth would harm the very people it intends to help—women. Forcing employers to pay women more would discourage them from hiring women, she believes. Companies would strive to keep the percentage of women performing any given job under the 70 percent that makes the job eligible for a comparable worth raise. Other women, in male-dominated professions, would have their salaries frozen at below the market price, she claims. This would discourage movement by women into traditionally male professions and make it more difficult for them to move out of traditionally feminine roles. Schlafly believes that comparable worth would also harm men, particularly men in blue-collar jobs, by freezing their salaries at an unfairly low level. Finally, Schlafly maintains, it is almost impossible to judge the objective "worth" of a job. What makes one job worth more than another? Skills? Mental demands? Physical conditions? Risk? Schlafly suggests that the best indication of the worth of a job is the salary it commands on the open market.

Gerald McEntee argues that Schlafly's fears are exaggerated and that policies of comparable worth are both workable and fair. Unlike Schlafly, McEntee does not see the differences in men's and women's pay as a result of the free market system. There is a gap between male and female salaries that cannot be accounted for by women's more recent entry into the job market or differences in skill and experience, he claims. This can only be due to sex discrimination, and policies of comparable worth are necessary to overcome this discrimination. Comparable worth does not require wages to be set by government authority; it simply requires each organization to pay their own workers comparable salaries for comparable work. Comparing the value of two different types of work, he adds, is not as difficult as it seems. Many companies already have evaluation systems that compare dissimilar jobs.

CHAPTER 7

Employee Rights and Duties

READINGS FOR CHAPTER SEVEN

David Ewing
An Employee Bill of Rights

George G. Brenkert
Privacy, Polygraphs and Work
294

Joseph R. Des Jardins and Ronald Duska
Drug Testing in Employment
301

Michael Waldholz
Drug Testing in the Workplace
309

Donald L. Martin
Is an Employee Bill of Rights Needed?
312

Ruth R. Faden and Tom L. Beauchamp
*The Right to Risk Information and the Right to Refuse
Health Hazards in the Workplace*
315

An Employee Bill of Rights

David Ewing*

For nearly two centuries Americans have enjoyed freedom of press, speech, and assembly, due process of law, privacy, freedom of conscience, and other important rights—in their homes, churches, political forums, and social and cultural life. But Americans have not enjoyed these civil liberties in most companies, government agencies, and other organizations where they work. Once a U.S. citizen steps through the plant or office door at 9 *a.m.*, he or she is nearly rightless until 5 *p.m.*, Monday through Friday. The employee continues to have political freedoms, of course, but these are not the significant ones now. While at work, the important relationships are with bosses, associates, and subordinates. Inequalities in dealing with these people are what really count for an employee.

To this generalization there are important exceptions. In some organizations, generous managements have seen fit to assure free speech, privacy, due process, and other concerns as privileges. But there is no guarantee the privileges will survive the next change of chief executive. As former Attorney General Ramsey Clark once said in a speech, "A right is not what someone gives you; it's what no one can take from you." Defined in this manner, rights are rare in business and public organizations.

In effect, U.S. society is a paradox. The Constitution and Bill of Rights light up the sky over political campaigners, legislators, civic leaders, families, church people, and artists. But not so over employees. The employee sector of our civil

liberties universe is more like a black hole, with rights so compacted, so imploded by the gravitational forces of legal tradition, that, like the giant black stars in the physical universe, light can scarcely escape.

Perhaps the most ironic thing is that only in recent years have Americans made many noises about this paradox. It is as if we took it for granted and assumed there was no alternative. "Organizations have always been this way and always have to be," we seem to say. One is reminded of an observation attributed to Marshall McLuhan: "Anybody's total surround, or environment, creates a condition of nonperception."

To put the situation in focus, let us make a brief review of rights in the workplace.

SPEECH

In many private and public organizations there is a well-oiled machinery for providing relief to an employee who is discharged because of his or her race, religion, or sex. But we have no mechanisms for granting similar relief to an employee who is discharged for exercising the right of free speech. The law states that all employers "may dismiss their employees at will...for good cause, for no cause, or even for cause morally wrong, without being thereby guilty of legal wrong."[1]

Of course, discharge is only the extreme weapon; many steps short of discharge may work well enough—loss of a raise in pay, demotion, assignment to the boondocks, or perhaps simply a cutback of normal and expected benefits.

Consider the case of a thirty-five-year-old business executive whom I shall call "Mike Z." He was a respected research manager in a large company. He believed that his company was making only superficial efforts to comply with newly enacted pollution laws. In a management meeting and later in social groups he spoke critically of top management's attitude. Soon strange things began to happen to him, different only in degree from what happens to a political dissenter in the Soviet Union. First, his place in the com-

Excerpted from *Freedom Inside the Organization* by David Ewing Copyright © 1977 by David W. Ewing. Reprinted by permission of the publisher, E.P. Dutton, a division of NAL Penguin, Inc.
*Organizational Behavior Area, Harvard Business School.

pany parking lot was canceled. Then his name was "accidentally" removed from the office building directory inside the main entrance. Soon routine requests he made to attend professional meetings began to get snarled up in red tape or were "lost." Next he found himself harassed by directives to rewrite routine reports. Then his budget for clerical service was cut, followed by a drastic slash in his research budget. When he tried to protest this treatment, he met a wall of top management silence. Rather than see his staff suffer further for his dissidence, he quit his job and moved his family to another city.

Mike Z. could be almost anyone in thousands of companies, government agencies, and other organizations. It should not be surprising, therefore, that when it comes to speaking out on issues of company policy or management practice, employees make about as much noise as fish swimming.

So well-established is the idea that any criticism of the company is "ratting" or "finking" that some companies hang out written prohibitions for all to see. For instance, a private bus company on the West Coast puts employees on notice with this rule:

> The company requires its employees to be loyal. It will not tolerate words or acts of hostility to the company, its officers, agents, or employees, its services, equipment or its condition, or...criticisms of the company to others than...superior officers.

CONSCIENTIOUS OBJECTION

There is very little protection in industry for employees who object to carrying out immoral, unethical, or illegal orders from their superiors. If the employee doesn't like what he or she is asked to do, the remedy is to pack up and leave. This remedy seems to presuppose an ideal economy, where there is another company down the street with openings for jobs just like the one the employee left. But what about the real world? Here resignation may mean having to uproot one's family and move to a strange city in another state. Or it may mean, for an employee in the semifi-

nals of a career, or for an employee with a specialized competence, not being able to find another suitable job anywhere.

In 1970 Shirley Zinman served as a secretary in a Philadelphia employment agency called LIB Services. One day she was instructed by her bosses to record all telephone conversations she might have with prospective clients. This was to be done for "training purposes," she was told, although the callers were not to be told that their words were being taped. The office manager would monitor the conversations on an extension in her office. Ms. Zinman refused to play along with this game, not only because it was unethical, in her view, but illegal as well—the telephone company's regulations forbade such unannounced telephone recordings.

So Ms. Zinman had to resign. She sought unemployment compensation. The state unemployment pay board refused her application. It reasoned that her resignation was not "compelling and necessitous." With the help of attorneys from the American Civil Liberties Union, she appealed her case to the Pennsylvania Commonwealth Court. In a ruling hailed by civil rights leaders, the court in 1973 reversed the pay board and held that Ms. Zinman was entitled to unemployment compensation because her objection to the unethical directive was indeed a "compelling" reason to quit her job.[2]

What this interesting case leaves unsaid is as important as what it does say: Resignation continues to be the accepted response for the objecting employee. The Pennsylvania court took a bold step in favor of employee rights, for prior to this decision there was little reason to think that the Shirley Zinmans of industry could expect any help at all from the outside world. But within the organization itself, an employee is expected to sit at the feet of the boss's conscience.

SECURITY AND PRIVACY

When employees are in their homes, before and after working hours, they enjoy well-established rights to privacy and to protection from arbitrary search and seizure of their papers and possessions. But no such rights protect them in the average company, government agency, or other organization; their superiors need only the flimsiest pretext to search their lockers, desks, and files. The boss can rummage through an employee's letters, memoranda, and tapes looking for evidence that (let us say) he or she is about to "rat" on the company. "Ratting" might include reporting a violation of safety standards to the Occupational Safety and Health Administration (which is provided for by law), or telling Ralph Nader about a product defect, or giving the mayor's office requested information about a violation of energy-use regulations.

CHOICE OF OUTSIDE ACTIVITIES AND ASSOCIATIONS

In practice, most business employees enjoy no right to work after hours for the political, social, and community organizations of their choice. To be sure, in many companies an enlightened management will encourage as much diversity of choice in outside activities as employees can make. As noted earlier, however, this is an indulgence which can disappear any time, for most states do not mandate such rights, and even in those that do, the rights are poorly protected. An employee who gets fired for his or her choice of outside activities can expect no damages for his loss even if he or she wins a suit against the employer. The employee may only "secure the slight satisfaction of seeing his employer suffer the statutory penalties."[3]

Ironically, however, a company cannot discriminate against people whose politics it dislikes when it *hires* them.[4] It has to wait a few days before it can exercise its prerogatives.

DUE PROCESS

"Accidents will occur in the best-regulated families," said Mr. Micawber in *David Copperfield.*

Similarly, accidents of administration occur even in the best-managed companies, with neurotic, inept, or distracted supervisors inflicting needless harm on subordinates. Many a subordinate who goes to such a boss to protest would be well-advised to keep one foot in the stirrups, for he is likely to be shown to the open country for his efforts.

This generalization does not hold for civil service employees in the federal government, who can resort to a grievance process. Nor does it hold for unionized companies, which also have grievance procedures. But it holds for *most* other organizations. A few organizations voluntarily have established a mechanism to ensure due process.

The absence of a right to due process is especially painful because it is the second element of constitutionalism in organizations. As we shall think of it in this book, employee constitutionalism consists of a set of clearly defined rights, and a means of protecting employees from discharge, demotion, or other penalties imposed when they assert their rights.

Why bother about rightlessness in corporations, government agencies, and other organizations? They are much smaller than state and federal governments, are they not? Must an organization that "rules" an employee only for forty or so hours per week be treated as a government?

For one answer, let us turn to the Founding Fathers. Of course, they did not know or conceive of the modern corporation and public agency, so we cannot read what their thoughts about all this might have been. Perhaps we can make a reasonable guess, however, by comparing some numbers.

If the original thirteen colonies were large and powerful enough to concern the Founding Fathers, it seems likely that those men, if here today, would want to extend their philosophy to other assemblages of equivalent size and magnitude. In the writings of James Madison, Thomas Jefferson, George Mason, Jonas Phillips,

Richard Henry Lee, Elbridge Gerry, Luther Martin, and others, there is no inference that human rights were seen as a good thing only some of the time or for some places. Instead, the Fathers saw rights as a universal need.[5]

In 1776, and in 1789, when the Bill of Rights (first ten amendments to the Constitution) was passed by Congress and sent to the states for ratification, trading companies and government agencies were tiny organizations incapable of harboring bureaucracy. Indeed, to use Mr. Micawber's phrase, there was hardly room in them to swing a cat, much less create layer on layer of hierarchy and wall after wall of departmental structure.

Today all that has changed. Some of our corporate and public organizations have larger "populations" than did the thirteen colonies. And a truly vast number of organizations have large enough "populations" to rank as real powers in people's everyday lives. For instance:

- AT&T has more than 939,000 employees, nearly twice the size of the largest colony, Virginia, which had about 493,000 inhabitants in 1776.
- General Motors, with 681,000 employees, is nearly two and one-half times the size of the second largest colony, Pennsylvania, which had a population of about 284,000 people in 1776.
- Westinghouse, the thirteenth largest corporate employer today with 166,000 employees, is four times the size of the thirteenth largest colony, Delaware, which had a population of 41,400. Westinghouse's "population" is also larger than that in 1776 of South Carolina, New Jersey, New Hampshire, Rhode Island, and Georgia.

In fact, 125 corporations have larger "populations" than did Delaware, the smallest colony, in 1776. But can employee workforces legitimately be compared with state populations? Of course, there are important differences—the twenty-four-hours-per-day jurisdiction of the

state as opposed to only eight hours per day for an employer, the fact that the state has courts and military forces while the employer does not, and others. Yet it is not an apples-and-oranges comparison. Decades ago, and long before corporations and public agencies achieved anything like their current size, political scientists were noting many important similarities between the governments of organizations and political governments. In 1908, for example, Arthur Bentley wrote:

> A corporation is government through and through...Certain technical methods which political government uses, as, for instance, hanging, are not used by corporations, generally speaking, but that is a detail.[6]

In numerous ways, sizable corporations, public agencies, and university administrations qualify as "minigovernments." They pay salaries and costs. They have medical plans. They provide for retirement income. They offer recreational facilities. They maintain cafeterias. They may assist an employee with housing, educational loans, personal training, and vacation plans. They schedule numerous social functions. They have "laws," conduct codes, and other rules. Many have mechanisms for resolving disputes. A few even keep chaplains on the payroll or maintain facilities for religious worship.

Accordingly, it seems foolish to dismiss minigovernments as possible subjects of rights, or to exclude employees from discussions of civil liberties. We have assumed that rights are not as important for employees as for political citizens. Our assumption is in error.

The bill of rights that follows is one person's proposal, a "working paper" for discussion, not a platform worked out in committee.

1. *No organization or manager shall discharge, demote, or in other ways discriminate against any employee who criticizes, in speech or press, the ethics, legality, or social responsibility of management actions.*

Comment: What this right does not say is as important as what it does say. Protection does not extend to employees who make nuisances of themselves or who balk, argue, or contest managerial decisions on normal operating and planning matters, such as the choice of inventory accounting method, whether to diversify the product line or concentrate it, whether to rotate workers on a certain job or specialize them, and so forth. "Committing the truth," as Ernest Fitzgerald called it, is protected only for speaking out on issues where we consider an average citizen's judgment to be as valid as an expert's—truth in advertising, public safety standards, questions of fair disclosure, ethical practices, and so forth.

2. *No employee shall be penalized for engaging in outside activities of his or her choice after working hours, whether political, economic, civic, or cultural, nor for buying products and services of his or her choice for personal use, nor for expressing or encouraging views contrary to top management's on political, economic, and social issues.*

Comment: Many companies encourage employees to participate in outside activities, and some states have committed this right to legislation. Freedom of choice of products and services for personal use is also authorized in various state statutes as well as in arbitrators' decisions. The third part of the statement extends the protection of the First Amendment to the employee whose ideas about government, economic policy, religion, and society do not conform with the boss's.

Note that this provision does not authorize an employee to come to work "beat" in the morning because he or she has been moonlighting. Participation in outside activities should enrich employees' lives, not debilitate them; if on-the-job performance suffers, the usual penalties may have to be paid.

3. *No organization or manager shall penalize an employee for refusing to carry out a directive that violates common norms of morality.*

Comment: The purpose of this right is to afford job security to subordinates who cannot perform an action because they consider it unethical or illegal. It is important that the conscientious objector in such a case hold to a view that has some public acceptance. Fad moralities—messages from flying saucers, mores of occult religious sects, and so on—do not justify refusal to carry out an order. Nor in any case is the employee entitled to interfere with the boss's finding another person to do the job requested.

4. *No organization shall allow audio or visual recordings of an employee's conversations or actions to be made without his or her prior knowledge and consent. Nor may an organization require an employee or applicant to take personality tests, polygraph examinations, or other tests that constitute, in his opinion, an invasion of privacy.*

Comment: This right is based on policies that some leading organizations have already put into practice. If an employee doesn't want his working life monitored, that is his privilege so long as he demonstrates (or, if an applicant, is willing to demonstrate) competence to do a job well.

5. *No employee's desk, files, or locker may be examined in his or her absence by anyone but a senior manager who has sound reason to believe that the files contain information needed for a management decision that must be made in the employee's absence.*

Comment: The intent of this right is to grant people a privacy right as employees similar to that which they enjoy as political and social citizens under the "searches and seizures" guarantee of the Bill of Rights (Fourth Amendment to the Constitution). Many leading organizations in business and government have respected the principle of this rule for some time.

6. *No employer organization may collect and keep on file information about an employee that is not relevant and necessary for efficient*

management. Every employee shall have the right to inspect his or her personnel file and challenge the accuracy, relevance, or necessity of data in it, except for personal evaluations and comments by other employees which could not reasonably be obtained if confidentiality were not promised. Access to an employee's file by outside individuals and organizations shall be limited to inquiries about the essential facts of employment.

Comment: This right is important if employees are to be masters of their employment track records instead of possible victims of them. It will help to eliminate surprises, secrets, and skeletons in the clerical closet.

7. *No manager may communicate to prospective employers of an employee who is about to be or has been discharged gratuitous opinions that might hamper the individual in obtaining a new position.*

Comment: The intent of this right is to stop blacklisting. The courts have already given some support for it.

8. *An employee who is discharged, demoted, or transferred to a less desirable job is entitled to a written statement from management of its reasons for the penalty.*

Comment: The aim of this provision is to encourage a manager to give the same reasons in a hearing, arbitration, or court trial that he or she gives the employee when the cutdown happens. The written statement need not be given unless requested; often it is so clear to all parties why an action is being taken that no document is necessary.

9. *Every employee who feels that he or she has been penalized for asserting any right described in this bill shall be entitled to a fair hearing before an impartial official, board, or arbitrator. The findings and conclusions of the hearing shall be delivered in writing to the employee and management.*

Comment: This very important right is the organizational equivalent of due process of law as we know it in political and community

life. Without due process in a company or agency, the rights in this bill would all have to be enforced by outside courts and tribunals, which is expensive for society as well as time-consuming for the employees who are required to appear as complainants and witnesses. The nature of a ''fair hearing'' is purposely left undefined here so that different approaches can be tried, expanded, and adapted to changing needs and conditions.

Note that the findings of the investigating official or group are not binding on top management. This would put an unfair burden on an ombudsperson or ''expedited arbitrator,'' if one of them is the investigator. Yet the employee is protected. If management rejects a finding of unfair treatment and then the employee goes to court, the investigator's statement will weigh against management in the trial. As a practical matter, therefore, employers will not want to buck the investigator-referee unless they fervently disagree with the findings.

Every sizable organization, whether in business, government, health, or another field, should have a bill of rights for employees. Only small organizations need not have such a statement—personal contact and oral communications meet the need for them. However, companies and agencies need not have identical bills of rights. Industry custom, culture, past history with employee unions and associations, and other considerations can be taken into account in the wording and emphasis given to different provisions.

NOTES

1. See Lawrence E. Blades, ''Employment at Will vs. Individual Freedom: On Limiting the Abusive Exercise of Employer Power,'' *Columbia Law Review* 67 (1967):1405.
2. 8 Pa. Comm. Ct. Reports 649,304 A. 2nd 380 (1973). Also see *New York Times,* August 26, 1973.
3. Blades, 1412.
4. See 299 F. Supp. 1100, cited in *Employee Rela-*

tions in Action, August 1971 (New York, N.Y., Man & Manager), pp. 1–2.

5. See, for example, Bernard Schwartz, *The Bill of Rights: A Documentary History.* Vol. 1 (Toronto and New York: Chelsea House Publishers in association with McGraw-Hill Book Company, 1971), pp. 435 ff.

6. Arthur Bentley, *The Process of Government,* cited in Arthur Selwyn Miller, *The Modern Corporate State* (Westport, Conn.: Greenwood Press, 1976), p. 188.

Privacy, Polygraphs and Work

George G. Brenkert*

The rights of prospective employees have been the subject of considerable dispute, both past and present. In recent years, this dispute has focused on the use of polygraphs to verify the claims which prospective employees make on employment application forms. With employee theft supposedly amounting to approximately ten billion dollars a year, with numerous businesses suffering sizeable losses and even being forced into bankruptcy by employee theft, significant and increasing numbers of employers have turned to the use of polygraphs.[1] Their right to protect their property is in danger, they insist, and the use of the polygraph to detect and weed out the untrustworthy prospective employee is a painless, quick, economical, and legitimate way to defend this right. Critics, however, have questioned both the reliability and validity of polygraphs, as well as objected to the use of polygraphs as demean-

*Department of Philosophy, the University of Tennessee.

ing, affronts to human dignity, violations of self-incrimination prohibitions, expressions of employers' mistrust, and violations of privacy.[2] Though there has been a great deal of discussion of the reliability and validity of polygraphs, there has been precious little discussion of the central moral issues at stake. Usually terms such as "dignity," "privacy," and "property rights" are simply bandied about with the hope that some favorable response will be evoked. The present paper seeks to redress this situation by discussing one important aspect of the above dispute—the supposed violation of personal privacy. Indeed, the violation of "a right to privacy" often appears to be the central moral objection to the use of polygraphs. However, the nature and basis of this claim have not yet been clearly established.[3] If they could be, there would be a serious reason to oppose the use of polygraphs on prospective employees.

There are three questions which must be faced in the determination of this issue. First, is the nature of the information which polygraphing seeks to verify, information which can be said to violate, or involve the violation of, a person's privacy? Second, does the use of the polygraph itself as the means to corroborate the responses of the job applicant violate the applicant's privacy? Third, even if—for either of the two preceding reasons—the polygraph does violate a person's privacy, might this violation still be justified by the appeal to more weighty reasons, e.g., the defense of property rights?

I

In order to determine what information might be legitimately private to an individual who seeks employment we must consider the nature of the employer/(prospective) employee relationship. The nature of this relationship depends upon the customs, conventions and rules of the society. These, of course, are in flux at any time—and particularly so in the present case. They may also need revision. Further, the nature of this relationship will depend upon its particular instances—e.g., that of the employer of five workers or of five thousand workers, the kind of work involved, etc. In essence, however, we have a complex relationship in which an employer theoretically contracts with a person(s) to perform certain services from which the employer expects to derive a certain gain for himself. In the course of the employee's performance of these services, the employer entrusts him with certain goods, money, etc.; in return for such services he delivers to the employee a certain remuneration and (perhaps) benefits. The goals of the employer and the employee are not at all, on this account, necessarily the same. The employee expects his remuneration (and benefits) even if the services, though adequately performed, do not result in the end the employer expected. Analogously, the employer expects to derive a certain gain for the services the employee has performed even if the employee is not (fully) satisfied with his work or remuneration. On the other hand, if the employer is significantly unable to achieve the ends sought through the contract with the employee, the latter may not receive his full remuneration (should the employer go bankrupt) and may even lose his job. There is, in short, a complicated mixture of trust and antagonism, connectedness and disparity of ends in the relation between employer and employee.

Given this (brief) characterization of the relationship between employer and employee, the information to which the employer qua employer is entitled about the (prospective) employee is that information which regards his possible acceptable performance of the services for which he might be hired. Without such information the employer could not fulfill the role which present society sanctions. There are two aspects of the information to which the employer is entitled given the employer/employee relationship. On the one hand, this information will relate to and vary in accordance with the services for which the person is to be hired. But in any case, it will be limited by those services and what they re-

quire. In short, one aspect of the information to which the employer is entitled is "job relevant" information. Admittedly the criterion of job relevancy is rather vague. Certainly there are few aspects of a person which might not affect his job performance—aspects including his sex life, etc. How then does the "job relevancy" criterion limit the questions asked or the information sought? It does so by limiting the information sought to that which is directly connected with the job description. If a typist is sought, it is job relevant to know whether or not a person can type—typing tests are legitimate. If a store manager is sought, it is relevant to know about his abilities to manage employees, stock, etc. That is, the description of the job is what determines the relevancy of the information to be sought. It is what gives the employer a right to know certain things about the person seeking employment. Accordingly, if a piece of information is not "job relevant" then the employer is not entitled qua employer to know it. Consequently, since sexual practices, political beliefs, associational activities, etc. are not part of the description of most jobs, that is, since they do not directly affect one's job performance, they are not legitimate information for an employer to know in the determination of the hiring of a job applicant.[4]

However, there is a second aspect to this matter. A person must be able not simply to perform a certain activity, or provide a service, but he must also be able to do it in an acceptable manner—i.e., in a manner which is approximately as efficient as others, in an honest manner, and in a manner compatible with others who seek to provide the services for which they were hired. Thus, not simply one's abilities to do a certain job are relevant, but also aspects of one's social and moral character are pertinent. A number of qualifications are needed for the purport of this claim to be clear. First, that a person must be able to work in an acceptable manner is not intended to legitimize the consideration of the prejudices of other employees. It is not legitimate to give weight in moral deliberations to the immoral and/or morally irrelevant beliefs which people hold concerning the characteristics of others. That one's present employees can work at a certain (perhaps exceptional) rate is a legitimate consideration in hiring other workers. That one's present employees have prejudices against certain religions, sexes, races, political views, etc. is not a morally legitimate consideration. Second, it is not, or should not be, the motives, beliefs, or attitudes underlying the job relevant character traits, e.g., honest, efficient, which are pertinent, but rather the fact that a person does or does not perform according to these desirable character traits. This is not to say, it should be noted, that a person's beliefs and attitudes about the job itself, e.g., how it is best to be done, what one knows or believes about the job, etc., are irrelevant. Rather it is those beliefs, attitudes and motives underlying one's desired character traits which are not relevant. The contract of the employer with the employee is for the latter to perform acceptably certain services—it is not for the employee to have certain underlying beliefs, motives, or attitudes. If I want to buy something from someone, this commercial relation does not entitle me to probe the attitudes, motives, and beliefs of the person beyond his own statements, record of past actions, and the observations of others. Even the used car salesman would correctly object that his right to privacy was being violated if he was required to submit to Rorschach tests, an attitude survey test, truth serums, and/or the polygraph in order to determine his real beliefs about selling cars. Accordingly, why the person acts the way in which he acts ought not to be the concern of the employer. Whether a person is a good working colleague simply because he is congenial, because his ego needs the approval of others, or because he has an oppressive superego is, in this instance, morally irrelevant. What is relevant is whether this person has, by his past actions, given some indication that he may work in a manner compatible with others.

Consequently, a great deal of the information which has been sought in preemployment screening through the use of polygraph tests has violated the privacy of individuals. Instances in which the sex lives, for example, of applicants have been probed are not difficult to find. However, privacy violations have occurred not simply in such generally atypical instances but also in standard situations. To illustrate the range of questions asked prospective employees and the violations of privacy which have occurred we need merely consider a list of some questions which one of the more prominent polygraph firms includes in its current tests:

> Have you ever taken any of the following without the advice of a doctor? If Yes, please check: Barbiturates, Speed, LSD, Tranquilizers, Amphetamines, Marijuana, Others.
>
> In the past five years about how many times, if any, have you bet on horse races at the race track?
>
> Do you think that policemen are honest?
>
> Did you ever think about committing a robbery?
>
> Have you been refused credit or a loan in the past five years?
>
> Have you ever consulted a doctor about a mental condition?
>
> Do you think that it is okay to get around the law if you don't actually break it?
>
> Do you enjoy stories of successful crimes and swindles?[5]

Such questions, it follows from the above argument, are for any standard employment violations of one's right to privacy. An employer might ask if a person regularly takes certain narcotic drugs, if he is considering him for a job which requires handling narcotics. An employer might ask if a person has been convicted of a larceny, etc. But whether the person enjoys stories about successful larcenists, whether a person has ever taken any prescription drugs without the advice of a doctor, or whether a person bets on the horses should be considered violations of one's rightful privacy.

The upshot of the argument in the first two sections is, then, that some information can be considered rightfully private to an individual. Such information is rightfully private or not depending on the relationship in which a person stands to another person or institution. In the case of the employer/employee relationship, I have argued that that information is rightfully private which does not relate to the acceptable performance of the activities as characterized in the job description. This excludes a good many questions which are presently asked in polygraph tests, but does not, by any means, exclude all such questions. There still remain many questions which an employer might conceivably wish to have verified by the use of the polygraph. Accordingly, I turn in the next section to the question whether the verification of the answers to legitimate questions by the use of the polygraph may be considered a violation of a person's right to privacy. If it is, then the violation obviously does not stem from the questions themselves but from the procedure, the polygraph test, whereby the answers to those questions are verified.

II

A first reason to believe that use of the polygraph occasions a violation of one's right to privacy is that, even though the questions to be answered are job relevant, some of them will occasion positive, lying reactions which are not necessarily related to any past misdeeds. Rather, the lying reaction indicated by the polygraph may be triggered because of unconscious conflicts, fears and hostilities a person has. It may be occasioned by conscious anxieties over other past activities and observations. Thus, the lying reaction indicated by the polygraph need not positively identify actual lying or the commission of illegal activities. The point, however, is not to question the validity of the polygraph. Rather, the point is that the validity of the polygraph can only be maintained by seeking to clarify whether or not such reactions really indicate lying and the commission of past misdeeds. But this can be done only by the polygraphist further probing into the person's background and inner thoughts. However, inasmuch as the questions can no longer be restrained in this situation by job relevancy considerations, but must explore other areas to which an employer is not necessarily entitled knowledge, to do this will violate a person's right to privacy.

A second reason why the polygraph must be said to violate a job applicant's right to privacy relates to the monitoring of a person's physiological responses to the questions posed to him. By measuring these responses, the polygraph can supposedly reveal one's mental processes. Now even though the questions posed are legitimate questions, surely a violation of one's right to privacy occurs. Just because I have something which you are entitled to see or know, it does not follow that you can use any means to fulfill that entitlement and not violate my privacy. Consider the instance of two good friends, one of whom has had some dental work done which puts him in a situation such that he can tune in the thoughts and feelings of his friend. Certain facts about, and emotional responses of, his friend— aspects which his friend (we will assume) would usually want to share with him—simply now stream into his head. Even though the friendship relation generally entitles its members to know personal information about the other person, the friend with the dental work is not entitled to such information in this direct and immediate way. This manner of gaining this information simply eliminates any private reserves of the person; it wholly opens his consciousness to the consciousness of another. Surely this would be a violation of his friend's right to privacy, and his friend would rightfully ask that such dental work be modified. Even friends do not have a right to learn in this manner of each other's inner thoughts and feelings.

Such fancy dental work may, correctly, be

said to be rather different from polygraphs. Still the point is that though one is entitled to some information about another, one is not entitled to use any means to get it. But why should the monitoring by an employer or his agent of one's physiological responses to legitimate questions be an invasion of privacy—especially if one has agreed to take the test? There are several reasons.

First, the claim that one freely agrees or consents to take the test is surely, in many cases, disingenuous.[6] Certainly a job applicant who takes the polygraph test is not physically forced or coerced into taking the exam. However, it is quite apparent that if he did not take the test and cooperate during the test, his application for employment would either not be considered at all or would be considered to have a significant negative aspect to it. This is surely but a more subtle form of coercion. And if this be the case, then one cannot say that the person has willingly allowed his reactions to the questions to be monitored. He has consented to do so, but he has consented under coercion. Had he a truly free choice, he would not have done so.

Now the whole point of the polygraph test is, of course, not simply to monitor physiological reactions but to use these responses as clues, indications, or revelations of one's mental processes and acts. The polygraph seeks to make manifest to others one's thoughts and ideas. However, unless we freely consent, we are entitled to the privacy of our thoughts, that is, we have a prima facie right not to have our thoughts exposed by others, even when the information sought is legitimate. Consider such analogous cases as a husband reading his wife's diary, a person going through a friend's desk drawers, a stranger reading personal papers on one's desk, an F.B.I. agent going through one's files. In each of these cases, a person attempts to determine the nature of someone else's thoughts by the use of clues and indications which those thoughts left behind. And, in each of these cases, though we may suppose that the person seeks to confirm answers to legitimate questions, we may also say

that, if the affected person's uncoerced consent is not forthcoming, his or her right to privacy is violated. Morally, however, there is no difference between ascertaining the nature of one's thoughts by the use of a polygraph, or reading notes left in a drawer, going through one's diary, etc. Hence, unless there are overriding considerations to consent to such revelations of one's thoughts, the use of the polygraph is a violation of one's right to privacy.[7]

Second, if we value privacy not simply as a barrier to the intrusion of others but also as the way by which we define ourselves as separate, autonomous persons, individuals with an integrity which lies at least in part in the ability to make decisions, to give or withhold information and access, then the polygraph strikes at this fundamental value.[8] The polygraph operates by turning part of us over which we have little or no control against the rest of us. If a person were an accomplished yogi, the polygraph would supposedly be useless—since that person's physiological reactions would be fully under his control. The polygraph works because most of us do not have that control. Thus, the polygraph is used to probe people's reactions which they would otherwise protect, not expose to others. It uses part of us to reveal the rest of us. It takes the "shadows" consciousness throws off within us and reproduces them for other people. As such, the use of the polygraph undercuts the decision-making aspect of a person. It circumvents the person. The person says such and such, but his uncontrolled reactions may say something different. He does not know—even when honest—what his reactions might say. Thus it undercuts and demeans that way by which we define ourselves as autonomous persons—in short, it violates our privacy. Suppose one said something to another—but his Siamese and undetached twin, who was given to absolute truth and who correctly knew every thought, past action, and feeling of the person said: "No, he does not really believe that." I think the person would rightfully complain that his twin had better remain silent. Just so, I have a right to complain when my own feelings are turned on me. This subtle form of self-incrimination is a form of invading one's privacy. An employer is entitled to know certain facts about one's background, but this relationship does not entitle him—or his agents—to probe one's emotional responses, feelings, and thoughts.

Thus, it follows that even if the only questions asked in a polygraph test are legitimate ones, the use of the polygraph for the screening of job applicants still violates one's privacy. In this case, the violation of privacy stems from the procedure itself, and not the questions. Accordingly, one can see the lameness of the defense of polygraphing which maintains that if a person has nothing to hide, he should not object to the polygraph tests. Such a defense is mistaken at least on two counts. First, just because someone believes something to be private does not mean that he believes that what is private is wrong, something to be ashamed about or to be hidden. Second, the polygraph test has been shown to violate a person's privacy, whether one person has really something to hide or not—whether he is dishonest or not. Consequently, if the question is simply whether polygraphing of prospective employees violates their privacy the answer must be affirmative.

III

There remains one possible defense of the use of polygraphs for screening prospective employees. This is to admit that such tests violate the applicant's privacy but to maintain that other considerations outweigh this fact. Specifically, in light of the great amount of merchandise and money stolen, the right of the employers to defend their property outweighs the privacy of the applicant. This defense is specious, I believe, and the following arguments seek to show why.

First, surely it would be better if people who steal or are dishonest were not placed in positions of trust. And if the polygraphs were used in only these cases, one might well maintain that the use of the polygraph, though it violates one's

privacy, is legitimate and justified. However, the polygraph cannot be so used, obviously, only in these cases—it must be used more broadly on both honest and dishonest applicants. Further, if a polygraph has a 90% validity then out of 1,000 interviewees, a full 100 will be misidentified.[9] Now if 10% of the interviewees are thieves, then 10 out of the 100 will steal, but 90 would not; in addition 90 out of the 900 would be thieves, and supposedly correctly identified. This means that 90 thieves would be correctly identified, 10 thieves would be missed, and 90 honest people would be said not to have cleared the test. Thus, for every thief "caught," one honest person would also be "caught"—the former would be correctly identified as one who would steal, while the latter could not be cleared of the suspicion that he too would steal. The point, then, is that this means of defending property rights is one that excludes not simply thieves but honest people as well—and potentially in equal numbers. Such a procedure certainly appears to constitute not simply a violation of privacy rights, but also, and more gravely, an injustice to those honest people stigmatized as not beyond suspicion and hobbled in their competition with others to get employment. If then using polygraph tests to defend property rights is not simply like preventing a thief from breaking into the safe, but more like keeping a thief from the safe plus binding the leg of an innocent bystander in his competition with others to gain employment, then one may legitimately doubt that this procedure to protect property rights is indeed defensible.[10]

Second, it has been claimed that just as the use of blood tests on suspected drunken drivers and the use of baggage searches at the airport are legitimate, so too is the polygraphing of prospective employees. Both of the former kinds of searches may also be said to violate a person's privacy; still they are taken to be justified whether the appeal is to the general good they produce or to the protection of the rights of other drivers or passengers and airline employees. However, neither the blood test nor the baggage search is really analogous to the use of the polygraph on job applicants. Blood tests are only administered to those drivers who have given police officers reason to believe that they (the drivers) are driving while under the influence of alcohol. The polygraph, however, is not applied only to those suspected of past thefts; it is applied to others as well. Further, the connection between driving while drunk and car accidents is quite direct; it immediately endangers both the safety and lives of others. The connection between polygraph tests of a diverse group of applicants (some honest and some dishonest) and future theft is not nearly so direct nor do the thefts endanger the lives of others. Baggage searches are a different matter. They are similar to polygraphing in that they are required of everyone. They are dissimilar in that they are made because of fears concerning the safety of other people. Further, surely there is a dissimilarity between officials searching one's baggage for lethal objects which one is presently trying to sneak on board, and employers searching one's mind for the true nature of one's past behavior which may or may not lead to future criminal intentions. Finally, there are signs at airports warning people, before they are searched, against carrying weapons on airplanes; such weapons could at that time be declared and sent, without prejudice, with the regular baggage. There is no similar aspect to polygraph tests. Thus, the analogies suggested do not hold. Indeed, they suggest that we allow for a violation of privacy only in very different circumstances than those surrounding the polygraphing of job applicants.

Third, the corporate defense of polygraphs seems one-sided in the sense that employers would not really desire the universalization of their demands. Suppose that the businesses in a certain industry are trying to get a new government contract. The government, however, has had difficulties with other corporations breaking the rules of other contracts. As a result it has lost large sums of money. In order to prevent this in the present case it says that it is going to set up devices to monitor the reactions of board members and top managers when a questionnaire is sent to them which they must answer. Any business, of course, need not agree to this procedure but if it does then it will be noted in their file regarding this and future government contracts. The questionnaire will include questions about the corporations' past fulfillment of contracts, competency to fulfill the present contract, loopholes used in past contracts, collusion with other companies, etc. The reactions of the managers and board members, as they respond to these questions, will be monitored and a decision on the worthiness of that corporation to receive the contract will be made in part on this basis.

There can be little doubt, I think, that the management and directors of the affected corporations would object to the proposal even though the right of the government to defend itself from the violation of its contracts and serious financial losses is at stake. It would be said to be an unjustified violation of the privacy of the decision-making process in a business; an illegitimate encroachment of the government on free enterprise. But surely if this is the legitimate response for the corporate job applicant, the same kind of response would be legitimate in the case of the individual job applicant.

Finally, it is simply false that there are not other measures which could be taken which could not help resolve the problem of theft. The fact that eighty percent of industry does not use the polygraph is itself suggestive that business does not find itself absolutely forced into the use of polygraphs. It might be objected that that does not indicate that certain industries might need polygraphs more than others—e.g., banks and drug companies more than auto plants and shipyards. But even granting this point there are other measures which businesses can use to avoid the problem of theft. Stricter inventory controls, different kinds of cash registers, educational programs, hot lines, incentives, etc. could all be used. The question is whether the employer, management, can be imaginative and innovative enough to move in these directions.

NOTES

1. Cf. Harlow Unger, "Lie Detectors: Business Needs Them to Avoid Costly Employee Rip-Offs," *Canadian Business*, Vol. 51 (April, 1978), p. 30. Other estimates may be found in "Outlaw Lie-Detector Tests?", *U.S. News & World Report*, Vol. 84, No. 4, (January 1978), p. 45, and Victor Lipman, "New Hiring Tool: Truth Tests," *Parade* (October 7, 1979), p. 19.

2. Both the AFL-CIO and the ACLU have raised these objections to the use of the polygraph for screening job applicants; cf. *AFL-CIO Executive Council Statements and Reports: 1956–1975* (Westport, Conn.: Greenwood Press, 1977), p. 1422. See also ACLU Policy #248.

3. See, for example, Alan F. Westin, *Privacy and Freedom* (New York: Atheneum, 1967), p. 238.

4. This would have to be qualified for security jobs and the like.

5. John E. Reid and Associates, *Reid Report* (Chicago: By the author, 1978), passim.

6. The reasons why people do not submit to the polygraph are many and various. Some might have something to hide; others may be scared of the questions, supposing that some of them will not be legitimate; some may feel that they are being treated like criminals; others may fear the jaundiced response of the employer to the applicant's honest answers to legitimate questions; finally some may even object to the polygraph on moral grounds, e.g., it violates one's right to privacy.

7. See Section III below.

8. Cf. Jeffrey H. Reiman, "Privacy, Intimacy, and Personhood," *Philosophy and Public Affairs*, Vol. VI (Fall, 1976).

9. Estimates of the validity of the polygraph range widely. Professor David Lykken has been reported as maintaining that the most prevalent polygraph test is correct only two-thirds of the time (cf. Bennett H. Beach, "Blood, Sweat and Fears," *Time*, September 8, 1980, p. 44). A similar figure of seventy percent is reported by Richard A. Sternbach et. al., "Don't Trust the Lie Detector," *Harvard Business Review*, Vol. XL (Nov.–Dec., 1962), p. 130. Operators of polygraphs, however, report figures as high as 95% accuracy; cf. Sternbach, p. 129.

10. This argument is suggested by a similar argument in David T. Lykken, "Guilty-Knowledge Test: The Right Way to Use a Lie Detector," *Psychology Today*, (March, 1975), p. 60.

Drug Testing in Employment

Joseph R. Des Jardins*
Ronald Duska†

According to one survey, nearly one-half of all *Fortune* 500 companies were planning to administer drug tests to employees and prospective employees by the end of 1987.[1] Counter to what seems to be the current trend in favor of drug testing, we will argue that it is rarely legitimate to override an employee's or applicant's right to privacy by using such tests or procedures.[2]

OPENING STIPULATIONS

We take privacy to be an "employee right" by which we mean a presumptive moral entitlement to receive certain goods or be protected from certain harms in the workplace.[3] Such a right creates a *prima facie* obligation on the part of the employer to provide the relevant goods or, as in this case, refrain from the relevant harmful treatment. These rights prevent employees from being placed in the fundamentally coercive position where they must choose between their job and other basic human goods.

Further, we view the employer-employee relationship as essentially contractual. The

Excerpted from "Drug Testing in Employment" by J.R. Des Jardins and R. Duska, *Business and Professional Ethics Journal* (forthcoming). Copyright by J.R. Des Jardins and R. Duska. Printed by permission of the authors.

*Center for Peace and Justice, Villanova University.
†Philosophy Department, Rosemont College.

employer-employee relationship is an economic one and, unlike relationships such as those between a government and its citizens or a parent and a child, exists primarily as a means for satisfying the economic interests of the contracting parties. The obligations that each party incurs are only those that it voluntarily takes on. Given such a contractual relationship, certain areas of the employee's life remain their own private concern and no employer has a right to invade them. On these presumptions we maintain that certain information about an employee is rightfully private, i.e. the employee has a right to privacy.

THE RIGHT TO PRIVACY

According to George Brenkert, a right to privacy involves a three-place relation between a person A, some information X, and another person B. The right to privacy is violated only when B deliberately comes to possess information X about A, and no relationship between A and B exists which would justify B's coming to know X about A.[4] Thus, for example, the relationship one has with a mortgage company would justify that company's coming to know about one's salary, but the relationship one has with a neighbor does not justify the neighbor's coming to know that information.

Hence, an employee's right to privacy is violated whenever personal information is requested, collected and/or used by an employer in a way or for any purpose that is *irrelevant to* or *in violation of* the contractual relationship that exists between employer and employee.

Since drug testing is a means for obtaining information, the information sought must be relevant to the contract in order for the drug testing not to violate privacy. Hence, we must first decide if knowledge of drug use obtained by drug testing is job relevant. In cases where the knowledge of drug use is *not* relevant, there appears to be no justification for subjecting employees to drug tests. In cases where information of drug use is job relevant, we need to consider if, when,

and under what conditions using a means such as drug testing to obtain that knowledge is justified.

IS KNOWLEDGE OF DRUG USE JOB RELEVANT INFORMATION?

There seem to be two arguments used to establish that knowledge of drug use is job relevant information. The first argument claims that drug use adversely affects job performance thereby leading to lower productivity, higher costs, and consequently lower profits. Drug testing is seen as a way of avoiding these adverse effects. According to some estimates twenty-five billion ($25,000,000,000) dollars are lost each year in the United States because of drug use.[5] This occurs because of loss in productivity, increase in costs due to theft, increased rates in health and liability insurance, and such. Since employers are contracting with an employee for the performance of specific tasks, employers seem to have a legitimate claim upon whatever personal information is relevant to an employee's ability to do the job.

The second argument claims that drug use has been and can be responsible for considerable harm to the employee him/herself, fellow employees, the employer, and/or third parties, including consumers. In this case drug testing is defended because it is seen as a way of preventing possible harm. Further, since employers can be held liable for harms done both to third parties, e.g. customers, and to the employee or his/her fellow employees, knowledge of employee drug use will allow employers to gain information that can protect themselves from risks such as liability. But how good are these arguments? We turn to examine the arguments more closely.

THE FIRST ARGUMENT: JOB PERFORMANCE AND KNOWLEDGE OF DRUG USE

The first argument holds that drug use leads to lower productivity and consequently implies that a knowledge of drug use obtained through drug testing will allow an employer to increase productivity. It is generally assumed that people using certain drugs have their performances affected by such use. Since enhancing productivity is something any employer desires, any use of drugs that reduces productivity affects the employer in an undesirable way, and that use is, then, job relevant. If such production losses can be eliminated by knowledge of the drug use, then knowledge of that drug use is job relevant information.

On the surface this argument seems reasonable. Obviously some drug use in lowering the level of performance can decrease productivity. Since the employer is entitled to a certain level of performance and drug use adversely affects performance, knowledge of that use seems job relevant.

But this formulation of the argument leaves an important question unanswered. To what level of performance are employers entitled? Optimal performance, or some lower level? If some lower level, what? Employers have a valid claim upon some *certain level* of performance, such that a failure to perform up to this level would give the employer a justification for disciplining, firing or at least finding fault with the employee. But that does not necessarily mean that the employer has a right to a maximum or optimal level of performance, a level above and beyond a certain level of acceptability. It might be nice if the employee gives an employer a maximum effort or optimal performance, but that is above and beyond the call of the employee's duty and the employer can hardly claim a right at all times to the highest level of performance of which an employee is capable.

That there are limits on required levels of performance and productivity becomes clear if we recognize that job performance is person-related. It is person-related because one person's best efforts at a particular task might produce results well below the norm, while another person's minimal efforts might produce results abnormally high when compared to the norm. For example a professional baseball player's performance on a ball field will be much higher than the average person's since the average person is unskilled at baseball. We have all encountered people who work hard with little or no results as well as people who work little with phenomenal results. Drug use by very talented people might diminish their performance or productivity, but that performance would still be better than the performance of the average person or someone totally lacking in the skills required. That being said, the important question now is whether the employer is entitled to an employee's maximum effort and best results, or merely to an effort sufficient to perform the task expected.

If the relevant consideration is whether the employee is producing as expected (according to the normal demands of the position and contract) not whether he/she is producing as much as possible, then knowledge of drug use is irrelevant or unnecessary. Let's see why.

If the person is producing what is expected, knowledge of drug use on the grounds of production is irrelevant since, *ex hypothesi* the production is satisfactory. If, on the other hand, the performance suffers, then, to the extent that it slips below the level justifiably expected, the employer has *prima facie* grounds for warning, disciplining or releasing the employee. But the justification for this is the person's unsatisfactory performance, not the person's use of drugs. Accordingly, drug use information is either unnecessary or irrelevant and consequently there are not sufficient grounds to override the right of privacy. Thus, unless we can argue that an employer is entitled to optimal performance, the argument fails.

This counter-argument should make it clear that the information which is job relevant, and consequently which is not rightfully private, is information about an employee's level of performance and not information about the underlying causes of that level. The fallacy of the argument which promotes drug testing in the name of increased productivity is the assumption that each employee is obliged to perform at an optimal, or at least, quite high level. But this is required under few, if any, contracts. What is required contractually is meeting the normally expected levels of production or performing the tasks in the job-description adequately (not optimally). If one can do that under the influence of drugs, then on the grounds of job performance at least, drug use is rightfully private. If one cannot perform the task adequately, then the employee is not fulfilling the contract, and knowledge of the cause of the failure to perform is irrelevant on the contractual model.

Of course, if the employer suspects drug use or abuse as the cause of the unsatisfactory performance, then she might choose to help the person with counseling or rehabilitation. However, this does not seem to be something morally required of the employer. Rather, in the case of unsatisfactory performance, the employer has a *prima facie* justification for dismissing or disciplining the employee.

THE SECOND ARGUMENT: HARM AND THE KNOWLEDGE OF DRUG USE TO PREVENT HARM

Even though the performance argument is inadequate, there is an argument that seems somewhat stronger. This is an argument that takes into account the fact that drug use often leads to harm. Using a type of Millian argument that allows interference with a person's rights in order to prevent harm, we could argue that drug testing might be justified if such testing led to knowledge that would enable an employer to prevent harm.

Drug use certainly can lead to harming others. Consequently, if knowledge of such drug use can prevent harm, then, knowing whether or not one's employee uses drugs might be a legitimate concern of an employer in certain circumstances. This second argument claims that knowledge of the employee's drug use is job relevant because

employees who are under the influence of drugs can pose a threat to the health and safety of themselves and others, and an employer who knows of that drug use and the harm it can cause has a responsibility to prevent it. Employers have both a general duty to prevent harm and the specific responsibility for harms done by their employees. Such responsibilities are sufficient reason for an employer to claim that information about an employee's drug use is relevant if that knowledge can prevent harm by giving the employer grounds for dismissing the employee or not allowing him/her to perform potentially harmful tasks. Employers might even claim a right to reduce unreasonable risks, in this case the risks involving legal and economic liability for harms caused by employees under the influence of drugs, as further justification for knowing about employee drug use.

But let us examine this more closely. Upon examination, certain problems arise, so that even if there is a possibility of justifying drug testing to prevent harm, some caveats have to be observed and some limits set out.

Jobs with Potential to Cause Harm

In the first place, it is not clear that every job is one with a potential to cause harm, or at least with potential to cause harm sufficient to override a *prima facie* right to privacy. To say that employers can use drug testing where that can prevent harm is not to say that every employer has the right to know about the drug use of every employee. Not every job poses a serious enough threat to justify an employer coming to know this information.

In deciding which jobs pose serious enough threats certain guidelines should be followed. First the potential for harm should be *clear* and *present*. Perhaps all jobs in some extended way pose potential threats to human well-being. We suppose an accountant's error could pose a threat of harm to someone somewhere. But some jobs like those of airline pilots, school bus drivers, public transit drivers and surgeons, are jobs in which unsatisfactory performance poses a clear and present danger to others. It would be much harder to make an argument that job performances by auditors, secretaries, executive vice-presidents for public relations, college teachers, professional athletes, and the like, could cause harm if those performances were carried on under the influence of drugs. They would cause harm only in exceptional cases.[6]

Not Every Person Is to Be Tested

But, even if we can make a case that a particular job involves a clear and present danger for causing harm if performed under the influence of drugs, it is not appropriate to treat everyone holding such a job the same. Not every job-holder is equally threatening. There is less reason to investigate an airline pilot for drug use if that pilot has a twenty-year record of exceptional service than there is to investigate a pilot whose behavior has become erratic and unreliable recently, or than one who reports to work smelling of alcohol and slurring his words. Presuming that every airline pilot is equally threatening is to deny individuals the respect that they deserve as autonomous, rational agents. It is to ignore previous history and significant differences. It is also probably inefficient and leads to the lowering of morale. It is the likelihood of causing harm, and not the fact of being an airline pilot *per se,* that is relevant in deciding which employees in critical jobs to test.

So, even if knowledge of drug use is justifiable to prevent harm, we must be careful to limit this justification to a range of jobs and people where the potential for harm is clear and present. The jobs must be jobs that clearly can cause harm, and the specific employee should not be someone who is reliable with a history of such reliability. Finally, the drugs being tested should be those drugs, the use of which in those jobs is really potentially harmful.

LIMITATIONS ON DRUG TESTING POLICIES

Even when we identify those jobs and individuals where knowledge of drug use would be job relevant information, we still need to examine whether some procedural limitations should not be placed upon the employer's testing for drugs. We have said that in cases where a real threat of harm exists and where evidence exists suggesting that a particular employee poses such a threat, an employer could be justified in knowing about drug use in order to prevent the potential harm. But we need to recognize that as long as the employer has the discretion for deciding when the potential for harm is clear and present, and for deciding which employees pose the threat of harm, the possibility of abuse is great. Thus, some policy limiting the employer's power is called for.

Just as criminal law places numerous restrictions protecting individual dignity and liberty on the state's pursuit of its goals, so we should expect that some restrictions be placed on an employer in order to protect innocent employees from harm (including loss of job and damage to one's personal and professional reputation). Thus, some system of checks upon an employer's discretion in these matters seems advisable. Workers covered by collective bargaining agreements or individual contracts might be protected by clauses in those agreements that specify which jobs pose a real threat of harm (e.g. pilots but not cabin attendants) and what constitutes a just cause for investigating drug use. Local, state, and federal legislatures might do the same for workers not covered by employment contracts. What needs to be set up is a just employment relationship—one in which an employee's expectations and responsibilities are specified in advance and in which an employer's discretionary authority to discipline or dismiss an employee is limited.

Beyond that, any policy should accord with the nature of the employment relationship. Since that relationship is a contractual one, it should meet the condition of a morally valid contract, which is informed consent. Thus, in general, we would argue that only methods that have received the informed consent of employees can be used in acquiring information about drug use.[7]

A drug-testing policy that requires all employees to submit to a drug test or to jeopardize their job would seem coercive and therefore unacceptable. Being placed in such a fundamentally coercive position of having to choose between one's job and one's privacy does not provide the conditions for a truly free consent. Policies that are unilaterally established by employers would likewise be unacceptable. Working with employees to develop company policy seems the only way to insure that the policy will be fair to both parties. Prior notice of testing would also be required in order to give employees the option of freely refraining from drug use. It is morally preferable to prevent drug use than to punish users after the fact, since this approach treats employees as capable of making rational and informed decisions.

Further procedural limitations seem advisable as well. Employees should be notified of the results of the test, they should be entitled to appeal the results (perhaps through further tests by an independent laboratory) and the information obtained through tests ought to be kept confidential. In summary, limitations upon employer discretion for administering drug tests can be derived from the nature of the employment contract and from the recognition that drug testing is justified by the desire to prevent harm, not the desire to punish wrong doing.

EFFECTIVENESS OF DRUG TESTING

Having declared that the employer might have a right to test for drug use in order to prevent harm, we still need to examine the second argument a little more closely.

It is important to keep in mind that: (1) if the knowledge doesn't help prevent the harm, the testing is not justified on prevention grounds; (2) if the testing doesn't provide the relevant knowledge it is not justified either; and finally, (3) even if it was justified, it would be undesirable if a more effective means of preventing harm were discovered.

Upon examination, the links between drug testing, knowledge of drug use, and prevention of harm are not as clear as they are presumed to be. As we investigate, it begins to seem that the knowledge of the drug use even though relevant in some instances is not the most effective means to prevent harm.

Let us turn to this last consideration first. Is drug testing the most effective means for preventing harm caused by drug use?

Consider. If someone exhibits obviously drugged or drunken behavior, then this behavior itself is grounds for preventing the person from continuing in the job. Administering urine or blood tests, sending the specimens out for testing and waiting for a response, will not prevent harm in this instance. Such drug testing because of the time lapse involved, is equally superfluous in those cases where an employee is in fact under the influence of drugs, but exhibits no or only subtly impaired behaviour.

Thus, even if one grants that drug testing somehow prevents harm an argument can be made that there might be much more effective methods of preventing potential harm such as administering dexterity tests of the type employed by police in possible drunk-driving cases, or requiring suspect pilots to pass flight simulator tests.[8] Eye-hand coordination, balance, reflexes, and reasoning ability can all be tested with less intrusive, more easily administered, reliable technologies which give instant results. Certainly if an employer has just cause for believing that a specific employee presently poses a real threat of causing harm, such methods are just more effective in all ways than are urinalysis and blood testing.

Even were it possible to refine drug tests so that accurate results were immediately available, that knowledge would only be job relevant if the drug use was clearly the cause of impaired job performance that could harm people. Hence, testing behavior still seems more direct and effective in preventing harm than testing for the presence of drugs *per se*.

In some cases, drug use might be connected with potential harms not by being causally connected to motor-function impairment, but by causing personality disorders (e.g. paranoia, delusions, etc.) that affect judgmental ability. Even though in such cases a *prima facie* justification for urinalysis or blood testing might exist, the same problems of effectiveness persist. How is the knowledge of the drug use attained by urinalysis and/or blood testing supposed to prevent the harm? Only if there is a causal link between the use and the potentially harmful behavior would such knowledge be relevant. Even if we get the results of the test immediately, there is the necessity to have an established causal link between specific drug use and anticipated harmful personality disorders in specific people.

But even when this link is established, it would seem that less intrusive means could be used to detect the potential problems, rather than relying upon the assumption of a causal link. Psychological tests of judgment, perception and memory, for example, would be a less intrusive and more direct means for acquiring the relevant information, which is, after all, the likelihood of causing harm and not the presence of drugs *per se*. In short, drug testing even in these cases doesn't seem to be very effective in preventing harm on the spot.

Still, this does not mean it is not effective at all. Where it is most effective in preventing harm is in its getting people to stop using drugs or in identifying serious drug addiction. Or to put it another way, urinalysis and blood tests for drug use are most effective in preventing potential harm when they serve as a deterrent to drug use *before* it occurs, since it is very difficult to prevent harm by diagnosing drug use *after* it has

occurred but before the potentially harmful behavior takes place.

Drug testing can be an effective deterrent when there is regular or random testing of all employees. This will prevent harm by inhibiting (because of the fear of detection) drug use by those who are occasional users and those who do not wish to be detected.

It will probably not inhibit or stop the use by the chronic addicted user, but it will allow an employer to discover the chronic user or addict, assuming that the tests are accurately administered and reliably evaluated. If the chronic user's addiction would probably lead to harmful behavior of others, the harm is prevented by taking that user off the job. Thus regular or random testing will prevent harms done by deterring the occasional user and by detecting the chronic user.

But we have said that testing without probable cause is unacceptable. Any type of regular testing of all employees is unacceptable. We have argued that testing employees without first establishing probable cause is an unjustifiable violation of employee privacy. Given this, and given the expense of general and regular testing of all employees (especially if this is done by responsible laboratories), it is more likely that random testing will be employed as the means of deterrence. But surely testing of randomly selected innocent employees is as intrusive to those tested as is regular testing. The argument that there will be fewer tests is correct on quantitative grounds, but qualitatively the intrusion and unacceptability are the same. The claim that employers should be allowed to sacrifice the well-being of (some few) innocent employees to deter (some equally few) potentially harmful employees seems, on the face of it, unfair. Just as we do not allow the state randomly to tap the telephones of just any citizen in order to prevent crime, so we ought not to allow employers to drug test all employees randomly to prevent harm. To do so is again to treat innocent employees solely as a means to the end of preventing potential harm.

This leaves only the use of regular or random drug testing as a deterrent in those cases where probable cause exists for believing that a particular employee poses a threat of harm. It would seem that in this case, the drug testing is acceptable. In such cases only the question of effectiveness remains: Are the standard techniques of urinalysis and blood testing more effective means for preventing harms than alternatives such as dexterity tests? It seems they are effective in different ways. The dexterity tests show immediately if someone is incapable of performing a task, or will perform one in such a way as to cause harm to others. The urinalysis and blood-testing will prevent harm indirectly by getting the occasional user to curtail their use, and by detecting the habitual or addictive user, which will allow the employer to either give treatment to the addictive personality or remove them from the job. Thus we can conclude that drug testing is effective in a limited way, but aside from inhibiting occasional users because of fear of detection, and discovering habitual users, it seems problematic that it does much to prevent harm that couldn't be achieved by other means.

In summary, then, we have seen that drug use is not always job relevant, and if drug use is not job relevant, information about it is certainly not job relevant. In the case of performance it may be a cause of some decreased performance, but it is the performance itself that is relevant to an employee's position, not what prohibits or enables him to do the job. In the case of potential harm being done by an employee under the influence of drugs, the drug use seems job relevant, and in this case drug testing to prevent harm might be legitimate. But how this is practical is another question. It would seem that standard motor dexterity or mental dexterity tests, immediately prior to job performance, are more efficacious ways of preventing harm, unless one concludes that drug use invariably and necessarily leads to harm. One must trust the individuals in any system in order for that system to work. One cannot police everything. It might work to ran-domly test people, to find drug users, and to weed out the few to forestall possible future harm, but are the harms prevented sufficient to over-ride the rights of privacy of the people who are innocent and to overcome the possible abuses we have mentioned? It seems not.

Clearly, a better method is to develop safety checks immediately prior to the performance of a job. Have a surgeon or a pilot or a bus driver pass a few reasoning and motor-skill tests before work. The cause of the lack of a skill, which lack might lead to harm, is really a secondary issue.

NOTES

[*Authors' note:* Versions of this paper were read to the Department of Philosophy at Southern Connecticut State College and to the Society of Business Ethics. The authors would like to thank those people, as well as Robert Baum and Norman Bowie, the editors of *Business and Professional Ethics Journal,* for their many helpful comments.]

1. *The New Republic,* March 31, 1986.
2. This trend primarily involves screening employees for such drugs as marijuana, cocaine, amphetamines, barbiturates, and opiates (e.g., heroin, methadone and morphine). While alcohol is also a drug that can be abused in the workplace, it seldom is among the drugs mentioned in conjunction with employee testing. We believe that testing which proves justified for controlled substances will, *a fortiori,* be justified for alcohol as well.
3. "A Defense of Employee Rights," Joseph Des Jardins and John McCall, *Journal of Business Ethics* 4, (1985). We should emphasize that our concern is with the *moral* rights of privacy for employees and not with any specific or prospective *legal* rights. Readers interested in pursuing the legal aspects of employee drug testing should consult: "Workplace Privacy Issues and Employer Screening Policies" by Richard Lehr and David Middlebrooks in *Employee Relations Law Journal* (Vol. 11, no. 3) pp. 407–21; and "Screening Workers for Drugs: A Legal and Ethical Framework" by Mark Rothstein, in *Employee Relations Law Journal* (Vol. 11, no. 3) pp. 422–36.

4. ''Privacy, Polygraphs, and Work,'' George Brenkert, *Journal of Business and Professional Ethics* vol. 1, no.1 (Fall 1981). For a more general discussion of privacy in the workplace see ''Privacy in Employment'' by Joseph Des Jardins, in *Moral Rights in the Workplace* edited by Gertrude Ezorsky, (SUNY Press, 1987). A good resource for philosophical work on privacy can be found in ''Recent Work on the Concept of Privacy'' by W.A. Parent, in *American Philosophical Quarterly* (Vol. 20, Oct. 1983) pp. 341–56.

5. *U.S. News & World Report* Aug. 1983; *Newsweek* May 1983.

6. Obviously we are speaking here of harms that go beyond the simple economic harm which results from unsatisfactory job performance. These economic harms were discussed in the first argument above. Further, we ignore such ''harms'' as providing bad role-models for adolescents, harms often used to justify drug tests for professional athletes. We think it unreasonable to hold an individual responsible for the image he/she provides to others.

7. The philosophical literature on informed consent is often concerned with ''informed consent'' in a medical context. For an interesting discussion of informed consent in the workplace, see Mary Gibson, *Worker's Rights* (Rowman and Allanheld, 1983) especially pp. 13–14 and 74–75.

8. For a reiteration of this point and a concise argument against drug testing see Lewis L. Maltby, ''Why Drug Testing Is a Bad Idea,'' *Inc.* June, 1987, pp. 152–153. ''But the fundamental flaw with drug testing is that it tests for the wrong thing. A realistic program to detect workers whose condition puts the company or other people at risk would test for the condition that actually creates the danger. The reason drunk or stoned airline pilots and truck drivers are dangerous is their reflexes, coordination, and timing are deficient. This impairment could come from many situations—drugs, alcohol, emotional problems—the list is almost endless. A serious program would recognize that the real problem is workers' impairment, and test for that. Pilots can be tested in flight simulators. People in other jobs can be tested by a trained technician in about 20 minutes—at the job site.'' p. 152.

Drug Testing in the Workplace: Whose Rights Take Precedence?

Michael Waldholz*

Amid growing national concern over substance abuse, drug testing in the workplace has become an explosive issue.

To those who support it, testing, which is commonly done through urinalysis, is often a question of protecting business interests. ''For us, it is the financial security of billions of dollars entrusted to us by clients,'' says Edwin A. Weihenmayer, vice president and director of the human-resources group at Kidder, Peabody & Co. The New York-based investment bank began drug testing this summer as part of a comprehensive drug-prevention program.

Critics, for their part, tend to view such measures as unnecessarily or even unconstitutionally invasive. ''For us, it just doesn't make good business sense to police our employees' private lives,'' says Lewis L. Maltby, vice president of Drexelbrook Engineering Co. The small instrumentation company in Horsham, Pa., has decided against drug tests.

What follows is a debate organized by *The Wall Street Journal* between the two executives.

MR. MALTBY: We've considered testing and totally rejected it. One reason is the accuracy problem. In an often-cited study, the U.S. Centers for Disease Control got false positive results of up to 66% from 13 randomly chosen private labs. The CDC said none of the labs were reliable. That isn't a very strong base to build a program on.

MR. WEIHENMAYER: You've hit on the one

---

*Staff reporter, *The Wall Street Journal*.

controversial aspect of drug-prevention programs. Our program consists of policy statements and a lot of communication: manager-awareness training, employee-assistance programs. And, yes, testing—of new hires, and just recently we began unannounced testing of current employees too.

We want to create a workplace mentality where people say, "If I work at Kidder, I don't do drugs." I see our workers accepting that objective, and I believe it's due to an umbrella of programs. It wouldn't be happening just with testing, but testing gives our program teeth.

Testing can be inaccurate if you use lousy labs, fail to monitor movement of the urine specimens, don't do reconfirmation tests. But we've addressed those problems. When an employee provides a sample, it is sealed and signed. Prescription-drug use is noted. Everywhere the sample moves, it's signed. If a test is positive for drugs, we feel we have an obligation to reconfirm. And if that's positive, we go back and give the employee a chance to explain any extenuating circumstance before we act.

MR. MALTBY: Ed is right: If the only test you use is the inexpensive test, which costs $15 or so but which is highly unreliable, you'll have serious problems. But the state-of-the-art test for reconfirmation costs from $75 to $100, which will multiply your costs an order of magnitude or so. Spending that much money isn't cost-justified for most companies. But unless you do, you're going to be firing people who shouldn't be fired.

MR. WEIHENMAYER: If it's an important business issue, you'll spend the money. We'll spend over $100,000 this year on our drug program. And that's just direct costs. A lot more cost is involved in dialoguing with our 7,000 employees, explaining why we test, answering all their questions. But I don't think you can put a price tag on the comfort that our clients have with the way we're processing and managing their money.

MR. MALTBY: I think we disagree on the relevance of the information you get from testing. Kidder tests, at least in part, to assure its cus-

tomers. Our only concern is job performance. But drug testing isn't a job-performance test. For instance, traces of drugs can remain in the system for days. I can't tell, if an employee takes a drug test on Monday, whether he is impaired now, whether he is sober as a judge or whether he had a couple of puffs on a joint Saturday night.

MR. WEIHENMAYER: We're concerned about performance. We're concerned about the effects of alcohol, but I can tell from someone's behavior if they come to work drunk. Not so with drugs. About 80% of performance problems from drugs are invisible. I equate our concern with that of the airline industry. When you walk on a plane, you don't want pilots to just appear drug free. You want to be absolutely sure they are.

We're also concerned about the potential pressures that result from drug use, whether it's done at work or not. Drug use can be expensive, and can exert financial demands—temptations—we don't want on employees who are dealing with transactions worth millions of dollars.

MR. MALTBY: I challenge the idea that you can't detect drug-related deterioration in job performance. In my experience, a really good supervisor who's paying attention is the best way to detect a problem. A supervisor should be watching if employees come in late, if they are sick often on Mondays, whether their error rate is up or their attention span is down. A well-tuned-in supervisor is a much better indicator of whether an employee has a problem than some testing program.

I really don't think, as Ed is saying, that for the sake of client perception you can fire someone for what they did on Saturday night if it's not affecting their job performance.

MR. WEIHENMAYER: I can tell you there are situations where supervisors were paying attention, where performance seemed fine, but that until an account problem surfaced through computer controls we didn't know we had a drug-related problem. We just aren't prepared to tolerate a problem until it arises, just as the airline industry can't tolerate drug use until a collision makes it visible.

Our program isn't designed to get rid of people. We invest a lot of money to find people and train them. And what we want to do is influence them toward working in our way, which is drug free. We want people to say, "I used marijuana casually, but this job is so important I quit." We can't afford to risk whatever results from that casual use, whether it affects the job or a person's financial integrity. Security in an industry dealing with billions of dollars demands that.

MR. MALTBY: We just don't think you need to test to keep the workplace drug free. After all, drugs are just a symptom of something else. What you really want is a committed, dedicated work force, people who like their jobs and care enough not to come to work stoned. What we do is select and nurture employees that are going to do a good job. We think if we do that, the drug problem takes care of itself.

We're incredibly careful about the people we hire. We do multiple reference checks, even for floor sweepers. And then we take a lot of time and trouble to really know our people. Our supervisors know their people's families; they work to build trust and rapport. If they have problems financial or otherwise, (the supervisors) want to know about it, and we have programs to provide them help. We've found that with that kind of trust people will confide in you when a problem arises, before they feel they must use drugs in a dangerous way. I think the proof is that we believe drug problems affect only about 1% of our work force.

MR. WEIHENMAYER: The relationship and concern expressed here is commendable, and everyone should strive for that. But the point is you think your drug incidence is 1%, but you don't know. Even if you do a thorough check, someone's going to get exposed to drugs after they join you.

MR. MALTBY: The implication is that we have employees running around with problems and we don't know it. We produce precision instrumentation for chemical plants and refineries. If we had drug problems at work, it would

affect our product and cause life-threatening problems, and we'd be up to our eyeballs in lawsuits.

MR. WEIHENMAYER: Our belief, put simply, is that certain industries require this type of assured security—pilots, air-traffic controllers, for instance. I think protecting a person's savings is crucial too. We want people to feel Kidder is doing everything possible to protect their savings. At the same time, we are trying to be very sensitive to the needs of our employees.

MR. MALTBY: You're saying you can have a testing program *and* the kind of employee relations I'm talking about. I say you can't. The two are inimical. Ours is based on a relationship that doesn't just come from a paycheck. When you say to an employee, "You're doing a great job; just the same, I want you to pee in this jar and I'm sending someone to watch you," you've undermined that trust.

MR. WEIHENMAYER: I'll grant you it makes it more difficult. It bothers us if they're bothered. That's why we spend so much time explaining our objectives. Also, when we test a department, everyone from top to bottom is tested. For most employees who test positive, we reexplain our policy, ask them to commit themselves to be drug free and to undergo periodic testing. The company makes available, at its expense, help if they feel they need it. But if they test positive again, they are subject to immediate termination.

We've had employees who say in good conscience they can't take the test. We treat that person with respect, but we explain that on this matter we have to call the shots. You may anguish a bit over the damage which is done, but it's extremely important for the program's integrity that everyone take the test.

We don't have watchers. It would make the program more accurate, but we have drawn the line because it would be too embarrassing.

MR. MALTBY: But that's the kind of swamp you get into with testing. Right now, the threat to the program is small. But as people learn how to beat the system, the only way you're going to keep people from monkeying around is to watch them.

MR. WEIHENMAYER: I don't think it will be a problem. Who is going to carry a urine sample around 365 days of the year?

Is an Employee Bill of Rights Needed?

Donald L. Martin*

The perception of the corporation as an industrial form of government in which management plays the role of the governor and labor the role of the governed has been particularly popular since the end of World War II. "Industrial democracy" has been the slogan of the labor movement in the industrial relations community. This analogy has recently given rise to demands for an "Employee Bill of Rights."[1] Such a bill would guarantee the worker the same *due process* that the Constitution guarantees the citizen. It would protect the worker from the arbitrary and inequitable exercise of managerial discretion.

WHERE THE INDUSTRIAL DEMOCRACY ANALOGY FALTERS

But, the industrial democracy analogy surely must be false. Two important considerations obviate it. First, a crucial distinction between government at any level and private economic organization, corporate or otherwise, is the right entrusted to government to exercise legitimate and reasonable force in its relations with its citizens. Second, the cost to a citizen of switching affiliation between governments is far greater than the cost to an employee of switching affiliations between firms. Since governments will surely violate public trust through their police powers, and since the costs to citizens of changing leaders or residences are relatively high, citizens will seek institutions to insulate themselves from the arbitrary and exploitative use of such powers by their elected and appointed representatives. These institutions include the first ten amendments to the United States Constitution (the Bill of Rights) and the Fourteenth Amendment (guaranteeing due process).

THE PROBLEM OF THE MONOPSONISTIC LABOR MARKET

Something close to an analogous use of exploitative power in the private sector occurs in the world of monopsonistic labor markets. In those labor markets, would-be employees have few, if any, alternative job opportunities, either because of an absence of immediate competitive employers or because of the presence of relatively high costs of moving to available job alternatives in other markets. With few or no job alternatives, workers are more likely to be the unwilling subjects of employer prejudice, oppression, and personal discretion than if labor market competition prevails.

No one would claim that the American economy is completely free of monopsony power. There is not a shred of evidence, on the other hand, that such power exists in the large American corporation of today. Indeed, there is impressive evidence to suggest that monopsony is not likely to be found in large, private corporations. Robert Bunting's examination of labor market concentration throughout the United States among large firms, for example, finds that employment concentration (measured by the fraction of total employees in a geographic area who are employed by the largest reporting firm in that area) is related inversely to labor market size, while firm size is correlated positively with labor market size.[2]

From *The Attack on Corporate America,* edited by M. Bruce Johnson, University of Miami Press. Copyright © 1978. Reprinted with permission.

*Formerly of the Law and Economics Center, University of Miami School of Law.

It is well known that monopsonistic powers reside in the collusive owners of professional sports teams, precisely because these powers are exempt from antitrust laws in the United States.[3] Professional sports firms, however, do not number among the large corporations at which "Employee Bill of Rights" proposals are directed.

Interestingly, monopsonistic power in the labor market may be a significant factor at the local government level. Evidence of monopsony exists in such fields as public education, fire and police protection, and nursing.[4]

THE NATURE OF EMPLOYER-EMPLOYEE AGREEMENTS

The Constitution of the United States does not extend the Bill of Rights and the due process clause of the Fourteenth Amendment to the private sector unless agents of the latter are performing public functions [*Marsh v. State of Alabama*, 66 S. Ct. 276 (1946)]. Instead of interpreting this limitation as an oversight of the founding fathers, the preceding discussion suggests that the distinctive treatment accorded governments reflects the conscious belief that market processes, more than political processes, yield a degree of protection to their participants that is closer to levels that those participants actually desire. It also suggests that this inherent difference justifies the institutionalization of civil liberties in one form of activity (political) and not in the other form (market).

This interpretation is consistent with the repeated refusal of the United States Supreme Court to interfere with the rights of employers and employees (corporate or otherwise) to make mutually agreeable arrangements concerning the exercise of civil liberties (otherwise protected under the Constitution) on the job or in connection with job-related activities. (The obvious legislative exceptions to this generalization are the Wagner Act of 1935 and the Taft-Hartley Act of 1947. These acts proscribe the free speech rights of employers with regard to their possible influ-ence over union elections on their own property, while allowing labor to use that same property for similar purposes.)

In the absence of monopsonistic power, the substantive content of an employer-employee relationship is the result of explicit and implicit bargaining that leaves both parties better off than they would be if they had not entered into the relationship. That both are better off follows because each is free to end the employment relationship at will—unless, of course, contractual relationships specify otherwise. Americans have demonstrated at an impressive rate a willingness to leave current employment for better pecuniary and nonpecuniary alternatives. During non-recessionary periods, employee resignations contribute significantly to turnover statistics. In an uncertain world, the workers who resign generate valuable information about all terms and conditions under which firms and would-be employees can reach agreement.

THE COSTS OF WORKPLACE CIVIL LIBERTIES

If information about each party to employment and information about potential and actual performance are costly, both firms *and* employees seek ways to economize. Indeed, the functions of a firm, from the viewpoint of employees, are to screen job applicants and to monitor on-the-job activities. A firm's final output is often a result of the joint efforts of workers rather than a result of the sum of the workers' separate efforts. This jointness of production makes individual effort difficult to measure, and on-the-job shirking becomes relatively inexpensive for any given employee. The reason is precisely that all employees must share the cost of one employee's "goldbricking." As a consequence, shirking, if done excessively, threatens the earning opportunities of other workers. Other white collar crimes, such as pilfering finished products or raw materials, have similar consequences.

To protect themselves from these threats, workers use the firm as a monitoring agent, implicitly authorizing it to direct work, manage tools, observe work practices and other on-the-job employee activities, and discipline transgressors. If employers function efficiently, the earnings of workers will be higher than if the monitoring function were not provided.[5]

Efficient *employer* activities, however, may appear to others, including some employees, to be flagrant violations of personal privacy from the perspective of the First, Fourth, Fifth, and Ninth Amendments to the Constitution. These employer activities, on the contrary, are the result of implied agreements between employers and employees, consummated by demand and supply forces in the labor market. The reduction in personal liberty that workers sustain in a firm has a smaller value for them, at the margin, than the increase in earning power that results. Thus, limitations on personal liberty in a firm, unlike such limitations in governments, are not manifestations of tyranny; they are, instead, the product of a mutually preferred arrangement.

It should not be surprising that higher-paying firms and firms entrusting more valuable decision-making responsibility to some employees would invest relatively more resources than would other firms in gathering potentially revealing information about the qualifications of prospective employees and about the actions of existing employees. Since the larger a firm is, by asset size or by employee number, the more likely it is to be a corporation, it should also not be surprising that corporations are among the firms that devote relatively large amounts of resources to gathering information of a personal nature about employees.

Prohibiting the gathering of such information by superimposing an ''Employee Bill of Rights'' on the employment relationship has the effect of penalizing a specific group of employees. This group is composed of those persons who cannot otherwise compete successfully for positions of responsibility, trust, or loyalty because the high cost of information makes it unprofitable for them to distinguish themselves from other workers without desirable job characteristics. Thus, federal protection of the civil liberties of employees in the marketplace may actually harm those who wish to waive such rights as a less expensive way of competing.

Under an ''Employee Bill of Rights,'' the process of searching for new employees and the process of managing existing employees are relatively more costly for an employer. This greater cost will be reflected not only in personnel policy but also in the cost of producing final outputs and in the prices consumers pay for them. An effect of an ''Employee Bill of Rights'' would be limited dimensions on which employees may compete with each other. Although there are precedents for such limitations (for example, federal minimum wage laws), it is important to recognize that this kind of protection may have unintended effects on the welfare of large numbers of employees. The anticompetitive effects of institutionalizing due process and civil liberties have long been recognized by trade unions. These effects constitute an important reason for the interest unions have in formalizing the procedures employers use in hiring, firing, promoting, demoting, rewarding, and penalizing union employees. It is false to argue, nevertheless, that an absence of formal procedures and rules in nonunionized firms is evidence that workers are at the mercy of unfettered employers, or that workers are more likely to be exploited if they are located in corporations rather than in noncorporate forms of organization.

Even the most powerful corporations must go to an effectively competitive labor market for their personnel. Prospective employees see arbitrary and oppressive personnel policies as relatively unattractive working conditions requiring compensation of pecuniary and nonpecuniary differentials over and above what they would receive from alternative employments. Those workers who want more certainty in the exercise of civil liberties pay for that certainty by forgoing these compensating differentials. This reasoning suggests that the degree of desired democracy in the labor market is amenable to the same forces that determine wages and working conditions. There is neither evidence nor persuasive arguments that suggest that workers in large corporations somehow have been excluded from the process that determines the degree of democracy they want.

NOTES

1. Ralph Nader, Mark Green and Joel Seligman, *Taming the Giant Corporation.* (New York: Norton, 1976), pp. 180–197.
2. Robert L. Bunting, *Employer Concentration in Local Labor Markets.* (Chapel Hill: The University of North Carolina Press, 1962). And "A Note on Large Firms and Labor Market Concentration," *Journal of Political Economy* 74 (August 1966), pp. 403–406.
3. James S. Mofsky, *Blue Sky Restrictions on New Business Promotions.* (New York: Matthew Bender, 1971).
4. Eugene J. Devine, *An Analysis of Manpower Shortages in Local Government.* (New York: Praeger, 1970).
5. Armen A. Alchian and Harold Demsetz, "Production, Information Costs, and Economic Organization," *American Economic Review* 62 (December 1972), pp. 777–795.

The Right to Risk Information and the Right to Refuse Health Hazards in the Workplace

Ruth R. Faden*

Tom L. Beauchamp †

In recent years, the right of employees to know about health hazards in the workplace has emerged as a major issue in occupational health policy.[1] This paper focuses on several philosophical and policy-oriented problems about the right to know and correlative duties to disclose. Also addressed are related rights, such as the right to refuse hazardous work and the right of workers to contribute to the development of safety standards in the workplace.

I

A general consensus has gradually evolved in government and industry that there is a right to know, and correlatively that there is both a moral and legal obligation to disclose relevant information to workers. The National Institute for Occupational Safety and Health (NIOSH) and other U.S. federal agencies informed the U.S. Senate as early as July 1977 that "workers have the right to know whether or not they are exposed to hazardous chemical and physical agents regulated by the Federal Government."[2] The Occupational Safety and Health Administration (OSHA) promulgated regulations guaranteeing workers access to medical and exposure records in 1980,[3] and then developed regulations in 1983 and 1986

From Ethical Theory and Business, Tom L. Beauchamp and Norman E. Bowie, eds., 3d edition (Englewood Cliffs, N.J.: Prentice-Hall, Inc., 1988), pp. 226–233. Copyright © 1982, 1987 by Ruth R. Faden and Tom L. Beauchamp. Reprinted with permission of the authors.
*Georgetown University and Department of Health Policy and Management, Johns Hopkins University.
†Senior research scholar, Kennedy Institute of Ethics, Georgetown University.

pertaining to the right to know about hazardous chemicals and requiring right-to-know training programs in many industries.[4] Legislation has also passed in numerous states and municipalities that are often more stringent than federal requirements.[5] For example, one of the earliest state bills, in New York, declared that employees and their representatives have a right to "*all* information relating to toxic substances"—a right that cannot be "waived as a condition of employment."[6] Many corporations—including Monsanto, DuPont, and Hercules—have also initiated right-to-know programs.

Although the general view that workers have some form of right to information about health hazards is now well established under law, there is no consensus about the nature and extent of an employer's moral or legal obligation to disclose such information. Considerable ambiguity also attends the nature and scope of the right—that is, which protections and actions the right entails, and to whom these rights apply.[7] For example, there is often a failure to distinguish between disclosing already available information, seeking information through literature searches or new research, and communicating about hazards through educational or other training programs. It is also often unclear whether there exists an affirmative duty to disclose information about health hazards to workers or merely a duty to honor worker-initiated or physician-initiated requests for access to records. What corporations owe their workers over and above the demands of federal and state requirements is likewise little discussed in the literature.

II

The belief that citizens and communities in general (and sometimes workers in particular) have a right to know about significant risks is reflected in a diverse set of recent laws and federal regulations in the United States. These include The Freedom of Information Act; The Federal Insecticide, Fungicide, and Rodenticide Amendments and Regulations; The Motor Vehicle and School Bus Safety Amendments; The Truth-in-Lending Act; The Pension Reform Act; The Real Estate Settlement Procedures Act; The Federal Food, Drug, and Cosmetic Act; The Consumer Product Safety Act; and The Toxic Substances Control Act. These acts commonly require manufacturers and other businesses to make available guidebooks, explanations of products, and warranties. Taken together, the implicit message of this corpus of legislation is that manufacturers and other businesses have a moral (and in some cases a legal) obligation to disclose information without which individuals could not adequately decide about matters of participation, usage, employment, or enrollment.[8]

Recent legal developments in the employee's right-to-know controversy have been consistent with this general trend toward disclosure and have included a more sweeping notion of corporate responsibility to provide adequate information to workers than had previously prevailed. These developments could have a pervasive and revolutionary effect on major American corporations. Until the 1983 final OSHA Hazard Communication Standard went into effect in 1986,[9] workers did not routinely receive extensive information from many employers. Now some corporations are beginning to establish model programs. For example, the Monsanto Company has a right-to-know program in which it distributes information on hazardous chemicals at its 53 plants, screens its employees, and both notifies and monitors past and current employees exposed to carcinogenic chemicals. Hercules Inc. has training sessions using videotapes with frank discussions of workers' anxieties. The tapes include depictions of dangers and of on-the-job accidents. Those employees who have seen the Hercules film are then instructed how to read safety data and how to protect themselves.[10]

That such programs are needed in many corporations is evident from the sobering statistics on worker exposure and injury and on dangerous chemicals in the workplace. The annual Registry of Toxic Effects of Chemical Substances lists over 25,000 hazardous chemicals, at least 8,000 of which are present in the workplace. As OSHA pointed out in the preamble to its final Hazard Communication Standard, an estimated 25 million largely uninformed workers in North America (1 in 4 workers) are exposed to toxic substances regulated by the federal government. About 6,000 American workers die from workplace injuries each year, and perhaps as many as 100,000 deaths annually are caused in some measure by workplace exposure and consequent disease. One percent of the labor force is exposed to known carcinogens, and over 44,000 U.S. workers are exposed *fulltime* to OSHA-regulated carcinogens.[11]

III

The most developed models of general disclosure obligations and the right to know are presently found in the extensive literature on informed consent, which also deals with informed refusal. This literature developed largely in the context of fiduciary relationships between physicians and patients, where there are broadly recognized moral and legal obligations to disclose known risks (and benefits) associated with a proposed treatment or research maneuver.

No parallel obligation has traditionally been recognized in nonfiduciary relationships, such as that between management and workers. Risks in this environment have traditionally been handled largely by workmen's compensation laws that were originally designed for problems of accident in instances of immediately assessable damage. Duties to warn or to disclose are irrelevant under the "no-fault" conception operative in workmen's compensation, and thus these duties went undeveloped.

However, needs for information in clinical medicine and in the workplace have become more similar in light of recent knowledge about occupational disease—in particular, knowledge about the serious long-term risks of injury, disease, and death from exposure to toxic substances. In comparison to traditional accident and safety issues, these recently discovered risks to health in the workplace carry with them *increased* need for information on the basis of which a person may wish to take various actions, including choosing to forego employment completely, to refuse certain work environments within a place of employment, to request improved protective devices, or to request lowered levels of exposure.

Employee-employer relationships—unlike physician-patient relationships—are often confrontational, with few goals shared in common, and therefore with undisclosed risk to workers a constant danger. This danger of harm to employees and their relative powerlessness in the employer-employee relationship may not be sufficient to justify employer disclosure obligations in *all* industries, but few would deny that placing relevant information in the hands of workers seems morally appropriate in at least some cases. By what criteria, then, shall such disclosure obligations be determined?

One plausible argument is the following: Because large employers, unions, and government agencies must deal with multiple employees and complicated causal conditions, no standard should be *more* demanding than the so-called objective reasonable person standard. This is the standard of what a fair and informed member of the relevant community believes is needed. Under this standard, no employer, union, or other party should be held responsible for disclosing information beyond that needed to make an informed choice about the adequacy of safety precautions, industrial hygiene, long-term hazards, and the like, as determined by what the reasonable person in the community would judge to be the worker's need for information material to a decision about employment or working conditions.

It does not follow, however, that this general standard of disclosure is adequate for all individual disclosures. At least in the case of serious hazards—such as those involved in short-term, but concentrated doses of radiation—a *subjective* standard may be more appropriate.[12] In cases where disclosures to *individual* workers may be expected to have significant subjective impact that varies with each individual, the reasonable person standard should perhaps be supplemented by a standard that takes account of each worker's personal informational needs. A viable alternative might be to include the following as a component of all general disclosures under the reasonable person standard: "If you are concerned about the possible effect of hazards on your individual health, and you seek clarification or personal information, a company physician may be consulted by making an appointment." Perhaps the most satisfactory solution to the problem of a general standard is a compromise between a reasonable-person and a subjective standard: Whatever a reasonable person would judge material to the decision-making process should be disclosed, and in addition any remaining information that is material to an individual worker should be provided through a process of asking whether he or she has any additional or special concerns.[13]

This standard is indifferent as to which groups of workers will be included. Former workers, for example, often have as much or even more need for the information than do presently employed workers. The federal government has the names of approximately 250,000 former workers whose risk of cancer, heart disease, and lung disease has been increased by exposure to asbestos, polyvinyl chloride, benzene, arsenic, betanaphthyalamine, and dozens of other chemicals. Employers have the names of several million such workers. Legislation has been in and out of the U.S. Congress to notify workers at greatest risk so that checkups and diagnosis of disease can be made before an advanced stage.[14] At this writing, neither industry nor the government has developed a systematic program, claiming that the expense of notification would be enormous, that many workers would be unduly alarmed, and that existing screening and surveillance programs should prove adequate to the task of monitoring and treating disease. Critics charge, however, that existing programs are far from adequate and that, in any event, there are duties to inform workers so that they can pursue potential problems at their own initiative.[15]

IV

Despite the apparent consensus on the appropriateness of having some form of right to know in the workplace, there are reasons why it will prove difficult to implement this right. There are, for example, complicated questions about the kinds of information to be disclosed, by whom, to whom, and under what conditions. Trade secrets have also been a long-standing thorn in the side of progress, because companies resist disclosing information about an ingredient or process that they claim is a trade-secret.[16]

There is also the problem of what to do if workers are inhibited from taking actions they otherwise would take because of economic or other constraints. For example, in industries where ten people stand in line for every available position, bargaining for increased protection is an unlikely event. However, we must set most of these problems aside here in order to consider perhaps the most perplexing difficulty about the right to know in the workplace: the right to refuse hazardous work assignments and to have effective mechanisms for workers to reduce the risks they face.

In a limited range of cases, it is possible for informed workers to reject employment because they regard health and safety conditions as unacceptable. This decision is most likely to be reached in a job market where workers have alternative employment opportunities or where a worker is being offered a new assignment with the option of remaining in his or her current job. More commonly, however, workers are not in a position to respond to information about health hazards by seeking employment elsewhere. For the information to be useful, it must be possible for workers to effect changes on the job.

The United States Occupational Safety and Health Act of 1970 (OSH Act)[17] confers a series of rights on employees that appear to give increased significance to the duty to disclose hazards in the workplace. Specifically, the OSH Act grants workers the right to request an OSHA inspection if they believe an OSHA standard has been violated or an imminent hazard exists. Under the Act, employees also have the right to "walk-around," that is, to participate in OSHA inspections of the worksite and to consult freely with the inspection officer. Most importantly, the OSH Act expressly protects employees who request an inspection or otherwise exercise their rights under the OSH Act from discharge or any discriminatory treatment in retaliation for legitimate safety and health complaints.[18]

While these worker rights under the OSH Act are important, they are not strong enough to assure that all workers have effective mechanisms for initiating inspections of suspected health hazards. Small businesses (those with fewer than ten workers) and federal, state, and municipal employees are not covered by the OSH Act. There are also questions about the ability of the Occupational Safety and Health Administration (OSHA) to enforce these provisions of the OSH Act. If workers are to make effective use of disclosed information about health hazards, they must have access to an effective and efficient regulatory system.

It is also essential that workers have an adequately protected right to refuse unsafe work. It is difficult to determine the extent to which this right is legally protected at the present time. Although the OSH Act does not grant a general right to refuse unsafe work,[19] provisions to this effect exist in some state occupational safety laws. In addition, the Secretary of Labor has issued a regulation that interprets the OSH Act as including a limited right to refuse unsafe work, a right that was upheld by the United States Supreme Court in 1980.[20] A limited right of refusal

is also protected in the Labor-Management Relations Act (LMRA) and implicitly in the National Labor Relations Act (NLRA).[21]

Unfortunately, these statutory protections vary significantly in the conditions under which they grant a right to refuse and in the consequences they permit to follow from such refusals. For example, the OSHA regulation allows workers to walk off the job where there is a "real danger of death or serious injury," while the LMRA permits refusals only under "abnormally dangerous conditions."[22] Thus, under the LMRA, the nature of the occupation determines the extent of danger justifying refusal, while under OSHA the character of the threat, or so-called "imminent danger," is determinative. By contrast, under the NLRA a walk-out by two or more workers may be justified for even minimal safety problems, so long as the action can be construed as a "concerted activity" for mutual aid and protection and there does not exist a no-strike clause in any collective bargaining agreements.[23] While the NLRA would appear to provide the broadest protection to workers, employees refusing to work under the NLRA may lose the right to be reinstated in their positions if permanent replacements can be found.[24]

The relative merits of the different statutes are further confused by questions of overlapping authority, called "preemption." It is not always clear (1) whether a worker is eligible to claim protection under a given law, (2) which law affords a worker maximum protections or remedies in a particular circumstance, and (3) whether or under what conditions a worker can seek relief under another law or through the courts, once a claim under a given law has not prevailed.

The current legal situation concerning the right to refuse hazardous work leaves many other questions unresolved as well. Consider, for example, whether a meaningful right to refuse hazardous work entails an obligation to continue to pay nonworking employees, or to award the employees back pay if the issue is resolved in their favor. On the one hand, workers without union strike benefits or other income protections would be unable to exercise their right to refuse unsafe work because of economic pressures. On the other hand, to permit such workers to draw a paycheck is to legitimate strike with pay, a practice generally considered unacceptable by management and by Congress. Also unresolved is whether the right to refuse unsafe work should be restricted to cases of obvious, imminent, and serious risks to health or life (the current OSHA and LMRA position) or should be expanded to include lesser risks and uncertain risks—for example, exposure to suspected toxic or carcinogenic substances that although not immediate threats, may prove more dangerous over time. If ''the right to know'' is to lead to meaningful worker action, workers must be able to remove themselves from exposure to suspected hazards, as well as obvious or known hazards.

Related to this issue is the question of the proper standard for determining whether a safety walkout is justified. At least three different standards have been applied in the past: a good-faith subjective standard, which requires only a determination that the worker honestly believes that the health hazard exists; a reasonable person standard, which requires that the belief be reasonable under the circumstances as well as sincerely held; and an objective standard, which requires evidence—generally established by expert witnesses—that the threat actually exists. Although the possibility of worker abuse of the right to refuse has been a major factor in a current trend to reject the good faith standard, recent commentary has argued that this trend raises serious equity issues in the proper balancing of this concern with the needs of workers confronted with basic self-preservation issues.[25]

No less important is whether the right to refuse hazardous work should be protected only until a formal review of the situation is initiated (at which time the worker must return to the job) or whether the walkout should be permitted until the alleged hazard is at least temporarily removed. So long as the hazards covered under a

right to refuse are restricted to risks that are obvious in the environment and that are easily established as health hazards, this issue is relatively easy to resolve. However, if the nature of the risk is less apparent, a major function of any meaningful right to refuse will be to call attention to an alleged hazard and to compel regulatory action. If this chain of events is set in motion, then requirements that workers continue to be exposed while OSHA or the NLRB conduct investigations may be unacceptable to workers and certainly will be unacceptable if the magnitude of potential harm is perceived to be significant. However, compelling employers to remove suspected hazards during the evaluation period may also result in intolerable economic burdens. We therefore need a delineation of the conditions under which workers may be compelled to return to work while an alleged hazard is being evaluated, and the conditions under which employers must be compelled to remove immediately alleged hazards.

V

Legal rights will be of no practical consequence if workers remain ignorant of their options. It is doubtful that many workers, particularly nonunion workers, are aware that they have a legally protected right to refuse hazardous work, let alone that there are at least three statutory provisions protecting that right.[26] Even if workers were aware of such a right, it is unlikely that they could weave their way through the maze of legal options unaided. If there is to be a meaningful right to know in the workplace, there will also have to be an adequate program to educate workers about their rights and how to exercise them, as well as adequate legal protection of this and related worker rights.

It is to be hoped that many corporations will follow the model guidelines and programs established by Monsanto and Hercules on the right to know and will make these rights as meaningful as possible by confirming a right to (at least temporarily) refuse work under unduly hazardous conditions. Potentially effective programs of information and training in hazards are as important for managers as for the workers they manage. In several recent court cases executives of corporations have been tried—and in some cases convicted—for murder because of negligence in causing the deaths of workers by failing to warn them of hazards. The Los Angeles District Attorney has announced that he will investigate all occupational deaths as possible homicides, and similar cases of criminal action have been prosecuted in Chicago.[27] A better system of corporate responsibility in disclosing risks thus stands to benefit management no less than employees.

NOTES

1. For developments in this area, see *Protecting Workplace Secrets, A Manager's Guide to Workplace Confidentiality* (New York: Joseph P. O'Reilly Executive Enterprises, 1985); Elihu D. Richter, "The Worker's Right to Know: Obstacles, Ambiguities, and Loopholes," *Journal of Health Politics, Policy and Law* 6 (1981): 340; George Miller, "The Asbestos Coverup," *Congressional Record*, May 17, 1979, pp. E2362–E2364, and "Asbestos Health Hazards and Company Morality," *Congressional Record*, May 24, 1979, pp. E2523–E2524; *The "Right to Know" Law: Special Report to the Governor and Legislature*, NY State Bureau of Toxic Substances, Department of Labor, March 1983.

2. NIOSH et al., "The Right to Know: Practical Problems and Policy Issues Arising from Exposures to Hazardous Chemical and Physical Agents in the Workplace," a report prepared at the request of the Subcommittee on Labor and Committee on Human Resources, U.S. Senate (Washington, D.C.: July 1977), 1, 5; Ilise L. Feitshans, "Hazardous Substances in the Workplace: How Much Does the Employee Have the Right to Know?" *Detroit Law Review* III (1985).

3. Occupational Safety and Health Administration, "Access to Employee Exposure and Medical Records—Final Rules," *Federal Register*, May 23, 1980, pp. 35212–35277. (Hereafter referred to as OSHA *Access* regulations.)

4. OSHA, *Access* regulations 29 CFR 1910.1200 et seq; printed in 48 FR 53278 (1983) and (1986). See also *United Steelworkers v. Auchter*, No. 83–3554 et al.; 763 F.2d 728 (3rd Cir. 1985).

5. See Barry Meier, "Use of Right-to-Know Rules Increasing," *Wall Street Journal*, May 23, 1986, p. 10; Vilma R. Hunt, "Perspective on Ethical Issues in Occupational Health," in *Biomedical Ethics Reviews 1984*, ed. J. Humber and R. Almeder (Clifton, N.J.: Humana Press, 1984), p. 194; and "Bhopal Has Americans Demanding the Right to Know," *Business Week*, February 18, 1985.

6. State of New York, 1979–1980 Regular Sessions, 7103-D, Article 28, para. 880.

7. 762 F.2d 728.

8. On this point, cf. Harold J. Magnuson, "The Right to Know," *Archives of Environmental Health* 32 (1977): 40–44.

9. 29 CFRs 1910. 1200; 48 FR 53,280 (1983). See also Mary Melville, "Risks on the Job: The Worker's Right to Know," *Environment* 23 (1981): 12–20, 42–45.

10. Laurie Hays, "New Rules on Workplace Hazards Prompt Intensified On the Job Training Programs," *Wall Street Journal*, July 8, 1986, p. 31; Cathy Trost, "Plans to Alert Workers to Health Risks Stir Fears of Lawsuits and High Costs," *Wall Street Journal*, March 28, 1986, p. 15.

11. See 48 CFR 53, 282 (1983); Office of Technology Assessment, *Preventing Illness and Injury in the Workplace* (Washington, D.C.: Government Printing Office, 1985); "Suit Challenges OSHA Limits on Worker's Right to Know Standards," *The Nation's Health* (July 1984): 1; U.S. Department of Labor, *"An Interim Report to Congress on Occupational Disease"* (Washington, D.C.: Government Printing Office, 1980), pp. 1–2; NIOSH et al., "The Right to Know," pp. 3–9.

12. For an account that in effect demands a subjective standard for carcinogens, see Andrea Hricko, "The Right to Know," in *Public Information in the Prevention of Occupational Cancer: Proceedings of a Symposium*, 2–3 December, 1976, ed. Thomas P. Vogl (Washington, D.C.: National Academy of Science, 1977), esp. p. 72.

13. As more and more data are gathered regarding the effects of workplace hazards on particular predisposing conditions, the need for disclosure of such information can be identified through pre-employment physical examinations without the worker's needing to ask questions.

14. High Risk Occupational Disease Notification and Prevention Act, HR 1309.

15. See Trost, "Plans to Alert Workers," p. 15; Peter Perl, "Workers Unwarned," *Washington Post,* January 14, 1985, pp. A1, A6.

16. OSHA initially asserted that by regulating the "worst" areas of illness, it had "preempted" (or replaced) state "Right-to-Know" laws when it promulgated OSHA's Hazard Communication Standard. OSHA also claimed that its broad definition of trade secret exemptions for employers superceded state trade secret laws. Connecticut, New York, and New Jersey joined with several other states and challenged both of these assertions in *United Steelworkers* v. *Auchter* (763 F.2d 728 (3rd Cir. 1985). The Steelworkers court held that OSH Act enabled the Secretary to promulgate *minimum* standards to protect workers, but that in the absence of coverage, states remain free to "fill the void" (between the need for regulation and actual hazards) with valid state laws. Consequently, insofar as OSHA's standard does not cover workers, there can be no "preemption" of state laws.

17. 29 U.S.C. S 651–658 (1970).

18. OSH Act 29 USC S 661 (c). Note, if the health or safety complaint is not determined to be legitimate, there are no worker protections.

19. Susan Preston, "A Right Under OSHA to Refuse Unsafe Work or A Hobson's Choice of Safety or Job?," *University of Baltimore Law Review* 8 (Spring 1979): 519–550.

20. The Secretary's interpretation of the OSH Act was upheld by the Supreme Court on February 26, 1980. *Whirlpool* v. *Marshall* 445 US 1 (1980).

21. Preston, "A Right Under OSHA to Refuse Unsafe Work," pp. 519–550.

22. 20 U.S.C. S143 (1976), and 29 CFR S 1977.12 (1978).

23. Nicholas Ashford and Judith P. Katz, "Unsafe Working Conditions: Employee Rights Under the Labor Management Relations Act and the Occupational Safety and Health Act," *Notre Dame Lawyer* 52 (June 1977): 802–837.

24. Preston, "A Right Under OSHA to Refuse Unsafe Work," p. 543.

25. Nancy K. Frank, "A Question of Equity: Workers' Right to Refuse Under OSHA Compared to the Criminal Necessity Defense," *Labor Law Journal* 31 (October 1980): 617–626.

26. In most states, these rights are not extended to public employees or domestic workers.

27. See *Illinois* v. *Chicago Magnet Wire Corporation,* No. 86–114, *Amicus Curiae* for The American Federation of Labor and Congress of Industrial Organizations; Jonathan Tasini, "The Clamor to Make Punishment Fit the Corporate Crime," *Business Week,* February 10, 1986, p. 73; Aric Press et al., "Murder in the Front Office," *Newsweek,* July 8, 1985; Bill Richards, "Ex-Officials Get 25-Year Sentences in Worker's Death," *Wall Street Journal,* July 2, 1985, p. 14; and *Illinois* v. *Chicago Magnet Wire Corporation,* No. 86–114, *Amicus Curiae* for The American Federation of Labor and Congress of Industrial Organizations.

[*Author's note:* We are indebted to Ilise Feitshans for helpful comments and criticisms on the 1987 revision. Parts of the earlier article had appeared in the *Canadian Journal of Philosophy,* Supplementary Volume, 1982.]

QUESTIONS FOR DISCUSSION

1. Ewing argues for an "Employee Bill of Rights" similar to the Bill of Rights guaranteed to U.S. citizens. How does the relationship between citizens and their government differ from the relationship between employees and their employer? How, if at all, does this affect Ewing's argument?

2. Brenkert argues that employers are entitled to "job relevant" information about their employees but that acquiring information that is not job relevant violates employee privacy. What does Brenkert mean by "job relevant" information? Do you agree? Why do Des Jardins and Duska argue that the information revealed by drug tests isn't really job relevant?

3. You are director of personnel for a large company that produces insecticides. The president of the company asks for your advice on instituting a drug-testing program. Should one be instituted, he wants to know? If not, why not? If so, what is the fairest possible way to do so? Having read all the readings in this chapter, draft a memo to the president with your answer.

4. Des Jardins and Duska argue that an employer is entitled to satisfactory job performance from employees but not to "peak" performance. Do you agree? What would be some of the implications of accepting the idea that employers are entitled to "peak" performance?

5. In the past decade, job security (protection against job loss) has become a central concern for employees, even more important than the traditional concerns of salary and benefits. How, if at all, does this affect Martin's thesis that working conditions are a result of mutually beneficial agreement and that employee rights are adequately protected?

CHAPTER 8

Whistle Blowing

READINGS FOR CHAPTER EIGHT

Richard T. De George
Whistle Blowing
325

Gene G. James
Whistle Blowing: Its Moral Justification
332

Whistle Blowing

Richard T. De George*

We shall restrict our discussion to a specific sort of whistle blowing, namely, *nongovernmental, impersonal, external whistle blowing.* We shall be concerned with (1) employees of profit-making firms, who, for moral reasons, in the hope and expectation that a product will be made safe, or a practice changed, (2) make public information about a product or practice of the firm that due to faulty design, the use of inferior materials, or the failure to follow safety or other regular procedures or state of the art standards (3) threatens to produce serious harm to the public in general or to individual users of a product. We shall restrict our analysis to this type of whistle blowing because, in the first place, the conditions that justify whistle blowing vary according to the type of case at issue. Second, financial harm can be considerably different from bodily harm. An immoral practice that increases the cost of a product by a slight margin may do serious harm to no individual, even if the total amount when summed adds up to a large amount, or profit. (Such cases can be handled differently from cases that threaten bodily harm.) Third, both internal and personal whistle blowing cause problems for a firm, which are for the most part restricted to those within the firm. External, impersonal whistle blowing is of concern to the general public, because it is the general public rather than the firm that is threatened with harm.

As a paradigm, we shall take a set of fairly clear-cut cases, namely, those in which serious bodily harm—including possible death—threatens either the users of a product or innocent bystanders because of a firm's practice, the design of its product, or the action of some person or persons within the firm. (Many of the famous whistle-blowing cases are instances of such situations.) We shall assume clear cases where serious, preventable harm will result unless a company makes changes in its product or practice.

Cases that are less clear are probably more numerous, and pose problems that are difficult to solve, for example, how serious is *serious,* and how does one tell whether a given situation is serious? We choose not to resolve such issues, but rather to construct a model embodying a number of distinctions that will enable us to clarify the moral status of whistle blowing, which may, in turn, provide a basis for working out guidelines for more complex cases.

Finally, the only motivation for whistle blowing we shall consider here is moral motivation. Those who blow the whistle for revenge, and so on, are not our concern in this discussion.

Corporations are complex entities. Sometimes those at the top do not want to know in detail the difficulties encountered by those below them. They wish lower-management to handle these difficulties as best they can. On the other hand, those in lower-management frequently present only good news to those above them, even if those at the top do want to be told about difficulties. Sometimes, lower-management hopes that things will be straightened out without letting their superiors know that anything has gone wrong. For instance, sometimes a production schedule is drawn up, which many employees along the line know cannot be achieved. Each level has cut off a few days of the production time actually needed, to make his projection look good to those above. Because this happens at each level, the final projection is weeks, if not months, off the mark. When difficulties develop in actual production, each level is further squeezed and is tempted to cut corners in order not to fall too far behind the overall schedule. The cuts may be that of not correcting defects in

Abridged with permission of Macmillan Publishing Company from *Business Ethics* (2nd edition) by Richard T. De George. Copyright © 1986 by Macmillan Publishing Company.

*Distinguished Professor of Philosophy, University of Kansas.

a design, or of allowing a defective part to go through, even though a department head and the workers in that department know that this will cause trouble for the consumer. Sometimes a defective part will be annoying; sometimes it will be dangerous. If dangerous, external whistle blowing may be morally mandatory.

The whistle blower usually fares very poorly at the hands of his company. Most are fired. In some instances, they have been blackballed in the whole industry. If they are not fired, they are frequently shunted aside at promotion time, and treated as pariahs. Those who consider making a firm's wrongdoings public must therefore be aware that they may be fired, ostracized, and condemned by others. They may ruin their chances of future promotion and security; and they also may make themselves a target for revenge. Only rarely have companies praised and promoted such people. This is not surprising, because the whistle blower forces the company to do what it did not want to do, even if, morally, it was the right action. This is scandalous. And it is ironic that those guilty of endangering the lives of others—even of indirectly killing them—frequently get promoted by their companies for increasing profits.

Because the consequences for the whistle blower are often so disastrous, such action is not to be undertaken lightly. Moreover, whistle blowing may, in some cases, be morally justifiable without being morally mandatory. The position we shall develop is a moderate one, and falls between two extreme positions: that defended by those who claim that whistle blowing is always morally justifiable, and that defended by those who say it is never morally justifiable.

WHISTLE BLOWING AS MORALLY PERMITTED

The kind of whistle blowing we are considering involves an employee somehow going public, revealing information or concerns about his or her firm in the hope that the firm will change its prod-uct, action, or policy, or whatever it is that the whistle blower feels will harm, or has harmed others, and needs to be rectified. We can assume that when one blows the whistle, it is not with the consent of the firm, but against its wishes. It is thus a form of disloyalty and of disobedience to the corporation. Whistle blowing of this type, we can further assume, does injury to a firm. It results in either adverse publicity or in an investigation of some sort, or both. If we adopt the principle that one ought not to do harm without sufficient reason, then, if the act of whistle blowing is to be morally permissible, some good must be achieved that outweighs the harm that will be done.

There are five conditions, which, if satisfied, change the moral status of whistle blowing. If the first three are satisfied, the act of whistle blowing will be morally justifiable and permissible. If the additional two are satisfied, the act of whistle blowing will be morally obligatory.

Whistle blowing is morally permissible if—

1. The firm, through its product or policy, will do serious and considerable harm to the public, whether in the person of the user of its product, an innocent bystander, or the general public.

Because whistle blowing causes harm to the firm, this harm must be offset by at least an equal amount of good, if the act is to be permissible. We have specified that the potential or actual harm to others must be serious and considerable. That requirement may be considered by some to be both too strong and too vague. Why specify "serious and considerable" instead of saying, "involve more harm than the harm that the whistle blowing will produce for the firm?" Moreover, how serious is "serious?" And how considerable is "considerable?"

There are several reasons for stating that the potential harm must be serious and considerable. First, if the harm is not serious and considerable, if it will do only slight harm to the public, or to the user of a product, the justification for whistle blowing will be at least problematic. We will not have a clear case. To assess the harm done to the firm is difficult; but though the harm may be rather vague, it is also rather sure. If the harm threatened by a product is slight or not certain, it might not be greater than the harm done to the firm. After all, a great many products involve some risk. Even with a well-constructed hammer, one can smash one's finger. There is some risk in operating any automobile, because no automobile is completely safe. There is always a trade-off between safety and cost. It is not immoral not to make the safest automobile possible, for instance, and a great many factors enter into deciding just how safe a car should be. An employee might see that a car can be made slightly safer by modifying a part, and might suggest that modification; but not making the modification is not usually grounds for blowing the whistle. If serious harm is not threatened, then the slight harm that is done, say by the use of a product, can be corrected after the product is marketed (e.g., as a result of customer complaint). Our society has a great many ways of handling minor defects, and these are at least arguably better than resorting to whistle blowing.

To this consideration should be added a second. Whistle blowing is frequently, and appropriately, considered an unusual occurrence, a heroic act. If the practice of blowing the whistle for relatively minor harm were to become a common occurrence, its effectiveness would be diminished. When serious harm is threatened, whistle blowers are listened to by the news media, for instance, because it is news. But relatively minor harm to the public is not news. If many minor charges or concerns were voiced to the media, the public would soon not react as it is now expected to react to such disclosures. This would also be the case if complaints about all sorts of perceived or anticipated minor harm were reported to government agencies, although most people would expect that government agencies would act first on the serious cases, and only later on claims of relatively minor harm.

There is a third consideration. Every time an employee has a concern about possible harm to the public from a product or practice we cannot assume that he or she makes a correct assessment. Nor can we assume that every claim of harm is morally motivated. To sift out the claims and concerns of the disaffected worker from the genuine claims and concerns of the morally motivated employee is a practical problem. It may be claimed that this problem has nothing to do with the moral permissibility of the act of whistle blowing; but whistle blowing is a practical matter. If viewed as a technique for changing policy or actions, it will be justified only if effective. It can be trivialized. If it is, then one might plausibly claim that little harm is done to the firm, and hence the act is permitted. But if trivialized, it loses its point. If whistle blowing is to be considered a serious act with serious consequences, it should be reserved for disclosing potentially serious harm, and will be morally justifiable in those cases.

Serious is admittedly a vague term. Is an increase in probable automobile deaths, from 2 in 100,000 to 15 in 100,000 over a one-year period, serious? Although there may be legitimate debate on this issue, it is clear that matters that threaten death are prima facie serious. If the threatened harm is that a product may cost a few pennies more than otherwise, or if the threatened harm is that a part or product may cause minor inconvenience, the harm—even if multiplied by thousands or millions of instances—does not match the seriousness of death to the user or the innocent bystander.

The harm threatened by unsafe tires, which are sold as premium quality but that blow out at 60 or 70 mph, is serious, for such tires can easily lead to death. The dumping of metal drums of toxic waste into a river, where the drums will rust, leak, and cause cancer or other serious ills to those who drink the river water or otherwise use it, threatens serious harm. The use of substandard concrete in a building, such that it is likely to collapse and kill people, poses a serious threat to people. Failure to x-ray pipe fittings, as required in building a nuclear plant, is a failure that might lead to nuclear leaks; this involves potential serious harm, for it endangers the health and lives of many.

The notion of *serious* harm might be expanded to include serious financial harm, and kinds of harm other than death and serious threats to health and body. But as we noted earlier, we shall restrict ourselves here to products and practices that produce or threaten serious harm or danger to life and health. The difference between producing harm and threatening serious danger is not significant for the kinds of cases we are considering.

2. Once an employee identifies a serious threat to the user of a product or to the general public, he or she should report it to his or her immediate superior and make his or her moral concern known. Unless he or she does so, the act of whistle blowing is not clearly justifiable.

Why not? Why is not the weighing of harm sufficient? The answer has already been given in part. Whistle blowing is a practice that, to be effective, cannot be routinely used. There are other reasons as well. First, reporting one's concerns is the most direct, and usually the quickest, way of producing the change the whistle blower desires. The normal assumption is that most firms do not want to cause death or injury, and do not willingly and knowingly set out to harm the users of their products in this way. If there are life-threatening defects, the normal assumption is, and should be, that the firm will be interested in correcting them—if not for moral reasons, at least for prudential reasons, viz., to avoid suits, bad publicity, and adverse consumer reaction. The argument from loyalty also supports the requirement that the firm be given the chance to rectify its action or procedure or policy before it is charged in public. Additionally, because whistle blowing does harm to the firm, harm in general is minimized if the firm is in-

formed of the problem and allowed to correct it. Less harm is done to the firm in this way, and if the harm to the public or the users is also averted, this procedure produces the least harm, on the whole.

The condition that one report one's concern to one's immediate superior presupposes a hierarchical structure. Although firms are usually so structured, they need not be. In a company of equals, one would report one's concerns internally, as appropriate.

Several objections may be raised to this condition. Suppose one knows that one's immediate superior already knows the defect and the danger. In this case reporting it to him or her would be redundant, and condition two would be satisfied. But one should not presume without good reason that one's superior does know. What may be clear to one individual may not be clear to another. Moreover, the assessment of risk is often a complicated matter. To a person on one level what appears as unacceptable risk may be defensible as legitimate to a person on a higher level, who may see a larger picture, and knows of offsetting compensations, and the like.

However, would not reporting one's concern effectively preclude the possibility of anonymous whistle blowing, and so put one in jeopardy? This might of course be the case; and this is one of the considerations one should weigh before blowing the whistle. We will discuss this matter later on. If the reporting is done tactfully, moreover, the voicing of one's concerns might, if the problem is apparent to others, indicate a desire to operate within the firm, and so make one less likely to be the one assumed to have blown the whistle anonymously.

By reporting one's concern to one's immediate superior or other appropriate person, one preserves and observes the regular practices of firms, which on the whole promote their order and efficiency; this fulfills one's obligation of minimizing harm, and it precludes precipitous whistle blowing.

3. If one's immediate superior does nothing effective about the concern or complaint, the employee should exhaust the internal procedures and possibilities within the firm. This usually will involve taking the matter up the managerial ladder, and, if necessary—and possible—to the board of directors.

To exhaust the internal procedures and possibilities is the key requirement here. In a hierarchically structured firm, this means going up the chain of command. But one may do so either with or without the permission of those at each level of the hierarchy. What constitutes exhausting the internal procedures? This is often a matter of judgment. But because going public with one's concern is more serious for both oneself and for the firm, going up the chain of command is the preferable route to take in most circumstances. This third condition is satisfied of course if, for some reason, it is truly impossible to go beyond any particular level.

Several objections may once again be raised. There may not be time enough to follow the bureaucratic procedures of a given firm; the threatened harm may have been done before the procedures are exhausted. If, moreover, one goes up the chain to the top and nothing is done by anyone, then a great deal of time will have been wasted. Once again, prudence and judgment should be used. The internal possibilities may sometimes be exhausted quickly, by a few phone calls or visits. But one should not simply assume that no one at any level within the firm will do anything. If there are truly no possibilities of internal remedy, then the third condition is satisfied.

As we mentioned, the point of the three conditions is essentially that whistle blowing is morally permissible if the harm threatened is serious, and if internal remedies have been attempted in good faith but without a satisfactory result. In these circumstances, one is morally justified in attempting to avert what one sees as serious harm, by means that may be effective, including blowing the whistle.

We can pass over as not immediately germane the questions of whether in nonserious matters one has an obligation to report one's moral concerns to one's superiors, and whether one fulfills one's obligation once one has reported them to the appropriate party.

WHISTLE BLOWING AS MORALLY REQUIRED

To say that whistle blowing is morally permitted does not impose any obligation on an employee. Unless two other conditions are met, the employee does not have a moral obligation to blow the whistle. To blow the whistle when one is not morally required to do so, and if done from moral motives (i.e., concern for one's fellow man) and at risk to oneself, is to commit a supererogatory act. It is an act that deserves moral praise. But failure to so act deserves no moral blame. In such a case, the whistle blower might be considered a moral hero. Sometimes he or she is so considered, sometimes not. If one's claim or concern turns out to be ill-founded, one's subjective moral state may be as praiseworthy as if the claim were well-founded, but one will rarely receive much praise for one's action.

For there to be an obligation to blow the whistle, two conditions must be met, in addition to the foregoing three.

4. The whistle blower must have, or have accessible, documented evidence that would convince a reasonable, impartial observer that one's view of the situation is correct, and that the company's product or practice poses a serious and likely danger to the public or to the user of the product.

One does not have an obligation to put oneself at serious risk without some compensating advantage to be gained. Unless one has documented evidence that would convince a reasonable, impartial observer, one's charges or claims, if made public, would be based essentially on one's word. Such grounds may be sufficient for a subjective feeling of certitude about one's charges, but they are not usually sufficient for others to act on one's claims. For instance, a newspaper is unlikely to print a story based simply on someone's undocumented assertion.

Several difficulties emerge. Should it not be the responsibility of the media or the appropriate regulatory agency or government bureau to carry out an investigation based on someone's complaint? It is reasonable for them to do so, providing they have some evidence in support of the complaint or claim. The damage has not yet been done, and the harm will not, in all likelihood, be done to the complaining party. If the action is criminal, then an investigation by a law-enforcing agency is appropriate. But the charges made by whistle blowers are often not criminal charges. And we do not expect newspapers or government agencies to carry out investigations whenever anyone claims that possible harm will be done by a product or practice. Unless harm is imminent, and very serious (e.g., a bomb threat), it is appropriate to act on evidence that substantiates a claim. The usual procedure, once an investigation is started or a complaint followed up, is to contact the party charged.

One does not have a moral obligation to blow the whistle simply because of one's hunch, guess, or personal assessment of possible danger, if supporting evidence and documentation are not available. One may, of course, have the obligation to attempt to get evidence if the harm is serious. But if it is unavailable—or unavailable without using illegal or immoral means—then one does not have the obligation to blow the whistle.

> 5. The employee must have good reason to believe that by going public the necessary changes will be brought about. The chance of being successful must be worth the risk one takes and the danger to which one is exposed.

Even with some documentation and evidence, a potential whistle blower may not be taken seriously, or may not be able to get the media or government agency to take any action. How far should one go, and how much must one try? The more serious the situation, the greater the effort required. But unless one has a reasonable expectation of success, one is not obliged to put oneself at great risk. Before going public, the potential whistle blower should know who (e.g., government agency, newspaper, columnist, TV reporter) will make use of his or her evidence, and how it will be handled. He or she should have good reason to expect that the action taken will result in the kind of change or result that he or she believes is morally appropriate.

The foregoing fourth and fifth conditions may seem too permissive to some and too stringent to others. They are too permissive for those who wish everyone to be ready and willing to blow the whistle whenever there is a chance that the public will be harmed. After all, harm to the public is more serious than harm to the whistle blower, and, in the long run, if everyone saw whistle blowing as obligatory, without satisfying the last two conditions, we would all be better off. If the fourth and fifth conditions must be satisfied, then people will only rarely have the moral obligation to blow the whistle.

If, however, whistle blowing were mandatory whenever the first three conditions were satisfied, and if one had the moral obligation to blow the whistle whenever one had a moral doubt or fear about safety, or whenever one disagreed with one's superiors or colleagues, one would be obliged to go public whenever one did not get one's way on such issues within a firm. But these conditions are much too weak, for the reasons already given. Other, stronger conditions, but weaker than those proposed, might be suggested. But any condition that makes whistle blowing mandatory in large numbers of cases, may possibly reduce the effectiveness of whistle blowing. If this were the result, and the practice were to become widespread, then it is doubtful that we would all be better off.

Finally, the claim that many people very often have the obligation to blow the whistle goes against the common view of the whistle blower as a moral hero, and against the commonly held feeling that whistle blowing is only rarely morally mandatory. This feeling may be misplaced. But a very strong argument is necessary to show that although the general public is morally mistaken in its view, the moral theoretician is correct in his or her assertion.

A consequence of accepting the fourth and fifth conditions stated is that the stringency of the moral obligation of whistle blowing corresponds with the common feeling of most people on this issue. Those in higher positions and those in professional positions in a firm are more likely to have the obligation to change a firm's policy or product—even by whistle blowing, if necessary—than are lower-placed employees. Engineers, for instance, are more likely to have access to data and designs than are assembly-line workers. Managers generally have a broader picture, and more access to evidence, than do nonmanagerial employees. Management has the moral responsibility both to see that the expressed moral concerns of those below them have been adequately considered and that the firm does not knowingly inflict harm on others.

The fourth and fifth conditions will appear too stringent to those who believe that whistle blowing is always a supererogatory act, that it is always moral heroism, and that it is never morally obligatory. They might argue that, although we are not permitted to do what is immoral, we have no general moral obligation to prevent all others from acting immorally. This is what the whistle blower attempts to do. The counter to that, however, is to point out that whistle blowing is an act in which one attempts to prevent harm to a third party. It is not implausible to claim both that we are morally obliged to prevent harm to others at relatively little expense to ourselves, and that we are morally obliged to prevent great harm to a great many others, even at considerable expense to ourselves.

The five conditions outlined can be used by an individual to help decide whether he or she is morally permitted or required to blow the whistle. Third parties can also use these conditions when attempting to evaluate acts of whistle blowing by others, even though third parties may have difficulty determining whether the whistle blowing is morally motivated. It might be possible successfully to blow the whistle anonymously. But anonymous tips or stories seldom get much attention. One can confide in a government agent, or in a reporter, on condition that one's name not be disclosed. But this approach, too, is frequently ineffective in achieving the results required. To be effective, one must usually be willing to be identified, to testify publicly, to produce verifiable evidence, and to put oneself at risk. As with civil disobedience, what captures the conscience of others is the willingness of the whistle blower to suffer harm for the benefit of others, and for what he or she thinks is right.

PRECLUDING THE NEED FOR WHISTLE BLOWING

The need for moral heroes shows a defective society and defective corporations. It is more important to change the legal and corporate structures that make whistle blowing necessary than to convince people to be moral heroes.

Because it is easier to change the law than to change the practices of all corporations, it should be illegal for any employer to fire an employee, or to take any punitive measures, at the time or later, against an employee who satisfies the first three aforementioned conditions and blows the whistle on the company. Because satisfying those conditions makes the action morally justifiable, the law should protect the employee in acting in accordance with what his or her conscience demands. If the whistle is falsely blown, the company will have suffered no great harm. If it is appropriately blown, the company should suffer the consequences of its actions being made public. But to protect a whistle blower by passing such a law is no easy matter. Employers can make life difficult for whistle blowers without firing them. There are many ways of passing over an employee. One can be relegated to the back room of the firm, or be given unpleasant jobs.

Employers can find reasons not to promote one or to give one raises. Not all of this can be prevented by law, but some of the more blatant practices can be prohibited.

Second, the law can mandate that the individuals responsible for the decision to proceed with a faulty product or to engage in a harmful practice be penalized. The law has been reluctant to interfere with the operations of companies. As a result, those in the firm who have been guilty of immoral and illegal practices have gone untouched even though the corporation was fined for its activity.

A third possibility is that every company of a certain size be required, by law, to have an inspector general or an internal operational auditor, whose job it is to uncover immoral and illegal practices. This person's job would be to listen to the moral concerns of employees, at every level, about the firm's practices. He or she should be independent of management, and report to the audit committee of the board, which, ideally, should be a committee made up entirely of outside board members. The inspector or auditor should be charged with making public those complaints that should be made public if not changed from within. Failure on the inspector's part to take proper action with respect to a worker's complaint, such that the worker is forced to go public, should be prima facie evidence of an attempt to cover up a dangerous practice or product, and the inspector should be subject to criminal charges.

In addition, a company that wishes to be moral, that does not wish to engage in harmful practices or to produce harmful products, can take other steps to preclude the necessity of whistle blowing. The company can establish channels whereby those employees who have moral concerns can get a fair hearing without danger to their position or standing in the company. Expressing such concerns, moreover, should be considered a demonstration of company loyalty and should be rewarded appropriately. The company might establish the position of ombudsman, to hear such complaints or moral concerns. Or an independent committee of the board might be established to hear such complaints and concerns. Someone might even be paid by the company to present the position of the would-be whistle blower, who would argue for what the company should do, from a moral point of view, rather than what those interested in meeting a schedule or making a profit would like to do. Such a person's success within the company could depend on his success in precluding whistle blowing, as well as the conditions that lead to it.

Whistle Blowing: Its Moral Justification

Gene G. James*

Whistle blowing may be defined as the attempt of an employee or former employee of an organization to disclose what he or she believes to be wrongdoing in or by the organization. Like blowing a whistle to call attention to a thief, whistle blowing is an effort to make others aware of practices one considers illegal or immoral. If the wrongdoing is reported to someone higher in the organization, the whistle blowing may be said to be *internal*. If the wrongdoing is reported to outside individuals or groups, such as reporters, public interest groups, or regulatory agencies, the whistle blowing is *external*. If the harm being reported is primarily harm to the whistle blower alone, such as sexual harassment, the whistle

Original essay. Copyright © 1990 by Gene G. James. Printed with permission of the author. This article is a revision of the earlier article "In Defense of Whistle Blowing" which appeared in the first edition of this book. Because the argument has been considerably revised and expanded, it seemed preferable to give it a new title to avoid confusion.
*Department of Philosophy, Memphis State University.

blowing may be said to be *personal*. If it is primarily harm to other people that is being reported, the whistle blowing is *impersonal*. Most whistle blowing is done by people currently employed by the organization on which they are blowing the whistle. However, people who have left an organization may also blow the whistle. The former may be referred to as *current* whistle blowing, the latter as *alumni* whistle blowing. If the whistle blower discloses his or her identity, the whistle blowing may be said to be *open;* if the whistle blower's identity is not disclosed, the whistle blowing is *anonymous*.

Whistle blowers almost always experience retaliation. If they work for private firms and are not protected by unions or professional organizations, they are likely to be fired. They are also likely to receive damaging letters of recommendation and may even be blacklisted so that they cannot find work in their profession. If they are not fired, they are still likely to be transferred, given less interesting work, denied salary increases and promotions, or demoted. Their professional competence is usually attacked. They are said to be unqualified to judge, misinformed, etc. Since their actions may threaten both the organization and their fellow employees, attacks on their personal lives are also frequent. They are called traitors, rat finks, disgruntled, known trouble makers, people who make an issue out of nothing, self-serving, and publicity seekers. Their life-styles, sex lives, and mental stability may be questioned. Physical assaults, abuse of their families, and even murder are not unknown as retaliation for whistle blowing.

WHISTLE BLOWING AND THE LAW[1]

The law does not at present offer whistle blowers very much protection. Agency law, the area of common law which governs relations between employees and employers, imposes a duty on employees to keep confidential any information learned through their employment that might be detrimental to their employers. However, this duty does not hold if the employee has knowledge that the employer either has committed or is about to commit a felony. In this case the employee has a positive obligation to report the offense. Failure to do so is known as misprision and makes one subject to criminal penalties.

One problem with agency law is that it is based on the assumption that unless there are statutes or agreements to the contrary, contracts between employees and employers can be terminated at will by either party. It therefore grants employers the right to discharge employees at any time for any reason or even for no reason at all. The result is that most employees who blow the whistle, even those who report felonies, are fired or suffer other retaliation. One employee of thirty years was even fired the day before his pension became effective for testifying under oath against his employer, without the courts doing anything to aid him.

This situation has begun to change somewhat in recent years. In *Pickering v. Board of Education* in 1968 the Supreme Court ruled that government employees have the right to speak out on policy issues affecting their agencies provided doing so does not seriously disrupt the agency. A number of similar decisions have followed, and the right of government employees to speak out on policy issues now seems firmly established. But employees in private industry cannot criticize company policies without risking being fired. In one case involving both a union and a company doing a substantial portion of its business with the federal government, federal courts did award back pay to an employee fired for criticizing the union and the company but did not reinstate or award him punitive damages.

A few state courts have begun to modify the right of employers to dismiss employees at will. Courts in Oregon and Pennsylvania have awarded damages to employees fired for serving on juries. A New Hampshire court granted damages to a woman fired for refusing to date her foreman. A West Virginia court reinstated a bank employee who reported illegal interest rates. The

Illinois Supreme Court upheld the right of an employee to sue when fired for reporting and testifying about criminal activities of a fellow employee. However, a majority of states still uphold the right of employers to fire employees at will unless there are statutes or agreements to the contrary. To my knowledge only one state, Michigan, has passed a law prohibiting employers from retaliating against employees who report violations of local, state, or federal laws.

A number of federal statutes contain provisions intended to protect whistle blowers. The National Labor Relations Act, Fair Labor Standards Act, Title VII of the 1964 Civil Rights Act, Age Discrimination Act, and the Occupational Safety and Health Act all have sections prohibiting employers from taking retaliatory actions against employees who report or testify about violations of the acts. Although these laws seem to encourage and protect whistle blowers, to be effective they must be enforced. A 1976 study[2] of the Occupational Safety and Health Act showed that only about 20 percent of the 2300 complaints filed in fiscal years 1975 and 1976 were judged valid by OSHA investigators. About half of these were settled out of court. Of the sixty cases taken to court at the time of the study in November 1976, one had been won, eight lost, and the others were still pending. A more recent study[3] showed that of the 3100 violations reported in 1979, only 270 were settled out of court and only sixteen litigated.

Since the National Labor Relations Act guarantees the right of workers to organize and bargain collectively, and most collective bargaining agreements contain a clause requiring employers to have just cause for discharging employees, these agreements would seem to offer some protection for whistle blowers. In fact, however, arbitrators have tended to agree with employers that whistle blowing is an act of disloyalty which disrupts business and injures the employer's reputation. Their attitude seems to be summed up in a 1972 case in which the arbitrator stated that one should not "bite the hand that feeds you and insist on staying for future banquets."[4] One reason for this attitude, pointed out by David Ewing, is that unions are frequently as corrupt as the organizations on which the whistle is being blown. Such unions he says, "are not likely to feed a hawk that comes to prey in their own barnyard."[5] The record of professional societies is not any better. They have generally failed to come to the aid or defense of members who have attempted to live up to their codes of professional ethics by blowing the whistle on corrupt practices.

THE MORAL JUSTIFICATION OF WHISTLE BLOWING

Under what conditions, if any, is whistle blowing morally justified? Some people have argued that whistle blowing is never justified because employees have absolute obligations of confidentiality and loyalty to the organization for which they work. People who argue this way see no difference between employees who reveal trade secrets by selling information to competitors and whistle blowers who disclose activities harmful to others.[6] This position is similar to another held by some business people and economists that the sole obligation of corporate executives is to make a profit for stockholders. If this were true, corporate executives would have no obligations to the public. However, no matter what one's special obligations, one is never exempt from the general obligations we have to our fellow human beings. One of the most fundamental of these obligations is to not cause avoidable harm to others. Corporate executives are no more exempt from this obligation than other people.

Just as the special obligations of corporate executives to stockholders cannot override their more fundamental obligations to others, the special obligations of employees to employers cannot override their more fundamental obligations. In particular, obligations of confidentiality and loyalty cannot take precedence over the fundamental duty to act in ways that prevent unnecessary harm to others. Agreements to keep something secret have no moral standing unless that which is to be kept secret is itself morally justifiable. For example, no one can have an obligation to keep secret a conspiracy to murder someone, because murder is an immoral act. It is for this reason also that employees have a legal obligation to report an employer who has committed or is about to commit a felony. Nor can one justify participation in an illegal or immoral activity by arguing that one was merely following orders. Democratic governments repudiated this type of defense at Nuremberg.

It has also been argued that whistle blowing is always justified because it is an exercise of the right to free speech. However, the right to free speech is not absolute. An example often used to illustrate this is that one does not have the right to shout "Fire" in a crowded theater because that is likely to cause a panic in which people may be injured. Analogously, one may have a right to speak out on a particular subject, in the sense that there are no contractual agreements which prohibit one from doing so, but it nevertheless be the case that it would be morally wrong for one to do so because it would harm innocent people, such as one's fellow workers and stockholders who are not responsible for the wrongdoing being disclosed. The mere fact that one has the right to speak out does not mean that one ought to do so in every case. But this kind of consideration cannot create an absolute prohibition against whistle blowing, because one must weigh the harm to fellow workers and stockholders caused by the disclosure against the harm to others caused by allowing the organizational wrong to continue. Furthermore, the moral principle that one must consider all people's interests equally prohibits giving priority to one's own group. There is, in fact, justification for not giving as much weight to the interests of the stockholders as to those of the public, because stockholders investing in corporate firms do so with the knowledge that they undergo financial risk if management acts in imprudent, illegal, or im-

moral ways. Similarly, if the employees of a company know that it is engaged in illegal or immoral activities and do not take action, including whistle blowing, to terminate the activities, then they too must bear some of the guilt for the actions. To the extent that these conditions hold, they nullify the principle that one ought to refrain from whistle blowing because speaking out would cause harm to the organization. Unless it can be shown that the harm to fellow workers and stockholders would be *significantly greater* than the harm caused by the organizational wrongdoing, the obligation to avoid unnecessary harm to the public must take precedence. Moreover, as argued above, this is true even when there are specific agreements which prohibit one from speaking out, because such agreements are morally void if the organization is engaged in illegal or immoral activities. In that case one's obligation to the public overrides one's obligation to maintain secrecy.

CRITERIA FOR JUSTIFIABLE WHISTLE BLOWING

The argument in the foregoing section is an attempt to show that unless special circumstances hold, one has a obligation to blow the whistle on illegal or immoral actions—an obligation that is grounded on the fundamental human duty to avoid preventable harm to others. In this section I shall attempt to spell out in greater detail the conditions under which blowing the whistle is morally obligatory. Since Richard De George has previously attempted to do this, I shall proceed by examining the criteria he has suggested.[7]

De George believes there are three conditions that must hold for whistle blowing to be morally permissible and two additional conditions that must hold for it to be morally obligatory. The three conditions that must hold for it to be morally permissible are:

1. The firm, through its product or policy, will do serious and considerable harm to the public, whether in the person of the user of its

product, an innocent bystander, or the general public.

2. Once an employee identifies a serious threat to the user of a product or to the general public, he or she should report it to his or her immediate superior and make his or her moral concern known. Unless he or she does so, the act of whistle blowing is not clearly justifiable.

3. If one's immediate superior does nothing effective about the concern or complaint, the employee should exhaust the internal procedures and possibilities within the firm. This usually will involve taking the matter up the managerial ladder, and, if necessary—and possible—to the board of directors.

The two additional conditions which De George thinks must hold for whistle blowing to be morally obligatory are:

4. The whistle blower must have, or have accessible, documented evidence that would convince a reasonable, impartial observer that one's view of the situation is correct and that the company's product or practice poses a serious and likely danger to the public or to the user of the product.

5. The employee must have good reason to believe that by going public the necessary changes will be brought about. The chance of being successful must be worth the risk one takes and the danger to which one is exposed.[8]

De George intends for the proposed criteria to apply to situations in which a firm's policies or products cause physical harm to people. Indeed, the first criterion he proposes is intended to restrict the idea of harm even more narrowly to threats of serious bodily harm or death.

De George apparently believes that situations which involve threats of serious bodily harm or death are so different from those involving other types of harm, that the kind of considerations which justify whistle blowing in the former situations could not possibly justify it in the latter. Thus, he says, referring to the former type of whistle blowing: "As a paradigm, we shall take a set of fairly clear-cut cases, namely, those in which serious bodily harm—including possible death—threatens either the users of a product or innocent bystanders."[9]

One problem in restricting discussion to clear-cut cases of this type, regarding which one can get almost universal agreement that whistle blowing is justifiable, is that it leaves us with no guidance when we are confronted with more usual situations involving other types of harm. Although De George states that his "analysis provides a model for dealing with other kinds of whistle blowing as well,"[10] his criteria in fact provide no help in deciding whether one should blow the whistle in situations involving such wrongs as sexual harassment, violations of privacy, industrial espionage, insider trading, and a variety of other harmful actions.

No doubt, one of the reasons De George restricts his treatment the way he does is to avoid having to define harm. This is indeed a problem. For if we fail to put any limitations on the idea of harm, it seems to shade into the merely offensive or distasteful and thus offer little help in resolving moral problems. But, on the other hand, if we restrict harm to physical injury, as De George does, it then applies to such a limited range of cases that it is of minimal help in most of the moral situations which confront us. One way of dealing with this problem is by correlating harm with violations of fundamental human rights such as the rights to due process, privacy, and property, in addition to the right to freedom from physical harm. Thus, not only situations which involve threats of physical harm, but also those involving actions such as sexual harassment which violates the right to privacy and causes psychological harm, compiling unnecessary records on people, and financial harm due to fraudulent actions, are situations which may justify whistle blowing.

A still greater problem with De George's analysis is that even in cases where there is a threat of serious physical harm or death, he believes that this only makes whistle blowing morally permissible, rather than creating a strong *prima facie* obligation in favor of whistle blowing. His primary reasons for believing this seem to be those stated in criterion 5. Unless one has reason to believe that the whistle blowing will eliminate the harm, and the cost to oneself is not too great, he does not believe whistle blowing is morally obligatory. He maintains that this is true even when the person involved is a professional whose code of ethics requires her or him to put the public good ahead of private good. He argued in an earlier article, for example, that:

> The myth that ethics has no place in engineering has...at least in some corners of the engineering profession...been put to rest. Another myth, however, is emerging to take its place—the myth of the engineer as moral hero.... The zeal...however, has gone too far, piling moral responsibility upon moral responsibility on the shoulders of the engineer. This emphasis...is misplaced. Though engineers are members of a profession that holds public safety paramount, we cannot reasonably expect engineers to be willing to sacrifice their jobs each day for principle and to have a whistle ever at their sides.[11]

He contends that engineers have only the obligation "to do their jobs the best they can."[12] This includes reporting their concerns about the safety of products to management, but does *not* include "the obligation to insist that their perceptions or...standards be accepted. They are not paid to do that, they are not expected to do that, and they have no moral or ethical obligation to do that."[13]

To take a specific case, De George maintains that even though some Ford engineers had grave misgivings about the safety of Pinto gas tanks, and several people had been killed when tanks exploded after rear-end crashes, the engineers did not have an obligation to make their misgivings public. De George's remarks are puzzling because the Pinto case would seem to be exactly the kind of clear-cut situation which he says provides the paradigm for justified whistle blowing. Indeed, if the Ford engineers did not have an obligation to blow the whistle, it is difficult to see what cases could satisfy his criteria. They knew that if Pintos were struck from the rear by vehicles traveling thirty miles per hour or more, their gas tanks were likely to explode, seriously injuring or killing people. They also knew that if they did not speak out, Ford would continue to market the Pinto. Finally, they were members of a profession whose code of ethics requires them to put public safety above all other obligations.

De George's remarks suggest that the only obligation the Ford engineers had was to do what management expected of them by complying with their job descriptions and that so long as they did that no one should find fault with them or hold them accountable for what the company did. It is true that when people act within the framework of an organization, it is often difficult to assess individual responsibility. But the fact that one is acting as a member of an organization does not relieve one of moral obligations. The exact opposite is true. Because most of the actions we undertake in organizational settings have more far-reaching consequences than those we undertake in our personal lives, our moral obligation to make sure that we do not harm others is *increased* when we act as a member of an organization. The amount of moral responsibility one has for any particular organizational action depends on the extent to which: (1) the consequences of the action are foreseeable, and (2) one's own action or failure to act is a cause of those consequences. It is important to include failure to act here, because frequently it is easier to determine what will happen if we do not act than if we do, and because we are morally responsible for not preventing harm as well as for causing it.

De George thinks that the Ford engineers would have had an obligation to blow the whistle only if they believed doing so would have been likely to prevent the harm involved. But we have an obligation to warn others of danger even if we believe they will ignore our warnings. This is especially true if the danger will come about partly because we did not speak out. De George admits that the public has a right to know about dangerous products. If that is true, then those who have knowledge about such products have an obligation to inform the public. This is not usurping the public's right to decide acceptable risk; it is simply supplying people with the information necessary to exercise that right.

De George's comments also seem to imply that in general it is not justifiable to ask people to blow the whistle if it would threaten their jobs. It is true that we would not necessarily be justified in demanding this if it would place them or their families' lives in danger. But this is *not* true if only their jobs are at stake. It is especially not true if the people involved are executives and professionals, who are accorded respect and high salaries, not only because of their specialized knowledge and skills, but also because of the special responsibilities we entrust to them. Frequently, as in the case of engineers, they also subscribe to codes of ethics which require them to put the public good ahead of their own or the organization's good. Given all this, it is difficult to understand why De George does not think the Ford engineers had an obligation to blow the whistle in the Pinto case.

The belief that whistle blowing is an act of disloyalty and disobedience seems to underlie De George's second and third criteria for justifiable whistle blowing: The whistle blower must have first reported the wrongdoing to his or her immediate superior and, if nothing was done, have taken the complaint as far up the managerial ladder as possible. Some of the problems with adopting these suggestions as general criteria for justified whistle blowing are: (1) It may be one's immediate supervisor who is responsible for the wrongdoing. (2) Organizations differ considerably in both their procedures for reporting, and how they respond to, wrongdoing. (3) Not all wrongdoing is of the same type. If the wrong-

doing is of a type that threatens people's health or safety, exhausting channels of protest within the organization may result in unjustified delay in correcting the problem. (4) Exhausting internal channels of protest may give people time to destroy evidence needed to substantiate one's allegations. (5) Finally, it may expose the employee to possible retaliation, against which she or he might have some protection if the wrongdoing were reported to an external agency.

His fourth criterion, that the whistle blower have documented evidence which would convince an impartial observer, is intended to reduce incidences of whistle blowing by curbing those who would blow the whistle on a mere suspicion of wrongdoing. It is true that one should not make claims against an organization based on mere guesses or hunches, because if they turn out to be false one will have illegitimately harmed the organization and innocent people affiliated with it. But, De George also wishes to curb whistle blowing, because he thinks that if it were widespread, that would reduce its effectiveness. De George's fourth and fifth criteria are, therefore, deliberately formulated in such a way that if they are satisfied, "people will only rarely have the moral obligation to blow the whistle."[14]

De George's fear, that unless strict criteria of justification are applied to whistle blowing it might become widespread, is unjustified. If it is true, as he himself claims, that there is a strong tradition in America against "ratting," that most workers consider themselves to have an obligation of loyalty to their organization, and that whistle blowers are commonly looked upon as traitors, then it is unlikely that whistle blowing will ever be a widespread practice. De George believes that if one is unable to document wrongdoing without recourse to illegal or immoral means, this relieves one of the obligation to blow the whistle. He argues:

> One does not have an obligation to blow the whistle simply because of one's hunch, guess, or personal assessment of possible danger, if supporting

evidence and documentation are not available. One may, of course, have the obligation to attempt to get evidence if the harm is serious. But if it is unavailable—or unavailable without using illegal or immoral means—then one does not have the obligation to blow the whistle.[15]

I have already indicated above that I do not think one has an obligation to blow the whistle on possible wrongdoing on the basis of a mere guess or hunch because this might harm innocent people. But if one has good reason to believe that wrongdoing is occurring even though one cannot document it without oneself engaging in illegal or immoral actions, this does not relieve one of the obligation to blow the whistle. Indeed, if this were true one would almost never have an obligation to blow the whistle, because employees are rarely in a position to satisfy De George's fourth criterion that the whistle blower "must have, or have accessible, documented evidence that would convince a reasonable, impartial observer that one's view of the situation is correct." Indeed, it is precisely because employees are rarely ever in a position to supply this type of documentation without themselves resorting to illegal or immoral actions, that they have an obligation to inform others who have the authority to investigate the possible wrongdoing. The attempt to secure such evidence on one's own may even thwart the gathering of evidence by the proper authorities. Thus, instead of De George's criterion being a necessary condition for justifiable whistle blowing, the attempt to satisfy it would prevent its occurrence. One has an obligation to gather as much evidence as one can so that authorities will have probable cause for investigation. But, if one is convinced that wrongdoing is occurring, one has an obligation to report it even if one is unable to adequately document it. One will have then done one's duty even if the authorities ignore the report.

The claim that it is usually necessary for the whistle blower to speak out openly for whistle blowing to be morally justified implies that anonymous whistle blowing is rarely, if ever, justified. Is this true? It has been argued that anonymous whistle blowing is never justified because it violates the right of people to face their accusers. But, as Frederick Elliston has pointed out, although people should be protected from false accusations, it is not necessary for the identity of whistle blowers to be known to accomplish this. "It is only necessary that accusations be properly investigated, proven true or false, and the results widely disseminated."[16]

Some people believe that because the whistle blower's motive is not known in anonymous whistle blowing, this suggests that the motive is not praiseworthy and in turn raises questions about the moral justification of anonymous whistle blowing. De George apparently believes this, because in addition to stating that only public whistle blowing by previously loyal employees who display their sincerity by their willingness to suffer is likely to be effective and morally justified, he mentions at several places that he is restricting his attention to whistle blowing for moral reasons. He says, e.g., that "the only motivation for whistle blowing we shall consider...is moral motivation."[17] However, in my opinion, concern with the whistle blower's motive is irrelevant to the moral justification of whistle blowing. It is a red herring which takes attention away from the genuine moral issue involved: whether the whistle blower's claim that the organization is doing something harmful to others is true. If the claim is true, then the whistle blowing is justified regardless of the motive. If the whistle blower's motives are not moral, that makes the act less praiseworthy, but this is a totally different issue. As De George states, whistle blowing is a "practical matter." But precisely because this is true, the justification of whistle blowing turns on the truth or falsity of the disclosure, not on the motives of the whistle blower. Anonymous whistle blowing is justified because it can both protect the whistle blower from unjust attacks and prevent those who are accused of wrongdoing from shifting the issue away from their wrongdoing by engaging in an irrelevant *ad hominem* attack on the whistle blower. Preoccupation with the whistle blower's motives facilitates this type of irrelevant diversion. It is only if the accusations prove false or inaccurate that the motives of the whistle blower have any moral relevance. For it is only then, and not before, that the whistle blower rather than the organization should be put on trial.

The view that whistle blowing is *prima facie* wrong because it goes against the tradition that "ratting" is wrong is indefensible because it falsely assumes both that we have a general obligation to not inform others about wrongdoing and that this outweighs our fundamental obligation to prevent harm to others. The belief that whistle blowers should suffer in order to show their moral sincerity, on the other hand, is not only false and irrelevant to the issue of the moral justification of whistle blowing, but is perverse. There are *no* morally justifiable reasons a person who discloses wrongdoing should be put at risk or made to suffer. The contradictory view stated by De George that "one does not have an obligation to put oneself at serious risk without some compensating advantage to be gained,"[18] is also false. Sometimes doing one's duty requires one to undertake certain risks. However, both individuals and society in general should attempt to reduce these risks to the minimum. In the next section I consider some of the actions whistle blowers can take to both make whistle blowing effective and avoid unnecessary risk. In the last section I briefly consider some of the ways society can reduce the need for whistle blowing.

FACTORS TO CONSIDER IN WHISTLE BLOWING

Since whistle blowing usually involves conflicting moral obligations and a wide range of variables and has far-reaching consequences for everyone concerned, the following is not intended as a recipe or how-to-do list. Like all compli-cated moral actions, whistle blowing cannot be reduced to such a list. Nevertheless, some factors can be stated which whistle blowers should consider in disclosing wrongdoing if they are to also act prudently and effectively.

Make Sure the Situation Is One That Warrants Whistle Blowing

Make sure the situation is one that involves illegal or immoral actions which harm others, rather than one in which you would be disclosing personal matters, trade secrets, customer lists, or similar material. If the disclosure would involve the latter as well, make sure that the harm to be avoided is great enough to offset the harm from the latter.

Examine Your Motives

Although it is not necessary for the whistle blower's motives to be praiseworthy for whistle blowing to be morally justified, examining your motives can help in deciding whether the situation is one that warrants whistle blowing.

Verify and Document Your Information

Try to obtain information that will stand up in regulatory hearings or court. If this is not possible, gather as much information as you can and indicate where and how additional information might be obtained. If the *only* way you could obtain either of these types of information would be through illegal procedures, make sure the situation is one in which the wrongdoing is so great that it warrants this risk. Although morality requires that in general we obey the law, it sometimes requires that we break it. Daniel Ellsberg's release of the Pentagon papers was a situation of this type in my opinion. If you do have to use illegal methods to obtain information, try to find alternative sources for any evidence you uncover so that it will not be challenged in legal hearings. Keep in mind also that if you use illegal methods to obtain information you are opening yourself to *ad hominem* attacks and possible prosecution. In general illegal methods should be avoided unless substantial harm to others is involved.

Determine the Type of Wrongdoing Involved and to Whom It Should Be Reported

Determining the exact nature of the wrongdoing can help you both decide what kind of evidence to obtain and to whom it should be reported. For example, if the wrongdoing consists of illegal actions such as the submission of false test reports to government agencies, bribery of public officials, racial or sexual discrimination, violation of safety, health, or pollution laws, then determining the nature of the law being violated will help indicate which agencies have authority to enforce the law. If, on the other hand, the wrongdoing is not illegal, but is nevertheless harmful to the public, determining this will help you decide whether you have an obligation to publicize the actions and if so how to go about it. The best place to report this type of wrongdoing is usually to a public interest group. Such an organization is more likely than the press to: (1) be concerned about and advise the whistle blower how to avoid retaliation, (2) maintain confidentiality if that is desirable, (3) investigate the allegations to try to substantiate them, rather than sensationalizing them by turning the issue into a ''personality dispute.'' If releasing information to the press is the best way to remedy the wrongdoing, the public interest group can help with or do this.

State Your Allegations in an Appropriate Way

Be as specific as possible without being unintelligible. If you are reporting a violation of law to a government agency, and it possible to do so, include technical data necessary for experts to verify the wrongdoing. If you are disclosing wrongdoing that does not require technical data to substantiate it, still be as specific as possible in stating the type of illegal or harmful activity involved, who is being harmed and how.

Stick to the Facts

Avoid name calling, slander, and being drawn into a mud-slinging contest. As Peter Raven-Hansen wisely points out: ''One of the most important points...is to focus on the disclosure.... This rule applies even when the whistle blower believes that certain individuals are responsible.... The disclosure itself usually leaves a trail for others to follow the miscreants.''[19] Sticking to the facts also helps the whistle blower minimize retaliation.

Decide Whether the Whistle Blowing Should Be Internal or External

Familiarize yourself with all available internal channels for reporting wrongdoing and obtain as much data as you can both on how people who have used these channels were treated by the organization and what was done about the problems they reported. If people who have reported wrongdoing in the past have been treated fairly and the problems corrected, use internal channels. If not, find out which external agencies would be the most appropriate to contact. Try to find out also how these agencies have treated whistle blowers, how much aid and protection they have given them, etc.

Decide Whether the Whistle Blowing Should Be Open or Anonymous

If you intend to blow the whistle anonymously, decide whether partial or total anonymity is required. Also document the wrongdoing as thoroughly as possible. Finally, since anonymity may be difficult to preserve, anticipate what you will do if your identity becomes known.

Decide Whether Current or Alumni Whistle Blowing Is Required

Sometimes it is advisable to resign one's position and obtain another before blowing the whistle. This is because alumni whistle blowing helps protect one from being fired, receiving damaging letters of recommendation, or even being blacklisted in one's profession. However, changing jobs should not be thought of as an alternative to whistle blowing. If one is aware of harmful practices, one has a moral obligation to try to do something about them, which cannot be escaped by changing one's job or location. Many times people who think the wrongdoing involved is personal, harming only them, respond to a situation by simply trying to remove themselves from it. They believe that ''personal whistle blowing is, in general, morally permitted but not morally required.''[20] For example, a female student subjected to sexual harassment, and fearful that she will receive low grades and poor letters of recommendation if she complains, may simply change departments or schools. However, tendencies toward wrongdoing are rarely limited to specific victims. By not blowing the whistle the student allows a situation to exist in which other students are likely to be harassed also.

Make Sure You Follow Proper Guidelines in Reporting the Wrongdoing

If you are not careful to follow any guidelines that have been established by organizations or external agencies for a particular type of whistle blowing, including using the proper forms, meeting deadlines, etc., wrongdoers may escape detection or punishment because of ''technicalities.''

Consult a Lawyer

Lawyers are advisable at almost every stage of whistle blowing. They can help determine if the wrongdoing violates the law, aid in documenting it, inform you of any laws you might break in documenting it, assist in deciding to whom to report it, make sure reports are filed correctly and promptly, and help protect you from retaliation. If you cannot afford a lawyer, talk with an appropriate public interest group that may be able to help. However, lawyers frequently view problems within a narrow legal framework, and decisions to blow the whistle are moral decisions, so in the final analysis you will have to rely on your own judgment.

Anticipate and Document Retaliation

Although not as certain as Newton's law of motion that for every action there is an equal reaction, whistle blowers whose identities are known can expect retaliation. Furthermore, it may be difficult to keep one's identity secret. Thus whether the whistle blowing is open or anonymous, personal or impersonal, internal or external, current or alumni, one should anticipate retaliation. One should, therefore, protect oneself by documenting every step of the whistle blowing with letters, tape recordings of meetings, etc. Without this documentation, the whistle blower may find that regulatory agencies and the courts are of little help in preventing or redressing retaliation.

BEYOND WHISTLE BLOWING

What can be done to eliminate the wrongdoing which gives rise to whistle blowing? One solution would be to give whistle blowers greater legal protection. Another would be to change the nature of organizations so as to diminish the need for whistle blowing. These solutions are of course not mutually exclusive.

Many people are opposed to legislation to protect whistle blowers because they think that it is unwarranted interference with the right to freedom of contract. However, if the right to freedom of contract is to be consistent with the public interest, it cannot serve as a shield for wrongdoing. It does this when threat of dismissal prevents people from blowing the whistle. The right of employers to dismiss at will has been previously restricted by labor laws which prevent employers from dismissing employees for union activities. It is ironic that we have restricted the right of employers to fire employees who are pursuing their economic self-interest but allowed them to fire employees acting in the public interest. The right of employers to dismiss employees in the interest of efficiency should be balanced against the right of the public to know about illegal, dangerous, and unjust practices of organizations. The most effective way to achieve this goal would be to pass a federal law protecting whistle blowers.

Laws protecting whistle blowers have also been opposed on the grounds that: (1) employees would use them to mask poor performance, (2) they would create an "informer ethos," and (3) they would take away the autonomy of business, strangling it in red tape.

The first objection is illegitimate because only those employees who could show that an act of whistle blowing preceded their being penalized or dismissed, and that their employment records were adequate up to the time of the whistle blowing, could seek relief under the law.

The second objection is more formidable but nevertheless invalid. A society that encourages snooping, suspicion, and mistrust does not conform to most people's idea of the good society. Laws which encourage whistle blowing for self-interested reasons, such as the federal tax law which pays informers part of any money that is collected, could help bring about such a society.[21] However, laws protecting whistle blowers from being penalized or dismissed are quite different. They do not reward the whistle blower; they merely protect him or her from unjust retaliation. It is unlikely that state or federal laws of this type would promote an informer society.

The third objection is also unfounded. Laws protecting whistle blowers would not require any positive duties on the part of organizations—only the negative duty of not retaliating against employees who speak out in the public interest.

However not every act of apparent whistle blowing should be protected. If (1) the whistle blower's accusations turn out to be false and, (2) it can be shown that she or he had no probable reasons for assuming wrongdoing, then the individual should not be shielded from being penalized or dismissed. Both of these conditions should be satisfied before this is allowed to occur. People who can show that they had probable reasons for believing that wrongdoing existed should be protected even if their accusations turn out to be false. If the accusation has not been disproved, the burden of proof should be on the organization to prove that it is false. If it has been investigated and proven false, then the burden of proof should be on the individual to show that she or he had probable reasons for believing wrongdoing existed. If it is shown that the individual did not have probable reasons for believing wrongdoing existed, and the damage to the organization from the false charge is great, it should be allowed to sue or seek other restitution. Since these provisions would impose some risks on potential whistle blowers, they would reduce the possibility of frivolous action. If, on the other hand, it is found that the whistle blower had probable cause for the whistle blowing and the organization has penalized or fired him or her, then that person should be reinstated, awarded damages, or both. If there is further retaliation, additional sizeable damages should be awarded.

What changes could be made in organizations to prevent the need for whistle blowing? Some of the suggestions which have been made are that organizations develop effective internal channels for reporting wrongdoing, reward people with salary increases and promotions for using these channels, and appoint senior executives, board members, ombudspersons, etc., whose primary obligations would be to investigate and eliminate organizational wrongdoing. These changes could be undertaken by organizations on their own or mandated by law. Other changes which might be mandated are requiring that certain kinds of records be kept, assessing larger fines for illegal actions, and making executives and other professionals personally liable for filing false reports, knowingly marketing dangerous products, failing to monitor how policies are being implemented, and so forth. Although these reforms could do much to reduce the need for whistle blowing, given human nature it is highly unlikely that this need can ever be totally eliminated. Therefore, it is important to have laws which protect whistle blowers and for us to state as clearly as we can both the practical problems and moral issues pertaining to whistle blowing.

NOTES

1. For discussion of the legal aspects of whistle blowing see Lawrence E. Blades, ''Employment at Will vs. Individual Freedom: On Limiting the Abusive Exercise of Employer Power,'' *Columbia Law Review,* vol. 67 (1967); Philip Blumberg, ''Corporate Responsibility and the Employee's Duty of Loyalty and Obedience: A Preliminary Inquiry,'' *Oklahoma Law Review,* vol. 24 (1967); Clyde W. Summers, ''Individual Protection Against Unjust Dismissal: Time for a Statue,'' *Virginia Law Review,* vol. 62 (1976); Arthur S. Miller, ''Whistle Blowing and the Law,'' in Ralph Nader, Peter J. Petkas, and Kate Blackwell, *Whistle Blowing,* New York: Grossman Publishers, 1972; Alan F. Westin, *Whistle Blowing!,* New York: McGraw-Hill, 1981. See also vol. 16, no. 2, Winter 1983, *University of Michigan Journal of Law Reform,* special issue, ''Individual Rights in the Workplace: The Employment-At-Will Issue.''

2. For a discussion of this study which was conducted by Morton Corn see Frank von Hipple, ''Professional Freedom and Responsibility: The Role of the Professional Society,'' *Newsletter on Science, Technology and Human Values,* vol. 22, January 1978.

3. See Westin, *Whistle Blowing!*

4. See Martin H. Marlin, ''Protecting the Whistleblower from Retaliatory Discharge,'' in the special issue of the *University of Michigan Journal of Law Reform.*

5. David W. Ewing, *Freedom inside the Organization,* New York: E. P. Dutton, 1977, pp. 165–166.

6. For a more detailed discussion of this argument see Gene G. James, ''Whistle Blowing: Its Nature and Justification,'' *Philosophy in Context,* vol. 10 (1980).

7. See Richard T. De George, 2d ed., *Business Ethics,* New York: Macmillan, 1986. Earlier versions of De George's criteria can be found in the first edition (1982), and in ''Ethical Responsibilities of Engineers in Large Organizations,'' *Business and Professional Ethics Journal,* vol. 1, no. 1, Fall 1981.

8. De George, *Business Ethics,* pp. 230–234.

9. *Ibid.,* p. 223.

10. *Ibid.,* p. 237.

11. De George, ''Ethical Responsibilities of Engineers,'' p. 1.

12. *Ibid.,* p. 5.

13. *Ibid.*

14. De George, *Business Ethics,* p. 235.

15. *Ibid.,* p. 234.

16. Frederick A. Elliston, ''Anonymous Whistleblowing,'' *Business and Professional Ethics Journal,* vol. 1, no. 2, Winter 1982.

17. De George, *Business Ethics,* p. 223.

18. *Ibid.,* p. 234.

19. Peter Raven-Hansen, ''Dos and Don'ts for Whistleblowers: Planning for Trouble,'' *Technology Review,* May 1980, p. 30. My discussion in this section is heavily indebted to this article.

20. De George, *Business Ethics,* p. 222.

21. People who blow the whistle on tax evaders in fact rarely receive any money because the law leaves payment to the discretion of the Internal Revenue Service.

QUESTIONS FOR DISCUSSION

1. ''Employees owe their employers loyalty and obedience, therefore they should never blow the whistle.'' Make a case for or against this statement, keeping in mind the arguments of De George and James.

2. De George believes that employees are obligated to blow the whistle only if they have documented evidence of a serious harm, and if they have reason to believe that whistle blowing will be effective in preventing the harm. Why does James think these criteria are too strict? Do you agree with De George or James, and why?

CHAPTER 9

The Quality of Working Life

READINGS FOR CHAPTER NINE

Richard E. Walton
Alienation and Innovation in the Workplace
347

Irving Bluestone
Labor's Stake in Improving the Quality of Working
Life
350

Mike Parker and Dwight Hansen
The Circle Game
355

Mitchell Fein
The Myth of Job Enrichment
361

Edward Cohen-Rosenthal
Should Unions Participate in Quality of Working Life
Activities?
366

Alienation and Innovation in the Workplace

Richard E. Walton*

Managers don't need anyone to tell them that employee alienation exists. Terms such as "blue-collar blues" and "salaried dropouts" are all too familiar. But are they willing to undertake the major innovations necessary for redesigning work organizations to deal effectively with the root causes of alienation? My purpose in this article is to urge them to do so, for two reasons: (1) The current alienation is not merely a phase that will pass in due time. (2) The innovations needed to correct the problem can simultaneously enhance the quality of work life (thereby lessening alienation) and improve productivity. I shall risk covering terrain already familiar to some readers in order to establish the fact that alienation is a basic, long-term, and mounting problem.

ANATOMY OF ALIENATION

There are two parts to the problem of employee alienation: (1) the productivity output of work systems and (2) the social costs associated with employee inputs. Regarding the first, U.S. productivity is not adequate to the challenges posed by international competition and inflation; it cannot sustain impressive economic growth. (I do not refer here to economic growth as something to be valued merely for its own sake—it is politically a precondition for the income redistribution that will make equality of opportunity pos-

sible in the United States.) Regarding the second, the social and psychological costs of work systems are excessive, as evidenced by their effects on the mental and physical health of employees and on the social health of families and communities.

Employee alienation *affects* productivity and *reflects* social costs incurred in the workplace. Increasingly, blue- and white-collar employees and, to some extent, middle managers tend to dislike their jobs and resent their bosses. Workers tend to rebel against their union leaders. They are becoming less concerned about the quality of the product of their labor and more angered about the quality of the context in which they labor.

In some cases, alienation is expressed by passive withdrawal—tardiness, absenteeism and turnover, and inattention on the job. In other cases, it is expressed by active attacks—pilferage, sabotage, deliberate waste, assaults, bomb threats, and other disruptions of work routines. Demonstrations have taken place and underground newspapers have appeared in large organizations in recent years to protest company policies. Even more recently, employees have cooperated with newsmen, congressional committees, regulatory agencies, and protest groups in exposing objectionable practices.

These trends all have been mentioned in the media, but one expression of alienation has been underreported: pilferage and violence against property and persons. Such acts are less likely to be revealed to the police and the media when they occur in a private company than when they occur in a high school, a ghetto business district, or a suburban town. Moreover, dramatic increases in these forms of violence are taking place at the plant level. This trend is not reported in local newspapers, and there is little or no appreciation of it at corporate headquarters. Local management keeps quiet because violence is felt to reflect unfavorably both on its effectiveness and on its plant as a place to work.

*Straus Professor of Business Administration, Harvard Business School.

ROOTS OF CONFLICT

The acts of sabotage and other forms of protest are overt manifestations of a conflict between changing employee attitudes and organizational inertia. Increasingly, what employees expect from their jobs is different from what organizations are prepared to offer them. These evolving expectations of workers conflict with the demands, conditions, and rewards of employing organizations in at least six important ways:

- Employees want challenge and personal growth, but work tends to be simplified and specialties tend to be used repeatedly in work assignments. This pattern exploits the narrow skills of a worker, while limiting his or her opportunities to broaden or develop.
- Employees want to be included in patterns of mutual influence; they want egalitarian treatment. But organizations are characterized by tall hierarchies, status differentials, and chains of command.
- Employee commitment to an organization is increasingly influenced by the intrinsic interest of the work itself, the human dignity afforded by management, and the social responsibility reflected in the organization's products. Yet organization practices still emphasize material rewards and employment security and neglect other employee concerns.
- What employees want from careers, they are apt to want *right now*. But when organizations design job hierarchies and career paths, they continue to assume that today's workers are as willing to postpone gratifications as yesterday's workers were.
- Employees want more attention to the emotional aspects of organization life, such as individual self-esteem, openness between people, and expressions of warmth. Yet organizations emphasize rationality and seldom legitimize the emotional part of the organizational experience.
- Employees are becoming less driven by competitive urges, less likely to identify competition as the "American way." Nevertheless, managers continue to plan career patterns, organize work, and design reward systems as if employees valued competition as highly as they used to.

The foregoing needs and desires that employees bring to their work are but a local reflection of more basic, and not readily reversible, trends in U.S. society. These trends are fueled by family and social experience as well as by social institutions, especially schools. Among the most significant are:

- *The rising level of education.* Employees bring to the workplace more abilities and, correspondingly, higher expectations than in the past.
- *The rising level of wealth and security.* Vast segments of today's society never have wanted for the tangible essentials of life: thus they are decreasingly motivated by pay and security, which are taken for granted.
- *The decreased emphasis given by churches, schools, and families to obedience to authority.* These socialization agencies have promoted individual initiative, self-responsibility and self-control, the relativity of values, and other social patterns that make subordinacy in traditional organizations an increasingly bitter pill to swallow for each successive wave of entrants to the U.S. work force.
- *The decline in achievement motivation.* For example, whereas the books my parents read in primary school taught them the virtues of hard work and competition, my children's books emphasize self-expression and actualizing one's potential. The workplace has not yet fully recognized this change in employee values.
- *The shifting emphasis from individualism to social commitment.* This shift is driven in part by a need for the direct gratifications of human connectedness (for example, as provided by communal living experiments). It also re-

sults from a growing appreciation of our interdependence, and it renders obsolete many traditional workplace concepts regarding the division of labor and work incentives.

I believe that protests in the workplace will mount even more rapidly than is indicated by the contributing trends postulated here. The latent dissatisfaction of workers will be activated as (1) the issues receive public attention and (2) some examples of attempted solutions serve to raise expectations (just as the blacks' expressions of dissatisfaction with social and economic inequities were triggered in the 1950s and women's discontent expanded late in the 1960s).

REVITALIZATION AND REFORM

It seems clear that employee expectations are not likely to revert to those of an earlier day. And the conflicts between these expectations and traditional organizations result in alienation. This alienation, in turn, exacts a deplorable psychological and social cost as well as causes worker behavior that depresses productivity and constrains growth. In short, we need major innovative efforts to redesign work organizations, efforts that take employee expectations into account.

Over the past two decades we have witnessed a parade of organization development, personnel, and labor relations programs that promised to revitalize organizations:

- *Job enrichment* would provide more varied and challenging content in the work.
- *Participative decision making* would enable the information, judgments, and concerns of subordinates to influence the decisions that affect them.
- *Management by objectives* would enable subordinates to understand and shape the objectives toward which they strive and against which they are evaluated.

- *Sensitivity training or encounter groups* would enable people to relate to each other as human beings with feelings and psychological needs.
- *Productivity bargaining* would revise work rules and increase management's flexibility with a quid pro quo whereby the union ensures that workers share in the fruits of the resulting productivity increases.

Each of the preceding programs by *itself* is an inadequate reform of the workplace and has typically failed in its more limited objectives. While application is often based on a correct diagnosis, each approach is only a partial remedy; therefore, the organizational system soon returns to an earlier equilibrium.

The lesson we must learn in the area of work reform is similar to one we have learned in another area of national concern. It is now recognized that a health program, a welfare program, a housing program, or an employment program alone is unable to make a lasting impact on the urban-poor syndrome. Poor health, unemployment, and other interdependent aspects of poverty must be attacked in a coordinated or systemic way.

So it is with meaningful reform of the workplace: we must think "systemically" when approaching the problem. We must coordinate into the redesign the way tasks are packaged into jobs, the way workers are required to relate to each other, the way performance is measured and rewards are made available, the way positions of authority and status symbols are structured, and the way career paths are conceived. Moreover, because these types of changes in work organizations imply new employee skills and different organizational cultures, transitional programs must be established.

Labor's Stake in Improving the Quality of Working Life

Irving Bluestone*

In the play *Fiddler on the Roof*, Tevye, bound by tradition, must face the challenge of changing times and circumstances. He finds himself compelled to grapple with new societal concepts of life as the generation he has helped spawn no longer pays obeisance to his traditions. In a sense, the industrial scene in these "modern times" in the United States is facing a similar challenge as changes in society demand a reassessment of the authoritarian practices of the past and present and influence certain basic shifts in managerial attitudes toward the workers and the structure of the work place.

In the ten-year period from 1970 to 1980 in the United States, for instance, the composition of the work force underwent significant change, and current forecasts presage a continuing transformation.

- Workers completing at least one year of college: blue collar—16 percent up from 7 percent in 1970; service—18 percent up from 8 percent in 1970; white collar—57 percent up from 45 percent in 1970. (Overall, workers today have about four more years of education than was true a generation ago.)
- The nature of the education process has changed, as students are more prone to question the authority of the teacher—even at the grade school level.
- Women as a proportion of the U.S. civilian

labor force have increased from 38.1 percent in 1970 to 42.2 percent in 1979. (It is estimated that, in 1980, 53 percent of all women were in the work force and this proportion will rise to 60 percent in the next several years.)
- A recent Conference Board study projects that 86 percent of U.S. families will have two incomes by 1990. There is a constant upward shift in the number of multiple income families.
- Persons age 45 and over as a percent of the civilian labor force have declined from 38.1 percent in 1970 to 30.8 percent in 1979 (to 30.3 percent in 1980).

Daniel Yankelovich, in his widely noted study, *The New Morality,* summed up his findings in part as follows:

Today's generation of young people is less fearful of economic insecurity than generations in the past. They want interesting and challenging work, but they assume that their employers cannot—or will not—provide it. By their own say-so, they are inclined to take "less crap" than older workers. They are not as automatically loyal to the organization as their fathers, and they are far more cognizant of their own needs and rights. Nor are they as awed by organizational and hierarchical authority. Being less fearful of discipline and the threat of losing their jobs, they feel free to express their discontent in myriad ways, from fooling around on the job to sabotage. They are better educated than their parents, even without a college degree. They want more freedom and opportunity and will struggle hard to achieve it. [1974, p. 37]

It is commonplace to hear business managers anchored in the customary management hierarchical structure—in which the boss makes the decisions and gives the orders, and the employees take the orders and do as they are told—complain that workers today:

- are less attentive to the quality of the product or service in the performance of their job;
- exhibit a surly, cynical attitude toward management;

From *The Quality of Working Life and the 1980's,* Harvey Kolodny and Hans van Beinum, eds. (Praeger Publishers, a division of Greenwood Press, New York, 1983), pp. 33–41. Copyright © 1983 by Praeger Publishers. Reprinted with permission.
*University Professor of Labor Studies, Wayne State University, and former vice-president of the United Auto Workers.

- run the gamut from apathy to rebelliousness;
- are more prone to unwarranted absenteeism and lateness;
- have no "loyalty" to the employer.

It is evident that these are the imputations of those managers who fail to comprehend the comparatively rapid changes occurring in society and the world of work and who have not yet realized the need to alter their own behavior in relation to their employees. Fortunately, however, an increasing number of business executives have perceived that the old authoritarian mode is not only morally and philosophically incompatible with a society rooted in democratic values, but is moreover antagonistic to their own self-interests.

Furthermore, world competition, not only from Japan and Europe but increasingly from developing nations as well, is compelling a reevaluation of the current system of business administration. Long term planning, the best uses of capital and investment, a review of research and development processes and programs, and the upgrading of managerial skills are some of the aspects of business administration coming under sharp scrutiny. No less so is the vitally important subject of the effective utilization of human resources. Every company proclaims that its employees are its most valuable resource. Most often, however, the proclamation is rhetoric without substance.

A primary function of unions is to make of this proclamation a reality. Toward this end a union represents workers in order to improve their living standards, enhance their job and income security, and establish enforceable negotiated work place rights for them. Essential to the purposes and goals of a union as well is to create a work place climate in which the workers will enjoy job satisfaction derived from recognition of their desire for dignity and self-realization—a knowledge that what they are as adult human beings counts more than being an extension of the tool, and that what they do is intrinsically meaningful.

The process of creating a work life of "quality" embraces those concepts that afford the opportunity for the employees at all levels—middle management, white collar, and blue collar—to be adult citizens in the work place as they are in society. To achieve this objective requires a departure from the all encompassing authoritarian managerial control of the decision-making process; it requires a system in which the employees participate significantly in the process of decision making.

For management this may be a disconcerting development since it represents a challenge to certain long established management prerogatives—especially those relating to decisions over the methods, means, and processes of production or, as the case may be, providing services. Yet the forces of change are impelling business executives to "think anew." For unions these recent developments should be viewed as a further step along the road of unionism's persistent historical goal—to bring a greater measure of democracy to the work place.

For both management and unions, the break with tradition does not come easy. For all that, it is, however, equally apparent that not all traditions are worthy of rigid preservation. From the point of view of the union, embracing the concept of improving the quality of work life raises anxieties, both expressed and latent, that should be thoroughly aired and dispelled.

First of all there is the problem of definition. What, after all, is the quality of working life (QWL)? Definitions abound, and the following are several of them for consideration:

> The essence of QWL is the opportunity for employees at all levels in an organization to have substantial influence over their work environment by participating in decisions related to their work, thereby enhancing their self-esteem and satisfaction from their work. [Greenberg and Glaser 1980, p. 19]

> Quality of work life is neither a single event nor a packaged program. It is a general label attached to

systematic programs that involve employees designing and carrying out improvements in their work conditions. The details vary widely. Sometimes QWL involves representative worker-management problem solving committees or task forces. Sometimes, it involves the creation of worker teams that might take on responsibility for quality control, for distribution of work assignments, and sometimes even for daily supervision.

QWL practices aim at extending growth, challenge, participation, responsibility and control to all employees. [Bell Telephone Magazine 1970, p. 15]

Improving the quality of work life is a people-oriented process dedicated to altering attitudes in the union-management relationship, developing mutual respect between management and labor and a cooperative effort toward achievement and mutually desirable and beneficial goals. Essential to its success is the meaningful involvement of workers in the decision-making process. Its primary thrust is to increase job satisfaction, self-worth, self-fulfillment at work and to enhance the dignity of the individual worker.

Improving the quality of work life is not a substitute for collective bargaining, but it can be complementary to collective bargaining subjects of mutual concern. It may cover a wide variety of non-controversial aspects of labor-management relations. It is not, and must not be, a management gimmick manipulated simply to increase production and profit.

It is essential to establish a relationship of co-equality between union and management in planning, designing and implementing the QWL program.

Fundamentally, improving the quality of work life is rooted in the democratic way of life. To the fullest extent possible, it means that the citizen as worker should be able to enjoy democratic values at the work place in the same sense that he enjoys democratic values as a citizen in a free society. [Bluestone, 1981]

Since QWL is a process derived largely from the unique circumstances existing in each individual situation, the definition will vary with the envisioned objectives. A fairly consistent thread runs through the various definitions, however, namely: the right of the employees to participate significantly in the decision-making process. This is as basic to the concept as it is foreign to the more familiar structure of work organization, and it therefore requires sincere, steadfast commitment on the part of both management and labor.

COMMITMENT TO THE QWL CONCEPT

A prerequisite to change in managerial behavior toward the employees is the commitment to the essential concept of QWL. It is not enough for management at all levels to be persuaded of the need and the justification for embarking on the QWL process. The union at its various levels of authority must likewise be convinced. While the cultural and societal changes described earlier provide motivation for managerial attitudinal change, principles of sound patterns of human behavior should impel it. In fact, however, it is the success of the QWL process where it currently exists that in the final analysis may be the more influential persuader. Concrete examples of vastly increased employee satisfaction through the QWL process and the resultant benefits to management, the workers, the union (and the community and consumers as well) serve to dispel doubts about the value of the QWL concept. In any event, firm commitment to the QWL process at the various levels of the management and the union hierarchies is a primary ingredient for the required initiative, its development, and its success.

COEQUAL STATUS

The constancy of the commitment is best assured within a climate in which both management and the union share coequal status responsibility in planning, designing, and implementing the QWL process. Without the cooperation of management, the union, no matter how deeply dedicated, will find it impossible to initiate, much less fully implement, the program. While management, on the other hand, might succeed in initially installing a QWL program without union cooperation, before long union opposition to such unilateral action will doom the program to ultimate failure. Moreover, a program that is designed and controlled solely by management, even with union acquiescence (but not union support) soon will lay itself open to abuse and exploitation by management itself, since there will be no countervailing force (the union) to protect the workers' interests and preserve the primary purpose of the QWL process: to enhance the dignity of the worker and provide the vehicle for worker self-fulfillment and self-satisfaction at work by assuring that the process remains primarily relevant to the needs of the workers.

SEPARATION OF QWL AND THE LABOR CONTRACT

One of the guidelines that the contracting parties accept as a matter of course when initiating the QWL process is that the negotiated labor contract provisions remain inviolate. Management should not contemplate that the mere agreement to undertake the QWL process through joint, cooperative endeavor means automatic change in the labor contract requirements. Maintaining a clear-cut separation between QWL and the negotiated labor contract is vitally important to both parties and to the workers. This is not to say the parties may not reach the conclusion that "bending" or even modifying certain negotiated contract provisions is desirable under given circumstances. It is up to the parties to the labor contract to reach such a decision, in which case, of course, they have the authority to act on their decision, subject to the usual ratification procedures.

BENEFITS OF QWL

By its very definition, the QWL process is designed for and on behalf of the worker. Its philosophic base, rooted in the principles of democ-

racy and participation, is people-oriented. From labor's point of view, therefore, the QWL process, properly effected, represents an extension of unionism's historic goals.

The benefits that workers and the union derive from the QWL process have also been manifested in other concrete ways—and are benefits of value to management as well.

Improved Product Quality

Workers know a great deal more about how to manage their jobs, and have greater concern for the quality of the product or service, than most managements are willing to give them credit for. If, like automatons, they are simply to be programmed and obey orders, they are deprived of the initiative to respond as problem solvers. As the Japanese system has proven to the chagrin of most industrialized nations, the floodgates of innovation and ingenuity, once opened to the workers, create near miracles of quality service— given the time, the opportunity, and the motivation. They recognize that good quality is tied inevitably to improved job security through assured sales.

It is well established that improved quality is a direct benefit derived from the QWL process— a benefit commonly desired by the workers, the union, the management, and, naturally, the consumer.

Reduced Absenteeism and Labor Turnover

The problem of unwarranted absenteeism is more often than not considered an issue solely of concern to management. Obviously, high unwarranted absentee rates are costly, jeopardize continuous high standards of quality excellence, and are disruptive of operations. For the workers who are present, absenteeism often means being moved from jobs that they find desirable to fill in on jobs with which they are not thoroughly familiar. They resent the reassignment and are critical of the union. Habitually absent workers are subject to disciplinary action, even discharge, creating grievance problems for the union representatives. An overall reduction in unwarranted absenteeism rates is desirable from the point of view of the workers and the union as well as management.

Successful QWL programs have demonstrated that increased job satisfaction results in a decline in such absenteeism rates—a mutually desirable objective.

Similarly, labor turnover, costly to management but also troublesome to the union, declines as the work place becomes more conducive to the fulfillment of employees' needs. Reduction in labor turnover makes for greater stability in the work force, which, in turn, makes for a more stable and effective union.

Reduction in Discharges, Disciplinary Layoffs, and Grievance Load

It is a truism that over time the QWL process results in a sharp reduction in the number of disciplinary actions assessed against employees and a notable decline in the number of written grievances. The change in managerial behavior and attitude appears to lengthen the managerial temper fuse; it causes management to seek out the causes of "employee discontent" rather than view only its results. The reasons for the reduction in the number of discharges and disciplinary layoffs may be inexplicable without in-depth research; nevertheless, it is a welcome fact.

The decline in the number of written grievances is attributable essentially to the fact that complaints at the work place are resolved more readily as they arise, through consultation and discussion between the union representative and floor supervision with the grievant. The process of change wrought by the parties' commitment to QWL influences the collective bargaining relationship. Issues that previously appeared hard core and controversial in nature become the targets of mutual problem solvers rather than problem creators—an altogether salutary development for all concerned.

Election of Union Officials

While it is not universally demonstrable, it is nevertheless a fact that, with few exceptions, union officials who are proponents of the QWL process and are actively involved in planning and implementing the program, are reelected to office. The acknowledged betterment in the quality of working life is the direct result of union effort as a coequal with management. The workers are quick to recognize and appreciate the union's role in bringing a better life into the work place. It is only natural, therefore, that at election time, they will vote for the incumbents who were prime movers in bringing it all to pass. The function of a union representative is to provide service to the constituents and advance their welfare. It is only natural that the constituents in turn support those union representatives who best fulfill that role in their behalf.

Reward System

Job satisfaction, enhanced dignity and self-realization, a feeling that one counts in the scheme of things, is for some reward enough. Financial reward or other types of reward systems may be the handmaiden to a successful QWL process. Profit sharing, gain sharing, paid time off, pay for knowledge, and so on, comprise some of the reward system approaches compatible with the QWL process—usually the subject of the customary collective bargaining procedures. Whatever may be negotiated between the parties will represent a mutually desirable and mutually agreeable pact, which both negotiating parties and the workers consider beneficial.

GUIDELINES

Among the guidelines that the parties might well consider adopting as they enter upon the cooperative process of QWL—over and above the separation of QWL from labor contract provisions and the coequal status position of the parties as noted earlier—are:

- The work pace should not be increased by reason of the QWL program. (Naturally, increased production due to technological change is another matter.)
- The program should be voluntary for all employees.
- The employee should experience genuinely that he is not simply the adjunct to the tool, but that his bent toward being creative, innovative, and inventive, plays a significant role in the production or service process.
- The employee should be assured that his participation in decision making will not erode his job security or that of his fellow workers.
- Job functions should be engineered to fit the employee; the current system is designed to make the employee fit the job on the theory that this is a more efficient production or service system and that, in any event, economic gain is the employee's only reason for working. This theory is, I believe, wrong on both counts.
- The employee should be assured the widest possible latitude of self-management, responsibility, and the opportunity for use of his "brain power." Gimmickry or manipulation of the employees must not be used.
- The changes in job content and function, the added responsibility and involvement in decision making should be accompanied by an appropriate reward system.
- The employees should be able to foresee opportunities for growth in their work and for promotion.
- The employees' role in the business should enable them to relate to the product being produced, or the services being rendered, and to its meaning in society; in a broader sense it should enable them as well to relate constructively to their role in society.

Achieving human dignity by bringing a meaningful measure of democratic values into the work place lies at the heart of the QWL process. And that, after all, is what unionism is all about. The marriage between unionism and its goals on the one hand and the QWL process on the other is a natural culmination of the historic march of labor toward a better life. Labor's stake in the success of the QWL process commands, therefore, that unions be in the forefront of advocacy; that, as has been so often true in the past, they become the initiators, the movers and doers in accelerating the process toward workers' participation in decision making and enjoying the better life.

NOTES

Bell Telephone Magazine 1970. "Quality of Work Life on the Bell System Drawing Board," edition 4.

Bluestone, Irving 1981. Unpublished paper distributed for classroom discussion to students in the Master of Arts in Industrial Relations program. Mich.: Wayne State University.

Greenberg, Paul D. and Edward Glaser 1980. *Some Issues in Joint Union-Management Quality of Worklife Improvement Efforts*. Kalamazoo, Mich.: W. E. Upjohn Institute for Employment Research.

Yankelovich, Daniel 1974. *The New Morality*. New York: McGraw-Hill.

The Circle Game

Mike Parker* and Dwight Hansen †

Every Wednesday, at a stamping plant in Dearborn, Michigan, twelve of the 120 workers and one of the five foremen interrupt what they are

From *The Progressive* (January 1983), pp. 32–35. Copyright © 1982, The Progressive, Inc. Reprinted by permission from *The Progressive,* Madison, WI 53703.
*Electrician and member of the United Auto Workers.
†Tool and die maker and member of the United Auto Workers.

doing and walk away from the assembly line where front sections for the Ford Escort are welded. For an hour, they brainstorm in a clean office lined with graphs and slogan-packed posters. "Circle 81," as this group calls itself, grapples with a single problem for several meetings. This time, it's how to keep the flanges on the front-end aprons from getting bent during production.

Each participant comes up with an idea to add to a list of possible solutions, and no suggestion is criticized or even discussed until the brainstorm has subsided. When the list has made the rounds, circle members rank the proposals according to handbook instructions the company has given the group's "facilitator." By consensus, members decide to have a chute realigned, so the aprons can slide smoothly off the line.

Circle 81 is pleased when, in this instance, the solution works out. One member is concerned about the worker who has had the job of hammering bent flanges back into shape, but the foreman offers reassurance: No jobs will be lost because of quality improvements. The Employee Involvement Circle, as it's known officially, puts another problem on its agenda and moves on.

In Flint, about fifty miles north, thirty-six female fashion models parade around in the latest styles while workers continue to turn out fifty-five cars an hour. A plant spokeswoman says Fashion Day would not have been possible at the Buick factory before General Motors brought in "quality-of-worklife" programs. But now, she says, "these people have become so trustworthy and so adept they can handle a show on the sideline. It doesn't take away from their work at all."

"It used to be like a concentration camp here when I first came six years ago," plant manager Lee Furse told the *Detroit Free Press*. "Now it's a fun place to work. For years we just hired the workers' hands. Now we treat them like people."

GM's quality-of-worklife (QWL) efforts and Ford's Employee Involvement Circles have counterparts at other companies, where they are variously known as Labor-Management Participation Teams or Quality Circles. Whatever they are called, the programs are part of a growing QWL movement—the centerpiece of the New Industrial Relations, the "non-adversarial relationship" heralded in some labor and business publications. QWL encompasses a vast range of schemes, from renamed employee suggestion systems to redrawn plant chain-of-command maps. Some programs concentrate on "hard" issues, such as product quality or productivity, while others focus on attitudes and factory relations. All bring workers and managers together to improve efficiency at the point of production.

Ten years ago, there was little interest in QWL except among a few academics, maverick business leaders, and unionists who drew their models from social democratic Scandinavia. In the last three years, however, QWL has swept through the nation's private and public sectors, thanks, in part, to support from most of organized labor. The United Auto Workers, the United Steelworkers, the Communication Workers of America, and several other AFL-CIO unions actively promote some form of QWL. Many labor leaders see QWL as a counterweight to contract concessions or as a demonstration of labor "statesmanship." Not surprisingly, then, it is the concession-wracked UAW that is blazing the QWL trail. GM and Ford have set up hundreds of circles and teams. GM has spent $1.6 million on QWL just at its plant in Tarrytown, New York.

Corporations have not been prompted to invest in QWL by some new-found concern for workers' needs, however. Big business has discovered that QWL is a convenient way to tighten control over the workforce. Nonetheless, union leaders are buying into the concept for their own reasons.

For many unionists, QWL is a job-security strategy. Workers at the Ford Rouge Glass Plant south of Detroit point to a recently completed construction project they helped salvage through

QWL. Management was about to scrap a planned improvement because outside bids were too high, but members of the employee involvement program said the job could be done with in-house labor. The work was finished on time and at about half the original projected cost, turning John Gutzman, president of the Maintenance and Construction unit of UAW Local 600, from a skeptic of QWL into a booster.

The construction project, Gutzman says, "is a good example of the positive benefits that can result when UAW members are given a voice in decision-making and when we all work together. The talent and potential of our membership is unlimited, and when this talent is tapped, we all benefit—as in the glass plant. The maintenance and construction unit members got a large amount of additional work which everyone enjoyed and really worked hard on. Management saved almost one-half of a million dollars and got a better quality job [and] the glass plant unit gained increased job security."

QWL can also be an inspiring personal experience for some workers. Carla, a custodial worker at a Detroit-area GM plant, describes an encounter with QWL-enlightened management as "the best thing that ever happened to me": "Imagine, I was sitting with the superintendent, and I'm just a janitor. He was asking *me* questions. We talked and we were equals. I really like it."

In fact, the promise of a new, personal relationship to one's work—of equality, respect, and dignity on the job—are QWL's strongest appeals to workers. But even when there is neither heightened personal fulfillment nor a big job-saving success story, QWL at least means a chance to get off the line for an hour to chat over coffee. And if only a fraction of the promises of QWL were to work out, it would be a giant step forward. Who could oppose the idea?

Not many have. One measure of QWL's popularity is that union leaders commonly invoke it at election time. According to *Fortune* magazine, "Leaders in quality-of-worklife plants find them-selves politically more popular than ever. To date [1981] according to UAW leaders, virtually every slate of the union's officers who campaigned by supporting an established quality-of-worklife effort has won." Even union dissidents are embracing QWL in surprising numbers, despite its emphasis on productivity and cooperation with management. Many QWL showcases involve locals with militant histories. Unionists with militant reputations are often selected to head QWL programs. Bob Evans coordinates QWL for Oldsmobile Local 652 in Lansing, Michigan, and Bob Roth, who had been fired five times for leading wildcat strikes, directs QWL for Buick Local 599 in Flint.

Its champions believe, for the most part, that QWL will significantly improve the lives of working people. Yet QWL eats away at the power of unions: The main point of QWL is to convince workers that their security and future are tied to the success of the company (or plant, or department) instead of to their union—or class. It pushes the message, *We* have to make *our* company profitable if we are to save our jobs.

Thus, UAW International Representative Al Hendricks told unionists in Ford Local 600 that *we* must make the company competitive with the Japanese in order to undercut GM and Chrysler—hardly the way to build trade union solidarity throughout the auto industry. Moreover, since the industry is set up so that divisions and individual plants bid on jobs from the parent company, QWL encourages UAW members at, say, the Ford Dearborn stamping plant to find a way to produce at lower cost than fellow unionists at the Ford Woodhaven stamping plant down the road. And jobs depend on such competition: The president of GM Buick Local 599, Al Christner, proudly explains how QWL enabled his division to underbid a GM Pontiac division, and GM Oldsmobile workers, long-time UAW activists, boast that their QWL program helped them win work from GM Buick.

The divisiveness does not stop there. Once workers are persuaded that job security depends on increasing *our* company's productivity, their attitudes change toward other workers in the plant. The older workers are now "slow," and employees who didn't mind "carrying" them in the past now see them as a drag on productivity. Production workers begin to bad-mouth "do-nothing" skilled workers. A Ford local president who supports QWL admits he has a problem with circle members who blame production snags on alcoholics and others with personal problems. Carla, the janitor and QWL enthusiast, acknowledges that custodial workers in her plant are capable of finishing their daily assignments in less than eight hours. "I don't want to give anything away and have sixty janitors mad," she says. "But I don't want to lie to these [management] people, if you are going to have trust and make changes." Carla says she feels "caught."

It may be that all of organized labor is caught in a QWL bind. While unions have historically defended workplaces from what bosses called "rationalization," when the word meant nothing more than speed-ups or job reductions, they now push that same old process in a new form. QWL paints productivity and competition as the paths to job security, and so anything that gets in the way is suspect, including union-negotiated work rules, "excessive" concern for the environment or workplace safety, and absenteeism.

Because it creates a competitive climate, QWL has turned out to be a favorite tool of union busters. The California Hospital Personnel Management Association conducts seminars on the use of QWL in the fight against unions. The Council on Union-Free Environment publishes a how-to pamphlet on starting "circle" programs and staving off unionization. And the National Association of Manufacturers estimates there are "roughly 32,000 quality circles in [South] Korea and 1,200 registered in Taiwan." To which the United Electrical Workers' *News* responded: "No better recommendation can be had for the enemies of trade union organization."

QWL is a sort of union version of Reaganomics: Help the company make more profits so that some of the wealth will trickle down in the form of more jobs. Indeed, UAW Vice President Donald Ephlin takes pleasure in noting the correlation between active QWL programs and local votes in favor of the Ford concessions contract— a pattern that also showed up in the GM contract vote. The case for concessions advanced by both the UAW leadership and the automakers echoes their endorsement of QWL; concessions, like QWL-induced efficiency, will save jobs in the face of the Japanese onslaught and stiffer domestic competition.

But QWL "victories" have not offset contract concessions. At the Ford Rouge plant, site of the successful Employee Involvement construction project, hourly employment is down more than 50 per cent in three years while Ford looks overseas for more parts. What's more, the concessions Ford is demanding are actually quality-of-worklife takebacks. The company is pressing to place more restrictions on workers' rights to change jobs; trying to change line rules in the name of efficiency; combining job classifications, and reducing the number of skilled jobs in the process. A union activist who supports QWL says Ford has become hard-nosed over grievances and is "refusing to move, particularly on terminations, because they have all the replacements they want on the layoff list." Management's "cooperative spirit" at the Rouge plant surfaces only when it serves to increase productivity, cut costs, or clamp down on absenteeism.

QWL is, in a sense, providing the ideological grease for concessions by sowing competitiveness. Ford is homing in on individual plants— even though contracts have long been signed— and threatening to ship work to other Ford factories if workers do not approve give-backs. (GM is pursuing the same strategy.) Among the reasons Local 1250 of the Cleveland engine plant refused to be taken for a ride was that Ford would not guarantee a new engine job in return for concessions. The company then assigned the work to its plant in Lima, Ohio, which had agreed to concessions. The UAW International stood by and watched.

The UAW response to the companies' divide-and-conquer strategy has, in fact, been to campaign for QWL programs. In throwing in its lot with QWL, the union tells workers to identify with the problems of plant management. And, far from breaking new ground, union backing for the concept reinforces a narrow, purely contractual vision of trade unionism engendered during the prosperity of the 1950s and 1960s. Consider how AFL-CIO Secretary-Treasurer Thomas Donahue reconciles QWL to trade unionism:

"The adversarial role, appropriate to the conflict of collective bargaining, ought to be limited to the period of negotiation. And during the lifetime of a contract so arrived at, it ought to be replaced by a period of cooperation, aimed at maximizing the potential success of the joint enterprise, i.e., the company's business or production."

Donahue's perspective raises an obvious question: Why don't unions just step aside between contracts and let managers manage? From the viewpoint of corporations, unions do serve a useful purpose from contract to contract—as conduits for workforce discipline and as efficient consolidators of such workplace discontent as is risked in a time of near-record unemployment. And if unionism is being turned into a management tool, QWL may be the tool's handle.

Can organized labor redeem QWL? Robert Cole, a sociologist at the University of Michigan, has spelled out a common union approach. Cole warns union leaders to make sure that "circles do not take up matters which fall under collective bargaining agreements." But he continues, "Now, you can tell this to the circle members and management and even get it in writing. But in some companies the local union found it had to insist on a union committee man being present at every meeting to be sure that this principle was maintained at least for the first several months before the ground rules were clear."

The message conveyed to the rank and file by having a union official assume the watchdog role is that the union itself is threatened, and scrambling to protect its position. Yet almost anything that affects working conditions at the plant level can be won in collective bargaining, either directly at contract time or in the continuing struggle to interpret the contract and set useful precedents. Union collaboration in setting up the circles therefore makes concrete the notion that a union defends the worker only at contract time. The ideology of QWL places management inside the workers' concept of "we" and simultaneously positions the union as "them." QWL success stories hint at union impotence: Why should it take a circle meeting to get splash shields installed so machine operators don't get sprayed with coolant?

What makes QWL different from yesterday's management fads is that QWL gives bosses a way around the union to the shop floor. This allows them to draw off those workers who are dissatisfied with their jobs but who have leadership skills and self-confidence—that is, potential union leaders. Quality circles become a Junior Achievement-style management training ground where people learn to think and act like managers. The more advanced QWL programs are explicitly organized so that, in the words of the former GM director of organizational development, "each team is like a small business."

The teams play in what one local union leader described as "a company ball game, with company umpires, on company turf."

The gloss of QWL appears to wear thin after a year or two. Some of the QWL success stories of a few years ago, such as Rushton Mine and Harmon Industries, have ended in bitterness on all sides. In Japan, some managers worry that quality circle activities are becoming ritualized and counterproductive. An expanding economy can paper over a lot of problems, but in bad times discussions cannot sustain enthusiasm. Sooner or later, QWL programs have to come up against the reality of capitalist industrial relations: Managers run the company, and their bottom line is profits; labor is a major production cost, and management's job is to cut it.

Some QWL consultants recognize that the attraction fades, and therefore have plans to expand and improve the process. (One cynical observer calls this "a bigger-participation fix.") Next steps include "gains sharing"—financial incentives for the suggestions generated by circles—and plant redesign. GM is experimenting with "pay-for-knowledge" systems and "self-managing" departments.

But increased participation is not the same thing as power. It is not even a step toward power when the participation undermines the only real power workers still have—the power to act collectively. Managers assume QWL programs will lead workers to cooperate in their own undoing because they are allowed to help in choosing the means. Business leaders are also betting that QWL will not raise expectations about the right to respect and dignity on the job, or if it does, that workers will not turn their anger and disappointment into anything more than cynicism.

Whether worker discontent is channeled into building a stronger union depends, in large measure, on whether the union has discredited itself during the QWL experience. An appropriate union response to QWL has to be determined by the specific situation; where a union has a solid reputation as an active fighter it can simply refuse to take part. The in-plant leaders of UAW Local 595 in Linden, New Jersey, turned their back on QWL and explained the decision with an educational campaign. Some locals of the International Association of Machinists (IAM) and the United Electrical Workers (UE) have entered into negotiations over QWL; their demands for the release of information on hazardous chemicals, investment, and production plans exposed the companies' hidden QWL agendas. One UE local ended a QWL program by publicizing the antiunion record of the company's QWL consult-

ant. The national leaders of both the IAM and the UE are against QWL. Says the IAM newspaper, "The simple reason is that we don't like cooperating on the shop floor while we're being mugged by management at the plant gate."

But these are exceptions. The argument that QWL will weaken unions has not seemed compelling to workers who are already alienated from their union; to them, QWL promises some relief. Union militants often face QWL programs imposed from above by their international leadership or already entered upon by past union officers. In these situations, direct opposition to QWL could easily be misunderstood and thus ineffective. On the other hand, the grudging support some unions have given QWL has reinforced the image of a union bureaucracy threatened by new approaches to shop-floor life.

One of the lessons of labor history is that skillful organizers find ways to bend to union purposes all manner of employer-initiated programs. Indeed, even pure company unions have been transformed into real ones in some industries. If a similar approach is to be tried on QWL, it will take aggressive organizing.

First, unions must try to convince workers in QWL circles to think of themselves as union representatives. Where election of representatives to circles is possible, it helps employees feel accountable to their fellow workers.

In one case, circle members were elected because there were more volunteers than management wanted. "People took it seriously," said Susan Greene, a circle participant at a Bell Telephone garage in Chicago. "We won some things at first, including a fan in the club room and a bike rack....But as time went on, people who were not on the circle began to get upset with our lack of progress and put pressure on us." When Bell tried to reduce overtime pay, the circle convened a meeting of all garage workers; they decided that the best protest would be a mass resignation. The experience demonstrated that a circle can be bent toward building worker solidarity.

Where elections are not possible because QWL programs are already in place, unions can still make workers "circle reps," and perhaps assign them union duties such as handling the first stages of grievance procedures. A model for this once existed in the auto industry, when "working stewards" (often called "blue button" or "line" stewards) tied the union to its grass-roots members.

Second, unions must develop plans to cope with technological advances and train circle representatives to protect workers from job cutbacks. QWL participants should be taught to see increased productivity in terms of its effect on the quantity and quality of work. The union can counter the tendency, inherent in QWL, for workers to identify with corporate management; cross-departmental and even cross-company meetings of unionized circle members can strengthen workers' identification with the union—and with each other.

Finally, unions should work to change the accepted jurisdiction of QWL circles, insisting, as the IAM does, that "every aspect of the employer-employee relationship is subject to negotiation through collective bargaining." A union that decides to buy into QWL would do well to make circles the vehicle for greater rank-and-file participation in the collective bargaining process.

Of course, none of these steps can be taken unless the unions are rebuilt to wage ideological war. Unions must not only be able to challenge this or that company's strategy; they must instill a collective union consciousness in the ranks. In short, unions must project a political program that offers workers a way out of their dead-end dependency on corporate profits as the source of job security.

The Myth of Job Enrichment

Mitchell Fein*

Practically all writing that deals with worker boredom and frustration starts with the idea that the nature of work in industry and offices degrades the human spirit, is antithetical to workers' needs and damages their mental health, and that the redesign of work is socially desirable and beneficial to workers. Curiously, however, this view is not supported by workers or their unions. If workers faced the dire consequences of deprivation projected by the behaviorists, they should be conscious of the need to redesign and enrich their jobs. (The term "behaviorist" is used in this article to include psychologists, social scientists, and others who favor the redesign of work and job enrichment as a way to enhance the quality of working life. Many behaviorists, in fact, may not hold these views. Still, there is a sharp difference of opinion between what workers say they want and what behaviorists say workers want.)

WHO SPEAKS FOR WORKERS?

Workers' feelings about their work and what goes on at the workplace are expressed quite freely by workers themselves and their spokesmen in the unions. Since no union has yet raised the issue of work boredom and the redesign of jobs, is it not reasonable to assume that the question is not important to workers? Workers are not bashful in their demands, and worker represen-

This article first appeared in the *The Humanist* issue of September/October 1973 and is reprinted by permission.

*Formerly in the Department of Industrial Engineering, New York University.

tatives are quite vocal in championing workers' needs. One might argue that workers do not comprehend the harm that is done to them by their work and that they must be shown that many of their problems and troubles really stem from the nature of their jobs. But that assumes that workers are naive or stupid, which is not the case.

The judgments of those advocating job changes derive from people whom Abraham Maslow would characterize as "superior people (called self-actualizers) who are also superior perceivers, not only of facts but of values,...their ultimate values [are then used] as possibly the ultimate values for the whole species."[1] These advocates of change maintain that healthy progress for people is toward self-fulfillment through work, and they see most jobs as dull, repetitive, seemingly meaningless tasks, offering little challenge or autonomy. They view the nature of work as the main deterrent to more fulfilling lives for the workers and the redesign of jobs as the keystone of their plans for accomplishing the desired changes.

Paul Kurtz has stated: "Humanists today attack all those social forces which seek to destroy man: they deplore the dehumanization and alienation of man within the industrial and technological society.... and the failure of modern man to achieve the full measure of his potential excellence. The problem for the humanist is to create the conditions that would emancipate man from oppressive and corruptive social organization, and from the denigration and perversion of his human talents..."[2] Humanists' goals and behaviorists' objectives appear similar. Both accept Maslow's self-actualization concepts as the preferred route to fulfillment. But by what divine right does one group assume that its values are superior to others and should be accepted as normal? Both the selection of goals and attitudes toward work are uniquely personal. The judges of human values have no moral right to press their normative concepts on others as preferable.

SATISFACTION AND ACHIEVEMENT

The fundamental question is whether or not the nature of work prevents people from achieving the full measure of their potential. When behaviorists view people at work, they see two main groups: those who are satisfied and those who are not. They examine the satisfied and like what they see. These are eager, energetic people, who are generally enthusiastic about their jobs and life in general. The behaviorists hold them up as ideal and prepare to convert the dissatisfied.

In contrasting the satisfied workers with the dissatisfied ones, behaviorists see the nature of the work performed as the main difference. So they propose to change the work of the dissatisfied to more closely resemble that performed by the satisfied. But there is a large "if" in this approach: What if the nature of the work is not the reason for the satisfaction?

It could very well be that the satisfied have more drive, which creates greater material wants and higher goals, which in turn motivates them to make more effective efforts in the workplace and to bid for more highly skilled jobs, and so on. Restructuring the work and creating new opportunities may make some people enthusiastic, but to what extent is the nature of the work the determinant of a person's drive?

There are no data that definitively show that restructuring and enriching jobs will increase the will to work or give workers greater satisfaction. Similarly, I have not seen any research data that show that a person with drive is deterred from reaching his potential by the nature of the work.

I believe that ethical considerations alone should keep behaviorists from setting up their values as the ideals for society. In addition, I will attempt to demonstrate that the behaviorists' views on redesigning jobs are misguided; they do not understand the work process in plants, and they misjudge workers' attitudes toward their jobs.

WORKERS' ATTITUDES TOWARD THEIR WORK

A 1972 Gallup Poll found that 80 to 90 percent of American workers are satisfied with their jobs. A 1973 poll by Thomas C. Sorenson found that from 82 to 91 percent of blue- and white-collar workers like their work. He asked, "If there were one thing you could change about your job, what would it be?" He found that "Astonishingly, very few mentioned making their jobs 'less boring' or 'more interesting.'"[3]

Behaviorists and humanists find it difficult to understand how workers can possibly say they like their work when it appears so barren to intellectuals. This view was recently expressed by the behavioral scientist David Sirota, after making a study in a garment plant. He was surprised to find that most sewing-machine operators found their work interesting. Since the work appeared highly repetitive to him, he had expected that they would say that they were bored and that their talents were not fully utilized. These workers' views are supported in a study by Emanuel Weintraub of 2,535 female sewing-machine operators in seventeen plants from Massachusetts to Texas. He found that "most of the operators like the nature of their work."[4] What the behaviorists find so difficult to comprehend is really quite simply explained: Workers have similar attitudes toward their work because *they are not a cross-section of the population, but rather a select group.*

There is greater choice in the selection of jobs by workers than is supposed. The selection process in factories and offices goes on without conscious direction by either workers or management. The data for white- and blue-collar jobs show that there is tremendous turnover in the initial employment period but that the turnover drops sharply with time on the job. What occurs is that a worker comes onto a new job, tries it out for several days or weeks, and decides whether or not the work suits his needs and desires. Impressions about a job are a composite of many factors: pay, proximity to home, nature of work, working conditions, attitude of supervision, congeniality of fellow workers, past employment history of the company, job security, physical demands, possibilities for advancement, and many others. Working conditions may be bad, but if the pay and job security are high, the job may be tolerable. To a married woman, the pay may be low, but if the job is close to home and working conditions are good, it may be desirable. There are numerous combinations of factors that influence a worker's disposition to stay on the job or not.

There is a dual screening process that sifts out many of those who will be dissatisfied with the work. The process operates as follows: The worker in the first instance decides whether or not to stay on the job; management then has the opportunity to determine whether or not to keep him beyond the trial period. The combination of the worker's choice to remain and management's decision regarding the worker's acceptability screens out many workers who might find the job unsatisfying.

Some workers find highly repetitive work in factories intolerable, so they become truck drivers, where they can be out on the road with no supervisor on their back all day. Others prefer to work in gas stations, warehouses, retail stores, and other such places. Increasingly workers are taking white-collar jobs that in many ways are similar to repetitive factory jobs but which have cleaner physical surroundings and better working conditions. In times of high unemployment, workers stay in safe jobs for continuity of income; but, as the job market improves, the rate of turnover increases and selection of jobs resumes.

There would undoubtedly be much greater dissatisfaction among workers if they were not free to make changes and selections in the work they do. Some prefer to remain in highly repetitive, low-skilled work even when they have an opportunity to advance to more highly skilled jobs through job bidding. A minority of workers strive to move into the more skilled jobs, such as machinists, maintenance mechanics, setup men, group leaders, and utility men, where work is discretionary and the workers have considerable autonomy in the tasks they perform.

The continued evaluation of workers by management and the mobility available to workers in the job market refine the selection process. A year or two after entering a plant, most workers are on jobs or job progressions that suit them or which they find tolerable.

However, the work force in the plant is not homogeneous. There are two main groups, the achievers and the nonachievers. Their attitudes toward work and their goals are vastly different. A minority of the work force, which I find to be 15 percent, have a drive for achievement and identify with their work. These workers' attitudes match the ideal projected by behaviorists. They dislike repetitive work and escape from it by moving into more skilled jobs, which have the autonomy and interest they look for in their work. Only a minority of jobs in industry and offices are in the skilled category, and fortunately only a minority of workers aspire to these jobs. About 85 percent of workers do not identify with their work, do not prefer more complicated and restructured jobs, and simply work in order to eat. Yet they, too, like their work and find it interesting.[5]

For different reasons, both groups of workers find their work interesting and satisfying. The work of the 85 percent who are nonachievers is interesting to them though boring to the other 15 percent. And the 15 percent who are achievers find their work interesting, though it is not sufficiently appealing for the majority to covet it. The selection process does amazingly well in matching workers and jobs.

What blinds behaviorists to this process is their belief that the achievement drive is an intrinsic part of human nature, that fulfillment at work is essential to sound mental health, and that, given the opportunity, workers would choose to become more involved in their work and take on larger and more complicated tasks.

Once behaviorists take this view, they cannot understand what really happens on the plant floor or why workers do one thing rather than another.

WHY DO BEHAVIORISTS CLAIM TO SPEAK FOR WORKERS?

Behaviorists' insistence that they know more about what workers want than workers themselves is largely based on a number of job-enrichment case histories and studies of workers over the past decade. It is claimed that these studies show that workers really want job enrichment and benefit from it. But when these studies are examined closely, four things are found. (1) What actually occurred was quite different from what was reported by the behaviorists. (2) Most of the studies were conducted with hand-picked employees, usually working in areas or plants isolated from the main operation, and they do not reflect a cross-section of the working population. Practically all are in nonunion plants. (3) Only a handful of job-enrichment cases have been reported in the past ten years, despite the behaviorists' claims of gains for employees and management obtained through job changes. (4) In all instances, the experiments were initiated by management, never by workers or unions.

The *Survey of Working Conditions,* conducted for the United States Department of Labor by the Survey Research Center of the University of Michigan, contained serious errors.[6] The General Foods-Topeka case reported by Richard E. Walton[7] omits important information that shows that the sixty-three workers for this plant were handpicked from seven hundred applicants. Texas Instruments, which conducted the longest and broadest experiments, only attracted 10 percent of its employees to the program.[8] The Texas Instruments cleaning-employees case, as well as others, was grossly misreported in HEW's *Work in America.*

There are no job-enrichment successes that bear out the predictions of the behaviorists, because the vast majority of workers reject the concept. A small proportion of workers who desire job changes are prevented from participating by the social climate in the plant. They find involvement by moving into skilled jobs. Perhaps behaviorists do not recognize the moral issues raised by their proposals to redesign work—for example: intrusion upon a person's right to personal decisions; exploitation of workers' job satisfaction for company gains; distortion of the truth.

The boundless wisdom of this country's founders in separating religion from government and public practices has been revealed in countless ways. But along comes a new faith that proclaims that people should derive satisfaction from their work. When up to 90 percent of workers are reported to be satisfied with their work, the behaviorists say that workers do not really know what satisfaction is and that they will lead them to a superior kind. This sounds oddly like the proselytizing of a missionary. If behaviorists called for making enriched work available for those who want it, I would support them because I believe a minority of workers do want it. But I oppose foisting these practices on workers who do not call for it. In any case, I believe the minority has all the enrichment they want.

Exploiting workers' job satisfaction for management's gain can backfire dangerously. Workers expect management to develop new approaches and production processes to increase productivity; they are prepared for continuous pressure for more output. But when these changes are designed primarily to create a more receptive worker attitude toward greater productivity, they may see that they have been "had." If management's gains are real, while workers' benefits are only in their minds, who has really benefited? The behaviorists now say that workers should also share in productivity gains. But these statements have come late and are couched in such vague terms as to be meaningless.

When a supposedly good thing must be put into fancy wrappings to enhance it, something is amiss. Why must the job-enrichment cases be distorted to make the final results appealing? Why must behaviorists use phrases such as "work humanization" to describe their proposals, as though work were now inhuman? Workers understand the meaning of money, job security, health benefits, and retirement without fancy explanations. If the enrichment and redesign of work is such a good thing, why is it rejected by those who would benefit from it? The so-called new industrial democracy is not really democracy but a new autocracy of "we know better than you what's good for you."

NOTES

1. Abraham Maslow, *The Farther Reaches of Human Nature* (New York: Viking, 1971), p. 10.
2. Paul Kurtz, "What Is Humanism?" in *Moral Problems in Contemporary Society: Essays in Humanistic Ethics,* ed. P. Kurtz (Buffalo: Prometheus Books, 1973), p. 11.
3. Thomas C. Sorenson, "Do Americans Like Their Jobs?" *Parade,* June 3, 1973.
4. Emanuel Weintraub, "Has Job Enrichment Been Oversold?" an address to the 25th annual convention of the American Institute of Industrial Engineers, May 1973, *Technical Papers,* p. 349.
5. A more complete discussion and supporting data for the 15/85 worker composition is contained in M. Fein's "Motivation for Work," in *Handbook of Work Organization and Society,* ed. Robert Dubin (Skokie, Ill.: Rand-McNally, 1973).
6. *Survey of Working Conditions* (Washington, D.C.: U.S. Dept. of Labor, 1971). These errors were disclosed in my analysis in "The Real Needs and Goals of Blue Collar Workers," *The Conference Board Record,* Feb. 1973.
7. Richard E. Walton, "How To Counter Alienation in the Plant," *Harvard Business Review,* Nov.–Dec. 1972, pp. 70–81.
8. Fein, "Motivation for Work."

Should Unions Participate in Quality of Working Life Activities?

Edward Cohen-Rosenthal*

Who would be against participating in a quality of working life effort? After all, being for a program aimed at improving the workplace is like supporting motherhood and apple pie. Yet when one searches for actual activity, the review does not reveal that quality of working life programs are the norm among companies and governments in the United States and Canada. The same is true among unions. There are a number of reasons for the scarcity of actual "quality of working life" or QWL programs. This is especially true when we define the topic to mean intentionally designed efforts to bring about increased labor-management cooperation to jointly solve the problem of improving organizational performance and employee satisfaction.

This article examines the issues of why organizations do or do not participate in quality of working life improvement programs. In exploring this topic, the perspective of the trade union is highlighted. At the outset, two caveats should be laid bare. First, though supportive, I do not believe that QWL programs are for everyone. There may be perfectly legitimate practical or philosophical reasons for non-participation. Secondly, I recognize that most workplaces do make some attempts to improve the quality of working life in one way or another. To focus on the more comprehensive and intentional efforts does not deny either the existence of alternative strategies or more isolated or informal efforts. Nor does it contest that other approaches may also have a positive impact.

Excerpted from "Should Unions Participate in Quality of Working Life Activities?", *Quality of Working Life: The Canadian Scene,* vol. 3, no. 4 (January 1980). Copyright © by Edward Cohen-Rosenthal. Reprinted by permission of the author.

*President, ECR Associates, and assistant to the president for educational programs, Bricklayers International Union.

WAYS TO THINK ABOUT POSSIBLE PARTICIPATION

The Theory of Competing Interests

Under our economic system, management has a responsibility to represent the interests of capital. The stockholders demand it. The management of a company is accountable for obtaining the best possible return on investment and managing the company in a manner which would guarantee it. If they did not, investors would put their money elsewhere and the company would go bankrupt. Unions are there to represent the interests of labor. They are the safeguard of the rights of workers in a workplace or company. Unions provide a collective voice for the demands and concerns of workers both for a fair share of the revenues of the company and for fair treatment at work. The workers demand it. Recognizing that management wants to get the most for its stockholders and labor for the employees, we have a classic presentation of the interests of labor pitted against the interests of capital. Many labor and management people alike are reluctant to blur the distinctions between the two roles.

Yet, the facts of the matter are that the two interests are not distinct but are interdependent. If the company goes bottom up then the workers have nothing. If the workers do not produce the products then the shareholders cannot obtain a return on their investment. Those involved with quality of working life look for the interdependencies as the grounds for activity while maintaining that there may be fundamental differences in orientation between the two parties.

Sometimes we make too much out of the adversarial nature of collective bargaining. Too often, the image is of two gunfighters squaring off against each other in a dusty Western town. In truth, collective bargaining is a method of conflict resolution. The aim is to reach a reasonable compromise. There are a set of rules and possible sanctions which each side can use. But it is their interdependence and need for compromise which compels them to come together and helps them come to an agreement.

Zero Sum Power Game

The power theory of why people balk at quality of working life programs is relatively simple. People who hold this view believe that there is only so much "power" in a situation. Therefore, the more one side has, the less the other side must have. Curiously, this belief tends to work in two directions. On the one hand, management is reluctant to involve the union for fear of enhancing its influence—and consequently diminishing management's authority. Yet at the same time, many unions are concerned because they do not want to allow more influence over the workers by management—and therefore weaken the union role. There is no way to buy out of this dilemma as long as power and authority are viewed as a struggle over a fixed power configuration. Yet the Maginot line view of industrial relations often is an imaginary view of the nature and possibilities of power and authority in the workplace.

The goal in the workplace in terms of power is the same as it is with any other power source. It is to provide the energy to make something happen. The power in the workplace can be employed to work together or it can be expended in fighting one another. Authority can be the kind associated with fear or it can be associated with positive attachment to the mutual goals of the union and the company. The aim in a QWL project is to create more power and greater authority by directing energies in a mutually beneficial manner. Often it is the workplaces with the greatest fights over turf power where QWL can have the greatest success by rechanneling the antagonistic energy into constructive activity.

Industrial Democracy

Since Sidney and Beatrice Webb at the turn of the century, industrial democracy has been a guiding phrase for trade unionists. There are many shapes to the call for greater industrial democracy. Collective bargaining has been correctly seen as a major step forward in the development of industrial democracy. Others have also employed the term in promoting equal employment opportunity. Co-determination is viewed as another avenue. All of the forms seek to broaden the franchise and improve the representation of workers. When Irving Bluestone of the United Automobile Workers discusses QWL, it is as much in terms of democratic rights as in any other manner. European trade unionists have used industrial democracy as a rallying cry for greater trade union and worker power in making decisions within corporations. Both union leaders and some managers have been attracted to new workplace change activities through a commitment to the idea of participation. They seek a new order of economic justice. An industrial democrat doesn't need justifications of productivity improvements or employee satisfaction. It's the moral justification which counts. Yet for the very same reasons, there are those who refuse to become involved with the slightest activity for fear that it will lead to ever increasing demands for industrial democracy and threaten the current power structure.

RISKS AND BENEFITS OF UNION PARTICIPATION IN QWL PROGRAMS

The following discussion of benefits and risks have been developed over the past few years as I have talked with and observed trade unionists and managers both considering and undertaking programs. To be fair, let's look at the possible pitfalls before assessing possible benefits.

Risks

There are a whole series of potentially negative problems which surround the issue of the union's role. My basic premise is that the union must maintain its clear identity as the representative of the workers. If this isn't clear, then problems are compounded. If the union becomes an apologist for management decisions or simply a prod for productivity (unfortunately, this has happened in some cases even without QWL), then it loses its authority as the workers' representative. This diminishes their effectiveness as a union and paradoxically makes them less useful to management. Involvement in quality of working life activities ought to be no preamble to softness in negotiations over traditional collective bargaining matters such as wages and benefits. Though an impact of QWL may be to increase the size of the pie available for negotiation, it rarely is the forum for the hard fights over who is to get what from whom. If the union allows communication to go directly to the membership without the union's involvement and acknowledgement of their role, then there is a danger of weakening union allegiance within the workforce. In almost all cases, employees like the new programs and if the union is perceived as an ogre or not heard from, then membership estrangement can occur. All of these matters have to do with maintaining an adequate perception of the union as the workers' voice.

A union needs to determine, before going into a program, whether the company is doing it for the legitimate purpose of improving the operation and morale at the worksite or for union busting. In a few cases, companies have instituted programs in their unionized plants and then transported their ideas to their non-union facilities as a way to contain union growth. However, more often than not, in developing QWL programs companies which have many unionized sections have ignored the unionized parts in favor of non-union facilities or new plants. This is probably the most insidious form of union busting since it provides the benefits of QWL to non-union and not to union employees. The lesson for a union is that you can get hurt by not doing it as much as by doing it.

Some unionists are concerned about the diverse nature of the treatment of employees in QWL programs thereby contradicting work rules developed in the union contract. There may be a long history of developing uniform rules to combat capriciousness in treatment and/or to encourage solidarity among workers in an industry. The issue of flexibility vs. protection is a difficult one. Some joint projects have sidestepped this issue by finding other areas of more common ground to attack.

A look at the record of the failures of union-management projects points out that the greatest problem is not the lack of sufficient results. It has to do with internal union politics. In some unions with powerful minority caucuses and fractured support, even the best program could provide ammunition for internal political opposition. Several projects I have run across in mining and woodworking were voted out in hastily called meetings packed with opponents.

There are other pitfalls to watch out for including possible violations of the contract, job loss due to increased productivity, speedup, arbitrary changes in job classifications and responsibilities without proper pay adjustments and loss of comparability in an industry. Another difficult question surrounds the potential liability of the union for the decisions it jointly entered into with management.

Benefits

Clearly there are many things that can go wrong with a quality of working life effort. If simple machines can go on the blink, then how many more possibilities are there for problems in complicated relationships, testing out new ground?

Each of the items mentioned above have remedies. Yet an honest appraisal would say that in certain situations a QWL initiative may not be possible. With proper and sustained attention, things can turn out quite well with many benefits to the company and the union. Here we concentrate on the positive impact on the union.

Given that the union is able to fend off all of the possible difficulties, especially the internal politics, then there are many benefits for the union. Some of these derive from the process directly through increased access to information and pre-notification of changes in work arrangements or machinery. Hopefully, the additional input can help avoid management errors or decisions which would have a negative impact on the membership.

Some of the other benefits come from increased representation of membership concerns. In almost all programs, grievances have gone down—sometimes dramatically. Those grievances which were filed were generally handled faster and at a lower step. This represents a substantial savings in time and money for both the union and the management especially in avoiding arbitration and labor board cases. The membership finds that their concerns are being resolved much more quickly. The grievances which disappear first are the petty grievances caused by poor communication and lack of respect. Another measure of member interest is attendance at union meetings. At present, most union meetings are chronically under-attended. In a number of cases, attendance at union meetings has gone up when a QWL project has been instituted.

Of course, there are a variety of other ways that a successful program better assists the membership. Their work satisfaction may increase. The union may be helping to address a broader range of personal concerns which extend beyond the economic. Workers tend to learn more under participative programs and health and safety is often improved. Stress caused by poor supervision and unnecessary ropes to jump may be alleviated. Better communication with fellow workers may result. The impact on stress and working conditions applies to union leaders as well as rank-and-file.

The increased visibility of the union in a joint project helps its image both internally and externally. The membership sees the union taking a lead on a variety of non-economic issues which affects them. The union is advocating another dimension of human dignity in addition to compensation justice. Often employees organize into a union because of the lack of respect and fair treatment they may receive. Too often, the questions of human dignity get sidetracked after an election is won. This kind of program fulfills the promises made in organizing. A cooperative spirit aimed at increased customer service and quality can also win applause in the industry and the public.

In a political organization like a union, elections are the true test of success. In the General Motors plants with joint QWL programs, every local UAW administration which stood for re-election won. This may be in part due to increased representation and it may also reflect some of the new skills of listening, problem solving and cooperation learned in the project. To my knowledge, nobody has lost an election solely because of QWL.

A final set of benefits has to do with the broad impacts of QWL programs. By helping improve the performance of the company, several benefits may be derived. There may be more money which could go for higher wages and benefits, or for modernization, expansion or health and safety improvement among other possibilities. Increasing the pool of money does not have to be done through the loss of jobs but rather the expansion of the market and cutting non-personnel costs. The improved condition of the company may result in saving jobs which may have been lost from falling into an uncompetitive position. In some cases, a QWL project has resulted in more jobs than before.

In the final analysis, real situations involve varying degrees of the benefits and the headaches. What will be the exact configuration in a local setting has to do with the conditions going in and the energy and imagination in the implementation.

CONCLUSION

The answer to the question of whether or not unions should participate in QWL programs is a definite maybe. Each union needs to weigh for itself its own situation. It needs to determine whether cooperation is consistent with the needs and goals of the membership and the values of the union. The situation surrounding the initiative needs to be examined and considered carefully to determine the sincerity of management and the possibilities of success. Internal union political situations need to be judged and accommodated. The potential benefits for the union, the membership, the company and the public need to be measured against the probable pitfalls. Sometimes the issue is not whether to respond to the initiatives of management but whether the union should take the issue up first. In this case, the motivation may be an ideological commitment to the spread of industrial democracy or a concern that the continued mismanagement of the company will seriously jeopardize the membership. A blind and naive adoption of quality of working life programs is ill advised. The answer to the initial question of whether one should be in favor of quality of working life improvements is of course yes. But the next questions are how, by whom and at what cost. Many roads and strategies can be employed in seeking a common goal of an effective, healthy and dignifying workplace.

QUESTIONS FOR DISCUSSION

1. How might an adversarial relationship between workers and employers protect workers? How might cooperation with management work against the interests of labor?
2. In what ways are the interests of workers and management interdependent? How might cooperation between workers and management benefit both?

CHAPTER 10

Hiring Practices: Preferential Hiring, Reverse Discrimination, and Comparable Worth

READINGS FOR CHAPTER TEN

William Bradford Reynolds
Equal Opportunity, Not Equal Results
372

Nancy Kubasek and Andrea M. Giampetro
Moving Forward on Reverse Discrimination
376

Laura M. Purdy
In Defense of Hiring Apparently Less Qualified Women
381

Gerald W. McEntee
Comparable Worth: A Matter of Simple Justice
385

Phyllis Schlafly
Comparable Worth: Unfair to Men and Women
388

Equal Opportunity, Not Equal Results

William Bradford Reynolds*

No one disputes that "affirmative action" is a subject of vital significance for our society. The character of our country is determined in large measure by the manner in which we treat our individual citizens—whether we treat them fairly or unfairly, whether we ensure equal opportunity to all individuals or guarantee equal results to selected groups. As the Assistant Attorney General, I am faced daily with what seem to have emerged on the civil rights horizon as the two predominant competing values that drive the debate on this issue—that is, the value of equal opportunity and the value of equal results—and I have devoted a great deal of time and attention to the very different meanings they lend to the phrase "affirmative action."

Typically—to the understandable confusion of almost everyone—"affirmative action" is the term used to refer to both of these contrasting values. There is, however, a world of difference between "affirmative action" as a measure for ensuring equality of opportunity and "affirmative action" as a tool for achieving equality of results.

In the former instance, affirmative steps are taken so that all individuals (whatever their race, color, sex, or national origin) will be given the chance to compete with all others on equal terms; each is to be given his or her place at the starting line without advantage or disadvantage. In the latter, by contrast, the promise of affirmative ac-

tion is that those who participate will arrive at the finish in prearranged places—places allocated by race or sex.

I have expressed on a number of occasions my conviction that the promise of equal results is a false one. We can never assure equal results in a world in which individuals differ greatly in motivation and ability; nor, in my view, is such a promise either morally or constitutionally acceptable. This was, in fact, well understood at the time that the concept of "affirmative action" was first introduced as a remedial technique in the civil rights arena. In its original formulation, that concept embraced only non-preferential affirmative efforts, in the nature of training programs and enhanced recruitment activities, aimed at opening wide the doors of opportunity to all Americans who cared to enter. Thus, President Kennedy's Executive Order 10925, one of the earliest to speak to the subject, stated that federal contractors should "take affirmative action to ensure that the applicants are employed, and that employees are treated during employment, without regard to their race, creed, color, or national origin."

This principle was understood by all at that time to mean simply that individuals previously neglected in the search for talent must be allowed to apply and be considered along with all others for available jobs or contracting opportunities, but that the hiring and selection decisions would be made from the pool of applicants without regard to race, creed, color, or national origin—and later sex. No one was to be afforded a preference, or special treatment, because of group membership; rather, all were to be treated equally as individuals based on personal ability and worth.

This administration's commitment is, of course, to this "original and undefiled meaning"—as Morris Abram, Vice Chairman of the Civil Rights Commission, calls it—of "affirmative action." Where unlawful discrimination exists, we see that it is brought to an abrupt and uncompromising halt; where that discrimination

---

Excerpted from "Equal Opportunity, Not Equal Rights" by William Bradford Reynolds, in Robert K. Fullinwider and Claudia Mills, eds., *The Moral Foundations of Civil Rights* (Totowa, N.J.: Rowman and Littlefield, Copyright © 1986). Reprinted with permission.
*Counselor to the United States Attorney General and Assistant Attorney General for Civil Rights under the Regan Administration.

has harmed any individual, we ensure that every victim of the wrongdoing receives "make-whole" relief; and affirmative steps are required in the nature of training programs and enhanced recruitment efforts to force open the doors of opportunity that have too long remained closed to far too many.

The criticism, of course, is that we do not go far enough. The remedial use of goals-and-timetables, quotas, or other such numerical devices—designed to achieve a particular balance as to race or sex in the work force—has been accepted by the lower federal courts as an available instrument of relief, and therefore, it is argued, such an approach should not be abandoned. There are several responses to this sort of argumentation.

The first is a strictly legal one and rests on the Supreme Court's recent decision in *Firefighters Local Union* v. *Stotts,* No. 82 - 206 (decided June 12, 1984). The Supreme Court in *Stotts* did not merely hold that federal courts are prohibited from ordering racially preferential layoffs to maintain a certain racial percentage, or that courts cannot disrupt bona fide seniority systems. To be sure, it did so rule; but the Court said much more, and in unmistakably forceful terms. As Justice Stevens remarked during his recent commencement address at Northwestern University, the decision represents "a far-reaching pronouncement concerning the limits on a court's power to prescribe affirmative action as a remedy for proven violations of Title VII of the Civil Rights Act." For the *Stotts* majority grounded the decision, at bottom, on the holding that federal courts are without *any* authority under Section 706(g)—the remedial provision of Title VII—to order a remedy, either by consent decree or after full litigation, that goes beyond enjoining the unlawful conduct and awarding "make-whole" relief for actual victims of the discrimination. Thus, quotas or other preferential techniques that, by design, benefit nonvictims because of race or sex cannot be part of Title VII relief ordered

in a court case, whether the context is hiring, promotion, or layoffs.

A brief review of the opinion's language is particularly useful to understanding the sweep of the decision. At issue in *Stotts* was a district court injunction ordering that certain white firefighters with greater seniority be laid off before blacks with less seniority in order to preserve a certain percentage of black representation in the fire department's work force. The Supreme Court held that this order was improper because "there was no finding that any of the blacks protected from layoff had been a victim of discrimination."[1] Relying explicitly on Section 706(g) of Title VII, the Court held that Congress intended to "provide make-whole relief only to those who have been actual victims of illegal discrimination."[2]

After *Stotts,* it is, I think, abundantly clear that Section 706(g) of Title VII does not tolerate remedial action by courts that would grant to non-victims of discrimination—at the expense of wholly innocent employees or potential employees—an employment preference based solely on the fact that they are members of a particular race or gender. Quotas, or any other numerical device based on color or sex, are by definition victim-blind: they embrace without distinction and accord preferential treatment to persons having no claim to "make-whole" relief. Accordingly, whether such formulas are employed for hiring, promotion, layoffs, or otherwise, they must fail under any reading of the statute's remedial provision.

There are equally strong policy reasons for coming to this conclusion. The remedial use of preferences has been justified by the courts primarily on the theory that they are necessary to cure "the effects of past discrimination" and thus, in the words of one Supreme Court Justice, to "get beyond" racism."[3] This reasoning is twice flawed.

First, it is premised on the proposition that any racial imbalance in the employer's work force is explainable only as a lingering effect on past racial discrimination. The analysis is no different where gender-based discrimination is involved. Yet, in either instance, equating "underrepresentation" of certain groups with discrimination against those groups ignores the fact that occupation selection in a free society is determined by a host of factors, principally individual interest, industry, and ability. It simply is not the case that applicants for any given job come proportionally qualified by race, gender, and ethnic origin in accordance with U.S. population statistics. Nor do the career interests of individuals break down proportionally among racial or gender groups. Accordingly, a selection process free of discrimination is no more likely to produce "proportional representation" along race or sex lines than it is to ensure proportionality among persons grouped according to hair color, shoe size, or any other irrelevant personal characteristic. No human endeavor, since the beginning of time, has attracted persons sharing a common physical characteristic in numbers proportional to the representation of such persons in the community. "Affirmative action" assumptions that one might expect otherwise in the absence of race or gender discrimination are ill-conceived.

Second, and more important, there is nothing *remedial*—let alone *equitable*—about a court order that *requires* the hiring, promotion, or retention of a person who has not suffered discrimination solely because that person is a member of the same racial or gender group as other persons who were victimized by the discriminatory employment practices. The rights protected under Title VII belong to individuals, not to groups. The Supreme Court made clear some years ago that "[t]he basic policy of [Title VII] requires that [courts] focus on fairness to individuals rather than fairness to classes."[4] The same message was again delivered in *Stotts*. As indicated, remedying a violation of Title VII requires that the individual victimized by the unlawful discrimination be restored to his or her "rightful place." It almost goes without saying, however, that a person who is *not* victimized by the employer's discriminatory practices has no claim to a "rightful place" in the employer's work force. And, according preferential treatment to *nonvictims* in no way remedies the injury suffered by persons who have in fact been discriminated against in violation of Title VII.

Moreover, racial quotas and other forms of preferential treatment unjustifiably infringe on the legitimate employment interests and expectations of third parties, such as incumbent employees, who are free of any involvement in the employer's wrongdoing. To be sure, awarding retroactive seniority and other forms of "rightful place" relief to individual victims of discrimination also unavoidably infringes upon the employment interests and expectations of innocent third parties. Indeed, this fact has compelled some, including Chief Justice Burger, to charge that granting rightful place relief to victims of racial discrimination is on the order of "robbing Peter to pay Paul."[5]

The legitimate "rightful place" claims of identifiable victims of discrimination, however, warrant imposition of a remedy that calls for a sharing of the burden by those innocent incumbent employees whose "places" in the work force are the product of, or at least enhanced by, the employer's unlawful discrimination. Restoring the victim of discrimination to the position he or she would have occupied but for the discrimination merely requires incumbent employees to surrender some of the largesse discriminatorily conferred upon them. In other words, there is justice in requiring Peter, as a kind of third-party beneficiary of the employer's discriminatory conduct, to share in the burden of making good on the debt to Paul created by that conduct. But, an incumbent employee should not be called upon as well to sacrifice or otherwise compromise legitimate employment interests in order to accommodate persons *never wronged* by the employer's unlawful conduct. An order directing Peter to pay Paul in the absence of any proof of a debt owing to Paul is without remedial justification and cannot be squared with basic notions of fairness.

Proponents of the so-called remedial use of class-based preferences often counter this point with a two-fold response. First, they note that the effort to identify and make whole all victims of the employer's discriminatory practices will never be 100 percent successful. While no one can dispute the validity of this unfortunate point, race- and gender-conscious preferences simply do not answer this problem. The injury suffered by a discriminatee who cannot be located is in no way ameliorated—much less remedied—by conferring preferential treatment on other, randomly selected members of his or her race or sex. A person suffering from appendicitis is not relieved of the pain by an appendectomy performed on the patient in the next room.

Second, proponents of judicially imposed numerical preferences also argue that they are necessary to ensure that the employer does not return to his or her discriminatory ways. The fallacy in this reasoning is self-evident. Far from *preventing* future discrimination, imposition of such remedial devices *guarantees* future discrimination. Only the color or gender of the ox being gored is changed.

It is against this backdrop that the Court's decision in *Stotts* assumes so much significance in the "affirmative action" debate. The inescapable consequence of *Stotts* is to move government at the federal, state, and local levels noticeably closer to the overriding objective of providing all citizens with a truly equal opportunity to compete on merit for the benefits that our society has to offer—an opportunity that allows an individual to go as far as the person's energy, ability, enthusiasm, imagination, and efforts will allow and not be hemmed in by the artificial allotment given to his or her group in the form of a numerical preference. The promise is that we might now be able to bring an end to that stifling process by which government and society view its citizens as possessors of racial or gender characteristics, not as the unique in-

dividuals they are; where advancements are viewed not as hard-won achievements, but as conferred "benefits."

The use of race or sex in an effort to restructure society along lines that better represent someone's preconceived notions of how our limited educational and economic resources should be allocated among the many groups in our pluralistic society necessarily forecloses opportunities to those having the misfortune—solely by reason of gender or skin color—to be members of a group whose allotment has already been filled. Those so denied, such as the more senior white Memphis firefighters laid off to achieve a more perfect racial balance in the fire department, are discriminated against every bit as much as the black Memphis firefighters originally excluded from employment. In our zeal to eradicate discrimination from society, we must be ever vigilant not to allow considerations of race or sex to intrude upon the decisional process of government. That was precisely the directive handed down by Congress in the Civil Rights Act of 1964, and, as *Stotts* made clear, the command has full application to the courts. Plainly, "affirmative action" remedies must be guided by no different principle. For the simple fact remains that wherever it occurs, and however explained, "no discrimination based on race [or sex] is benign. . . . no action disadvantaging a person because of color [or gender] is affirmative."[6]

NOTES

1. Slip opinion at p. 16.
2. Slip opinion at p. 17.
3. *University of California Regents* v. *Bakke,* 438 U.S. 265, 407 (Justice Blackmun, concurring).
4. *Los Angeles Department of Water & Power* v. *Manhart,* 435 U.S. 702, 708 (1978).
5. *Franks* v. *Bowman Transportation Co.,* 424 U.S. 747, 781 (1976) (Justice Burger, dissenting).
6. *United Steelworkers of America, AFL-CIO* v. *Weber,* 443 U.S. 193, 254 (1979) (Justice Rehnquist, dissenting).

Moving forward on Reverse Discrimination

Nancy Kubasek* and Andrea M. Giampetro †

During 1986, the U.S. Supreme Court finally agreed to consider the legality of affirmative action plans. In seventeen separate opinions handed down in four cases, this country's highest court concluded that race-conscious remedies granted to those who have not proven that they were the victims of specific acts of racial discrimination are not unconstitutional.[1]

An end to the debate over the legality of a remedy, however, does not necessarily signify the end of the debate over the desirability of the remedy. Although the Supreme Court's decision may silence some who oppose affirmative action and may change the behavior of others, the debates over affirmative action will not cease; rather, their focus will change. Those who are opposed to the use of nonvictim-specific race-conscious remedies will still continue to oppose their use. But the opponents of affirmative action will now focus their efforts on raising philosophical objections to affirmative action. They will no longer try to use legal precedents to argue that such programs are unlawful; instead, they will question the fairness or justice of using such legally available remedies.

What are these philosophical objections to affirmative action? How should the proponents of affirmative action respond to these objections? Are affirmative action programs philosophically unjustifiable?

*Department of Legal Studies, Bowling Green University.
†Department of Business Law, Loyola College/ Baltimore.

OPPONENTS' ARGUMENTS

Many of those who are philosophically opposed to affirmative action do not see any distinction between discrimination against minorities and discrimination in favor of minorities. They call the latter reverse discrimination, claiming that discrimination has been reversed and is now being used to prevent qualified whites from getting the jobs to which they are entitled, just as discrimination used to prevent blacks from obtaining the jobs to which they were entitled. To evaluate this reverse discrimination objection fairly, we must state it in its strongest form. The reverse discrimination argument is that since the time of Aristotle, the concept of distributive justice has required that equals be treated equally and unequals be treated unequally. This means that individuals are not to be denied benefits or forced to bear burdens based on irrelevant characteristics. Such actions would be arbitrary discrimination, which violates the concept of distributive justice.

It is now generally agreed that race is an irrelevant characteristic for purposes of distributing the benefits of education and employment. Therefore, affirmative action in the form of preferential treatment or reverse discrimination is violative of the principle of distributive justice because it distributes benefits and burdens on the basis of an irrelevant characteristic: race. Discrimination in employment or education based on race is arbitrary discrimination regardless of which race is being singled out.

Further, the ideal of equality is that all share the benefits and burdens of citizenship. The law governs all citizens equally, with all citizens regarding all others as having the same rights and protections. No inequalities not absolutely necessary for the functioning of society and the benefit of all are tolerable. Justice is equal treatment under the law for all citizens. Injustice occurs when all are not treated equally under the law. Reverse discrimination, or preferential treatment, violates equality because it treats one group of citizens differently; it destroys the protections of the law for one group of citizens. The very fact that we can talk about *preferential* treatment implies that before such treatment there was equality.

COMPENSATORY JUSTICE

Reverse discrimination also violates the principle of compensatory justice. Compensatory justice requires that when one is unjustly deprived of something that he rightfully possesses, he is entitled to compensation for his loss from the one who harmed him. This principle does not allow one to randomly seek compensation from those who did not harm him; they are as innocent as the one originally harmed. Preferential treatment policies, which require a minority to be hired, promoted, or admitted to a program instead of a more qualified nonminority, provide compensation for the allegedly wronged minority at the expense of the rejected innocent nonminority.

One approach to the foregoing philosophical objection to reverse discrimination is to point out that when so-called reverse discrimination occurs and blacks are given preferential treatment, the relevant basis for the discrimination is not race, which is arguably an arbitrary characteristic. Rather, it is the wrongs and losses blacks have suffered and the special needs they have that now form the relevant characteristics on which the discrimination is based. In other words, the reason for preferring blacks is not that they are black, which is why they have been denied housing and employment in the past. Instead, blacks are being treated differently because they have been victimized by a history of slavery and discrimination. We are preferring people with a history of suffering that makes them different from others, and different in a manner relevant to the preference they are now receiving. Therefore, the discrimination is not arbitrary. Race, when explicitly used as a classification, is being used for administrative convenience. Because there is a high correlation between being black and being a victim of invidious discrimination, race is a valid administrative tool for discerning who has suffered a history of slavery and discrimination.

One may, however, accept race as the relevant characteristic yet still find the reverse discrimination objection untenable. To accept the reverse discrimination objection, one must see blacks and nonminorities as equal in all relevant respects—including having the equal opportunity to compete for positions of power and prestige in our society.

Thus, in order to accept the reverse discrimination objection, one must define equality as meaning simply the absence of overt bars to quality education, housing, and employment. If one accepts this definition, one can then point to the civil rights laws prohibiting discrimination and say that these laws now ensure equal opportunity for all. Blacks and whites are therefore equals and must be treated equally.

Supporters of affirmative action, however, subscribe to a different definition of equality. As Justice Blackmun pointed out in *Bakke:* "In order to get past racism, we must take into account race. There is no other way. In order to treat people equally, we must treat them differently."

There is a plethora of evidence to support the proposition that when we are talking about competition in America among members of different races, equality, or equality of opportunity, means more than the elimination of overt barriers. As Lyndon Johnson said in a 1965 commencement address at Howard University, "You do not take a person who for years has been hobbled by chains and liberate him, bring him up to the starting line of a race, and then say, 'You are free to compete against all the others,' and still justly believe that you have been completely fair."

SEGREGATION FACTOR

A major factor affecting blacks' access to training, education, health care, and employment opportunities is the pattern of housing that exists and has existed in this country. In today's society, housing not only provides needed shelter from the elements but also significantly influences one's ability to get a decent education and a prestigious job. It affects one's self-concept, which in turn further affects one's ability to compete for the economic goods available in our society.

We have a situation today in which the older inner cities are populated by poorly educated and economically disadvantaged persons, a large proportion of whom are minority families. The suburbs are primarily populated by whites who are looking for better health care, quality education, and personal safety. Increasingly, industrial parks are also moving out to the more attractive suburbs. There is little affordable housing accessible to minorities near these suburban industrial centers.

When there is a concentration of minority families in the inner cities and a loss of taxpaying families and industries to the suburbs, the tax base in the city becomes eroded. This makes it difficult for the government to meet the physical and social needs of the remaining residents, thus worsening the conditions under which they live and lessening their "equal opportunities" to develop themselves so they can realistically become competitive with nonminorities.

SCHOOL SEGREGATION

An additional problem caused by segregated housing is that it tends to result in a large number of schools being primarily minority or nonminority, despite the fact that intentional school segregation in most states is still unlawful. While school districts cannot be drawn so as to segregate the races, there are many instances where any way the districts are drawn, schools will be predominantly black or white due to segregated housing patterns. Most of the schools that are primarily black are located in lower-income areas of the inner cities. In such lower-income

schools with their large classes, it is not uncommon for the teachers to contribute to the low student achievement levels by having low expectations. When teachers expect little from their students, a self-fulfilling prophecy may be put into effect. Thus, lower-income black competitors will be competing with an academic disadvantage as a result of their having attended segregated schools in economically depressed neighborhoods.

Even many blacks who have been relatively successful in the economic competition feel that after a certain level of success, their chances for continued progress are slim, to a large extent because top-level white management people do not feel comfortable working with blacks. This discomfort arises to a great extent from a lack of early experiences in interacting with blacks on any sort of equal basis.

These lower-level minority managers believe that the general cultural and social separation of the races has a significant impact on such conditions as the existence of only four black senior executives in the largest thousand United States corporations in 1985. As one black female executive explained, "People in the senior ranks might have gone to the same prep schools, fraternity, and church. Put yourself in corporate America's shoes—you hire those who you feel comfortable with." Institutions tend to perpetuate themselves unless something interferes with the process. Thus, the all-white executive suites will tend to stay that way unless forced to change.

The impact of not growing up in an interactive environment with members of the white community will often preclude blacks from even getting inside the corporate door, because potential minority candidates often do not know that many contests exist. This is because many jobs are filled through informal social contacts. A job opening occurs and the person responsible for filling the position asks a few of his colleagues if they know of anyone who might be good for the job. These white males will usually respond with recommendations for people like themselves, other white males with whom they socialize. Those people will be contacted and one of them hired. Even if the job is minimally advertised to meet EEOC regulations, the hiring decision has, in effect, already been made. Whites are generally the ones in powerful positions who can affect who is hired. If blacks do not have white friends, they will never find out about a large number of job opportunities and may never really be considered for many jobs for which they apply.

UNEQUALS TREATED UNEQUALLY

It is apparent that blacks do not have the equal opportunity to compete for the desirable economic goods that one gets by acquiring a position of power and prestige. As several commentators have correctly pointed out, whites could never be kicked around in the way blacks have. Whites today who complain about reverse discrimination have not been ''beaten, lynched, denied the right to use a bathroom, a place to sleep or eat, forced to take the dirtiest jobs or denied work at all, forced to attend dilapidated and mind-killing schools, subjected to brutal unequal justice or stigmatized as an inferior being.''

Since blacks are so clearly not the equals of whites in terms of their opportunities and treatment, preferential treatment of blacks is not a violation of distributive justice because equals are not being treated unequally. Unequals are being treated unequally, which is what distributive justice requires. Thus the argument that preferential treatment policies violate the principles of distributive justice cannot withstand careful examination and must be rejected.

Reverse discrimination does not violate the principle of compensatory justice either. While it is true that whites who may never have directly discriminated against the blacks receiving preferential treatment will be denied jobs or admission to programs that they would have received in the absence of preferential treatment policies, whites are not necessarily being unjustly forced to compensate the policies' beneficiaries. All that these white ''victims'' really lose is the expectation that they maintain the same positions that societal discrimination has helped them to acquire. The reverse discrimination that nonminorities suffer only partially offsets the advantages they have received for years.

This point becomes more clear when we examine the case of a typical reverse discrimination claim. When a nonminority applicant is not admitted to a professional school because preferential policies require admission of a minority, it is not the most qualified white who is being denied admission. It is the white who was barely qualified to meet the admissions standards. Chances are good, therefore, that this complaining applicant is able to meet the standards only because initial conditions were unfair. Were it not for the educational and housing advantages that this white applicant received, at the expense of minorities, he would not have met the standards for admission in the first place. While this is not necessarily true in every instance, when it is true it provides added support for the argument that ''innocent'' whites are not being forced to compensate minorities.

Thus, because the preferred treatment of minorities does not require compensation from those who are denied positions given to minorities, ''reverse discrimination'' does not violate the principle of compensatory justice either.

Many of those who are philosophically opposed to affirmative action believe that we should base employment and admission decisions solely on merit. Obviously, affirmative action is to some extent inconsistent with the merit system. And this merit system is deeply embedded into our culture. Most of us accept unquestionably the idea that no matter how oppressed our backgrounds, we can attain any position if we develop our talents and work hard. Affirmative action, however, gives some people a head start. These people may subsequently attain positions ahead of individuals who are more qualified.

Let us consider an example of the merit objection, if for no other reason than to entertain the reader who values highly logical reasoning. Clarence Pendleton, Jr., of the U.S. Commission on Civil Rights, relies on a merit objection when he speaks against affirmative action. He says: "I think [the fact that over 60 percent of most professional football teams and about 80 percent of basketball teams are black] deals with market forces. I think people have ability and you put down your money and take your pick." Apparently, in Pendleton's eyes, blacks have merit at sports so teams pick them. It follows, then, that blacks do not have merit regarding other types of employment, so employers do not pick them. Is that what he has in mind? His analysis is unclear but still illustrative of the merit objection.

What is wrong with the merit objection? One major problem with the merit objection is that when we befriend merit, we inaccurately assume that a merit system has always existed; merit accepts the status quo. But a true merit system has not, does not, and will never prevail. Many jobs simply require "knowing somebody." The saying "It's not what you know, it's who you know" is not just a trite, old statement. Since human beings make employment decisions, it is impossible to prevent human bias from being a factor. Blacks have been ostracized from the buddy system. The merit objection fails to recognize this fact.

Even if the "old-boy network" did not exist, can we really measure merit for most jobs? To go back to Clarence Pendleton's example, we do have a pretty good way to measure the merit of a baseball player. We can look at his batting average. What comparable statistics do we have to measure someone's abilities as a manager? Or a chief executive officer? For most of the more prestigious positions in our society, there is no objective way to measure merit.

Another inadequacy of the merit objection is that it ignores the possibility that our need to compensate blacks for past unequal treatment is greater than our need to consider merit. A closely related consequentialist response is that while it may be unjust to the more meritorious individual who was denied a job or admission to a professional program, this temporary injustice will provide the best overall consequences for society and this outweighs the injustice to the individuals.

Finally, some argue that the merit objection is inadequate because race and merit are not mutually exclusive. Some writers define merit in such a way that race is an element of merit. If we value the goal of having blacks contribute to society, race becomes a "plus" or meritorious factor in employment and admission decisions. Did the fact that Sandra Day O'Connor was a woman and Thurgood Marshall was a black contribute to their being named to the Supreme Court? Should it have? Probably, if we believe that it is important that society's institutions, including its workplaces, reflect society, the minority status of candidates in these and many other situations is indeed important. For example, when establishing standards for admission to professional programs, a diverse student body may be desirable, and thus race will become a meritorious condition when someone is of a race not highly represented in the program.

In some cases, when one examines the job description, race may be directly implicated as a meritorious characteristic. Police work provides such an example. Black policemen are much more likely to obtain needed information from inner-city residents than are white policemen. This is especially true where there have been racial conflicts in a particular community. Thus, if we had a predominantly white police force in an area with a large black population, being black would be a characteristic to search for in new recruits.

It is interesting to note that affirmative action programs are more abhorrent to some people than programs like welfare, which require the outright giving of money to individuals, not simply the giving of opportunities. In fact, some who raise the merit objection propose to replace them with monetary compensation for proven victims of racial discrimination. The reason for this apparent inconsistency is rooted in our attitudes toward merit and charity. Americans, as a group, are highly individualistic and believe that it is of utmost importance to reward merit. However, we also have some sympathy for those who have met with misfortune and are willing to accept our generosity.

Welfare is, to some people, charity. The reason welfare is more acceptable than affirmative action is that welfare recipients do not participate in society the way we do; they are accepting our help because they have failed and we are generous enough to give them some aid so that they can survive. Our generosity, however, is not cost-free. Society typically scorns welfare recipients, and they know it. The same is not as true for those who benefit from affirmative action programs, because the benefits are not as tangible as, for instance, food stamps. Hence, they are not visible. With affirmative action, we give opportunity and mobility, not "charity." We allow "less deserving" people to participate in society in the same way we do. What is even worse to some opponents of affirmative action is that not only do some minorities participate, but they may actually be successful. And such participation and success is something they do not deserve.

While there may be practical problems in the implementation of certain affirmative action programs, and these should be addressed, we should recognize that from a philosophical perspective, such programs are not objectionable. Thus preferential treatment policies should not be abandoned. Perhaps with the use of affirmative action, it may one day no longer be true that blacks are unequal to whites and therefore do not need such programs to compete in the economic game.

NOTE

1. The four cases are: *Wygant v. Jackson Board of Education*, 54, U.S.L.W. 4479 (U.S. May 19, 1986);

Sheet Metal Workers, Local 28 v. EEOC, 1, 54, U.S.L.W. 4984 (U.S. July 2, 1986); *International Association of Firefighters, Local 93 v. Cleveland*, 54, U.S.L.W. 5005 (U.S. July 2, 1986); *Blazemore v. Friday*, 54, U.S.L.W. 4972 (U.S. July 1, 1986).

In Defense of Hiring Apparently Less Qualified Women

Laura M. Purdy*

A Man's mind—what there is of it—has always the advantage of being masculine—as the smallest birchtree is of higher kind than the most soaring palm—and even his ignorance is of a sounder quality.

George Elliot, *Middlemarch*, ch. 2

There are relatively few women in academe, and it is reasonable to believe that discrimination—conscious and unconscious, subtle and overt, individual and institutional—is responsible for this state of affairs.[1] Affirmative action programs have been promoted to try to neutralize this discrimination. One form requires academic departments to search actively for female candidates; if a woman with qualifications at least as good as those of the leading male contender is found, she is to be hired.

Does this policy create new and serious injustice, as some contend?[2] If a woman and a man were equally qualified, and one could be sure that prejudice against women played no part in the decision to hire, such a policy would certainly be an imposition on the department's freedom to hire the most compatible-seeming colleague. (This is not to say that such an imposition could never be justified: we might, for example,

Excerpted from "In Defense of Hiring Apparently Less Qualified Women" by Laura M. Purdy. *Journal of Social Philosophy*, Vol. 15 (Summer 1984), pp. 26–33. Reprinted with permission of the author and publisher.
*Department of Philosophy, Wells College.

believe that the importance of creating role models for female students justifies some loss of freedom on the part of departments.) However, it is widely conceded that there is prejudice against women among academics, with the result that women are not getting the appointments they deserve. My intent here is to consider how this happens. I will argue that women are often not perceived to be as highly qualified as they really are. Thus when the qualifications of candidates are compared, a woman may not be thought equally (or more highly) qualified, even when she is. Affirmative action programs which require hiring of equally qualified women will therefore be ineffective: the hiring of women perceived to be less qualified is needed if discrimination against women is to cease.

Some people think that the latter course is both unnecessary and unfair. Alan Goldman, for instance, maintains that it is unnecessary because the procedural requirements of good affirmative action programs are sufficient to guarantee equal opportunity. He also believes it to be unfair because it deprives the most successful new Ph.D.'s of their just reward—a good job.[3] I will argue that neither of these claims is true and that there is a good case for hiring women perceived to be less well qualified than their male competitors.

The general difficulty of forming accurate assessments of candidates' merit is well-known, and it is probable that the better candidate has sometimes been taken for the worse. It is reasonable to believe, however, that the subjective elements in evaluations lead to systematic lowering of women's perceived qualifications. I have two arguments for this claim. The first is that past prejudice biases the evidence and the second is that present prejudice biases perception of the evidence. Let us examine each in turn.

Why then may women be better qualified than their records suggest? One principal reason is that many men simply do not take women seriously:

You might think that the evaluation of a specific performance would be an objective process, judged on characteristics of performance itself rather than on assumptions about the personality or ability of the performer. Yet performance is rarely a totally objective process. Two people may view the same event and interpret it differently. In the same way, it is possible for someone to view two people acting in exactly the same way and yet come to different conclusions about that behavior.[4]

Studies by Rosenthal and Jacobson provide experimental support for this claim. They found that students reported one group of rats to run mazes faster than another identical group, when they had previously been told that the first group was brighter. Ann Sutherland Harris quite plausibly concludes that such studies have important implications for women:

> If male scholars believe that women are intellectually inferior to men—less likely to have original contributions to make, less likely to be logical, and so on—will they not also find the evidence to support their beliefs in the women students in their classes, evidence of a far more sophisticated nature than the speed at which one rat finds its way through a maze? Their motives will be subconscious. Indeed, they will firmly believe that their judgment is rational and objective.[5]

What grounds are there for maintaining that this does not occur whenever women are evaluated? Other studies suggest additional hurdles for women that bias the evidence upon which they are judged. For instance, male students (though not female ones) rate identical course syllabi higher when the professor is said to be a man.[6]

Sociologist Jessie Bernard suggests that bias occurs whether women present accepted ideas or novel ones. In one study, a man and a woman taught classes using the same material. The man engaged the students' interest: he was thought both more biased and more authoritative than the equally competent woman. According to Bernard, she was taken less seriously because she did not "look the part."[7] To support her position that novel ideas are less well received from women than men, Bernard mentions the case of Agnes Pockels, whose discoveries in physics were ignored for years. She cites this as an example of the general inability to see women in "the idea-man or instrumental role. We are simply not used to looking for innovation and originality from women."[8] The consequences of failing to take new ideas seriously may be even more detrimental to women than the failure to be taken seriously as a teacher. Bernard argues: "The importance of priority...highlights the importance of followers, or, in the case of science, of the public qualified to judge innovations. If an innovation is not recognized—even if recognition takes the form of rejection and a fight—it is dead."[9]

Additional persuasive evidence that women's ideas are not taken seriously by men comes from a study by Daryl and Sandra Bem, replicating a previous study by Philip Goldberg with women. A number of scholarly articles were submitted to a group of undergraduate men, who were to judge how good they were. Each paper was read by each man, but the paper read by half the students was attributed to a man, that read by the other half, to a woman. The results were striking: the "man's" article was rated higher than the "woman's" in most cases.[10] Does this prejudice continue to operate at more advanced levels?

One significant study showed more papers by women were chosen for presentation at the annual meeting of a national professional organization when they were submitted anonymously.[11] This suggests that whether a woman's work is published or not will also depend more on the reviewers' conception of women than upon the merits of the piece—at least until blind reviewing becomes the rule. Furthermore, there is evidence that even when a woman is recognized as having done a good job at some task, her performance is more likely than a man's to be attributed to factors other than ability. Hence others are less likely to expect future repeated success on her part.[12] And, unsuccess-

ful performance by a male is more likely than that of a female to be attributed to bad luck.[13] Studies have also shown that male applicants for scholarship funds were judged more intelligent and likeable than their female counterparts,[14] and that males were favored over females for study abroad programs.[15] In addition, until very recently, recommendations written for women were more likely to mention personal appearance in an undermining way (as well as marital status) than those written for men.[16] These facts have obvious repercussions for candidates' overall records. Hence if the hypotheses considered so far here are true, then women are systematically undervalued with respect to some of the most widely-used indicators of quality.

[Women also] run the risk of having their already undervalued qualifications devalued again when they are candidates for a position. This conclusion is supported by a study which showed that the same dossier was often ranked higher by academic departments when it was attributed to a man than when it was attributed to a woman.[17] Research on interviews also suggests that both men and women are systematically biased against women.[18]

I have been arguing that women are likely to be more highly qualified than they seem. This fact alone would support a policy of hiring women perceived to be less qualified. However, I think there is another sound argument for such a policy. Women may sometimes be less qualified than their male competitors because as students they faced stumbling-blocks the men did not. Hence some women probably deserve their weak recommendations and dearth of publications because their work is less fully developed and their claims less well supported than a man's might be. This can occur because women's social role often precludes opportunities for informal constructive criticism; it may also be the result of the lack of a mentor to push her to her limits. Finally, a woman is likely to have had to work in a debilitating environment of lowered expectations.[19]

Goldman argues that it would be wrong to hire such a woman if there were a more qualified candidate: "...the white male who has successfully met the requirements necessary to attaining maximal competence attains some right to that position. It seems unjust for society to set standards of achievement and then to thwart the expectations of those who have met those standards."[20]

But surely hiring is ultimately intended to produce the best scholar and teacher, not to reward the most successful graduate student. Consequently, if there are grounds for believing that women turn into the former, despite not having been the latter according to the traditional criteria, it is reasonable to hold that they should sometimes be hired anyway. And there are such grounds.

The obstacles encountered by women in academe are well-documented and there is no need to elaborate at length upon them here. What matters is the nature of the person they create. Until very recently, at every stage of schooling, fewer girls than boys continued.[21] There is considerable evidence that women graduate students have higher academic qualifications than their male counterparts.[22] This appears to be because only the very highly qualified get into graduate school.[23] Harris argues that it "...is worth remembering that women candidates for graduate school are the survivors of a long sifting process—only the very best of the good students go on to graduate school."[24] A report issued by women at the University of Chicago supports this claim—the grade averages of women students entering graduate school were significantly higher than those of men.[25]

Once there, women have somewhat higher attrition rates than men. But Harris thinks that this is "largely explained by the lack of encouragement and the actual discouragement experienced by women graduate students for their career plans....It is not surprising that some women decide that they are not cut out to be scholars and teachers."[26] She argues that if women were

not highly committed, the attrition rate would be much higher: "...only the hardiest survive."[27]

In light of all these facts, a temporary policy of hiring women perceived to be less well qualified would be reasonable, to see if the hypothesis that they will bloom is borne out. Such a policy is less risky than it might seem since junior faculty members are on probation and can be fired if they do not start to fulfill their promise.

In conclusion, there are good grounds for at least a trial of the policy I am proposing with regard to hiring in academe, since existing affirmative action programs have not been and cannot be effective.[28] I have tried to show why women may often seem less qualified than they really are, and why they may be more promising than they seem. Unless faculty members take these factors into account, no improvements in the position of women can be expected, for women are likely to seem less worthy of being hired than their male competitors when they are judged in the usual manner. Requiring departments to hire women perceived to be less well qualified may well turn out to be the most efficacious way to force departments to recognize and remedy the situation. It might also have a more generally beneficial side-effect of promoting faculty members' awareness of their own biases as they struggle to distinguish between truly mediocre women and those merely perceived to be so!

NOTES

1. The general trend continues to be that the more prestigious the post or institution, the fewer women there are to be found. See, for instance, "Status of Female Faculty Members, 1979–80," *The Chronicle of Higher Education,* 29 September 1980.
2. See Alan Goldman, "Affirmative Action," *Philosophy and Public Affairs,* Vol. 5, n. 2 (Winter 1976), 178.
3. Ibid.
4. Kay Deaux, *The Behavior of Women and Men,*

(Monterey, Ca.: Brooks/Cole Publishing Co., 1976), p. 24.

5. Ann Sutherland Harris reports this study in "The Second Sex in Academe" in *And Jill Came Tumbling After: Sexism in American Education,* ed. Judith Stacey et al., (New York: 1974), p. 299.

6. Jessie Bernard, *Academic Women,* (New York: Meridian Press, 1965), pp. 255–57. "The 'teachers' were selected by the department as being of about equal competence in communications skills. They were given two written lectures to deliver to sections of Sociology I . . . both young people were given the lectures in advance, and they agreed on how to interpret all major points in their presentations, which were to be identical. One spoke to each section and a week later each spoke to the other section" (p. 256).

7. Ibid.

8. Ibid.

9. Ibid.

10. Reported by Deaux, p. 25.

11. This study appeared in "On Campus with Women," March 1977, Association of American Colleges, and was reported in *Ms.,* Vol. 7, n. 5 (November 1978), 87. *Ms.* writes: "In 1973, at the last annual conference held before the policy was initiated, 6.3 percent of the papers selected were from women scholars. In 1975, 17 percent of the papers selected were from women scholars." The organization in question is the Archaeological Institute of America.

12. Veronica F. Nieva and Barbara Gutek, "Sex Effects on Evaluation," *Academy of Management Review,* Vol. 5, n. 2 (1980), p. 267.

13. Ibid., p. 270.

14. Ibid., p. 268.

15. Ibid.

16. Jennie Farley, "Academic Recommendations: Males and Females as Judges and Judged," *AAUP Bulletin,* Vol. 64, n. 2 (May 1978), p. 84.

17. L. S. Fidell, "Empirical Verification of Sex Discrimination in Hiring Practices in Psychology," *American Psychologist,* Vol. 60 (1970), 1049–98.

18. Robert L. Dipboye, Richard D. Arvey, and David E. Terpstra, "Sex and Physical Attractiveness of Raters and Applicants as Determinants of Resume Evaluations," *Journal of Applied Psychology,* Vol. 62, n. 3 (June 1977), p. 288. This study was limited to undergraduate students, however, so it

should not be assumed that it can be generalized to the educated population we are concerned with here.

19. Nieva and Gutek, p. 271.

20. Goldman, p. 191.

21. See Harris and Barnard in Stacey et al., pp. 302–5.

22. Harris, pp. 304–5.

23. Ibid.

24. Ibid.

25. Ibid.

26. Ibid.

27. Ibid. My own experience at the prestigious Ivy League institution where I took my Ph.D. was far from encouraging. When I arrived, there were no women faculty members. The class before mine, numbering about 10, contained no women, and I was the only woman in my class of about 10. Twice in my first year I was present in groups addressed by professors as "Gentlemen." One of these occasions was especially fraught with emotion. I and four men gathered at a professor's office to return one of the crucial 4-hour field exams required of first-year students. The professor beamed at us and said, "Well, we'll see how you did, gentlemen!"

28. See *Sex Discrimination in Higher Education,* ed. Jennie Farley, (Ithaca: ILR Publications, 1981).

Comparable Worth: A Matter of Simple Justice

Gerald W. McEntee*

On December 31, 1985, the American Federation of State, County, and Municipal Employees (AFSCME) and the state of Washington reached a historic comparable worth agreement.

This article first appeared in *The Humanist* issue of May/June 1986 and is reprinted with permission.
*President, American Federation of State, County and Municipal Employees.

They negotiated a settlement of the *AFSCME* v. *Washington State* pay equity lawsuit. The $106.5 million payout is historic because it is the largest comparable worth settlement in history, and it ended over a decade of resistance by the state to rectify sex-based wage discrimination in its wage scales, as documented by Washington's own studies.

In spite of this historic ruling, however, there is evidence that public sector employers still practice intentional wage discrimination and job segregation policies that funnel women into lower-paying, female-dominated jobs. Is this segregation intentional? And are the pay scales for these particular jobs based on sex-based wage discrimination?

AFSCME believes that the answer to both is ''yes.''

Take the Washington State example. According to the state's own studies, a laundry operator working in a large state institution should have been paid more than a farm equipment operator. But the salaries for farm equipment operators were seventeen pay grades higher than those of the laundry workers. The difference? One job was male-dominated; the other, female-dominated.

Also in Washington, clerk-typists working in state government and beginning warehouse workers were rated at the same level. But typists earned salaries ten pay grades below those of warehouse workers.

In both the public and the private sector workforce, these examples of pay discrimination are repeated hundreds of times in various job classifications. This translates into a national problem for working women, who still earn only sixty-four cents for every dollar working men earn, in spite of increased education and growing workforce participation by women.

The Washington State settlement capped off a year of comparable worth successes for AFSCME. Comparable worth moved from the courts to the bargaining table and state legislatures in 1985. Public employers are beginning to negotiate with their employees and their unions to work out practical and affordable solutions to the historic problem of sex-based wage discrimination.

However, in spite of the gains made on the comparable worth front this past year, the debate over this method of eradicating sex-based wage discrimination continues. Unfortunately, the discussion too often remains mired in the same kind of mean-spirited arguments used against every major piece of civil rights legislation. Opponents include U.S. Civil Rights Commission Chairman Clarence Pendleton, Phyllis Schlafly, and President Reagan. They have constructed their own definition of what comparable worth is, how it can be accomplished, how much it will cost, and what its effects will be. Their dire predictions fly in the face of the experience of AFSCME and public sector employers across the country. Many employers have voluntarily begun to correct disparities in their wage scales due to sex discrimination. The main arguments of comparable worth opponents are the following:

The gap between men's earnings and women's earnings is due to women's more recent entry into the workforce and their lesser education, training, and experience. Once you have allowed for legitimate differences in pay between men and women, such as seniority, experience, and collective bargaining agreements, there is still a gap that has remained constant for most of the years women have been in the workforce. At least half of this gap is due to sex discrimination by employers. AFSCME defines pay equity, or comparable worth, as a means of closing the gap between men's salaries and women's salaries that can be attributed only to sex discrimination.

Instituting comparable worth will upset the free market economy and require new laws and government wage-setting boards. The U.S. economy is partly controlled by minimum wage laws, civil rights laws, child labor laws, and the Equal Pay Act of 1963. AFSCME contends that the so-called free market has historically discriminated against women. Otherwise, nurses would be handsomely paid, because over the years they have been in critically short supply. But in 1981, for example, full-time registered nurses earned an average of only $331 a week—less than ticket agents and drafters.

Similarly, laws requiring women to be paid the same as men if they are doing comparable work are already on the books—all that remains is the will to enforce the law. In 1981, the Supreme Court ruled that the prohibition of T*itle* VII of the 1964 Civil Rights Act against discrimination in wage compensation was not limited to the claims of working women for equal pay for equal work. The Court made it clear that T*itle* VII prohibits all forms of discrimination in wage setting, including instances in which the male and female jobs being compared are dissimilar.

No advocate of comparable worth has urged that a government board set wages. Comparable worth requires only that *each individual employer* remove sex bias from his or her wage scale. If, say, a truck driver and a secretary within the same organization are evaluated as doing comparable work, they should be paid comparably.

Dissimilar jobs—like apples and oranges—cannot be compared. Think again. You *can* compare apples and oranges on a basis of their weight, their color, and their percentages of vitamins and fluid. Likewise, jobs have certain common characteristics: training, experience, responsibility, working conditions, and other criteria. Employers have been comparing jobs for as long as they have been hiring workers. Two-thirds of all workers are covered by some form of job evaluation system. The federal government has had an evaluation system to compare dissimilar jobs for one hundred years.

Comparable worth costs too much. AFSCME's on-the-job experience has shown that comparable worth has never cost more than 4 percent of a jurisdiction's payroll. In its first four

years of implementation on the state level in Minnesota (which is now implementing pay equity on the county and local level), comparable worth was expected to cost 4 percent of the state's total payroll. Actually, it will cost about 3.5 percent.

Interestingly, the same cost argument was made during the debate over civil rights legislation in the 1960s. Critics charged that paying blacks more would reduce the salaries of white workers. Critics of comparable worth argue that paying women more will reduce men's salaries.

Charging that pay equity will cost too much is an empty argument; it is inflammatory rhetoric designed to alienate women from men. Just because it carries a price, we should not be diverted from our goal of ending discrimination.

Unions promote pay equity because they want to keep women segregated in traditionally female-dominated jobs. Sex segregation in the workforce is a fact of life. A recent National Academy of Sciences report found that, despite recent progress, most American women who are employed will continue to work in largely low-paying occupations dominated by women for the foreseeable future.

Fifty-one percent of AFSCME's members are working women. The concerns of the union's women members are part of the union's overall agenda for the 1980s. Career ladders and career development programs are two of the contract provisions AFSCME negotiates to help move women into better-paying, more skilled jobs.

At the same time, a worker should be paid fairly for his or her work. Today, nearly 60 percent of mothers in families with children under eighteen are working; 80 percent of all working women are segregated into only twenty of the jobs listed by the *Dictionary of Occupational Titles.* Comparable worth is a means to bring the wages of working women into the mainstream. There are side benefits, also. For example, in Minnesota, during the first four years of pay equity, there has been an increase of 19 percent in the number of women entering nontraditional jobs.

AFSCME believes that comparable worth is the civil rights issue of the eighties. By using collective bargaining and legislative lobbying, AFSCME is pursuing the vestiges of sex-based wage discrimination. Its pay equity lawsuits on behalf of workers in Hawaii, Connecticut, New York City, Philadelphia, and Nassau County, New York, are making their way through the federal courts. Tens of thousands of workers—both women and men—in female-dominated jobs across the country are beginning to be paid based upon fairness and worth. It's a matter of simple justice.

Comparable Worth: Unfair to Men and Women

Phyllis Schlafly*

My name is Phyllis Schlafly, president of Eagle Forum, a national profamily organization. I am a lawyer, writer, and homemaker.

We oppose the concept called *comparable worth* for two principal reasons: (*a*) it's unfair to men and (*b*) it's unfair to women.

The comparable worth advocates are trying to freeze the wages of blue-collar men while forcing employers to raise the wages of *some* white- and pink-collar women above marketplace rates. According to the comparable worth rationale, blue-collar men are overpaid and their wages

From *The Humanist,* May/June 1986. Testimony to the Compensation and Employee Benefits Subcommittee of the House Post Office and Civil Service Committee, May 30, 1985. Reprinted with permission of the author.

*Lawyer, syndicated columnist, and president of Eagle Forum.

should be frozen until white- and pink-collar women have their wages artificially raised to the same level. The proof that this is really what the comparable worth debate is all about is in both their rhetoric and their statistics.

I've been debating feminists and listening to their arguments for more than a decade. It is impossible to overlook their rhetoric of envy. I've heard feminist leaders say hundreds of times, ''It isn't fair that the man with a high school education earns more money than the women who graduated from college or nursing or secretarial school.''

That complaint means that the feminists believe that truck drivers, electricians, plumbers, mechanics, highway workers, maintenance men, policemen, and firemen earn more money than feminists think they are worth. And how do the feminists judge ''worth''? By paper credentials instead of by apprenticeship and hard work and by ignoring physical risk and unpleasant working conditions.

So the feminists have devised the slogan *comparable worth* to make the blue-collar man feel guilty for earning more money than women with paper credentials and to trick him into accepting a government-enforced wage freeze while all available funds are used to raise the wages of *some* women.

Statistical proof that the aim of comparable worth is to reduce the relative earning power of blue-collar men is abundantly available in the job evaluations commissioned and approved by the comparable worth advocates. You can prove this to yourself by making a job-by-job examination of *any* study or evaluation made with the approval of comparable worth advocates; it is always an elaborate scheme to devalue the blue-collar man.

For example, look at the Willis evaluation used in the famous case called *AFSCME* v. *State of Washington*. Willis determined that the electricians and truck drivers were over valued by the state and that their ''worth'' was really far less than the ''worth'' of a registered nurse. More precisely, Willis produced an evaluation chart on which the registered nurse was worth 573 points, whereas the electrician was worth only 193 points (one-third of the nurse), while the truck driver was only worth 97 points (one-sixth of the nurse).

The federal court accepted the Willis evaluation as though it were some kind of divine law (refusing to listen to the Richard Jeanneret "PAQ" evaluation which produced very different estimates of "worth"). The federal court decision (unless it is overturned on appeal) means that the electricians and the truck drivers will probably have their salaries frozen until the state finds a way to pay the registered nurse three times and six times as much, respectively. [In a September 4, 1985, decision, the Ninth U.S. Circuit Court of Appeals overturned the decision.]

How do jobs get certain points? The evaluator invents them. The comparable worth advocates hire under contract an evaluator who is obligated (*a*) to ignore all marketplace factors and (*b*) to produce a point scheme to "prove" discrimination against women.

One of the techniques by which this is done is the devaluing of the physical and working-condition factors so important in blue-collar jobs. This devaluation of blue-collar jobs is always an inevitable result of integrating white-collar and blue-collar jobs in the same evaluation. If the federal white-collar and blue-collar pay classifications were integrated, the blue-collar employees would be tremendously devalued because the federal white-collar pay system accords less than 5 percent of the possible points to "physical demands" and "working environment" combined.

The comparable worth advocates and evaluators join in a chorus to claim that it's so "scientific" because "worth" is based on education, training, skills, experience, effort, responsibility, and working conditions. The fact is that, once you throw out marketplace factors, the evaluation is completely subjective and wholly reflective of the bias of the evaluator.

The Willis evaluation determined that the "mental demands" on a nurse are worth 122 points, whereas the mental demands on an electrician are worth only 30 points, and the mental demands on a truck driver are worth only 10 points. That's the view of the profeminist evaluator. For a contrary view, ask the electrician and the truck driver about the worth of their mental demands.

Comparable worth evaluations must be recognized as a racket to get people with your own biases on the evaluation team or to saddle the evaluator with a contract that binds him or her to produce the results you predetermine.

Not only is the comparable worth concept wholly subjective but it is also wholly arbitrary. It proposes to raise only *some* women's pay at the expense of men and other women. This arbitrariness is shown by the fact that *only* those jobs where 70 percent or more of the employees are female would be eligible for comparable worth raises. This was made clear in a devastating analysis of the Wisconsin governor's evaluation made by the Wisconsin Association of Manufacturers and Commerce.

The Wisconsin Governor's Task Force Study lists the job called *institution aide* as having a "C-W Gap" of $5,132. But the employees in this position would not get a comparable worth raise because only 67 percent of the 116 employees are women and institution aide cannot be designated a "woman's job" unless it meets the 70 percent test.

Now suppose that the state needs two more institution aides. If it hires two women, it will cross the 70 percent threshold. The state will then have to give all institution aides a raise, and it will therefore cost the state $595,000 to hire two women. The personnel manager can easily manipulate the system, depending on whether he is profeminist or probudget-cutting.

Or, look at the position called *nursing assistant 3*. Because it has 70 percent women, all 104 employees would be scheduled to get a raise of $3,626 to close the so-called C-W Gap. If the personnel manager simply hires one male or fires two females, he or she can avoid comparable worth raises for all and save $377,136 in his budget.

The entire concept of comparable worth hangs on comparisons between male-dominated jobs and female-dominated jobs, so it is impossible to escape the arbitrary nature of the 70 percent.

In addition, comparable worth is unfair to women in that its effect is to squeeze lower-skilled women out of the job market altogether. The respected economist June O'Neill has written lengthy treatises to show how and why this is the result. Clarence Pendleton, chairman of the U.S. Commission on Civil Rights, put this same point succinctly when he said, "Comparable worth would do to low-skilled women what the minimum wage did to black teenagers."

But that's not the only way comparable worth is unfair to women. It also hurts the women who have moved into nontraditional jobs.

When the Illinois nurses sued the state of Illinois, claiming they should be paid equally with the (mostly male) electricians and stationary engineers, eleven female state employees in nontraditional jobs tried to enter the lawsuit as intervenors. They all work in a job classification called *correctional officer,* which is a euphemism for *prison guard.* The evaluation said that these "male-dominated" jobs are not "worth" as much as they are now paid. Illinois was paying prison guards $145 a month more than entry-level secretaries, but the comparable worth evaluation gave secretaries twelve more comparable worth points than prison guards.

The women prison guards claimed that the present system of compensation properly rewards them for their special skills, performance of particularly difficult, dangerous, and unpleasant work, their willingness to challenge stereotypes and perform nontraditional jobs, and the nondiscriminatory market forces of supply and demand. Put another way, the state has found that it must pay more to hire prison guards than office personnel because of the risks on the job and the unpleasant work.

Ask yourself the question, how many women would be willing to be a prison guard if the pay were the same or less than the pay of a secretary?

Women are already flooding into the so-called traditional "women's jobs" by the millions. If the pay is raised for those jobs, even more women will seek those jobs and abandon plans to go into nontraditional lines of work. At the same time, business will eliminate jobs in order to cut costs, and low-skilled women will be laid off. That's why Clarence Pendleton says that comparable worth for women is as self-defeating as saying, twenty years ago, that the way to improve the economic lot of blacks would be to raise the pay of redcaps.

We are all aware that comparable worth has in recent months become a controversial issue in the media. The profeminist bias of the media has meant a pro-comparable-worth bias on most television programs.

So it was with particular interest that I discovered a confidential and copyrighted memorandum on comparable worth distributed by the legal department of the National Association of Broadcasters for the benefit of its television and radio station members. This memorandum warns stations to "think very carefully before undertaking any formal study of the relationship between the 'value' or 'difficulty' of the positions held by their employees and the salaries they receive." Be sure to consult your lawyer, the memorandum says. "If an employer's only motive is to protect itself against the hazards of new theories of wage discrimination like comparable worth, it is fair to say that a job evaluation study is far more likely to be a burden than a boon."

That's good advice—not only for television and radio broadcasters but for any employer, including the federal government and state governments.

QUESTIONS FOR DISCUSSION

1. In basketball, when a member of the team makes a foul, the entire team must pay a penalty, and the opposing team gets two foul shots. Does this analogy help illuminate the affirmative action controversy at all? How is the situation of the two basketball teams and their players similar to the situation of white males and minorities and females? Dissimilar? Explain.

2. How do the theories of Rawls, Nozick, and Smart (from Chapter 1) illuminate the debate about affirmative action?

3. How does a believer in wage discrimination explain the discrepancy between men's and women's salaries? How does a believer in strictly market forces explain it? Would it be possible for both of these explanations to be correct? Take each explanation in turn, and discuss how you think men and women would fare both with and without a policy of comparable worth.

Work in the Corporation

CASES FOR PART THREE

Martha W. Elliott and Tom L. Beauchamp
DuPont's Policy of Exclusion from the Workplace
394

Roger Boisjoly and Ellen Foster Curtis
Roger Boisjoly and the Challenger Disaster: A Case Study in Management Practice, Corporate Loyalty, and Business Ethics
397

John Simmons
The Eastern Airlines Union–Management Experiment
404

Linda Greenhouse
High Court Backs a Preference Plan for Blacks in Jobs: United Steelworkers of America v. Weber
410

DuPont's Policy of Exclusion from the Workplace

Martha W. Elliott* and Tom L. Beauchamp †

In January 1981 the *New York Times* reviewed a new and startling development in the workplaces of the nation. Some fertile women workers chose to undergo voluntary sterilization rather than give up high-paying jobs that involved exposure to chemicals potentially harmful to a developing fetus. Disclosure of this practice precipitated discussion of a new civil rights issue with "questions . . . raised about whether a company should be allowed to discriminate against a woman to protect her unborn child, or whether the practice of keeping a woman out of certain well-paying jobs because she was fertile was simply another form of sex discrimination in the workplace."[1]

Some background information is necessary for understanding this issue. The causes of congenital (or "birth") defects in humans are not well understood. Four to six percent are known to be caused by specific drugs and environmental chemicals, but the causes of at least 65 to 70 percent are unknown. It *is* known, however, that of the 28,000 toxic substances listed by the National Institute of Occupational Safety and Health (NIOSH) 56 are known animal mutagens (that is, they cause chromosomal damage to either the ova *or* the sperm cells), and 471 are known animal teratogens (that is, they can damage the developing fetus).[2] As the 1960s' thalidomide tragedy showed, a substance can be perfectly harmless to the mother, while at the same time

Excerpted from "DuPont's Policy of Exclusion from the Workplace," *Case Studies in Business, Society, and Ethics,* (Englewood Cliffs, N.J.: Prentice-Hall Inc., 1983). Copyright © Tom L. Beauchamp. Reprinted with permission.
*Department of Social Work, Johns Hopkins Hospital.
†Senior research scholar, Kennedy Institute of Ethics, Georgetown University.

having devastating effects on the developing fetus. (Doctors prescribed thalidomide for pregnant women as a tranquilizer, but found that the drug caused such fetal defects as severely shortened and often useless arms and legs.)

Exposure to mutagenic or teratogenic substances in the workplace is complicated by the fact that chemicals and other toxic substances usually do not occur singly, but in combination. Also, the average worker does not have knowledge of the chemical makeup of many products. Furthermore, the period of maximum hazard of the developing fetus occurs during the third and fourth weeks of pregnancy, which is often before the woman is even aware of her pregnancy. The United States government (FDA and EPA, in particular) requires animal testing of drugs to insure that any new product to which pregnant women may be exposed is harmless to the fetus.

Industries such as chemical plants and zinc smelters with high concentrations of lead have coped with this potential threat to the fetus in various ways. The most common strategy is simply to make jobs that involve the risk of exposure "off limits" to women "of child-bearing potential." That is, fertile women in their late teens, twenties, thirties, and forties are banned from those particular positions. (Ironically, lead poses an equal danger to the male reproductive system.) Since a woman is assumed fertile until proven otherwise, this sweeping policy affects a large portion of the female workforce.[3] This policy, entitled "protective exclusion," has aroused the ire of the women's movement and civil libertarians, who see these policies as one more form of sex discrimination.

Charges of discrimination are made credible for several reasons. Jobs that *are* open to "women of child-bearing potential" are almost always lower-paying jobs. In addition, women's groups have noted a shortage of well-supported evidence about exposure to certain alleged toxic hazards and a general lack of consensus in government and industry about proper levels of unsafe exposure. The most significant charge of discrimination rests on evidence of the *male's* contribution to birth defects. As noted earlier, mutagenic substances affect the sperm as well as the egg. This can result in sterility for the man, but also can produce mutated sperm and ultimately a malformed fetus. Thus, any policy designed to protect the fetus must include considerations of the sperm and egg that form it. This would logically include a more expansive protective policy than the mere exclusion of women from the workplace.

Du Pont de Nemours & Co., the largest chemical manufacturer in the United States, has been concerned about these issues since a high incidence of bladder tumors appeared at its large Chambers work plant in Southern New Jersey in the 1930s. Du Pont has issued perhaps the most explicit policy statement about hazards to women and fetuses. If a chemical is found to be or is suspected of being an "embryotoxin" (toxic to the fetus), the first step is to use engineering and administrative procedures to eliminate the risk or to reduce it to an acceptable level. Engineering procedures might, for example, involve special ventilation equipment; administrative procedures might involve management of the length of exposure time or the required use of protective clothing. However, where no "acceptable exposure level" has been determined or where engineering and administrative procedures are inadequate to control exposure, the Du Pont policy reads: "females of child bearing capacity shall be excluded from work areas."[4]

Du Pont has rejected the suggestion that a woman be apprised of the health risk and sign a waiver if she chooses to accept the risk. The Du Pont position is that the exclusionary policy is to protect the fetus, not the woman. Bruce Karrh, medical director of Du Pont, holds that "the primary issue...is not whether the exclusion from the workplace is necessary to protect the adult female or male, but whether it is a necessary step to protect the embryo or fetus."[5]

Du Pont holds that "...the waiver of subsequent claims by the female worker would be of

no legal significance because the deformed fetus, if born, may have its own rights as a person which could not be waived by the mother."[6]

Women's groups continue, however, to view "protective exclusion" as sex discrimination, especially since there is growing evidence that the reproductive systems of men are also adversely affected by certain industrial chemicals. A discussion between Dr. Donald Whorton, one of the first to study testicular toxins in the workplace, and Dr. William N. Rom illustrates the problem many women's groups find with policies of female exclusion:

DR. WHORTON: ...In a situation in which there is testicular toxicity, why would you be removing the women?

DR. ROM: Because it may affect both sexes.

DR. WHORTON: But you would remove the men before the women, wouldn't you?

DR. ROM: Somebody has to work there.[7]

The Coalition for the Reproductive Rights of Women, a group organized to fight discrimination against women of childbearing age, points out that exclusionary protections are unusually broad, especially since not all women want or plan to have children. An attorney for the women's rights project of the American Civil Liberties Union has criticized the notion that women should be protected "against their wishes" and states that "we insist that the cost of safety cannot be equality. Another solution should be found."[8]

Du Pont sees the sex of the excluded party as irrelevant, on grounds that the sole issue is that of protecting the susceptible fetus. The company also notes that implementation of [this policy] is far more costly to the company than a policy that would allow women to make their own choices. However, women's advocates take the view that companies such as Du Pont are simply remiss in developing technological solutions for the control of embryotoxins. A common union complaint is that industry makes the worker safe for the workplace, even to the point of exclusion, rather than making the workplace safe for the worker. These women view with suspicion management contentions that acceptable levels of exposure cannot be achieved.

Growing evidence that toxic substances pose a threat to the *future* fetus, as well as to the *existing* one, through mutation of the sperm and egg, indicates that this issue is not likely to prove amenable to simple solution.[9]

All these issues are further complicated because information that a chemical may be embryotoxic often is not available well in advance of policy decisions. In the case of a chemical used by Du Pont in some resins and elastomers, Du Pont was informed by a supplier in March 1981 that it was possibly teratogenic. The data was preliminary and needed corroboration by a study designed to show if teratogenicity occurs. Rather than wait for such a study to be completed, Du Pont immediately determined a level of exposure considered to pose "no risk." Du Pont then promptly advised all employees working with the chemical of the preliminary findings and determined that the jobs of about fifty women involved unacceptable levels of exposure. About one-half were found to be of childbearing capability and were excluded. All excluded women were moved to comparable positions without penalty in wages or benefits.

Du Pont's Haskell Laboratory simultaneously instituted an animal study to corroborate the preliminary work. The supplier's follow-up study and the Du Pont study both found no teratogenic effect in the animals studied. The supplier's earlier study results apparently contained experimental error. Du Pont notified its employees of the new findings and no longer excluded women of childbearing capability. Return preference was given to women formerly removed from these jobs. During this period, Du Pont made its plant physicians available for counseling employees and for consultations with the personal physicians of employees.[10]

NOTES

1. Philip Shabecoff, "Industry and Women Clash over Hazards in the Workplace," *New York Times*, January 3, 1981.
2. Earl A. Molander, "Regulating Reproductive Risks in the Workplace," in his *Responsive Capitalism: Case Studies in Corporate Social Conduct* (New York: McGraw-Hill Book Co., 1980), p. 9.
3. Albert Rosenfeld, "Fertility May be Hazardous to Your Job," *Saturday Review* **6** (9), p. 12.
4. Bruce W. Karrh, "A Company's Duty to Report Health Hazards," *Bulletin of the New York Academy of Medicine* **54** (September 1978), esp. pp. 783, 785, and Molander, "Regulating Reproductive Risks," p. 16.
5. Bruce W. Karrh, "Occupational Medicine," (Editorial) *Journal of the American Medical Association* **245** (June 5, 1981), p. 2207; see also his "Evaluation and Control of Embryotoxic Agents" (1979), available from Du Pont.
6. Molander, "Regulating Reproductive Risks," p. 16.
7. M. Donald Whorton, "Considerations about Reproductive Hazards," in Jeffrey S. Lee and William N. Rom, eds., *Legal and Ethical Dilemmas in Occupational Health* (Ann Arbor: Butterworth Group), p. 412.
8. Shabecoff, "Industry and Women Clash."
9. Sources: M. Donald Whorton, *et al.*, "Testicular Function among Cabaryl-Exposed Employees," *Journal of Toxicology and Environmental Health* **5** (1979), pp. 929–941; H. Northrop, "Predictive Value of Animal Toxicology," a paper presented at the "Symposium on Reproductive Health Policies in the Workplace," Pittsburgh, Pennsylvania, May 10, 1982; Vilma R. Hunt, "The Reproductive System Sensitivity through the Life Cycle," a paper presented at the American Conference of Governmental Industrial Hygienists, "Symposium: Protection of the Sensitive Individual," Tucson, Arizona, November 9, 1981.
10. The final two paragraphs are based on personal correspondence of August 24, 1982, from Nancy K. Tidonia of Du Pont's Public Affairs Department to Tom L. Beauchamp.

[*Authors' note:* This case was revised by Linda Kern.]

Roger Boisjoly and the Challenger Disaster: A Case Study in Management Practice, Corporate Loyalty, and Business Ethics

Russell P. Boisjoly* and Ellen Foster Curtis*

INTRODUCTION

On January 28, 1986, the space shuttle *Challenger* exploded 73 seconds into its flight, killing the seven astronauts aboard. As the nation mourned the tragic loss of the crew members, the Rogers Commission was formed to investigate the causes of the disaster. (W. P. Rogers was the head of the congressional commission appointed by President Reagan in 1986 to investigate the *Challenger* accident.) The commission concluded that the explosion occurred due to seal failure in one of the solid rocket booster joints. Testimony given by Roger Boisjoly, senior scientist and acknowledged rocket seal expert, indicated that top management at NASA and Morton Thiokol, Inc. had been aware of problems with the O-ring seals, but agreed to launch against the recommendation of Boisjoly and other engineers. Boisjoly had alerted management to problems with the O-rings as early as January 1985, yet several shuttle launches prior to the *Challenger* had been approved without correcting the hazards.

The management process at NASA and Morton Thiokol the year prior to the launch, and Thiokol's postdisaster treatment of Boisjoly and his associates, demonstrate a dramatic change in the corporate environment. Management's willingness to accept previously unacceptable risks increased, which contributed to a communications breakdown between technical experts, their supervisors, and top-level decision makers. This created conflicts about the corporate loyalty of the dissenting engineers, the welfare of the astronauts and the public, and the personal morality of the engineers, as well as the managers who made the launch decision and exacted retribution from the so-called whistle blowers.

The following case study focuses on Roger Boisjoly's attempt to prevent the *Challenger* launch, the scenario that resulted in the launch decision, and Boisjoly's quest to set the record straight despite enormous negative personal and professional consequences. A brief epilogue further analyzes some of the ethical questions raised throughout the case.

PREVIEW FOR DISASTER

On January 24, 1985, Roger Boisjoly, senior scientist at Morton Thiokol, watched the launch of Flight 51-C of the space shuttle program. He was at Cape Canaveral to inspect the solid rocket boosters from Flight 51-C following their recovery in the Atlantic Ocean and to conduct a training session at Kennedy Space Center (KSC) on the proper methods of inspecting the booster joints. While watching the launch, he noted that the temperature that day was much cooler than recorded at other launches, but was still much warmer than the 18 degree temperature encountered three days earlier when he arrived in Orlando. The unseasonably cold weather of the past several days had produced the worst citrus crop failures in Florida history.

When he inspected the solid rocket boosters several days later, Boisjoly discovered evidence that both the primary and secondary O-ring seals on a field joint had been compromised by hot combustion gases (that is, hot gas blow-by had occurred) which had also eroded part of the primary O-ring. This was the first time that a primary seal on a field joint had been penetrated. When he discovered the large amount of blackened grease between the primary and secondary seals, his concern heightened. The blackened grease was discovered over 60-degree and 110-degree arcs, respectively, on two of the seals, with the larger arc indicating greater hot gas blow-by. Postflight calculations indicated that the ambient temperature of the field joints at launch time was 53 degrees. This evidence, coupled with his recollection of the low temperature the day of the launch and the citrus crop damage caused by the cold spell, led to his conclusion that the severe hot gas blow-by may have been caused by, and related to, low temperature. After reporting these findings to his superiors, Boisjoly presented them to engineers and management at NASA's Marshall Space Flight Center (MSFC). As a result of his presentation at MSFC, Roger Boisjoly was asked to participate in the Flight Readiness Review (FRR) on February 12, 1985 for Flight 51-E which was scheduled for launch in April 1985. This FRR represents the first public association of low temperature with blow-by on a field joint, a condition that was considered an "acceptable risk" by Larry Mulloy, NASA's manager for the Booster Project, and other NASA officials.

Roger Boisjoly had twenty-five years of experience as an engineer in the aerospace industry. Among his many notable assignments were the performance of stress and deflection analysis on the flight control equipment of the Advanced Minuteman Missile at Autonetics and his service as a lead engineer on the lunar module of Apollo at Hamilton Standard. He moved to Utah in 1980 to take a position in the Applied Mechanics Department as a staff engineer at the Wasatch Division of Morton Thiokol. He was considered the leading expert in the United States on O-rings and rocket joint seals and received plaudits for his work on the joint seal problems from Joe C. Kilminster, vice president of Space Booster Programs, Morton Thiokol (Kilminster, July 1985). His commitment to the company and the community was further demonstrated by his service as mayor of Willard, Utah, from 1982 to 1983.

The tough questioning he had received at the February 12 FRR convinced Boisjoly of the need for further evidence linking low temperature and hot gas blow-by. He worked closely with Arnie Thompson, supervisor of Rocket Motor Cases, who conducted subscale laboratory tests in March 1985, to further test the effects of temperature on O-ring resiliency. The bench tests that were performed provided powerful evidence to support Boisjoly's and Thompson's theory: Low temperatures greatly and adversely affected the ability of O-rings to create a seal on solid rocket booster joints. If temperature was too low (and they did not know what the threshold temperature would be), it was possible that neither the primary nor secondary O-rings would seal!

One month later the postflight inspection of Flight 51-B revealed that the primary seal of a booster nozzle joint did not make contact during its 2-minute flight. If this damage had occurred in a field joint, the secondary O-ring may have failed to seal, causing the loss of the flight. As a result, Boisjoly and his colleagues became increasingly concerned about shuttle safety. This evidence from the inspection of Flight 51-B was presented at the FRR for Flight 51-F on July 1, 1985; the key engineers and managers at NASA and Morton Thiokol were now aware of the critical O-ring problems and the influence of low temperature on the performance of the joint seals.

During July 1985, Boisjoly and his associates voiced their desire to devote more effort and resources to solving the problems of O-ring erosion. In his activity reports dated July 22 and 29, 1985, Boisjoly expressed considerable frustration with the lack of progress in this area, despite the fact that a Seal Erosion Task Force had been informally appointed on July 19. Finally, Boisjoly wrote the following memo, labeled "Company Private," to R. K. Lund, vice president of engineering for Morton Thiokol, to express the extreme urgency of his concerns. Here are some excerpts from that memo:

> This letter is written to insure that management is fully aware of the seriousness of the current O-Ring erosion problem. . . . The mistakenly accepted po-

sition on the joint problem was to fly without fear of failure... is now drastically changed as a result of the SRM 16A [Solid Rocket Motor] nozzle joint erosion which eroded a secondary O-Ring with the primary O-Ring never sealing. If the same scenario should occur in a field joint (and it could), then it is a jump ball as to the success or failure of the joint.... The result would be a catastrophe of the highest order—loss of human life.

It is my honest and real fear that if we do not take immediate action to dedicate a team to solve the problem, with the field joint having the number one priority, then we stand in jeopardy of losing a flight along with all the launch pad facilities (Boisjoly, July 1985).

On August 20, 1985, R. K. Lund formally announced the formation of the Seal Erosion Task Team. The team consisted of five full-time engineers from the 2500 employed by Morton Thiokol on the Space Shuttle Program. The events of the next five months would demonstrate that management had not provided the resources necessary to carry out the enormous task of solving the seal erosion problem.

On October 3, 1985, the Seal Erosion Task Force met with Joe Kilminster to discuss the problems they were having in gaining organizational support necessary to solve the O-ring problems. Boisjoly later stated that Kilminster summarized the meeting as a "good bullshit session." Once again frustrated by bureaucratic inertia, Boisjoly wrote in his activity report dated October 4th:

> ...NASA is sending an engineering representative to stay with us starting Oct. 14th. We feel that this is a direct result of their feeling that we (MTI) are not responding quickly enough to the seal problem...upper management apparently feels that the SRM program is ours for sure and the customer be damned. (Boisjoly, October 1985)

Boisjoly was not alone in his expression of frustration. Bob Ebeling, department manager, Solid Rocket Motor Igniter and Final Assembly, and a member of the Seal Erosion Task Force, wrote in a memo to Allan McDonald, manager of the

Solid Rocket Motor Project, "HELP! The seal task force is constantly being delayed by every possible means....We wish we could get action by verbal request, but such is not the case. This is a red flag." (McConnell, 1987).

The October 30 launch of Flight 61-A of the *Challenger* provided the most convincing, and yet to some the most contestable, evidence to date that low temperature was directly related to hot gas blow-by. The left booster experienced hot gas blow-by in the center and aft field joints without any seal erosion. The ambient temperature of the field joints was estimated to be 75 degrees at launch time based on postflight calculations. Inspection of the booster joints revealed that the blow-by was less severe than that found on Flight 51-C because the seal grease was a grayish black color, rather than the jet black hue of Flight 51-C. The evidence was now consistent with the bench tests for joint resiliency conducted in March. The actual flight data revealed greater hot gas blow-by for the O-rings on Flight 51-C which had an ambient temperature of 53 degrees than for Flight 61-A which had an ambient temperature of 75 degrees. Those who rejected this line of reasoning concluded that temperature must be irrelevant, since hot gas blow-by had occurred even at room temperature (75 degrees). This difference in interpretation would receive further attention on January 27, 1986.

During the next two-and-one-half months, little progress was made in obtaining a solution to the O-ring problems. Roger Boisjoly made the following entry into his log on January 13, 1986, "O-ring resiliency tests that were requested on September 24, 1985 are now scheduled for January 15, 1986."

THE DAY BEFORE THE DISASTER

At 10 a.m. on January 27, 1986, Arnie Thompson received a phone call from Boyd Brinton, Thiokol's manager of Project Engineering at MSFC, relaying the concerns of NASA's Larry

Wear, also at MSFC, about the 18-degree temperature forecast for the launch of Flight 51-L, the *Challenger,* scheduled for the next day. This phone call precipitated a series of meetings within Morton Thiokol, at the Marshall Space Flight Center, and at the Kennedy Space Center, which culminated in a three-way telecon involving three teams of engineers and managers beginning at 8:15 p.m. EST.

Joe Kilminster, vice president, Space Booster Programs, of Morton Thiokol began the telecon by turning the presentation of the engineering charts over to Roger Boisjoly and Arnie Thompson. They presented thirteen charts which resulted in a recommendation against the launch of the *Challenger.* Boisjoly demonstrated their concerns with the performance of the O-rings in field joints during the initial phases of *Challenger*'s flight with charts showing the effects of primary O-ring erosion, and its timing, on the ability to maintain a reliable secondary seal. The tremendous pressure and release of power from the rocket boosters create rotation in the joint such that the metal moves away from the O-rings so that they cannot maintain contact with the metal surfaces. If, at the same time, erosion occurs in the primary O-ring for any reason, then there is a reduced probability of maintaining a secondary seal. It is highly probable that as the ambient temperature drops, the primary O-ring will not seat; that there will be hot gas blow-by and erosion of the primary O-ring; and that a catastrophe will occur when the secondary O-ring fails to seal.

Bob Lund presented the final chart that included the Morton Thiokol recommendations that the ambient temperature including wind must be such that the seal temperature would be greater than 53 degrees to proceed with the launch. Since the overnight low was predicted to be 18 degrees, Bob Lund recommended against launch on January 28, 1986 or until the seal temperature exceeded 53 degrees.

NASA's Larry Mulloy bypassed Bob Lund and directly asked Joe Kilminster for his reac-tion. Kilminster stated that he supported the position of his engineers and he would not recommend launch below 53 degrees.

George Hardy of MSFC said he was "appalled at that recommendation," according to Allan McDonald's testimony before the Rogers Commission. Nevertheless, Hardy would not recommend to launch if the contractor was against it. After Hardy's reaction, Stanley Reinartz, manager of Shuttle Project Office at MSFC, objected by pointing out that the solid rocket motors were qualified to operate between 40 and 90 degrees Fahrenheit.

Larry Mulloy, citing the data from Fight 61-A which indicated to him that temperature was not a factor, strenuously objected to Morton Thiokol's recommendation. He suggested that Thiokol was attempting to establish new Launch Commit Criteria at 53 degrees and that they couldn't do that the night before a launch. In exasperation Mulloy asked, "My God, Thiokol, when do you want me to launch? Next April?" (McConnell, 1987). Although other NASA officials also objected to the association of temperature with O-ring erosion and hot gas blow-by, Roger Boisjoly was able to hold his ground and demonstrate with the use of his charts and pictures that there was indeed a relationship: The lower the temperature, the higher the probability of erosion and blow-by and the greater the likelihood of an accident. Finally, Joe Kilminster asked for a 5-minute caucus off-net.

According to Boisjoly's testimony before the Rogers Commission, Jerry Mason, senior vice president of Wasatch Operations for Morton Thiokol, began the caucus by saying that "a management decision was necessary." Sensing that an attempt would be made to overturn the no-launch decision, Thompson took a pad of paper and tried to sketch out the problem with the joint, while Boisjoly laid out the photos of the compromised joints from Flights 51-C and 61-A. When they became convinced that no one was listening, they ceased their efforts. As Boisjoly would later testify, "There was not one positive pro-launch statement ever made by anybody'' (Boisjoly, 1986).

According to Boisjoly, after he and Thompson made their last attempts to stop the launch, Jerry Mason asked rhetorically, ''Am I the only one who wants to fly?'' Mason turned to Bob Lund and asked him to ''take off his engineering hat and put on his management hat.'' The four managers held a brief discussion and voted unanimously to recommend *Challenger*'s launch.

Joe Kilminster revised the initial engineering recommendations so that they would support management's decision to launch. Of the nine rationales presented that evening, only one objectively could support the launch decision; although one other rationale could be considered a neutral statement of engineering fact, the other seven rationales were negative, antilaunch, statements. After hearing Kilminster's presentation, which was accepted without a single probing question, George Hardy asked him to sign the chart and telefax it to Kennedy Space Center and Marshall Space Flight Center. At 11 p.m. EST the teleconference ended.

Aside from the four senior Morton Thiokol executives present at the teleconference, all others were excluded from the final decision. The process represented a radical shift from previous NASA policy. Until that moment, the burden of proof had always been on the engineers to prove beyond a doubt that it was safe to launch. NASA, with their objections to the original Thiokol recommendation against the launch, and Mason, with his request for a ''management decision,'' shifted the burden of proof in the opposite direction. Morton Thiokol was expected to prove that launching *Challenger* would not be safe (Boisjoly, 1986).

The change in the decision so deeply upset Boisjoly that he returned to his office and made the following journal entry: ''I sincerely hope that this launch does not result in a catastrophe. I personally do not agree with some of the statements made in Joe Kilminster's written summary

stating that SRM-25 is okay to fly'' (Boisjoly, 1987).

THE DISASTER AND ITS AFTERMATH

On January 28, 1986, a reluctant Roger Boisjoly watched the launch of the *Challenger*. As the vehicle cleared the tower, Bob Ebeling whispered, ''we've just dodged a bullet.'' (The engineers who opposed the launch assumed that O-ring failure would result in an explosion almost immediately after engine ignition.) To continue in Boisjoly's words, ''At approximately $T + 60$ seconds Bob told me he had just completed a prayer of thanks to the Lord for a successful launch. Just thirteen seconds later we both saw the horror of the destruction as the vehicle exploded'' (Boisjoly, 1987).

Morton Thiokol formed a failure investigation team on January 31, 1986 to study the causes of the *Challenger* explosion. Roger Boisjoly and Arnie Thompson were part of the team that was sent to the MSFC in Huntsville, Alabama. Boisjoly's first inkling of a division between himself and management came on February 13, when he was informed that he was to testify before the Rogers Commission the next day. He had very little time to prepare for his testimony. Five days later, two commission members held a closed session with Kilminster, Boisjoly, and Thompson. During the interview Boisjoly gave his memos and activity reports to the commissioners. After that meeting, Kilminster chastised Thompson and Boisjoly for correcting his interpretation of the technical data. Their response was that they would continue to correct his version if it was technically incorrect.

Boisjoly's February 25 testimony before the commission, rebutting the general manager's statement that the initial decision by the Thiokol participants against the launch was not unanimous, drove a wedge further between him and Morton Thiokol management. Boisjoly was flown to MSFC before he could hear the NASA testimony about the preflight telecon. The next day, he was removed from the failure investigation team and returned to Utah.

Beginning in April, Boisjoly began to believe that for the previous month he had been used solely for public relations purposes. Although given the title of seal coordinator for the redesign effort, he was isolated from NASA and the seal redesign effort. His design information had been changed without his knowledge and presented without his feedback. On May 1, 1986, in a briefing preceding closed sessions before the Rogers Commission, Ed Garrison, president of Aerospace Operations for Morton Thiokol, chastised Boisjoly for "airing the company's dirty laundry" with the memos he had given the commission. The next day, Boisjoly testified about the change in his job assignment. Commission chairman Rogers criticized Thiokol management:

> "...if it appears that you're punishing the two people or at least two of the people who are right about the decision and objected to the launch which ultimately resulted in criticism of Thiokol and then they're demoted or feel that they are being retaliated against, that is a very serious matter. It would seem to me, just speaking for myself, they should be promoted, not demoted or pushed aside" (Rogers, 1986).

Boisjoly now sensed a major rift developing within the corporation. Some coworkers perceived that his testimony was damaging the company image. In an effort to clear the air, he and McDonald requested a private meeting with the company's three top executives, which was held on May 16, 1986. According to Boisjoly, management was unreceptive throughout the meeting. The CEO told McDonald and Boisjoly that the company "was doing just fine until Al and I testified about our job reassignments" (Boisjoly, 1987). McDonald and Boisjoly were nominally restored to their former assignments, but Boisjoly's position became untenable as time went passed. On July 21, 1986, Roger Boisjoly requested an extended sick leave from Morton Thiokol.

EPILOGUE—ETHICAL ANALYSIS AND IMPLICATIONS

Roger Boisjoly's experience before, during, and after the *Challenger* tragedy raises ethical questions which can be applied generally to other management situations. Some of those questions concern the moral obligations of engineers and managers, the link imposed by technology on the relationship between engineering and business ethics, and the issues of corporate loyalty and whistleblowing.

Most codes of ethics adopted by engineering professional societies agree with Cicero that "the engineer shall hold paramount the health, safety, and welfare of the public in the performance of his professional duties" (Broome, 1986). New technologies will tie the ethics of engineering more closely to business ethics as corporate tragedies force recognition that traditional ethical standards alone cannot answer the questions posed by a more complex world. Entrenched corporate cultures, failure of managers to ask hard questions, and ethical illiteracy make new technologies difficult to manage. The dangers present in technology are usually forewarned, as in the *Challenger* case, but managers apparently refuse to consider them or are not diligent enough in their efforts to recognize them. The following is one explanation for the occurrence of corporate tragedies:

> Most of us are unaware that we have the following unspoken compact with life: "The world is inherently orderly and predictable. It will behave as it always has; the worst will not happen to me." Imagine the shock to an individual or a corporation when something so terrible and unpredictable happens that it shatters our belief in the orderliness of the world" (Pastin, 1986).

Mark Pastin goes on to state "an accident or disaster differs from a tragedy in that tragedy violates ground rules" (Pastin, 1986). In this sense, the *Challenger* explosion was a corporate and national tragedy: NASA and Morton Thiokol violated a basic ground rule by shifting the burden of proof during the prelaunch teleconference. In making their "management decision" to launch, the executives indicated their belief that the worst could not happen and expressed a willingness to accept risks that they had previously considered unacceptable. One explanation for this "risk taking," given by Howard Schwartz, is that NASA began to view itself as the ideal organization that did not make mistakes. According to Schwartz, "The organization ideal is an image of perfection. It is, so to speak, an idea of God. God does not make mistakes. Having adopted the idea of NASA as the organization ideal it follows that the individual will believe that, if NASA has made a decision, that decision will be correct" (Schwartz, 1987). In his testimony before the Rogers Commission, Roger Boisjoly indicated the extent to which NASA procedure had changed: "This was a meeting (the night before the launch) where the determination was to launch, and it was up to us to prove beyond the shadow of a doubt that it was not safe to do so. This is the total reverse to what the position usually is in a preflight conversation or a flight readiness review" (Boisjoly, 1986). As Schwartz indicates: "If it was a human decision, engineering standards of risk should prevail in determining whether it is safe to launch. On the other hand, if the decision was a NASA decision, it is simply safe to launch, since NASA does not make mistakes" (Schwartz, 1987).

Roger Boisjoly's dilemma became more complicated after the *Challenger* explosion. Boisjoly's repeated efforts to alert management to the problems facing the Seal Task Force, and his attempts to prevent the launch, illustrate his desire to effect changes within normal corporate channels, without violating the "rules." In doing so, he became the "loyal opposition." Thiokol management did not question his loyalty until the government hearings, when, in their eyes, he became a "whistle blower." At that critical juncture, Boisjoly, by testifying as he did, contradicted the company line and made documents available to the Rogers Commission. As discussed above, the personal cost to Boisjoly has been extremely high. His professional position, relationships, and health have suffered. Still, his belief in the moral imperative of his actions prompted him to make the following statement in a speech given to engineering students at Massachusetts Institute of Technology on January 7, 1987:

"I have been asked by some if I would testify again if I knew in advance of the potential consequences to me and my career. My answer is always an immediate 'yes.' I couldn't live with any self respect if I tailored my actions based upon the personal consequences as a result of my honorable actions..." (Boisjoly, 1987).

The case of Roger Boisjoly and the *Challenger* disaster illustrates the need for protection of individual employee rights, as well as the public safety. Currently, only twenty-one states have legislation protecting corporate and government whistleblowers. [Utah's law (Thiokol is located in Utah) protects public employees only.] The *Challenger* disaster has focused enough attention on the need to protect the rights of whistle blowers that on June 4, 1987, NASA announced a formal policy designed to protect individuals like Roger Boisjoly who have information that should be brought to the attention of top-level decision makers. The future struggle facing engineering managers will be the need to balance technological advancement with their moral obligations to the public, while fostering corporate loyalty and protecting individual employee rights.

BIBLIOGRAPHY

[*Authors' note:* For a more detailed analysis of the ethical issues raised by Roger Boisjoly's actions and experiences, see Russell P. Boisjoly, Ellen Foster Curtis, and Eugene Mellican, "Roger Boisjoly and the *Challenger* Disaster: The Ethical Dimensions," *Journal of Business Ethics,* forthcoming.]

Boisjoly, R. M. Applied Mechanics Memorandum to Robert K. Lund, Vice President, Engineering, Wasatch Division, Morton Thiokol, Inc. July 31, 1985.

————. Activity Report, SRM Seal Erosion Task Team Status. October 4, 1985.

————. *Testimony Before the Presidential Commission on Space Shuttle Challenger Accident*. Washington, D.C. February 25, 1986.

————. "Ethical Decisions: Morton Thiokol and the Shuttle Disaster." Speech given at Massachusetts Institute of Technology, January 7, 1987.

Broome, T. "The Slippery Ethics of Engineering." *Washington Post*, December 28, 1986, D3.

Kilminster, J. C. Memorandum (E000-FY86-003) to Robert Lund, Vice President, Engineering, Wasatch Division, Morton Thiokol, Inc. July 5, 1985.

McConnell, M. *Challenger, A Major Malfunction: A True Story of Politics, Greed, and the Wrong Stuff*. Garden City, N.J.: Doubleday and Company, Inc., 1987.

Pastin, M. *The Hard Problems of Management: Gaining the Ethics Edge*. San Francisco: Jossey-Bass, 1986.

Rogers, W. P. *Proceedings Before the Presidential Commission on the Space Shuttle Accident*. Washington, D.C. May 2, 1986.

Schwartz, H. S. "On the Psychodynamics of Organizational Disaster: The Case of the Space Shuttle Challenger." *The Columbia Journal of World Business*. Spring 1987.

The Eastern Airlines Union— Management Experiment

John Simmons*

Over the past decade, Eastern Airlines, under the leadership of Frank Borman, has survived many troubles, although things seemed to be im-

Excerpted from "The Eastern Airlines Union-Management Experiment," *The Boston Globe* (March 30, 1986) by John Simmons. Copyright © 1986 by John Simmons. Reprinted by permission of the author.

*Department of Labor-Management Relations, University of Massachusetts/Amherst, and president, Participation Associates.

proving last year. The first two quarters of 1985, in fact, were Eastern's most profitable. The price of its stock had risen from $3.50 to $11 a share, and forecasters predicted a $90 million net profit for the year. Then, in September 1985, the company was hit heavily in the fare wars—and the final quarter of 1985 became the worst in Eastern's history. The red ink continued into 1986, and late last month the airline had to fight for its life.

Lenders who held $2.5 billion in debt gave the airline until February 28 to obtain wage cuts and changes in work rules or benefits from Eastern's three unions. If the concessions weren't agreed upon, the bankers would put Eastern into default. All three of the airline unions were up in arms, but during the last week in February the pilots' and transport workers' unions seemed close to accepting the company's demands. Only the machinists' union, led by Charles E. Bryan, refused to accept the concessions. At a four-hour meeting of Eastern's board of directors that ended in the early hours of February 24, Bryan offered to cut wages by 15 percent (instead of the requested 20 percent), but he refused to accept work changes and insisted on the removal of Borman as chief executive. This was unacceptable to the board, and faced with the prospect of being put in default, the directors approved a buy-out bid from Texas Air Corporation, which also owns Continental Airlines and New York Air.

Two facts put a special twist on this story. Eastern Airlines is the largest American corporation to institute systems whereby top management, union leaders, and the rank and file join to manage the operation. Thanks to this system, the company survived several crises in the past few years. Deepening trust, cooperation, and worker participation helped pull the company from near bankruptcy in 1983 to a $289 million turnaround in operating profit in 1984. But successful, long-lasting revolutions of this kind require shifts in basic behaviors throughout the vast organization. Old behaviors take time to change. And Eastern did not have enough time.

The second fact is that Eastern Airlines is run by Frank Borman, former test pilot and astronaut, a man whose idea of relaxation is to get into a speedboat and roar down Biscayne Bay at 50 miles an hour. Borman likes a crisis; he was accused by some employees of practicing management by roller coaster, but the company needed stability, not crisis. Borman also likes adventure—and he has had the courage to make management history. "It is a hell of a thing we are doing," he said of worker participation. "I'll tell you, it is exciting."

While wage concessions and an improved economy helped Eastern in the past few years, an explosion of energy and ideas among employees across the organization fueled its momentary comeback. It was often a matter of simple changes. For example:

- SkyDrol is a special hydraulic fluid used in the landing gears and wing flaps of Eastern jets. Recently a stock clerk at the Miami base checked on the price the airline was paying a vendor for a 42-gallon drum. Then he asked a friend at another carrier what they were paying and learned that it was $200 less. Bud Staley, steward of the machinists' union, took this information to the purchasing manager, who renegotiated the price. Since Eastern buys 700 barrels a year, a savings of $140,000 was realized. Staley says that it used to be "them" and "us"; that idea, he says, was replaced by, "Everyone cares about this company."

- In 1984, Roy Hrytzay, manager of the print shop, concluded that most of Eastern's forms could be printed in-house if he had an efficient form printer and a collator for carbon forms. The "Farm-In Task Force" accepted his proposal to spend $600,000 for the equipment to do the job. Hrytzay estimated the cost saving to be $576,000 in the first three years.

- When Eastern flights arrived in Atlanta in 1984, supervisors were no longer there to manage plane turnaround procedures. The union ramp crews that dock, unload, and clean the planes were carrying out their duties with peer leaders heading each crew. The result was faster turnaround time, a 15 percent reduction in lost baggage, and the elimination from the company payroll of six supervisory positions. (As part of the employee-involvement and wage-concession programs, the extraneous supervisors were guaranteed new jobs elsewhere through company attrition and turnover.) Recently a turnaround record was set by the ramp crew at Columbia, South Carolina. The plane was at the gate one minute and 39 seconds while 24 passengers boarded and their bags were loaded. Several months ago, before talk of a takeover, Pat Levi, then director for employee involvement, summed things up: "You are looking at a more responsible work force today, simply because they are more aware than before."

The systems of cooperation seem wonderfully simple down at the grass-roots level. But they were constantly threatened—often by their greatest advocates. Borman himself, although temperamentally and ideologically predisposed to endorse participative management, faltered in his leadership. Some of the same qualities that made him a leader of vision and energy—decisiveness, the ability to act, impatience, fearlessness, and a deep respect for the individual—are also the qualities that may have prevented him from becoming part of the new participatory culture at Eastern.

The union leaders, too, who were the first to demand greater influence by the workers in a cooperative venture, have found that the habits of participative management are not easy to get used to. Since Eastern's new approach was based on nonadversarial relationships, it violated every practice and position of traditional union strategy and behavior. And the rank and file, despite increased cost-effectiveness in the company and generally improved morale, still felt jerked around by management and union leadership.

The success of participation was also threatened from the outside. Eastern did have some miraculous results due to the new systems. But the greater miracle was that Eastern was able to institute these systems while tap dancing to the tune of deregulation, with the advent of low-cost competitors such as People Express. In 1978, when the airlines were deregulated, commercial aviation became one of the most volatile industries in America.

For the past 10 years, the most visible figure at Eastern has been Frank Borman, who joined the company in 1970 as a senior vice president and became chief executive officer in late 1975. Like most CEOs, Borman is assertive, energetic, and confident. He is far more progressive than his predecessors, but he is fundamentally an old-style CEO.

When Borman became chairman of the board of Eastern Airlines in 1975, he began to change what he saw as "corrosive" influences in the organization. Under his predecessor, Eddie Rickenbacker, management by fear had cascaded down the organizational levels, all the way from the top to the union members. This created a climate that Eastern employees have been reacting to ever since. "We spent 20 years making animals out of them," Borman said in an interview about a year ago. "They were trained to treat themselves and their efforts as commodities. Then how can you wonder why they feel the way they do?"

Borman was the beginning of the new culture. Before him, because golf was a favorite pastime for Eastern executives, the company held two or three big country-club memberships. "We had [an advertising] contract with Jack Nicklaus, not so much because he sold tickets," Borman said in an interview, "but because guys liked to play golf with him." The corporate officers all had leased cars; the top two had Mercedes. These cars were depreciated at an enormous rate and then sold to the officers individually after they'd been driving them a year. A corporate jet was parked outside the executive office building in Miami and used for personal trips. Offended by

the values represented by these practices, Borman eliminated the frills. In 1976, Eastern became the first major airline to have profit sharing for all employees instead of bonuses for executives.

But Borman's approach to changing the organizational culture was not enough to weather the storms wrought by deregulation and new competitors, because the approach was not part of a shared vision of how people would like to be managed. There was no strategy for changing the basic assumptions and ways of doing business, just Borman's sense that he didn't like certain hierarchical practices and their underlying values. Borman undertook changing the organization without understanding where it was going or how to get there, and without information about the experiences of other companies trying to make similar changes. There was little chance that such an effort could succeed.

Although his attitude prepared the way for the restructuring of Eastern, Borman was not the one who proposed substantive organizational changes. Those came in December 1983 from union leadership.

The year 1983 was a bad one for Eastern. Along with the rest of the industry, the company had never regained its equilibrium after the 1978 deregulation. The recession that had begun in 1981 continued to take its toll. In March of 1983, Borman caved in to a strike threat from International Association of Machinists president Bryan, whose union represents mechanics, ramp crews, and baggage handlers, giving the machinists the wage increase they demanded. This outraged pilots, flight attendants, and noncontract employees, bitterly divided Eastern's unions, and deepened the antagonism between employees and management. Middle managers were particularly demoralized; their rate of wage increases in the previous five years had been 12 percent less than that given to the pilots during the same period.

That summer the recession hit Eastern hard. One Sunday evening in late September, Borman walked into an Eastern TV studio and taped a message to be shown to employees the next day. He said that in 12 days Eastern would declare bankruptcy. Some employees believed him, and some did not. Consumers did; nearly $2 million worth of tickets bought for holiday travel were returned in the next three days. Those tickets represented the cash that Eastern needed to operate.

If the firm had not been in trouble before, it certainly was then—and Bryan knew it as well as Borman did. Leaders of all three unions—machinists, pilots, and flight attendants—hurriedly signed an agreement with Borman to "do whatever is necessary to maintain the financial health of the company." Holiday travelers stopped asking for ticket refunds, and travel agents started booking Eastern flights again. While Borman got his agreement, employees were fed up with management by crisis—especially since many of them believed that Borman had created the crisis to begin with.

The unions then sat down with management. Management wanted wage concessions; in return, the unions insisted on influence. Union members and their leaders believed that the company was mismanaged; they pointed to four years of growing losses plus the industry's worst debt-equity ratio and a poor record of labor relations.

At a meeting in November 1983, Bryan, representing IAM and supported by the pilots and flight attendants, offered a 24-point plan under which employees would share in managerial decision-making and ownership. In return for concessions equal to 18 to 22 percent of their wages, the unions wanted two more board seats (in addition to the two seats employee representatives had contracted to get in April 1983); 25 percent of the common stock; the expansion of an employee-involvement program (so-called action teams, overseen by a council composed in equal parts of management and labor); and the right to review corporate decisions, including all financial information.

According to one observer, Borman "went through the roof." He had no real alternative, however; he negotiated some modifications and in early December 1983 accepted the union proposal. Eastern had a new flight plan, one that no American firm had ever charted before. Management and the unions thought that getting the plan on paper had been rough, but that was nothing compared with keeping it aloft.

After years of negotiating on the basis of adversarial relations, a company does not become cooperative overnight. A worker does not suddenly trust his or her supervisor or union representative. The leader of one union does not suddenly trust the leader of another union, and no union leader suddenly trusts the CEO. Management does not suddenly trust workers and union leaders. Behavior is learned over many years through the reality of the corporate culture. In their experience in corporate America, most people have been taught one basic truth: The less you trust, the longer you survive.

The agreement of December 1983 was Eastern's only formal strategy for change. Workers got more influence through the action teams, and the unions got decision-making power through the board and stock ownership. Such innovations cannot thrive, however, without radical changes in attitude, from the bottom up to the top. All the employees must look at the way they work and ask, "Is this behavior consistent with how we would like to behave? Is it consistent with the values of participatory management, emphasizing trust, respect for the individual, cooperation, honesty, and participation?"

Eastern had plenty of work to do—in reorienting the company and in getting back on its feet—and very little time. In the first four months, participatory management clearly resulted in improved productivity, but no one realized that such a system requires constant work at the human level.

Some events did reflect positive shifts in attitude. In May of 1984, Bryan drew up a list of changes that had been made since the December 1983 agreement. Four vice presidents had left because they could not stomach the participation system. Union representatives were regularly attending meetings on corporate forecasting and planning. Borman was delegating more authority. He no longer ran the regular morning conference on operations. The former "extreme adversaries" in the legal department were acting as "allies in every regard," Bryan said—for example, by bringing more work in-house, which, the union believed, led to more job security. Management had made a "total commitment" to go all out to change "the whole image of the management-labor relationship." Management was sending all press releases and communications with the employees to the union leaders for their review before distribution, "to be sure...[they] won't be offensive," as Bryan put it.

But other events reflected a lack of change that proved fatal. In May 1984, six months after the agreement, a crucial meeting was mismanaged. It was to have been a new kind of event, not simply an old-style business meeting. This special two-day conference, away from corporate headquarters, had been planned to bring labor and management together outside the bargaining room for the first time so they could discuss their mutual concerns for the future. It was to have been a first step toward developing mutual trust as well as the vision of the new Eastern.

It became an old-style meeting. With the consent of both Borman and the union, management planners changed the agenda. Instead of working on cementing trust, the joint group tackled the long-term financial plan. Management felt that understanding the numbers was more important than building relationships.

According to Borman, the meeting was a disaster because the pilots and machinists fought it out—but he did not fully understand how to correct it. Not enough trust had been established to launch any kind of cooperative effort, not only between labor and management but also among the unions. Changing agendas was a critical error that a well-thought-out plan for major change would have exposed. Borman and his advisers assumed that they had sufficiently "fixed" the union-management relationship. After all, hadn't the machinists given the company $50 million in documented productivity increases in the first four months of the year? It was time, according to traditional management logic, to get on with building the "system," to get the unions to buy into the corporate plan for the future.

They did not understand that in a culture based on participation, relationship-building is a never-ending process that must be a top priority. New structures cannot work without changes in attitudes.

In the meantime, there was trouble within each union. Moving from an adversarial to a cooperative approach with management is high risk for any union leader, because no one can be sure of what it means. Even more important, union leaders know they get elected because they are good fighters. Bob Callahan, president of the Transport Workers' Union, said in an interview in May 1984 that he believed strongly in the Eastern slogan of "working together," but he added, "I also believe, relative to my group, that [cooperation] is going to be such a political liability for me that I will be unelectable in three years."

On June 19, 1984, the pilots' Master Executive Council, the senior-management decision-making group, fired George Smith, its chairman. This act was a major setback to building a cooperative effort between labor and management. "I had not been belligerent enough in my dealings with management of Eastern," Smith said.

Both union leadership and senior management of Eastern are responsible for not having understood the process of organizational change. Had they started the trust-building process immediately after the December 1983 agreement, they might have solved the problems of the following years. Instead, those problems, fed by suspicion and frustration, grew into full-fledged crises.

The three union leaders and Borman never met together privately to begin cementing relationships. And there were few one-on-one meetings because neither side ever asked for them. Borman and the union leaders never went fishing, never shared so much as a beer after work.

All three unions have experienced serious internal problems in shifting to a more cooperative approach. Like management, they have no guidelines or manuals for change. The leaders have had their own trouble in expanding their management techniques beyond the adversarial approach. In some ways it was easier to develop a cooperative approach with higher-ups than with "brothers and sisters."

IAM leader Bryan, who refused to accept management's terms on February 24, isolated himself, rarely using a team approach. Not until May 1985 did he begin to look at his own management style and explore better ways to manage the union. And according to one participant, in October 1985 Bryan stormed out of what had been a reasonably relaxed session at a retreat with Borman and other senior managers after an executive vice president suggested quietly that Bryan would be easier to talk to if he didn't make speeches all the time.

At the same time, the rank and file wondered whether the traditional structures of the old system could serve them in the new system. Trust in union leadership was not high. Smith's termination was not an isolated event. The pilots had five negotiating committees in three years, a rate of change that did not foster trust in their constituency and did not contribute to a partnership with management. In May of 1985, Callahan's Transport Workers' Union members voted down, four to one, the contract he had recommended.

Despite problems with union leadership and in the marketplace, however, ultimate responsibility for the success or failure of Eastern and its new management approach lies in great measure with Frank Borman. Participation does not mean only that people work together; it means that people learn *how* to work together. It means that people—from corporate suites to ramp crews—must learn how to change. Thus, if Borman advocated participation for the airline's hard-working mechanics, he had to advocate participation for the CEO as well.

As time went on, Borman did, in fact, grow more open to examining his own behavior, and he encouraged others to examine theirs. This was crucial in the establishment of the new attitudes, habits, and structure at Eastern. In a large and decentralized organization, the greatest power a CEO has lies more in example and persuasion than in direct exercise of authority. The CEO chooses the senior vice presidents, helps run the board of directors, is involved at many different levels with the outside world, and provides leadership for the nation's economy.

Borman's puzzle, like that of any CEO, was to figure out *how* to provide leadership. A CEO sets objectives and provides a model of behavior, implying that the model is to be followed. If the behavior is participatory, the CEO can demonstrate his personal commitment to consensus decision-making, delegation, sharing of responsibility, and cutting out levels of management.

Borman has begun his own re-education. When asked in an interview what advice he would give to chief executives who want to institute participatory management at other corporations, he replied, "Start at the top." People throughout the organization, he said, need to understand that there is "absolute support from the senior management."

Next, he advised putting in place "a structure that does not simply start and stop." Meetings can be useful, he said, but not if they are isolated cheerleading sessions with no connection to daily behavior on the job. And the other side of this notion is the understanding that the process of transformation must continue even when the company's fortunes improve. In good times you cannot let people think, "Everything's in shape. We can go back to our old ways."

In the interview, Borman listed nine additional points for CEOs considering a move to new management philosophy:

- Recognize that the purpose is to "change the culture." It is "not a program you put in place and ask, 'How do I measure the results tomorrow?'"
- Be prepared "to listen to some of your very, very dear strategies challenged by people who were formerly adversaries."
- The new partnership with the unions is like a good marriage; you have to keep working at it "on a daily basis."
- You must lead the transition to the new culture "by setting the example, not simply by fiat."
- You must maintain the belief "on faith" that such a long-term effort is the right thing to do.
- "Be prepared to spend some money on it." At Eastern, Borman said, 32 of the company's most talented people led the change full-time.
- If people cannot adapt to the new approach, Borman warned, "You are going to have to get rid of them."
- You must bring new team-building skills to management—and reinforce their use so that they "take."
- You have to be "fully committed to it."

First, last, and foremost, participative management is a partnership. The recent crisis at Eastern, culminating in the probable sale to Texas Air, seems to be the final chapter in an ambitious, failed partnership among workers, union leaders, and management. It is most dramatically the failure of a thorny partnership between Borman and Bryan.

That ending came in a bitter meeting of the board that ended after 2 a.m. on February 24, at which many of the players reverted to their least constructive roles. Borman was again using the pressure of imminent disaster to ask for sacrifices from workers. Again, unions were in conflict with one another. Bryan held out for terms that seemed unfair to many—smaller wage concessions than the other unions had agreed to and the demand for Borman's resignation. The future under Texas Air chairman Frank Lorenzo

looks bleak. Sources say that Bryan recently requested a meeting with Lorenzo and that in response Lorenzo told Eastern management: "I don't talk to union leaders."

Eastern came close to making the new system work. The partnership had produced extraordinary results at the base of the organization. The action teams were able to work together; upper management and union leadership were not.

In the final meeting, frustrated hopes exploded. For participation to have taken hold, the company needed systems in motion from top to bottom. It needed stability, not repeated crisis.

Eastern had changed the management philosophy, but it had not been able to change leadership behavior quickly enough. The partnership had failed.

High Court Backs a Preference Plan for Blacks in Jobs: United Steelworkers of America v. Weber

Linda Greenhouse*

WASHINGTON, June 27, 1979—The Supreme Court ruled today that private employers can legally give special preferences to black workers to eliminate "manifest racial imbalance" in traditionally white-only jobs.

In a 5-to-2 decision that was greeted as an important victory by civil rights leaders, the Court held that voluntary affirmative action plans, even those containing numerical quotas, do not automatically violate the Civil Rights Acts of 1964.

*Reporter, *The New York Times*.

Title VII of that act bars discrimination in employment on the basis of race.

The majority opinion, written by Associate Justice William J. Brennan Jr., reversed two lower Federal courts, which had held that Title VII outlawed a special training program designed to increase the number of blacks in skilled craft jobs in a Louisiana steel mill.

WHITE WORKER'S ARGUMENT

The majority rejected the argument of a white worker, Brian F. Weber, that the training program constituted illegal "reverse discrimination" against whites by reserving half the places for black workers.

"It would be ironic indeed," Justice Brennan wrote, "if a law triggered by a nation's concern over centuries of racial injustice and intended to improve the lot of those who had 'been excluded from the American dream for so long' constituted the first legislative prohibition of all voluntary, private, race-conscious efforts to abolish traditional patterns of racial segregation and hierarchy."

The majority was joined by Associate Justices Potter Stewart, Byron R. White, Thurgood Marshall and Harry A. Blackmun, who also filed a concurring opinion. Chief Justice Warren E. Burger and Associate Justice William H. Rehnquist both filed dissenting opinions.

A CLEAR MAJORITY

The decision in *United Steelworkers of America v. Weber* (No. 78–432) stopped short of giving blanket approval of any conceivable affirmative action plan. Nevertheless, it commanded a clear, if narrow, majority, without the confusion and ambiguity engendered by the six opinions in last year's case of Allan P. Bakke. In that decision, handed down a year ago tomorrow, the Court struck down a rigid quota system for admission to a California state medical school but also suggested that affirmative action programs could be justified under other circumstances.

The Bakke case turned on the Court's analysis of the equal protection clause of the Fourteenth Amendment to the United States Constitution. Today's opinion did not involve the Constitution at all. The Court viewed the affirmative action plan as a voluntary agreement between private parties whose behavior is not regulated by the Constitution. The Justices therefore addressed only the question of whether Congress meant to bar this kind of voluntary action when it outlawed discrimination in employment on the basis of race.

Justice Brennan conceded that the literal language of Title VII would seem to outlaw racial preferences as well as race discrimination in hiring. That argument, he said, "is not without force." But such a literal interpretation, he continued, "is misplaced," and ignores both the historical context in which Congress enacted the law and the intention of the legislators who voted for it to improve the economic condition of blacks in America.

An interpretation of Title VII that "forbade all race-conscious affirmative action," Justice Brennan wrote, "would bring about an end completely at variance with the purpose of the statute and must be rejected."

The two dissenters sharply disputed this conclusion. Chief Justice Burger called it "contrary to the explicit language of the statute and arrived at by means wholly incompatible with long-established principles of separation of powers."

In enacting Title VII, the Chief Justice said, "Congress expressly *prohibited* the discrimination against Brian Weber the Court approves now." In unusually acerbic language, Chief Justice Burger accused the majority of "totally rewriting a crucial part of Title VII to reach a desirable result."

Justice Rehnquist, frequently the Court's most rhetorically flamboyant member, was even more biting in a 37-page dissent also signed by the Chief Justice. The majority opinion itself ran 13 pages.

Justice Rehnquist quoted at length from the floor debates, committee reports, and other legislative history of Title VII to show that "Congress meant to outlaw *all* racial discrimination, recognizing that no discrimination based on race is benign, that no action disadvantaging a person because of his color is affirmative.''

He wrote that the majority opinion ''introduces into Title VII a tolerance for the very evil that the law was intended to eradicate, without offering even a clue as to what the limits on that tolerance may be.''

The challenged affirmative action program was part of a nationwide agreement reached in 1974 through collective bargaining between Kaiser and the United Steelworkers. It covered 15 Kaiser plants around the country and was designed to remedy the almost complete absence of black workers from skilled jobs in the aluminum industry.

AGREEMENT ON TRAINING

The agreement called for the creation of special training programs, open to blacks and whites on a 50-50 basis and remaining in operation until the number of blacks in skilled jobs reached the proportion of blacks in the labor force from which the individual plants recruited.

At Kaiser's plant in Gramercy, Louisiana, where Mr. Weber works, the area's work force was 39 percent black. But blacks made up less than 2 percent—five out of 273—of the skilled workers at the plant.

There were 13 openings in the new training program at the Gramercy plant. Mr. Weber had insufficient seniority to get one of the six places reserved for whites. However, two of the blacks accepted had less seniority than he did, and he brought a lawsuit in Federal District Court charging violation of Title VII.

The district court held that the training program was unlawful under Title VII because the black workers whom it benefited had not themselves been the victims of illegal discrimination by Kaiser.

On appeal, the United States Court of Appeals for the Fifth Circuit affirmed. In a 2-to-1 opinion, that court held that Title VII made affirmative action programs permissible only to remedy discrimination against individual employees, not as a response to a perception of general societal discrimination.

That opinion was viewed by the federal Government and the civil rights movement as a serious threat to all voluntary affirmative action plans. In order to satisfy the Fifth Circuit's requirement that an affirmative action plan be a remedy for past discrimination, an employer would have to admit that it had discriminated and thereby invite Title VII lawsuits from blacks.

Failure to admit past discrimination, on the other hand, would invite ''reverse discrimination'' suits from whites. Given such a dilemma, employers could be expected to abandon the effort and wait for the Government to sue them.

The Supreme Court agreed to take the case last December and heard arguments in March. The union, the company and the Federal government all argued for reversal, but the union and the government were in nearly total disagreement about the approach the Court should take.

The union contended that Title VII, while prohibiting the government from ordering affirmative action plans, nonetheless permitted voluntary action. The government argued that Title VII did authorize the Federal courts to impose affirmative action plans, and that employers could therefore legally devise their own whenever the low numbers of blacks on their employment rolls raised the possibility of a government enforcement suit.

EXCERPTS FROM HIGH COURT'S OPINIONS

From Majority Opinion by Justice Brennan

We emphasize at the outset the narrowness of our inquiry. Since the Kaiser-USWA plan does not involve state action, this case does not present an alleged violation of the Equal Protection Clause of the Constitution. Further, since the Kaiser-USWA plan was adopted voluntarily, we are not concerned with what Title VII requires or with what a court might order to remedy a past proven violation of the act. The only question before us is the narrow statutory issue of whether Title VII forbids private employers and unions from voluntarily agreeing upon bona fide affirmative action plans that accord racial preferences in the manner and for the purpose provided in the Kaiser-USWA plan. That question was expressly left open in *McDonald v. Santa Fe Trail Trans. Co.,* which held, in a case not involving affirmative action, that Title VII protects whites as well as blacks from certain forms of racial discrimination.

Respondent argues that Congress intended in Title VII to prohibit all race-conscious affirmative action plans. Respondent's argument rests upon a literal interpretation of Sec. 703 (a) and (d) of the Act. Those sections make it unlawful to "discriminate...because of...race" in hiring and in the selection of apprentices for training programs. Since, the argument runs, *McDonald v. Santa Fe Trans. Co.,* supra, settled that Title VII forbids discrimination against whites as well as blacks, and since the Kaiser-USWA affirmative action plan operates to discriminate against white employees solely because they are white, it follows that the Kaiser-USWA plan violates Title VII.

Affirmative Action Plan Respondent's argument is not without force. But it overlooks the significance of the fact that the Kaiser-USWA plan is an affirmative action plan voluntarily adopted by private parties to eliminate traditional patterns of racial segregation. In this context respondent's reliance upon a literal construction of Sec. 703 (a) and (d) and upon McDonald is misplaced. The prohibition against racial discrimination in Sec. 703 (a) and (d) of Title VII must therefore be read against the background of the legislative history of Title VII and the historical context from which the Act arose. Examination of those sources makes clear that an interpretation of the sections that forbade all race-

conscious affirmative action would "bring about an end completely at variance with the purpose of the statute" and must be rejected.

Congress' primary concern in enacting the prohibition against racial discrimination in Title VII of the Civil Rights Act of 1964 was with "the plight of the Negro in our economy" (remarks of Senator Humphrey). Before 1964, blacks were largely relegated to "unskilled and semiskilled jobs." Because of automation the number of such jobs was rapidly decreasing. As a consequence "the relative position of the Negro worker (was) steadily worsening. In 1947 the nonwhite unemployment rate was only 64 percent higher than the white rate; in 1962 it was 124 percent higher." Congress considered this a serious social problem.

Congress feared that the goals of the Civil Rights Act—the integration of blacks into the mainstream of American society—could not be achieved unless this trend were reversed. And Congress recognized that that would not be possible unless blacks were able to secure jobs "which have a future."

Title VII Prohibition Accordingly, it was clear to Congress that "the crux of the problem [was] to open employment opportunities for Negroes in occupations which have been traditionally closed to them," and it was to this problem that Title VII's prohibition against racial discrimination in employment was primarily addressed.

It plainly appears from the House Report accompanying the Civil Rights Act that Congress did not intend wholly to prohibit private and voluntary affirmative action efforts as one method of solving this problem.

Given this legislative history, we cannot agree with respondent that Congress intended to prohibit the private sector from taking effective steps to accomplish the goal that Congress designed Title VII to achieve. The very statutory words intended as a spur or catalyst to cause "employers and unions to self-examine and to self-evaluate their employment practices and to endeavor to eliminate, so far as possible, the last vestiges of an unfortunate and ignominious page in this country's history,'' *Albemarle v. Moody,* cannot be interpreted as an absolute prohibition against all private, voluntary, race-conscious affirmative action efforts to hasten the elimination of such vestiges. It would be ironic indeed if a law triggered by a Nation's concern over centuries of racial injustice and intended to improve the lot of those who had ''been excluded from the American dream for so long'' constituted the first legislative prohibition of all voluntary, private, race-conscious efforts to abolish traditional patterns of racial segregation and hierarchy.

History of Section 703   Our conclusion is further reinforced by examination of the language and legislative history of Section 703 (j) of Title VII. Opponents of Title VII raised two related arguments against the bill. First, they argued that the Act would be interpreted to require employers with racially imbalanced work forces to grant preferential treatment to racial minorities in order to integrate. Second, they argued that employers with racially imbalanced work forces would grant preferential treatment to racial minorities, even if not required to do so by the Act. Had Congress meant to prohibit all race-conscious affirmative action, as respondent urges, it easily could have answered both objections by providing that Title VII would not require or permit racially preferential integration efforts. But Congress did not choose such a course. Rather, Congress added Section 703 (j), which addresses only the first objection. The section provides that nothing contained in Title VII ''shall be interpreted to require any employer...to grant preferential treatment...to any group because of the race...of such...group on account of'' a de facto racial imbalance in the employer's work force. The section does not state that ''nothing in Title VII shall be interpreted to permit'' voluntary affirmative efforts to correct racial imbalances. The natural infer-

ence is that Congress chose not to forbid all voluntary race-conscious affirmative action.

The reasons for this choice are evident from the legislative record. Title VII could not have been enacted into law without substantial support from legislators in both Houses who traditionally resisted federal regulation of private business. Those legislators demanded as a price for their support that ''management prerogatives and union freedoms...be left undisturbed to the greatest extent possible.'' Section 703 (j) was proposed by Senator Dirksen to allay any fears that the Act might be interpreted in such a way as to upset this compromise. In view of this legislative history and in view of Congress' desire to avoid undue federal regulation of private businesses, use of the word ''require'' rather than the phrase ''require or permit'' in Section 703 (j) fortifies the conclusion that Congress did not intend to limit traditional business freedom to such a degree as to prohibit all voluntary, race-conscious affirmative action.

Limits of Prohibition   We therefore hold that Title VII's prohibition in Sec. 703 (a) and (d) against racial discrimination does not condemn all private, voluntary, race-conscious affirmative action plans.

We need not today define in detail the line of demarcation between permissible and impermissible affirmative action plans. It suffices to hold that the challenged Kaiser-USWA affirmative action plan falls on the permissible side of the line. The purposes of the plan mirror those of the statute. Both were designed to break down old patterns of racial segregation and hierarchy. Both were structured to ''open employment opportunities for Negroes in occupations which have been traditionally closed to them.''

At the same time the plan does not unnecessarily trammel the interests of the white employees. The plan does not require the discharge of white workers and their replacement with new black hirees. Nor does the plan create an absolute bar to the advancement of white employees; half of those trained in the program will be white. Moreover, the plan is a temporary measure; it is not intended to maintain racial balance, but simply to eliminate a manifest racial imbalance. Preferential selection of craft trainees at the Gramercy plant will end as soon as the percentage of black skilled craft workers in the Gramercy plant approximates the percentage of blacks in the local labor force.

We conclude, therefore, that the adoption of the Kaiser-USWA plan for the Gramercy plant falls within the area of discretion left by Title VII to the private sector voluntarily to adopt affirmative action plans designed to eliminate conspicuous racial imbalance in traditionally segregated job categories. Accordingly, the judgment of the Court of Appeals for the Fifth Circuit is reversed.

From Dissenting Opinion by Justice Rehnquist

We have never wavered in our understanding that Title VII "prohibits all racial discrimination in employment, without exception for any particular employees."

Today, however, the Court behaves as if it had been handed a note indicating that Title VII would lead to a result unacceptable to the Court if interpreted here as it was in our prior decisions. Accordingly, without even a break in syntax, the Court rejects "a literal construction of Sec. 703 (a)" in favor of newly discovered "legislative history," which leads it to a conclusion directly contrary to that compelled by the "uncontradicted legislative history" unearthed in McDonald and our other prior decisions.

Thus, by a tour de force reminiscent not of jurists such as Hale, Holmes, and Hughes, but of escape artists such as Houdini, the Court eludes clear statutory language, "uncontradicted" legislative history, and uniform precedent in concluding that employers are, after all, permitted to consider race in making employment decisions.

Were Congress to act today specifically to prohibit the type of racial discrimination suffered by Weber, it would be hard pressed to draft language better tailored to the task than that found in Sec. 703 (d) of Title VII:

"It shall be an unlawful employment practice for any employers, labor organization, or joint labor-management committee controlling apprenticeship or other training or retraining, including on-the-job training programs to discriminate against any individual because of his race, color, religion, sex, or national origin in admission to, or employment in, any program established to provide apprenticeship or other training." 43 U.S.C. Sec. 2000e-2 (d). Equally suited to the task would be Sec. 703 (a) (2), which makes it unlawful for an employer to classify his employees "in any way which would deprive or tend to deprive any individual of employment opportunities or otherwise adversely affect his status as an employee, because of such individual's race, color, religion, sex, or national origin."

Entirely consistent with these two express prohibitions is the language of Sec. 703 (j) of Title VII, which provides that the Act is not to be interpreted "to require any employer...to grant preferential treatment to any individual or to any group because of the race...of such individual or group" to correct a racial imbalance in the employer's work force. Seizing on the word "require," the Court infers that Congress must have intended to "permit" this type of racial discrimination. Not only is this reading of Sec. 703 (j) outlandish in the light of the flat prohibitions of Sec. 703 (a) and (d), but it is totally belied by the Act's legislative history.

Quite simply, Kaiser's racially discriminatory admission quota is flatly prohibited by the plain language of Title VII.

From Dissenting Opinion by Chief Justice Burger

The Court reaches a result I would be inclined to vote for were I a member of Congress considering a proposed amendment of Title VII. I cannot join the Court's judgment, however, because it is contrary to the explicit language of the statute and arrived at by means wholly incompatible with long-established principles of separation of powers. Under the guise of statutory "construction," the Court effectively rewrites Title VII to achieve what it regards as a desirable result.

Often we have difficulty interpreting statutes either because of imprecise drafting or because legislative compromises have produced genuine ambiguities. But here there is no lack of clarity, no ambiguity. The quota embodied in the collective-bargaining agreement between Kaiser and the Steelworkers unquestionably discriminates on the basis of race against individual employees seeking admission to on-the-job training programs. And, under the plain language of Section 703 (d), that is "an unlawful employment practice."

Oddly, the Court seizes upon the very clarity of the statute almost as a justification for evading the unavoidable impact of its language. The Court blandly tells us that Congress could not really have meant what it said, for a "literal construction" would defeat the "purpose" of the statute—at least the Congressional "purpose" as five Justices divine it today.

Arguably, Congress may not have gone far enough in correcting the effects of past discrimination when it enacted Title VII. But that statute was conceived and enacted to make discrimination against any individual illegal, and I fail to see how "voluntary compliance" with the no-discrimination principle that is the heart and soul of Title VII as currently written will be achieved by permitting employers to discriminate against some individuals to give preferential treatment to others.

It is often observed that hard cases make bad law. I suspect there is some truth to that adage, for the "hard" cases always tempt judges to exceed the limits of their authority, as the Court does today by totally rewriting a crucial part of Title VII to reach a desirable result.

QUESTIONS FOR DISCUSSION

1. Do you think that Du Pont was justified in excluding women of childbearing age from working with mutagenic and teratogenic chemicals? Defend your answer. Did Du Pont's exclusionary policy violate the rights of women? Men? Explain. Do you think Du Pont's rationale for not excluding men was a good one?

2. Do you regard Roger Boisjoly as a loyal or disloyal employee? To whom do employees owe loyalty? Would Boisjoly have been justified in blowing the whistle to someone outside the company? Did he have an obligation to do so? Why or why not?

3. What can we learn about worker/management cooperation from the case of Eastern Airlines? About the relationship between workers and unions? Do you think that management and unions at Eastern should have worked harder to sustain cooperation?

4. Do you believe that the training program and selection process of Kaiser Aluminum were justified? Defend your answer.

5. Many of you have worked or will work with people whom you feel less qualified than you are, but who nevertheless have seniority. Is seniority a qualification for a job? What role do you think it should play in the hiring and promotion process? Why might it have played such a central role in the controversy over affirmative action?

SUPPLEMENTARY READING FOR PART THREE

Blackstone, William T., and Robert D. Heslep, eds. *Social Justice and Preferential Treatment*. Athens: University of Georgia Press, 1977.

Bok, Sissela. *Secrets*. New York: Pantheon Books, 1983.

Cohen, Marshall, Thomas Nagel, and Thomas Scanlon, eds. *Equality and Preferential Treatment*. Princeton, N.J.: Princeton University Press, 1977.

Davis, Louis E., and Albert Cherns, eds. *The Quality of Working Life,* vols. 1 and 2. New York: Free Press, 1975.

De George, Richard T. "Ethical Responsibilities of Engineers in Large Organizations." *Business and Professional Ethics Journal,* vol. 1, *1,* Fall 1981, pp. 1–14.

Elliston, Frederick, et al. *Whistleblowing: Managing Dissent in the Workplace*. New York: Praeger, 1985.

Ewing, David. *Do It My Way or You're Fired: Employee Rights and the Changing Role of Management Prerogative*. New York: Wiley, 1983.

———. *Freedom Inside the Organization*. New York: Dutton, 1977.

Ezorsky, Gertrude. *Moral Rights in the Workplace*. Albany: SUNY Press, 1987.

Fairfield, Roy P., ed. *Humanizing the Workplace*. New York: Prometheus Books, 1974.

Fullinwider, Robert K. *The Reverse Discrimination Controversy*. Totowa, N.J.: Rowman and Littlefield, 1980.

———, and Claudia Mills, eds. *The Moral Foundations of Civil Rights*. Totowa, N.J.: Rowman and Littlefield, 1986.

Gold, Michael Evan. *A Dialogue on Comparable Worth*. Ithaca, N.Y.: Cornell University Press, 1983.

Graebner, William. "Doing the World's Unhealthy Work: The Fiction of Free Choice." *Hastings Center Report* 14 (August 1984).

Gross, Barry R., ed. *Reverse Discrimination*. Buffalo, N.Y.: Prometheus Books, 1977.

Heisler, W. J., and John W. Houck, eds. *A Matter of Dignity: Inquiries into the Humanization of Work*. Notre Dame and London: University of Notre Dame Press, 1977.

Hoffman, W. Michael, and Thomas J. Wyly, eds. *The Work Ethic in Business: Proceedings of the Third National Conference on Business Ethics*. Cambridge, Mass.: Oelgeschlager, Gunn & Hain, 1981.

Kolodny, Harvey, and Hans van Beinum, eds. *The Quality of Working Life and the 1980's*. New York: Praeger Publishers, 1983.

Nelkin, Dorothy, and Michael S. Brown. *Workers at Risk: Voices from the Workplace*. Chicago: University of Chicago Press, 1984.

"Paying Women What They're Worth," *Report from the Center for Philosophy and Public Policy,* vol. 3, 1983.

Terkel, Studs. *Working*. New York: Pantheon Books, 1974.

Thomson, Judith Jarvis. "The Right to Privacy," *Philosophy and Public Affairs,* vol. 4, Summer, 1975.

Westin, Alan F. *Privacy and Freedom*. New York: Atheneum Publishers, 1976.

———. *Whistle Blowing!* New York: McGraw-Hill, 1981.

———, and Stephen Salisbury, eds. *Individual Rights in the Corporation*. New York: Pantheon Books, 1980.

Whyte, William H., Jr. *The Organization Man*. New York: Simon and Schuster, 1956.

Work. The Philosophical Forum, vol. 10, *2, 3,* Winter/Summer, 1978/1979. A special issue edited in cooperation with the Society for Philosophy and Public Affairs.

The Corporation in Society

In Part Three we examined some aspects of the relationship of business to one of its most important internal constituencies, its employees. Here we turn attention to the relationship between business and its external constituencies—that is, between business and its environment. In Chapter 11, we examine the relationship between business and consumers by looking at some of the ethical aspects of marketing and production; Chapter 12 explores some ethical dimensions of the relation of business to the natural environment; in Chapter 13 we raise questions about the appropriate roles of government and business in the regulation of corporate behavior; and Chapter 14 takes up some of the ethical problems raised by multinational business operations.

BUSINESS AND CONSUMERS

Business organizations exist by selling goods and services to consumers. Consumers, therefore, are one of business' most important constituencies, literally essential for its survival. Traditionally, the relationship between business and consumers in U.S. society has been defined by the free market, which links business and consumers in what is intended to be a mutually beneficial relationship. Business is free to make as large a profit as possible on its transactions with consumers; but—the theory goes—business succeeds only by giving consumers what they want. Both consumer and business interests are protected by the "invisible hand" of the market. Presumably an unsatisfactory or undesirable product, or one offered at an unreasonable price, will not sell. In such a system it is often said that "the consumer is king," and sellers must serve the consumer or go out of business.

This system can work in practice, however, only if two conditions are met: (1) there is no deception, and the consumer receives adequate and accurate information about products on the market to make rational market decisions; and (2) the consumer is free to choose what to buy. Does the real world really meet these conditions, however? This question is the takeoff point for some of the most important debates about business and consumer relations in business ethics.

One business activity which has led thinkers to question the accuracy of the traditional picture of business and consumer relations is advertising or marketing. Advertising of some kind is necessary to convey information to consumers and to make them aware of what products are available. But how much information is really conveyed in such slogans as "Coke is the real thing" or "This Bud's for you"? It is not surprising that many observers of advertising conclude that its main purpose is not to inform but to persuade.

Advertisers have been accused not only of failing to inform the public but of creating needs and desires which the consumer otherwise would not have had. This is the charge made by John Kenneth Galbraith in his article, "The Dependence Effect." Galbraith argues that in the United States the manufacture of consumer demands is as important as, if not more important than, the manufacture of products which satisfy those demands. The same companies that satisfy wants, he claims, also *create* those wants by advertising, establishing a self-perpetuating cycle of desire and satisfaction. If consumers truly wanted all the products on the market, Galbraith claims, such creation of desires would not be necessary. Genuine desires originate with the consumer and do not need to be created from outside. Galbraith might regard the extensive advertising campaign for cigarettes as an example of this want creation.

If Galbraith is correct, consumers are being manipulated into buying things they do not really want or need. The consumer is not the "king" in this picture, but a pawn. Recalling our discussion of Kant in the general introduction, we might say that if Galbraith is correct then consumers are being treated by producers as means to an end rather than as ends in themselves. For rather than responding to consumer needs, producers are creating needs and looking on the consumer as nothing more than an instrument for making profits. Creation of consumer needs is also bad, according to Galbraith, because it encourages the excessive consumption of private goods which are not really essential, and diverts spending away from public goods like clean air, livable cities, parks, and public transportation. People would get a great deal of satisfaction from such public goods, Galbraith believes, but since there is comparatively little advertising to persuade us to spend our money on public goods, private goods tend to dominate. Galbraith feels that although our society is rich in private goods, it is poor in public goods.

But does advertising really manipulate us in the way that Galbraith claims? F. A. Von Hayek does not think so. Von Hayek agrees that many of our wants are created by production. Living in a society in which many material goods are available generates wants we would not have if we were raised in a different sort of society. But, he claims, this does not mean these wants are not urgent or important. Most of what we regard as our "highest" desires—for art, literature, education—are instilled in us by our culture. If only internally generated wants or needs were legitimate, we would have to conclude that the only important desires are for food, sex, and shelter. Advertising is only one cultural element that shapes our desires, Von Hayek concludes. It cannot, by itself, *determine* our wants.

Advertisers and salespeople have also been accused of deceiving and manipulating the public through techniques such as "puffery" or exaggeration, failure to tell the whole truth about a product, misleading pricing and packaging, and appeals to emotion rather than to rational judgment. In his article, David Holley reviews and analyzes a number of such practices. Sales techniques are unethical, Holley argues, if they undermine the possibility of a fair and free exchange between buyer and seller. If a consumer is led by a deceptive sales practice to buy a product, for example, he or she purchases that product on a false basis. Deception makes it impossible for the free market to satisfy the consumer's needs. Because the product is not what the consumer intended to buy when he or she made the purchase, the consumer's freedom has been violated.

Theodore Levitt argues that the problem of deception is more complex than people like Holley would have us believe. He claims that, although deliberate falsification is wrong, distortion and exaggeration are part of the legitimate business of an advertiser or seller. Like poetry, advertising uses symbol, metaphor, and hyperbole to influence the emotions of the reader or listener. Our lives would be impoverished without such symbols. Even more importantly, Levitt argues, consumers *want* the illusions created by advertising; these are part of what they pay for when they buy a product. The purchaser of a sports car, for example, desires much more than motive power—she or he also wants success, desirability, or power. It is partly because the sports car is associated with these images that it satisfies the consumer.

Another important issue raised by the relationship between business and consumers is that of product safety. If a manufacturer has a responsibility to consumers not to market unsafe products, how far does this responsibility extend? Who should assume the liability if a consumer is injured by a defective product? Here, as in the case of advertising, it is unclear whether the market system by itself really protects the interests of the consumers. If they had adequate information consumers could freely choose the risks they wish to run, and products considered too risky would be driven off the market. But in most cases manufacturers need not make explicit the potential hazards of what they sell.

Most consumers lack the expertise to assess the safety of today's technologically sophisticated products, and must rely at least to some extent on the impression they are given by sellers. Many purchases are "one-shot" deals, which means that the consumer has no opportunity to benefit from his or her experience in the future. And although we are likely to hear about seriously dangerous products, their danger does not attract attention until some consumers are injured.

Our growing lack of confidence in the market system to protect consumer safety is demonstrated by the increase in consumer protection legislation, and by the establishment of two major consumer protection agencies in the last decade—the Consumer Product Safety Commission and the National Highway Traffic Safety Administration. Some observers of this trend claim that we have moved from a stance of "let the buyer beware" to one of "let the manufacturer/ seller beware." Moreover, many feel that the responsibility of manufacturers to consumers goes beyond obedience to federal safety regulations. Ford, for example, was asked to pay substantial amounts in settlements for accidents due to the placement of the Pinto's gas tank, even though there were no federal standards for fuel-system integrity at the time the Pinto was produced. One might argue that the manufacturer has an obligation to the consumer to make a product that can be used safely for the purposes for which the consumer has been led to believe it can be used, regardless of federal standards.

No product can be absolutely risk-free, however; some theorists hold that the most that can be demanded of manufacturers is that they exercise "due care" to make all products "reasonably" safe. The National Commission on Product Safety (NCPS) has suggested that risks are reasonable when consumers are aware of them, able to assess their probability and severity, know how to cope with them if they do arise, and voluntarily accept them to receive benefits they could not get otherwise. Risks which could easily be prevented, or which consumers would be willing to pay to prevent if given the choice, the NCPS concluded, are not reasonable. In part, it was the failure of Ford to exercise due care in making a safe product which is at issue in the Pinto case included in this book. But the case is an unusual one because in it Ford is accused of *criminal* homicide—of knowingly choosing not to exercise due care and trading human lives for profit.

It may seem fair that manufacturers should assume liability for consumer injuries caused by failure to exercise due care. But in recent years the courts have extended the liability of manufacturers to include all cases in which injuries result from defects in the manufacturing process, even if the manufacturer could not have foreseen or prevented the injury. This doctrine is called "strict products liability." Proponents of the doctrine argue that manufacturers are best able to bear the costs of injuries because they can distribute them to others, and that forcing manufacturers to assume liability is likely to reduce the frequency of accidents in the future. These are essentially utilitarian arguments. But do they constitute a justification for strict products liability? George Brenkert is one thinker who does not find them convincing, although he supports the doctrine of strict products liability.

Brenkert questions whether holding manufacturers strictly liable really will reduce the number of accidents and, if it will, whether it is the only way or the best way to do so. And even if a policy of strict products liability would reduce accidents, Brenkert argues, it does not follow that the doctrine is just. Similarly, that manufacturers are best able to bear the costs of injuries does not mean that it is just that they pay those costs.

Nevertheless, Brenkert believes that in the context of a free enterprise system, the doctrine of strict products liability is a just one. Essential to the functioning of a free enterprise system, he argues, is equal opportunity. However unintentionally, a manufacturer whose defective product has injured a consumer has interfered with that consumer's equal opportunity to participate in the system. Just as a team may be penalized for hurting an opposing player's ability to compete, even if the injury was an accident, a manufacturer may be required to compensate a consumer in-

jured by a defective product, whether the defect was foreseen or not. Brenkert concludes that for this reason it is just
to place the burden of liability on the manufacturer.

BUSINESS AND THE ENVIRONMENT

Some of the most urgent questions faced by society today
are those raised by the increasing contamination and depletion of our natural resources. The air pollution which is
present in all major United States cities increases the incidence of respiratory disease, heart disease, and lung cancer. Toxic wastes like those dumped in Love Canal by
Hooker Chemical Company find their way into drinking water and pose serious threats to human life and health. The
earth's protective ozone layer is deteriorating, leaving us
vulnerable to harmful effects from beyond the atmosphere.
Researchers predict that if the exponentially rising rate of
use of fossil fuels continues, estimated reserves will be de-
pleted in about a hundred years.

In Chapter 11 we look at some environmental problems
raised by the activities of commercial and industrial enterprises. Business is by no means the sole polluter, nor is it
the sole consumer of natural resources. But there are several important reasons for focusing on business-related environmental issues.

One reason is that the structure of the free enterprise system itself has been accused of encouraging pollution. At one
time air and water were thought of as unlimited and "free"
goods, available for anyone's use without charge. The effects—in terms of pollution—of any particular business' use
of air or water were negligible, and we were confident of the
ability of the environment to absorb them. Today, we realize that the environment can't absorb them. Air and water
pollution are costs of production that business has "exter-
nalized," or passed on to society as a whole. Market forces
encourage this conversion of private to public costs. However, as increasing pollution and the depletion of natural
resources force us to adopt what Kenneth Boulding has
called a "spaceship earth" mentality, it seems clear that

pollution must be made less desirable by forcing polluters to internalize environmental costs. It is not surprising that business is resisting such attempts, and that some business-people view environmental protection measures as contrary to their interests.

A second reason for examining business' role in the environmental crisis is the pervasiveness of the value placed on consumption, which is an integral part of our business society. Although Americans comprise only 6 percent of the world's population, we consume 35 percent of the world's annual energy resources. We also have the highest gross national product of any country in the world. The link between standard of living, economic growth as measured by the GNP, and high levels of pollution and consumption of natural resources cannot be denied. Business has developed into a powerful force in our society because of its ability to satisfy the appetite for consumption. Whether business is responsible for the pervasiveness of consumption as a social value, as Galbraith would suggest, is not clear. But it is clear that the environmental protection movement presents a challenge to private consumption, and therefore to a very important aspect of business activity.

Some thinkers hold that pollution is wrong because it violates the rights of nature to be respected. They argue that these rights ought to be protected by the recognition of legal rights for natural entities such as forests, lakes, and streams. Others, like William T. Blackstone in this text, claim that pollution is wrong because it violates the *human* right to a livable environment. Blackstone claims that each of us possesses the basic rights necessary for us to live human lives and to fulfill our capacities as rational and free beings. Such inalienable rights have traditionally included equality, liberty, happiness, life, and property.

But these basic rights cannot be exercised, Blackstone argues, without a livable environment. He concludes that the right to a livable environment, a right which has emerged as a result of changing environmental conditions, is also an inalienable right on an equal footing with the rights to life, liberty, and property. One might argue along Blackstone's lines that the violation of Niagara Falls residents' right to a livable environment is part of what is at issue in the Love Canal case. Recognition of the right to a livable environment as a legal as well as a moral right, Blackstone suggests, could be an important tool in solving some of our environmental problems.

But what constitutes a livable environment, and how far ought we to go to protect people's rights to one? As we noted above, it seems clear that pollution control and conservation of natural resources will have a significant cost to both business and consumers. In his article, Robert W. Lee criticizes the EPA for what he believes are arbitrary rules that fail to consider costs and recommends abolishing the agency. Lee believes that the environment has not improved in the past few years, although costs have skyrocketed. Environmentalism, he suggests, is at bottom a cloak for people who want to undermine capitalism and bring business under rigid federal control. The costs of what Lee calls "environmental extremism" include higher prices of consumer goods, higher energy costs, increased unemployment, and the slowdown of economic growth.

Larry Ruff's "The Economic Common Sense of Pollution" echoes some of Lee's claims in a more moderate voice. Ruff suggests that we should strive, not for *no* pollution, but for an "optimum" level of pollution at which the costs of further pollution abatement exceed the benefits. The best way to regulate pollution control, Ruff argues, is to place a price on the right to pollute. Prices would be set by the combined efforts of a pollution control board that measures the costs and benefits of pollution, and a popular referendum. Such a price-based system would allow anyone to pollute as long as he or she paid the price, and, Ruff believes, would lead people to regulate their pollution in the most efficient possible way.

Both Lee and Ruff argue against environmental regulation that has a negative impact on traditional economic indicators such as the Consumer Price Index or the Gross National Product (GNP). Are these indicators a true measurement of the well-being of society, however? In his article Kenneth Boulding challenges the usefulness of the GNP as a social indicator. When the environment becomes polluted, Boulding explains, the cost of cleaning it up is added to the national product but the pollution is not subtracted, so that the gross national product is higher than it would have been had there been no pollution at all. But this increased GNP does not reflect an increase in social well-being. This and other examples, Boulding argues, indicate that the GNP is not an accurate measure of the welfare of society. He suggests that the economy, as measured by the GNP, may have to be adapted or constricted to enhance the quality of life on "spaceship earth."

In "At the Shrine of Our Lady of Fatima," Mark Sagoff challenges the view that environmental issues should be dealt with on purely economic grounds. The cost of environmental protection is one element to be included in the political calculus, but only one, he claims. The American people are not only consumers; they are also citizens, and their interests as citizens may be quite different than their interests as consumers. As consumers, we think about how to get the best deal for ourselves. As citizens, our interests are wider: We think about the community as a whole. Sagoff points out that, as citizens, we may vote for a bottle bill because it helps the community, even though as consumers we hate the process of collecting and returning bottles. As consumers, we may try to sneak out of a speeding ticket by bribing a police officer but, as citizens, support legislation that cracks down on police corruption. It is because we frequently have different interests as consumers and as citizens that our society has a political as well as an economic arena. And it is for this reason, Sagoff argues, that we should resist reducing all political issues to economic ones. Because our interests go beyond the economic, we cannot expect market or cost-benefit analysis to answer all our political questions. This does not mean that Sagoff rejects cost-benefit analysis altogether. It is an excellent tool, he argues, for deciding how to reach our goals, once we have chosen them as citizens. But, he claims, cost-benefit analysis should not be used to set those goals. We want to achieve our political aims as efficiently as possible. But economic efficiency is a means rather than an end in itself.

BUSINESS AND GOVERNMENT

Thus far we have explored the notion that business has obligations to its multiple "stakeholders," and we have examined some of the specific responsibilities of business toward its employees, consumers, and society at large. How can we best ensure that business discharges these obligations? This question inevitably raises issues regarding the relationship between business and government. In the Pinto case, for example, part of the strength of Ford's defense was the fact that the company did not violate any government regulations in producing the Pinto. We might indict not only Niagara Falls' Board of Education and Hooker Chemical Company, but also the state of New York and the United States government for their part in the Love Canal tragedy. And Congress is considering legislation as one way of dealing with ethical problems raised by cigarette advertising.

Should we use extensive government regulations to enforce responsible business behavior? Or can and should business organizations regulate themselves? Although there are a number of important issues surrounding the relationship between business and government, we focus here on the so-called social regulations which are designed to make business carry out ethical obligations to its various constituencies.

American business has never been unregulated; but in recent years the "invisible hand" of market forces has been increasingly supported by the visible—and sometimes heavy—hand of government. As George Steiner explains in his article, the past two decades have seen a shift from industry-oriented regulations designed mainly to promote competition to regulations which cut across industry lines and are intended to improve the quality of life.

The new regulations are concerned with one function of corporate activity, such as product safety, environmental protection, or worker health and safety, and not with the organization as a whole. They are numerous, specific, and detailed. Important benefits can be and have been produced by the new regulations. Some of them are cited by Steven Kelman in his article: significant improvements in the quality of air in major urban areas, a 50 percent reduction in accidental workplace deaths, decreases in racial and sexual discrimination in the workplace.

But substantial costs have resulted as well. Steiner, a critic of the new regulatory policies, believes that the costs of the policies outweigh their benefits. He points out that they are expensive to implement and enforce, that they reduce efficiency, and that the high costs of conforming to them must be passed on to society as a whole in the form of higher prices. Much of the new regulation is cumbersome and contradictory. And Steiner believes that the extensive government regulation has upset the balance of power between government and business, interfering with the freedom of private enterprise.

Steven Kelman claims that Steiner and other opponents of the new regulation have vastly exaggerated its costs and failed to consider the savings it can provide. But even if this were not true, he argues, many of the new regulations ought to remain in force. The regulations are directed at preventing serious harms, and thus far they have been effective in doing so. Persons have a right to safe products, a clean environment, and humane working conditions, Kelman argues, and this right should be protected even if it is costly to do so. Readers will see some similarities between Kelman's position and that of Sagoff in Chapter 12. Readers may also recognize some of Kelman's arguments from his article on cost-benefit analysis in Chapter 3.

Because government regulation is costly, cumbersome, and undesirable to most businesspeople, some thinkers have pointed to forms of self-regulation as a possible key to responsible business behavior. Norman Bowie suggests industrywide codes of ethics as an alternative to government regulation. Such codes could protect businesses from unethical acts on the part of competitors and enhance the public confidence, which is necessary for business' survival. If a code is adopted by an entire industry, no one firm puts itself at a competitive disadvantage by obeying it. If they are clearly and precisely written, if they are supplemented by effective interpretive and enforcement procedures, and if they are truly taken seriously by top management, Bowie believes, industrywide codes can be effective.

Ian Maitland is more skeptical about the possibility of effective self-regulation through codes. Individual firms that adopt codes of conduct that go beyond industry standards, he argues, place themselves at a competitive disadvantage. Our economy thus openly discourages responsible behavior at the level of the firm. Industrywide codes of conduct such as those suggested by Bowie avoid this problem, he admits, but run into others. The same competitiveness that makes responsible action so difficult for a single firm is also the economy's major mechanism for protecting consumers. Traditionally, we have been suspicious of cooperation among competitors because we have feared that cooperation gives firms an opportunity to evade the discipline of the market and take advantage of consumers. Our suspicion is reflected in a wide range of antitrust laws. Until we are prepared to view cooperation as a positive phenomenon, Maitland suggests, we will find it hard to make industrywide self-regulation work. Maitland finds businesswide self-regulation administered by representatives of the business community as a whole to be the most promising form of self-regulation.

Advocates of self-regulation generally do not argue that there should be *no* government regulation of business. Although we expect individual persons to regulate their behavior, we also back up our expectations with legal statutes and sanctions. But when government does not bear the sole responsibility for corporate behavior, regulations can be less numerous and less specific, and business has more freedom. Perhaps government regulation and self-regulation are best regarded as complementary rather than as opposed.

BUSINESS IN A MULTINATIONAL SETTING

Multinationals and the Third World

Multinational corporations are business organizations that maintain extensive operations in more than one country. Multinational business faces many of the same ethical issues as domestic business, but the fact that multinationals conduct business across national and cultural lines raises special problems. Legal and cultural standards may differ from culture to culture. Practices that are benign in the United States may be inappropriate or even unethical in other contexts. Because they are so extensive, multinational corporations do not come under the complete control of any one government, and some fear that their interests diverge from those of both their home and host countries.

Extensive investment by multinational corporations can help the economies of developing nations, but as Louis Turner points out in his article on multinationals and the Third World, such investment can have harmful effects as well. Multinational investment can lead to extensive dependence on foreign capital and technology, leaving the developing nation powerless and vulnerable. Many multinationals establish foreign operations to get cheap labor or to engage in hazardous production processes without the expense of conforming to U.S. health and safety regulations. The natural desire of multinational corporations to do business in a secure investment climate sometimes leads them to support authoritarian and repressive regimes. Multinational industry can stifle local enterprise and submerge the characteristic culture of the nations in which the industry operates. Finally, successful private enterprise does not always lead to the satisfaction of the needs of developing countries.

Richard De George suggests that some of the dilemmas that appear to face multinational corporations doing business in the Third World in fact arise from assuming that U.S. standards are universal moral standards. There are important differences in culture and values between First- and Third-World countries, De George believes, and these should be respected. In spite of these differences, however,

De George believes that there are universal moral norms that can be applied across cultures, and he offers seven principles that might serve as guidelines for evaluating the actions of multinational corporations.

The crisis caused by marketing infant formula in Third-World countries is one illustration of the kinds of challenges faced by multinational corporations. In a First-World market, infant formula is a safe product that makes an important contribution to mothers' quality of life. But its introduction into the Third World led to widespread infant malnutrition and even death among users. James Post examines Nestle's contribution to the infant formula controversy and suggests some ethical guidelines for marketing First World products in the Third World.

Bribery

One ethical challenge faced by managers of multinationals abroad is the widespread occurrence of bribery and extortion. In the United States, bribery is illegal and almost universally regarded as unethical. But in some countries, claim U.S. managers, bribery is a way of life, necessary to conducting business. Is it morally permissible to bribe if bribery is a common practice in the culture in which you are doing business? What, really, is wrong with bribery?

Scott Turow explains that the essence of bribery is the attempt to corrupt a public official's impartial judgment, giving the briber an unfair advantage over others. Managers of multinationals who bribe to secure a contract are trying to "buy" the loyalty of foreign officials, loyalty that the officials actually owe to their public. It is easy to see that the practice of bribery is hostile to a free market system. In a free market system, companies compete to offer consumers the best product at the best price. Bribery shifts the terms of competition from quality and price to the size of the sum of money paid to a government official. Widespread bribery would make fair competition impossible. Bribery also injures the consumer, because the selection of an item on any basis other than quality and price often leads to the purchase of an inferior product.

In 1977 Congress passed the Foreign Corrupt Practices Act, which makes payments to foreign political officials to secure or retain business illegal. Its passage has been quite controversial. Although it is generally conceded that bribery is unethical, some argue that the act is an inappropriate response. Mark Pastin and Michael Hooker go so far as to claim that the act itself is immoral.

Pastin and Hooker argue on "end point" or utilitarian grounds that the act is wrong because it does not benefit the majority of the people it affects. In fact, they claim, the Foreign Corrupt Practices Act has serious and far-reaching negative consequences for American business, including loss of sales, loss of jobs, and a weakened ability to compete in foreign markets. Often, they suggest, the only way to secure a *superior* product for a client is to offer a larger bribe than a competing company which makes an inferior product. And a law forbidding American companies to offer bribes does not stop foreign officials from accepting bribes from non-American businesses.

Pastin and Hooker also offer a "rule assessment" or deontological argument against the act, suggesting that it places U.S. business in a conflict of obligations. By cutting into corporate profits, the act forces organizations to break their promise (1) to shareholders to maximize return on investment and (2) to employees to provide job security.

Robert Frederick believes that Hooker and Pastin's position is not persuasive and that the act has a firm ethical foundation. Accurate end-point, or utilitarian, assessment of the act, he points out, requires objective empirical evidence that Hooker and Pastin do not provide. Does the act really have a serious negative impact on U.S. firms' foreign operations? Frederick cites studies that claim it does not. He also points out that loss of business by U.S. firms is balanced by the gains for the country whose firm does get the business. This means there is no decrease in *total* utility when a U.S. firm fails to gain a contract, as Hooker and Pastin imply. From the perspective of rule assessment, Frederick argues, Hooker and Pastin's argument is also faulty. The obligation of U.S. corporations to provide jobs and make a profit for shareholders does *not* include furthering the interest of these groups by illegal or immoral means.

It is common for managers of U.S. multinationals to assume that bribery is standard practice in many countries and that they will have little choice but to adopt the practice also. Henry Lane and Donald Simpson challenge this "conventional wisdom," suggesting that managers frequently create situations in which bribes are demanded by assuming bribery is necessary to do business. From their interviews with managers of multinational firms, and from their own experience, Lane and Simpson conclude that bribery is not as common as it sometimes seems and that it is possible to refrain from the practice and still operate profitably abroad.

Multinational Investment in South Africa

Are multinational corporations obligated to use their power to correct injustice in the societies in which they operate? Should they refrain entirely from investing in countries whose political climate their home country regards as immoral?

South Africa has been condemned by many throughout the world for its policy of systematic racial segregation and repression known as *apartheid*. Although there are 19 million blacks and only 4.5 million whites in the country, blacks are permitted to live only on 13 percent of the land and earn less than 20 percent of the national income. Blacks are not permitted to vote, own property, or organize politically. They hold only low-paying, low-status jobs and are forced to use segregated facilities. These policies are enforced by various authoritarian political measures, including "banning" and detention without trial. It seems clear that the involvement of U.S. firms in South Africa strengthens its economy, thus preserving the stability of the government. If this is so, is it possible for U.S. multinationals to operate ethically in South Africa, or should they pull out altogether? Precisely this issue is faced by Texaco and Standard Oil of California in the case, "A South African Investment."

Kenneth Carstens argues that there is no moral justification for doing business in South Africa, since it gives both symbolic and material support to the regime of apartheid. The usual justification for staying in is that U.S. business can use its power to exert positive pressure for change only as long as the business maintains a presence in the country. Another frequent argument is that it is the black population that would suffer the most if U.S. business pulled out and the economy became shaky. Carstens argues that not only has there been no positive move toward change in the past 30 years, the apartheid regime has consolidated. South African laws make it extremely difficult for U.S. corporations to do anything significant to improve the plight of the black population. Moreover, he points out that the vast majority of black leaders have spoken out in favor of economic sanctions against the regime. Blacks are willing to suffer now, he claims, if it will help them overturn the policies that have kept them oppressed and impoverished for decades. Change will only come to South Africa if real economic pressure is applied in the form of sanctions.

In contrast to Carstens, Patricia Werhane argues that it is possible to do business ethically in South Africa. As long as U.S. companies can contribute to the welfare of black South Africans by providing a model of fairness, she argues, their presence is justifiable. She admits that this position is a morally ''mixed'' one, a position of ''moral risk,'' since the presence of U.S. companies in the country strengthens the South African economy, and thus apartheid. Still, she argues, this morally ambiguous position is permissible, since there is no option available that will produce a purely positive result, and since, by pulling out of South Africa, U.S. companies give up any opportunity to make a positive difference in the country. Werhane recommends the adoption of the Sullivan Principles, guidelines drawn up (but since repudiated) by the Reverend Leon Sullivan for conducting business ethically in South Africa, as a necessary, though not necessarily sufficient, step for U.S. business.

CHAPTER 11

The Consumer

READINGS FOR CHAPTER ELEVEN

John Kenneth Galbraith
The Dependence Effect
438

F. A. von Hayek
The Non Sequitor of the "Dependence Effect"
442

Theodore Levitt
The Morality (?) of Advertising
445

David M. Holley
A Moral Evaluation of Sales Practices
452

George G. Brenkert
Strict Products Liability and Compensatory Justice
460

The Dependence Effect

John Kenneth Galbraith*

The theory of consumer demand, as it is now widely accepted, is based on two broad propositions, neither of them quite explicit but both extremely important for the present value system of economists. The first is that the urgency of wants does not diminish appreciably as more of them are satisfied or, to put the matter more precisely, to the extent that this happens it is not demonstrable and not a matter of any interest to economists or for economic policy. When man has satisfied his physical needs, then psychologically grounded desires take over. These can never be satisfied or, in any case, no progress can be proved. The concept of satiation has very little standing in economics. It is neither useful nor scientific to speculate on the comparative cravings of the stomach and the mind.

The second proposition is that wants originate in the personality of the consumer or, in any case, that they are given data for the economist. The latter's task is merely to seek their satisfaction. He has no need to inquire how these wants are formed. His function is sufficiently fulfilled by maximizing the goods that supply the wants.

The notion that wants do not become less urgent the more amply the individual is supplied is broadly repugnant to common sense. It is something to be believed only by those who wish to believe. Yet the conventional wisdom must be tackled on its own terrain. Intertemporal comparisons of an individual's state of mind do rest on doubtful grounds. Who can say for sure that the deprivation which afflicts him with hunger is more painful than the deprivation which afflicts him with envy of his neighbour's new car? In the time that has passed since he was poor his soul may have become subject to a new and deeper searing. And where a society is concerned, comparisons between marginal satisfactions when it is poor and those when it is affluent will involve not only the same individual at different times but different individuals at different times. The scholar who wishes to believe that with increasing affluence there is no reduction in the urgency of desires and goods is not without points for debate. However plausible the case against him, it cannot be proved. In the defence of the conventional wisdom this amounts almost to invulnerability.

However, there is a flaw in the case. If the individual's wants are to be urgent they must be original with himself. They cannot be urgent if they must be contrived for him. And above all they must not be contrived by the process of production by which they are satisfied. For this means that the whole case for the urgency of production, based on the urgency of wants, falls to the ground. One cannot defend production as satisfying wants if that production creates the wants.

Were it so that man on arising each morning was assailed by demons which instilled in him a passion sometimes for silk shirts, sometimes for kitchenware, sometimes for chamber-pots, and sometimes for orange squash, there would be every reason to applaud the effort to find the goods, however odd, that quenched this flame. But should it be that his passion was the result of his first having cultivated the demons, and should it also be that his effort to allay it stirred the demons to ever greater and greater effort, there would be question as to how rational was his solution. Unless restrained by conventional attitudes, he might wonder if the solution lay with more goods or fewer demons.

So it is that if production creates the wants it seeks to satisfy, or if the wants emerge *pari passu* with the production, then the urgency of the wants can no longer be used to defend the ur-

*Warburg Professor Emeritus of Economics, Harvard University.

gency of the production. Production only fills a void that it has itself created.

The even more direct link between production and wants is provided by the institutions of modern advertising and salesmanship. These cannot be reconciled with the notion of independently determined desires, for their central function is to create desires—to bring into being wants that previously did not exist.[1] This is accomplished by the producer of the goods or at his behest. A broad empirical relationship exists between what is spent on production of consumers' goods and what is spent in synthesizing the desires for that production. A new consumer product must be introduced with a suitable advertising campaign to arouse an interest in it. The path for an expansion of output must be paved by a suitable expansion in the advertising budget. Outlays for the manufacturing of a product are not more important in the strategy of modern business enterprise than outlays for the manufacturing of demand for the product. None of this is novel. All would be regarded as elementary by the most retarded student in the nation's most primitive school of business administration. The cost of this want formation is formidable. In 1956 total advertising expenditure—though, as noted, not all of it may be assigned to the synthesis of wants—amounted to about ten thousand million dollars. For some years it had been increasing at a rate in excess of a thousand million dollars a year. Obviously, such outlays must be integrated with the theory of consumer demand. They are too big to be ignored.

But such integration means recognizing that wants are dependent on production. It accords to the producer the function both of making the goods and of making the desires for them. It recognizes that production, not only passively through emulation, but actively through advertising and related activities, creates the wants it seeks to satisfy.

The businessman and the lay reader will be puzzled over the emphasis which I give to a seemingly obvious point. The point is indeed obvious. But it is one which, to a singular degree, economists have resisted. They have sensed, as the layman does not, the damage to established ideas which lurks in these relationships. As a result, incredibly, they have closed their eyes (and ears) to the most obtrusive of all economic phenomena, namely modern want creation.

This is not to say that the evidence affirming the dependence of wants on advertising has been entirely ignored. It is one reason why advertising has so long been regarded with such uneasiness by economists. Here is something which cannot be accommodated easily to existing theory. More previous scholars have speculated on the urgency of desires which are so obviously the fruit of such expensively contrived campaigns for popular attention. Is a new breakfast cereal or detergent so much wanted if so much must be spent to compel in the consumer the sense of want? But there has been little tendency to go on to examine the implications of this for the theory of consumer demand and even less for the importance of production and productive efficiency. These have remained sacrosanct. More often the uneasiness has been manifested in a general disapproval of advertising and advertising men, leading to the occasional suggestion that they shouldn't exist. Such suggestions have usually been ill received.

And so the notion of independently determined wants still survives. In the face of all the forces of modern salesmanship it still rules, almost undefiled, in the textbooks. And it still remains the economist's mission—and on few matters is the pedagogy so firm—to seek unquestioningly the means for filling these wants. This being so, production remains of prime urgency. We have here, perhaps, the ultimate triumph of the conventional wisdom in its resistance to the evidence of the eyes. To equal it one must imagine a humanitarian who was long ago persuaded of the grievous shortage of hospital facilities in the town. He continues to importune the passers-by for money for more beds and refuses to notice that the town doctor is deftly knocking over pedestrians with his car to keep up the occupancy.

And in unravelling the complex we should always be careful not to overlook the obvious. The fact that wants can be synthesized by advertising, catalysed by salesmanship, and shaped by the discreet manipulations of the persuaders shows that they are not very urgent. A man who is hungry need never be told of his need for food. If he is inspired by his appetite, he is immune to the influence of Messrs. Batten, Barton, Durstine and Osborn. The latter are effective only with those who are so far removed from physical want that they do not already know what they want. In this state alone men are open to persuasion.

The general conclusion of these pages is of such importance for this essay that it had perhaps best be put with some formality. As a society becomes increasingly affluent, wants are increasingly created by the process by which they are satisfied. This may operate passively. Increases in consumption, the counterpart of increases in production, act by suggestion or emulation to create wants. Or producers may proceed actively to create wants through advertising and salesmanship. Wants thus come to depend on output. In technical terms it can no longer be assumed that welfare is greater at an all-round higher level of production than at a lower one. It may be the same. The higher level of production has, merely, a higher level of want creation necessitating a higher level of want satisfaction. There will be frequent occasion to refer to the way wants depend on the process by which they are satisfied. It will be convenient to call it the Dependence Effect.

The final problem of the productive society is what it produces. This manifests itself in an implacable tendency to provide an opulent supply of some things and a niggardly yield of others. This disparity carries to the point where it is a cause of social discomfort and social unhealth. The line which divides our area of wealth from our area of poverty is roughly that which divides privately produced and marketed goods and services from publicly rendered services. Our wealth in the first is not only in startling contrast with the meagreness of the latter, but our wealth in privately produced goods is, to a marked degree, the cause of crisis in the supply of public services. For we have failed to see the importance, indeed the urgent need, of maintaining a balance between the two.

This disparity between our flow of private and public goods and services is no matter of subjective judgment. On the contrary, it is the source of the most extensive comment which only stops short of the direct contrast being made here. In the years following World War II, the papers of any major city—those of New York were an excellent example—told daily of the shortages and shortcomings in the elementary municipal and metropolitan services. The schools were old and overcrowded. The police force was under strength and underpaid. The parks and playgrounds were insufficient. Streets and empty lots were filthy, and the sanitation staff was under-equipped and in need of men. Access to the city by those who work there was uncertain and painful and becoming more so. Internal transportation was overcrowded, unhealthful, and dirty. So was the air. Parking on the streets had to be prohibited, and there was no space elsewhere. These deficiencies were not in new and novel services but in old and established ones. Cities have long swept their streets, helped their people move around, educated them, kept order, and provided horse rails for vehicles which sought to pause. That their residents should have a non-toxic supply of air suggests no revolutionary dalliance with socialism.

The contrast was and remains evident not alone to those who read. The family which takes its mauve and cerise, air-conditioned, power-steered, and power-braked car out for a tour passes through cities that are badly paved, made hideous by litter, blighted buildings, billboards, and posts for wires that should long since have been put underground. They pass on into a countryside that has been rendered largely invisible by commercial art. (The goods which the latter advertise have an absolute priority in our value system. Such aesthetic considerations as a view of the countryside accordingly come second. On such matters we are consistent.) They picnic on exquisitely packaged food from a portable ice-box by a polluted stream and go on to spend the night at a park which is a menace to public health and morals. Just before dozing off on an air-mattress, beneath a nylon tent, amid the stench of decaying refuse, they may reflect vaguely on the curious unevenness of their blessings. Is this, indeed, the American genius?

The case for social balance has, so far, been put negatively. Failure to keep public services in mini-mal relation to private production and use of goods is a cause of social disorder or impairs economic per-formance. The matter may now be put affirmatively. By failing to exploit the opportunity to expand pub-lic production we are missing opportunities for en-joyment which otherwise we might have had. Pre-sumably a community can be as well rewarded by buying better schools or better parks as by buying bigger cars. By concentrating on the latter rather than the former it is failing to maximize its satisfactions. As with schools in the community, so with public services over the country at large. It is scarcely sen-sible that we should satisfy our wants in private goods with reckless abundance, while in the case of public goods, on the evidence of the eye, we practice ex-treme self-denial. So, far from systematically exploit-ing the opportunities to derive use and pleasure from these services, we do not supply what would keep us out of trouble.

The conventional wisdom holds that the com-munity, large or small, makes a decision as to how much it will devote to its public services. This decision is arrived at by democratic pro-cess. Subject to the imperfections and uncertain-ties of democracy, people decide how much of their private income and goods they will surren-der in order to have public services of which they are in greater need. Thus there is a balance, how-ever rough, in the enjoyments to be had from private goods and services and those rendered by public authority.

It will be obvious, however, that this view de-pends on the notion of independently determined consumer wants. In such a world one could with

some reason defend the doctrine that the con-sumer, as a voter, makes an independent choice between public and private goods. But given the dependence effect—given that consumer wants are created by the process by which they are satisfied—the consumer makes no such choice. He is subject to the forces of advertising and emulation by which production creates its own demand. Advertising operates exclusively, and emulation mainly, on be-half of privately produced goods and services.[2] Since management and emulative effects operate on behalf of private production, public services will have an inherent tendency to lag behind. Car de-mand which is expensively synthesized will inev-itably have a much larger claim on income than parks or public health or even roads where no such influence operates. The engines of mass commu-nication, in their highest state of development, as-sail the eyes and ears of the community on behalf of more beer but not of more schools. Even in the conventional wisdom it will scarcely be contended that this leads to an equal choice between the two.

The competition is especially unequal for new products and services. Every corner of the pub-lic psyche is canvassed by some of the nation's most talented citizens to see if the desire for some merchantable product can be cultivated. No sim-ilar process operates on behalf of the nonmer-chantable services of the state. Indeed, while we take the cultivation of new private wants for granted we would be measurably shocked to see it applied to public services. The scientist or en-gineer or advertising man who devotes himself to developing a new carburetor, cleanser, or de-pilatory for which the public recognizes no need and will feel none until an advertising campaign arouses it, is one of the valued members of our society. A politician or a public servant who dreams up a new public service is a wastrel. Few public offences are more reprehensible.

So much for the influences which operate on the decision between public and private produc-tion. The calm decision between public and private consumption pictured by the conventional wisdom is, in fact, a remarkable example of the error which arises from viewing social behavior out of context. The inherent tendency will always be for public services to fall behind private production. We have here the first of the causes of social imbalance.

NOTES

1. Advertising is not a simple phenomenon. It is also important in competitive strategy and want creation is, ordinarily, a complementary result of efforts to shift the demand curve of the individual firm at the expense of others or (less importantly, I think) to change its shape by increasing the degree of product differentiation. Some of the failure of economists to identify advertising with want creation may be attributed to the undue attention that its use in purely competitive strategy has attracted. It should be noted, however, that the competitive manipulation of consumer desire is only possible, at least on any appreciable scale, when such need is not strongly felt.
2. Emulation does operate between communities. A new school or a new highway in one community does exert pressure on others to remain abreast. However, as compared with the pervasive effects of emulation in extending the demand for privately produced consumers' goods there will be agreement, I think, that this intercommunity effect is probably small.

The *Non Sequitur* of the "Dependence Effect"

F. A. von Hayek*

For well over a hundred years the critics of the free enterprise system have resorted to the argument that if production were only organized

Excerpted from "The *Non Sequitur* of the 'Dependence Effect'" by F. A. von Hayek, *Southern Economic Journal* (April 1961). Copyright © 1961. Reprinted by permission of the publisher.
*Professor Emeritus of Economics, University of Chicago and University of Freiburg.

rationally, there would be no economic problem. Rather than face the problem which scarcity creates, socialist reformers have tended to deny that scarcity existed. Ever since the Saint-Simonians their contention has been that the problem of production has been solved and only the problem of distribution remains. However absurd this contention must appear to us with respect to the time when it was first advanced, it still has some persuasive power when repeated with reference to the present.

The latest form of this old contention is expounded in *The Affluent Society* by Professor J. K. Galbraith. He attempts to demonstrate that in our affluent society the important private needs are already satisfied and the urgent need is therefore no longer a further expansion of the output of commodities but an increase of those services which are supplied (and presumably can be supplied only) by government. Though this book has been extensively discussed since its publication in 1958, its central thesis still requires some further examination.

I believe the author would agree that his argument turns upon the "Dependence Effect" [p. 438 of this book]. The argument of this chapter starts from the assertion that a great part of the wants which are still unsatisfied in modern society are not wants which would be experienced spontaneously by the individual if left to himself, but are wants which are created by the process by which they are satisfied. It is then represented as self-evident that for this reason such wants cannot be urgent or important. This crucial conclusion appears to be a complete *non sequitur* and it would seem that with it the whole argument of the book collapses.

The first part of the argument is of course perfectly true: we would not desire any of the amenities of civilization—or even of the most primitive culture—if we did not live in a society in which others provide them. The innate wants are probably confined to food, shelter, and sex. All the rest we learn to desire because we see others enjoying various things. To say that a desire is not important because it is not innate is to say that the whole cultural achievement of man is not important.

This cultural origin of practically all the needs of civilized life must of course not be confused with the fact that there are some desires which aim, not as a satisfaction derived directly from the use of an object, but only from the status which its consumption is expected to confer. In a passage which Professor Galbraith quotes, Lord Keynes seems to treat the latter sort of Veblenesque conspicuous consumption as the only alternative "to those needs which are absolute in the sense that we feel them whatever the situation of our fellow human beings may be." If the latter phrase is interpreted to exclude all the needs for goods which are felt only because these goods are known to be produced, these two Keynesian classes describe of course only extreme types of wants, but disregard the overwhelming majority of goods on which civilized life rests. Very few needs indeed are "absolute" in the sense that they are independent of social environment or of the example of others, and that their satisfaction is an indispensable condition for the preservation of the individual or of the species. Most needs which make us act are needs for things which only civilization teaches us to exist at all, and these things are wanted by us because they produce feelings or emotions which we would not know if it were not for our cultural inheritance. Are not in this sense probably all our esthetic feelings "acquired tastes"?

How complete a *non sequitur* Professor Galbraith's conclusion represents is seen most clearly if we apply the argument to any product of the arts, be it music, painting, or literature. If the fact that people would not feel the need for something if it were not produced did prove that such products are of small value, all those highest products of human endeavor would be of small value. Professor Galbraith's argument could be easily employed without any change of the essential terms, to demonstrate the worthlessness of literature or any other form of art. Surely an individual's want for literature is not

original with himself in the sense that he would experience it if literature were not produced. Does this then mean that the production of literature cannot be defended as satisfying a want because it is only the production which provokes the demand? In this, as in the case of all cultural needs, it is unquestionably, in Professor Galbraith's words, "the process of satisfying the wants that creates the wants." There have never been "independently determined desires for" literature before literature has been produced and books certainly do not serve the "simple mode of enjoyment which requires no previous conditioning of the consumer." Clearly my taste for the novels of Jane Austen or Anthony Trollope or C. P. Snow is not "original with myself." But is it not rather absurd to conclude from this that it is less important than, say, the need for education? Public education indeed seems to regard it as one of its tasks to instill a taste for literature in the young and even employs producers of literature for that purpose. Is this want creation by the producer reprehensible? Or does the fact that some of the pupils may possess a taste for poetry only because of the efforts of their teachers prove that since "it does not arise in spontaneous consumer need and the demand would not exist were it not contrived, its utility or urgency, ex contrivance, is zero?"

The appearance that the conclusions follow from the admitted facts is made possible by an obscurity of the wording of the argument with respect to which it is difficult to know whether the author is himself the victim of a confusion or whether he skillfully uses ambiguous terms to make the conclusion appear plausible. The obscurity concerns the implied assertion that the wants of the consumers are determined by the producers. Professor Galbraith avoids in this connection any terms as crude and definite as "determine." The expressions he employs, such as that wants are "dependent on" or the "fruits of" production, or that "production creates the wants" do, of course, suggest determination but avoid saying so in plain terms. After what has already been said it is of course obvious that the knowledge of what is being produced is one of the many factors on which it depends what people will want. It would scarcely be an exaggeration to say that contemporary man, in all fields where he has not yet formed firm habits, tends to find out what he wants by looking at what his neighbours do and at various displays of goods (physical or in catalogues or advertisements) and then choosing what he likes best.

In this sense the tastes of man, as is also true of his opinions and beliefs and indeed much of his personality, are shaped in a great measure by his cultural environment. But though in some contexts it would perhaps be legitimate to express this by a phrase like "production creates the wants," the circumstances mentioned would clearly not justify the contention that particular producers can deliberately determine the wants of particular consumers. The efforts of all producers will certainly be directed towards that end; but how far any individual producer will succeed will depend not only on what he does but also on what the others do and on a great many other influences operating upon the consumer. The joint but uncoordinated efforts of the producers merely create one element of the environment by which the wants of the consumers are shaped. It is because each individual producer thinks that the consumers can be persuaded to like his products that he endeavours to influence them. But though this effort is part of the influences which shape consumers' tastes, no producer can in any real sense "determine" them. This, however, is clearly implied in such statements as that wants are "both passively and deliberately the fruits of the process by which they are satisfied." If the producer could in fact deliberately determine what the consumers will want, Professor Galbraith's conclusions would have some validity. But though this is skillfully suggested, it is nowhere made credible, and could hardly be made credible because it is not true. Though the range of choice open to the consumers is the joint result of, among other things, the efforts of all producers who vie with each other

in making their respective products appear more attractive than those of their competitors, every particular consumer still has the choice between all those different offers.

A fuller examination of this process would, of course, have to consider how, after the efforts of some producers have actually swayed some consumers, it becomes the example of the various consumers thus persuaded which will influence the remaining consumers. This can be mentioned here only to emphasize that even if each consumer were exposed to pressure of only one producer, the harmful effects which are apprehended from this would soon be offset by the much more powerful example of his fellows. It is of course fashionable to treat this influence of the example of others (or, what comes to the same thing, the learning from the experience made by others) as if it amounted all to an attempt of keeping up with the Joneses and for that reason was to be regarded as detrimental. It seems to me that not only the importance of this factor is usually greatly exaggerated but also that it is not really relevant to Professor Galbraith's main thesis. But it might be worthwhile briefly to ask what, assuming that some expenditure were actually determined solely by a desire of keeping up with the Joneses, that would really prove? At least in Europe we used to be familiar with a type of persons who often denied themselves even enough food in order to maintain an appearance of respectability or gentility in dress and style of life. We may regard this as a misguided effort, but surely it would not prove that the income of such persons was larger than they knew how to use wisely. That the appearance of success, or wealth, may to some people seem more important than many other needs, does in no way prove that the needs they sacrifice to the former are unimportant. In the same way, even though people are often persuaded to spend unwisely, this surely is no evidence that they do not still have important unsatisfied needs.

Professor Galbraith's attempt to give an apparent scientific proof for the contention that the need for the production of more commodities has greatly decreased seems to me to have broken down completely. With it goes the claim to have produced a valid argument which justifies the use of coercion to make people employ their income for those purposes of which he approves. It is not to be denied that there is some originality in this latest version of the old socialist argument. For over a hundred years we have been exhorted to embrace socialism because it would give us more goods. Since it has so lamentably failed to achieve this where it has been tried, we are now urged to adopt it because more goods after all are not important. The aim is still progressively to increase the share of the resources whose use is determined by political authority and the coercion of any dissenting minority. It is not surprising, therefore, that Professor Galbraith's thesis has been most enthusiastically received by the intellectuals of the British Labour Party where his influence bids fair to displace that of the late Lord Keynes. It is more curious that in this country it is not recognized as an outright socialist argument and often seems to appeal to people on the opposite end of the political spectrum. But this is probably only another instance of the familiar fact that on these matters the extremes frequently meet.

The Morality (?) of Advertising

Theodore Levitt*

This year Americans will consume about $20 billion of advertising, and very little of it because we want it. Wherever we turn, advertising will be forcibly thrust on us in an intrusive orgy of abrasive sound and sight, all to induce us to do something we might not ordinarily do, or to induce us to do it differently. This massive and persistent effort crams increasingly more commercial noise into the same, few, strained 24 hours of the day. It has provoked a reaction as predictable as it was inevitable: a lot of people want the noise stopped, or at least alleviated.

And they want it cleaned up and corrected. As more and more products have entered the battle for the consumer's fleeting dollar, advertising has increased in boldness and volume. Last year, industry offered the nation's supermarkets about 100 new products a week, equal, on an annualized basis, to the total number already on their shelves. Where so much must be sold so hard, it is not surprising that advertisers have pressed the limits of our credulity and generated complaints about their exaggerations and deceptions.

Only classified ads, the work of rank amateurs, do we presume to contain solid, unembellished fact. We suspect all the rest of systematic and egregious distortion, if not often of outright mendacity.

The attack on advertising comes from all sectors. Indeed, recent studies show that the people most agitated by advertising are precisely those in the higher income brackets whose affluence is generated by the industries that create the ads.[1] While these studies show that only a modest group of people are preoccupied with advertising's constant presence in our lives, they also show that distortion and deception are what bother people most.

This discontent has encouraged Senator Philip Hart and Senator William Proxmire to sponsor consumer-protection and truth-in-advertising legislation. People, they say, want less fluff and more fact about the things they buy. They want description, not distortion, and they want some relief from the constant, grating, vulgar noise.

Legislation seems appropriate because the natural action of competition does not seem to work,

*Carter Professor of Business Administration, Harvard Business School, and editor, *Harvard Business Review*.

or at least not very well. Competition may ultimately flush out and destroy falsehood and shoddiness, but "ultimately" is too long for the deceived—not just the deceived who are poor, ignorant, and dispossessed, but also all the rest of us who work hard for our money and can seldom judge expertly the truth of conflicting claims about products and services.

The consumer is an amateur, after all; the producer is an expert. In the commercial arena, the consumer is an impotent midget. He is certainly not king. The producer is a powerful giant. It is an uneven match. In this setting, the purifying power of competition helps the consumer very little—especially in the short run, when his money is spent and gone, from the weak hands into the strong hands. Nor does competition among the sellers solve the "noise" problem. The more they compete, the worse the din of advertising.

A BROAD VIEWPOINT REQUIRED

Most people spend their money carefully. Understandably, they look out for larcenous attempts to separate them from it. Few men in business will deny the right, perhaps even the wisdom, of people today asking for some restraint on advertising, or at least for more accurate information on the things they buy and for more consumer protection.

Yet, if we speak in the same breath about consumer protection and about advertising's distortions, exaggerations, and deceptions, it is easy to confuse two quite separate things—the legitimate purpose of advertising and the abuses to which it may be put. Rather than deny that distortion and exaggeration exist in advertising, in this article I shall argue that embellishment and distortion are among advertising's legitimate and socially desirable purposes; and that illegitimacy in advertising consists only of falsification with larcenous intent. And while it is difficult, as a practical matter, to draw the line between legitimate distortion and essential falsehood, I want

to take a long look at the distinction that exists between the two. This I shall say in advance—the distinction is not as simple, obvious, or great as one might think.

The issue of truth versus falsehood, in advertising or in anything else, is complex and fugitive. It must be pursued in a philosophic mood that might seem foreign to the businessman. Yet the issue at base *is* more philosophic than it is pragmatic. Anyone seriously concerned with the moral problems of a commercial society cannot avoid this fact. I hope the reader will bear with me—I believe he will find it helpful, and perhaps even refreshing.

What Is Reality?

What, indeed? Consider poetry. Like advertising, poetry's purpose is to influence an audience; to affect its perceptions and sensibilities; perhaps even to change its mind. Like rhetoric, poetry's intent is to convince and seduce. In the service of that intent, it employs without guilt or fear of criticism all the arcane tools of distortion that the literary mind can devise. Keats does not offer a truthful engineering description of his Grecian urn. He offers, instead, with exquisite attention to the effects of meter, rhyme, allusion, illusion, metaphor, and sound, a lyrical, exaggerated, distorted, and palpably false description. And he is thoroughly applauded for it, as are all other artists, in whatever medium, who do precisely this same thing successfully.

Commerce, it can be said without apology, takes essentially the same liberties with reality and literality as the artist, except that commerce calls its creations advertising, or industrial design, or packaging. As with art, the purpose is to influence the audience by creating illusions, symbols, and implications that promise more than pure functionality. Once, when asked what his company did, Charles Revson of Revlon, Inc. suggested a profound distinction: "In the factory we make cosmetics; in the store we sell hope." He obviously has no illusions. It is not cosmetic chemicals women want, but the seductive charm promised by the alluring symbols with which these chemicals have been surrounded—hence the rich and exotic packages in which they are sold, and the suggestive advertising with which they are promoted.

Commerce usually embellishes its products thrice: first, it designs the product to be pleasing to the eye, to suggest reliability, and so forth; second, it packages the product as attractively as it feasibly can; and then it advertises this attractive package with inviting pictures, slogans, descriptions, songs, and so on. The package and design are as important as the advertising.

The Grecian vessel, for example, was used to carry liquids, but that function does not explain why the potter decorated it with graceful lines and elegant drawings in black and red. A woman's compact carries refined talc, but this does not explain why manufacturers try to make these boxes into works of decorative art.

Neither the poet nor the ad man celebrates the literal functionality of what he produces. Instead, each celebrates a deep and complex emotion which he symbolizes by creative embellishment—a content which cannot be captured by literal description alone. Communication, through advertising or through poetry or any other medium, is a creative conceptualization that implies a vicarious experience through a language of symbolic substitutes. Communication can never be the real thing it talks about. Therefore, all communication is in some inevitable fashion a departure from reality.

Everything Is Changed...

Poets, novelists, playwrights, composers, and fashion designers have one thing more in common. They all deal in symbolic communication. None is satisfied with nature in the raw, as it was on the day of creation. None is satisfied to tell it exactly "like it is" to the naked eye, as do the classified ads. It is the purpose of all art to alter nature's surface reality, to reshape, to embellish, and to augment what nature has so crudely fashioned, and then to present it to the same applauding humanity that so eagerly buys Revson's exotically advertised cosmetics.

Few, if any, of us accept the natural state in which God created us. We scrupulously select our clothes to suit a multiplicity of simultaneous purposes, not only for warmth, but manifestly for such other purposes as propriety, status, and seduction. Women modify, embellish, and amplify themselves with colored paste for the lips and powders and lotions for the face; men as well as women use devices to take hair off the face and others to put it on the head. Like the inhabitants of isolated African regions, where not a single whiff of advertising has ever intruded, we all encrust ourselves with rings, pendants, bracelets, neckties, clips, chains, and snaps.

Man lives neither in sackcloth nor in sod huts—although these are not notably inferior to tight clothes and overheated dwellings in congested and polluted cities. Everywhere man rejects nature's uneven blessings. He molds and repackages to his own civilizing specifications an otherwise crude, drab, and generally oppressive reality. He does it so that life may be made for the moment more tolerable than God evidently designed it to be. As T. S. Eliot once remarked, "Human kind cannot bear very much reality."

...Into Something Rich and Strange

No line of life is exempt. All the popes of history have countenanced the costly architecture of St. Peter's Basilica and its extravagant interior decoration. All around the globe, nothing typifies man's materialism so much as the temples in which he preaches asceticism. Men of the cloth have not been persuaded that the poetic self-denial of Christ or Buddha—both men of sackcloth and sandals—is enough to inspire, elevate, and hold their flocks together. To amplify the temple in men's eyes, they have, very realistically, systematically sanctioned the embellishment of the houses of the gods with the same kind of luxurious design and expensive decoration that Detroit puts into a Cadillac.

One does not need a doctorate in social anthropology to see that the purposeful transmutation of nature's primeval state occupies all people in all cultures and all societies at all stages of development. Everybody everywhere wants to modify, transform, embellish, enrich, and reconstruct the world around him—to introduce into an otherwise harsh or bland existence some sort of purposeful and distorting alleviation. Civilization is man's attempt to transcend his ancient animality; and this includes both art and advertising.

Let us assume for the moment that there is no objective, operational difference between the embellishments and distortions of the artist and those of the ad man—that both men are more concerned with creating images and feelings than with rendering objective, representational, and informational descriptions. The greater virtue of the artist's work must then derive from some subjective element. What is it?

It will be said that art has a higher value for many because it has a higher purpose. True, the artist is interested in philosophic truth or wisdom, and the ad man is selling his goods and services. Michelangelo, when he designed the Sistine chapel ceiling, had some concern with the inspirational elevation of man's spirit, whereas Edward Levy, who designs cosmetics packages, is interested primarily in creating images to help separate the unwary consumer from his loose change.

But this explanation of the difference between the value of art and the value of advertising is not helpful at all. For is the presence of a "higher" purpose all that redeeming?

Perhaps not; perhaps the reverse is closer to the truth. While the ad man and designer seek only to convert the audience to their commercial custom, Michelangelo sought to convert its soul. Which is the greater blasphemy? Who commits the greater affront to life—he who dabbles with man's erotic appetites, or he who meddles with man's soul? Which act is the easier to judge and justify?

THE AUDIENCE'S DEMANDS

This compulsion to rationalize even art is a highly instructive fact. It tells one a great deal about art's purposes and the purposes of all other communication. As I have said, the poet and the artist each seek in some special way to produce an emotion or assert a truth not otherwise apparent. But it is only in communion with their audiences that the effectiveness of their efforts can be tested and truth revealed. It may be academic whether a tree falling in the forest makes a noise. It is *not* academic whether a sonnet or a painting has merit. Only an audience can decide that.

Where have we arrived? Only at some common characteristics of art and advertising. Both are rhetorical, and both literally false; both expound an emotional reality deeper than the "real"; both pretend to "higher" purposes, although different ones; and the excellence of each is judged by its effect on its audience—its persuasiveness, in short. I do not mean to imply that the two are fundamentally the same, but rather that they both represent a pervasive, and I believe *universal,* characteristic of human nature—the human audience *demands* symbolic interpretation in everything it sees and knows. If it doesn't get it, it will return a verdict of "no interest."

To get a clearer idea of the relation between the symbols of advertising and the products they glorify, something more must be said about the fiat the consumer gives to industry to "distort" its messages.

Symbol and Substance

As we have seen, man seeks to transcend nature in the raw everywhere. Everywhere, and at all times, he has been attracted by the poetic imagery of some sort of art, literature, music, and mysticism. He obviously wants and needs the promises, the imagery, and the symbols of the poet and the priest. He refuses to live a life of primitive barbarism or sterile functionalism.

Consider a sardine can filled with scented powder. Even if the U.S. Bureau of Standards were to certify that the contents of this package are identical with the product sold in a beautiful paisley-printed container, it would not sell. The Boston matron, for example, who has built herself a deserved reputation for pinching every penny until it hurts, would unhesitatingly turn it down. While she may deny it, in self-assured and neatly cadenced accents, she obviously desires and needs the promises, imagery, and symbols produced by hyperbolic advertisements, elaborate packages, and fetching fashions.

The need for embellishment is not confined to personal appearance. A few years ago, an electronics laboratory offered a $700 testing device for sale. The company ordered two different front panels to be designed, one by the engineers who developed the equipment and one by professional industrial designers. When the two models were shown to a sample of laboratory directors with Ph.D.'s, the professional design attracted twice the purchase intentions that the engineer's design did. Obviously, the laboratory director who has been baptized into science at M.I.T. is quite as responsive to the blandishments of packaging as the Boston matron.

And, obviously, both these customers define the products they buy in much more sophisticated terms than the engineer in the factory. For a woman, dusting powder in a sardine can is not the same product as the identical dusting powder in an exotic paisley package. For the laboratory director, the test equipment behind an engineer-designed panel just isn't as "good" as the identical equipment in a box designed with finesse.

But all promises and images, almost by their very nature, exceed their capacity to live up to themselves. As every eager lover has ever known, the consummation seldom equals the promises which produced the chase. To forestall and suppress the visceral expectation of disappointment that life has taught us must inevitably come, we use art, architecture, literature, and the rest, and advertising as well, to shield ourselves, in advance of experience, from the stark and plain reality in which we are fated to live. I agree that we wish for unobtainable unrealities, "dream castles." But why promise ourselves reality, which we already possess? What we want is what we do *not* possess!

Everyone in the world is trying in his special personal fashion to solve a primal problem of life—the problem of rising above his own negligibility, of escaping from nature's confining, hostile, and unpredictable reality, of finding significance, security, and comfort in the things he must do to survive. Many of the so-called distortions of advertising, product design, and packaging may be viewed as a paradigm of the many responses that man makes to the conditions of survival in the environment. Without distortion, embellishment, and elaboration, life would be drab, dull, anguished, and at its existential worst.

But still, the critics may say, commercial communications tend to be aggressively deceptive. Perhaps, and perhaps not. The issue at stake here is more complex than the outraged critic believes. Man wants and needs the elevation of the spirit produced by attractive surroundings, by handsome packages, and by imaginative promises. He needs the assurances projected by well-known brand names, and the reliability suggested by salesmen who have been taught to dress by Oleg Cassini and to speak by Dale Carnegie. Of course, there are blatant, tasteless, and willfully deceiving salesmen and advertisers, just as there are blatant, tasteless, and willfully deceiving artists, preachers, and even professors. But, before talking blithely about deception, it is helpful to make a distinction between things and descriptions of things.

The Question of Deceit

Poetic descriptions of things make no pretense of being the things themselves. Nor do advertisements, even by the most elastic standards. Advertisements are the symbols of man's aspirations. They are not the real things, nor are they intended to be, nor are they accepted as such by the public. A study some years ago by the Center for Research in Marketing, Inc. concluded that deep down inside the consumer understands this perfectly well and has the attitude that an advertisement is an ad, not a factual news story.

Even Professor Galbraith grants the point when he says that "...because modern man is exposed to a large volume of information of varying degrees of unreliability...he establishes a system of discounts which he applies to various sources almost without thought....The discount becomes nearly total for all forms of advertising. The merest child watching television dismisses the health and status-giving claims of a breakfast cereal as 'a commercial.'"[2]

This is not to say, of course, that Galbraith also discounts advertising's effectiveness. Quite the opposite: "Failure to win belief does not impair the effectiveness of the management of demand for consumer products. Management involves the creation of a compelling image of the product in the mind of the consumer. To this he responds more or less automatically under circumstances where the purchase does not merit a great deal of thought. For building this image, palpable fantasy may be more valuable than circumstantial evidence."[3]

Linguists and other communications specialists will agree with the conclusion of the Center for Research in Marketing that "advertising is a symbol system existing in a world of symbols. Its reality depends upon the fact that it is a symbol...the content of an ad can never be real, it can only say something about reality, or create a relationship between itself and an individual which has an effect on the reality life of an individual."

Consumer, Know Thyself!

Consumption is man's most constant activity. It is well that he understands himself as a consumer.

The object of consumption is to solve a problem. Even consumption that is viewed as the creation of an opportunity—like going to medical school or taking a singles-only Caribbean tour—has as its purpose the solving of a problem. At a minimum, the medical student seeks to solve the problem of how to lead a relevant and comfortable life, and the lady on the tour seeks to solve the problem of spinsterhood.

The "purpose" of the product is not what the engineer explicitly says it is, but what the consumer implicitly demands that it shall be. Thus the consumer consumes not things, but expected benefits—not cosmetics, but the satisfactions of the allurements they promise; not quarter-inch drills, but quarter-inch holes; not stock in companies, but capital gains; not numerically controlled milling machines, but trouble-free and accurately smooth metal parts; not low-cal whipped cream, but self-rewarding indulgence combined with sophisticated convenience.

The significance of these distinctions is anything but trivial. Nobody knows this better, for example, than the creators of automobile ads. It is not the generic virtues that they tout, but more likely the car's capacity to enhance its user's status and his access to female prey.

Whether we are aware of it or not, we in effect expect and demand that advertising create these symbols for us to show us what life *might* be, to bring the possibilities that we cannot see before our eyes and screen out the stark reality in which we must live. We insist, as Gilbert put it, that there be added a "touch of artistic verisimilitude to an otherwise bald and unconvincing narrative."

Understanding the Difference

In a world where so many things are either commonplace or standardized, it makes no sense to refer to the rest as false, fraudulent, frivolous, or immaterial. The world works according to the aspirations and needs of its actors, not according to the arcane or moralizing logic of detached critics who pine for another age—an age which, in any case, seems different from today's largely because its observers are no longer children shielded by protective parents from life's implacable harshness.

To understand this is not to condone much of the vulgarity, purposeful duplicity, and scheming half-truths we see in advertising, promotion, packaging, and product design. But before we condemn, it is well to understand the difference between embellishment and duplicity and how extraordinarily uncommon the latter is in our times. The noisy visibility of promotion in our intensely communicating times need not be thoughtlessly equated with malevolence.

Thus the issue is not the prevention of distortion. It is, in the end, to know what kinds of distortions we actually want so that each of our lives is, without apology, duplicity, or rancor, made bearable. This does not mean we must accept out of hand all the commercial propaganda to which we are each day so constantly exposed, or that we must accept out of hand the equation that effluence is the price of affluence, or the simple notion that business cannot and government should not try to alter and improve the position of the consumer vis-à-vis the producer. It takes a special kind of perversity to continue any longer our shameful failure to mount vigorous, meaningful programs to protect the consumer, to standardize product grades, labels, and packages, to improve the consumer's information-getting process, and to mitigate the vulgarity and oppressiveness that is in so much of our advertising.

But the consumer suffers from an old dilemma. He wants "truth," but he also wants and needs the alleviating imagery and tantalizing promises of the advertiser and designer.

Business is caught in the middle. There is hardly a company that would not go down in ruin if it refused to provide fluff, because nobody will buy pure functionality. Yet, if it uses too much fluff and little else, business invites possibly ruinous legislation. The problem, therefore, is to find a middle way. And in this search, business can do a great deal more than it has been either accustomed or willing to do:

It can exert pressure to make sure that no single industry "finds reasons" why it should be exempt from legislative restrictions that are reasonable and popular.

It can work constructively with government to develop reasonable standards that will assure a more amenable commercial environment.

It can support legislation to provide the consumer with the information he needs to make easy comparison with products, packages, and prices.

It can support and help draft improved legislation on quality stabilization.

It can support legislation that gives consumers easy access to strong legal remedies where justified.

It can support programs to make local legal aid easily available, especially to the poor and undereducated who know so little about their rights and how to assert them.

Finally, it can support efforts to moderate and clean up the advertising noise that dulls our senses and assaults our sensibilities.

It will not be the end of the world or of capitalism for business to sacrifice a few commercial freedoms so that we may more easily enjoy our own humanity. Business can and should, for its own good, work energetically to achieve this end. But it is also well to remember the limits of what is possible. Paradise was not a free-goods society. The forbidden fruit was gotten at a price.

NOTES

1. See Raymond A. Bauer and Stephen A. Greyser, *The Consumer View* (Boston, Division of Research, Harvard Business School, 1968); see also Gary A. Steiner, *The People Look at Television* (New York, Alfred A. Knopf, Inc., 1963).
2. John Kenneth Galbraith, *The New Industrial State* (Boston, Houghton-Mifflin Company, 1967), pp. 325–326.
3. *Ibid.*, p. 326.

A Moral Evaluation of Sales Practices

David M. Holley*

In this paper I will attempt to develop a framework for evaluating the morality of various sales practices. Although I recognize that much of the salesforce in companies is occupied exclusively or primarily with sales to other businesses, my discussion will focus on sales to the individual consumer. Most of what I say should apply to any type of sales activity, but the moral issues arise most clearly in cases in which a consumer may or may not be very sophisticated in evaluating and responding to a sales presentation.

My approach will be to consider first the context of sales activities, a market system of production and distribution. Since such a system is generally justified on teleological grounds, I describe several conditions for its successful achievement of key goals. Immoral sales practices are analyzed as attempts to undermine these conditions.

Excerpted from "A Moral Evaluation of Sales Practices" by David M. Holley, *Business and Professional Ethics Journal*, Vol. 5, No. 1, circa 1987, pp. 3–21. Copyright © David M. Holley. Reprinted by permission of the author.
*Department of Philosophy and Religion, Grand Canyon College.

I

The primary justification for a market system is that it provides an efficient procedure for meeting people's needs and desires for goods and services.[1] This appeal to economic benefits can be elaborated in great detail, but at root it involves the claim that people will efficiently serve each other's needs if they are allowed to engage in voluntary exchanges.

A crucial feature of this argument is the condition that the exchange be voluntary. Assuming that individuals know best how to benefit themselves and that they will act to achieve such benefits, voluntary exchange can be expected to serve both parties. On the other hand, if the exchanges are not made voluntarily, we have no basis for expecting mutually beneficial results. To the extent that mutual benefit does not occur, the system will lack efficiency as a means for the satisfaction of needs and desires. Hence, this justification presupposes that conditions necessary for the occurrence of voluntary exchange are ordinarily met.

What are these conditions? For simplicity's sake, let us deal only with the kind of exchange involving a payment of money for some product or service. We can call the person providing the product the *seller* and the person making the monetary payment the *buyer*. I suggest that voluntary exchange occurs only if the following conditions are met:

1. Both buyer and seller understand what they are giving up and what they are receiving in return.
2. Neither buyer nor seller is compelled to enter into the exchange as a result of coercion, severely restricted alternatives, or other constraints on the ability to choose.
3. Both buyer and seller are able at the time of the exchange to make rational judgments about its costs and benefits.

I will refer to these three conditions as the knowledge, noncompulsion, and rationality conditions, respectively.[2] If the parties are uninformed, it is possible that an exchange might accidentally turn out to benefit them. But given the lack of information, they would not be in a position to make a rational judgment about their benefit, and we cannot reasonably expect beneficial results as a matter of course in such circumstances. Similarly, if the exchange is made under compulsion, then the judgment of personal benefit is not the basis of the exchange. It is possible for someone to be forced or manipulated into an arrangement that is in fact beneficial. But there is little reason to think that typical or likely.[3]

It should be clear that all three conditions are subject to degrees of fulfillment. For example, the parties may understand certain things about the exchange but not others. Let us posit a theoretical situation in which both parties are fully informed, fully rational, and enter into the exchange entirely of their own volition. I will call this an *ideal exchange*. In actual practice there is virtually always some divergence from the ideal. Knowledge can be more or less adequate. Individuals can be subject to various irrational influences. There can be borderline cases of external constraints. Nevertheless, we can often judge when a particular exchange was adequately informed, rational, and free from compulsion. Even when conditions are not ideal, we may still have an *acceptable exchange*.

With these concepts in mind, let us consider the obligations of sales personnel. I suggest that the primary duty of salespeople to customers is to avoid undermining the conditions of acceptable exchange. It is possible by act or omission to create a situation in which the customer is not sufficiently knowledgeable about what the exchange involves. It is also possible to influence the customer in ways that short-circuit the rational decision-making process. To behave in such ways is to undermine the conditions that are presupposed in teleological justifications of the market system. Of course, an isolated act is not sufficient to destroy the benefits of the system. But the moral acceptability of the system may become questionable if the conditions of acceptable exchange are widely abused. The individual who attempts to gain personally by undermining these conditions does that which, if commonly practiced, would produce a very different system from the one that supposedly provides moral legitimacy to that individual's activities.

II

If a mutually beneficial exchange is to be expected, the parties involved must be adequately informed about what they are giving up and what they are receiving. In most cases this should create no great problem for the seller[4], but what about the buyer? How is she to obtain the information needed? One answer is that the buyer is responsible for doing whatever investigation is necessary to acquire the information. The medieval principle of *caveat emptor* encouraged buyers to take responsibility for examining a purchase thoroughly to determine whether it had any hidden flaws. If the buyer failed to find defects, that meant that due caution had not been exercised.

If it were always relatively easy to discover defects by examination, then this principle might be an efficient method of guaranteeing mutual satisfaction. Sometimes, however, even lengthy investigation would not disclose what the buyer wants to know. With products of great complexity, the expertise needed for an adequate examination may be beyond what could reasonably be expected of most consumers. Even relatively simple products can have hidden flaws that most people would not discover until after the purchase, and to have the responsibility for closely examining every purchase would involve a considerable amount of a highly treasured modern commodity, the buyer's time. Furthermore, many exchange situations in our context involve products that cannot be examined in this way—goods that will be delivered at a later time or sent through the mail, for example. Finally, even if we assume that most buyers, by exercising enough caution, can protect their interests, the system of *caveat emptor* would take advantage of those least able to watch out for themselves. It would in effect justify mistreatment of a few for a rather questionable benefit.

In practice the buyer almost always relies on the seller for some information, and if mutually beneficial exchanges are to be expected, the information needs to meet certain standards of both quality and quantity. With regard to quality, the information provided should not be deceptive. This would include not only direct lies but also truths that are intended to mislead the buyer. Consider the following examples:

1. An aluminum siding salesperson tells customers that they will receive "bargain factory prices" for letting their homes be used as models in a new advertising campaign. Prospective customers will be brought to view the houses, and a commission of $100 will be paid for each sale that results. In fact, the price paid is well above market rates, the workmanship and materials are substandard, and no one is ever brought by to see the houses.[5]
2. A used car salesperson turns back the odometer reading on automobiles by an average of 25,000 to 30,000 miles per car. If customers ask whether the reading is correct, the salesperson replies that it is illegal to alter odometer readings.
3. A salesperson at a piano store tells an interested customer that the "special sale" will be good only through that evening. She neglects to mention that another "special sale" will begin the next day.
4. A telephone salesperson tells people who answer the phone that they have been selected to receive a free gift, a brand new freezer. All they have to do is buy a year's subscription to a food plan.
5. A salesperson for a diet system proclaims that under this revolutionary new plan the pounds

will melt right off. The system is described as a scientific advance that makes dieting easy. In fact, the system is a low-calorie diet composed of foods and liquids that are packaged under the company name but are no different from standard grocery store items.

The possibilities are endless, and whether or not a lie is involved, each case illustrates a salesperson's attempt to get a customer to believe something that is false in order to make the sale. It might be pointed out that these kinds of practices would not deceive a sophisticated consumer. Perhaps so, but whether they are always successful deceptions is not the issue. They are attempts to mislead the customer, and given that the consumer must often rely on information furnished by the salesperson, they are attempts to subvert the conditions under which mutually beneficial exchange can be expected. The salesperson attempts to use misinformation as a basis for customer judgment rather than allowing that judgment to be based on accurate beliefs. Furthermore, if these kinds of practices were not successful fairly often, they would probably not be used.

In the aluminum siding case, the customer is led to believe that there will be a discount in exchange for a kind of service, allowing the house to be viewed by prospective customers. This leaves the impression both that the job done will be of high quality and that the price paid will be offset by commissions. The car salesperson alters the product in order to suggest false information about the extent of its use. With such information, the customer is not able to judge accurately the value of the car. The misleading reply to inquiries is not substantially different from a direct lie. The piano salesperson deceives the customer about how long the product will be obtainable at a discount price. In this case the deception occurs through an omission. The telephone solicitor tries to give the impression that there has been a contest of some sort and that the freezer is a prize. In this way, the nature of the exchange is obscured.

The diet-system case raises questions about how to distinguish legitimate ''puffery'' from deception. Obviously, the matter will depend to some extent on how gullible we conceive the customer to be. As described, the case surely involves an attempt to get the customer to believe that dieting will be easier under this system and that what is being promoted is the result of some new scientific discovery. If there were no prospect that a customer would be likely to believe this, we would probably not think the technique deceptive. But in fact a number of individuals are deceived by claims of this type.

Some writers have defended the use of deceptive practices in business contexts on the grounds that there are specific rules applying to these contexts that differ from the standards appropriate in other contexts. It is argued, for example, that deception is standard practice, understood by all participants as something to be expected and, therefore, harmless, or that it is a means of self-defense justified by pressures of the competitive context.[6] To the extent that claims about widespread practice are true, people who know what is going on may be able to minimize personal losses, but that is hardly a justification of the practice. If I know that many people have installed devices in their cars that can come out and puncture the tires of the car next to them, that may help keep me from falling victim, but it does not make the practice harmless. Even if no one is victimized, it becomes necessary to take extra precautions, introducing a significant disutility into driving conditions. Analogously, widespread deception in business debases the currency of language, making business communication less efficient and more cumbersome.

More importantly, however, people are victimized by deceptive practices, and the fact that some may be shrewd enough to see through clouds of misinformation does not alter the deceptive intent. Whatever may be said with regard to appropriate behavior among people who ''know the rules,'' it is clear that many buyers are not aware of having entered into some special domain where deception is allowed. Even if this is naive, it does not provide a moral justification for subverting those individuals' capacity for making a reasoned choice.

Only a few people would defend the moral justifiability of deceptive sales practices. However, there may be room for much more disagreement with regard to how much information a salesperson is obligated to provide. In rejecting the principle of *caveat emptor,* I have suggested that there are pragmatic reasons for expecting the seller to communicate some information about the product. But how much? When is it morally culpable to withhold information? Consider the following cases:

1. An automobile dealer has bought a number of cars from another state. Although they appear to be new or slightly used, these cars have been involved in a major flood and were sold by the previous dealer at a discount rate. The salesperson knows the history of the cars and does not mention it to customers.

2. A salesperson for an encyclopedia company never mentions the total price of a set unless he has to. Instead he emphasizes the low monthly payment involved.

3. A real estate agent knows that one reason the couple selling a house with her company want to move is that the neighbors often have loud parties and neighborhood children have committed minor acts of vandalism. The agent makes no mention of this to prospective customers.

4. An admissions officer for a private college speaks enthusiastically about the advantages of the school. He does not mention the fact that the school is not accredited.

5. A prospective retirement home resident is under the impression that a particular retirement home is affiliated with a certain church. He makes it known that this is one of the fea-

tures he finds attractive about the home. Though the belief is false, the recruiters for the home make no attempt to correct the misunderstanding.

In all these cases the prospective buyer lacks some piece of knowledge that might be relevant to the decision to buy. The conditions for ideal exchange are not met. Perhaps, however, there can be an acceptable exchange. Whether or not this is the case depends on whether the buyer has adequate information to decide if the purchase would be beneficial. In the case of the flood-damaged autos, there is information relevant to evaluating the worth of the car that the customer could not be expected to know unless informed by the seller. If this information is not revealed, the buyer will not have adequate knowledge to make a reasonable judgment. Determining exactly how much information needs to be provided is not always clear-cut. We must in general rely on our assessments of what a reasonable person would want to know. As a practical guide, a salesperson might consider, ''What would I want to know if I were considering buying this product?''

Surely a reasonable person would want to know the total price of a product. Hence the encyclopedia salesperson who omits this total is not providing adequate information. The salesperson may object that this information could be inferred from other information about the monthly payment, length of term, and interest rate. But if the intention is not to have the customer act without knowing the full price, then why shouldn't it be provided directly? The admissions officer's failure to mention that the school is unaccredited also seems unacceptable when we consider what a reasonable person would want to know. There are some people who would consider this a plus, since they are suspicious about accrediting agencies imposing some alien standards (e.g., standards that conflict with religious views). But regardless of how

one evaluates the fact, most people would judge it to be important for making a decision.

The real estate case is more puzzling. Most real estate agents would not reveal the kind of information described, and would not feel they had violated any moral duties in failing to do so. Clearly, many prospective customers would want to be informed about such problems. However, in most cases failing to know these facts would not be of crucial importance. We have a case of borderline information. It would be known by all parties to an ideal exchange, but we can have an acceptable exchange even if the buyer is unaware of it. Failure to inform the customer of these facts is not like failing to inform the customer that the house is on the sight of a hazardous waste dump or that a major freeway will soon be adjacent to the property.

It is possible to alter the case in such a way that the information should be revealed or at least the buyer should be directed another way. Suppose the buyer makes it clear that his primary goal is to live in a quiet neighborhood where he will be undisturbed. The ''borderline'' information now becomes more central to the customer's decision. Notice that thinking in these terms moves us away from the general standard of what a reasonable person would want to know to the more specific standard of what is relevant given the criteria of this individual. In most cases, however, I think that a salesperson would be justified in operating under general ''reasonable person'' standards until particular deviations become apparent.[7]

The case of the prospective retirement home resident is a good example of how the particular criteria of the customer might assume great importance. If the recruiters, knowing what they know about this man's religious preferences, allow him to make his decision on the basis of a false assumption, they will have failed to support the conditions of acceptable exchange. It doesn't really matter that the misunderstanding was not caused by the salespeople. Their allowing it to be part of the basis for a decision borders on deception. If the misunderstanding was not on a matter of central importance to the individual's evaluation, they might have had no obligation to correct it. But the case described is not of that sort.

Besides providing nondeceptive and relatively complete information, salespeople may be obligated to make sure that their communications are understandable. Sales presentations containing technical information that is likely to be misunderstood are morally questionable. However, it would be unrealistic to expect all presentations to be immune to misunderstanding. The salesperson is probably justified in developing presentations that would be intelligible to the average consumer of the product he or she is selling and making adjustments in cases where it is clear that misunderstanding has occurred.

III

The condition of uncompelled exchange distinguishes business dealings from other kinds of exchanges. In the standard business arrangement, neither party is forced to enter the negotiations. A threat of harm would transform the situation to something other than a purely business arrangement. Coercion is not the only kind of compulsion, however. Suppose I have access to only one producer of food. I arrange to buy food from this producer, but given my great need for food and the absence of alternatives, the seller is able to dictate the terms. In one sense I choose to make the deal, but the voluntariness of my choice is limited by the absence of alternatives.

Ordinarily, the individual salesperson will not have the power to take away the buyer's alternatives. However, a clever salesperson can sometimes make it seem as if options are very limited and can use the customer's ignorance to produce the same effect. For example, imagine an individual who begins to look for a particular item at a local store. The salesperson extolls the line carried by his store, warns of the deficiencies of alternative brands, and warns about the

dishonesty of competitors, in contrast to his store's reliability. With a convincing presentation, a customer might easily perceive the options to be very limited. Whether or not the technique is questionable may depend on the accuracy of the perception. If the salesperson is attempting to take away a legitimate alternative, that is an attempt to undermine the customer's voluntary choice.

Another way the condition of uncompelled choice might be subverted is by involving a customer in a purchase without allowing her to notice what is happening. This would include opening techniques that disguise the purpose of the encounter so there can be no immediate refusal. The customer is led to believe that the interview is about a contest or a survey or an opportunity to make money. Not until the end does it become apparent that this is an attempt to sell something, and occasionally if the presentation is smooth enough, some buyers can be virtually unaware that they have bought anything. Obviously, there can be degrees of revelation, and not every approach that involves initial disguise of certain elements that might provoke an immediate rejection is morally questionable. But there are enough clear cases in which the intention is to get around, as much as possible, the voluntary choice of the customer. Consider the following examples:

1. A seller of children's books gains entrance to houses by claiming to be conducting an educational survey. He does indeed ask several "survey" questions, but he uses these to qualify potential customers for his product.

2. A salesperson alludes to recent accidents involving explosions of furnaces and, leaving the impression of having some official government status, offers to do a free safety inspection. She almost always discovers a "major problem" and offers to sell a replacement furnace.

3. A man receives a number of unsolicited books and magazines through the mail. Then he is

sent a bill and later letters warning of damage to his credit rating if he does not pay.

These are examples of the many variations on attempts to involve customers in exchanges without letting them know what is happening. The first two cases involve deceptions about the purpose of the encounter. Though they resemble cases discussed earlier that involved deception about the nature or price of a product, here the salesperson uses misinformation as a means of limiting the customer's range of choice. The customer does not consciously choose to listen to a sales presentation but finds that this is what is happening. Some psychological research suggests that when people do something that appears to commit them to a course of action, even without consciously choosing to do so, they will tend to act as if such a choice had been made in order to minimize cognitive dissonance. Hence, if a salesperson successfully involves the customer in considering a purchase, the customer may feel committed to give serious thought to the matter. The third case is an attempt to get the customer to believe that an obligation has been incurred. In variations on this technique, merchandise is mailed to a deceased person to make relatives believe that some payment is owed. In each case, an effort is made to force the consumer to choose from an excessively limited range of options.

IV

How can a salesperson subvert the rationality condition? Perhaps the most common way is to appeal to emotional reactions that cloud an individual's perception of relevant considerations. Consider the following cases:

1. A man's wife has recently died in a tragic accident. The funeral director plays upon the husband's love for his wife and to some extent his guilt about her death to get him to purchase a very expensive funeral.
2. A socially insecure young woman has bought a series of dance lessons from a local studio.

During the lessons, an attractive male instructor constantly compliments her on her poise and natural ability and tries to persuade her to sign up for more lessons.[8]
3. A life insurance salesperson emphasizes to a prospect the importance of providing for his family in the event of his death. The salesperson tells several stories about people who put off this kind of preparation.
4. A dress salesperson typically tells customers how fashionable they look in a certain dress. Her stock comments also include pointing out that a dress is slimming or sexy or "looks great on you."
5. A furniture salesperson regularly tells customers that a piece of furniture is the last one in stock and that another customer recently showed great interest in it. He sometimes adds that it may not be possible to get any more like it from the factory.

These cases remind us that emotions can be important motivators. It is not surprising that salespeople appeal to them in attempting to get the customer to make a purchase. In certain cases the appeal seems perfectly legitimate. When the life insurance salesperson tries to arouse the customer's fear and urges preparation, it may be a legitimate way to get the customer to consider something that is worth considering. Of course, the fact that the fear is aroused by one who sells life insurance may obscure to the customer the range of alternative possibilities in preparing financially for the future. But the fact that an emotion is aroused need not make the appeal morally objectionable.

If the appeal of the dress salesperson seems more questionable, this is probably because we are not as convinced of the objective importance of appearing fashionable, or perhaps because repeated observations of this kind are often insincere. But if we assume that the salesperson is giving an honest opinion about how the dress looks on a customer, it may provide some input for the individual who has a desire to achieve a particular effect. The fact that such remarks appeal to one's vanity or ambition does not in itself make the appeal unacceptable.

The furniture salesperson's warnings are clearly calculated to create some anxiety about the prospect of losing the chance to buy a particular item unless immediate action is taken. If the warnings are factually based, they would not be irrelevant to the decision to buy. Clearly, one might act impulsively or hastily when under the spell of such thoughts, but the salesperson cannot be faulted for pointing out relevant considerations.

The case of the funeral director is somewhat different. Here there is a real question of what benefit is to be gained by choosing a more expensive funeral package. For most people, minimizing what is spent on the funeral would be a rational choice, but at a time of emotional vulnerability it can be made to look as if this means depriving the loved one or the family of some great benefit. Even if the funeral director makes nothing but true statements, they can be put into a form designed to arouse emotions that will lessen the possibility of a rational decision being reached.

The dance studio case is similar in that a weakness is being played upon. The woman's insecurity makes her vulnerable to flattery and attention, and this creates the kind of situation in which others can take advantage of her. Perhaps the dance lessons fulfill some need, but the appeal to her vanity easily becomes a tool to manipulate her into doing what the instructor wants.

The key to distinguishing between legitimate and illegitimate emotional appeals lies in whether the appeal clouds one's ability to make a decision based on genuine satisfaction of needs and desires. Our judgment about whether this happens in a particular case will depend in part on whether we think the purchase likely to benefit the customer. The more questionable the benefits, the more an emotional appeal looks like manipulation rather than persuasion. When questionable benefits are combined with some spe-cial vulnerability on the part of the consumer, the use of the emotional appeal appears even more suspect.

V

I have attempted to provide a framework for evaluating the morality of a number of different types of sales practices. The framework is based on conditions for mutually beneficial exchange and ultimately for an efficient satisfaction of economic needs and desires. An inevitable question is whether this kind of evaluation is of any practical importance.

If we set before ourselves the ideal of a knowledgeable, unforced, and rational decision on the part of a customer, it is not difficult to see how some types of practices would interfere with this process. We must, of course, be careful not to set the standards too high. A customer may be partially but adequately informed to judge a purchase's potential benefits. A decision may be affected by nonrational and even irrational factors and yet still be rational enough in terms of being plausibly related to the individual's desires and needs. There may be borderline cases in which it is not clear whether acting in a particular way would be morally required or simply overscrupulous, but that is not an objection to this approach, only a recognition of a feature of morality itself.[9]

NOTES

1. The classic statement of the argument from economic benefits is found in Adam Smith, *The Wealth of Nations* (1776) (London: Methusen and Co. Ltd., 1930). Modern proponents of this argument include Ludwig von Mises, Friedrich von Hayek, and Milton Friedman.
2. One very clear analysis of voluntariness making use of these conditions may be found in John Hospers' *Human Conduct: Problems of Ethics,* 2nd ed. (New York: Harcourt Brace Jovanovich, 1982), pp. 385–388.
3. I will refer to the three conditions indifferently as conditions for voluntary exchange or conditions for

mutually beneficial exchange. By the latter designation I do not mean to suggest that they are either necessary or sufficient conditions for the occurrence of mutual benefit, but that they are conditions for the reasonable expectation of mutual benefit.

4. There are cases, however, in which the buyer knows more about a product than the seller. For example, suppose Cornell has found out that land Fredonia owns contains minerals that make it twice as valuable as Fredonia thinks. The symmetry of my conditions would lead me to conclude that Cornell should give Fredonia the relevant information unless perhaps Fredonia's failure to know was the result of some culpable negligence.

5. This case is described in Warren Magnuson and Jean Carper, *The Dark Side of the Market-Place* (Englewood Cliffs, N.J.: Prentice Hall, 1968), pp. 3–4.

6. Albert Carr, "Is Business Bluffing Ethical?" *Harvard Business Review* 46 (January–February 1968): 143–153. See also Thomas L. Carson,. Richard E. Wokutch, and Kent F. Murrmann, "Bluffing in Labor Negotiations: Legal and Ethical Issues," *Journal of Business Ethics* 1 (1982): 13–22.

7. My reference to a reasonable person standard should not be confused with the issue facing the FTC of whether to evaluate advertising by the reasonable consumer or ignorant consumer standard as described in Ivan Preston, "Reasonable Consumer or Ignorant Consumer: How the FTC Decides," *Journal of Consumer Affairs* 8 (Winter 1974): 131–143. There the primary issue is with regard to whom the government should protect from claims that might be misunderstood. My concern here is with determining what amount of information is necessary for informed judgment. In general I suggest that a salesperson should begin with the assumption that information a reasonable consumer would regard as important needs to be revealed and that when special interests and concerns of the consumer come to light they may make further revelations necessary. This approach parallels the one taken by Tom Beauchamp and James Childress regarding the information that a physician needs to provide to obtain informed consent. See their *Principles of Biomedical Ethics,* 2nd ed. (New York: Oxford University Press, 1983), pp. 74–79.

8. This is adapted from a court case quoted in Braybrooke, pp. 68–70.

9. This paper was written during a sabbatical leave from Friends University at the Center for the Study of Values, University of Delaware. I wish to thank Friends University for the leave and Dr. Norman Bowie for his hospitality during my stay at the Center.

Strict Products Liability and Compensatory Justice

George G. Brenkert*

I

Strict products liability is the doctrine that the seller of a product has legal responsibilities to compensate the user of that product for injuries suffered because of a defective aspect of the product, even when the seller has not been negligent in permitting that defect to occur.[1] Thus, even though a manufacturer, for example, has reasonably applied the existing techniques of manufacture and has anticipated and cared for nonintended uses of the product, he may still be held liable for injuries a product user suffers if it can be shown that the product was defective when it left the manufacturer's hands.[2]

To say that there is a crisis today concerning this doctrine would be to utter a commonplace which few in the business community would deny. The development of the doctrine of strict products liability, according to most business people, threatens many businesses financially.[3]

Written for the first edition of this book. Copyright © 1984 by George G. Brenkert. Reprinted by permission of the author.

*Department of Philosophy, the University of Tennessee.

Furthermore, strict products liability is said to be a morally questionable doctrine, since the manufacturer or seller has not been negligent in permitting the injury-causing defect to occur. On the other hand, victims of defective products complain that they deserve full compensation for injuries sustained in using a defective product whether or not the seller is at fault. Medical expenses and time lost from one's job are costs no individual should have to bear by himself. It is only fair that the seller share such burdens.

In general, discussions of this crisis focus on the limits to which a business ought to be held responsible. Much less frequently, discussions of strict products liability consider the underlying question of whether the doctrine of strict products liability is rationally justifiable. But unless this question is answered it would seem premature to seek to determine the limits to which business ought to be held liable in such cases. In the following paper I discuss this underlying philosophical question and argue that there is a rational justification for strict products liability which links it to the very nature of the free enterprise system.

II

It should be noted at the outset that strict products liability is not absolute liability. To hold a manufacturer legally (and morally) responsible for any and all injuries which product users might sustain would be morally perverse. First, it would deny the product user's own responsibility to take care in his actions and to suffer the consequences when he does not. It would therefore constitute an extreme form of moral and legal paternalism.

Second, if the product is not defective, there is no significant moral connection between anything the manufacturer has done or not done and the user's injuries other than the production and sale of the product. This provides no basis for holding the manufacturer responsible for the user's injuries. If, because of my own carelessness,

I cut myself with my new pocket knife, the fact that I just bought my knife from Blade Manufacturing Company provides no moral reason to hold Blade Manufacturing responsible for my injury.

Finally, though the manufacturer's product might be said to have harmed the person,[4] it is wholly implausible, when the product is not defective and the manufacturer not negligent, to say that the manufacturer has harmed the user. Thus, there would seem to be no moral basis upon which to maintain that the manufacturer has any liability to the product user. Strict products liability, on the other hand, holds that the manufacturer can be held liable when the product can be shown to be defective, even though the manufacturer himself has not been negligent.[5]

Two justifications of strict products liability are predominant in the literature. Both, I believe, are untenable. They are:

1. To hold producers strictly liable for defective products will cut down on the number of accidents and injuries which occur by forcing manufacturers to make their products safer.[6]
2. The manufacturer is best able to distribute to others the costs of injuries which users of his defective products suffer.[7]

There are several reasons why the first justification is unacceptable. First, it has been argued plausibly that almost everything that can be attained through the use of strict liability to force manufacturers to make their products safer can also be attained in other ways through the law.[8] Hence, to hold manufacturers strictly liable will not necessarily help reduce the number of accidents. The incentive to produce safer products already exists, without invoking the doctrine of strict products liability.

Second, at least some of the accidents which have been brought under strict liability have been caused by features of the products which the manufacturers could not have foreseen or controlled. At the time the product was designed and manufactured, the technological knowledge required to discover the hazard and take steps to minimize its effects was not available. It is doubtful that in such cases the imposition of strict liability upon the manufacturer could reduce accidents.[9] Thus, again, this justification for strict products liability fails.[10]

Third, the fact that the imposition of legal restraints and/or penalties would have a certain positive effect—for example, reduce accidents—does not show that the imposition of those penalties would be just. It has been pointed out before that the rate of crime might be cut significantly if the law would imprison the wives and children of men who break the law. Regardless of how correct that claim may be, to use these means in order to achieve a significant reduction in the crime rate would be unjust. Thus, the fact—if fact it be—that strict liability would cut down on the amount of dangerous and/or defective products placed on the market, and thus reduce the number of accidents and injuries, does not justify the imposition of strict liability on manufacturers.

Finally, the above justification is essentially a utilitarian appeal which emphasizes the welfare of the product users. It is not obvious, however, that those who use this justification have ever undertaken the utilitarian analysis which would show that greater protection of the product user's safety would further the welfare of product users. If emphasis on product user safety would cut down on the number and variety of products produced, the imposition of strict liability might not enhance product user welfare; rather, it might lower it. Furthermore, if the safety of product users is the predominant concern, massive public and private education safety campaigns might do as much or more to lower the level of accidents and injuries as strict products liability.

The second justification given for strict products liability is also utilitarian in nature. Among the factors cited in favor of this justification are the following:

1. "An individual harmed by his or her use of a defective product is often unable to bear the loss individually."
2. "Distribution of losses among all users of a product would minimize both individual and aggregate loss."
3. "The situation of producers and marketers in the marketplace enables them conveniently to distribute losses among all users of a product by raising prices sufficiently to compensate those harmed (which is what in fact occurs where strict liability is in force)."[11]

This justification is also defective.

First, the word "best" in the phrase "best able to distribute to others the cost" is usually understood in a nonmoral sense; it is used to signify that the manufacturer can most efficiently pass on the costs of injuries to others. Once this use of "best" is recognized, surely we may ask why these costs ought to be passed on to other consumers and/or users of the same product or line of products. Even if the imposition of strict liability did maximize utility, it might still be unjust to use the producer as the distributor of losses.[12] Indeed, some have objected that to pass along the costs of such accidents to other consumers of a manufacturer's products is unjust to them.[13] The above justification is silent with regard to these legitimate objections.

Second, manufacturers may not always be in the best (that is, most efficient and economical) position to pass costs on to customers. Even in monopoly areas, there are limitations. Furthermore, some products are subject to an elastic demand, preventing the manufacturer from passing along the costs.[14] Finally, the present justification could justify far more than is plausible. If the reason for holding the manufacturer liable is that the manufacturer is the "best" administrator of costs, one might plausibly argue that the manufacturer should pay for injuries suffered not only when he is not negligent but also when the product is not defective. Theoretically, at least, this argument could be extended from cases of strict liability to that of absolute liability.

Whether this argument holds up depends upon contingent facts concerning the nature and frequency of injuries people suffer using products, the financial strength of businesses, and the kinds and levels of products liability insurance available to them. It does not depend on any morally significant elements in the relationship between the producer and the product user. Such an implication, I believe, undercuts the purported moral nature of this justification and reveals it for what it is: an economic, not a moral, justification.

Accordingly, neither of the major current justifications for the imposition of strict liability appears to be acceptable. If this is the case, is strict products liability a groundless doctrine, willfully and unjustly imposed on manufacturers?

III

This question can be asked in two different ways. On the one hand, it can be asked within the assumptions of the free enterprise system. On the other hand, it could be raised with the premise that the fundamental assumptions of that socioeconomic system are also open to revision and change. In the following, I will discuss the question *within* the general assumptions of the free enterprise system. Since these assumptions are broadly made in legal and business circles it is interesting to determine what answer might be given within these constraints. Indeed, I suggest that only within these general assumptions can strict products liability be justified.

To begin with, it is crucial to remember that what we have to consider is the relationship between an entity doing business and an individual.[15] The strict liability attributed to business would not be attributed to an individual who happened to sell some product he had made to his neighbor or a stranger. If Peter sold an article he had made to Paul and Paul hurt himself because the article had a defect which occurred

through no negligence of Peter's, we would not normally hold Peter morally responsible to pay for Paul's injuries.

Peter did not claim, we may assume, that the product was absolutely risk-free. Had he kept it, he himself might have been injured by it. Paul, on the other hand, bought it. He was not pressured, forced, or coerced to do so. Peter mounted no advertising campaign. Though Paul might not have been injured if the product had been made differently, he supposedly bought it with open eyes. Peter did not seek to deceive Paul about its qualities. The product, both its good and bad qualities, became his when he bought it.

In short, we assume that both Peter and Paul are morally autonomous individuals capable of knowing their own interests, that such individuals can legitimately exchange their ownership of various products, that the world is not free of risks, and that not all injuries one suffers in such a world can be blamed on others. To demand that Peter protect Paul from such dangers and/or compensate him for injuries resulting from such dangers is to demand that Peter significantly reduce the risks of the product he offers to Paul and to protect Paul from encountering those risks. However, this demand smacks of paternalism and undercuts our basic moral assumptions about such relations. Hence, in such a case, Peter is not morally responsible for Paul's injuries or, because of this transaction, obligated to aid him. Perhaps Peter owes Paul aid because Paul is an injured neighbor or person. Perhaps for charitable reasons Peter ought to help Paul. But Peter has no moral obligation stemming from the sale itself to provide aid.

It is different for businesses. They have been held to be legally and morally obliged to pay the victim for his injuries. Why? What is the difference? The difference is that when Paul is hurt by a defective product from corporation X, he is hurt by something produced in a socioeconomic system purportedly embodying free enterprise. In other words, among other things:

1. Each business and/or corporation produces articles or services it sells for profit.
2. Each member of this system competes with other members of the system in trying to do as well as it can for itself not simply in each exchange, but through each exchange for its other values and desires.
3. Competition is to be "open and free, without deception or fraud."
4. Exchanges are voluntary and undertaken when each party believes it can benefit thereby. One party provides the means for another party's ends if the other party will provide the first party the means to its ends.[16]
5. The acquisition and disposition of ownership rights—that is, of private property—is permitted in such exchanges.
6. No market or series of markets constitutes the whole of a society.
7. Law, morality, and government play a role in setting acceptable limits to the nature and kinds of exchange in which people may engage.[17]

What is it about such a system which would justify claims of strict products liability against businesses? Calabresi has suggested that the free enterprise system is essentially a system of strict liability.[18] Thus the very nature of the free enterprise system justifies such liability claims. His argument has two parts. First, he claims that "bearing risks is both the function of, and justification for, private enterprise in a free enterprise society."[19] "Free enterprise is prized, in classical economics, precisely because it fosters the creation of entrepreneurs who will take such uninsurable risks, who will, in other words, gamble on uncertainty and demonstrate their utility by surviving—by winning more than others."[20]

Accordingly, the nature of private enterprise requires individual businesses to assume the burden of risk in the production and distribution of its products. However, even if we grant that this characterization of who must bear the risks "in deciding what goods are worthy of producing and

what new entrants into an industry are worth having" is correct, it would not follow that individual businesses ought to bear the burden of risk in cases of accidents.

Calabresi himself recognizes this. Thus in the second part of his argument he maintains that there is a close analogy which lets us move from the regular risk-bearing businesses must accept in the marketplace to the bearing of risks in accidents: "although...[the above characterization] has concerned *regular* entrepreneurial-product risks, not accident risks, the analogy is extremely close."[21] He proceeds to draw the analogy, however, in the following brief sentence: "As with product-accident risks, our society starts out by allocating ordinary product-production risks in ways which try to maximize the chances that incentives will be placed on those most suited to 'manage' these risks."[22] In short, he asserts that the imposition of strict products liability on business will be the most effective means of reducing such risks.

But such a view does not really require, as we have seen in the previous section, any assumptions about the nature of the free enterprise system. It could be held independently of such assumptions. Further, this view is simply a form of the first justificatory argument we discussed and rejected in the previous section. We can hardly accept it here just by attaching it to the nature of free enterprise.

Nevertheless, Calabresi's initial intuitions about a connection between the assumptions of the free enterprise system and the justification of strict products liability are correct. However, they must be developed in the following, rather different, manner. In the free enterprise system, each person and/or business is obligated to follow the rules and understandings which define this socioeconomic system. Following the rules is expected to channel competition among individuals and businesses to socially positive results. In providing the means to fulfill the ends of others, one's own ends also get fulfilled.

Though this does not happen in every case, it

is supposed to happen most of the time. Those who fail in their competition with others may be the object of charity, but not of other duties. Those who succeed, qua members of this socio-economic system, do not have moral duties to aid those who fail. Analogously, the team which loses the game may receive our sympathy but the winning team is not obligated to help it to win the next game or even to play it better. Those who violate the rules, however, may be punished or penalized, whether or not the violation was intentional and whether or not it redounded to the benefit of the violator. Thus, a team may be assessed a penalty for something that a team member did unintentionally to a member of the other team but which injured the other team's chances of competition in the game by violating the rules.

This point may be emphasized by another instance involving a game that brings us closer to strict products liability. Imagine that you are playing table tennis with another person in his newly constructed table tennis room. You are both avid table tennis players and the game means a lot to both of you. Suppose that after play has begun, you are suddenly and quite obviously blinded by the light over the table—the light shade has a hole in it which, when it turned in your direction, sent a shaft of light unexpectedly into your eyes. You lose a crucial point as a result. Surely it would be unfair of your opponent to seek to maintain his point because he was faultless—after all, he had not intended to blind you when he installed that light shade. You would correctly object that he had gained the point unfairly, that you should not have to give up the point lost, and that the light shade should be modified so that the game can continue on a fair basis. It is only fair that the point be played over.

Businesses and their customers in a free enterprise system are also engaged in competition with each other.[23] The competition here, however, is multifaceted as each tries to gain the best agreement he can from the other with regard to

the buying and selling of raw materials, products, services, and labor. Such agreements must be voluntary. The competition which leads to them cannot involve coercion. In addition, such competition must be fair and ultimately result in the benefit of the entire society through the operation of the proverbial invisible hand.

Crucial to the notion of fairness of competition are not simply the demands that the competition be open, free, and honest, but also that each person in a society be given an equal opportunity to participate in the system in order to fulfill his or her own particular ends. Friedman formulates this notion in the following manner:

> ...the priority given to equality of opportunity in the hierarchy of values...is manifested particularly in economic policy. The catchwords were free enterprise, competition, laissez-faire. Everyone was to be free to go into any business, follow any occupation, buy any property, subject only to the agreement of the other parties to the transaction. Each was to have the opportunity to reap the benefits if he succeeded, to suffer the costs if he failed. There were to be no arbitrary obstacles. Performance, not birth, religion, or nationality, was the touchstone.[24]

What is obvious in Friedman's comments is that he is thinking primarily of a person as a producer. Equality of opportunity requires that one not be prevented by arbitrary obstacles from participating (by engaging in a productive role of some kind or other) in the system of free enterprise, competition, and so on in order to fulfill one's own ends ("reap the benefits"). Accordingly, monopolies are restricted, discriminatory hiring policies have been condemned, and price collusion is forbidden.

However, each person participates in the system of free enterprise *both* as a worker/producer *and* as a consumer. The two roles interact; if the person could not consume he would not be able to work, and if there were no consumers there would be no work to be done. Even if a particular individual is only (what is ordinarily considered) a consumer, he or she plays a theoretically significant role in the competitive free enterprise system. The fairness of the system depends upon what access he or she has to information about goods and services on the market, the lack of coercion imposed on that person to buy goods, and the lack of arbitrary restrictions imposed by the market and/or government on his or her behavior.

In short, equality of opportunity is a doctrine with two sides which applies both to producers and to consumers. If, then, a person as a consumer or a producer is injured by a defective product—which is one way his activities might arbitrarily be restricted by the action of (one of the members of) the market system—surely his free and voluntary participation in the system of free enterprise will be seriously affected. Specifically, his equal opportunity to participate in the system in order to fulfill his own ends will be diminished.

Here is where strict products liability enters the picture. In cases of strict liability the manufacturer does not intend for a certain aspect of his product to injure someone. Nevertheless, the person is injured. As a result, he is at a disadvantage both as a consumer and as a producer. He cannot continue to play either role as he might wish. Therefore, he is denied that equality of opportunity which is basic to the economic system in question just as surely as he would be if he were excluded from employment by various unintended consequences of the economic system which nevertheless had racially or sexually prejudicial implications. Accordingly, it is fair for the manufacturer to compensate the person for his losses before proceeding with business as usual. That is, the user of a manufacturer's product may justifiably demand compensation from the manufacturer when its product can be shown to be defective and has injured him and harmed his chances of participation in the system of free enterprise.

Hence, strict liability finds a basis in the notion of equality of opportunity which plays a central role in the notion of a free enterprise system. That is why a business which does *not* have to pay for the injuries an individual suffers in the use of a defective article made by that business is felt to be unfair to its customers. Its situation is analogous to that of a player's unintentional violation of a game rule which is intended to foster equality of competitive opportunity.

A soccer player, for example, may unintentionally trip an opposing player. He did not mean to do it; perhaps he himself had stumbled. Still, he has to be penalized. If the referee looked the other way, the tripped player would rightfully object that he had been treated unfairly. Similarly, the manufacturer of a product may be held strictly liable for a product of his which injures a person who uses that product. Even if he is faultless, a consequence of his activities is to render the user of his product less capable of equal participation in the socioeconomic system. The manufacturer should be penalized by way of compensating the victim. Thus, the basis upon which manufacturers are held strictly liable is compensatory justice.

In a society which refuses to resort to paternalism or to central direction of the economy and which turns, instead, to competition in order to allocate scarce positions and resources, compensatory justice requires that the competition be fair and losers be protected.[25] Specifically, no one who loses should be left so destitute that he cannot reenter the competition. Furthermore, those who suffer injuries traceable to defective merchandise or services which restrict their participation in the competitive system should also be compensated.

Compensatory justice does not presuppose negligence or evil intentions on the part of those to whom the injuries might ultimately be traced. It is not perplexed or incapacitated by the relative innocence of all parties involved. Rather, it is concerned with correcting the disadvantaged situation an individual experiences due to accidents or failures which occur in the normal working of that competitive system. It is on this basis that other compensatory programs which alleviate the disabilities of various minority groups are founded. Strict products liability is also founded on compensatory justice.

An implication of the preceding argument is that business is not morally obliged to pay, as such, for the physical injury a person suffers. Rather, it must pay for the loss of equal competitive opportunity—even though it usually is the case that it is because of a (physical) injury that there is a loss of equal opportunity. Actual legal cases in which the injury which prevents a person from going about his or her daily activities is emotional or mental, as well as physical, support this thesis. If a person were neither mentally nor physically harmed, but still rendered less capable of participating competitively because of a defective aspect of a product, there would still be grounds for holding the company liable.

For example, suppose I purchased and used a cosmetic product guaranteed to last a month. When used by most people it is odorless. On me, however, it has a terrible smell. I can stand the smell, but my co-workers and most other people find it intolerable. My employer sends me home from work until it wears off. The product has not harmed me physically or mentally. Still, on the above argument, I would have reason to hold the manufacturer liable. Any cosmetic product with this result is defective. As a consequence my opportunity to participate in the socioeconomic system is curbed. I should be compensated.

IV

There is another way of arriving at the same conclusion about the basis of strict products liability. To speak of business or the free enterprise system, it was noted above, is to speak of the voluntary exchanges between producer and customer which take place when each party believes he has an opportunity to benefit. Surely customers and producers may miscalculate their benefits; something they voluntarily agreed to buy

or sell may turn out not to be to their benefit. The successful person does not have any moral responsibilities to the unsuccessful person—at least as a member of this economic system. If, however, fraud is the reason one person does not benefit, the system is, in principle, undermined. If such fraud were universalized, the system would collapse. Accordingly, the person committing the fraud does have a responsibility to make reparations to the one mistreated.

Consider once again the instance of a person who is harmed by a product he bought or used, a product that can reasonably be said to be defective. Has the nature of the free enterprise system also been undermined or corrupted in this instance? Producer and consumer have exchanged the product but it has not been to their mutual benefit; the manufacturer may have benefited, but the customer has suffered because of the defect. Furthermore, if such exchanges were universalized, the system would also be undone.

Suppose that whenever people bought products from manufacturers the products turned out to be defective and the customers were always injured, even though the manufacturers could not be held negligent. Though one party to such exchanges might benefit, the other party always suffered. If the rationale for this economic system—the reason it was adopted and is defended—were that in the end both parties share the equal opportunity to gain, surely it would collapse with the above consequences. Consequently, as with fraud, an economic system of free enterprise requires that injuries which result from defective products be compensated. The question is: Who is to pay for the compensation?

There are three possibilities. The injured party could pay for his own injuries. However, this is implausible since what is called for is compensation and not merely payment for injuries. If the injured party had simply injured himself, if he had been negligent or careless, then it is plausible that he should pay for his own injuries. No compensation is at stake here. But in the present case the injury stems from the actions of a particular manufacturer who, albeit unwittingly, placed the defective product on the market and stands to gain through its sale.

The rationale of the free enterprise system would be undermined, we have seen, if such actions were universalized, for then the product user's equal opportunity to benefit from the system would be denied. Accordingly, since the rationale and motivation for an individual to be part of this socioeconomic system is his opportunity to gain from participation in it, justice requires that the injured product user receive compensation for his injuries. Since the individual can hardly compensate himself, he must receive compensation from some other source.

Second, some third party—such as government—could compensate the injured person. This is not wholly implausible if one is prepared to modify the structure of the free enterprise system. And, indeed, in the long run this may be the most plausible course of action. However, if one accepts the structure of the free enterprise system, this alternative must be rejected because it permits the interference of government into individual affairs.[26]

Third, we are left with the manufacturer. Suppose a manufacturer's product, even though the manufacturer wasn't negligent, always turned out to be defective and injured those using his products. We might sympathize with his plight, but he would either have to stop manufacturing altogether (no one would buy such products) or else compensate the victims for their losses. (Some people might buy and use his products under these conditions.) If he forced people to buy and use his products he would corrupt the free enterprise system. If he did not compensate the injured users, they would not buy and he would not be able to sell his products. Hence, he could partake of the free enterprise system— that is, sell his products—only if he compensated his user/victims. Accordingly, the sale of this hypothetical line of defective products would be voluntarily accepted as just or fair only if com-

pensation were paid the user/victims of such products by the manufacturer.

The same conclusion follows even if we consider a single defective product. The manufacturer put the defective product on the market. Because of his actions others who seek the opportunity to participate on an equal basis in this system in order to benefit therefrom are unable to do so. Thus, a result of his actions, even though unintended, is to undermine the system's character and integrity. Accordingly, when a person is injured in his attempt to participate in this system, he is owed compensation by the manufacturer. The seller of the defective article must not jeopardize the equal opportunity of the product user to benefit from the system. The seller need not guarantee that the buyer/user will benefit from the purchase of the product; after all, the buyer may miscalculate or be careless in the use of a nondefective product. But if he is not careless or has not miscalculated, his opportunity to benefit from the system is illegitimately harmed if he is injured in its use because of the product's defectiveness. He deserves compensation.

It follows from the arguments in this and the preceding section that strict products liability is not only compatible with the system of free enterprise but that if it were not attributed to the manufacturer the system itself would be morally defective. And the justification for requiring manufacturers to pay compensation when people are injured by defective products is that the demands of compensatory justice are met.[27]

NOTES

1. This characterization of strict products liability is adapted from Alvin S. Weinstein et al., *Products Liability and the Reasonably Safe Product* (New York: John Wiley & Sons, 1978), ch. 1. I understand the seller to include the manufacturer, the retailer, distributors, and wholesalers. For the sake of convenience, I will generally refer simply to the manufacturer.

2. Cf. John W. Wade, ''On Product 'Design Defects'

and Their Actionability,'' 33 *Vanderbilt Law Review* 553 (1980); Weinstein et al., *Products Liability and the Reasonably Safe Product,* pp. 8, 28–32; Reed Dickerson, ''Products Liability: How Good Does a Product Have to Be?'' 42 *Indiana Law Journal* 308–316 (1967). Section 402A of the Restatement (Second) of Torts characterizes the seller's situation in this fashion: ''the seller has exercised all possible care in the preparation and sale of his product.''

3. Cf. John C. Perham, ''The Dilemma in Product Liability,'' *Dun's Review,* 109 (1977), pp. 48–50, 76, W. Page Keeton, ''Products Liability–Design Hazards and the Meaning of Defect,'' 10 *Cumberland Law Review* 293–316 (1979); Weinstein et al., *Products Liability and the Reasonably Safe Product,* ch. 1.

4. More properly, of course, the person's use of the manufacturer's product harmed the product user.

5. Clearly one of the central questions confronting the notion of strict liability is what is to count as ''defective.'' With few exceptions, it is held that a product is defective if and only if it is unreasonably dangerous. There have been several different standards proposed as measures of the defectiveness or unreasonably dangerous nature of a product. However, in terms of logical priorities, it really does not matter what the particular standard for defectiveness is unless we know whether we may justifiably hold manufacturers strictly liable for defective products. That is why I concentrate in this paper on the justifiability of strict products liability.

6. Michel A. Coccia, John W. Dondanville, and Thomas R. Nelson, *Product Liability: Trends and Implications* (New York: American Management Association, 1970), p. 13; W. Page Keeton, ''The Meaning of Defect in Products Liability Law—A Review of Basic Principles,'' 45 *Missouri Law Review* 580 (1980); William L. Prosser, ''The Assault Upon the Citadel (Strict Liability to the Consumer),'' 69 *The Yale Law Journal* 119 (1960).

7. Coccia, Dondanville, and Nelson, *Product Liability: Trends and Implications,* p. 13; Keeton, ''The Meaning of Defect in Products Liability Law—A Review of Basic Principles,'' pp. 580–581; David G. Owen, ''Rethinking the Policies of Strict Products Liability,'' 33 *Vanderbilt Law Review* 686 (1980); Prosser, ''The Assault Upon the Citadel (Strict Liability to the Consumer),'' p. 1120.

8. Marcus L. Plant, ''Strict Liability of Manufacturers for Injuries Caused by Defects in Products—An Opposing View,'' 24 *Tennessee Law Review* 945 (1957); Prosser, ''The Assault Upon the Citadel (Strict Liability to the Consumer),'' pp. 1114, 1115, 1119.

9. Keeton, ''The Meaning of Defect in Products Liability Law—A Review of Basic Principles,'' pp. 594–595; Weinstein et al., *Products Liability and the Reasonably Safe Product,* p. 55.

10. An objection might be raised that such accidents ought not to fall under strict products liability and hence do not constitute a counterexample to the above justification. This objection is answered in Sections III and IV.

11. These three considerations are formulated by Michael D. Smith, ''The Morality of Strict Liability in Tort,'' *Business and Professional Ethics Newsletter,* 3(1979), p. 4. Smith himself, however, was drawing upon Guido Calabresi, ''Some Thoughts on Risk Distribution and the Law of Torts,'' 70 *Yale Law Journal* 499–553 (1961).

12. Smith, ''The Morality of Strict Liability in Tort,'' p. 4. Cf. George P. Fletcher, ''Fairness and Utility in Tort Theory,'' 85 *Harvard Law Review* 537–573 (1972).

13. Rev. Francis E. Lucey, S. J., ''Liability Without Fault and the Natural Law,'' 24 *Tennessee Law Review* 952–962 (1957); Perham, ''The Dilemma in Product Liability,'' pp. 48–49.

14. Plant, ''Strict Liability of Manufacturers for Injuries Caused by Defects in Products—An Opposing View,'' pp. 946–947. By ''elastic demand'' is meant ''a slight increase in price will cause a sharp reduction in demand or will turn consumers to a substitute product'' (pp. 946–947).

15. Cf. Prosser, ''The Assault Upon the Citadel (Strict Liability to the Consumer),'' pp. 1140–1141; Wade, ''On Product 'Design Defects' and Their Actionability,'' p. 569; Coccia, Dondanville, and Nelson, *Product Liability: Trends and Implications,* p. 19.

16. F. A. Hayek emphasizes this point in ''The Moral Element in Free Enterprise,'' in *Studies in Philosophy, Politics, and Economics* (New York: Simon and Schuster, 1967), p. 229.

17. Several of these characteristics have been drawn

from Milton Friedman and Rose Friedman, *Free to Choose* (New York: Avon Books, 1980).

18. Calabresi, "Product Liability: Curse or Bulwark of Free Enterprise," 27 *Cleveland State Law Review* 325 (1978).

19. *Ibid.*, p. 321.

20. *Ibid.*

21. *Ibid.*, p. 324.

22. *Ibid.*

23. Cf. H. B. Acton, *The Morals of Markets* (London: Longman Group Limited, 1971), pp. 1–7, 33–37; Milton Friedman and Rose Friedman, *Free to Choose.*

24. Milton Friedman and Rose Friedman, *Free to Choose,* pp. 123–124.

25. I have drawn heavily, in this paragraph, on the fine article by Bernard Boxhill, "The Morality of Reparation," reprinted in *Reverse Discrimination,* ed. Barry R. Gross (Buffalo, New York: Prometheus Books, 1977), pp. 270–278.

26. Cf. Calabresi, "Product Liability: Curse or Bulwark of Free Enterprise," pp. 315–319.

27. I would like to thank the following for providing helpful comments on earlier versions of this paper: Betsy Postow, Jerry Phillips, Bruce Fisher, John Hardwig, and Sheldon Cohen.

QUESTIONS FOR DISCUSSION

1. The CEO of Consumer Products Unlimited opened the annual meeting with a speech about CPU's commitment to "serving the needs of the consumer." At the same meeting, she announced the introduction of a new bath soap into the company's product line, which already contained 11 soaps. She explained that it had the same formula as three of CPU's other soaps, but would have a French name, would cost more, and would appeal to a more sophisticated consumer. The marketing division, she said, was already beginning an aggressive ad campaign. Do consumers *need* CPU's new soap? Do they want it? If not, why not? If so, in what sense? Would CPU's ads be deceptive if they claimed that the soap contained "unique European skin-care ingredients?"

2. Galbraith claims that U.S. society is rich in private goods, such as those produced by CPU, but poor in public goods such as clean air, parks, and public transportation. According to Galbraith, does this mean that people want public goods less than they want private goods? Explain. Would it make sense to conduct advertising campaigns for public goods? Why or why not?

3. Explain when a manufacturer is liable under the doctrine of strict products liability, and when he is not. What is the point of Brenkert's table-tennis analogy? Are there any other appropriate sports analogies that illuminate strict products liability?

The Environment

READINGS FOR CHAPTER TWELVE

William T. Blackstone
Ethics and Ecology
472

Kenneth E. Boulding
Fun and Games with the Gross National Product: The Role of Misleading Indicators in Social Policy
477

Robert W. Lee
Conservatives Consider the Crushing Cost of Environmental Extremism
482

Larry E. Ruff
The Economic Common Sense of Pollution
487

Mark Sagoff
At the Shrine of Our Lady of Fátima, or Why Political Questions Are Not All Economic
494

Ethics and Ecology

William T. Blackstone*

Much has been said about the right to a decent or livable environment. In his 22 January 1970 state of the union address, President Nixon stated: "The great question of the seventies is, shall we surrender to our surroundings, or shall we make our peace with Nature and begin to make the reparations for the damage we have done to our air, our land, and our water?...Clean air, clean water, open spaces—these would once again be the birthright of every American; if we act now, they can be." It seems, though, that the use of the term *right* by President Nixon, under the rubric of a "birthright" to a decent environment, is not a strict sense of the term. That is, he does not use this term to indicate that one has or should have either a legal right or a moral right to a decent environment. Rather he is pointing to the fact that in the past our environmental resources have been so abundant that all Americans did in fact inherit a livable environment, and it would be *desirable* that this state of affairs again be the case. Pollution and the exploitation of our environment is precluding this kind of inheritance.

Few would challenge the desirability of such a state of affairs or of such a "birthright." What we want to ask is whether the right to a decent environment can or ought to be considered a right in a stricter sense, either in a legal or moral sense. In contrast to a merely desirable state of affairs, a right entails a correlative duty or obligation on the part of someone or some group to accord one a certain mode of treatment or to act in a certain way.[1] Desirable states of affairs do not entail such correlative duties or obligations.

THE RIGHT TO A LIVABLE ENVIRONMENT AS A HUMAN RIGHT

Let us first ask whether the right to a livable environment can properly be considered to be a human right. For the purposes of this paper, however, I want to avoid raising the more general question of whether there are any human rights at all. Some philosophers do deny that any human rights exist.[2] In two recent papers I have argued that human rights do exist (even though such rights may properly be overridden on occasion by other morally relevant reasons) and that they are universal and inalienable (although the actual exercise of such rights on a given occasion is alienable).[3] My argument for the existence of universal human rights rests, in the final analysis, on a theory of what it means to be human, which specifies the capacities for rationality and freedom as essential, and on the fact that there are no relevant grounds for excluding any human from the opportunity to develop and fulfill his capacities (rationality and freedom) as a human.

If the right to a livable environment were seen as a basic and inalienable human right, this could be a valuable tool (both inside and outside of legalistic frameworks) for solving some of our environmental problems, both on a national and on an international basis. Are there any philosophical and conceptual difficulties in treating this right as an inalienable human right? Traditionally we have not looked upon the right to a decent environment as a human right or as an inalienable right. Rather, inalienable human or natural rights have been conceived in somewhat different terms; equality, liberty, happiness, life, and property. However, might it not be possible to view the right to a livable environment as being entailed by, or as constitutive of, these basic human or natural rights recognized in our polit-

Excerpted from "Ethics and Ecology" by William T. Blackstone, in *Philosophy and Environmental Crisis,* edited by William T. Blackstone. Copyright © 1974, the University of Georgia Press. Reprinted by permission of the University of Georgia Press.

*Formerly at the Department of Philosophy, University of Georgia.

CHAPTER 12: THE ENVIRONMENT

ical tradition? If human rights, in other words, are those rights which each human possesses in virtue of the fact that he is human and in virtue of the fact that those rights are essential in permitting him to live a human life (that is, in permitting him to fulfill his capacities as a rational and free being), then might not the right to a decent environment be properly categorized as such a human right? Might it not be conceived as a right which has emerged as a result of changing environmental conditions and the impact of those conditions on the very possibility of human life and on the possibility of the realization of other rights such as liberty and equality? Let us explore how this might be the case.

Given man's great and increasing ability to manipulate the environment, and the devastating effect this is having, it is plain that new social institutions and new regulative agencies and procedures must be initiated on both national and international levels to make sure that the manipulation is in the public interest. It will be necessary, in other words, to restrict or stop some practices and the freedom to engage in those practices. Some look upon such additional state planning, whether national or international, as unnecessary further intrusion on man's freedom. Freedom is, of course, one of our basic values, and few would deny that excessive state control of human action is to be avoided. But such restrictions on individual freedom now appear to be necessary in the interest of overall human welfare and the rights and freedoms of *all* men. Even John Locke with his stress on freedom as an inalienable right recognized that this right must be construed so that it is consistent with the equal right to freedom of others. The whole point of the state is to restrict unlicensed freedom and to provide the conditions for equality of rights for all. Thus it seems to be perfectly consistent with Locke's view and, in general, with the views of the founding fathers of this country to restrict certain rights or freedoms when it can be shown that such restriction is necessary to insure the

equal rights of others. If this is so, it has very important implications for the rights to freedom and to property. These rights, perhaps properly seen as inalienable (though this is a controversial philosophical question), are not properly seen as unlimited or unrestricted. When values which we hold dear conflict (for example, individual or group freedom and the freedom of all, individual or group rights and the rights of all, and individual or group welfare and the welfare of the general public) something has to give; some priority must be established. In the case of the abuse and waste of environmental resources, less individual freedom and fewer individual rights for the sake of greater public welfare and equality of rights seem justified. What in the past had been properly regarded as freedoms and rights (given what seemed to be unlimited natural resources and no serious pollution problems) can no longer be so construed, at least not without additional restrictions. We must recognize both the need for such restrictions and the fact that none of our rights can be realized without a livable environment. Both public welfare and equality of rights now require that natural resources not be used simply according to the whim and caprice of individuals or simply for personal profit. This is not to say that all property rights must be denied and that the state must own all productive property, as the Marxist argues. It is to insist that those rights be qualified or restricted in the light of new ecological data and in the interest of the freedom, rights, and welfare of all.

The answer then to the question, Is the right to a livable environment a human right? is yes. Each person has this right *qua* being human and because a livable environment is essential for one to fulfill his human capacities. And given the danger to our environment today and hence the danger to the very possibility of human existence, access to a livable environment must be conceived as a right which imposes upon everyone a correlative moral obligation to respect.

THE RIGHT TO A LIVABLE ENVIRONMENT AS A LEGAL RIGHT

If the right to a decent environment is to be treated as a legal right, then obviously what is required is some sort of legal framework which gives this right a legal status. Such legal frameworks have been proposed. Sen. Gaylord Nelson, originator of Earth Day, proposed a Constitutional Amendment guaranteeing every American an inalienable right to a decent environment.[4] Others want to formulate an entire "environmental bill of rights" to assist in solving our pollution problems. Such a bill of rights or a constitutional revision would provide a legal framework for the enforcement of certain policies bearing on environmental issues. It would also involve the concept of "legal responsibility" for acts which violate those rights. Such legal responsibility is beginning to be enforced in the United States.

Others propose that the right to a decent environment also be a cardinal tenet of international law. Pollution is not merely a national problem but an international one. The population of the entire world is affected by it, and a body of international law, which includes the right to a decent environment and the accompanying policies to save and preserve our environmental resources, would be an even more effective tool than such a framework at the national level. Of course, one does not have to be reminded of the problems involved in establishing international law and in eliciting obedience to it. Conflicts between nations are still settled more by force than by law or persuasion. The record of the United Nations attests to this fact. In the case of international conflict over environmental interests and the use of the environment, the possibility of international legal resolution, at least at this stage of history, is somewhat remote; for the body of enforceable international law on this topic is meager indeed. This is not to deny that this is the direction in which we should (and must) move.

A good case can be made for the view that not all moral or human rights should be legal rights and that not all moral rules should be legal rules. It may be argued that any society which covers the whole spectrum of man's activities with legally enforceable rules minimizes his freedom and approaches totalitarianism. There is this danger. But just as we argued that certain traditional rights and freedoms are properly restricted in order to insure the equal rights and welfare of all, so also it can plausibly be argued that the human right to a livable environment should become a legal one in order to assure that it is properly respected. Given the magnitude of the present dangers to the environment and to the welfare of all humans, and the ingrained habits and rules, or lack of rules, which permit continued waste, pollution, and destruction of our environmental resources, the legalized status of the right to a livable environment seems both desirable and necessary.

It is essential that government step in to prevent the potentially dire consequences of industrial pollution and the waste of environmental resources. Such government regulations need not mean the death of the free enterprise system. The right to private property can be made compatible with the right to a livable environment, for if uniform antipollution laws were applied to all industries, then both competition and private ownership could surely continue. But they would continue within a quite different set of rules and attitudes toward the environment. This extension of government would not be equivalent to totalitarianism. In fact it is necessary to insure equality of rights and freedom, which is essential to a democracy.

ECOLOGY AND ECONOMIC RIGHTS

We suggested above that it is necessary to qualify or restrict economic or property rights in the light of new ecological data and in the interest of the freedom, rights, and welfare of all. In part, this suggested restriction is predicated on the assumption that we cannot expect private business to provide solutions to the multiple pollution problems for which they themselves are responsible. Some companies have taken measures to limit the polluting effect of their operations, and this is an important move. But we are deluding ourselves if we think that private business can function as its own pollution police. This is so for several reasons: the primary objective of private business is economic profit. Stockholders do not ask of a company, ''Have you polluted the environment and lowered the quality of the environment for the general public and for future generations?'' Rather they ask, ''How high is the annual dividend and how much higher is it than the year before?'' One can hardly expect organizations whose basic norm is economic profit to be concerned in any great depth with the long-range effects of their operations upon society and future generations or concerned with the hidden cost of their operations in terms of environmental quality to society as a whole. Second, within a free enterprise system companies compete to produce what the public wants at the lowest possible cost. Such competition would preclude the spending of adequate funds to prevent environmental pollution, since this would add tremendously to the cost of the product—unless all other companies would also conform to such antipollution policies. But in a free enterprise economy such policies are not likely to be self-imposed by businessmen. Third, the basic response of the free enterprise system to our economic problems is that we must have greater economic growth or an increase in gross national product. But such growth many ecologists look upon with great alarm, for it can have devastating long-range effects upon our environment. Many of the products of uncontrolled growth are based on artificial needs and actually detract from, rather than contribute to, the quality of our lives. A stationary economy, some economists and ecologists suggest, may well be best for the quality of man's environment and of his life in the long run. Higher GNP does not automatically result in an increase in social well-being, and it should not be used as a measuring

rod for assessing economic welfare. This becomes clear when one realizes that the GNP

aggregates the dollar value of all goods and services produced—the cigarettes as well as the medical treatment of lung cancer, the petroleum from offshore wells as well as the detergents required to clean up after oil spills, the electrical energy produced and the medical and cleaning bills resulting from the air-pollution fuel used for generating the electricity. The GNP allows no deduction for negative production, such as lives lost from unsafe cars or environmental destruction perpetrated by telephone, electric and gas utilities, lumber companies, and speculative builders.[5]

To many persons, of course, this kind of talk is not only blasphemy but subversive. This is especially true when it is extended in the direction of additional controls over corporate capitalism. (Some ecologists and economists go further and challenge whether corporate capitalism can accommodate a stationary state and still retain its major features.[6]) The fact of the matter is that the ecological attitude forces one to reconsider a host of values which have been held dear in the past, and it forces one to reconsider the appropriateness of the social and economic systems which embodied and implemented those values. Given the crisis of our environment, there must be certain fundamental changes in attitudes toward nature, man's use of nature, and man himself. Such changes in attitudes undoubtedly will have far-reaching implications for the institutions of private property and private enterprise and the values embodied in these institutions. Given the crisis we can no longer look upon water and air as free commodities to be exploited at will. Nor can the private ownership of land be seen as a lease to use that land in any way which conforms merely to the personal desires of the owner. In other words, the environmental crisis is forcing us to challenge what had in the past been taken to be certain basic rights of man or at least to restrict those rights. And it is forcing us to challenge institutions which embodied those rights.

ETHICS AND TECHNOLOGY

I have been discussing the relationship of ecology to ethics and to a theory of rights. Up to this point I have not specifically discussed the relation of technology to ethics, although it is plain that technology and its development is responsible for most of our pollution problems. This topic deserves separate treatment, but I do want to briefly relate it to the thesis of this work.

It is well known that new technology sometimes complicates our ethical lives and our ethical decisions. Whether the invention is the wheel or a contraceptive pill, new technology always opens up new possibilities for human relationships and for society, for good and ill. The pill, for example, is revolutionizing sexual morality, for its use can preclude many of the bad consequences normally attendant upon premarital intercourse. *Some* of the strongest arguments against premarital sex have been shot down by this bit of technology (though certainly not all of them). The fact that the use of the pill can prevent unwanted pregnancy does not make premarital sexual intercourse morally right, nor does it make it wrong. The pill is morally neutral, but its existence does change in part the moral base of the decision to engage in premarital sex. In the same way, technology at least in principle can be neutral—neither necessarily good nor bad in its impact on other aspects of the environment. Unfortunately, much of it is bad—very bad. But technology can be meshed with an ecological attitude to the benefit of man and his environment.

I am not suggesting that the answer to technology which has bad environmental effects is necessarily more technology. We tend too readily to assume that new technological developments will always solve man's problems. But this is simply not the case. One technological innovation often seems to breed a half-dozen additional ones which themselves create more environmental problems. We certainly do not solve pollution problems, for example, by changing from power plants fueled by coal to power plants fueled by nuclear energy, if radioactive waste from the latter is worse than pollution from the former. Perhaps part of the answer to pollution problems is less technology. There is surely no real hope of returning to nature (whatever that means) or of stopping *all* technological and scientific development, as some advocate. Even if it could be done, this would be too extreme a move. The answer is not to stop technology, but to guide it toward proper ends, and to set up standards of antipollution to which all technological devices must conform. Technology has been and can be used to destroy and pollute an environment, but it can also be used to save and beautify it.

NOTES

1. This is a dogmatic assertion in this context. I am aware that some philosophers deny that rights and duties are correlative. Strictly interpreted this correlativity thesis is false, I believe. There are duties for which there are no correlative rights. But space does not permit discussion of this question here.
2. See Kai Nielsen's "Scepticism and Human Rights," *Monist,* 52, no. 4 (1968): 571–594.
3. See my "Equality and Human Rights," *Monist,* 52, no. 4 (1968): 616–639; and my "Human Rights and Human Dignity," in Laszlo and Gotesky, eds., *Human Dignity.*
4. *Newsweek,* 4 May 1970, p. 26.
5. See Melville J. Ulmer, "More Than Marxist," *New Republic,* 26 December 1970, p. 14.
6. See Murdock and Connell, "All about Ecology," *Center Magazine,* 3, no. 1 (January–February 1970): 63.

Fun and Games with the Gross National Product: The Role of Misleading Indicators in Social Policy

Kenneth E. Boulding *

The Gross National Product is one of the great inventions of the twentieth century, probably almost as significant as the automobile and not quite so significant as TV. The effect of *physical* inventions is obvious, but social inventions like the GNP change the world almost as much.

The idea of the total product of society is fairly old, certainly dating back to Adam Smith, but the product's measurement is very much a matter of the second half of the 1900s, which I suppose we can call the fortieth half-century. Before 1929 we did not really have any adequate measure of Gross National Product, although its measurement was pioneered by Simon Kuznets and others at the National Bureau of Economic Research from 1919 on. We began to get theories which used it in the '30s, and the cumulative effect has been substantial.

The danger of measures is precisely that they become ideals. You see it even in the thermostat. If we had no Fahrenheit, we would not be stabilizing our room temperature too high. There is a magic about the number 70, and we tend to stabilize the temperature at it, when for the sake of health it might be better at 64 degrees. Certainly, one should never underestimate the power of magic numbers. We are really all Pythagore-

ans. Once we get a number, we sit down and worship it.

This may seem to be a long way from the GNP. Actually, I am trying to illustrate this: when you measure something, you inevitably affect people's behavior; and as a measure of the total gross output of the economy, the GNP has had an enormous impact on behavior.

A fascinating book, *The Fiscal Revolution in America* (University of Chicago Press, 1969), has been written by Herbert Stein. Stein has done an extremely interesting study, an intellectual history explaining the great change in economic policy from the administration of Herbert Hoover to that of John F. Kennedy.

In the depths of the depression, Hoover engineered a tax increase which exacerbated the depression. That dark hour in the global economy contributed to the rise of Adolf Hitler who precipitated World War II. Had it not been for all those developments we might not have had today's Russian problem; we might not even have had Vietnam. Hoover never knew what hit him because he did not have a Council of Economic Advisers. We did not know much economics in those days. We did not know about the GNP.

Kennedy, in a much milder situation, fostered a tax cut which was an enormous success. As a result, we have had the bloated '60s, the decade without a depression. That should go down in the history books as something spectacular. It is the longest boom ever enjoyed in the United States. Economics has had something to do with it. So has the GNP.

These days, if the GNP starts to go down, an economic adviser will go to the President and say, "Oh, look, Mr. President. The GNP dropped half a point. We have to do something about this." This is the beauty of having social cybernetics, an information system that we can use to our advantage.

I suspect that without economics we might have had a Great Depression in the 1950s and '60s. The rate of return on investment in eco-

*Professor Emeritus of Economics, University of Colorado.

nomics may be at least 10,000 percent per annum, because we have not put much into it and we have gotten a lot out of it. On the other hand, this very success worries me. I have revised some folk wisdom lately; one of my edited proverbs is "Nothing fails like success," because you do not learn anything from it. The only thing we ever learn from is failure. Success only confirms our superstitions.

For some strange reason which I do not understand at all a small subculture arose in western Europe which legitimated failure. Science is the only subculture in which failure is legitimate. When astronomers Albert A. Michelson and Edward W. Morley did an experiment which proved to be a dud (in some eyes), they did not just bury it the way the State Department does. Instead, they shouted the results from the housetops, and revised the whole image of the universe. In political life—and to a certain extent in family life—when we make an Edsel, we bury it. We do not learn from our mistakes. Only in the scientific community is failure legitimated. The very success of the GNP and the success of economics should therefore constitute a solemn warning.

I am something of an ecologist at heart, mainly because I am really a preacher, and we know that all ecologists are really preachers under the skin. They are great viewers with alarm. Is there any more single-minded, simple pleasure than viewing with alarm? At times it is even better than sex.

I propose, then, to view the GNP with alarm.

The Gross National Product is supposed to be a measure of economic success, or economic welfare, or something like that. Of course, it is not. So we have to modify it.

In the first place, the Gross National Product is too gross. It includes a number of things which should be netted out. If we are going to get the net benefit of our economic activity, we have to net the national product, and the real question is how net can we make it? We get first what we call the Net National Product, which technically is the Gross National Product minus depreciation.

The GNP is like the Red Queen in *Alice Through the Looking Glass:* it runs as fast as it can to stay where it is. It includes all the depreciation of capital, so we net that out.

We really ought to net out all sorts of other things such as the military, which is also in the GNP and does not produce much. The world war industry is really a self-contained exercise in mutual masochism. The war industry of each country depends on the other's war industry, and it is a largely self-contained system. It has little to do with defense. It is extremely expensive and very dangerous, and we certainly ought to net it out of the product. That takes out about 10 percent.

Things like commuting and pollution also should be netted out. When somebody pollutes something and somebody else cleans it up, the cleanup is added to the national product and the pollution is not subtracted; that, of course, is ridiculous. In fact, I have been conducting a mild campaign to call the GNP the Gross National Cost rather than the product. It really represents what we have to produce, first to stay where we are and second to get a little farther along.

I have been arguing for years (and nobody has paid the slightest attention) that the real measure of economic welfare is not income at all. It is the state or condition of the person, or of the society. Income is just the unfortunate price that we have to pay because the state is corruptible. We have breakfast, and breakfast depreciates; so we must have lunch. The sole reason for lunch is metabolism, and metabolism is decay. Most change is truly decay. Consumption is decay—your automobile wearing out, your clothes becoming threadbare. It is burning up the gasoline. It is eating up the food. Consumption is a bad, not a good thing; production is what we must undergo because of consumption. Things will not stay as they are because of a reality which I sometimes call the Law of Moth and Rust. What causes our illusion that welfare is measured by the Gross National Product or anything else related to income (that is, any flow variable)? The more there is, the more is consumed; therefore, the more we must produce to replace what has been consumed. The bigger the capital stock, the more it will be consumed; hence, the more you have to produce to replace it and, of course, add to it if you want to increase it. In this sense the GNP has a kind of rough relationship with the stock or state, but I think it should always be regarded as a cost rather than a product.

All of economics, the whole GNP mentality, assumes that economic activity is a throughput, a linear process from the mine to the garbage dump.

The ultimate physical product of economic life is garbage. The system takes ores and fossil fuels (and in a boom the unemployed) out of the earth, chews them up in the process of production, and eventually spews them out into sewers and garbage dumps. We manage to have a state or condition in the middle of the throughput in which we are well fed and well clothed, in which we can travel, in which we have buildings in which we are protected from the atrocious climate and enabled to live in the temperate zone. Just imagine how the GNP would fall and welfare would rise if man abandoned the temperate zone and moved into the tropics. An enormous amount of the GNP is heating this building because the plain truth is that nature is very disagreeable. It is cold, damp, and miserable, and the main effort of human activity is to get away from it. As a matter of fact, we do not even like pure air. Otherwise we would not smoke. All of this indicates that a great deal of man's activity is directed toward what we might call desired pollution.

The throughput is going to come to an end. We are approaching the end of an era. People have been saying it for a long time, but nobody has ever believed them. Very often they were wrong in their forecasts, but this time I suspect they are right. We really are approaching the end of the era of expanding man.

Up to now, man has psychologically lived on a flat earth—a great plain, in fact a "darkling plain" where "ignorant armies clash by night," as Matthew Arnold says. Man has always had somewhere to go. There has always been a Kansas somewhere to beckon him as a virgin land of promise. There is no longer any Kansas. The photographs of the earth by astronauts in lunar orbit symbolize the end of this era. Clearly the earth is a beautiful little spaceship, all blue and green and white, with baroque cloud patterns on it, and its destination unknown. It is getting pretty crowded and its resources rather limited.

The problem of the present age is that of the transition from the Great Plains into the spaceship or into what Barbara Ward and I have been calling spaceship earth. We do not have any mines and we do not have any sewers in a spaceship. The water has to go through the algae to the kidneys to the algae to the kidneys, and so on, and around and around and around. If the earth is to become a spaceship, we must develop a cyclical economy within which man can maintain an agreeable state.

Under such circumstances the idea of the GNP simply falls apart. We need a completely different set of concepts for that eventuality, and we are still a long way from it technologically because we never had to worry about it. We always have had an unlimited Schmoo, Al Capp's delightful cartoon creature that everlastingly gets its kicks from being the main course for gluttonous man. We could just rip the earth apart and sock it away. We used to think Lake Erie was a great lake; now it smells like the Great Society. We used to think the oceans were pretty big, but events like the oil leakage in California have spotlighted that fallacy. Suddenly, it is becoming obvious that the Great Plains has come to an end and that we are in a very crowded spaceship. This is a fundamental change in human consciousness, and it will require an adjustment of our ethical, religious, and national systems which may be quite traumatic.

On the whole, human society has evolved in response to a fairly unlimited environment. That is not true of all societies, of course. It is not so true of the Indian village, but the societies that are mainly cyclical are almost uniformly disagreeable. Even the societies which are cyclical (where you return the night soil to the farms) are not really circular. They rely on water and solar energy coming down from somewhere and going out to somewhere. There is some sort of an input-output.

Up to now we have not even begun to solve the problem of a high-level circular economy. In fact, we have not even been interested in it. We did not have to be, because it was so far off in the future. Now it is still a fair way off. Resources for the Future says, "We're all right, Jack. We've got a hundred years." Its report points to our fossil fuels and our ores, and reassures us that they will be adequate for a century. After that, the deluge. I would not be a bit surprised if we run out of pollutable reservoirs before our mines and ores are exhausted. There are some signs of this happening in the atmosphere, in the rivers, and in the oceans.

My IBM spies tell me that a fundamental doctrine applied to computers is called the Gigo Principle, standing for "garbage in, garbage out." It is a basic law that what you put in you have to take out. This is throughput. Otherwise, we have to recycle everything, and we have not begun to consider the problems of a high-level, recycled economy. I am pretty sure there is no nonexistence theorem about it. I am certain that a recycling technology is possible which, of course, must have an input of energy. Nobody is going to repeal the second law of thermodynamics, not even the Democrats. This means that if we are to avoid the increase of material entropy, we must have an input of energy into the system. The present system has an enormous input of energy in fossil fuels which cannot last very long unless we go to nuclear fusion. In that case there is an awful lot of water around, and it would last a long time.

Fission is not any good; it is just messy. I understand that if we began using uranium to produce all our power requirements in this country,

we would run out of it in ten years. So actually nuclear energy is not a great source of energy; this planet's coal probably has more. Nuclear energy is not a great new field opened up. I suspect it could turn out to be rather dangerous nonsense.

What does this leave us with? The good old sun. At the most pessimistic, you might say we have to devise a basic economy which relies on the input of solar energy for all its energy requirements. As we know, there is a lot of solar energy.

On the other hand, what we do not know is how many people this spaceship earth will support at a high level. We do not know this even to order of magnitude. I suggest that this is one of the major research projects for the next generation, because the whole future of man depends on it. If the optimum population figure is 100 million, we are in for a rough time. It could be as low as that if we are to have a really high-level economy in which everything is recycled. Or it could be up to 10 billion. If it is up to 10 billion, we are okay, Jack—at least for the time being. A figure somewhere between 100 million and 10 billion is a pretty large area of ignorance. I have a very uneasy feeling that it may be towards the lower level, but we do not really know that.

We do not really know the limiting factor. I think we can demonstrate, for instance, that in all probability the presently underdeveloped countries are not going to develop. There is not enough of anything. There is not enough copper. There is not enough of an enormous number of elements which are essential to the developed economy. If the whole world developed to American standards overnight, we would run out of everything in less than 100 years.

Economic development is the process by which the evil day is brought closer when everything will be gone. It will result in final catastrophe unless we treat this interval in the history of man as an opportunity to make the transition to the spaceship earth.

When we get to $10,000 per capita, what does it really mean? Does it simply mean that we are exhausting the resources of the earth at a much more rapid rate? Of course, we have a process here of increased efficiency in exploitation of the earth, not exploitation of man. We go on, we become terribly rich, and suddenly it is all gone. We may have a process of this sort.

What may happen is that we are going to have to face something of this sort in the next 500 years. Unquestionably, we will have to aim for much lower levels of growth, because the cyclical process costs more than the throughput does. However, if we devote our knowledge industries to solution of the problem of the cyclical economy, maybe it will turn out all right.

The idea that we are moving into a world of absolutely secure and effortless abundance is nonsense. This is an illusion of the young who are supported by their parents. Once they have children of their own, they realize that abundance is an illusion. It is a plausible illusion, because we have had an extraordinary two centuries. We have had an extraordinary period of economic growth and of the discovery of new resources.

But this is not a process that can go on forever, and we do not know how abundant this spaceship is going to be. Nobody here now is going to live to see the spaceship, because it is certainly 100 years—perhaps 500 years—off. I am sure it will be no longer than 500 years off, and that is not a tremendously long period of historic time.

An extraordinary conference was held in December [1968] on the Ecological Consequences of International Development. It was an antidevelopment gathering of ecologists, who presented 60 developmental horror stories, among them predictions that the Aswan Dam is going to ruin Egypt, the Kariba Dam will ruin central Africa, DDT will ruin us all, insecticides will ruin the cotton crops, thallium will ruin Israel, and so on all down the line. Some of these forecasts I take with a little grain of ecological salt. The cumulative effect, however, is significant, and suggests that no engineer should be allowed into the world without an ecologist in attendance as a priest. The most dangerous thing in the world

is the completely untrammeled engineer. A friend of mine was at the Aswan Dam talking to the Russian engineer in charge. He asked him about all the awful ecological consequences: snails, erosion, evaporation, and such. The engineer replied, "Well, that is not my business. My job is just to build the dam."

We are all like that, really. I have recently discovered the real name of the devil, which is something terribly important to know. The real name of the devil is *suboptimization*, finding out the best way to do something which should not be done at all. The engineers, the military, the governments, and the corporations are all quite busy at this. Even professors try to find the best way of giving a Ph.D. degree, which to my mind should not be done at all. We are all suboptimizers.

The problem of how to prevent suboptimization is, I think, the great problem of social organization. The only people who have thought about it are the economists, and they have the wrong answer, which was perfect competition. Nobody else has any answer at all. Obviously, the deep, crucial problem of social organization is how to prevent people from doing their best when the best in the particular, in the small, is not the best in the large.

The answer to this problem lies mainly in the ecological point of view, which is perhaps the most fundamental thing we can teach anybody. I am quite sure that it has to become the basis of our educational system.

I have added a verse to a long poem I wrote at that ecological conference. There are some who may still shrug off its somber tone, but the wise man—and nation—will take heed.

With development extended to the whole of planet earth
What started with abundance may conclude in dismal dearth.
And it really will not matter then who started it or ran it
If development results in an entirely plundered planet.

Conservatives Consider the Crushing Cost of Environmental Extremism

Robert W. Lee *

There is certainly nothing wrong with environmentalism, but there is a great deal wrong with the sort of "environmentalism" to which our nation has been subjected in recent years. It is one thing to strive to be good stewards of the land, air, and water through the application of sensible, cost-effective policies based on marketplace and common-law incentives for polluters to "clean up their act." It is quite another to impose on industry and individuals the sort of draconian, often counterproductive, schemes which have become a hallmark of federal intervention in the field of environmentalism since 1970.

There is substantial doubt whether federal policies have resulted in a net improvement in the quality of the national environment, but there is no question at all that they have led to a massive increase in the size and expense of government and its control of the private sector, while seriously encroaching on the personal freedom of individual Americans. Some observers believe such results were the primary objectives from the start, with scare stories about environment being cranked up as an excuse to achieve them.

Gary Allen reported in *American Opinion* for May 1970, more than thirteen years ago: "Through the use of highly emotional rhetoric, and by playing upon fears of impending social and environmental chaos, the Left is hoping to convert sincere and legitimate concern over the quality of our environment into acceptance of government control of that environment.... The objective is federal control of the environment in which we all must live." Which might explain why, no matter what the immediate ecological grievance has been, private property and individual enterprise have always been branded the culprits while more government was offered as the solution. Every new regulation has in some way controlled and manipulated one or more aspects of our social or economic life while decreasing our individual freedom. Gary Allen was, alas, right on target.

The average American has paid for all of this government regulation as a *taxpayer* (to finance the bureaucracy itself) and as a *consumer* (since the cost of regulations imposed by the bureaucracy boosted the price of nearly every commodity). In addition, there have been such less-obvious costs as those suffered when plans to build factories and other important projects were delayed or abandoned, along with the jobs they would have created, after government red tape made such endeavors unbearably frustrating and financially unrewarding.

While it is impossible to settle an exact figure for the total financial burden which American industry has suffered from overzealous, often malicious, environmentalism during the past decade, the direct cost undoubtedly exceeds half a trillion dollars, while the indirect cost may be three or four times that amount. One study released in the late Seventies concluded that pollution controls alone had already cost our country approximately ten percent of its industrial capacity. Another study by a prominent accounting firm, evaluating the impact of regulation on forty-eight major companies during 1977, had discovered: "The complexities and volume of EPA [*Environmental Protection Agency*] regulations made it necessary for [*the 48*] companies to incur $36 million [*in expenses*]...solely to maintain internal environmental programs and to keep current with existing regulations and practices and to prepare for new regulations." Needless to say, those millions of dollars were *not* devoted to increased economic productivity, job creation, new plants and equipment.

In 1980, direct environmental controls added approximately $400 to the annual expenses of a family of four. That figure is predicted to reach $638 within five years. The Council on Environmental Quality speculates that the cost of administering the Clean Air Act will total $300 billion for the period 1979 through 1988. And, no less a "Liberal" than the late Nelson Rockefeller estimated the cost of implementing the Water Pollution Control Act at *three trillion dollars*. And each new car is saddled with close to $700 in anti-pollution paraphernalia, while homes cost two to three thousand dollars more due to direct federal, state, and local environmental regulations.

The increased cost of local utilities is also attributable in large part to regulatory excesses, as indicated by this "Dear Customer" explanation sent to those serviced by Utah Power and Light Company in the spring of 1978: "Through 1977, we spent a total of $140,000,000 for pollution control equipment. In the next five years, we'll spend $190,000,000! More in five years than in all the other years we've been in business! About 25 percent of all of the dollars in our generating plant construction program go for this purpose." The situation is typical for utilities nationwide.

And, a key factor helping to bring our steel industry to its knees has been the enormous cost of meeting pristine environmental standards. For instance, it may be relatively cost-effective to remove, say, ninety-five percent of pollutants from industrial exhaust, but it costs billions to remove each percentage point thereafter. One study commissioned by the E.P.A. itself revealed that it costs twenty-six cents per kilogram to eliminate ninety percent of the pollutants from making carbon steel, but $4.98 to remove ninety-seven percent and $32.20 to get rid of ninety-nine percent. On one occasion, the E.P.A. approved regulations prohibiting steel plants

from emitting "any visible emissions" whatsoever, despite the fact that it cost $1,200 per pound per hour to remove the first ninety-nine percent of such visible emissions, and a mind-boggling $400,000 per pound per hour to remove that last one percent.

Scores of similar statistics, from dozens of other industries, could be cited. And remember, we are considering only the cost of *environmental* regulation, which is but a fraction of the *total* regulatory burden that is estimated to exceed $135 billion annually. In many (perhaps most) cases, the cost of fighting pollution the federal way exceeds the cost of the damage supposedly inflicted by the pollution being fought.

It is important to keep some sort of perspective regarding the extent of man-made pollution. For instance, during all of his earthly existence, man has yet to equal the particulate and noxious-gas levels of the combined volcanic eruptions on Krakatoa, Indonesia (1883), Katmai, Alaska (1912), and Hekla, Iceland (1947). Indeed, nature contributes approximately sixty percent of all particulates in the atmosphere, sixty-five percent of the sulfur dioxide, seventy percent of the hydrocarbons, ninety-three percent of the carbon monoxide, ninety percent of the ozone, and ninety-nine percent of the nitrogen oxides. While environmentalists become frenzied about the ten million tons of man-made pollutants injected into the atmosphere by Americans each year, they largely ignore the 1.6 *billion* tons of methane gas emitted each year by swamps, and the 170 million tons of hydrocarbons released annually by forests and other forms of vegetation. On one occasion, officials of a major city on the West Coast became agitated about the extent to which the disposal of human waste might be "polluting" the Pacific Ocean, oblivious to the fact that similar waste from gray whales, or even schools of anchovies, far exceed any such contribution which residents of the city could conceivably make.

Although trees and other greeneries contribute some 3.5 billion tons of carbon monoxide to the atmosphere each year, compared to mankind's 270 million tons, environmentalists continually attack the automobile as a deadly polluter. Professor E.J. Mishan of the London School of Economics, for instance, once described the private automobile as a disaster for the human race which pollutes air, clogs streets, destroys natural beauty, etc., etc. Which is verbal pollution of the worst sort. As Professor Hans Sennholz has noted in rebuttal, "The automobile has meant high standards of living, great individual mobility and productivity, and access to the countryside for recreation and enjoyment. In rural America it is the only means of transportation that assures employment and income. Without it, the countryside would surely be depopulated and our cities far more congested than now."

A balanced perspective of the pollution picture could lead to reasonable, cost-effective programs to moderate man-made pollution. Unfortunately, the environmental field is today dominated by special interests and advocates of big government who willfully distort and exaggerate the problem in order to justify their efforts to undermine the Free Market economic system and increase government control over our lives.

Consider, for instance, the National Environmental Policy Act of 1969, and how it came about. On January 28, 1969, a Union Oil Company well on a lease in the Santa Barbara Channel blew out. Within ten days, it discharged 235,000 gallons of oil into the Pacific Ocean, fouled thirty miles of beach, and damaged some boats and wildlife. Environmentalist organizations and radical politicians, bolstered by the "Liberal" news media, labeled the event an ecological catastrophe. *Life* magazine reported that the Channel was "a sea gone dead." And news commentators routinely referred to the "hundreds of thousands" of birds killed by the blowout. Yet, it was subsequently established that only "an estimated 600 birds were affected by the oil." (*Energy Crisis In America;* Washing-

ton, *Congressional Quarterly,* 1973) And, when all the facts were in, there had been no increase in mortality among whales or seals and no long-lasting ill effects on other animal or vegetable life. Nature accomplished most of the cleanup (and man the rest) in short order.

Yet, in the wake of the Santa Barbara oil spill, and the wildly exaggerated reports about the damage it had supposedly inflicted on the environment, our fickle Congress approved the National Environmental Policy Act in December of that year.

The new law contained a number of loosely worded provisions which sounded humanitarian and harmless to most observers. But it gave environmental activists the legal foothold they needed to make court challenges against business activities nationwide. Indeed, this new law defined "environment" in such vague terms that the courts had virtually unlimited authority to nullify or modify at whim various laws passed by Congress, actions by Executive agencies, etc. During the previous 182 years of our history (from 1789 to 1971), the Supreme Court had heard only four cases relating to the environment, all of which had been brought by state governments. But, by the end of 1971, more than one hundred sixty cases based on the 1969 Act were pending in federal courts, nearly all of which were filed by activist lawyers representing radical environmentalist groups. As author Dan Smoot noted in his best-selling book *The Business End of Government* (Boston, Western Islands, 1973): "Within 18 months that law had been responsible for stopping the building of nuclear power plants; for preventing oil exploration on the outer-continental shelf; for sharply curtailing oil production in offshore fields already explored and tapped; for prohibiting the building of the Alaska pipeline; for preventing the leasing of oil-shale lands; and for reducing the production of coal."

The impact of the 1969 law on construction of the Alaska pipeline is especially revealing as an example of the high price we pay for environmental extremism. On September 11, 1969, Alaska auctioned off $900 million worth of oil leases to a consortium of oil companies anxious to develop an eight-hundred-mile pipeline to tap the rich oil-reserves (estimated at ten billion barrels) of the Prudhoe Bay area of Alaska's North Slope. Originally, the consortium planned to spend $1 billion and have perhaps two million barrels of oil flowing daily within three years. But the National Environmental Policy Act was used as the basis for years of legal harassment which delayed the project for more than four years, assuring (among other things) that no Alaska oil was available when the energy crunch of 1973–1974 was inflicted on the nation.

It was in the midst of that "energy crisis" (November 13, 1973) that Congress, at long last, put an end to the obstruction by approving the pipeline project and banning further lawsuits on environmental grounds. The projected cost of the pipeline had been swollen by all of this to around $4 billion. Harassed every foot of the way, the project was completed within four years and oil began to flow on June 20, 1977.

Note that, had the pipeline been completed within a forty-three month time span following its instigation in 1969, it would have been carrying oil by the spring of 1973, in plenty of time to blunt the fuel shortage. The environmentalist "victory" in delaying the pipeline not only gave the American people memorably long gas lines and the many other inconveniences associated with the shortage, but forced us to pay an additional $25 billion to $30 billion in inflated oil prices to the bandits of O.P.E.C. as well. And, when all was said and done, *none* of the horror stories predicted for Alaska's flora and fauna which had been concocted to justify the delays (such as the claim that hot oil flowing through the pipeline would melt the permafrost) came to pass. The horror claims were an outright fraud.

The momentum ignited by the Santa Barbara oil spill eventually led to the first so-called Earth Day, an event organized by the radical and anti-capitalist student activists associated with the ecology movement, as a mass protest against "destruction of the world's life-giving resources."

It was less than three months after Earth Day (July 9, 1970) that President Richard Nixon transmitted his "reorganization Plan Number 3" to Congress, announcing that he would create the Environmental Protection Agency as an umbrella agency to consolidate and administer federal anti-pollution programs. Congress concurred in the plan on October 2, 1970, and—following a sixty-day planning period—the E.P.A. formally began operating on December 2, 1970, with a Budget of $303 million and staff of 3,860. My how Topsy has grown! For Fiscal Year 1983, the agency's budget was $3.7 *billion* and its staff equivalent to 10,925 full-time employees.

According to the American Legislative Exchange Council, the E.P.A. has spawned an average of ninety regulations each year since its inception. In some instances, the heavy-handed manner in which those edicts have been administered has itself discouraged advances in pollution control. As explained by Richard L. Stroup and John A. Baden of the Center for Political Economy and Natural Resources at Montana State University:

"An industry that develops a new technique for reducing harmful discharges may be unwilling to use it because it may lead to a tightening of emission standards for the entire industry. For example, the EPA discovered that cement plants were capable of filtering out significant levels of harmful particulate emissions. As a result, the agency imposed emission levels for cement plants that were more stringent than emission levels for electric power plants. In other words, electric power plants were allowed to pollute more. Angered by the supposed inequities sanctioned by the EPA, a Portland cement plant challenged the agency's rate structure in court. In denying the challenge, the court argued that if an industry can more effectively control emissions, it should be required to do so. Because of such cases, many critics accuse the EPA of penalizing innovation, leading to continued rather than reduced pollution levels.'' (*Natural Resources: Bureaucratic Myths And Environmental Management,* San Francisco, Pacific Institute For Public Policy Research, 1983)

There is simply no way to do justice here to the havoc wrought by E.P.A.'s edicts. A few randomly selected samples must suffice.

Consider, for instance, the so-called "significant deterioration" clean-air standard which demands that the "significant deterioration" of air quality will not be allowed in an area *even when the new level of air quality remains above federal standards*. That draconian standard is nowhere to be found in the Clean Air Act of 1970. It was promulgated by a federal court, incorporated into E.P.A. guidelines, and upheld by the Supreme Court in June of 1973. The anti-growth implications of the standard are obvious, and ominous, as noted by syndicated columnist M. Stanton Evans in *Human Events* for August 28, 1976: "The impact of this ultra-purist ruling is felt mainly in rural areas that are planning any kind of economic development—industry, shopping centers, a housing complex. It is an obvious barrier to growth and economic progress, mandating that any area now consisting of sylvan glades or open fields remain that way. It is a de facto 'no growth' policy for America, a form of backdoor land control."

Another area of regulatory overkill is that of pesticides. In 1975, E.P.A. officials alleged that hundreds of thousands of farm workers were injured each year by pesticides and that hundreds had died. When pressed for specifics, the agency eventually admitted that its claims were baseless. An E.P.A. spokesman confessed: "We used these statistics in good faith, thinking they were accurate, and they turned out not to be accurate. They cannot possibly be substantiated."

The E.P.A.'s ban on D.D.T. (except in "extreme emergencies," as defined by the bureaucrats, not the actual circumstances of the case) enabled Tussock moths to defoliate nearly seven hundred thousand acres of forest land in Washington, Oregon, and northern Idaho a decade ago.

It was the only pesticide proven effective against the destructive creatures. The E.P.A.'s own Hearing Examiner had reported in early 1972 (following eighty-one days of Hearings, involving 125 witnesses, and ten thousand pages of testimony) that "DDT as offered under the registrations involved herein is not misbranded. DDT is not a carcinogenic hazard to man. The uses of DDT under the registrations involved here do not have a deleterious effect on freshwater fish, estuarine organisms, wild birds or other wildlife. …in my opinion, the evidence in this proceeding supports the conclusion that there is a present need for the essential uses of DDT."

Yet, six months later, then-E.P.A. Administrator William Ruckelshaus banned the pesticide except for emergencies, and his successor (Russell Train) refused to grant an emergency exception so it could be used in time to save those Western forests from the ravages of the Tussock moth.

Similar environmental extremism, this time at the state level, seriously exaggerated the threat posed to fruit and vegetable crops in California by the Mediterranean fruit fly during 1980 and 1981. The Medflies, which were first discovered in the state in June of 1980, were quickly eradicated in the Los Angeles area, but proved to be tenacious in the north. Plans to spray infested areas from the air with the effective pesticide malathion were brought to a halt when environmental groups, bolstered by support from then-Governor Jerry Brown, instigated a storm of protest that such aerial spraying would be "death from the sky." This despite the fact that the substance had long been used safely to spray mosquitos on the East Coast; had been found non-carcinogenic by two separate National Cancer Institute studies; and, had been found by California's own Health Service Department to be the "least toxic of the organo-phosphate pesticides" which "degrades and disappears relatively rapidly after application."

Governor Brown refused to take effective action as the Medfly infestation spread, until at last the Reagan Agriculture Department (on July 10, 1981) threatened a statewide quarantine of California produce unless aerial spraying was begun. The infestation, you see, was on the verge of moving beyond California and threatening the long-term production of more than two hundred varieties of fruits and vegetables nationwide. Governor Brown reluctantly backed down and allowed the aerial spraying to begin on July fourteenth. Within one month, the infestation was under control, and total victory over the Medfly was formally declared on September twenty-third. Nevertheless, the damage to crops from the environmentalist delay totaled approximately $100 million.

The E.P.A. should be abolished. It cannot be adequately moderated. President Reagan initially appointed Anne Burford to administer the agency under a mandate which could be summarized as: Stop the war against private industry and try to persuade companies to improve their record, reserving federal coercion for the recalcitrant few which refuse to cooperate. Mrs. Burford worked admirably to abide by that humane and reasonable guideline. For her efforts, she was brutally savaged by environmental extremists within Congress and the "Liberal" press until, at last, she felt compelled to resign.

The Burford mandate has apparently been abandoned even by President Reagan himself, who selected as her successor William Ruckelshaus, the original E.P.A. Administrator who banned D.D.T. and otherwise set the agency rolling along its destructive course. On April 6, 1983, the post-Burford E.P.A. returned to form by proposing a truly asinine national emission standard for radionuclides. As explained by Representative John T. Myers (R.-Indiana): "Both the National Commission on Radiation Protection and the International Commission on Radiological Protection have proposed and support a maximum radiation exposure limit for the public of 500 millirems per year annual dose equivalent to the whole body, gonads, or bone marrow, and 1,500 millirems per year to other organs. EPA

would reduce the 500/1,500 millirem exposure limit to 10 millirems per year to the whole body, gonads, or bone marrow and 30 millirems to other organs—a reduction of 98 percent.... The absurd stringency of this proposed standard is most apparent when one considers that the average radiation exposure to all of us in the United States from environmental sources is 100 to 200 millirems per year and that the dose from only one round-trip intercontinental flight can exceed a 10 millirem whole body limit. Implementation of these standards will result in the unnecessary expenditure of hundreds of millions of tax and industry dollars, will seriously impair vital national defense activities, and will provide no benefits to the health or safety of the American public."

So it is again business as usual at the E.P.A., and so it will likely remain until the American people recognize the extent to which this outrageous regulatory monster is ripping them off as taxpayers, consumers, and free citizens.

The Economic Common Sense of Pollution

Larry E. Ruff *

We are going to make very little real progress in solving the problem of pollution until we recognize it for what, primarily, it is: an economic problem, which must be understood in economic terms. Of course, there are *noneconomic* aspects of pollution, as there are with all economic problems, but all too often, such secondary matters dominate discussion. Engineers, for example, are

Excerpted from "The Economic Sense of Pollution" by Larry E. Ruff, *The Public Interest*, No. 19 (Spring 1970), pp. 69–85. Copyright © 1970 by National Affairs, Inc. Reprinted with permission of the publisher.

*Formerly in the Department of Economics, University of California/San Diego.

certain that pollution will vanish once they find the magic gadget or power source. Politicians keep trying to find the right kind of bureaucracy; and bureaucrats maintain an unending search for the correct set of rules and regulations. Those who are above such vulgar pursuits pin their hopes on a moral regeneration or social revolution, apparently in the belief that saints and socialists have no garbage to dispose of. But as important as technology, politics, law, and ethics are to the pollution question, all such approaches are bound to have disappointing results, for they ignore the primary fact that pollution is an economic problem.

MARGINALISM

One of the most fundamental economic ideas is that of *marginalism,* which entered economic theory when economists became aware of the differential calculus in the 19th century and used it to formulate economic problems as problems of "maximization." The standard economic problem came to be viewed as that of finding a level of operation of some activity which would maximize the net gain from that activity, where the net gain is the difference between the benefits and the costs of the activity. As the level of activity increases, both benefits and costs will increase; but because of diminishing returns, costs will increase faster than benefits. When a certain level of the activity is reached, any further expansion increases costs more than benefits. At this "optimal" level, "marginal cost"— or the cost of expanding the activity—equals "marginal benefit," or the benefit from expanding the activity. Further expansion would cost more than it is worth, and reduction in the activity would reduce benefits more than it would save costs. The net gain from the activity is said to be maximized at this point.

This principle is so simple that it is almost embarrassing to admit it is the cornerstone of economics. Yet intelligent men often ignore it in discussion of public issues. Educators, for example, often suggest that, if it is better to be literate than illiterate, there is no logical stopping point in supporting education. Or scientists have pointed out that the benefits derived from "science" obviously exceed the costs and then have proceeded to infer that their particular project should be supported. The correct comparison, of course, is between *additional* benefits created by the proposed activity and the *additional* costs incurred.

The application of marginalism to questions of pollution is simple enough conceptually. The difficult part lies in estimating the cost and benefits functions, a question to which I shall return. But several important qualitative points can be made immediately. The first is that the choice facing a rational society is *not* between clean air and dirty air, or between clear water and polluted water, but rather between various *levels* of dirt and pollution. The aim must be to find that level of pollution abatement where the costs of further abatement begin to exceed the benefits.

The second point is that the optimal combination of pollution control methods is going to be a very complex affair. Such steps as demanding a 10 per cent reduction in pollution from all sources, without considering the relative difficulties and costs of the reduction, will certainly be an inefficient approach. Where it is less costly to reduce pollution, we want a greater reduction, to a point where an additional dollar spent on control anywhere yields the same reduction in pollution levels.

MARKETS, EFFICIENCY, AND EQUITY

A second basic economic concept is the idea— or the ideal—of the self-regulating economic system. Adam Smith illustrated this ideal with the example of bread in London: the uncoordinated, selfish actions of many people—farmer, miller, shipper, baker, grocer—provide bread for the city dweller, without any central control and at the lowest possible cost. Pure self-interest, guided only by the famous "invisible hand" of competition, organizes the economy efficiently.

The logical basis of this rather startling result is that, under certain conditions, competitive prices convey all the information necessary for making the optimal decision. A builder trying to decide whether to use brick or concrete will weigh his requirements and tastes against the prices of the materials. Other users will do the same, with the result that those whose needs and preferences for brick are relatively the strongest will get brick. Further, profit-maximizing producers will weigh relative production costs, reflecting society's productive capabilities, against relative prices, reflecting society's tastes and desires, when deciding how much of each good to produce. The end result is that users get brick and cement in quantities and proportions that reflect their individual tastes and society's production opportunities. No other solution would be better from the standpoint of all the individuals concerned.

This suggests what it is that makes pollution different. The efficiency of competitive markets depends on the identity of *private* costs and *social* costs. As long as the brick-cement producer must compensate somebody for every cost imposed by his production, his profit-maximizing decisions about how much to produce, and how, will also be socially efficient decisions. Thus, if a producer dumps wastes into the air, river, or ocean; if he pays nothing for such dumping; and if the disposed wastes have no noticeable effect on anyone else, living or still unborn; then the private and social costs of disposal are identical and nil, and the producer's private decisions are socially efficient. *But if these wastes do affect others, then the social costs of waste disposal are not zero. Private and social costs diverge, and private profit-maximizing decisions are not socially efficient.* Suppose, for example, that cement production dumps large quantities of dust into the air, which damages neighbors, and that the brick-cement producer pays these neighbors nothing. In the social sense, cement will be over-produced relative to brick and other products because users of the products will make decisions based on market prices which do not reflect true social costs. They will use cement when they should use brick, or when they should not build at all.

This divergence between private and social costs is the fundamental cause of pollution of all types, and it arises in any society where decisions are at all decentralized—which is to say, in any economy of any size which hopes to function at all. Even the socialist manager of the brick-cement plant, told to maximize output given the resources at his disposal, will use the People's Air to dispose of the People's Wastes; to do otherwise would be to violate his instructions. And if instructed to avoid pollution "when possible," he does not know what to do: how can he decide whether more brick or cleaner air is more important for building socialism? The capitalist manager is in exactly the same situation. Without prices to convey the needed information, he does not know what action is in the public interest, and certainly would have no incentive to act correctly even if he did know.

ESTIMATING THE COSTS OF POLLUTION

Both in theory and practice, the most difficult part of an economic approach to pollution is the measurement of the cost and benefits of its abatement. Only a small fraction of the costs of pollution can be estimated straightforwardly. If, for example, smog reduces the life of automobile tires by 10 per cent, one component of the cost of smog is 10 per cent of tire expenditures. It has been estimated that, in a moderately polluted area of New York City, filthy air imposes extra costs for painting, washing, laundry, etc., of $200 per person per year. Such costs must be included in any calculation of the benefits of pollution abatement, and yet they are only a part of the relevant costs—and often a small part. Accordingly it rarely is possible to justify a measure like river pollution control solely on the basis of costs to individuals or firms of treating water because it usually is cheaper to process only the water that is actually used for industrial or municipal purposes, and to ignore the river itself.

The costs of pollution that cannot be measured so easily are often called "intangible" or "noneconomic," although neither term is particularly appropriate. Many of these costs are as tangible as burning eyes or a dead fish, and all such costs are relevant to a valid economic analysis. Let us therefore call these costs "nonpecuniary."

The only real difference between nonpecuniary costs and the other kind lies in the difficulty of estimating them. If pollution in Los Angeles harbor is reducing marine life, this imposes costs on society. The cost of reducing commercial fishing could be estimated directly: it would be the fixed cost of converting men and equipment from fishing to an alternative occupation, plus the difference between what they earned in fishing and what they earn in the new occupation, plus the loss to consumers who must eat chicken instead of fish. But there are other, less straightforward costs: the loss of recreation opportunities for children and sportsfishermen and of research facilities for marine biologists, etc. Such costs are obviously difficult to measure and may be very large indeed; but just as surely as they are not zero, so too are they not infinite. Those who call for immediate action and damn the cost, merely because the spiney starfish and furry crab populations are shrinking, are putting an infinite marginal value on these creatures. This strikes a disinterested observer as an overestimate.

The above comments may seem crass and insensitive to those who, like one angry letter-writer to the Los Angeles *Times,* want to ask: "If conservation is not for its own sake, then what in the world *is* it for?" Well, what *is* the purpose of pollution control? Is it for its own sake? Of course not. If we answer that it is to make the air and water clean and quiet, then the question arises: what is the purpose of clean air and water? If the answer is, to please the nature gods, then it must be conceded that all pollution must cease immediately because the cost of angering the gods is presumably infinite. But if the answer is that the purpose of clean air and water is to further human enjoyment of life on this planet, then we are faced with the economists' basic question: given the limited alternatives that a niggardly nature allows, how can we best further human enjoyment of life? And the answer is, by making intelligent marginal decisions on the basis of costs and benefits. Pollution control is for lots of things: breathing comfortably, enjoying mountains, swimming in water, for health, beauty, and the general delectation. But so are many other things, like good food and wine, comfortable housing and fast transportation. The question is not which of these desirable things we should have, but rather what combination is most desirable. To determine such a combination, we must know the rate at which individuals are willing to substitute more of one desirable thing for less of another desirable thing. Prices are one way of determining those rates.

But if we cannot directly observe market prices for many of the costs of pollution, we must find another way to proceed. One possibility is to infer the costs from other prices, just as we infer the value of an ocean view from real estate prices. In principle, one could estimate the value people put on clean air and beaches by observing how much more they are willing to pay for property in nonpolluted areas. Such information could be obtained; but there is little of it available at present.

Another possible way of estimating the costs of pollution is to ask people how much they would be willing to pay to have pollution reduced. A resident of Pasadena might be willing to pay $100 a year to have smog reduced 10 or 20 per cent. In Barstow, where the marginal cost of smog is much less, a resident might not pay $10 a year to have smog reduced 10 per cent. If we knew how much it was worth to everybody, we could add up these amounts and obtain an estimate of the cost of a marginal amount of pollution. The difficulty, of course, is that there is no way of guaranteeing truthful responses. Your response to the question, how much is pollution costing *you,* obviously will depend on what you think will be done with this information. If you think you will be compensated for these costs, you will make a generous estimate; if you think that you will be charged for the control in proportion to these costs, you will make a small estimate.

Let us assume that, somehow, we have made an estimate of the social cost function for pollution, including the marginal cost associated with various pollution levels. We now need an estimate of the benefits of pollution—or, if you prefer, of the costs of pollution abatement. So we set the Pollution Control Board (PCB) to work on this task.

The PCB has a staff of engineers and technicians, and they begin working on the obvious question: for each pollution source, how much would it cost to reduce pollution by 10 per cent, 20 per cent, and so on. If the PCB has some economists, they will know that the cost of reducing total pollution by 10 per cent is *not* the total cost of reducing each pollution source by 10 per cent. Rather, they will use the equimarginal principle and find the pattern of control such that an additional dollar spent on control of any pollution source yields the same reduction. This will minimize the cost of achieving any given level of abatement. In this way the PCB can generate a "cost of abatement" function, and the corresponding marginal cost function.

Once cost and benefit functions are known, the PCB should choose a level of abatement that maximizes net gain. This occurs where the marginal cost of further abatement just equals the marginal benefit. If, for example, we could reduce pollution damages by $2 million at a cost of $1 million, we should obviously impose that $1 million cost. But if the damage reduction is only $½ million, we should not and in fact should reduce control efforts.

This principle is obvious enough but is often overlooked. One author, for example, has written that the national cost of air pollution is $11 billion a year but that we are spending less than $50 million a year on control; he infers from this that "we could justify a tremendous strengthening of control efforts on purely economic grounds."

That *sounds* reasonable, if all you care about are sounds. But what is the logical content of the statement? Does it imply we should spend $11 billion on control just to make things even? Suppose we were spending $11 billion on control and thereby succeeded in reducing pollution costs to $50 million. Would this imply we were spending too *much* on control? Of course not. We must compare the *marginal* decrease in pollution costs to the *marginal* increase in abatement costs.

PUTTING A PRICE ON POLLUTION

Once the optimal pollution level is determined, all that is necessary is for the PCB to enforce the pattern of controls which it has determined to be optimal. But now a new problem arises: how should the controls be enforced?

There is a very simple way to accomplish this. *Put a price on pollution.* A price-based control mechanism would differ from an ordinary market transaction system only in that the PCB would set the prices, instead of their being set by demand-supply forces, and that the state would force payment. Under such a system, anyone could emit any amount of pollution so long as he pays the price which the PCB sets to approximate the marginal social cost of pollution. Under this circumstance, private decisions based on self-interest are efficient. If pollution consists of many components, each with its own social cost, there should be different prices for each component. Thus, extremely dangerous materials must have an extremely high price, perhaps stated in terms of "years in jail" rather than "dollars," although a sufficiently high dollar price is essentially the same thing. In principle, the prices should vary with geographical location, season of the year, direction of the wind, and even day of the week, although the cost of too many variations may preclude such fine distinctions.

Once the prices are set, polluters can adjust to them any way they choose. Because they act on self-interest they will reduce their pollution by every means possible up to the point where further reduction would cost more than the price. Because all face the same price for the same type of pollution, the marginal cost of abatement is the same everywhere. If there are economies of scale in pollution control, as in some types of liquid waste treatment, plants can cooperate in establishing joint treatment facilities. In fact, some enterprising individual could buy these wastes from various plants (at negative prices—i.e., they would get paid for carting them off), treat them, and then sell them at a higher price, making a profit in the process. (After all, this is what rubbish removal firms do now.) If economies of scale are so substantial that the provider of such a service becomes a monopolist, then the PCB can operate the facilities itself.

Obviously, such a scheme does not eliminate the need for the PCB. The board must measure the output of pollution from all sources, collect the fees, and so on. But it does not need to know anything about any plant except its total emission of pollution. It does not control, negotiate, threaten, or grant favors. It does not destroy incentive because development of new control methods will reduce pollution payments.

As a test of this price system of control, let us consider how well it would work when applied to automobile pollution, a problem for which direct control is usually considered the only feasible approach. If the price system can work here, it can work anywhere.

Suppose, then, that a price is put on the emissions of automobiles. Obviously, continuous metering of such emissions is impossible. But it should be easy to determine the average output of pollution for cars of different makes, models, and years, having different types of control devices and using different types of fuel. Through graduated registration fees and fuel taxes, each car owner would be assessed roughly the social cost of his car's pollution, adjusted for whatever control devices he has chosen to install and for his driving habits. If the cost of installing a device, driving a different car, or finding alternative means of transportation is less than the price

he must pay to continue his pollution, he will presumably take all the necessary steps. But each individual remains free to find the best adjustment to his particular situation. It would be remarkable if everyone decided to install the same devices which some states currently require; and yet that is the effective assumption of such requirements.

Even in the difficult case of auto pollution, the price system has a number of advantages. Why should a person living in the Mojave desert, where pollution has little social cost, take the same pains to reduce air pollution as a person living in Pasadena? Present California law, for example, makes no distinction between such areas; the price system would. And what incentive is there for auto manufacturers to design a less polluting engine? The law says only that they must install a certain device in every car. If GM develops a more efficient engine, the law will eventually be changed to require this engine on all cars, raising costs and reducing sales. But will such development take place? No collusion is needed for manufacturers to decide unanimously that it would be foolish to devote funds to such development. But with a pollution fee paid by the consumer, there is a real advantage for any firm to be first with a better engine, and even a collusive agreement wouldn't last long in the face of such an incentive. The same is true of fuel manufacturers, who now have no real incentive to look for better fuels. Perhaps most important of all, the present situation provides no real way of determining whether it is cheaper to reduce pollution by muzzling cars or industrial plants. The experts say that most smog comes from cars; but *even if true, this does not imply that it is more efficient to control autos rather than other pollution sources.* How can we decide which is more efficient without mountains of information? The answer is, by making drivers and plants pay the same price for the same pollution, and letting self-interest do the job.

In situations where pollution outputs can be measured more or less directly (unlike the automobile pollution case), the price system is clearly superior to direct control. A study of possible control methods in the Delaware estuary, for example, estimated that, compared to a direct control scheme requiring each polluter to reduce his pollution by a fixed percentage, an effluent charge which would achieve the same level of pollution abatement would be only half as costly—a saving of about $150 million. Such a price system would also provide incentive for further improvements, a simple method of handling new plants, and revenue for the control authority.

In general, the price system allocates costs in a manner which is at least superficially fair: those who produce and consume goods which cause pollution, pay the costs. But the superior efficiency in control and apparent fairness are not the only advantages of the price mechanism. Equally important is the ease with which it can be put into operation. It is not necessary to have detailed information about all the techniques of pollution reduction, or estimates of all costs and benefits. Nor is it necessary to determine whom to blame or who should pay. All that is needed is a mechanism for estimating, if only roughly at first, the pollution output of all polluters, together with a means of collecting fees. Then we can simply pick a price—any price—for each category of pollution, and we are in business. The initial price should be chosen on the basis of some estimate of its effects but need not be the optimal one. If the resulting reduction in pollution is not "enough," the price can be raised until there is sufficient reduction. A change in technology, number of plants, or whatever, can be accommodated by a change in the price, even without detailed knowledge of all the technological and economic data. Further, once the idea is explained, the price system is much more likely to be politically acceptable than some method of direct control. Paying for a service, such as garbage disposal, is a well-established tradition, and is much less objectionable than having a bureaucrat nosing around and giving arbitrary orders. When businessmen, consumers, and politicians

understand the alternatives, the price system will seem very attractive indeed.

An important part of this method of control obviously is the mechanism that sets and changes the pollution price. Ideally, the PCB could choose this price on the basis of an estimate of the benefits and costs involved, in effect imitating the impersonal workings of ordinary market forces. But because many of the costs and benefits cannot be measured, a less "objective," more political procedure is needed. This political procedure could take the form of a referendum, in which the PCB would present to the voters alternative schedules of pollution prices, together with the estimated effects of each. The strongest argument for the price system is not found in idle speculation but in the real world, and in particular, in Germany. The Rhine River in Germany is a dirty stream, recently made notorious when an insecticide spilled into the river and killed millions of fish. One tributary of the Rhine, a river called the Ruhr, is the sewer for one of the world's most concentrated industrial areas. The Ruhr River valley contains 40 per cent of German industry, including 80 per cent of coal, iron, steel and heavy chemical capacity. The Ruhr is a small river, with a low flow of less than half the flow on the Potomac near Washington. The volume of wastes is extremely large—actually exceeding the flow of the river itself in the dry season! *Yet people and fish swim in the Ruhr River*.

This amazing situation is the result of over forty years of control of the Ruhr and its tributaries by a hierarchy of regional authorities. These authorities have as their goal the maintenance of the quality of the water in the area at minimum cost, and they have explicitly applied the equimarginal principle to accomplish this. Water quality is formally defined in a technological rather than an economic way; the objective is to "not kill the fish." Laboratory tests are conducted to determine what levels of various types of pollution are lethal to fish, and from these figures an index is constructed which measures the "amount of pollution" from each source in terms of its fish-killing capacity. This index is different for each source, because of differences in amount and composition of the waste, and geographical locale. Although this physical index is not really a very precise measure of the real economic *cost* of the waste, it has the advantage of being easily measured and widely understood. Attempts are made on an *ad hoc* basis to correct the index if necessary—if, for example, a nonlethal pollutant gives fish an unpleasant taste.

Once the index of pollution is constructed, a price is put on the pollution, and each source is free to adjust its operation any way it chooses. Geographical variation in prices, together with some direct advice from the authorities, encourage new plants to locate where pollution is less damaging. For example, one tributary of the Ruhr has been converted to an open sewer; it has been lined with concrete and landscaped, but otherwise no attempt is made to reduce pollution in the river itself. A treatment plant at the mouth of the river processes all these wastes at low cost. Therefore, the price of pollution on this river is set low. This arrangement, by the way, is a rational, if perhaps unconscious, recognition of marginal principles. The loss caused by destruction of *one* tributary is rather small, if the nearby rivers are maintained, while the benefit from having this inexpensive means of waste disposal is very large. However, if *another* river were lost, the cost would be higher and the benefits lower; one open sewer may be the optimal number.

The revenues from the pollution charges are used by the authorities to measure pollution, conduct tests and research, operate dams to regulate stream flow, and operate waste treatment facilities where economies of scale make this desirable. These facilities are located at the mouths of some tributaries, and at several dams in the Ruhr. If the authorities find pollution levels are getting too high, they simply raise the price, which causes polluters to try to reduce their wastes, and provides increased revenues to use on further treatment. Local governments influence the authorities, which helps to maintain recreation values, at least in certain stretches of the river.

This classic example of water management is obviously not exactly the price system method discussed earlier. There is considerable direct control, and the pollution authorities take a very active role. Price regulation is not used as much as it could be; for example, no attempt is made to vary the price over the season, even though high flow on the Ruhr is more than ten times larger than low flow. If the price of pollution were reduced during high flow periods, plants would have an incentive to regulate their production and/or store their wastes for release during periods when the river can more easily handle them. The difficulty of continuously monitoring wastes means this is not done; as automatic, continuous measurement techniques improve and are made less expensive, the use of variable prices will increase. Though this system is not entirely regulated by the price mechanism, prices are used more here than anywhere else, and the system is much more successful than any other. So, both in theory and in practice, the price system is attractive, and ultimately must be the solution to pollution problems.

At the Shrine of Our Lady of Fátima, or Why Political Questions Are Not All Economic

Mark Sagoff *

Lewiston, New York, a well-to-do community near Buffalo, is the site of the Lake Ontario Ordinance Works, where the federal government, years ago, disposed of the residues of the Man-

Excerpted from "At the Shrine of Our Lady of Fátima or Why Political Questions are Not all Economic" by Mark Sagoff, 23 *Arizona Law Review*, No. 1283 (1981). Copyright © 1981 by the Arizona Board of Regents. Reprinted by permission.

*Research associate, Center for Philosophy and Public Policy, University of Maryland.

hattan Project. These radioactive wastes are buried but are not forgotten by the residents, who say that when the wind is southerly radon gas blows through the town. Several parents at a recent conference I attended there described their terror on learning that cases of leukemia had been found among area children. They feared for their own lives as well. At the other sides of the table, officials from New York State and from local corporations replied that these fears were ungrounded. People who smoke, they said, take greater risks than people who live close to waste disposal sites. One speaker talked in term s of "rational methodologies of decision making." This aggravated the parents' rage and frustration.

The speaker suggested that the townspeople, were to make their own decision in a free market, would choose to live near the hazardous waste facility, if they knew the scientific facts. He told me later they were irrational—he said, "neurotic"—because they refused to recognize or to act upon their own interests. The residents of Lewiston were unimpressed with his analysis of their "willingness to pay" to avoid this risk or that. They did not see what risk-benefit analysis had to do with the issues they raised.

If you take the Military Highway (as I did) from Buffalo to Lewiston, you will pass through a formidable wasteland. Landfills stretch in all directions, where enormous trucks—tiny in that landscape—incessantly deposit sludge which great bulldozers, like yellow ants, then push into the ground. These machines are the only signs of life, for in the miasma that hangs in the air, no birds, not even scavengers, are seen. Along colossal power lines which criss-cross this dismal land, the dynamos at Niagara send electric power south, where factories have fled, leaving their remains to decay. To drive along this road is to feel, oddly, the mystery and awe one experiences in the presence of so much power and decadence.

Henry Adams had a similar response to the dynamos on display at the Paris Exposition of 1900. To him "the dynamo became a symbol of infinity."[1] To Adams, the dynamo functioned as the modern equivalent of the Virgin, that is, as the center and focus of power. "Before the end, one began to pray to it; inherited instinct taught the natural expression of man before silent and infinite force."[2]

Adams asks in his essay "The Dynamo and the Virgin" how the products of modern industrial civilization will compare with those of the religious culture of the Middle Ages. If he could see the landfills and hazardous waste facilities bordering the power stations and honeymoon hotels of Niagara Falls he would know the answer. He would understand what happens when efficiency replaces infinity· as the central conception of value. The dynamos at Niagara will not produce another Mont-Saint-Michel. "All the steam in the world," Adams wrote, "could not, like the Virgin, build Chartres."[3]

At the Shrine of Our Lady of Fátima, on a plateau north of the Military Highway, a larger than life sculpture of Mary looks into the chemical air. The original of this shrine stands in central Portugal, where in May, 1917, three children said they saw a Lady, brighter than the sun, raised on a cloud in an evergreen tree.[4] Five months later, on a wet and chilly October day, the Lady again appeared, this time before a large crowd. Some who were skeptical did not see the miracle. Others in the crowd reported, however, that "the sun appeared and seemed to tremble, rotate violently and fall, dancing over the heads of the throng...."[5]

The Shrine was empty when I visited it. The cult of Our Lady of Fátima, I imagine, has only a few devotees. The cult of Pareto optimality, however, has many. Where some people see only environmental devastation, its devotees perceive efficiency, utility, and the maximization of wealth. They see the satisfaction of wants. They envision the good life. As I looked over the smudged and ruined terrain I tried to share that vision. I hoped that Our Lady of Fátima, worker of miracles, might serve, at least for the moment, as the Patroness of cost-benefit analysis. I thought of all the wants and needs that are satisfied in a landscape of honeymoon cottages, commercial strips, and dumps for hazardous waste. I saw the miracle of efficiency. The prospect, however, looked only darker in that light.

I

This essay concerns the economic decisions we make about the environment. It also concerns our political decisions about the environment. Some people have suggested that ideally these should be the same, that all environmental problems are problems in distribution. According to this view there is an environmental problem only when some resource is not allocated in equitable and efficient ways.[6]

This approach to environmental policy is pitched entirely at the level of the consumer. It is his or her values that count, and the measure of these values is the individual's willingness to pay. The problem of justice or fairness in society becomes, then, the problem of distributing goods and services so that more people get more of what they want to buy. A condo on the beach. A snowmobile for the mountains. A tank full of gas. A day of labor. The only values we have, on this view, are those which a market can price.

How much do you value open space, a stand of trees, an "unspoiled" landscape? Fifty dollars? A hundred? A thousand? This is one way to measure value. You could compare the amount consumers would pay for a townhouse or coal or a landfill and the amount they would pay to preserve an area in its "natural" state. If users would pay more for the land with the house, the coal mine, or the landfill, than without—less construction and other costs of development—then the efficient thing to do is to improve the land and thus increase its value. That is why we have so many tract developments. And pizza stands. And gas stations. And strip mines.

And landfills. How much did you spend last year to preserve open space? How much for pizza and gas? "In principle, the ultimate measure of environmental quality," as one basic text assures us, "is the value people place on these...services or their *willingness to pay*."[7]

Willingness to pay. What is wrong with that? The rub is this: not all of us think of ourselves simply as *consumers*. Many of us regard ourselves *as citizens* as well. We act as consumers to get what we want *for ourselves*. We act as citizens to achieve what we think is right or best *for the community*. The question arises, then, whether what we want for ourselves individually as consumers is consistent with the goals we would set for ourselves collectively as citizens. Would I vote for the sort of things I shop for? Are my preferences as a consumer consistent with my judgments as a citizen?

They are not. I am schizophrenic. Last year, I fixed a couple of tickets and was happy to do so since I saved fifty dollars. Yet, at election time, I helped to vote the corrupt judge out of office. I speed on the highway; yet I want the police to enforce laws against speeding. I used to buy mixers in returnable bottles—but who can bother to return them? I buy only disposables now, but, to soothe my conscience, I urge my state senator to outlaw one-way containers. I love my car; I hate the bus. Yet I vote for candidates who promise to tax gasoline to pay for public transportation. I send my dues to the Sierra Club to protect areas in Alaska I shall never visit. And I support the work of the American League to Abolish Capital Punishment although, personally, I have nothing to gain one way or the other. (When I hang, I will hang myself.) And of course I applaud the Endangered Species Act, although I have no earthly use for the Colorado squawfish or the Indiana bat. I support almost any political cause that I think will defeat my consumer interests. This is because I have contempt for—although I act upon—those interests. I have an "Ecology Now" sticker on a car that leaks oil everywhere it's parked.

The distinction between consumer and citizen preferences has long vexed the theory of public finance. Should the public economy serve the same goals as the household economy? May it serve, instead, goals emerging from our association as citizens? The question asks if we may collectively strive for and achieve only those items we individually compete for and consume. Should we aspire, instead, to public goals we may legislate as a nation?

The problem, insofar as it concerns public finance, is stated as follows by R. A. Musgrave, who reports a conversation he had with Gerhard Colm.

> He [Colm] holds that the individual voter dealing with political issues has a frame of reference quite distinct from that which underlies his allocation of income as a consumer. In the latter situation the voter acts as a private individual determined by self-interest and deals with his personal wants; in the former, he acts as a political being guided by his image of a good society. The two, Colm holds, are different things.[8]

Are these two different things? Stephen Marglin suggests that they are. He writes:

> The preferences that govern one's unilateral market actions no longer govern his actions when the form of reference is shifted from the market to the political arena. The Economic Man and the Citizen are for all intents and purposes two different individuals. It is not a question, therefore, of rejecting individual...preference maps; it is, rather, that market and political preference maps are inconsistent.[9]

Marglin observes that if this is true, social choices optimal under one set of preferences will not be optimal under another. What, then, is the meaning of "optimality"? He notices that if we take a person's true preferences to be those expressed in the market, we may, then, neglect or reject the preferences that person reveals in advocating a political cause or position.

II

On February 19, 1981, President Reagan published Executive Order 12,291 requiring all administrative agencies and departments to support every new major regulation with a cost-benefit analysis establishing that the benefits of the regulation to society outweigh its costs.[10] The Order directs the Office of Management and Budget (OMB) to review every such regulation on the basis of the adequacy of the cost-benefit analysis supporting it. This is a departure from tradition. Traditionally, regulations have been reviewed not by OMB but by the courts on the basis of their relation not to cost-benefit analysis but to authorizing legislation.

A month earlier, in January 1981, the Supreme Court heard lawyers for the American Textile Manufacturers Institute argue against a proposed Occupational Safety and Health Administration (OSHA) regulation which would have severely restricted the acceptable levels of cotton dust in textile plants.[11] The lawyers for industry argued that the benefits of the regulation would not equal the costs. The lawyers for the government contended that the law required the tough standard. OSHA, acting consistently with Executive Order 12,291, asked the Court not to decide the cotton dust case, in order to give the agency time to complete the cost-benefit analysis required by the textile industry. The Court declined to accept OSHA's request and handed down its opinion on June 17, 1981.[12]

The Supreme Court, in a 5–3 decision, found that the actions of regulatory agencies which conform to the OSHA law need not be supported by cost-benefit analysis. In addition, the Court asserted that Congress in writing a statute, rather than the agencies in applying it, has the primary responsibility for balancing benefits and costs. The Court said:

> When Congress passed the Occupational Health and Safety Act in 1970, it chose to place preeminent value on assuring employees a safe and healthful working environment, limited only by the fea-

sibility of achieving such an environment. We must measure the validity of the Secretary's actions against the requirements of that Act.[13]

The opinion upheld the finding of the Appeals Court that "Congress itself struck the balance between costs and benefits in the mandate to the agency."[14]

The Appeals Court opinion in *American Textile Manufacturers* vs. *Donovan* supports the principle that legislatures are not necessarily bound to a particular conception of regulatory policy. Agencies that apply the law, therefore, may not need to justify on cost-benefit grounds the standards they set. These standards may conflict with the goal of efficiency and still express our political will as a nation. That is, they may reflect not the personal choices of self-interested individuals, but the collective judgments we make on historical, cultural, aesthetic, moral, and ideological grounds.

The appeal of the Reagan Administration to cost-benefit analysis, however, may arise more from political than economic considerations. The intention, seen in the most favorable light, may not be to replace political or ideological goals with economic ones but to make economic goals more apparent in regulation. This is not to say that Congress should function to reveal a collective willingness-to-pay just as markets reveal an individual willingness-to-pay. It is to suggest that Congress should do more to balance economic with ideological, aesthetic, and moral goals. To think that environmental or worker safety policy can be based exclusively on aspiration for a "natural" and "safe" world is as foolish as to hold that environmental law can be reduced to cost-benefit accounting. The more we move to one extreme, as I found in Lewiston, the more likely we are to hear from the other.

III

There are some who believe, on principle, that worker safety and environmental quality ought to be protected only insofar as the benefits of protection balance the costs. On the other hand, people argue, also on principle, that neither worker safety nor environmental quality should be treated merely as a commodity, to be traded at the margin for other commodities, but should be valued for its own sake. The conflict between these two principles is logical or moral, to be resolved by argument or debate. The question whether cost-benefit analysis should play a decisive role in policymaking is not to be decided by cost-benefit analysis. A contradiction between principles—between contending visions of the good society—cannot be settled by asking how much partisans are willing to pay for their beliefs.

The role of the *legislator,* the political role, may be more important to the individual than the role of *consumer.* The person, in other words, is not to be treated as merely a bundle of preferences to be juggled in cost-benefit analyses. The individual is to be respected as an advocate of ideas which are to be judged in relation to the reasons for them. If health and environmental statutes reflect a vision of society as something other than a market by requiring protections beyond what are efficient, then this may express not legislative ineptitude but legislative responsiveness to public values. To deny this vision because it is economically inefficient is simply to replace it with another vision. It is to insist that the ideas of the citizen be sacrificed to the psychology of the consumer.

We hear on all sides that government is routinized, mechanical, entrenched, and bureaucratized; the jargon alone is enough to dissuade the most mettlesome meddler. Who can make a difference? It is plain that for many of us the idea of a national political community has an abstract and suppositional quality. We have only our private conceptions of the good, if no way exists to arrive at a public one. This is only to note the continuation, in our time, of the trend Benjamin Constant described in the essay, *De La Liberte des Anciens Comparee a Celle des Modernes.*[15] Constant observes that the modern world, as opposed to the ancient, emphasizes civil over political liberties, the rights of privacy and property over those of community and participation.

Nowhere are the rights of the moderns, particularly the rights of privacy and property, less helpful than in the area of the natural environment. Here the values we wish to protect—cultural, historical, aesthetic, and moral—are public values; they depend not so much upon what each person wants individually as upon what he or she believes we stand for collectively. We refuse to regard worker health and safety as commodities; we regulate hazards as a matter of right. Likewise, we refuse to treat environmental resources simply as public goods in the economist's sense. Instead, we prevent significant deterioration of air quality not only as a matter of individual self-interest but also as a matter of collective self-respect. How shall we balance efficiency against moral, cultural, and aesthetic values in policy for the workplace and the environment? No better way has been devised to do this than by legislative debate ending in a vote. This is not the same thing as a cost-benefit analysis terminating in a bottom line.

IV

It is the characteristic of cost-benefit analysis that it treats all value judgments other than those made on its behalf as nothing but statements of preference, attitude, or emotion, insofar as they are value judgments. The cost-benefit analyst regards as true the judgment that we should maximize efficiency The analyst believes that this view can be backed by reasons; the analyst does not regard it as a preference or want for which he or she must be willing to pay. The cost-benefit analyst, however, tends to treat all other normative views and recommendations as if they were nothing but subjective reports of mental states. The analyst supposes in all such cases that "this is right" and "this is what we ought to do" are equivalent to "I want this" and "this is what I prefer." Value judgments are beyond crit-

icism if, indeed, they are nothing but expressions of personal preference; they are incorrigible since every person is in the best position to know what he or she wants. All valuation, according to this approach, happens *in foro interno;* debate *in foro publico* has no point. On this approach, the reasons that people give for their views, unless these people are welfare economists, do not count; what counts is how much they are willing to pay to satisfy their wants. Those who are willing to pay the most, for all intents and purposes, have the right view; theirs is the more informed opinion, the better aesthetic judgment, and the deeper moral insight.

The assumption that valuation is subjective, that judgments of good and evil are nothing but expressions of desire and aversion, is not unique to economic theory.[16] There are psychotherapists—Carl Rogers is an example—who likewise deny the objectivity or cognitivity of valuation.[17] For Rogers, there is only one criterion of worth: it lies in "the subjective world of the individual. Only he knows it fully."[18] The therapist shows his or her client that a "value system is not necessarily something imposed from without, but is something experienced."[19] Therapy succeeds when the client "perceives himself in such a way that no self-experience can be discriminated as more or less worthy of positive self-regard than any other...."[20] The client then "tends to place the basis of standards within himself, recognizing that the 'goodness' or 'badness' of any experience or perceptual object is not something inherent in that object, but is a value placed in it by himself."[21]

Rogers points out that "some clients make strenuous efforts to have the therapist exercise the valuing function, so as to provide them with guides for action."[22] The therapist, however, "consistently keeps the locus of evaluation with the client."[23] As long as the therapist refuses to "exercise the valuing function" and as long as he or she practices an "unconditional positive regard"[24] for all the affective states of the client, then the therapist remains neutral among the client's values or "sensory and visceral experiences."[25] The role of the therapist is legitimate, Rogers suggests, because of this value neutrality. The therapist accepts all felt preferences as valid and imposes none on the client.

Economists likewise argue that their role as policymakers is legitimate because they are neutral among competing values in the client society. The political economist, according to James Buchanan, "is or should be ethically neutral: the indicated results are influenced by his own value scale only insofar as this reflects his membership in a larger group."[26] The economist might be most confident of the impartiality of his or her policy recommendations if he or she could derive them formally or mathematically from individual preferences. If theoretical difficulties make such a social welfare function impossible,[27] however, the next best thing, to preserve neutrality, is to let markets function to transform individual preference orderings into a collective ordering of social states. The analyst is able then to base policy on preferences that exist in society and are not necessarily his own.

Economists have used this impartial approach to offer solutions to many outstanding social problems, for example, the controversy over abortion. An economist argues that "there is an optimal number of abortions, just as there is an optimal level of pollution, or purity.... Those who oppose abortion could eliminate it entirely, if their intensity of feeling were so strong as to lead to payments that were greater at the margin than the price anyone would pay to have an abortion."[28] Likewise economists, in order to determine whether the war in Vietnam was justified, have estimated the willingness to pay of those who demonstrated against it.[29] Likewise it should be possible, following the same line of reasoning, to decide whether Creationism should be taught in the public schools, whether black and white people should be segregated, whether the death penalty should be enforced, and whether the square root of six is three. All of these questions depend upon how much people

are willing to pay for their subjective preferences or wants—or none of them do. This is the beauty of cost-benefit analysis: no matter how relevant or irrelevant, wise or stupid, informed or uninformed, responsible or silly, defensible or indefensible wants may be, the analyst is able to derive a policy from them—a policy which is legitimate because, in theory, it treats all of these preferences as equally valid and good.

V

Consider, by way of contrast, a Kantian conception of value.[30] The individual, for Kant, is a judge of values, not a mere haver of wants, and the individual judges not for himself or herself merely, but as a member of a relevant community or group. The central idea in a Kantian approach to ethics is that some values are more reasonable than others and therefore have a better claim upon the assent of members of the community as such.[31] The world of obligation, like the world of mathematics or the world of empirical fact, is intersubjective, it is public not private, so that objective standards of argument and criticism apply. Kant recognizes that values, like beliefs, are subjective states of mind, but he points out that like beliefs they have an objective content as well; therefore they are either correct or mistaken. Thus Kant discusses valuation in the context not of psychology but of cognition. He believes that a person who makes a value judgment—or a policy recommendation—claims to know what is right and not just what is *preferred*. A value judgment is like an empirical or theoretical judgment in that it claims to be *true*, not merely to be *felt*.

We have, then, two approaches to public policy before us. The first, the approach associated with normative versions of welfare economics, asserts that the only policy recommendation that can or need be defended on objective grounds is efficiency or wealth-maximization. Every policy decision after that depends only on the preponderance of feeling or preference, as expressed in willingness to pay. The Kantian approach, on the other hand, assumes that many policy recommendations other than that one may be justified or refuted on objective grounds. It would concede that the approach of welfare economics applies adequately to some questions, e.g., those which ordinary consumer markets typically settle. How many yo-yos should be produced as compared to how many frisbees? Shall pens have black ink or blue? Matters such as these are so trivial it is plain that markets should handle them. It does not follow, however, that we should adopt a market or quasi-market approach to every public question.

A market or quasi-market approach to arithmetic, for example, is plainly inadequate. No matter how much people are willing to pay, three will never be the square root of six. Similarly, segregation is a national curse and the fact that we are willing to pay for it does not make it better but only makes us worse. Similarly, the case for abortion must stand on the merits; it cannot be priced at the margin. Similarly, the war in Vietnam was a moral debacle and this can be determined without shadow-pricing the willingness to pay of those who demonstrated against it. Similarly, we do not decide to execute murderers by asking how much bleeding hearts are willing to pay to see a person pardoned and how much hard hearts are willing to pay to see him hanged. Our failures to make the right decisions in these matters are failures in arithmetic, failures in wisdom, failures in taste, failures in morality—but not market failures. There are no relevant markets to have failed. What separates these questions from those for which markets are appropriate is this. They involve matters of knowledge, wisdom, morality, and taste that admit of better or worse, right or wrong, true or false—and these concepts differ from that of economic optimality. Surely environmental questions—the protection of wilderness, habitats, water, land, and air as well as policy toward environmental safety and health—involve moral and aesthetic principles and not just economic ones. This is consis-

tent, of course, with cost-effectiveness and with a sensible recognition of economic constraints.

The neutrality of the economist, like the neutrality of Rogers' therapist, is legitimate if private preferences or subjective wants are the only values in question. A person should be left free to choose the color of his or her necktie or necklace—but we cannot justify a theory of public policy or private therapy on that basis. If the patient seeks moral advice or tries to find reasons to justify a choice, the therapist, according to Rogers' model, would remind him or her to trust his visceral and sensory experiences. The result of this is to deny the individual status as a cognitive being capable of responding intelligently to reasons; it reduces him or her to a bundle of affective states. What Rogers' therapist does to the patient the cost-benefit analyst does to society as a whole. The analyst is neutral among our "values"—having first imposed a theory of what value is. This is a theory that is impartial among values and for that reason fails to treat the persons who have them with respect or concern. It does not treat them even as persons but only as locations at which wants may be found. And thus we may conclude that the neutrality of economics is not a basis for its legitimacy. We recognize it as an indifference toward value—an indifference so deep, so studied, and so assured that at first one hesitates to call it by its right name.

VI

The residents of Lewiston at the conference I attended demanded to know the truth about the dangers that confronted them and the reasons for these dangers. They wanted to be convinced that the sacrifice asked of them was legitimate even if it served interests other than their own. One official from a large chemical company dumping wastes in the area told them, in reply, that corporations were people and that people could talk to people about their feelings, interests, and needs. This sent a shiver through the audience. Like Joseph K. in *The Trial*,[32] the residents of Lewiston asked for an explanation, justice, and truth, and they were told that their wants would be taken care of. They demanded to know the reasons for what was continually happening to them. They were given a personalized response instead.

"At the rate of progress since 1900," Henry Adams speculates in his *Education,* "every American who lived into the year 2000 would know how to control unlimited power."[33] Adams thought that the Dynamo would organize and release as much energy as the Virgin. Yet in the 1980s, the citizens of Lewiston, surrounded by dynamos, high tension lines, and nuclear wastes, are powerless. They do not know how to criticize power, resist power, or justify power—for to do so depends on making distinctions between good and evil, right and wrong, innocence and guilt, justice and injustice, truth and lies. These distinctions cannot be made out and have no significance within an emotive or psychological theory of value. To adopt this theory is to imagine society as a market in which individuals trade voluntarily and without coercion. No individual, no belief, no faith has authority over them. To have power to act as a nation, however, we must be able to act, at least at times, on a public philosophy, conviction, or faith. We cannot replace with economic analysis the moral function of public law.

NOTES

1. H. Adams, *The Education of Henry Adams* 380 (1970, 1961).
2. *Id.*
3. *Id.* at 388.
4. For an account, see J. Pelletier, *The Sun Danced At Fatima* (1951).
5. *New Catholic Encyclopedia* 856 (1967).
6. See, e.g., W. Baxter, *People or Penguins: The Case For Optimal Pollution* chap. 1 (1974). See generally A. Freeman III, R. Haveman, A. Kneese, *The Economics of Environmental Policy* (1973).
7. Freeman et al., note 6 *supra* at 23.
8. R. Musgrave, *The Theory of Public Finance* 87–88 (1959).
9. Marglin, "The Social Rate of Discount and the Optimal Rate of Investment," 77 *Q. J. of Econ.* 98 (1963).
10. See 46 *Fed. Reg.* 13193 (February 19, 1981). The Order specifies that the cost-benefit requirement shall apply "to the extent permitted by law."
11. *American Textile Mfgrs. Inst.* v. *Bingham,* 617 F.2d 636 (D.C. Cir. 1979) *cert.* granted *sub nom.* [1980]; *American Textile Mfgrs.* v. *Marshall,* 49 U.S.L.W. 3208.
12. *Textile Mfgrs.* v. *Donovan,* 101 S.Ct. 2478 (1981).
13. *Id.* U.S.L.W. (1981), 4733–34.
14. *Ibid.,* 4726–29.
15. *De la Liberte des Anciens Comparee a Celle des Modernes* (1819).
16. This is the emotive theory of value. For the classic statement, see C. Stevenson, *Ethics and Language* chaps. 1, 2 (1944). For criticism, see Blanshard, "The New Subjectivism in Ethics" 9 *Philosophy and Phenomenological Research* 504 (1949).
17. My account is based on C. Rogers, *On Becoming a Person* (1961); C. Rogers, *Client Centered Therapy* (1965); and Rogers, "A Theory of Therapy, Personality, and Interpersonal Relationships, as Developed in the Client Centered Framework" 3 *Psychology: A Study of a Science* 184 (S. Koch ed., 1959).
18. Rogers, note 17 *supra* at 210.
19. C. Rogers, *Client Centered Therapy* 150 (1965).
20. Rogers, note 17 *supra* at 208.
21. Rogers, note 19 *supra* at 139.
22. *Id.* at 150.
23. *Id.*
24. Rogers, note 17 *supra* at 208.
25. *Id.* at 523–24.
26. Buchanan, "Positive Economics, Welfare Economics, and Political Economy" 2 *J. L. and Econ.* 124, 127 (1959).
27. K. Arrow, *Social Choice and Individual Values* i–v (2d ed., 1963).
28. H. Macaulay and B. Yandle, *Environmental Use and the Market* 120–21 (1978).
29. Cicchetti, Freeman, Haveman, and Knetsch, "On the Economics of Mass Demonstrations: A Case

Study of the November 1969 March on Washington, 61 *Am. Econ. Rev.* 719 (1971).

30. I. *Kant, Foundations of the Metaphysics of Morals* (R. Wolff, ed., L. Beck trans., 1969). I follow the interpretation of Kantian ethics of W. Sellars, *Science and Metaphysics* chap. VII (1968) and

Sellars, "On Reasoning about Values" 17 *Am. Phil. Q.* 81 (1980).

31. See A. Macintyre, *After Virtue* 22 (1981).

32. F. Kafka, *The Trial* (rev. ed. trans. 1957).

33. H. Adams, note 1 *supra* at 476.

QUESTIONS FOR DISCUSSION

1. Do you think that people have a "right to a livable environment"? If not, why not? If so, how would you go about defending such a right?

2. What does "spaceship earth" mean? How does this conception of the environment differ from what Boulding calls the "frontier mentality," and why does it dictate a reassessment of our traditional conceptions of economic and social well-being?

3. What does Ruff mean by an "optimum" level of pollution? How would he go about determining this level? Would Sagoff agree? Why or why not? Is there any way of reconciling the ideas of Ruff and Sagoff?

4. What does Sagoff mean when he says that we are "citizens" as well as "consumers"? What does this distinction imply about the use of economic decision making in the political arena?

CHAPTER 13

Regulation

READINGS FOR CHAPTER THIRTEEN

Norman E. Bowie
Business Codes of Ethics: Window Dressing or Legitimate Alternative to Government Regulation?
505

Ian Maitland
The Limits of Business Self-Regulation
509

George A. Steiner
New Patterns in Government Regulation of Business
518

Steven Kelman
Regulation That Works
525

Business Codes of Ethics: Window Dressing or Legitimate Alternative to Government Regulation?

Norman E. Bowie*

The problem is to find some mechanism for ensuring that *all* corporations adhere to the minimum conditions of business ethics. Most corporations believe that it is clearly in the enlightened self-interest of the free enterprise system to ensure adherence to ethical standards through self-regulation. Unethical conditions should not be allowed to develop to the point where government regulation takes over. Government regulation of corporate ethics is viewed on a scale from distrust to horror. There are several reasons why government regulation is opposed. These include:

1. A recognition that government regulation would diminish the power and the prestige of corporate officials.
2. A fear that government officials would interfere with incentives and efficiency and hence reduce profit.
3. A judgment that government officials do not understand business and hence that its regulations would be unrealistic and hence unworkable.
4. A judgment that government officials are in no position to comment on the ethics of others.
5. A judgment that the federal government is already too powerful in a pluralistic society so that it is inappropriate to increase the power of government in this way.

From *Ethical Theory and Business,* edited by Tom L. Beauchamp and Norman E. Bowie (Englewood Cliffs, N.J.: Prentice-Hall, 1979). Reprinted by permission of the author.

*Director, Center for the Study of Values, University of Delaware.

6. A judgment that government regulation violates the legitimate freedom and moral rights of corporations.

When compared to the spectre of government regulations, codes of ethics at least deserve a second look. Codes of good business practice do serve a useful function and are not new. After all, one of the purposes of the Better Business Bureau is to protect both the consumer and the legitimate business operator from the "fly-by-night operator." The lesson we learn from the Better Business Bureau is that business ethics is not simply in the interest of the consumer, it is in the vital interest of the business community as well. Business activity depends on a high level of trust and confidence. If a firm or industry loses the confidence of the public, it will have a difficult time in selling its products. An important result follows from the argument that business codes are in the general interest of business. To be effective, codes of business ethics must be adopted industry-wide. Otherwise, it is not to the competitive advantage of the individual firm to follow them. For example, it would not make sense for Bethlehem Steel to initiate the installation of anti-pollution devices for their own plants. In the absence of similar initiatives on the part of other steel companies, Bethlehem's steel would become more expensive and hence Bethlehem would suffer at the hands of its competitors.

An industry-wide code based on rational self-interest would help rebut a frequent criticism of the codes of individual firms. Often the cynical reaction of the public to any individual code is that it is a mere exercise in public relations. An individual code by a particular firm on matters of industry-wide significance runs the danger of being nothing but window dressing if the firm is not to be at a competitive disadvantage. However an industry-wide code designed to protect legitimate businesses from the unethical acts of their competitors is not mere public relations; it is designed to preserve the trust and confidence of the public which is necessary for the survival of the industry itself. For the purpose of protecting the consumer and hence ultimately for the protection of industry itself, industry-wide codes of ethics are in theory a viable alternative to government regulation.

If industry-wide codes of ethics make sense on grounds of self-interest, why don't we have more successful examples? Two factors explain the basic situation. The first has to do with the scope of the regulations, and the second has to do with enforcement.

First, it is hard to make regulations flexible enough to meet a wide variety of situations, especially new situations, and yet simple enough to guide people's behavior in ways that will hold them accountable. Many criticize professional codes of ethics because they are too broad and amorphous. For example, consider four of the first six standards of the Public Relations Society of America.

1. A member has a general duty of fair dealing towards his clients or employees, past and present, his fellow members and the general public.
2. A member shall conduct his professional life in accord with the public welfare.
3. A member has the affirmative duty of adhering to generally accepted standards of accuracy, truth, and good taste.
4. A member shall not engage in any practice which tends to corrupt the integrity of channels of public communication.

By using such terms as "fair dealing," "public welfare," "generally accepted standards," and "corrupt the integrity" the code of standards of the PRSA could be charged with being too general and vague.

Before giving up on codes on this account, a few comments about the nature of language are in order. Except in the use of proper names, language is always general and is always in need of interpretation. Consider a municipal law: "No vehicles are allowed in the park." What counts

as a vehicle? A bicycle? A skateboard? A baby carriage? Moreover, whenever we have a definition, there are certain borderline cases. When is a person bald or middle-aged? I used to think 35 was middle-aged. Now I am not so sure. The point of these comments is to show that some of the criticisms of business codes are really not criticisms of the codes but of language itself.

One should note, however, that none of these remarks refutes the criticism that business codes of ethics are too general and amorphous. Indeed these codes must be supplemented by other forms of self-regulation. First, the codes must provide procedures for interpreting what the code means and what it requires. Just as the Constitution needs the Supreme Court, a code of business ethics needs something similar. A serious code of business ethics can have its vagueness and generality corrected in ways not dissimilar from the mechanisms used by the law to correct vagueness problems in statutes and precedents. Perhaps a professional association could serve as the necessary analogue. Business codes of ethics do not have unique problems here.

Now we come to the second basic factor underlying the lack of successful existing codes of ethics: the difficulty of adequate enforcement procedures. There is a validity to the saying that a law which is unenforceable is really not a law at all. Any code of ethics worth having is worth enforcing and enforcing effectively.

First, the codes must be taken seriously in the sense that failure to follow them will carry the same penalties that failure to meet other company objectives carries. The trouble with many corporate codes of ethics is that employees see the codes as peripheral to their main concerns. After all, what is important is the bottom line. Experience demonstrates that when the crunch comes, ethics takes a back seat.

If they were philosophers, the employees could put their point in the form of a syllogism. (1) If management is serious about a policy, management will enforce it; (2) management doesn't enforce its codes of ethics; (3) therefore management isn't really serious about its codes of ethics.

If codes of ethics are to work they must be enforced, and the first step in getting them enforced is to get them taken seriously by the management. How is that to be done? Phillip T. Drotning of Standard Oil of Indiana puts it this way:

> Several generations of corporate history have demonstrated that any significant corporate activity must be locked into the mainstream of corporate operations or it doesn't get done. Social policies will remain placebos for the tortured executive conscience until they are implemented with the same iron fisted management tools that are routinely employed in other areas of activity to measure performance, secure accountability, and distribute penalties and rewards.[1]

In a home where discipline is taken seriously a certain atmosphere pervades. I submit that in a company where ethics is taken seriously, a certain atmosphere will also pervade. Since I do not work in a business corporation, I cannot identify all the signs which indicate that the right atmosphere exists, but I can mention some possibilities discussed in the literature. These include:

1. Recognition that ethical behavior transcends the requirements of the law. The attitude that if it's not illegal it's okay is wrong. It's wrong first because at most the law prescribes minimum standards of ethical behavior. The public desires higher standards and the desire of the public is legitimate although I will not argue for this point here. Moreover, the attitude "if it's not illegal, it's okay" is wrong because it is ultimately self-defeating. By depending upon the law, one is encouraging the government regulations most business persons strongly object to. The American Institute for Certified Public Accountants recognizes this point when it describes its code of professional ethics as a voluntary assumption of self-discipline above and beyond the requirements of law.

2. A high level officer, presumably a vice-president, with suitable staff support, being empowered to interpret and enforce the code. This vice-president should have the same status as the vice-presidents for marketing, production, personnel, etc. The vice-president should also be responsible for measuring performance.

3. Utilization of the device of the corporate social audit as part of the measurement of performance. The corporate social audit has come to have a number of different meanings. What I have in mind, however, is a revision of the corporation's profit and loss statement and balance sheet. Following the ideas of David Linowes, on the credit side all voluntary expenditures not required by law aimed at improving the employees and the public would be entered. On the debit side would be known expenditures which a reasonably prudent socially aware management would make, but didn't make. Such debit entries represent lost opportunities which the company should not have lost.

I recognize that many of these suggestions are highly controversial and I do not want the discussion to shift away from our main topic. This discussion does reiterate, however, an important point made before. Codes of ethics by themselves are not sufficient devices to provide the climate for a desirable record on business ethics. Codes of ethics must be buttressed by internal mechanisms within the corporation if they are to be effective. They must be adequately interpreted and effectively enforced.

Given these criticisms, we should remind ourselves why written codes, both legal and moral, are viewed as desirable despite their inadequacies. Laws or codes of conduct provide more stable permanent guides to right or wrong than do human personalities. As you recall, God recognized that the charismatic leadership of Moses needed to be replaced by the Ten Commandments. Codes of ethics or rules of law provide guidance especially in ethically ambiguous situations. When one is tempted to commit a wrong act, laws also provide the basis for appeal in interpersonal situations. Professor Henry P. Sims, Jr., Professor of Organizational Behavior at Penn State, has done some research with graduate students confronted with decision-making opportunities. His results show that a clear company policy forbidding kickbacks lowers the tendency of the graduate students to permit kickbacks. A business code of ethics can provide an independent ground of appeal when one is urged by a friend or associate to commit an unethical act. "I'm sorry, but company policy strictly forbids it," is a gracious way of ending a conversation about a "shady" deal.

Codes of ethics have another advantage. They not only guide the behavior of average citizens or employees, they control the power of the leaders and employers. For Plato, questions of political morality were to be decided by philosopher kings. Plato had adopted this approach after observing the bad decisions of the Athenian participatory democracy. Aristotle, however, saw the danger that Plato's elitism could easily lead to tyranny. The actions of human beings needed to be held in check by law. The English and American tradition is similar. One means for controlling the king or other governing officials is through a constitution. The Bill of Rights of our own Constitution protects the individual from the tyranny of the majority. A strict company code of ethics would help provide a needed defense for an employee ordered by a superior to do something immoral. "I'm sorry but company regulations forbid that" does have some bite to it.

Finally, during the time when conflicting standards of ethics are being pushed on the business community, a code of ethics would help clarify the ethical responsibilities of business. One of the most frustrating aspects of the current debate about business ethics is that no one knows what the rules are. Most business leaders recognize that the social responsibilities of business must expand and that businessmen and women will be held to higher ethical standards than in the past. However there are some obvious limits. A blanket ethical demand that business solve all social problems is arbitrary and unrealistic. Business codes of ethics acceptable both to the business community and to the general public would help bring some order out of the chaos.

Let me conclude by providing some suggestions for writing an effective code of ethics. I am taking these suggestions directly from an article by Neil H. Offen, Senior Vice-President and Legal Counsel of the Direct Selling Association.

1. Be clear on your objectives, and make sure of your constituent's support. It is important to get the commitment from the president of each company.
2. Set up a realistic timetable for developing and implementing your code.
3. Know the costs of running a code program, and be sure you have long-term as well as short-term funding.
4. Make sure to provide for changing the code to meet new situations and challenges. It should be a living document.
5. Gear your code to the problems faced by your industry or profession.
6. Be aware of the latest developments and trends in the area of self-regulation. Pay particular attention to FTC, Justice Department, and Congressional activities.
7. Make sure legal counsel is consulted and the code is legally defensible.
8. Get expert advice on how to promote the code and how to go about educating the public.
9. Watch your rhetoric. Don't promise more than you can deliver.
10. Write it as simply as possible. Avoid jargon and gobbledygook.
11. Be totally committed to being responsive and objective.
12. Select an independent administrator of unquestionable competence and integrity.

13. Be patient, maintain your perspective, and don't lose your sense of humor.[2]

NOTES

1. Phillip T. Drotning, "Organizing the Company for Social Action," in S. Prakash Sethi, *The Unstable Ground: Corporate Social Policy in a Dynamic Society* (Los Angeles: Melville Publishing Co., 1974), p. 259.
2. Neil H. Offen, "Commentary on Code of Ethics of Direct Selling Association," in *The Ethical Basis of Economic Freedom* (Chapel Hill, N.C.: American Viewpoint, Inc., 1976), pp. 274–75.

The Limits of Business Self-Regulation

Ian Maitland*

In a liberal democracy, there are limits to the extent to which socially responsible behavior can be ordered by law. Beyond a certain point, the costs of expanding the apparatus of state control become prohibitive—in terms of abridged liberties, bureaucratic hypertrophy, and sheer inefficiency. This fact probably accounts for the lasting appeal of the concept of self-regulation— the idea that we would be better off if we could rely on the promptings of a corporate "conscience" to regulate corporate behavior instead of the heavy hand of government regulation.

To its advocates, the virtues of self-regulation —or "corporate social responsibility"—seem

Excerpted from "The Limits of Business Self-Regulation" by Ian Maitland. Copyright © 1985 by the Regents of the University of California. Reprinted/Condensed from the *California Management Review,* Vol. 27, No. 3 (Spring 1985). Reprinted by permission of The Regents.
*Carlson School of Management, Strategic Management and Organization, University of Minnesota.

self-evident. It promises simultaneously to allay business fears of further government encroachment and to restore the public's faith in business. What is more, it asks of business only that it behave in its own enlightened self-interest. While this entails a radical break with the way managers have conceived of their role in the past, it does not make any impossible or self-contradictory demands that an imaginative manager cannot adapt to. In any case, such things as the new awareness of the fragility of the physical environment, the quantum leap in the power of large corporations, and a New American Ideology, all demand no less.

The period from the mid-1950s to the mid-1970s saw a stream of proposals for the moral reconstruction of the corporation. The principal obstacle to self-regulation was diagnosed as managers' single-minded preoccupation with profit maximization. This, in turn, was attributed to intellectual shortcomings—managers' insularity, their failure to keep up with changing values, their inability to see their role in a system-wide perspective, and their attachment to an outmoded ideology which defined the public interest as the unintended outcome of the pursuit of selfish interests. Also implicated were the organizational structure and culture of the modern corporation which supposedly embodied and perpetuated this orientation to profit. The advocates of self-regulation saw their task as being the proselytizing and scolding of managers into a broader definition of their role and the drawing up of blueprints for the socially responsible corporation.

This most recent wave of enthusiasm for self-regulation has largely receded, leaving behind it few enduring achievements. By and large, the exhortations appear to have fallen on deaf ears, or at best to have had only a marginal impact on corporate conduct. The primacy of profit maximization remains unchallenged and we continue to rely—and will do so for the foreseeable future—on legal compulsion administered by the state to regulate the undesirable consequences of economic activity.

If the marriage between the corporation and self-regulation was made in heaven, why has it not been consummated? The failure of self-regulation to live up to its promise is attributable to factors that have, for the most part, been overlooked by its advocates. In their attempts to make over managers' value systems and restructure the modern corporation, they have largely neglected the very real limits on managers' discretion that result from the operation of a market economy. As a consequence of these limits, managers are largely *unable* to consider their firms' impact on society or to subordinate profit-maximization to social objectives, no matter how well-intentioned they are.

A GAME THEORETIC ANALYSIS OF SELF-REGULATION

The crux of this argument is the recognition that an individual firm's interests as a competitor in the marketplace often diverge from its interests as a part of the wider society (or, for that matter, as a part of the business community). In this latter role, the firm is likely to welcome a cleaner environment, but as a competitor in the marketplace it has an interest in minimizing its own pollution abatement costs. It may philosophically favor a free market, but it will probably lobby in favor of protection for itself. This observation is a commonplace one, but its implications are rarely fully explored.

The firm's interests as part of a broader group typically take the form of collective or public goods. Using a rational choice model of behavior, Mancur Olson has demonstrated that it is not in the interest of a group member (let us say, the firm) to contribute to the costs of providing such goods.[1] Public goods (e.g., a cleaner environment or the free market) are goods that are available to all firms irrespective of whether or not they have contributed to their upkeep or refrained from abusing them. Since their availability is not contingent on a firm having contributed, each firm has a rational incentive to free-

ride, i.e., to leave the costs of providing them to other firms. However, if each firm succumbs to this temptation, as it must if it acts in its own rational self-interest, then the public good will not be provided at all. Thus, even when they are in agreement, "rational, self-interested individuals will not act to achieve their common or group interests."[2] In a rational world, Olson concludes, "it is certain that a collective good will *not* be provided unless there is coercion or some outside inducement."[3]

The typical objectives of business self-regulation and responsible corporate behavior—such as a cleaner environment—are public goods. Olson's theory therefore provides a basis for explaining why business self-regulation appears so hard to achieve.

Russell Hardin has pointed out that the logic underlying Olson's theory of collective action is identical to that of an n-person prisoner's dilemma (PD).[4] The strategy of not contributing toward the cost of a public good dominates the strategy of paying for it, in the sense that no matter what other firms do, any particular firm will be better off if it does not contribute.

Both Olson's theory and the PD have been criticized on the grounds that their assumptions regarding human motivations (i.e., that they are invariably rational and self-interested) are unduly strict. A modified version of the PD relaxes its harsh motivational assumptions. Ford Runge (following A.K. Sen) has argued that what appears to be a prisoner's dilemma proves, on closer inspection, to be an "assurance problem" (AP).[5] According to this theory, the group member (i.e., firm) does not withhold its contribution to a public good based on a rational calculation of the costs and benefits involved (as with the PD) but rather does so because it is unable to obtain the necessary assurance that other firms will contribute their fair share. In other words, the AP substitutes the more lenient assumption that firms prefer equal or fair shares for the PD's assumption that they invariably try to maximize their individual net gain. Under the AP, we can expect firms to regulate their own behavior in some larger interest so long as they are confident that other firms are doing the same.

But in a market economy, where decision making is highly dispersed, the prediction of other firms' behavior becomes problematic. As a consequence, no individual firm can be sure that it is not placing itself at a competitive disadvantage by unwittingly interpreting its own obligations more strictly than its competitors do theirs. In these circumstances, all firms are likely to undertake less self-regulation than they would in principle be willing (indeed, eager) to accept.

In spite of their differences, both the PD and the AP involve problems of collective action. In the case of the PD, the problem is that it is always in the rational interest of each firm to put its own individual interests ahead of its collective interests. In the case of the AP, the problem is that of coordinating firms' expectations regarding fair shares.

The sub-optimal supply of business self-regulation can be explained largely in terms of the barriers to collective action by firms. There are three levels of self-regulation: the firm level (corporate social responsibility); the industry level (industry self-regulation); and the level of the economy (business-wide self-regulation). It is only at the third level that the necessary collective action is likely to be of a socially benign variety.

THREE LEVELS OF SELF-REGULATION

Corporate Social Responsibility

Contemporary advocates of corporate social responsibility acknowledge the difficulties of implementing it, but they go on to proclaim its inevitability anyway. In their view, it has to work because nothing else will; at best, the law elicits grudging and literal compliance with certain minimal standards when what is needed is corporations' spontaneous and whole-hearted identification with the *goals* of the law.[6] As

Christopher Stone says, there are clear advantages to "encouraging people to act in socially responsible ways because they believe it the 'right thing' to do, rather than because (and thus, perhaps, only to the extent that) they are ordered to do so."[7]

Advocates of social responsibility have offered a number of prescriptions for curing firms' fixation on profit maximization. The weakness of these proposals lies in their assumption that social responsibility can be produced by manipulating the corporation. They overlook the extent to which the firm's behavior is a function of market imperatives rather than of managers' values or corporate structure.

The irony is that corporate "irresponsibility" is largely a product of our own making. The principal means we (the people) rely on to regulate corporate conduct in the public interest—namely the competitive market—undercuts the ability of firms to regulate themselves in cases of market failure. In effect, we have sought to make the logic of the prisoner's dilemma work for us (much as the D.A. does in the paradigmatic case of the PD).[8] We have isolated firms from one another so that they cannot coordinate their behavior to our detriment. While we have been successful at creating truly competitive markets, we have in the process limited firms' capacity to take into consideration anything but profits.

This point is illustrated by cases where competitive pressures have prevented firms from acting responsibly even where it would be in their economic interest to do so. Robert Leone has described how aerosol spray manufacturers were reluctant to abandon the use of fluorocarbon propellants (which were suspected of depleting the ozone layer in the stratosphere) even though the alternative technology was cheaper. The problem was that "any individual company that voluntarily abandoned the use of such propellants ran the risk of a sizable loss of market share as long as competitors still offered aerosol versions of their products [which the public valued for their convenience]."[9] In situations of this kind it is not unusual for responsible firms, aware of their own helplessness, to solicit regulation in order to prevent themselves being taken advantage of by competitors who do not share their scruples about despoiling the environment or injuring the industry's reputation. Thus aerosol manufacturers did not oppose the ban on fluorocarbons in spite of the tenuous scientific evidence of their dangers. Similarly, following the Tylenol poisonings, the pharmaceutical industry sought and obtained from the FDA a uniform national rule on tamper-resistant packaging, because no individual firm had wanted to unilaterally incur the expense of such packaging.[10] The list of examples is endless.

In a market economy, firms are usually *unable* to act in their own collective interests because "responsible" conduct risks placing the firms that practice it at a competitive disadvantage unless other firms follow suit. Where there is no well-defined standard that enjoys general acceptance, it will take some sort of tacit or overt coordination by firms to supply one. Even if that coordination survives the attentions of the Antitrust Division and the FTC, compliance will still be problematic because of the free-rider problem. Arrow has pointed out that a "code [of behavior] may be of value to...all firms if all firms maintain it, and yet it will be to the advantage of any one firm to cheat—in fact the more so, the more other firms are sticking to it."[11] We are therefore faced with the paradox that the voluntary compliance of the majority of firms may depend on the coercive imposition of the code of behavior on the minority of free riders. Thus, although it is fashionable to view voluntarism and coercion as opposites—and to prefer the former for being more humane and, ultimately, effective—they are more properly seen as interdependent.[12]

Industry Self-Regulation

If responsible corporate conduct must ultimately be backed by coercion, there remains the question of who is to administer the coercion. Is self-regulation by a trade association or other industry body a practical alternative to government regulation? The classic solution to the public goods dilemma is "mutual coercion, mutually agreed upon."[13] The possibility of "permitting businesses to coerce themselves" has been raised by Thomas Schelling who adds that such an approach "could appeal to firms which are prepared to incur costs but only on condition that their competitors do also."[14]

The record of industry self-regulation in the United States suggests that it does indeed commonly arise in response to the public goods problem. David A. Garvin explains the development of self-regulation in the advertising industry in this way.[15] Michael Porter has noted that self-regulation may be of particular importance to an emerging industry which is trying to secure consumer acceptance of its products. At this stage of its life cycle, an industry's reputation could be irretrievably injured by the actions of a single producer.[16] Thus the intense self-regulation in the microwave industry is understandable in terms of the industry's need to "overcome the inherent suspicion with which many people view 'new' technology like microwave ovens."[17] Nevertheless, industry self-regulation remains the exception in the United States. This is so because it is a two-edged sword: the powers to prevent trade abuses are the same powers that would be needed to restrain trade.

Because of the potential anti-competitive implications of industry self-regulation, its scope has been strictly limited. Anti-trust laws have significantly circumscribed the powers of trade associations. Legal decisions have proscribed industry-wide attempts to eliminate inferior products or impose ethical codes of conduct. Major oil firms were frustrated by the anti-trust statutes when they tried to establish an information system to rate the quality of oil tankers in an attempt to reduce the incidence of oil spills from substandard vessels.[18] Airlines have had to petition the civil Aeronautics Board for antitrust immunity so that they could discuss ways of co-ordinating their schedules in order to reduce peak-hour overcrowding at major airports.[19]

In short, industry or trade associations appear to hold out little promise of being transformed into vehicles for industry self-regulation. The fear is too entrenched that industry self-regulation, however plausible its initial rationale, will eventually degenerate into industry protectionism.

Business Self-Regulation

If self-regulation at the level of the individual firm is of limited usefulness because of the free-rider problem, and if industry self-regulation is ruled out by anti-trust considerations, we are left with self-regulation on a business-wide basis, presumably administered by a confederation or peak organization. An "encompassing" business organization of this sort would be less vulnerable to the anti-trust objections that can be levelled at industry associations. This is so because the diversity of its membership would inhibit such an organization from aligning itself with the sectional interests of particular firms or industries. Because it would embrace, for example, both producers and consumers of steel, it would be unable to support policies specifically favoring the steel industry (such as a cartel or tariffs) without antagonizing other parts of its membership that would be injured by such policies. A business peak organization would thus be constrained to adopt a pro-competitive posture.[20]

How might a peak organization contribute to resolving the assurance problem and the prisoner's dilemma? In the case of the AP, we saw that the principal impediment to cooperation is the difficulty of predicting others' behavior—without which coordination is impossible. By defining a code of responsible corporate conduct—and/or making authoritative rulings in particular cases—a peak organization might substantially remove this difficulty. In particular, if it is equipped to *monitor* compliance with the code, it could provide cooperating firms with the necessary assurance that they were not shouldering an unfair burden.

The point here is not that a peak organization would necessarily be more competent to make ethical judgments or that its code would be ethically superior; it is that the code would be a *common* one that would enable firms to coordinate their behavior. As we have seen, where there is a multiplicity of standards, there is effectively no standard at all, because no firm can be confident that its competitors are playing by the same rules.

A common external code would also help defuse two contentious issues in top management's relations with the firm's stockholders. First, managers would be at least partly relieved of the task of making subjective (and often thankless) judgments about the firm's obligations to various stakeholders—a task for which they are generally not equipped by training, by aptitude, or by inclination. Second, such a code would permit them to heed society's demands that the firm behave responsibly while at the same time protecting them from the charge that their generosity at the stockholders' expense was jeopardizing the firm's competitive position.[21]

So far we have assumed that each firm *wants* to cooperate (i.e., to contribute to the realization of the public good, in this case by acting responsibly) provided other firms do the same. As long as there is some means of coordinating their behavior, then firms can be counted on to cooperate. What happens if we allow for the likelihood that, while most firms may be disposed to comply with the code, some number of opportunistic firms will choose to defect?

A code of conduct—even if only morally binding—can be expected to exert a powerful constraining influence on the behavior of would-be defectors. Such a code would embody "good practice" and so would serve as a standard against which corporate behavior could be judged in individual cases. Consequently, firms which violated the code would be isolated and the spotlight of public indignation would be turned on them. In the cases where moral suasion failed, the code would still offer certain advantages (at least from business's standpoint). First, an adverse ruling by the peak organization would serve to distance the business community as a whole from the actions of a deviant firm and so would counter the impression that business was winking at corporate abuses.[22] Second, the standards defined by the peak organization might become the basis for subsequent legislation or regulatory rule-making. By setting the agenda in this fashion, the peak organization might forestall more extreme or onerous proposals.

However, the defection of even a handful of firms (if it involved repeated or gross violation of the code) would undermine the social contract on which the consent of the majority was based. Their continued compliance would likely be conditional on the code being effectively policed. Therefore, it seems inconceivable that business self-regulation could be based on moral suasion alone.

Thus, if we modify the AP to reflect the real-world probability that some number of opportunistic firms will disregard the code, the case for investing the peak organization with some powers of compulsion becomes unanswerable. The case is stronger still if we accept the axiom of the PD that firms will invariably defect when it is in their narrow self-interest to do so. Some form of sovereign to enforce the terms of the social contract then becomes indispensable.

THE CONSEQUENCES OF PEAK ORGANIZATION

Peak (or "encompassing") organizations are not merely larger special interest organizations. By virtue of the breadth and heterogeneity of their membership, they are transformed into a qualitatively different phenomenon. Indeed, peak organizations are likely to exert pressure on the behavior of their members in the direction of the public interest.

In the interests of its own stability, any organization must resist efforts by parts of its membership to obtain private benefits at the expense of other parts. It follows that the more inclusive or encompassing the organization, the larger the fraction of society it represents, and so the higher the probability that it will oppose self-serving behavior (by sections of its membership) that inflicts external costs on the rest of society.

The officers of business peak organizations in Germany, Japan, and Sweden have a quasi-public conception of their role that is far removed from the American interest group model. According to Andrew Shonfield, Germany's two business *Spitzenverbände* "have typically seen themselves as performing an important public role, as guardians of the long-term interests of the nation's industries."[23] The same finding is reported by an American scholar who evidently has difficulty in taking at face value the claims made by leaders of the BDI (Confederation of German Industry): "To avoid giving an impression that it is an interest group with base, selfish and narrow aims, the BDI constantly identifies its own goals with those of the entire nation."[24] Finally, David Bresnick recently studied the role of the national confederation of employers and trade unions of six countries in the formation and implementation of youth employment policies. In Germany, these policies were largely made and administered by the confederations themselves. In Bresnick's words, "The system in Germany has evolved with minimal government regulation and maximum protection of the interests of the young, while promoting the interests of the corporations, trade unions and the society in general. It has reduced the government role to one of occasional intervenor. It has taken the government out of the business of tax collector and achieved a degree of social compliance that is extraordinary."[25]

A similar account is given by Ezra Vogel of the role of the Japanese business peak organization, *Keidanren*.[26] Keidanren concentrates on issues of interest to the business community as a whole and "cannot be partial to any single group or any industrial sector.'' Vogel reports that Japanese business leaders are surprised at ''the extent to which American businessmen thought only of their own company and were unprepared to consider business problems from a broader perspective.'' In Japan, this ''higher level of aggregation of interests within the business community tends to ensure that the highest level politicians also think in comparably broad terms.''[27]

Perhaps the fullest account of the role played by a peak organization in the regulatory process is to be found in Steven Kelman's comparative case-study of occupational safety and health rule making in Sweden and the United States.[28] Remarkably, Kelman found that the content of the regulations in the two countries was rather similar and in both cases tended to favor more protective alternatives over less protective ones. But the resemblances ended there. According to Kelman:

- The regulations were fought persistently in the U.S. but accepted meekly in Sweden.
- OSHA was bound by a detailed set of procedural requirements while ASV (its Swedish counterpart) was bound by virtually none.
- OSHA adopted a far more punitive approach to compliance than ASV did.
- Lawyers and courts were pervasively involved in both rule making and compliance in the United States and virtually uninvolved in Sweden.[29]

In short, American business got a set of regulations no less strict than the Swedish ones, but only after a rancorous and costly rule-making process. What is more, the American regulations were then administered in a more coercive, inflexible, and adversarial manner. In his introduction to Kelman's study, James Q. Wilson notes the irony of the finding that social democratic Sweden showed ''a willingness to accommodate business views, an inclination to make policy behind closed doors, and a readiness to accept business assurances of compliance that, if they oc-

curred in this country, would bring forth immediate charges of collusive behavior and irresistible demands for congressional investigations.''[30]

PROSPECTS

What are the prospects of system of business self-regulation administered by a peak organization taking root in the U.S.? What incentives would an American peak organization be able to rely on to secure firms' compliance with its standards and rulings? We have seen that, by itself, recognition of the mutuality of gains to be had from a peak organization cannot guarantee such compliance. In order to overcome the free-rider problem, the would-be peak organization must be able to offer firms private benefits or ''selective incentives'' that are unavailable outside the organization but that are sufficiently attractive to induce firms to comply.[31]

Students of organizations have identified an array of incentives—both positive and negative—that have been used to attract and hold members. These include: selective access to information (e.g., about government actions, technical developments, and commercial practices) under the organization's control; regulation of jurisdictional disputes between members; predatory price-cutting; boycotts; withdrawal of credit; public disparagement; fines; social status; and conviviality. But, in the absence of major external threats, organizations relying on such incentives have typically recruited only a fraction of their potential members.[32]

Associations have been much more successful when they have enlisted the government to underwrite their agreements for them. And, in fact, in Western Europe, it appears that ''many of the peak associations...reached their hegemonic status with major contributions from the more or less official recognition of key government agencies.''[33]

What form would such public support have to take in the U.S.? It might involve waiving antitrust laws in the case of the peak organization, e.g., by permitting it to punish free-riding behavior by imposing fines or administering boycotts. Government might grant it certain prerogatives—e.g., privileged access to key policy deliberations or agency rule-making, which it might in turn use to obtain leverage over recalcitrant firms. The government might require—as in Japan[34]—that every firm be a registered member of the peak organization. All these actions would serve to strengthen the peak organization vis-à-vis its members.

However, the chances are slight that actions of this kind could be taken in the U.S. In the first place, as Salisbury says, "American political culture is so rooted in individualist assumptions that [interest] groups have no integral place."[35] In contrast with Europe, associations have not been officially incorporated into the process of policy formation; bureaucrats in the U.S. deal directly with constituent units (individual firms, hospitals, universities, etc.) not with associations.[36] Given the dubious legitimacy of interest organizations in general, it seems improbable that semi-official status or privileged access would be granted to a peak organization.

A second obstacle is the structure of American government. The fragmentation of power in the American system—federalism, separation of powers, legislators nominated and elected from single-member districts—has created multiple points of access for interests that want to influence the policy process. Wilson has persuasively argued that a country's interest group structure is largely a reflection of its political structure. Thus a centralized, executive-led government is likely to generate strong national interest associations and, conversely, "the greater decentralization and dispersion of political authority in the United States helps explain the greater variety of politically active American voluntary associations."[37] In the American context, then, it is virtually inconceivable that a peak organization could secure a monopolistic or privileged role in public policymaking in even a few

key areas; but without superior access of this sort it is deprived of one of the few resources available to influence its members' behavior.

CONCLUSION

This article has examined the ways it might be possible for firms to coordinate their behavior (both in their own larger interests and the public interest) while at the same time minimizing the risk that this coordination would be exploited for anti-social purposes. Such a benign outcome could be obtained by permitting collective action to be administered by a business-wide peak organization. At this level of coordination, a competitive market economy could coexist with effective self-regulation. However, the United States—given its distinctive political institutions—is not likely to provide a congenial soil for such an organization to take root.

NOTES

1. Mancur Olson, *The Logic of Collective Action,* (Cambridge, MA: Harvard University Press, 1965).
2. Ibid., p. 2.
3. Ibid., p. 44.
4. Russell Hardin, "Collective Action as an Agreeable n-Prisoner's Dilemma," *Behavioral Science,* vol. 16 (1971), pp. 472–79.
5. C. Ford Runge, "Institutions and the Free Rider: The Assurance Problem in Collective Action," *Journal of Politics,* vol. 46 (1984), pp. 154–81.
6. Cf. Henry Mintzberg, "The Case for Corporate Social Responsibility," *Journal of Business Strategy,* vol. 14 (1983), pp. 3–15.
7. Christopher Stone, *Where the Law Ends,* (New York, NY: Harper Torchbooks, 1975), p. 112.
8. In the prisoner's dilemma, two prisoners are interrogated separately about an armed robbery they are charged with committing. Given the strength of the case against them, each can expect to get one year in jail for fire-arms possession, but only so long as neither confesses. The D.A. offers each of them a deal: if either turns state's evidence against the other, all charges against him will be

dropped, but his partner will be convicted and will face a ten-year sentence. However, if *both* confess, both will be convicted and will receive reduced sentences of six years each. Plainly, what is in the narrow self-interest of each prisoner (each is better off confessing no matter what his partner does) is in conflict with what is in their collective interest (between them they serve a total of only two years if neither squeals). See Russell Hardin, op. cit., p. 2.

9. Robert A. Leone, "Competition and the Regulatory Boom," in Dorothy Tella, ed., *Government Regulation of Business: Its Growth, Impact, and Future,* (Washington, D.C.: Chamber of Commerce of the United States, 1979), p. 34.

10. Susan Bartlett Foote, "Corporate Responsibility in a Changing Legal Environment," *California Management Review,* vol. 26 (1984), pp. 217–28.

11. Kenneth J. Arrow, "Social Responsibility and Economic Efficiency," *Public Policy,* vol. 21 (1973), p. 315.

12. See Thomas Schelling on "the false dichotomy of voluntarism and coercion," in "Command and Control," in James W. McKie, ed., *Social Responsibility and the Business Predicament,* (Washington, D.C.: Brookings, 1974), p. 103.

13. The phrase is from Garrett Hardin's "The Tragedy of the Commons," *Science,* vol. 162 (1968), p. 1247.

14. Schelling, op. cit., p. 103.

15. David Garvin, "Can Industry Self-Regulation Work?" *California Management Review,* vol. 25 (1983), p. 42.

16. Michael Porter, *Competitive Strategy,* (New York, NY: Free Press, 1980), p. 230.

17. Thomas P. Grumbly, "Self-Regulation: Private Vice and Public Virtue Revisited," in Eugene Bardach and Robert Kagan, eds., *Social Regulation: Strategies for Reform* (San Francisco, CA: Institute for Contemporary Studies, 1982), p. 97.

18. Garvin, op. cit., p. 155, 156.

19. Christopher Conte, "Transport Agency's Dole Vows to Restrict Traffic at 6 Busy Airports if Carriers Don't," *Wall Street Journal,* August 16, 1984, p. 10.

20. Mancur Olson, *The Rise and Decline of Nations,* (New Haven, CT: Yale University Press, 1982), pp. 47–48.

21. These objections lie at the heart of the complaint that the doctrine of corporate social responsibility provides no operational guidelines to assist managers in making responsible choices. The most sophisticated (but, I think, ultimately unsuccessful) attempt to supply an objective, external standard (located in what they call the public policy process) is Lee Preston and James Post, *Private Management and Public Policy,* Englewood Cliffs, NJ: Prentice-Hall, 1975).

22. See on this point the remarks of Walter A. Haas, Jr., of Levi Strauss quoted in Leonard Silk and David Vogel, *Ethics and Profits* (New York, NY: Simon & Schuster, 1976), pp. 25–27.

23. Andrew Shonfield, *Modern Capitalism,* (New York and London: Oxford University Press, 1965), p. 245.

24. Gerard Baunthal, *The Federation of German Industries in Politics,* (Ithaca, NY: Cornell University Press, 1965), pp. 56–57.

25. David Bresnick, "The Youth Employment Policy Dance: Interest Groups in the Formulation and Implementation of Public Policy," paper presented at the American Political Science Association meetings in Denver, September 2–5, 1982, p. 33.

26. Ezra Vogel, *Japan as Number 1,* (New York, NY: Harper Colophon, 1979), chapter 5.

27. Ibid.

28. Steven Kelman, *Regulating America, Regulating Sweden: A Comparative Study of Occupational Safety and Health Policy,* (Cambridge, MA: MIT Press, 1981).

29. Ibid., p. 6.

30. Ibid., p. x.

31. This is, of course, the essence of the argument in Olson's *Logic,* op. cit. This section draws heavily on James Q. Wilson, *Political Organizations,* (New York: Basic Books, 1973); Robert H. Salisbury, "Why No Corporatism in America?," in Philippe Schmitter and Gerhard Lehmbruch, *Trends Toward Corporatist Intermediation,* (Beverly Hills: Sage, 1979); and Philippe Schmitter and Donald Brand, "Organizing Capitalists in the United States: The Advantages and Disadvantages of Exceptionalism," presented at a workshop at the International Institute of Management, Berlin, November 14–16, 1979.

32. Wilson, op. cit., pp. 146–47, 34, 153–56 and passim.

33. Salisbury, op. cit., p. 215. See also Wilson, op. cit., p. 82.
34. Vogel, *Japan as Number 1,* op. cit., p. 112.
35. Salisbury, op. cit., p. 222.
36. Schmitter and Brand, op. cit., p. 71.
37. Wilson, op. cit., p. 83; see generally chapter 5.

New Patterns in Government Regulation of Business

George A. Steiner*

A new wave of government regulation of business began in 1962. The purpose of this article is primarily to illustrate the dimensions of this new wave and their significance to individual businesses and the evolution of the business institution. These dimensions are not presented in any particular order of importance. They are not mutually exclusive. All are interrelated.

Not only has the volume of regulation grown dramatically during the past sixteen years but also, when aggregated with past governmental regulations, the result is an extraordinary total body of federal regulations affecting business.[1] So huge is this body of regulation that one executive lamented, and probably correctly: "The volume of laws and regulations is such that no one can comply faithfully with all rules. No large organization can effectively police all its employees."[2]

It is not easy to portray the sheer volume of regulations to which business is subject. One dimension, of course, is federal expenditure for regulatory activities, most of which goes to pay

Excerpted from "New Patterns in Government Regulation of Business," published in *MSU Business Topics,* Autumn 1978. Reprinted by permission of publisher.
*Kunin Professor of Business and Society, and Professor of Management Emeritus, University of California/Los Angeles.

employees to regulate business. From 1974 to 1978, federal expenditures (for consumer safety and health; job safety and other working conditions; energy; financial reporting and other financial controls; and industry-specific regulation) increased 85 percent, from $2.030 billion to $3.764 billion.[3]

In 1975 there appeared in the *Federal Register* 177 proposed rules and 2,865 proposed amendments to existing rules. During the same period, the *Federal Register* printed 309 final rules and 7,305 final rule amendments. In 1975, therefore, federal agencies had under consideration more than 10,000 regulations. This was an increase of 14 percent over 1974. The number of pages in the *Federal Register* rose from more than 20,000 in 1970 to more than 60,000 in 1975, an increase of more than 200 percent.[4]

As late as the mid-1950s, the federal government assumed major regulatory responsibility in only four areas: antitrust, financial institutions, transportation, and communications. In 1976, 83 federal agencies were involved in regulating private business activity. Of these, 34 had been created after 1960.[5] Included in the former group are agencies such as the Interstate Commerce Commission, Civil Aeronautics Board, Federal Trade Commission, Federal Communications Commission, Federal Reserve Board, and Securities and Exchange Commission. In the latter group are the newer agencies, such as the Environmental Protection Agency, Equal Employment Opportunity Commission, Consumer Product Safety Commission, and Occupational Safety and Health Administration.

THE GROWING COSTS OF REGULATION

Federal expenditures for regulatory employees, noted above, are merely the tip of the iceberg of the total cost of these regulations. There is, of course, no reliable single measure of cost; a number of types of cost must be considered.

In 1975 the Ford administration made an official estimate that the annual cost to consumers of unnecessary and wasteful regulatory policies was $2,000 per family. The total cost, therefore, was estimated to be $130 billion. The Center for the Study of American Business, Washington University, St. Louis, Missouri, calculated that in fiscal 1979 the aggregate cost of government regulation would be $102.7 billion. By comparison, the total costs in fiscal 1977 were $79.1 billion.[6] While these numbers cannot, of course, be exact, they do reveal the magnitude of the cost.

There are many cost estimates of particular types of regulations. For example, the Federal Council on Environmental Quality has calculated that pollution control for the 1970s will cost more than $287 billion.[7] A more recent estimate of the ten-year cost of pollution control for the 1974–1983 decade is $217.7 billion.[8]

Murray Weidenbaum has calculated that federally mandated safety and environmental features increase the price of the average passenger car by $666.[9] General Motors has reported that in 1977 it spent $1.258 billion on research, development, and administrative expenses in response to government regulations. This figure did not include installation of federally mandated parts, such as emission-control systems and safety devices. Beyond these costs, GM states that the fuel economy standards coming into effect between now and the early 1980s could add another $800 or more to the average retail price of cars.[10]

Also to be considered are expenses incurred to comply with data requirements. The Office of Management and Budget, in its first report to the Congress on President Carter's effort to cut paperwork, calculated that Americans now spend 785 million hours a year filling out about 4,000 federal forms at a cost of $100 billion.[11] This is not all, of course, carried on by business. To illustrate the impact on one company, which probably is reasonably typical, Standard Oil of Indiana says it files 1,000 forms annually with 35 federal agencies. To do this work the company employs 100 persons at a cost of about $3 mil-

lion a year.[12] Even small companies must bear heavy reporting burdens.[13]

Foundries have closed down because they could not meet costs imposed by the Environmental Protection Agency, OSHA, and other government agency regulations. The cost of meeting pollution standards has weakened the competitive position of heavy industries in foreign markets. Costs added to products to meet government regulations have been inflationary. According to Paul MacAvoy, the reallocation of investment from productivity increasing projects to projects meeting government regulations has probably reduced overall GNP growth by one-quarter to one-half of a percentage point per year. This means, to him, that our economy is operating at 6 to 7 percent below its capacity potential because of controls.[14] A major cost of regulation is its contribution to inflation, reduced productivity, and a slower GNP rate of growth.[15]

A primary and unanswered question concerns the justification for these regulatory costs. There are, of course, offsetting benefits, a point which will be discussed later, but there are also many illustrations of costs being incurred which exceed benefits. To illustrate, Irving Shapiro, chairman of the board of Du Pont, says that his company spent $1.2 million to reduce particulate emissions in one plant by 94 percent. He said this was a justified expenditure. However, federal regulations required an additional reduction of particulates by 3 percent. The costs of meeting this standard totaled $1.8 million. According to Shapiro, there was no detectable difference in air quality between the 94 and 97 percent reduction. This was equivalent, he said, to paying 80 cents for a dozen eggs and an additional $1.20 for a piece of eggshell.[16]

A recent government-sponsored poll of 57 chief executive officers and top government liaison staff officers found that 86 percent believed that government regulations added more to product and service costs than the benefits they supposedly provided were worth.[17]

OLD AND NEW REGULATION

It is important to observe that there are major differences between the old and new models of regulation. The new model might be called *functional social* regulation in contrast to the older *industrial* regulation. All regulation, of course, is social in that it is ultimately concerned with social welfare, but there are basic distinctions between the models.

The old style of regulation was concerned with one industry, such as railroads, airlines, drugs, and so on. The focus was on such matters as markets, rates, and obligations to serve the public. There were regulations that cut across industry lines but the main focus was on industrial segments. In contrast, the newer functional regulations cut across industrial lines. They are broader in scope and are concerned with one function in an organization, not the entirety of the organization. As a result, of course, the newer regulations affect far more industries and companies than older regulations and, therefore, more customers.

Several important implications for business exist in this new pattern, aside from the number of regulations which must be followed. The old cliché about an industry capturing the agency that regulates it is obsolete. What industry is going to capture OSHA? It would be impractical for an industry to try to dominate a functional regulatory agency such as the Consumer Product Safety Commission or EPA. On the contrary, these agencies can dominate a company's affairs in their realm of functional authority and do so with limited understanding of their impact on the total operation of the company. Older industry regulatory agencies are more or less concerned with the total operation of an industry and the companies in it. Newer functional regulatory agencies are only concerned with a specific part of an industry's operations. Weidenbaum concludes that, far from being dominated by an industry, the newer type of regulatory activity is more likely to ignore the needs of various industries, including their service to the public, to further the agency's objectives.[18]

PURPOSES, POLICIES, AND METHODS OF NEWER REGULATIONS

Newer regulations have different purposes and apply different policies and methods. There are several aspects of this dimension. First, in a simplistic way, the purposes of the new legislation differ from the older regulatory agencies. For example, the older independent regulatory agencies, such as the Civil Aeronautics Board, the Federal Trade Commission, and so on, were designed to prevent monopoly; increase competition; save free enterprise from big business; establish uniform standards of safety, security, communications, and financial practice; and prevent abuses of managerial practices.

The newer regulations are the results of pressures to improve the quality of life. The purposes of the newer regulations are to clean up the environment, employ minorities, assure greater safety and health of workers, provide more information to consumers, protect consumers from shoddy products, and so on.

Second, in the achievement of their purposes the newer agencies do not establish policy to guide private industry in its operations, but specify in detail what shall be done. The National Highway Traffic Safety Administration, which now administers the Motor Vehicle Safety Standards Act of 1966, is very specific about safety features which automobiles must have. This is what Charles Schultze calls a "command and control" method of regulation. He points out that once a decision is made to intervene in the market, the current pattern of regulation is not to seek to alter incentives in the marketplace, modify information flows, or change institutional structures. Rather, direct intervention, the command and control technique, is almost always chosen. Seldom do we try other alternatives, "regardless of whether that mode of response fits the problem."[19]

A third dimension of the new regulations is that legislation is lengthy and specific. Government regulatory legislation in the past established broad policies, with comparatively little specific guidance, and gave the regulatory agency wide powers to set detailed regulations in conformance with the public interest and the policy guidelines drawn by the Congress. Today's legislation tends to be lengthy and detailed. The EPA, for example, administers statutes that run into hundreds of pages of detailed specifications. The Clean Air Act sets specific pollution-reduction targets and timetables and leaves the EPA little discretion.

Two significant results ensue. First, government today is an active managerial partner with business executives. This partnership extends all the way from the governance of corporations to the specific ways in which products are produced and distributed. Many business managers today are in fact acting as agents of the government without being under contract.[20] Second, government is losing the power of motivated individuals in the decentralized market process. As Schultze has put it:

> Regardless of the circumstances...new social intervention has almost always been output-oriented, giving short shrift to the process-oriented alternative. And this has proven a costly bias. It has, with no offsetting gain, forfeited the strategic advantages of market-like arrangements. It has led to ineffective and inefficient solutions to important social problems. It has taxed, well beyond its limit, the ability of government to make complex output decisions. And it has stretched thin the delicate fabric of political consensus by unnecessarily widening the scope of activities it must cover.[21]

NONSENSE REGULATIONS

One significant dimension of federal regulation is the growth of nonsense regulations.[22] OSHA regulates trivia in exquisite detail, as the following examples from the *Code of Federal Regulations* of 1 July 1975 reveal:

Section 1910.35(b): Exit access is that portion of a means of egress which leads to the entrance to an exit.

Section 1910.25(d)(vii): [out of 21 pages of fine print devoted to ladders] when ascending or descending, the user should face the ladder; ...(d)(2)(xx): The bracing on the back leg of step ladders is designed solely for increasing stability and not for climbing.

Section 1910.244(a)(2)(vii): Jacks which are out of order shall be tagged accordingly, and shall not be used until repairs are made.

Such trivia has little to do with the important causes of industrial accidents and worker illness. Many silly rules on worker safety have been eliminated or modified, but many remain.[23]

Nonsense regulations are not, of course, confined to OSHA. Other regulatory agencies are just as guilty of this shortcoming.

CONFLICTS AMONG REGULATIONS

There have always been conflicts among government regulations, but the number, intensity, and incidence have been mounting. Cases have arisen in which the EPA has demanded that a plant convert from coal to oil to reduce atmospheric pollution. At the same time, power plants have been ordered to convert from oil to coal by the Department of Energy to reduce oil consumption. Antipollution requirements have forced some companies to abandon marginal plants, a policy which conflicts with federal goals of reduced unemployment.[24]

NEW TECHNOLOGICAL ISSUES

The new policy regulations are raising significant and controversial technological issues. For example, we all want clean air, clean water, less noise, and protection of workers from carcinogens. In dealing with such matters the question of standards arises. Generally speaking, the costs of eliminating 90 percent of hazardous effluent from a belching smokestack are not great in light of total costs of production. Each additional percentage point of air purification, however, can be achieved only by accelerating costs, until the last few percentage points become prohibitively expensive.

Extremely sensitive issues arise with respect to equating statistical loss of life with costs of controls. Sam Peltzman, for instance, concluded that Federal Drug Administration regulations which delay the introduction of new drugs on the market save fewer lives than would a quicker introduction of the drugs.[25] Of course, different lives are involved. How should the cost-benefit equation be balanced?

With growing scientific knowledge, more and more hazards to life are becoming apparent. Decisions about technical matters, such as whether to put fluorocarbons or another substance in spray-propelled fluids, no longer are being left to private industry. No one knows in all cases what a rational decision is or how it should be made.

New biological, chemical, and other findings are continuously raising difficult technical questions. They reflect, of course, a growing awareness of hazards to human life and a national policy to reduce them. The policy is not a question here, but the fact is that new regulations do become embroiled in controversial technical issues undreamed of in the past.

BUREAUCRATIC IMPERIALISM

Bureaucrats tend to be arbitrary, authoritarian, arrogant, and uncompromising in making and applying rules. Furthermore, a certain antipathy toward business exists in the U.S. federal bureaucracy, and in recent years this tendency seems to have increased. Irving Kristol, who has been observing the scene for some time, has concluded:

> Here we must be candid as well as careful. Though officialdom will deny it—sometimes naively, sometimes not—it is a fact that most of those holding career jobs in EPA, OSHA, and other newer regulatory agencies have an ideological animus against

the private economic sector....They are not in those jobs because they could not find any others. Most of them, in truth, are sufficiently educated and intelligent to find better-paying jobs in the world of business. But they are not much interested in money. They are idealistic—that is, they are concerned with exercising power so as to create "a better world."[26]

Another characteristic of some officials is a reluctance, if not lack of interest, to consider the cost of their regulations. Weidenbaum quotes a member of the CPSC: "When it involves a product that is unsafe, I don't care how much it costs the company to correct the problem."[27] Such an attitude can lead not only to ignoring alternative solutions to a problem but also to severe injury to the regulated. Weidenbaum cites the example of an offending company that had not pasted a label on its product bearing the correct statement required by a regulation ("cannot be made non-poisonous"). The company was forced to destroy the contents. "If you do not care about costs," noted Weidenbaum, "apparently you do not think about such economical solutions as pasting a new label on the can."[28]

A more serious illustration of the unfortunate results of such an attitude concerns the Marlin Toy Products Company of Horicon, Wisconsin. The CPSC mistakenly put the company's toy on its ban list. When the error was called to its attention, the agency refused to issue a retraction, and the company was forced out of business.[29]

INCREASING BUSINESS DISRESPECT FOR LAW

Regulations that are trivial, seemingly contrary to common sense, arbitrarily imposed and administered, and difficult to understand tend to erode respect for the law and willingness to comply with it. This trend is exacerbated when those to whom a rule applies do not know of its existence. The chief executive of Citicorp expresses deep concern about the latter situation in these words:

What worries me is that General Motors and Citibank have a fighting chance of obeying all the new regulatory laws because we have the staff and the big-time lawyers to do so. But most small business people do not. They cannot even find out what the law is. There are, for example, 1,200 interpretations by the Federal Reserve staff of the Truth in Lending Act. Now 90% of the more than 14,000 commercial banks in the country have fewer than 100 employees. If you gave every staff member those regulations and started them reading, they wouldn't be finished by next year.[30]

Declining respect for the law, if such is really present in the United States today, is the result of a great many forces. The regulatory experience is one of those forces. The great volume of penetrating, detailed, and often petty regulations lays a fertile groundwork for the development of some form of payoff, both large and small, to government officials either to get needed action or to avoid paying the costs of regulation.

Thomas Ehrlich, dean of the Law School at Stanford University, has used the term *legal pollution* to describe what he calls the growing feeling that it is virtually impossible to move "without running into a law or a regulation or a legal problem."[31]

CONFLICTS AMONG ECONOMIC, LEGAL, AND POLITICAL RATIONALITY

A major pattern in federal regulation is the significant shift which has taken place from market to political-legal decisions. More and more governmental regulatory decisions are supplanting market decisions, and less reliance is being placed on the market mechanism in achieving the objectives of society.

Associated with this phenomenon is the conflict which often occurs among economic, political, and legal rationality. What is politically rational may not be, and frequently is not, economically rational. The obvious result, therefore, is the injection of more and more irrationality into the private market mechanism. A theme discussed by Schultze is the tendency of govern-

ment to intervene in resource allocation decisions in order to achieve equity and income distribution goals.[32] The failure to disentangle the two may lead to irrational economic decisions because of what politicians see as politically rational actions. The problem in devising an energy program is a case in point.

As implementation and adjudication of regulations move into courts of law, a further potential conflict with economic rationality arises. Courts have their own rationality rooted, of course, in the law. Rationality concerns adherence to legal precedents, seeking a balance among many competing values and interests, and a bias toward exploration of all matters in a case with equal thoroughness and diligence, irrespective of their relative importance in economic life.[33] It is not at all surprising, therefore, that many legal decisions may not square with the logic of the economic market mechanism.

Within a particular government regulatory agency the rationality of politics and law may collide with economic rationality. A former U.S. tariff commissioner, a trained economist, has lamented the difficulties in behaving like an economist in a government agency.[34]

THE REGULATORY COST-BENEFIT EQUATION

Regulations have protected and subsidized business interests as well as consumer and general public interests. Regulation has helped society achieve economic and social goals. It has helped to improve the position of minorities, achieve cleaner air, hold business accountable, prevent abuses of the market mechanism, prevent monopoly, reduce industrial accidents, and so on. The list of pluses of government regulation is long.

On the other hand, there are substantial costs of regulation, using cost in a broad sense. Many, but by no means all, have been discussed here.

In the aggregate, the costs of today's government regulations seem greater than the benefits.

Twenty-five years ago the power scale between business and government was balanced reasonably well.[35] Five years ago, the balance seemed to be reasonable.[36] Today, the overall balance is significantly upset in favor of government.

NOTES

1. It is recognized, of course, that there is a vast and growing volume of state and local regulation of business. Limited space forces me to deal only with federal controls.

2. Eleanore Carruth, "The 'Legal Explosion' Has Left Business Shell-Shocked" *Fortune* 87 (April 1973): 65.

3. Murray L. Weidenbaum, "A Fundamental Reform of Government Regulation," in George A. Steiner, ed., *Business and Its Changing Environment* (Los Angeles: UCLA Graduate School of Management, 1978), p. 189.

4. William Lilley III and James C. Miller III, "The New Social Regulation," *Public Interest* 45 (Spring 1977): 5–51.

5. Charles L. Schultze, The *Public Use of Private Interest* (Washington, D.C.: The Brookings Institution, 1977), p. 7.

6. Reported in the *New York Times,* 13 April 1978.

7. Council on Environmental Quality, *Environmental Quality* (Washington, D.C.: U.S. Government Printing Office, 1972), pp. 277–78.

8. Ibid., p. 534.

9. If 11 million cars are sold this year, as expected, the compliance cost to American consumers will be $7 billion. In addition, weight added to cars by such equipment is increasing fuel consumption by $3 billion annually. Murray Weidenbaum, quoted in the *New York Times,* 13 April 1978.

10. Reported in *Time,* 5 June 1978.

11. *Time,* 10 July 1978, p. 26. See also Paul H. Weaver, "That Crusade against Federal Paperwork Is a Paper Tiger," *Fortune* 94 (November 1976): 118–21, 206–10.

12. Don Dedera, "Paperwork! It's Costing Us All a Bundle!" *Exxon USA,* Fourth Quarter 1977.

13. The owner of a small automobile repair shop in California reported that last year he spent 270 hours completing 548 government mandated forms at a conservatively calculated cost of $3,904. A California legislative survey calculated that each small business in California spends an average of $4,000 a year completing government forms. Ibid.

14. Paul W. MacAvoy, "The Existing Condition of Regulation and Regulatory Reform," in Chris Argyris et al., *Regulating Business: The Search for an Optimum* (San Francisco: Institute for Contemporary Studies, 1978), p. 3.

15. See John G. Myers, Leonard I. Nakamura, and Normal R. Madrid, "The Impact of OPEC, FEA, EPA, and OSHA on Productivity and Growth," *Conference Board Record* 13 (April 1976): 61–64. By presidential order, initiated in 1974, the executive branch of the federal government now must evaluate the effects of all major legislation on regulatory proposals in the areas of prices and costs. This is called an Inflationary Impact Statement. See Robert F. Kamm, Stephen F. Nagy, and Joseph Nemec, "Complying with Proposed Regulations: Estimating Industry's Costs," *Business Horizons* 20 (August 1977): 86–91. I have seen no studies relating to the effects of such statements.

16. Irving S. Shapiro, an excerpt of remarks presented at the Southern Governors' Conference, San Antonio, Texas, 29 August 1977, found in *Across the Board* 15 (January 1978): 37.

17. John F. Steiner, "Government Regulation of Business: An Overview," *Los Angeles Business and Economics* 3 (Fall 1977): 7.

18. Weidenbaum, "Business, Government, and the Public," in *Business and Its Changing Environment,* pp. 14–15.

19. Schultze, *Public Use of Private Interest,* p. 13.

20. Weidenbaum, "Business, Government, and the Public."

21. Schultze, *Public Use of Private Interest.*

22. Ibid.

23. "Interview with Eula Bingham, Head of the Occupational Safety and Health Administration," *U.S. News & World Report,* 16 January 1978, p. 65.

24. Murray L. Weidenbaum, "The Costs of Government Regulation," Publication No. 12, Center for the Study of American Business, Washington University (St. Louis: February 1977).

25. Sam Peltzman, "An Evaluation of Consumer Protection Legislation: The 1962 Drug Amendments," *Journal of Political Economy* 81 (September/October 1973): 1049–91.

26. Irving Kristol, "A Regulated Society?" *Regulation* 1 (July/August 1977): 13.
27. Murray L. Weidenbaum, "The Case for Economizing on Government Controls," *Journal of Economic Issues* 11 (June 1975): 207.
28. Ibid.
29. Comptroller General of the United States, *Banning of Two Toys and Certain Aerosol Spray Adhesives*, MWD-75-65 (Washington, D.C.: U.S. General Accounting Office, 1975).
30. Walter B. Wriston, quoted in *Time*, 1 May 1978, p. 44.
31. "Complaints about Lawyers," interview with Thomas Ehrlich, *U.S. News & World Report*, 21 July 1975, p. 46.
32. Schultze, *Public Use of Private Interest*.
33. Norman Kangun and R. Charles Moyer, "The Failings of Regulation," *MSU Business Topics* 24 (Spring 1976): 5–14.
34. Penelope Hartland-Thunberg, "Tales of a Onetime Tariff Commissioner," *Challenge* 19 (July–August 1977): 6–12.
35. George A. Steiner, *Government's Role in Economic Life* (New York: John Wiley & Sons, 1953).
36. George A. Steiner, *Business and Society*, 1st ed. (New York: Random House, 1971).

Regulation that Works

Steven Kelman*

The last decade has seen dramatic restrictions in the freedom of action society chooses to allow to business firms. A series of laws in areas like environmental protection, occupational safety and health, consumer product safety and equal opportunity has restricted the prerogatives of business firms to pursue production, hiring

Excerpted from "Regulation that Works," published in *The New Republic*, Nov. 25, 1978. Copyright © 1978 The New Republic, Inc., New York. Reprinted by permission of *The New Republic*.

*Kennedy School of Government, Harvard University.

and marketing practices that would have continued without these laws. Business and conservatives have now launched a counterattack against these changes. Cleverly exploiting various popular resentments, the counterattacking forces seek to lump "excessive government regulation" together with themes as diverse as high taxes and school busing to generate an all-embracing demand to "get the government out of our hair." To hear the critics of the new government regulatory programs tell it, nothing less fundamental than our very freedom is at stake in the battle against meddlesome bureaucrats. And now, with national concern over inflation growing, we are being told that the new regulatory programs are an important cause of the increased cost of living, and must be reduced for that reason as well.

One fact it is important to get clear from the beginning is that the alleged popular ground swell against government regulation of business does not exist. A recent Louis Harris survey asked Americans, "In the future, do you think there should be more government regulation of business, less government regulation, or the same amount there is now?" By 53 percent to 30 percent, those polled favored either more regulation or the same amount as now, over less regulation. In fact, almost as many respondents (24 percent) favored more regulation as favored less regulation (30 percent). Repeated polls have shown wide popular support for measures to make workplaces safe, and to clean up the environment.

This absence of any ground swell against the new regulatory thrust of the last decade is reassuring, because the conservative and business counterattack is, I believe, largely wrong. New regulatory programs neither threaten freedom nor contribute significantly to inflation. On the whole, the new regulation is a good thing. Certainly there have been excesses by bureaucrats, but what is more impressive than these excesses is the unfinished work the new agencies still have before them to deal with the injustices that prompted their creation in the first place.

There are two kinds of activities often lumped together as "government regulation." When denouncing the "costs of government regulation," opponents of the new regulatory agencies tend to forget this distinction. An older generation of liberals, fond of asserting that regulatory agencies always get captured by those they regulate, also ignore this distinction.

Most of the regulatory agencies established before the last decade were set up to regulate prices and conditions of entry in various industries. The grandfather of such agencies was the Interstate Commerce Commission, established in 1887 to regulate railroads. There is a lively dispute among historians about whether the ICC, when it was established, was an attempt to tame a powerful and oppressive industry, or a government-sanctioned effort by the railroads themselves to set up a cartel to avoid price competition. It is much clearer, however, that other agencies regulating market conditions in various industries, such as the Civil Aeronautics Board and the Federal Communications Commission, *were* originally established at the behest of industries seeking to avoid "excessive" competition. These agencies, by maintaining artificially high prices in various industries, have been very costly to consumers and to the economy as a whole. But you do not hear the voices of business complaining about them. Indeed, when proposals are made to deregulate surface transportation, airlines, or television, the main opponents of such proposals have been the industries being "regulated."

The situation is very different, both politically and conceptually, for the regulatory agencies—which have blossomed especially during the last decade—intended to regulate non-market behavior by business firms. Usually they regulate acts that injure third parties. These "social" regulatory agencies include the Environmental Protection Agency, the Occupational Safety and Health Administration, the National Highway Transportation Safety Board, the Consumer Product Safety Commission, and the Equal Employment Opportunity Commission. These agencies generally came into being despite genuine business resistance. Business representatives certainly have ample opportunity to participate in developing the regulations these agencies promulgate, but there are other organized constituencies interested in their work as well (environmentalists at EPA, trade unions at OSHA, civil rights and women's groups at EEOC, for instance). Few reasonable people believe the social regulatory agencies have been "captured" by business—least of all, as the current attacks demonstrate, business itself.

The conceptual basis for the social regulatory agencies also is different from that of agencies intended to limit or replace the free market. In any society, one of the basic tasks of government and the legal system is to decide which acts of individuals are so harmful to others that they cannot be freely permitted (and which harmful acts may rightfully be performed, even though others are indeed harmed). The social regulatory agencies are engaged in this age-old task. There is nothing conceptually new about their activities. What *is* new is that they have redefined certain acts by business firms previously regarded as acceptable, and determined that they are henceforth unacceptable.

Government has never left businessmen "unregulated," as business spokesmen now wistfully, but erroneously, imagine. The voluminous case and statute law of property, contracts and torts along with large chunks of the criminal law, comprise an elaborate system—far more complex and intricate than any OSHA standard—regulating acts that injure property holders, as well as acts by property holders that injure others. A starving person does not have the freedom to injure a rich man by appropriating the rich man's money in order to buy food. People do not have the freedom to injure a landowner by trespassing on his land. Furthermore, the process by which these older rules were elucidated and enforced through litigation was much more cumbersome and arbitrary than the rulemaking of today's regulatory agencies.

The plethora of regulations regarding property that has grown up over the centuries is not some sort of natural order, onto which new regulations of business behavior in areas like safety, health, environmental protection, consumer fraud, and discrimination represent an unnatural intrusion. As long as the regulations were restricting the freedom of non-property-holders to injure *them,* businessmen raised no chorus of complaints about an oppressive government stifling freedom. The chorus of complaints from business has begun only as regulations have begun increasingly to restrict the freedom of business firms to injure others.

The harms that social regulations of the last decade were intended to curb were not insignificant. Urban air had become unhealthy as well as unpleasant to breathe. Rivers were catching on fire. Many working people were dying from exposure to chemicals on their jobs. Firms were selling products of whose hazards consumers were ignorant. And the nation faced a legacy of racial and sexual discrimination. Frequently the harm was borne disproportionately by the more disadvantaged members of society, while the more advantaged produced the harm. The social regulation of the past decade grew largely, then, out of a sense of fairness—a view that people, frequently disadvantaged people, were being victimized by others in unacceptable ways.

The impact of the new agencies in alleviating these injuries has begun to be felt. Racial and sexual discrimination have decreased, partly thanks to broader social trends, but partly thanks to government efforts. There has been a vast increase in the amount of information manufacturers are required to tell consumers about their products, and surveys indicate that many consumers use this information in making purchasing decisions.

Since the much-maligned OSHA and its sister agency regulating coal mining safety have come into existence, the number of accidental workplace deaths has been cut almost in half. Worker exposures to harmful amounts of coal dust and chemicals like vinyl chloride, asbestos and lead have been reduced, and this will reduce the toll of occupational sickness and death in the years to come. Improvements in emergency medical care and some changes in workforce composition since 1970 may be partially responsible for the dramatic reduction in workplace deaths. But today's figures don't even reflect the reduction in deaths due to occupational disease, which will be felt mainly in future years because of the frequently lengthy period separating exposure to harmful levels of chemical and death or illness due to that exposure.

Environmental regulation has produced significant improvements in the quality of air in the United States. Without regulation the situation would have gotten worse because economic growth tends to increase the level of pollution. Carbon monoxide levels in eight representative cities declined 46 percent between 1972 and 1976. Carbon monoxide levels that had been found in urban air were enough to increase the incidence of heart attacks and of painful angina attacks among people with heart disease. There has been a major decline in heart attack deaths in the United States during the 1970s. No one yet knows why, but I predict that studies will show that improvement in air quality has played a role in this decline. Another common air pollutant, sulfur dioxide, which definitely causes respiratory illness and death and is suspected of causing cancer, has now declined to a point where almost every place in the country is in compliance with EPA standards.

The critics ask: have the benefits outweighed the costs? Are they feeding inflation, for example? Allegations that health, safety, environmental and antidiscrimination regulations are a major cause of inflation are little short of grotesque. Much of the business thunder about regulation begins by citing some overall figure for the "cost of regulation," and then goes on to zero in on agencies like OSHA and EPA. These agencies are chosen, however, only because business dislikes them especially, not because they are major contributors to the "cost of regulation." Most of the cost of regulation is imposed by the market-fixing agencies, like the ICC, that the business world likes. Murray Weidenbaum, director of the Center for the Study of American Business and an adjunct scholar at the American Enterprise Institute, estimated that in 1976 federal regulation in the areas he examined cost $62.3 billion to comply with. But of this sum, approximately $26 billion—or 42 percent—was the estimated impact on consumer prices of tariff protection against imports and of price and entry regulations by the ICC, CAB and FCC. (The largest figure in this category was the cost of ICC regulation of transportation). Another $18 billion—29 percent of the estimated total cost—represented the alleged cost of federal paperwork. Certainly there are plenty of pointless federal paperwork requirements. But few of these relate to what would normally be thought of as "government regulation." Much federal paperwork takes the form of reports for statistical purposes and of requirements for federal contractors or other citizens receiving federal benefits.

Only five percent of Weidenbaum's estimated total—$3.2 billion in 1976—was spent on complying with OSHA regulations. Another $7.8 billion allegedly was spent to comply with EPA regulations—less than 13 percent of the total. (Weidenbaum also estimated a $3.7 billion retail cost for auto safety and emissions requirements.)

Even these modest figures do not reflect the direct savings that result from some of these regulations. The actual monetary cost of pollution abatement measures, for example, is the cost to firms of capital equipment, energy and maintenance, *minus* the savings in medical bills, damaged crops, premature corrosion of property, laundering expenses and so forth, that would otherwise be borne by victims of pollution. Most accounts of the "inflationary impact" of government regulation do not calculate such savings.

More fundamentally, these estimates of the "cost" of regulation ignore widespread benefits that do not have a direct monetary value, but are real nonetheless. In the case of pollution control, for example, the air smells a bit better for five million people; 100,000 people get to see mountains in the distance which they would not have seen had the air not been as clean; and 50 lives are saved. There is no way of objectively determining whether these non-priced benefits justify the net monetary costs.

The costs and benefits of the business behavior now coming under regulation have not been distributed randomly. Much of the new social regulation benefits more disadvantaged groups in society. To put it somewhat simply—but not, in my view, unfairly—those who argue, say, that OSHA should "go soft" on its health regulations in order to spare the country the burden of additional costs, are saying that some workers should die so that consumers can pay a few bucks less for the products they purchase, and stockholders can make a somewhat higher return on their investments. It is hard to see why workers exposed to health hazards should be at the front line of the battle against inflation, however the overall costs and benefits tally up.

There are, to be sure, those sudden friends of the poor who allege that environmental regulation has significantly added to unemployment, or who point out that regulation-induced price increases weigh most heavily on the poor. But studies have concluded that, on balance, environmental legislation has probably created many more jobs than it has cost. And one must wonder whether there aren't more direct ways to help the poor than to eliminate the health, safety, and environmental regulations that slightly increase the costs of goods they buy.

None of this means that every regulation promulgated by social regulatory agencies in the last few years is justified. In some instances, as with some affirmative action requirements, regulations may have gone beyond their conceptual justifications. In other instances the administrative burden, the paperwork requirements or the monetary costs of regulating may be too great to justify the benefits, however real, received by those whom the regulations are intended to protect. Offhand, for example, it appears to me that the costs of retrofitting older urban subway systems to accommodate the handicapped, only a small number of whom could be expected to use those systems anyway, appear unjustified, even though failure to retrofit does indeed injure some disadvantaged people. Questions like this should be considered case-by-case, but with sympathy for those people injured by the failure to regulate.

The thrust of the current movement against social regulation in the United States is a wish by the strong to regain prerogatives whose disappearance, for the most part, is one of the most welcome events of the past decade. Individual regulations can and should be criticized. But the assault on the concept of regulation must be resisted if we are to continue to be a decent people living in a decent society.

QUESTIONS FOR DISCUSSION

1. Kelman and Steiner have quite different positions on the "costs" and "benefits" of government regulation. Why is this? Why does Steiner regard recent trends in regulation as "new," and Kelman regard them as a continuation of government's traditional role in society? Do you agree more with Steiner or with Kelman?
2. Taking into account the arguments of Kelman, Steiner, Bowie, and Maitland, explain the advantages of self-regulation over government regulation. What are the advantages of government regulation over self-regulation?
3. What is a "prisoner's dilemma"? An "assurance problem"? How, in Maitland's view, are these relevant to the issue of the self-regulation of business? What possible ways are there to get around these problems?

CHAPTER 14

Multinational Business

Section A   Multinationals in Less Developed Countries

Louis Turner
There's No Love Lost Between Multinational Companies and the Third World
531

Richard T. De George
Ethical Dilemmas for Multinational Enterprise: A Philosophical Overview
536

James E. Post
Ethical Dilemmas of Multinational Enterprises: An Analysis of Nestle's Traumatic Experience with the Infant Formula Controversy
541

Section B   Bribery

Scott Turow
What's Wrong with Bribery
549

Mark Pastin and Michael Hooker
Ethics and the Foreign Corrupt Practices Act
551

Robert E. Frederick
Bribery and Ethics: A Reply to Pastin and Hooker
555

Henry W. Lane and Donald G. Simpson
Bribery in International Business: Whose Problem Is It?
561

Section C   South Africa

Kenneth N. Carstens
A Case for Sanctions against South Africa
569

Patricia H. Werhane
Moral Justifications for Doing Business in South Africa
576

Section A
Multinationals in Less Developed Countries

There's No Love Lost between Multinational Companies and the Third World

Louis Turner*

Managers of multinational corporations excel at such tasks as transferring products, technology, and advanced management thinking to all quarters of the globe. In doing so, they tend to assume that the problems of New Delhi, Lagos, or Rio de Janeiro can be solved by hardware and concepts developed in Frankfurt or Detroit. Critics deny this. They argue that the impact of such corporations in the Third World is, in fact, harmful in that they exacerbate the tensions found within such societies and help create the kind of tragically polarized societies which we can see throughout Latin America. What is good for General Motors is probably, in the long run, not so good for Gabon and Guatemala.

To take a simple example: The Swiss company, Nestlé, introduced powdered milk as a baby food into West Africa as an alternative to breast feeding. Emulating Western fashion, local mothers adopted bottle feeding wholeheartedly. The result was increased infant mortality: To combat their extreme poverty, mothers were diluting the milk to the point that a bottle had virtually no nutrition.

In earlier times, few managers worried about such niceties. The bulk of corporations in the

Third World were looking for minerals or tropical produce which they would ship back to the industrialized world as fast as possible. Rather than contribute to the wider development of the societies in which they found themselves, they created "enclaves," virtual states-within-states, in which their rule was law. Due to their influence, some countries with diversified agricultural economies became dependent on single crops; the Central American "banana republics" and the rubber economies of Malaya and Liberia are examples. Even if such countries were formally independent, they were in fact shackled by their nearly total dependence on the benevolence of companies such as Firestone and United Fruit. Political leaders and local entrepreneurs either flourished or were overthrown at the whim of these companies, thus stifling the development of local economic and political initiative. On occasions, the companies even tried to redraw political boundaries, as when the Belgian mining company, Union Minière, helped finance the attempted breakaway of Katanga soon after the ex-Belgian Congo (now Zaire) attained independence.

Today, despite the abortive coup attempts of ITT in Chile, the situation is less stark. As Third World economies have grown, they have become more diversified, reducing their dependence on single companies and forcing managements to become more circumspect in their outward behaviour. In the aftermath of the Independence Era, governments have been growing in self-confidence and experience, and they are now willing to attack corporations which get out of line. Obviously the example of OPEC (Organization of Petroleum Exporting Countries) has been extremely important, as it has shown how relatively powerless the oil giants actually are. Since the oil producers began their onslaught, the bauxite producers have started to follow suit, with significant actions also coming from the governments of Malaysia (rubber) and Morocco (phosphates). However, despite this Third World militancy, the multinationals remain formidable adversaries.

Excerpted from "There's No Love Lost between Multinational Companies and the Third World," published in *Business and Society Review*, Autumn 1974. Reprinted by permission of the publisher. Copyright © 1974, Warren, Gorham and Lamont Inc. All rights reserved.

*Research scholar, Royal Institute of International Affairs, London.

SQUEEZING OUT LOCAL ENTREPRENEURS

For one thing, the multinationals are still very large by Third World standards. They possess the technical and marketing skills that countries trying to industrialize desperately need. The result is often a dependence on foreign companies to a degree embarrassing to see. Take the case of Unilever's subsidiary in Nigeria, the United Africa Co. (UAC), which originally entered that country to produce palm oil needed for the manufacture of margarine. By natural expansion it diversified into shipping and a general import-export trade aimed at the Nigerian market. As the country grew, so did the UAC, establishing itself in all the new markets created by Nigeria's fledgling industrialization. By the mid-1960s, it was four times the size of the next largest company, and one could almost claim that the industrialization of Nigeria was the industrialization of UAC. From its start as an agricultural and trading company, it moved into textiles, sugar, beer, cement, cigarettes, building contracting, radio assembly, plastic products, bicycle and truck assembly, etc. In any sector which mattered, the company was involved.

UAC is generally credited with having used its power responsibly; but, in microcosm, its history reflects what has been happening throughout the Third World. In the case of Latin America, foreign industrialists were squeezing local competitors out of all key industries as early as the nineteenth century. Every time there was a slump, it would be the undercapitalized local businessmen who would go to the wall, leaving the multinationals to emerge ever more dominant. Only during the two world wars, when European and American companies had other things on their minds, did local entrepreneurs have a chance to flourish—but this was not enough. Today, it is virtually meaningless to talk of Third World entrepreneurship in the sense in which Carnegie or Rockefeller were entrepreneurs. What we find instead is Third World planners

and businessmen passively accepting technologies which have been developed by the multinationals, perhaps modifying them slightly for local needs, but certainly not trying to produce innovations which might challenge the foreigners' sway. This approach has probably contributed to the long-term political stagnation found in many Third World countries. Furthermore, it is culturally dangerous in that it assumes that products produced by the multinationals are suitable for Third World needs. In many cases, this is blatantly untrue.

The vast majority of multinationals are just not interested in the Third World except as a convenient residual market in which extra profits can be made once a product has proved itself in the American and European arenas. I once tested this belief by reading a couple of hundred company reports, looking for examples of involvement with the Third World which the companies might want to emphasize. It was a depressing experience. The majority of companies gave Third World activities no coverage at all, instead stressing things like the companies' contribution to the American space program. Otherwise, apart from CPC (the Corn Products Corp.), which had its chairman pictured knee-deep in a paddy field, the reports boasted of products like refrigerator fronts of Formica-based laminate (American Cyanamid in Argentina), car radios (Bosch in Brazil), or the lighting, traffic lights, and illustrated fountains along eighteen miles of road in the oil-rich Trucial States (Philips). Nothing about searches for nutritionally enriched forms of tropical fruits and vegetables; virtually nothing about the search for cures for tropical diseases; nothing about the search for labor-intensive industries which might well mop up the vast armies of the unemployed found everywhere in the poor countries. Instead, the companies listed trivial products which can contribute nothing to the long-term development of the Third World, but which are symptomatic of the overall corrupting effect which the multinationals tend to have on Third World elites.

CORRUPTING THE ELITE

These elites should be concerned with the majority of their countrymen who are still in the countryside working outside the market economy (if working at all—only some 2 percent of Nigeria's 63 million population is earning a wage or salary). They ought to be thinking of ways to cope with spiraling urban unemployment (some estimates suggest that 20 percent of the world's potential work force is without a job). Above all, they ought to be preaching austerity, since the task of pulling the world's poorest 40 percent above their current near-starvation level is one which will take decades, if not centuries.

The multinationals have very little constructive to offer. What they are good at is identifying and filling gaps in the markets of industrialized consumer societies; but, as Galbraith has pointed out, private enterprise does not lead automatically to the satisfaction of wider social needs. A dynamic auto industry, for instance, does not guarantee a good educational or health system; in the Third World, such an industry may even harm the interests of the bottom 40 percent of the population, since the elites will divert precious resources to building the roads and importing the gasoline which a flourishing auto industry demands. Thus the inequality of such societies increases, precisely the danger which the World Bank is starting to warn against. It contends that social inequality is growing noticeably within the Third World, even within rapidly growing economies like Brazil's. And it is starting to argue that the classic measurement of growth, G.N.P., is (by itself) a misleading indicator of development, that slower growing countries which put more stress on reducing social inequalities may well produce stabler societies in the long run.

The multinationals, whether they know it or not, are firmly on the side of inequality, forming a deadly alliance with corruptible Third World elites. The latter have been brought up to believe that one should envy the slick consumer society of the West, and they see the multinationals as the organizations which will deliver the goods. The elites want record players, refrigerators, cars, television, telephones, etc., and the multinationals are only too happy to deliver them. There are some managers who are aware that none of this is helping the starving and unemployed at the bottom of the pile. Sometimes they make token protests, but the elites prevail, since national pride tells them that their country is not modern unless it has things like an airport, an airline, a car industry, and a Hilton hotel. They can be extremely insistent on getting them. For instance, a Fiat manager once told me of the efforts they made in the late 1960s to persuade various national governments that truck plants were far better investments than car plants for countries at a low level of development. The technologies involved in assembling trucks are simpler, less import-intensive and more labor-intensive, and produce products which are of direct use in activities like farming and civil engineering. Their arguments were to no avail; the government officials insisted on having a car plant.

While the multinationals are not all to blame, clearly they are a vital part of the process which corrupts the elites. Hollywood films, television programs, and advertising are all instrumental in creating a certain image of Western society. The expatriate managers of multinational subsidiaries are a flesh and blood demonstration of this way of life. Highly paid (by local standards), they provide a model to the indigenous managers (who are increasingly replacing them) and to local officials. Their replacement can cause problems. In Africa, for instance, local replacements have been expecting not only similar levels of pay to those of the expatriate managers, but even some of the latters' ''perks,'' like the free trip to Europe every eighteen months. From the start, local managers have expectations which can be satisfied only at the expense of the less powerful in their societies. In East Africa they have coined the name *Wa-Benzi* for the African elite which rides about in Mercedes-Benzes while the peasants and unemployed starve.

Another insidious effect arises from tourism, an industry in which multinationals are playing an increasing role. Tourists are flying more and more to exotic (i.e., poor) Third World destinations like the Pacific Islands, the Caribbean, and North and East Africa. Although many tourist resorts are "golden ghettos," located away from the centers of population, the social harm done by this industry is extraordinarily difficult to avoid. The local population learns to despise and cheat tourists, whose wealth appears limitless and who normally have no clear idea how much anything costs. Prostitution springs up, as seen in the Boys' towns, like Tijuana, along the U.S.-Mexican border. Even more grotesque are government attempts to build an image of friendliness toward tourists, launching "Be-Nice" campaigns and going so far as to have school children taught that tourists are friends who must be smiled at and treated well. Such campaigns are necessary in the sense that expressions of hostility may keep tourists from returning. But there is something intensely degrading about nations like Jamaica, Barbados, and the Bahamas launching such programs, particularly when they are part of a culture steeped deeply in the slave trade, with all its connotations of black servitude.

REAL DEVELOPMENT DOES NOT PAY

Despite everything, we should not be too harsh on the multinationals, since they are merely symbols for the general capitalist system, of which most of us are just as much a part. Asking them to contribute positively to the development of the Third World is to ask them to perform a task for which they were not designed. They are motivated by money, and yet we critics are asking them to develop goods for part of the world which is still predominantly outside the market economy. A bank, the Barclay's, lost $4.2 million in the early 1960s when its managers in West Africa were instructed to lend much more adventurously in rural areas. They managed to pull in small savings, but the amounts were so small,

and so expensive to collect, that normal banking practices seemed almost irrelevant. Undoubtedly there was an overall social gain for Nigeria in the attempts to attract rural savings into productive investments, but a profit-oriented institution was obviously not the right vehicle for extending the experiment. Likewise, tractor manufacturers are searching for a mini-tractor which can compete effectively with the traditional ox and plough. Ford, for instance, spent at least six years trying to develop a simple, one-speed, seven-horse-power, rope-started model which could be easily assembled by local dealers, but after field-testing in Jamaica, Mexico, and Peru, and market-testing in Jamaica, they finally concluded that the returns were not going to be enough to justify their utilizing a disproportionately high number of their executives on this product.

One is tempted to argue that there is little that the multinationals can do in key fields like population control, tropical diseases, and tropical agriculture—just the areas which would do most for that bottom 40 percent of the Third World. This is simply because on the scale on which most multinationals work, there just is not sufficient money to be made, and the risks are horrendous. So a pharmaceutical company will always choose to investigate a possible cure for arthritis, rather than a simple, self-administered, long-action contraceptive using materials indigenous, say, to India. A cure for arthritis would be an instant gold mine; a long-action contraceptive for India would run the risk that the company might have to sell to the Indian government at a loss, or might have its patents ignored. Either way, the product aimed at the Third World is just not an acceptable risk.

The multinationals play safe. They develop products for the U.S. and Europe and are pleasantly surprised if they find Third World markets as well. Obviously, the formula sometimes works well for the poor. The discovery of DDT, for instance, did, with all its side effects, eradicate malaria. On balance, though, the multinationals are happiest doing business with urbanized, west ernized elites—the soldiers who will buy their weapons, the managers who will buy their consumer goods. It would be nice if all the people of the Third World were as rich as those of Rio de Janeiro and Sao Paulo; unfortunately, they are not. Multinationals have a lot to contribute to these cities, but virtually nothing for the peasants living in grinding poverty in Brazil's northeast.

THE EVILS OF "DEPENDENCIA"

Finally, if we are looking at the cultural impact of multinationals, we must examine arguments stemming from Latin America about "Dependencia"—the contention that many of the ills of that continent can be blamed on the polarization of societies by overdependence on foreign markets, technology and culture. If this is indeed true of Latin America, what chance have the less developed continents of Africa and Asia?

This argument is difficult to substantiate conclusively, but it is not dissimilar to the charges raised by Ralph Nader and Mark Green about the effect of corporate domination of U.S. communities. They have written that when a community's economy is controlled by national or multinational conglomerates, the overall well-being of the community is threatened. Civic leadership suffers since corporate officials do not identify with communities which are merely one step on the career ladder. The independent middle classes are eliminated and income becomes less equitably distributed. Local society becomes more polarized. They cite the words of C. Wright Mills: "Big business tends to depress, while small business tends to raise the level of civic welfare."

On the international level, one can make a similar argument. Multinationals certainly prefer to do business with authoritarian regimes, which can guarantee a "secure" investment climate. They are happier investing in Brazil or Spain than in radical states like Allende's Chile or Nyerere's Tanzania. Nor do they show much sympathy toward democracies like Italy and India where underlying social tensions interfere with the smooth running of the economy. Governments encourage multinationals to invest by repressing potential troublemakers. Taiwan, Singapore, and Malaysia vie with each other by guaranteeing foreign investors freedom from trade union activities.

On a deeper level, reliance on multinationals saps a nation's vitality. Multinationals do not encourage indigenous research and development, almost always choosing to locate these facilities in North America or Europe. Local businessmen become mere intermediaries, adapting foreign technologies (if at all) to local conditions. Where countries are industrializing, multinationals move in to snuff out local competition before it has any chance of getting established.

THE AMERICAN LESSON

The degree of dominance exercised, however benevolently, by companies like UAC in Nigeria is a phenomenon which no Western commentator is entitled to gloss over. It is totally unlike anything in the history of the United States or Europe. To begin to comprehend it, imagine the United States as a Third World country winning its independence from a technically sophisticated Great Britain whose per capita GNP was ten times as great as that of ours, and which possessed companies fully capable of operating in the American market. The first result would have been that the incredible flowering of American entrepreneurial talent in the nineteenth century would have been nipped in the bud. Cyrus McCormick, Francis Cabot Lowell, Cornelius Vanderbilt, John D. Rockefeller, and J.P. Morgan would, at best, have ended up as talented managers for some British conglomerate. After all, who would need to design an American reaper when perfectly adequate British designs already existed and could be imported or assembled under license? Public ire in the late nineteenth century would not have focused on "the trusts," but would have vented itself against a handful of British giants, one of which might well have owned not just the oil industry, but the key American railroads and transatlantic shipping lines as well. Congress would have been in the pay of the British, and independent presidents would have invited bombardment by the British navy or coups from the British intelligence service.

This is a fair picture of what multinational investment has meant to many Third World countries. Clearly, the American political tradition would have been totally different had it sprung from such a background. For one thing, political divisions would have been far deeper than they are. Labor disputes and left-wing politics would be tinged with greater intensity, for there would be a xenophobic element to all controversies. Radical critics would face a much less powerful middle class, since the entrepreneurial element of U.S. society would be much smaller. Above all, the unifying belief in the American dream would not exist. How could there be a feeling of hope and optimism in a society where material "success" means working for some giant foreign company? The forces of the left would thus be relatively strong, forcing foreign corporate interests into relatively extreme defensive action. The likelihood of coups, armed repression, and terrorist tactics would be high.

So, we come to the harsh conclusion that multinational investment in the Third World has long-term harmful social and cultural effects. The multinational managers who complain about political chaos in Latin America are deluding themselves, since they are an integral part of the problem. This is not to claim that the majority of such managers are not perfectly well-meaning citizens; nor is it to deny that many of the products of their companies are of vital importance in the Third World. But we would do well to look more sympathetically at alternative approaches to development, while agreeing sadly with the words of George Bernard Shaw:

> Capitalism is not an orgy of human villainy, but a utopia that has dazzled and misled very amiable and public spirited men. The upholders of capital-

ism are dreamers and visionaries who, instead of doing good with evil intentions like Mephistopheles, do evil with the best of intentions.

Ethical Dilemmas for Multinational Enterprise: A Philosophical Overview

Richard T. De George*

First World multinational corporations (MNCs) are both the hope of the Third World and the scourge of the Third World. The working out of this paradox poses moral dilemmas for many MNCs. I shall focus on some of the moral dilemmas that many American MNCs face.

Third World countries frequently seek to attract American multinationals for the jobs they provide and for the technological transfers they promise. Yet when American MNCs locate in Third World countries, many Americans condemn them for exploiting the resources and workers of the Third World. While MNCs are a means for improving the standard of living of the underdeveloped countries, MNCs are blamed for the poverty and starvation such countries suffer. Although MNCs provide jobs in the Third World, many criticize them for transferring these jobs from the United States. American MNCs usually pay at least as high wages as local industries, yet critics blame them for paying the workers in underdeveloped countries less than they pay American workers for comparable work. When American MNCs pay higher than

---

From *Ethics and the Multinational Enterprise,* edited by W. Michael Hoffman, Ann E. Lange and David A. Fedo (Lanham, MD: University Press of America, 1986). Copyright © 1986 by University Press of America. Reprinted by permission of the publisher.
*Distinguished Professor of Philosophy, University of Kansas.

local wages, local companies criticize them for skimming off all the best workers and for creating an internal brain-drain. Multinationals are presently the most effective vehicle available for the development of the Third World. At the same time, critics complain that the MNCs are destroying the local cultures and substituting for them the tinsel of American life and the worst aspects of its culture. American MNCs seek to protect the interests of their shareholders by locating in an environment in which their enterprise will be safe from destruction by revolutions and confiscation by socialist regimes. When they do so, critics complain that the MNCs thrive in countries with strong, often right-wing, governments.[1]

The dilemmas the American MNCs face arise from conflicting demands made from opposing, often ideologically based, points of view. Not all of the demands that lead to these dilemmas are equally justifiable, nor are they all morally mandatory. We can separate the MNCs that behave immorally and reprehensibly from those that do not by clarifying the true moral responsibility of MNCs in the Third World. To help do so, I shall state and briefly defend five theses.

Thesis 1: Many of the moral dilemmas MNCs face are false dilemmas which arise from equating United States standards with morally necessary standards.

Many American critics argue that American multinationals should live up to and implement the same standards abroad that they do in the United States and that United States mandated norms should be followed.[2] This broad claim confuses morally necessary ways of conducting a firm with United States government regulations. The FDA sets high standards that may be admirable. But they are not necessarily morally required. OSHA specifies a large number of rules which in general have as their aim the protection of the worker. However, these should not be equated with morally mandatory rules. United States wages are the highest in the world. These also

should not be thought to be the morally necessary norms for the whole world or for United States firms abroad. Morally mandatory standards that no corporation—United States or other—should violate, and moral minima below which no firm can morally go, should not be confused either with standards appropriate to the United States or with standards set by the United States government. Some of the dilemmas of United States multinationals come from critics making such false equations.

This is true with respect to drugs and FDA standards, with respect to hazardous occupations and OSHA standards, with respect to pay, with respect to internalizing the costs of externalities, and with respect to foreign corrupt practices. By using United States standards as moral standards, critics pose false dilemmas for American MNCs. These false dilemmas in turn obfuscate the real moral responsibilities of MNCs.

Thesis 2: Despite differences among nations in culture and values, which should be respected, there are moral norms that can be applied to multinationals.

I shall suggest seven moral guidelines that apply in general to any multinational operating in Third World countries and that can be used in morally evaluating the actions of MNCs. MNCs that respect these moral norms would escape the legitimate criticisms contained in the dilemmas they are said to face.

1. *MNCs should do no intentional direct harm.* This injunction is clearly not peculiar to multinational corporations. Yet it is a basic norm that can be usefully applied in evaluating the conduct of MNCs. Any company that does produce intentional direct harm clearly violates a basic moral norm.

2. *MNCs should produce more good than bad for the host country.*
   This is an implementation of a general utilitarian principle. But this norm restricts the

extent of that principle by the corollary that, in general, more good will be done by helping those in most need, rather than by helping those in less need at the expense of those in greater need. Thus the utilitarian analysis in this case does not consider that more harm than good might justifiably be done to the host country if the harm is offset by greater benefits to others in developed countries. MNCs will do more good only if they help the host country more than they harm it.

3. *MNCs should contribute by their activities to the host country's development.*

   If the presence of an MNC does not help the host country's development, the MNC can be correctly charged with exploitation, or using the host country for its own purposes at the expense of the host country.

4. *MNCs should respect the human rights of its employees.*

   MNCs should do so whether or not local companies respect those rights. This injunction will preclude gross exploitation of workers, set minimum standards for pay, and prescribe minimum standards for health and safety measures.

5. *MNCs should pay their fair share of taxes.*
   Transfer pricing has as its aim taking advantage of different tax laws in different countries. To the extent that it involves deception, it is itself immoral. To the extent that it is engaged in to avoid legitimate taxes, it exploits the host country, and the MNC does not bear its fair share of the burden of operating in that country.

6. *To the extent that local culture does not violate moral norms, MNCs should respect the local culture and work with it, not against it.*
   MNCs cannot help but produce some changes in the cultures in which they operate. Yet, rather than simply transferring American ways into other lands, they can consider changes in operating procedures, plant planning, and the like, which take into account local needs and customs.

7. *MNCs should cooperate with the local government in the development and enforcement of just background institutions.*
   Instead of fighting a tax system that aims at appropriate redistribution of incomes, instead of preventing the organization of labor, and instead of resisting attempts at improving the health and safety standards of the host country, MNCs should be supportive of such measures.

Thesis 3: Wholesale attacks on multinationals are most often overgeneralizations. Valid moral evaluations can be best made by using the above moral criteria for context-and-corporation-specific studies and analysis.

Broadside claims, such that all multinationals exploit underdeveloped countries or destroy their culture, are too vague to determine their accuracy. United States multinationals have in the past engaged—and some continue to engage—in immoral practices. A case by case study is the fairest way to make moral assessments. Yet we can distinguish five types of business operations that raise very different sorts of moral issues: 1) banks and financial institutions; 2) agricultural enterprises; 3) drug companies and hazardous industries; 4) extractive industries; and 5) other manufacturing and service industries.

If we were to apply our seven general criteria in each type of case, we would see some of the differences among them. Financial institutions do not generally employ many people. Their function is to provide loans for various types of development. In the case of South Africa they do not do much—if anything—to undermine apartheid, and by lending to the government they usually strengthen the government's policy of apartheid. In this case, an argument can be made that they do more harm than good—an argument that several banks have seen to be valid, causing them to discontinue their South African operations even before it became financially dangerous to continue lending money to that government. Financial institutions can help and have helped development tremendously. Yet the servicing of debts that many Third World countries face condemns them to impoverishment for the foreseeable future. The role of financial institutions in this situation is crucial and raises special and difficult moral problems, if not dilemmas.

Agricultural enterprises face other demands. If agricultural multinationals buy the best lands and use them for export crops while insufficient arable land is left for the local population to grow enough to feed itself, then MNCs do more harm than good to the host country—a violation of one of the norms I suggested above.

Drug companies and dangerous industries pose different and special problems. I have suggested that FDA standards are not morally mandatory standards. This should not be taken to mean that drug companies are bound only by local laws, for the local laws may require less than morality requires in the way of supplying adequate information and of not producing intentional, direct harm.[3] The same type of observation applies to hazardous industries. While an asbestos company will probably not be morally required to take all the measures mandated by OSHA regulations, it cannot morally leave its workers completely unprotected.[4]

Extractive industries, such as mining, which remove minerals from a country, are correctly open to the charge of exploitation unless they can show that they do more good than harm to the host country and that they do not benefit only either themselves or a repressive elite in the host country.

Other manufacturing industries vary greatly, but as a group they have come in for sustained charges of exploitation of workers and the undermining of the host country's culture. The above guidelines can serve as a means of sifting the valid from the invalid charges.

Thesis 4: On the international level and on the national level in many Third World countries the lack of adequate just background institutions makes the use of clear moral norms all the more necessary.

American multinational corporations operating in Germany and Japan, and German and Japanese multinational corporations operating in the United States, pose no special moral problems. Nor do the operations of Brazilian multinational corporations in the United States or Germany. Yet First World multinationals operating in Third World countries have come in for serious and sustained moral criticism. Why?

A major reason is that in the Third World the First World's MNCs operate without the types of constraints and in societies that do not have the same kinds of redistributive mechanisms as in the developed countries. There is no special difficulty in United States multinationals operating in other First World countries because in general these countries *do* have appropriate background institutions.[5]

More and more Third World countries are developing controls on multinationals that insure the companies do more good for the country than harm.[6] Authoritarian regimes that care more for their own wealth than for the good of their people pose difficult moral conditions under which to operate. In such instances, the guidelines above may prove helpful.

Just as in the nations of the developed, industrial world the labor movement serves as a counter to the dominance of big business, consumerism serves as a watchdog on practices harmful to the consumer, and big government serves as a restraint on each of the vested interest groups, so international structures are necessary to provide the proper background constraints on international corporations.

The existence of MNCs is a step forward in the unification of mankind and in the formation of a global community. They provide the economic base and substructure on which true international cooperation can be built. Because of their special position and the special opportunities they enjoy, they have a special responsibility to promote the cooperation that only they are able to accomplish in the present world.

Just background institutions would preclude

any company's gaining a competitive advantage by engaging in immoral practices. This suggests that MNCs have more to gain than to lose by helping formulate voluntary, UN (such as the code governing infant formulae),[7] and similar codes governing the conduct of all multinationals. A case can also be made that they have the moral obligation to do so.

Thesis 5: The moral burden of MNCs do not exonerate local governments from responsibility for what happens in and to their country. Since responsibility is linked to ownership, governments that insist on part or majority ownership incur part or majority responsibility.

The attempts by many underdeveloped countries to limit multinationals have shown that at least some governments have come to see that they can use multinationals to their own advantage. This may be done by restricting entry to those companies that produce only for local consumption, or that bring desired technology transfers with them. Some countries demand majority control and restrict the export of money from the country. Nonetheless, many MNCs have found it profitable to engage in production under the terms specified by the host country.

What host countries cannot expect is that they can demand control without accepting correlative responsibility. In general, majority control implies majority responsibility. An American MNC, such as Union Carbide, which had majority ownership of its Indian Bhopal plant, should have had primary control of the plant. Union Carbide, Inc. can be held liable for the damage the Bhopal plant caused because Union Carbide, Inc. did have majority ownership.[8] If Union Carbide did not have effective control, it is not relieved of its responsibility. If it could not exercise the control that its responsibility demanded, it should have withdrawn or sold off part of its holdings in that plant. If India had had majority ownership, then it would have had primary responsibility for the safe operation of the plant.

This is compatible with maintaining that if a company builds a hazardous plant, it has an obligation to make sure that the plant is safe and that those who run it are properly trained to run it safely. MNCs cannot simply transfer dangerous technologies without consideration of the people who will run them, the local culture, and similar factors. Unless MNCs can be reasonably sure that the plants they build will be run safely, they cannot morally build them. To do so would be to will intentional, direct harm.

The theses and guidelines that I have proposed are not a panacea. But they suggest how moral norms can be brought to bear on the dilemmas American multinationals face and they suggest ways out of apparent or false dilemmas. If MNCs observed those norms, they could properly avoid the moral sting of their critics' charges, even if their critics continued to level charges against them.

NOTES

1. The literature attacking American MNCs is extensive. Many of the charges mentioned in this paper are found in Richard J. Barnet and Ronald E. Muller, *Global Reach: The Power of the Multinational Corporations,* New York: Simon & Schuster, 1974, and in Pierre Jalee, *The Pillage of the Third World,* translated from the French by Mary Klopper, New York and London: Modern Reader Paperbacks, 1968.

2. The position I advocate does not entail moral relativism, as my third thesis shows. The point is that although moral norms apply uniformly across cultures, U.S. standards are not the same as moral standards, should themselves be morally evaluated, and are relative to American conditions, standard of living, interests, and history.

3. For a fuller discussion of multinational drug companies see Richard T. De George, *Business Ethics,* 2nd ed., New York: Macmillan, 1986, pp. 363–367.

4. For a more detailed analysis of the morality of exporting hazardous industries, see my *Business Ethics,* 367–372.

5. This position is consistent with that developed by John Rawls in his *A Theory of Justice,* Cambridge,

Mass.: Harvard University Press, 1971, even though Rawls does not extend his analysis to the international realm. The thesis does not deny that United States, German, or Japanese policies on trade restrictions, tariff levels, and the like can be morally evaluated.

6. See, for example, Theodore H. Moran, "Multinational Corporations: A Survey of Ten Years' Evidence," Georgetown School of Foreign Service, 1984.

7. For a general discussion of UN codes, see Wolfgang Fikentscher, "United Nations Codes of Conduct: New Paths in International Law," *The American Journal of Comparative Law,* 30 (1980), pp. 577–604.

8. The official Indian Government report on the Bhopal tragedy has not yet appeared. The Union Carbide report was partially reprinted in the *New York Times,* March 21, 1985, p. 48. The major *New York Times* reports appeared on December 9, 1984, January 28, 30, and 31, and February 3, 1985.

Ethical Dilemmas of Multinational Enterprises: An Analysis of Nestle's Traumatic Experience with the Infant Formula Controversy

James E. Post*

INTRODUCTION

Among the many different types of dilemmas faced by multinational enterprises are those related to its marketing of consumer products. It has now become apparent that the marketing of

Excerpted from "Ethical Dilemmas of Multinational Enterprise: An Analysis of Nestle's Traumatic Experience with the Infant Formula Controversy" by James E. Post, in *Ethics and the Multinational Enterprise* edited by W. Michael Hoffman, Ann E. Lange, and David A. Fedo (Lanham, MD: University Press of America, 1986). Copyright © 1986 by James E. Post. Reprinted by permission of the author.

*Department of Management Policy, Boston University.

First World foods in Third World nations poses a special type of concern to the populations and governments of host nations, and to the would-be marketers themselves. While there are a number of products that one can cite as illustrative of the generic issue, none has so sharply and clearly defined it as the controversy surrounding the marketing and promotion of infant formula in the developing world.

My perspective on the infant formula controversy, industry, and on Nestle in particular, is derived from more than a decade of research. In addition to field research on infant formula marketing in Latin America, Africa, and Southern Asia, I have served as a consultant to the World Health Organization (WHO) in the development of the international marketing code, and testified at congressional and United States Senate hearings on these issues. Most recently, it has included about 18 months of service on the Nestle Infant Formula Audit Commission, which was created to monitor the company's compliance with marketing policies that were drafted for the purpose of implementing the WHO Code.

Rest assured, this is no apologia for Nestle. I know that some of their managers disagree with my interpretation of the evidence. That troubles me little, for I cannot think of an ethical dilemma that does not breed some disagreement among caring participants. Were it otherwise, I doubt it could be called a dilemma. Among the various types of ethical dilemmas confronting the managers of multinational enterprises (MNEs) are those tied to the introduction of products developed and used in one social environment into a significantly different environment. I prefer to term this the introduction of First World Products in Third World Markets.

The infant formula situation involves a product which is not defective in itself. This distinguishes it from such cases as the dumping of products which are unsafe or deemed unacceptable for sale in the United States, but are accepted for sale in another nation (e.g., Tris-treated sleepwear).

Infant formula is also not harmful to the consumer (user) when used properly under appropriate conditions. This distinguishes it from products such as tobacco, which are, in the view of most health professionals, per se dangerous to all users.

Infant formula is the *definitive* example, however, of a First World product which is safe when used properly, but which is *demanding*. That is, when risk conditions are present, it can be—and is—potentially harmful to users.

The fundamental ethical dilemma for MNE managers, then, is whether such a product can be marketed when it cannot be guaranteed, or reasonably expected, that it will be used by people who meet the minimum conditions necessary for safe use.

EVOLUTION OF A PUBLIC ISSUE

The criticism of the infant formula manufacturers for their aggressive marketing behavior in developing nations became a serious issue in 1970. Prior to that time, individual physicians and health workers had criticized promotional practices, but there was nothing to suggest an organized campaign of criticism. In 1970, however, the Protein-Calorie Advisory Group (PAG) of the United Nations held a meeting in Bogota to discuss the problem of infant malnutrition and disease in developing nations. Participants pointed a finger of blame at the industry, charging that it pushed its products to mothers, many of whom lived in circumstances that made the use of such products a highly risky adventure. First, infant formula must be sold in powdered form in tropical environments, requiring that the mother mix the powder with locally available water. When water supplies are of poor quality, as so often is the case in the developing nations, infants are exposed to disease. Second, since the product must be mixed, preparation instructions are important, and mothers must be able to read. Unfortunately, the rate of illiteracy is very high in many developing nations. Thirdly, since infant

formulas are relatively expensive to purchase, there is a temptation to overdilute the powder with water. This effort to "stretch" its uses enables the mother to go a few extra days without buying a new supply. Unfortunately, overdiluted formula preparations provide very poor nutrition to the baby. Thus mothers who came to the health clinics with malnourished babies often reported that a five day supply of formula had been stretched to ten days or more. Having decided to bottlefeed their babies in order to improve their chances for a healthy life, many mothers discovered to their horror that they had actually been starving their little ones. Because corporate advertising by the infant formula companies had promoted the idea that bottlefeeding was better than breastfeeding, a view with which doctors disagreed, there was a sharp condemnation of the industry and its behavior at the Bogota meeting.

Management scholars now understand that public issues often proceed through a predictable series of phases in their evolution. Some refer to this as the "public issue life cycle," modelled after the product life cycle described in marketing research. The public issue life cycle can be thought of as a measure of continuing public concern about an underlying problem.

Phase I of the issue life cycle involved rising awareness and sensitivity to the facts of the issue. In the infant formula controversy, this phase began with the PAG Meeting in 1970 and continued for several years. An important element in the process of rising awareness was the activity of journalist Peter Muller who, with support from the British charity group, War on Want, travelled to Africa in the early 1970s to study allegations of marketing abuses. Muller wrote several articles and a pamphlet which War on Want published in 1974 under the title, *The Baby Killer*. These publications began to draw the attention of a broader public to the problem of sick and dying children, and the connection between commercial practices and this tragedy.

Because Nestle was, and still is, the industry's largest producer and seller of infant formula products, Muller encountered many examples of Nestle advertising and promotional practices in Africa. Indeed, Nestle employees were willing to speak with Muller, while those of other companies were often much less willing. Not surprisingly, then, *The Baby Killer* pamphlet included Nestle actions as examples of unethical industry behavior. This became very important, because a Swiss public action group, Third World Action Group, reprinted the Muller pamphlet in Switzerland under the new title, *Nestle Kills Babies!*

Nestle immediately sued the group for defamation, and in 1975 the case came to trial in Switzerland. Because the trial involved several hearings, with experts from developing nations brought in to testify, the media began to show increasing interest in the story. It became quite clear that although the trial involved only Nestle and the defendants, the entire infant formula industry was being examined and criticized for their actions in the developing nations. Thus, the trial was a turning point in two important ways. First, public interest in the issue expanded greatly as the newspaper stories began to carry the details of what one doctor called ''commerciogenic malnutrition''—malnutrition brought about because of corporate commercial practices. Second, the infant formula industry began to respond as an industry, having formed an international association, known as the International Council of Infant Foods Industries (ICIFI). The council, whose existence was announced in Switzerland at the time of the trial, made an immediate effort to develop an international code of marketing which addressed some of the most criticized marketing practices. In this Phase II of the life cycle, both the critics, the media, and the industry recognized that the issue had become an important political matter, as well as a public health concern.

Between 1975 and 1978, the infant formula controversy became increasingly politicized. The media in Europe and the United States paid increasing attention to the conflict. Each newspaper or magazine story brought about more awareness in the general public. The critics highlighted the terrible tragedy of dying and sick children, while the companies, including Nestle, tried to respond to the criticism individually and through ICIFI. The political pressure mounted against the industry. In 1977, an official consumer boycott of Nestle and its products was begun in the United States. Interest in the boycott spread quickly, in part because many member churches of the National Council of Churches had been concerned about the problems of world hunger. The Nestle boycott gave church leaders an opportunity to educate their congregations about the problem of world hunger and suggest a practical course of action that would pressure companies to act responsibly in dealing with the poor and needy of the Third World. The National Council of Churches had been concerned about many corporate responsibility issues, and had a special research and action unit known as the Interfaith Center on Corporate Responsibility (ICCR). ICCR became actively involved in the boycott campaign, and helped spread the message of consumer action to hundreds of thousands of people in the United States.

The high point of Phase II of the infant formula controversy occurred when boycott sponsors were able to convince the staff of United States Senator Edward Kennedy to hold hearings into the infant formula marketing controversy. These hearings were held in May, 1978 in Washington, DC, and occurred at a time when Senator Kennedy was widely rumored to be considering a campaign for the presidency against incumbent President Jimmy Carter. The media followed Kennedy's every action. On the day of the public hearing, every American television network had cameras in the hearing room, and many famous reporters sat at special tables to hear the testimony of witnesses. The witnesses were heard in three groups. First, people who had worked in developing nations told a tale of human tragedy and marketing abuses by the companies. The second panel consisted of experts in public health (Pan American Health Organization, World Health Organization), medicine, and the author of this paper, who was an expert on the industry. The third panel consisted of the company representatives. Nestle was represented by the head of its Brazilian operation, and the three American companies were represented by senior executives from their corporate headquarters.

The Kennedy hearings were a landmark in the history of this controversy. They represented the highest level of media attention and political attention that had been achieved in nearly eight years of conflict. Critics had to be pleased with their success. Moreover, Nestle behaved in a way that actually strengthened the claims of the boycott supporters and organizers. The company's representative charged that the consumer boycott was a conspiracy of church organizations and an indirect attack on the free enterprise system. Senator Kennedy exploded in anger at the charge that the churchmen and health workers were part of a conspiracy to undermine the free enterprise system. The Nestle statement was a political disaster. Every television program featured the testimony and the reaction from the political leaders in attendance. Nestle was denounced for its statement and its foolishness.

Phase III of an evolving public issue occurs when some governmental or other formal action begins to develop. In a single nation, this may take the form of a regulatory standard, a piece of legislation, or a government program. In the infant formula controversy, formal action took the form of an international code of marketing conduct which industry and national governments would support. Following the Kennedy hearings, the Director-General of the World Health Organization agreed to convene a meeting of interested parties to lay the groundwork for international action. An important meeting took place in 1979, with delegates calling upon WHO to draft an international marketing code. The code development process took several years, required extensive negotiation, and even-

tually produced a document that was adopted by the World Health Assembly (the governing body of WHO) in 1981. Throughout this process, Nestle and other industry members actively participated in the discussions and lobbied for particular terms and provisions. In advance of the World Health Assembly vote, Nestle was the only company to publicly state that it would follow the code if it was adopted.

Phase IV of a public issue involves the process of implementing the new policy throughout the organizations involved. This is called "institutionalizing" the policy action. Nestle considered how to implement the WHO Code's provisions following the World Health Assembly's adoption. But there existed a number of very serious obstacles. Many of the Code's terms were imprecise, leaving unanswered questions about the proper interpretations. WHO was reluctant to provide continuing interpretation and reinterpretation of the Code's terms, as this would require a staff of lawyers and a continuing commitment. In addition, the Nestle boycott continued in both the United States and Europe. Critics continued to pressure the company, and offered alternative interpretations of various code provisions. WHO had no desire to get further drawn into the dispute between the company and its adversaries. Thus, Nestle was left to negotiate proper interpretations with members of what was now called the International Nestle Boycott Committee (INBC).

Since 1981, Nestle has continued to pursue a process of institutionalizing the provisions of the WHO Code by transforming those requirements into policy instructions for its own sales and marketing personnel. A number of innovations have been created to assist this process. These will be discussed below. In early 1984, the international boycott group suspended the Nestle boycott, following extensive negotiations about such critical issues as product labelling, marketing in health facilities, gifts to medical personnel, and provisions of free supplies to health institutions. By October 1984, the INBC leaders had concluded that Nestle's commitment to implement the policies had proceeded well enough to permit them to terminate the boycott. Its conclusion was announced at a joint press conference attended by boycott leaders and senior Nestle managers. Nearly fifteen years after the first formal complaints began, Nestle had managed to close the controversy over its marketing activities.

ETHICAL ISSUES AND LESSONS

Throughout this long conflict, Nestle has faced a variety of difficult ethical issues. Some of the broad issues and lessons are summarized below.

All businesses which sell their products in developing nations must consider two basic questions: (1) Is the product an appropriate one for the people in that country? and (2) Are the proposed tactics for marketing the product proper for selling the products but not misleading consumers for whom the product is not appropriate? As Nestle discovered, both questions are easily overlooked by managers when they are concerned with sales and profits.

Managers should recognize the following points about the appropriateness of products in developing nation markets.

1. Products which are appropriate and acceptable in one social environment may be inappropriate in the social environment of another nation.

Infant formula products are demanding products. There must be pure water with which to prepare them, refrigeration to safely store unused prepared formula, and customers must be able to read instructions and have the income to purchase adequate quantities of the products. The greater the existence of these *risk factors*, the less appropriate the product becomes for marketing. This phenomenon applies to many other consumer products as well.

2. Good products, made without defects, may still be inappropriate because of the inherent riskiness of the environment in which those products are to be used.

Nestle and its competitors often stated that the market they sought to reach consisted only of those who could safely use the product, and who had adequate income. However, the evidence from many developing nations continuously showed that vast numbers of the population did not meet the necessary requirements for safe use of the product. By selling formula products to such people, managers could know with virtual certainty that there would be overdilution, improper mixing, or contamination with impure water. As Nestle discovered, many people would denounce and criticize any company that sought to sell its infant formula products under such conditions. When a large part of the population cannot safely use a product, *and* the company cannot effectively segment the market to ensure that only qualified consumers purchase and use it, there may be no choice for the business but to halt sales in that community.

3. Companies may not close their eyes once a product is sold. There is a continuing responsibility to monitor product use, resale, and consumption to determine who is actually using the product, and how. Post-marketing reviews are a necessary step in this process.

Repeatedly, Nestle and its industry colleagues claimed that they had no desire or intention to see unqualified consumers use their formula products. In 1978 at the United States Senate hearings, representatives from Nestle, Abbott Laboratories, American Home Products, and Bristol-Myers were asked whether they conducted any post-marketing research studies to determine who actually used their products. Each company representative answered that his company did no such research and did not know who actually used its products. Naturally, critics attacked the companies for such a careless attitude toward learning the true facts surrounding their products.

4. Products which have been sold to consumers who cannot safely use them must be demarketed. Demarketing may involve withdrawal or recall of products, limitations of the selling of the product, or even a halting of future sales.

The infant formula controversy raised the issue of whether, and when, companies should demarket products which have been commercially successful, but also harmful to innocent consumers. Nestle and its competitors gradually changed their marketing practices, and recognized that infant formula was not the same "mass market" product that it had once been. The World Health Organization Code specifically indicated that marketing had to be done in ways that guaranteed that the users of formula products had proper information to use the product safely, and to make an intelligent choice about whether or not infant formula was even an appropriate product for them to use. Much of this is to be done by insisting that companies not market directly to mothers, but channel product supplies and advice through health institutions which can ensure that unbiased health information is received by the mother.

5. Marketing strategies must be appropriate to the circumstances of consumers, the social and economic environment in which they live, and to political realities.

Consumer advertising to people for whom product use is highly risky is unacceptable and unethical marketing behavior. Critics of the infant formula industry continued to find evidence of highly aggressive and misleading advertising by companies for many years after the issue became well known. Mass marketing became an unacceptable and inappropriate marketing strategy for infant formula products. The companies, however, had difficulty segmenting their markets and drawing back from the mass market approach. It was only through an industry-wide effort, and then the WHO Code, that managers began to accept that it was more appropriate to focus marketing promotions through the health care system then to consumers directly.

6. Marketing techniques are inappropriate when they exploit a condition of consumer vulnerability.

Many firms in the industry used "milk nurses" during the 1960s and 1970s. These were sales personnel who dressed in nurses uniforms and visited new mothers in hospitals. They would try to encourage the mother to allow their babies to be fed formula, rather than breastfeed, in order to encourage formula adoptions. Since a mother loses the ability to breastfeed after several days of not doing so, such a decision would then require that the baby continue to be fed from a bottle for the next six months. This would be good for formula sales, if the mother could afford to buy it, but might be bad for the baby if the mother had to find a cheaper substitute product to put in the bottle. In South America, for example, members of my own research team saw mothers feeding a mixture of corn starch and water to babies because they had no money to buy formula. Mothers who have given birth are quite vulnerable, and the use of the milk nurses took advantage of that vulnerability in ways that were unethical and unfair. Actions which exploit consumer vulnerability and result in harm are inappropriate marketing tactics.

7. Marketing strategies should be formulated in such a way as to permit flexibility and adjustment to new circumstances.

In the early 1970s, Nestle management knew that critics had a legitimate concern for the sales practices of the industry, but were unable to change their marketing activities in response. The company seemed to be "locked in" to a strategy of resistance, denial, and anger at such charges. In retrospect, it seems that Nestle needed time to change its marketing strategy from a mass-market, consumer-advertising approach, to one which emphasized promotion through the medical and health care system. It took Nestle much longer to change its marketing strategy than it took many of its competitors. This may have been because of pressures from field managers or from the product marketing staff, which denied the truth of the critics' charges. Whatever the case, the company was injured by its slow response to criticism, and its seeming inability to find an alternative way to continue marketing its products. A company which can only market its products in one way is very vulnerable to public issues and political pressures.

CONCLUSION

Nestle's traumatic experience with the infant formula controversy has finally come to an end, but the impact is likely to last for many years. The company suffered a major blow to its reputation and to the morale of its people. It is traumatic and difficult for people to be told they are working for a company which "kills babies." Today, Nestle's senior management is again working to restore the company's economic and cultural fabric. Its future success will depend upon much more than sales and profits. Nestle has been a successful institution as well as a successful business. Institutions represent a structure of values, and it is this structure which was most sharply affected by the long controversy over infant formula.

If a historian writes the history of Nestle one hundred years from now, will he or she include

a reference to the infant formula controversy? Very likely yes. The conflict continued for more than ten years, cost the company many millions of dollars of revenue, expenses, and profits, and damaged or destroyed the careers of a number of its promising managers. It is impossible to say how long it will take for the company to regain its good name and for the public to once again think of Nestle as a good corporate citizen.

Multinational corporations must learn to anticipate conflicts of the sort faced by Nestle, and be prepared to respond in ways that not only justify what the company is doing but also deal with the legitimate concerns of the critics. Union Carbide cannot forget its experience in Bhopal, India; Unilever cannot ignore its experience with Persil in England; Johnson & Johnson cannot forget its experience with Tylenol in the United States; and Nestle cannot forget its experience with infant formula. Each of these experiences involved a company with a good reputation, successful business strategies, and a major public credibility problem. The resolution of each dilemma required a careful integration of public affairs strategies with the business strategy for the company. And each situation demanded and required that the company's managers recognize the *common interest* that existed between the corporation and the public. In the long run, there is no other way to harmonize the legitimate interests of companies with the legitimate interests of the public.

Section B
Bribery

What's Wrong with Bribery

Scott Turow*

The question on the floor is what is wrong with bribery? I am not a philosopher and thus my answer to that question may be less systematic than others, but it is certainly no less deeply felt. As a federal prosecutor I have worked for a number of years now in the area of public corruption. Over that course of time, perhaps out of instincts of self-justification, or, so it seems, sharpened moral insights, I have come to develop an abiding belief that bribery is deeply immoral.

We all know that bribery is unlawful and I believe that the legal concepts in this area are in fact grounded in widely accepted moral intuitions. Bribery as defined by the state of Illinois and construed by the United States Court of Appeals for the Seventh Circuit in the case of *United States* v. *Isaacs,* in which the former Governor of Illinois, Otto Kerner, was convicted for bribery, may be said to take place in these instances: Bribery occurs when property or personal advantage is offered, without the authority of law, to a public official with the intent that the public official act favorably to the offeror at any time or fashion in execution of the public official's duties.

Under this definition of bribery, the crime consists solely of an unlawful offer, made or accepted with a prohibited state of mind. No particular act need be specified; and the result is immaterial.

This is merely a matter of definition. Oddly the moral underpinnings of bribery are clearer in the context of another statute—the criminal law against mail

Found in *Journal of Business Ethics,* Vol. 4, No. 4 (1985), pp. 249–251. Copyright © 1985 by D. Reidel Publishing Company. Reprinted by permission of Kluwer Academic Publishers.

*Deputy Chief at the Criminal Receiving and Appellate Division of the U.S. Attorney's office and author of *One L* and *Presumed Innocent.*

fraud. Federal law has no bribery statute of general application; it is unlawful of course to bribe federal officials, to engage in a pattern of bribery, or to engage in bribery in certain other specified contexts, e.g., to influence the outcome of a sporting contest. But unlike the states, the Congress, for jurisdictional reasons, has never passed a general bribery statute, criminalizing *all* instances of bribery. Thus, over time the federal mail fraud statute has come to be utilized as the vehicle for some bribery prosecutions. The theory, adopted by the courts, goes to illustrate what lawyers have thought is wrong with bribery.

Mail fraud/bribery is predicated on the theory that someone—the bribee's governmental or private employer—is deprived, by a bribe, of the recipient's undivided loyalties. The bribee comes to serve two masters and as such is an 'unfaithful servant.' This breach of fiduciary duty, when combined with active efforts at concealment becomes actionable under the mail fraud law, assuming certain other jurisdictional requisites are met. Concealment, as noted, is another essential element of the crime. An employee who makes no secret of his dual service cannot be called to task; presumably his employer is thought to have authorized and accepted the divided loyalties. For this reason, the examples of maitre d's accepting payments from customers cannot be regarded as fully analogous to instances of bribery which depend on persons operating under false pretenses, a claimed loyalty that has in truth been undermined.

Some of the stricter outlines of what constitutes bribery, in the legal view, can be demonstrated by example. Among the bribery prosecutions with which I have spent the most time is a series of mail fraud/bribery cases arising out of corruption at the Cook County Board of Appeals. The Board of Appeals is a local administrative agency, vested with the authority to review and revise local real estate property tax assessments. After a lengthy grand jury investigation, it became clear that the Board of Appeals was a virtual cesspool, where it was commonplace for lawyers practicing before the Board to make regular cash payments to some decisionmakers. The persons accused of bribery at the Board generally relied on two defenses. Lawyers and tax consultants who made the payments often contended that the payments were, in a fashion, a necessity; the Board was so busy, so overcome by paperwork, and so many other people were paying, that the only way to be sure cases would be examined was to have an 'in' with an official whom payments had made friendly. The first argument also suggests the second: that the payments, whatever their nature, had accomplished nothing untoward, and that any tax reduction petition granted by the bribed official actually deserved the reduction it received.

Neither contention is legally sufficient to remove the payments from the category of bribery. Under the definition above, any effort to cause favorable action constitutes bribery, regardless of the supposedly provocative circumstances. And in practice juries had great difficulty accepting the idea that the lawyers involved had been 'coerced' into making the boxcar incomes—sometimes $300 000 to $400 000 a year—that many of the bribers earned. Nor is the merits of the cases involved a defense, under the above definitions. Again, in practical terms, juries seemed reluctant to believe that lawyers would be passing the Board's deputy commissioners cash under the table if they were really convinced of their cases' merits. But whatever the accuracy of that observation, it is clear that the law prohibits a payment, even to achieve a deserved result.

The moral rationale for these rules of law seems clear to me. Fundamentally, I believe that any payment to a governmental official for corrupt purposes is immoral. The obligation of government to deal with like cases alike is a principal of procedural fairness which is well recognized. But this principal is more than a matter of procedure; it has a deep moral base. We recognize that the equality of humans, their fundamental dignity as beings, demands that each stand as an equal before the government they have joined to create, that each, as Ronald Dworkin has put, has a claim to government's equal concern and respect. Bribery asks that that principal be violated, that some persons be allowed to stand ahead of others, that like cases not be treated alike, and that some persons be preferred. This I find morally repugnant.

Moreover, for this reason, I cannot accept the idea that bribery, which is wrong here, is somehow more tolerable abroad. Asking foreign officials to act in violation of moral principles must, as an abstract matter, be no less improper than asking that of members of our own government; it even smacks of imperialist attitudes. Furthermore, even dealing with the question on this level assumes that there are societies which unequivocally declare that governmental officials may properly deal with the citizenry in a random and unequal fashion. I doubt, in fact, whether any such sophisticated society exists; more than likely, bribery offends the norms and mores of the foreign country as well.

Not only does bribery violate fundamental notions of equality, but it also endangers the vitality of the institution affected. Most bribery centers on persons in discretionary or decision-making positions. Much as we want to believe that bribery invites gross deviations in duty, a prosecutor's experience is that in many cases there are no objectively correct decisions for the bribed official to make. We discovered that this was the case in the Board of Appeals prosecutions where a variety of competing theories of real estate valuation guaranteed that there was almost always some justification, albeit often thin, for what had been done. But it misses the point to look solely at the ultimate actions of the bribed official. Once the promise of payment is accepted, the public official is no longer the impartial decision-maker he is supposed to be. Whatever claims he might make, it is difficult to conceive of a public official who could convince anyone that he entirely disregarded a secret 'gift' from a person affected by his judgments.

Indeed, part of the evil of bribery inheres in the often indetectable nature of some of its results. Once revealed, the presence of bribery thus robs persons affected of a belief in the integrity of *all* prior decisions. In the absolute case, bribery goes to dissolve the social dependencies that require discretionary decision-making at certain junctions in our social scheme. Bribery, then, is a crime against trust; and to the extent that trust, a belief in the good faith of discretionary decision-makers, is essential to certain bureaucratic and governmental structures, bribery is deeply corrosive.

Because of its costs, the law usually deems bribery to be without acceptable justification. Again, I think this is in line with moral intuitions. Interestingly, the law does not regard extortion and bribery as mutually exclusive; extortion requires an apprehension of harm, bribery desire to influence. Often, in fact, the two are coincident. Morally—and legally, perhaps—it would seem that bribery can be justified only if the bribe-giver is truly without alternatives, including the alternative of refusing payment and going to the authorities. Moreover, the briber should be able to show not merely that it was convenient or profitable to pay the bribe, but that the situation presented a choice of evils in which the bribe somehow avoided a greater peril. The popular example in our discussions has been bribing a Nazi camp guard in order to spare concentration camp internees.

Ethics and the Foreign Corrupt Practices Act

Mark Pastin* and Michael Hooker†

Not long ago it was feared that as a fallout of Watergate, government officials would be hamstrung by artificially inflated moral standards. Re-

---

Excerpted from "Ethics and the Foreign Corrupt Practices Act" by Mark Pastin and Michael Hooker, in *Business Horizons* (December 1980). *Business Horizons:* Copyright © 1980, by the Foundation for the School of Business at Indiana University. Reprinted by permission.

*Director, Lincoln Center for Ethics, Arizona State University.

†President, University of Maryland, Baltimore.

cent events, however, suggest that the scapegoat of post-Watergate morality may have become American business rather than government officials.

One aspect of the recent attention paid to corporate morality is the controversy surrounding payments made by American corporations to foreign officials for the purpose of securing business abroad. Like any law or system of laws, the Foreign Corrupt Practices Act (FCPA), designed to control or eliminate such payments, should be grounded in morality, and should therefore be judged from an ethical perspective. Unfortunately, neither the law nor the question of its repeal has been adequately addressed from that perspective.

HISTORY OF THE FCPA

On December 20, 1977 President Carter signed into law S.305, the Foreign Corrupt Practices Act (FCPA), which makes it a crime for American corporations to offer or provide payments to officials of foreign governments for the purpose of obtaining or retaining business. The FCPA also establishes record keeping requirements for publicly held corporations to make it difficult to conceal political payments proscribed by the Act. Violators of the FCPA, both corporations and managers, face severe penalties. A company may be fined up to $1 million, while its officers who directly participated in violations of the Act or had reason to know of such violations, face up to five years in prison and/or $10,000 in fines. The Act also prohibits corporations from indemnifying fines imposed on their directors, officers, employees, or agents. The Act does not prohibit "grease" payments to foreign government employees whose duties are primarily ministerial or clerical, since such payments are sometimes required to persuade the recipients to perform their normal duties.

At the time of this writing, the precise consequences of the FCPA for American business are unclear, mainly because of confusion surrounding the government's enforcement intentions. Vigorous objections have been raised against the Act by corporate attorneys and recently by a few government officials. Among the latter is Frank A. Weil, former Assistant Secretary of Commerce, who has stated, "The questionable payments problem may turn out to be one of the most serious impediments to doing business in the rest of the world."[1]

The potentially severe economic impact of the FCPA was highlighted by the fall 1978 report of the Export Disincentives Task Force, which was created by the White House to recommend ways of improving our balance of trade. The Task Force identified the FCPA as contributing significantly to economic and political losses in the United States. Economic losses come from constricting the ability of American corporations to do business abroad, and political losses come from the creation of a holier-than-thou image.

The Task Force made three recommendations in regard to the FCPA:

- The Justice Department should issue guidelines on its enforcement policies and establish procedures by which corporations could get advance government reaction to anticipated payments to foreign officials.
- The FCPA should be amended to remove enforcement from the SEC, which now shares enforcement responsibility with the Department of Justice.
- The administration should periodically report to Congress and the public on export losses caused by the FCPA.

In response to the Task Force's report, the Justice Department, over SEC objections, drew up guidelines to enable corporations to check any proposed action possibly in violation of the FCPA. In response to such an inquiry, the Justice Department would inform the corporation of its enforcement intentions. The purpose of such an arrangement is in part to circumvent the intent of the law. As of this writing, the SEC appears to have been successful in blocking publication of the guidelines, although Justice recently reaffirmed its intention to publish guidelines. Being more responsive to political winds, Justice may be less inclined than the SEC to rigidly enforce the Act.

Particular concern has been expressed about the way in which bookkeeping requirements of the Act will be enforced by the SEC. The Act requires that company records will "accurately and fairly reflect the transactions and dispositions of the assets of the issuer." What is at question is the interpretation the SEC will give to the requirement and the degree of accuracy and detail it will demand. The SEC's post-Watergate behavior suggests that it will be rigid in requiring the disclosure of all information that bears on financial relationships between the company and any foreign or domestic public official. This level of accountability in record keeping, to which auditors and corporate attorneys have strongly objected, goes far beyond previous SEC requirements that records display only facts material to the financial position of the company.

Since the potential consequences of the FCPA for American businesses and business managers are very serious, it is important that the Act have a rationale capable of bearing close scrutiny. In looking at the foundation of the FCPA, it should be noted that its passage followed in the wake of intense newspaper coverage of the financial dealings of corporations. Such media attention was engendered by the dramatic disclosure of corporate slush funds during the Watergate hearings and by a voluntary disclosure program established shortly thereafter by the SEC. As a result of the SEC program, more than 400 corporations, including 117 of the Fortune 500, admitted to making more than $300 million in foreign political payments in less than ten years.

Throughout the period of media coverage leading up to passage of the FCPA, and especially during the hearings on the Act, there was in all public discussions of the issue a tone of righteous moral indignation at the idea of American companies making foreign political payments. Such payments were ubiquitously termed "bribes," although many of these could more accurately be called extortions, while others were more akin to brokers' fees or sales commissions.

American business can be faulted for its reluctance during this period to bring to public attention the fact that in a very large number of countries, payments to foreign officials are virtually required for doing business. Part of that reluctance, no doubt, comes from the awkwardly difficult position of attempting to excuse bribery or something closely resembling it. There is a popular abhorrence in this country of bribery directed at domestic government officials, and that abhorrence transfers itself to payments directed toward foreign officials as well.

Since its passage, the FCPA has been subjected to considerable critical analysis, and many practical arguments have been advanced in favor of its repeal.[2] However, there is always lurking in back of such analyses the uneasy feeling that no matter how strongly considerations of practicality and economics may count against this law, the fact remains that the law protects morality in forbidding bribery. For example, Gerald McLaughlin, professor of law at Fordham, has shown persuasively that where the legal system of a foreign country affords inadequate protection against the arbitrary exercise of power to the disadvantage of American corporations, payments to foreign officials may be required to provide a compensating mechanism against the use of such arbitrary power. McLaughlin observes, however, that "this does not mean that taking advantage of the compensating mechanism would necessarily make the payment moral."[3]

The FCPA, and questions regarding its enforcement or repeal, will not be addressed adequately until an effort has been made to come to terms with the Act's foundation in morality. While it may be very difficult, or even impossible, to legislate morality (that is, to change the moral character and sentiments of people by passing laws that regulate their behavior), the existing laws undoubtedly still reflect the moral beliefs we hold. Passage of the FCPA in Congress was eased by the simple connection most Congressmen made between bribery, seen as morally repugnant, and the Act, which is designed to prevent bribery.

Given the importance of the FCPA to American business and labor, it is imperative that attention be given to the question of whether there is adequate moral justification for the law.

ETHICAL ANALYSIS OF THE FCPA

The question we will address is not whether each payment prohibited by the FCPA is moral or immoral, but rather whether the FCPA, given all its consequences and ramifications, is itself moral. It is well known that morally sound laws and institutions may tolerate some immoral acts. The First Amendment's guarantee of freedom of speech allows individuals to utter racial slurs. And immoral laws and institutions may have some beneficial consequences, for example, segregationist legislation bringing deep-seated racism into the national limelight. But our concern is with the overall morality of the FCPA.

The ethical tradition has two distinct ways of assessing social institutions, including laws: *End-Point Assessment* and *Rule Assessment*. Since there is no consensus as to which approach is correct, we will apply both types of assessment of the FCPA.

The End-Point approach assesses a law in terms of its contribution to general social well-being. The ethical theory underlying End-Point Assessment is utilitarianism. According to utilitarianism, a law is morally sound if and only if the law promotes the well-being of those affected by the law to the greatest extent practically achievable. To satisfy the utilitarian principle, a law must promote the well-being of those affected by it at least as well as any alternative law that we might propose, and better than no law at all. A conclusive End-Point Assessment of a law requires specification of what constitutes the welfare of those affected by the law, which the liberal tradition generally sidesteps by identifying an individual's welfare with what he takes to be in his interests.

Considerations raised earlier in the paper suggest that the FCPA does not pass the End-Point test. The argument is not the too facile one that we could propose a better law. (Amendments to the FCPA are now being considered.[4]) The argument is that it may be better to have *no* such law than to have the FCPA. The main domestic consequences of the FCPA seem to include an adverse effect on the balance of payments, a loss of business and jobs, and another opportunity for the SEC and the Justice Department to compete. These negative effects must be weighed against possible gains in the conduct of American business within the United States. From the perspective of foreign countries in which American firms do business, the main consequence of the FCPA seems to be that certain officials now accept bribes and influence from non-American businesses. It is hard to see that who pays the bribes makes much difference to these nations.

Rule Assessment of the morality of laws is often favored by those who find that End-Point Assessment is too lax in supporting their moral codes. According to the Rule Assessment approach: A law is morally sound if and only if the law accords with a code embodying correct ethical rules. This approach has no content until the rules are stated, and different rules will lead to different ethical assessments. Fortunately, what we have to say about Rule Assessment of the FCPA does not depend on the details of a particular ethical code.

Those who regard the FCPA as a worthwhile expression of morality, despite the adverse effects on American business and labor, clearly subscribe to a rule stating that it is unethical to bribe. Even if it is conceded that the payments proscribed by the FCPA warrant classifications as bribes, citing a rule prohibiting bribery does not suffice to justify the FCPA.

Most of the rules in an ethical code are not *categorical* rules; they are *prima facie* rules. A categorical rule does not allow exceptions, whereas a prima facie rule does. The ethical rule that a person ought to keep promises is an example of a prima facie rule. If I promise to loan you a book on nuclear energy and later find out that you are a terrorist building a private atomic bomb, I am ethically obligated not to keep my promise. The rule that one ought to keep promises is "overridden" by the rule that one ought to prevent harm to others.

A rule prohibiting bribery is a prima facie rule. There are cases in which morality requires that a bribe be paid. If the only way to get essential medical care for a dying child is to bribe a doctor, morality requires one to bribe the doctor. So adopting an ethical code which includes a rule prohibiting the payment of bribes does not guarantee that a Rule Assessment of the FCPA will be favorable to it.

The fact that the FCPA imposes a cost on American business and labor weighs against the prima facie obligation not to bribe. If we suppose that American corporations have obligations, tantamount to promises, to promote the job security of their employees and the investments of shareholders, these obligations will also weigh against the obligation not to bribe. Again, if government legislative and enforcement bodies have an obligation to secure the welfare of American business and workers, the FCPA may force them to violate their public obligations.

The FCPA's moral status appears even more dubious if we note that many of the payments prohibited by the Act are neither bribes nor share features that make bribes morally reprehensible. Bribes are generally held to be malefic if they persuade one to act against his good judgement, and consequently purchase an inferior product. But the payments at issue in the FCPA are usually extorted *from the seller*. Further it is arguable that not paying the bribe is more likely to lead to purchase of an inferior product than paying the bribe. Finally, bribes paid to foreign officials may not involve deception when they accord with recognized local practices.

In conclusion, neither End-Point nor Rule Assessment uncovers a sound moral basis for the FCPA. It is shocking to find that a law prohibiting bribery has no clear moral basis, and may even be an immoral law. However, this is precisely what examination of the FCPA from a moral perspective reveals. This is symptomatic of the fact that moral conceptions which were appropriate to a simpler world are not adequate to the complex world in which contemporary business functions. Failure to appreciate this point often leads to righteous condemnation of business, when it should lead to careful reflection on one's own moral preconceptions.

NOTES

1. *National Journal,* June 3, 1978: 880.
2. David C. Gustman, "The Foreign Corrupt Practices Act of 1977," *The Journal of International Law and Economics,* Vol. 13, 1979; 367–401, and Walter S. Surrey, "The Foreign Corrupt Practices Act: Let the Punishment Fit the Crime," *Harvard International Law Journal,* Spring 1979: 203–303.
3. Gerald T. McLaughlin, "The Criminalization of Questionable Foreign Payments by Corporations," *Fordham Law Review,* Vol. 46: 1095.
4. "Foreign Bribery Law Amendments Drafted," *American Bar Association Journal,* February 1980: 135.

Bribery and Ethics: A Reply to Pastin and Hooker

Robert E. Frederick*

In their article on the Foreign Corrupt Practices Act, Mark Pastin and Michael Hooker used both "end-point assessment" and "rule assessment"

Original essay. Copyright © 1990 by Robert E. Frederick. Printed by permission of the author.

*Assistant director, Center for Business Ethics, Bentley College.

to evaluate the FCPA from a moral point of view.[1] They argue that neither method of assessment supports the FCPA and hence that it "has no clear moral basis, and may even be an immoral law."[2] It seems to me, however, that Pastin and Hooker's arguments are not compelling and that there is a sense in which the FCPA does have a sound moral basis. Thus in the remainder of this paper I will give reasons why I think Pastin and Hooker are mistaken. I will begin with their end-point assessment of the FCPA and then turn to the rule assessment. In the final section I will have some brief comments about extortion and the FCPA.

I

End-point assessment is based on the moral theory of utilitarianism. If we use end-point assessment to evaluate a law, then according to Pastin and Hooker it is a morally sound law "if and only if the law promotes the well-being of those affected by the law to the greatest extent practically achievable."[3] They argue that the FCPA has not promoted the well-being of those affected by the law to the greatest extent practically achievable, since it has led to a loss of business and jobs, it has unfavorably affected the balance of payments, and it is a source of discord between government agencies.[4] Hence, they suggest that the FCPA does not pass the end-point test of moral soundness.

It is difficult to judge the strength of this argument against the FCPA, since it is very difficult to find and evaluate objective empirical evidence that either confirms or disconfirms the economic harm allegedly caused by the FCPA. There is anecdotal evidence that the FCPA has caused some firms a loss of business.[5] In a 1983 study of the data, however, John L. Graham finds that "the FCPA has not had a negative effect on U.S. trade," and in a 1987 analysis of U.S. trade in the Mideast, Kate Gillespie concludes that "The FCPA potential to hurt U.S. exports remains unproved."[6] These studies do not show that the FCPA has promoted the well-being of those affected by it to the greatest extent practically achievable, so they do not show that the FCPA passes the end-point assessment test of moral soundness. Perhaps the best we can say about the studies is that they seem to show, not that we are economically any better off for having the FCPA on the books, but rather that we are not any worse off.

Let us suppose, however, that there is good evidence that the FCPA has caused a loss of U.S. exports and a loss of jobs in U.S. export-related industries. Would this show that the FCPA does not pass the end-point assessment? It seems to me it would not. One of the central tenets of utilitarianism is that the well-being of any one person or group of persons is not to count more or be of more moral weight than the well-being of some other person or group of persons. Thus the well-being of people in the United States does not count more than the well-being of people in France or Uganda or China. Now, if the FCPA causes a U.S. firm to lose an export contract, then some foreign competitor must have gotten that contract. Thus it could be that a loss of exports and jobs in the United States would be offset by an increase in exports and jobs in some foreign country. Assuming the people receiving the goods are as well off with either vendor, and since the well-being of people in the United States does not count more than the well-being of people in the country that got the contract, the net effect of the FCPA on economic well-being, once we consider *everyone* affected by it, might be entirely neutral.

If this argument is correct, it shows that from a utilitarian point of view the FCPA is morally neutral. It neither harms nor enhances total economic well-being. Thus, as long as we consider only economic well-being, end-point assessment does not provide moral grounds for either favoring or opposing the law. Of course, it is possible that the FCPA affects well-being in noneconomic ways. For example, one might argue that insofar as the FCPA discourages the corrupt practice of bribery, people both in the United States and abroad are better off. But it seems to me that considerations of well-being, although important, do not address the central moral issues raised by the FCPA. For that we have to turn to rule assessment.

II

Pastin and Hooker claim that a law passes the rule assessment test of moral soundness "if and only if the law accords with a code embodying correct moral rules."[7] They then try to show that the FCPA does not pass the rule assessment test regardless of the actual content of the moral code. This may seem a little extreme, since it may be that the correct moral code contains a rule such as "under no circumstances is bribery morally permissible." But Pastin and Hooker circumvent this problem by claiming that the rule against bribery is always a prima facie rule, i.e., it can be overridden by other moral considerations in appropriate circumstances. They then seem to claim that in the arena of international competition other moral considerations frequently override the rule. And since the FCPA makes no allowance for such instances—it prohibits bribes even in cases where it is morally permissible to offer a bribe—it does not accord with the moral code and does not pass the end-point assessment.

But is the rule against bribery a prima facie rule? And even if it is, are there moral considerations that frequently override it? I will try to show that for certain types of bribery the moral rule against bribery is not a prima facie rule and that in other cases the considerations Pastin and Hooker mention are not overriding. I will begin with a brief description of what I take to be a central case of bribery, and then, using that case as a focal point for discussion, I will say something about why I think bribery is morally wrong.

Suppose you find yourself in the following situation: You are taking a difficult course required for your major. You work hard, go to class, do all the homework, and are well satisfied with the B you receive for a final grade. You happen to find out, however, that an acquaintance of yours made an A in the course even though he missed most of the classes, didn't do the homework, and didn't even show up for the final exam. You know this person is no genius, so you wonder how he did it. You are so curious, in fact, that you decide to ask him. "Well," he replies, "let's just say I know how to spread some money around where it will do the most good."

You are outraged, since the clear implication is that your acquaintance bribed the professor to give him an A. But exactly why are you outraged? Exactly what is wrong with bribery?

The best way to begin to answer that question is to get as clear as we can about the main characteristics of a central case of bribery, such as the one just described. The first thing to note is that the above situation is a kind of social practice which is governed in all essential respects by an agreement or understanding between the participants. This understanding, parts of which may be explicit and parts implicit, is voluntary, at least in the sense that no one is threatened with unjustifiable harm if they do not take the class, and the understanding does not require that any of the participants engage in morally impermissible behavior. In addition, the agreement defines the role, position, or function of each participant in the practice and delineates the kinds of behaviors that are acceptable or unacceptable for each role or position in certain circumstances. For example, even though it may never be explicitly stated, it is a part of the understanding, and undoubtedly a part of your expectations for the course, that all students will be graded solely on the amount and quality of work that they do.

The understanding can be broken in a number of ways, some of which are innocuous and do not involve immoral behavior. But the case of bribery in question is not innocuous. It is an attempt by one student to gain an unfair advantage over the other students by offering the professor something of value in return for the professor violating the understanding by giving the student special treatment. It is, in effect, an attempt by one of the participants to subvert the original understanding by entering into a new one with terms that are incompatible with the terms of the original.

If we put all these things together we can give a complete, although somewhat complex, characterization of central cases of bribery:

> In central cases bribery is a violation of an understanding or agreement which defines a social practice. It is an attempt by one person(s) X to secure an unfair advantage over another person(s) Y by giving a third person(s) Z something of value in exchange for Z giving favorable treatment to X by violating some prima facie duty Z has in virtue of Z's position, role, or function in a morally permissible understanding in which X, Y, and Z are all voluntary participants.

Thus, if my analysis is correct, central cases of bribery always involve social practices in which there are voluntary and morally permissible agreements or understandings, always involve a three-term relationship, and are always attempts to gain an unfair advantage. Noncentral cases of bribery deviate from central cases in that they apparently either do not involve morally permissible agreements, or voluntary agreements, or there is no three-term relationship, or they are not attempts to gain an unfair advantage.

We are finally in a position to say something about what is wrong with central cases of bribery. To give someone an unfair advantage is to give them special treatment that others do not receive, treatment that cannot be justified under the terms of the original understanding, and treatment that the other parties of the understanding would not acquiesce to if they were to know about it. And to give someone such an advantage is, it seems reasonable to say, morally wrong. To paraphrase Aristotle, it is not to treat equals equally. Hence to *accept* a bribe is morally wrong. This does not explain why *offering* a bribe is morally wrong. But I suggest, as a general moral principle, that if one person attempts to get another person to do something morally wrong, then the attempt is also morally wrong. Hence, if I attempt to bribe you to do something that is morally wrong, my attempt to bribe you is morally wrong regardless of whether you accept the bribe or not.

If the rule against bribery is a prima facie rule, then, even for central cases of bribery, there must be some possible circumstances in which it can be overridden. But what circumstances might those be? Under what conditions is it morally permissible to give someone an unfair advantage over others? It seems to me there are no such conditions. It is never morally permissible to give someone an unfair advantage, nor is it morally permissible to induce someone to provide an unfair advantage. Hence, for central cases, the rule against bribery is not a prima facie rule. Thus, the FCPA does have a clear moral basis since it prohibits a type of bribery that is always morally wrong.

III

There are two ways that Pastin and Hooker might respond. We concede, they might say, that central cases of bribery are always wrong. Given your characterization of central cases it could hardly be otherwise. Yet in foreign competition such cases hardly ever occur. Noncentral cases are much more common, and in these cases the rule against bribery is prima facie. Their second response would probably be to point out, as they do in their article, that many of the payments prohibited by the FCPA are not bribes at all, but extortions. And, they might continue, since the FCPA as it is presently formulated prohibits noncentral cases of bribery, and since it prohibits most types of extortion, it lacks a completely

sound moral basis. The reason is that in many instances it is morally permissible to pay bribes in noncentral cases, or to make extortion payments. Thus, the FCPA does not pass the rule assessment test after all, since the FCPA is not in *complete* accord with the correct moral code.

To some extent I am sympathetic with these responses. They do show, I believe, that there are considerations in favor of *revising* the law.[8] This is not too surprising, since there are many laws that could be improved. But it is important to see that, as long as the FCPA is on the books in its present form, the responses I have attributed to Pastin and Hooker give no justification whatever for violating the law by offering a bribe. Let me explain.

Suppose for a moment that we have not made the distinction between central and noncentral cases of bribery, and suppose Pastin and Hooker are correct about the rule against bribery always being a prima facie rule. If it is, then if one has other moral obligations that override the obligation not to bribe, it is morally permissible to offer a bribe. So, in order to determine whether it is permissible, we need to know something about what kinds of obligations might override the rule against bribery.

It is beyond the scope of this article to examine all the different obligations that might override the rule against bribery, but Pastin and Hooker do mention one that deserves discussion. It is the obligation businesspeople have to protect the financial interests of corporate investors. Pastin and Hooker seem to say that in order to protect these interests businesspeople must sometimes offer bribes. I believe, however, that this mistakes the obligations businesspeople actually have. Except in very unusual circumstances they are only obligated to protect the interests of investors *within* the limits established by law. They simply have no obligation to protect those interests by breaking the law. Thus, investors can have no *moral* complaint against a businessperson if they suffer a financial loss because the businessperson refused to break a law.

There are occasions on which it is morally permissible or obligatory to break the law. If the law is flagrantly unjust, or if following the law is likely to cause severe and irremediable harm, then our moral obligations may outweigh our legal ones. But it has not been established that the FCPA is flagrantly unjust or that following it is likely to cause severe and irremediable harm. Hence, there is no justification for concluding that businesspeople are morally required to violate the FCPA by offering bribes, even assuming the rule against bribery is always prima facie.[9]

IV

One aspect of the FCPA that I have only touched on is the prohibition of most types of extortion payments. Typically extortion is an attempt by one person(s) X to gain from another person(s) Y something of value to which X has no rightful claim by an actual or implied threat to harm unjustifiably Y's legitimate interests unless Y yields the thing of value to X. For example, if your professor makes it known to you that she will not grade your work fairly unless you give her $100, then she is attempting extortion.

Although there are clear differences between extortion and central cases of bribery, extortion and noncentral cases of bribery are often confused. For example, an illustration Pastin and Hooker use—''bribing'' a doctor to get essential medical treatment for a child—seems to me a form of extortion instead of bribery.[10]

It is important to distinguish carefully between extortion and bribery, since the moral relationships in extortion are quite different from the moral relationships in bribery. For example, in extortion, but not in bribery, there is a threat to vital interests. And since, I believe, it is always morally wrong to threaten unjustifiably vital interests, demanding extortion is always morally wrong. But it is sometimes morally permissible to make an extortion payment provided that no other reasonable alternative is available to protect threatened vital interests. Paying the doctor

to treat the child is a good example. Thus, there is a sense, absent in cases of bribery, in which someone making an extortion payment is a victim of morally improper behavior.

Pastin and Hooker appear to argue that since it is at least sometimes morally permissible to make extortion payments, and since the FCPA prohibits most types of extortion payments, the FCPA is defective from a moral point of view. But I suggest that we look at the FCPA in a different light. Businesspeople who are forced to make extortion payments to protect threatened interests are victims of a corrupt and immoral practice. We do have moral obligations to protect people from such victimization. How should we do it? It is unlikely that businesspeople acting individually would be able to prevent extortion. What is needed is concerted action, and one effective way to achieve concerted action is through regulation and law.[11] If the FCPA prohibition of extortion payments is strictly enforced, then U.S. firms will not do business in countries where extortion is common. And if we can encourage other countries strictly to enforce laws against extortion, or to pass such laws if they do not have them, then businesspeople in those countries will respond similarly. This will eventually bring pressure on the remaining countries where extortion is common, since it will close them off from products and services that are needed for their economies. And this, in turn, should make them much more likely to enforce laws against demanding extortion. Thus, instead of the FCPA being morally defective, if it is strictly enforced, and if other countries enforce similar laws, the FCPA can advance a worthwhile moral purpose by helping stop the victimization imposed by extortion.

It would be naive to think that extortion can be completely eliminated via the sort of concerted action I have proposed, but I believe it is morally unacceptable to take no action against it at all. Enforcing the FCPA and similar laws is one way to help the international business community avoid falling victim to extortionists' demands. Hence, in my view the FCPA should not be revised to permit extortion payments. If anything, the prohibition of such payments should be strengthened.

There is one misunderstanding I would like to forestall. It might be suggested that prohibiting extortion payments is *imposing* morality. As long as we are concerned with a rule assessment of the FCPA, this is a completely mistaken view. The correct moral code, on which rule assessment is based, is a moral code that applies to everyone at all times. It exempts no one. Thus if a practice is a violation of the code, as I have claimed demanding extortion always is, to refuse to pay extortion is not in any sense imposing morality. It is refusing to participate in and make possible behavior prohibited by the moral code, behavior that is immoral for anyone in any country.

In conclusion I would like to emphasize that my analysis and discussion of bribery and extortion is by no means complete. I have not tried to address many issues that could be raised, and with many others I have undoubtedly raised more questions than I have answered. But I do think I have shown that Pastin and Hooker are incorrect in claiming that the FCPA does not pass either end-point or rule assessment tests of moral soundness. The FCPA may not be a perfect law, but it is not entirely without moral justification.[12]

NOTES

1. Mark Pastin and Michael Hooker, ''Ethics and the Foreign Corrupt Practices Act,'' in *Business Ethics: Readings and Cases in Corporate Morality,* ed. W. Michael Hoffman and Jennifer Mills Moore, 2d ed. (New York: McGraw-Hill Book Company, 1989), pp. 551.
2. Ibid., p. 555.
3. Ibid., p. 553.
4. It is beyond my expertise to say whether, in this case, discord between agencies is a good thing or a bad one, so I will not comment on it.
5. Suk H. Kim, ''On Repealing the Foreign Corrupt Practices Act: Survey and Assessment,'' *Columbia Journal of World Business,* Fall 1981, pp. 16–20. Also see Justin G. Longenecker, Joseph A. McKinney, and Carlos W. Moore, ''The Ethical Issue of International Bribery: A Survey of Attitudes among U.S. Business Professionals,'' *Journal of Business Ethics,* vol. 7, no. 5, May 1988, pp. 341–346.
6. John L. Graham, ''Foreign Corrupt Practices: A Manager's Guide,'' *Columbia Journal of World Business,* Fall 1983, p. 89. Kate Gillespie, ''Middle East Response to the Foreign Corrupt Practices Act,'' *California Management Review,* vol. 29, no. 4, Summer 1987, p. 28.
7. Pastin and Hooker, p. 554.
8. I will argue later that the FCPA prohibition of extortion payments should not be revised.
9. The same sort of argument applies against making extortion payments. However, extortion is more complex, since in some cases severe harm may be caused by refusing to make an extortion payment. The FCPA makes provision for some of these cases. In the final section I will suggest one way such harm might be avoided.
10. There are a number of more difficult cases. For example, it is often said that in some countries bribery is a common practice. But are payments made in such countries bribes or extortion payments? Can bribery be a common practice, or after a certain point does it become institutionalized extortion?
11. Longenecker, McKinney, and Moore, p. 346.
12. My thanks to W. Michael Hoffman and Jennifer Mills Moore for their comments on an earlier draft of this paper.

Bribery in International Business: Whose Problem Is It?

Henry W. Lane* and Donald G. Simpson*

INTRODUCTION

No discussion of problems in international business seems complete without reference to familiar complaints about the questionable business practices North American executives encounter in foreign countries, particularly developing nations. Beliefs about the pervasiveness of dishonesty and the necessity of engaging in such practices as bribery vary widely however, and these differences often lead to vigorous discussions that generate more heat than light. Pragmatists or "realists" may take the attitude that "international business is a rough game and no place for the naive idealist or the faint-hearted. Your competitors use bribes and unless you are willing to meet this standard, competitive practice you will lose business and, ultimately, jobs for workers at home. Besides, it is an accepted business practice in those countries, and when you are in Rome you have to do as the Romans do." "Moralists", on the other hand, believe that cultural relativity is no excuse for unethical behavior. "As Canadians or Americans we should uphold our legal and ethical standards anywhere in the world; and any good American or Canadian knows that bribery, by any euphemism, is unethical and wrong. Bribery increases a product's cost and often is used to secure import licenses for products that no longer can be sold in the developed world. Such corrupting practices also contribute to the moral disintegration of individuals and eventually societies."

The foregoing comments represent extreme polar positions but we are not using these stereotypes to create a 'straw-man' or a false dichotomy about attitudes toward practices like bribery. These extreme viewpoints, or minor variations of them, will be encountered frequently as one meets executives who have experience in developing countries. Some 'realists' and 'moralists' undoubtedly are firm believers in their positions, but many other executives probably gravitate toward one of the poles because they have not found a realistic alternative approach to thinking about the issue of bribery, never mind finding an answer to the problem.

The impetus for this article came from discussions with executives and government officials in Canada and in some developing nations about whether a North American company could conduct business successfully in developing countries without engaging in what would be considered unethical or illegal practices. It was apparent from these talks that the question was an important one and of concern to business executives, but not much practical, relevant information existed on the issue. There was consensus on two points: first, there are a lot of myths surrounding the issue of pay-offs and, second, if anyone had some insights into the problem, executives would appreciate hearing them.

In this article we would like to share what we have learned about the issue during the two years we have been promoting business (licensing agreements, management contracts, joint ventures) between Canadian and African companies. Our intention is not to present a comprehensive treatment of the subject of bribery nor a treatise on ethical behavior. Our intention is to present a practical discussion of some dimensions of the problem based on our experience, discussions and, in some cases investigation of specific incidents.

Excerpted from "Bribery in International Business: Whose Problem Is It?" by Henry W. Lane and Donald G. Simpson in *The Journal of Business Ethics*, vol. 3, no. 1, February 1984, pp. 35–43. Copyright © 1984 by D. Reidel Publishing Company. Reprinted by permission of Kluwer Academic Publishers.

*Promoter of projects for Canadian business ventures.

THE PROBLEM IS MULTI-FACETED

It can be misleading to talk about bribery in global terms without considering some situational specifics such as country, type of business and company. Our discussions with businessmen indicate that the pay-off problem is more prevalent in some countries than in others. Executives with extensive experience probably could rank countries on a scale reflecting the seriousness of the problem. Also, some industries are probably more susceptible to pay-off requests than others. Large construction projects, turn-key capital projects, and large commodity or equipment contracts are likely to be most vulnerable because the scale of the venture may permit the easy disguise of pay-offs, and because an individual, or small group of people, may be in a strategic position to approve or disapprove the project. These projects or contracts are undoubtedly obvious targets also because the stakes are high, the competition vigorous and the possibility that some competitors may engage in pay-offs increased. Finally, some companies may be more vulnerable due to a relative lack of bargaining power or because they have no policies to guide them in these situations. If the product or technology is unique, or clearly superior, and it is needed, the company is in a relatively strong position to resist the pressure. Similarly, those firms with effective operational policies against pay-offs are in a position of strength. Many senior executives have stated, with pride, that their companies have reputations for not making pay-offs and, therefore, are not asked for them. These were executives of large, successful firms that also had chosen not to work in some countries where they could not operate comfortably. These executives often backed up their claims with specific examples in which they walked away from apparently lucrative deals where a pay-off was a requirement.

Two other elements of the situational context of a pay-off situation that vary are the subtlety of the demand and the amount of money in-volved. All pay-off situations are not straight-forward and unambiguous which may make a clear response more difficult.

Finally, pay-offs range in size from the small payments that may help getting through customs without a hassle up to the multi-million dollar bribes that make headlines and embarass governments. The pay-off situations we discuss in this article are more significant than the former, but much smaller and far less dramatic than the latter. These middle-range pay-offs (tens of thousands of dollars) may pose a problem for corporations. They are too big to be ignored but possibly not big enough to be referred to corporate headquarters unless the firm has clear guidelines on the subject. Regional executives or lower level managers may be deciding whether or not these 'facilitating payments' are just another cost of doing business in the developing world.

ON THE OUTSIDE LOOKING IN (THE NORTH AMERICAN PERSPECTIVE)

''It's a corrupt, pay-off society. The problem has spread to all levels. On the face it looks good, but underneath it's rotten.'' Comments such as these are often made by expatriate businessmen and government officials alike. The North American executive may arrive in a Third World country with a stereotype of corrupt officials and is presented with the foregoing analysis by people-on-the-spot who, he feels, should know the situation best. His fears are confirmed.

This scenario may be familiar to some readers. It is very real to us because we have gone through that process. Two cases provide examples of the stories a businessman may likely be told in support of the dismal analysis.

The New Venture: Company Y, a wholly-owned subsidiary of a European multinational, wished to manufacture a new product for export. Government permission was required and Company Y submitted the necessary applications. Sometime later one of Company Y's executives (a local national) informed the Managing Director that the application was approved and the consultant's fee must be paid. The Managing Director knew nothing about a consultant or such a fee. The executive took his boss to a meeting with the consultant—a government official who sat on the application review committee. Both the consultant and the executive claimed to remember the initial meeting at which agreement was reached on the $10,000 fee. A few days later the Managing Director attended a cocktail party at the home of a high ranking official in the same agency. This official recommended that the fee be paid. The Managing Director decided against paying the fee and the project ran into unexpected delays. At this point the Managing Director asked the parent company's legal department for help. Besides the delay, the situation was creating a problem between the Managing Director and his executives as well as affecting the rest of the company. He initially advised against payment but after watching the company suffer, acquiesced with the approval of the parent company. The fee was re-negotiated downward and the consultant paid. What was the result? Nothing! The project was not approved.

The Big Sale: Company Z, which sold expensive equipment, established a relationship with a well placed government official on the first trip to the country. This official, and some other nationals, assured Company Z representatives that they would have no trouble getting the contract. On leaving the country, Company Z representatives had a letter of intent to purchase the equipment. On the second trip Company Z representatives brought the detailed technical specifications for a certain department head to approve. The department head refused to approve the specifications and further efforts to have the government honour its promise failed. The deal fell through. Company Z's analysis of the situation, which became common knowledge in business and government circles, was that a competitor paid the department head to approve its equipment and that the government reneged on its obligation to purchase Company Z equipment.

The Big Sale Re-visited: After the representatives of Company Z received what they described as a letter of intent to purchase the equipment they returned home. On the second visit they had to deal with the department head to receive his approval for the technical specifications.

While in the country, the visiting executive may even have met Company Z's agent in the 'Big Sale' who confirms the story. Corruption is rampant, and in the particular case of the 'Big Sale' he claims to know that the department head received the money and from whom. The case is closed! An honest North American company cannot function in this environment—or so it seems.

At the meeting they told the department head that he need not worry about the details and just sign-off on the necessary documents. If he had any questions regarding the equipment he could inspect it in two weeks time in their home country. The department head's initial responses were: (1) he would not rubber stamp anything, and (2) how could this complex equipment which was supposedly being custom made for his country's needs be inspected in two weeks when he had not yet approved the specifications.

As he reviewed the specifications he noticed a significant technical error and brought it to the attention of Company Z's representatives. They became upset with this 'interference' and inferred that they would use their connections in high places to ensure his compliance. When asked again to sign the documents he refused, and the company reps left saying that they would have him removed from his job.

After this meeting the Premier of the country became involved and asked the company officials to appear before him. They arrived with the Premier's nephew for a meeting with the Premier and his top advisors. The Premier told his nephew that he had no business being there and directed him to leave. The company officials then had to face the Premier and his advisors alone.

The Premier asked if the company had a contract and that if it had, it would be honoured. The company had to admit that it had no contract. As far as the Premier was concerned the issue was settled.

However, the case was not closed for the Company Z representatives. They felt they had been promised the deal and that the department had reneged. They felt that someone had paid-off the department head and they were quite bitter. In discussions with their local embassy officials and with government officials at home they presented their analysis of the situation. The result was strained relations and the department head got a reputation for being dishonest.

ON THE INSIDE LOOKING OUT (THE DEVELOPING COUNTRY'S PERSPECTIVE)

During his visit the executive may have met only a few nationals selected by his company or government representatives. He probably has not discussed bribery with them because of its sensitive nature. If the businessmen and the officials he met were dishonest, they would not admit it; if they were honest he probably felt they would resent the discussion. Also, he may not have had enough time to establish the type of relationship in which the subject could be discussed frankly. It is almost certain that he did not speak with the people in the government agencies who allegedly took the pay-offs. What would he say if he did meet them? And more than likely he would not be able to get an appointment with them if he did want to pursue the matter further. So the executive is convinced that corruption is widespread having heard only one side of the horror stories.

Had the visitor been able to investigate the viewpoints of the nationals what might he have heard? "I would like to find a person from the developed world that I can trust. You people brought corruption here. We learned the concept from you. You want to win all the time, and you are impatient so you bribe. You offer bribes to the local people and complain that business is impossible without bribing."

Comments like these are made by local businessmen and government officials alike. If the visiting executive heard these comments he would be confused and would wonder whether or not these people were talking about the same country. Although skeptical, his confidence in the accuracy of his initial assessment would have been called into question. Had he been able to

stay longer in the country, he might have met an old friend who knew the department head who allegedly was paid-off in the Big Sale. His friend would have made arrangements for the visitor to hear the other side of the story.

Well, the other side of the story certainly has different implications about whose behaviour may be considered questionable. The situation is now very confusing. Is the department head honest or not? The executive's friend has known the department head for a long time and strongly believes he is honest; and some other expatriate government officials have basically corroborated the department head's perception of the matter. But the businessmen and government officials who first told the story seemed reputable and honest. Who should be believed? As the visiting executive has learned, you have to decide on the truth for yourself.

PATTERNS OF BEHAVIOUR

The preceding vignettes illustrate our position that bribery and corruption is a problem for North American and Third World businessmen alike. We also have observed two recurring behavioural patterns in these real, but disguised, situations. The first is the predisposition of the North American businessman to accept the premise that bribery is the way of life in the developing world and a necessity in business transactions. The second behavioural pattern occurs in situations where payments are requested and made.

We believe that many executives visit Third World countries with an expectation to learn that bribery is a problem. This attitude likely stems from a number of sources. First, in many cases it may be true. In some countries it may be impossible to complete a transaction without a bribe and the horror stories about the widespread disappearance of honesty are valid. However, in some instances the expectations are conditioned by the "conventional wisdom" available in international business circles. This conventional wisdom develops from situations like the ones we have described. As these situations are passed from individual to individual accuracy may diminish and facts be forgotten. This is not done intentionally but happens since it is rare that the story tellers have the complete story or all the facts. Unverified stories of bribery and corruption circulate through the business and government communities and often become accepted as true and factual. The obvious solution, and difficulty, is learning how to distinguish fact from fiction.

Another factor influencing initial expectations are the unfavourable impressions of developing countries and their citizens that are picked up from the media. Often only the sensational, and negative, news items from these countries are reported in North America. We learn of bombings, attacks on journalists and tourists, alleged (and real) coup d'états, and major scandals. These "current events" and the "conventional wisdom" combined with an executive's probable lack of knowledge of the history, culture, legal systems or economic conditions of a country all contribute to the development of unfavourable stereotypes that predispose the executive toward readily accepting reports that confirm his already drawn conclusions: all Latin American or African countries, for example, are the same and corruption is to be expected.

The stories that constitute "evidence" of corruption may be tales of bribery like the "New Venture" or the "Big Sale," or they may take other forms. The story we have heard most often has the 'protect yourself from your local partner' theme. It goes like this: "If you are going to invest in this country, particularly in a joint venture, you have to find a way to protect yourself from your partner. He is likely to strip all the company's assets and leave you nothing but a skeleton. Just look what happened to Company A."

On hearing the "evidence," particularly from expatriates in the foreign country, a visiting businessman most likely accepts it without further investigation. He has forgotten the old adage about there being two sides to every story. His conclusion and conviction are most likely based on incomplete and biased data.

Is there another viewpoint? Certainly! Many nationals have expressed it to us: "The Europeans and North Americans have been taking advantage of us for decades, even centuries. The multi-nationals establish a joint venture and then strip the local company bare through transfer pricing, management fees and royalties based on a percentage of sales rather than profits. They have no interest in the profitability of the company or its long-term development."

The situation is ironic. Some local investors are desperately looking for an honest North American executive whom they can trust at the same time the North American is searching for them. Our experience indicates that this search process is neither straightforward, nor easy. And while the search continues, if it does, it is difficult for the North American to maintain a perspective on the situation and remember that there are locals who may share his values and who are equally concerned about unethical and illegal practices.

In summary, we would characterize the first observed pattern of behavior as a preparedness to accept "evidence" of corruption and the simultaneous failure to examine critically the "evidence" or its source.

The second behavioral pattern appears in the actual pay-off process. The request very likely comes from a low- or middle-level bureaucrat who says that his boss must be paid for the project to be approved or for the sale to be finalized. Alternatively, it may be your agent who is providing similar counsel. In either case you are really not certain who is making the demand.

Next, the pay-off is made. You give your contact the money, but you never really know where it goes.

Your expectations are obvious. You have approached this transaction from a perspective of economic rationality. You have provided a benefit and expect one in return. The project will be approved or the sale consummated.

The results, however, may be very different than expected. As in the case of the 'New Venture', nothing may happen. The only outcome is indignation, anger, and perhaps the loss of a significant amount of money. Now is the time for action, but what recourse do you have? Can you complain? You may be guilty of bribing a government official. And, you certainly are reluctant to admit that you have been duped. Since your direct options are limited, your primary action may be to spread the word: "This is a corrupt, pay-off society."

WHY DOES IT HAPPEN?

There are numerous explanations for corruption in developing nations. First, and most obvious is that some people are simply dishonest. A less pejorative explanation is that the cost of living in these countries may be high and salaries low. Very often a wage earner must provide for a large extended family. The businessman is viewed opportunistically as a potential source of extra income to improve the standard of living. Finally, some nationals may believe strongly that they have a right to share some of the wealth controlled by multi-national corporations.

Besides being familiar to many readers, these explanations all share another common characteristic. They all focus on "the other person"—the local national. Accepting that there may be some truth in the previous explanations, let us, however, turn our focus to the visiting North American to see what we find. We could find a greedy, dishonest expatriate hoping to make a killing. But, let us give him the same benefit of the doubt we have accorded to the local nationals so far.

On closer examination we may find a situation in which the North American executive is vulnerable. He has entered an action vacuum and is at a serious disadvantage. His lack of knowledge of systems and procedures, laws, institutions, and the people can put him in a dependent position. Un-

familiarity with the system and/or people makes effective, alternative action such as he could take at home difficult. A strong relationship with a reputable national could help significantly in this situation. Quite often the national knows how to fight the system and who to call in order to put pressure on the corrupt individual. This potential resource should not be dismissed lightly. Although the most powerful and experienced MNC's may also be able to apply this pressure, most of us must be realistic and recognize that no matter how important we think we are, we may not be among those handful of foreigners that can shake the local institutions.

Time also can be a factor. Often the lack of time spent in the country either to establish relationships, or to give the executive the opportunity to fight the system contributes to the problem. Because the North American businessman believes that time is money and that his time, in particular, is very valuable, he operates on a tight schedule with little leeway for unanticipated delays. The payoff appears to be a cost-effective solution. In summary the executive might not have the time, knowledge, or contacts to fight back and sees no alternative other than pay or lose the deal.

SOME REAL BARRIERS

If, as we think, there are many honest businessmen in North America and in the developing world looking for mutually profitable arrangements and for reliable, honest partners, why is it difficult for them to find each other? We believe a significant reason is the inability of both sides to overcome two interrelated barriers—time and trust.

Trust is a critical commodity for business success in developing countries. The North American going to invest in a country far from home needs to believe he will not be cheated out of his assets. The national has to believe that a joint venture, for example, will be more than a mechanism for the North American to get rich at his expense. But, even before the venture is established trust may be essential if the perspective partners are ever to meet. This may require the recommendation of a third party respected by both sides.

Establishing good relationships with the right people requires an investment of time, money and energy. An unwillingness of either party to make this investment is often interpreted as a lack of sincerity or interest. The executive trying to do business in four countries in a week (the "5 day wonder") is still all too common a sight. Similarly the successful local businessman may have an equally hectic international travel schedule. Both complain that if the other was really serious he would find time to meet. Who should give in? In our opinion the onus is on whichever party is visiting to build into his schedule the necessary time to work on building a relationship or to find a trusted intermediary. Also both parties must be realistic about the elapsed time required to establish a good relationship and negotiate a mutually satisfactory deal. This will involve multiple trips by each party to the other's country and could easily take 12 to 18 months.

THE COST OF BRIBERY

The most quantifiable costs are the financial ones. The cost of the "service" is known. The costs of not bribing are also quantifiable: the time and money that must be invested in long term business development in the country, or the value of the lost business. However, there are other costs that must be considered.

1. You may set a precedent and establish that you and/or your company are susceptible to pay-off demands.
2. You may create an element in your organization that believes pay-offs are standard operating procedure and over which you may eventually lose control.
3. You or your agents may begin using bribery and corruption as a personally non-threatening, convenient excuse to dismiss failure. You may not address some organiza-

tional problems of adapting to doing business in the developing world.
4. There are also personal costs. Ultimately you will have to accept responsibility for your decisions and action, and those of your subordinates. At a minimum it may involve embarrassment, psychological suffering and a loss of reputation. More extreme consequences include the loss of your job and jail sentences.

CONCLUSION

It is clear that bribery can be a problem for the international executive. Assuming you do not want to participate in the practice, how can you cope with the problem?

1. Do not ignore the issue. Do as many North American companies have done. Spend time thinking about the tradeoffs and your position prior to the situation arising.
2. After thinking through the issue establish a corporate policy. We would caution, however, that for any policy to be effective, it must reflect values that are important to the company's senior executives. The policy must also be used. Window dressing will not work.
3. Do not be too quick to accept the "conventional wisdom." Examine critically the stories of bribery and the source of the stories. Ask for details. Try to find out the other side of the story and make enquiries of a variety of sources.
4. Protect yourself by learning about the local culture and by establishing trusting relationships with well-respected local businessmen and government officials.
5. Do not contribute to the enlargement of myths by circulating unsubstantiated stories.

Finally, we would offer the advice that when in Rome do as the *better* Romans do. But, we would add, do not underestimate the time, effort, and expense it may take to find the better Romans and establish a relationship with them.

Section C
South Africa

A Case for Sanctions against South Africa

Kenneth N. Carstens*

Virtually everyone agrees that apartheid is morally repugnant in both theory and practice. The psychic and physical violence of apartheid was once generally confined to the effects of racially discriminatory laws and institutions, which included the killing and disabling of blacks[1] by easily preventable diseases, starvation, malnutrition, beatings, etc. This whole range of "institutional violence" continues unabated in 1988. In addition, the overt violence of security forces killing and wounding unarmed people began in 1960, if not earlier. Such violence has provoked not only rage but increasingly well-organized and widespread non-violent resistance by blacks in the ghettos and by most of the main non-racial churches—especially after virtually all genuine political opposition was prohibited by the regime in February 1988. Official violence also provoked a rising spiral of counter violence, which began with symbolic acts of sabotage in 1961; by 1988, shoot-outs between guerrillas and and security forces were virtually weekly occurrences and road-blocks sprouted even in white neighborhoods. The government itself has repeatedly said that South Africa is at war in a "revolutionary climate"—for which, of course, it blames not its own apartheid but "communism". This "war" is likely to continue until genuine democracy is achieved or, in the more distant future, until the white-controlled government is overthrown, with unpredictable consequences. (Even if the regime should succeed in its current strategy of coopting a sufficient minority of blacks to perpetuate white control indefinitely, what it calls the war will undoubtedly continue.)

I will be arguing that sanctions[2] are the most effective means by which the rest of the world can support the moderate opposition, promote non-racial democracy and shorten instead of prolong the bloodshed and destruction.

A NOTE ON APARTHEID AND DEMOCRACY

The bedrock of apartheid is white political control. And since the whites are an ever-shrinking minority of 14% of the population, even such attenuated democratic rights as the two black minorities—the Coloureds (9%) and the Asians (3%)—now have could not have been extended to them until the "reform" Constitution of 1983, which further entrenched white political power, was in place. Extending even those attenuated political rights to the African majority (74%) is called "suicide" by the regime.

Consequently, the only reforms seriously considered by the apartheid regime—and the only reforms they are ever likely to consider—would be such as left white control entrenched for the foreseeable future. Even the most daring reforms yet proposed by the regime—such as appointing an African Cabinet Minister—would leave the African majority without a single freely elected representative in the national government. Once the *principle* of democracy is conceded to Africans, white control—apartheid—will be doomed. Some in the governing circles concede that some such scenario is inevitable; therefore they support the considerable efforts being exerted to slow down the process by dividing the majority along tribal, regional and class lines (hitherto mainly in the bantustans or "homelands"—i.e., tribal reservations, more recently in a policy re-

Excerpted and revised from "A Case for Sanctions against South Africa" by Kenneth N. Carstens, in *Ethics and the Multinational Enterprise,* edited by W. Michael Hoffman, Ann E. Lange, and David A. Fedo (Lanham, MD: University Press of America, 1986). Copyright © 1986 by Kenneth N. Carstens. Reprinted by permission of the author.

*Executive director, International Aid and Defense Fund for Southern Africa.

versal also in the encouragement of an African middle class). Official policy is to promote and institutionalize these divisions as ends in themselves—that is, as a *permanent* alternative to democracy in a unitary state. As the reforming State President, P.W. Botha, repeatedly asserts —echoing the white supremacists in Rhodesia in the 1970s: "One-person-one-vote is not negotiable."

That official policy has, however, been compromised, if not contradicted, by one set of Botha's reforms, viz., those which permitted some Africans some form of home ownership outside the bantustans, which halted, at least in theory, the process of denationalizing Africans, and which abolished the pass laws. On the practical level, the end of the pass laws meant giving with one hand but taking with the other. For with their abolition came an unprecedented security clampdown and then a State of Emergency which was lifted in March 1986 only to be reimposed in June 1986. So the evil of having hundreds of thousands of short-term prisoners who violated the pass laws was replaced with the evil of tens of thousands of more overtly political prisoners, nearly 40% of them children, who were and are routinely tortured and brutalized, and detained for months and in some cases for years without even the perfunctory charges and trial to which a pass-law offender was entitled. On the theoretical level, however, this set of reforms has conceded the permanence of at least some Africans in the "white" areas—which may seem to be an arcane point, since most Africans were already there and most had been there for generations. But the official ideology, blind to facts, had resolutely denied the permanence of Africans in "white" and especially urban areas.

This suggests that official policy, and not merely some influential *verligtes,* foresees (albeit in the far-distant future) having to concede the democratic principle—not, if they can possibly help it, to all Africans, but only to certain "qualified" Africans in urban areas.

This is the crucial area of disagreement between the right-wing ruling Nationalist Party and the lunatic-right official opposition Conservative Party. The main area of agreement between them is security: they believe fervently in crushing— with the utmost brutality, it seems—every form of opposition, whether violent or nonviolent, and whether internal or in the neighboring states. It is this *de facto* consensus on what the regime calls war that lends additional urgency to the need for sanctions; for without them the spiral of violence, brutality and bitterness would have no constraints.

FOREIGN INVESTMENT AND APARTHEID: FALSE HOPES

In order to consolidate white political power, a sustained assault on such vestigial rights as blacks possessed was already well under way in the 1950s, but its violent and homicidal operations were largely systemic and largely obscure to those especially foreigners, who were not themselves the actual victims of apartheid. Nevertheless, foreign investors could not have been unaware that the unusually high profits available in South Africa were not unrelated to the growing powerlessness, poverty, and suffering of blacks on whose exploitation and repression those profits depended. In the early 1950s, the United States financial stake in apartheid was less than $200 million and was unchallenged on moral and political grounds. In 1983, according to the columnist Jack Anderson, the United States Consulate in Johannesburg reported to the State Department that the United States stake in apartheid was over $14.6 billion. This includes loans, direct investment, and some but not all indirect investment.[3] Direct investment alone in 1985 was over $2 billion, a ten-fold increase over three decades. The US stake in apartheid had by then already begun to decrease.

The justification for this large (in South African terms) stake in apartheid is that prosperity in general and American business in particular has been and remains a positive force for change and exercises a moderating influence. Much is also made of the desirable changes which were promised by the government and which are already visible, if not to South African blacks, at least to some American business and political leaders who have a distinct interest in seeing such changes occur in order to justify their policies and profits. In trying to assess the changes during the period in which the United States' financial stake had so vastly increased, as well as those currently under way, we should recognize that changes of great significance to right-wing white South Africans like State President P. W. Botha—who defines change, controls it, and has instant access to the world's news media—matter very little to the voiceless, voteless millions of Africans. For example, of vast significance to Botha but irrelevant to most blacks is the repeal of the Immorality Act, which now permits them to have sexual intercourse with whites.

What matters to the black majority is not that a few of the lucky ones have well-paid jobs and use "whites-only" toilets; it is not even that black workers (and *not* United States business interests, as is often asserted) forced the government by dint of repeated and costly strikes to "concede" the right of blacks to form their own trade unions which in fact already existed. What does matter to the blacks is that there are literally millions more of them living below the poverty level today than in the 1950s; that many more today than in the 1950s are dying of starvation and disease while whites live off the fat of the land; that 3.5 million blacks have been forcibly removed, many from ancestral lands and modest livelihoods to resettlement camps which have become death camps for thousands of them; that even those who cling to life are stripped of dignity and hope; that instead of seeing their children grow and learn like white children, they see their children arrested, whipped, beaten, and brutalized, if not killed, by white soldiers and police; that instead of children's laughter there is rage—which this time, it seems, will not be quelled as in the children's uprising of 1976. Is

this the utopia for which they must thank thirty years of American investment? Is this the change which two billion dollars will buy—levels of fear, frustration, desperation, degradation, violence, and death beyond the worst nightmares of the 1950s?

There is an argument which emphasizes the *symbolic* significance and potential for future progress in some changes which, in terms of their practical consequences, are purely rhetorical or cosmetic. It is a hopeful sign, it is argued, that whites now speak of a "non-racial society," "an end to discrimination," and "power-sharing," etc., even if many white leaders do not really mean what they say in these terms. The argument suggests that if whites can utter today what was yesterday unthinkable, tomorrow they may be willing to do it. The fact is, however, that whites have been using euphemisms like "separate development" and telling each other and the world lies about apartheid for thirty years—and look at the results. The extent to which language is misused and devalued by public figures is hardly a hopeful index to desirable change.

But the basic fallacy in this "let's be hopeful and upbeat" line of reasoning is the false premise that the government which invented and painstakingly built apartheid will now or soon begin to dismantle it. Has there ever been a class or group of people who have been persuaded by rational argument or moral insight to surrender their hold on privilege and power? Has it not always had to be taken from them by the application of some kind of force, whether military or economic? Was it morality, or economic pressure backed up with military force, that freed the slaves in the United States in the nineteenth century? Is it reasonable, in any event, to expect white South Africans (of whom I am one) to be the first in history to do the right thing solely because it is right or because reason reveals that there is no morally responsible alternative?

Those who continue to look to the architects and builders of apartheid to dismantle it are either deceived or trying to deceive; they are either ill-informed or they share P. W. Botha's definition of change, which is well exemplified in his "reform" Constitution of 1983.[4] This Constitution was framed under Botha's direction, and it made him both head of government and head of state, conferring on him as President powers so great that even his own right-wingers have correctly described them as dictatorial. His powers extend not only through the whole government bureaucracy, but also over Parliament, which he has the power to dissolve and whose legislative functions he can manipulate. The President is not even elected by popular vote of the three minorities represented in Parliament (26% of all South Africans), but by an electoral college dominated by Botha's own ruling white Nationalist Party. "Reforms" of this and other parts of the system proposed in 1988 will not in the least affect white power.

Parliament consists of three houses: the white Assembly with 178 members, the Coloured House of Representatives with 85 members, and the Indian House of Delegates with 45 members. Legislation is divided into "general affairs" and "own affairs," the latter being defined as affairs relating only to the minority racial group concerned. It is the exclusive privilege of the President to decide which matters are of general concern and which are "own affairs," and his decision is final. An "own affairs" matter can be debated only in the house to which he assigns it. Matters which the President defines as "common concerns" go to all three houses. If there is disagreement between the three houses, the President's Council resolves the disagreement.

What of the Africans, who constitute, after all, 74% of the population? The "control and administration" of African affairs "shall vest in the State President." Along with the considerable diminution of the democratic powers of Parliament, this fact was one of the main reasons that the overwhelming majority of the South African population rejected the "reform" Constitution. Some 82% of the Coloured and Indian people,

whom it was supposed to have enfranchised, rejected it. The depth of the reaction against it can also be gauged by the unprecedented intensity of the demonstrations and protests which began with the introduction of the new Constitution in September 1984. (The new Constitution was not the sole cause of the uprising of 1984, but it became the symbolic focus of it.) By mid-1988, with unimaginably Draconian State of Emergency powers behind them, the security forces and their vigilantes had killed probably many more than the official death count of well over 3,000 black—and hardly any white—demonstrators, bystanders and other opponents, had wounded many thousands and had detained tens of thousands (nearly 40% of all categories were children). Yet all this killing and brutality did not succeed in crushing the sustained, nationwide wave of protest and resistance which had already begun to redirect its actions into less visible (and therefore less dangerous) channels as early as 1986. What the killing and brutality of the regime did—and continues to do—was to fuel black rage and outrage and determination.

However, two out of three white voters approved the Constitution. Voters representing little more than 10% of the population as a whole, therefore, approved the new constitution, which entrenches white power more deeply than either of the earlier South African constitutions and is the most racially divisive of them all—and certainly the least democratic. That the United States State Department should have welcomed it as "a step in the right direction" is ironic, deplorable, and a clear indication of the kind of change United States policy is promoting in South Africa—namely, new facades on the superstructure, but with the same foundations of apartheid, and with repressive laws and brutal actions still propping it up. This is also the kind of change in which United States businesses have been investing for thirty years. As the United States Senate Committee on Foreign Relations stated in a report entitled *United States Corporate Interests in South Africa:* "The net effect of

American investment has been to strengthen the economic and military self-sufficiency of South Africa's apartheid regime.''

MOTIVES FOR CHANGE

Real changes, however, are under way in the United States if not in South Africa. Is it possible that a mixture of self-interest, political pressures, and perhaps even a grain or two of morality (one does not want to be too sanguine!) has persuaded United States businesses to pursue a more responsible policy than the United States government? (In fact, even the Reagan Administration was forced in 1986 to impose symbolic sanctions, with substantive sanctions looking likely in 1988.) On February 27, 1986, the *Wall Street Journal* reported that ''blue-chip United States companies...are pulling out (of South Africa) at an accelerating rate'' due to ''the twin pressures of unrest there and political harassment (sic) at home.'' The report added that ''many large United States companies are developing contingency plans to get out.'' Figures cited in the report suggest the beginning of a trend which by mid-1988 had reduced the number of U.S. companies doing business openly in South Africa by nearly half. These developments are taking place in a context of a growing national divestment movement in which hundreds, if not thousands, of divestment actions have been taken by groups ranging from national, regional, and local church bodies and trade unions to universities, journals, and family trusts. Moreover, by June 1988, well over 100 state, county, city, and town authorities had committed themselves to divestment and/or selective purchasing actions which are exerting a very considerable financial and public relations pressure on corporations which might otherwise have less sensitive consciences on the matter.

While those departures from South Africa are to be welcomed as long overdue, the reasons cited for the exodus—instability there and political harassment here—lend support to the suspicion that a social conscience has not yet evolved in firms that do business with apartheid. Moral considerations generally remain absent from the plans, decisions, and actions of these firms even though the *language* of morality has found its way into their public relations statements and programs in South Africa and here. Fear of lower profits and of being tarred with the apartheid brush are not ranked among the most noble motives for ''pulling out.''

Better reasons for disinvestment and other sanctions against apartheid were being given thirty years ago by such leaders as South Africa's first Nobel Peace laureate, Albert Luthuli, President of the African National Congress of South Africa (ANC). As the non-violent campaigns for basic human rights were being suppressed with traditional white South African severity, Luthuli warned that soon the only recourse left to the black majority would be counterviolence. South Africa was set on a course leading inexorably towards a disastrous cycle of violence and counterviolence, he said, from which the black majority was vainly trying to steer South Africa. For decades, the Africans had sought to turn the government towards a rational solution, first by patient reasoning and then by boycotts, demonstrations, and campaigns of civil disobedience. The response had been whips, clubs, and guns wielded with brutal effect by the police, while racist and Draconian laws multiplied on the statute books, and torture became as routine as imprisonment. Why, asked Luthuli, did Britain and America misuse their moral authority and economic power in tacit approval of this disastrous road of violence and death? He pleaded with them to use their power for freedom and democracy instead by withdrawing investment and imposing sanctions. If the West did not end its *de facto* support of apartheid, Luthuli argued, they would in effect be endorsing counterviolence, which was a last resort the ANC had been struggling for years to avoid.

Luthuli's arguments were clinched by the police massacre of scores of African children, women, and men at Sharpeville in 1960 and the launching of the ANC's campaign of sabotage in 1961—the week after Luthuli had reiterated his plea and warning in his Nobel Peace Prize acceptance speech in Oslo. Three years later, Martin Luther King, Jr., on his way to Oslo to receive his own Nobel Peace Prize, stopped in London and in a powerful speech also advocated withdrawal of American investment from South Africa and economic sanctions as the one hope for achieving change non-violently.

Every credible black leader in South Africa has reiterated the pleas and the warnings of Luthuli and King: Mandela, Sobukwe, Biko, Boesak, Tutu, and Barayi—the leader of the new and significant Congress of South African Trade Unions.[5] Their pleas for sanctions and their warnings of the dreadful alternatives to sanctions are more compelling and urgent now than when they were ignored thirty years ago. There is every sign that the momentum which the cycle of violence is gaining will increase. For the intransigence and brutality of the regime, its false promises of change, and its summary executions on ghetto streets have succeeded in replacing the patient endurance and persistent goodwill of the black people with rage and frustration fueled by fear—and hope.

THE MORAL ARGUMENT FOR DIVESTMENT, DISINVESTMENT, AND SANCTIONS

Even before the regime promulgated its total powers of censorship of everything from advertisements to pictures—let alone news—there were more than 100 laws in South Africa which restricted the freedom of the press and distorted the flow of news and information. Nevertheless, on the basis of facts provided by the South African government itself, unaninimity as to the nature of the apartheid system has been reached by all reasonable people. I know of no American businessperson on public record who does not condemn apartheid as evil. Surely such people

must also agree that it is morally indefensible to associate oneself individually, or collectively as a corporation, with evil. Obviously when one associates one's individual or corporate self with evil, one is associating one's name, one's reputation, one's values, one's religion, and one's nationality with that evil. The onus, therefore, is on business to justify associating itself with the unambiguous evil of apartheid.

In addition to the acquiescence in and involuntary symbolic contributions to the system of injustice which simply being there entails, there is further moral blame in being there for profit, since the wealth of the few is related to the powerlessness and poverty of the many, and any investment gives the investor a tangible interest in this inequitable system and in its perpetuation in some form related to the present one. Many contribute involuntarily to the perpetuation of apartheid. The law sees to this. To ensure that the investor's interest in apartheid is given full force and effect, such laws as the Petroleum Producers Act of 1977, the National Supplies Procurement Act of 1977, the Official Secrets Act of 1956 as amended in 1972, and the Key Points Act of 1980 as amended in 1984 are on the statute books. Lest moral or other considerations should tempt a businessperson to act inconsistently with the *de facto* interest in the preservation of the status quo, these acts prohibit the following: (1) withholding supplies and services from the security forces; (2) shifting resources from such supplies or services to their more profitable lines or customers; (3) divulging information to an unauthorized person "in any manner or for any purpose prejudicial to the safety or interests of the Republic" of South Africa; and (4) not taking adequate steps to provide security in cooperation with the military authorities and under regulations drawn up by the Minister of Defense. Such laws were reinforced yet further by the State of Emergency which began in June 1986.

Thus, being there as an investor or trader, whether individual or corporate, not only becomes inseparable from *symbolic* support of apartheid, but also inevitably gives *material* support to the system in the form of taxes and the legal regulation of the sale of products and services. There simply is no choice in the matter. It is, after all, the government and not the black majority which sets the terms and conditions for investment and trade—and much more so in South Africa's much-touted "free-market" economy than Americans suspect. Thus, one's identification with apartheid has gone beyond the vitally important realm of symbols to the equally important practical level of guns, butter, technology, skills, and taxes, all of which are vitally necessary to defend the system which those who invest in it deplore as evil.

As if to reinforce the logic of established facts and the moral logic of sanctions, as well as to underline the obviously desperate need apartheid has for all the taxes, all the computers, and all the bullets and biscuits and symbols of legitimacy which American businesses can provide, the apartheid government has fiercely opposed the sanctions movement in America and elsewhere by short-wave radio broadcasts, by glossy propaganda, by costly public relations firms and lobbyists, and by savage laws against its advocacy within South Africa. Could an impartial observer escape the conclusion that foreign investors are either suffering from self-delusion of pathological proportions or are in shameful collusion with the apartheid government if they try to deny such facts and such logic?

Nevertheless, some well-meaning people do still ask whether sanctions would not "hurt those we want to help." Albert Luthuli and the many who have echoed his arguments over the past thirty years concede that there *may* be some additional suffering for at least a few in the short term. After all, if an American factory closes down in Port Elizabeth, the few blacks employed there will obviously lose their jobs, even though the longer-term effect will in fact create more jobs as high-tech imports are replaced by cruder local goods and as the capital-intensive foreign investment is perforce replaced by labor-intensive enterprises. But Luthuli and the others who advocate sanctions have said: "Our people are suffering more than you can know at present. That suffering shows no sign of lessening and even less of ending. We are prepared to suffer a little more—indeed, we are prepared to suffer a lot more in the short-term if we can see an end to the suffering. We would rather suffer far more now and have some hope for the future and for our children than keep our suffering at this level in perpetuity with no hope for the future."

For those concerned lest "we hurt those we want to help," the question is this: whom do you want to help? What is the normal, rational way of helping anyone other than infants and the insane? Is it not to give them that for which they themselves have asked? The apartheid government spends millions every year to ensure that you know what *they* are asking for, namely, more and more investments, loans, and trade. Genuine black South African leaders do not have the millions to ensure that you hear their requests, but you have nevertheless heard that both of South Africa's Nobel Peace laureates, Albert Luthuli and Desmond Tutu, have asked you to disinvest, as has every leader whom common sense and elementary facts would identify as credible.

So the question is, Whom do you want to "help" or "hurt?" There is absolutely no way in which support for the evil system of apartheid can be defended on moral grounds. There is equally no way in which one can invest in South Africa, trade with South Africa, or make loans to South Africa without supporting apartheid—and lest such a way should be found, the South African government has enacted statute after statute to *ensure* that support will be exacted. However, there is no law to compel anyone to invest there. That is a free choice, and with it goes what cannot be bought or enacted by law, namely, the symbolic legitimation and moral support of an evil system.

Every investment in or loan to South Africa and every business deal with South Africa is an explicit moral and political statement. Disinvestment and refusal to do business with South Africa are equally explicit moral and political statements. One course of action is morally wrong. The other is morally right. There is no neutral ground.

NOTES

1. I use the term "blacks" to denote collectively Africans, Coloureds, and Asians. The last official census was in 1985, the corrected results of which were as follows (including the population of what South Africa but not a single other government calls the "independent" reservations or bantustans of Bophuthatswana, Ciskei, Transkei, and Venda):

African	24,901,139	74.1%
Coloured	2,881,362	8.6%
Asian	878,300	2.6%
Black subtotal	28,660,801	85.3%
White	4,961,062	14.7%
Total	33,621,863	100.0%

2. I use the term "sanctions" to denote all political and economic measures short of military action. Most often, I will use it to refer to economic measures such as boycotts, divestment (the selling of shares held in a company operating in South Africa) and, more especially, disinvestment (the withdrawal of a company or other investor from South Africa).

3. *Washington Post,* 30 July 1983.

4. Republic of South Africa Constitution Act of 1983 and the Constitution Amendment Act of 1984.

5. As Americans discovered in their war of independence, every country has its collaborators, and South Africa is no exception. Bantustan leaders, despite impressive titles like "Chief Minister" and "President," are in fact civil servants of the South African government which controls every important aspect of even the four "independent" bantustans, both directly and by providing an average of 77% of their budgets. The bantustan leaders, together with their urban counterparts, are seen as second only to black police and informers among the collaborators. Paraded as the "real leaders,"

they are frequently quoted and interviewed on the state-controlled Radio South Africa (which beams short-wave broadcasts to North America daily at 0200 G.M.T.) as well as on television. Their support of more foreign investment and trade is often highlighted during these broadcasts.

[Author's note: The views expressed in this paper are those of the author and not necessarily those of the International Defense and Aid Fund for Southern Africa, of which the author is the executive director.]

Moral Justifications for Doing Business in South Africa

Patricia H. Werhane*

INTRODUCTION

It is commonly argued that because of the abhorrent nature of apartheid and other injustices committed by the South African government and South African law, it is morally objectionable to do business with or in South Africa. Indeed, according to this perspective, one is morally required *not* to do business with or in South Africa since to do so would appear to be in support of the principles of apartheid. Doing business with or in South Africa supports a government committed to injustices and provides it with financial and technical resources to strengthen its hold on South African nonwhite people. Thus businesses currently dealing with South Africa should withdraw their operations from that country.

On the other side, corporations doing business with and in South Africa argue that if they

From *Ethics and the Multinational Enterprise,* edited by W. Michael Hoffman, Ann E. Lange, and David A. Fedo (Lanham, MD: University Press of America, 1986). Copyright © 1986 by Patricia H. Werhane. Reprinted by permission of the author.

*Department of Philosophy, Loyola University of Chicago.

do not trade with this country, other nations will do so, thus depriving American business of profits while not depriving South Africa of industry. American corporations further point out that such businesses provide jobs for nonwhite South Africans, jobs they otherwise might have, but perhaps under less auspicious working conditions or poorer wages. Worse, it is very costly for shareholders if American companies withdraw from South Africa, because under South African law, companies can neither withdraw their assets nor expect any form of reparations when leaving that country.

American companies, then, appear to be faced with the dilemma of engaging in practices which are often questioned on ethical grounds by the American public and some of their shareholders, or sacrificing economic gains and thus not honoring their fiduciary commitments to the same shareholders. Note the schizophrenic position of transnational corporations vis-a-vis their shareholders. Some shareholders object on *moral* grounds to transnational South African operations, while others would object on fiscal ones to losses on major earnings which might be created by withdrawal. No wonder institutional shareholders have problems developing a policy toward owning shares in such corporations, and no wonder corporations have trouble deciding whether or not to leave South Africa!

In this paper I shall argue that this dilemma is misconstrued. What appears to be a clear-cut case of ethics versus economics is much more complicated in its implications. While it may be ethically questionable to do business *with* South Africa, a question I shall not consider in this paper, businesses currently operating *in* that country can defend their existence there under certain ethically specified conditions. Such business operations might be justified if and where these companies engage in what I shall call moral risk in their business affairs in South Africa. Moral risk does not entail an *ad hoc* exportation of American customs and business practices nor does it require merely following the accepted

practices of South African businesspersons and corporations. Rather, moral risk requires a careful analysis of what is not merely accepted practice, but also what is morally acceptable. And the business practices one adopts must also meet one's own moral standards and pass tests of ethical acceptability from a more universal perspective. It will turn out that in many instances one can continue to do business in South Africa without either sacrificing one's own principles or insulting the host nation.

THREE OPTIONS FOR MULTINATIONAL ENTERPRISES IN SOUTH AFRICA

Why is the case for or against doing business in South Africa so complex? Transnational corporations are faced with three kinds of choices, each of which has its positive and negative aspects. First, transnationals can simply remain in South Africa, doing business in the way that other white South African businesses do. This choice can be defended on a number of grounds. As I mentioned earlier, there are the obvious utilitarian arguments that American businesses profit from their South African operations, and since their operations would be replaced by businesses from South Africa or other countries if these corporations withdrew, the reasons for withdrawing are moot. Furthermore, following what I shall call the "Negative Harm Principle," the notion that a business dealing is morally permissible if it is not illegal so long as it does not deliberately or knowingly harm some person, some institution, or some nation, the operations of American transnational corporations are morally permissible. This is because (1) these corporations provide jobs, (2) they do not permit working conditions or wage scales which are worse than other South African companies, and (3) if these companies repatriated their operations, they would be replaced by other companies from other countries so that any positive benefit that might be accrued from their withdrawal is lost. Moreover, (4) since South Africa is a relatively wealthy "Westernized" country compared at least to other African nations, by and large transnational business operations in that country do not produce consequences often seen as heinous by critics of transnationals operating in the Third World. For example, there is little evidence that transnationals have imported radical economic, social, or cultural changes incompatible with the South African way of life. They have not exploited the agriculture of the country by replacing important food crops with exportable but locally useless products. They have not exploited the labor force with wages abnormally lower or higher than the South African norm or with temporary employment. At the same time, American transnationals have provided employment for decent wages and, with the exception of the mining industries, decent working conditions. In other words, American transnationals operating in South Africa have not aggravated or altered the social, psychological, economic, or ecological balance (or imbalance) of South Africa.[1]

This choice, to remain in South Africa under the *status quo,* however, has a number of difficulties including (1) moral objections of shareholders part of whom are institutional shareholders and (2) acquiescence to a system of apartheid neither approved nor practiced in the home country of the transnational. To support these objections, critics of transnational operations in South Africa argue that merely not deliberately creating cultural, economic, or physical harm is not enough justification for supporting any operation which cooperates with a government in a society which abets and aggrandises apartheid. To exist in South Africa and to contribute to its economy is to offer economic support for an inherently evil social and political structure and thereby to cause and to contribute positive harm. One cannot morally justify continuing to do business in South Africa on the basis of the Negative Harm Principle since merely not intentionally or deliberately causing harm is not enough in this case to prevent American transnationals from

contributing to positive harm. It seems obvious, then, according to these critics, that doing business in South Africa is simply the wrong thing to do, and the alternate, withdrawing economic operations, is the right thing to do even though this creates economic hardships for some transnationals and their shareholders.

Aside from the deleterious economic effects of withdrawing from South Africa, a choice which itself has moral components, e.g., corporate fiduciary responsibility to shareholders, this choice is not a perfect one either. It is not a perfect decision first because American transnational corporations provide needed jobs for nonwhite South Africans. Now *if* other corporations take over American transnational operations when American companies leave, these jobs would continue, but under South African legal guidelines. Second, by withdrawing, American transnationals are giving up an opportunity to do positive good, not merely positive economic good, but also to serve as an example of how private enterprises can work efficiently and without deliberate injustice.

This brings us to the third most difficult choice: to stay in South Africa and not merely avoid deliberately causing harm, but also serve as a positive model for private enterprise at its most fair. This choice is the most interesting and the most challenging, and according to some critics, the least perfect, since it is, at best, a mixed moral action which cannot avoid the result of contributing economically to white South Africa.

MORAL RISK

We must now ask why this third option is a viable option and perhaps even the best sort of choice, all things considered. Under what conditions could one continue to do business in South Africa without overwhelming moral impunity? The responses to these questions entail what I shall call "moral risk." Moral risk is entailed in any decision-making process in which one becomes engaged when the particular moral dilemma one faces (1) has neither a positive nor a negative alternative that is clear-cut, (2) has no alternative that will produce a positive result (e.g., Sophie's Choice), (3) is characterized by the fact that not choosing itself is a contributory negative choice (German acquiescence to Nazism in World War II), and/or (4) results in any possible action having both contributory and deleterious effects. In these sorts of situations, because choosing not to choose (or simply, not choosing) is itself an effective choice, one needs to engage in serious moral deliberation. This deliberation calls for moral creativity and entails moral risk because of the ambiguous nature of any decision one is to make. Notice, again, that I have termed this ''risk'' in ethical decision making, because no choice one makes will be perfectly good. Since any choice one makes will have some negative consequences, *how* one chooses is of upmost importance. The structure of one's decision requires not merely drawing straws, but setting up guidelines, formal guidelines, for such decisions. These guidelines in turn must meet the following requirements: (1) universalizability, (2) respect for equal rights of all persons, (3) respect for individual, institutional, cultural, or national customs, mores, or ideologies, (4) respect for the Negative Harm Principle, and (5) when possible creation of positive benefits. Let us briefly discuss each of these.

The universalizability principle in these sorts of instances is to be interpreted as the evaluation of the decision in terms of whether I would expect others to make this sort of decision under these circumstances, all things considered. Without evaluating a choice by this principle, albeit qualified, the choice has no status as a moral choice since it cannot be justified except as my subjective preference. Yet the universalizability principle is a qualified principle, qualified by the particular situation and by the kind of decision to be made. Secondly, a decision, however universalizable, which does not respect persons and their rights and interests, has difficulty as a *moral* decision. The South African government, for ex-

ample, appeals to the principle of universalizability in its governmental policies, since it advocates apartheid as the proper way for all nations to divide and govern races. Yet these policies fail on the grounds that they do not respect persons or respect persons equally. In much of moral decision making, of course, it is not simply the respect for persons which is at issue, but conflicts between rights or interests of persons or persons and institutions. Giving the benefit of the doubt, this is, in part, the issue in South Africa where there is a conflict between the rights of white and nonwhite South Africans. And a solution to apartheid which abrogates the rights of *white* South Africans would not be an acceptable one either.

Third, as Michael Walzer cogently argues, respect for individual and national autonomy is essential if one is to value human freedom. Therefore, such autonomy can be violated only where there is a clear-cut and radical violation of people's rights.[2] Fourth, a decision which creates harm to the present *status quo* is always questionable unless it can be demonstrated that violent and continued disrespect for persons requires it, or that in the long run positive benefits will accrue. Simply not creating harm may not, in every case, be the best choice. Fifth, any decision which produces positive benefits is more justified than one which does not, although I would place respect for persons as a more important criterion for a decision than the creation of positive benefits. South Africa claims to have the highest standard of living in Africa for blacks. Yet human rights are consistently and deliberately violated in such a way that the alleged economic benefits do not morally outweigh the violations of human rights.

MORAL RISK AND MULTINATIONALS IN SOUTH AFRICA

Turning now to the choice of whether and how to continue to do business in South Africa, the criteria for this decision are complex, because individual, institutional, and national considerations must be taken into account. In criticizing South African apartheid policies, we can apply the principles of universalizability and respect for persons. Can these same principles be evoked and in what ways to *justify* doing business in South Africa? It would appear that one *can* justify such operations only if one can create a situation which improves the moral condition of black South Africans by enhancing their rights and interests in such a way that would be an acceptable practice in other similar business situations. At the same time, one cannot simply disregard the autonomy of South Africa as a nation, although its consistent practice of rights violations might warrant some sort of intervention at some point. But this is surely not the responsibility of a transnational corporation nor would we want to grant such corporations this power. Moreover, from a practical standpoint, no business will be allowed to engage in practices which are clearly antithetical to South African autonomy. Finally, if doing business in South Africa does not improve the moral as well as the economic condition of black South Africans and indeed causes undue harm, one has no justification for remaining in that country since one is merely abetting apartheid without any balancing contribution.

The issue is, then, can one continue in South Africa while enhancing rights of nonwhite South Africans without alienating the South African government to the point of being expelled? Note that no business has the moral obligation to do more than it can—its primary responsibilities are to its shareholders, its customers, and its employees. So if a corporation could create a nondiscriminatory climate within its corporation which enhanced the moral and working conditions of its employees and if it produces goods or provides services which are not harmful to blacks and the black economy, such a corporation would be making moral progress both on an individual level with its employees and as a model for morally decent private enterprise. It is ob-

vious that American transnational corporations which actively endorse and practice the Sullivan Principles are engaging in moral creativity and contributing positively to the moral improvement of nonwhite South Africans. Such principles specify positive nondiscriminatory actions only within the corporation so that adopting them does not blatantly insult the South African government. These principles allow companies not to compromise their moral standards within the confines of the company, and at the same time allow them to engage in economically successful operations. Of course, putting these principles into practice uniformly and consistently is critical.

Merely adopting the Sullivan Principles, however, does not get a corporation off the "moral hook." For one may always ask whether these principles are adequate. What is the role of the transnational in a positive cultural change? Can a transnational do more, and should it? Moreover, no transnational corporation has adopted the Sullivan Principles solely because of their contribution to black South African life. The Sullivan Principles are adopted in large measure to protect transnationals from shareholder criticism and to respond to American public pressure without having to withdraw from that country. And as we have repeatedly noted, these operations increase the GNP of South Africa and help to maintain it as perhaps the strongest and most stable country in Africa. So transnationals face two constant moral risks—the risk of not doing enough, morally, and the risk of contributing more to apartheid than in helping its foes. Why, then, continue?

Although I cannot answer that question directly, I can illustrate what is at stake with another, more difficult example. During World War II, the German theologian Dietrich Bonhoeffer actively and publicly fought Nazism. According to a widespread but undocumented rumor, during the war Bonhoeffer's followers infiltrated concentration camps not as inmates but as guards. In trying to undermine the system, some of these followers were forced to participate in the actual deaths of inmates in order to protect their identity and continue with their mission. Were their actions good or evil? Was it better to do nothing than to engage in activities, some of which were abhorrent, that were aimed at creating changes? There is no simple answer. But if moral improvement of a society can take place best within that society, then it is not clear that Bonhoeffer's followers acted wrongly even though their individual actions contributed to evil. Perhaps it is an exaggerated analogy to compare the actions of Bonhoeffer and his followers to transnational operations in South Africa since the motives of the transnationals are not pure. Yet to withdraw from an opportunity to contribute to positive change in a situation as abhorrent as apartheid is perhaps not the best ethical decision either.

In conclusion, the Negative Harm Principle is not always enough to prevent harm from occurring as a result of one's well-intentioned actions. At the same time, positive moral action often requires making choices which are, at best, ambiguous. Doing business in South Africa in the way in which South Africans do embodies the Negative Harm Principle and contributes to positive harm. At the same time, withdrawing from South Africa makes no positive contribution in a situation where such a contribution is possible. The difficult decision of choosing to remain in South Africa with a specific moral agenda, then, is ethically risky but not as wrong as it may seem.

NOTES

1. For a discussion of the "traditional evils" often committed by transnationals see Richard J. Barnet and Ronald E. Muller, *Global Reach* (New York: Simon and Schuster, 1974), especially Chapter 13.
2. See Michael Walzer, *Just and Unjust Wars* (New York: Basic Books, 1977), especially pp. 88–106.

QUESTIONS FOR DISCUSSION

1. What are some of the most important ethical problems facing multinational corporations operating in the Third World, according to Turner? Do you think that the principles offered by De George might help resolve some of these dilemmas? Explain.
2. Were the marketing practices of infant formula manufacturers in the Third World deceptive? Explain. Did they create a need for an otherwise unnecessary product? Defend your answer. (You may wish to look back at the Galbraith and Holley articles in Chapter 11 in answering this question.)
3. What does Werhane mean by a position of "moral risk," and why does she think this position is appropriate for U.S. companies operating in South Africa? Why does Carstens disagree? What is your position?

The Corporation in Society

CASES FOR PART FOUR

John Robinson
Tobacco Advertising,
Taxes Come under Attack in Congress
584

W. Michael Hoffman
The Ford Pinto
587

Timothy S. Mescon and George S. Vozikis
Hooker Chemical and the Love Canal
594

Manuel G. Velasquez,
with an update by Timothy Smith
A South African Investment
599

Tobacco Advertising, Taxes Come under Attack in Congress

John Robinson*

WASHINGTON—Like many former smokers, Rep. Michael L. Synar, Oklahoma's snappy young bachelor congressman, remembers the precise date he kicked his cigarette habit: Oct. 17, 1980.

That it also happened to be his 30th birthday seems now of only middling importance in his life, considering the prominence he has achieved since then in driving antismoking initiatives through Congress.

Among the brace of bills designed to curb the tobacco industry, Synar's legislation to ban all media advertising and promotion of tobacco products has become a major point of contention between pro-tobacco and anti-tobacco partisans this year on Capitol Hill.

Although few people will predict the outcome on any of the tobacco legislation, it is increasingly perceived on Capitol Hill that the tobacco lobby has lost some of the clout that once gave it an aura of invincibility when it came to industry interests.

Recent House passage of a bill to limit smoking on airlines as well as the success of other antismoking bills here and in state legislatures has reinforced the perception.

The assault on advertising is being waged on several fronts. Rep. Brian Donnelly (D-Mass.) and Sen. Bill Bradley (D-N.J.) have produced bills similar to the Synar legislation to deny cigarette advertisers a tax deduction for the cost of promoting tobacco products.

Excerpted from "Tobacco Advertising, Taxes Come under Attack in Congress" by John Robinson, in *The Boston Globe* (September 21, 1987). Reprinted courtesy of *The Boston Globe*.

*Staff writer, *The Boston Globe*.

Donnelly's bill also would include advertising and promotion of beer, wine and distilled spirits. He estimated the Treasury would gain at least $5 billion over three years as a result of his legislation.

"Why should taxpayers subsidize promotion of these products that harm people?" Donnelly asked. "The federal health costs of cigarette-related illnesses is $8 billion, and more than that for alcohol-related illnesses."

Only the prospect of a rise in the cigarette excise tax from the current 16 cents a pack to 32 cents is viewed with as much alarm by pro-tobacco interests as the proposed advertising curb. Either approach—outright ban or a limitation of the tax deduction—likely would have a profound impact on the young, believed to be most vulnerable to advertising claims and most sensitive to the price of cigarettes.

"My thing has been to focus on the children," said Synar, who has helped push through Congress two health-labeling bills that were hotly opposed by the tobacco lobby, one of the oldest and richest in the Capitol.

"Sixty percent of all adult smokers started before age 14; 90 percent of all smokers began before age 19," said Synar. "If adults want to ignore widely available evidence that cigarettes are a health hazard that's fine with me. But the children can't make decisions on a factual basis."

Among his bill's 40 cosponsors are Massachusetts representatives Chester G. Atkins and Edward J. Markey. The bill also has picked up the support of the chairman of the Energy and Commerce subcommittee on health and the environment, Henry A. Waxman (D-Calif.).

By attacking the marketing and pricing of tobacco products, the two initiatives strike at a key aspect of the tobacco business.

The last time federal excise taxes were raised on cigarettes, from 8 cents to 16 cents a pack in 1983, consumption declined 5 percent. Although the drop was especially pronounced among young people, it is clear that the price increases also cost the industry long-term customers, according to some researchers.

Congress, like its counterparts at the state and local levels and even many private enterprises, increasingly is sensing grass-roots pressure to curb the use of tobacco products, and further restrictions seem inevitable.

"The pressure on members, especially those who have been ambivalent about tobacco issues, has increased tremendously," said a Health and Environment staffer. "It's no longer easy, if you have no parochial stake in tobacco politics, to take a 'bye' on a tobacco bill."

Some dedicated antismokers, such as Sen. John Kerry, whose private Senate office contains no ashtrays in a signal of his disapproval of smoking, are hesitant about banning advertising because of their concern for First Amendment guarantees of free expression.

But many of them support other restrictions, most notably on smoking in public places. "I think I would ban all smoking on airlines, for instance," Kerry said.

When the House passed a bill in July to curb smoking on airlines, it was hailed by antismoking advocates as another example of the diminished clout on Capitol Hill of the once-mighty tobacco lobby.

The bill is expected to receive Senate attention this month.

Similar legislation has been introduced to limit smoking on buses and trains, and in virtually all government-owned or controlled buildings.

The trend on Capitol Hill mirrors legislative efforts on the local and state level to curb tobacco use, particularly smoking.

Younger congressmen, even those who represent tobacco states, are beginning to show what many observers believe is a generational antipathy toward tobacco and a greater sensitivity to the health issues involved with smoking.

Rep. James Cooper, for instance, whose Tennessee district includes some 8,800 tobacco farmers on 14,000 state-designated tobacco allotments, drew the ire of tobacco companies last winter when he told a meeting of the Tobacco Institute that "tobacco smoke is obnoxious; it's like body odor."

Freshman North Carolina congressman David E. Price, while in step with his state's delegation in opposing legislation aimed at tobacco use, acknowledged his concern for health consequences. "But I draw the line at the economic issues," he said.

"Tobacco is the major cash crop in our state, even where diversification has taken place," said Price, a former Duke University professor who beat conservative Republican William W. Cobey Jr. last November. "There is no ready substitute for it."

More than 605,000 acres are devoted to tobacco cultivation in the United States. Much of the farming is small-scale and goes to support poor rural dwellers for whom the semiperishable crop is the mainstay of their annual incomes.

Cooper was an original cosponsor of the tobacco labeling bill that was opposed by the industry, but he is holding back on Synar's advertising ban and the excise tax until the committee finishes work.

The United States is the world's leading tobacco exporter as well as the largest importer, according to the Department of Agriculture. The country is the third-largest producer of tobacco, after China and India, both of which are self-sufficient in tobacco.

But many legislators see tobacco as a product for which alternatives must be found. Otherwise, they say, tobacco farmers who fail to anticipate change could find themselves in the situation of workers in sunset industries who get caught without a job or a marketable skill.

"There has been a change in demand for tobacco, but an even sharper drop in demand for US tobacco products because other countries are becoming competitive on quality," according to Dallas Smith, a spokesman for the US Department of Agriculture.

Consumption of all tobacco products in the United States, including chewing tobacco, snuff, cigars and smoking tobacco, declined last year, according to the USDA's Economic Research Service.

Prices of tobacco, accordingly, have declined and tobacco acreage allotments were reduced between 35 percent and 40 percent in the small-plot farms in Kentucky and Tennessee.

Cigarette consumption declined almost 2 percent last year to 584 billion cigarettes because of higher prices, anti-smoking activity and restrictions on where people may smoke. A decade ago, US cigarette consumption stood at 617 billion. The trend is expected to continue.

Revisions last year in the commodity support program to adjust to the shifting demand were designed to increase exports of US tobacco, raising fears among antismoking advocates that the industry is looking overseas to promote products that are considered unhealthy for Americans to consume.

The politics of tobacco have changed dramatically, observers say, since the day when the lobbyists got virtually everything they wanted out of a Congress top-heavy with senior officials from the Tobacco Belt.

Resentment has been growing because of what an increasing number of officials view as the arrogance of the industry in promoting its products and programs.

Lawmakers are particularly irritated by the industry's spurning last year of a small, directed tax proposed by Rep. Charles Rose to pay for tobacco price supports in favor of a billion-dollar bailout authored by Sen. Jesse Helms (R-N.C.).

"What they're doing is playing North Carolina politics, pitting Republicans against Democrats in order to get the best deal for themselves," said Donnelly. "Even people who aren't directly involved in the issue don't like that."

Other legislators complain that the industry has shown bad faith in its agreements to regulate its own promotional activities.

They point as an example to the youthful-looking models in cigarette advertisements that conform to the letter of restrictions against using teen-age models but seem to violate the spirit of curbs to avoid appealing directly to the youth.

Anger is rising, too, over the industry's continued high pitch to minority communities, which sorely need revenues for local and national publications but which also face disproportionate rates of alcohol- and tobacco-related illnesses.

"There is a good case to be made for tobacco," said Cooper. "That is that this is America and people ought to have the freedom to do what they want to do as long as it does not hurt others. But that depends on everybody getting the information they need to make the right choices."

IF MONEY IS MEASURE OF MUSCLE

WASHINGTON—Smoking is down, but profits are up and so are political contributions from tobacco growers, cigarette manufacturers and the network of interests that are tied to the leaf.

The word on Capitol Hill is that the once herculean tobacco lobby is losing its punch. But money is the muscle behind lobbying, and by that gauge tobacco is as powerful as ever, perhaps more so.

In the last election cycle, for example, Philip Morris, the nation's largest cigarette manufacturer, ranked second among all corporate contributors to election campaigns, according to records on file with the Federal Election Commission, having handed out $559,505.

RJR-Nabisco spent $229,725, ranking 30th among corporate givers, according to FEC records.

The Tobacco Institute, the principal industry trade association, contributed $222,114 in the 1985–86 cycle, according to the FEC.

Together, the three giants of the tobacco industry have directed nearly $2.2 million into political campaigns since 1980, according to figures compiled by the Almanac of Federal Political Action Committees.

But spending by tobacco PACs can be deceptive. Both Philip Morris and RJR-Nabisco, which together account for about two-thirds of the cigarette market, are gargantuan conglomerates, embracing a far-flung array of interests.

Congressmen reported last July before a House vote on banning cigarette smoking on airlines that lobbyists from retail outlets and soft drink companies owned by one or another tobacco conglomerate pressed the pro-tobacco line as if their corporate lives depended on the outcome.

In addition, the well-heeled network of tobacco retainers from Washington's top law firms to the nation's premier advertising agencies are also freewheeling contributors to political campaigns.

There are, for instance, 23 tobacco companies or associations listed in the 1987 edition of *Washington Representatives*. All of them have either PACs or wealthy lawyers representing their interests on Capitol Hill.

Finally, congressional observers report, billboard companies have become surrogates for tobacco interests since advertising was banned from television and billboards became a primary advertising outlet for cigarettes.

The Outdoor Advertising Association PAC, representing 200 companies that own advertising billboards, is recognized as one of the most effective lobbying groups in the Capitol, spending in the $100,000-plus category in each election cycle.

The Outdoor Advertising Association's PAC contributions have been nearly doubling each cycle since 1980, and there is no indication the pace has subsided.

The Ford Pinto

W. Michael Hoffman*

I

On August 10, 1978, a tragic automobile accident occurred on U.S. Highway 33 near Goshen, Indiana. Sisters Judy and Lynn Ulrich (ages 18 and 16, respectively) and their cousin

Written for the first edition of this book. Copyright © 1984 by W. Michael Hoffman.
*Director, Center for Business Ethics, Bentley College.

Donna Ulrich (age 18) were struck from the rear in their 1973 Ford Pinto by a van. The gas tank of the Pinto ruptured, the car burst into flames, and the three teenagers were burned to death.

Subsequently an Elkhart County grand jury returned a criminal homicide charge against Ford, the first ever against an American corporation. During the following twenty-week trial, Judge Harold R. Staffeldt advised the jury that Ford should be convicted of reckless homicide if it were shown that the company had engaged in "plain, conscious and unjustifiable disregard of harm that might result (from its actions) and the disregard involves a substantial deviation from acceptable standards of conduct."[1]

The key phrase around which the trial hinged, of course, is "acceptable standards." Did Ford knowingly and recklessly choose profit over safety in the design and placement of the Pinto's gas tank? Elkhart County prosecutor Michael A. Cosentino and chief Ford attorney James F. Neal battled dramatically over this issue in a rural Indiana courthouse. Meanwhile, American business anxiously awaited the verdict which could send warning ripples through boardrooms across the nation concerning corporate responsibility and product liability.

II

As a background to this trial some discussion of the Pinto controversy is necessary. In 1977 the magazine *Mother Jones* broke a story by Mark Dowie, general manager of *Mother Jones* business operations, accusing Ford of knowingly putting on the road an unsafe car—the Pinto—in which hundreds of people have needlessly suffered burn deaths and even more have been scarred and disfigured from burns. In his article "Pinto Madness" Dowie charges that:

- Fighting strong competition from Volkswagen for the lucrative small-car market, the Ford Motor Company rushed the Pinto into production in much less than the usual time.

- Ford engineers discovered in preproduction crash tests that rear-end collisions would rupture the Pinto's fuel system extremely easily.
- Because assembly-line machinery was already tooled when engineers found this defect, top Ford officials decided to manufacture the car anyway—exploding gas tank and all—even though Ford owned the patent on a much safer gas tank.
- For more than eight years afterward, Ford successfully lobbied, with extraordinary vigor and some blatant lies, against a key government safety standard that would have forced the company to change the Pinto's fire-prone gas tank.

By conservative estimates Pinto crashes have caused 500 burn deaths to people who would not have been seriously injured if the car had not burst into flames. The figure could be as high as 900. Burning Pintos have become such an embarrassment to Ford that its advertising agency, J. Walter Thompson, dropped a line from the ending of a radio spot that read "Pinto leaves you with that warm feeling."

Ford knows that the Pinto is a firetrap, yet it has paid out millions to settle damage suits out of court, and it is prepared to spend millions more lobbying against safety standards. With a half million cars rolling off the assembly lines each year, Pinto is the biggest-selling subcompact in America, and the company's operating profit on the car is fantastic. Finally, in 1977, new Pinto models have incorporated a few minor alterations necessary to meet that federal standard Ford managed to hold off for eight years. Why did the company delay so long in making these minimal, inexpensive improvements?

- Ford waited eight years because its internal "cost-benefit analysis," which places a dollar value on human life, said it wasn't profitable to make the changes sooner.[2]

Several weeks after Dowie's press conference on the article, which had the support of Ralph Nader and auto safety expert Byron Bloch, Ford issued a news release attributed to Herbert T. Misch, vice president of Environmental and Safety Engineering, countering points made in the *Mother Jones* article. Their statistical studies conflict significantly with each other. For example, Dowie states that more than 3,000 people were burning to death yearly in auto fires; he claims that, according to a National Highway Traffic Safety Administration (NHTSA) consultant, although Ford makes 24 percent of the cars on American roads, these cars account for 42 percent of the collision-ruptured fuel tanks.[3] Ford, on the other hand, uses statistics from the Fatality Analysis Reporting System (FARS) maintained by the government's NHTSA to defend itself, claiming that in 1975 there were 848 deaths related to fire-associated passenger-car accidents and only 13 of these involved Pintos; in 1976, Pintos accounted for only 22 out of 943. These statistics imply that Pintos were involved in only 1.9 percent of such accidents, and Pintos constitute about 1.9 percent of the total registered passenger cars. Furthermore, fewer than half of those Pintos cited in the FARS study were struck in the rear.[4] Ford concludes from this and other studies that the Pinto was never an unsafe car and has not been involved in some 70 burn deaths annually, as *Mother Jones* claims.

Ford admits that early-model Pintos did not meet rear-impact tests at 20 mph but denies that this implies that they were unsafe compared with other cars of that type and era. In fact, according to Ford, some of its tests were conducted with experimental rubber "bladders" to protect the gas tank, in order to determine how best to have its future cars meet a 20-mph rear-collision standard which Ford itself set as an internal performance goal. The government at that time had no such standard. Ford also points out that in every model year the Pinto met or surpassed the government's own standards, and

it simply is unreasonable and unfair to contend that a car is somehow unsafe if it does not meet standards proposed for future years or embody the technological improvements that are introduced in later model years.[5]

Mother Jones, on the other hand, presents a different view of the situation. If Ford was so concerned about rear-impact safety, why did it delay the federal government's attempts to impose standards? Dowie gives the following answer:

The particular regulation involved here was Federal Motor Vehicle Safety Standard 301. Ford picked portions of Standard 301 for strong opposition way back in 1968 when the Pinto was still in the blueprint stage. The intent of 301, and the 300 series that followed it, was to protect drivers and passengers after a crash occurs. Without question the worst post-crash hazard is fire. So Standard 301 originally proposed that all cars should be able to withstand a fixed barrier impact of 20 mph (that is, running into a wall at that speed) without losing fuel.

When the standard was proposed, Ford engineers pulled their crash-test results out of their files. The front ends of most cars were no problem— with minor alterations they could stand the impact without losing fuel. "We were already working on the front end," Ford engineer Dick Kimble admitted. "We knew we could meet the test on the front end." But with the Pinto particularly, a 20 mph rear-end standard meant redesigning the entire rear end of the car. With the Pinto scheduled for production in August of 1970, and with $200 million worth of tools in place, adoption of this standard would have created a minor financial disaster. So Standard 301 was targeted for delay, and with some assistance from its industry associates, Ford succeeded beyond its wildest expectations: the standard was not adopted until the 1977 model year.[6]

Ford's tactics were successful, according to Dowie, not only due to their extremely clever lobbying, which became the envy of lobbyists all over Washington, but also because of the pro-industry stance of NHTSA itself.

Furthermore, it is not at all clear that the Pinto was as safe as comparable cars with regard to the positioning of its gas tank. Unlike the gas tank in the Capri, which rode over the rear axle, a "saddle-type" fuel tank on which Ford owned the patent, the Pinto tank was placed just behind the rear bumper. According to Dowie,

Dr. Leslie Ball, the retired safety chief for the NASA manned space program and a founder of the International Society of Reliability Engineers, recently made a careful study of the Pinto. "The release to production of the Pinto was the most reprehensible decision in the history of American engineering," he said. Ball can name more than 40 European and Japanese models in the Pinto price and weight range with safer gas-tank positioning.

Los Angeles auto safety expert Byron Bloch has made an in-depth study of the Pinto fuel system. "It's a catastrophic blunder," he says. "Ford made an extremely irresponsible decision when they placed such a weak tank in such a ridiculous location in such a soft rear end. It's almost designed to blow up—premeditated."[7]

Although other points could be brought out in the debate between *Mother Jones* and Ford, perhaps the most intriguing and controversial is the cost-benefit analysis study that Ford did entitled "Fatalities Associated with Crash-Induced Fuel Leakage and Fires" released by J. C. Echold, director of automotive safety for Ford. This study apparently convinced Ford and was intended to convince the federal government that a technological improvement costing $11 per car which would have prevented gas tanks from rupturing so easily was not cost effective for society. The costs and benefits are broken down in the following way:

Benefits

Savings:	180 burn deaths, 180 serious burn injuries, 2,100 burned vehicles
Unit Cost:	$200,000 per death, $67,000 per injury, $700 per vehicle
Total Benefit:	180 × $200,000 +180 × $67,000 + 2,100 × $700 = *$49.5 million*

Costs

Sales:	11 million cars, 1.5 million light trucks
Unit Cost:	$11 per car, $11 per truck
Total Cost:	11,000,000 × $11 + 1,500,000 × $11 = *$137 million*

And where did Ford come up with the $200,000 figure as the cost per death? This came from a NHTSA study which broke down the estimated social costs of a death as follows:

Component	1971 Costs
Future productivity losses	
Direct	$132,000
Indirect	41,300
Medical costs	
Hospital	700
Other	425
Property damage	1,500
Insurance administration	4,700
Legal and court	3,000
Employer losses	1,000
Victim's pain and suffering	10,000
Funeral	900
Assets (lost consumption)	5,000
Miscellaneous	200
Total per fatality	$200,725

(Although this analysis was on all Ford vehicles, a breakout of just the Pinto could be done.) *Mother Jones* reports it could not find anybody who could explain how the $10,000 figure for "pain and suffering" had been arrived at.[8]

Although Ford does not mention this point in its news release defense, one might have replied that it was the federal government, not Ford, that set the figure for a burn death. Ford simply carried out a cost-benefit analysis based on that figure. *Mother Jones*, however, in addition to insinuating that there was industry-agency (NHTSA) collusion, argues that the $200,000 figure was arrived at under intense pressure from the auto industry to use cost-benefit analysis in determining regulations. *Mother Jones* also questions Ford's estimate of burn injuries: "All independent experts estimate that for each person who dies by an auto fire, many more are left with charred hands, faces and limbs." Referring to the Northern California Burn Center, which estimates the ratio of burn injuries to deaths at ten to one instead of one to one, Dowie states that "the true ratio obviously throws the company's calculations way off."[9] Finally, *Mother Jones* claims to have obtained "confidential" Ford documents which Ford did not send to Washington, showing that crash fires could largely be prevented by installing a rubber bladder inside the gas tank for only $5.08 per car, considerably less than the $11 per car Ford originally claimed was required to improve crashworthiness.[10]

Instead of making the $11 improvement, installing the $5.08 bladder, or even giving the consumer the right to choose the additional cost for added safety, Ford continued, according to *Mother Jones*, to delay the federal government for eight years in establishing mandatory rear-impact standards. In the meantime, Dowie argues, thousands of people were burning to death and tens of thousands more were being badly burned and disfigured for life, while many of these tragedies could have been prevented for only a slight cost per vehicle. Furthermore, the delay also meant that millions of new unsafe vehicles went on the road, "vehicles that will be crashing, leaking fuel and incinerating people well into the 1980s."[11]

In concluding his article Dowie broadens his attack beyond just Ford and the Pinto.

> Unfortunately, the Pinto is not an isolated case of corporate malpractice in the auto industry. Neither is Ford a lone sinner. There probably isn't a car on the road without a safety hazard known to its manufacturer....
>
> Furthermore, cost-valuing human life is not used by Ford alone. Ford was just the only company careless enough to let such an embarrassing cal-

culation slip into public records. The process of willfully trading lives for profits is built into corporate capitalism. Commodore Vanderbilt publicly scorned George Westinghouse and his "foolish" air brakes while people died by the hundreds in accidents on Vanderbilt's railroads.[12]

Ford has paid millions of dollars in Pinto jury trials and out-of-court settlements, especially the latter. *Mother Jones* quotes Al Slechter in Ford's Washington office as saying: "We'll never go to a jury again. Not in a fire case. Juries are just too sentimental. They see those charred remains and forget the evidence. No sir, we'll settle."[13] But apparently Ford thought such settlements would be less costly than the safety improvements. Dowie wonders if Ford would continue to make the same decisions "were Henry Ford II and Lee Iacocca serving twenty-year terms in Leavenworth for consumer homicide."[14]

III

On March 13, 1980, the Elkhart County jury found Ford not guilty of criminal homicide in the Ulrich case. Ford attorney Neal summarized several points in his closing argument before the jury. Ford could have stayed out of the small-car market, which would have been the "easiest way," since Ford would have made more profit by sticking to bigger cars. Instead, Ford built the Pinto "to take on the imports, to save jobs for Americans and to make a profit for its stockholders."[15] The Pinto met every fuel-system standard of any federal, state, or local government, and was comparable to other 1973 subcompacts. The engineers who designed the car thought it was a good, safe car and bought it for themselves and their families. Ford did everything possible to recall the Pinto quickly after NHTSA ordered it to do so. Finally, and more specifically to the case at hand, Highway 33 was a badly designed highway, and the girls were fully stopped when a 4,000-pound van rammed into the rear of their Pinto at at least 50 miles an hour. Given the same circumstances, Neal stated, any

car would have suffered the same consequences as the Ulrich's Pinto.[16] As reported in the *New York Times* and *Time,* the verdict brought a "loud cheer" from Ford's board of directors and undoubtedly at least a sigh of relief from other corporations around the nation.

Many thought this case was that of a David against a Goliath because of the small amount of money and volunteer legal help Prosecutor Cosentino had in contrast to the huge resources Ford poured into the trial. In addition, it should be pointed out that Cosentino's case suffered from a ruling by Judge Staffeldt that Ford's own test results on pre-1973 Pintos were inadmissible. These documents confirmed that Ford knew as early as 1971 that the gas tank of the Pinto ruptured at impacts of 20 mph and that the company was aware, because of tests with the Capri, that the over-the-axle position of the gas tank was much safer than mounting it behind the axle. Ford decided to mount it behind the axle in the Pinto to provide more trunk space and to save money. The restrictions of Cosentino's evidence to testimony relating specifically to the 1973 Pinto severely undercut the strength of the prosecutor's case.[17]

Whether this evidence would have changed the minds of the jury will never be known. Some, however, such as business ethicist Richard De George, feel that this evidence shows grounds for charges of recklessness against Ford. Although it is true that there were no federal safety standards in 1973 to which Ford legally had to conform and although Neal seems to have proved that all subcompacts were unsafe when hit at 50 mph by a 4,000-pound van, the fact that the NHTSA ordered a recall of the Pinto and not other subcompacts is, according to De George, "*prima facie* evidence that Ford's Pinto gas tank mounting was substandard."[18] De George argues that these grounds for recklessness are made even stronger by the fact that Ford did not give the consumer a choice to make the Pinto gas tank safer by installing a rubber bladder for a rather modest fee.[19] Giving the consumer such a choice, of course, would have made the Pinto gas tank problem known and therefore probably would have been bad for sales.

Richard A. Epstein, professor of law at the University of Chicago Law School, questions whether Ford should have been brought up on criminal charges of reckless homicide at all. He also points out an interesting historical fact. Before 1966 an injured party in Indiana could not even bring civil charges against an automobile manufacturer solely because of the alleged "uncrashworthiness" of a car; one would have to seek legal relief from the other party involved in the accident, not from the manufacturer. But after *Larson v. General Motors Corp.* in 1968, a new era of crashworthiness suits against automobile manufacturers began. "Reasonable" precautions must now be taken by manufacturers to minimize personal harm in crashes.[20] How to apply criteria of reasonableness in such cases marks the whole nebulous ethical and legal arena of product liability.

If such a civil suit had been brought against Ford, Epstein believes, the corporation might have argued, as it did to a large extent in the criminal suit, that the Pinto conformed to all current applicable safety standards and with common industry practice. (Epstein cites that well over 90 percent of United States standard production cars had their gas tanks in the same position as the Pinto.) But in a civil trial the adequacy of industry standards are ultimately up to the jury, and had civil charges been brought against Ford in this case the plaintiffs might have had a better chance of winning.[21] Epstein feels that a criminal suit, on the other hand, had no chance from the very outset, because the prosecutor would have had to establish criminal intent on the part of Ford. To use an analogy, if a hunter shoots at a deer and wounds an unseen person, he may be held civilly responsible but not criminally responsible because he did not intend to harm. And even though it may be more difficult to determine the mental state of a corporation (or its principal agents), it seems clear

to Epstein that the facts of this case do not prove any such criminal intent even though Ford may have known that some burn deaths and injuries could have been avoided by a different placement of its Pinto gas tank and that Ford consciously decided not to spend more money to save lives.[22] Everyone recognizes that there are trade-offs between safety and costs. Ford could have built a "tank" instead of a Pinto, thereby considerably reducing risks, but it would have been relatively unaffordable for most and probably unattractive to all potential consumers.

To have established Ford's reckless homicide it would have been necessary to establish the same of Ford's agents, since a corporation can only act through its agents. Undoubtedly, continues Epstein, the reason why the prosecutor did not try to subject Ford's officers and engineers to fines and imprisonment for their design choices is "the good faith character of their judgment, which was necessarily decisive in Ford's behalf as well."[23] For example, Harold C. MacDonald, Ford's chief engineer on the Pinto, testified that he felt it was important to keep the gas tank as far from the passenger compartment as possible, as it was in the Pinto. And other Ford engineers testified that they used the car for their own families. This is relevant information in a criminal case which must be concerned about the intent of the agents.

Furthermore, even if civil charges had been made in this case, it seems unfair and irrelevant to Epstein to accuse Ford of trading cost for safety. Ford's use of cost-benefit formulas, which must assign monetary values to human life and suffering, is precisely what the law demands in assessing civil liability suits. The court may disagree with the decision, but to blame industry for using such a method would violate the very rules of civil liability. Federal automobile officials (NHTSA) had to make the same calculations in order to discharge their statutory duties. In allowing the Pinto design, are not they too (and in turn their employer, the United States) just as guilty as Ford's agents?[24]

IV

The case of the Ford Pinto raises many questions of ethical importance. Some people conclude that Ford was definitely wrong in designing and marketing the Pinto. The specific accident involving the Ulrich girls, because of the circumstances, was simply not the right one to have attacked Ford on. Other people believe that Ford was neither criminally nor civilly guilty of anything and acted completely responsibly in producing the Pinto. Many others, I suspect, find the case morally perplexing, too complex to make sweeping claims of guilt or innocence.

Was Ford irresponsible in rushing the production of the Pinto? Even though Ford violated no federal safety standards or laws, should it have made the Pinto safer in terms of rear-end collisions, especially regarding the placement of the gas tank? Should Ford have used cost-benefit analysis to make decisions relating to safety, specifically placing dollar values on human life and suffering? Knowing that the Pinto's gas tank could have been made safer by installing a protective bladder for a relatively small cost per consumer, perhaps Ford should have made that option available to the public. If Ford did use heavy lobbying efforts to delay and/or influence federal safety standards, was this ethically proper for a corporation to do? One might ask, if Ford was guilty, whether the engineers, the managers, or both are to blame. If Ford had been found guilty of criminal homicide, was the proposed penalty stiff enough ($10,000 maximum fine for each of the three counts equals $30,000 maximum), or should agents of the corporation such as MacDonald, Iacocca, and Henry Ford II be fined and possibly jailed?

A number of questions concerning safety standards are also relevant to the ethical issues at stake in the Ford trial. Is it just to blame a corporation for not abiding by "acceptable standards" when such standards are not yet determined by society? Should corporations like Ford play a role in setting such standards? Should individual juries be determining such standards state by state, incident by incident? If Ford should be setting safety standards, how does it decide how safe to make its product and still make it affordable and desirable to the public without using cost-benefit analysis? For that matter, how does anyone decide? Perhaps it is putting Ford, or any corporation, in a catch-22 position to ask it both to set safety standards and to make a competitive profit for its stockholders.

Regardless of how we answer these and other questions it is clear that the Pinto case raises fundamental issues concerning the responsibilities of corporations, how corporations should structure themselves in order to make ethical decisions, and how industry, government, and society in general ought to interrelate to form a framework within which such decisions can properly be made in the future.

NOTES

1. *The Indianapolis Star,* Sunday, Mar. 9, 1980, Section 3, p. 2.
2. Mark Dowie, "Pinto Madness," *Mother Jones,* September–October, 1977, pp. 18, 20. Subsequently Mike Wallace for "Sixty Minutes" and Sylvia Chase for "20-20" came out with similar exposés.
3. *Ibid.,* p. 30.
4. Ford news release (Sept. 9, 1977), pp. 1–3.
5. *Ibid.,* p. 5.
6. Dowie, p. 29.
7. *Ibid.,* pp. 22–23.
8. *Ibid.,* pp. 24, 28.
9. *Ibid.,* p. 28.
10. *Ibid.,* pp. 28–29.
11. *Ibid.,* p. 30.
12. *Ibid.,* p. 32. Dowie might have cited another example which emerged in the private correspondence which transpired almost a half-century ago between Lammot du Pont and Alfred P. Sloan, Jr., then president of GM. Du Pont was trying to convince Sloan to equip GM's lowest-priced cars, Chevrolets, with safety glass. Sloan replied by saying: "It is not my responsibility to sell safety

glass.... You can say, perhaps, that I am selfish, but business is selfish. We are not a charitable institution—we are trying to make a profit for our stockholders." [Quoted in Morton Mintz and Jerry S. Cohen, *Power, Inc.* (New York: The Viking Press, 1976), p. 110.]

13. *Ibid.*, p. 31.

14. *Ibid.*, p. 32.

15. Transcript of report of proceedings in *State of Indiana v. Ford Motor Company,* Cause No. 11-431, Monday, Mar. 10, 1980, pp. 6202–6203. How Neal reconciled his "easiest way" point with his "making more profit for stockholders" point is not clear to this writer.

16. *Ibid.*, pp. 6207–6209.

17. *Chicago Tribune*, Oct. 13, 1979, p. 1, and Section 2, p. 12; *New York Times*, Oct. 14, 1979, p. 26; *The Atlanta Constitution*, Feb. 7, 1980.

18. Richard De George, "Ethical Responsibilities of Engineers in Large Organizations: The Pinto Case," *Business and Professional Ethics Journal,* vol. 1., No. 1 (Fall 1981), p. 4. *The New York Times*, Oct. 26, 1978, p. 103, also points out that during 1976 and 1977 there were thirteen fiery fatal rear-end collisions involving Pintos, more than double that of other United States comparable cars, with VW Rabbits and Toyota Corollas having none.

19. *Ibid.*, p. 5.

20. Richard A. Epstein, "Is Pinto a Criminal?", *Regulation*, March–April, 1980, pp. 16–17.

21. A California jury awarded damages of $127.8 million (reduced later to $6.3 million on appeal) in a Pinto crash in which a youth was burned over 95 percent of his body. See *New York Times*, Feb. 8, 1978, p. 8.

22. Epstein, p. 19.

23. *Ibid.*, pp. 20–21.

24. *Ibid.*, pp. 19–21.

Hooker Chemical and the Love Canal

Timothy S. Mescon* and George S. Vozikis †

Just prior to the turn of the century, Colonel William Love arrived in Niagara Falls, New York, with a dream. Love envisioned a canal that would connect the upper and lower Niagara Rivers across the peninsula, drop it over a 300-foot Niagara escarpment, and bring a new source of electrical power to the area. Love envisioned a model industrial city emerging in this beautiful upstate New York area. Initial support was slow in developing, so Love started digging the canal by himself until financial backers were identified. Unfortunately, the combination of an economic depression, which dried up Colonel Love's sources of funds, and the invention of alternating current (which meant that electricity could be transmitted over distances) brought an abrupt halt to Colonel Love's dream. The canal served as a swimming hole in the summer and as a skating rink in the winter for over 30 years until it was acquired by Hooker Electrochemical Company in 1942.

HOOKER CHEMICAL—A BRIEF HISTORY

Elon Huntington Hooker was the founder of the Development and Funding Company [1906], which was the predecessor of the Hooker Electrochemical Company, later renamed Hooker Chemical Company.

During both World Wars, Hooker Electro-

Excerpted from "Hooker Chemical and the Love Canal," published in *Management Policy and Strategy,* 2d ed., edited by George A. Steiner et al. (New York: Macmillan Publishing Co., Inc., 1982). Reprinted by permission of Timothy S. Mescon.

*Franklin Perdue School of Business, Salisbury State University.

†Department of Management, Memphis State University.

chemical Company was instrumental in America's effort to achieve independence in the field of industrial chemistry. The company built and ran five defense plants for the government, turning out scores of chemicals useful in products from synthetic rubber to waterproof tents. The company also participated in the Manhattan District Atomic Project. In the decade following World War II, the company's sales grew from $15 million to $54 million. The company was also producing more than 100 chemicals in three locations. In 1958, the company incorporated. Ten years later, Occidental Petroleum Corporation acquired the company through a stock exchange. One dollar invested in the Hooker Company in 1905 had grown to $3077. Today, Hooker is the tenth largest chemical company in the nation, with 1979 sales of $1.7 billion. Hooker Chemical Corporation has 30 plants in 11 countries, and employs more than 110,000 workers. Few Americans are ever out of reach of Hooker's products. The company's chemicals can be found in toothpaste, soap, gasolines, tires, inks, and diapers, to name just a few products.

THE LOVE CANAL

Between the years 1942–53 Hooker disposed its chemical wastes in the Love Canal. The Love Canal was considered an ideal landfill site for chemical residues and numerous other wastes for two basic reasons: (1) at the time, the canal area was sparsely populated, and (2) the soil was an impervious clay that was characteristic of the land in that part of New York state. Such impervious clay created a natural ''vault'' which would hold the chemical residues and other industrial wastes.

The sections of the canal used by Hooker were isolated as needed. The chemical wastes were transported to the site in drums and were then placed, either in the old canal bed or a new excavation, and covered with several feet of clay material.

By 1952, the Board of Education of the City of Niagara Falls wanted the Love Canal site for a school, and Hooker found itself facing the threat of seizure of the land by the law of eminent domain. Resulting from the persistence of the School Board in 1953 Hooker deeded the land to the city for $1. The deed contained the following admonition:

> Prior to the delivery of this instrument of conveyance, the grantee herein has been advised by the grantor that the premises above described have been filled, in whole or in part, to the present grade level thereof with waste products resulting from the manufacturing of chemicals by the grantor at its plant in the City of Niagara Falls, New York, and the grantee assumes all risk and liability incident to the use thereof. It is, therefore, understood and agreed that, as a part of the consideration for this conveyance and as a condition thereof, no claim, suit, action or demand of any nature whatsoever shall ever be made by the grantee, its successors or assigns, against the grantor, including death resulting therefrom, or loss of or damage to property caused by, in connection with or by reason of the presence of said industrial wastes. It is further agreed as a condition hereof that each subsequent conveyance of the aforesaid lands shall be made subject to the foregoing provisions and conditions.

After acquiring the land, the School Board subdivided it and built a school adjacent to the central portion of the canal. The northern part of the land was deeded to the city and the southern portion was eventually sold to a private developer. In time, despite the warning issued by Hooker, houses and shopping centers sprang up in the area (no homes, however, were built directly on the Love Canal property). The basements of many of these houses expanded into the impervious clay. When the construction crews removed the topsoil covering the surface of the Love Canal, rain and snow began to seep into the canal gradually forcing a chemical mixture, leachate, to flow out of sealed containers.

As early as 1958 some children playing above the Love Canal dump site had to be treated for chemical burns; this, however, was merely a minor indication of the problems to come. Throughout the 1970s heavy rains accelerated the erosion of the more than 199,900 tons of contaminated waste representing 150 chemical compounds in the area [EPA Hits Hooker, 1979]. As the waste oozed to the surface, some ominous statistics also began to emerge. An unusually high percentage of miscarriages, serious birth defects, liver abnormalities, chromosome breakdown, and cancer was detected in the area. Additionally, a strong smell emitted from the chemicals prompted one local resident to claim, "The whole area stinks" [Molotsky, 1979].

THE CONFLICT

On May 21, 1980, President Carter signed an emergency order under which the federal government and the state of New York will share the ($3–$5 million) cost of relocating 710 Love Canal area families to other housing. This move will be in addition to the 239 other families who were forced to abandon their homes in 1978 after toxic fumes were discovered in their basements and traces of trichlorophenal (which breaks down into dioxin and can cause cancer, nervous system depression, liver and kidney damage, and irritate skin and mucous membranes) were found in nearby drainage ditches. President Carter's action followed the release of a study conducted by the Environmental Protection Agency (EPA) that examined 36 residents in the area and concluded that 11 showed signs of chromosome breakdown.

In December 1979 the EPA filed a complaint against Hooker Chemical, the city of Niagara Falls and the Niagara Falls Board of Education. In part, the complaint stated,

> Hooker neither warned residents and developers in the vicinity that contact with materials at the canal could be injurious, nor did it take any action to prevent future injuries due to exposure of the wastes. [What Hooker Told Whom, When About Love Canal, 1980]

Only two of the nine school board members who accepted the deed to the land in 1953 can be found. Although the transference of the deed took place almost 30 years ago, Irma Runals, one of the school board members, who insists that Hooker warned no one of any dangers said, "By golly, you certainly would remember that" [Molotsky, 1979].

Minutes collected from the Board of Education meetings held in 1957 prior to the subdivision of the land, however, indicate that representatives from Hooker did indeed urge the Board not to approve construction on the land.

Arthur Chambers, appearing before the Board on November 7, 1957, as a representative of Hooker's Legal Department,

> reminded the board that...the land was not suitable for construction where underground facilities are necessary. It was their (Hooker's) intent that the property be used for a school and for parking. He referred to the moral obligation on the part of the Board of Education in the event the property is sold." [What Hooker Told Whom, When About Love Canal, 1980]

On November 22, Chambers reappeared before the Board and warned,

> there are dangerous chemicals buried there in drums, in loose form, in solids and liquids. It was understood the land would be used for a park or some surface activity if it was developed. [What Hooker Told Whom, When About Love Canal, 1980]

A 1979 study conducted by the American Institute of Chemical Engineers told a Senate environmental subcommittee that the original dump site was *well within federal guidelines* set in 1976 by the Resource Conservation and Recovery Act. According to the researchers, "the problem at Love Canal was a lack of remedial work" [Love Canal Lessons, 1980].

The Resource Conservation and Recovery Act was designed to control the treatment of hazardous wastes from their generation to their ultimate disposal. This 1976 law deals primarily with the regulation of *new* waste-disposal sites. To date, EPA officials have been somewhat reluctant to regulate dumps already in existence because the law requires that there be an "imminent hazard" to public health before the government can step in. (Hazardous wastes are defined by the EPA as those that are flammable, corrosive, or toxic to humans, or that react violently with chemicals. Some 36 million tons of hazardous wastes are manufactured each year.)

For its part, Hooker, which has not officially owned the land for 20 years, does not consider that it had any responsibility in the matter. The company did, however, volunteer to share the cost of the consulting engineers' study and to contribute one third of the original estimate for the cost of a remedial program.

The other two-thirds of the cost of recapping the southern portion of the canal was to be assumed by the school board and the city. However, because of the school board's inability to raise the necessary funds and the delay in rectifying the existing situation, a state of emergency was declared and the federal and state governments assumed the costs of the remedial program. According to sources at Hooker, the company is still willing to share the cost, as long as the school board and the local government also participate.

HOOKER'S PAST RECORD

Although Hooker does not claim responsibility for the Love Canal situation, it has admitted to falsifying records concerning releases of toxic waste in upstate New York and the pollution of wells on Long Island. An internal memo at Hooker's Durex division also disclosed that "Hooker had instructed supervisors on how to hide toxic waste and spills inside the plant from New York State Department of Environmental Control inspectors" [Galdston, 1979, p. 27].

Other dumping and storage acts on Hooker's part seem to solidify critics' concerns. Recent disclosures include the dumping of Kepone (a known carcinogen) into the James River in Virginia, runoff from improperly stored barrels of Mirex (a carcinogen) into Lake Ontario, which prompted health officials to bar all commercial and private fishing on the lake, and the release of Mirex being stored in rotting barrels into Lake Michigan.

A company report titled "Operation Bootstrap" indicates that Hooker employees frequently handled carcinogenic chemicals with little personal protection. "Operation Bootstrap" also revealed that a variety of dangerous gases (chlorine, phosphorous, chlorides, mercury, and so on) were being released into the air outside of the company's Niagara Falls facility. Moreover, in April 1979, Hooker employees showed a Buffalo, New York, newspaper reporter their "Hooker bumps," which were red bumps on their necks and faces caused by contact with trichlorophenal in the plant [Galdston, 1979, p. 27]. One outspoken critic has stated, "Of the 5500 chemical companies in the United States, Hooker Chemical Company has thus far been most frequently, almost consistently, associated with the worst instances of illegal and inadequate toxic waste dumping" [Galdston, 1979, p. 25].

AND NOW...

Currently, 44 states are pursuing plans for action in the waste disposal area. While Love Canal presents a serious problem, many experts are divided on whether the Love Canal is more the exception rather than the rule. Carl A. Goslini of the Chemical Manufacturers Association attempts to dispel the notion that chemical companies dump their wastes in clandestine manner by stating: "94 percent of all solid chemical (industrial) waste generated by the 54 largest chemical producers in the last 30 years repose in facilities owned by them. Of the remainder, 5 percent are in known other sites, only 1 percent in unknown facilities" [Evans, 1980].

Love Canal is only one of an estimated 100,000 industrial waste dumps in the United

States. Additionally, there are some 18,500 municipal sites for the disposal of solid wastes and 23,000 sewage-sludge dumps; 1200 of these dumps have been classified as "dangerous" by the EPA [Hazardous Wastes—How Dangerous?, 1979]. The EPA estimates that the cost of cleaning up the most dangerous dumps could exceed $3 billion and that as much as $22 billion will be required to neutralize all *potentially* hazardous sites.

In the meantime Hooker is continuing with its clean-up program. The leachate that seeped out of the canal is being rechanneled into an underground tank from which it will be pumped through a charcoal filtering system to remove the toxic chemicals prior to being sent to the city waste-treatment plant. Finally a new clay cap is being placed over the entire site [McWilliams, 1979].

> One significant effect of the Love Canal situation has been the focusing of national attention on the whole subject of industrial waste disposal. In common with other corporations, Occidental had been concentrating on this problem, applying its research facilities and devoting money toward the development of a solution. But more is needed. It will take a strenuous effort by industry, government, and the academic community to solve the problem, but solve it we must so that we can continue to benefit from the contribution the chemical industry makes to our lives. And, equally important, so that there be no Love Canals tomorrow [McWilliams, 1979].

NOTES

"A Formula to Settle Toxic Dump Problems," *Business Week,* 14 January 1980, p. 34.

"An Alarming Silence on Chemical Wastes," *Business Week,* 7 May 1979, pp. 44–46.

"A Review of Hooker's Chemical Disposal Sites in the Niagara Frontier," *Hooker Chemical Company,* March 1979, pp. 3–4.

Beck, Melinda, "A Caustic Report on Chemical Dumps," *Newsweek,* October 22, 1979, p. 51.

Dionne, E. J. Jr. "New York Survey Lists Industrial Poisons," *New York Times,* 9 August 1978, p. 1:3.

"EPA Hits Hooker with Suits Asking $118MM for Clean Up of Hazardous Waste Dumps," *Chemical Marketing Reporter,* vol. 216, no. 26, December 24, 1979, p. 47.

Evans, M. Stenton. "... And Government Overreacts," *The Phoenix Gazette,* June 2, 1980, p. A-6.

Galdston, K. "Hooker Chemical's Nightmarish Pollution Record," *Business and Society Review,* Summer 1979, pp. 25–28.

Hammer, Stephen. "The Invisible Friend," *Oxy Today and Yesterday #9,* 1977, pp. 17–21.

"Hazardous Wastes—How Dangerous?" *U.S. News & World Report,* November 5, 1979, p. 46.

"Hooker Beset by Disposal Problems, Sees Troubles Mount on Long Island," *Chemical Marketing Reporter,* 11 June 1979, pp. 3–24.

"Hooker and Velsicol Outline Cleanup Actions," *Chemical Week,* 4 April 1979.

"Hooker Tells Its Side of the Story," *Chemical Week,* 27 June 1979, p. 34.

"Love Canal Lessons," *The Wall Street Journal,* May 22, 1980, p. 24.

McNeil, Donald G., Jr. "Health Chief Calls Niagara Falls Waste Site A Peril," *New York Times,* 3 August 1978, p. 1–6.

McWilliams, Bruce. "Special Report: Love Canal," *Oxy Today #13,* 1979, p. 5.

Molosky, Irvin. "A Love Canal Warning No One Can Recall," *New York Times,* April 14, 1979, p. 22L.

"New Rule Asked For Controlling Unsafe Wastes." *New York Times,* 15 December 1978, p. 20.

Simon, Ellis. "Everyone Denies Liability in N.Y. Chemical Disaster." *Business Insurance,* 25 December 1978, p. 1.

Thomas, Robert E. *Salt and Water, Power and People.* New York, Hooker Electro Company, 1955.

"Upstate Waste Site May Endanger Lives." *New York Times,* 2 August 1978, p. 1.

"What Hooker Told Whom, When About Love Canal." *The Wall Street Journal,* June 19, 1980, p. 18.

A South African Investment

Manuel G. Velasquez*

In April 1977, the Interfaith Center on Corporate Responsibility announced that some of its subscribing members owned stock in Texaco, Inc. and in Standard Oil Co. of California (SoCal), and that these members would introduce shareholders' resolutions at the next annual stockholders' meeting of Texaco and SoCal that would require that these companies and their affiliates terminate their operations in South Africa. The effort to get Texaco and SoCal out of South Africa was primarily directed and coordinated by Tim Smith, project director of the Interfaith Center on Corporate Responsibility. The stockholders' resolution that Tim Smith would have the Interfaith shareholders introduce at the annual meetings of Texaco and SoCal read as follows:

> Whereas in South Africa the black majority is controlled and oppressed by a white minority that comprises 18 percent of the population;
>
> Whereas South Africa's apartheid system legalizes racial discrimination in all aspects of life and deprives the black population of their most basic human rights, such as, Africans cannot vote, cannot collectively bargain, must live in racially segregated areas, are paid grossly discriminatory wages, are assigned 13 percent of the land while 87

percent of the land is reserved for the white population;

> Whereas black opposition to apartheid and black demands for full political, legal, and social rights in their country has risen dramatically within the last year;
>
> Whereas widespread killing, arrests, and repression have been the response of the white South African government to nationwide demonstrations for democratic rights;
>
> Whereas Prime Minister Vorster has openly declared his intention to maintain apartheid and deny political rights to South African blacks;
>
> Whereas we believe that U.S. business investments in the Republic of South Africa, including our company's operations, provide significant economic support and moral legitimacy to South Africa's apartheid government;
>
> Therefore be it resolved: that the shareholders request the Board of Directors to establish the following as corporate policy:
>
> "Texaco [and Standard Oil of California] and any of its subsidiaries or affiliates shall terminate its present operations in the Republic of South Africa as expeditiously as possible unless and until the South African government has committed itself to ending the legally enforced form of racism called apartheid and has taken meaningful steps toward the achievement of full political, legal, and social rights for the majority population (African, Asian, colored)."

The resolution was occasioned by the fact that Texaco and SoCal were the joint owners of Caltex Petroleum Co. (each owns 50 percent of Caltex), an affiliate that operates oil refineries in South Africa and that in 1973 was worth about $100 million. In 1975 Caltex announced that it was planning to expand its refinery plant in Milnerto, South Africa, from a capacity of 58,000 barrels a day to an increased capacity of 108,000 barrels a day. The expansion would cost $135 million and would increase South Africa's *total* refining capacity by 11 percent. Caltex would be obliged by South African law to bring in at least $100 million of these investment funds from outside the country.

From *Business Ethics: Concepts and Cases,* 2d ed., by Manuel G. Velasquez (Englewood Cliffs, N.J.: (Prentice-Hall, 1988), pp. 123–131. Copyright © 1988 by Prentice-Hall. Reprinted with permission of the publisher. Quotation from Timothy Smith, "Whitewash for Apartheid from Twelve U.S. Firms," *Business and Society Review* (Summer 1977), pp. 59–60. Copyright © 1977. Reprinted by permission of *Business and Society Review.* Quotation from Timothy Smith, "South Africa: The Churches vs. the Corporations," *Business and Society Review* (Fall, 1975). Copyright © 1975. Reprinted by permission of *Business and Society Review.*

*Director, Center for Applied Ethics, University of Santa Clara.

The management of Texaco and SoCal were both opposed to the resolution that would have required them to pull out of South Africa and to abandon their Caltex expansion plans, which, by some estimates, promised an annual return of 20 percent on the original investment. They therefore recommended that stockholders vote against the resolution. The managements of both Texaco and SoCal argued that Caltex was committed to improving the economic working conditions of its black employees and that their continued presence in South Africa did not constitute an "endorsement" of South Africa's "policies." The commitment of Caltex to improving the condition of its employees was evidenced, the companies claimed, by its adherence to the 1977 "Sullivan principles."

Early in 1977, Caltex was one of several dozen corporations who had adopted a code of conduct drafted by the Reverend Dr. Leon Sullivan, a civil rights activist who is a minister of Philadelphia's large Zion Baptist Church. The Code was based on these six principles that the corporations affirmed for their plants:[1]

1. Nonsegregation of the races in all eating, comfort, and work facilities.
2. Equal and fair employment practices for all employees.
3. Equal pay for all employees doing equal or comparable work for the same period of time.
4. Initiation of and development of training programs that will prepare, in substantial numbers, blacks and other nonwhites for supervisory, administrative, clerical, and technical jobs.
5. Increasing the number of blacks and other nonwhites in management and supervisory positions.
6. Improving the quality of employees' lives outside the work environment in such areas as housing, transportation, schooling, recreation, and health facilities.

These companies agree to further implement these principles. Where implementation requires a modification of existing South African working conditions, we will seek such modification through appropriate channels.

The code had been approved by the South African government since the principles were to operate within "existing South African working conditions," that is, within South African laws. South African laws requiring separate facilities and South African laws prohibiting blacks from becoming apprentices, for example, would continue to apply where in force.[2] Also, the principle of equal pay for equal work would probably require few changes where blacks and whites did not have equal work.

Caltex, however, was apparently committed to improving the economic position of its workers. It had moved 40 percent of its 742 black workers into refinery jobs formerly held by whites, although most blacks had remained in the lower six job categories (a total of 29 had moved into the top four white-collar and skilled categories).[3] The company had also kept its wages well above the averages determined in studies conducted by the South African University of Port Elizabeth. A basic argument that Texaco and SoCal advanced in favor of remaining in South Africa, then, was that their continued presence in South Africa advanced the economic welfare of blacks.

Texaco believes that continuation of Caltex's operations in South Africa is in the best interests of Caltex's employees of all races in South Africa. . . . In management's opinion, if Caltex were to withdraw from South Africa in an attempt to achieve political changes in that country, as the proposal directs, . . . such withdrawal would endanger prospects for the future of all Caltex employees in South Africa regardless of race. We are convinced that the resulting dislocation and hardship would fall most heavily on the nonwhite communities. In this regard, and contrary to the implications of the stockholders' statement, Caltex employment policies include equal pay for equal work and the same level of benefit plans for all employees as well as a continuing and successful program to advance employees to positions of responsibility on the basis of ability, not race. [Statement of Texaco management][4]

It is undeniable that the presence of foreign corporations in South Africa had helped to improve the real earnings of black industrial workers. Between 1970 and 1975, black incomes in Johannesburg rose 118 percent, while between 1975 and 1980 black per capita income was expected to rise 30 percent. In addition, the gap between black and white incomes in South Africa had narrowed. Between 1970 and 1976, the gap in industry narrowed from 1:5.8 to 1:4.4; in construction from 1:6.6 to 1:5.2; and in the mining sector from 1:19.8 to 1:7.7.[5] If the flow of foreign investment came to a halt, however, the South African normal yearly growth rate of 6 percent would drop to about 3 percent and the results would undoubtedly hit blacks the hardest.[6] Unemployment would rise (American companies employ 60,000 blacks), and whatever benefits blacks had gained would be lost.

Tim Smith and the Interfaith stockholders were aware of these facts. The basic issue for them, however, was not whether Caltex adhered to the six Sullivan principles or whether its presence in South Africa improved the economic position of blacks:

> The issue in South Africa at this time is black political power; it is not slightly higher wages or better benefits or training programs, unless these lead to basic social change. As one South African church leader put it, "These [six] principles attempt to polish my chains and make them more comfortable. I want to cut my chains and cast them away."... We must look not just at wages but at the transfer of technology, the taxes paid to South Africa, the effect of U.S. foreign policy, and the provision of strategic products to the racist government. If these criteria become part of the "principles" of U.S. investors, it should be clear that on balance many of the corporations strengthen and support white minority rule. This form of support should be challenged, and American economic complicity in apartheid ended. [Statement of Tim Smith][7]

In short, the issue was one of human rights. The white South African government was committed to denying blacks their basic rights, and the continued presence of American companies supported this system of white rule.

> Nonwhites in South Africa are rightless persons in the land of their birth.... [The black African] has no rights in "white areas." He cannot vote, cannot own land, and may not have his family with him unless he has government permission....The two major black political parties have been banned and hundreds of persons detained for political offenses...strikes by Africans are illegal, and meaningful collective bargaining is outlawed....by investing in South Africa, American companies inevitably strengthen the status quo of [this] white supremacy....The leasing of a computer, the establishment of a new plant, the selling of supplies to the military—all have political overtones....And among the country's white community, the overriding goal of politics is maintenance of white control. In the words of Prime Minister John Vorster during the 1970 election campaign: "We are building a nation for whites only. Black people are entitled to political rights but only over their own people—not my people." [Statement of Tim Smith][8]

There was no doubt that the continuing operations of Caltex provided some economic support for the South African government. South African law required oil refineries in South Africa to set aside a percentage of their oil for government purchase. In 1975, about 7 percent of Caltex's oil sales went to the government of South Africa. As a whole, the South African economy relied on oil for 25 percent of its energy needs. Moreover, Caltex represented almost 11 percent of the total U.S. investment in South Africa. If Caltex closed down its operations in South Africa, this would certainly have had great impact on the economy especially if other companies then lost confidence in the South African economy and subsequently also withdrew from South Africa. Finally, Caltex also supported the South African government through corporate taxes.

At each of the Texaco and Socal shareholder's meetings held in May, 1977, the resolutions of the Interfaith Center on Corporate Responsibility received less than five per cent of the shares voted. The Caltex plant in South Africa completed its expansion as planned. But conditions in South Africa continued to deteriorate for the oil industry.

In 1978, the O.P.E.C. nations announced that all of their members had at last unanimously agreed to embargo oil shipments to South Africa. Concerned about the increasingly sensitive vulnerability of its strategic oil supplies, the South African government, now under the leadership of Prime Minister P. W. Botha, responded by tightening its regulation of the oil industry. The National Supplies Procurement Act was strengthened to give the government authority to force foreign-owned companies to produce strategically important petroleum products. The Act also prohibited oil companies from restricting sales of oil products to any credit-worthy customers, including any branch of government. And the Official Secrets Act made it a crime for anyone within South Africa to release any information whatsoever on the petroleum industry or the operations of any oil enterprise.

Because it was important that foreign companies remain in South Africa, however, the government became more receptive to the lobbying efforts of American companies. Business lobbying efforts were instrumental in the 1979 repeal of laws that had denied legal status to unions for Africans and of laws that hindered Africans from being trained or promoted for skilled jobs. Starting in the early 1980s, American Businesses began lobbying for the repeal of the hated "influx control laws" (laws requiring black Africans within white South Africa to carry a "pass book" detailing their residence and employer and prohibiting non-employed black Africans from remaining in white South Africa for longer than seventy-two hours) and for granting blacks some form of political representation in the South African government. Several of the

social aspects of apartheid (such as the "Immorality Act" which made interracial sexual intercourse a criminal offense until 1985 and the "petty apartheid laws" which required enforced segregation of the races) were eventually lifted or attenuated.

Although the 1977 defeat of their resolution was disappointing, anti-apartheid activists determined to press on with their battle. In May 1983, activists introduced another shareholder resolution to be considered at the Texaco and Socal shareholders' meetings, this time asking that Caltex not sell petroleum products to the police or military of South Africa. The managers of both Texaco and Socal objected to the resolution, claiming that this new resolution asked them to violate the laws of South Africa. According to the managers, South Africa's National Supplies Procurement Act gave the South African government the authority to require any business to supply it with goods. Moreover, the Price Control Act of 1964 also gave the government the authority to prohibit companies from placing restrictions on the sale of their goods. The South African government had exercised this authority, the managers said, when it earlier had "directed Caltex to refrain from imposing any conditions or reservations of whatever nature in respect to the use, resale, or further distribution of petroleum products and, also, from refusing to sell except subject to such conditions."[9] Consequently, they held, the resolution in effect asked them to commit a serious crime: "It would be a crime under South Africa's law were Caltex-South Africa to undertake a commitment to not supply petroleum products for use by the South African military or any other branch of the South African government."[10] The Securities and Exchange Commission (SEC), which regulates the submission of shareholders' resolutions, agreed with the companies. The SEC therefore allowed Socal to remove the resolution from its proxy ballots on the grounds that the resolution might be asking the company to do something illegal. Although Texaco was allowed to do the same, Texaco managers decided to let the resolution be voted upon by its shareholders.

At the May, 1983 shareholders' meetings, the resolution received the support of 7.4 per cent of the Texaco shares voted, an unusually high level of support, but not sufficient to require the company to implement the resolution.

Encouraged by the gradually increasing levels of shareholder support their resolutions were drawing, the anti-apartheid forces were more determined than ever to press on with their efforts. In June, 1983, Bishop Desmond Tutu, a moderate black South African religious leader, had outlined four principles that he urged foreign companies in South Africa to follow. Foreign companies, he said, should tell the government of South Africa that they would remain in the country only if they were permitted to (1) ensure their black workers could live with their families, (2) recognize black labor unions, (3) oppose influx control over labor, and (4) enforce fair labor practices and invest in black education. These four principles, activists felt, went beyond the Sullivan principles because they required companies to work for change *outside* the company. Consequently, in 1984, and again in 1985, they brought a resolution before the shareholders of Texaco and Socal (now renamed "Chevron") that read as follows:

WHEREAS, the system of apartheid assigns the non-white majority of South Africa to perpetual and enforced inferiority by excluding them from full participation in the social and economic system and political processes by which their lives are controlled, thus effectively denying them their economic and political rights;

WHEREAS, laws such as the Group Areas Act which assigns 87% of the land to 16% of the population and the various influx control laws which regulate the movement of blacks within the country form the basic legal structure of apartheid;

WHEREAS, Texaco Inc. [and Chevron], through Caltex, is one of the largest U.S. investors in South Africa, with assets of approximately 300 million;

WHEREAS, Caltex is engaged in South Africa, through subsidiaries in refining crude oil, manufacturing and blending lubricants, and marketing petroleum products, including retail gasoline sales. Caltex holds an estimated 20 percent share of the petroleum market in South Africa. The oil industry plays an extremely strategic role in South Africa today, and oil is deemed a "munition of war" under South African Law;

WHEREAS, the operations of Caltex in South Africa are subject to the National Supplies Procurement Act No. 89 of 1970, and the Price Control Act No. 25 of 1964. Caltex has been given a directive under these laws that it may not refuse to supply petroleum products to any credit-worthy South African citizen or organization, and the Government has power to demand the supply and delivery of such products. The South African Government has directed Caltex to refrain from imposing any conditions or reservations of whatever nature in respect of the use, resale or further distribution of petroleum products. Caltex cannot impose any restrictions on its sales to the military or police;

WHEREAS, the size of Texaco's investment, strategic role in the economy, and sales to the military and police in South Africa invest Texaco with special social responsibility for the impact of its operations in South Africa;

WHEREAS, Texaco has stated that "We believe our affiliate is making an important positive contribution to improving economic and social opportunities for its present and future employees";

WHEREAS, Bishop Tutu, General Secretary of the South African Council of Churches, recently outlined several conditions of the investment which would enable Caltex and other U.S. companies to make such a "positive contribution to improving economic and social opportunities," these conditions include:

1. House the workforce in family-type accommodations as family units near the place of work of the breadwinner.
2. Recognizing black trade unions as long as they are representative.
3. Recognizing the right of the worker to sell labor wherever the best price can be obtained, calling for labor mobility, and opposing any ultimate implementation of influx control, and

4. Enforcing fair labor practices and investing massively in black education and training.

RESOLVED, Shareholders request the Board of Directors to:

1. Implement and/or increase activity on each of the four Tutu conditions and report to shareholders annually how the Company's presence is, on balance, a positive influence for improving the quality of life for non-white South Africans; Or,
2. If the South African Government does not within 24 months take steps to rescind the Group Areas Act and the influx control laws as steps toward the dismantling of apartheid, begin the process of withdrawal from South Africa.

Although the resolutions failed in both years, they were again supported by a surprisingly large number of votes. By the end of 1985, it was clear that South Africa was at a crisis point and that the pressure on companies would continue.[11] Hundreds of blacks had been killed in the unrest that had erupted in September 1984 when a new constitution had established a three-part government with representation for whites, Indians, and coloreds, but not for blacks. In 1985 martial law was imposed on the country. Freed from the fear of civil restraints, the police brutally abused blacks. Thousands were imprisoned without charges, dozens were shot and killed in "incidents." Black townships assigned as living areas for blacks in white South Africa became dangerous "no go" areas for whites. The press and television were banned from photographing "any public disturbance." The economy was undergoing a severe recession. Sporadic black boycotts of white businesses broke out. Black unemployment climbed to 35 percent, while the costs of basic goods and services rose sharply. In an effort to show that black Africans were not completely disenfranchised, Prime Minister Botha had earlier established elected community councils to govern the black townships. But in most townships council members were forced to resign under pressure from other blacks who

held that the councils were a cover for the basic fact that blacks still had no political rights in the three-part government that had been imposed on them.

Several major Western nations imposed economic sanctions against South Africa, and Western banks began to refuse to renew loans to private companies as they came due. The South African government responded by imposing a moratorium on the repayment of its foreign debt on September 1, 1985. The government also announced that foreign companies wishing to sell their assets in South Africa would have to be paid in "financial rands," special currency that could not be converted into a foreign currency unless another foreign investor wanted to buy the South African assets. It thus became more difficult for firms to leave South Africa.

Update and Opinion

Timothy Smith*

The campaign pressing the U.S. oil industry to withdraw from South Africa has grown considerably. For example, in 1987–1988 the shareholder resolutions to Texaco and Chevron were no longer sponsored solely by church investors but by some of the largest institutional investors in the country. The resolution to Texaco included as sponsors the N.Y. State Common Retirement Fund, and the resolution to Chevron included TIAA-CREF.

The heat is on Caltex, Mobil, and Royal Dutch Shell to leave South Africa. This pressure is no longer primarily from shareholder resolutions. It also comes from:

• Increased sanctions by the U.S. government

Written for this volume, and printed with permission of the author.
*Executive director, Interfaith Center on Corporate Responsibility.

- Over 35 cities and states passing laws refusing to buy products from companies with South African ties
- Huge pension funds deciding to divest stock in companies in South Africa
- Continued bad publicity, and a consumer boycott of Shell, which sends a message to all the oil companies in South Africa

In short Caltex's connection with apartheid South Africa is beginning to hit Texaco and Chevron's bottom line. Interestingly both managements still argue that they are a force for social change in South Africa. Their public defense, however, consistently ignores:

- The millions of dollars of taxes they pay the racist Pretoria government
- The failure of their lobbying for change in moving South Africa toward majority rule
- Their help with South Africa's refining of oil and then being forced to sell it to that government, including the police and military

Church investors have therefore targeted the oil companies in South Africa for a special campaign aimed at what ICCR has called corporate "Partners in Apartheid," and ICCR has charged that Caltex helps oil the wheels of apartheid.

Meanwhile the South African economy continues to deteriorate, and the social and political situation remains extremely volatile. Over 150 U.S. companies have decided to sell their South African investments.

The challenge to Texaco and Chevron is to do the same.

NOTES

1. Jack Magarrell, "U.S. Adopts Stand on Apartheid: Backed on Many Campuses," *The Chronicle of Higher Education*, 12 March 1979.
2. See Herman Nickel, "The Case for Doing Business in South Africa," *Fortune*, 19 June 1968, p. 72.
3. Investor Responsibility Research Center, *Analysis E Supplement No. 9*, 7 April 1977, p. E 114.
4. *Texaco Proxy Statement*, 1977, item 3.
5. Nickel, "Doing Business in South Africa," p. 64.
6. *Ibid.*, p. 63.
7. Timothy Smith, "Whitewash for Apartheid from Twelve U.S. Firms," *Business and Society Review*, Summer 1977, pp. 59, 60.
8. Timothy Smith, "South Africa: The Churches vs. the Corporations," *Business and Society Review*, 1971, pp. 54, 55, 56.
9. Investor Responsibility Research Center, Inc., *Corporate Activity in South Africa*, 1984, Analysis G, supplement no. 2, April 10, 1984.
10. *The Corporate Examiner*, vol. 14, no. 5, 1985, p. 2.
11. Investor Responsibility Research Center, Inc., *U.S. Corporate Activity in South Africa*, 1986 Analysis B, January 28, 1986.

QUESTIONS FOR DISCUSSION

1. Is cigarette advertising generally deceptive? Does it create needs in consumers? Explain. Does the fact that cigarette smoking is addictive affect your response to these questions? How would Galbraith, Von Hayek, Holley, and Levitt assess cigarette advertising?
2. No product can be absolutely safe, but we still want reasonably safe products. How safe is safe enough? Some have suggested that a product is safe enough if its risks are "acceptable." What criteria should be used to determine "acceptable risk"? Who should make these judgments—corporations, regulatory agencies,

consumers? Or do you think that the free market alone should be allowed to decide safety factors? Defend your answer.

3. Why do you think Hooker Chemical *sold* the Love Canal to the school board rather than allowing it to be seized by eminent domain? Which party (or parties) would you hold responsible for the injuries done to the residents around Love Canal? Does the Hoffman/Fisher article (in Part Two) illuminate this case in any way?

4. You are a shareholder in Texaco and/or Standard Oil, committed to the principle of ethical investment. How would you vote on the various shareholder resolutions related to South Africa? Defend your answer.

SUPPLEMENTARY READING FOR PART FOUR

Attfield, Robin. *The Ethics of Environmental Concern*. New York: Columbia University Press, 1983.

Barbour, Ian G., ed. *Western Man and Environmental Ethics*. Reading, Mass.: Addison-Wesley, 1973.

Barnet, Richard J., and Ronald E. Muller. *Global Reach: The Power of the Multinational Corporation*. New York: Simon and Schuster, 1974.

Beauchamp, Tom. "Manipulative Advertising," *Business and Professional Ethics Journal* 3, Spring/Summer 1984.

Blackstone, William T., ed. *Philosophy and the Environmental Crisis*. Athens, Ga.: University of Georgia Press, 1974.

Corporate Social Reporting in the United States. Report of the Task Force on Corporate Social Performance. Washington, D.C.: U.S. Department of Commerce, July 1979.

Elliot, Robert, and Arran Gare, eds. *Environmental Philosophy*. University Park, Penn.: The Pennsylvania State University Press, 1983.

Galbraith, John Kenneth. *The Affluent Society*. Boston: Houghton Mifflin, 1958.

Goodpaster, K. E., and K. M. Sayre. *Ethics and Problems of the 21st Century*. Notre Dame, Ind.: University of Notre Dame, 1979.

Hoffman, W. Michael, Ann E. Lange, and David A. Fedo, eds. *Ethics and the Multinational Enterprise: Proceedings of the Sixth National Conference on Business Ethics*. Lanham, Md.: University Press of America, 1986.

Krauthammer, Charles, et al. "Does Business Love Foreign Dictators?" *Business and Society Review* 41, Spring 1982.

Leape, Jonathan, et al. *Business in the Shadow of Apartheid: U.S. Firms in South Africa*. Lexington, Mass.: Lexington Books, 1985.

Ledogar, Robert J. *Hungry for Profits*. New York: IDOC/North America, 1975.

Lilly, William, III, and James C. Miller III. "The New Social Regulation," *Public Interest*, vol. 45, Spring 1977, pp. 5–51.

Lowrance, William W. *Of Acceptable Risk*. Los Altos, Calif.: William Kaufman, Inc., 1976.

Mishan, E. J. *The Economic Growth Debate*. London: George Allen & Unwin, 1977.

Posner, Richard A. "Strict Liability: A Comment," *The Journal of Legal Studies*, vol. 2, January 1973.

Preston, Ivan L. *The Great American Blow-Up: Puffery in Advertising and Selling*. Madison, Wisc.: The University of Wisconsin Press, 1975.

Regan, Tom, ed. *Earthbound: New Introductory Essays in Environmental Ethics*. New York: Random House, 1984.

Scherer, Donald, and Thomas Attig, eds. *Ethics and the Environment*. Englewood Cliffs, N.J.: Prentice-Hall, 1983.

Schudson, Michael. *Advertising, the Uneasy Persuasion*. New York: Basic Books, 1984.

Sethi, S. Prakash, ed. *The South African Quagmire*. Cambridge, Mass.: Ballinger, 1987.

Smith, Michael D. "The Morality of Strict Liability in Tort," *Business and Professional Ethics Journal,* vol. 3: December, 1979.

Stone, Christopher D. *Should Trees Have Standing?* Los Altos, Calif.: William Kaufman, Inc., 1972.

Tavis, Lee, ed. *Multinational Managers and Poverty in the Third World.* Notre Dame, Ind.: Notre Dame University Press, 1982.

Turner, Louis. *Multinationals and the Third World.* New York: Hill and Wang, 1973.

''Unsafe Products: The Great Debate over Blame and Punishment,'' *Business Week,* April 30, 1984.

VanDeVeer, Donald, and Christine Pierce, eds. *People, Penguins, and Plastic Trees: Basic Issues in Environmental Ethics.* Belmont, Calif.: Wadsworth, 1986.

Weidenbaum, Murray L. *Business, Government and the Public,* 2d ed. Englewood Cliffs, N.J.: Prentice-Hall, 1981.

The Future Corporate Ethos

In Parts One and Four we explored some of the most important dilemmas faced by American business today. In this final part of the text we look toward the future of the American corporation. In particular, we wish to ask how the business organization of the future will meet the ethical challenges posed to it by society. Its ability to meet these challenges could prove to be crucial for business' very survival.

Observers of business sometimes speak as if business had no normative role to play in society, but this view is misleading. The legitimacy of business—the public's acceptance of its right to exist and its belief in the "rightness" of business as an institution—has always rested on business' connection with our highest social values and on its perceived contribution to what we view as the good life or the good society. While business has been essentially a profit-making institution, society has encouraged business to strive for profits in the belief that its doing so would promote the general welfare. Maximizing profits, then, has been the way in which business has discharged its social responsibilities. The "invisible hand" of the market system, it has been assumed, would function automatically to harmonize self-interest and bring about the good of society as a whole. And indeed business has made enormous contributions to American society. It has supported fundamental social values such as freedom of opportunity, productivity, growth, efficiency, and material well-being. It has encouraged enterprise and creativity. No society has a higher standard of living or such an abundance of goods and services.

The legitimacy of business still rests on public confidence in its contribution to a good society. In the past two decades, however, this confidence has eroded, and our conception of a good society has undergone some transformation. Observers of the American scene have concluded that business could be facing a genuine crisis in legitimacy.

Increasingly, people are challenging the belief that economic well-being is identical with social well-being, or that the former leads automatically to the latter. On the contrary, many now feel that some of the same values which contributed to our economic success—growth, productivity, consumption, the profit motive—have led to unacceptably high social costs. Americans have lost confidence in the ability of the market system automatically to bring about the general welfare. Rather than encouraging business in the single-minded pursuit of profit and waiting for social well-being to follow, the public is demanding that business broaden the scope of its concerns and assume a more active role in solving social problems and in working for a good society. The social responsibility of business today, the American public seems to be saying, no longer ends with its economic responsibility.

The view that business should assume social as well as economic responsibilities and take an active role in working toward social goals represents a challenge to the traditional understanding of the nature and functions of business. As we have worked through this text, we have seen the impact of this challenge in nearly every aspect of business activity. Traditionally, business organizations have been understood to be the private property of their shareholders. Managers were viewed as agents of the shareholders, bound by an agreement to serve their interests as the shareholders themselves would serve them—which, presumably, was to make a profit. As we have seen, however, the increasing separation of ownership and control and the decreasing confidence in the market system to contribute to public welfare have undermined the idea that management's sole responsibility is to shareholders. Business is now expected to exercise responsibility toward a range of "stakeholders," including consumers, employees, and the public at large.

Increasingly, society expects corporations not only to supply goods to consumers, but also to exercise care and foresight to make sure that the product is safe for consumer use. Manufacturers' liability for defective products has been extended to include even situations in which manufacturers could not have foreseen and prevented accidents. Society now demands that business avoid undue pollution and depletion of natural resources, and that it operate as much as possible in harmony with the natural environment. Business has been asked not simply to invest where it is most profitable, but to be sensitive to the social consequences of investment and to use its economic power to alleviate social injustice. It is expected not merely to provide jobs for members of the community, but also to offer a safe, healthy, and fulfilling work environment. Many thinkers have called for restrictions on the corporation's freedom to hire and fire and on the obedience and loyalty it demands from its employees. Increasingly, business organizations are being asked to adopt hiring policies which help solve problems of institutional racism. As the duties of business organizations are broadened to include social responsibilities, employees who resist or reveal illegal or unethical acts on the part of their employers may in fact be acting in the best interests of the corporation.

Many of the responsibilities corporations are being asked to assume are duties which, until now, have been associated with government. Traditionally, it has been government's job to promote social welfare; the job of business was to make money. Ironically, government has also traditionally been expected to keep its interference with business at a minimum, passing only those regulations necessary to preserve freedom of competition. As public dissatisfaction with business performance has increased, however, the relationship between business and government has shifted. Business is now subject to a multiplicity of "social regulations," many of which it feels are unfair and unnecessary. The restrictions placed on business by these regulations constitute a powerful argument for complying voluntarily with society's new demands.

How is business to respond effectively to public expectations, however, when all institutional attitudes and forces encourage corporate managers to place profits first? Today's manager is rewarded with success and esteem not for cutting down on the pollution of a local river or for improving employee satisfaction, but for maximizing profits. Indeed, as we have seen in many of the cases included in the text, pressures to sacrifice ethical concerns to profits are often severe. The corporation can create a closed context in which behavior that might be condemned elsewhere is found acceptable.

Christopher Stone argues that neither restrictions from outside nor internal structural reforms will succeed in getting the corporation to assume the new social responsibilities as long as the values, attitudes, and customs of the corporation remain unchanged. For this reason, Stone believes we must reform the "corporate culture"; we must attempt to change the things the corporation cares about.

Stone recognizes that a corporation cannot sustain a number of competing aims, and he believes that business must remain essentially a profit-oriented institution. While he accepts the corporate orientation toward profit, Stone does not believe that we should permit any and all acts—acts that harm others, for example—in the name of profit. He feels that business can be made to strive for profit within the limits required by ethics, and he lists a number of attitudes he would like to see adopted by corporations, not in place of, but in conjunction with, their profit orientation. Already, Stone notes, different corporations and industries possess recognizably different cultures. Precisely because a corporation is a culture of its own defined by norms, values, and mores which powerfully influence behavior, there is hope for change. Such change is necessary, Stone believes, if business is to ensure its legitimacy and integrity in the future.

Mark Pastin offers an "ideal" of what he believes business should be like, but is not: experimental, creative, and free thinking. This ideal is not offered as wishful thinking, but "to foster a realistic raising of our sights." Pastin argues that ethics is one excellent way of presenting this ideal, because by searching for appropriate ethics a corporation uncovers the "ground rules" upon which it operates, thereby opening it up to possible change.

Based on his participation in a three-year international corporate study which attempted to find connections between high ethical and high economic performance, Pastin presents four principles which serve to ground his ideal for business. First, firms should interact with and incorporate the interests of their "stakeholder" groups. Second, fairness in treating others' interests equally with one's own should be fundamental. Third, firms should highlight individual responsibility. And finally, finding the "purpose" or value of a firm and acting out of it is more basic than merely setting goals. Using these principles, Pastin argues, will encourage the firm to ask the hard questions which are necessary for it to develop into what it should be.

Michael Hoffman contends that much corporate wrongdoing is due to the fact that business has paid too little attention to developing an ethical corporate culture. Concern over "individual integrity" is important, but more effort must be directed toward "institutional integrity" which demands the institutionalizing of ethics into the corporation.

Based on a survey conducted by the Center for Business Ethics, Hoffman concludes that, for various reasons, many more corporations during the 1980s have taken steps to institutionalize ethics than in the past; however, more progress is necessary. Although over two-thirds of the major U.S. corporations have codes of ethics, far too few have established ethics committees, ethics ombudsmen, and ethics judiciary boards. This is also true, Hoffman argues, for other important strategies and structures for developing the ethical corporation such as ethics training programs for employees, social (ethical) audits, and changes in corporate governance—especially those relating to boards of directors.

Even those corporations who have taken the above steps have not done them satisfactorily, according to Hoffman. Codes of ethics are not communicated well and do not provide adequate guidelines for ethical decision making. Membership on committees is not representative of the entire corporation but consists usually of appointed upper level executives or board members. Ethics training programs concentrate on managers, rarely on hourly employees. Social audits are seldom disclosed to anyone other than those at the highest levels of the company. And in all but a handful of corporations, governance changes totally omit ethics officers on boards, worker participation plans, and employee bills of rights. Hoffman believes that these problems, among others, must be dealt with for the successful emergence of ethical corporations, but he is optimistic that corporations will continue to make progress toward this goal.

There may be good reason for this optimism since many corporations at the time of this writing are actively involved in setting up business ethics programs. To cite just two examples, as of January 1988, over forty defense contractors have signed the *Defense Industry Initiatives on Business Ethics and Conduct*. This document contains six principles of business ethics and a program for their implementation. And in February 1988, The Business Roundtable, one of the most influential business groups in America, published a report on policy and practice in company conduct entitled *Corporate Ethics: A Prime Business Asset*. This report states in its Introduction:

> The question of ethics in business conduct has become one of the most challenging issues confronting the corporate community in this era. Major corporations throughout the U.S. are vigorously addressing the challenge . . . The corporate community should continue to refine and improve performance and manage change effectively through programs in corporate ethics.

The Proctor and Gamble Rely case demonstrates a socially responsible corporate action and a promising ethical decision-making strategy. It also presents an interesting contrast to the more traditional business responses to social concerns exemplified by Ford with its Pinto and Firestone with its 500 radial tire. These corporate social responses, along with the respective and negative social ramifications on these corporations, should serve as lessons for future corporate ethical development.

CHAPTER 15

Developing the Moral Corporation

READINGS FOR CHAPTER FIFTEEN

Christopher D. Stone
The Culture of the Corporation
618

Mark Pastin
Lessons for High-Profit, High-Ethics Companies:
An Agenda for Managerial Action
626

W. Michael Hoffman
Developing the Ethical Corporation
630

The Culture of the Corporation

Christopher D. Stone*

Can we change those things that the corporation cares about? We can restructure the corporation's information processes so as to make it gather and channel vital data to those in a position to do something about it. But what is there to guarantee that the person in authority, supplied the information, will act upon it? What if he doesn't care that his company is running the risk of imposing long-range health hazards on the public? We can make companies install special officers in charge of particular problem areas. But what is there to guarantee that, the special executive having been instituted, the other officers will not undermine him in all the subtle ways available to them? We can provide arrangements to protect, and thus encourage, potential "whistle blowers" to come forward with information about the dangers and abuses that they see on their jobs. But what amount of protection will get the workers to come forward if they simply don't give a damn in the first place?

I do not want to leave the impression that "internal reform" measures cannot be rested upon anything firmer than the corporation's good intentions. On the contrary, there are any number of ways to link legal penalties (and rewards) to bona fide compliance, both of the company and of key individuals.

But we have to recognize too that, in the last analysis, the most these measures can do is *reduce* the resistance of the preexistent corporate cultures. So long as the underlying attitudes are left untouched, some measure of resistance—of

circumvention, disregard, and foot dragging—is inevitable.

Should we hold out any hope of altering the very attitudes of corporate America? *Is there any chance at all?*

The answer, I am afraid, is that we are very limited in what we can do. It isn't just a matter of autonomy: No organization, of course, is going to hand control over gladly. There is, even beyond this, simply a limit to how many different, potentially competing aims and attitudes any institution can entertain. Universities aim to educate; armies, to fight; hospitals, to treat and cure. These shared, mutually understood goals provide a context against which commands are interpreted and actions synchronized. They provide a post against which the institution can measure its "success" and stabilize itself.

To be realistic, with the American business corporation the dominant orientation of the institution is going to remain toward profit, expansion, and prestige. Those who labor in it are going to remain concerned about providing for their wives and kids, about the approval of their peers, about "moving up" in the organization. What ideas can we gather up in our entire society that are powerful enough to set in competition with these, with "self-interest" as so many centuries of the culture have defined it?

To recognize these basic constraints is not to say we are powerless, however. We live with the fact that human beings are dominated by certain ego-centered goals/drives (sexual gratification, power, self-preservation). But through various acculturating mechanisms we have been able, not to do away with these forces, but at least to put constraints on them. On a parity of reasoning, even if we accept profit *orientation* as a basic and inalterable fact of American corporate life, we don't have to accept, or expect, sheer corporate hedonism. What I am asking of our chemical companies, for example, is not that they abandon profits. Producing fertilizers and chemicals that will get the world fed would be, and should be, a profitable activity. But what

Excerpted from Chapter 20, "The Culture of the Corporation," from *Where the Law Ends,* by Christopher D. Stone. Copyright © 1975 by Christopher D. Stone. Reprinted by permission of Harper & Row Publishers, Inc., New York.
*Crocker Professor of Law, University of Southern California.

we want, too, is that the companies will manifest enough concern about the effects their products are having on the health of the field workers who use them, that they will accept the internal structures we deem appropriate; that in cooperation with the imposed systems they will perform some amount of follow-up; that, if suspicious circumstances are apparent, they will undertake appropriate studies and notify health authorities; that they will make data available to interested parties—rather than cover up the apparent risks and deny their very possibility.

We could, in fact, attempt a listing of various attitudes desirable in connection with each of the various social roles that the corporation plays.

The corporation as citizen:

- to be concerned with obeying the laws (even if it can get away with law breaking profitably)
- to aid in the making of laws, as by volunteering information within its control regarding additional measures that may need to be imposed on industry
- to heed the fundamental moral rules of the society not to engage in deception, corruption, and the like
- as a citizen abroad, to act decently to host country citizens, and not inimically to U.S. foreign policy

The corporation as producer:
- to aim for safe and reliable products at a fair price

The corporation as employer:
- to be concerned with the safety of the work environment
- to be concerned with the emotional well-being of its workers
- not to discriminate

The corporation as resource manager:
- not to contribute unduly to the depletion of resources
- to manifest some concern for the aesthetics of land management

The corporation as an investment:
- to safeguard the interests of investors

- to make full and fair disclosures of its economic condition

The corporation as neighbor:
- to be concerned with pollution
- to conduct safe and quiet operations

The corporation as competitor:
- not to engage in unfair competition, on the one hand, or cozy restrictions of competition, on the other

The corporation as social designer:
- to be innovative and responsive in the introduction of new products and methods
- not to close its eyes to the fact that the movies it turns out, the shows it produces, the styles it sets, have an impact on the quality of our lives, and to concern itself with the impact responsibly

Some will say it is unlikely that corporations will ever do these sorts of things—that is, go much beyond whatever the law, and market competition, can absolutely force from them. How much do ordinary citizens meet some of these standards—report favorable errors on their tax returns, for example? Indeed, if Christianity "hasn't been tried yet" why should we suppose that it is corporations who are finally going to get it off the ground?

The possibility of something better is inherent, oddly enough, in the very development decried by Adolf Berle and Gardner Means in their famous *The Modern Corporation and Private Property* (1932). Berle and Means first called public attention to the fact that as the industrial sector was evolving from sole proprietorships to larger and larger corporations, the owners of the property in the traditional sense—the investors— were no longer the true managers of the companies. Formerly, the owner-investor had been his own manager, or had exercised tight control over the hired officers. But now the officers— the men who were calling the shots—were emerging with relative independence from the stockholders as the latter became increasingly passive and dispersed. The investors, moreover, were losing their link to the underlying corporate property; they sold their shares and bought stock in a new enterprise with perfect fluidity.

This situation, Berle and Means saw, contained the germs of a sort of "irresponsibility" that had not existed on such a scale before. But they were thinking of the relations between the managers and stockholders. This is the relationship that was of paramount concern to those analyzing the "corporation problem" in the thirties, when widespread tragedy to investors was very much a part of the intellectual and moral climate, rather than "consumerism," "environmentalism," and the like. And from this perspective, they were clearly right. But from the other perspective— that of the management's relations to interests "outside" the corporation—the same historical development provides at least a new wedge of hope for greater managerial accountability. For when the interests of management and ownership are one (as, most purely, in the case of a sole proprietorship) all the compromises management makes with profits come out of its own pockets. If the people who own the business decide to install an unrequired pollution filter, or establish day care for mother-workers, or go out of their way to investigate the health hazards of their products, *they* pay. But it is not so in the giant, broadly held companies. There, the "charitable" gestures of management do not come out of their own pockets. Thus, in theory—and I think in practice as well—the giant, broadly held company is more likely to be socially accountable, and less likely to engage in sharp, irresponsible conduct, than the small, closely held concern that served as Berle and Means's historical model.

WHY AREN'T CORPORATIONS MORE MORAL?

"Well, then," someone may ask, "why isn't the corporation more responsible than it is?" The answers are not all obvious; they are, moreover, important because any program to change cor-

porate attitudes has to begin by identifying the particular asocial attitudes that we are up against.

The first point to remember is that while the corporation is *potentially* immune from a single-minded profit orientation, in any particular company that potentiality is able to become reality only after some satisfactory level of profits has been achieved. A corporation that is operating "on the margin" is going to cut as many corners as it can get away with on worker safety, product quality, and everything else.

Then, too, it would be a mistake to believe that the desire to turn profits is the only attitude that causes us problems. We know, for example, that many companies—especially the major dominant companies—go through periods in which they are well enough off that they could put a little something extra into, say, environmental protection, and not have to face (what is a real rarity) a shareholder coup d'état. The true range of attitudes we have to confront is much deeper and more complex than "profits"—but not necessarily any the less intractable.

One range of attitudes we might call "profit-connected." Even when the company is achieving enough profits that the managers can protect their own tenure, they may continue to pursue much the same course of conduct, but now as a reflection of other motives. Prestige in the business world comes of being connected with a firm listed on the New York Stock Exchange, one whose sales are rising, or which appears in the *Fortune* 500. The problem here is a lack of most other measures of success, other guarantors of prestige, than those which can be read off the company's ledgers.

Some other of the attitudes we are up against are even further removed from profits. Consider corporate insensitivity to their workers. The received wisdom on "blue-collar blues" is a purely economic one: that the worker is crushed in the corporation's never-ending push for profits. In part, this is true. But any bureaucracy, and not only the modern corporation, evolves toward depersonalized relationships. Its very "success" depends upon the mobilization of personalities into roles—the better for the synchronization of behavior. Thus, if corporations appear insensitive (to the world as well as to their workers) they may be insensitive for many of the same reasons that many nonprofit bureaucracies are insensitive (a hospital is the first example that comes to my mind). I am not saying that we therefore give up on attempts to sensitize them. I am just suggesting that if we are going to confront such problems, we have to be prepared to deal with subtler and more pervasive features than "capitalist greed."

In such actions as sabotage, we are involved, too, in very complex matters of group dynamics. In an institutional framework, men do things they ordinarily wouldn't. (The army is a dramatic example.) One reason for this is that the usual restraints on antisocial behavior operate through a self-image: "I can't see myself doing *that*." In an institutional setting, however, *that* isn't being done *by me,* but *through me* as an actor, a role player in an unreal "game" that everyone is "playing." The evidence in the electrical equipment industry's price-fixing case is shot through with this flavor of a huge game. So, too, is the entire Watergate affair. The Equity Funding scandal went so far as to involve role playing in the most literal sense—"forgery parties" at which people played the roles necessary to fake dossiers.

What I am getting at is that behavior that may seem on the surface to spring from profits or even venality may actually involve, and have to be dealt with as, something as far removed from venality as play. An ideal examination of "the culture of the corporation" (which I can present here only in outline) would try to identify a whole range of underlying institutional attitudes and forces, and proceed to identify the particular sorts of undesired corporate behavior that constitute their symptoms. These attitudes would include, for example: a desire for profits, expansion, power; desire for security (at corporate as well as individual levels); the fear of failure (par-

ticularly in connection with shortcomings in corporate innovativeness); group loyalty identification (particularly in connection with citizenship violations and the various failures to "come forward" with internal information); feelings of omniscience (in connection with inadequate testing); organizational diffusion of responsibility (in connection with the buffering of public criticism); corporate ethnocentrism (in connection with limits on concern for the public's wants and desires).

WHAT CAN BE DONE?

This definition of the corporate culture is barely even a first step. And we have to face the fact that we really know very little about how to change it. There are, it is true, plenty of people (industrial and management psychologists, for example) who study and attempt to alter attitudes within this matrix. Much thought has gone into motivating workers toward increased productivity. Sensitivity training has been invoked with executives to eliminate "interpersonal frictions" that threaten the corporation's "solidarity."

But how about calling to question the organization's own values? How about motivating workers to recognize and report clues that a substance they are working with may kill fish, or farm workers? Or to adopt a more positive attitude toward the law—even when the chances of the company's getting caught are slim? What I have discovered is that there is almost no literature available on these matters; when industrial psychologists have been called into a company, it is always by management with an eye toward getting some group to perform more "effectively" from the point of management's pre-established aims—not to challenge those aims, or to try to work into the organization "extraneous" values favored by the society at large.

Thus, to a large extent, the territory we are striking out into is unmarked. To map our way, we ought to begin by learning more about why different corporations—like different political administrations—seem to permeate themselves with their own characteristic attitudes toward law abidance and "good citizenship" generally. "Law-breaking," some sociologists have observed, "can become a normative pattern within certain corporations, and violation norms may be shared between corporations and their executives." The atmosphere becomes one in which the participants (as at Equity Funding) "learn the necessary values, motives, rationalizations and techniques favorable to particular kinds of crime."

One would want to know, too, why different industries manage to evolve their own customs, habits, and attitudes. For example, the most recent and provocative survey I have seen involves a comparison of worker safety records in coal mines owned and operated by traditional coal mining companies with those owned and operated by steel firms.[1] The differences are striking. The ten major mining concerns experienced an average 0.78 deaths per million man-hours worked; but in the mines operated by the steel companies, there were on average only 0.36 fatalities per million man-hours. The injury statistics were more discrepant still. The ten major mining companies experienced, on average, 40.61 injuries per million man-hours; the steel-company-operated coal mines averaged 7.50. There are several possible explanations for these striking discrepancies. But one of the most common factors cited was simply an attitudinal one—that the steel companies have just not evolved what was called "a 'coal mentality' that accepts a great loss of life and limb as the price of digging coal."

> ...Traditionally the steel companies' top corporate executives, being used to a relatively good safety record in their steel mills, have never been willing to tolerate poor safety performance in their mines.... "There's a paternalistic attitude [in the steel companies] that you don't find prevalent in [coal,]" admits the head of one large commercial coal operation.[2]

Why is it that different corporations, and different industries, exhibit these differences in attitude? Can we identify the variables that make

some more responsible than others, and put this knowledge to work by directly manipulating those variables? We simply do not know the answer to these and many similar questions. But even in the absence of this knowledge we do have some good clues as to how attitudinal changes can be brought about—clues that suggest two broad approaches suited to two distinguishable situations.

The key characteristic of the first situation is that the attitudes we want to inculcate can be connected with, and find support in, norms and/or subgroups that preexist in the organization. An example of this is provided in the aftermath of the electrical equipment conspiracy cases.

Price-fixing in the industry—certainly in the heavy-equipment section of the industry—had become so widespread as to constitute something of a behavioral norm. To change this corporate culture that had grown up within it, Westinghouse appointed an outside advisory panel.

The advisory panel insisted not merely on the company's instructing its employees that price-fixing was illegal. Despite all the industry protests about the "vagueness" of the antitrust laws, none of those involved in the secret meetings had any doubts about the illegality of price-fixing. And that knowledge, of itself, obviously had not pulled enough freight. Instead, the panel decided to aim for an affirmative demonstration "that competition, properly pursued, can produce far more consistent profits than... conspiracy."[3]

In-house programs were established—management courses, workshops, conferences—all adopting the positive approach that the company's business success in the future, over the long haul, depended "to a considerable degree on the adoption... of policies of vigorous (and even aggressive) flexible, competitive initiative."[4]

The presentation, in other words, was not that the company had to "submit" to a stronger, outside force—that is, the government. Rather, the price-fixing was depicted as itself a foreign element, inimical to the more fundamental corporate ideal of increasing one's share of the market through better salesmanship, superior design, and the like—the norm of competition. In fact, I am authoritatively informed that at discussions among employees, a sentiment emerged that the price-fixing had been "the sales force's thing: a way to avoid the hard work of really going after sales." The same source reports that the design engineers actually resented what had been going on. Their self-esteem had been based on their ability to build better mousetraps; suddenly they discovered that their share of the market for heavy equipment had been fixed at a ratio that had no real bearing on their own contribution.

This brings me to the second point. Securing conformity to the compliance norm was not based solely on demonstrating its link to a preexistent, supposedly dominant, corporate *ideal*. In addition, there already existed within the organization certain *groups* potentially more supportive of the desired attitude than the corporation as a whole. Part of the trick of changing the attitude manifested by the corporation as a whole is to locate the critical support group and strengthen its hand. (The engineers have already been mentioned.) In the example at hand, lawyers were particularly crucial. Company lawyers "look bad," both among their peers and their co-workers, when something like widespread price-fixing is revealed to have been going on under their noses. What is more, along with their other functions, they, in particular, symbolize law abidance within the organization. In such a context, making the desired attitude more acceptable involves placing the symbolic custodian of the attitude more prominently in the corporate hierarchy. This was accomplished in the Westinghouse situation by requiring other employees to, for example, file reports with the lawyers whenever certain questionable activity was undertaken.

In a second class of situation, however, the problem of dealing with the corporate culture is stickier. I am thinking now of the cases where the attitudes the society wants to inculcate are at odds with all the dominant norms of the corporation and can find no alliance with any of the attitudinal groups I mentioned (the work group, industry, business community).

For example, where worker-safety problems are concerned, we can at least consider mobilizing some internal alliance with the unions; for product quality and safety, with the engineers; for resource conservation (as through recycling energy), with the investors. But consider, by contrast, the problem of getting "insiders" to give notice of the company's pollution; to halt industrial espionage and campaign law violations; to keep clear of political adventures in foreign countries; to exercise concern for land use aesthetics. In these cases, the attitudes desired by the "outside" world have barely a toehold on the "inside."

When we move into this area what we are faced with is nothing less than providing the organization with a new *internal rhetoric*—the special "vocabulary of motives" that every culture, and every cultural subgroup, provides its members with as its own "legitimate" reasons for doing things. These varying vocabularies involve more than just different ways of interpreting and explaining an act already completed. The range of available motives imposes boundaries on the alternatives a member of the group is prepared to consider. Today, a lower-level executive who recommended against a program on the grounds that "it will cause a lot of noise in the neighborhood" would be rather unlikely to get his recommendation advanced very far up the corporate hierarchy—unless he could convincingly append something about "we are likely to get fined (or zoned out)."

That is why any program to shift basic corporate attitudes has to involve, not replacing the profit motive ("will it sell?"), but at least providing respectable alternate vocabularies that can effectively be invoked, within some range of profit constraint, in special circumstances.

How can such a change be brought about?

A good deal depends upon the sort of gradual social evolution that is out of the control of any of us. As the general public becomes more and more informed and concerned about the environment, for example, some of that concern will gradually work its way through the corporation's walls, with the result that explanations today unacceptable—"out of place"—will become persuasive in time.

On the other hand, while much is in the hands of this sort of evolution, there are some deliberate measures that we can take. These possibilities include the following.

REWARDS FOR EXCELLENCE

At present, just about the only positive reward corporations achieve is in the form of profits (or sales, or other measures of financial growth). Essentially, all other social feedback is negative—public criticisms or legal punishments for doing things badly. This need not be the case. During World War II, for example, "E" awards were bestowed on defense companies that had exceeded their allotted production. The presentation of the "E" to a qualifying corporation was the occasion of a high ceremony, at which government representatives, executives, and workers joined. The company would get a flag, and each of the workers an "E" pin. Why should not the Environmental Protection Agency, for example, be authorized to give out its own Environmental Protection "E"'s to companies that accelerate beyond their "cleanup" timetables, or come up with ingenious new environment-protecting methods?

THE SOCIAL AUDIT

A great deal has been written recently about devising a "social audit" for corporations to supplement their traditional financial audits. Their aim would be to represent on paper the total social costs and benefits of a corporation's activities, over and above those that are now reflected in its financial statements.

The problem with the traditional statements is that they developed to reflect the interests of the financial community. Investors—and potential investors—have no particular need for a breakdown of figures displaying, for example, how much the company has put into quality-control systems or how much it has done to increase minority worker mobility. A paper company's statement will reflect the cost of the lumber it consumes; but if it uses the local river as a sewer to carry away waste, and does not have to pay for the damages this causes downstream, those social costs will nowhere appear on the company's books. They don't affect earnings.

A reporting system that measured these hidden costs and benefits would be—if we had it—quite interesting. But at present, the details of how to implement it are wanting. Much of the value of a true audit, for example, is that it has a set, prescribed structure, designed to display the answers to a series of questions which are the same for all companies.[5] This the social auditors are nowhere near achieving. And it may well be beyond their grasp.

Against this background, I am inclined to agree with the suggestion of Bauer and Fenn that, at least while we are seeing what, if anything, corporate social audits may develop into, management ought to be encouraged to make them up for their own internal use only.[6] I myself have doubts as to how successfully and far the social audit can evolve even in such a private and nurtured atmosphere. But to my mind, the key point is that even if these experiments never do produce anything terribly useful informationally, along the lines of a true audit, there is still a chance of success from our present viewpoint: from the point of developing a new internal vocabulary of motive that might compete with "profitability" and the profit constellation (sales, costs, etc.). What new constellations of motive would evolve, one cannot say. I would rather suspect that, in contrast with the true audit, different companies would design incommensurable categories and structures, each appropriate to its own fields of operation, capital intensivity, and so forth. Then these categories, in turn, could be worked into the internal evaluation process, so that those divisions and persons who performed in the appropriate way would stand a chance of reward.

INTERCHANGES

There is no more primitive way to alter intergroup attitudes (hopefully, for the better) than to bring the groups together. On an intracorporate scale, there have been a number of experiments in "sensitivity" confrontations among executives and, to a lesser extent I believe, among management and workers.

But insofar as the boundary between the corporation and the outside world is concerned, the exchanges could barely be worse. The government, for its part, relies largely on lawsuits and the threat of suits—certainly a less than ideal way to communicate values. The public at large—or, at least, the activist groups that purport to speak for it—maintain a shrill criticism that is just overstated enough that managers (even otherwise sympathetic managers) can find grounds to dismiss it in their own minds. The corporate response to the public is either a cynical PR bluff, or a defensiveness no less shrill and hysterical than the criticisms it receives. In a recent interview, Union Oil Company's president dismissed the environmental movement as "a question of people being irrational." Then, thinking a little further he added darkly, "It's more than that, actually. I don't know who's behind the Sierra Club, but it obviously isn't people of good will."[7]

What is called for, obviously, is some improved modes of communication and understanding—in both directions. Public criticism of corporate behavior certainly should be maintained. But it should be informed enough, and even sympathetic enough, that it does not induce so extreme and inflexible a defensiveness.

PUBLIC EDUCATION

Part of the problem corporate reformers face in changing the corporate culture has been mentioned: that the shriller their criticisms, the more the corporate community inclines to discount them as "one-sided" and ill-informed. The reform movement has some particularly sensitive problems, too, in taking its case to the public. How the issues are handled is important, not only because of the obvious implications for garnering legislative support, but because the reactions of the outside world are themselves one of the more significant determinants of the corporation's internal culture.

Altering corporate behavior may involve reexamining the views that prevail in the outside world. And in this regard, one has to be struck by the fact that while the public may be periodically exercised over corporations, corporate wrong-doing simply doesn't command the same dread and fascination as crimes committed by tangible human beings.

I strongly suspect—although I cannot prove—that where a corporation rather than an identifiable person is the wrongdoer, the hostility that is aroused is less even where the offense is more or less the same. For example, if we are subjected to the noise of a motorcyclist driving up and down our street at night, I think a deeper and more complex level of anger is tapped in us than if we are subjected to the same disturbance (decibelically measured) from an airline's operations overhead. It is not just that the one seems "uncalled for" while the other seems incidental to commerce and progress. It is also that where a tangible person is involved, we can picture him (even if that means only to fantasize him); whereas when the nuisances we are subjected to are corporate, there is no tangible target to fix our anger upon. And it all seems so hopeless anyway. The consequence, if I am right, is that while various small groups are turning increased publicity onto corporate wrongdoing, they are still a long way from bringing about effective changes in corporate laws and corporate performance. A reform movement, to be effective, needs both widespread indignation and widespread hope to sustain itself. Neither by itself will do. So long as the public continues to perceive the wrongs corporations do as impersonal, market-dictated, and somehow inevitable, the reformers will have as little success forcing a change in corporate consciousness as they will in marshaling a public opposition that can seriously challenge the corporation's legislative clout. In all events, those of us who aim to change things have a job to sort out and deal with the various reasons why corporate reform movements have not been more successful after so many decades of agitation. One principal reason, I am sure, is that the public little cares to be reminded, over and over, that it is being victimized by impersonal forces, without being told what it can do about it. I like to think that some of the ideas in this paper, expanded upon by others, will suggest the steps we might now begin to consider.

NOTES

1. "Coal-Mines Study Shows Record Can Be Improved When Firms Really Try," *Wall Street Journal,* January 18, 1973, p. 1, col. 6.
2. Ibid., p. 7.
3. Richard Austin Smith, *Corporations in Crisis* (New York: Doubleday, 1964), p. 165.
4. A Report from the Board of Advice to Westinghouse Electric Corporation (1962), p. 10.
5. "Enter the Social Auditors," *London Sunday Times,* June 21, 1973, p. 72, col. 5.
6. Raymond A. Bauer and Dan H. Fenn, "What Is a Corporate Social Audit?," *Harvard Business Review* 51 (January–February 1973): 43–44.
7. Digby Diehl, "Q & A: Fred L. Hartley," *West Magazine (Los Angeles Sunday Times),* February 20, 1972, p. 30.

Lessons from High-Profit, High-Ethics Companies: An Agenda for Managerial Action

Mark Pastin*

The great end of life is not knowledge but action.

—Thomas Huxley, *Technical Education*

I offer an ideal. It is an ideal for business and business organizations. What should business be like?

Business should be experimental, always seeking nonconformist ideas that will break open or create markets. It should be a hotbed of creativity, harboring no respect for bureaucratic power struggles. It should (to borrow a thought from Steve Jobs) be our internal Ellis Island, embracing those rejected by academies, governments, and accrediting bodies—and anxious to get ahead by producing results. Business should have a voracious appetite for social problems that it can solve profitably. It should be confident in its ability to produce prosperity and unembarrassed in resisting governmental meddling. Free thinking should find its true home and chance of finding application in business.

Things have never been this way, unless by exception. We think of Apple Computer as a free-spirited company even though it strictly enforces its antielitist dress code, antidefense ideology, and mandated gestures towards "team spirit." And Apple does deserve credit, if only for being nonconformist about what it is conformist about. We could list many reasons why business is, and

Excerpted from "Lessons from High-Profit, High-Ethics Companies: An Agenda for Managerial Action" in *The Hard Problems of Management: Gaining the Ethics Edge,* Chapter 11, pp. 218–228, by Mark Pastin (San Francisco: Jossey-Bass, Inc., 1986). Copyright © 1986. Reprinted by permission of the publisher and author.

*Director, Lincoln Center for Ethics, Arizona State University.

has been, less than it might and should be. These reasons would range from greed to improper education for managers to the demands of intense competition. But the better we explain why things must be as they are, the further we are from having them be otherwise. The value of an ideal is that it shifts attention away from what we know does not work and onto what we want to accomplish.

The thinking manager uses ethics to produce constructive explosion. The purpose of such explosion is to allow the firm to peek over the edge of the world as it is into the domain of how it can and should be. Most of us live with the disappointment that things will not turn out as we once had hoped; that is why the Eastern philosophy of lowering our expectations, and thus our exposure to disappointment, is popular with so many these days. Organizations do the same thing. They lower their sights to reduce the risk of disappointment; they thereby ensure slow catabolism—a diet of day-to-day death. The hard part about consulting to organizations is not addressing the problems, but convincing them that there is a chance for things to be very much better. My purpose in stating an ideal is not to foster a Pollyannaish optimism, but to foster a realistic raising of our sights.

There is a chance to close the gap between business as it is and business as it reasonably might be. And ethics is one way of seeing where that chance is. It does so by allowing managers to penetrate to the ground rules the organization really operates on. This in turn opens the possibility of *choosing* these ground rules or choosing to replace them. It is often necessary to explode the old rules to make way for new rules, but it is irresponsible to explode the old rules unless you have something to offer in place of them. We thus need an ideal—a picture of what could replace the old rules.

I express this ideal as a set of principles for high-ethics, high-profit organizations. To have ethics is to have ground rules. What then are the ground rules of the *high*-ethics organiza-

tion? I offer these principles to answer this question.

When I speak of principles for high-ethics organizations, I offer principles for high-ethics, *high-profit* organizations. High-ethics, low-profit organizations do not persist, and high-profit, low-ethics firms should not. These principles are based on the research, consulting, and thought that have guided my argument. The research included a three-year international study of twenty-five firms recognized for both their economic and ethical performance. The firms studied included Cadbury Schweppes, 3M, Arco, Motorola, Hilby Wilson Inc., Northern Chemical Company, Interwestern Management, Apple Computer, and many other fine firms; additionally, we studied several public (governor's office; mayor's office) and semipublic (chamber of commerce; industry association) organizations.

The study was conducted by leading management researchers, practicing managers, and management consultants. The objective was to discover what connections, if any, there are between high ethical performance and high economic performance. The participants carried trial versions of our principles back to our organizations or consulting practices to sort out the wishful thinking from the substantive lessons. We finally settled on a set of principles that work synergistically to promote good ethics and good economics. These principles are good ethics by our standards.

I believe that the ideal embodied in the principles is a practical one. I believe that this ideal is within the reach of able managers because I, and the other participants, have seen these principles work, albeit not all at one time in one organization. When I say that these principles express an ideal, I do not mean something removed from action, for all responsible action is practically motivated as much by ideals as by interests. Ideals are no more or less than the formal statements of guiding purposes.

The agenda for thinking managers is to take these principles to work and start the process of testing them against hard problems, revising or rejecting them, and trying again. Above all, the thinking manager will carry these principles as questions, not as question killers, and will persistently seek criticism, new principles, and new questions.

The principles are formulated as principles for high-ethics *firms*. Although the study focused more on private than on public organizations, I can suggest with measured confidence that these principles also provide the basis for high-ethics, high-effectiveness public organizations.

Most firms are a closed "reality." Managers are comfortable dealing with peer managers and often not entirely comfortable even with this group. In high-ethics firms managers deal comfortably with the extremely diverse groups who do or should take an interest in the firm's activities.

Principle 1. High-ethics firms are at ease interacting with diverse internal and external stakeholder groups. The ground rules of these firms make the good of these stakeholder groups part of the firm's own good.

The high-ethics firm knows that its success depends on many stakeholder groups not ordinarily encompassed in business thinking. This goes beyond being close to customers, suppliers, employees, and so on. It is an *attitude* of looking inside and outside the firm to see whose interests can be folded into the firm's purpose and activities. It is an attitude of recognizing the perspective most unlike one's own and of seeking to internalize it.

Control Data took note of the unemployed minority youth in neighborhoods where it operated. It knew that these kids were unlikely to acquire the skills necessary to participate in the emerging information economy and started intensive computer training programs for them. Motorola recognized that cost-effective *quality* health care was a priority for its employees and tackled the issue; it shared proprietary cost-reduction and quality-assurance programs with health care providers. Diesel Engines recognized that clean air was a priority for many stakeholder groups; it adopted a strategy to clean the air and enhance its competitive position at one and the same time. Interwestern Management knows that every employee is an individual and wants to be treated as such; its ground rules emphasize autonomy and uniqueness in all aspects of the business and make a virtue of individualism.

Principle 1 suggests that you look at the true stakeholders in your firm, ask whether your firm has any reasonable idea of how its actions look in the eyes of the stakeholders, and ask whether the firm has overlooked ways of folding stakeholder perspectives into the firm's thought and actions. It also suggests getting some first-hand knowledge of the stakeholders and allowing them some first-hand knowledge of the firm.

Nothing makes most managers more uncomfortable than issues of justice or fairness. In high-ethics firms, however, fairness is the bread and butter of management.

Principle 2. High-ethics firms are obsessed with fairness. Their ground rules emphasize that the other person's interests count as much as their own.

These firms waste little energy managing conflicts; thus they appear to be undermanaged. The amount of control and management that you need is proportional to the number of people who feel unfairly treated. A paradigmatic example is Cadbury Schweppes. It has achieved labor peace in a hostile labor environment by assiduously maintaining fairness in dealing with employees at all levels. Despite bargaining with over twenty unions, it has better labor-management relations than any nonunionized U.S. firm we know of, and it does this with a lean management cadre. Hilby Wilson, Inc., a land syndication company, succeeds with a similar approach. It offers no deal that it would not invest in as an outsider. Its ground rules emphasize putting its own interests on the line before asking anyone else to do so.

Its deals quickly sell themselves. Little management and no marketing function are needed. Jaguar PLC and R. L. Carol succeed by attending mainly to a tough-minded, competitive style of fairness.

Principle 2 suggests that you find the groups within and outside of your firm who may feel unfairly treated by the firm. Look at the firm's actions from their viewpoints, and make adjustments to achieve fairness. Observe situations in which managers spend their time managing conflicts of interest, and ask how conflict and its management could be reduced or eliminated by taking a new view of fairness. This does not mean giving turkeys to the poor at Christmas. It means having the basic confidence that you treat people well and that you can restore fairness when imbalances inevitably occur. Fairness includes fairness to yourself and to the firm. You and the firm have a right to fair treatment and should forthrightly seek it.

Responsibility is impossible to pinpoint in most firms; it stares you in the eye in high-ethics firms.

Principle 3. In high-ethics firms, responsibility is individual rather than collective, with individuals assuming personal responsibility for actions of the firm. These firms' ground rules mandate that individuals are responsible to themselves.

This principle, whose influence has been evident throughout this book, was the most surprising and paradoxical finding of our research project. The emphasis on individual responsibility is a surprising contrast to the nearly unanimous call for collective responsibility in the current management literature. It is paradoxical in that individuals in these firms claim personal responsibility for the actions of the firm itself.

Consider a discussion that we had with line workers at Jaguar PLC. We refer to the new, post-1980 Jaguar, liberated from both British

Leyland and the British government and a strong economic and ethical performer. Workers scorned the "we are all one" mentality and personalized actions and responsibility for them. A typical comment: "I am the emblem man; every emblem you see on a Jaguar is mine." An individualistic view. On the other hand, the emblem man said, "That door is crooked; I don't know how that got by me." Joseph Yiu, one of Motorola's best managers, frequently expounds his philosophy, which views every last action of Motorola as one of his actions; he seriously believes that he runs the company from his midmanagement position. In short, we found individualized responsibility, with individuals taking a broad view of what they individually do and an equally broad view of their responsibilities.

Principle 3 suggests that you first look at the degree to which you accept responsibility for what happens in the firm. Then consider what others consider themselves responsible for. Adopt an attitude which says: "If it happens here, I did it. I did it by doing *A*, *B*, and *C*." Although this attitude is naturally infectious, it is still worth promoting. Promote it by reviewing the tasks that make up various jobs in order to find their creative component and by drawing attention to that component by every means possible. Let it be known that people create in countless forms in every aspect of their work, and watch the responsibility flow.

The glue that holds the high-ethics firm together is not culture, goals, superordinate goals, participation, employee stock ownership, or leadership. It is purpose.

Principle 4. The high-ethics firm sees its activities in terms of a purpose. This purpose is a way of operating that members of the firm value. And purpose ties the firm to its environment.

We describe the glue of high-ethics firms as purpose, not goals, to underscore an important point. Goals are future-oriented, inviting members of the firm to see present activities in terms of a speculative future good. This does not work. High-ethics, high-profit firms invite members of the firm to see their activities as valuable *in themselves* and *to the world at large*.

3M is, perhaps, the best example of a firm held together by purpose. 3M's purpose is to innovate. *Being* innovative is not a goal, although 3M has goals reflecting its commitment to innovation. *Becoming* innovative is a goal, a goal 3M neither has nor needs. Innovation is a way of life at 3M enjoyed by 3M managers and employees *day to day*. And 3M people see innovation as socially important. At one time, Apple Computer was held together by the purpose of making computers an integral part of the life of common folk; Apple people believed they were leading this process and that it was vitally important that they succeed. The Eagle team at Data General operated from the purpose of being at the creative edge of new computer technology and succeeded against stiff odds.

Principle 4 suggests that you take an honest look at the issue of how many members of your firm view themselves as engaged in work that truly matters. From those to whom the work matters, find out why. From those to whom the work does not matter, find out what does matter, and see if there is a possible alignment with the work of the firm. Purpose is hard to find for two reasons—there is not that much around, and what is around is buried beneath layers of belief, rationalization, and fear of disclosure. The only way to find purpose is to learn to persist in asking why, to try to see the pattern and underlying assumptions, and to become an excellent reverse engineer. But find it you must if you seek the alignment and self-motivation that produces the most ethical and effective action.

The ethical firm operates on ground rules that deal fairly with diverse constituencies, promote individual responsibility, and enact a purpose. This is fairly complicated. A simpler formulation says that the ethical firm thrives on individuality, rather than suppressing it, and uses a grounding purpose to focus and multiply the efforts of individuals. The mark of unethical firms is that individuals lose part of themselves to belong to the firm. The mark of the ethical firm is that individuals gain new dimensions through the firm, without giving anything away. In this firm, ethical conduct is natural and needs no support from codes, slogans, and phony ceremonies.

We do not offer these four principles as answers. Being a thinking manager and trying to build a high-ethics, high-profit firm or work unit is a bootstrapping operation. You start by questioning the accepted answers: Ask hard questions about the accepted answers, try out some new answers, and then start asking why once again. Since you must stand somewhere to start asking questions, I offer the above principles for you to use in raising some critical questions. Treat these principles, and the ethics they embody, as a ladder to climb up on and then to kick away once you have achieved a better view.

Developing the Ethical Corporation

W. Michael Hoffman*

Over the past several months, the public has been informed of a rash of very questionable corporate activities. Such reports include the check-kiting scam in E.F. Hutton, defense contract fraud by such corporations as General Dynamics and General Electric, failure by the Bank of Boston to report large cash deposits made by reputed leaders of organized crime, failure by Eli Lilly to report deaths of patients who took Oraflex, the investigation of Cartier regarding

Excerpted from "Developing the Ethical Corporation" by W. Michael Hoffman, in *Bell Atlantic Quarterly*, Vol. 3, No. 1 (Spring 1986). Copyright © 1986. Reprinted by permission of the publisher.

*Director, Center for Business Ethics, Bentley College.

collusion with customers to avoid sales tax by mailing empty boxes out of state, alleged cover-up by A. H. Robins of the dangers of the Dalkon Shield, cyanide poisoning of employees within Film Recovery Systems, and unfair takeover tactics by Texaco. Some would also mention the lack of adequate safety standards by Union Carbide, leading to the tragedy in Bhopal.

Do these recent disclosures indicate that, generally speaking, corporations are just not interested in ethics, that ultimately corporate greed simply takes priority over moral responsibility? I suspect the majority of the public would answer yes, especially when a *New York Times* poll reported this past summer that 55 percent think most U.S. corporate executives are not honest. But this negative public opinion of the ethical standards of business did not originate with these new scandals. Such reports simply add fuel to an already burning fire whose sparks were generated over a decade ago by corporate bribery and illegal campaign contributions. A poll by Yankelovich, Skelly, and White reported that in 1968, 70 percent believed business tried to strike a balance between profits and the public interest, compared with only 15 percent believing so ten years later. A Harris poll reported that in 1966, 55 percent had respect for and confidence in business leaders, whereas more recently only 20 percent say that they do. And in 1977, a Gallup poll taken for the Center for Business Ethics found that big business was rapidly becoming, in the public's view, the biggest threat to the country's future.

These opinions are not without foundation—a foundation that was given even more support in a recent survey of the 1984 *Fortune* 500 largest industrial corporations by the Center for Policy Research. According to the survey, roughly two-thirds of these companies have been involved in illegal behavior over the past ten years based on an examination of public records. Furthermore, this survey did not even include unethical acts as judged by prevailing community standards; it focused exclusively on illegal acts

such as price-fixing, overcharging, violation of environmental regulations and antitrust laws, bribes, fraud, patent infringements, and violations of various other market regulations. It is also worth noting that the 100 largest corporations accounted for 55 percent of these illegal offenses.

It has been argued that focusing on the morality of institutions depersonalizes the issue, obscuring the primary role of individuals. E.F. Hutton and General Dynamics and the rest are blamed only because certain individuals committed wrongful actions; hence we should focus our attention on developing individual integrity which will lead to institutional integrity. Although there is some truth to this claim, it nevertheless overlooks the essential dynamics and reciprocity between individuals and organizations. Individuals do not operate in a vacuum. Just as organizations are made up of individuals, individuals are dependent on organizations. Individuals gain meaning, direction, and purpose by belonging to and acting out of organizations, out of social cultures that are formed around common goals, shared beliefs, and collective duties. As the philosopher John Dewey has put it, "Apart from ties which bind [the individual] to others, [the individual] is nothing." Corporations, like other social organizations, can and do influence individual decisions and actions. Corporations are social cultures with character—character that can exercise good or bad influences depending on goals, policies, structures, strategies, and other characteristics that formalize relations among the individuals who make up corporations. Therefore, when 60 to 70 percent of the managers of two major corporations feel pressure to sacrifice their own personal ethical integrity for corporate goals, as *Business Week* has reported, it is necessary and appropriate that we direct our attention to issues of corporate integrity.

I am convinced that a major reason why we have witnessed outbreaks of corporate wrongdoing, recently as well as in the past, is not that business people are less ethical than others, but rather that business gives so little thought to developing a moral corporate culture within which individuals can act ethically. Causes of unethical actions are quite often systemic and not simply the result of rotten apples in the corporate barrel. Ethical people can be brought down by serving in a bad organization, just as people with questionable ethical integrity can be uplifted or at least held in check by serving in a good one. Corporations should examine themselves to see if their structures and relations, which systematically bind and move their collections of individuals, are compatible with ethical behavior. And if they are not, then certain steps ought to be taken to change or supplement them.

Have corporations been taking any steps to incorporate ethical values and concerns into their operations? The Center for Business Ethics, having been asked this question often by many different people and groups, made it a lead question in a lengthy questionnaire to the 1984 *Fortune* 500 industrial and 500 service companies. Of the 279 responding companies (a 28 percent survey response), 223 (almost 80 percent) indicated that they were taking steps to incorporate ethics (Table 1). Furthermore, the goal of being a socially responsible corporation was listed more often than any other as the primary reason for building ethics into the organization, by far taking precedence over the goal of simply complying with state and federal guidelines. These findings help to corroborate what I felt I was learning piecemeal as director of the Center, namely that more and more of America's major corporations are trying in various ways to institutionalize ethics. Cautiously generalizing from this survey, I believe a truly significant number of attempts are underway to develop ethical corporations.

However, the survey also indicates that most of these corporate attempts need to go much further before they will be successful. (The following results are summarized on Table 2.) Although 93 percent of the responding companies taking ethical steps have written codes of ethics in place—representing almost a 40 percent rise over a study for the Conference Board 20 years ago—only 18 percent have ethics committees, only 8 percent have ethics ombudsmen, and only three companies said they have judiciary boards. It is difficult to understand how codes can be overseen and enforced adequately without a committee or ombudsman assigned to that task or how alleged violations of codes can be adjudicated effectively and fairly without a board committee for that purpose. Furthermore, the communica-

TABLE 1		
HAS YOUR COMPANY BEEN TAKING STEPS TO INCORPORATE ETHICAL VALUES AND CONCERNS INTO THE DAILY OPERATIONS OF YOUR ORGANIZATION?		
	Number	Percent
No	56	20.1%
Yes	223	79.9%
Total	279	100.0%

Results for the combined industrial and service corporations.
Source: Center for Business Ethics Questionnaire Survey, 1985.

TABLE 2

SOME WAYS THAT ETHICAL VALUES CAN BE INCORPORATED INTO THE CORPORATE ENVIRONMENT ARE LISTED BELOW. WHICH OF THESE DOES YOUR COMPANY USE?

	Yes		No	
	Number	Percent	Number	Percent
Code of conduct	208	93.3%	15	6.7%
Ethics committee	40	17.9	183	82.1
Judiciary board	3	1.3	220	98.7
Ombudsman	17	7.6	206	92.4
Employee training in ethics	99	44.4	124	55.6
Social auditing and reporting	98	43.9	125	56.1
Changes in corporate structure	46	20.6	177	79.4
None of the above	2	0.9	221	99.1

The total number of responses = 223. Results for the combined industrial and service corporations.

Source: Center for Business Ethics Questionnaire Survey, 1985.

tion of the codes seemed suspect, according to the survey. Almost all the companies communicate them to their employees through printed materials, but only 40 percent do so through advice from a superior, 34 percent through an entrance interview, and 21 percent through workshops or seminars. Only 11 percent post them in the workplace. Writing a code of ethics is an important first step toward building an ethical corporation, but it is just that—a first step. To be effective, it must be backed up by other kinds of support structures throughout the organization to insure its adequate communication, oversight, enforcement, adjudication, and review.

Some corporate codes of ethics are better than others. Of those with which I am familiar, some consist of just a set of specific rules, a list of do's and don'ts usually corresponding to clearly illegal or unethical actions such as bribery, price-fixing, conflicts of interest, improper use of company funds, improper accounting practices, and the acceptance of gifts. Other codes consist largely of general statements putting forth the corporate goals and responsibilities, a kind of credo expressing the company's philosophy and values. The better

codes consist of both. Rules of conduct without a general credo lack a framework of meaning and purpose; credos without rules of conduct lack specific content.

Codes of ethics also should not be written to imply that whatever is not strictly prohibited is thereby allowed. There is no way that all ethical or unethical conduct can be exhaustively listed and mandated through a code, nor ought it to be. Business ethics, like all areas of ethics, has its grey areas that require individual discretion. A good corporate code of ethics should include certain managerial and employee guidelines for ethical decision making. Such guidelines might include the principles and factors that one ought to think about before arriving at a decision. They might include sources both inside and outside the corporation through which advice and counsel could be offered. They could even include cases based on history that might clarify a future ethical dilemma. Whatever these guidelines include, they should make one aware that there may very well be some difficult ethical judgments to make—for which one is accountable—that will have to be made from the spirit of the code, rather than from its letter. This will also place a greater sense of personal ethical responsibility on corporate employees and send a clear message that corporate integrity is in this way dependent on individual integrity.

But recognition of the importance of individual integrity and its accompanying responsibilities must be backed up by strong corporate support. The employee must believe that the corporation will stand behind individual decisions made in keeping with or out of respect for the ethics code. The code, therefore, should have clear support from the very top of the corporation, preferably from the board of directors. In fact, a corporate ethics committee should probably be chaired by a member of the board, or at least report directly to a member of the board. Equally important is that everyone in the corporation should be brought into efforts to develop the ethical corporation. Unfortunately, the profile of the relatively few ethics committees suggests that they are strongly oriented toward upper management, designed without much input or representation from lower-level employees. Only 23 percent have managers below the level of the board or executive officers as members of the ethics committees, and only 8 percent have non-managers as members. Furthermore, most of the members are appointed; only 8 percent have any elected members. And finally, only 40 percent of these ethics committees handle infractions of the code, and 23 percent respond to employee complaints. A corporate code of ethics lacks overall effectiveness if it is simply handed down and run from on high, so to speak. Corporations must find ways for all their members to feel they have played and continue to play some role in the on-going design and maintenance of the code. The code, of course, will also lack effectiveness and meaning if no appropriately representative committee or board actually addresses employee concerns about the code or potential code violations.

There are other steps corporations should take and, in some cases, have been taking, to institutionalize ethics. One is the implementation of an ethics training or development program for corporate employees. The Center's survey revealed that more than 44 percent of those corporations taking ethical steps have some form of ethics training, with 53 percent stating that they use a workshop or seminar as one method. Although specific ethics workshops seem far preferable to other methods, just as with codes, some are better than others. I have participated as a consultant in some ethics workshops that consisted of only a three-hour module of a week-long educational program for upper management. Such modules are not long enough to accomplish anything significant, and they are often poorly conceived in terms of their integration into the rest of the program and the preparation of their participants prior to the workshop. As with any educational program, they require sufficient time for presentation of issues and cases, discussion and debate, and follow-up sessions.

A successful ethics workshop program should also include all levels of the corporation, not just upper management; yet the Center's survey revealed that only 35 percent of those companies engaged in ethics training involved hourly workers. In fact, ethics workshops should mix different levels of the corporation, from hourly workers to executive officers to, perhaps, members of the board, to promote better understanding and communication among all members of the corporation relating to the ethical commitments of the organization. This, in turn, would build a stronger and more unified ethical corporate culture.

Another corporate step toward institutionalizing ethics is the social audit or report, which analyzes the firm's activities in a number of ethically sensitive areas. Although it poses problems, a social audit can help in determining where the most important ethical issues and problems are in one's business. It makes little sense to implement answers to a company's ethical problems before making sure what the problems are; if a program for institutionalizing ethics is going to work effectively, some procedure to determine areas of ethical strain and perhaps to measure progress seems necessary. The Center's survey showed that 43 percent of those corporations taking ethical steps perform a social audit including areas such as equal opportunity employment, compliance, community involvement, safety, quality of products and service, protection of the environment, and conduct in multinational operations.

Although the issue of disclosure is controversial, I believe corporations ought to disclose the results of their social audit more widely both within and without the organization. The Center's survey found that social audit information in most cases is located in internal memoranda and circulated only at the highest levels of the company. Only 22 percent disclose their social audits to the general public and to shareholders. I would argue that wider dissemination of such information will strengthen the commitment and performance of a corporation's ethics program and provide opportunity both from within and without for suggestions for improvement. Furthermore, assuming corporations are performing responsibly, it would seem they would improve their ethical image by disclosing audit information to all employees, stockholders, and the general public. It also seems correct to me that a necessary criterion for being an ethical corporation is the disclosure of information to "stakeholders" socially affected by corporate activities.

Finally, a corporate program for institutionalizing ethics might very well demand internal structural changes that clearly would create and define the appropriate ethical role and make-up of the governance system—especially that of the board of directors, which is ultimately responsible for the ethical integrity of the corporation. Many argue that boards have not understood or carried out their responsibilities to oversee and insure the ethical activities of their companies, nor is their insider-dominated membership and leadership conducive to such an ethical role. The Center's survey discovered that almost 80 per-

cent of the companies taking ethical steps have made no changes in corporate structure to accommodate their ethical efforts. And of the 20 percent that have, only 39 percent have made changes in the role of the board, only 41 percent in the inclusion of outside directors, and only 2 percent in the representation of an ethics officer on the board. Furthermore, of the 20 percent that have made some structural changes, only 24 percent moved toward worker participation in decision making and only 7 percent introduced an employee bill of rights.

I am convinced that certain structural reforms need to be made in most corporate organizations to insure that there is appropriate ethical focus, information flow, and oversight, starting with the board and proceeding down through the corporate hierarchy. Boards need to be more informed, more representative, and more independent of the influence of corporate officers. Only then will they effectively discharge one of their primary responsibilities, namely, the establishment of a corporate ethical culture. Changes also need to be made in the traditional reliance on hierarchical top-down chains of responsibility and decision making. Flatter organizations and bottom-up structures allow for increased responsibility and participatory decision making at lower levels in the organization. At all levels, or perhaps better said in all areas of the organization, ethical responsibilities and guidelines for ethical action should be clearly stated, communicated, and overseen with participation from all affected parties. And such responsibilities should be complemented by equally important statements of rights for all employees. Only when such corporate structural changes are initiated will a foundation be laid for the development of the ethical corporation.

I believe corporations are interested in ethics and not just profit, despite the barrage of recently publicized unethical activities listed at the beginning of this article. Business people do not want to see themselves or be seen by others in this way. Nor are people in business inherently less ethical than people in other professions. The ethical problems that occur in corporations, as with other organizations, quite often are systemic. Attention must be paid to the ethical goals, mechanisms, and structure of the system within which individuals operate if actions emanating from the system are to be ethical.

As the survey by the Center for Business Ethics shows, corporations are paying more attention to the institutionalization of ethics within their organizational systems. This is happening, in part, because business has become aware of the enormous costs of unethical activity: White-collar crime is estimated to cost business $200 billion annually; fines and penalties run into the millions; resulting governmental regulations even now cost business over $100 billion annually in compliance expenses; and the damage to a firm's public image probably has economic ramifications that are more costly than any of the above. I am convinced that corporations are also paying more attention to ethics because they feel it is the right thing to do. It is unfair and naive for anyone to believe that most people working in the corporate world are not themselves concerned, even outraged, about unethical practices occurring in their profession.

However, as the Center's survey also reveals, more work is needed toward building ethical corporations. This would include, in most cases, improved codes, more ethics committees, judiciary boards, and ombudsmen with better oversight and enforcement functions. It would also include more ethics training for all corporate employees, more social reporting with wider disclosure, and more changes in corporate structure—such as more diverse representation on all committees, including the board, and different governance strategies to provide more responsiveness to and responsibility for ethical concerns up and down the organization.

It is impossible totally to prevent unscrupulous people from committing wrongful acts in any organization, but by working toward the development of the ethical corporation, business leaders can lessen such acts and strengthen individual integrity. My experience as director of the Center for Business Ethics for the past decade has convinced me that significant progress has been and will continue to be made toward this worthwhile goal.

NOTES

For more detailed information on the Center for Business Ethics survey see "Are Corporations Institutionalizing Ethics?" *Journal of Business Ethics,* vol. 5, 2, April 1986.

Hoffman, W. Michael, Jennifer Mills Moore, and David A. Fedo, editors. *Corporate Governance and Institutionalizing Ethics: Proceedings of the Fifth National Conference on Business Ethics.* Lexington, Massachusetts: D.C. Heath and Company, 1984.

Hoffman, W. Michael. "What Is Necessary for Corporate Moral Excellence?" *Journal of Business Ethics,* vol. 5, 3, June 1986.

QUESTION FOR DISCUSSION

1. Stone, Pastin, and Hoffman all have suggestions for developing a moral corporation. Stone talks about changing attitudes and values; Pastin urges the adoption of ethical ground rules or principles; and Hoffman recommends the institutionalization of definite strategies and structures. Based on these suggestions and ideas from other readings in the text, map out a specific plan for developing a moral corporate culture. Do you think that such a goal is important for corporations to be working toward? Why or why not?

The Future Corporate Ethos

CASE FOR PART FIVE

Archie B. Carroll and Elizabeth Gatewood
The Proctor & Gamble Rely Case:
A Social Response Pattern for the 1980s?
638

The Procter & Gamble *Rely* Case: A Social Response Pattern for the 1980s?

Archie B. Carroll* and Elizabeth Gatewood†

In recent times it has become popular for corporations to espouse socially responsible policies. More corporate annual reports than ever before contain discussions on the subject. The recurring theme of these reports is that business as a social institution must satisfy both the economic and social needs of the society in which it functions. For example, Edward G. Harness, Chairman of the Board of Procter & Gamble (P&G) believes that:

> Company management must consistently demonstrate a superior talent for keeping profit and growth objectives as first priorities. However, it also must have enough breadth to recognize that enlightened self-interest requires the company to fill any reasonable expectation placed upon it by the community and the various concerned publics. Keeping priorities straight and maintaining the sense of civic responsibility will achieve important secondary objectives of the firm. Profitability and growth go hand in hand with fair treatment of employees, of direct customers, of consumers, and of the community (Harness, 1980).

Corporations have increasingly recognized the importance of social issues to the performance of the operations of their firms. On the other hand, although awareness has occurred it has not always been translated into meaningful action. A first step for corporations that have recognized the necessity for dealing with social issues is to develop a philosophy of response to guide its future actions. In the development of this philosophy, it may be worthwhile to review other companies' responses to a social issue in the hope of choosing a philosophy that will be most beneficial to the company.

This article will describe Procter & Gamble's response to the Rely tampon issue and contrast it with the responses of two other companies to product liability issues. P&G's unprecedented action, in effect de-marketing in a couple of weeks a product they had spent $74 million and 20 years of research and marketing preparations, may well set the tone for corporate social response strategies, in general, and product liability strategies, in particular, for the 1980s (Yoshihara and Moreland, 1980). P&G's response will be depicted and analyzed in terms of conceptual schemes of social responsiveness provided by several writers.

SOCIAL RESPONSE STRATEGIES

There are a number of strategies business could adopt toward social issues. These strategies range from a negative to a positive response. Several writers have described various conceptual frameworks for classifying corporate social responses. For example, Ian Wilson asserts there are four possible business strategies—reaction, defense, accommodation, and proaction (1975). Terry McAdam has, likewise, described four social responsibility philosophies that mesh well with Wilson's strategies and describe the range of responsiveness. These philosophies are (1) "Fight all the way," (2) "Do only what is required," (3) "Be progressive," and (4) "Lead the industry" (McAdam, 1973). Keith Davis and Robert Blomstrom, too, describe alternative responses to societal pressures as follows: (a) withdrawal, (b) public relations approach, (c) legal approach, (d) bargaining, and (e) problem solv-

Excerpted from "The Procter & Gamble *Rely* Case: A Social Response Pattern for the 1980s" by Archie B. Carroll and Elizabeth Gatewood, in *Proceedings: Academy of Management, 41st Conference,* 1981. Copyright © 1981. Reprinted with permission of the authors and the Academy of Management, Mississippi State University.

*Georgia Power Company Professor of Management and Corporate Public Affairs, University of Georgia.

†Director of Research & Experiential Education, Small Business Development Center, University of Georgia.

ing (1975). Archie Carroll in his presentation of a conceptual model of corporate social performance arranges these philosophies of response along a continuum from negative to positive responses (1979).

Procter & Gamble's removal of its product from the market in the Rely issue seems to have moved, in a time period of about four months from the first awareness of toxic shock syndrome, along the continuum from a negative to a positive response. We will use Wilson's categories as a basis for describing the different stages of P&G's social response since his framework seems the most appropriate to the issue at hand.

PROCTER & GAMBLE'S SOCIAL RESPONSE

Reaction Phase (June through August, 1980)

Although doctors say they are now increasingly convinced that toxic shock syndrome has been present for decades (Severo, 1980), Procter & Gamble first became aware of it on June 13, 1980, when the Center for Disease Control (CDC) in Atlanta contacted P&G and other major tampon manufacturers and requested data concerning tampon usage. At that time, there were no data to suggest a link between toxic shock syndrome and the usage of tampons.

On June 19, 1980; the CDC contacted tampon manufacturers once again to invite them to a June 25–26 meeting. Manufacturers were asked to provide market histories and market-share data on their brands. The CDC's actions were prompted by the findings of their first investigation which showed an apparent statistical link between toxic shock and tampon usage.

Although the CDC's June study did not link any specific tampon to the occurrence of the disease, studies done by the state health departments of Wisconsin and Minnesota showed a statistical link to Rely brand tampons (Severo,

1980). In June when P&G was notified of a possible problem with its product, it began to collect information about toxic shock and tampon usage, in general, and Rely, in particular. Information collected from health departments and individual physicians appeared to confirm no correlation between any specific tampon brand and toxic shock syndrome. During July and August, P&G's reaction was to begin laboratory testing with the suspected bacteria and to assemble a panel of scientific experts. P&G's microbiologists tested the suspected bacteria on Rely, and the results seemed to indicate that the material in Rely did not encourage the growth of the bacteria.

Defense Phase (September 15 to 17, 1980)

On Monday, September 15, the CDC announced the results of a study of cases of toxic shock syndrome sufferers in July and August. In the sample of 42 women, 71% had used the Rely tampon (*Wall Street Journal,* 1980). The results of this study prompted the scheduling of a meeting between P&G, the Food and Drug Administration (FDA), and CDC officials.

The results of the CDC's second study put P&G on the defensive. In an attempt to retain a product for which they had spent more than 20 years of research and marketing preparations, P&G announced in a news release that the company had examined a summary of the CDC's data and believed the information too limited and fragmentary for any conclusions to be drawn (P&G, 1980).

Edward G. Harness, chairman and chief executive of Procter & Gamble, recalls he was "determined to fight for a brand, to keep an important brand from being hurt by insufficient data in the hands of a bureaucracy" (Rotbart and Prestbo, 1980).

When the 13 P&G representatives met face to face on September 16 with 12 FDA and 3 CDC officials, P&G arrived with a number of questions concerning the CDC study. P&G contended that the extensive news coverage of toxic shock cases may have biased the results of the survey; they challenged the study's interviewing techniques and quibbled with some of the data. But Procter & Gamble also arrived with a proposed warning label they were willing to put on their packages. The meeting ended with the FDA allowing P&G one week to study the CDC's findings and respond (Rotbart and Prestbo, 1980).

Accommodation Phase (September 18 to 22, 1980)

By September 18, P&G had halted production of the Rely tampon, perhaps because of the uncertainty about the necessity of a warning label, perhaps under the deluge of negative publicity. On September 19, the Utah State Health Department reported results from a study they performed which confirmed the CDC's September report statistically linking Rely and toxic shock syndrome.

Procter & Gamble's previously recruited group of independent physicians, microbiologists, and epidemiologists were unable to positively refute the latest studies, although they agreed with P&G that no direct evidence linked toxic shock to Rely more than any other tampon brand. "That was the turning point," Mr. Harness said. "I knew Sunday night what we had to do." Consequently, P&G announced on September 22 its voluntary suspension of sale of its product from the market (Rotbart and Prestbo, 1980).

Proaction Phase (September 23, 1980 on)

"We didn't know enough about toxic shock to act, and yet we knew too much not to act," Mr. Harness states. On September 23, the FDA and P&G began the drafting of a consent agreement. P&G had already started pulling back some 400,000 cases of Rely by this time (Rotbart and Prestbo, 1980). Under the agreement, Procter &

Gamble denied any violation of federal law or any product defect, but agreed to buy back any unused product the customer still had, including P&G's $10 million introductory promotion free samples. They also pledged their research expertise to the CDC to investigate toxic shock syndrome, and agreed to finance and direct a large educational program about the disease, as well as issue a warning to women not to use Rely. According to Chairman Harness, "This is being done despite the fact that we know of no defect in Rely tampons and despite evidence that the withdrawal of Rely won't eliminate the occurrence of toxic shock syndrome" (P&G, 1980).

As a result of the consent decree worked out between P&G and the FDA, Procter & Gamble launched a broad educational campaign to inform women about toxic shock syndrome, the link between this disease and tampons, and the greater statistical link with the Rely brand. It also informed consumers about the voluntary withdrawal of Rely and the details of the refund offer.

The program was designed to communicate with a broad base of women very quickly. The plan established a reach objective (percent of women who would receive at least one message) of 90% of all women in the target audience. This is 7% higher than Rely's normal reach and also greater than any other tampon brand. The program ran for four weeks in all key media elements—network television, radio, and newspaper. The retrieval advertisements appeared on 203 television market areas in the United States, covering virtually all households with televisions. The advertisement aired on 350 radio stations in the United States, reaching 87% of the households. Newspaper advertisements of 1,000 lines ran in 1,200 newspapers in the United States (Consent Agreement, 1980). The program is unprecedented in both its scope and the speed with which the company reacted to adverse findings from the scientific community.

One can see the striking contrast of the P&G social response most vividly when it is compared to the kind of response made by the Firestone Company and Ford Motor Company when they faced possible product recalls due to problems with their products several years ago. The Firestone 500 tire and Ford Pinto were kept on the market long after consumer groups, government agencies, and lawsuits had attacked them. Ford's and Firestone's responses seem to have never progressed past the defense phase.

FIRESTONE'S SOCIAL RESPONSE PATTERN

Firestone's social response would likely be classified by Wilson as falling in the reaction-defense categories. McAdam may choose to classify it as "fighting all the way" at worst or "doing only what is required" at best.

The Firestone 500 series of steel-belted radials were, according to federal authorities, prone to blowouts, tread separations, and other dangerous deformities. They have been the target of thousands of consumer complaints. Associated with the tire were at least 34 deaths and hundreds of accidents, according to Firestone's own reports supplied to Congressional investigators and other sources.

Firestone contended there was nothing defective in the tire design despite numerical evidence that the tire's readjustment rate—7.4%—was more than double that of competitive steel-belted lines. Firestone chose to lay the blame on the customer. According to Firestone, "practically all the tire failures can be blamed on consumer neglect and abuse . . . Consumers damage their tires by overloading them, banging them against the curb, failing to keep them adequately inflated, and driving at excessive speeds" (Louis, 1978).

Firestone repeatedly tried to block investigation of its tire, as well as to publicly question the motives of the investigators. Firestone attempted to suppress the results of a survey of tire owners conducted by the Traffic Safety Administration by petitioning in U.S. District Court for a re-straining order. "It was a phony survey," John E. Floberg, Firestone's vice president and general counselor, was quoted as saying. "We had no choice but trying to get it squelched" (Louis, 1978).

Firestone's attack also took other forms. When the Traffic Safety Administration requested answers to a long list of questions concerning steel-belted radial tires, Firestone responded by insisting that it could not supply all the information requested without spending months researching and compiling. Information requested dealt with any and all complaints about failures of the tire, a list of all lawsuits against Firestone arising from these failures, and detailed accounts of any changes in the methods used to manufacture radials.

Firestone continued to stall long after the agency ran out of patience and demanded answers to twenty-seven specific questions under penalty of prosecution. Firestone objected to almost all of the questions and continued to insist it would require an inordinate amount of time and effort to gather the information. It also questioned the Traffic Safety Administration's authority to demand the information. One of the arguments Firestone offered was that the agency was asking Firestone to analyze documents and compile new ones when the agency only had the authority to request the company to make existing documents available for inspection. Firestone also argued it was only responsible for making documents available for inspection at Ford headquarters, and the Traffic Safety Administration was asking it to send copies of certain documents. It also objected to the agency's request for information about tires produced more than three years ago, on the grounds that such tires do not fall under the control of the agency.

THE FORD PINTO RESPONSE

The Ford Pinto social response was similar to Firestone's but was raised to a new level of sophistication and effectiveness. According to one observer, for more than eight years Ford successfully lobbied against a government safety standard (Federal Motor Vehicle Safety Standard 301) that would have forced a redesign of the Pinto's fire-prone gas tank. This occurred despite the fact that by a conservative estimate the Pinto had been responsible for 500 burn deaths to people who would not have been seriously injured by the impact of the accident. The figure could be as high as 900 deaths. Ford delayed those eight years because its cost-benefit analysis showed it was not profitable to make the redesign (Dowie, 1977). Ford's response would appear to fall into McAdam's "fight all the way" category or Wilson's "defense" posture.

Ford used several techniques to thwart passage of the Federal Motor Vehicle Act 301. Among the successful techniques were (a) make your arguments in succession, so the feds can be working on disproving only one at a time; (b) claim the real problem is Y not X (i.e., "the problem is people not cars"); (c) no matter how ridiculous each argument is, accompany it with thousands of pages of highly technical assertions it will take the government months or, preferably, years to treat (Dowie, 1977).

Ford managed to use all three techniques with great success. In 1968, using argument (b) they asserted that auto fires were not the real problem. They only constituted a tiny proportion of the matters that NHTSA should be concerned with. After months of studies, Transportation officials found that auto fires were much more a problem than they had previously conceived— 400,000 cars were burning every year resulting in 3,000 deaths. It was also found that of the collision-ruptured fuel-tank cases, 42% were Ford Motor Company products, although they produce only 24% of the cars on the American road.

Ford officials then parried with technique (a)— bringing up a new argument. This argument went something like this. Yes, burn accidents happen, but rear-end accidents seldom occur. Again Transportation officials were forced to spend months analyzing accident reports to refute Ford's latest argument.

Ford then switched to tactic (b) again. The people killed in those fiery collisions would have died from the force of the impact. The fire was a non-determining factor. This argument resulted in a new round of testing and analysis of collision reports. In the end this argument was again refuted (Dowie, 1977).

Among other arguments offered by Ford to NHTSA, and accompanied by thousands of pages of reports, studies, and charts, was that the federal testing criteria were unfair and that design changes required to meet the proposed standards would take forty-three months. Along with the gargantuan amount of paperwork, Ford also used a certain amount of political pressure. Henry Ford warned, "If we can't meet the standards when they are published, we will have to close down" (Dowie, 1977).

DISCUSSION

Procter & Gamble's response in the Rely tampon issue, an unparalleled response to a product liability issue, is in striking contrast to Ford's and Firestone's responses to similar product liability problems. Years after Ford and Firestone were aware of possible defects in their products they were still fighting to keep the products on the market, never moving beyond a defensive response. P&G traversed the range of responses to arrive at proaction within a very short time. The decision to withdraw Rely took less than one week, the actual pulling the product off the market another two weeks or so.

The public and consumer response to the manner in which P&G, Firestone, and Ford handled the issues provides a vivid contrast. The prompt withdrawal of Rely and the vigorous and effective information program pursued by P&G helped offset the negative publicity surrounding the company and the product. Research carried out by the firm Leo Shapiro and Associates during two different periods of the crisis, reports a change of attitude by consumers from a negative to a positive feeling about P&G. George Rosenblaum, the research firm's president, says the first survey immediately following the withdrawal announcement uncovered a sour reaction to Rely. The second survey in mid-October revealed admiration for P&G's quick action (Rotbart and Prestbo, 1980).

Firestone is still suffering the effects of negative publicity from congressional hearings and courtroom cases, reported on the air and in print. The negative publicity has resulted in the loss of Firestone customers to competing brands. The company has experienced difficulty in selling other radial lines, although none of them has been judged defective. Despite extra-heavy advertising and promotion, and the creation of a special warranty, Firestone's share of the multibillion radial-tire market has slipped by about a half percent. A company officer says the drain on sales already has amounted to scores of millions of dollars (Louis, 1978).

Ford has also received its share of bad publicity with quotes such as safety expert Dr. Leslie Ball's appearing in print. "The release to production of the Pinto was the most reprehensible decision in the history of American engineering" (Dowie, 1977). Dr. Ball lists more than forty European or Japanese models with safer gas tank positioning, all competing in the same price and weight range as the Pinto. The effect of the negative publicity concerning the Pinto on consumer demand for the product is difficult to establish, but it is during the same time period that foreign imports were able to capture such a large proportion of the American small-car market.

CONCLUSION

A number of observers have outlined possible responses businesses may adopt in social responsibility issues. Although we have only discussed the responses of three companies to product liability problems there seem to be some conclusions that can be drawn. Although there are a number of responses available to a company, whatever response is chosen seems to have an effect on how the company and product is viewed by customers and the general public.

Managers who are faced with similar product liability issues would do well to review the responses of other companies and their ultimate effects when choosing their own philosophy of response. The business which vacillates or chooses not to act in a socially responsible manner may court customer dissatisfaction and public disfavor. Society seems to expect business to act in a socially responsible manner in product liability issues. If business fails to do so, it may find that it is compelled to do so by a government regulatory agency. The end result will be that business will be forced to respond in a manner dictated by the political process as opposed to responding in a manner tailored to its individual case. For chief executives caught up in product safety controversy the advice of P&G's Edward Harness is, "Keep the ball in your own court, if you can. Do it right before somebody else does it wrong for you" (Rotbart and Prestbo, 1980).

NOTES

Ackerman, Robert, "How Companies Respond to Social Demands," *Harvard Business Review* (July–August, 1973), pp. 88–98.

Carroll, Archie B., "A Three-Dimensional Conceptual Model of Corporate Social Performance," *Academy of Management Review,* 1979, Vol. 4, No. 4, pp. 497–505.

Consent Agreement signed between Procter & Gamble and the Food and Drug Administration, 1980.

Davis, Keith and Blomstrom, Robert, *Business and Society: Environment and Responsibility,* (3rd ed.), New York: McGraw-Hill, 1975, pp. 85–86.

Dowie, Mark, "How Ford Put Two Million Firetraps on Wheels," *Business and Society Review,* Fall 1977, No. 23, pp. 26–55.

Harness, Edward G., "Views on Corporate Responsibility," *Corporate Ethics Digest,* Vol. 1, No. 3, 1980.

Louis, Arthur M., "Lessons from the Firestone Fracas," *Fortune,* August 28, 1978, p. 45.

McAdam, Terry W., "How to Put Corporate Responsibility into Practice," *Business and Society Review/Innovation,* 1973, pp. 6, 8–16.

Procter & Gamble News Releases, Cincinnati, Ohio, September 17 and 22, 1980.

Rotbart, Dean and Prestbo, John A., "Killing a Product," *Wall Street Journal,* November 3, 1980, p. 21.

QUESTIONS FOR DISCUSSION (Case for Part Five)

1. Do you believe that Procter & Gamble's social response to the 1980 Rely crisis was appropriate? Do you believe that the steps Procter & Gamble took serve as a good model for business ethical decision making? Should it have considered other factors or taken other steps as well?
2. Do some research on Johnson & Johnson's response to the 1982 and 1986 Tylenol crises and compare Johnson & Johnson's actions to Procter & Gamble's actions in the Rely crisis. Do some research on A. H. Robins' response to the Dalkon Shield crisis and compare Robins' actions to Ford's actions in the Pinto crisis and Firestone's actions in the 500 radial crisis.

SUPPLEMENTARY READING FOR PART FIVE

Blanchard, Kenneth, and Norman Vincent Peale. *The Power of Ethical Management.* New York: William Morrow and Company, 1988.

Corporate Ethics. New York: The Conference Board. Research Report No. 900, 1987.

Corporate Ethics: A Prime Business Asset. A Report on Policy and Practice in Company Conduct. New York: The Business Roundtable, 1988.

Deal, Terrance E., and Allan A. Kennedy. *Corporate Cultures: The Rituals of Corporate Life.* Reading, Mass.: Addison-Wesley, 1982.

Defense Industry Initiatives on Business Ethics and Conduct. Washington, D.C.: Ethics Resource Center, 1988.

Ethics in American Business: An Opinion Survey of Key Business Leaders on Ethical Standards and Behavior. New York: The Touche Ross Foundation, 1988.

Freeman, R. Edward, and Daniel R. Gilbert, Jr. *Corporate Strategy and the Search for Ethics.* Englewood Cliffs, N.J.: Prentice-Hall, 1988.

Freudberg, David. *The Corporate Conscience.* New York: AMACOM, 1986.

Hennessy, Edward L. "Business Ethics: Is It a Priority for Corporate America?" *The Magazine for Corporate Executives,* October 1986.

Hoffman, W. Michael. "What Is Necessary for Corporate Moral Excellence?" *Journal of Business Ethics,* vol. 5, *3,* June 1986.

———, Jennifer Mills Moore, and David A. Fedo, eds. *Corporate Governance and Institutionalizing Ethics,* Lexington, Mass.: D.C. Heath, 1984.

Jackall, Robert. *Moral Mazes.* New York: Random House, 1986.

Jones, Donald G., ed. *Doing Ethics in Business.* Cambridge, Mass.: Oelgeschlager, Gunn & Hain, 1982.

Linowes, David F. *The Corporate Conscience.* New York: Hawthorne Books, 1974.

McCoy, Charles S. *Management of Values.* Marshfield, Mass.: Pitman, 1985.

Miller, Lawrence M. *American Spirit: Visions of a New Corporate Culture.* New York: William Morrow and Company, 1984.

Mintz, Morton. *At Any Cost: Corporate Greed, Women and the Dalkon Shield.* New York: Pantheon, 1985.

Pastin, Mark. *The Hard Problems of Management: Gaining the Ethics Edge.* San Francisco: Jossey-Bass, 1986.

Peters, Thomas J., and Robert H. Waterman, Jr. *In Search of Excellence: Lessons from America's Best-Run Companies.* New York: Harper and Row, 1982.

Stone, Christopher D. *Where the Law Ends: The Social Control of Corporate Behavior*. New York: Harper & Row, 1975.

Tuleja, Tad. *Beyond the Bottom Line*. New York: Facts on File Publications, 1985.

FURTHER SUGGESTED READING ON BUSINESS ETHICS

The following list represents some of the leading anthologies, texts, case books, and monographs on business ethics which are relevant to a number of the specific issues explored in this text.

Allen, William R., and Louis K. Bragaw, Jr., eds. *Social Forces and the Manager*. New York: John Wiley & Sons, 1982.

Aram, John D., ed. *Managing Business and Public Policy,* 2d ed. Marshfield, Mass.: Pitman, 1986.

Barry, Vincent, ed. *Moral Issues in Business*. Belmont, Calif.: Wadsworth Publishing Company, 1979, 1983, 1986.

Beauchamp, Tom, and Norman Bowie, eds. *Ethical Theory and Business*. Englewood Cliffs, N.J.: Prentice-Hall, 1979, 1983, 1988.

Behrman, Jack N., ed. *Essays on Ethics in Business and the Professions*. Englewood Cliffs, N.J.: Prentice-Hall, 1988.

Bond, Kenneth M. *Bibliography of Business Ethics and Business Moral Values,* 4th ed., January 1988. Published by Creighton University, Omaha, Nebraska and also distributed by the Center for Business Ethics, Bentley College, Waltham, Mass.

Bowie, Norman. *Business Ethics*. Englewood Cliffs, N.J.: Prentice-Hall, 1982.

Braybrooke, David. *Ethics in the World of Business*. Totowa, N.J.: Rowman & Allanheld, 1983.

Buchholz, Rogene, *Fundamental Concepts and Problems in Business Ethics*. Englewood Cliffs, N.J.: Prentice-Hall, 1989.

Buono, Anthony F., and Larry Nichols. *Corporate Policy, Values and Social Responsibility*. New York: Praeger, 1985.

Cavanagh, Gerald F. *American Business Values*, 2d ed. Englewood Cliffs, N.J.: Prentice-Hall, 1984.

———, and Arthur F. McGovern. *Ethical Dilemmas in the Modern Corporation*. Englewood Cliffs, N.J.: Prentice-Hall, 1988.

Davis, Keith, William C. Frederick, and Robert L. Blomstrom, eds. *Business and Society: Concepts and Policy Issues*. New York: McGraw-Hill, 1985.

De George, Richard T. *Business Ethics*. New York: Macmillan, 1982, 1986.

———, and Joseph A. Pichler, eds. *Ethics, Free Enterprise and Public Policy*. New York: Oxford University Press, 1978.

Des Jardins, Joseph R., and John J. McCall, *Contemporary Issues in Business*. Belmont, Calif.: Wadsworth, 1985.

Dickie, Robert B., and Leroy S. Rouner, eds. *Corporations and the Common Good*. Notre Dame, Ind.: University of Notre Dame Press, 1986.

Donaldson, Thomas. *Corporations and Morality*. Englewood Cliffs, N.J.: Prentice-Hall, 1982.

———, ed. *Case Studies in Business Ethics*. Englewood Cliffs, N.J.: Prentice-Hall, 1984.

———, and Patricia H. Werhane, eds. *Ethical Issues in Business: A Philosophical Approach*. Englewood Cliffs, N.J.: Prentice-Hall, 1979, 1983, 1988.

Goodpaster, Kenneth E. *Ethics in Management, Harvard Business School Case Studies*. Boston: Harvard Business School, 1984.

Green, Mark, ed. *The Big Business Reader*. New York: The Pilgrim Press, 1983.

Ethics for Executives Series. Reprints from *Harvard Business Review.* Boston, Mass: Harvard University Press.

Ethics for Executives: Part II. A *Harvard Business Review* reprint series. Boston, Mass.: Harvard University Press.

Heilbroner, Robert L., and Paul London, eds. *Corporate Social Policy.* Reading, Mass.: Addison-Wesley, 1975.

Hoffman, W. Michael, et al., eds. *Proceedings of the National Conferences on Business Ethics,* 7 vols. Center for Business Ethics, Waltham, Mass., 1977–1989.

Jones, Donald G., and Patricia Bennett. *A Bibliography of Business Ethics 1981–1985.* Lewiston, N.Y.: The Edwin Mellon Press, 1986.

Luthans, Fred, and Richard M. Hodgetts, eds. *Social Issues in Business.* New York: Macmillan, 1972, 1976, 1980, 1984.

Matthews, John B., Kenneth E. Goodpaster, and Laura L. Nash. *Policies and Persons: A Case Book in Business Ethics.* New York: McGraw-Hill, 1985.

Molander, Earl A., and David L. Arthur. *Responsive Capitalism: Case Studies in Corporate Social Conduct.* New York: McGraw-Hill, 1980.

Partridge, Scott H. *Cases in Business and Society.* Englewood Cliffs, N.J.: Prentice-Hall, 1982.

Regan, Tom, ed. *Just Business.* New York: Random House, 1984.

Sethi, S. Prakash. *Up Against the Corporate Wall,* 4th ed. Englewood Cliffs: N.J.: Prentice-Hall, 1982.

———, and Cecilia M. Falbe, eds. *Business and Society.* Lexington, Mass.: Lexington Books, 1987.

Snoeyenbos, Milton, Robert Almeder, and James Humber, eds. *Business Ethics.* New York: Prometheus, 1983.

Solomon, Robert C., and Kristine R. Hanson. *Above the Bottom Line: An Introduction to Business Ethics.* New York: Harcourt Brace Jovanovich, 1983.

———. *It's Good Business.* New York: Atheneum, 1985.

Stone, Christopher D. *Where the Law Ends.* New York: Harper & Row, 1975.

Sturdivant, Frederick D. *Business and Society: A Managerial Approach,* rev. ed. Homewood, Ill.: Richard D. Irvin, 1981.

Velasquez, Manuel G. *Business Ethics: Concepts and Cases.* Englewood Cliffs, N.J.: Prentice-Hall, 1982, 1988.

Walton, Clarence, ed. *The Ethics of Corporate Conduct.* Englewood Cliffs, N.J.: Prentice-Hall, 1974.

Werhane, Patricia H. *Persons, Rights & Corporations.* Englewood Cliffs, N.J.: Prentice-Hall, 1985.

Westin, Alan F., and John D. Aram. *Managerial Dilemmas: Cases in Social, Legal, and Technological Change.* Cambridge, Mass.: Ballinger, 1988.

Williams, Oliver F., and John W. Houck, eds. *The Judeo-Christian Vision and the Modern Corporation.* Notre Dame, Ind.: University of Notre Dame Press, 1982.